OXFORI

OXFORD-DUDEN PICTORIAL ENGLISH DICTIONARY

THE OXFORD-DUDEN PICTORIAL ENGLISH DICTIONARY

OXFORD UNIVERSITY PRESS

Oxford University Press, Walton Street, Oxford OX2 6DP
Oxford New York Toronto
Delhi Bombay Calcutta Madras Karachi
Kuala Lumpur Singapore Hong Kong Tokyo
Nairobi Dar es Salaam Cape Town
Melbourne Auckland Madrid

and associated companies in
Berlin Ibadan

Oxford is a trade mark of Oxford University Press

First published 1981
First issued as a paperback 1984

Edited by John Pheby, Oxford, with the assistance of Roland Breitsprecher, Michael Clark, Judith Cunningham, Derek Jordan, and Werner Scholze-Stubenrecht
Illustrations by Jochen Schmidt, Mannheim

British Library Cataloguing in Publication Data
Data available

Library of Congress Cataloging in Publication Data
Data available
ISBN 0-19-864155-9 (pbk.)

13 15 17 19 20 18 16 14 12

Printed in Hong Kong

Foreword

This pictorial dictionary is based on the Oxford–Duden Pictorial German–English Dictionary published in 1980. It was produced by the German Section of the Oxford University Press Dictionary Department in cooperation with the Dudenredaktion of the Bibliographisches Institut, Mannheim, and with the assistance of various British companies, institutions, and specialists. Numerous modifications of the text and illustrations of the original work have been carried out, especially regarding the depiction of everyday objects and situations, in order to allow greater scope for the treatment of these objects and situations in the context of English-speaking countries.

There are certain kinds of information which can be conveyed more readily and clearly by pictures than by definitions and explanations alone: an illustration will help the reader to visualize the object denoted by the word and to form an impression of the way in which objects function in their own technical field or in the everyday life of English-speaking countries. The layout of the illustrations and the text will be particularly useful to the learner. Each double page of the dictionary contains a list of the vocabulary of a subject together with a picture illustrating this vocabulary. This arrangement, and the presence of an alphabetical index, allows the book to be used in two ways: either as a key to the vocabulary of a subject or as an alphabetical dictionary in which the reader is referred to the section or sections in which the word is illustrated.

Oxford, 1981 J.P.

Abbreviations

Am.	*American usage*
c.	*castrated (animal)*
coll.	*colloquial*
f.	*female (animal)*
form.	*formerly*
joc.	*jocular*
m.	*male (animal)*
poet.	*poetic*
sg.	*singular*
sim.	*similar*
y.	*young (animal)*

Contents

The arabic numerals are the numbers of the pictures.

Atom, Universe, Earth
Atom I 1
Atom II 2
Astronomy I 3
Astronomy II 4
Astronomy III 5
Moon Landing 6
The Atmosphere 7
Meteorology I 8
Meteorology II and Climatology 9
Meteorological Instruments 10
Physical Geography I 11
Physical Geography II 12
Physical Geography III 13
Map I 14
Map II 15

Man and his Social Environment
Man I 16
Man II 17
Man III 18
Man IV 19
Man V 20
First Aid 21
Doctor I 22
Doctor II 23
Dentist 24
Hospital I 25
Hospital II 26
Hospital III 27
Infant Care and Layette 28
Children's Clothes 29
Ladies' Wear I (Winter Wear) 30
Ladies' Wear II (Summer Wear) 31
Underwear, Nightwear 32
Men's Wear 33
Hairstyles and Beards 34
Headgear 35
Jewellery (*Am.* Jewelry) 36
Types of Dwelling 37
Roof and Boiler Room 38
Kitchen 39
Kitchen Utensils and Appliances 40
Hall 41
Living Room (Lounge) 42
Bedroom 43
Dining Room 44
Tableware and Cutlery 45
Flat (Apartment) 46
Children's Room (Nursery) 47
Kindergarten (Day Nursery) 48
Bathroom and Toilet 49
Household Appliances and Utensils 50

Nature as Environment, Agriculture, and Forestry
Flower Garden 51
Fruit and Vegetable Garden 52
Indoor Plants (Houseplants) 53
Propagation of Plants 54
Market Garden (*Am.* Truck Garden, Truck Farm) 55
Garden Tools 56
Vegetables (Vegetable Plants) 57
Soft Fruit and Pomes 58
Drupes and Nuts 59
Garden Flowers 60
Weeds 61
Farm Buildings (*Am.* Farmstead) 62
Agriculture (Farming) 63
Agricultural Machinery I 64
Agricultural Machinery II 65
Agricultural Implements 66
Overhead Irrigation 67
Arable Crops 68
Fodder Plants (Forage Plants) 69
Breeds of Dog 70
Horse I 71
Horse II 72
Domestic Animals 73
Poultry Farming, Egg Production 74
Rearing (*Am.* Raising) of Livestock 75
Dairy 76
Bees and Beekeeping (Apiculture) 77
Wine Growing (Viniculture, Viticulture) 78
Wine Cellar 79
Garden and Field Pests 80
House Insects, Food Pests, and Parasites 81
Forest Pests 82
Pest Control 83
Forestry I 84
Forestry II 85
Hunting 86
Hunting Weapons, Hunting Equipment 87
Game 88
Fish Farming (Fish Culture, Pisciculture) and Angling 89
Sea Fishing 90

Trades, Crafts, and Industry
Mills 91
Malting and Brewing I 92
Brewing II 93
Slaughterhouse (Abattoir) 94

Meat Joints 95
Butcher's Shop 96
Bakery 97
Grocer's Shop (*Am.* Grocery Store) 98
Supermarket 99
Shoemaker (Bootmaker) 100
Shoes (Footwear) 101
Needlework 102
Dressmaker 103
Tailor 104
Ladies' Hairdresser 105
Men's Hairdresser (Barber) 106
Tobacco and Smoking Requisites 107
Goldsmith, Silversmith 108
Watchmaker, Clockmaker 109
Clocks and Watches 110
Optician 111
Optical Instruments I 112
Optical Instruments II 113
Photography I 114
Photography II 115
Photography III 116
Cine Film 117
Building Site (Construction Site) I 118
Building Site (Construction Site) II 119
Carpenter 120
Roof, Timber Joints 121
Roof and Roofer 122
Floor, Ceiling, Staircase Construction 123
Glazier 124
Plumber 125
Plumber, Gas Fitter, Heating Engineer 126
Electrician 127
Paperhanger 128
Painter 129
Cooper and Tank Construction Engineer 130
Furrier 131
Joiner I 132
Joiner II 133
Do-it-yourself 134
Turner (Ivory Carver) 135
Basket Maker 136
Blacksmith (Smith) I 137
Blacksmith (Smith) II (Farm Vehicle Engineering) 138
Hammer Forging (Smith Forging) and Drop Forging 139
Metalworker 140
Gas Welder 141
Arc Welder 142
Sections, Bolts, and Machine Parts 143
Coal Mine 144
Mineral Oil (Oil, Petroleum) 145
Offshore Drilling 146
Iron and Steel Works 147
Iron Foundry and Rolling Mill 148
Machine Tools I 149
Machine Tools II 150
Drawing Office 151
Power Plant (Power Station) I 152
Power Plant (Power Station) II 153
Nuclear Energy 154
Modern Sources of Energy 155
Coking Plant 156
Sawmill 157
Quarry 158
Brickworks (Brickyard, Brickfield) 159
Cement Works (Cement Factory) 160
Porcelain and China Manufacture 161
Glass Production 162
Cotton Spinning I 163
Cotton Spinning II 164
Weaving I 165
Weaving II 166
Knitting 167
Finishing of Textile Fabrics 168
Synthetic (Man-made) Fibres (*Am.* Fibers) I 169
Synthetic (Man made) Fibres (*Am.* Fibers) II 170
Weaves and Knits 171
Papermaking I 172
Papermaking II 173

Printing Industry

Composing Room (Case Room) I 174
Composing Room (Case Room) II 175
Composing Room (Case Room) III (Phototypesetting, Photocomposition, Photosetting, Filmsetting) 176
Photomechanical Reproduction 177
Electrotyping and Block Making 178
Offset Platemaking 179
Offset Printing 180
Letterpress Printing 181
Photogravure (Gravure Printing, Intaglio Printing) 182
Bookbinding I 183
Bookbinding II 184
Bookbinding III 185

Transport, Communications, and Information Technology

Horse-drawn Carriages 186
Bicycle 187
Motorcycles, Bicycles, Scooters, Mopeds 188
Motorcycle 189
Internal Combustion Engines 190
Motor Car (*Am.* Automobile) I 191
Motor Car (*Am.* Automobile) II 192
Motor Car (*Am.* Automobile) III 193
Lorries (*Am.* Trucks), Vans, Buses 194
Garage (*Am.* Shop) 195
Service Station 196
Tram (*Am.* Streetcar, Trolley), Interurban Electric Train 197

Cross-section of a Street 198
Refuse Disposal (*Am.* Garbage Disposition), Street Cleaning 199
Road Construction I (Road Building, Road Making) 200
Road Construction II (Road Building, Road Making) 201
Railway Line (*Am.* Railroad Track) I 202
Railway Line (*Am.* Railroad Track) II (Signalling Equipment) 203
Station Hall 204
Station Platform 205
Goods Station (Freight Depot) 206
Railway Vehicles (Rolling Stock) I 207
Railway Vehicles (Rolling Stock) II 208
Railway Vehicles (Rolling Stock) III 209
Railway Vehicles (Rolling Stock) IV 210
Railway Vehicles (Rolling Stock) V 211
Railway Vehicles (Rolling Stock) VI 212
Railway Vehicles (Rolling Stock) VII 213
Mountain Railways (*Am.* Mountain Railroads) and Cableways 214
Bridges 215
Rivers and River Engineering 216
Waterway and Hydraulic Engineering 217
Types of Historical Ship 218
Sailing Ship I 219
Sailing Ship II 220
Types of Ship 221
Shipbuilding 222
Motor Ship 223
Navigation 224
Docks, Port, Harbour (*Am.* Harbor) I 225
Docks, Port, Harbour (*Am.* Harbor) II 226
Salvage (Salving) and Towage 227
Life Saving 228
Aircraft I 229
Aircraft II 230
Aircraft III 231
Aircraft IV 232
Airport 233
Space Flight I 234
Space Flight II 235
Post Office I 236
Post Office II (Telephones and Telegraphy) 237
Broadcasting (Radio and Television) I 238
Broadcasting (Radio and Television) II 239
Broadcasting III (Television Engineering) 240
Music Systems (Audio Systems) 241
Teaching Equipment and Information Technology 242
Audiovision (AV) 243
Computer Centre (*Am.* Center) 244

Office, Bank, Stock Exchange

Office I 245
Office II 246
Office III 247
Office IV 248
Office V 249
Bank 250
Stock Exchange 251

Community

Money (Coins and Notes, *Am.* Coins and Bills) 252
Flags 253
Heraldry, Crowns and Coronets 254
Armed Forces I (Army) 255
Armed Forces II (Air Force I) 256
Armed Forces III (Air Force II) 257
Warships I 258
Warships II (Modern Fighting Ships) 259
School I (Primary School) 260
School II (Secondary School, High School) 261
University 262
Election 263
Police 264
Café 265
Restaurant 266
Hotel 267
Town (Town Centre, *Am.* Downtown) 268
Water Supply 269
Fire Service (*Am.* Fire Department) 270
Department Store 271
Park 272

Recreation, Games, Sport

Children's Playground 273
Spa 274
Roulette 275
Board Games and Party Games 276
Billiards 277
Camping and Caravanning (*Am.* Trailering) 278
Surf Riding (Surfing), Skin Diving 279
Bathing Beach 280
Swimming Bath (Leisure Centre, *Am.* Center) 281
Swimming 282
Rowing and Canoeing 283
Sailing (Yachting) I 284
Sailing (Yachting) II 285
Motorboats (Powerboats), Water Skiing 286
Gliding (Soaring) 287
Aerial Sports (Airsports) 288
Horsemanship, Equestrian Sport 289
Cycle Racing and Motorsports 290
Ball Games I (Football, Association Football, Soccer) 291

Ball Games II 292
Ball Games III 293
Fencing 294
Free Exercise 295
Apparatus Gymnastics I 296
Apparatus Gymnastics II (Women's Gymnastics) 297
Athletics (Track and Field Events) 298
Weightlifting and Combat Sports 299
Mountaineering 300
Winter Sports I (Skiing) 301
Winter Sports II 302
Winter Sports III 303
Countryside in Winter 304
Various Sports 305

Entertainment, Culture, and Art
Carnival 306
Circus 307
Fair, Fairground 308
Flea Market 309
Films (Motion Pictures) I 310
Films (Motion Pictures) II 311
Films (Motion Pictures) III 312
Films (Motion Pictures) IV 313
Ballet 314
Theatre (*Am.* Theater) I 315
Theatre (*Am.* Theater) II 316
Discotheque 317
Nightclub 318
Bullfighting, Rodeo 319
Musical Notation I 320
Musical Notation II 321
Musical Instruments I 322
Musical Instruments II 323
Musical Instruments III 324
Musical Instruments IV 325
Musical Instruments V 326
Fabulous Creatures (Fabled Beings) 327
Prehistory 328
Chivalry 329
Church I 330
Church II 331
Church III 332
Art I 333
Art II 334
Art III 335
Art IV 336
Art V 337
Artist's Studio 338
Sculptor's Studio 339
Graphic Art 340
Script I 341
Script II 342
Colour (*Am.* Color) 343
Mathematics I 344
Mathematics II 345
Mathematics III (Geometry I) 346
Mathematics IV (Geometry II) 347
Mathematics V (Sets) 348
Chemistry Laboratory I 349
Chemistry Laboratory II 350
Crystals, Crystallography 351
Ethnology I 352
Ethnology II 353
Ethnology III 354
Historical Costumes 355

Animals and Plants
Zoo (Zoological Gardens) 356
Invertebrates 357
Articulates 358
Birds I 359
Birds II (Indigenous Birds, Endemic Birds) 360
Birds III (Passerines) 361
Birds IV (Birds of Prey) 362
Birds V (Exotic Birds) 363
Fish, Amphibia, and Reptiles 364
Lepidoptera (Butterflies and Moths) 365
Mammals I 366
Mammals II 367
Mammals III 368
Deep-sea Fauna 369
General Botany 370
Deciduous Trees 371
Conifers 372
Ornamental Shrubs and Trees I 373
Ornamental Shrubs and Trees II 374
Meadow Flowers and Wayside Flowers (Wild Flowers) I 375
Meadow Flowers and Wayside Flowers (Wild Flowers) II 376
Plants of Forest, Marsh, and Heathland 377
Alpine Plants, Aquatic Plants (Water Plants), and Marsh Plants 378
Poisonous Plants 379
Medicinal Plants 380
Edible Fungi (Esculent Fungi) 381
Tropical Plants used as Stimulants, Spices, and Flavourings (*Am.* Flavorings) 382
Plants used in Industry 383
Southern Fruits (Tropical, Subtropical, and Mediterranean Fruits) 384

1 Atom I

1–8 atom models
1 model of the hydrogen (H) atom
2 atomic nucleus, a proton
3 electron
4 electron spin
5 model of the helium (He) atom
6 electron shell
7 Pauli exclusion principle (exclusion principle, Pauli principle)
8 complete electron shell of the Na atom (sodium atom)
9–14 molecular structures (lattice structures)
9 crystal of sodium chloride (of common salt)
10 chlorine ion
11 sodium ion
12 crystal of cristobalite
13 oxygen atom
14 silicon atom
15 **energy levels** (possible quantum jumps) of the hydrogen atom
16 atomic nucleus (proton)
17 electron
18 ground state level
19 excited state
20–25 quantum jumps (quantum transitions)
20 Lyman series
21 Balmer series
22 Paschen series
23 Brackett series
24 Pfund series
25 free electron
26 Bohr–Sommerfeld model of the H atom
27 energy levels of the electron
28 **spontaneous decay** of radioactive material
29 atomic nucleus
30–31 alpha particle (α, alpha radiation, helium nucleus)
30 neutron
31 proton
32 beta particle (β, beta radiation, electron)
33 gamma radiation (γ, a hard X-radiation)
34 **nuclear fission:**
35 heavy atomic nucleus
36 neutron bombardment
37–38 fission fragments
39 released neutron
40 gamma radiation (γ)
41 **chain reaction**
42 incident neutron
43 nucleus prior to fission
44 fission fragment
45 released neutron
46 repeated fission
47 fission fragment
48 **controlled chain reaction in a nuclear reactor**
49 atomic nucleus of a fissionable element
50 neutron bombardment
51 fission fragment (new atomic nucleus)
52 released neutron
53 absorbed neutrons
54 moderator, a retarding layer of graphite
55 extraction of heat (production of energy)
56 X-radiation
57 concrete and lead shield
58 **bubble chamber** for showing the tracks of high-energy ionizing particles
59 light source
60 camera
61 expansion line
62 path of light rays
63 magnet
64 beam entry point
65 reflector
66 chamber

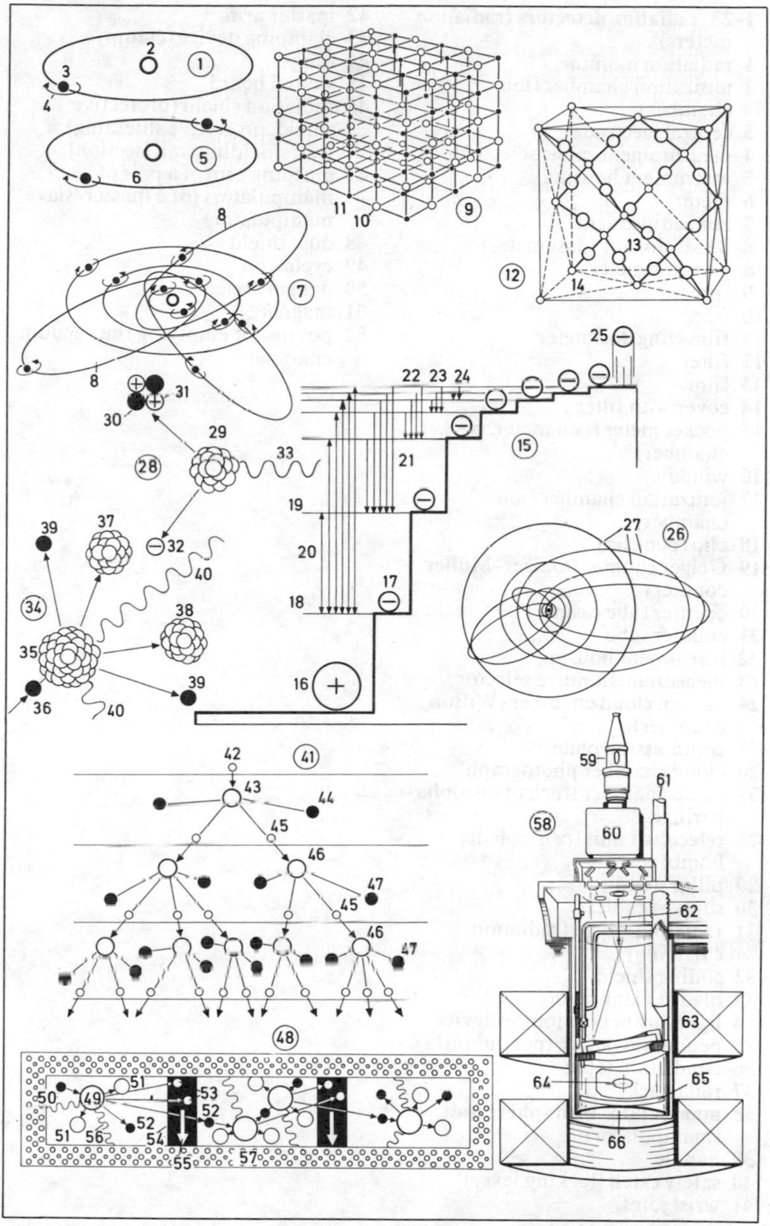

2 Atom II

1–23 radiation detectors (radiation meters)
1 radiation monitor
2 ionization chamber (ion chamber)
3 central electrode
4 measurement range selector
5 instrument housing
6 meter
7 zero adjustment
8–23 dosimeter (dosemeter)
8 film dosimeter
9 filter
10 film
11 film-ring dosimeter
12 filter
13 film
14 cover with filter
15 pocket meter (pen meter, pocket chamber)
16 window
17 ionization chamber (ion chamber)
18 clip (pen clip)
19 Geiger counter (Geiger-Müller counter)
20 counter tube casing
21 counter tube
22 instrument housing
23 measurement range selector
24 Wilson cloud chamber (Wilson chamber)
25 compression plate
26 cloud chamber photograph
27 cloud chamber track of an alpha particle
28 **telecobalt unit** (*coll.* cobalt bomb)
29 pillar stand
30 support cables
31 radiation shield (radiation shielding)
32 sliding shield
33 bladed diaphragm
34 light-beam positioning device
35 pendulum device (pendulum)
36 irradiation table
37 rail (track)
38 **manipulator with sphere unit** (manipulator)
39 handle
40 safety catch (locking lever)
41 wrist joint
42 master arm
43 clamping device (clamp)
44 tongs
45 slotted board
46 radiation shield (protective shield, protective shielding), a lead shielding wall [section]
47 grasping arm of a pair of manipulators (of a master/slave manipulator)
48 dust shield
49 **cyclotron**
50 danger zone
51 magnet
52 pumps for emptying the vacuum chamber

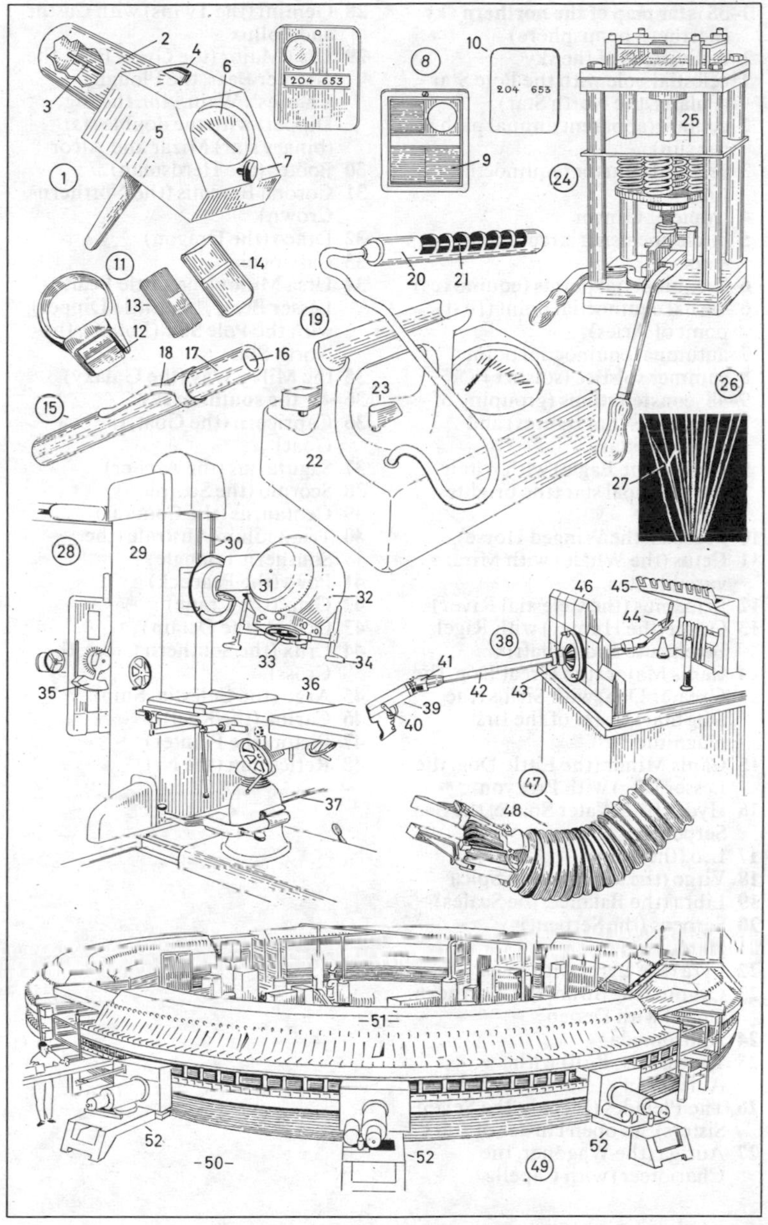
1
2
3
4
5
6
7
8
204 653
9
10
204 653
11
12
13
14
15
16
17
18
19
20
21
22
23
24
25
26
27
28
29
30
31
32
33
34
35
36
37
38
39
40
41
42
43
44
45
46
47
48
49
50
51
52
52
52

3 Astronomy I

1–35 star map of the northern sky (northern hemisphere)
1–8 divisions of the sky
1 celestial pole with the Pole Star (Polaris, the North Star)
2 ecliptic (apparent annual path of the sun)
3 celestial equator (equinoctial line)
4 tropic of Cancer
5 circle enclosing circumpolar stars
6–7 equinoctial points (equinoxes)
6 vernal equinoctial point (first point of Aries)
7 autumnal equinoctial point
8 summer solstice (solstice)
9–48 constellations (grouping of fixed stars into figures) **and names of stars**
9 Aquila (the Eagle) with Altair the principal star (the brightest star)
10 Pegasus (the Winged Horse)
11 Cetus (the Whale) with Mira, a variable star
12 Eridamus (the Celestial River)
13 Orion (the Hunter) with Rigel, Betelgeuse and Bellatrix
14 Canis Major (the Great Dog, the Greater Dog) with Sirius (the Dog Star), a star of the first magnitude
15 Canis Minor (the Little Dog, the Lesser Dog) with Procyon
16 Hydra (the Water Snake, the Sea Serpent)
17 Leo (the Lion)
18 Virgo (the Virgin) with Spica
19 Libra (the Balance, the Scales)
20 Serpens (the Serpent)
21 Hercules
22 Lyra (the Lyre) with Vega
23 Cygnus (the Swan, the Northern Cross) with Deneb
24 Andromeda
25 Taurus (the Bull) with Aldebaran
26 The Pleiades (Pleiads, the Seven Sisters), an open cluster of stars
27 Auriga (the Wagoner, the Charioteer) with Capella
28 Gemini (the Twins) with Castor and Pollux
29 Ursa Major (the Great Bear, the Greater Bear, the Plough, Charles's Wain, *Am.* the Big Dipper) with the double star (binary star) Mizar and Alcor
30 Boötes (the Herdsman)
31 Corona Borealis (the Northern Crown)
32 Draco (the Dragon)
33 Cassiopeia
34 Ursa Minor (the Little Bear, Lesser Bear, *Am.* Little Dipper) with the Pole Star (Polaris, the North Star)
35 the Milky Way (the Galaxy)
36–48 the southern sky
36 Capricorn (the Goat, the Sea Goat)
37 Sagittarius (the Archer)
38 Scorpio (the Scorpion)
39 Centaurus (the Centaur)
40 Triangulum Australe (the Southern Triangle)
41 Pavo (the Peacock)
42 Grus (the Crane)
43 Octans (the Octant)
44 Crux (the Southern Cross, the Cross)
45 Argo (the Celestial Ship)
46 Carina (the Keel)
47 Pictor (the Painter)
48 Reticulum (the Net)

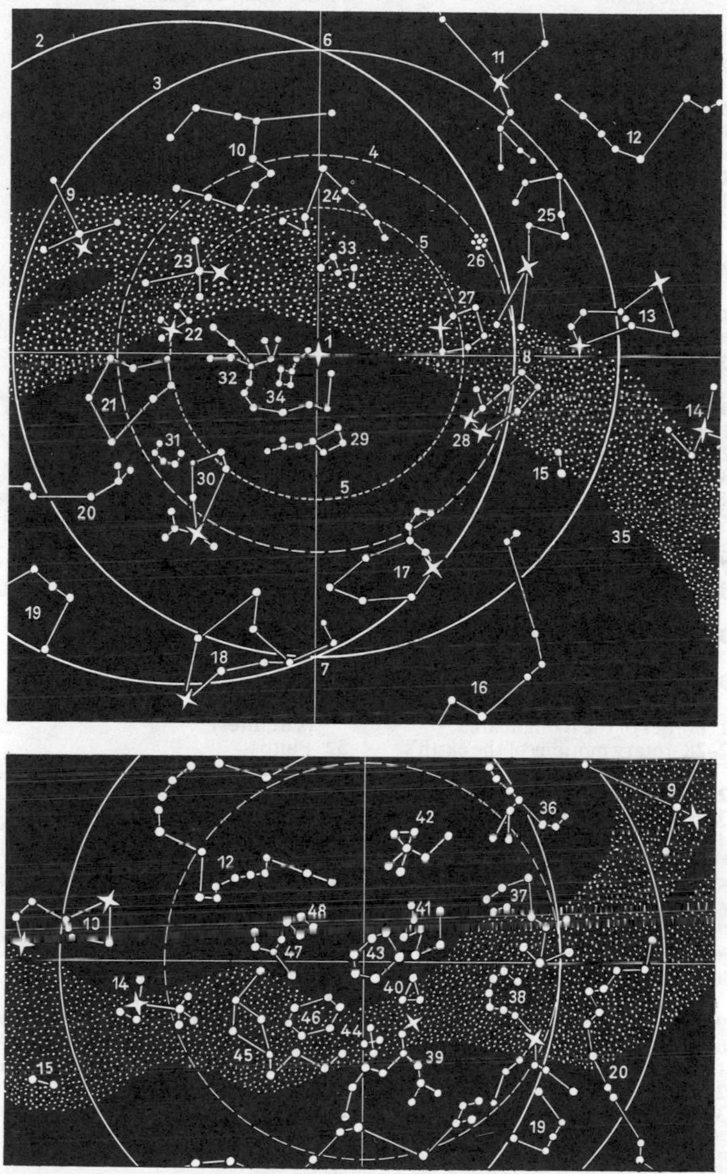
2
3
6
4
5
7
8
1
9
10
11
12
13
14
15
16
17
18
19
20
21
22
23
24
25
26
27
28
29
30
31
32
33
34
35
36
37
38
39
40
41
42
43
44
45
46
47
48

4 Astronomy II

1–9 the moon
1 moon's path (moon's orbit round the earth)
2–7 lunar phases (moon's phases, lunation)
2 new moon
3 crescent (crescent moon, waxing moon)
4 half-moon (first quarter)
5 full moon
6 half-moon (last quarter, third quarter)
7 crescent (crescent moon, waning moon)
8 the earth (terrestrial globe)
9 direction of the sun's rays
10–21 apparent path of the sun at the beginning of the seasons
10 celestial axis
11 zenith
12 horizontal plane
13 nadir
14 east point
15 west point
16 north point
17 south point
18 apparent path of the sun on 21 December
19 apparent path of the sun on 21 March and 23 September
20 apparent path of the sun on 21 June
21 border of the twilight area
22–28 rotary motions of the earth's axis
22 axis of the ecliptic
23 celestial sphere
24 path of the celestial pole (precession and nutation)
25 instantaneous axis of rotation
26 celestial pole
27 mean axis of rotation
28 polhode
29–35 solar and lunar eclipse [not to scale]
29 the sun
30 the earth
31 the moon
32 solar eclipse
33 area of the earth in which the eclipse appears total
34–35 lunar eclipse
34 penumbra (partial shadow)
35 umbra (total shadow)
36–41 the sun
36 solar disc (disk) (solar globe, solar sphere)
37 sunspots
38 cyclones in the area of sunspots
39 corona (solar corona), observable during total solar eclipse or by means of special instruments
40 prominences (solar prominences)
41 moon's limb during a total solar eclipse
42–52 planets (planetary system, solar system) [not to scale] and planet symbols
42 the sun
43 Mercury
44 Venus
45 Earth, with the moon, a satellite
46 Mars, with two moons (satellites)
47 asteroids (minor planets)
48 Jupiter, with 14 moons (satellites)
49 Saturn, with 10 moons (satellites)
50 Uranus, with five moons (satellites)
51 Neptune, with two moons (satellites)
52 Pluto
53–64 signs of the zodiac (zodiacal signs)
53 Aries (the Ram)
54 Taurus (the Bull)
55 Gemini (the Twins)
56 Cancer (the Crab)
57 Leo (the Lion)
58 Virgo (the Virgin)
59 Libra (the Balance, the Scales)
60 Scorpio (the Scorpion)
61 Sagittarius (the Archer)
62 Capricorn (the Goat, the Sea Goat)
63 Aquarius (the Water Carrier, the Water Bearer)
64 Pisces (the Fish)

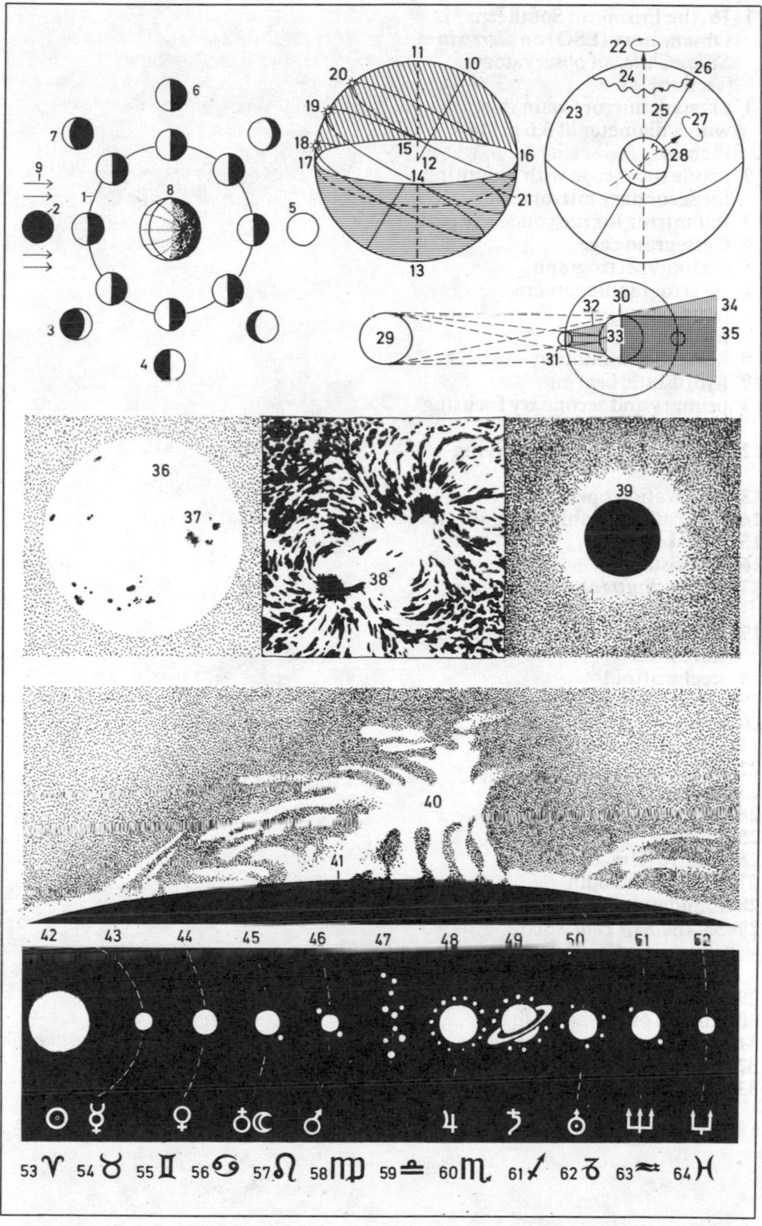
1
2
3
4
5
6
7
8
9
10
11
12
13
14
15
16
17
18
19
20
21
22
23
24
25
26
27
28
29
30
31
32
33
34
35
36
37
38
39
40
41
42
43
44
45
46
47
48
49
50
51
52
53 ♈ 54 ♉ 55 ♊ 56 ♋ 57 ♌ 58 ♍ 59 ♎ 60 ♏ 61 ♐ 62 ♑ 63 ♒ 64 ♓

5 Astronomy III

1-16 the European Southern Observatory (ESO) on *Cerro la Silla, Chile*, an observatory [section]
1 primary mirror (main mirror) with a diameter of 3.6 m (144 inches)
2 prime focus cage with mounting for secondary mirrors
3 flat mirror for the coudé ray path
4 Cassegrain cage
5 grating spectrograph
6 spectrographic camera
7 hour axis drive
8 hour axis
9 horseshoe mounting
10 hydrostatic bearing
11 primary and secondary focusing devices
12 observatory dome (revolving dome)
13 observation opening
14 vertically movable dome shutter
15 wind screen
16 siderostat
17-28 the *Stuttgart* Planetarium [section]
17 administration, workshop, and store area
18 steel scaffold
19 glass pyramid
20 revolving arched ladder
21 projection dome
22 light stop
23 planetarium projector
24 well
25 foyer
26 theatre (*Am.* theater)
27 projection booth
28 foundation pile
29-33 the *Kitt Peak* solar observatory near *Tucson, Ariz.* [section]
29 heliostat
30 sunken observation shaft
31 water-cooled windshield
32 concave mirror
33 observation room housing the spectrograph

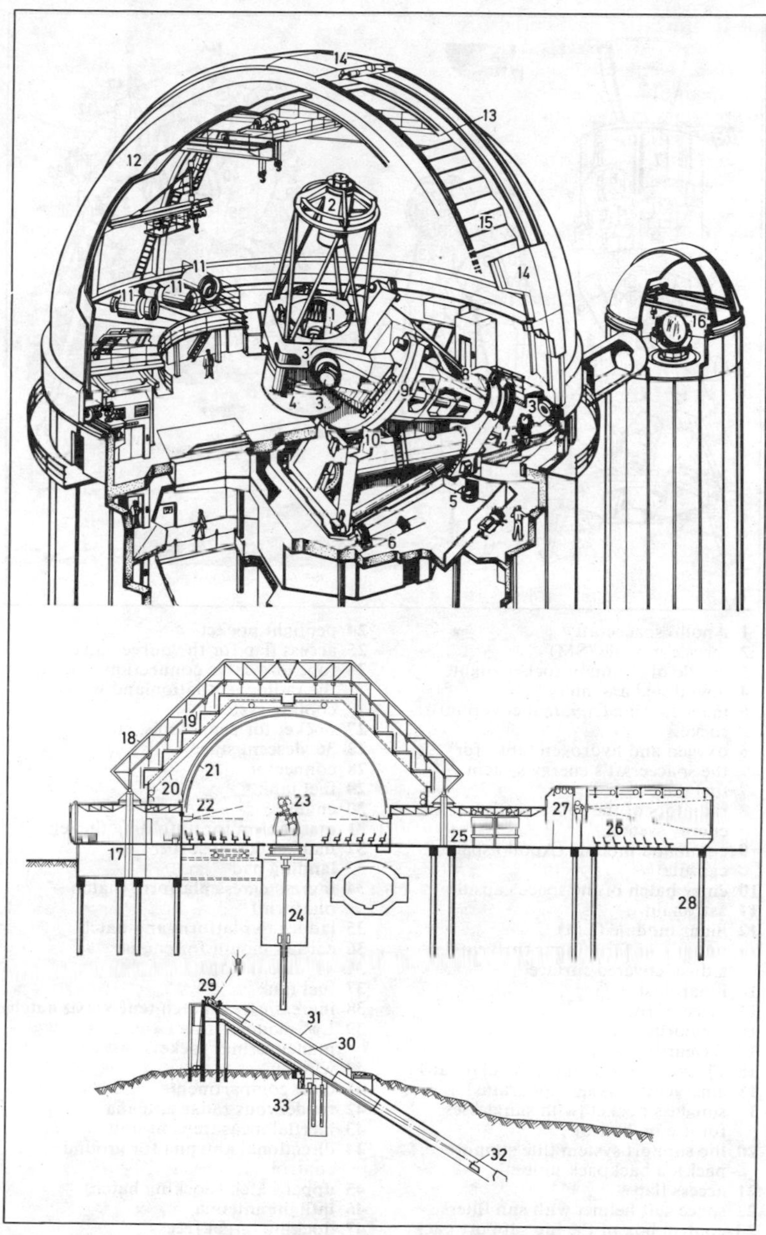
14
13
12
2
15
14
11
11
11
1
16
3
8
9
4
3
3
7
10
5
6
18
19
21
20
22
23
27
26
25
17
24
28
29
31
30
33
32

6 Moon Landing

1 Apollo spacecraft
2 service module (SM)
3 nozzle of the main rocket engine
4 directional antenna
5 manoeuvring (*Am.* maneuvering) rockets
6 oxygen and hydrogen tanks for the spacecraft's energy system
7 fuel tank
8 radiators of the spacecraft's energy system
9 command module (Apollo space capsule)
10 entry hatch of the space capsule
11 astronaut
12 lunar module (LM)
13 moon's surface (lunar surface), a dust-covered surface
14 lunar dust
15 piece of rock
16 meteorite crater
17 the earth
18-27 space suit (extra-vehicular suit)
18 emergency oxygen apparatus
19 sunglass pocket [with sunglasses for use on board]
20 life support system (life support pack), a backpack unit
21 access flap
22 space suit helmet with sun filters
23 control box of the life support pack
24 penlight pocket
25 access flap for the purge valve
26 tube and cable connections for the radio, ventilation,and water-cooling systems
27 pocket for pens, tools, etc.
28-36 descent stage
28 connector
29 fuel tank
30 engine
31 mechanism for unfolding the legs
32 main shock absorber
33 landing pad
34 ingress/egress platform (hatch platform)
35 ladder to platform and hatch
36 cardan mount for engine
37-47 ascent stage
37 fuel tank
38 ingress/egress hatch (entry/exit hatch)
39 LM manoeuvring (*Am.* maneuvering) rockets
40 window
41 crew compartment
42 rendezvous radar antenna
43 inertial measurement unit
44 directional antenna for ground control
45 upper hatch (docking hatch)
46 inflight antenna
47 docking target recess

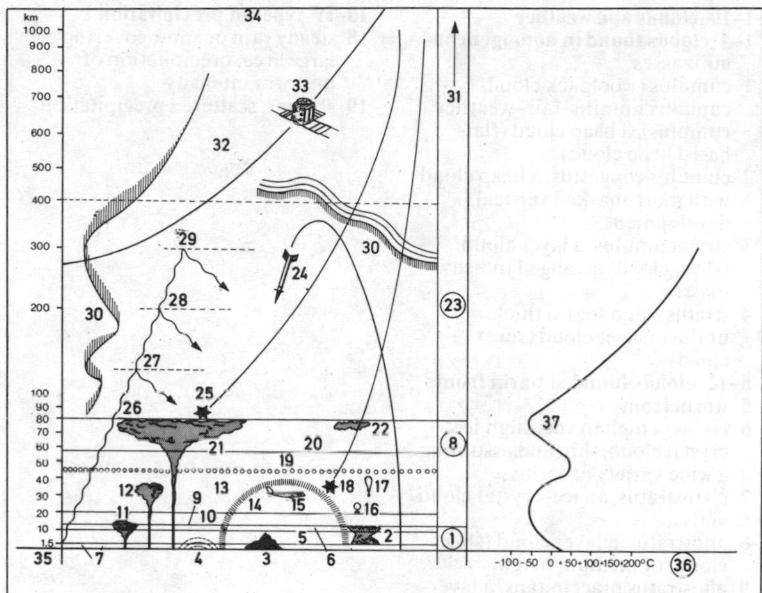

1 the troposphere
2 thunderclouds
3 the highest mountain, *Mount Everest* [8,882m]
4 rainbow
5 jet stream level
6 zero level (inversion of vertical air movement)
7 ground layer (surface boundary layer)
8 the stratosphere
9 tropopause
10 separating layer (layer of weaker air movement)
11 atomic explosion
12 hydrogen bomb explosion
13 ozone layer
14 range of sound wave propagation
15 stratosphere aircraft
16 manned balloon
17 sounding balloon
18 meteor
19 upper limit of ozone layer
20 zero level
21 eruption of Krakatoa
22 luminous clouds (noctilucent clouds)
23 the ionosphere
24 range of research rockets
25 shooting star
26 short wave (high frequency)
27 E-layer (Heaviside-Kennelly Layer)
28 F_1-layer
29 F_2-layer
30 aurora (polar light)
31 the exosphere
32 atom layer
33 range of satellite sounding
34 fringe region
35 altitude scale
36 temperature scale (thermometric scale)
37 temperature graph

8 Meteorology I

1–19 clouds and weather
1–4 clouds found in homogeneous air masses
1 cumulus (woolpack cloud, cumulus humilis, fair-weather cumulus), a heap cloud (flat-based heap cloud)
2 cumulus congestus, a heap cloud with more marked vertical development
3 stratocumulus, a layer cloud (sheet cloud) arranged in heavy masses
4 stratus (high fog), a thick, uniform layer cloud (sheet cloud)
5–12 clouds found at warm fronts
5 warm front
6 cirrus, a high to very high ice-crystal cloud, thin and assuming a wide variety of forms
7 cirrostratus, an ice-crystal cloud veil
8 altostratus, a layer cloud (sheet cloud) of medium height
9 altostratus praecipitans, a layer cloud (sheet cloud) with precipitation in its upper parts
10 nimbostratus, a rain cloud, a layer cloud (sheet cloud) of very large vertical extent which produces precipitation (rain or snow)
11 fractostratus, a ragged cloud occurring beneath nimbostratus
12 fractocumulus, a ragged cloud like 11 but with billowing shapes
13–17 clouds at cold fronts
13 cold front
14 cirrocumulus, thin fleecy cloud in the form of globular masses; *covering the sky:* mackerel sky
15 altocumulus, a cloud in the form of large globular masses
16 altocumulus castellanus and altocumulus floccus, species of 15
17 cumulonimbus, a heap cloud of very large vertical extent, to be classified under 1–4 in the case of tropical storms
18–19 types of precipitation
18 steady rain or snow covering a large area, precipitation of uniform intensity
19 shower, scattered precipitation

black arrow = cold air white arrow = warm air

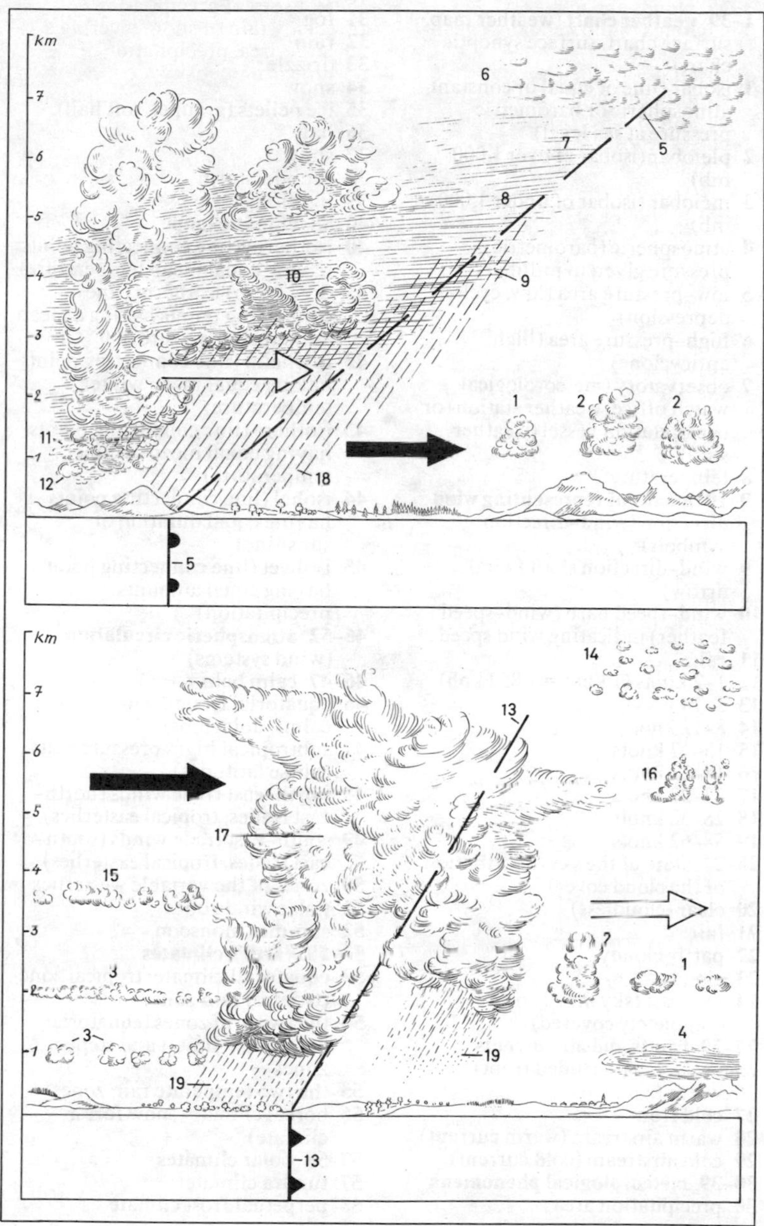
km
7
6
5
4
3
2
1
6
7
5
8
9
10
1
2
2
11
12
18
5
km
7
6
5
4
3
2
1
14
13
16
17
15
3
3
2
1
4
19
19
13

9 Meteorology II and Climatology

1–39 weather chart (weather map, surface chart, surface synoptic chart)
1 isobar (line of equal or constant atmospheric or barometric pressure at sea level)
2 pleiobar (isobar of over 1,000 mb)
3 meiobar (isobar of under 1,000 mb)
4 atmospheric (barometric) pressure given in millibars
5 low-pressure area (low, cyclone, depression)
6 high-pressure area (high, anticyclone)
7 observatory (meteorological watch office, weather station) or ocean station vessel (weather ship)
8 temperature
9–19 means of representing wind direction (wind-direction symbols)
9 wind-direction shaft (wind arrow)
10 wind-speed barb (wind-speed feather) indicating wind speed
11 calm
12 1–2 knots (1 knot = 1.852 kph)
13 3–7 knots
14 8–12 knots
15 13–17 knots
16 18–22 knots
17 23–27 knots
18 28–32 knots
19 58–62 knots
20–24 state of the sky (distribution of the cloud cover)
20 clear (cloudless)
21 fair
22 partly cloudy
23 cloudy
24 overcast (sky mostly or completely covered)
25–29 fronts and air currents
25 occlusion (occluded front)
26 warm front
27 cold front
28 warm airstream (warm current)
29 cold airstream (cold current)
30–39 meteorological phenomena
30 precipitation area
31 fog
32 rain
33 drizzle
34 snow
35 ice pellets (graupel, soft hail)
36 hail
37 shower
38 thunderstorm
39 lightning
40–58 climatic map
40 isotherm (line connecting points having equal mean temperature)
41 0 °C (zero) isotherm (line connecting points having a mean annual temperature of 0 °C)
42 isocheim (line connecting points having equal mean winter temperature)
43 isothere (line connecting points having equal mean summer temperature)
44 isohel (line connecting points having equal duration of sunshine)
45 isohyet (line connecting points having equal amounts of precipitation)
46–52 atmospheric circulation (wind systems)
46–47 calm belts
46 equatorial trough (equatorial calms, doldrums)
47 subtropical high-pressure belts (horse latitudes)
48 north-east trade winds (north-east trades, tropical easterlies)
49 south-east trade winds (south-east trades, tropical easterlies)
50 zones of the variable westerlies
51 polar wind zones
52 summer monsoon
53–58 earth's climates
53 equatorial climate: tropical zone (tropical rain zone)
54 the two arid zones (equatorial dry zones): desert and steppe zones
55 the two temperate rain zones
56 boreal climate (snow forest climate)
57–58 polar climates
57 tundra climate
58 perpetual frost climate

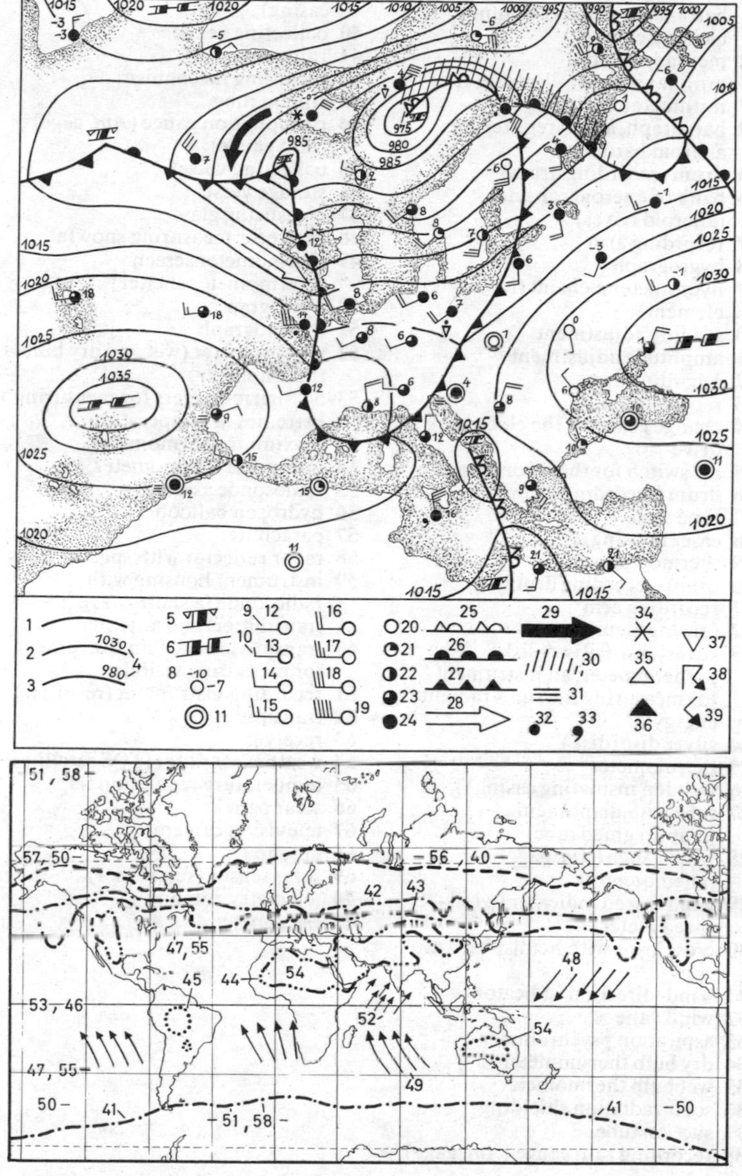
1
2
3
4
5
6
8
9
10
11
12
13
14
15
16
17
18
19
20
21
22
23
24
25
26
27
28
29
30
31
32
33
34
35
36
37
38
39
51, 58
57, 50
56, 40
42
43
47, 55
45
44
54
48
53, 46
52
49
47, 55
50
41
51, 58
41
50

10 Meteorological Instruments

1 mercury barometer, a siphon barometer, a liquid-column barometer
2 mercury column
3 millibar scale (millimetre, *Am.* millimeter, scale)
4 barograph, a self-registering aneroid barometer
5 drum (recording drum)
6 bank of aneroid capsules (aneroid boxes)
7 recording arm
8 hygrograph
9 hygrometer element (hair element)
10 reading adjustment
11 amplitude adjustment
12 recording arm
13 recording pen
14 change gears for the clockwork drive
15 off switch for the recording arm
16 drum (recording drum)
17 time scale
18 case (housing)
19 thermograph
20 drum (recording drum)
21 recording arm
22 sensing element
23 silver-disc (silver-disk) pyrheliometer, an instrument for measuring the sun's radiant energy
24 silver disc (disk)
25 thermometer
26 wooden insulating casing
27 tube with diaphragm (diaphragmed tube)
28 wind gauge (*Am.* gage) (anemometer)
29 wind-speed indicator (wind-speed meter)
30 cross arms with hemispherical cups
31 wind-direction indicator
32 wind vane
33 aspiration psychrometer
34 dry bulb thermometer
35 wet bulb thermometer
36 solar radiation shielding
37 suction tube
38 recording rain gauge (*Am.* gage)
39 protective housing (protective casing)
40 collecting vessel
41 rain cover
42 recording mechanism
43 siphon tube
44 precipitation gauge (*Am.* gage) (rain gauge)
45 collecting vessel
46 storage vessel
47 measuring glass
48 insert for measuring snowfall
49 thermometer screen (thermometer shelter)
50 hygrograph
51 thermograph
52 psychrometer (wet and dry bulb thermometer)
53-54 thermometers for measuring extremes of temperature
53 maximum thermometer
54 minimum thermometer
55 radiosonde assembly
56 hydrogen balloon
57 parachute
58 radar reflector with spacing lines
59 instrument housing with radiosonde (a short-wave transmitter) and antenna
60 transmissometer, an instrument for measuring visibility
61 recording instrument (recorder)
62 transmitter
63 recciver
64 weather satellite (ITOS satellite)
65 temperature regulation flaps
66 solar panel
67 television camera
68 antenna
69 solar sensor (sun sensor)
70 telemetry antenna
71 radiometer

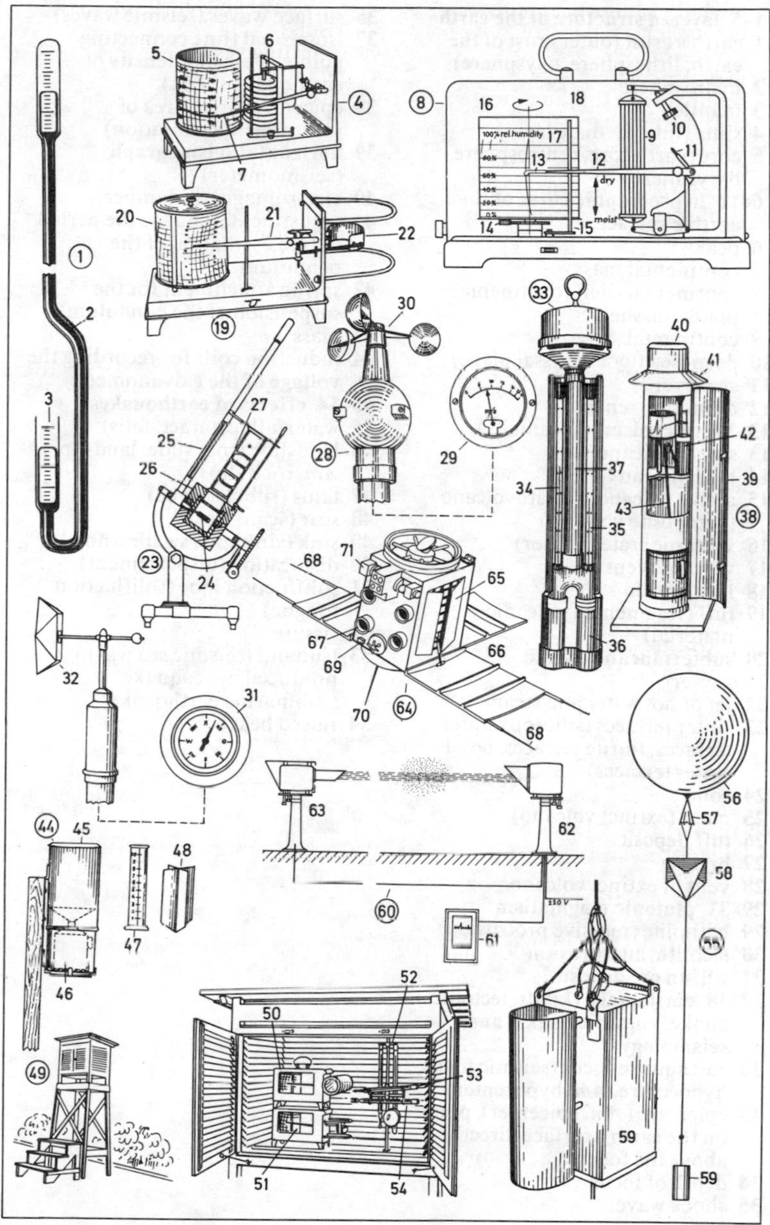
100% rel. humidity
80%
60%
40%
20%
0%
dry
moist
230 V

11 Physical Geography I

1–5 layered structure of the earth
1 earth's crust (outer crust of the earth, lithosphere, oxysphere)
2 hydrosphere
3 mantle
4 sima (intermediate layer)
5 core (earth core, centrosphere, barysphere)
6–12 hypsographic curve of the earth's surface
6 peak
7 continental mass
8 continental shelf (continental platform, shelf)
9 continental slope
10 deep-sea floor (abyssal plane)
11 sea level
12 deep-sea trench
13–28 volcanism (vulcanicity)
13 shield volcano
14 lava plateau
15 active volcano, a stratovolcano (composite volcano)
16 volcanic crater (crater)
17 volcanic vent
18 lava stream
19 tuff (fragmented volcanic material)
20 subterranean volcano
21 geyser
22 jet of hot water and steam
23 sinter terraces (siliceous sinter terraces, fiorite terraces, pearl sinter terraces)
24 cone
25 maar (extinct volcano)
26 tuff deposit
27 breccia
28 vent of extinct volcano
29–31 plutonic magmatism
29 batholite (massive protrusion)
30 lacolith, an intrusion
31 sill, an ore deposit
32–38 earthquake (*kinds:* tectonic quake, volcanic quake) **and seismology**
32 earthquake focus (seismic focus, hypocentre, *Am.* hypocenter)
33 epicentre (*Am.* epicenter), point on the earth's surface directly above the focus
34 depth of focus
35 shock wave
36 surface waves (seismic waves)
37 isoseismal (line connecting points of equal intensity of earthquake shock)
38 epicentral area (area of macroseismic vibration)
39 horizontal seismograph (seismometer)
40 electromagnetic damper
41 adjustment knob for the period of free oscillation of the pendulum
42 spring attachment for the suspension of the pendulum
43 mass
44 induction coils for recording the voltage of the galvanometer
45–54 effects of earthquakes
45 waterfall (cataract, falls)
46 landslide (rockslide, landslip, *Am.* rock slip)
47 talus (rubble, scree)
48 scar (scaur, scaw)
49 sink (sinkhole, swallowhole)
50 dislocation (displacement)
51 solifluction lobe (solifluction tongue)
52 fissure
53 tsunami (seismic sea wave) produced by seaquake (submarine earthquake)
54 raised beach

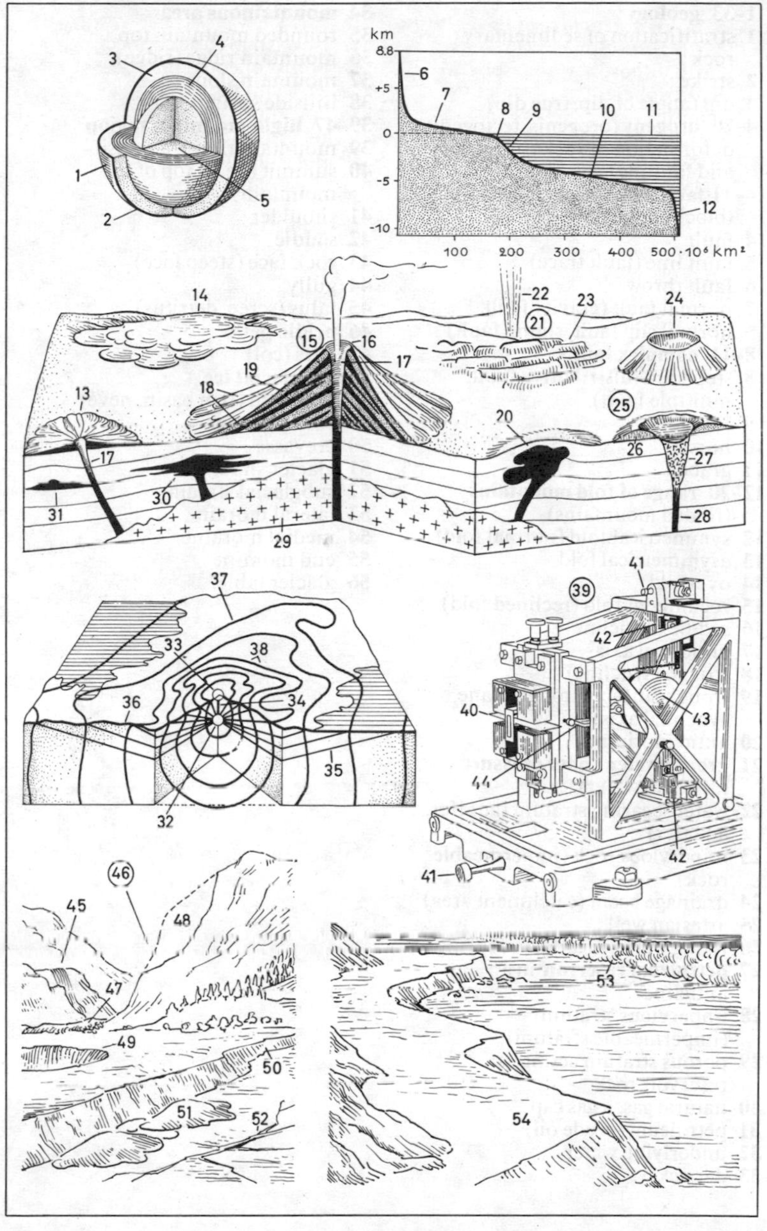
km
8.8
+5
0
-5
-10
100
200
300
400
500 · 10⁶ km²
1
2
3
4
5
6
7
8
9
10
11
12
13
14
15
16
17
18
19
20
21
22
23
24
25
26
27
28
29
30
31
32
33
34
35
36
37
38
39
40
41
42
43
44
45
46
47
48
49
50
51
52
53
54

12 Physical Geography II

1–33 geology
1 stratification of sedimentary rock
2 strike
3 dip (angle of dip, true dip)
4–20 orogeny (orogenis, tectogenis, deformation of rocks by folding and faulting)
4–11 fault-block mountains (block mountains)
4 fault
5 fault line (fault trace)
6 fault throw
7 normal fault (gravity fault, normal slip fault, slump fault)
8–11 complex faults
8 step fault (distributive fault, multiple fault)
9 tilt block
10 horst
11 graben
12–20 range of fold mountains (folded mountains)
12 symmetrical fold (normal fold)
13 asymmetrical fold
14 overfold
15 recumbent fold (reclined fold)
16 saddle (anticline)
17 anticlinal axis
18 trough (syncline)
19 trough surface (trough plane, synclinal axis)
20 anticlinorium
21 **groundwater under pressure** (artesian water)
22 water-bearing stratum (aquifer, aquafer)
23 impervious rock (impermeable rock)
24 drainage basin (catchment area)
25 artesian well
26 rising water, an artesian spring
27 **petroleum reservoir** in an anticline
28 impervious stratum (impermeable stratum)
29 porous stratum acting as reservoir rock
30 natural gas, a gas cap
31 petroleum (crude oil)
32 underlying water
33 derrick

34 **mountainous area**
35 rounded mountain top
36 mountain ridge (ridge)
37 mountain slope
38 hillside spring
39–47 high-mountain region
39 mountain range, a massif
40 summit (peak, top of the mountain)
41 shoulder
42 saddle
43 rock face (steep face)
44 gully
45 talus (scree, detritus)
46 bridle path
47 pass (col)
48–56 glacial ice
48 firn field (firn basin, nevé)
49 valley glacier
50 crevasse
51 glacier snout
52 subglacial stream
53 lateral moraine
54 medial moraine
55 end moraine
56 glacier table

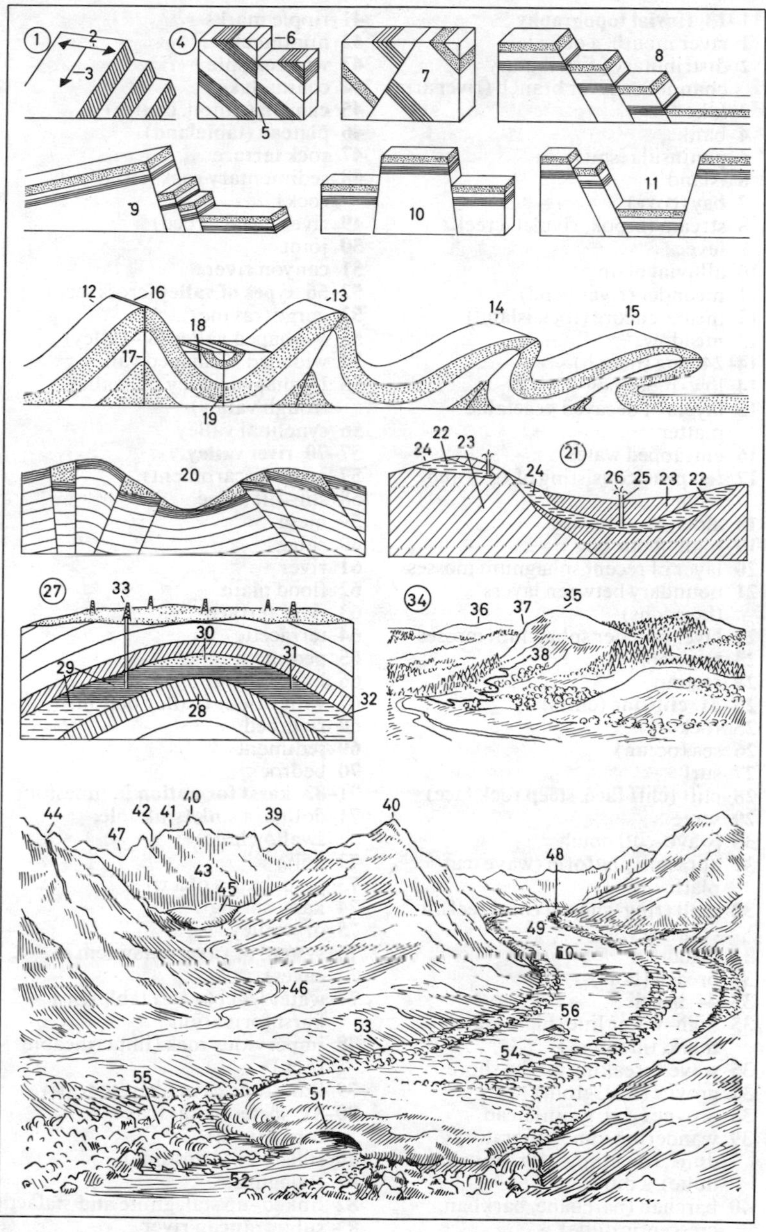
1
2
3
4
5
6
7
8
9
10
11
12
13
14
15
16
17
18
19
20
21
22
23
24
25
26
27
28
29
30
31
32
33
34
35
36
37
38
39
40
41
42
43
44
45
46
47
48
49
50
51
52
53
54
55
56

13 Physical Geography III

1–13 fluvial topography
1 river mouth, a delta
2 distributary (distributary channel), a river branch (river arm)
3 lake
4 bank
5 peninsula (spit)
6 island
7 bay (cove)
8 stream (brook, rivulet, creek)
9 levee
10 alluvial plain
11 meander (river bend)
12 meander core (rock island)
13 meadow
14–24 bog (marsh)
14 low-moor bog
15 layers of decayed vegetable matter
16 entrapped water
17 fen peat [consisting of rush and sedge]
18 alder-swamp peat
19 high-moor bog
20 layer of recent sphagnum mosses
21 boundary between layers (horizons)
22 layer of older sphagnum mosses
23 bog pool
24 swamp
25–31 cliffline (cliffs)
25 rock
26 sea (ocean)
27 surf
28 cliff (cliff face, steep rock face)
29 scree
30 [wave-cut] notch
31 abrasion platform (wave-cut platform)
32 atoll (ring-shaped coral reef), a coral reef
33 lagoon
34 breach (hole)
35–44 beach
35 high-water line (high-water mark, tidemark)
36 waves breaking on the shore
37 groyne (*Am.* groin)
38 groyne (*Am.* groin) head
39 wandering dune (migratory dune, travelling, *Am.* traveling, dune), a dune
40 barchan (barchane, barkhan, crescentic dune)
41 ripple marks
42 hummock
43 wind cripple
44 coastal lake
45 **canyon** (cañon, coulee)
46 plateau (tableland)
47 rock terrace
48 sedimentary rock (stratified rock)
49 river terrace (bed)
50 joint
51 canyon river
52–56 types of valley [cross section]
52 gorge (ravine)
53 V-shaped valley (V-valley)
54 widened V-shaped valley
55 U-shaped valley (U-valley, trough valley)
56 synclinal valley
57–70 river valley
57 scarp (escarpment)
58 slip-off slope
59 mesa
60 ridge
61 river
62 flood plain
63 river terrace
64 terracette
65 pediment
66 hill
67 valley floor (valley bottom)
68 riverbed
69 sediment
70 bedrock
71–83 karst formation in limestone
71 dolina, a sink (sinkhole, swallowhole)
72 polje
73 percolation of a river
74 karst spring
75 dry valley
76 system of caverns (system of caves)
77 water level (water table) in a karst formation
78 impervious rock (impermeable rock)
79 limestone cave (dripstone cave)
80–81 speleothems (cave formations)
80 stalactite (dripstone)
81 stalagmite
82 linked-up stalagmite and stalactite
83 subterranean river

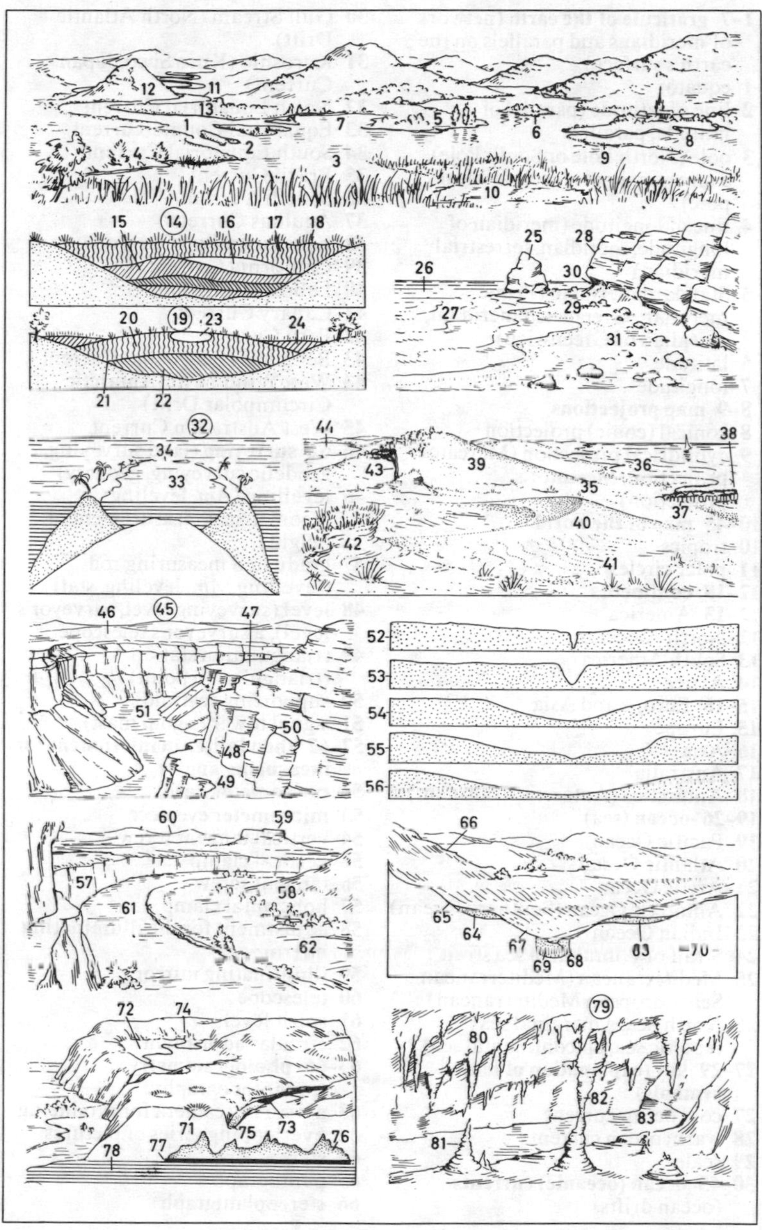

1
2
3
4
5
6
7
8
9
10
11
12
13
14
15
16
17
18
19
20
21
22
23
24
25
26
27
28
29
30
31
32
33
34
35
36
37
38
39
40
41
42
43
44
45
46
47
48
49
50
51
52
53
54
55
56
57
58
59
60
61
62
63
64
65
66
67
68
69
70
71
72
73
74
75
76
77
78
79
80
81
82
83

14 Map I

1–7 graticule of the earth (network of meridians and parallels on the earth's surface)
1 equator
2 line of latitude (parallel of latitude, parallel)
3 pole (North Pole or South Pole), a terrestrial pole (geographical pole)
4 line of longitude (meridian of longitude, meridian, terrestrial meridian)
5 Standard meridian (Prime meridian, Greenwich meridian, meridian of Greenwich)
6 latitude
7 longitude
8–9 map projections
8 conical (conic) projection
9 cylindrical projection (Mercator projection, Mercator's projection)
10–45 map of the world
10 tropics
11 polar circles
12–18 continents
12–13 America
12 North America
13 South America
14 Africa
15–16 Europe and Asia
15 Europe
16 Asia
17 Australia
18 Antarctica (Antarctic Continent)
19–26 ocean (sea)
19 Pacific Ocean
20 Atlantic Ocean
21 Arctic Ocean
22 Antarctic Ocean (Southern Ocean)
23 Indian Ocean
24 Strait of Gibraltar, a sea strait
25 Mediterranean (Mediterranean Sea, European Mediterranean)
26 North Sea, a marginal sea (epeiric sea, epicontinental sea)
27–29 key (explanation of map symbols)
27 cold ocean current
28 warm ocean current
29 scale
30–45 ocean (oceanic) currents (ocean drifts)
30 Gulf Stream (North Atlantic Drift)
31 Kuroshio (Kuro Siwo, Japan Current)
32 North Equatorial Current
33 Equatorial Countercurrent
34 South Equatorial Current
35 Brazil Current
36 Somali Current
37 Agulhas Current
38 East Australian Current
39 California Current
40 Labrador Current
41 Canary Current
42 Peru Current
43 Benguela (Benguella) Current
44 West Wind Drift (Antarctic Circumpolar Drift)
45 West Australian Current
46–62 surveying (land surveying, geodetic surveying, geodesy)
46 levelling (*Am.* leveling) (geometrical measurement of height)
47 graduated measuring rod (levelling, *Am.* leveling, staff)
48 level (surveying level, surveyor's level), a surveyor's telescope
49 triangulation station (triangulation point)
50 supporting scaffold
51 signal tower (signal mast)
52–62 theodolite, an instrument for measuring angles
52 micrometer head
53 micrometer eyepiece
54 vertical tangent screw
55 vertical clamp
56 tangent screw
57 horizontal clamp
58 adjustment for the illuminating mirror
59 illuminating mirror
60 telescope
61 spirit level
62 circular adjustment
63–66 photogrammetry (phototopography)
63 air survey camera for producing overlapping series of pictures
64 stereoscope
65 pantograph
66 stereoplanigraph

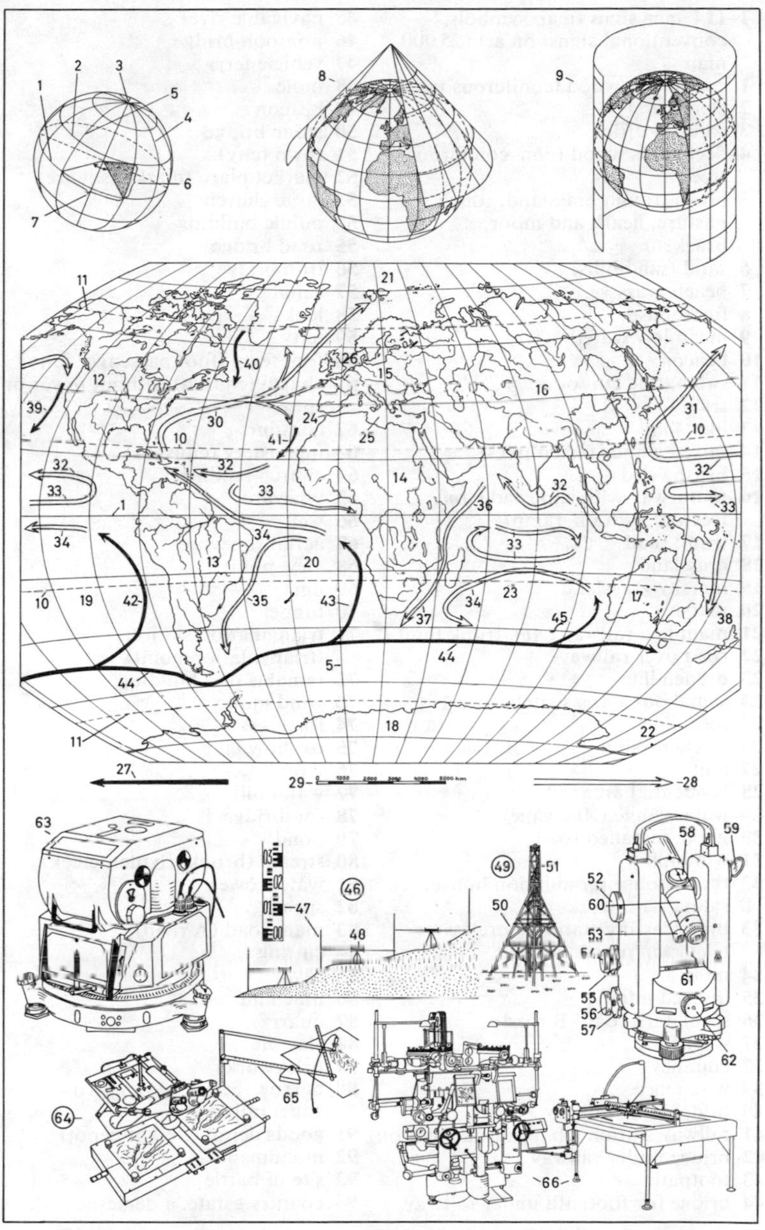
1
2
3
4
5
6
7
8
9
10
11
12
13
14
15
16
17
18
19
20
21
22
23
24
25
26
27
28
29
30
31
32
33
34
35
36
37
38
39
40
41
42
43
44
45
46
47
48
49
50
51
52
53
54
55
56
57
58
59
60
61
62
63
64
65
66
0 1000 2000 3000 4000 5000 km

15 Map II

1–114 map signs (map symbols, conventional signs) on a 1 : 25 000 map
1 coniferous wood (coniferous trees)
2 clearing
3 forestry office
4 deciduous wood (non–coniferous trees)
5 heath (rough grassland, rough pasture, heath and moor, bracken)
6 sand (sand hills)
7 beach grass
8 lighthouse
9 mean low water
10 beacon
11 submarine contours
12 train ferry
13 lightship
14 mixed wood (mixed trees)
15 brushwood
16 motorway with slip road (*Am.* freeway with on–ramp)
17 trunk road
18 grassland
19 marshy grassland
20 marsh
21 main line railway (*Am.* trunk line)
22 road over railway
23 branch line
24 signal box (*Am.* switch tower)
25 local line
26 level crossing
27 halt
28 residential area
29 water gauge (*Am.* gage)
30 good, metalled road
31 windmill
32 thorn house (graduation house, salina, salt–works)
33 broadcasting station (wireless or television mast)
34 mine
35 disused mine
36 secondary road (B road)
37 works
38 chimney
39 wire fence
40 bridge over railway
41 railway station (*Am.* railroad station)
42 bridge under railway
43 footpath
44 bridge for footpath under railway
45 navigable river
46 pontoon bridge
47 vehicle ferry
48 mole
49 beacon
50 stone bridge
51 town (city)
52 market place (market square)
53 large church
54 public building
55 road bridge
56 iron bridge
57 canal
58 lock
59 jetty
60 foot ferry (foot passenger ferry)
61 chapel (church) without tower or spire
62 contours
63 monastery (convent)
64 church landmark
65 vineyard
66 weir
67 aerial ropeway
68 view point
69 dam
70 tunnel
71 triangulation station (triangulation point)
72 remains of a building
73 wind pump
74 fortress
75 ox–bow lake
76 river
77 watermill
78 footbridge
79 pond
80 stream (brook, rivulet, creek)
81 water tower
82 spring
83 main road (A road)
84 cutting
85 cave
86 lime kiln
87 quarry
88 clay pit
89 brickworks
90 narrow–gauge (*Am.* narrow gage) railway
91 goods depot (freight depot)
92 monument
93 site of battle
94 country estate, a demesne

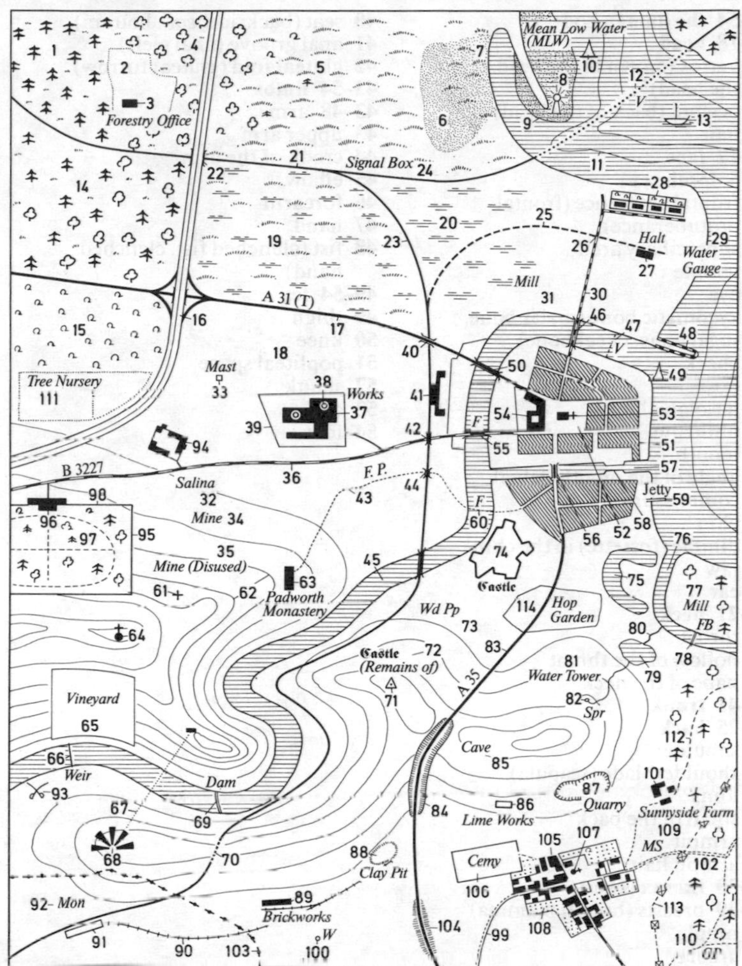

95 wall
96 stately home
97 park
98 hedge
99 poor or unmetalled road
100 well
101 farm
102 unfenced path (unfenced track)
103 district boundary
104 embankment
105 village
106 cemetery
107 church (chapel) with spire
108 orchard
109 milestone
110 guide post
111 tree nursery
112 ride (aisle, lane, section line)
113 electricity transmission line
114 hop garden

16 Man I

1–54 the human body
1–18 head
1 vertex (crown of the head, top of the head)
2 occiput (back of the head)
3 hair
4–17 face
4–5 forehead
4 frontal eminence (frontal protuberance)
5 superciliary arch
6 temple
7 eye
8 zygomatic bone (malar bone, jugal bone, cheekbone)
9 cheek
10 nose
11 nasolabial fold
12 philtrum
13 mouth
14 angle of the mouth (labial commissure)
15 chin
16 dimple (fossette) in the chin
17 jaw
18 ear
19–21 neck
19 throat
20 hollow of the throat
21 nape of the neck
22–41 trunk
22–25 back
22 shoulder
23 shoulderblade (scapula)
24 loins
25 small of the back
26 armpit
27 armpit hair
28–30 thorax (chest)
28–29 breasts (breast, mamma)
28 nipple
29 areola
30 bosom
31 waist
32 flank (side)
33 hip
34 navel
35–37 abdomen (stomach)
35 upper abdomen
36 abdomen
37 lower abdomen
38 groin
39 pudenda (vulva)
40 seat (backside, *coll.* bottom)
41 anal groove (anal cleft)
42 gluteal fold (gluteal furrow)
43–54 limbs
43–48 arm
43 upper arm
44 crook of the arm
45 elbow
46 forearm
47 hand
48 fist (clenched fist, clenched hand)
49–54 leg
49 thigh
50 knee
51 popliteal space
52 shank
53 calf
54 foot

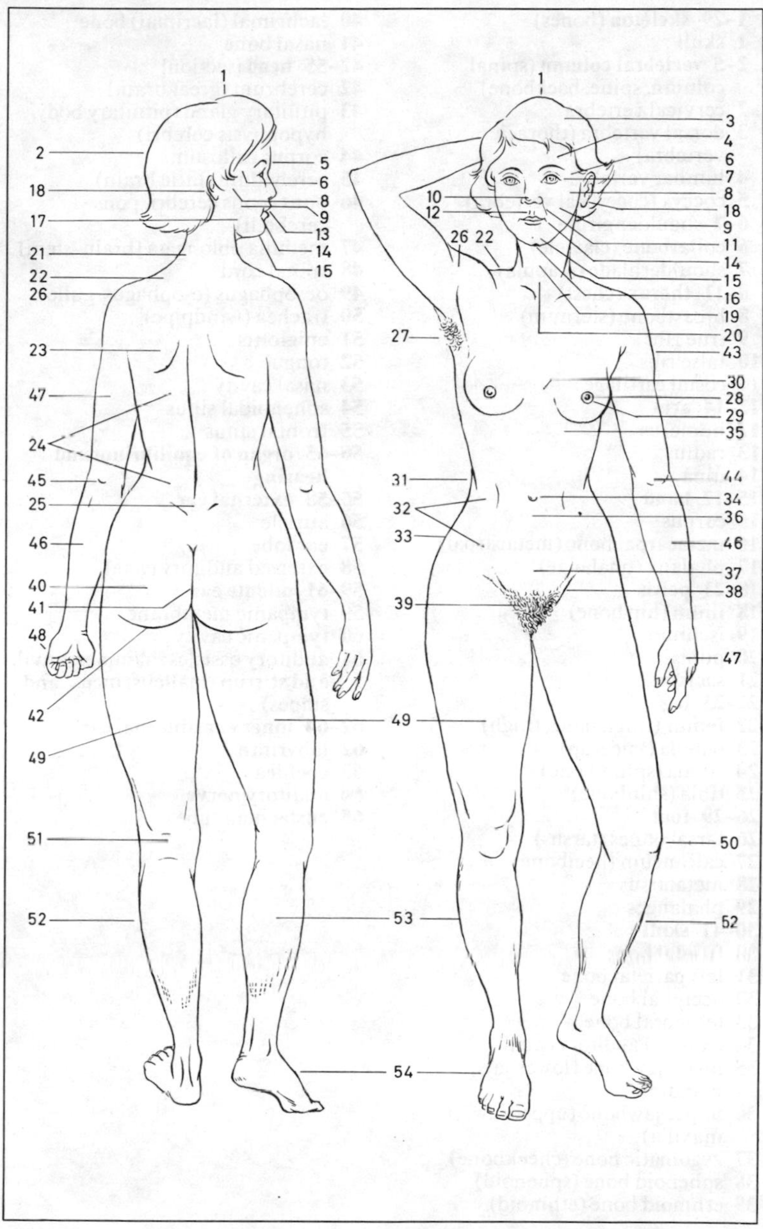
1
2
18
17
21
22
26
5
6
8
9
13
14
15
23
47
24
45
25
46
40
41
48
42
49
51
52
53
54
1
3
4
6
7
8
18
9
11
14
15
16
19
20
10
12
26 22
27
43
30
28
29
35
31
32
33
44
34
36
46
37
38
39
47
49
50
52

17 Man II

1–29 skeleton (bones)
1 skull
2–5 vertebral column (spinal column, spine, backbone)
2 cervical vertebra
3 dorsal vertebra (thoracic vertebra)
4 lumbar vertebra
5 coccyx (coccygeal vertebra)
6–7 shoulder girdle
6 collarbone (clavicle)
7 shoulderblade (scapula)
8–11 thorax (chest)
8 breastbone (sternum)
9 true ribs
10 false ribs
11 costal cartilage
12–14 arm
12 humerus
13 radius
14 ulna
15–17 hand
15 carpus
16 metacarpal bone (metacarpal)
17 phalanx (phalange)
18–21 pelvis
18 ilium (hip bone)
19 ischium
20 pubis
21 sacrum
22–25 leg
22 femur (thigh bone, thigh)
23 patella (kneecap)
24 fibula (splint bone)
25 tibia (shinbone)
26–29 foot
26 tarsal bones (tarsus)
27 calcaneum (heelbone)
28 metatarsus
29 phalanges
30–41 skull
30 frontal bone
31 left parietal bone
32 occipital bone
33 temporal bone
34 external auditory canal
35 lower jawbone (lower jaw, mandible)
36 upper jawbone (upper jaw, maxilla)
37 zygomatic bone (cheekbone)
38 sphenoid bone (sphenoid)
39 ethmoid bone (ethmoid)
40 lachrimal (lacrimal) bone
41 nasal bone
42–55 head [section]
42 cerebrum (great brain)
43 pituitary gland (pituitary body, hypophysis cerebri)
44 corpus callosum
45 cerebellum (little brain)
46 pons (pons cerebri, pons cerebelli)
47 medulla oblongata (brain-stem)
48 spinal cord
49 oesophagus (esophagus, gullet)
50 trachea (windpipe)
51 epiglottis
52 tongue
53 nasal cavity
54 sphenoidal sinus
55 frontal sinus
56–65 organ of equilibrium and hearing
56–58 external ear
56 auricle
57 ear lobe
58 external auditory canal
59–61 middle ear
59 tympanic membrane
60 tympanic cavity
61 auditory ossicles: hammer, anvil, and stirrup (malleus, incus, and stapes)
62–64 inner ear (internal ear)
62 labyrinth
63 cochlea
64 auditory nerve
65 eustachian tube

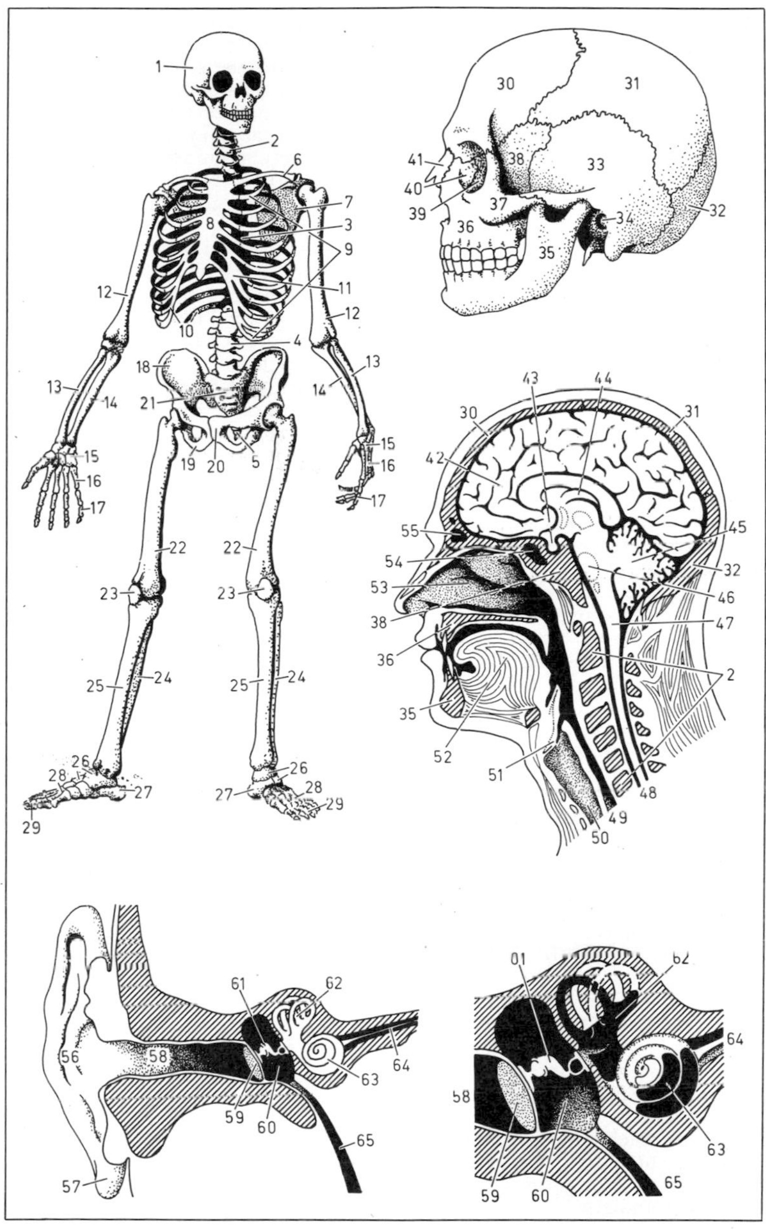
1
2
3
4
5
6
7
8
9
10
11
12
13
14
15
16
17
18
19
20
21
22
23
24
25
26
27
28
29
30
31
32
33
34
35
36
37
38
39
40
41
42
43
44
45
46
47
48
49
50
51
52
53
54
55
56
57
58
59
60
61
62
63
64
65

18 Man III

1–21 blood circulation (circulatory system)
1 common carotid artery, an artery
2 jugular vein, a vein
3 temporal artery
4 temporal vein
5 frontal artery
6 frontal vein
7 subclavian artery
8 subclavian vein
9 superior vena cava
10 arch of the aorta (aorta)
11 pulmonary artery [with venous blood]
12 pulmonary vein [with arterial blood]
13 lungs
14 heart
15 inferior vena cava
16 abdominal aorta (descending portion of the aorta)
17 iliac artery
18 iliac vein
19 femoral artery
20 tibial artery
21 radial artery
22–33 nervous system
22 cerebrum (great brain)
23 cerebellum (little brain)
24 medulla oblongata (brain-stem)
25 spinal cord
26 thoracic nerves
27 brachial plexus
28 radial nerve
29 ulnar nerve
30 great sciatic nerve [lying posteriorly]
31 femoral nerve (anterior crural nerve)
32 tibial nerve
33 peroneal nerve
34–64 musculature (muscular system)
34 sternocleidomastoid muscle (sternomastoid muscle)
35 deltoid muscle
36 pectoralis major (greater pectoralis muscle, greater pectoralis)
37 biceps brachii (biceps of the arm)
38 triceps brachii (triceps of the arm)
39 brachioradialis
40 flexor carpi radialis (radial flexor of the wrist)
41 thenar muscle
42 serratus anterior
43 obliquus externus abdominis (external oblique)
44 rectus abdominis
45 sartorius
46 vastus lateralis and vastus medialis
47 tibialis anterior
48 tendo calcanaeus (Achilles' tendon)
49 abductor hallucis (abductor of the hallux), a foot muscle
50 occipitalis
51 splenius of the neck
52 trapezius
53 infraspinatus
54 teres minor (lesser teres)
55 teres major (greater teres)
56 extensor carpi radialis longus (long radial extensor of the wrist)
57 extensor communis digitorum (common extensor of the digits)
58 flexor carpi ulnaris (ulnar flexor of the wrist)
59 latissimus dorsi
60 gluteus maximus
61 biceps femoris (biceps of the thigh)
62 gastrocnemius, medial and lateral heads
63 extensor communis digitorum (common extensor of the digits)
64 peroneus longus (long peroneus)

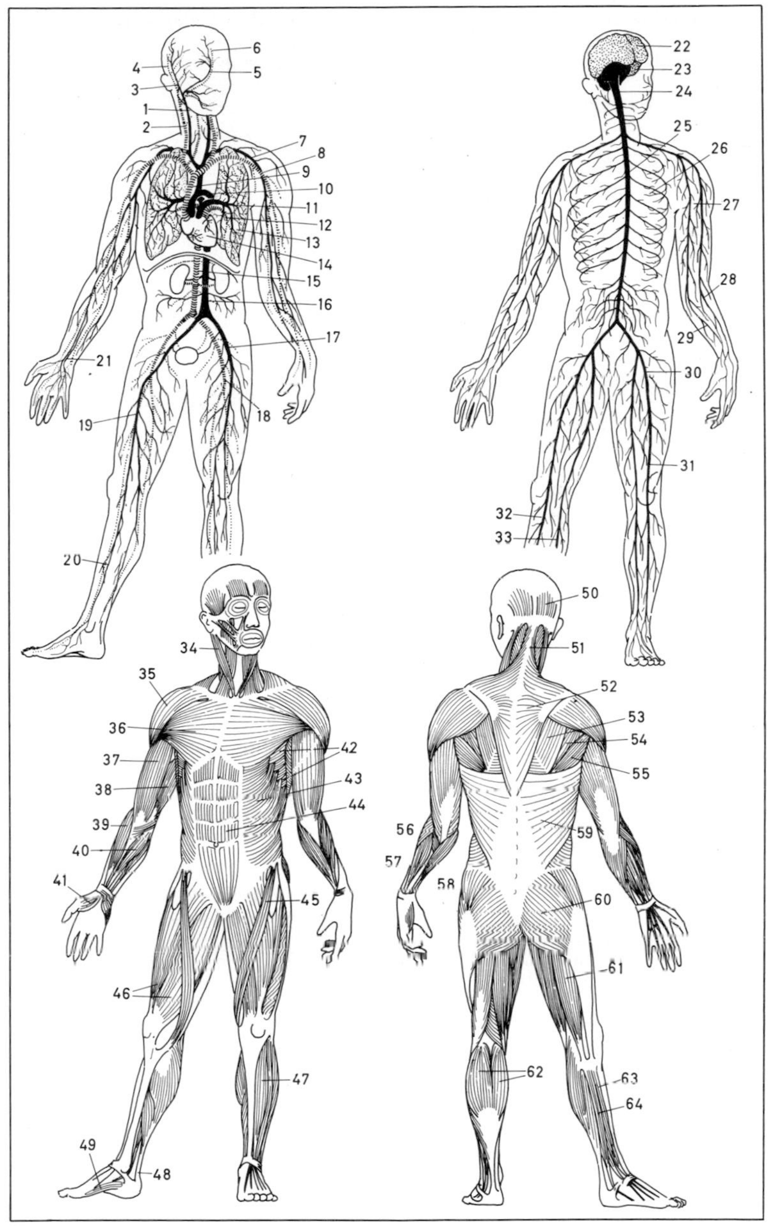
1
2
3
4
5
6
7
8
9
10
11
12
13
14
15
16
17
18
19
20
21
22
23
24
25
26
27
28
29
30
31
32
33
34
35
36
37
38
39
40
41
42
43
44
45
46
47
48
49
50
51
52
53
54
55
56
57
58
59
60
61
62
63
64

19 Man IV

1-13 head and neck
1 sternocleidomastoid muscle (sternomastoid muscle)
2 occipitalis
3 temporalis (temporal, temporal muscle)
4 occipito frontalis (frontalis)
5 orbicularis oculi
6 muscles of facial expression
7 masseter
8 orbicularis oris
9 parotid gland
10 lymph node (submandibular lymph gland)
11 submandibular gland (submaxillary gland)
12 muscles of the neck
13 Adam's apple (laryngeal prominence) [in men only]
14-37 mouth and throat
14 upper lip
15 gum
16-18 teeth (set of teeth)
16 incisors
17 canine tooth (canine)
18 premolar (bicuspid) and molar teeth (premolars and molars)
19 angle of the mouth (labial commissure)
20 hard palate
21 soft palate (velum palati, velum)
22 uvula
23 palatine tonsil (tonsil)
24 pharyngeal opening (pharynx, throat)
25 tongue
26 lower lip
27 upper jaw (maxilla)
28-37 tooth
28 periodontal membrane (periodontium, pericementum)
29 cement (dental cementum, crusta petrosa)
30 enamel
31 dentine (dentin)
32 dental pulp (tooth pulp, pulp)
33 nerves and blood vessels
34 incisor
35 molar tooth (molar)
36 root (fang)
37 crown
38-51 eye
38 eyebrow (supercilium)
39 upper eyelid (upper palpebra)
40 lower eyelid (lower palpebra)
41 eyelash (cilium)
42 iris
43 pupil
44 eye muscles (ocular muscles)
45 eyeball
46 vitreous body
47 cornea
48 lens
49 retina
50 blind spot
51 optic nerve
52-63 foot
52 big toe (great toe, first toe, hallux, digitus I)
53 second toe (digitus II)
54 third toe (digitus III)
55 fourth toe (digitus IV)
56 little toe (digitus minimus, digitus V)
57 toenail
58 ball of the foot
59 lateral malleolus (external malleolus, outer malleolus, malleolus fibulae)
60 medial malleolus (internal malleolus, inner malleolus, malleolus tibulae, malleolus medialis)
61 instep (medial longitudinal arch, dorsum of the foot, dorsum pedis)
62 sole of the foot
63 heel
64-83 hand
64 thumb (pollex, digitus I)
65 index finger (forefinger, second finger, digitus II)
66 middle finger (third finger, digitus medius, digitus III)
67 ring finger (fourth finger, digitus anularis, digitus IV)
68 little finger (fifth finger, digitus minimus, digitus V)
69 radial side of the hand
70 ulnar side of the hand
71 palm of the hand (palma manus)
72-74 lines of the hand
72 life line (line of life)
73 head line (line of the head)
74 heart line (line of the heart)
75 ball of the thumb (thenar eminence)
76 wrist (carpus)
77 phalanx (phalange)
78 finger pad
79 fingertip
80 fingernail (nail)
81 lunule (lunula) of the nail
82 knuckle
83 back of the hand (dorsum of the hand, dorsum manus)

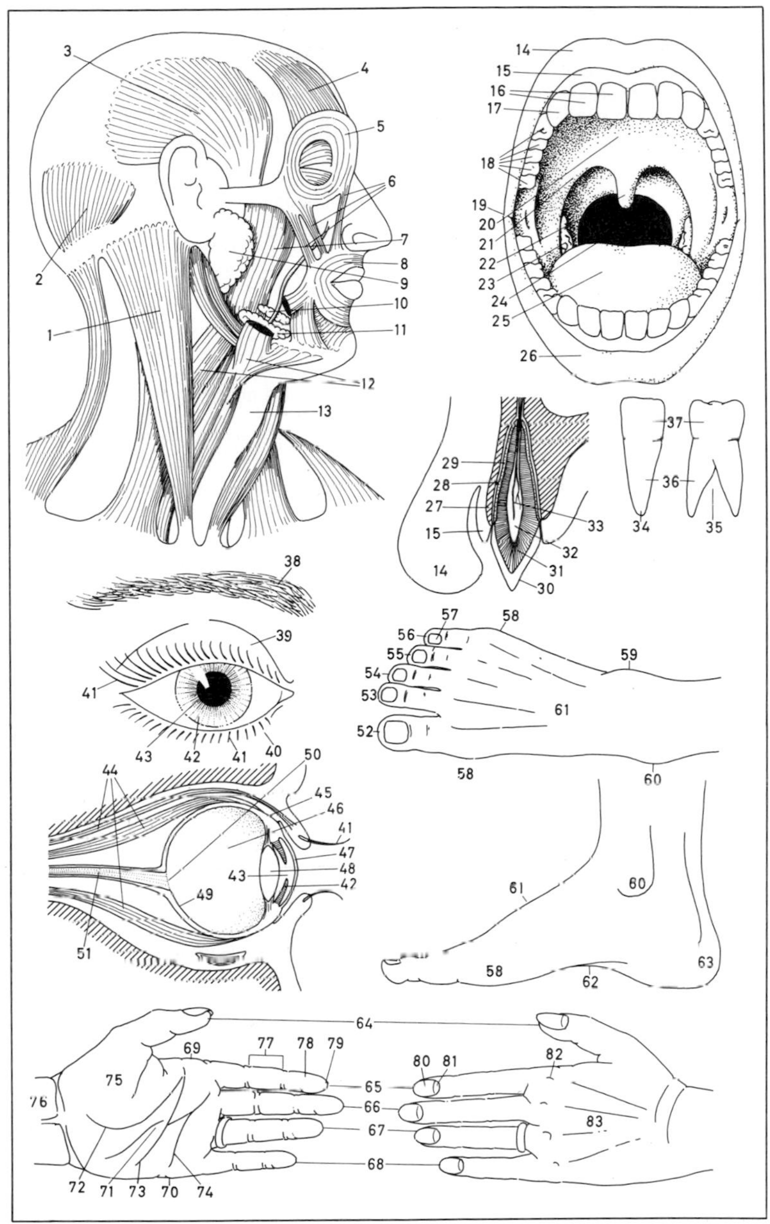
1
2
3
4
5
6
7
8
9
10
11
12
13
14
15
16
17
18
19
20
21
22
23
24
25
26
27
28
29
30
31
32
33
34
35
36
37
38
39
40
41
42
43
44
45
46
47
48
49
50
51
52
53
54
55
56
57
58
59
60
61
62
63
64
65
66
67
68
69
70
71
72
73
74
75
76
77
78
79
80
81
82
83

1-57 internal organs [front view]
1 thyroid gland
2–3 larynx
2 hyoid bone (hyoid)
3 thyroid cartilage
4 trachea (windpipe)
5 bronchus
6-7 lung
6 right lung
7 upper pulmonary lobe (upper lobe of the lung) [section]
8 heart
9 diaphragm
10 liver
11 gall bladder
12 spleen
13 stomach
14-22 intestines (bowel)
14-16 small intestine (intestinum tenue)
14 duodenum
15 jejunum
16 ileum
17-22 large intestine (intestinum crassum)
17 caecum (cecum)
18 appendix (vermiform appendix)
19 ascending colon
20 transverse colon
21 descending colon
22 rectum
23 oesophagus (esophagus, gullet)
24-25 heart
24 auricle
25 anterior longitudinal cardiac sulcus
26 diaphragm
27 spleen
28 right kidney
29 suprarenal gland
30-31 left kidney [longitudinal section]
30 calyx (renal calyx)
31 renal pelvis
32 ureter
33 bladder
34-35 liver [from behind]
34 falciform ligament of the liver
35 lobe of the liver
36 gall bladder
37-38 common bile duct
37 hepatic duct (common hepatic duct)
38 cystic duct
39 portal vein (hepatic portal vein)
40 oesophagus (esophagus, gullet)
41-42 stomach
41 cardiac orifice
42 pylorus
43 duodenum
44 pancreas
45-57 heart (longitudinal section]
45 atrium
46-47 valves of the heart
46 tricuspid valve (right atrioventricular valve)
47 bicuspid valve (mitral valve, left atrioventricular valve)
48 cusp
49 aortic valve
50 pulmonary valve
51 ventricle
52 ventricular septum (interventricular septum)
53 superior vena cava
54 aorta
55 pulmonary artery
56 pulmonary vein
57 inferior vena cava
58 peritoneum
59 sacrum
60 coccyx (coccygeal vertebra)
61 rectum
62 anus
63 anal sphincter
64 perineum
65 pubic symphisis (symphisis pubis)
66-77 male sex organs [longitudinal section]
66 penis
67 corpus cavernosum and spongiosum of the penis (erectile tissue of the penis)
68 urethra
69 glans penis
70 prepuce (foreskin)
71 scrotum
72 right testicle (testis)
73 epididymis
74 spermatic duct (vas deferens)
75 Cowper's gland (bulbourethral gland)
76 prostate (prostate gland)
77 seminal vesicle
78 bladder
79-88 female sex organs [longitudinal section]
79 uterus (matrix, womb)
80 cavity of the uterus
81 fallopian tube (uterine tube, oviduct)
82 fimbria (fimbriated extremity)
83 ovary
84 follicle with ovum (egg)
85 os uteri externum
86 vagina
87 lip of the pudendum (lip of the vulva)
88 clitoris

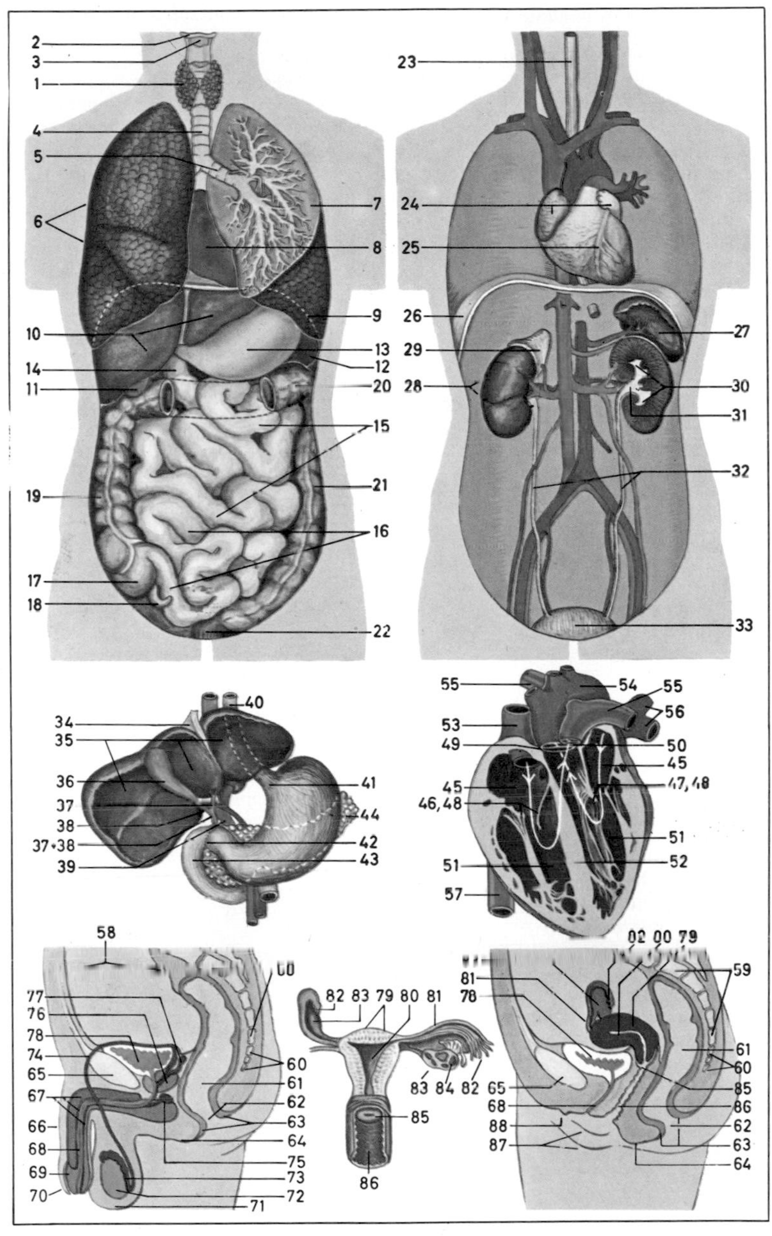

1
2
3
4
5
6
7
8
9
10
11
12
13
14
15
16
17
18
19
20
21
22
23
24
25
26
27
28
29
30
31
32
33
34
35
36
37
38
37+38
39
40
41
42
43
44
45
46, 48
47, 48
49
50
51
52
53
54
55
56
57
58
59
60
61
62
63
64
65
66
67
68
69
70
71
72
73
74
75
76
77
78
79
80
81
82
83
84
85
86
87
88

21 First Aid

1–13 emergency bandages
1 arm bandage
2 triangular cloth used as a sling (an arm sling)
3 head bandage (capeline)
4 first aid kit
5 first aid dressing
6 sterile gauze dressing
7 adhesive plaster (sticking plaster)
8 wound
9 bandage
10 emergency splint for a broken limb (fractured limb)
11 fractured leg (broken leg)
12 splint
13 headrest
14–17 measures for stanching the blood flow (tying up of, ligature of, a blood vessel)
14 pressure points of the arteries
15 emergency tourniquet on the thigh
16 walking stick used as a screw
17 compression bandage
18–23 rescue and transport of an injured person
18 Rautek grip (for rescue of victim of a car accident)
19 helper
20 injured person (casualty)
21 chair grip
22 carrying grip
23 emergency stretcher of sticks and a jacket
24–27 the positioning of an unconscious person and artificial respiration (resuscitation)
24 coma position
25 unconscious person
26 mouth-to-mouth resuscitation (*variation:* mouth-to-nose resuscitation)
27 resuscitator (respiratory apparatus, resuscitation apparatus), a respirator (artificial breathing device)
28–33 methods of rescue in ice accidents
28 person who has fallen through the ice
29 rescuer
30 rope
31 table (or similar device)
32 ladder
33 self-rescue
34–38 rescue of a drowning person
34 method of release (release grip, release) to free rescuer from the clutch of a drowning person
35 drowning person
36 lifesaver
37 chest grip, a towing grip
38 tired swimmer grip (hip grip)

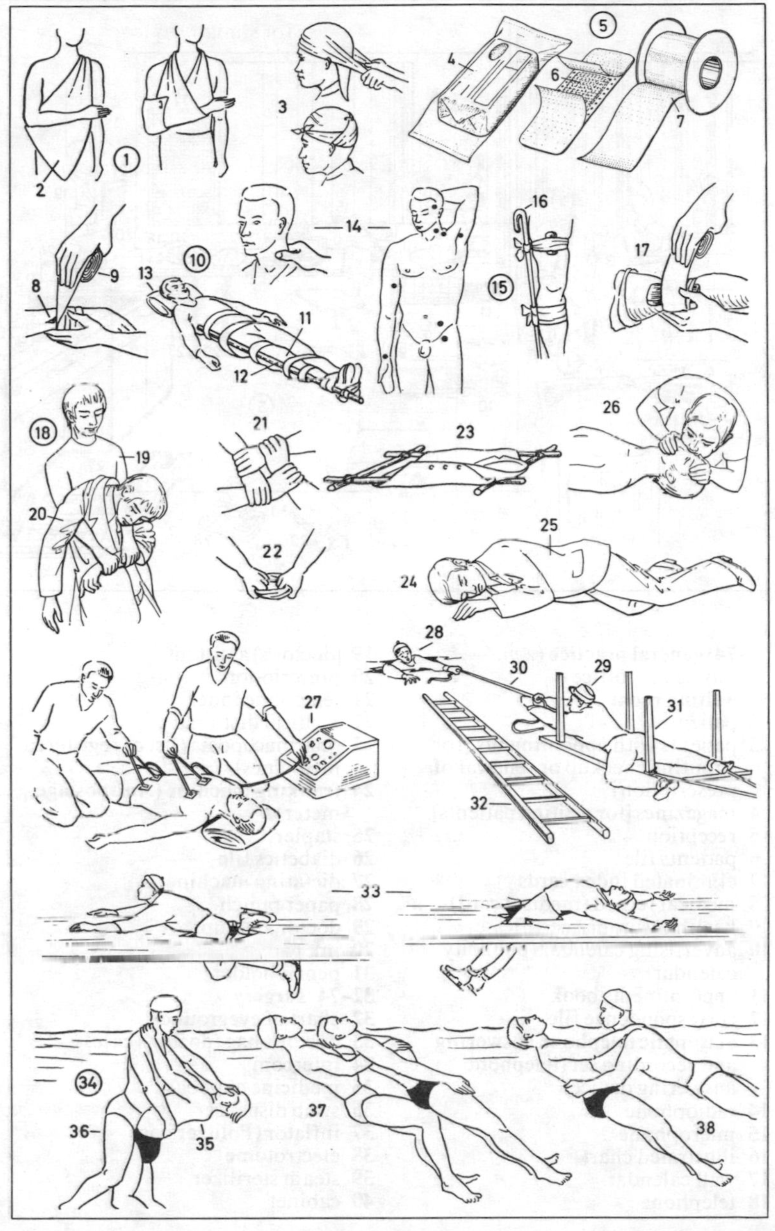
1
2
3
4
5
6
7
8
9
10
11
12
13
14
15
16
17
18
19
20
21
22
23
24
25
26
27
28
29
30
31
32
33
34
35
36
37
38

22 Doctor I

1–74 general practice (*Am.* physician's office)
1 waiting room
2 patient
3 patients with appointments (for a routine checkup or renewal of prescription)
4 magazines [for waiting patients]
5 reception
6 patients file
7 eliminated index cards
8 medical record (medical card)
9 health insurance certificate
10 advertising calendar (publicity calendar)
11 appointments book
12 correspondence file
13 automatic telephone answering and recording set (telephone answering device)
14 radiophone
15 microphone
16 illustrated chart
17 wall calendar
18 telephone
19 [doctor's] assistant
20 prescription
21 telephone index
22 medical dictionary
23 pharmacopoeia (list of registered medicines)
24 franking machine (*Am.* postage meter)
25 stapler
26 diabetics file
27 dictating machine
28 paper punch
29 doctor's stamp
30 ink pad
31 pencil holder
32–74 surgery
32 chart of eyegrounds
33 doctor's bag (doctor's case)
34 intercom
35 medicine cupboard
36 swab dispenser
37 inflator (Politzer bag)
38 electrotome
39 steam sterilizer
40 cabinet

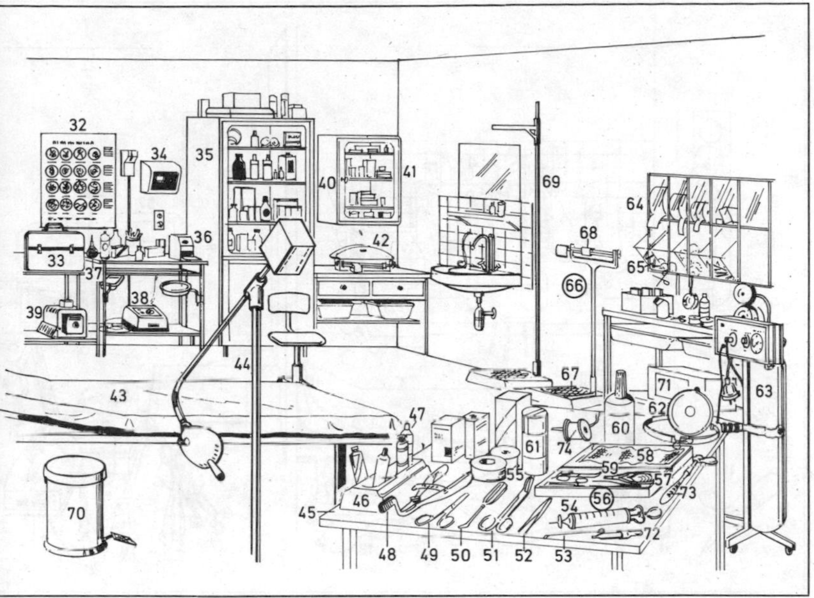

41 medicine samples
42 baby scales
43 examination couch
44 directional lamp
45 instrument table
46 tube holder
47 tube of ointment
48–50 instruments for minor surgery
48 mouth gag
49 Kocher's forceps
50 scoop (curette)
51 angled scissors
52 forceps
53 olive-pointed (bulb-headed) probe
54 syringe for irrigations of the ear or bladder
55 adhesive plaster (sticking plaster)
56 surgical suture material
57 curved surgical needle
58 sterile gauze
59 needle holder
60 spray for disinfecting the skin
61 thread container
62 ophthalmoscope
63 freezer for cryosurgery
64 dispenser for plasters and small pieces of equipment
65 disposable hypodermic needles and syringes
66 scales, sliding-weight scales
67 weighing platform
68 sliding weight (jockey)
69 height gauge (*Am.* gage)
70 waste bin (*Am.* trash bin)
71 hot-air sterilizer
72 pipette
73 percussor
74 aural speculum (auriscope, aural syringe)

23 Doctor II

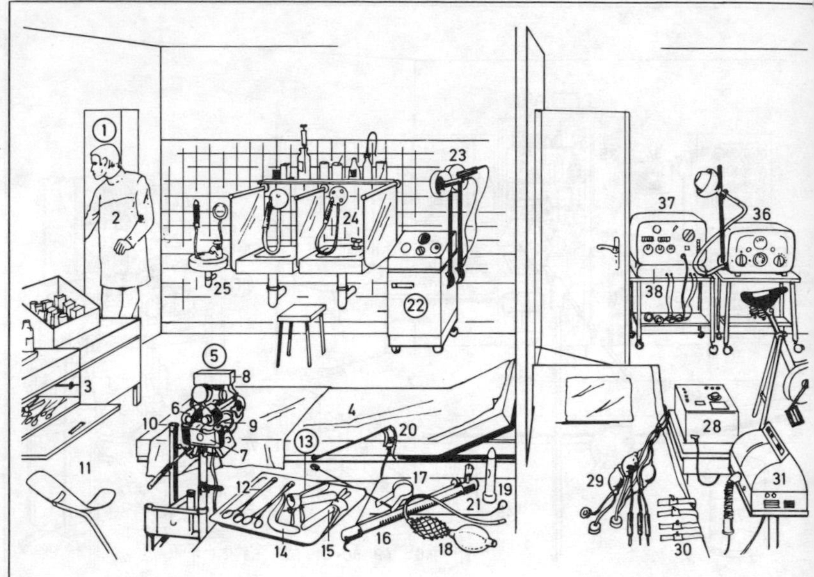

1 consulting room
2 general practitioner
3–21 instruments for gynecological and proctological examinations
3 warming the instruments up to body temperature
4 examination couch
5 colposcope
6 binocular eyepiece
7 miniature camera
8 cold light source
9 cable release
10 bracket for the leg support
11 leg support (leg holder)
12 holding forceps (sponge holder)
13 vaginal speculum
14 lower blade of the vaginal speculum
15 platinum loop (for smears)
16 rectoscope
17 biopsy forceps used with the rectoscope (proctoscope)
18 insufflator for proctoscopy (rectoscopy)
19 proctoscope (rectal speculum)
20 urethroscope
21 guide for inserting the proctoscope
22 diathermy unit (short-wave therapy apparatus)
23 radiator
24 inhaling apparatus (inhalator)
25 basin (for sputum)
26–31 ergometry
26 bicycle ergometer
27 monitor (visual display of the ECG and of pulse and respiratory rates when performing work)
28 ECG (electrocardiograph)
29 suction electrodes
30 strap-on electrodes for the limbs
31 spirometer (for measuring respiratory functions)
32 measuring the blood pressure

33 sphygmomanometer
34 inflatable cuff
35 stethoscope
36 microwave treatment unit
37 faradization unit (application of low-frequency currents with different pulse shapes)
38 automatic tuner
39 short-wave therapy apparatus
40 timer
41–59 laboratory
41 medical laboratory technician
42 capillary tube stand for blood sedimentation
43 measuring cylinder
44 automatic pipette
45 kidney dish
46 portable ECG machine for emergency use
47 automatic pipetting device
48 constant temperature water bath
49 tap with water jet pump
50 staining dish (for staining blood smears, sediments and other smears)
51 binocular research microscope
52 pipette stand for photometry
53 computer and analyser for photometry
54 photometer
55 potentiometric recorder
56 transforming section
57 laboratory apparatus (laboratory equipment)
58 urine sediment chart
59 centrifuge

24 Dentist

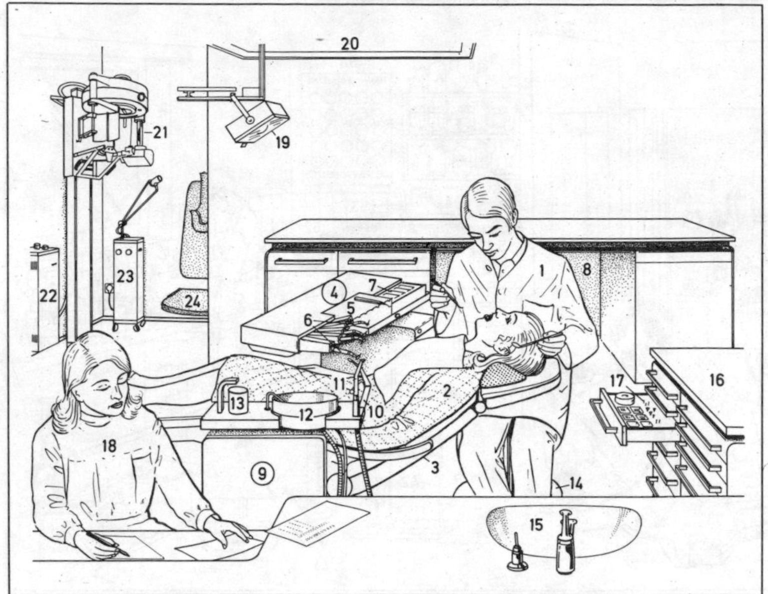

1 dentist (dental surgeon)
2 patient
3 dentist's chair
4 dental instruments
5 instrument tray
6 drills with different handpieces
7 medicine case
8 storage unit (for dental instruments)
9 assistant's unit
10 multi-purpose syringe (for cold and warm water, spray or air)
11 suction apparatus
12 basin
13 water glass, filled automatically
14 stool
15 washbasin
16 instrument cabinet
17 drawer for drills
18 dentist's assistant
19 dentist's lamp
20 ceiling light
21 X-ray apparatus for panoramic pictures
22 X-ray generator
23 microwave treatment unit, a radiation unit
24 seat
25 denture (set of false teeth)
26 bridge (dental bridge)
27 prepared stump of the tooth
28 crown (*kinds:* gold crown, jacket crown)
29 porcelain tooth (porcelain pontic)
30 filling
31 post crown
32 facing
33 diaphragm
34 post
35 carborundum disc (disk)
36 grinding wheel
37 burs
38 flame-shaped finishing bur
39 fissure burs
40 diamond point
41 mouth mirror
42 mouth lamp

43 cautery
44 platinum-iridium electrode
45 tooth scalers
46 probe
47 extraction forceps
48 tooth-root elevator
49 bone chisel
50 spatula
51 mixer for filling material
52 synchronous timer
53 hypodermic syringe for injection of local anaesthetic
54 hypodermic needle
55 matrix holder
56 impression tray
57 spirit lamp

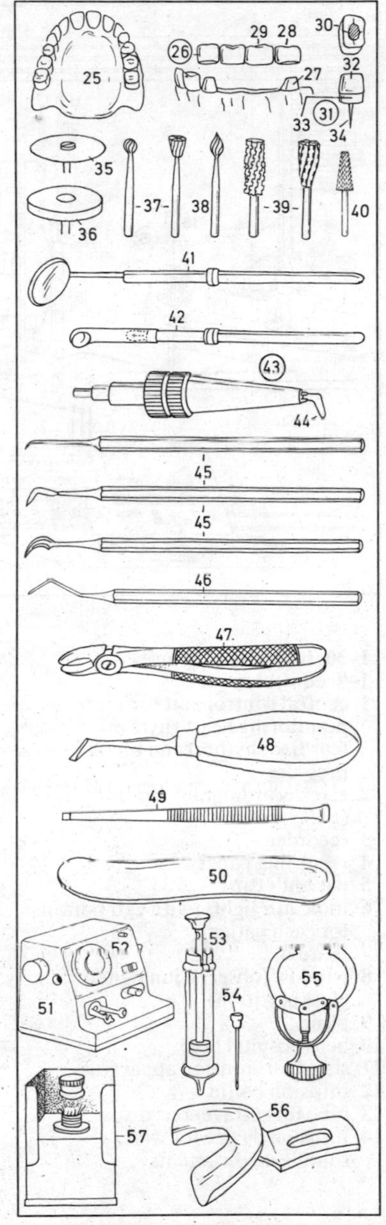

25 Hospital I

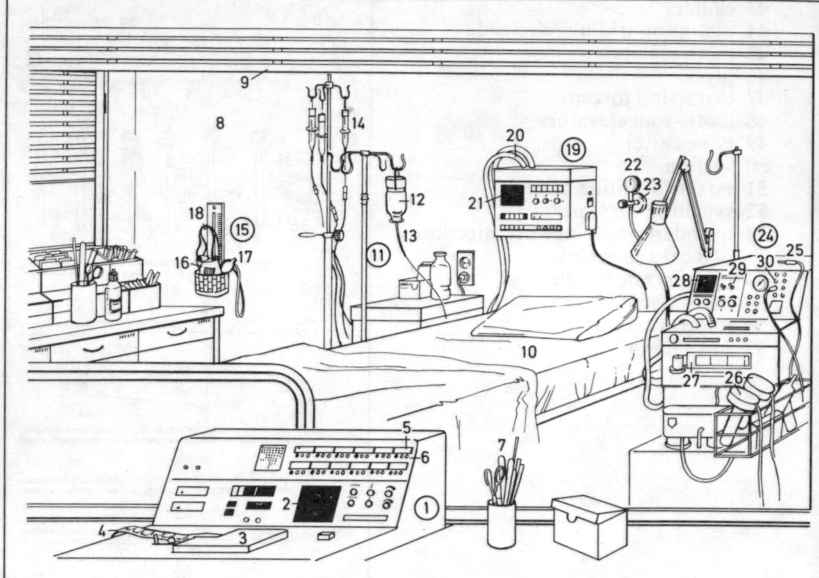

1–30 intensive care unit

1–9 control room

1 central control unit for monitoring heart rhythm (cardiac rhythm) and blood pressure
2 electrocardiogram monitor (ECG monitor)
3 recorder
4 recording paper
5 patient's card
6 indicator lights (with call buttons for each patient)
7 spatula
8 window (observation window, glass partition)
9 blind
10 bed (hospital bed)
11 stand for infusion apparatus
12 infusion bottle
13 tube for intravenous drips
14 infusion device for water-soluble medicaments
15 sphygmomanometer
16 cuff
17 inflating bulb
18 mercury manometer
19 bed monitor
20 connecting lead to the central control unit
21 electrocardiogram monitor (ECG monitor)
22 manometer for the oxygen supply
23 wall connection for oxygen treatment
24 mobile monitoring unit
25 electrode lead to the short-term pacemaker
26 electrodes for shock treatment
27 ECG recording unit
28 electrocardiogram monitor (ECG monitor)
29 control switches and knobs (controls) for adjusting the monitor

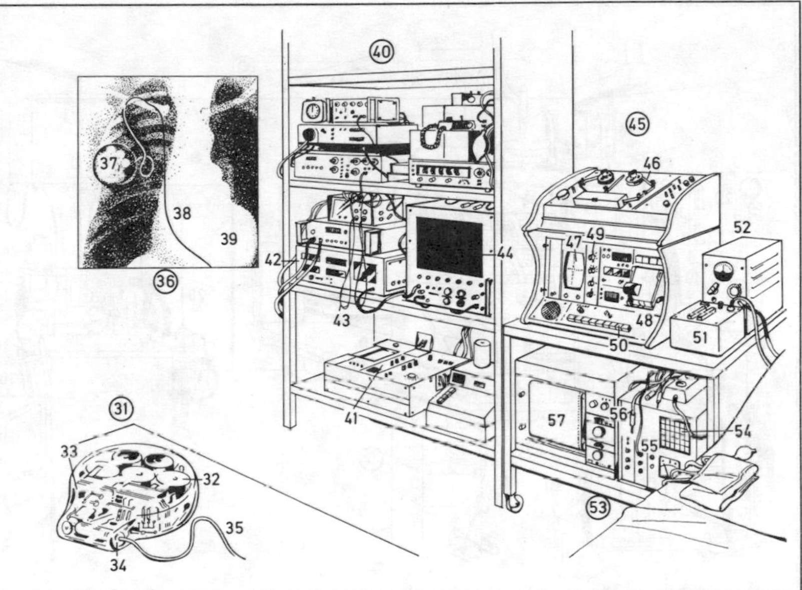

30 control buttons for the pacemaker unit
31 **pacemaker** (cardiac pacemaker)
32 mercury battery
33 programmed impulse generator
34 electrode exit point
35 electrode
36 implantation of the pacemaker
37 internal cardiac pacemaker (internal pacemaker, pacemaker)
38 electrode inserted through the vein
39 cardiac silhouette on the X-ray
40 **pacemaker control unit**
41 electrocardiograph (ECG recorder)
42 automatic impulse meter
43 ECG lead to the patient
44 monitor unit for visual monitoring of the pacemaker impulses
45 long-term ECG analyser
46 magnetic tape for recording the ECG impulses during analysis
47 ECG monitor
48 automatic analysis on paper of the ECG rhythm
49 control knob for the ECG amplitude
50 program selector switches for the ECG analysis
51 charger for the pacemaker batteries
52 battery tester
53 pressure gauge (*Am.* gage) for the right cardiac catheter
54 trace monitor
55 pressure indicator
56 connecting lead to the paper recorder
57 paper recorder for pressure traces

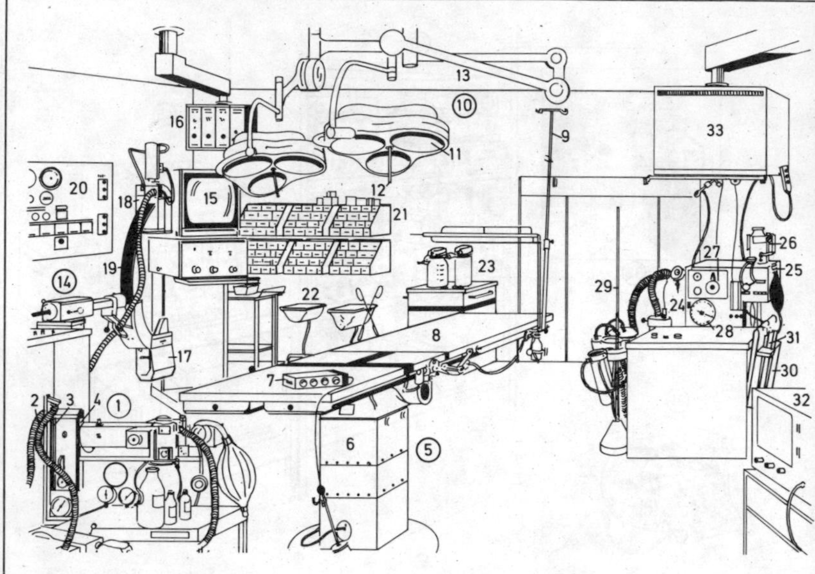

1-54 surgical unit
1-33 operating theatre (*Am.* theater)
1 anaesthesia and breathing apparatus (respiratory machine)
2 inhalers (inhaling tubes)
3 flowmeter for nitrous oxide
4 oxygen flow meter
5 pedestal operating table
6 table pedestal
7 control device (control unit)
8 adjustable top of the operating table
9 stand for intravenous drips
10 swivel-mounted shadow-free operating lamp
11 individual lamp
12 handle
13 swivel arm
14 mobile fluoroscope
15 monitor of the image converter
16 monitor [back]
17 tube
18 image converter
19 C-shaped frame
20 control panel for the air-conditioning
21 surgical suture material
22 mobile waste tray
23 containers for unsterile (unsterilized) pads
24 anaesthesia and respiratory apparatus
25 respirator
26 fluothane container (halothane container)
27 ventilation control knob
28 indicator with pointer for respiratory volume
29 stand with inhalers (inhaling tubes) and pressure gauges (*Am.* gages)
30 catheter holder
31 catheter in sterile packing

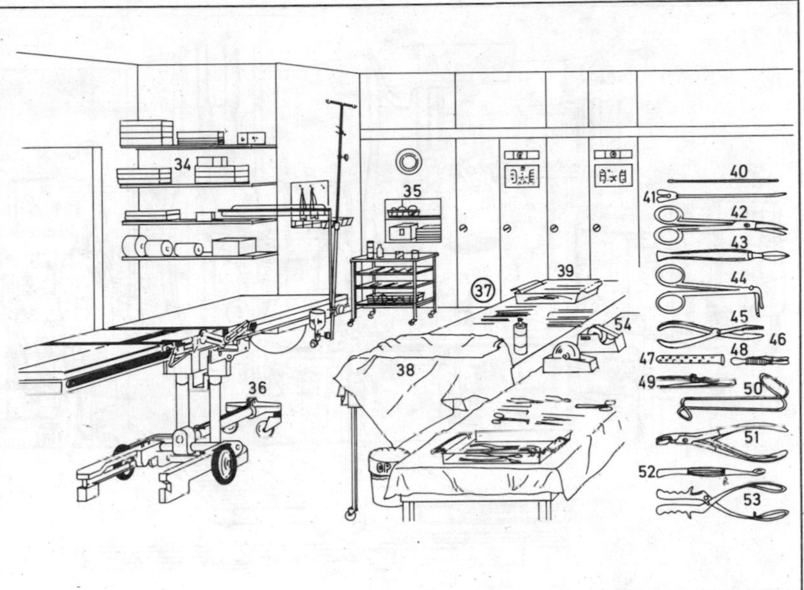

32 sphygmograph
33 monitor
34–54 preparation and sterilization room
34 dressing material
35 small sterilizer
36 carriage of the operating table
37 mobile instrument table
38 sterile cloth
39 instrument tray
40–53 surgical instruments
40 olive-pointed (bulb-headed) probe
41 hollow probe
42 curved scissors
43 scalpel (surgical knife)
44 ligature-holding forceps
45 sequestrum forceps
46 jaw
47 drainage tube
48 surgeon's tourniquet
49 artery forceps
50 blunt hook
51 bone nippers (bone-cutting forceps)
52 scoop (curette) for erasion (curettage)
53 obstetrical forceps
54 roll of plaster

27 Hospital III

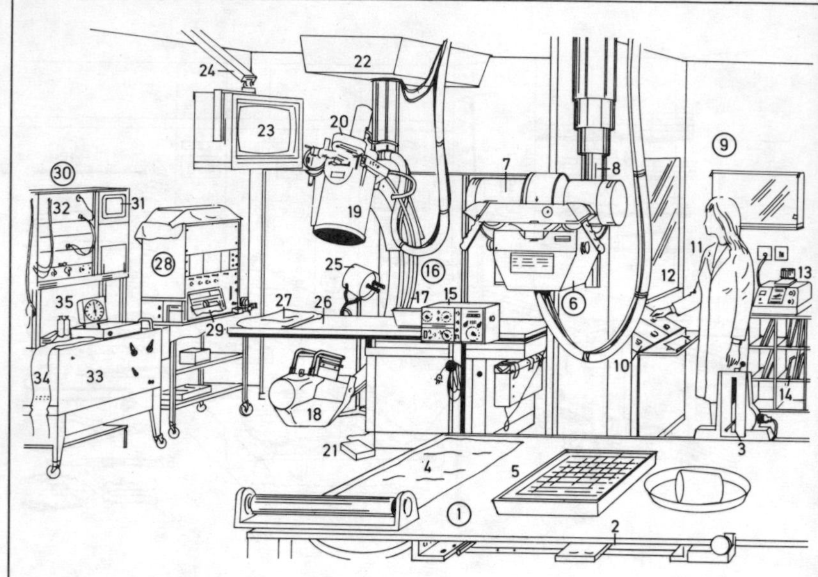

1–35 X-ray unit
1 X-ray examination table
2 support for X-ray cassettes
3 height adjustment of the central beam for lateral views
4 compress for pyelography and cholecystography
5 instrument basin
6 X-ray apparatus for pyelograms
7 X-ray tube
8 telescopic X-ray support
9 central X-ray control unit
10 control panel (control desk)
11 radiographer (X-ray technician)
12 window to the angiography room
13 oxymeter
14 pyelogram cassettes
15 contrast medium injector
16 X-ray image intensifier
17 C-shaped frame
18 X-ray head with X-ray tube
19 image converter with converter tube
20 film camera
21 foot switch
22 mobile mounting
23 monitor
24 swivel-mounted monitor support
25 operating lamp
26 angiographic examination table
27 pillow
28 eight-channel recorder
29 recording paper
30 catheter gauge (*Am.* gage) unit for catheterization of the heart
31 six-channel monitor for pressure graphs and ECG
32 slide-in units of the pressure transducer
33 paper recorder unit with developer for photographic recording
34 recording paper
35 timer

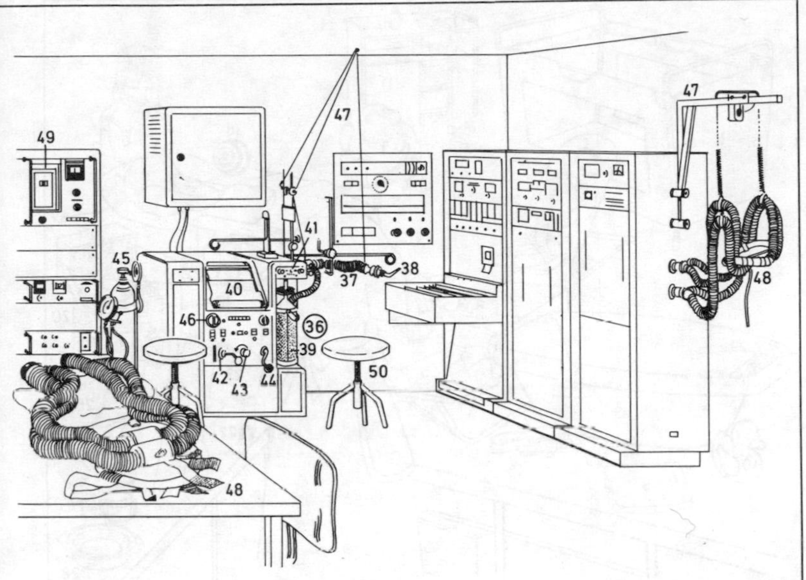

36–50 spirometry
36 spirograph for pulmonary function tests
37 breathing tube
38 mouthpiece
39 soda-lime absorber
40 recording paper
41 control knobs for gas supply
42 O_2-stabilizer
43 throttle valve
44 absorber attachment
45 oxygen cylinder
46 water supply
47 tube support
48 mask
49 CO_2 consumption meter
50 stool for the patient

28 Infant Care and Layette

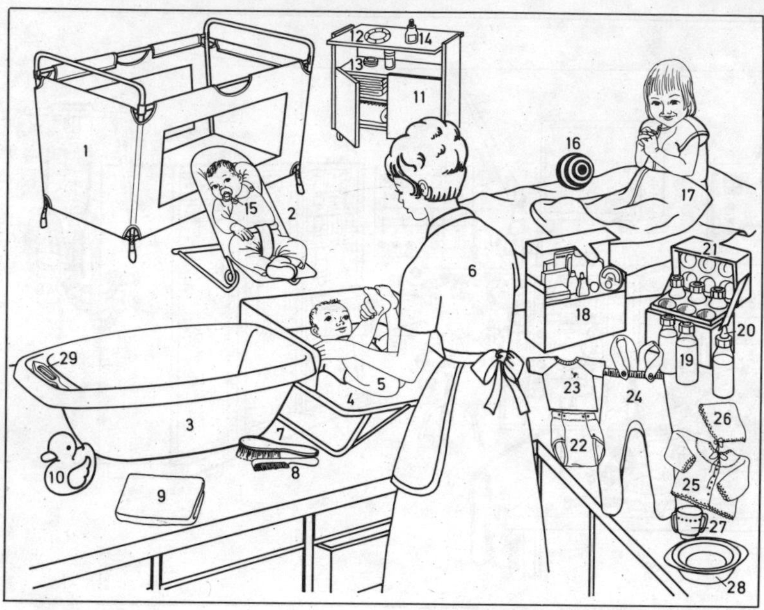

1 collapsible cot
2 bouncing cradle
3 baby bath
4 changing top
5 baby (new-born baby)
6 mother
7 hairbrush
8 comb
9 hand towel
10 toy duck
11 changing unit
12 teething ring
13 cream jar
14 box of baby powder
15 dummy
16 ball
17 sleeping bag
18 layette box
19 feeding bottle
20 teat
21 bottle warmer
22 rubber baby pants for disposable nappies (*Am.* diapers)
23 vest
24 leggings
25 baby's jacket
26 hood
27 baby's cup
28 baby's plate, a stay-warm plate
29 thermometer

30 bassinet, a wicker pram
31 set of bassinet covers
32 canopy
33 baby's high chair, a folding chair
34 pram (baby-carriage)[with windows]
35 folding hood
36 window
37 pushchair (*Am.* stroller)
38 foot-muff (*Am.* foot-bag)
39 play pen
40 floor of the play pen
41 building blocks (building bricks)
42 small child
43 bib
44 rattle (baby's rattle)
45 bootees
46 teddy bear
47 potty (baby's pot)
48 carrycot
49 window
50 handles

29 Children's Clothes

1–12 baby clothes
1 pram suit
2 hood
3 pram jacket (matinée coat)
4 pompon (bobble)
5 bootees
6 sleeveless vest
7 envelope-neck vest
8 wrapover vest
9 baby's jacket
10 rubber baby pants
11 playsuit
12 two-piece suit
13–30 infants' wear
13 child's sundress, a pinafore dress
14 frilled shoulder strap
15 shirred top
16 sun hat
17 one-piece jersey suit
18 front zip
19 catsuit (playsuit)
20 motif (appliqué)
21 romper
22 playsuit (romper suit)
23 coverall (sleeper and strampler)
24 dressing gown (bath robe)
25 children's shorts
26 braces (*Am.* suspenders)
27 children's T-shirt
28 jersey dress (knitted dress)
29 embroidery
30 children's ankle socks
31–47 school children's wear
31 raincoat (loden coat)
32 leather shorts (lederhosen)
33 staghorn button
34 braces (*Am.* suspenders)
35 flap
36 girl's dirndl
37 cross lacing
38 snow suit (quilted suit)
39 quilt stitching (quilting)
40 dungarees (bib and brace)
41 bib skirt (bib top pinafore)
42 tights
43 sweater (jumper)
44 pile jacket
45 leggings
46 girl's skirt
47 child's jumper
48–68 teenagers' clothes
48 girl's overblouse (overtop)
49 slacks
50 girl's skirt suit
51 jacket
52 skirt
53 knee-length socks
54 girl's coat
55 tie belt
56 girl's bag
57 woollen (*Am.* woolen) hat
58 girl's blouse
59 culottes
60 boy's trousers
61 boy's shirt
62 anorak
63 inset pockets
64 hood drawstring (drawstring)
65 knitted welt
66 parka coat (parka)
67 drawstring (draw cord)
68 patch pockets

1
2
3
4
5
6
7
8
9
10
11
12
13
14
15
16
17
18
19
20
21
22
23
24
25
26
27
28
29
30
31
32
33
34
35
36
37
38
39
40
41
42
43
44
45
46
47
48
49
50
51
52
53
54
55
56
57
58
59
60
61
62
63
64
65
66
67
68

30 Ladies' Wear I (Winter Wear)

1 mink jacket
2 cowl neck jumper
3 cowl collar
4 knitted overtop
5 turndown collar
6 turn-up (turnover) sleeve
7 polo neck jumper
8 pinafore dress
9 blouse with revers collar
10 shirt-waister dress, a button-through dress
11 belt
12 winter dress
13 piping
14 cuff
15 long sleeve
16 quilted waistcoat
17 quilt stitching (quilting)
18 leather trimming
19 winter slacks
20 striped polo jumper
21 boiler suit (dungarees, bib and brace)
22 patch pocket
23 front pocket
24 bib
25 wrapover dress (wrap-around dress)
26 shirt
27 peasant-style dress
28 floral braid
29 tunic (tunic top, tunic dress)
30 ribbed cuff
31 quilted design
32 pleated skirt
33 two-piece knitted dress
34 boat neck, a neckline
35 turn-up
36 kimono sleeve
37 knitted design
38 lumber-jacket
39 cable pattern
40 shirt-blouse
41 loop fastening
42 embroidery
43 stand-up collar
44 cossack trousers
45 two-piece combination (shirt top and long skirt)
46 tie (bow)
47 decorative facing
48 cuff slit
49 side slit
50 tabard
51 inverted pleat skirt
52 godet
53 evening gown
54 pleated bell sleeve
55 party blouse
56 party skirt
57 trouser suit (slack suit)
58 suede jacket
59 fur trimming
60 fur coat (*kinds:* Persian lamb, broadtail, mink, sable)
61 winter coat (cloth coat)
62 fur cuff (fur-trimmed cuff)
63 fur collar (fur-trimmed collar)
64 loden coat
65 cape
66 toggle fastenings
67 loden skirt
68 poncho-style coat
69 hood

1
2
3
4
5
6
7
8
9
10
11
12
13
14
15
16
17
18
19
20
21
22
23
24
25
26
27
28
29
30
31
32
33
34
35
36
37
38
39
40
41
42
43
44
45
46
47
48
49
50
51
52
53
54
55
56
57
58
59
60
61
62
63
64
65
66
67
68
69

31 Ladies' Wear II (Summer Wear)

1 skirt suit
2 jacket
3 skirt
4 inset pocket
5 decorative stitching
6 dress and jacket combination
7 piping
8 pinafore dress
9 summer dress
10 belt
11 two-piece dress
12 belt buckle
13 wrapover (wrap-around) skirt
14 pencil silhouette
15 shoulder buttons
16 batwing sleeve
17 overdress
18 kimono yoke
19 tie belt
20 summer coat
21 detachable hood
22 summer blouse
23 lapel
24 skirt
25 front pleat
26 dirndl (dirndl dress)
27 puffed sleeve
28 dirndl necklace
29 dirndl blouse
30 bodice
31 dirndl apron
32 lace trimming (lace), cotton lace
33 frilled apron
34 frill
35 smock overall
36 house frock (house dress)
37 poplin jacket
38 T-shirt
39 ladies' shorts
40 trouser turn-up
41 waistband
42 bomber jacket
43 stretch welt
44 Bermuda shorts
45 saddle stitching
46 frill collar
47 knot
48 culotte
49 twin set
50 cardigan
51 sweater
52 summer (lightweight) slacks
53 jumpsuit
54 turn-up
55 zip
56 patch pocket
57 scarf (neckerchief)
58 denim suit
59 denim waistcoat
60 jeans (denims)
61 overblouse
62 turned-up sleeve
63 stretch belt
64 halter top
65 knitted overtop
66 drawstring waist
67 short-sleeved jumper
68 V-neck (vee-neck)
69 turndown collar
70 knitted welt
71 shawl

1
2
3
4
5
6
7
8
9
10
11
12
13
14
15
16
17
18
19
20
21
22
23
24
25
26
27
28
29
30
31
32
33
34
35
36
37
38
39
40
41
42
43
44
45
46
47
48
49
50
51
52
53
54
55
56
57
58
59
60
61
62
63
64
65
66
67
68
69
70
71

32 Underwear, Nightwear

1–15 ladies' underwear (ladies' underclothes, lingerie)
1 brassière (bra)
2 pantie-girdle
3 pantie-corselette
4 longline brassière (longline bra)
5 stretch girdle
6 suspender
7 vest
8 pantie briefs
9 ladies' knee-high stocking
10 long-legged (long leg) panties
11 long pants
12 tights (pantie-hose)
13 slip
14 waist slip
15 bikini briefs
16–21 ladies' nightwear
16 nightdress (nightgown, nightie)
17 pyjamas (*Am.* pajamas)
18 pyjama top
19 pyjama trousers
20 housecoat
21 vest and shorts set [for leisure wear and as nightwear]
22–29 men's underwear (men's underclothes)
22 string vest
23 string briefs
24 front panel
25 sleeveless vest
26 briefs
27 trunks
28 short-sleeved vest
29 long johns
30 braces (*Am.* suspenders)
31 braces clip
32–34 men's socks
32 knee-length sock
33 elasticated top
34 long sock
35–37 men's nightwear
35 dressing gown
36 pyjamas (*Am.* pajamas)
37 nightshirt
38–47 men's shirts
38 casual shirt
39 belt
40 cravat
41 tie
42 knot
43 dress shirt
44 frill (frill front)
45 cuff
46 cuff link
47 bow-tie

1
2
3
4
5
6
7
8
9
10
11
12
13
14
15
16
17
18
19
20
21
22
23
24
25
26
27
28
29
30
31
32
33
34
35
36
37
38
39
40
41
42
43
44
45
46
47

33 Men's Wear

1-67 men's fashion
1 single-breasted suit, a men's suit
2 jacket
3 suit trousers
4 waistcoat (vest)
5 lapel
6 trouser leg with crease
7 dinner dress, an evening suit
8 silk lapel
9 breast pocket
10 dress handkerchief
11 bow-tie
12 side pocket
13 tailcoat (tails), evening dress
14 coat-tail
15 white waistcoat (vest)
16 white bow-tie
17 casual suit
18 pocket flap
19 front yoke
20 denim suit
21 denim jacket
22 jeans (denims)
23 waistband
24 beach suit
25 shorts
26 short-sleeved jacket
27 tracksuit
28 tracksuit top with zip
29 tracksuit bottoms
30 cardigan
31 knitted collar
32 men's short-sleeved pullover (men's short-sleeved sweater)
33 short-sleeved shirt
34 shirt button
35 turn-up
36 knitted shirt
37 casual shirt
38 patch pocket
39 casual jacket
40 knee-breeches
41 knee strap
42 knee-length sock
43 leather jacket
44 bib and brace overalls
45 adjustable braces (*Am.* suspenders)
46 front pocket
47 trouser pocket
48 fly
49 rule pocket
50 check shirt
51 men's pullover
52 heavy pullover
53 knitted waistcoat (vest)
54 blazer
55 jacket button
56 overall
57 trenchcoat
58 coat collar
59 coat belt
60 poplin coat
61 coat pocket
62 fly front
63 car coat
64 coat button
65 scarf
66 cloth coat
67 glove

1
2
3
4
5
6
7
8
9
10
11
12
13
14
15
16
17
18
19
20
21
22
23
24
25
26
27
28
29
30
31
32
33
34
35
36
37
38
39
40
41
42
43
44
45
46
47
48
49
50
51
52
53
54
55
56
57
58
59
60
61
62
63
64
65
66
67

34 Hairstyles and Beards

1–25 men's beards and hairstyles (haircuts)
1 long hair worn loose
2 allonge periwig (full-bottomed wig), a wig; *shorter and smoother:* bob wig, toupet
3 curls
4 bag wig (purse wig)
5 pigtail wig
6 queue (pigtail)
7 bow (ribbon)
8 handlebars (handlebar moustache, *Am.* mustache)
9 centre (*Am.* center) parting
10 goatee (goatee beard), chintuft
11 closely-cropped head of hair (crew cut)
12 whiskers
13 Vandyke beard (stiletto beard, bodkin beard), with waxed moustache (*Am.* mustache)
14 side parting
15 full beard (circular beard, round beard)
16 tile beard
17 shadow
18 head of curly hair
19 military moustache (*Am.* mustache) (English-style moustache)
20 partly bald head
21 bald patch
22 bald head
23 stubble beard (stubble, short beard bristles)
24 side-whiskers (sideboards, sideburns)
25 clean shave
26 Afro look (for men and women)
27–38 ladies' hairstyles (coiffures, women's and girls' hairstyles)
27 ponytail
28 swept-back hair (swept-up hair, pinned-up hair)
29 bun (chignon)
30 plaits (bunches)
31 chaplet hairstyle (Gretchen style)
32 chaplet (coiled plaits)
33 curled hair
34 shingle (shingled hair, bobbed hair)
35 pageboy style
36 fringe (*Am.* bangs)
37 earphones
38 earphone (coiled plait)

1
2
3
4
5
6
7
8
9
10
11
12
13
14
15
16
17
18
19
20
21
22
23
24
25
26
27
28
29
30
31
32
33
34
35
36
37
38

35 Headgear

1–21 ladies' hats and caps
1 milliner making a hat
2 hood
3 block
4 decorative pieces
5 sombrero
6 mohair hat with feathers
7 model hat with fancy appliqué
8 linen cap (jockey cap)
9 hat made of thick candlewick yarn
10 woollen (*Am.* woolen) hat (knitted hat)
11 mohair hat
12 cloche with feathers
13 large men's hat made of sisal with corded ribbon
14 trilby-style hat with fancy ribbon
15 soft felt hat
16 Panama hat with scarf
17 peaked mink cap
18 mink hat
19 fox hat with leather top
20 mink cap
21 slouch hat trimmed with flowers

22–40 men's hats and caps
22 trilby hat (trilby)
23 loden hat (Alpine hat)
24 felt hat with tassels (Tyrolean hat, Tyrolese hat)
25 corduroy cap
26 woollen (*Am.* woolen) hat
27 beret
28 bowler hat
29 peaked cap (yachting cap)
30 sou'wester (southwester)
31 fox cap with earflaps
32 leather cap with fur flaps
33 musquash cap
34 astrakhan cap, a real or imitation astrakhan cap
35 boater
36 (grey, *Am.* gray, or black) top hat made of silk taffeta; *collapsible:* crush hat (opera hat, claque)
37 sun hat (lightweight hat) made of cloth with small patch pocket
38 wide-brimmed hat
39 toboggan cap (skiing cap, ski cap)
40 workman's cap

36 Jewellery (*Am.* Jewelry)

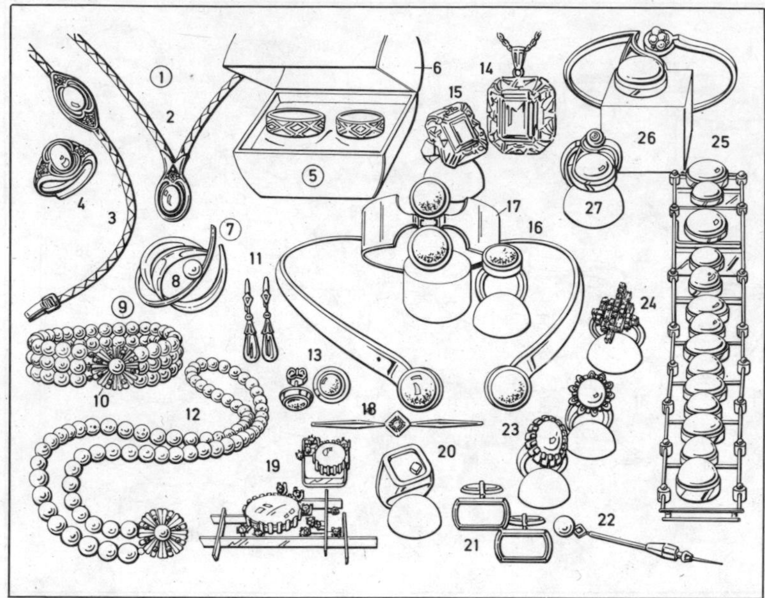

1 set of jewellery (*Am.* jewelry)
2 necklace
3 bracelet
4 ring
5 wedding rings
6 wedding ring box
7 brooch, a pearl brooch
8 pearl
9 cultured pearl bracelet
10 clasp, a white gold clasp
11 pendant earrings (drop earrings)
12 cultured pearl necklace
13 earrings
14 gemstone pendant
15 gemstone ring
16 choker (collar, neckband)
17 bangle
18 diamond pin
19 modern-style brooches
20 man's ring
21 cuff links
22 tiepin
23 diamond ring with pearl
24 modern-style diamond ring
25 gemstone bracelet
26 asymmetrical bangle
27 asymmetrical ring
28 ivory necklace
29 ivory rose
30 ivory brooch
31 jewel box (jewel case)
32 pearl necklace
33 bracelet watch
34 coral necklace
35 charms
36 coin bracelet
37 gold coin
38 coin setting
39 link
40 signet ring
41 engraving (monogram)
42–86 cuts and forms

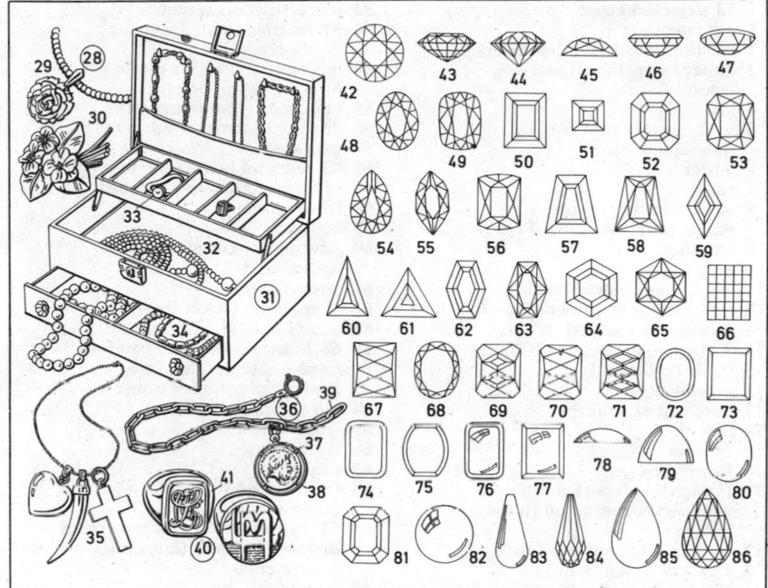

42–71 faceted stones
42–43 standard round cut
44 brilliant cut
45 rose cut
46 flat table
47 table en cabochon
48 standard cut
49 standard antique cut
50 rectangular step-cut
51 square step-cut
52 octagonal step-cut
53 octagonal cross-cut
54 standard pear-shape (pendeloque)
55 marquise (navette)
56 standard barrel-shape
57 trapezium step-cut
58 trapezium cross-cut
59 rhombus step-cut
60–61 triangular step-cut
62 hexagonal step-cut
63 oval hexagonal cross-cut
64 round hexagonal step-cut
65 round hexagonal cross-cut
66 chequer-board cut
67 triangle cut
68–71 fancy cuts
72–77 ring gemstones
72 oval flat table
73 rectangular flat table
74 octagonal flat table
75 barrel-shape
76 antique table en cabochon
77 rectangular table en cabochon
78–81 cabochons
78 round cabochon (simple cabochon)
79 high dome (high cabochon)
80 oval cabochon
81 octagonal cabochon
82–86 spheres and pear-shapes
82 plain sphere
83 plain pear-shape
84 faceted pear-shape
85 plain drop
86 faceted briolette

37 Types of Dwelling

1-53 detached house
1 basement
2 ground floor (*Am.* first floor)
3 upper floor (first floor, *Am.* second floor)
4 loft
5 roof, a gable roof (saddle roof, saddleback roof)
6 gutter
7 ridge
8 verge with bargeboards
9 eaves, rafter-supported eaves
10 chimney
11 gutter
12 swan's neck (swan-neck)
13 rainwater pipe (downpipe, *Am.* downspout, leader)
14 vertical pipe, a cast-iron pipe
15 gable (gable end)
16 glass wall
17 base course (plinth)
18 balcony
19 parapet
20 flower box
21 French window (French windows) opening on to the balcony
22 double casement window
23 single casement window
24 window breast with window sill
25 lintel (window head)
26 reveal
27 cellar window (basement window)
28 rolling shutter
29 rolling shutter frame
30 window shutter (folding shutter)
31 shutter catch
32 garage with tool shed
33 espalier
34 batten door (ledged door)
35 fanlight with mullion and transom
36 terrace
37 garden wall with coping stones
38 garden light
39 steps
40 rockery (rock garden)
41 outside tap (*Am.* faucet) for the hose
42 garden hose
43 lawn sprinkler
44 paddling pool
45 stepping stones
46 sunbathing area (lawn)
47 deck-chair
48 sunshade (garden parasol)
49 garden chair
50 garden table
51 frame for beating carpets
52 garage driveway
53 fence, a wooden fence
54-57 housing estate (housing development)
54 house on a housing estate (on a housing development)
55 pent roof (penthouse roof)
56 dormer (dormer window)
57 garden
58-63 terraced house [one of a row of terraced houses], **stepped**
58 front garden
59 hedge
60 pavement (*Am.* sidewalk, walkway)
61 street (road)
62 street lamp (street light)
63 litter bin (*Am.* litter basket)
64-68 house divided into two flats (*Am.* house divided into two apartments, duplex house)
64 hip (hipped) roof
65 front door
66 front steps
67 canopy
68 flower window (window for house plants)
69-71 pair of semi-detached houses divided into flour flats (*Am.* apartments)
69 balcony
70 sun lounge (*Am.* sun parlor)
71 awning (sun blind, sunshade)
72-76 block of flats (*Am.* apartment building, apartment house) with access balconies
72 staircase
73 balcony
74 studio flat (*Am.* studio apartment)
75 sun roof, a sun terrace
76 open space
77-81 multi-storey block of flats (*Am.* multistory apartment building, multistory apartment house)
77 flat roof
78 pent roof (shed roof, lean-to roof)
79 garage
80 pergola
81 staircase window
82 high-rise block of flats (*Am.* high-rise apartment building, high-rise apartment house)
83 penthouse
84-86 weekend house, a timber house
84 horizontal boarding
85 natural stone base course (natural stone plinth)
86 strip windows (ribbon windows)

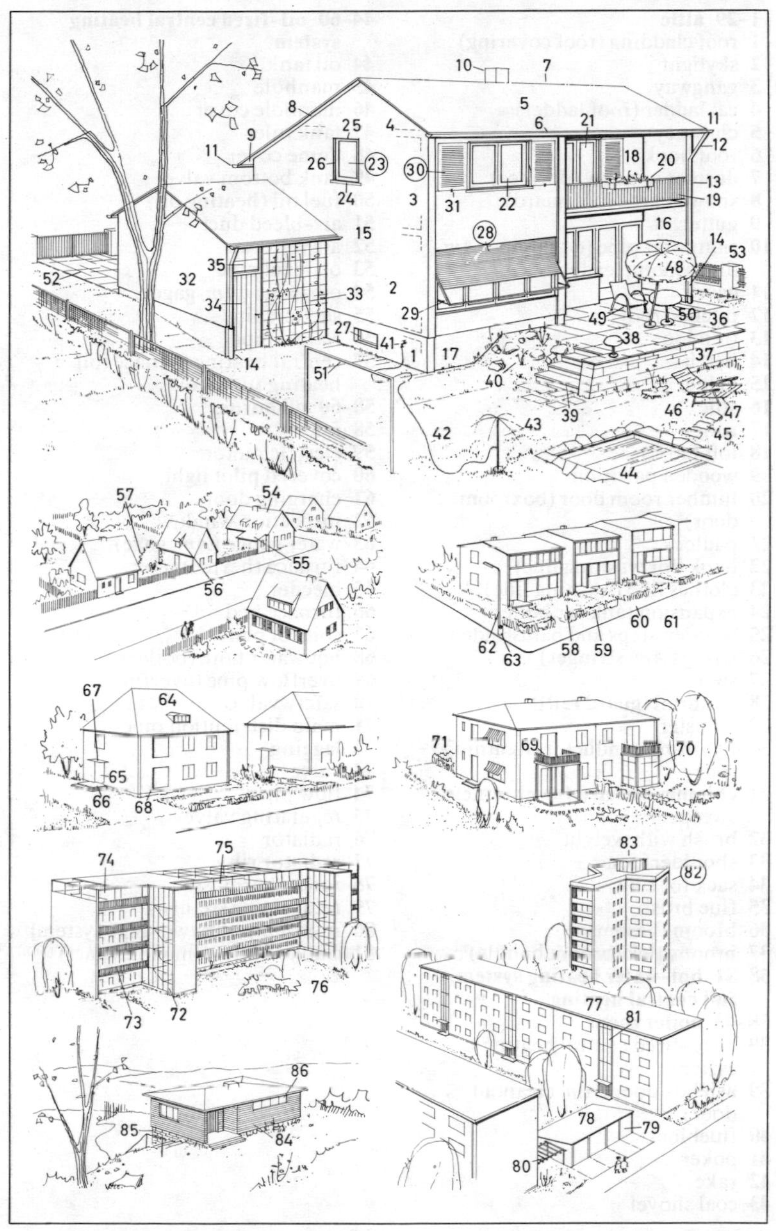
1
2
3
4
5
6
7
8
9
10
11
12
13
14
15
16
17
18
19
20
21
22
23
24
25
26
27
28
29
30
31
32
33
34
35
36
37
38
39
40
41
42
43
44
45
46
47
48
49
50
51
52
53
54
55
56
57
58
59
60
61
62
63
64
65
66
67
68
69
70
71
72
73
74
75
76
77
78
79
80
81
82
83
84
85
86

38 Roof and Boiler Room

1–29 attic
1 roof cladding (roof covering)
2 skylight
3 gangway
4 cat ladder (roof ladder)
5 chimney
6 roof hook
7 dormer window (dormer)
8 snow guard (roof guard)
9 gutter
10 rainwater pipe (downpipe, *Am.* downspout, leader)
11 eaves
12 pitched roof
13 trapdoor
14 hatch
15 ladder
16 stile
17 rung
18 loft (attic)
19 wooden partition
20 lumber room door (boxroom door)
21 padlock
22 hook [for washing line]
23 clothes line (washing line)
24 expansion tank for boiler
25 wooden steps and balustrade
26 string (*Am.* stringer)
27 step
28 handrail (guard rail)
29 baluster
30 lightning conductor (lightning rod)
31 **chimney sweep** (*Am.* chimney sweeper)
32 brush with weight
33 shoulder iron
34 sack for soot
35 flue brush
36 broom (besom)
37 broomstick (broom handle)
38–81 hot-water heating system, full central heating
38–43 boiler room
38 coke-fired central heating system
39 ash box door (*Am.* cleanout door)
40 flueblock
41 poker
42 rake
43 coal shovel
44–60 oil-fired central heating system
44 oil tank
45 manhole
46 manhole cover
47 tank inlet
48 dome cover
49 tank bottom valve
50 fuel oil (heating oil)
51 air-bleed duct
52 air vent cap
53 oil level pipe
54 oil gauge (*Am.* gage)
55 suction pipe
56 return pipe
57 central heating furnace (oil heating furnace)
58–60 oil burner
58 fan
59 electric motor
60 covered pilot light
61 charging door
62 inspection window
63 water gauge (*Am.* gage)
64 furnace thermometer
65 bleeder
66 furnace bed
67 control panel
68 hot water tank (boiler)
69 overflow pipe (overflow)
70 safety valve
71 main distribution pipe
72 lagging
73 valve
74 flow pipe
75 regulating valve
76 radiator
77 radiator rib
78 room thermostat
79 return pipe (return)
80 return pipe [in two-pipe system]
81 smoke outlet (smoke extract)

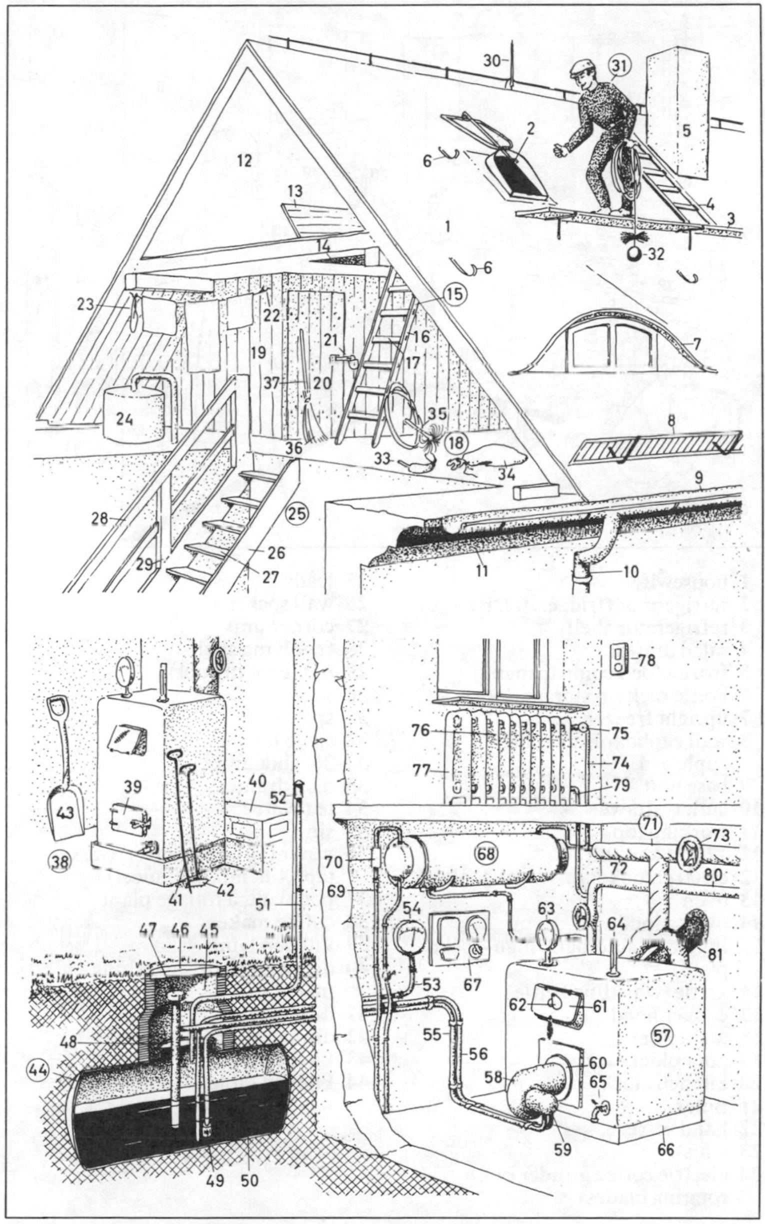

1
2
3
4
5
6
7
8
9
10
11
12
13
14
15
16
17
18
19
20
21
22
23
24
25
26
27
28
29
30
31
32
33
34
35
36
37
38
39
40
41
42
43
44
45
46
47
48
49
50
51
52
53
54
55
56
57
58
59
60
61
62
63
64
65
66
67
68
69
70
71
72
73
74
75
76
77
78
79
80
81

39 Kitchen

1 housewife
2 refrigerator (fridge, *Am.* icebox)
3 refrigerator shelf
4 salad drawer
5 frozen food compartment
6 bottle rack (in storage door)
7 upright freezer
8 wall cupboard, a kitchen cupboard
9 base unit
10 cutlery drawer
11 working top
12–17 cooker unit
12 electric cooker (*also:* gas cooker)
13 oven
14 oven window
15 hotplate (automatic high-speed plate)
16 kettle (whistling kettle)
17 cooker hood
18 pot holder
19 pot holder rack
20 kitchen clock
21 timer
22 hand mixer
23 whisk
24 electric coffee grinder (with rotating blades)
25 lead
26 wall socket
27 corner unit
28 revolving shelf
29 pot (cooking pot)
30 jug
31 spice rack
32 spice jar
33–36 sink unit
33 dish drainer
34 tea plate
35 sink
36 water tap (*Am.* faucet) (mixer tap, *Am.* mixing faucet)
37 pot plant, a foliage plant
38 coffee maker
39 kitchen lamp
40 dishwasher (dishwashing machine)
41 dish rack
42 dinner plate
43 kitchen chair
44 kitchen table

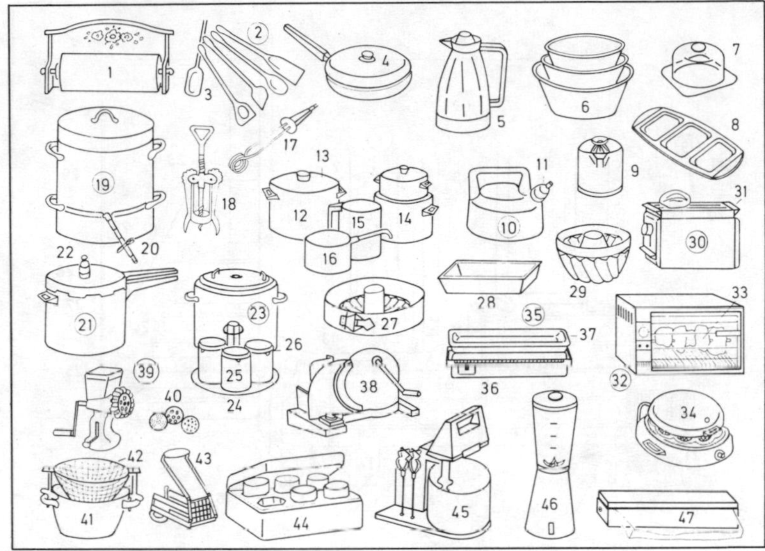

1 general-purpose roll holder with kitchen roll (paper towels)
2 set of wooden spoons
3 mixing spoon
4 frying pan
5 Thermos jug
6 set of bowls
7 cheese dish with glass cover
8 three-compartment dish
9 lemon squeezer
10 whistling kettle
11 whistle
12–16 pan set
12 pot (cooking pot)
13 lid
14 casserole dish
15 milk pot
16 saucepan
17 immersion heater
18 corkscrew [with levers]
19 juice extractor
20 tube clamp (tube clip)
21 pressure cooker
22 pressure valve
23 fruit preserver
24 removable rack
25 preserving jar
26 rubber ring
27 spring form
28 cake tin
29 cake tin
30 toaster
31 rack for rolls
32 rotisserie
33 spit
34 electric waffle iron
35 sliding-weight scales
36 sliding weight
37 scale pan
38 food slicer
39 mincer (*Am.* meat chopper)
40 blades
41 chip pan
42 basket
43 potato chipper
44 yoghurt maker
45 mixer
46 blender
47 bag sealer

41 Hall

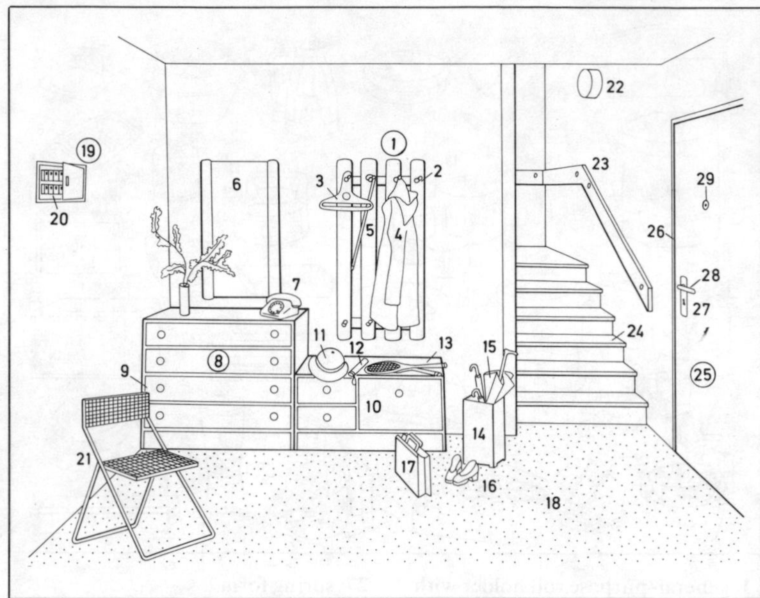

1–29 hall (entrance hall)
1 coat rack
2 coat hook
3 coat hanger
4 rain cape
5 walking stick
6 hall mirror
7 telephone
8 chest of drawers for shoes, etc.
9 drawer
10 seat
11 ladies' hat
12 telescopic umbrella
13 tennis rackets (tennis racquets)
14 umbrella stand
15 umbrella
16 shoes
17 briefcase
18 fitted carpet
19 fuse box
20 miniature circuit breaker
21 tubular steel chair
22 stair light
23 handrail
24 step
25 front door
26 door frame
27 door lock
28 door handle
29 spyhole

1 wall units
2 side wall
3 bookshelf
4 row of books
5 display cabinet unit
6 cupboard base unit
7 cupboard unit
8 television set (TV set)
9 stereo system (stereo equipment)
10 speaker (loudspeaker)
11 pipe rack
12 pipe
13 globe
14 brass kettle
15 telescope
16 mantle clock
17 bust
18 encyclopaedia [in several volumes]
19 room divider
20 drinks cupboard
21-26 upholstered suite (seating group)
21 armchair
22 arm
23 seat cushion (cushion)
24 settee
25 back cushion
26 [round] corner section
27 scatter cushion
28 coffee table
29 ashtray
30 tray
31 whisky (whiskey) bottle
32 soda water bottle (soda bottle)
33-34 dining set
33 dining table
34 chair
35 net curtain
36 indoor plants (houseplants)

43 Bedroom

1 wardrobe (*Am.* clothes closet)
2 linen shelf
3 cane chair
4–13 double bed (*sim.*: double divan)
4–6 bedstead
4 foot of the bed
5 bed frame
6 headboard
7 bedspread
8 duvet, a quilted duvet
9 sheet, a linen sheet
10 mattress, a foam mattress with drill tick
11 [wedge-shaped] bolster
12–13 pillow
12 pillowcase (pillowslip)
13 tick
14 bookshelf [attached to the headboard]
15 reading lamp
16 electric alarm clock
17 bedside cabinet
18 drawer
19 bedroom lamp
20 picture
21 picture frame
22 bedside rug
23 fitted carpet
24 dressing stool
25 dressing table
26 perfume spray
27 perfume bottle
28 powder box
29 dressing-table mirror (mirror)

1–11 dining set
1 dining table
2 table leg
3 table top
4 place mat
5 place (place setting, cover)
6 soup plate (deep plate)
7 dinner plate
8 soup tureen
9 wineglass
10 dining chair
11 seat
12 lamp (pendant lamp)
13 curtains
14 net curtain
15 curtain rail
16 carpet
17 wall unit
18 glass door
19 shelf
20 sideboard
21 cutlery drawer
22 linen drawer
23 base
24 round tray
25 pot plant
26 china cabinet (display cabinet)
27 coffee set (coffee service)
28 coffee pot
29 coffee cup
30 saucer
31 milk jug
32 sugar bowl
33 dinner set (dinner service)

45 Tableware and Cutlery

1 dining table
2 tablecloth, a damask cloth
3–12 place (place setting, cover)
3 bottom plate
4 dinner plate
5 deep plate (soup plate)
6 dessert plate (dessert bowl)
7 knife and fork
8 fish knife and fork
9 serviette (napkin, table napkin)
10 serviette ring (napkin ring)
11 knife rest
12 wineglasses
13 place card
14 soup ladle
15 soup tureen (tureen)
16 candelabra
17 sauceboat (gravy boat)
18 sauce ladle (gravy ladle)
19 table decoration
20 bread basket
21 roll
22 slice of bread
23 salad bowl
24 salad servers
25 vegetable dish
26 meat plate (*Am.* meat platter)
27 roast meat (roast)
28 fruit dish
29 fruit bowl
30 fruit (stewed fruit)
31 potato dish
32 serving trolley
33 vegetable plate (*Am.* vegetable platter)
34 toast
35 cheeseboard
36 butter dish
37 open sandwich
38 filling
39 sandwich
40 fruit bowl
41 almonds (*also:* potato crisps, peanuts)
42 oil and vinegar bottle
43 ketchup (catchup, catsup)
44 sideboard
45 electric hotplate
46 corkscrew
47 crown cork bottle-opener (crown cork opener), a bottle-opener

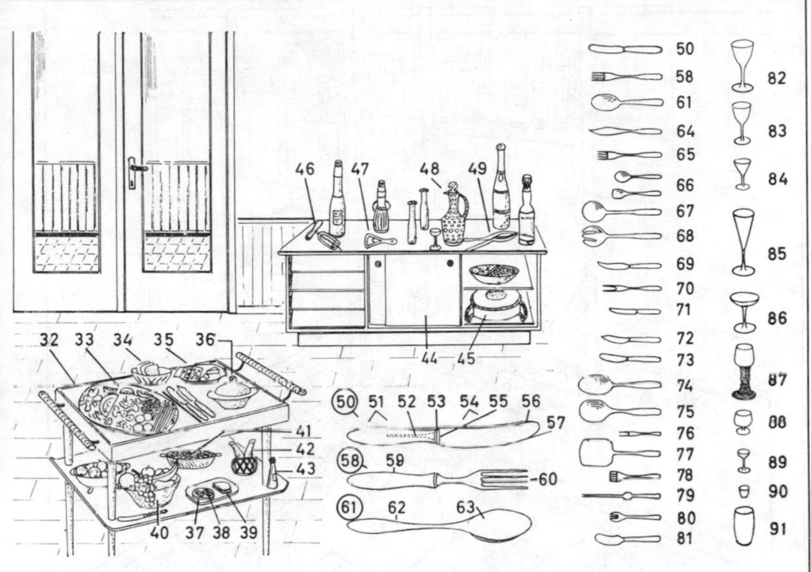

48 liqueur decanter
49 nutcrackers (nutcracker)
50 knife
51 handle
52 tang (tongue)
53 ferrule
54 blade
55 bolster
56 back
57 edge (cutting edge)
58 fork
59 handle
60 prong (tang, tine)
61 spoon; *here:* dessert spoon
62 handle
63 bowl
64 fish knife
65 fish fork
66 dessert spoon (fruit spoon)
67 salad spoon
68 salad fork
69–70 carving set (serving cutlery)
69 carving knife
70 serving fork
71 fruit knife
72 cheese knife
73 butter knife
74 vegetable spoon, a serving spoon
75 potato server (serving spoon for potatoes)
76 cocktail fork
77 asparagus server (asparagus slice)
78 sardine server
79 lobster fork
80 oyster fork
81 caviare knife
82 white wine glass
83 red wine glass
84 sherry glass (madeira glass)
85–86 champagne glasses
85 tapered glass
86 champagne glass, a crystal glass
87 rummer
88 brandy glass
89 liqueur glass
90 spirit glass
91 beer glass

46 Flat (Apartment)

1 wall units (shelf units)
2 wardrobe door (*Am.* clothes closet door)
3 body
4 side wall
5 trim
6 two-door cupboard unit
7 bookshelf unit (bookcase unit) [with glass door]
8 books
9 display cabinet
10 card index boxes
11 drawer
12 decorative biscuit tin
13 soft toy animal
14 television set (TV set)
15 records (discs)
16 bed unit
17 scatter cushion
18 bed unit drawer
19 bed unit shelf
20 magazines
21 desk unit (writing unit)
22 desk
23 desk mat (blotter)
24 table lamp
25 wastepaper basket
26 desk drawer
27 desk chair
28 arm
29 kitchen unit
30 wall cupboard
31 cooker hood
32 electric cooker
33 refrigerator (fridge, *Am.* icebox)
34 dining table
35 table runner
36 oriental carpet
37 standard lamp

1 children's bed, a bunk-bed
2 storage box
3 mattress
4 pillow
5 ladder
6 soft toy elephant, a cuddly toy animal
7 soft toy dog
8 cushion
9 fashion doll
10 doll's pram
11 sleeping doll
12 canopy
13 blackboard
14 counting beads
15 toy horse for rocking and pulling
16 rockers
17 children's book
18 compendium of games
19 ludo
20 chessboard
21 children's cupboard
22 linen drawer
23 drop-flap writing surface
24 notebook (exercise book)
25 school books
26 pencil (*also:* crayon, felt tip pen, ballpoint pen)
27 toy shop
28 counter
29 spice rack
30 display
31 assortment of sweets (*Am.* candies)
32 bag of sweets (*Am.* candies)
33 scales
34 cash register
35 toy telephone
36 shop shelves (goods shelves)
37 wooden train set
38 dump truck, a toy lorry (toy truck)
39 tower crane
40 concrete mixer
41 large soft toy dog
42 dice cup

48 Kindergarten (Day Nursery)

1–20 pre-school education (nursery education)
1 nursery teacher
2 nursery child
3 handicraft
4 glue
5 watercolour (*Am.* watercolor) painting
6 paintbox
7 paintbrush
8 glass of water
9 jigsaw puzzle (puzzle)
10 jigsaw puzzle piece
11 coloured (*Am.* colored) pencils (wax crayons)
12 modelling (*Am.* modeling) clay (plasticine)
13 clay figures (plasticine figures)
14 modelling (*Am.* modeling) board
15 chalk (blackboard chalk)
16 blackboard
17 counting blocks
18 felt pen (felt tip pen)
19 shapes game
20 group of players
21–32 toys
21 building and filling cubes
22 construction set
23 children's books
24 doll's pram, a wicker pram
25 baby doll
26 canopy
27 building bricks (building blocks)
28 wooden model building
29 wooden train set
30 rocking teddy bear
31 doll's pushchair
32 fashion doll
33 child of nursery school age
34 cloakroom

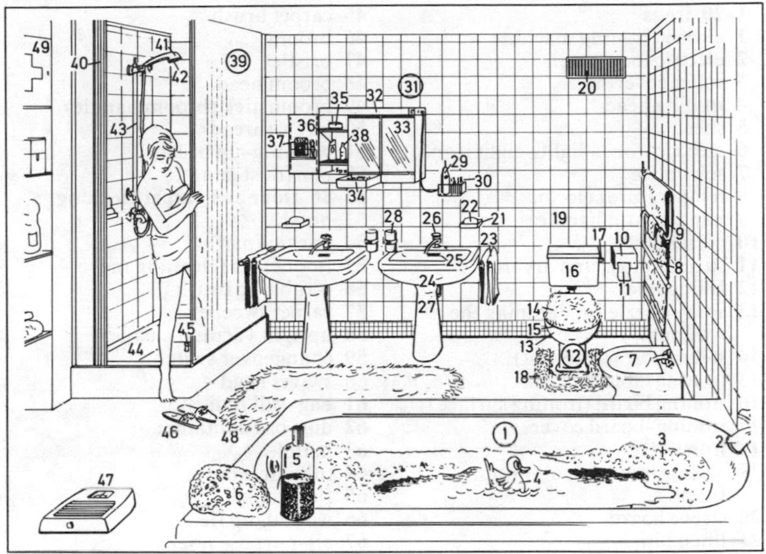

1 bath
2 mixer tap (*Am.* mixing faucet) for hot and cold water
3 foam bath (bubble bath)
4 toy duck
5 bath salts
6 bath sponge (sponge)
7 bidet
8 towel rail
9 terry towel
10 toilet roll holder (*Am.* bathroom tissue holder)
11 toilet paper (*coll.* loo paper, *Am.* bathroom tissue), a roll of crepe paper
12 toilet (lavatory, W.C., *coll.* loo)
13 toilet pan (toilet bowl)
14 toilet lid with terry cover
15 toilet seat
16 cistern
17 flushing lever
18 pedestal mat
19 tile
20 ventilator (extraction vent)
21 soap dish
22 soap
23 hand towel
24 washbasin
25 overflow
26 hot and cold water tap
27 washbasin pedestal with trap (anti-syphon trap)
28 tooth glass (tooth mug)
29 electric toothbrush
30 detachable brush heads
31 mirrored bathroom cabinet
32 fluorescent lamp
33 mirror
34 drawer
35 powder box
36 mouthwash
37 electric shaver
38 aftershave lotion
39 shower cubicle
40 shower curtain
41 adjustable shower head
42 shower nozzle
43 shower adjustment rail
44 shower base
45 waste pipe (overflow)
46 bathroom mule
47 bathroom scales
48 bath mat
49 medicine cabinet

50 Household Appliances and Utensils

1–20 irons
1 electric ironing machine
2 electric foot switch
3 roller covering
4 ironing head
5 sheet
6 electric iron, a lightweight iron
7 sole-plate
8 temperature selector
9 handle (iron handle)
10 pilot light
11 steam, spray, and dry iron
12 filling inlet
13 spray nozzle for damping the washing
14 steam hole (steam slit)
15 ironing table
16 ironing board (ironing surface)
17 ironing-board cover
18 iron well
19 aluminium (*Am.* aluminum) frame
20 sleeve board
21 linen bin
22 dirty linen
23–34 washing machines and driers
23 washing machine (automatic washing machine)
24 washing drum
25 safety latch (safety catch)
26 program selector control
27 front soap dispenser [with several compartments]
28 tumble drier
29 drum
30 front door with ventilation slits
31 work top
32 airer
33 clothes line (washing line)
34 extending airer
35 stepladder (steps), an aluminium (*Am.* aluminum) ladder
36 stile
37 prop
38 tread (rung)
39–43 shoe care utensils
39 tin of shoe polish
40 shoe spray, an impregnating spray
41 shoe brush
42 brush for applying polish
43 tube of shoe polish
44 clothes brush
45 carpet brush
46 broom
47 bristles
48 broom head
49 broomstick (broom handle)
50 screw thread
51 washing-up brush
52 pan (dust pan)
53–86 floor and carpet cleaning
53 brush
54 bucket (pail)
55 floor cloth (cleaning rag)
56 scrubbing brush
57 carpet sweeper
58 upright vacuum cleaner
59 changeover switch
60 swivel head
61 bag-full indicator
62 dust bag container
63 handle
64 tubular handle
65 flex hook
66 wound-up flex
67 all-purpose nozzle
68 cylinder vacuum cleaner
69 swivel coupling
70 extension tube
71 floor nozzle (*sim.:* carpet beater nozzle)
72 suction control
73 bag-full indicator
74 sliding fingertip suction control
75 hose (suction hose)
76 combined carpet sweeper and shampooer
77 electric lead (flex)
78 plug socket
79 carpet beater head (*sim.:* shampooing head, brush head)
80 all-purpose vacuum cleaner (dry and wet operation)
81 castor
82 motor unit
83 lid clip
84 coarse dirt hose
85 special accessory (special attachment) for coarse dirt
86 dust container
87 shopper (shopping trolley)

1
2
3
4
5
6
7
8
9
10
11
12
13
14
15
16
17
18
19
20
21
22
23
24
25
26
27
28
29
30
31
32
33
34
35
36
37
38
39
40
41
42
43
44
45
46
47
48
49
50
51
52
53
54
55
56
57
58
59
60
61
62
63
64
65
66
67
68
69
70
71
72
73
74
75
76
77
78
79
80
81
82
83
84
85
86
87

51 Flower Garden

1–35 flower garden
1 pergola
2 deck-chair
3 lawn rake (wire-tooth rake)
4 garden rake
5 Virginia creeper (American ivy, woodbine), a climbing plant (climber, creeper)
6 rockery (rock garden)
7 rock plants; *varieties:* stonecrop (wall pepper), houseleek, dryas, aubretia
8 pampas grass
9 garden hedge
10 blue spruce
11 hydrangeas
12 oak (oak tree)
13 birch (birch tree)
14 garden path
15 edging
16 garden pond
17 flagstone (stone slab)
18 water lily
19 tuberous begonias
20 dahlias
21 watering can (*Am.* sprinkling can)
22 weeding hoe
23 lupin
24 marguerites (oxeye daisies, white oxeye daisies)
25 standard rose
26 gerbera
27 iris
28 gladioli
29 chrysanthemums
30 poppy
31 blazing star
32 snapdragon (antirrhinum)
33 lawn
34 dandelion
35 sunflower

1–32 allotment (fruit and vegetable garden)
1, 2, 16, 17, 29 dwarf fruit trees (espaliers, espalier fruit trees)
1 quadruple cordon, a wall espalier
2 vertical cordon
3 tool shed (garden shed)
4 water butt (water barrel)
5 climbing plant (climber, creeper, rambler)
6 compost heap
7 sunflower
8 garden ladder (ladder)
9 perennial (flowering perennial)
10 garden fence (paling fence, paling)
11 standard berry tree
12 climbing rose (rambling rose) on the trellis arch
13 bush rose (standard rose tree)
14 summerhouse (garden house)
15 Chinese lantern (paper lantern)
16 pyramid tree (pyramidal tree, pyramid), a free-standing espalier
17 double horizontal cordon
18 flower bed, a border
19 berry bush (gooseberry bush, currant bush)
20 concrete edging
21 standard rose (standard rose tree)
22 border with perennials
23 garden path
24 allotment holder
25 asparagus patch (asparagus bed)
26 vegetable patch (vegetable plot)
27 scarecrow
28 runner bean (*Am.* scarlet runner), a bean plant on poles (bean poles)
29 horizontal cordon
30 standard fruit tree
31 tree stake
32 hedge

53 Indoor Plants (Houseplants)

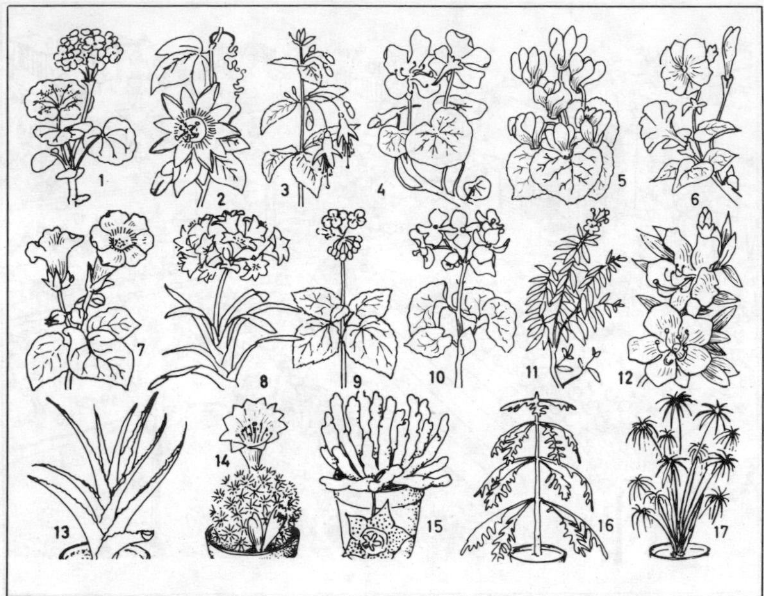

1 pelargonium (crane's bill), a geranium
2 passion flower (Passiflora), a climbing plant (climber, creeper)
3 fuchsia, an anagraceous plant
4 nasturtium (Indian cress, tropaeolum)
5 cyclamen, a primulaceous herb
6 petunia, a solanaceous herb
7 gloxinia (Sinningia), a gesneriaceous plant
8 Clivia minata, an amaryllis (narcissus)
9 African hemp (Sparmannia), a tiliaceous plant, a linden plant
10 begonia
11 myrtle (common myrtle, Myrtus)
12 azalea, an ericaceous plant
13 aloe, a liliaceous plant
14 globe thistle (Echinops)
15 stapelia (carrion flower), an asclepiadaceous plant
16 Norfolk Island Pine (an araucaria, grown as an ornamental)
17 galingale, a cyperacious plant of the sedge family

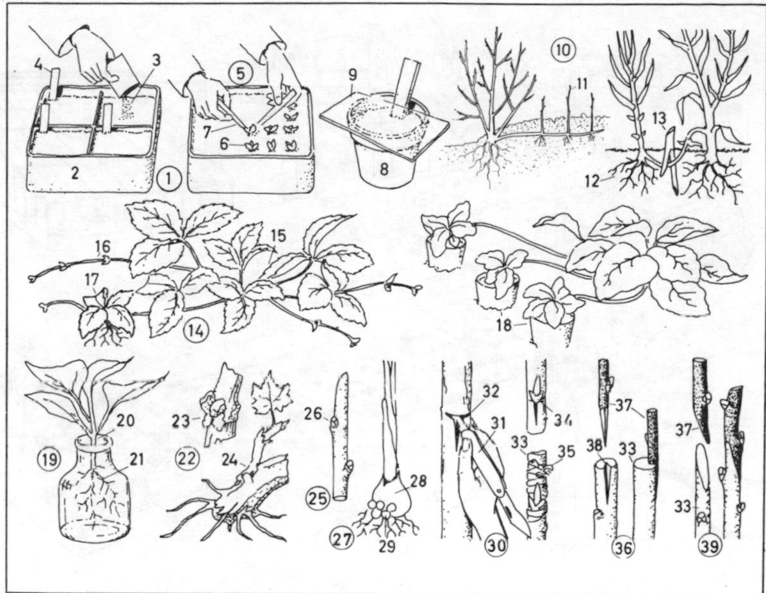

1 seed sowing (sowing)
2 seed pan
3 seed
4 label
5 pricking out (pricking off, transplanting)
6 seedling (seedling plant)
7 dibber (dibble)
8 flower pot (pot)
9 sheet of glass
10 propagation by layering
11 layer
12 layer with roots
13 forked stick used for fastening
14 propagation by runners
15 parent (parent plant)
16 runner
17 small rooted leaf cluster
18 setting in pots
19 cutting in water
20 cutting (slip, set)
21 root
22 bud cutting on vine tendril
23 scion bud, a bud
24 sprouting (shooting) cutting
25 stem cutting (hardwood cutting)
26 bud
27 propagation by bulbils (brood bud bulblets)
28 old bulb
29 bulbil (brood bud bulblet)
30–39 grafting (graftage)
30 budding (shield budding)
31 budding knife
32 T-cut
33 support (stock, rootstock)
34 inserted scion bud
35 raffia layer (bast layer)
36 side grafting
37 scion (shoot)
38 wedge-shaped notch
39 splice graft (splice grafting)

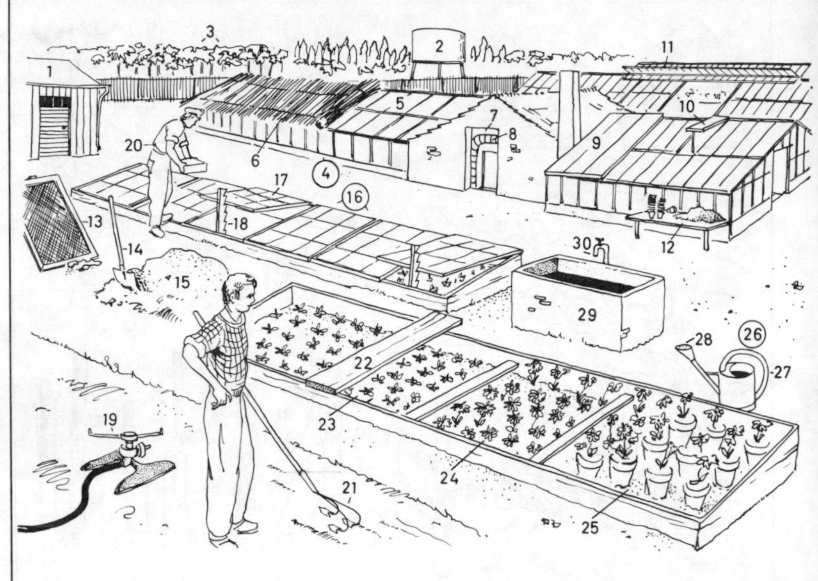

1–51 market garden (*Am.* truck garden, truck farm)
1 tool shed
2 water tower (water tank)
3 market garden (*Am.* truck garden, truck farm), a tree nursery
4 hothouse (forcing house, warm house)
5 glass roof
6 matting, e.g. straw matting, reed matting
7 boiler room (boiler house)
8 heating pipe (pressure pipe)
9 shading panel (shutter)
10–11 ventilators (vents)
10 ventilation window (window vent, hinged ventilator)
11 ridge vent
12 potting table (potting bench)
13 riddle (sieve, garden sieve, upright sieve)
14 garden shovel (shovel)
15 heap of earth (composted earth, prepared earth, garden mould, *Am.* mold)
16 hotbed (forcing bed, heated frame)
17 hotbed vent (frame vent)
18 vent prop
19 sprinkler (sprinkling device)
20 gardener (nursery gardener, grower, commercial grower)
21 cultivator (hand cultivator, grubber)
22 plank
23 pricked-out seedlings (pricked-off seedlings)
24 forced flowers [forcing]
25 potted plants (plants in pots, pot plants)
26 watering can (*Am.* sprinkling can)
27 handle
28 rose
29 water tank

Market Garden (*Am.* Truck Garden, Truck Farm) 55

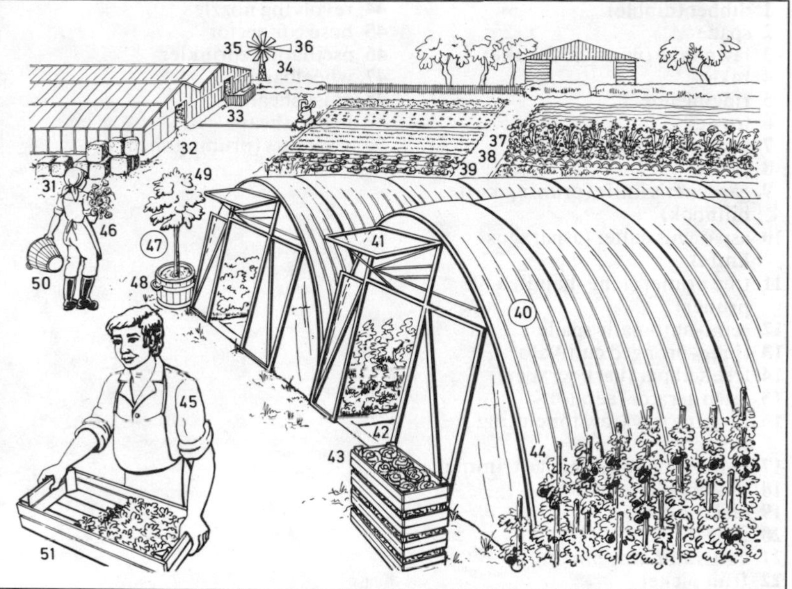

30 water pipe
31 bale of peat
32 warm house (heated greenhouse)
33 cold house (unheated greenhouse)
34 wind pump; *sim.:* wind generator (aerogenerator)
35 wind wheel
36 wind vane
37 shrub bed, a flower bed
38 hoop edging
39 vegetable plot
40 plastic tunnel (polythene greenhouse)
41 ventilation flap
42 central path
43 vegetable crate
44 tomato plant
45 nursery hand
46 nursery hand
47 tub plant
48 tub
49 orange tree
50 wire basket
51 seedling box

56 Garden Tools

1 dibber (dibble)
2 spade
3 lawn rake (wire-tooth rake)
4 rake
5 ridging hoe
6 trowel
7 combined hoe and fork
8 sickle
9 gardener's knife (pruning knife, billhook)
10 asparagus cutter (asparagus knife)
11 tree pruner (long-handled pruner)
12 semi-automatic spade
13 three-pronged cultivator
14 tree scraper (bark scraper)
15 lawn aerator (aerator)
16 pruning saw (saw for cutting branches)
17 battery-operated hedge trimmer
18 motor cultivator
19 electric drill
20 gear
21 cultivator attachment
22 fruit picker
23 tree brush (bark brush)
24 sprayer for pest control
25 lance
26 hose reel (reel and carrying cart)
27 garden hose
28 motor lawn mower (motor mower)
29 grassbox
30 two-stroke motor
31 electric lawn mower (electric mower)
32 electric lead (electric cable)
33 cutting unit
34 hand mower
35 cutting cylinder
36 blade
37 riding mower
38 brake lock
39 electric starter
40 brake pedal
41 cutting unit
42 tip-up trailer
43 revolving sprinkler, a lawn sprinkler
44 revolving nozzle
45 hose connector
46 oscillating sprinkler
47 wheelbarrow
48 grass shears
49 hedge shears
50 secateurs (pruning shears)

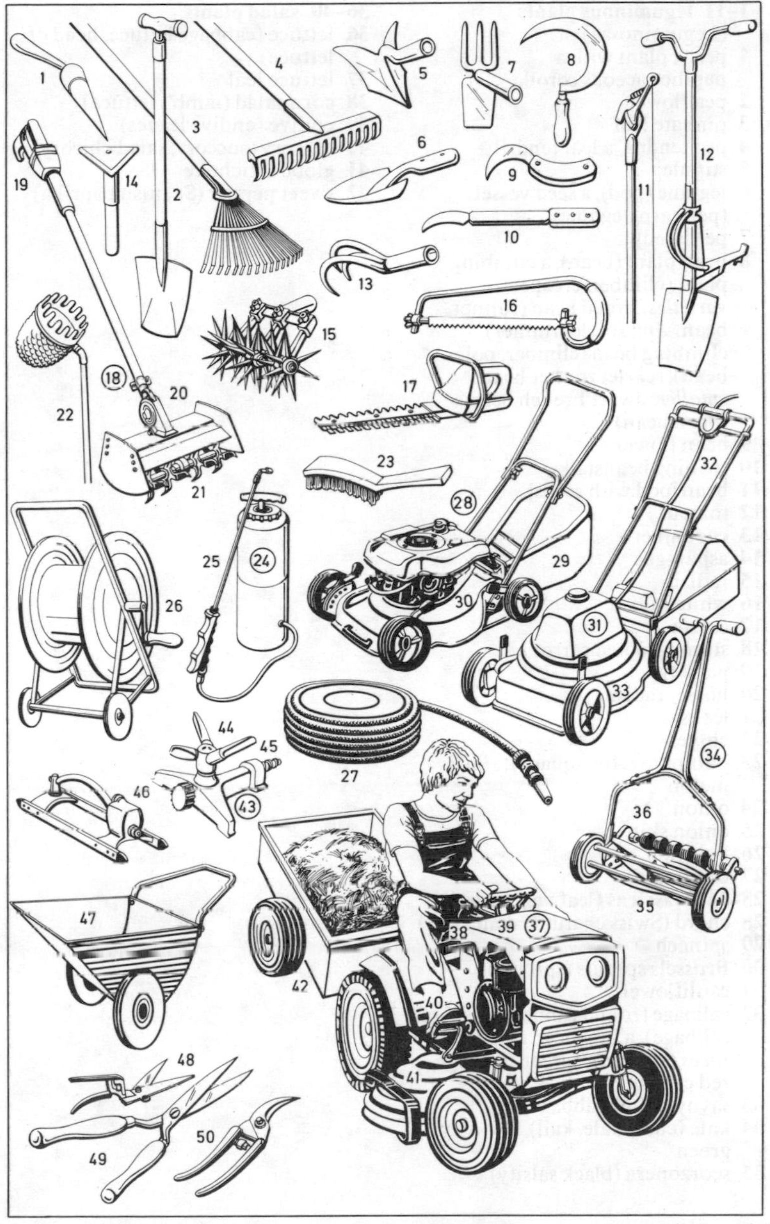

57 Vegetables (Vegetable Plants)

1–11 leguminous plants (Leguminosae)
1 pea, a plant with a papilionaceous corolla
2 pea flower
3 pinnate leaf
4 pea tendril, a leaf tendril
5 stipule
6 legume (pod), a seed vessel (pericarp, legume)
7 pea [seed]
8 bean plant (bean), a climbing plant (climber, creeper); *varieties:* broad bean (runner bean, *Am.* scarlet runner), climbing bean (climber, pole bean), scarlet runner bean; *smaller:* dwarf French bean (bush bean)
9 bean flower
10 twining beanstalk
11 bean [pod with seeds]
12 tomato
13 cucumber
14 asparagus
15 radish
16 white radish
17 carrot
18 stump-rooted carrot
19 parsley
20 horse-radish
21 leeks
22 chives
23 pumpkin (*Am.* squash); *sim.:* melon
24 onion
25 onion skin
26 kohlrabi
27 celeriac
28–34 brassicas (leaf vegetables)
28 chard (Swiss chard, seakale beet)
29 spinach
30 Brussels sprouts (sprouts)
31 cauliflower
32 cabbage (round cabbage, head of cabbage), a brassica; *cultivated races (cultivars):* green cabbage, red cabbage
33 savoy (savoy cabbage)
34 kale (curly kale, kail), a winter green
35 scorzonera (black salsify)
36–40 salad plants
36 lettuce (cabbage lettuce, head of lettuce)
37 lettuce leaf
38 corn salad (lamb's lettuce)
39 endive (endive leaves)
40 chicory (succory, salad chicory)
41 globe artichoke
42 sweet pepper (Spanish paprika)

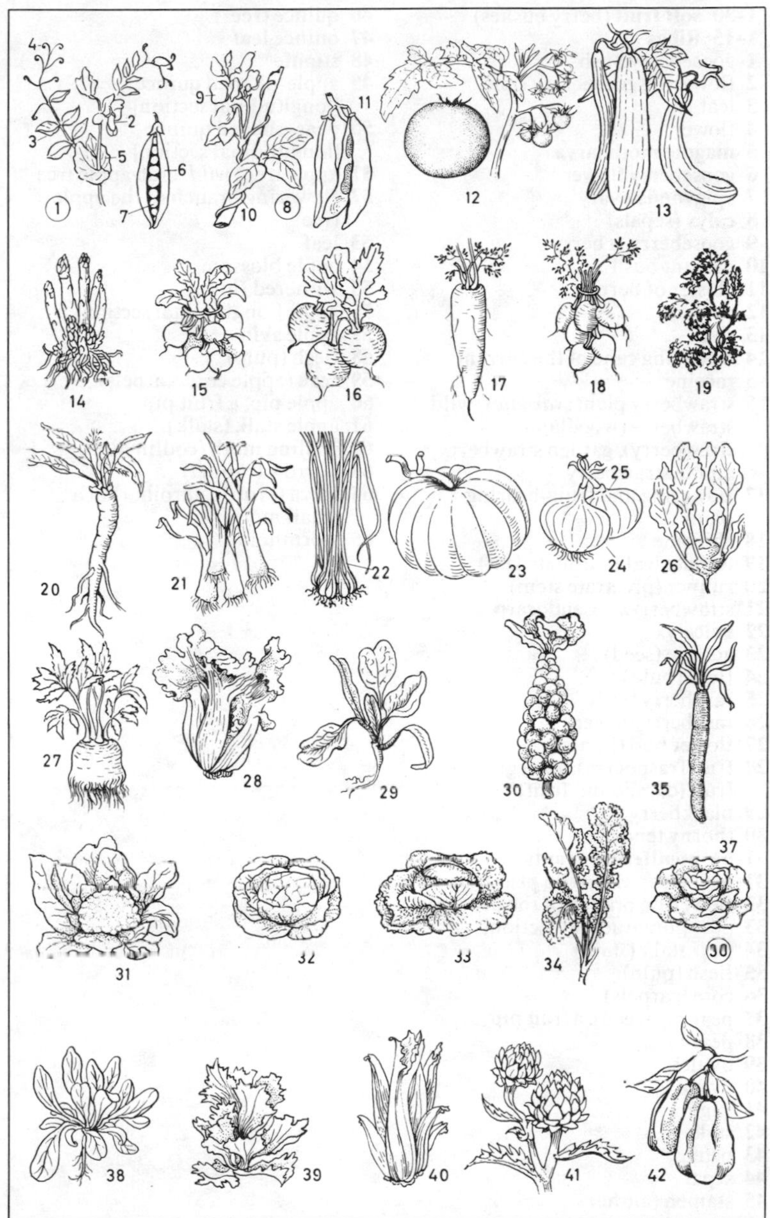

4
2
3
5
6
1
7
9
10
8
11
12
13
14
15
16
17
18
19
20
21
22
23
25
24
26
27
28
29
30
35
37
31
32
33
34
30
38
39
40
41
42

58 Soft Fruit and Pomes

1–30 soft fruit (berry bushes)
1–15 Ribes
1 gooseberry bush
2 flowering gooseberry cane
3 leaf
4 flower
5 magpie moth larva
6 gooseberry flower
7 epigynous ovary
8 calyx (sepals)
9 gooseberry, a berry
10 currant bush
11 cluster of berries
12 currant
13 stalk
14 flowering cane of the currant
15 raceme
16 strawberry plant; *varieties:* wild strawberry (woodland strawberry), garden strawberry, alpine strawberry
17 flowering and fruit-bearing plant
18 rhizome
19 ternate leaf (trifoliate leaf)
20 runner (prostrate stem)
21 strawberry, a pseudocarp
22 epicalyx
23 achene (seed)
24 flesh (pulp)
25 raspberry bush
26 raspberry flower
27 flower bud (bud)
28 fruit (raspberry), an aggregate fruit (compound fruit)
29 blackberry
30 thorny tendril
31–61 pomiferous plants
31 pear tree; *wild:* wild pear tree
32 flowering branch of the pear tree
33 pear [longitudinal section]
34 pear stalk (stalk)
35 flesh (pulp)
36 core (carpels)
37 pear pip (seed), a fruit pip
38 pear blossom
39 ovules
40 ovary
41 stigma
42 style
43 petal
44 sepal
45 stamen (anther)
46 quince tree
47 quince leaf
48 stipule
49 apple-shaped quince [longitudinal section]
50 pear-shaped quince [longitudinal section]
51 apple tree; *wild:* crab apple tree
52 flowering branch of the apple tree
53 leaf
54 apple blossom
55 withered flower
56 apple [longitudinal section]
57 apple skin
58 flesh (pulp)
59 core (apple core, carpels)
60 apple pip, a fruit pip
61 apple stalk (stalk)
62 codling moth (codlin moth)
63 burrow (tunnel)
64 larva (grub, caterpillar) of a small moth
65 wormhole

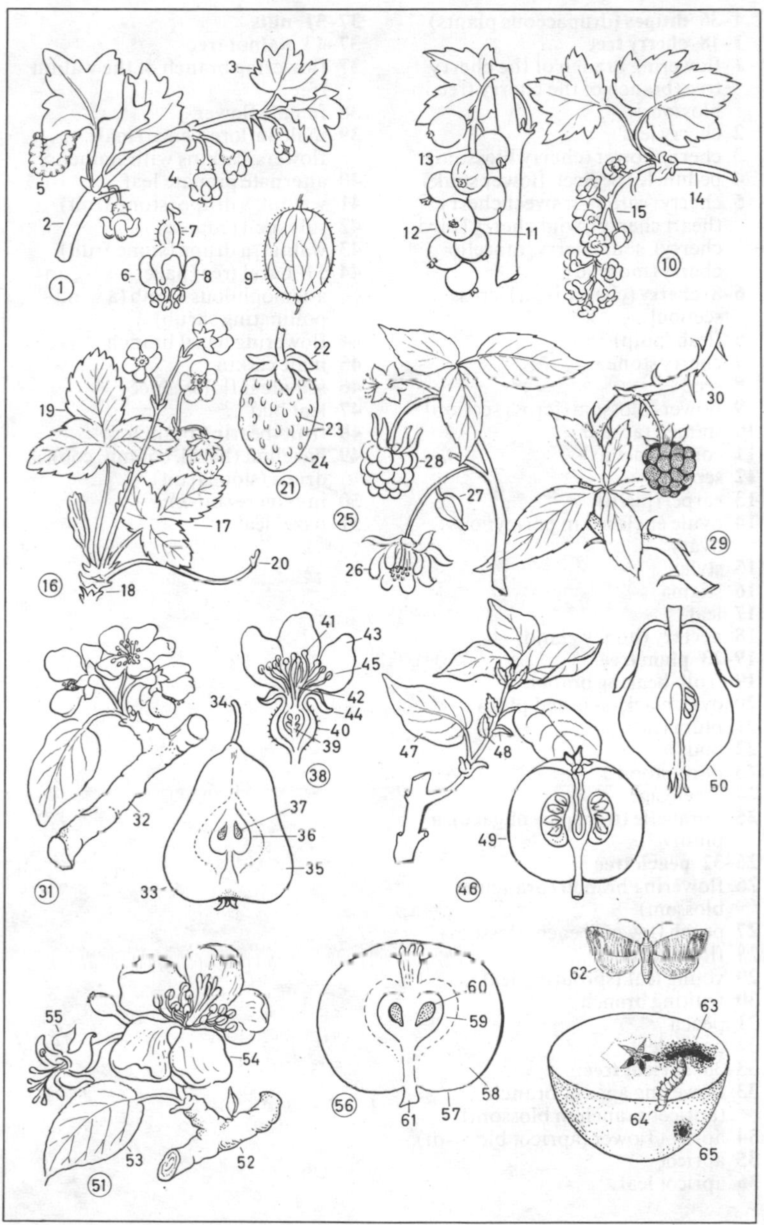
1
2
3
4
5
6
7
8
9
10
11
12
13
14
15
16
17
18
19
20
21
22
23
24
25
26
27
28
29
30
31
32
33
34
35
36
37
38
39
40
41
42
43
44
45
46
47
48
49
50
51
52
53
54
55
56
57
58
59
60
61
62
63
64
65

59 Drupes and Nuts

1–36 drupes (drupaceous plants)
1–18 cherry tree
1 flowering branch of the cherry tree (branch of the cherry tree in blossom)
2 cherry leaf
3 cherry flower (cherry blossom)
4 peduncle (pedicel, flower stalk)
5 cherry; *varieties:* sweet cherry (heart cherry), wild cherry (bird cherry), sour cherry, morello cherry (morello)
6–8 cherry (cherry fruit) [cross section]
6 flesh (pulp)
7 cherry stone
8 seed
9 flower (blossom) [cross section]
10 stamen (anther)
11 corolla (petals)
12 sepal
13 carpel (pistil)
14 ovule enclosed in perigynous ovary
15 style
16 stigma
17 leaf
18 nectary (honey gland)
19–23 plum tree
19 fruit-bearing branch
20 oval, black-skinned plum
21 plum leaf
22 bud
23 plum stone
24 greengage
25 mirabelle (transparent gage), a plum
26–32 peach tree
26 flowering branch (branch in blossom)
27 peach flower (peach blossom)
28 flower shoot
29 young leaf (sprouting leaf)
30 fruiting branch
31 peach
32 peach leaf
33–36 apricot tree
33 flowering apricot branch (apricot branch in blossom)
34 apricot flower (apricot blossom)
35 apricot
36 apricot leaf
37–51 nuts
37–43 walnut tree
37 flowering branch of the walnut tree
38 female flower
39 male inflorescence (male flowers, catkins with stamens)
40 alternate pinnate leaf
41 walnut, a drupe (stone fruit)
42 soft shell (cupule)
43 walnut, a drupe (stone fruit)
44–51 hazel tree (hazel bush), an anemophilous shrub (a wind-pollinating shrub)
44 flowering hazel branch
45 male catkin
46 female inflorescence
47 leaf bud
48 fruit-bearing branch
49 hazelnut (hazel, cobnut, cob), a drupe (stone fruit)
50 involucre (husk)
51 hazel leaf

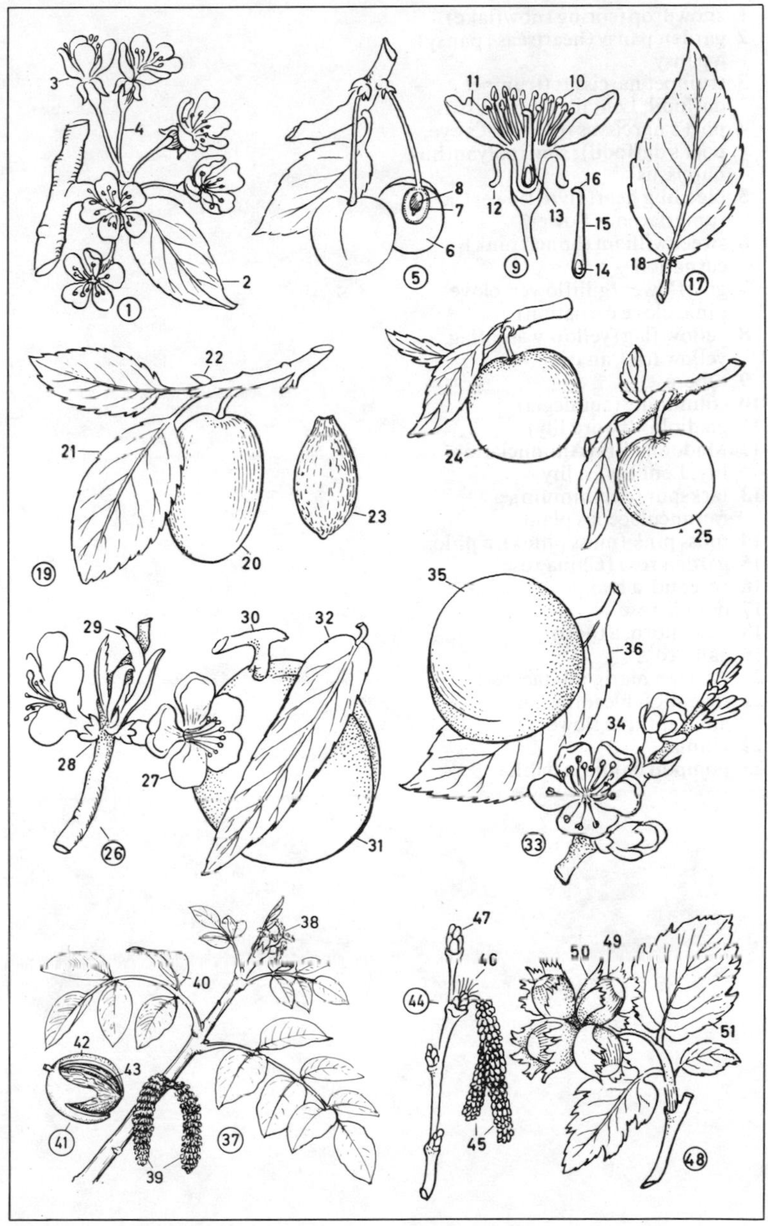
1
2
3
4
5
6
7
8
9
10
11
12
13
14
15
16
17
18
19
20
21
22
23
24
25
26
27
28
29
30
31
32
33
34
35
36
37
38
39
40
41
42
43
44
45
46
47
48
49
50
51

60 Garden Flowers

1 snowdrop (spring snowflake)
2 garden pansy (heartsease pansy), a pansy
3 trumpet narcissus (trumpet daffodil, Lent lily), a narcissus
4 poet's narcissus (pheasant's eye, poet's daffodil); *sim.*: polyanthus narcissus
5 bleeding heart (lyre flower), a fumariaceous flower
6 sweet william (bunch pink), a carnation
7 gillyflower (gilliflower, clove pink, clove carnation)
8 yellow flag (yellow water flag, yellow iris), an iris
9 tuberose
10 columbine (aquilegia)
11 gladiolus (sword lily)
12 Madonna lily (Annunciation lily, Lent lily), a lily
13 larkspur (delphinium), a ranunculaceous plant
14 moss pink (moss phlox), a phlox
15 garden rose (China rose)
16 rosebud, a bud
17 double rose
18 rose thorn, a thorn
19 gaillardia
20 African marigold (tagetes)
21 love-lies-bleeding, an amaranthine flower
22 zinnia
23 pompon dahlia, a dahlia

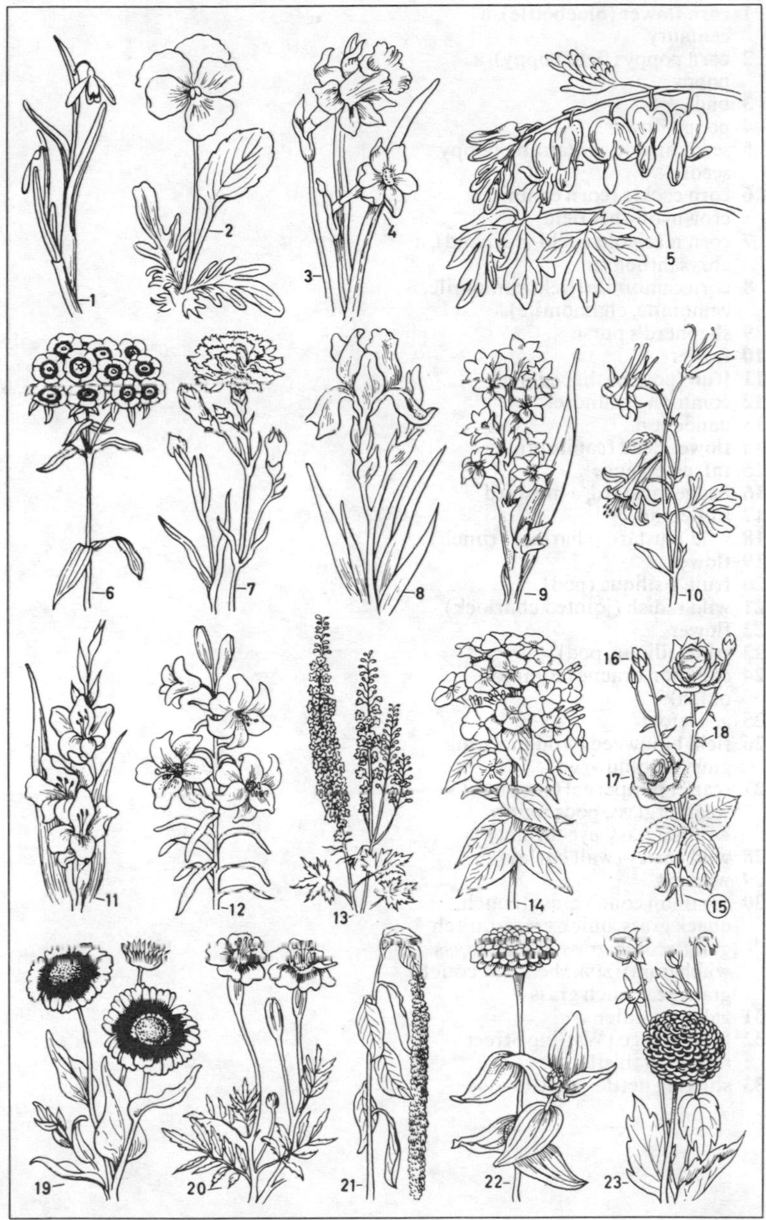
1
2
3
4
5
6
7
8
9
10
11
12
13
14
15
16
17
18
19
20
21
22
23

61 Weeds

1 corn flower (bluebottle), a centaury
2 corn poppy (field poppy), a poppy
3 bud
4 poppy flower
5 seed capsule containing poppy seeds
6 corn cockle (corn campion, crown-of-the-field)
7 corn marigold (field marigold), a chrysanthemum
8 corn camomile (field camomile, camomile, chamomile)
9 shepherd's purse
10 flower
11 fruit (pouch-shaped pod)
12 common groundsel
13 dandelion
14 flower head (capitulum)
15 infructescence
16 hedge mustard, a mustard
17 stonecrop
18 wild mustard (charlock, runch)
19 flower
20 fruit, a siliqua (pod)
21 wild radish (jointed charlock)
22 flower
23 fruit (siliqua, pod)
24 common orache (common orach)
25 goosefoot
26 field bindweed (wild morning glory), a bindweed
27 scarlet pimpernel (shepherd's weatherglass, poor man's weatherglass, eye-bright)
28 wild barley (wall barley)
29 wild oat
30 common couch grass (couch, quack grass, quick grass, quitch grass, scutch grass, twitch grass, witchgrass); *sim.:* bearded couch grass, sea couch grass
31 gallant soldier
32 field eryngo (Watling Street thistle), a thistle
33 stinging nettle, a nettle

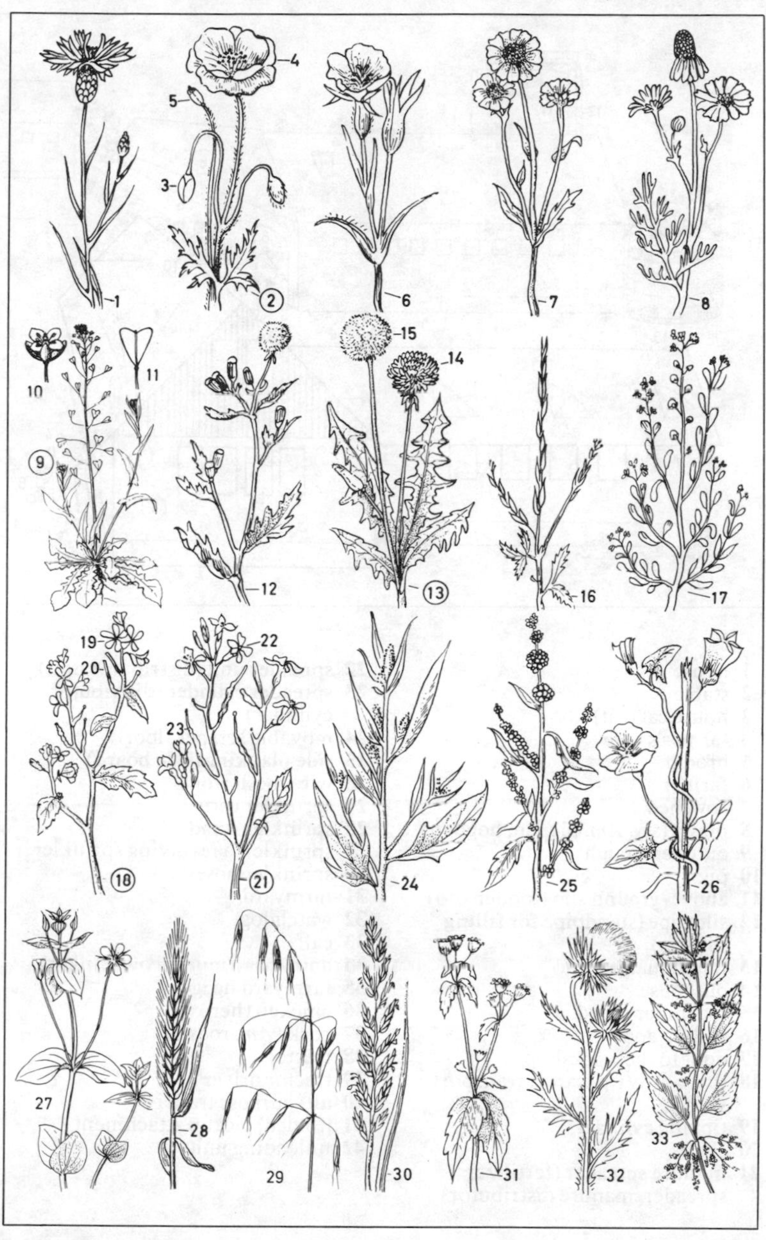
1
2
3
4
5
6
7
8
9
10
11
12
13
14
15
16
17
18
19
20
21
22
23
24
25
26
27
28
29
30
31
32
33

62 Farm Buildings (*Am.* Farmstead)

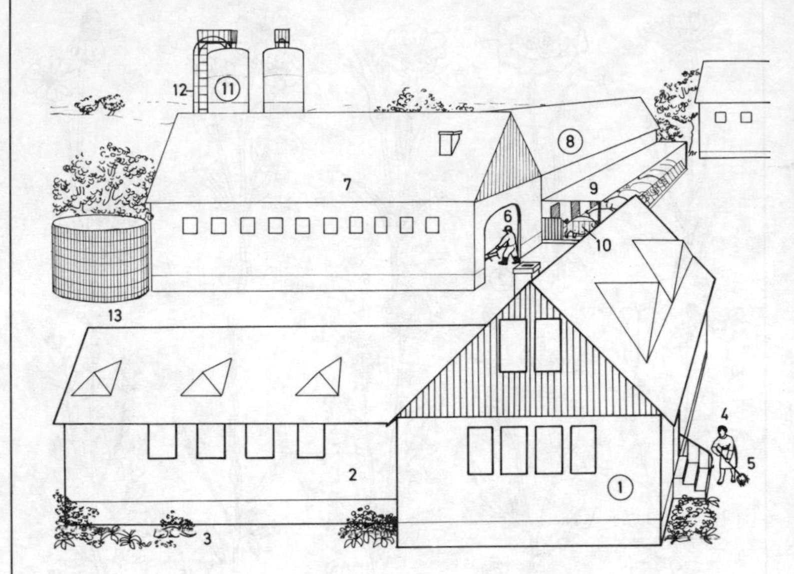

1 house
2 stable
3 house cat (cat)
4 farmer's wife
5 broom
6 farmer
7 cowshed
8 pigsty (sty, *Am.* pigpen, hogpen)
9 outdoor trough
10 pig
11 above-ground silo (fodder silo)
12 silo pipe (standpipe for filling the silo)
13 liquid manure silo
14 outhouse
15 machinery shed
16 sliding door
17 door to the workshop
18 three-way tip-cart, a transport vehicle
19 tipping cylinder
20 shafts
21 manure spreader (fertilizer spreader, manure distributor)
22 spreader unit (distributor unit)
23 spreader cylinder (distributor cylinder)
24 movable scraper floor
25 side planking (side board)
26 wire mesh front
27 sprinkler cart
28 sprinkler stand
29 sprinkler, a revolving sprinkler
30 sprinkler hoses
31 farmyard
32 watchdog
33 calf
34 dairy cow (milch-cow, milker)
35 farmyard hedge
36 chicken (hen)
37 cock (*Am.* rooster)
38 tractor
39 tractor driver
40 all-purpose trailer
41 [folded] pickup attachment
42 unloading unit

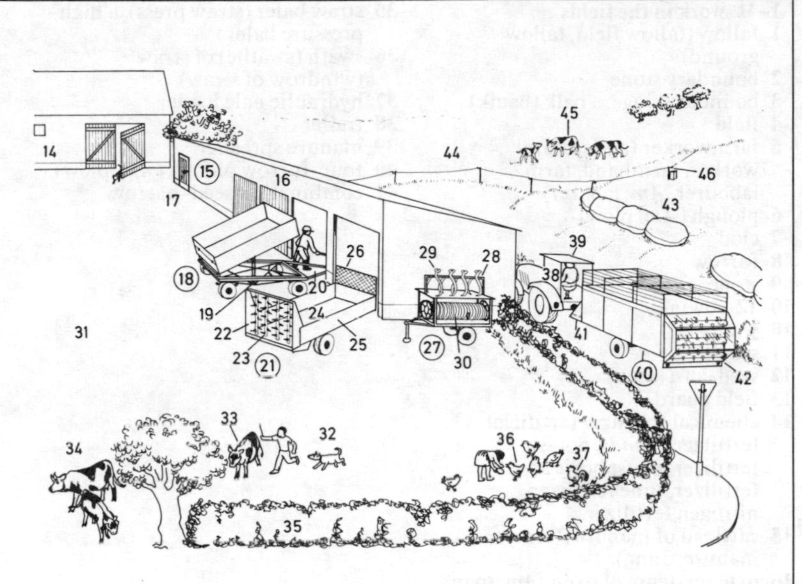

43 polythene silo, a fodder silo
44 meadow
45 grazing cattle
46 electrified fence

63 Agriculture (Farming)

1–41 work in the fields
1 fallow (fallow field, fallow ground)
2 boundary stone
3 boundary ridge, a balk (baulk)
4 field
5 farmworker (agricultural worker, farmhand, farm labourer, *Am.* laborer)
6 plough (*Am.* plow)
7 clod
8 furrow
9 stone
10–12 sowing
10 sower
11 seedlip
12 seed corn (seed)
13 field guard
14 chemical fertilizer (artificial fertilizer); *kinds:* potash fertilizer, phosphoric acid fertilizer, lime fertilizer, nitrogen fertilizer
15 cartload of manure (farmyard manure, dung)
16 oxteam (team of oxen, *Am.* span of oxen)
17 fields (farmland)
18 farm track (farm road)
19–30 hay harvest (haymaking)
19 rotary mower with swather (swath reaper)
20 connecting shaft (connecting rod)
21 power take-off (power take-off shaft)
22 meadow
23 swath (swathe)
24 tedder (rotary tedder)
25 tedded hay
26 rotary swather
27 trailer with pickup attachment
28 fence rack (rickstand), a drying rack for hay
29 rickstand, a drying rack for hay
30 hay tripod
31–41 grain harvest and seedbed preparation
31 combine harvester
32 cornfield
33 stubble field
34 bale of straw
35 straw baler (straw press), a high-pressure baler
36 swath (swathe) of straw (windrow of straw)
37 hydraulic bale loader
38 trailer
39 manure spreader
40 four-furrow plough (*Am.* plow)
41 combination seed-harrow

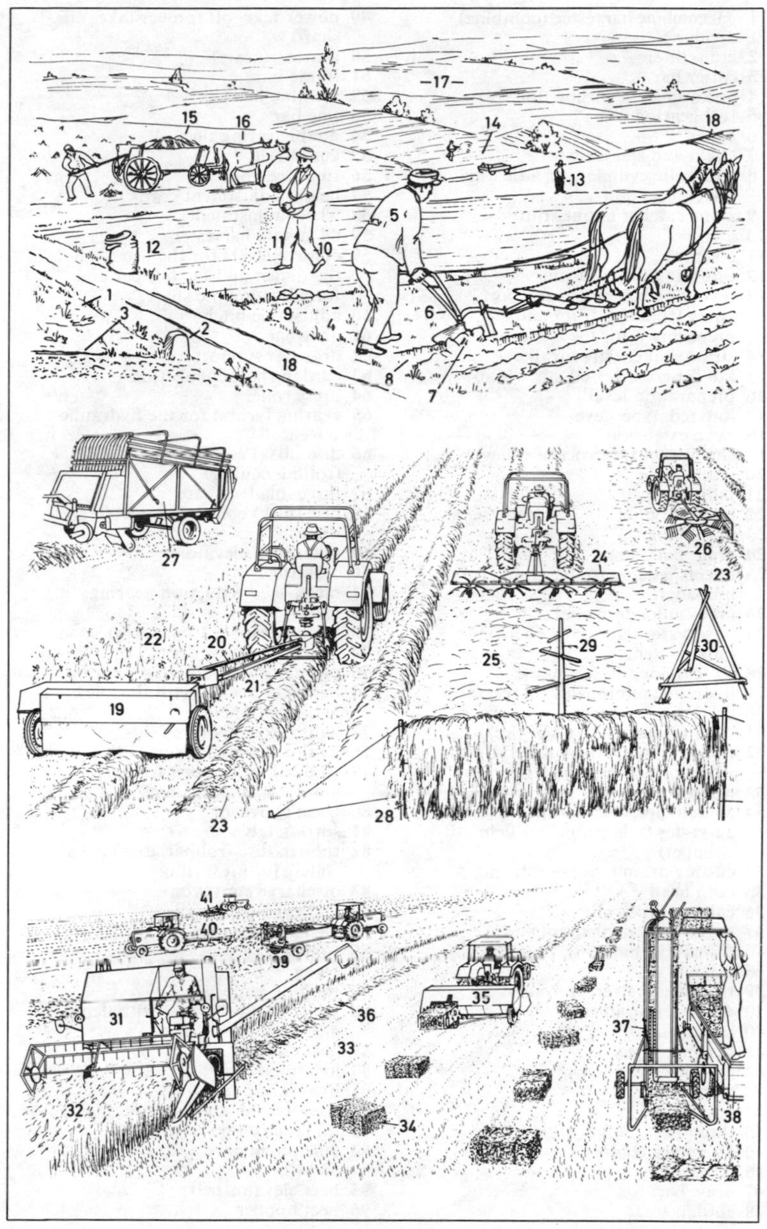
-17-
15
16
14
18
-13
5
11
10
12
1
3
9
6
2
4
18
8
7
27
24
26
23
22
20
29
30
25
21
19
28
23
41
40
39
31
36
35
33
37
32
34
38

64 Agricultural Machinery I

1-33 combine harvester (combine)
1 divider
2 grain lifter
3 cutter bar
4 pickup reel, a spring-tine reel
5 reel gearing
6 auger
7 chain and slat elevator
8 hydraulic cylinder for adjusting the cutting unit
9 stone catcher (stone trap)
10 awner
11 concave
12 threshing drum (drum)
13 revolving beater [for freeing straw from the drum and preparing it for the shakers]
14 straw shaker (strawwalker)
15 fan for compressed-air winnowing
16 preparation level
17 louvred-type sieve
18 sieve extension
19 shoe sieve (reciprocating sieve)
20 grain auger
21 tailings auger
22 tailings outlet
23 grain tank
24 grain tank auger
25 augers feeding to the grain tank unloader
26 grain unloader spout
27 observation ports for checking tank contents
28 six-cylinder diesel engine
29 hydraulic pump with oil reservoir
30 driving axle gearing
31 driving wheel tyre (*Am.* tire)
32 rubber-tyred (*Am.* rubber-tired) wheel on the steering axle
33 driver's position
34-39 self-propelled forage harvester (self-propelled field chopper)
34 cutting drum (chopper drum)
35 corn head
36 cab (driver's cab)
37 swivel-mounted spout (discharge pipe)
38 exhaust
39 rear-wheel steering system
40-45 rotary swather
40 cardan shaft
41 running wheel
42 double spring tine
43 crank
44 swath rake
45 three-point linkage
46-58 rotary tedder
46 tractor
47 draw bar
48 cardan shaft
49 power take-off (power take-off shaft)
50 gearing (gears)
51 frame bar
52 rotating head
53 tine bar
54 double spring tine
55 guard rail
56 running wheel
57 height adjustment crank
58 wheel adjustment
59-84 potato harvester
59 control levers for the lifters of the digger and the hopper and for adjusting the shaft
60 adjustable hitch
61 drawbar
62 drawbar support
63 cardan shaft connection
64 press roller
65 gearing (gears) for the hydraulic system
66 disc (disk) coulter (*Am.* colter) (rolling coulter)
67 three-bladed share
68 disc (disk) coulter (*Am.* colter) drive
69 open-web elevator
70 agitator
71 multi-step reduction gearing
72 feeder
73 haulm stripper (flail rotor)
74 rotary elevating drum
75 mechanical tumbling separator
76 haulm conveyor with flexible haulm strippers
77 haulm conveyor agitator
78 haulm conveyor drive with V-belt
79 studded rubber belt for sorting vines, clods and stones
80 trash conveyor
81 sorting table
82 rubber-disc (rubber-disk) rollers for presorting
83 discharge conveyor
84 endless-floor hopper
85-96 beet harvester
85 topper
86 feeler
87 topping knife
88 feeler support wheel with depth adjustment
89 beet cleaner
90 haulm elevator
91 hydraulic pump
92 compressed-air reservoir
93 oil tank (oil reservoir)
94 tensioning device for the beet elevator
95 beet elevator belt
96 beet hopper

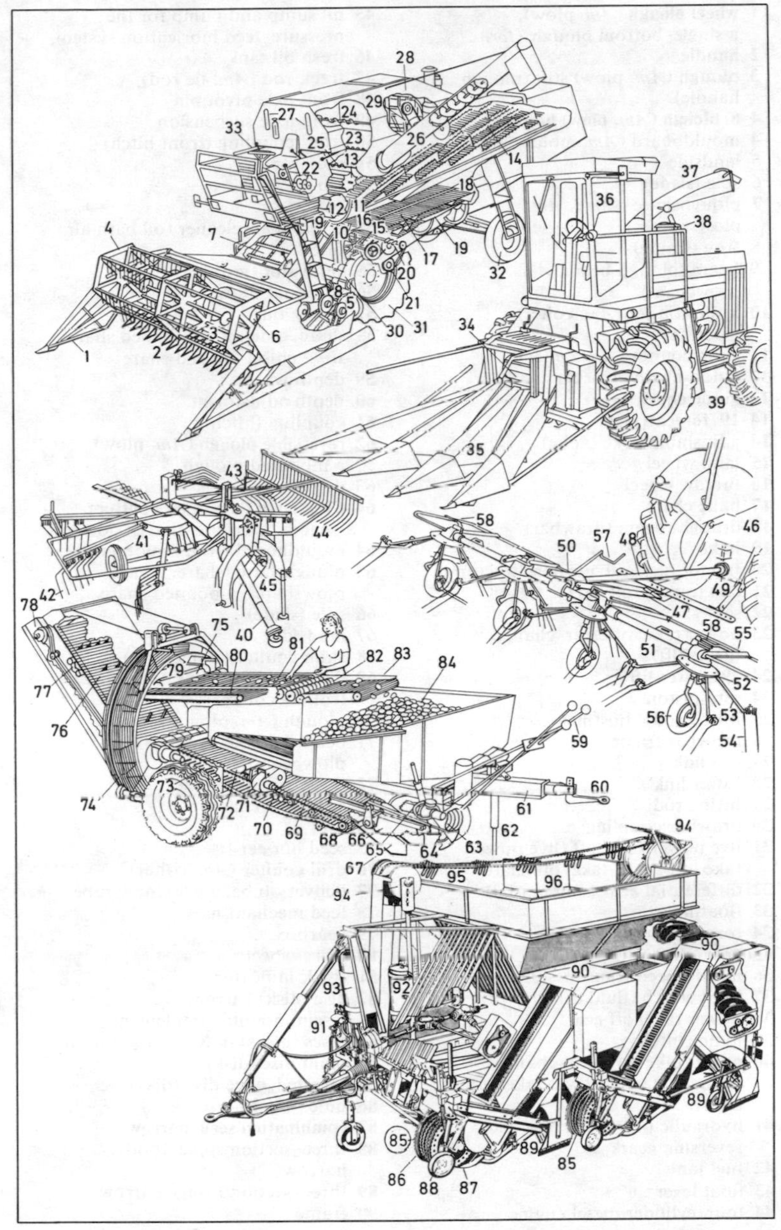
1
2
3
4
5
6
7
8
9
10
11
12
13
14
15
16
17
18
19
20
21
22
23
24
25
26
27
28
29
30
31
32
33
34
35
36
37
38
39
40
41
42
43
44
45
46
47
48
49
50
51
52
53
54
55
56
57
58
59
60
61
62
63
64
65
66
67
68
69
70
71
72
73
74
75
76
77
78
79
80
81
82
83
84
85
86
87
88
89
90
91
92
93
94
95
96

65 Agricultural Machinery II

1 **wheel plough** (*Am.* plow), a single-bottom plough *[form.]*
2 handle
3 plough (*Am.* plow) stilt (plough handle)
4-8 **plough** (*Am.* **plow) bottom**
4 mouldboard (*Am.* moldboard)
5 landside
6 sole (slade)
7 ploughshare (share, *Am.* plowshare)
8 frog (frame)
9 beam (plough beam, *Am.* plowbeam)
10 knife coulter (*Am.* colter), a coulter
11 skim coulter (*Am.* colter)
12 guide-chain crossbar
13 guide chain
14-19 **forecarriage**
14 adjustable yoke (yoke)
15 land wheel
16 furrow wheel
17 hake chain
18 draught beam (drawbar)
19 hake
20 **tractor** (general-purpose tractor)
21 cab frame (roll bar)
22 seat
23 power take-off gear-change (gearshift)
24-29 **power lift**
24 ram piston
25 lifting rod adjustment
26 drawbar frame
27 top link
28 lower link
29 lifting rod
30 drawbar coupling
31 live power take-off (live power take-off shaft, take-off shaft)
32 differential gear (differential)
33 floating axle
34 torque converter lever
35 gear-change (gearshift)
36 multi-speed transmission
37 fluid clutch (fluid drive)
38 power take-off gear
39 main clutch
40 power take-off gear-change (gearshift) with power take-off clutch
41 hydraulic power steering and reversing gears
42 fuel tank
43 float lever
44 four-cylinder diesel engine
45 oil sump and pump for the pressure-feed lubrication system
46 fresh oil tank
47 track rod (*Am.* tie rod)
48 front axle pivot pin
49 front axle suspension
50 front coupling (front hitch)
51 radiator
52 fan
53 battery
54 oil bath air cleaner (oil bath air filter)
55 **cultivator** (grubber)
56 sectional frame
57 spring tine
58 share, a diamond-shaped share; *sim.:* chisel-shaped share
59 depth wheel
60 depth adjustment
61 coupling (hitch)
62 **reversible plough** (*Am.* plow), a mounted plough
63 depth wheel
64–67 **plough** (*Am.* **plow) bottom,** a general-purpose plough bottom
64 mouldboard (*Am.* moldboard)
65 ploughshare (share, *Am.* plowshare), a pointed share
66 sole (slade)
67 landside
68 skim coulter (*Am.* colter)
69 disc (disk) coulter (*Am.* colter) (rolling coulter)
70 plough (*Am.* plow) frame
71 beam (plough beam, *Am.* plowbeam)
72 three-point linkage
73 swivel mechanism
74 **drill**
75 seed hopper
76 drill coulter (*Am.* colter)
77 delivery tube, a telescopic tube
78 feed mechanism
79 gearbox
80 drive wheel
81 track indicator
82 **disc (disk) harrow,** a semimounted implement
83 discs (disks) in X-configuration
84 plain disc (disk)
85 serrated-edge disc (disk)
86 quick hitch
87 **combination seed-harrow**
88 three-section spike-tooth harrow
89 three-section rotary harrow
90 frame

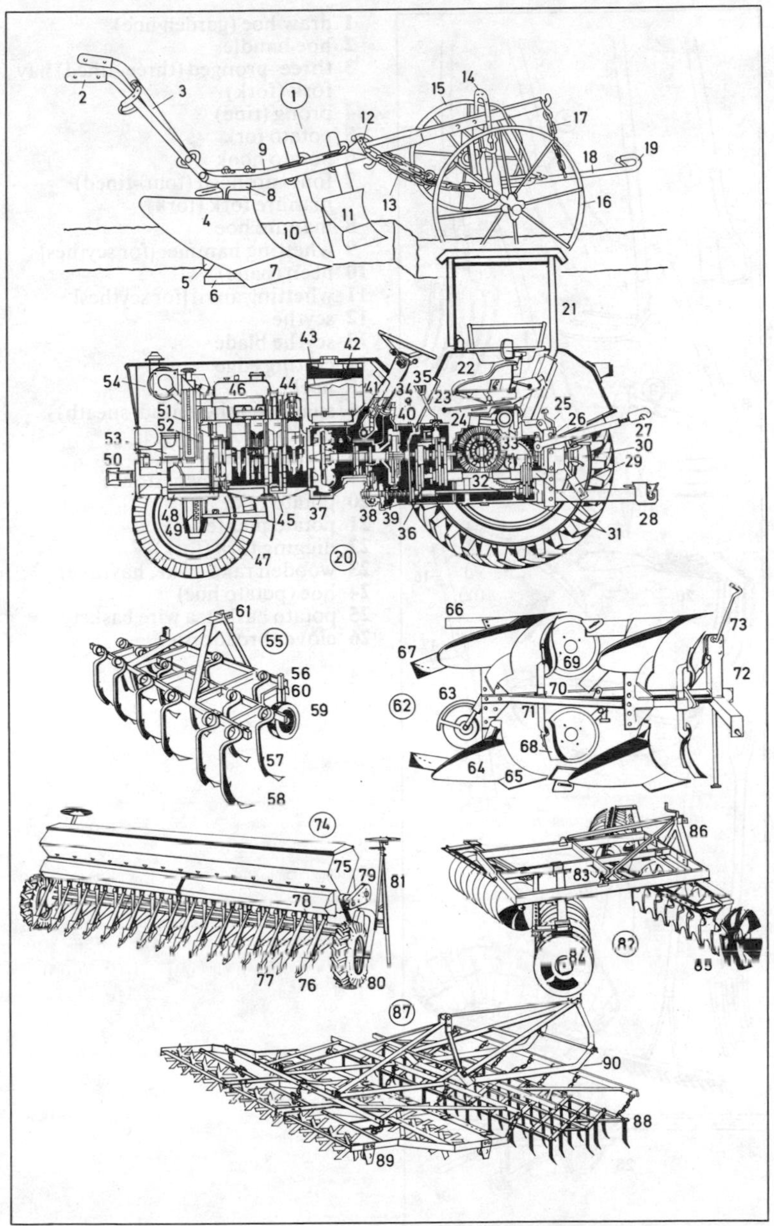
1
2
3
4
5
6
7
8
9
10
11
12
13
14
15
16
17
18
19
20
21
22
23
24
25
26
27
28
29
30
31
32
33
34
35
36
37
38
39
40
41
42
43
44
45
46
47
48
49
50
51
52
53
54
55
56
57
58
59
60
61
62
63
64
65
66
67
68
69
70
71
72
73
74
75
76
77
78
79
80
81
82
83
84
85
86
87
88
89
90

66 Agricultural Implements

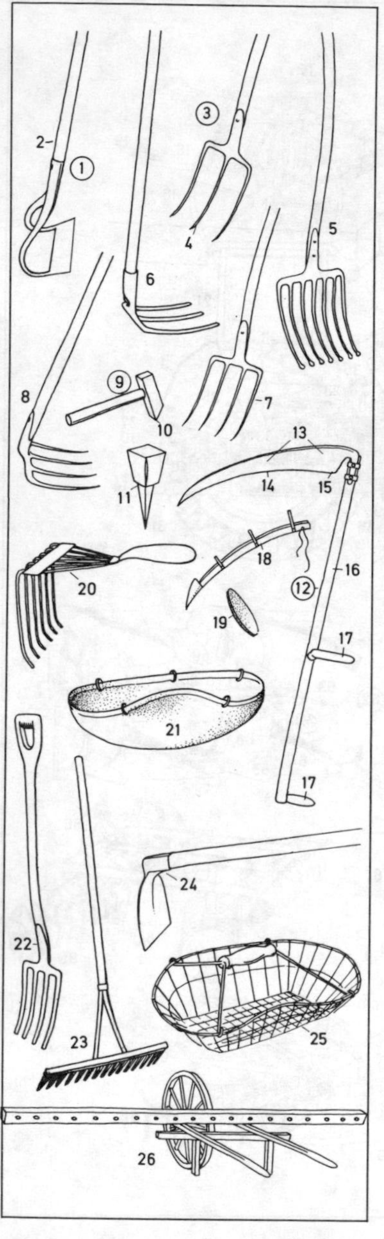

1 draw hoe (garden hoe)
2 hoe handle
3 three-pronged (three-tined) hay fork (fork)
4 prong (tine)
5 potato fork
6 potato hook
7 four-pronged (four-tined) manure fork (fork)
8 manure hoe
9 whetting hammer [for scythes]
10 peen (pane)
11 whetting anvil [for scythes]
12 scythe
13 scythe blade
14 cutting edge
15 heel
16 snath (snathe, snead, sneath)
17 handle
18 scythe sheath
19 whetstone (scythestone)
20 potato rake
21 potato planter
22 digging fork (fork)
23 wooden rake (rake, hayrake)
24 hoe (potato hoe)
25 potato basket, a wire basket
26 clover broadcaster

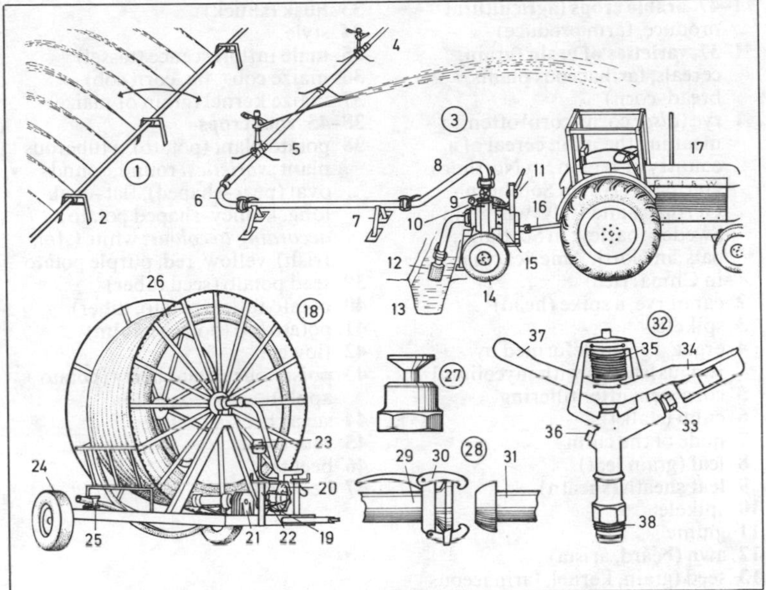

1 oscillating spray line
2 stand (steel chair)
3 portable irrigation system
4 revolving sprinkler
5 standpipe coupler
6 elbow with cardan joint (cardan coupling)
7 pipe support (trestle)
8 pump connection
9 delivery valve
10 pressure gauge (*Am.* gage) (manometer)
11 centrifugal evacuating pump
12 basket strainer
13 channel
14 chassis of the p.t.o.-driven pump (power take-off-driven pump)
15 p.t.o.-driven (power take-off-driven) pump
16 cardan shaft
17 tractor
18 long-range irrigation unit
19 drive connection
20 turbine
21 gearing (gears)
22 adjustable support
23 centrifugal evacuating pump
24 wheel
25 pipe support
26 polyester pipe
27 sprinkler nozzle
28 quick-fitting pipe connection with cardan joint
29 M-cardan
30 clamp
31 V-cardan
32 revolving sprinkler, a field sprinkler
33 nozzle
34 breaker
35 breaker spring
36 stopper
37 counterweight
38 thread

68 Arable Crops

1–47 arable crops (agricultural produce, farm produce)
1–37 varieties of grain (grain, cereals, farinaceous plants, bread-corn)
1 rye (*also:* corn, 'corn' often meaning the main cereal of a country or region; in Northern Germany: rye; in Southern Germany and Italy: wheat; in Sweden: barley; in Scotland: oats; in North America: maize; in China: rice)
2 ear of rye, a spike (head)
3 spikelet
4 ergot, a grain deformed by fungus [shown with mycelium]
5 corn stem after tillering
6 culm (stalk)
7 node of the culm
8 leaf (grain leaf)
9 leaf sheath (sheath)
10 spikelet
11 glume
12 awn (beard, arista)
13 seed (grain, kernel, farinaceous grain)
14 embryo plant
15 seed
16 embryo
17 root
18 root hair
19 grain leaf
20 leaf blade (blade, lamina)
21 leaf sheath
22 ligule (ligula)
23 wheat
24 spelt
25 seed; *unripe:* green spelt, a soup vegetable
26 barley
27 oat panicle, a panicle
28 millet
29 rice
30 rice grain
31 maize (Indian corn, *Am.* corn); *varieties:* popcorn, dent corn, flint corn (flint maize, *Am.* Yankee corn), pod corn (*Am.* cow corn, husk corn), soft corn (*Am.* flour corn, squaw corn), sweet corn
32 female inflorescence
33 husk (shuck)
34 style
35 male inflorescence (tassel)
36 maize cob (*Am.* corn cob)
37 maize kernel (grain of maize)
38–45 root crops
38 potato plant (potato), a tuberous plant; *varieties:* round, round-oval (pear-shaped), flat-oval, long, kidney-shaped potato; *according to colour:* white (*Am.* Irish), yellow, red, purple potato
39 seed potato (seed tuber)
40 potato tuber (potato, tuber)
41 potato top (potato haulm)
42 flower
43 poisonous potato berry (potato apple)
44 sugar beet, a beet
45 root (beet)
46 beet top
47 beet leaf

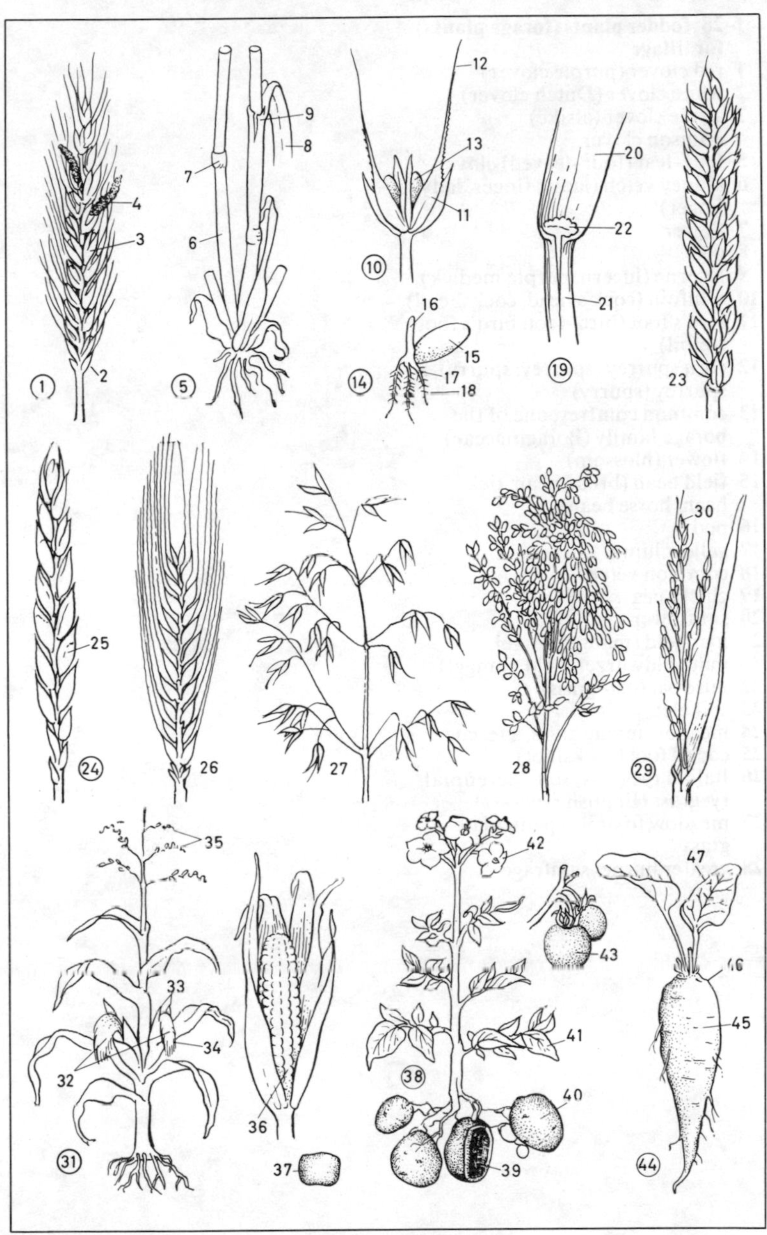
1
2
3
4
5
6
7
8
9
10
11
12
13
14
15
16
17
18
19
20
21
22
23
24
25
26
27
28
29
30
31
32
33
34
35
36
37
38
39
40
41
42
43
44
45
46
47

69 Fodder Plants (Forage Plants)

1–28 fodder plants (forage plants) for tillage

1 red clover (purple clover)
2 white clover (Dutch clover)
3 alsike clover (alsike)
4 crimson clover
5 four-leaf (four-leaved) clover
6 kidney vetch (lady's finger, lady-finger)
7 flower
8 pod
9 lucerne (lucern, purple medick)
10 sainfoin (cock's head, cockshead)
11 bird's foot (bird-foot, bird's foot trefoil)
12 corn spurrey (spurrey, spurry), a spurrey (spurry)
13 common comfrey, one of the borage family (Boraginaceae)
14 flower (blossom)
15 field bean (broad bean, tick bean, horse bean)
16 pod
17 yellow lupin
18 common vetch
19 chick-pea
20 sunflower
21 mangold (mangelwurzel, mangoldwurzel, field mangel)
22 false oat (oat-grass)
23 spikelet
24 meadow fescue grass, a fescue
25 cock's foot (cocksfoot)
26 Italian ryegrass; *sim.:* perennial ryegrass (English ryegrass)
27 meadow foxtail, a paniculate grass
28 greater burnet saxifrage

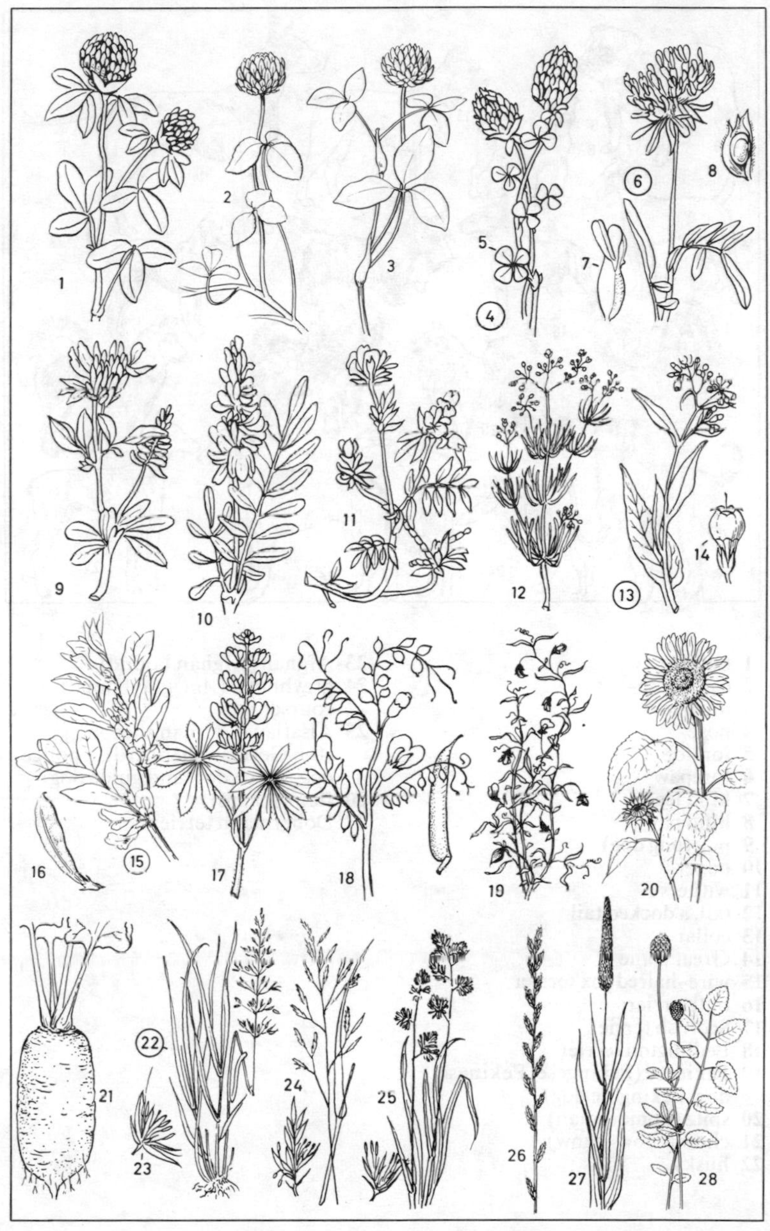
1
2
3
4
5
6
7
8
9
10
11
12
13
14
15
16
17
18
19
20
21
22
23
24
25
26
27
28

70 Breeds of Dog

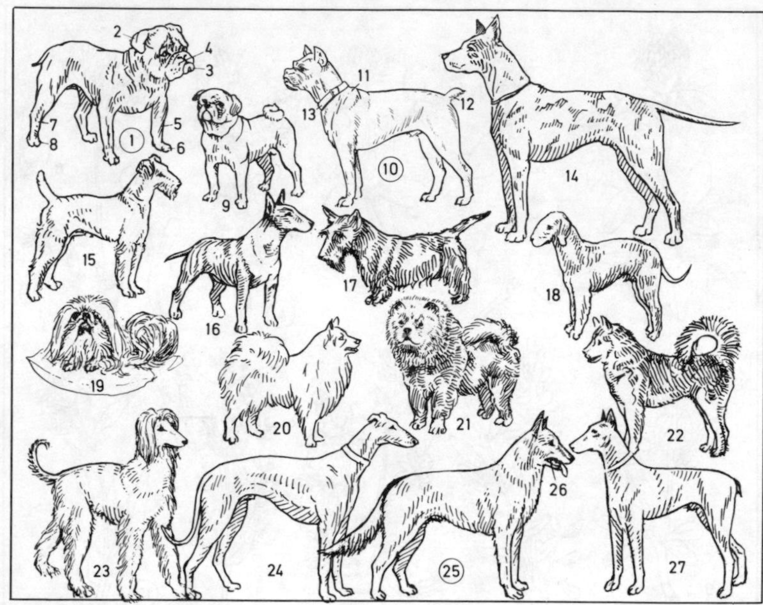

1 bulldog
2 ear, a rose-ear
3 muzzle
4 nose
5 foreleg
6 forepaw
7 hind leg
8 hind paw
9 pug (pug dog)
10 boxer
11 withers
12 tail, a docked tail
13 collar
14 Great Dane
15 wire-haired fox terrier
16 bull terrier
17 Scottish terrier
18 Bedlington terrier
19 Pekinese (Pekingese, Pekinese dog, Pekingese dog)
20 spitz (Pomeranian)
21 chow (chow-chow)
22 husky
23 Afghan (Afghan hound)
24 greyhound (*Am.* grayhound), a courser
25 Alsatian (German sheepdog, *Am.* German shepherd), a police dog, watch dog, and guide dog
26 flews (chaps)
27 Dobermann terrier

28 dog brush
29 dog comb
30 lead (dog lead, leash); *for hunting:* leash
31 muzzle
32 feeding bowl (dog bowl)
33 bone
34 Newfoundland dog
35 schnauzer
36 poodle; *sim. and smaller:* pygmy (pigmy) poodle
37 St. Bernard (St. Bernard dog)
38 cocker spaniel
39 dachshund, a terrier
40 German pointer
41 English setter
42 trackhound
43 pointer, a trackhound

71 Horse I

1–6 equitation (high school riding, haute école)
1 piaffe
2 walk
3 passage
4 levade (pesade)
5 capriole
6 courbette (curvet)
7–25 harness
7–13 bridle
7–11 headstall (headpiece, halter)
7 noseband
8 cheek piece (cheek strap)
9 browband (front band)
10 crownpiece
11 throatlatch (throatlash)
12 curb chain
13 curb bit
14 hasp (hook) of the hame (*Am.* drag hook)
15 pointed collar, a collar
16 trappings (side trappings)
17 saddle-pad
18 girth
19 backband
20 shaft chain (pole chain)
21 pole
22 trace
23 second girth (emergency girth)
24 trace
25 reins (*Am.* lines)
26–36 breast harness
26 blinker (*Am.* blinder, winker)
27 breast collar ring
28 breast collar (Dutch collar)
29 fork
30 neck strap
31 saddle-pad
32 loin strap
33 reins (rein, *Am.* line)
34 crupper (crupper-strap)
35 trace
36 girth (belly-band)
37–49 saddles
37–44 stock saddle (*Am.* western saddle)
37 saddle seat
38 pommel horn (horn)
39 cantle
40 flap (*Am.* fender)
41 bar
42 stirrup leather
43 stirrup (stirrup iron)
44 blanket
45–49 English saddle (cavalry saddle)
45 seat
46 cantle
47 flap
48 roll (knee roll)
49 pad
50–51 spurs
50 box spur (screwed jack spur)
51 strapped jack spur
52 curb bit
53 gag bit (gag)
54 currycomb
55 horse brush (body brush, dandy brush)

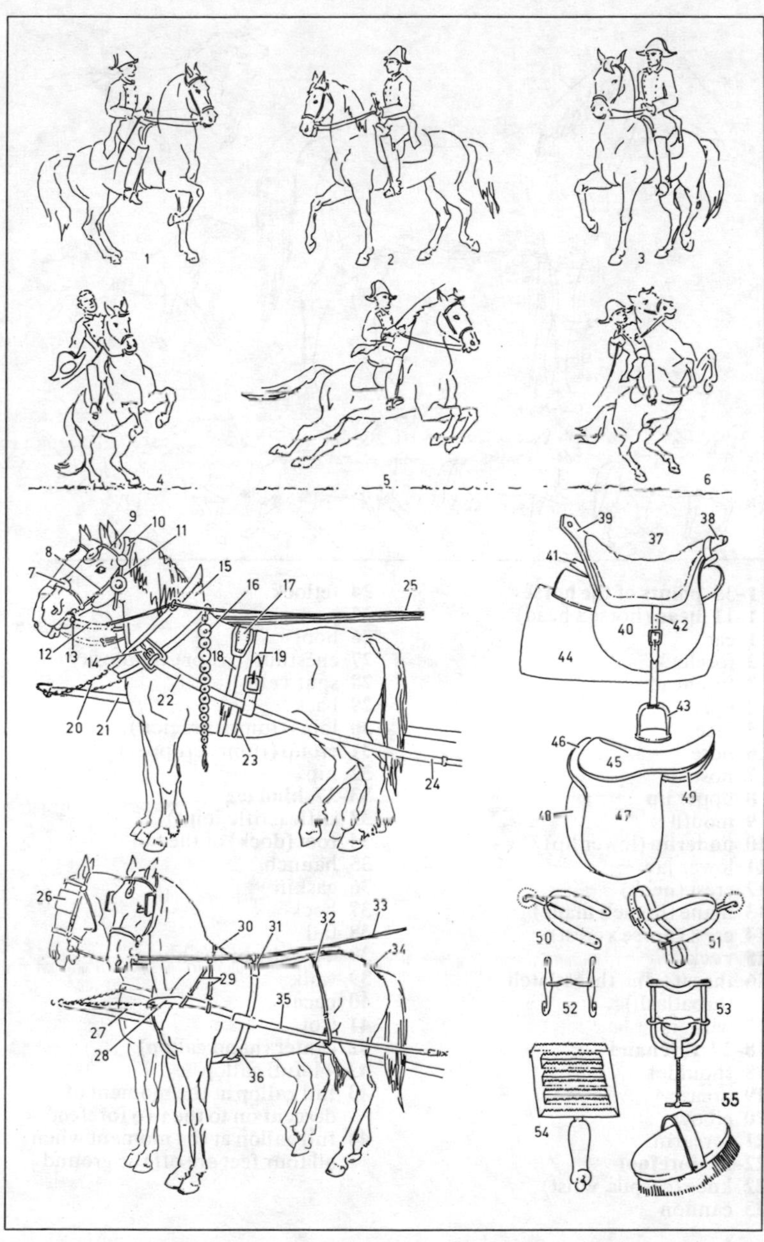
1
2
3
4
5
6
7
8
9
10
11
12
13
14
15
16
17
18
19
20
21
22
23
24
25
26
27
28
29
30
31
32
33
34
35
36
37
38
39
40
41
42
43
44
45
46
47
48
49
50
51
52
53
54
55

72 Horse II

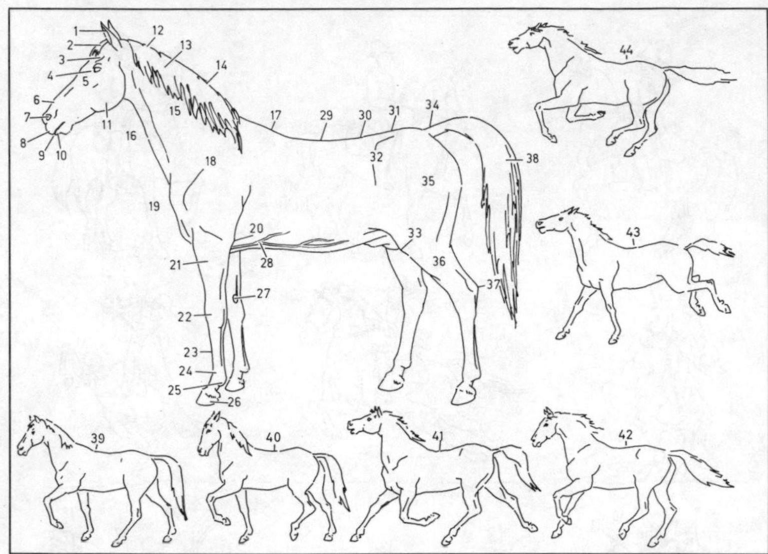

1–38 points of the horse
1–11 head (horse's head)
1 ear
2 forelock
3 forehead
4 eye
5 face
6 nose
7 nostril
8 upper lip
9 mouth
10 underlip (lower lip)
11 lower jaw
12 crest (neck)
13 mane (horse's mane)
14 crest (horse's crest)
15 neck
16 throat (*Am.* throatlatch, throatlash)
17 withers
18–27 forehand
18 shoulder
19 breast
20 elbow
21 forearm
22–26 forefoot
22 knee (carpus, wrist)
23 cannon
24 fetlock
25 pastern
26 hoof
27 chestnut (castor), a callosity
28 spur vein
29 back
30 loins (lumbar region)
31 croup (rump, crupper)
32 hip
33–37 hind leg
33 stifle (stifle joint)
34 root (dock) of the tail
35 haunch
36 gaskin
37 hock
38 tail
39–44 gaits of the horse
39 walk
40 pace
41 trot
42 canter (hand gallop)
43–44 full gallop
43 full gallop at the moment of descent on to the two forefeet
44 full gallop at the moment when all four feet are off the ground

Abbreviations:
– *m.* = male; *c.* = castrated; *f.* = female; *y.* = young

1–2 cattle

1 cow, a ruminant; *m.* bull; *c.* ox; *f.* cow; *y.* calf

2 horse; *m.* stallion; *c.* gelding; *f.* mare; *y.* foal

3 donkey

4 pack saddle (carrying saddle)

5 pack (load)

6 tufted tail

7 tuft

8 mule, a cross between a male donkey and a mare

9 pig, a cloven-hoofed animal; *m.* boar; *f.* sow; *v.* piglet

10 pig's snout (snout)

11 pig's ear

12 curly tail

13 sheep; *m.* ram; *c.* wether; *f.* ewe; *y.* lamb

14 goat

15 goat's beard

16 dog, a Leonberger; *m.* dog; *f.* bitch; *y.* pup (puppy, whelp)

17 cat, an Angora cat (Persian cat); *m.* tom (tom cat)

18–36 small domestic animals

18 rabbit; *m.* buck; *f.* doe

19–36 poultry (domestic fowl)

19–26 chicken

19 hen

20 crop (craw)

21 cock (*Am.* rooster); *c.* capon

22 cockscomb (comb, crest)

23 lap

24 wattle (gill, dewlap)

25 falcate (falcated) tail

26 spur

27 guinca fowl

28 turkey; *m.* turkey cock (gobblcr); *f.* turkey hen

29 fan tail

30 peacock

31 peacock's feather

32 eye (ocellus)

33 pigeon; *m.* cock pigeon

34 goose; *m.* gander; *y.* gosling

35 duck; *m.* drake; *y.* duckling

36 web (palmations) of webbed foot (palmate foot)

74 Poultry Farming (Poultry Keeping), Egg Production

1–27 poultry farming (intensive poultry management)
1–17 straw yard (strawed yard) system
1 fold unit for growing stock (chick unit)
2 chick
3 brooder (hover)
4 adjustable feeding trough
5 pullet fold unit
6 drinking trough
7 water pipe
8 litter
9 pullet
10 ventilator
11–17 broiler rearing (rearing of broiler chickens)
11 chicken run (*Am.* fowl run)
12 broiler chicken (broiler)
13 mechanical feeder (self-feeder, feed dispenser)
14 chain
15 feed supply pipe
16 mechanical drinking bowl (mechanical drinker)
17 ventilator
18 battery system (cage system)
19 battery (laying battery)
20 tiered cage (battery cage, stepped cage)
21 feeding trough
22 egg collection by conveyor
23–27 mechanical feeding and dunging (manure removal, droppings removal)
23 rapid feeding system for battery feeding (mechanical feeder)
24 feed hopper
25 endless-chain conveyor (chain feeder)
26 water pipe (liquid feed pipe)
27 dunging chain (dunging conveyor)
28 [cabinet type] setting and hatching machine
29 ventilation drum [for the setting compartment]
30 hatching compartment (hatcher)
31 metal trolley for hatching trays
32 hatching tray
33 ventilation drum motor
34–53 egg production
34 egg collection system (egg collection)
35 multi-tier transport
36 collection by pivoted fingers
37 drive motor
38 sorting machine
39 conveyor trolley
40 fluorescent screen
41 suction apparatus (suction box) for transporting eggs
42 shelf for empty and full egg boxes
43 egg weighers
44 grading
45 egg box
46 fully automatic egg-packing machine
47 radioscope box
48 radioscope table
49–51 feeder
49 suction transporter
50 vacuum line
51 supply table
52 automatic counting and grading
53 packing box dispenser
54 leg ring
55 wing tally (identification tally)
56 bantam
57 laying hen
58 hen's egg (egg)
59 eggshell, an egg integument
60 shell membrane
61 air space
62 white [of the egg] (albumen)
63 chalaza (*Am.* treadle)
64 vitelline membrane (yolk sac)
65 blastodisc (germinal disc, cock's tread, cock's treadle)
66 germinal vesicle
67 white
68 yolk

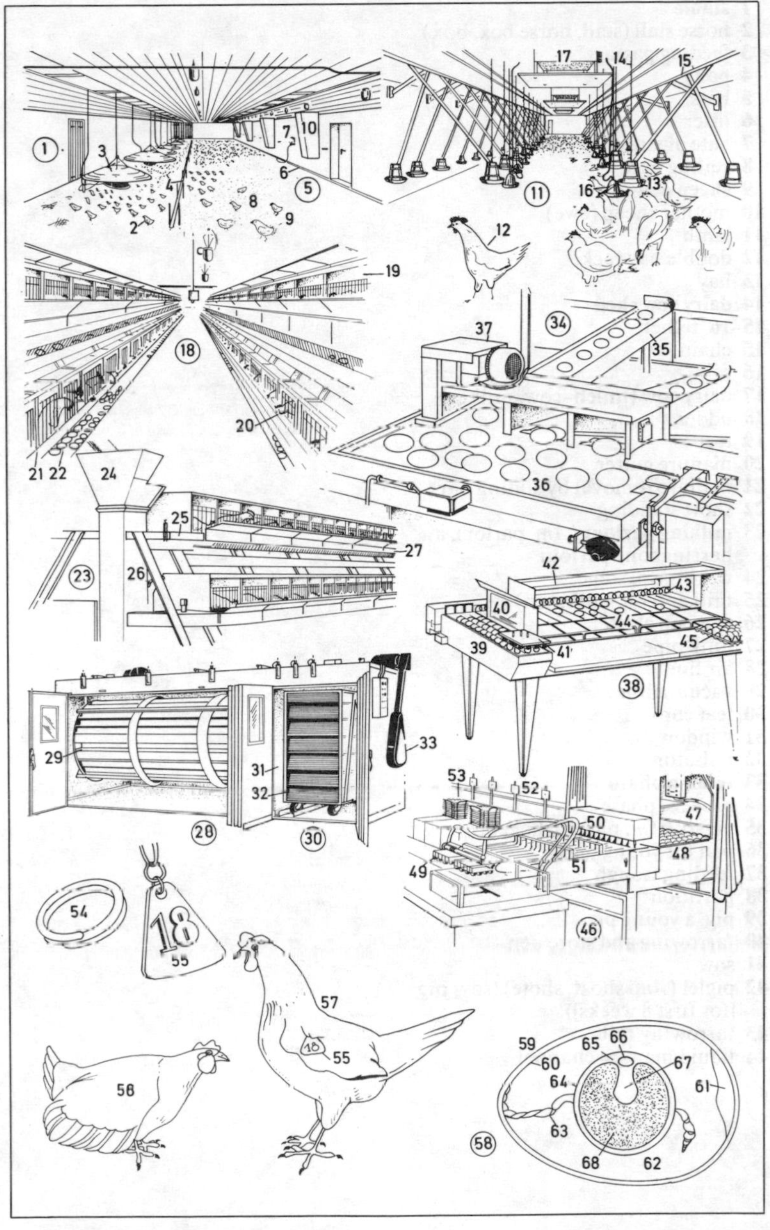
1
2
3
4
5
6
7
8
9
10
11
12
13
14
15
16
17
18
19
20
21
22
23
24
25
26
27
28
29
30
31
32
33
34
35
36
37
38
39
40
41
42
43
44
45
46
47
48
49
50
51
52
53
54
55
18
56
57
58
59
60
61
62
63
64
65
66
67
68

75 Rearing (*Am.* Raising) of Livestock

1 **stable**
2 horse stall (stall, horse box, box)
3 feeding passage
4 pony
5 bars
6 litter
7 bale of straw
8 ceiling light
9 **sheep pen**
10 mother sheep (ewe)
11 lamb
12 double hay rack
13 hay
14 **dairy cow shed**
15–16 tether
15 chain
16 rail
17 dairy cow (milch-cow, milker)
18 udder
19 teat
20 manure gutter
21 manure removal by sliding bars
22 short standing
23 **milking parlour** (*Am.* parlor), a herringbone parlour
24 working passage
25 milker (*Am.* milkman)
26 teat cup cluster
27 milk pipe
28 air line
29 vacuum line
30 teat cup
31 window
32 pulsator
33 release phase
34 squeeze phase
35 **pigsty** (*Am.* pigpen, hogpen)
36 pen for young pigs
37 feeding trough
38 partition
39 pig, a young pig
40 farrowing and store pen
41 sow
42 piglet (*Am.* shoat, shote) (sow pig [for first 8 weeks])
43 farrowing rails
44 liquid manure channel

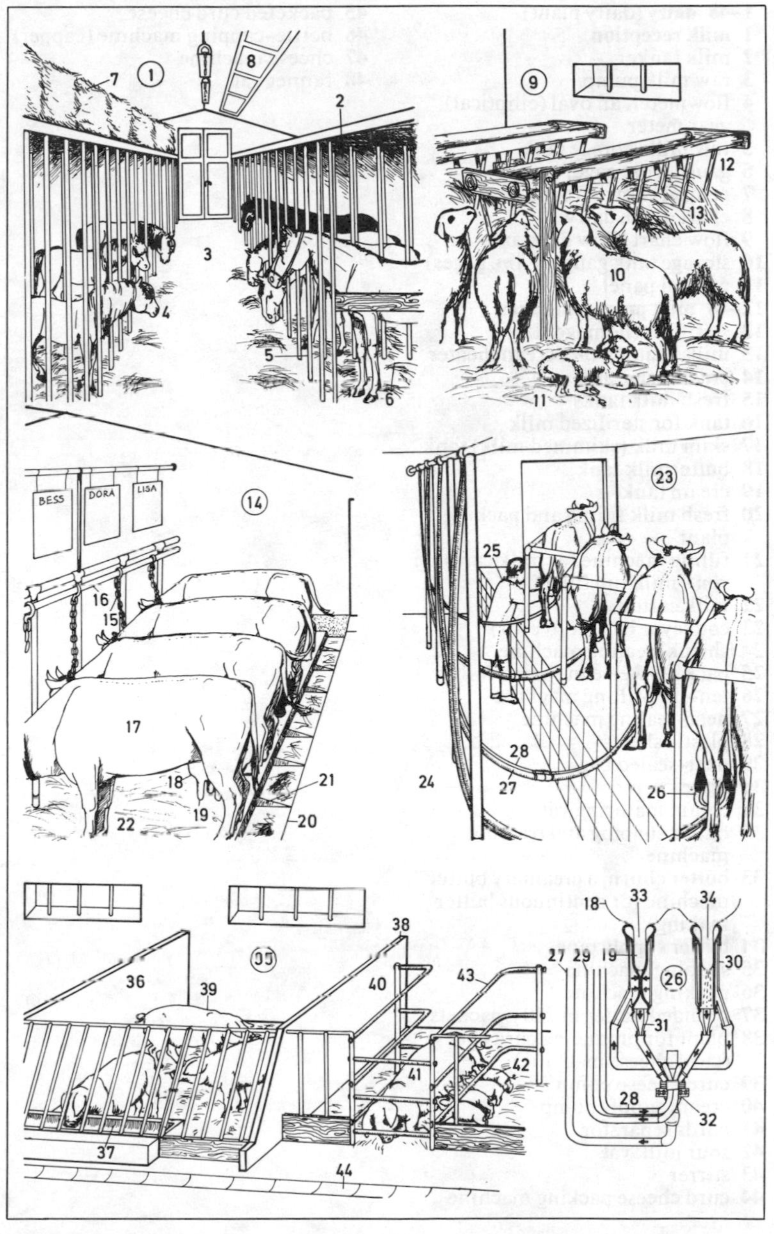
BESS
DORA
LISA

1–48 dairy (dairy plant)
1 milk reception
2 milk tanker
3 raw milk pump
4 flowmeter, an oval (elliptical) gear meter
5 raw milk storage tank
6 gauge (*Am.* gage)
7 central control room
8 chart of the dairy
9 flow chart (flow diagram)
10 storage tank gauges (*Am.* gages)
11 control panel
12–48 milk processing area
12 sterilizer (homogenizer)
13 milk heater; *sim.:* cream heater
14 cream separator
15 fresh milk tanks
16 tank for sterilized milk
17 skim milk (skimmed milk) tank
18 buttermilk tank
19 cream tank
20 fresh milk filling and packing plant
21 filling machine for milk cartons; *sim.:* milk tub filler
22 milk carton
23 conveyor belt (conveyor)
24 shrink-sealing machine
25 pack of twelve in shrink foil
26 ten-litre filling machine
27 heat-sealing machine
28 plastic sheets
29 heat-sealed bag
30 crate
31 cream maturing vat
32 butter shaping and packing machine
33 butter churn, a creamery butter machine for continuous butter making
34 butter supply pipe
35 shaping machine
36 packing machine
37 branded butter in 250 g packets
38 plant for producing curd cheese (curd cheese machine)
39 curd cheese pump
40 cream supply pump
41 curds separator
42 sour milk vat
43 stirrer
44 curd cheese packing machine
45 packeted curd cheese
46 bottle-capping machine (capper)
47 cheese machine
48 rennet vat

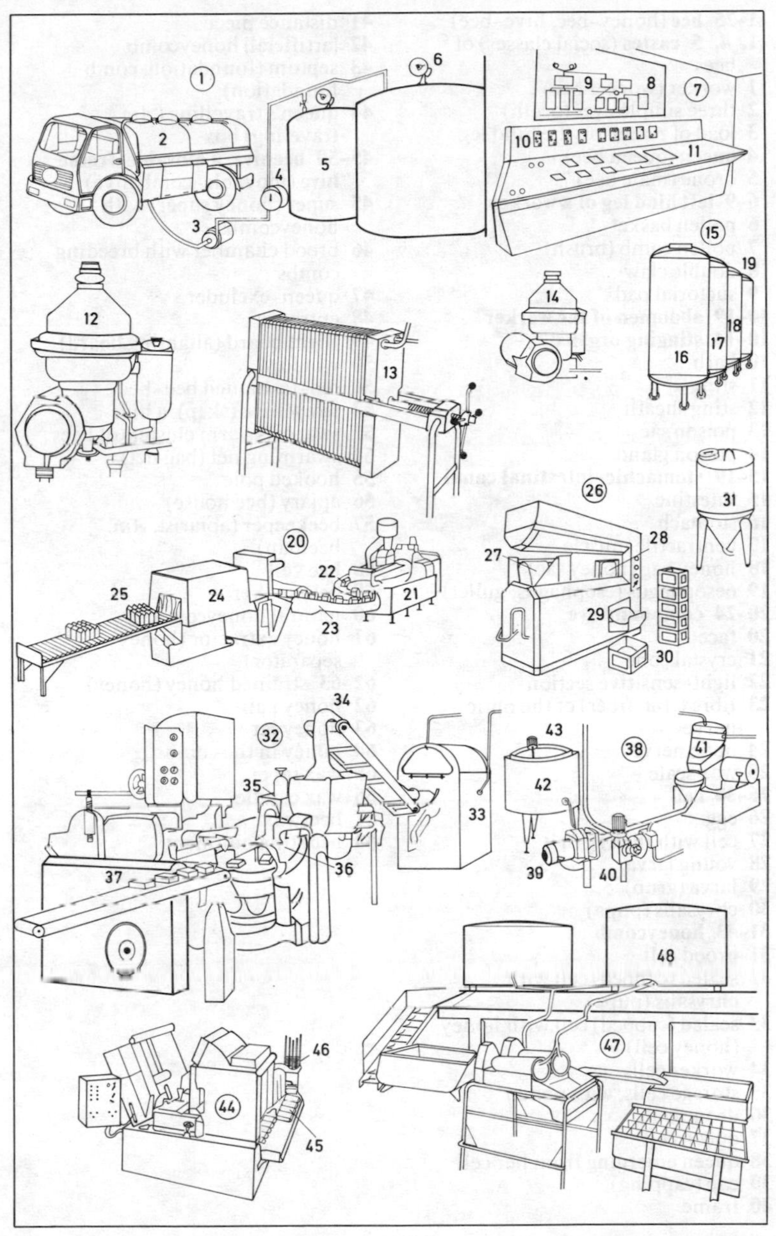
1
2
3
4
5
6
7
8
9
10
11
12
13
14
15
16
17
18
19
20
21
22
23
24
25
26
27
28
29
30
31
32
33
34
35
36
37
38
39
40
41
42
43
44
45
46
47
48

77 Bees and Beekeeping (Apiculture)

1–25 bee (honey–bee, hive–bee)
1, 4, 5 castes (social classes) of bees
1 worker (worker bee)
2 three simple eyes (ocelli)
3 load of pollen on the hind leg
4 queen (queen bee)
5 drone (male bee)
6–9 left hind leg of a worker
6 pollen basket
7 pollen comb (brush)
8 double claw
9 suctorial pad
10–19 abdomen of the worker
10–14 stinging organs
10 barb
11 sting
12 sting sheath
13 poison sac
14 poison gland
15–19 stomachic–intestinal canal
15 intestine
16 stomach
17 contractile muscle
18 honey bag (honey sac)
19 oesophagus (esophagus, gullet)
20–24 compound eye
20 facet
21 crystal cone
22 light–sensitive section
23 fibre (*Am.* fiber) of the optic nerve
24 optic nerve
25 wax scale
26–30 cell
26 egg
27 cell with the egg in it
28 young larva
29 larva (grub)
30 chrysalis (pupa)
31–43 honeycomb
31 brood cell
32 sealed (capped) cell with chrysalis (pupa)
33 sealed (capped) cell with honey (honey cell)
34 worker cells
35 storage cells, with pollen
36 drone cells
37 queen cell
38 queen emerging from her cell
39 cap (capping)
40 frame
41 distance piece
42 [artificial] honeycomb
43 septum (foundation, comb foundation)
44 queen's travelling (*Am.* traveling) box
45–50 beehive, a movable–frame hive (movable–comb hive)
45 super (honey super) with honeycombs
46 brood chamber with breeding combs
47 queen–excluder
48 entrance
49 flight board (alighting board)
50 window
51 old–fashioned bee shed
52 straw hive (skep), a hive
53 swarm (swarm cluster) of bees
54 swarming net (bag net)
55 hooked pole
56 apiary (bee house)
57 beekeeper (apiarist, *Am.* beeman)
58 bee veil
59 bee smoker
60 natural honeycomb
61 honey extractor (honey separator)
62–63 strained honey (honey)
62 honey pail
63 honey jar
64 honey in the comb
65 wax taper
66 wax candle
67 beeswax
68 bee sting ointment

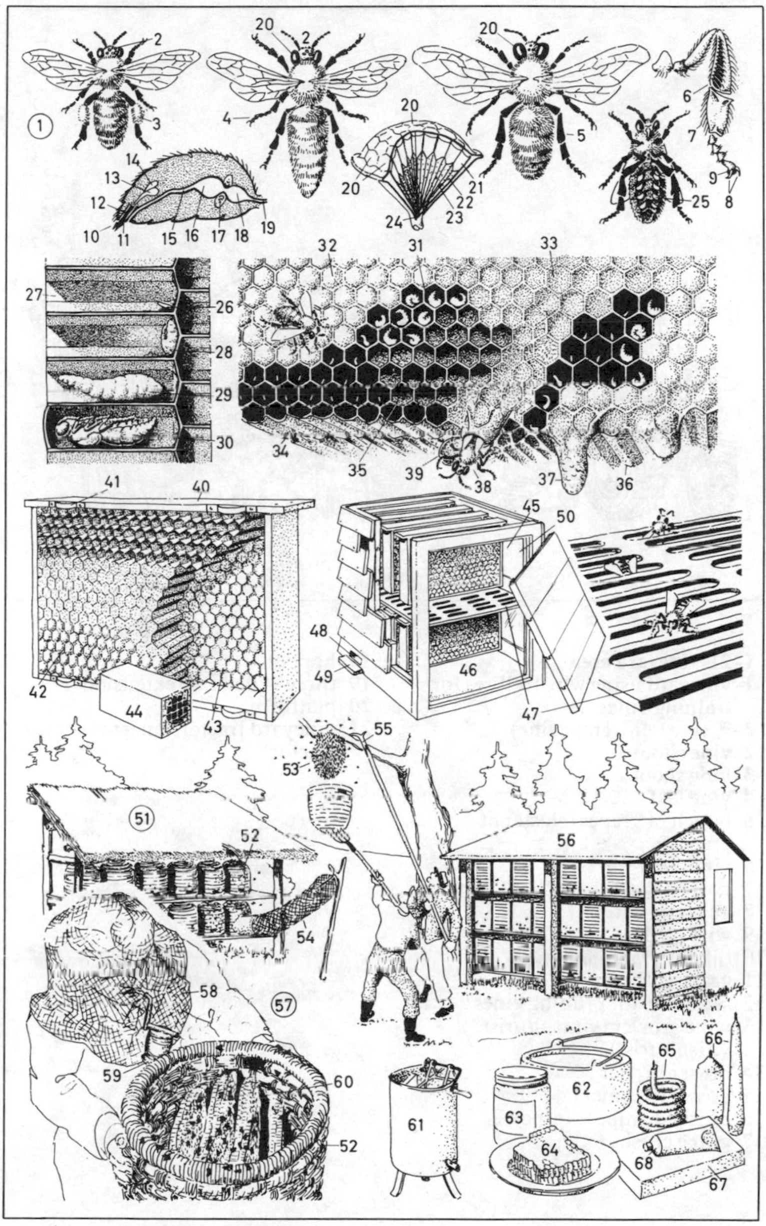
1
2
3
4
5
6
7
8
9
10
11
12
13
14
15
16
17
18
19
20
21
22
23
24
25
26
27
28
29
30
31
32
33
34
35
36
37
38
39
40
41
42
43
44
45
46
47
48
49
50
51
52
53
54
55
56
57
58
59
60
61
62
63
64
65
66
67
68

78 Wine Growing (Viniculture, Viticulture)

1–21 vineyard area
1 vineyard using wire trellises for training vines
2–9 vine (*Am.* grapevine)
2 vine shoot
3 long shoot
4 vine leaf
5 bunch of grapes (cluster of grapes)
6 vine stem
7 post (stake)
8 guy (guy wire)
9 wire trellis
10 tub for grape gathering
11 grape gatherer
12 secateurs for pruning vines
13 wine grower (viniculturist, viticulturist)
14 dosser carrier
15 dosser (pannier)
16 crushed grape transporter
17 grape crusher
18 hopper
19 three-sided flap extension
20 platform
21 vineyard tractor, a narrow-track tractor

1–22 wine cellar (wine vault)
1 vault
2 wine cask
3 wine vat, a concrete vat
4 stainless steel vat (*also:* vat made of synthetic material)
5 propeller-type high-speed mixer
6 propeller mixer
7 centrifugal pump
8 stainless steel sediment filter
9 semi-automatic circular bottling machine
10 semi-automatic corking machine
11 bottle rack
12 cellarer's assistant
13 bottle basket
14 wine bottle
15 wine jug
16 wine tasting
17 head cellarman
18 cellarman
19 wineglass
20 inspection apparatus [for spot-checking samples]
21 horizontal wine press
22 humidifier

80 Garden and Field Pests

1–19 fruit pests
1 gipsy (gypsy) moth
2 batch (cluster) of eggs
3 caterpillar
4 chrysalis (pupa)
5 small ermine moth, an ermine moth
6 larva (grub)
7 tent
8 caterpillar skeletonizing a leaf
9 fruit surface eating tortrix moth (summer fruit tortrix moth)
10 appleblossom weevil, a weevil
11 punctured, withered flower (blossom)
12 hole for laying eggs
13 lackey moth
14 caterpillar
15 eggs
16 winter moth, a geometrid
17 caterpillar
18 cherry fruit fly, a borer
19 larva (grub, maggot)
20–27 vine pests
20 downy mildew, a mildew, a disease causing leaf drop
21 grape affected with downy mildew
22 grape-berry moth
23 first-generation larva of the grape-berry moth (*Am.* grape worm)
24 second-generation larva of the grape-berry moth (*Am.* grape worm)
25 chrysalis (pupa)
26 root louse, a grape phylloxera
27 root gall (knotty swelling of the root, nodosity, tuberosity)
28 brown-tail moth
29 caterpillar
30 batch (cluster) of eggs
31 hibernation cocoon
32 woolly apple aphid (American blight), an aphid
33 gall caused by the woolly apple aphid
34 woolly apple aphid colony
35 San-José scale, a scale insect (scale louse)
36 larvae (grubs) [*male* elongated, *female* round]

37–55 field pests
37 click beetle, a snapping beetle (*Am.* snapping bug)
38 wireworm, larva of the click beetle
39 flea beetle
40 Hessian fly, a gall midge (gall gnat)
41 larva (grub)
42 turnip moth, an earth moth
43 chrysalis (pupa)
44 cutworm, a caterpillar
45 beet carrion beetle
46 larva (grub)
47 large cabbage white butterfly
48 caterpillar of the small cabbage white butterfly
49 brown leaf-eating weevil, a weevil
50 feeding site
51 sugar beet eelworm, a nematode (a threadworm, hairworm)
52 Colorado beetle (potato beetle)
53 mature larva (grub)
54 young larva (grub)
55 eggs

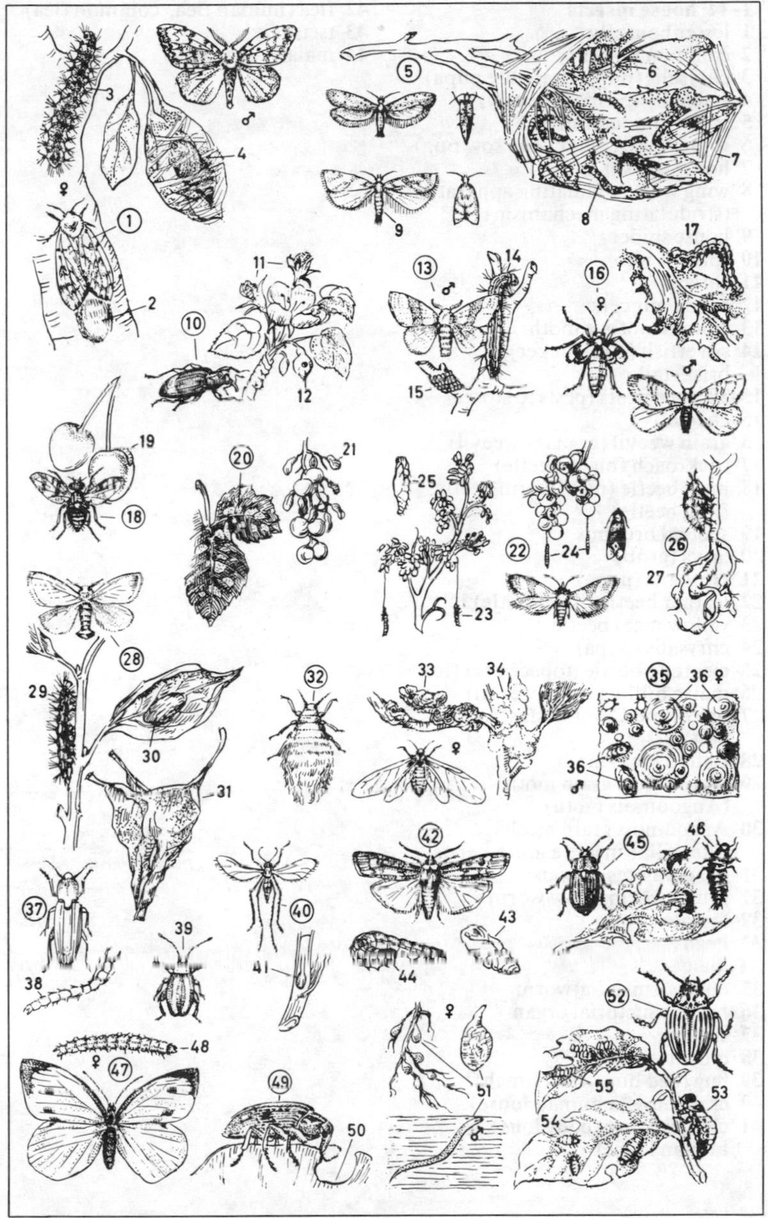
1
2
3
4
5
6
7
8
9
10
11
12
13
14
15
16
17
18
19
20
21
22
23
24
25
26
27
28
29
30
31
32
33
34
35
36
37
38
39
40
41
42
43
44
45
46
47
48
49
50
51
52
53
54
55

81 House Insects, Food Pests, and Parasites

1–14 house insects
1 lesser housefly
2 common housefly
3 chrysalis (pupa, coarctate pupa)
4 stable fly (biting housefly)
5 trichotomous antenna
6 wood louse (slater, *Am.* sow bug)
7 house cricket
8 wing with stridulating apparatus (stridulating mechanism)
9 house spider
10 spider's web
11 earwig
12 caudal pincers
13 clothes moth, a moth
14 silverfish (*Am.* slicker), a bristletail
15–30 food pests (pests to stores)
15 cheesefly
16 grain weevil (granary weevil)
17 cockroach (black beetle)
18 meal beetle (meal worm beetle, flour beetle)
19 spotted bruchus
20 larva (grub)
21 chrysalis (pupa)
22 leather beetle (hide beetle)
23 yellow meal beetle
24 chrysalis (pupa)
25 cigarette beetle (tobacco beetle)
26 maize billbug (corn weevil)
27 one of the Cryptolestes, a grain pest
28 Indian meal moth
29 Angoumois grain moth (Angoumois moth)
30 Angoumois grain moth caterpillar inside a grain kernel
31–42 parasites of man
31 round worm (maw worm)
32 female
33 head
34 male
35 tapeworm, a flatworm
36 head, a suctorial organ
37 sucker
38 crown of hooks
39 bug (bed bug, *Am.* chinch)
40 crab louse (a human louse)
41 clothes louse (body louse, a human louse)
42 flea (human flea, common flea)
43 tsetse fly
44 malaria mosquito

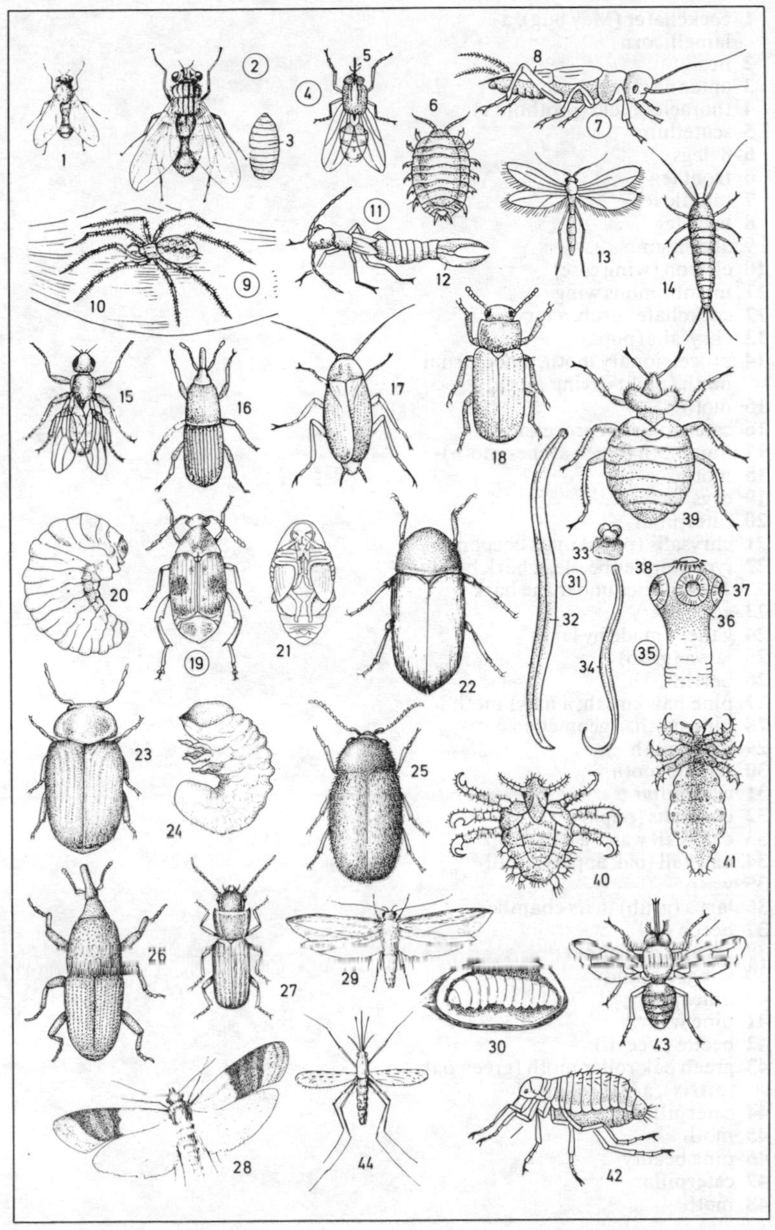
1
2
3
4
5
6
7
8
9
10
11
12
13
14
15
16
17
18
19
20
21
22
23
24
25
26
27
28
29
30
31
32
33
34
35
36
37
38
39
40
41
42
43
44

82 Forest Pests

1 cockchafer (May bug), a lamellicorn
2 head
3 antenna (feeler)
4 thoracic shield (prothorax)
5 scutellum
6–8 legs
6 front leg
7 middle leg
8 back leg
9 abdomen
10 elytron (wing case)
11 membranous wing
12 cockchafer grub, a larva
13 chrysalis (pupa)
14 processionary moth, a nocturnal moth (night-flying moth)
15 moth
16 caterpillars in procession
17 nun moth (black arches moth)
18 moth
19 eggs
20 caterpillar
21 chrysalis (pupa) in its cocoon
22 typographer beetle, a bark beetle
23–24 galleries under the bark
23 egg gallery
24 gallery made by larva
25 larva (grub)
26 beetle
27 pine hawkmoth, a hawkmoth
28 pine moth, a geometrid
29 male moth
30 female moth
31 caterpillar
32 chrysalis (pupa)
33 oak-gall wasp, a gall wasp
34 oak gall (oak apple), a gall
35 wasp
36 larva (grub) in its chamber
37 beech gall
38 spruce-gall aphid
39 winged aphid
40 pineapple gall
41 pine weevil
42 beetle (weevil)
43 green oak roller moth (green oak tortrix), a leaf roller
44 caterpillar
45 moth
46 pine beauty
47 caterpillar
48 moth

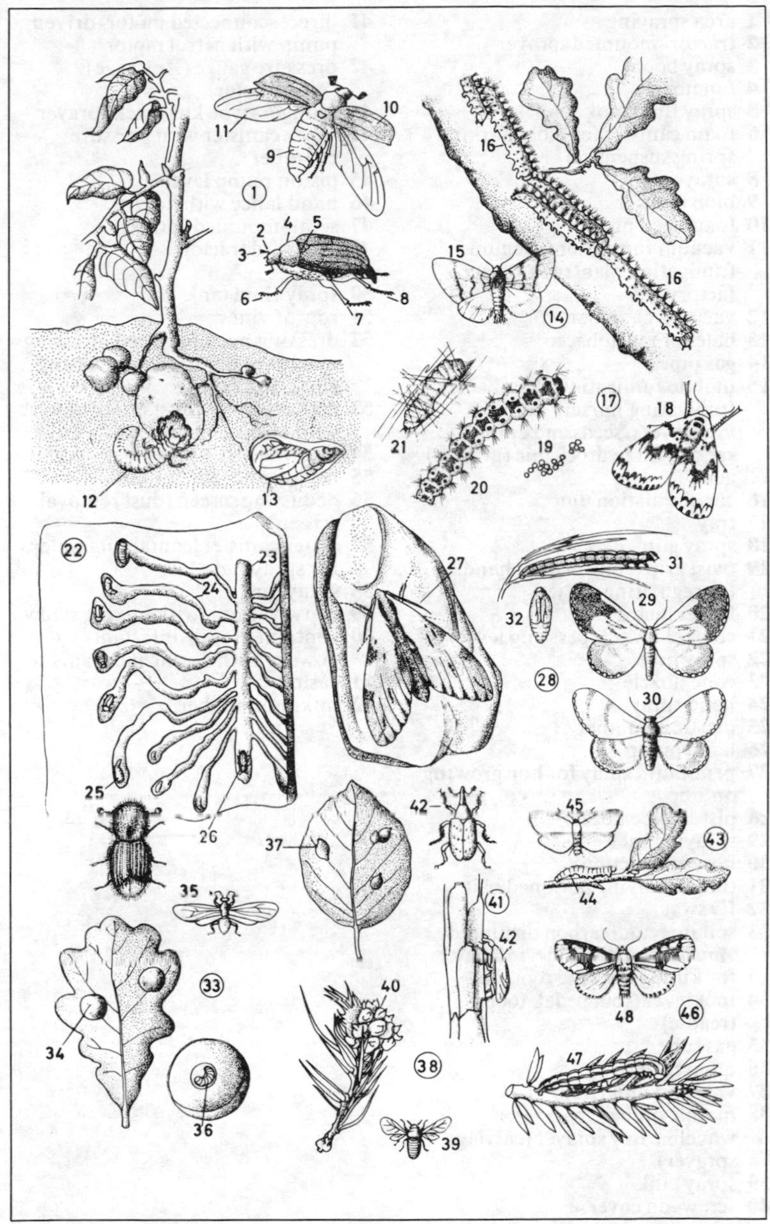
11
10
9
1
2
4
5
3
6
7
8
12
13
16
15
16
14
17
18
21
19
20
22
23
24
27
31
32
29
28
30
25
26
42
45
43
44
37
35
41
42
33
40
34
36
38
39
48
46
47

83 Pest Control

1 area spraying
2 tractor-mounted sprayer
3 spray boom
4 fan nozzle
5 spray fluid tank
6 foam canister for blob marking
7 spring suspension
8 spray
9 blob marker
10 foam feed pipe
11 vacuum fumigator (vacuum fumigation plant) of a tobacco factory
12 vacuum chamber
13 bales of raw tobacco
14 gas pipe
15 mobile fumigation chamber for fumigating nursery saplings, vine layers, seeds,and empty sacks with hydrocyanic (prussic) acid
16 gas circulation unit
17 tray
18 spray gun
19 twist grip (control grip, handle) for regulating the jet
20 finger guard
21 control lever (operating lever)
22 spray tube
23 cone nozzle
24 hand spray
25 plastic container
26 hand pump
27 pendulum spray for hop growing on slopes
28 pistol-type nozzle
29 spraying tube
30 hose connection
31 tube for laying poisoned bait
32 fly swat
33 soil injector (carbon disulphide, *Am.* carbon disulfide, injector) for killing the vine root louse
34 foot lever (foot pedal, foot treadle)
35 gas tube
36 mousetrap
37 vole and mole trap
38 mobile orchard sprayer, a wheelbarrow sprayer (carriage sprayer)
39 spray tank
40 screw-on cover
41 direct-connected motor-driven pump with petrol motor
42 pressure gauge (*Am.* gage) (manometer)
43 plunger-type knapsack sprayer
44 spray canister with pressure chamber
45 piston pump lever
46 hand lance with nozzle
47 semi-mounted sprayer
48 vineyard tractor
49 fan
50 spray fluid tank
51 row of vines
52 dressing machine (seed-dressing machine) for dry-seed dressing (seed dusting)
53 dedusting fan (dust removal fan) with electric motor
54 bag filter
55 bagging nozzle
56 dedusting screen (dust removal screen)
57 water canister [containing water for spraying]
58 spray unit
59 conveyor unit with mixing screw
60 container for disinfectant powder with dosing mechanism
61 castor
62 mixing chamber

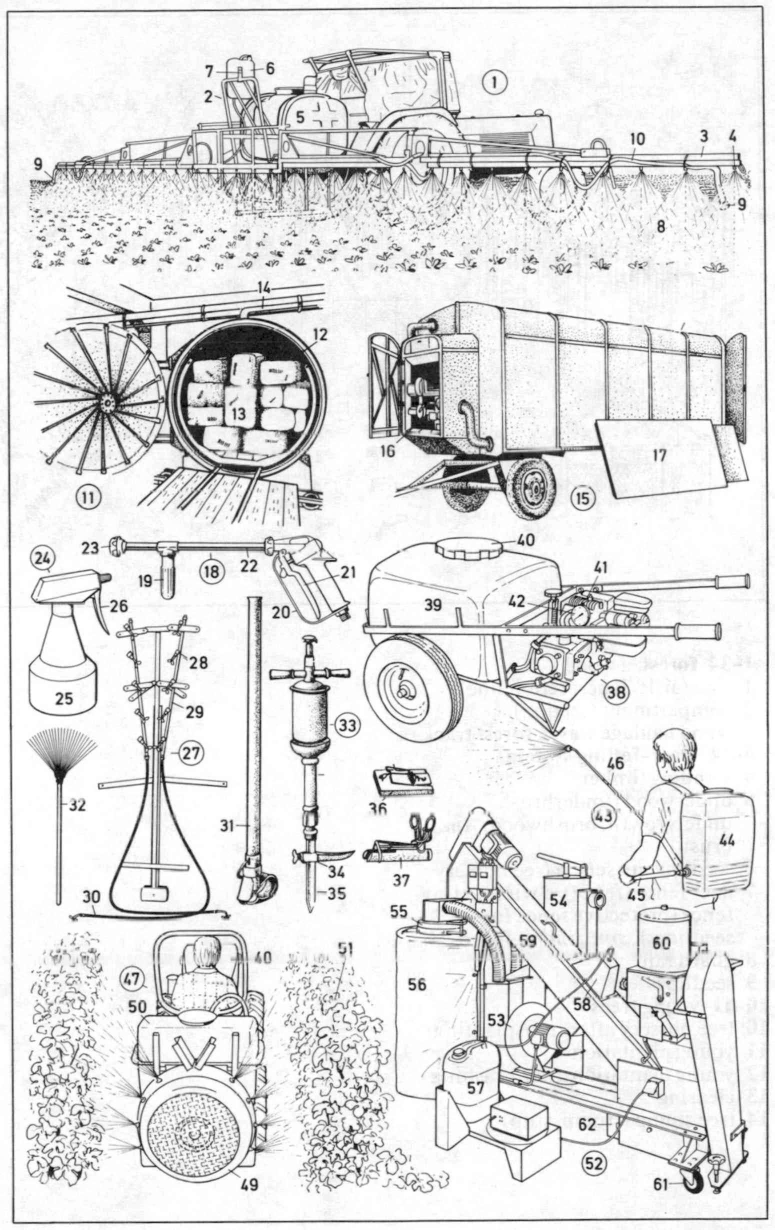
1
2
3
4
5
6
7
8
9
10
11
12
13
14
15
16
17
18
19
20
21
22
23
24
25
26
27
28
29
30
31
32
33
34
35
36
37
38
39
40
41
42
43
44
45
46
47
49
50
51
52
53
54
55
56
57
58
59
60
61
62

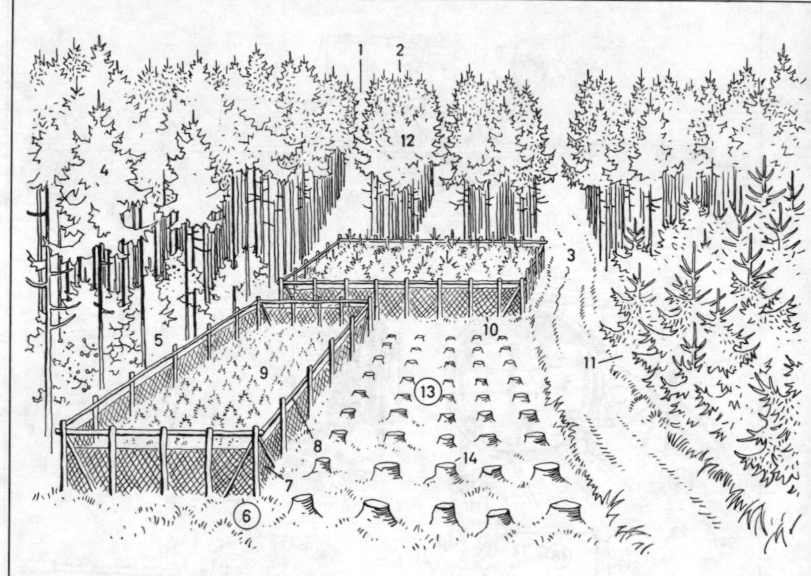

1–34 forest, a wood
1 ride (aisle, lane, section line)
2 compartment (section)
3 wood haulage way, a forest track
4–14 clear-felling system
4 standing timber
5 underwood (underbrush, undergrowth, brushwood, *Am.* brush)
6 seedling nursery, a tree nursery
7 deer fence (fence), a wire netting fence (protective fence for seedlings); *sim.:* rabbit fence
8 guard rail
9 seedlings
10–11 young trees
10 tree nursery after transplanting
11 young plantation
12 young plantation after brashing
13 clearing
14 tree stump (stump, stub)

15–37 wood cutting (timber cutting, tree felling, *Am.* lumbering)
15 timber skidded to the stack (stacked timber, *Am.* yarded timber)
16 stack of logs, one cubic metre (*Am.* meter) of wood
17 post (stake)
18 forest labourer (woodsman, *Am.* logger, lumberer, lumberjack, lumberman, timberjack) turning (*Am.* canting) timber
19 bole (tree trunk, trunk, stem)
20 feller numbering the logs
21 steel tree calliper (caliper)
22 power saw (motor saw) cutting a bole
23 safety helmet with visor and ear pieces
24 annual rings
25 hydraulic felling wedge
26 protective clothing [orange top, green trousers]
27 felling with a power saw (motor saw)
28 undercut (notch, throat, gullet, mouth, sink, kerf, birdsmouth)
29 back cut
30 sheath holding felling wedge
31 log
32 free-cutting saw for removing underwood and weeds
33 circular saw (or activated blade) attachment
34 power unit (motor)
35 canister of viscous oil for the saw chain
36 petrol canister (*Am.* gasoline canister)
37 felling of small timber (of small-sized thinnings) (thinning)

85 Forestry II

1 axe (*Am.* ax)
2 edge (cutting edge)
3 handle (helve)
4 felling wedge (falling wedge) with wood insert and ring
5 riving hammer (cleaving hammer, splitting hammer)
6 lifting hook
7 cant hook
8 barking iron (bark spud)
9 peavy
10 slide calliper (caliper) (calliper square)
11 billhook, a knife for lopping
12 revolving die hammer (marking hammer, marking iron, *Am.* marker)
13 power saw (motor saw)
14 saw chain
15 safety brake for the saw chain, with finger guard
16 saw guide
17 accelerator lock
18 snedding machine (trimming machine, *Am.* knotting machine, limbing machine)
19 feed rolls
20 flexible blade
21 hydraulic arm
22 trimming blade
23 debarking (barking, bark stripping) of boles
24 feed roller
25 cylinder trimmer
26 rotary cutter
27 short-haul skidder
28 loading crane
29 log grips
30 post
31 Ackermann steering system
32 log dump
33 number (identification number)
34 skidder
35 front blade (front plate)
36 crush-proof safety bonnet (*Am.* safety hood)
37 Ackermann steering system
38 cable winch
39 cable drum
40 rear blade (rear plate)
41 boles with butt ends held off the ground
42 haulage of timber by road
43 tractor (tractor unit)
44 loading crane
45 hydraulic jack
46 cable winch
47 post
48 bolster plate
49 rear bed (rear bunk)

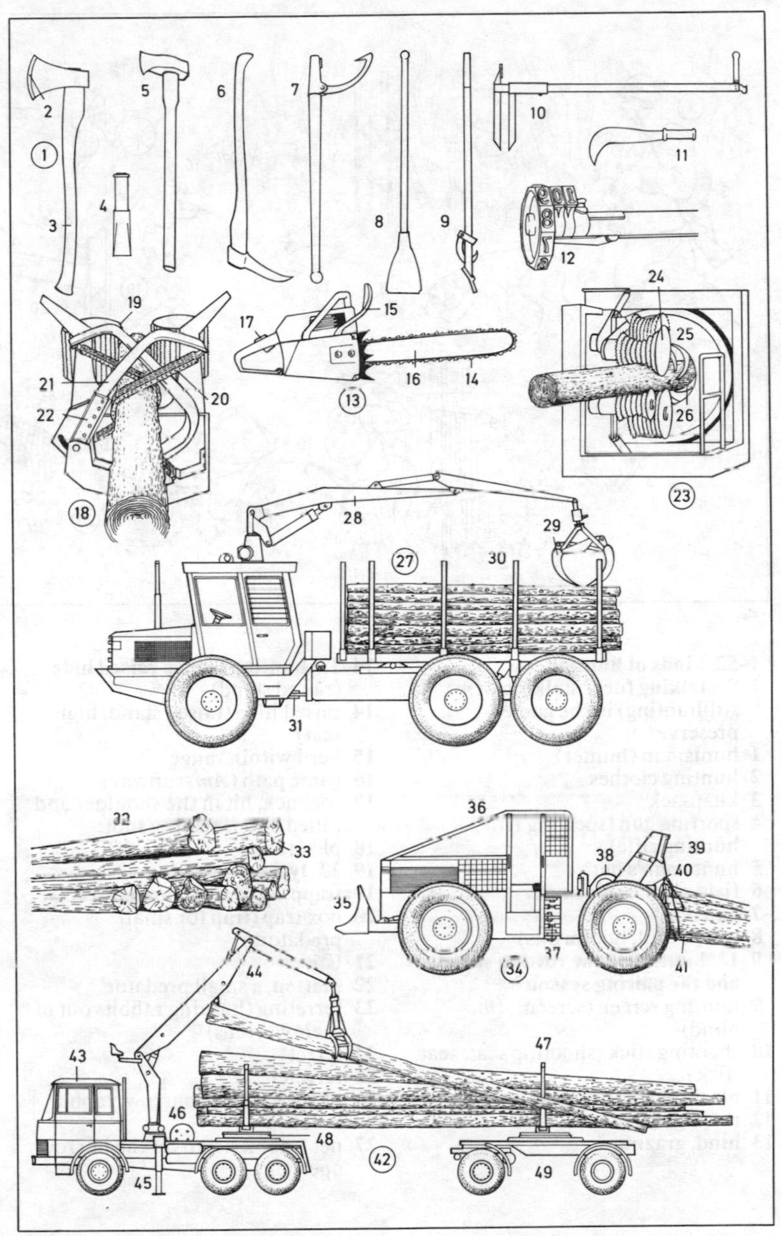
1
2
3
4
5
6
7
8
9
10
11
12
13
14
15
16
17
18
19
20
21
22
23
24
25
26
27
28
29
30
31
32
33
34
35
36
37
38
39
40
41
42
43
44
45
46
47
48
49

86 Hunting

1–52 kinds of hunting
1–8 stalking (deer stalking, *Am.* stillhunting) in the game preserve
1 huntsman (hunter)
2 hunting clothes
3 knapsack
4 sporting gun (sporting rifle, hunting rifle)
5 huntsman's hat
6 field glasses, binoculars
7 gun dog
8 track (trail, hoofprints)
9–12 hunting in the rutting season and the pairing season
9 hunting screen (screen, *Am.* blind)
10 shooting stick (shooting seat, seat stick)
11 blackcock, displaying
12 rutting stag
13 hind, grazing
14–17 hunting from a raised hide (raised stand)
14 raised hide (raised stand, high seat)
15 herd within range
16 game path (*Am.* runway)
17 roebuck, hit in the shoulder and killed by a finishing shot
18 phaeton
19–27 types of trapping
19 trapping of small predators
20 box trap (trap for small predators)
21 bait
22 marten, a small predator
23 ferreting (hunting rabbits out of their warrens)
24 ferret
25 ferreter
26 burrow (rabbit burrow, rabbit hole)
27 net (rabbit net) over the burrow opening

28 feeding place for game (winter feeding place)
29 poacher
30 carbine, a short rifle
31 boar hunt
32 wild sow (sow, wild boar)
33 boarhound (hound, hunting dog; *collectively:* pack, pack of hounds)
34–39 beating (driving, hare hunting)
34 aiming position
35 hare, furred game, ground game
36 retrieving
37 beater
38 bag (kill)
39 cart for carrying game
40 waterfowling (wildfowling, duck shooting, *Am.* duck hunting)
41 flight of wild ducks, winged game
42–46 falconry (hawking)
42 falconer
43 reward, a piece of meat
44 falcon's hood
45 jess
46 falcon, a hawk, a male hawk (tiercel) swooping (stooping) on a heron
47–52 shooting from a butt
47 tree to which birds are lured
48 eagle owl, a decoy bird (decoy)
49 perch
50 decoyed bird, a crow
51 butt for shooting crows or eagle owls
52 gun slit

87 Hunting Weapons, Hunting Equipment

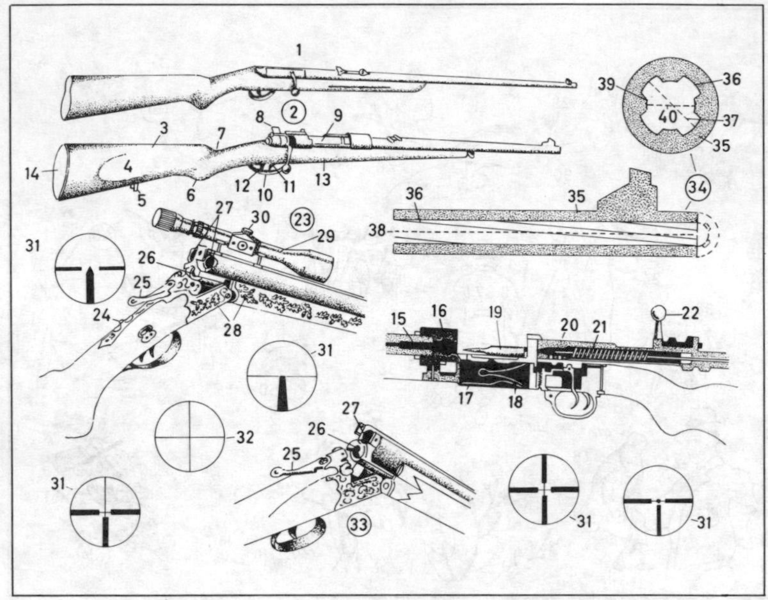

1–40 sporting guns (sporting rifles, hunting rifles)
1 single-loader (single-loading rifle)
2 repeating rifle, a small-arm (fire-arm), a repeater (magazine rifle, magazine repeater)
3, 4, 6,13 stock
3 butt
4 cheek [on the left side]
5 sling ring
6 pistol grip
7 small of the butt
8 safety catch
9 lock
10 trigger guard
11 second set trigger (firing trigger)
12 hair trigger (set trigger)
13 foregrip
14 butt plate
15 cartridge chamber
16 receiver
17 magazine
18 magazine spring
19 ammunition (cartridge)
20 chamber
21 firing pin (striker)
22 bolt handle (bolt lever)
23 triple-barrelled (triple-barreled) rifle, a self-cocking gun
24 reversing catch (*in various guns:* safety catch)
25 sliding safety catch
26 rifle barrel (rifled barrel)
27 smooth-bore barrel
28 chasing
29 telescopic sight (riflescope, telescope sight)
30 graticule adjuster screws
31–32 graticule (sight graticule)
31 various graticule systems
32 cross wires (*Am.* cross hairs)
33 over-and-under shotgun
34 rifled gun barrel
35 barrel casing
36 rifling
37 rifling calibre (*Am.* caliber)
38 bore axis
39 land
40 calibre (bore diameter, *Am.* caliber)

41–48 hunting equipment
41 double-edged hunting knife
42 [single-edged] hunting knife
43–47 calls for luring game (for calling game)
43 roe call
44 hare call
45 quail call
46 stag call
47 partridge call
48 bow trap (bow gin), a jaw trap
49 small-shot cartridge
50 cardboard case
51 small-shot charge
52 felt wad
53 smokeless powder (*different kind:* black powder)
54 cartridge
55 full-jacketed cartridge
56 soft-lead core
57 powder charge
58 detonator cap
59 percussion cap
60 hunting horn
61–64 rifle cleaning kit
61 cleaning rod
62 cleaning brush
63 cleaning tow
64 pull-through (*Am.* pull-thru)
65 sights
66 notch (sighting notch)
67 back sight leaf
68 sight scale division
69 back sight slide
70 notch [to hold the spring]
71 front sight (foresight)
72 bead
73 **ballistics**
74 azimuth
75 angle of departure
76 angle of elevation
77 apex (zenith)
78 angle of descent
79 ballistic curve

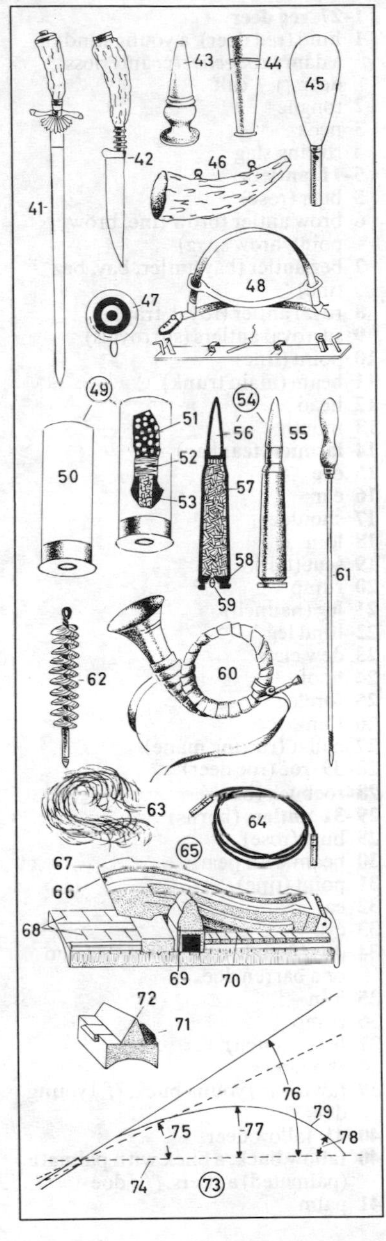

1–27 red deer
1 hind (red deer), a young hind or a dam; *collectively:* anterless deer, *(y.)* calf
2 tongue
3 neck
4 rutting stag
5–11 antlers
5 burr (rose)
6 brow antler (brow tine, brow point, brow snag)
7 bez antler (bay antler, bay, bez tine)
8 royal antler (royal, tray)
9 surroyal antlers (surroyals)
10 point (tine)
11 beam (main trunk)
12 head
13 mouth
14 larmier (tear bag)
15 eye
16 ear
17 shoulder
18 loin
19 scut (tail)
20 rump
21 leg (haunch)
22 hind leg
23 dew claw
24 hoof
25 foreleg
26 flank
27 collar (rutting mane)
28–39 roe (roe deer)
28 roebuck (buck)
29–31 antlers (horns)
29 burr (rose)
30 beam with pearls
31 point (tine)
32 ear
33 eye
34 doe (female roe), a female fawn or a barren doe
35 loin
36 rump
37 leg (haunch)
38 shoulder
39 fawn, *(m.)* young buck, *(f.)* young doe
40–41 fallow deer
40 fallow buck, a buck with palmate (palmated) antlers, *(f.)* doe
41 palm
42 red fox, *(m.)* dog, *(f.)* vixen, *(y.)* cub
43 eyes
44 ear
45 muzzle (mouth)
46 pads (paws)
47 brush (tail)
48 badger, *(f.)* sow
49 tail
50 paws
51 wild boar, *(m.)* boar, *(f.)* wild sow (sow), *(y.)* young boar
52 bristles
53 snout
54 tusk
55 shield
56 hide
57 dew claw
58 tail
59 hare, *(m.)* buck, *(f.)* doe
60 eye
61 ear
62 scut (tail)
63 hind leg
64 foreleg
65 rabbit
66 blackcock
67 tail
68 falcate (falcated) feathers
69 hazel grouse (hazel hen)
70 partridge
71 horseshoe (horseshoe marking)
72 wood grouse (capercaillie)
73 beard
74 axillary marking
75 tail (fan)
76 wing (pinion)
77 common pheasant, a pheasant, *(m.)* cock pheasant (pheasant cock), *(f.)* hen pheasant (pheasant hen)
78 plumicorn (feathered ear, ear tuft, ear, horn)
79 wing
80 tail
81 leg
82 spur
83 snipe
84 bill (beak)

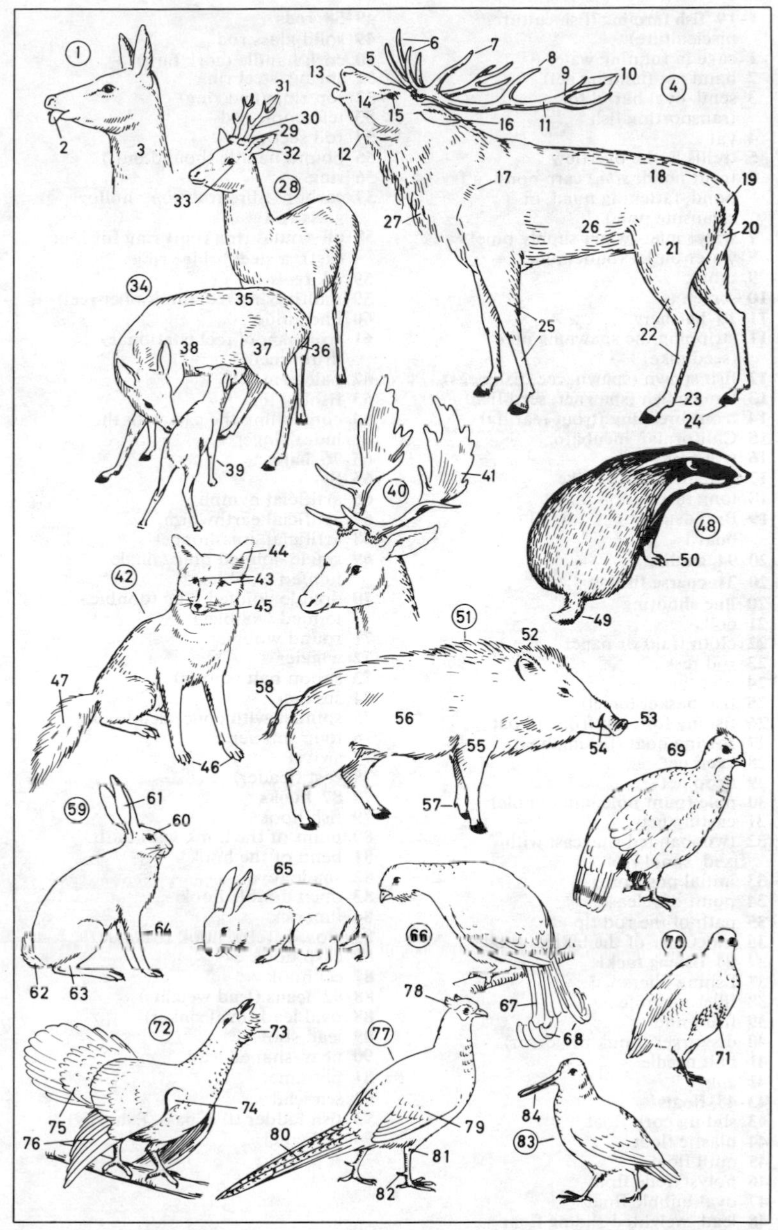
1
2
3
4
5
6
7
8
9
10
11
12
13
14
15
16
17
18
19
20
21
22
23
24
25
26
27
28
29
30
31
32
33
34
35
36
37
38
39
40
41
42
43
44
45
46
47
48
49
50
51
52
53
54
55
56
57
58
59
60
61
62
63
64
65
66
67
68
69
70
71
72
73
74
75
76
77
78
79
80
81
82
83
84

89 Fish Farming (Fish Culture, Pisciculture) and Angling

1-19 fish farming (fish culture, pisciculture)
1 cage in running water
2 hand net (landing net)
3 semi-oval barrel for transporting fish
4 vat
5 trellis in the overflow
6 trout pond; *sim.:* carp pond, a fry pond, fattening pond, or cleansing pond
7 water inlet (water supply pipe)
8 water outlet (outlet pipe)
9 monk
10 screen
11-19 hatchery
11 stripping the spawning pike (seed pike)
12 fish spawn (spawn, roe, fish eggs)
13 female fish (spawner, seed fish)
14 trout breeding (trout rearing)
15 Californian incubator
16 trout fry
17 hatching jar for pike
18 long incubation tank
19 Brandstetter egg-counting board
20-94 angling
20-31 coarse fishing
20 line shooting
21 coils
22 cloth (rag) or paper
23 rod rest
24 bait tin
25 fish basket (creel)
26 fishing for carp from a boat
27 rowing boat (fishing boat)
28 keep net
29 drop net
30 pole (punt pole, quant pole)
31 casting net
32 two-handed side cast with fixed-spool reel
33 initial position
34 point of release
35 path of the rod tip
36 trajectory of the baited weight
37-94 fishing tackle
37 fishing pliers
38 filleting knife
39 fish knife
40 disgorger (hook disgorger)
41 bait needle
42 gag
43-48 floats
43 sliding cork float
44 plastic float
45 quill float
46 polystyrene float
47 oval bubble float
48 lead-weighted sliding float
49-58 rods
49 solid glass rod
50 cork handle (cork butt)
51 spring-steel ring
52 top ring (end ring)
53 telescopic rod
54 rod section
55 bound handle (bound butt)
56 ring
57 carbon-fibre rod; *sim.:* hollow glass rod
58 all-round ring (butt ring for long cast), a steel bridge ring
59-64 reels
59 multiplying reel (multiplier reel)
60 line guide
61 fixed-spool reel (stationary-drum reel)
62 bale arm
63 fishing line
64 controlling the cast with the index finger
65-76 baits
65 fly
66 artificial nymph
67 artificial earthworm
68 artificial grasshopper
69 single-jointed plug (single-jointed wobbler)
70 double-jointed plug (double-jointed wobbler)
71 round wobbler
72 wiggler
73 spoon bait (spoon)
74 spinner
75 spinner with concealed hook
76 long spinner
77 swivel
78 cast (leader)
79-87 hooks
79 fish hook
80 point of the hook with barb
81 bend of the hook
82 spade (eye)
83 open double hook
84 limerick
85 closed treble hook (triangle)
86 carp hook
87 eel hook
88-92 leads (lead weights)
88 oval lead (oval sinker)
89 lead shot
90 pear-shaped lead
81 plummet
92 sea lead
93 fish ladder (fish pass, fish way)
94 stake net

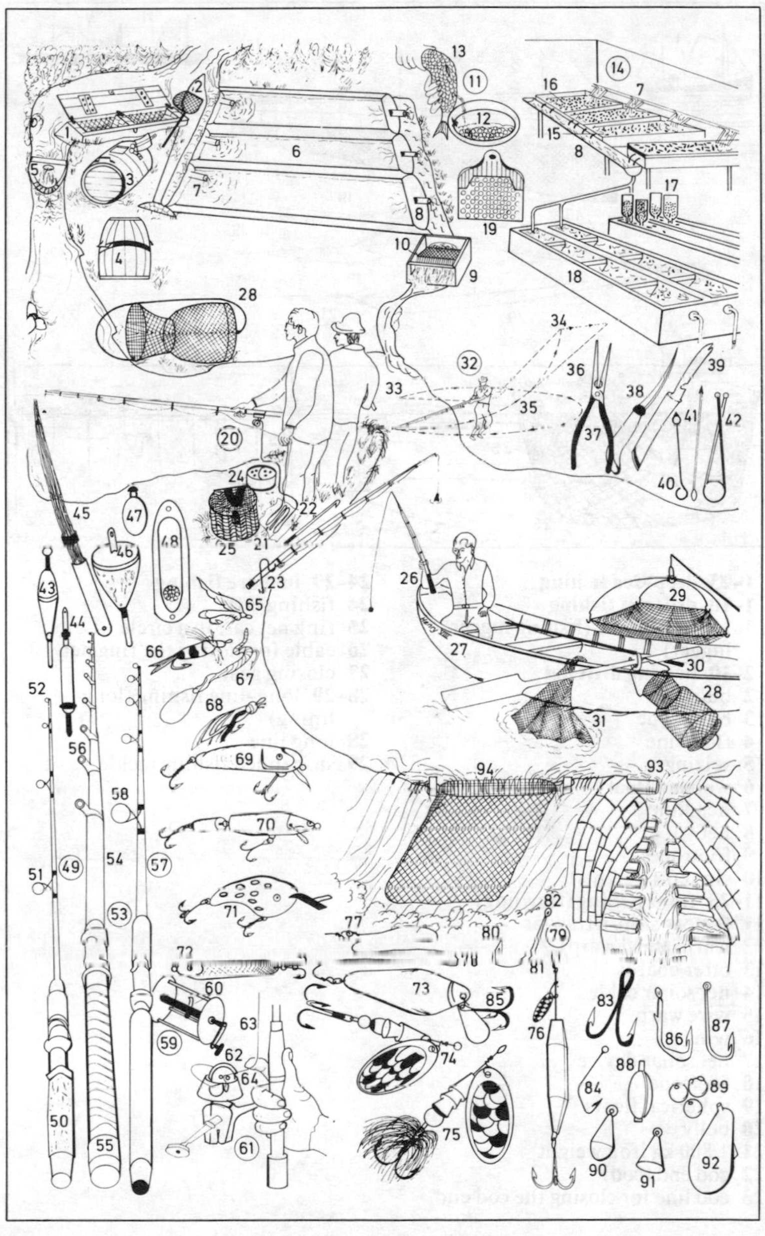
13
14
1
2
11
12
16
7
15
8
6
5
3
7
8
19
17
4
10
9
18
28
34
32
36
38
39
33
35
20
37
41
42
24
40
45
47
22
46
48
25
21
23
26
29
43
65
44
27
66
30
67
28
52
68
31
56
69
94
93
58
70
54
57
49
51
53
71
82
77
80
79
72
78
81
60
73
85
83
63
76
86
87
59
62
74
64
88
84
89
50
55
75
61
90
91
92

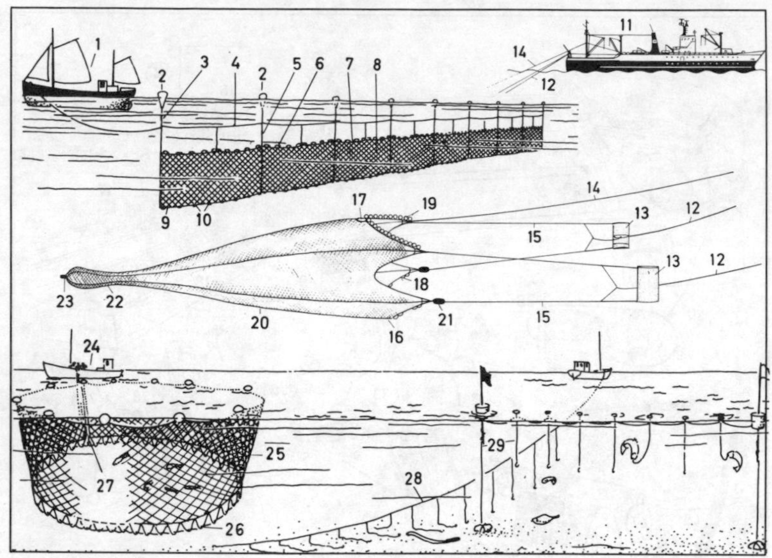

1–23 deep-sea fishing
1–10 drift net fishing
1 herring lugger (fishing lugger, lugger)
2–10 herring drift net
2 buoy
3 buoy rope
4 float line
5 seizing
6 wooden float
7 headline
8 net
9 footrope
10 sinkers (weights)
11–23 trawl fishing (trawling)
11 factory ship, a trawler
12 warp (trawl warp)
13 otter boards
14 net sonar cable
15 wire warp
16 wing
17 net sonar device
18 footrope
19 spherical floats
20 belly
21 1,800 kg iron weight
22 cod end (cod)
23 cod line for closing the cod end

24–29 inshore fishing
24 fishing boat
25 ring net cast in a circle
26 cable for closing the ring net
27 closing gear
28–29 long-line fishing (long-lining)
28 long line
29 suspended fishing tackle

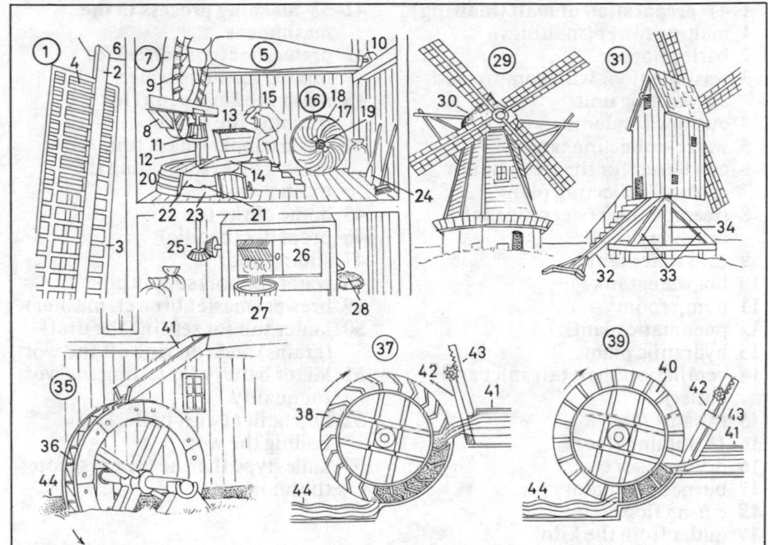

1–34 windmill
1 windmill vane (windmill sail, windmill arm)
2 stock (middling, back, radius)
3 frame
4 shutter
5 wind shaft (sail axle)
6 sail top
7 brake wheel
8 brake
9 wooden cog
10 pivot bearing (step bearing)
11 wallower
12 mill spindle
13 hopper
14 shoe (trough, spout)
15 miller
16 millstone
17 furrow (flute)
18 master furrow
19 eye
20 hurst (millstone casing)
21 set of stones (millstones)
22 runner (upper millstone)
23 bed stone (lower stone, bedder)
24 wooden shovel
25 bevel gear (bevel gearing)
26 bolter (sifter)
27 wooden tub (wooden tun)
28 flour
29 smock windmill (Dutch windmill)
30 rotating (revolving) windmill cap
31 post windmill (German windmill)
32 tailpole (pole)
33 base
34 post
35–44 watermill
35 overshot mill wheel (high-breast mill wheel), a mill wheel (waterwheel)
36 bucket (cavity)
37 middleshot mill wheel (breast mill wheel)
38 curved vane
39 undershot mill wheel
40 flat vane
41 headrace (discharge flume)
42 mill weir
43 overfall (water overfall)
44 millstream (millrace, *Am.* raceway)

1–41 preparation of malt (malting)
1 malting tower (maltings)
2 barley hopper
3 washing floor with compressed-air washing unit
4 outflow condenser
5 water-collecting tank
6 condenser for the steep liquor
7 coolant-collecting plant
8 steeping floor (steeping tank, dressing floor)
9 cold water tank
10 hot water tank
11 pump room
12 pneumatic plant
13 hydraulic plant
14 ventilation shaft (air inlet and outlet)
15 exhaust fan
16–18 kilning floors
16 drying floor
17 burner ventilator
18 curing floor
19 outlet from the kiln
20 finished malt collecting hopper
21 transformer station
22 cooling compressors
23 green malt (germinated barley)
24 turner (plough)
25 central control room with flow diagram
26 screw conveyor
27 washing floor
28 steeping floor
29 drying kiln
30 curing kiln
31 barley silo
32 weighing apparatus
33 barley elevator
34 three-way chute (three-way tippler)
35 malt elevator
36 cleaning machine
37 malt silo
38 corn removal by suction
39 sacker
40 dust extractor
41 barley reception

42–53 mashing process in the mashhouse
42 premasher (converter) for mixing grist and water
43 mash tub (mash tun) for mashing the malt
44 mash copper (mash tun, *Am.* mash kettle) for boiling the mash
45 dome of the tun
46 propeller (paddle)
47 sliding door
48 water (liquor) supply pipe
49 brewer (master brewer, masher)
50 lauter tun for settling the draff (grains) and filtering off the wort
51 lauter battery for testing the wort for quality
52 hop boiler (wort boiler) for boiling the wort
53 ladle-type thermometer (scoop thermometer)

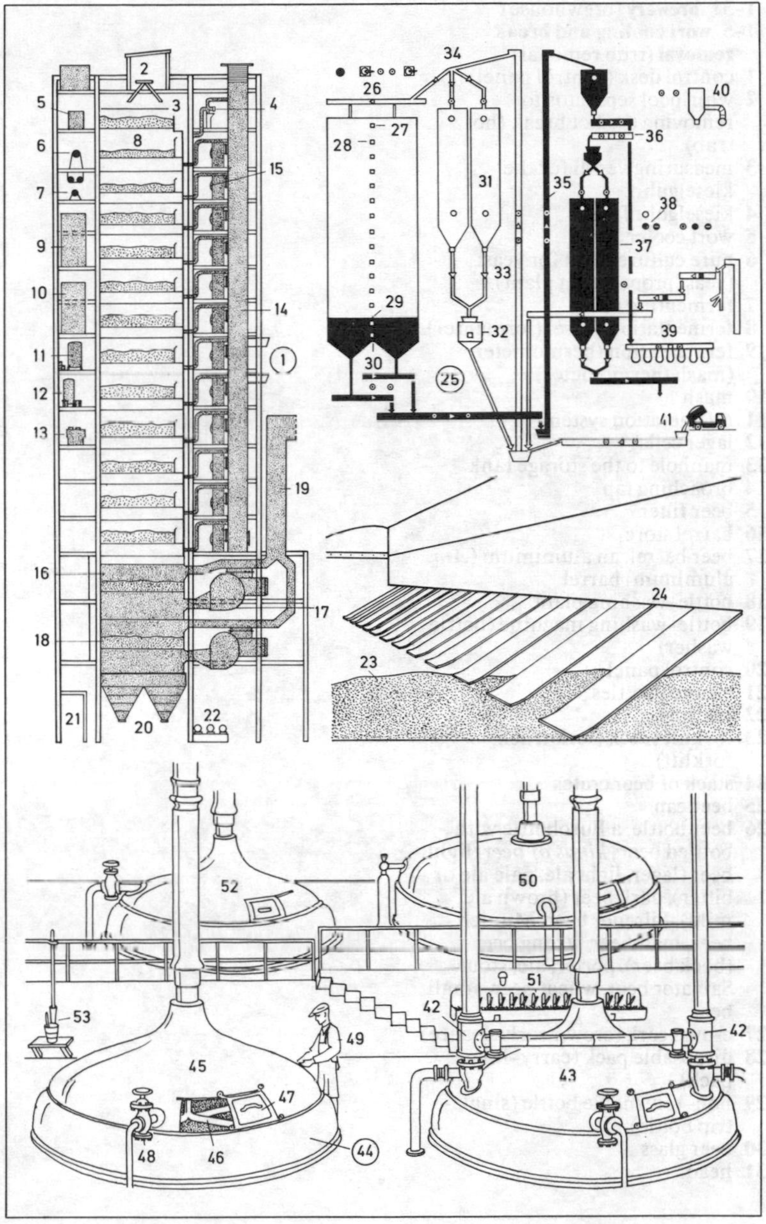
1
2
3
4
5
6
7
8
9
10
11
12
13
14
15
16
17
18
19
20
21
22
23
24
25
26
27
28
29
30
31
32
33
34
35
36
37
38
39
40
41
42
43
44
45
46
47
48
49
50
51
52
53

93 Brewing II

1–31 brewery (brewhouse)
1–5 wort cooling and break removal (trub removal)
1 control desk (control panel)
2 whirlpool separator for removing the hot break (hot trub)
3 measuring vessel for the kieselguhr
4 kieselguhr filter
5 wort cooler
6 pure culture plant for yeast (yeast propagation plant)
7 fermenting cellar
8 fermentation vessel (fermenter)
9 fermentation thermometer (mash thermometer)
10 mash
11 refrigeration system
12 lager cellar
13 manhole to the storage tank
14 broaching tap
15 beer filter
16 barrel store
17 beer barrel, an aluminium (*Am.* aluminum) barrel
18 bottle-washing plant
19 bottle-washing machine (bottle washer)
20 control panel
21 cleaned bottles
22 bottling
23 forklift truck (fork truck, forklift)
24 stack of beer crates
25 beer can
26 beer bottle, a Eurobottle with bottled beer; *kinds of beer:* light beer (lager, light ale, pale ale or bitter), dark beer (brown ale, mild), Pilsener beer, Munich beer, malt beer, strong beer (bock beer), porter, ale, stout, Salvator beer, wheat beer, small beer
27 crown cork (crown cork closure)
28 disposable pack (carry-home pack)
29 non-returnable bottle (single-trip bottle)
30 beer glass
31 head

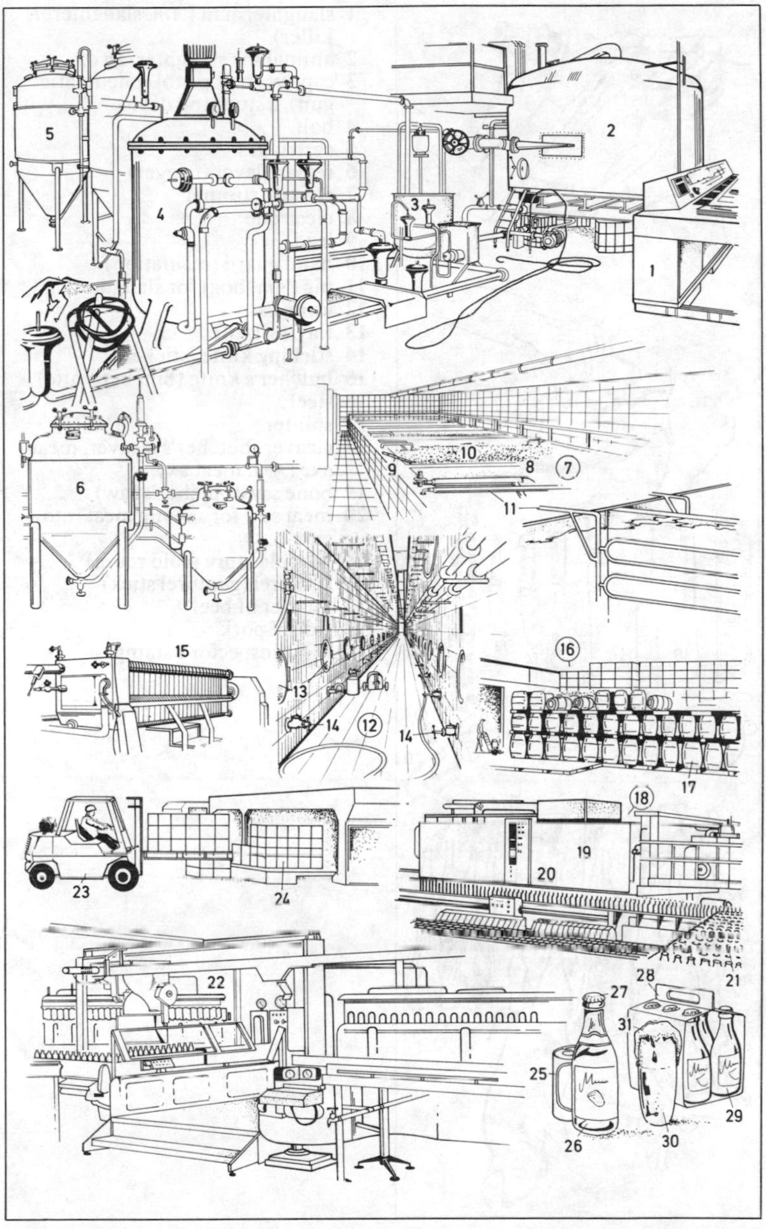
1
2
3
4
5
6
7
8
9
10
11
12
13
14
14
15
16
17
18
19
20
21
22
23
24
25
26
27
28
29
30
31

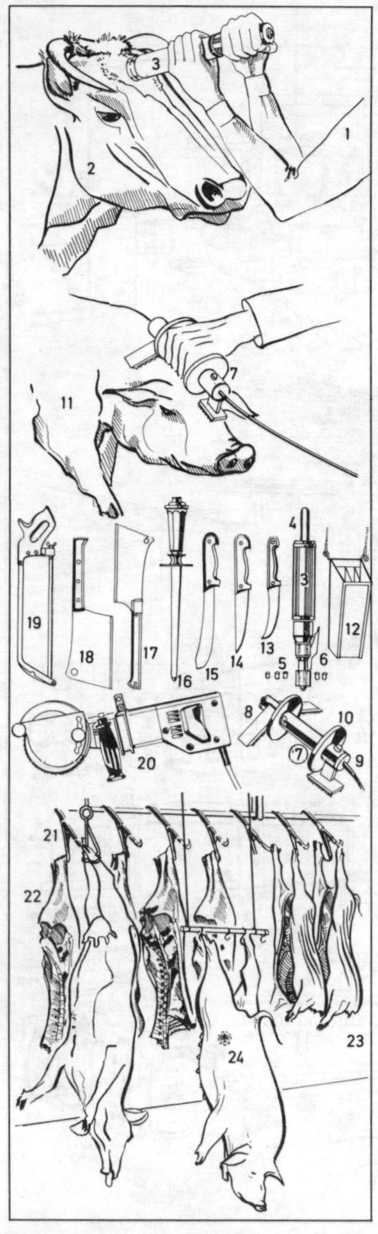

1 slaughterman (*Am.* slaughterer, killer)
2 animal for slaughter, an ox
3 captive-bolt pistol (pneumatic gun), a stunning device
4 bolt
5 cartridges
6 release lever (trigger)
7 electric stunner
8 electrode
9 lead
10 hand guard (insulation)
11 pig (*Am.* hog) for slaughter
12 knife case
13 flaying knife
14 sticking knife (sticker)
15 butcher's knife (butcher knife)
16 steel
17 splitter
18 cleaver (butcher's cleaver, meat axe (*Am.* meat ax))
19 bone saw (butcher's saw)
20 meat saw for sawing meat into cuts
21-24 cold store (cold room)
21 gambrel (gambrel stick)
22 quarter of beef
23 side of pork
24 meat inspector's stamp

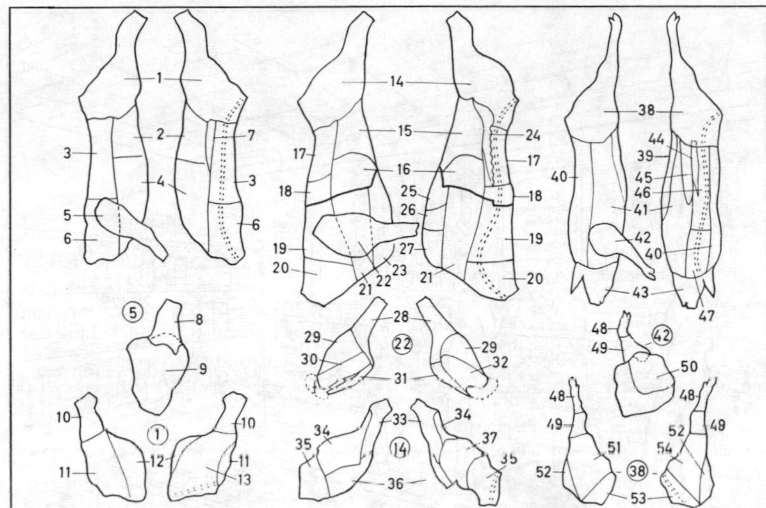

left: meat side;
right: bone side

1–13 ***animal*: calf; *meat*: veal**
1 leg with hind knuckle
2 flank
3 loin and rib
4 breast (breast of veal)
5 shoulder with fore knuckle
6 neck with scrag (scrag end)
7 best end of loin (of loin of veal)
8 fore knuckle
9 shoulder
10 hind knuckle
11 roasting round (oyster round)
12 cutlet for frying or braising
13 undercut (fillet)
14–37 ***animal*: ox; *meat*: beef**
14 round with rump and shank
15–16 flank
15 thick flank
16 thin flank
17 sirloin
18 prime rib (fore ribs, prime fore rib)
19 middle rib and chuck
20 neck
21 flat rib
22 leg of mutton piece (bladebone) with shin
23 brisket (brisket of beef)
24 fillet (fillet of beef)
25 hind brisket
26 middle brisket
27 breastbone
28 shin
29 leg of mutton piece
30 bladebone [meat side]
31 part of top rib
32 bladebone [bone side]
33 shank
34 silverside
35 rump
36 thick flank
37 top side
38–54 ***animal*: pig; *meat*: pork**
38 leg with knuckle and trotter
39 ventral part of the belly
40 back fat
41 belly
42 bladebone with knuckle and trotter
43 head (pig's head)
44 fillet (fillet of pork)
45 leaf fat (pork flare)
46 loin (pork loin)
47 spare rib
48 trotter
49 knuckle
50 butt
51 fore end (ham)
52 round end for boiling
53 fat end
54 gammon steak

96 Butcher's Shop

1–30 butcher's shop

1–4 meat

1 ham on the bone

2 flitch of bacon

3 smoked meat

4 piece of loin (piece of sirloin)

5 lard

6–11 sausages

6 price label

7 mortadella

8 scalded sausage; *kinds:* Vienna sausage (Wiener), Frankfurter sausage (Frankfurter)

9 collared pork (*Am.* headcheese)

10 ring of Lyoner sausage

11 pork sausages; *also:* beef sausages

12 cold shelves

13 meat salad (diced meat salad)

14 cold meats (*Am.* cold cuts)

15 pâté

16 mince (mincemeat, minced meat)

17 knuckle of pork

18 basket for special offers

19 price list for special offers

20 special offer

21 freezer

22 pre-packed joints

23 deep-frozen ready-to-eat meal

24 chicken

25 canned food

26 can

27 canned vegetables

28 canned fish

29 salad cream

30 soft drinks

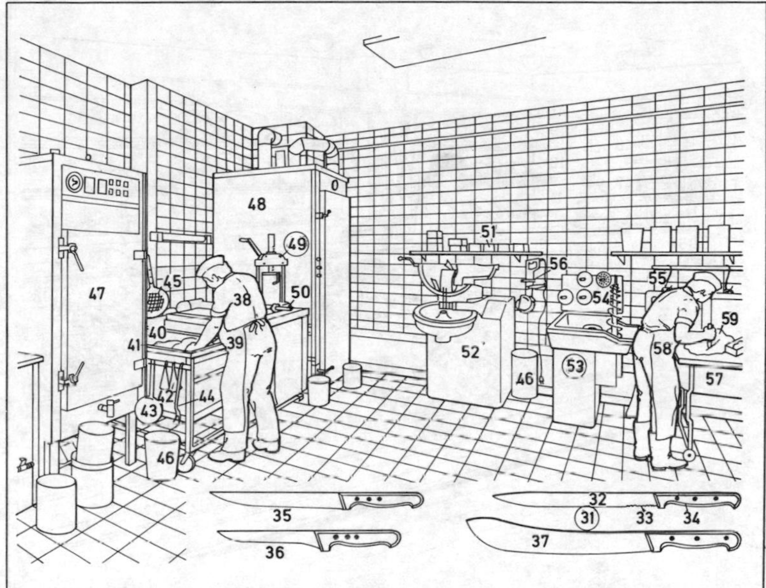

31–59 manufacture of sausages
31–37 butcher's knives
31 slicer
32 knife blade
33 saw teeth
34 knife handle
35 carver (carving knife)
36 boning knife
37 butcher's knife (butcher knife)
38 butcher (master butcher)
39 butcher's apron
40 meat-mixing trough
41 sausage meat
42 scraper
43 skimmer
44 sausage fork
45 scalding colander
46 waste bin (*Am.* trash bin)
47 cooker, for cooking with steam or hot air
48 smoke house
49 sausage filler (sausage stuffer)
50 feed pipe (supply pipe)
51 containers for vegetables
52 mincing machine for sausage meat
53 mincing machine (meat mincer, mincer, *Am.* meat grinder)
54 plates (steel plates)
55 meathook (butcher's hook)
56 bone saw
57 chopping board
58 butcher, cutting meat
59 piece of meat

97 Bakery

1–54 baker's shop
1 shop assistant (*Am.* salesgirl, saleslady)
2 bread (loaf of bread, loaf)
3 crumb
4 crust (bread crust)
5 crust (*Am.* heel)
6–12 kinds of bread (breads)
6 round loaf, a wheat and rye bread
7 small round loaf
8 long loaf (bloomer), a wheat and rye bread
9 white loaf
10 pan loaf, a wholemeal rye bread
11 yeast bread (*Am.* stollen)
12 French loaf (baguette, French stick)
13–16 rolls
13 brown roll
14 white roll
15 finger roll
16 rye-bread roll
17–47 cakes (confectionery)
17 cream roll
18 vol-au-vent, a puff pastry (*Am.* puff paste)
19 Swiss roll (*Am.* jelly roll)
20 tartlet
21 slice of cream cake
22–24 flans (*Am.* pies) and gateaux (torten)
22 fruit flan (*kinds:* strawberry flan, cherry flan, gooseberry flan, peach flan, rhubarb flan)
23 cheesecake
24 cream cake (*Am.* cream pie) (*kinds:* butter-cream cake, Black Forest gateau)
25 cake plate
26 meringue
27 cream puff
28 whipped cream
29 doughnut (*Am.* bismarck)
30 Danish pastry
31 saltstick (saltzstange) (*also:* caraway roll, caraway stick)
32 croissant (crescent roll, *Am.* crescent)
33 ring cake (gugelhupf)
34 slab cake with chocolate icing
35 streusel cakes
36 marshmallow

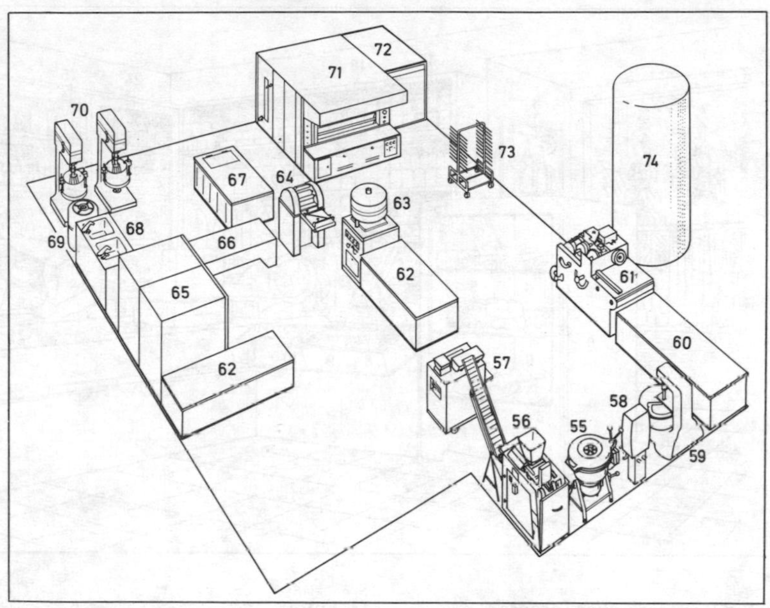

37 coconut macaroon
38 pastry whirl
39 iced bun
40 sweet bread
41 plaited bun (plait)
42 Frankfurter garland cake
43 slices (*kinds:* streusel slices, sugared slices, plum slices)
44 pretzel
45 wafer (*Am.* waffle)
46 tree cake (baumkuchen)
47 flan case
48–50 wrapped bread
48 wholemeal bread (*also:* wheatgerm bread)
49 pumpernickel (wholemeal rye bread)
50 crispbread
51 gingerbread (*Am.* lebkuchen)
52 flour (*kinds:* wheat flour, rye flour)
53 yeast (baker's yeast)
54 rusks (French toast)
55–74 bakery (bakehouse)
55 kneading machine (dough mixer)
56–57 bread unit
56 divider
57 moulder (*Am.* molder)
58 premixer
59 dough mixer
60 workbench
61 roll unit
62 workbench
63 divider and rounder (rounding machine)
64 crescent-forming machine
65 freezers
66 oven [for baking with fat]
67–70 confectionery unit
67 cooling table
68 sink
69 boiler
70 whipping unit [with beater]
71 reel oven (oven)
72 fermentation room
73 fermentation trolley
74 flour silo

98 Grocer's Shop (*Am.* Grocery Store)

1–87 grocer's shop (grocer's, delicatessen shop, *Am.* grocery store, delicatessen store), a retail shop (*Am.* retail store)
1 window display
2 poster (advertisement)
3 cold shelves
4 sausages
5 cheese
6 roasting chicken (broiler)
7 poulard, a fattened hen
8–11 baking ingredients
8 raisins; *sim.:* sultanas
9 currants
10 candied lemon peel
11 candied orange peel
12 computing scale, a rapid scale
13 shop assistant (*Am.* salesclerk)
14 goods shelves (shelves)
15–20 canned food
15 canned milk
16 canned fruit (cans of fruit)
17 canned vegetables
18 fruit juice
19 sardines in oil, a can of fish
20 canned meat (cans of meat)
21 margarine
22 butter
23 coconut oil, a vegetable oil
24 oil; *kinds:* salad oil, olive oil, sunflower oil, wheatgerm oil, ground-nut oil
25 vinegar
26 stock cube
27 bouillon cube
28 mustard
29 gherkin (pickled gherkin)
30 soup seasoning
31 shop assistant (*Am.* salesgirl, saleslady)
32–34 pastas
32 spaghetti
33 macaroni
34 noodles
35–39 cereal products
35 pearl barley
36 semolina
37 rolled oats (porridge oats, oats)
38 rice
39 sago
40 salt
41 grocer (*Am.* groceryman), a shopkeeper (tradesman, retailer, *Am.* storekeeper)

42 capers
43 customer
44 receipt (sales check)
45 shopping bag
46–49 wrapping material
46 wrapping paper
47 adhesive tape
48 paper bag
49 cone-shaped paper bag
50 blancmange powder
51 whole-fruit jam (preserve)
52 jam
53–55 sugar
53 cube sugar
54 icing sugar (*Am.* confectioner's sugar)
55 refined sugar in crystals
56–59 spirits
56 whisky (whiskey)
57 rum
58 liqueur
59 brandy (cognac)
60–64 wine in bottles (bottled wine)
60 white wine
61 Chianti
62 vermouth
63 sparkling wine
64 red wine
65–68 tea, coffee, etc.
65 coffee (pure coffee)
66 cocoa
67 coffee
68 tea bag
69 electric coffee grinder
70 coffee roaster
71 roasting drum
72 sample scoop
73 price list
74 freezer
75–86 confectionery (*Am.* candies)
75 sweet (*Am.* candy)
76 drops
77 toffees
78 bar of chocolate
79 chocolate box
80 chocolate, a sweet
81 nougat
82 marzipan
83 chocolate liqueur
84 Turkish delight
85 croquant
86 truffle
87 soda water

99 Supermarket

1–96 supermarket, a self-service food store
1 shopping trolley
2 customer
3 shopping bag
4 entrance to the sales area
5 barrier
6 sign (notice) banning dogs
7 dogs tied by their leads
8 basket
9 bread and cake counter (bread counter, cake counter)
10 display counter for bread and cakes
11 kinds of bread (breads)
12 rolls
13 croissants (crescent rolls, *Am.* crescents)
14 round loaf
15 gateau
16 pretzel [made with yeast dough]
17 shop assistant (*Am.* salesgirl, saleslady)
18 customer
19 sign listing goods
20 fruit flan
21 slab cake
22 ring cake
23 cosmetics gondola, a gondola (sales shelves)
24 canopy
25 hosiery shelf
26 stockings (nylons)
27–35 toiletries (cosmetics)
27 jar of cream (*kinds:* moisturising cream, day cream, night-care cream, hand cream)
28 packet of cotton wool
29 talcum powder
30 packet of cotton wool balls
31 toothpaste
32 nail varnish (nail polish)
33 shaving cream
34 bath salts
35 sanitary articles
36–37 pet foods
36 complete dog food
37 packet of dog biscuits
38 bag of cat litter
39 cheese counter
40 whole cheese
41 Swiss cheese (Emmental cheese) with holes
42 Edam cheese, a round cheese
43 gondola for dairy products
44 long-life milk; *also:* pasteurized milk, homogenized milk
45 plastic milk bag
46 cream

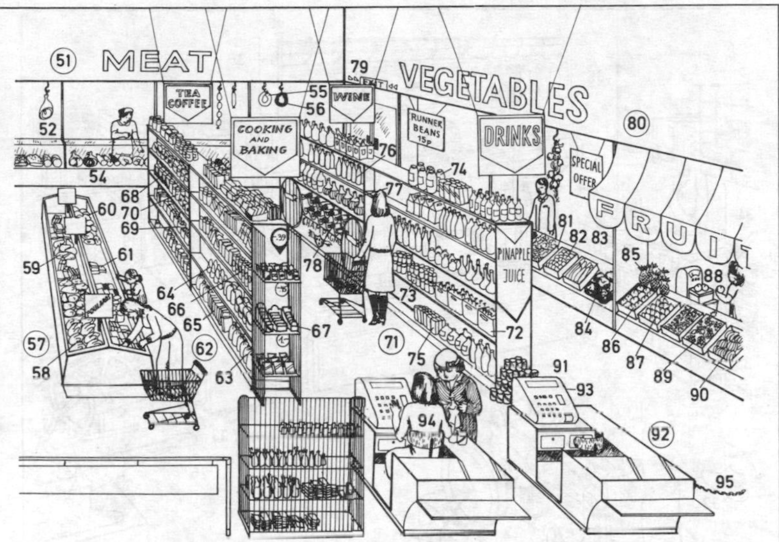

47 butter
48 margarine
49 box of cheeses
50 box of eggs
51 **fresh meat counter** (meat counter)
52 ham on the bone
53 meat (meat products)
54 sausages
55 ring of pork sausage
56 ring of blood sausage
57 freezer
58–61 **frozen food**
58 poulard
59 turkey leg (drumstick)
60 boiling fowl
61 frozen vegetables
62 **gondola for baking ingredients and cereal products**
63 wheat flour
64 sugar loaf
65 packet of noodles
66 salad oil
67 packet of spice
68–70 **tea, coffee, etc.**
68 coffee
69 packet of tea
70 instant coffee
71 **drinks gondola**
72 soft drinks
73 can of beer (canned beer)
74 bottle of fruit juice (bottled fruit juice)
75 can of fruit juice (canned fruit juice)
76 bottle of wine
77 bottle of Chianti
78 bottle of champagne
79 emergency exit
80 **fruit and vegetable counter**
81 vegetable basket
82 tomatoes
83 cucumbers
84 cauliflower
85 pineapple
86 apples
87 pears
88 scales for weighing fruit
89 grapes (bunches of grapes)
90 bananas
91 can
92 **checkout**
93 cash register
94 cashier
95 chain

100 Shoemaker (Bootmaker)

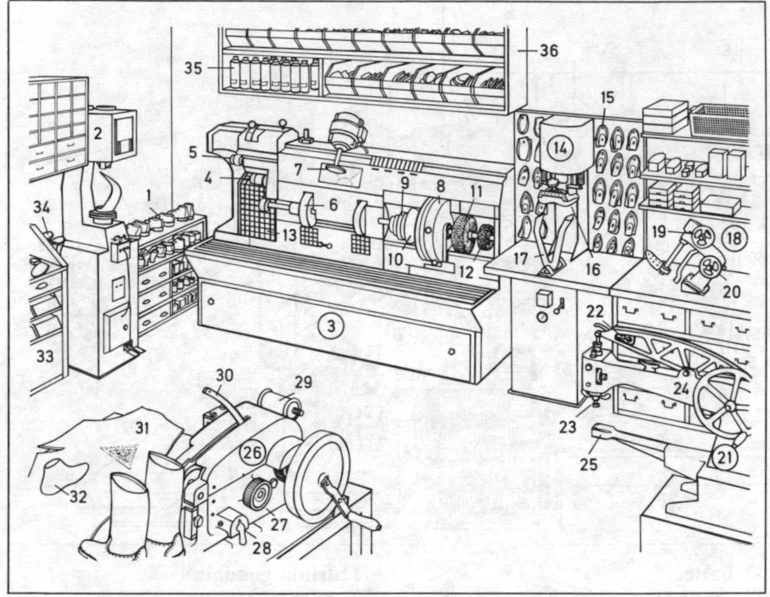

1–68 shoemaker's workshop (bootmaker's workshop)
1 finished (repaired) shoes
2 auto-soling machine
3 finishing machine
4 heel trimmer
5 sole trimmer
6 scouring wheel
7 naum keag
8 drive unit (drive wheel)
9 iron
10 buffing wheel
11 polishing brush
12 horsehair brush
13 extractor grid
14 automatic sole press
15 press attachment
16 pad
17 press bar
18 stretching machine
19 width adjustment
20 length adjustment
21 stitching machine
22 power regulator (power control)
23 foot
24 handwheel
25 arm
26 sole stitcher (sole-stitching machine)
27 foot bar lever
28 feed adjustment (feed setting)
29 bobbin (cotton bobbin)
30 thread guide (yarn guide)
31 sole leather
32 [wooden] last
33 workbench
34 last
35 dye spray
36 shelves for materials

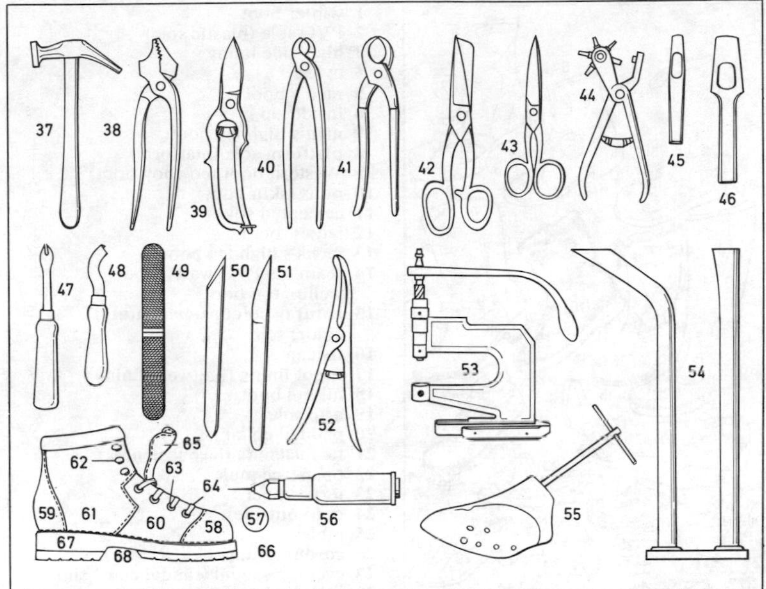

37 shoemaker's hammer
38 shoemaker's pliers (welt pincers)
39 sole-leather shears
40 small pincers (nippers)
41 large pincers (nippers)
42 upper-leather shears
43 scissors
44 revolving punch (rotary punch)
45 punch
46 punch with handle
47 nail puller
48 welt cutter
49 shoemaker's rasp
50 cobbler's knife (shoemaker's knife)
51 skiving knife (skife knife, paring knife)
52 toecap remover
53 eyelet, hook, and press-stud setter
54 stand with iron lasts
55 width-setting tree
56 nail grip
57 boot
58 toecap
59 counter
60 vamp
61 quarter
62 hook
63 eyelet
64 lace (shoelace, bootlace)
65 tongue
66 sole
67 heel
68 shank (waist)

101 Shoes (Footwear)

1 winter boot
2 PVC sole (plastic sole)
3 high-pile lining
4 nylon
5 men's boot
6 inside zip
7 men's high leg boot
8 platform sole (platform)
9 Western boot (cowboy boot)
10 pony-skin boot
11 cemented sole
12 ladies' boot
13 mens's high leg boot
14 seamless PVC waterproof wellington boot
15 natural-colour (*Am.* natural-color) sole
16 toecap
17 tricot lining (knitwear lining)
18 hiking boot
19 grip sole
20 padded collar
21 tie fastening (lace fastening)
22 open-toe mule
23 terry upper
24 polo outsole
25 mule
26 corduroy upper
27 evening sandal (sandal court shoe)
28 high heel (stiletto heel)
29 court shoe (*Am.* pump)
30 moccasin
31 shoe, a tie shoe (laced shoe, Oxford shoe, *Am.* Oxford)
32 tongue
33 high-heeled shoe (shoe with raised heel)
34 casual
35 trainer (training shoe)
36 tennis shoe
37 counter (stiffening)
38 natural-colour (*Am.* natural-color) rubber sole
39 heavy-duty boot (*Am.* stogy, stogie)
40 toecap
41 slipper
42 woollen (*Am.* woolen) slip sock
43 knit stitch (knit)
44 clog
45 wooden sole
46 soft-leather upper
47 sabot
48 toe post sandal
49 ladies' sandal
50 surgical footbed (sock)
51 sandal
52 shoe buckle (buckle)
53 sling-back court shoe (*Am.* sling pump)
54 fabric court shoe
55 wedge heel
56 baby's first walking boot

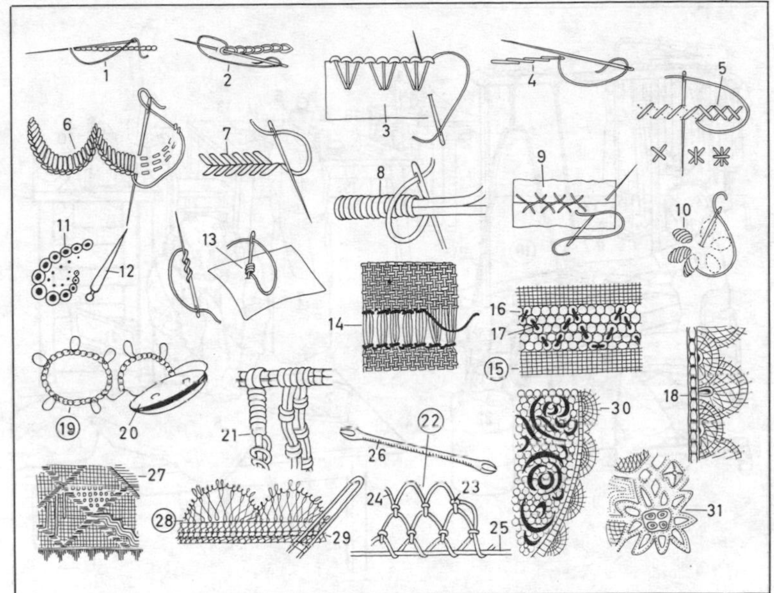

1 backstitch seam
2 chain stitch
3 ornamental stitch
4 stem stitch
5 cross stitch
6 buttonhole stitch (button stitch)
7 fishbone stitch
8 overcast stitch
9 herringbone stitch (Russian stitch, Russian cross stitch)
10 satin stitch (flat stitch)
11 eyelet embroidery (broderie anglaise)
12 stiletto
13 French knot (French dot, knotted stitch, twisted knot stitch)
14 hem stitch work
15 tulle work (tulle lace)
16 tulle background (net background)
17 darning stitch
18 pillow lace (bobbin lace, bone lace); *kinds:* Valenciennes, Brussels lace
19 tatting
20 tatting shuttle (shuttle)
21 knotted work (macramé)
22 filet (netting)
23 netting loop
24 netting thread
25 mesh pin (mesh gauge)
26 netting needle
27 open work
28 gimping (hairpin work)
29 gimping needle (hairpin)
30 needlepoint lace (point lace, needlepoint); *kinds:* reticella lace, Venetian lace, Alençon lace; *sim.* with metal thread: filigree work
31 braid embroidery (braid work)

1–27 dressmaker's workroom
1 dressmaker
2 tape measure (measuring tape), a metre (*Am.* meter) tape measure
3 cutting shears
4 cutting table
5 model dress
6 dressmaker's model (dressmaker's dummy, dress form)
7 model coat
8 sewing machine
9 drive motor
10 drive belt
11 treadle
12 sewing machine cotton (sewing machine thread) [on bobbin]
13 cutting template
14 seam binding
15 button box
16 remnant
17 movable clothes rack
18 hand-iron press
19 presser (ironer)
20 steam iron
21 water feed pipe
22 water container
23 adjustable-tilt ironing surface
24 lift device for the iron
25 steam extractor
26 foot switch controlling steam extraction
27 pressed non-woven woollen (*Am.* woolen) fabric

1–32 tailor's workroom
1 triple mirror
2 lengths of material
3 suiting
4 fashion journal (fashion magazine)
5 ashtray
6 fashion catalogue
7 workbench
8 wall shelves (wall shelf unit)
9 cotton reel
10 small reels of sewing silk
11 hand shears
12 combined electric and treadle sewing machine
13 treadle
14 dress guard
15 band wheel
16 bobbin thread
17 sewing machine table
18 sewing machine drawer
19 seam binding
20 pincushion
21 marking out
22 tailor
23 shaping pad
24 tailor's chalk (French chalk)
25 workpiece
26 steam press (steam pressing unit)
27 swivel arm
28 pressing cushion (pressing pad)
29 iron
30 hand-ironing pad
31 clothes brush
32 pressing cloth

105 Ladies' Hairdresser

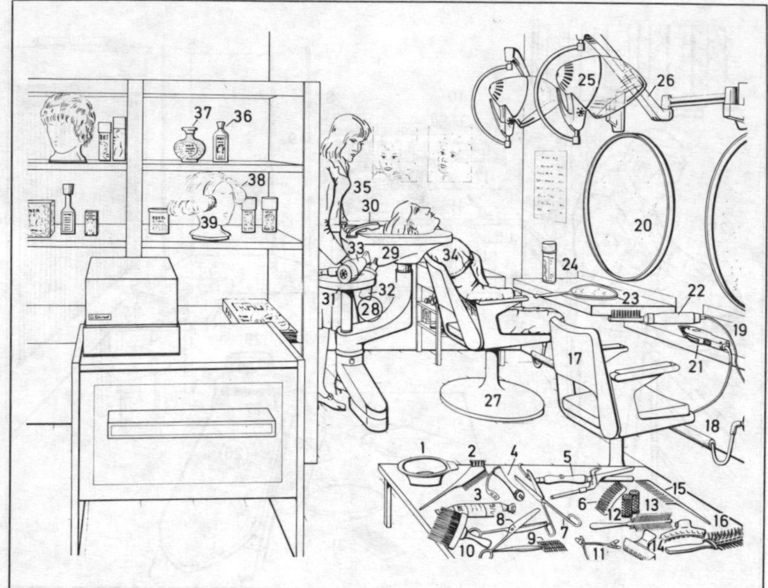

1–39 ladies' hairdressing salon and beauty salon (*Am.* beauty parlor, beauty shop)

1–16 hairdresser's tools

1 bowl containing bleach
2 detangling brush
3 bleach tube
4 curler [used in dyeing]
5 curling tongs (curling iron)
6 comb (back comb, side comb)
7 haircutting scissors
8 thinning scissors (*Am.* thinning shears)
9 thinning razor
10 hairbrush
11 hair clip
12 roller
13 curl brush
14 curl clip
15 dressing comb
16 stiff-bristle brush
17 adjustable hairdresser's chair
18 footrest
19 dressing table
20 salon mirror (mirror)
21 electric clippers
22 warm-air comb
23 hand mirror (hand glass)
24 hair spray (hair-fixing spray)
25 drier, a swivel-mounted drier
26 swivel arm of the drier
27 round base
28 shampoo unit
29 shampoo basin
30 hand spray (shampoo spray)
31 service tray
32 shampoo bottle
33 hair drier (hand hair drier, hand-held hair drier)
34 cape (gown)
35 hairdresser
36 perfume bottle
37 bottle of toilet water
38 wig
39 wig block

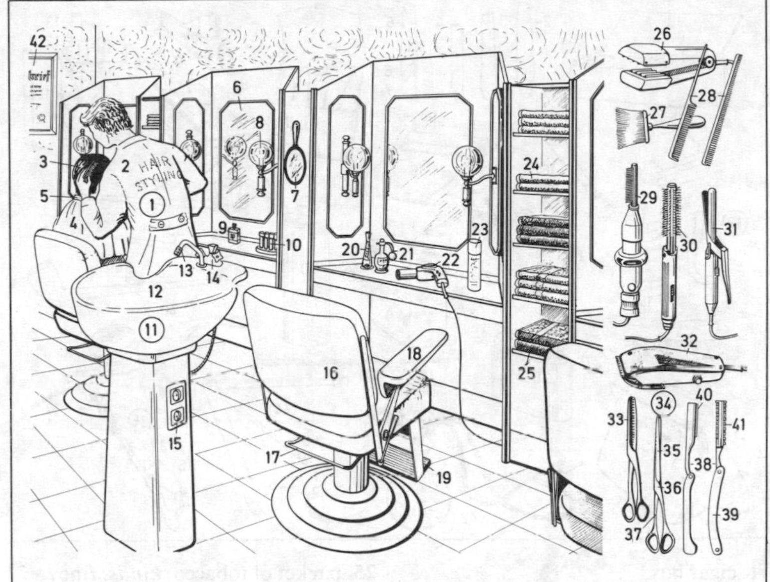

1-42 men's salon (men's hairdressing salon, barber's shop, *Am.* barbershop)
1 hairdresser (barber)
2 overalls (hairdresser's overalls)
3 hairstyle (haircut)
4 cape (gown)
5 paper towel
6 salon mirror (mirror)
7 hand mirror (hand glass)
8 light
9 toilet water
10 hair tonic
11 shampoo unit
12 shampoo basin
13 hand spray (shampoo spray)
14 mixer tap (*Am.* mixing faucet)
15 sockets, e.g. for hair drier
16 adjustable hairdresser's chair (barber's chair)
17 height-adjuster bar (height adjuster)
18 armrest
19 footrest
20 shampoo
21 perfume spray
22 hair drier (hand hair drier, hand-held hair drier)
23 setting lotion in a spray can
24 hand towels for drying hair
25 towels for face compresses
26 crimping iron
27 neck brush
28 dressing comb
29 warm-air comb
30 warm-air brush
31 curling tongs (hair curler, curling iron)
32 electric clippers
33 thinning scissors (*Am.* thinning shears)
34 haircutting scissors; *sim.*: styling scissors
35 scissor-blade
36 pivot
37 handle
38 open razor (straight razor)
39 razor handle
40 edge (cutting edge, razor's edge, razor's cutting edge)
41 thinning razor
42 diploma

107 Tobacco and Smoking Requisites

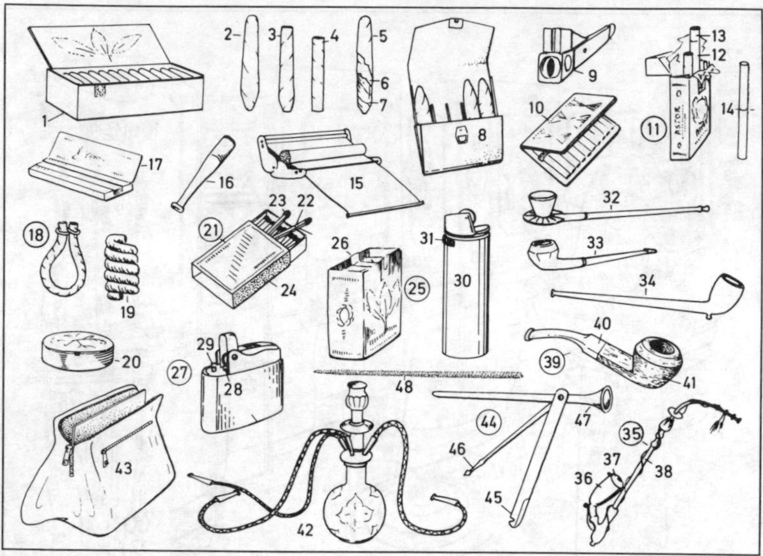

1 cigar box
2 cigar; *kinds:* Havana cigar (Havana), Brazilian cigar, Sumatra cigar
3 cigarillo
4 cheroot
5 wrapper
6 binder
7 filler
8 cigar case
9 cigar cutter
10 cigarette case
11 cigarette packet (*Am.* pack)
12 cigarette, a filter-tipped cigarette
13 cigarette tip; *kinds:* cork tip, gold tip
14 Russian cigarette
15 cigarette roller
16 cigarette holder
17 packet of cigarette papers
18 pigtail (twist of tobacco)
19 chewing tobacco; *a piece:* plug (quid, chew)
20 snuff box, containing snuff
21 matchbox
22 match
23 head (match head)
24 striking surface
25 packet of tobacco; *kinds:* fine cut, shag, navy plug
26 revenue stamp
27 petrol cigarette lighter (petrol lighter)
28 flint
29 wick
30 gas cigarette lighter (gas lighter), a disposable lighter
31 flame regulator
32 chibonk (chibonque)
33 short pipe
34 clay pipe (Dutch pipe)
35 long pipe
36 pipe bowl (bowl)
37 bowl lid
38 pipe stem (stem)
39 briar pipe
40 mouthpiece
41 sand-blast finished or polished briar grain
42 hookah (narghile, narghileh), a water pipe
43 tobacco pouch
44 smoker's companion
45 pipe scraper
46 pipe cleaner
47 tobacco presser
48 pipe cleaner

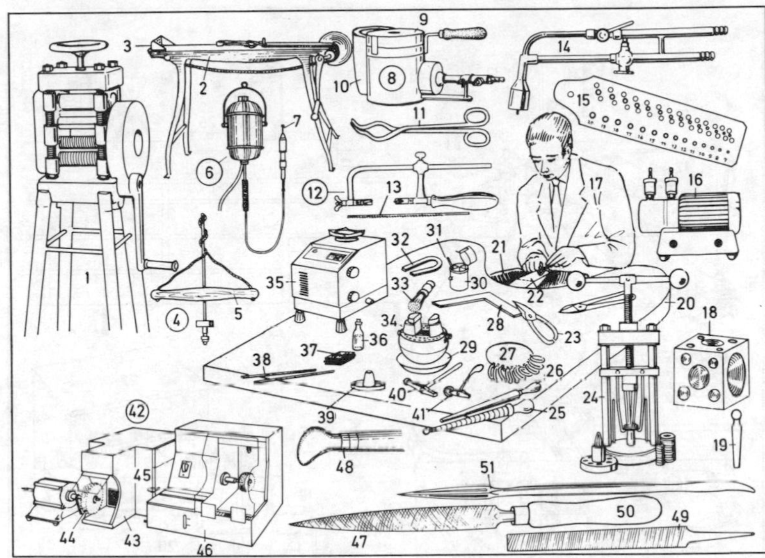

1 wire and sheet roller
2 drawbench (drawing bench)
3 wire (gold or silver wire)
4 archimedes drill (drill)
5 crossbar
6 suspended (pendant) electric drilling machine
7 spherical cutter (cherry)
8 melting pot
9 fireclay top
10 graphite crucible
11 crucible tongs
12 piercing saw (jig saw)
13 piercing saw blade
14 soldering gun
15 thread tapper
16 blast burner (blast lamp) for soldering
17 goldsmith
18 swage block
19 punch
20 workbench (bench)
21 bench apron
22 needle file
23 metal shears
24 wedding ring sizing machine
25 ring gauge (*Am.* gage)
26 ring-rounding tool
27 ring gauge (*Am.* gage)
28 steel set-square
29 leather pad
30 box of punches
31 punch
32 magnet
33 bench brush
34 engraving ball (joint vice, clamp)
35 gold and silver balance (assay balance), a precision balance
36 soldering flux (flux)
37 charcoal block
38 stick of solder
39 soldering borax
40 shaping hammer
41 chasing (enchasing) hammer
42 polishing and burnishing machine
43 dust exhauster (vacuum cleaner)
44 polishing wheel
45 dust collector (dust catcher)
46 buffing machine
47 round file
48 bloodstone (haematite, hematite)
49 flat file
50 file handle
51 polishing iron (burnisher)

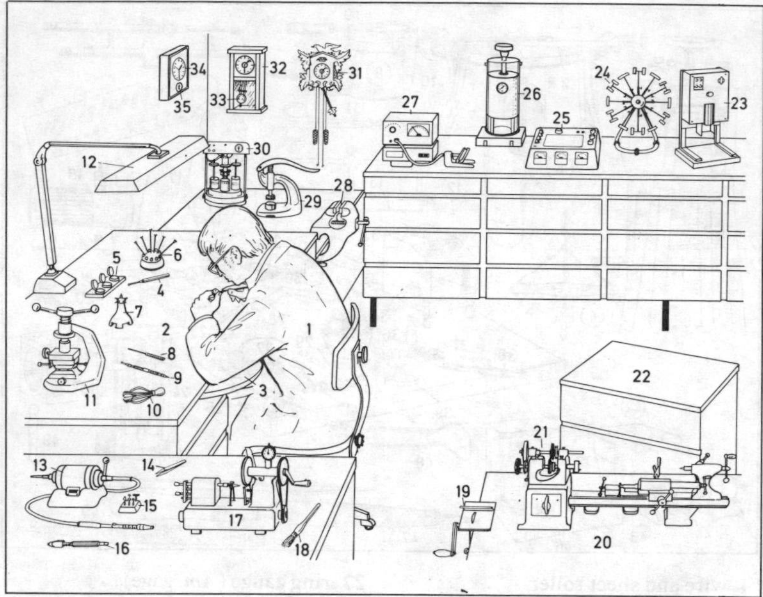

1 watchmaker; *also:* clockmaker
2 workbench
3 armrest
4 oiler
5 oil stand
6 set of screwdrivers
7 clockmaker's anvil
8 broach, a reamer
9 spring pin tool
10 hand-removing tool
11 watchglass-fitting tool
12 workbench lamp, a multi-purpose lamp
13 multi-purpose motor
14 tweezers
15 polishing machine attachments
16 pin vice (pin holder)
17 burnisher, for burnishing, polishing, and shortening of spindles
18 dust brush
19 cutter for metal watch straps
20 precision bench lathe (watchmaker's lathe)
21 drive-belt gear
22 workshop trolley for spare parts
23 ultrasonic cleaner
24 rotating watch-testing machine for automatic watches
25 watch-timing machine for electronic components
26 testing device for waterproof watches
27 electronic timing machine
28 vice (*Am.* vise)
29 watchglass-fitting tool for armoured (*Am.* armored) glasses
30 [automatic] cleaning machine for conventional cleaning
31 cuckoo clock (Black Forest clock)
32 wall clock (regulator)
33 compensation pendulum
34 kitchen clock
35 timer

1 electronic wristwatch
2 digital readout, a light-emitting diode (LED) readout; *also:* liquid crystal readout
3 hour and minute button
4 date and second button
5 strap (watch strap)
6 tuning fork principle (principle of the tuning fork watch)
7 power source (battery cell)
8 transformer
9 tuning fork element (oscillating element)
10 wheel ratchet
11 wheels
12 minute hand
13 hour hand
14 principle of the electronic quartz watch
15 quartz
16 integrated circuit
17 oscillation counter
18 decoder
19 calendar clock (alarm clock)
20 digital display with flip-over numerals
21 second indicator
22 stop button
23 forward and backward wind knob
24 grandfather clock
25 face
26 clock case
27 pendulum
28 striking weight
29 time weight
30 sundial
31 hourglass (egg timer)
32-43 components of an automatic watch (automatic wristwatch)
32 weight (rotor)
33 stone (jewel, jewelled bearing), a synthetic ruby
34 click
35 click wheel
36 clockwork (clockwork mechanism)
37 bottom train plate
38 spring barrel
39 balance wheel
40 escape wheel
41 crown wheel
42 winding crown
43 drive mechanism

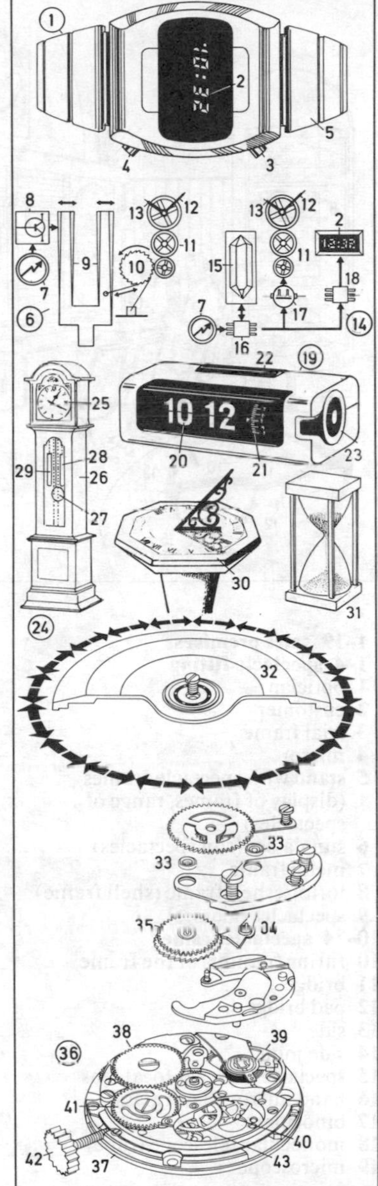

111 Optician

1–19 sales premises
1–4 spectacle fitting
1 optician
2 customer
3 trial frame
4 mirror
5 stand with spectacle frames (display of frames, range of spectacles)
6 sunglasses (sun spectacles)
7 metal frame
8 tortoiseshell frame (shell frame)
9 spectacles (glasses)
10–14 spectacle frame
10 fitting (mount) of the frame
11 bridge
12 pad bridge
13 side
14 side joint
15 spectacle lens, a bifocal lens
16 hand mirror (hand glass)
17 binoculars
18 monocular telescope (tube)
19 microscope

20–47 optician's workshop
20 workbench
21 universal centring (centering) apparatus
22 centring (centering) suction holder
23 sucker
24 edging machine
25 formers for the lens edging machine
26 inserted former
27 rotating printer
28 abrasive wheel combination
29 control unit
30 machine part
31 cooling water pipe
32 cleaning fluid
33 focimeter (vertex refractionometer)
34 metal-blocking device
35 abrasive wheel combination and forms of edging
36 roughing wheel for preliminary surfacing

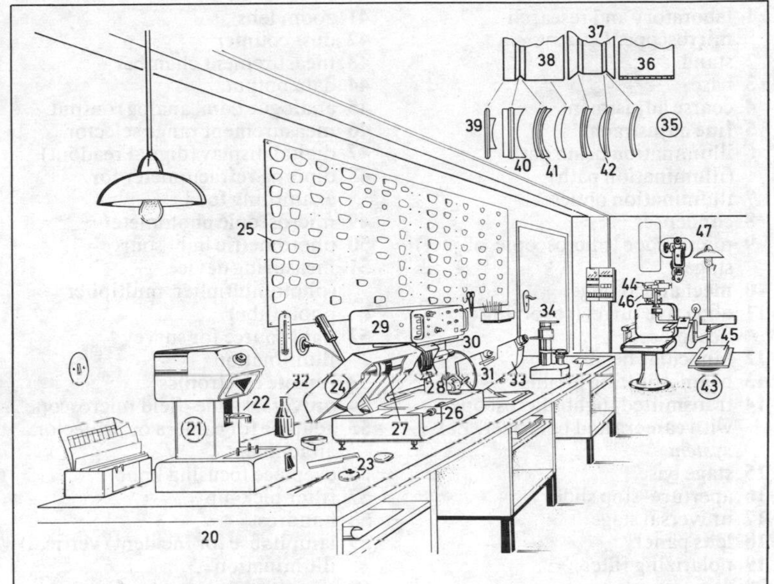

37 fining lap for positive and negative lens surfaces
38 fining lap for special and flat lenses
39 plano-concave lens with a flat surface
40 plano-concave lens with a special surface
41 concave and convex lens with a special surface
42 convex and concave lens with a special surface
43 ophthalmic test stand
44 phoropter with ophthalmometer and optometer (refractometer)
45 trial lens case
46 collimator
47 acuity projector

112 Optical Instruments I

1 laboratory and research microscope, *Leitz system*
2 stand
3 base
4 coarse adjustment
5 fine adjustment
6 illumination beam path (illumination path)
7 illumination optics
8 condenser
9 microscope (microscopic, object) stage
10 mechanical stage
11 objective turret (revolving nosepiece)
12 binocular head
13 beam-splitting prisms
14 transmitted-light microscope with camera and polarizer, *Zeiss system*
15 stage base
16 aperture-stop slide
17 universal stage
18 lens panel
19 polarizing filter
20 camera
21 focusing screen
22 discussion tube arrangement
23 wide-field metallurgical microscope, a reflected-light microscope (microscope for reflected light)
24 matt screen (ground glass screen, projection screen)
25 large-format camera
26 miniature camera
27 base plate
28 lamphouse
29 mechanical stage
30 objective turret (revolving nosepiece)
31 surgical microscope
32 pillar stand
33 field illumination
34 photomicroscope
35 miniature film cassette
36 photomicrographic camera attachment for large-format or television camera
37 surface-finish microscope
38 light section tube
39 rack and pinion
40 zoom stereomicroscope
41 zoom lens
42 dust counter
43 measurement chamber
44 data output
45 analogue (*Am.* analog) output
46 measurement range selector
47 digital display (digital readout)
48 dipping refractometer for examining food
49 microscopic photometer
50 photometric light source
51 measuring device (photomultiplier, multiplier phototube)
52 light source for survey illumination
53 remote electronics
54 universal wide-field microscope
55 adapter for camera or projector attachment
56 eyepiece focusing knob
57 filter pick-up
58 handrest
59 lamphouse for incident (vertical) illumination
60 lamphouse connector for transillumination
61 wide-field stereomicroscope
62 interchangeable lenses (objectives)
63 incident (vertical) illumination (incident top lighting)
64 fully automatic microscope camera, a camera with photomicro mount adapter
65 film cassette
66 universal condenser for research microscope 1
67 universal-type measuring machine for photogrammetry (phototheodolite)
68 photogrammetric camera
69 motor-driven level, a compensator level
70 electro-optical distance-measuring instrument
71 stereometric camera
72 horizontal base
73 one-second theodolite

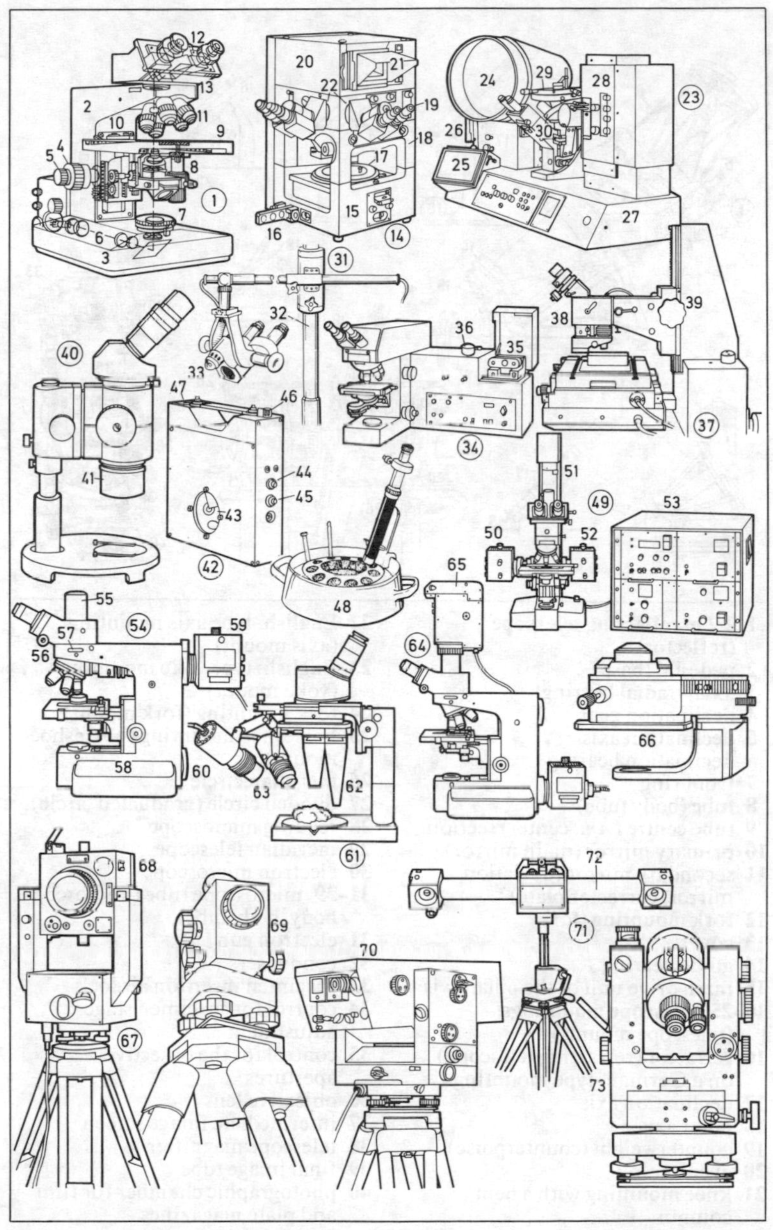
1
2
3
4
5
6
7
8
9
10
11
12
13
14
15
16
17
18
19
20
21
22
23
24
25
26
27
28
29
30
31
32
33
34
35
36
37
38
39
40
41
42
43
44
45
46
47
48
49
50
51
52
53
54
55
56
57
58
59
60
61
62
63
64
65
66
67
68
69
70
71
72
73

113 Optical Instruments II

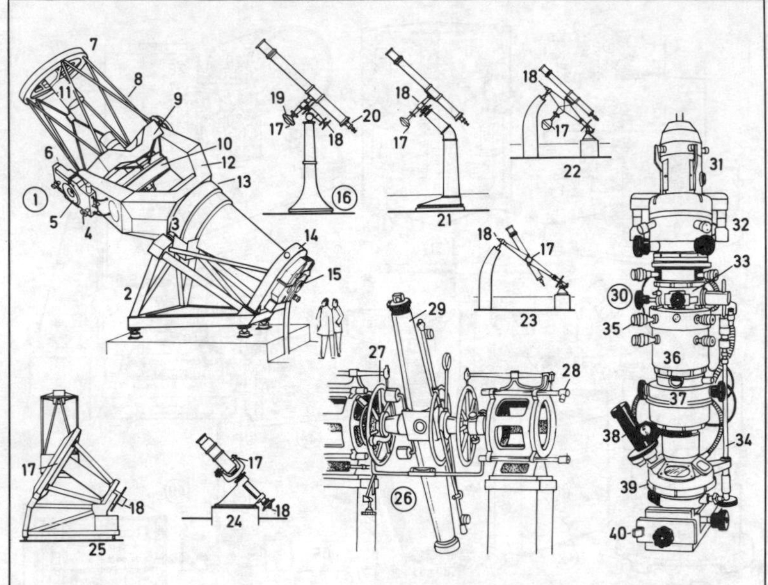

1 **2.2 m reflecting telescope** (reflector)
2 pedestal (base)
3 axial-radial bearing
4 declination gear
5 declination axis
6 declination bearing
7 front ring
8 tube (body tube)
9 tube centre (*Am.* center) section
10 primary mirror (main mirror)
11 secondary mirror (deviation mirror, corrector plate)
12 fork mounting (fork)
13 cover
14 guide bearing
15 main drive unit of the polar axis
16–25 **telescope mountings** (telescope mounts)
16 refractor (refracting telescope) on a German-type mounting
17 declination axis
18 polar axis
19 counterweight (counterpoise)
20 eyepiece
21 knee mounting with a bent column
22 English-type axis mounting (axis mount)
23 English-type yoke mounting (yoke mount)
24 fork mounting (fork mount)
25 horseshoe mounting (horseshoe mount)
26 meridian circle
27 divided circle (graduated circle)
28 reading microscope
29 meridian telescope
30 electron microscope
31–39 microscope tube (microscope body, body tube)
31 electron gun
32 condensers
33 specimen insertion air lock
34 control for specimen stage adjustment
35 control for the objective apertures
36 objective lens
37 intermediate image screen
38 telescope magnifier
39 final image tube
40 photographic chamber for film and plate magazines

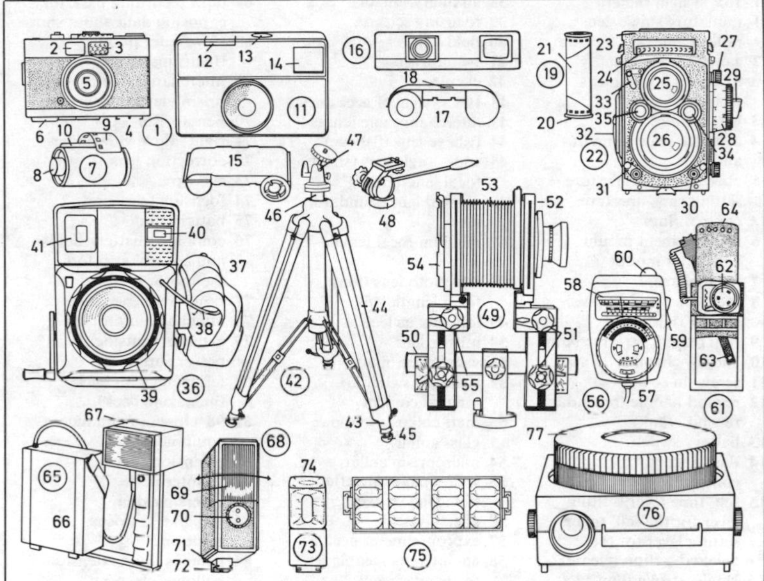

1 miniature camera (35 mm camera)
2 viewfinder eyepiece
3 meter cell
4 accessory shoe
5 flush lens
6 rewind handle (rewind, rewind crank)
7 miniature film cassette (135 film cassette, 35 mm cassette)
8 film spool
9 film with leader
10 cassette slit (cassette exit slot)
11 cartridge-loading camera
12 shutter release (shutter release button)
13 flash cube contact
14 rectangular viewfinder
15 126 cartridge (instamatic cartridge)
16 pocket camera (subminiature camera)
17 110 cartridge (subminiature cartridge)
18 film window
19 120 rollfilm
20 rollfilm spool
21 backing paper
22 twin-lens reflex camera
23 folding viewfinder hood (focusing hood)
24 meter cell
25 viewing lens
26 object lens
27 spool knob
28 distance setting (focus setting)
29 exposure meter using needle-matching system
30 flash contact
31 shutter release
32 film transport (film advance, film wind)
33 flash switch
34 aperture-setting control
35 shutter speed control
36 large-format hand camera (press camera)
37 grip (handgrip)
38 cable release
39 distance-setting ring (focusing ring)
40 rangefinder window
41 multiple-frame viewfinder (universal viewfinder)
42 tripod
43 tripod leg
44 tubular leg
45 rubber foot
46 central column
47 ball and socket head
48 cine camera pan and tilt head
49 large-format folding camera
50 optical bench
51 standard adjustment
52 lens standard
53 bellows
54 camera back
55 back standard adjustment
56 hand-held exposure meter (exposure meter)
57 calculator dial
58 scales (indicator scales) with indicator needle (pointer)
59 range switch (high/low range selector)
60 diffuser for incident light measurement
61 probe exposure meter for large-format cameras
62 meter
63 probe
64 dark slide
65 battery-portable electronic flash (battery-portable electronic flash unit)
66 powerpack unit (battery)
67 flash head
68 single-unit electronic flash (flashgun)
69 swivel-mounted reflector
70 photodiode
71 foot
72 hot-shoe contact
73 flash cube unit
74 flash cube
75 flash bar
76 slide projector
77 rotary magazine

115 Photography II

1-105 system camera
1 miniature single–lens reflex camera
2 camera body
3-8 lens, a normal lens (standard lens)
3 lens barrel
4 distance scale in metres and feet
5 aperture ring (aperture-setting ring, aperture control ring)
6 front element mount with filter mount
7 front element
8 focusing ring (distance-setting ring)
9 ring for the carrying strap
10 battery chamber
11 screw-in cover
12 rewind handle (rewind, rewind crank)
13 battery switch
14 flash socket for F and X contact
15 self-time lever (setting lever for the self-timer, setting lever for the delayed-action release)
16 single-stroke film advance lever
17 exposure counter (frame counter)
18 shutter release (shutter release button)
19 shutter speed setting knob (shutter speed control)
20 accessory shoe
21 hot-shoe flash contact
22 viewfinder eyepiece with correcting lens
23 camera back
24 pressure plate
25 take-up spool of the rapid-loading system
26 transport sprocket
27 rewind release button (reversing clutch)
28 film window
29 rewind cam
30 tripod socket (tripod bush)
31 reflex system (mirror reflex system)
32 lens
33 reflex mirror
34 film window
35 path of the image beam
36 path of the sample beam
37 meter cell
38 auxiliary mirror
39 focusing screen
40 field lens
41 pentaprism
42 eyepiece
43–105 system of accessories
43 interchangeable lenses
44 fisheye lens (fisheye)
45 wide-angle lens (short focal length lens)
46 normal lens (standard lens)
47 medium focal length lens
48 telephoto lens (long focal length lens)
49 long-focus lens
50 mirror lens
51 viewfinder image
52 signal to switch to manual control
53 matt collar (ground glass collar)
54 microprism collar
55 split-image rangefinder (focusing wedges)
56 aperture scale
57 exposure meter needle
58-66 interchangeable focusing screens
58 all-matt screen (ground glass screen) with microprism spot
59 all-matt screen (ground glass screen) with microprism spot and split-image rangefinder
60 all-matt screen (ground glass screen) without focusing aids
61 matt screen (ground glass screen) with reticule
62 microprism spot for lenses with a large aperture
63 microprism spot for lenses with an aperture of f = 1 : 3.5 or larger
64 Fresnel lens with matt collar (ground glass collar) and split-image rangefinder
65 all-matt screen (ground glass screen) with finely matted central spot and graduated markings
66 matt screen (ground glass screen) with clear spot and double cross hairs
67 data recording back for exposing data about shots
68 viewfinder hood (focusing hood)
69 interchangeable pentaprism viewfinder
70 pentaprism
71 right-angle viewfinder
72 correction lens
73 eyecup
74 focusing telescope
75 battery unit
76 combined battery holder and control grip for the motor drive
77 rapid-sequence camera
78 attachable motor drive
79 external (outside) power supply
80 ten meter film back (magazine back)
81-98 close-up and macro equipment
81 extension tube
82 adapter ring
83 reversing ring
84 lens in retrofocus position
85 bellows unit (extension bellows, close-up bellows attachment)
86 focusing stage
87 slide-copying attachment
88 slide-copying adapter
89 micro attachment (photomicroscope adapter)
90 copying stand (copy stand, copypod)
91 spider legs
92 copying stand (copy stand)
93 arm of the copying stand (copy stand)
94 macrophoto stand
95 stage plates for the macrophoto stand
96 insertable disc (disk)
97 Lieberkühn reflector
98 mechanical stage
99 table tripod (table-top tripod)
100 rifle grip
101 cable release
102 double cable release
103 camera case (ever-ready case)
104 lens case
105 soft–leather lens pouch

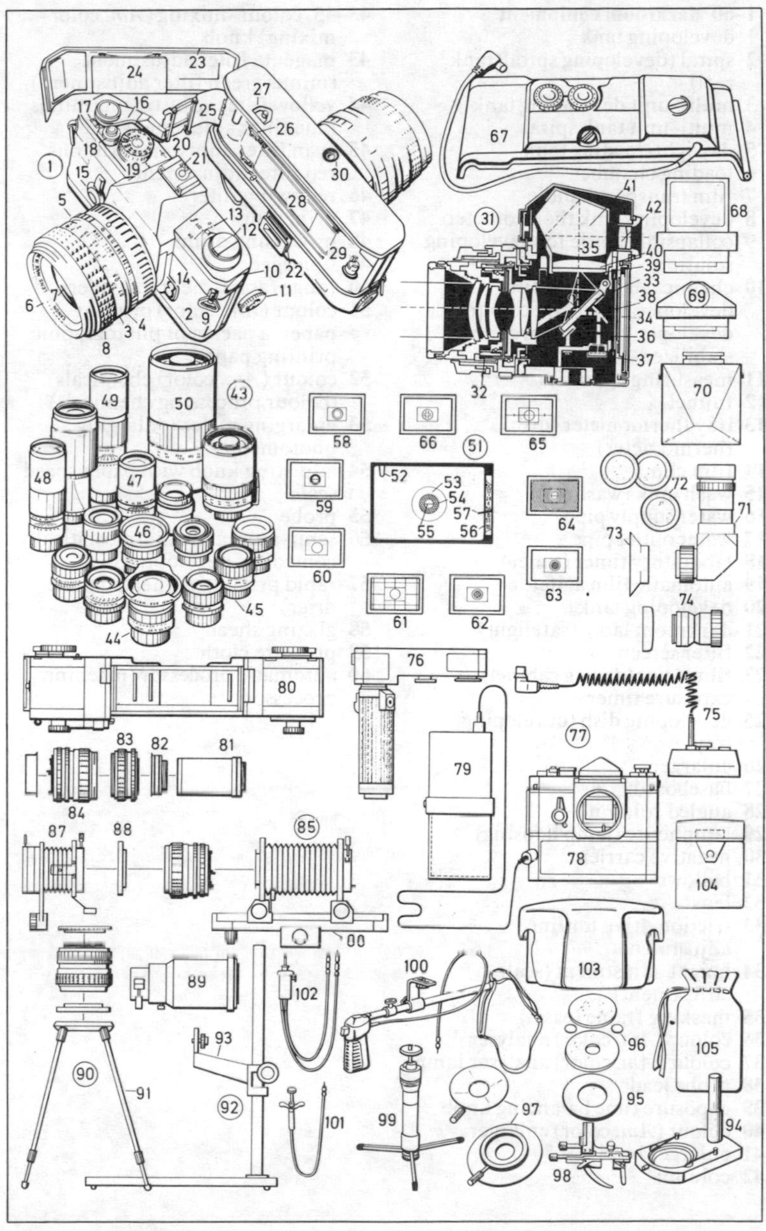

1-60 darkroom equipment
1 developing tank
2 spiral (developing spiral, tank reel)
3 multi-unit developing tank
4 multi-unit tank spiral
5 daylight-loading tank
6 loading chamber
7 film transport handle
8 developing tank thermometer
9 collapsible bottle for developing solution
10 chemical bottles for first developer, stop bath, colour developer, bleach-hardener, stabilizer
11 measuring cylinders
12 funnel
13 tray thermometer (dish thermometer)
14 film clip
15 wash tank (washer)
16 water supply pipe
17 water outlet pipe
18 laboratory timer (timer)
19 automatic film agitator
20 developing tank
21 darkroom lamp (safelight)
22 filter screen
23 film drier (drying cabinet)
24 exposure timer
25 developing dish (developing tray)
26 enlarger
27 baseboard
28 angled column
29 lamphouse (lamp housing)
30 negative carrier
31 bellows
32 lens
33 friction drive for fine adjustment
34 height adjustment (scale adjustment)
35 masking frame (easel)
36 colour (*Am.* color) analyser
37 colour (*Am.* color) analyser lamp
38 probe lead
39 exposure time balancing knob
40 colour (*Am.* color) enlarger
41 enlarger head
42 column
43-45 colour-mixing (*Am.* color-mixing) knob
43 magenta filter adjustment (minus green filter adjustment)
44 yellow filter adjustment (minus blue filter adjustment)
45 cyan filter adjustment (minus red filter adjustment)
46 red swing filter
47 print tongs
48 processing drum
49 squeegee
50 range (assortment) of papers
51 colour (*Am.* color) printing paper, a packet of photographic printing paper
52 colour (*Am.* color) chemicals (colour processing chemicals)
53 enlarging meter (enlarging photometer)
54 adjusting knob with paper speed scale
55 probe
56 semi-automatic thermostatically controlled developing dish
57 rapid print drier (heated print drier)
58 glazing sheet
59 pressure cloth
60 automatic processor (machine processor)

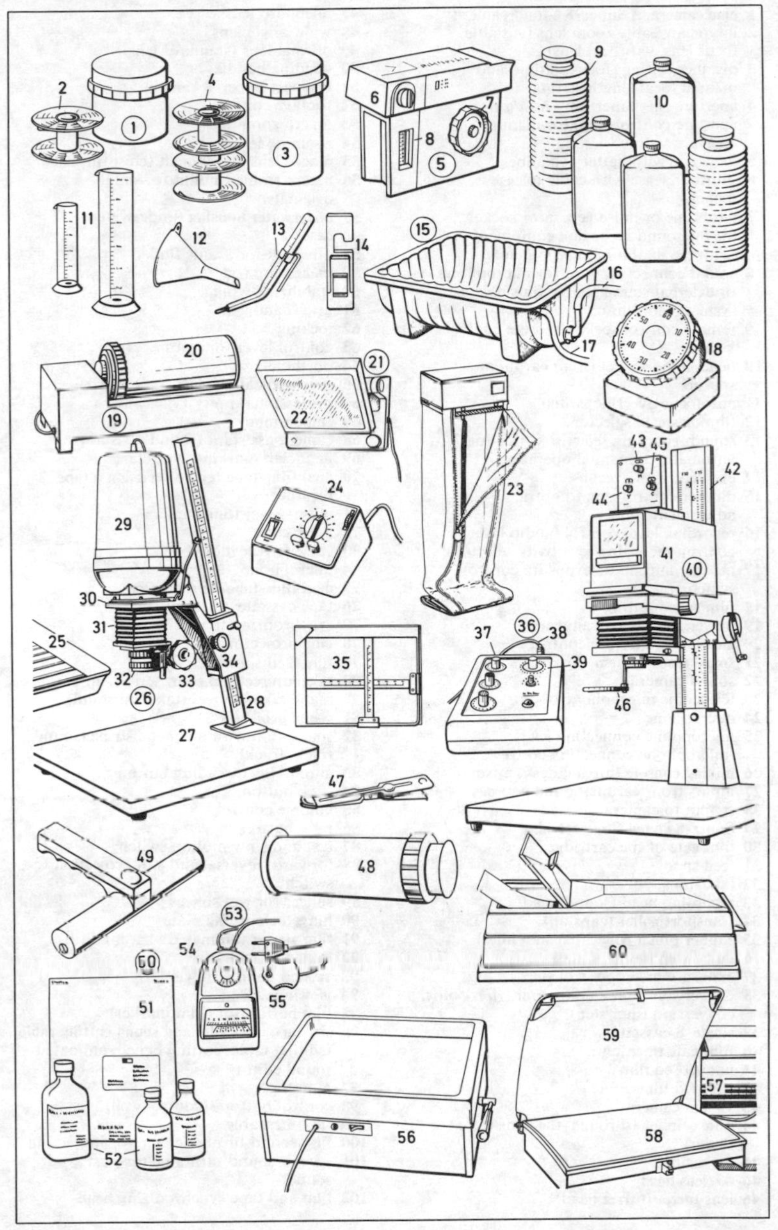

1
2
3
4
5
6
7
8
9
10
11
12
13
14
15
16
17
18
19
20
21
22
23
24
25
26
27
28
29
30
31
32
33
34
35
36
37
38
39
40
41
42
43
44
45
46
47
48
49
50
51
52
53
54
55
56
57
58
59
60

117 Cine Film

1 **cine camera,** a Super-8 sound camera
2 interchangeable zoom lens (variable focus lens, varifocal lens)
3 distance setting (focus setting) and manual focal length setting
4 aperture ring (aperture-setting ring, aperture control ring) for manual aperture setting
5 handgrip with battery chamber
6 shutter release with cable release socket
7 pilot tone or pulse generator socket for the sound recording equipment (with the dual film-tape system)
8 sound connecting cord for microphone or external sound source (in single-system recording)
9 remote control socket (remote control jack)
10 headphone socket (*sim.:* earphone socket)
11 autofocus override switch
12 filming speed selector
13 sound recording selector switch for automatic or manual operation
14 eyepiece with eyecup
15 diopter control ring (dioptric adjustment ring)
16 recording level control (audio level control, recording sensitivity selector)
17 manual/automatic exposure control switch
18 film speed setting
19 power zooming arrangement
20 automatic aperture control
21 **sound track system**
22 sound camera
23 telescopic microphone boom
24 microphone
25 microphone connecting lead (microphone connecting cord)
26 **mixing console** (mixing desk, mixer)
27 inputs from various sound sources
28 output to camera
29 **Super-8 sound film cartridge**
30 film gate of the cartridge
31 feed spool
32 take-up spool
33 recording head (sound head)
34 transport roller (capstan)
35 rubber pinch roller (capstan idler)
36 guide step (guide notch)
37 exposure meter control step
38 conversion filter step (colour, *Am.* color, conversion filter step)
39 **single-8 cassette**
40 film gate opening
41 unexposed film
42 exposed film
43 **16 mm camera**
44 reflex finder (through-the-lens reflex finder)
45 magazine
46-49 **lens head**
46 lens turret (turret head)
47 telephoto lens
48 wide-angle lens
49 normal lens (standard lens)
50 winding handle
51 **compact Super-8 camera**
52 footage counter
53 macro zoom lens
54 zooming lever
55 macro lens attachment (close-up lens)
56 macro frame (mount for small originals)
57 **underwater housing** (underwater case)
58 direct-vision frame finder
59 measuring rod
60 stabilizing wing
61 grip (handgrip)
62 locking bolt
63 control lever (operating lever)
64 porthole
65 **synchronization start** (sync start)
66 professional press-type camera
67 cameraman
68 camera assistant (sound assistant)
69 handclap marking sync start
70 **dual film-tape recording using a tape recorder**
71 pulse-generating camera
72 pulse cable
73 cassette recorder
74 microphone
75 **dual film-tape reproduction**
76 tape cassette
77 synchronization unit
78 cine projector
79 film feed spool
80 take-up reel (take-up spool), an automatic take-up reel (take-up spool)
81 **sound projector**
82 sound film with magnetic stripe (sound track, track)
83 automatic-threading button
84 trick button
85 volume control
86 reset button
87 fast and slow motion switch
88 forward, reverse, and still projection switch
89 splicer for wet splices
90 hinged clamping plate
91 **film viewer** (animated viewer editor)
92 foldaway reel arm
93 rewind handle (rewinder)
94 viewing screen
95 film perforator (film marker)
96 **six-turn able film and sound cutting table** (editing table, cutting bench, animated sound editor)
97 monitor
98 control buttons (control well)
99 film turntable
100 first sound turntable, e.g. for live sound
101 second sound turntable for post-sync sound
102 film and tape synchronizing head

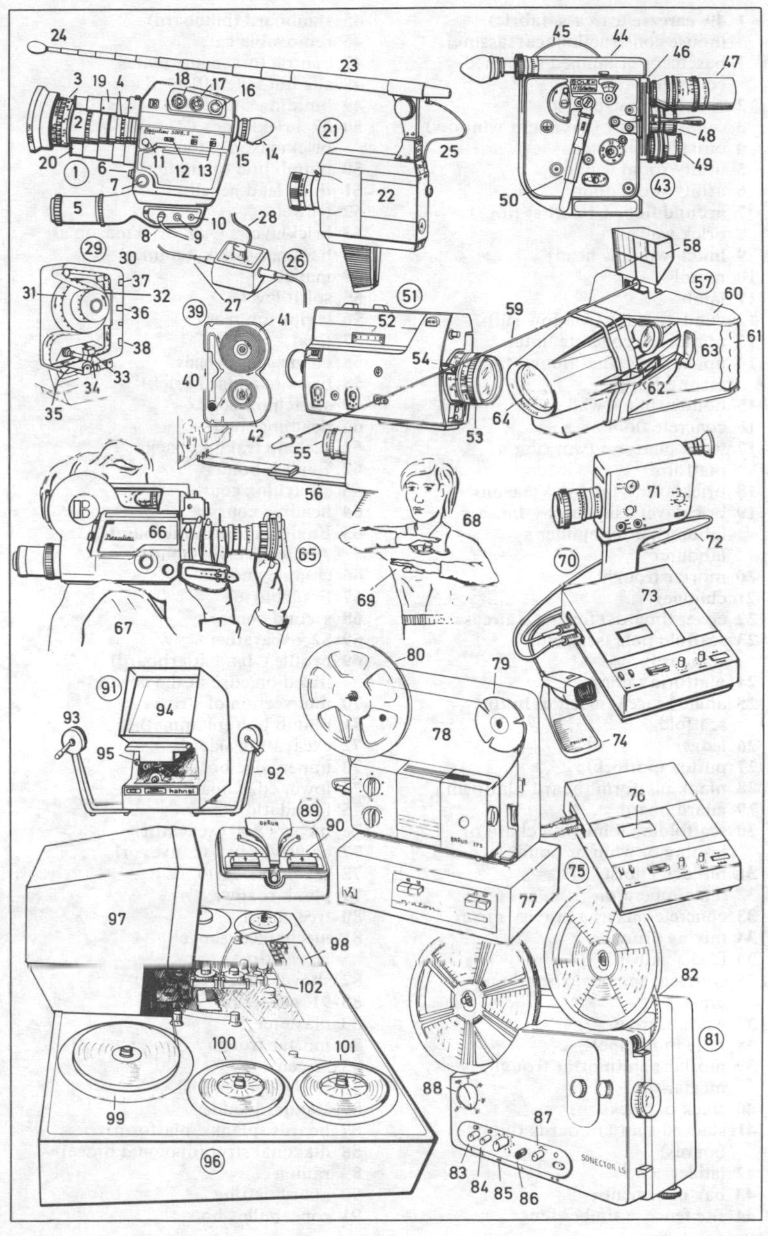
1
2
3
4
5
6
7
8
9
10
11
12
13
14
15
16
17
18
19
20
21
22
23
24
25
26
27
28
29
30
31
32
33
34
35
36
37
38
39
40
41
42
43
44
45
46
47
48
49
50
51
52
53
54
55
56
57
58
59
60
61
62
63
64
65
66
67
68
69
70
71
72
73
74
75
76
77
78
79
80
81
82
83
84
85
86
87
88
89
90
91
92
93
94
95
96
97
98
99
100
101
102
Beaulieu
hahnel
BRAUN
SONECTOR LS

1-49 carcase (carcass, fabric) [house construction, carcassing]
1 basement of tamped (rammed) concrete
2 concrete base course
3 cellar window (basement window)
4 outside cellar steps
5 utility room window
6 utility room door
7 ground floor (*Am.* first floor)
8 brick wall
9 lintel (window head)
10 reveal
11 jamb
12 window ledge (window sill)
13 reinforced concrete lintel
14 upper floor (first floor, *Am.* second floor)
15 hollow-block wall
16 concrete floor
17 work platform (working platform)
18 bricklayer (*Am.* brickmason)
19 bricklayer's labourer (*Am.* laborer); *also:* builder's labourer
20 mortar trough
21 chimney
22 cover (boards) for the staircase
23 scaffold pole (scaffold standard)
24 platform railing
25 angle brace (angle tie) in the scaffold
26 ledger
27 putlog (putlock)
28 plank platform (board platform)
29 guard board
30 scaffolding joint with chain or lashing or whip or bond
31 builder's hoist
32 mixer operator
33 concrete mixer, a gravity mixer
34 mixing drum
35 feeder skip
36 concrete aggregate [sand and gravel]
37 wheelbarrow
38 hose (hosepipe)
39 mortar pan (mortar trough, mortar tub)
40 stack of bricks
41 stacked shutter boards (lining boards)
42 ladder
43 bag of cement
44 site fence, a timber fence
45 signboard (billboard)
46 removable gate
47 contractors' name plates
48 site hut (site office)
49 building site latrine
50-57 bricklayer's (*Am.* brickmason's) **tools**
50 plumb bob (plummet)
51 thick lead pencil
52 trowel
53 bricklayer's (*Am.* brickmason's) hammer (brick hammer)
54 mallet
55 spirit level
56 laying-on trowel
57 float
58-68 masonry bonds
58 brick (standard brick)
59 stretching bond
60 heading bond
61 racking (raking) back
62 English bond
63 stretching course
64 heading course
65 English cross bond (Saint Andrew's cross bond)
66 chimney bond
67 first course
68 second course
69-82 excavation
69 profile (*Am.* batterboard) [fixed on edge at the corner]
70 intersection of strings
71 plumb bob (plummet)
72 excavation side
73 upper edge board
74 lower edge board
75 foundation trench
76 navvy (*Am.* excavator)
77 conveyor belt (conveyor)
78 excavated earth
79 plank roadway
80 tree guard
81 mechanical shovel (excavator)
82 shovel bucket (bucket)
83-91 plastering
83 plasterer
84 mortar trough
85 screen
86-89 ladder scaffold
86 standard ladder
87 boards (planks, platform)
88 diagonal strut (diagonal brace)
89 railing
90 guard netting
91 rope-pulley hoist

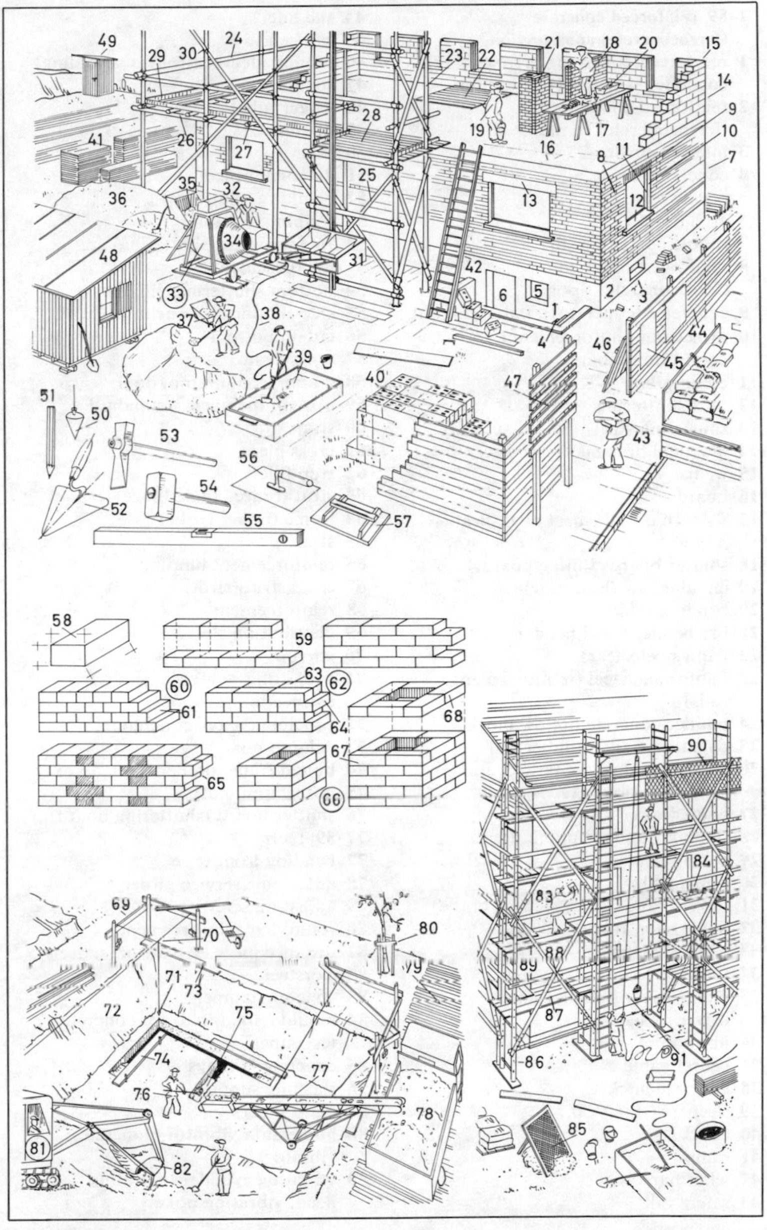

1 2 3 4 5 6 7 8 9 10 11 12 13 14 15 16 17 18 19 20 21 22 23 24 25 26 27 28 29 30 31 32 33 34 35 36 37 38 39 40 41 42 43 44 45 46 47 48 49 50 51 52 53 54 55 56 57 58 59 60 61 62 63 64 65 66 67 68 69 70 71 72 73 74 75 76 77 78 79 80 81 82 83 84 85 86 87 88 89 90 91

119 Building Site (Construction Site) II

1-89 reinforced concrete (ferroconcrete) construction
1 reinforced concrete (ferroconcrete) skeleton construction
2 reinforced concrete (ferroconcrete) frame
3 inferior purlin
4 concrete purlin
5 ceiling joist
6 arch (flank)
7 rubble concrete wall
8 reinforced concrete (ferroconcrete) floor
9 concreter (concretor), flattening out
10 projecting reinforcement (*Am.* connection rebars)
11 column box
12 joist shuttering
13 shuttering strut
14 diagonal bracing
15 wedge
16 board
17 sheet pile wall (sheet pile, sheet piling)
18 shutter boards (lining boards)
19 circular saw (buzz saw)
20 bending table
21 bar bender (steel bender)
22 hand steel shears
23 reinforcing steel (reinforcement rods)
24 pumice concrete hollow block
25 partition wall, a timber wall
26 concrete aggregate [gravel and sand of various grades]
27 crane track
28 tipping wagon (tipping truck)
29 concrete mixer
30 cement silo
31 tower crane (tower slewing crane)
32 bogie (*Am.* truck)
33 counterweight
34 tower
35 crane driver's cabin (crane driver's cage)
36 jib (boom)
37 bearer cable
38 concrete bucket
39 sleepers (*Am.* ties)
40 chock
41 ramp
42 wheelbarrow
43 safety rail
44 site hut
45 canteen
46 tubular steel scaffold (scaffolding)
47 standard
48 ledger tube
49 tie tube
50 shoe
51 diagonal brace
52 planking (platform)
53 coupling (coupler)
54-76 formwork (shuttering) and reinforcement
54 bottom shuttering (lining)
55 side shutter of a purlin
56 cut-in bottom
57 cross beam
58 cramp iron (cramp, dog)
59 upright member, a standard
60 strap
61 cross piece
62 stop fillet
63 strut (brace, angle brace)
64 frame timber (yoke)
65 strap
66 reinforcement binding
67 cross strut (strut)
68 reinforcement
69 distribution steel
70 stirrup
71 projecting reinforcement (*Am.* connection rebars)
72 concrete (heavy concrete)
73 column box
74 bolted frame timber (bolted yoke)
75 nut (thumb nut)
76 shutter board (shuttering board)
77-89 tools
77 bending iron
78 adjustable service girder
79 adjusting screw
80 round bar reinforcement
81 distance piece (separator, spacer)
82 Torsteel
83 concrete tamper
84 mould (*Am.* mold) for concrete test cubes
85 concreter's tongs
86 sheeting support
87 hand shears
88 immersion vibrator (concrete vibrator)
89 vibrating cylinder (vibrating head, vibrating poker)

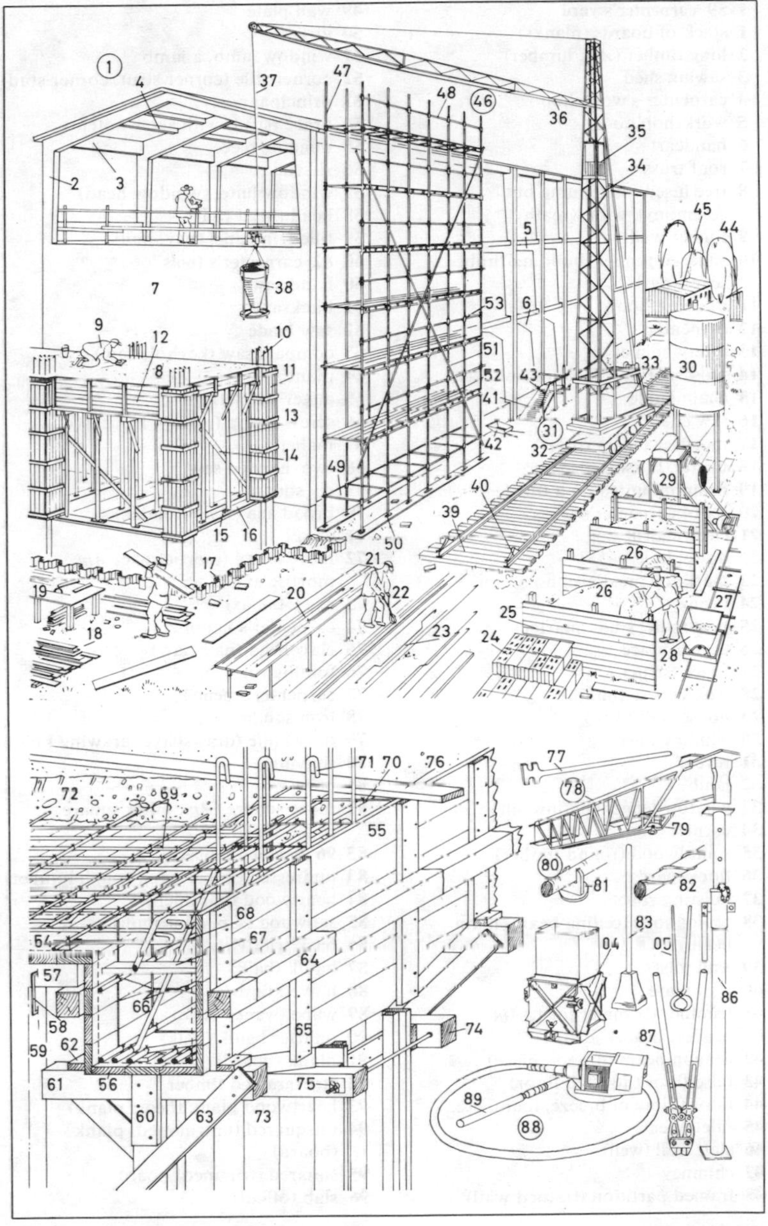
1
4
37
47
48
46
36
35
34
2
3
45
44
5
38
7
53
6
9
10
12
8
11
51
52
43
33
30
41
13
31
42
32
14
29
49
40
39
15
16
50
17
21
26
19
22
20
26
27
25
23
24
28
18
71
70
76
77
72
69
78
55
79
80
81
82
68
83
67
64
04
05
64
57
66
86
58
65
74
87
62
59
61
56
75
89
60
63
73
88

120 Carpenter

1-59 carpenter's yard
1 stack of boards (planks)
2 long timber (*Am.* lumber)
3 sawing shed
4 carpenter's workshop
5 workshop door
6 handcart
7 roof truss
8 tree [used for topping out ceremony], with wreath
9 timber wall
10 squared timber (building timber, scantlings)
11 drawing floor
12 carpenter
13 safety helmet
14 cross-cut saw, a chain saw
15 chain guide
16 saw chain
17 mortiser (chain cutter)
18 trestle (horse)
19 beam mounted on a trestle
20 set of carpenter's tools
21 electric drill
22 dowel hole
23 mark for the dowel hole
24 beams
25 post (stile, stud, quarter)
26 corner brace
27 brace (strut)
28 base course (plinth)
29 house wall (wall)
30 window opening
31 reveal
32 jamb
33 window ledge (window sill)
34 cornice
35 roundwood (round timber)
36 floorboards
37 hoisting rope
38 ceiling joist (ceiling beam, main beam)
39 wall joist
40 wall plate
41 trimmer (trimmer joist, *Am.* header, header joist)
42 dragon beam (dragon piece)
43 false floor (inserted floor)
44 floor filling of breeze, loam, etc.
45 fillet (cleat)
46 stair well (well)
47 chimney
48 framed partition (framed wall)
49 wall plate
50 girt
51 window jamb, a jamb
52 corner stile (corner strut, corner stud)
53 principal post
54 brace (strut) with skew notch
55 nogging piece
56 sill rail
57 window lintel (window head)
58 head (head rail)
59 filled-in panel (bay, pan)

60-82 carpenter's tools
60 hand saw
61 bucksaw
62 saw blade
63 compass saw (keyhole saw)
64 plane
65 auger (gimlet)
66 screw clamp (cramp, holdfast)
67 mallet
68 two-handed saw
69 try square
70 broad axe (*Am.* broadax)
71 chisel
72 mortise axe (mortice axe, *Am.* mortise ax)
73 axe (*Am.* ax)
74 carpenter's hammer
75 claw head (nail claw)
76 folding rule
77 carpenter's pencil
78 iron square
79 drawknife (drawshave, drawing knife)
80 shaving
81 bevel
82 mitre square (*Am.* miter square, miter angle)

83-96 building timber
83 undressed timber (*Am.* rough lumber)
84 heartwood (duramen)
85 sapwood (sap, alburnum)
86 bark (rind)
87 baulk (balk)
88 halved timber
89 wane (waney edge)
90 quarter baulk (balk)
91 plank (board)
92 end-grained timber
93 heartwood plank (heart plank)
94 unsquared (untrimmed) plank (board)
95 squared (trimmed) board
96 slab (offcut)

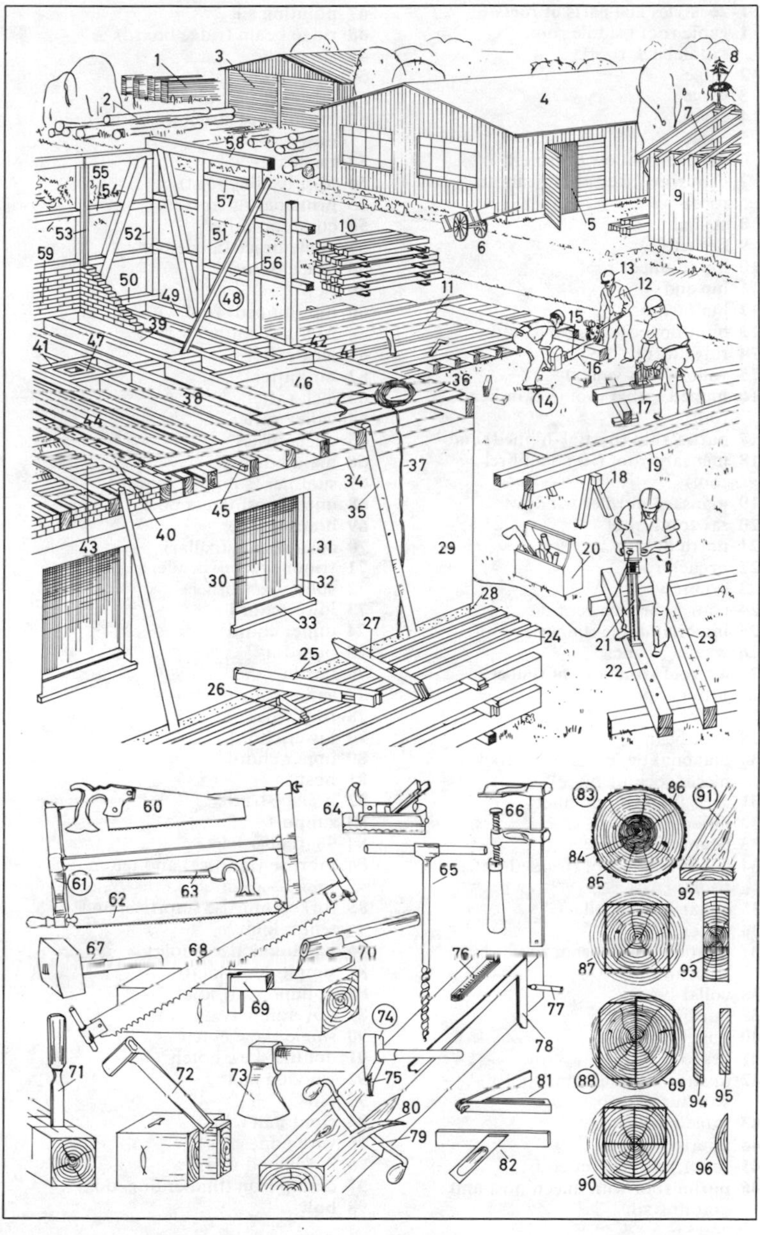
1
2
3
4
5
6
7
8
9
10
11
12
13
14
15
16
17
18
19
20
21
22
23
24
25
26
27
28
29
30
31
32
33
34
35
36
37
38
39
40
41
42
43
44
45
46
47
48
49
50
51
52
53
54
55
56
57
58
59
60
61
62
63
64
65
66
67
68
69
70
71
72
73
74
75
76
77
78
79
80
81
82
83
84
85
86
87
88
89
90
91
92
93
94
95
96

121 Roof, Timber Joints

1-26 styles and parts of roofs
1 gable roof (saddle roof, saddleback roof)
2 ridge
3 verge
4 eaves
5 gable
6 dormer window (dormer)
7 pent roof (shed roof, lean-to roof)
8 skylight
9 fire gable
10 hip (hipped) roof
11 hip end
12 hip (arris)
13 hip (hipped) dormer window
14 ridge turret
15 valley (roof valley)
16 hipped-gable roof (jerkin head roof)
17 partial-hip (partial-hipped) end
18 mansard roof (*Am.* gambrel roof)
19 mansard dormer window
20 sawtooth roof
21 north light
22 broach roof
23 eyebrow
24 conical broach roof
25 imperial dome (imperial roof)
26 weather vane
27-83 roof structures of timber
27 rafter roof
28 rafter
29 roof beam
30 diagonal tie (cross tie, sprocket piece, cocking piece)
31 arris fillet (tilting fillet)
32 outer wall
33 beam head
34 collar beam roof (trussed-rafter roof)
35 collar beam (collar)
36 rafter
37 strutted collar beam roof structure
38 collar beams
39 purlin
40 post (stile, stud)
41 brace
42 unstrutted (king pin) roof structure
43 ridge purlin
44 inferior purlin
45 rafter head (rafter end)
46 purlin roof with queen post and pointing sill
47 pointing sill
48 ridge beam (ridge board)
49 simple tie
50 double tie
51 purlin
52 purlin roof structure with queen post
53 tie beam
54 joist (ceiling joist)
55 principal rafter
56 common rafter
57 angle brace (angle tie)
58 brace (strut)
59 ties
60 hip (hipped) roof with purlin roof structure
61 jack rafter
62 hip rafter
63 jack rafter
64 valley rafter
65 queen truss
66 main beam
67 summer (summer beam)
68 queen post (truss post)
69 brace (strut)
70 collar beam (collar)
71 trimmer (*Am.* header)
72 solid–web girder
73 lower chord
74 upper chord
75 boarding
76 purlin
77 supporting outer wall
78 roof truss
79 lower chord
80 upper chord
81 post
82 brace (strut)
83 support
84-98 timber joints
84 mortise (mortice) and tenon joint
85 forked mortise (mortice) and tenon joint
86 halving (halved) joint
87 simple scarf joint
88 oblique scarf joint
89 dovetail halving
90 single skew notch
91 double skew notch
92 wooden nail
93 pin
94 clout nail (clout)
95 wire nail
96 hardwood wedges
97 cramp iron (timber dog, dog)
98 bolt

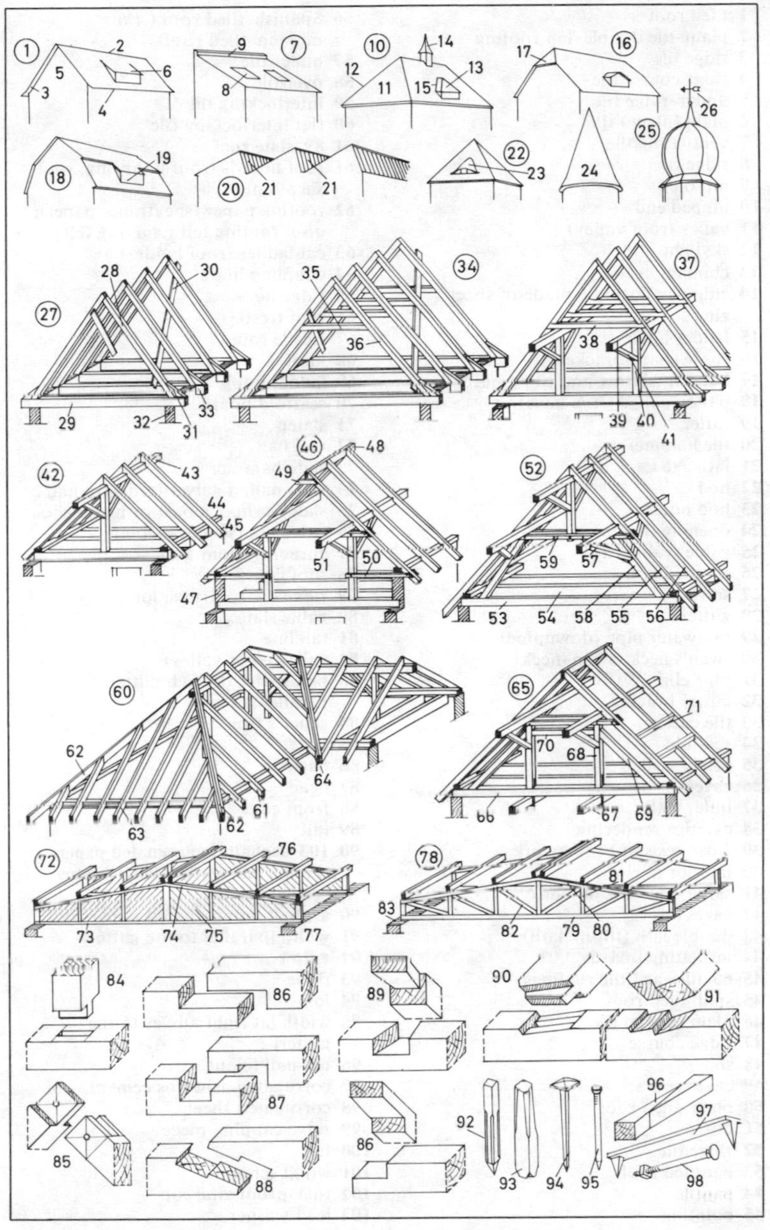
1
2
3
4
5
6
7
8
9
10
11
12
13
14
15
16
17
18
19
20
21
21
22
23
24
25
26
27
28
29
30
31
32
33
34
35
36
37
38
39
40
41
42
43
44
45
46
47
48
49
50
51
52
53
54
55
56
57
58
59
60
61
62
62
63
64
65
66
67
68
69
70
71
72
73
74
75
76
77
78
79
80
81
82
83
84
85
86
86
87
88
89
90
91
92
93
94
95
96
97
98

122 Roof and Roofer

1 tiled roof
2 plain-tile double-lap roofing
3 ridge tile
4 ridge course tile
5 under-ridge tile
6 plain (plane) tile
7 ventilating tile
8 ridge tile
9 hip tile
10 hipped end
11 valley (roof valley)
12 skylight
13 chimney
14 chimney flashing, made of sheet zinc
15 ladder hook
16 snow guard bracket
17 battens (slating and tiling battens)
18 batten gauge (*Am.* gage)
19 rafter
20 tile hammer
21 lath axe (*Am.* ax)
22 hod
23 hod hook
24 opening (hatch)
25 gable (gable end)
26 toothed lath
27 soffit
28 gutter
29 rainwater pipe (downpipe)
30 swan's neck (swan-neck)
31 pipe clip
32 gutter bracket
33 tile cutter
34 scaffold
35 safety wall
36 eaves
37 outer wall
38 exterior rendering
39 frost-resistant brickwork
40 inferior purlin
41 rafter head (rafter end)
42 eaves fascia
43 double lath (tilting lath)
44 insulating boards
45-60 tiles and tile roofings
45 split-tiled roof
46 plain (plane) tile
47 ridge course
48 slip
49 eaves course
50 plain-tiled roof
51 nib
52 ridge tile
53 pantiled roof
54 pantile
55 pointing
56 Spanish-tiled roof (*Am.* mission-tiled roof)
57 under tile
58 over tile
59 interlocking tile
60 flat interlocking tile
61-89 slate roof
61 roof boards (roof boarding, roof sheathing)
62 roofing paper (sheathing paper); *also:* roofing felt (*Am.* rag felt)
63 cat ladder (roof ladder)
64 coupling hook
65 ridge hook
66 roof trestle
67 trestle rope
68 knot
69 ladder hook
70 scaffold board
71 slater
72 nail bag
73 slate hammer
74 slate nail, a galvanized wire nail
75 slater's shoe, a bast or hemp shoe
76 eaves course (eaves joint)
77 corner bottom slate
78 roof course
79 ridge course (ridge joint)
80 gable slate
81 tail line
82 valley (roof valley)
83 box gutter (trough gutter, parallel gutter)
84 slater's iron
85 slate
86 back
87 head
88 front edge
89 tail
90-103 asphalt-impregnated paper roofing and corrugated asbestos cement roofing
90 asphalt-impregnated paper roof
91 width [parallel to the gutter]
92 gutter
93 ridge
94 join
95 width [at right angles to the gutter]
96 felt nail (clout nail)
97 corrugated asbestos cement roof
98 corrugated sheet
99 ridge capping piece
100 lap
101 wood screw
102 rust-proof zinc cup
103 lead washer

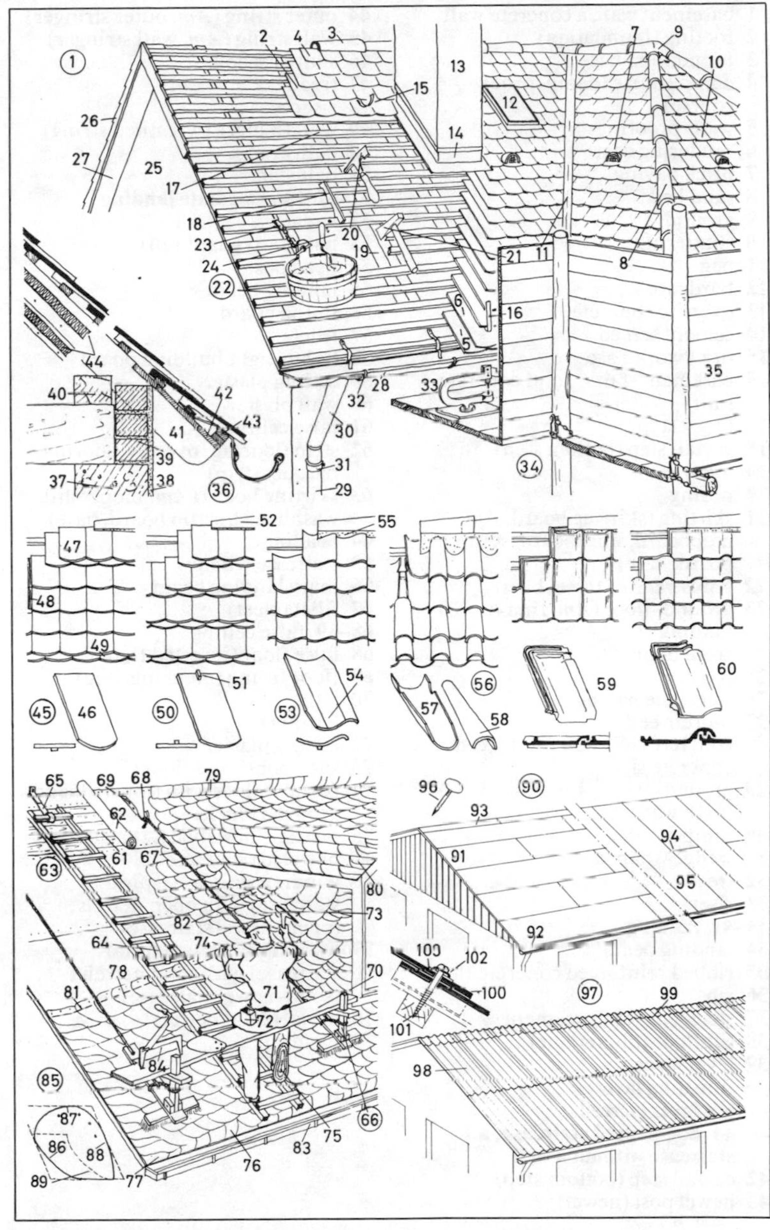
1
2
3
4
26
7
9
10
13
12
15
14
27
25
17
18
20
23
24
19
21
11
8
22
6
16
5
44
40
42
43
41
39
37
38
36
28
33
32
30
31
29
34
35
52
55
47
48
49
51
54
56
59
60
45
46
50
53
57
58
65
69
68
79
62
61
67
63
96
90
93
91
94
95
80
73
82
64
74
92
100
102
100
70
78
71
81
72
97
99
101
84
98
85
87
66
86
88
75
83
76
89
77

123 Floor, Ceiling, Staircase Construction

1 basement wall, a concrete wall
2 footing (foundation)
3 foundation base
4 damp course (damp-proof course)
5 waterproofing
6 rendering coat
7 brick paving
8 sand bed
9 ground
10 shuttering
11 peg
12 hardcore
13 oversite concrete
14 cement screed
15 brickwork base
16 basement stairs, solid concrete stairs
17 block step
18 curtail step (bottom step)
19 top step
20 nosing
21 skirting (skirting board, *Am.* mopboard, washboard, scrub board, base)
22 balustrade of metal bars
23 ground-floor (*Am.* first-floor) landing
24 front door
25 foot scraper
26 flagstone paving
27 mortar bed
28 concrete ceiling, a reinforced concrete slab
29 ground-floor (*Am.* first-floor) brick wall
30 ramp
31 wedge-shaped step
32 tread
33 riser
34–41 landing
34 landing beam
35 ribbed reinforced concrete floor
36 rib
37 steel-bar reinforcement
38 subfloor (blind floor)
39 level layer
40 finishing layer
41 top layer (screed)
42–44 dog-legged staircase, a staircase without a well
42 curtail step (bottom step)
43 newel post (newel)
44 outer string (*Am.* outer stringer)
45 wall string (*Am.* wall stringer)
46 staircase bolt
47 tread
48 riser
49 wreath piece (wreathed string)
50 balustrade
51 baluster
52–62 intermediate landing
52 wreath
53 handrail (guard rail)
54 head post
55 landing beam
56 lining board
57 fillet
58 lightweight building board
59 ceiling plaster
60 wall plaster
61 false ceiling
62 strip flooring (overlay flooring, parquet strip)
63 skirting board (*Am.* mopboard, washboard, scrub board, base)
64 beading
65 staircase window
66 main landing beam
67 fillet (cleat)
68–69 false ceiling
68 false floor (inserted floor)
69 floor filling (plugging, pug)
70 laths
71 lathing
72 ceiling plaster
73 subfloor (blind floor)
74 parquet floor with tongued-and-grooved blocks
75 quarter-newelled (*Am.* quarter-neweled) staircase
76 winding staircase (spiral staircase) with open newels (open-newel staircase)
77 winding staircase (spiral staircase) with solid newels (solid-newel staircase)
78 newel (solid newel)
79 handrail

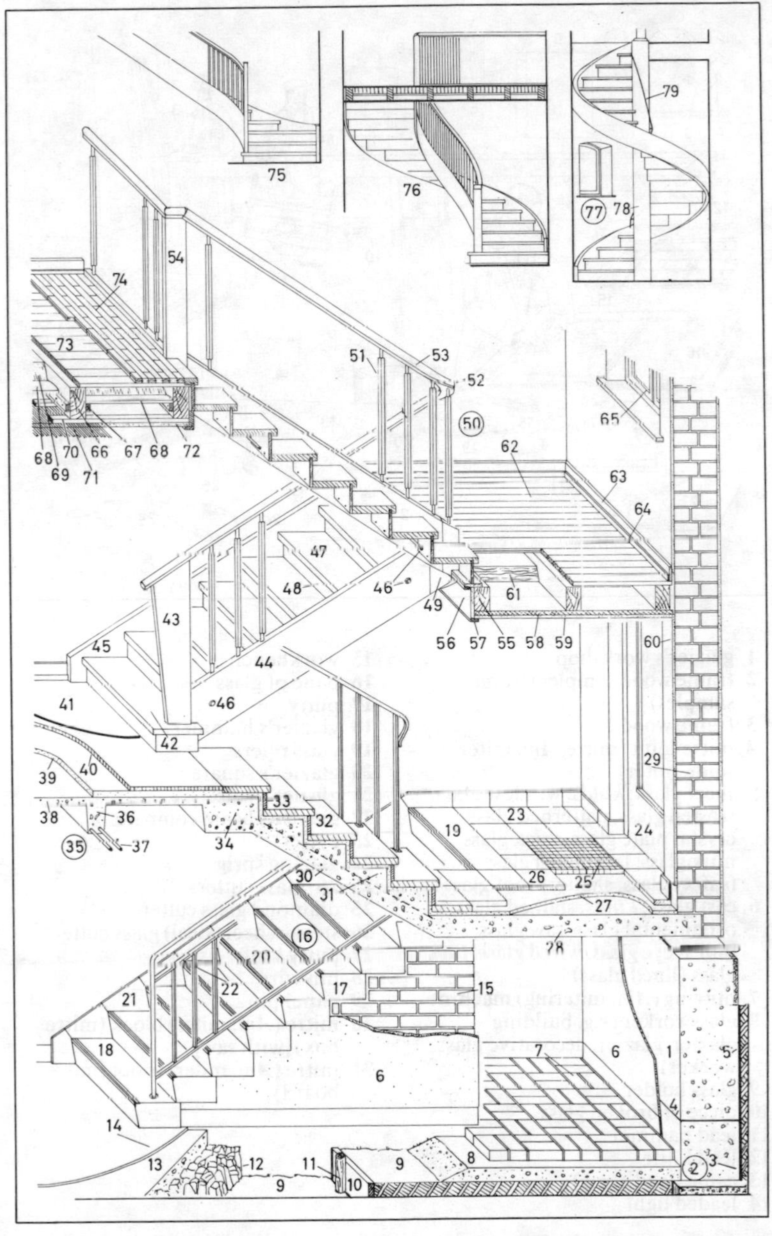
75
76
79
77
78
54
74
73
51
53
52
50
68
70
66
67
68
72
69
71
65
62
63
64
47
48
46
49
61
43
56
57
55
58
59
60
45
44
41
46
42
39
40
29
33
38
36
32
23
19
24
35
37
34
30
26
25
31
27
28
16
20
22
17
15
21
18
6
7
6
1
5
14
4
13
12
11
9
10
8
9
2
3

124 Glazier

1 glazier's workshop
2 frame wood samples (frame samples)
3 frame wood
4 mitre joint (mitre, *Am.* miter joint, miter)
5 sheet glass; *kinds:* window glass, frosted glass, patterned glass, crystal plate glass, thick glass, milk glass, laminated glass (safety glass, shatterproof glass)
6 cast glass; *kinds:* stained glass, ornamental glass, raw glass, bull's-eye glass, wired glass, line glass (lined glass)
7 mitring (*Am.* mitering) machine
8 glassworker (*e.g.* building glazier, glazier, decorative glass worker)
9 glass holder
10 piece of broken glass
11 lead hammer
12 lead knife
13 came (lead came)
14 leaded light
15 workbench
16 pane of glass
17 putty
18 glazier's hammer
19 glass pliers
20 glazier's square
21 glazier's rule
22 glazier's beam compass
23 eyelet
24 glazing sprig
25–26 glass cutters
25 diamond glass cutter
26 steel-wheel (steel) glass cutter
27 putty knife
28 pin wire
29 panel pin
30 mitre (*Am.* miter) block (mitre box) [with saw]
31 mitre (*Am.* miter) shoot (mitre board)

1 metal shears (tinner's snips, *Am.* tinner's shears)
2 elbow snips (angle shears)
3 gib
4 lapping plate
5–7 propane soldering apparatus
5 propanc soldering iron, a hatchet iron
6 soldering stone, a sal-ammoniac block
7 soldering fluid (flux)
8 beading iron for forming reinforcement beading
9 angled reamer
10 workbench (bench)
11 beam compass (trammel, *Am.* beam trammel)
12 electric hand die
13 hollow punch
14 chamfering hammer
15 beading swage (beading hammer)
16 abrasive-wheel cutting-off machine
17 plumber
18 mallet
19 mandrel
20 socket (tinner's socket)
21 block
22 anvil
23 stake
24 circular saw (buzz saw)
25 flanging, swaging, and wiring machine
26 sheet shears (guillotine)
27 screw-cutting machine (thread-cutting machine, die stocks)
28 pipe-bending machine (bending machine, pipe bender)
29 welding transformer
30 bending machine (rounding machine) for shaping funnels

126 Plumber, Gas Fitter, Heating Engineer

1 gas fitter and plumber
2 stepladder
3 safety chain
4 stopcock
5 gas meter
6 bracket
7 service riser
8 distributing pipe
9 supply pipe
10 pipe-cutting machine
11 pipe repair stand
12–25 gas and water appliances
12–13 geyser, an instantaneous water heater
12 gas water heater
13 electric water heater
14 toilet cistern
15 float
16 bell
17 flush pipe
18 water inlet
19 flushing lever (lever)
20 radiator
21 radiator rib
22 two-pipe system
23 flow pipe
24 return pipe
25 gas heater
26–37 plumbing fixtures
26 trap (anti-syphon trap)
27 mixer tap (*Am.* mixing faucet) for washbasins
28 hot tap
29 cold tap
30 extendible shower attachment
31 water tap (pillar tap) for washbasins
32 spindle top
33 shield
34 draw-off tap (*Am.* faucet)
35 supatap
36 swivel tap
37 flushing valve
38–52 fittings
38 joint with male thread
39 reducing socket (reducing coupler)
40 elbow screw joint (elbow coupling)
41 reducing socket (reducing coupler) with female thread
42 screw joint
43 coupler (socket)
44 T-joint (T-junction joint, tee)
45 elbow screw joint with female thread
46 bend
47 T-joint (T-junction joint, tee) with female taper thread
48 ceiling joint
49 reducing elbow
50 cross
51 elbow joint with male thread
52 elbow joint
53–57 pipe supports
53 saddle clip
54 spacing bracket
55 plug
56 pipe clips
57 two-piece spacing clip
58–86 plumber's tools, gas fitter's tools
58 gas pliers
59 footprints
60 combination cutting pliers
61 pipe wrench
62 flat-nose pliers
63 nipple key
64 round-nose pliers
65 pincers
66 adjustable S-wrench
67 screw wrench
68 shifting spanner
69 screwdriver
70 compass saw (keyhole saw)
71 hacksaw frame
72 hand saw
73 soldering iron
74 blowlamp (blowtorch) [for soldering]
75 sealing tape
76 tin-lead solder
77 club hammer
78 hammer
79 spirit level
80 steel-leg vice (*Am.* vise)
81 pipe vice (*Am.* vise)
82 pipe-bending machine
83 former (template)
84 pipe cutter
85 hand die
86 screw-cutting machine (thread-cutting machine)

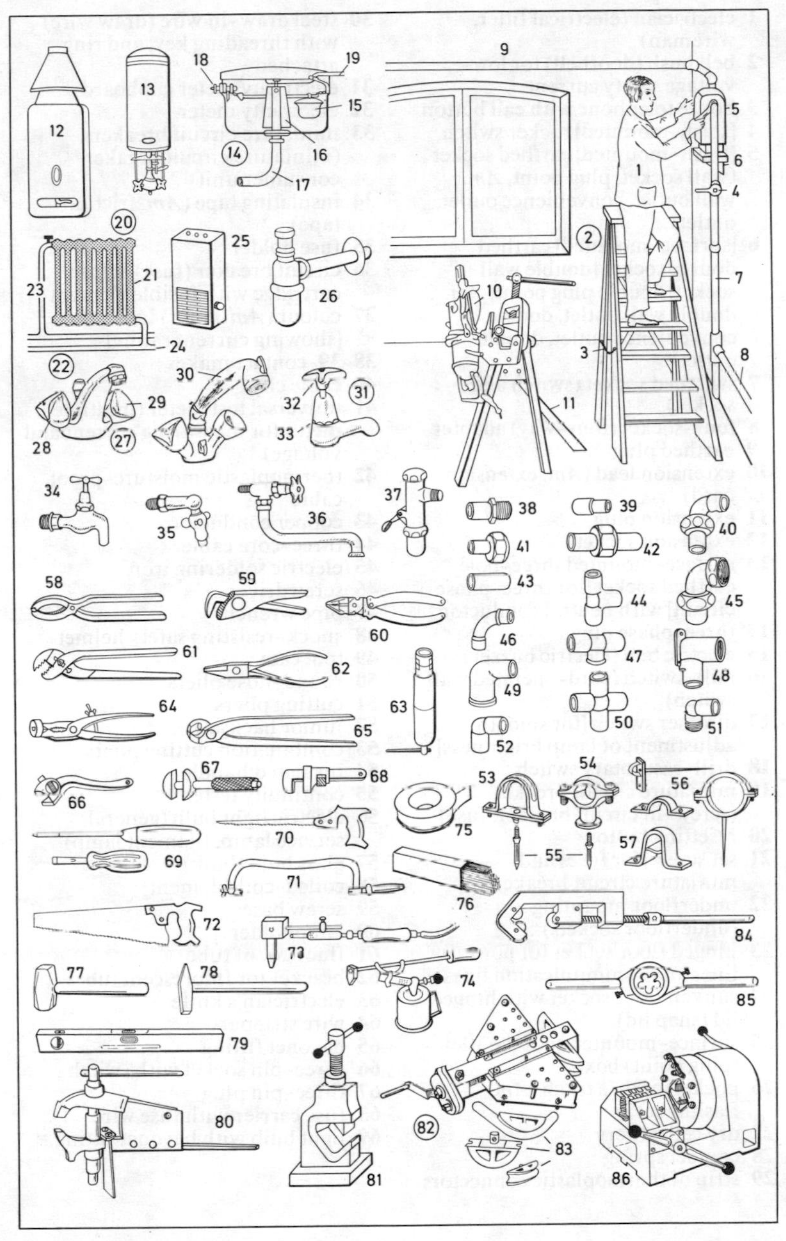
1
2
3
4
5
6
7
8
9
10
11
12
13
14
15
16
17
18
19
20
21
22
23
24
25
26
27
28
29
30
31
32
33
34
35
36
37
38
39
40
41
42
43
44
45
46
47
48
49
50
51
52
53
54
55
56
57
58
59
60
61
62
63
64
65
66
67
68
69
70
71
72
73
74
75
76
77
78
79
80
81
82
83
84
85
86

127 Electrician

1 electrician (electrical fitter, wireman)
2 bell push (doorbell) for low-voltage safety current
3 house telephone with call button
4 [flush-mounted] rocker switch
5 [flush-mounted] earthed socket (wall socket, plug point, *Am.* wall outlet, convenience outlet, outlet)
6 [surface-mounted] earthed double socket (double wall socket, double plug point, *Am.* double wall outlet, double convenience outlet, double outlet)
7 switched socket (switch and socket)
8 four-socket (four-way) adapter
9 earthed plug
10 extension lead (*Am.* extension cord)
11 extension plug
12 extension socket
13 surface-mounted three-pole earthed socket [for three-phase circuit] with neutral conductor
14 three-phase plug
15 electric bell (electric buzzer)
16 pull-switch (cord-operated wall switch)
17 dimmer switch [for smooth adjustment of lamp brightness]
18 drill-cast rotary switch
19 miniature circuit breaker (screw-in circuit breaker, fuse)
20 resetting button
21 set screw [for fuses and miniature circuit breakers]
22 underfloor mounting (underfloor sockets)
23 hinged floor socket for power lines and communication lines
24 sunken floor socket with hinged lid (snap lid)
25 surface-mounted socket outlet (plug point) box
26 pocket torch, a torch (*Am.* flashlight)
27 dry cell battery
28 contact spring
29 strip of thermoplastic connectors
30 steel draw-in wire (draw wire) with threading key, and ring attached
31 electricity meter cupboard
32 electricity meter
33 miniature circuit breakers (miniature circuit breaker consumer unit)
34 insulating tape (*Am.* friction tape)
35 fuse holder
36 circuit breaker (fuse), a fuse cartridge with fusible element
37 colour (*Am.* color) indicator [showing current rating]
38-39 contact maker
40 cable clip
41 universal test meter (multiple meter for measuring current and voltage)
42 thermoplastic moisture-proof cable
43 copper conductor
44 three-core cable
45 electric soldering iron
46 screwdriver
47 pipe wrench
48 shock-resisting safety helmet
49 tool case
50 round-nose pliers
51 cutting pliers
52 junior hacksaw
53 combination cutting pliers
54 insulated handle
55 continuity tester
56 electric light bulb (general service lamp, filament lamp)
57 glass bulb (bulb)
58 coiled-coil filament
59 screw base
60 lampholder
61 fluorescent tube
62 bracket for fluorescent tubes
63 electrician's knife
64 wire strippers
65 bayonet fitting
66 three-pin socket with switch
67 three-pin plug
68 fuse carrier with fuse wire
69 light bulb with bayonet fitting

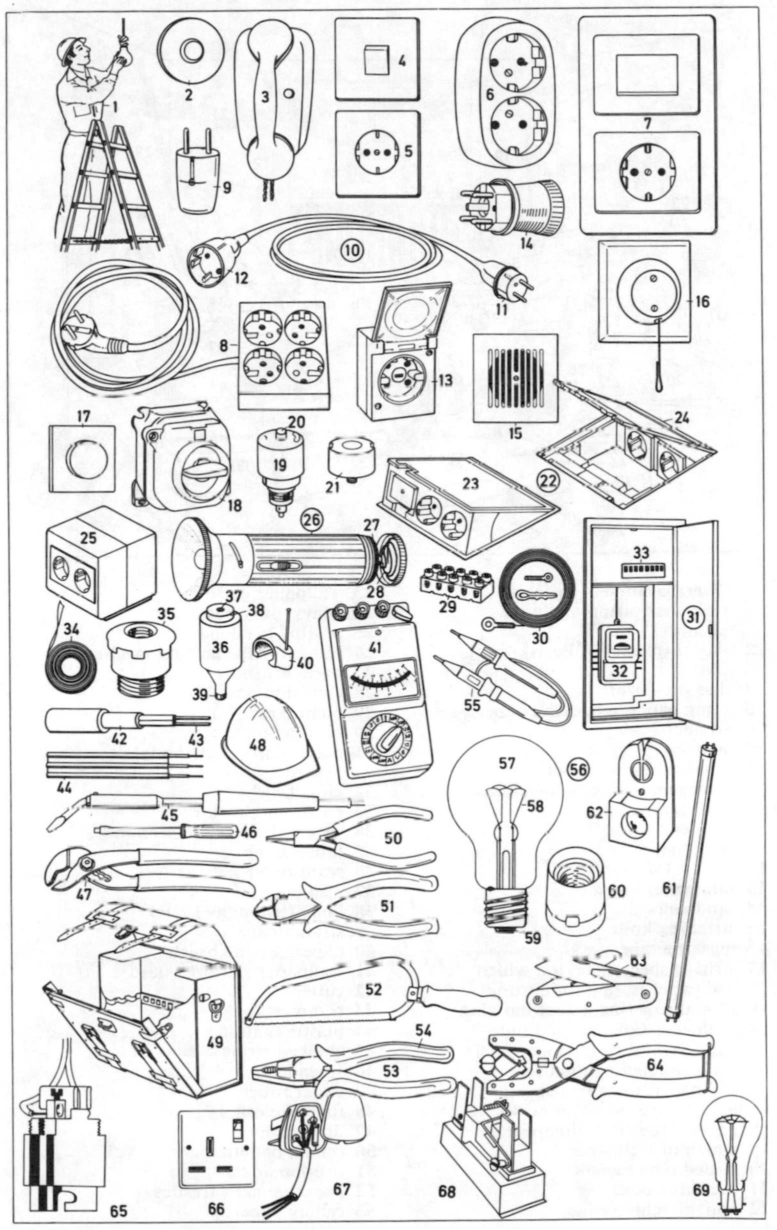

1
2
3
4
6
7
5
9
14
10
12
11
16
8
13
15
24
17
20
19
21
23
22
18
26
27
25
33
28
29
37
38
35
34
36
40
41
30
31
55
32
39
42
43
48
57
56
44
58
45
62
46
50
47
60
61
51
59
63
52
54
64
49
53
65
66
67
68
69

128 Paperhanger

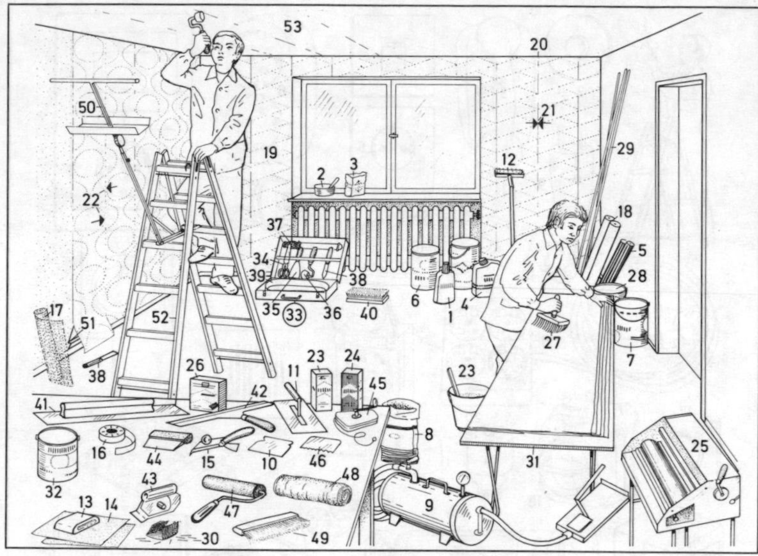

1-17 preparation of surfaces
1 wallpaper-stripping liquid (stripper)
2 plaster (plaster of Paris)
3 filler
4 glue size (size)
5 lining paper, a backing paper
6 primer
7 fluate
8 shredded lining paper
9 wallpaper-stripping machine (stripper)
10 scraper
11 smoother
12 perforator
13 sandpaper block
14 sandpaper
15 stripping knife
16 masking tape
17 strip of sheet metal [on which wallpaper ist laid for cutting]
18-53 wallpapering (paper hanging)
18 wallpaper (*kinds:* wood pulp paper, wood chip paper, fabric wallhangings, synthetic wallpaper, metallic paper, natural (*e.g.* wood or cork) paper, tapestry wallpaper)
19 length of wallpaper
20 butted paper edges
21 matching edge
22 non-matching edge
23 wallpaper paste
24 heavy-duty paste
25 pasting machine
26 paste [for the pasting machine]
27 paste brush
28 emulsion paste
29 picture rail
30 beading pins
31 pasteboard (paperhanger's bench)
32 gloss finish
33 paperhanging kit
34 shears (bull-nosed scissors)
35 filling knife
36 seam roller
37 hacking knife
38 knife (trimming knife)
39 straightedge
40 paperhanging brush
41 wallpaper-cutting board
42 cutter
43 trimmer
44 plastic spatula
45 chalked string
46 spreader
47 paper roller
48 flannel cloth
49 dry brush
50 ceiling paperhanger
51 overlap angle
52 paperhanger's trestles
53 ceiling paper

1 painting
2 painter
3 paintbrush
4 emulsion paint (emulsion)
5 stepladder
6 can (tin) of paint
7-8 cans (tins) of paint
7 can (tin) with fixed handle
8 paint kettle
9 drum of paint
10 paint bucket
11 paint roller
12 grill [for removing excess paint from the roller]
13 stippling roller
14 varnishing
15 oil-painted dado
16 canister for thinner
17 flat brush for larger surfaces (flat wall brush)
18 stippler
19 fitch
20 cutting-in brush
21 radiator brush (flay brush)
22 paint scraper
23 scraper
24 putty knife
25 sandpaper
26 sandpaper block
27 floor brush
28 sanding and spraying
29 grinder
30 sander
31 pressure pot
32 spray gun
33 compressor (air compressor)
34 flow coating machine for flow coating radiators, etc.
35 hand spray
36 airless spray unit
37 airless spray gun
38 efflux viscometer
39 seconds timer
40 lettering and gilding
41 lettering brush (signwriting brush, pencil)
42 tracing wheel
43 stencil knife
44 oil gold size
45 gold leaf
46 outline drawing
47 mahlstick
48 pouncing
49 pounce bag
50 gilder's cushion
51 gilder's knife
52 sizing gold leaf
53 filling in the letters with stipple paint
54 gilder's mop

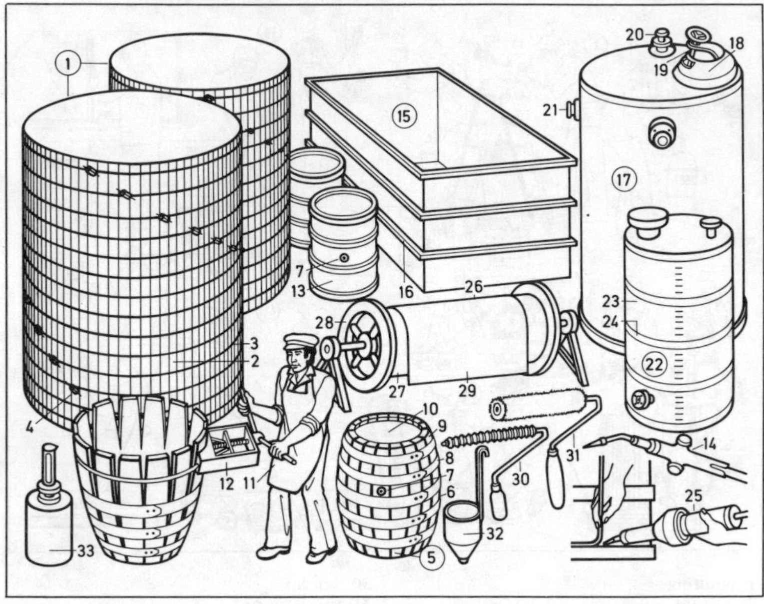

1–33 cooper's and tank construction engineer's workshops
1 tank
2 circumference made of staves (staved circumference)
3 iron rod
4 turnbuckle
5 barrel (cask)
6 body of barrel (of cask)
7 bunghole
8 band (hoop) of barrel
9 barrel stave
10 barrelhead (heading)
11 cooper
12 trusser
13 drum
14 gas welding torch
15 staining vat, made of thermoplastics
16 iron reinforcing bands
17 storage container, made of glass fibre (*Am.* glass fiber) reinforced polyester resin
18 manhole
19 manhole cover with handwheel
20 flange mount
21 flange-type stopcock
22 measuring tank
23 shell (circumference)
24 shrink ring
25 hot-air gun
26 roller made of glass fibre (*Am.* glass fiber) reinforced synthetic resin
27 cylinder
28 flange
29 glass cloth
30 grooved roller
31 lambskin roller
32 ladle for testing viscosity
33 measuring vessel for hardener

1–25 furrier's workroom
1 furrier
2 steam spray gun
3 steam iron
4 beating machine
5 cutting machine for letting out furskins
6 uncut furskin
7 let-out strips (let-out sections)
8 fur worker
9 fur-sewing machine
10 blower for letting out
11–21 furskins
11 mink skin
12 fur side
13 leather side
14 cut furskin
15 lynx skin before letting out
16 let-out lynx skin
17 fur side
18 leather side
19 let-out mink skin
20 lynx fur, sewn together (sewn)
21 broadtail
22 fur marker
23 fur worker
24 mink coat
25 ocelot coat

132 Joiner I

1–73 joiner's workshop
1–28 joiner's tools
1 wood rasp
2 wood file
3 compass saw (keyhole saw)
4 saw handle
5 [square-headed] mallet
6 try square
7–11 chisels
7 bevelled-edge chisel (chisel)
8 mortise (mortice) chisel
9 gouge
10 handle
11 framing chisel (cant chisel)
12 glue pot in water bath
13 glue pot (glue well), an insert for joiner's glue
14 handscrew
15–28 planes
15 smoothing plane
16 jack plane
17 toothing plane
18 handle (toat)
19 wedge
20 plane iron (cutter)
21 mouth
22 sole
23 side
24 stock (body)
25 rebate (rabbet) plane
26 router plane (old woman's tooth)
27 spokeshave
28 compass plane
29–37 woodworker's bench
29 foot
30 front vice (*Am.* vise)
31 vice (*Am.* vise) handle
32 vice (*Am.* vise) screw
33 jaw
34 bench top
35 well
36 bench stop (bench holdfast)
37 tail vice (*Am.* vise)
38 cabinet maker (joiner)
39 trying plane
40 shavings
41 wood screw
42 saw set
43 mitre (*Am.* miter) box
44 tenon saw
45 thicknesser (thicknessing machine)
46 thicknessing table with rollers
47 kick-back guard
48 chip-extractor opening
49 chain mortising machine (chain mortiser)
50 endless mortising chain
51 clamp (work clamp)
52 knot hole moulding (*Am.* molding) machine
53 knot hole cutter
54 quick-action chuck
55 hand lever
56 change-gear handle
57 sizing and edging machine
58 main switch
59 circular-saw (buzz saw) blade
60 height (rise and fall) adjustment wheel
61 V-way
62 framing table
63 extension arm (arm)
64 trimming table
65 fence
66 fence adjustment handle
67 clamp lever
68 board-sawing machine
69 swivel motor
70 board support
71 saw carriage
72 pedal for raising the transport rollers
73 block board

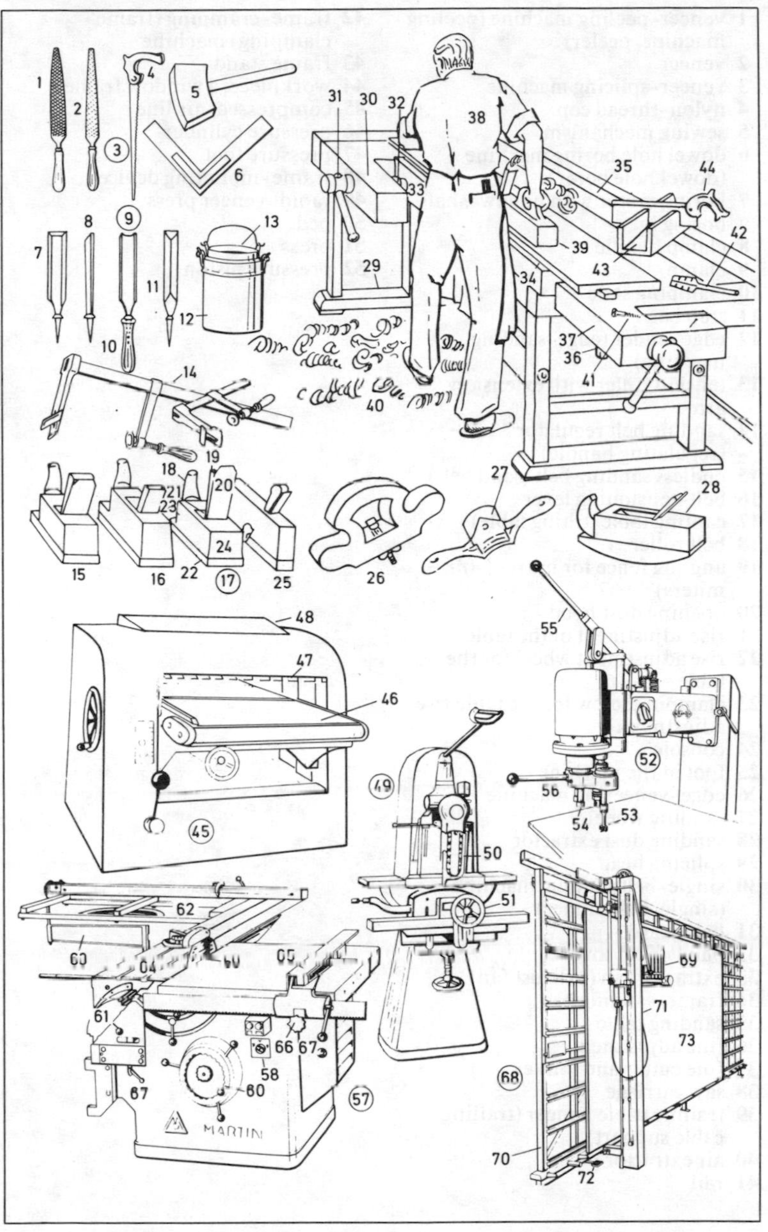
1
2
3
4
5
6
7
8
9
10
11
12
13
14
15
16
17
18
19
20
21
22
23
24
25
26
27
28
29
30
31
32
33
34
35
36
37
38
39
40
41
42
43
44
45
46
47
48
49
50
51
52
53
54
55
56
57
58
60
61
62
64
65
66
67
68
69
70
71
72
73
MARTIN

133 Joiner II

1 veneer-peeling machine (peeling machine, peeler)
2 veneer
3 veneer-splicing machine
4 nylon-thread cop
5 sewing mechanism
6 dowel hole boring machine (dowel hole borer)
7 boring motor with hollow-shaft boring bit
8 clamp handle
9 clamp
10 clamping shoe
11 stop bar
12 edge sander (edge-sanding machine)
13 tension roller with extension arm
14 sanding belt regulator (regulating handle)
15 endless sanding belt (sand belt)
16 belt-tensioning lever
17 canting table (tilting table)
18 belt roller
19 angling fence for mitres (*Am.* miters)
20 opening dust hood
21 rise adjustment of the table
22 rise adjustment wheel for the table
23 clamping screw for the table rise adjustment
24 console
25 foot of the machine
26 edge-veneering machine
27 sanding wheel
28 sanding dust extractor
29 splicing head
30 single-belt sanding machine (single-belt sander)
31 belt guard
32 bandwheel cover
33 extractor fan (exhaust fan)
34 frame-sanding pad
35 sanding table
36 fine adjustment
37 fine cutter and jointer
38 saw carriage
39 trailing cable hanger (trailing cable support)
40 air extractor pipe
41 rail
42 frame-cramping (frame-clamping) machine
43 frame stand
44 workpiece, a window frame
45 compressed-air line
46 pressure cylinder
47 pressure foot
48 frame-mounting device
49 rapid-veneer press
50 bed
51 press
52 pressure piston

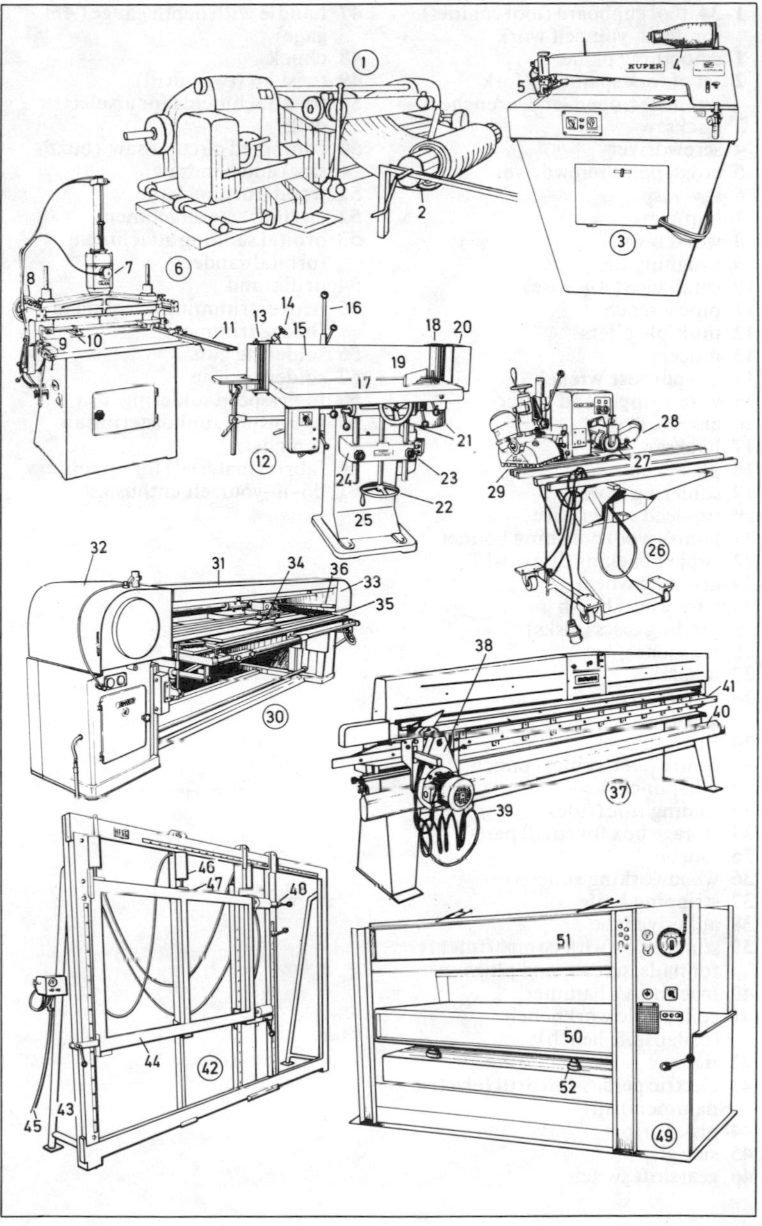
1
2
3
4
5
KUPER
6
7
8
9
10
11
12
13
14
15
16
17
18
19
20
21
22
23
24
25
26
27
28
29
30
31
32
33
34
35
36
37
38
39
40
41
42
43
44
45
46
47
48
49
50
51
52

1-34 tool cupboard (tool cabinet) for do-it-yourself work
1 smoothing plane
2 set of fork spanners (fork wrenches, open-end wrenches)
3 hacksaw
4 screwdriver
5 cross-point screwdriver
6 saw rasp
7 hammer
8 wood rasp
9 roughing file
10 small vice (*Am.* vise)
11 pipe wrench
12 multiple pliers
13 pincers
14 all-purpose wrench
15 wire stripper and cutter
16 electric drill
17 hacksaw
18 plaster cup
19 soldering iron
20 tin-lead solder wire
21 lamb's wool polishing bonnet
22 rubber backing disc (disk)
23 grinding wheel
24 wire wheel brush
25 sanding discs (disks)
26 try square
27 hand saw
28 universal cutter
29 spirit level
30 firmer chisel
31 centre (*Am.* center) punch
32 nail punch
33 folding rule (rule)
34 storage box for small parts
35 tool box
36 woodworking adhesive
37 stripping knife
38 adhesive tape
39 storage box with compartments for nails, screws, and plugs
40 machinist's hammer
41 collapsible workbench (collapsible bench)
42 jig
43 electric percussion drill (electric hammer drill)
44 pistol grip
45 side grip
46 gearshift switch
47 handle with depth gauge (*Am.* gage)
48 chuck
49 twist bit (twist drill)
50-55 attachments for an electric drill
50 combined circular saw (buzz saw) and bandsaw
51 wood-turning lathe
52 circular saw attachment
53 orbital sanding attachment (orbital sander)
54 drill stand
55 hedge-trimming attachment (hedge trimmer)
56 soldering gun
57 soldering iron
58 high-speed soldering iron
59 upholstery, upholstering an armchair
60 fabric (material) for upholstery
61 do-it-yourself enthusiast

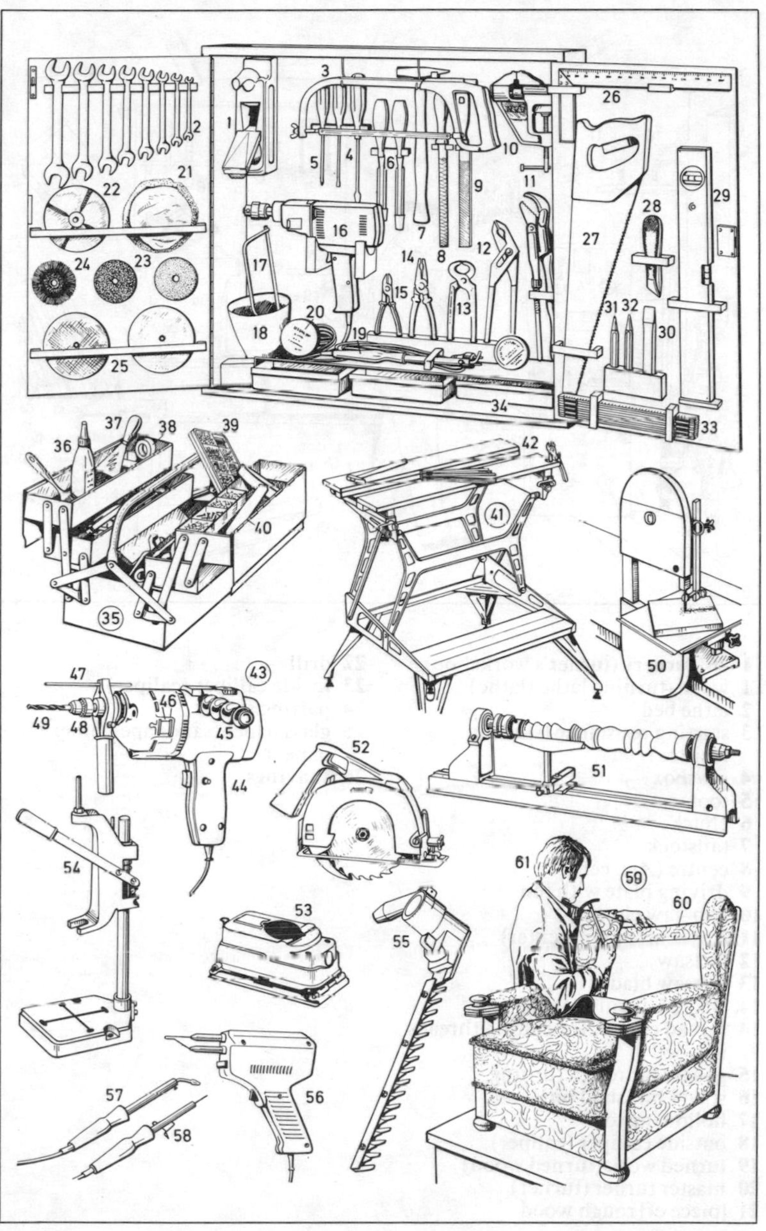
1
2
3
4
5
6
7
8
9
10
11
12
13
14
15
16
17
18
19
20
21
22
23
24
25
26
27
28
29
30
31
32
33
34
35
36
37
38
39
40
41
42
43
44
45
46
47
48
49
50
51
52
53
54
55
56
57
58
59
60
61

135 Turner (Ivory Carver)

1–26 turnery (turner's workshop)
1 wood-turning lathe (lathe)
2 lathe bed
3 starting resistance (starting resistor)
4 gearbox
5 tool rest
6 chuck
7 tailstock
8 centre (*Am.* center)
9 driving plate with pin
10 two-jaw chuck
11 live centre (*Am.* center)
12 fretsaw
13 fretsaw blade
14, 15, 24 turning tools
14 thread chaser, for cutting threads in wood
15 gouge, for rough turning
16 spoon bit (shell bit)
17 hollowing tool
18 outside calliper (caliper)
19 turned work (turned wood)
20 master turner (turner)
21 [piece of] rough wood
22 drill
23 inside calliper (caliper)
24 parting tool
25 glass paper (sandpaper, emery paper)
26 shavings

1–40 basket making (basketry, basketwork)
1–4 weaves (strokes)
1 randing
2 rib randing
3 oblique randing
4 randing, a piece of wickerwork (screen work)
5 weaver
6 stake
7 workboard; *also:* lapboard
8 screw block
9 hole for holding the block
10 stand
11 chip basket (spale basket)
12 chip (spale)
13 soaking tub
14 willow stakes (osier stakes)
15 willow rods (osier rods)
16 basket, a piece of wickerwork (basketwork)
17 border
18 woven side
19 round base
20 woven base
21 slath
22–24 covering a frame
22 frame
23 end
24 rib
25 upsett
26 grass; *kinds:* esparto grass, alfalfa grass
27 rush (bulrush, reed mace)
28 reed
29 raffia (bast)
30 straw
31 bamboo cane
32 rattan (ratan) chair cane
33 basket maker
34 bending tool
35 cutting point (bodkin)
36 rapping iron
37 pincers
38 picking knife
39 shave
40 hacksaw

137 Blacksmith (Smith) I

1–8 hearth (forge) with blacksmith's fire
1 hearth (forge)
2 shovel (slice)
3 swab
4 rake
5 poker
6 blast pipe (tue iron)
7 chimney (cowl, hood)
8 water trough (quenching trough, bosh)
9 power hammer
10 ram (tup)
11–16 anvil
11 anvil
12 flat beak (beck, bick)
13 round beak (beck, bick)
14 auxiliary table
15 foot
16 upsetting block
17 swage block
18 tool-grinding machine (tool grinder)
19 grinding wheel
20 block and tackle
21 workbench (bench)
22–39 blacksmith's tools
22 sledge hammer
23 blacksmith's hand hammer
24 flat tongs
25 round tongs
26 parts of the hammer
27 peen (pane, pein)
28 face
29 eye
30 haft
31 cotter punch
32 hardy (hardie)
33 set hammer
34 sett (set, sate)
35 flat-face hammer (flatter)
36 round punch
37 angle tongs
38 blacksmith's chisel (scaling hammer, chipping hammer)
39 moving iron (bending iron)

1 compressed-air system
2 electric motor
3 compressor
4 compressed-air tank
5 compressed-air line
6 percussion screwdriver
7 pedestal grinding machine (floor grinding machine)
8 grinding wheel
9 guard
10 trailer
11 brake drum
12 brake shoe
13 brake lining
14 testing kit
15 pressure gauge (*Am.* gage)
16 brake-testing equipment, a rolling road
17 pit
18 braking roller
19 meter (recording meter)
20 precision lathe for brake drums
21 lorry wheel
22 boring mill
23 power saw, a hacksaw (power hacksaw)
24 vice (*Am.* vise)
25 saw frame
26 coolant supply pipe
27 riveting machine
28 trailer frame (chassis) under construction
29 inert-gas welding equipment
30 rectifier
31 control unit
32 CO_2 cylinder
33 anvil
34 hearth (forge) with blacksmith's fire
35 trolley for gas cylinders
36 vehicle under repair, a tractor

139 Hammer Forging (Smith Forging) and Drop Forging

1 continuous furnace with grid hearth for annealing of round stock
2 discharge opening (discharge door)
3 gas burners
4 charging door
5 counterblow hammer
6 upper ram
7 lower ram
8 ram guide
9 hydraulic drive
10 column
11 short-stroke drop hammer
12 ram (tup)
13 upper die block
14 lower die block
15 hydraulic drive
16 frame
17 anvil
18 forging and sizing press
19 standard
20 table
21 disc (disk) clutch
22 compressed-air pipe
23 solenoid valve
24 air-lift gravity hammer (air-lift drop hammer)
25 drive motor
26 hammer (tup)
27 foot control (foot pedal)
28 preshaped (blocked) workpiece
29 hammer guide
30 hammer cylinder
31 anvil
32 mechanical manipulator to move the workpiece in hammer forging
33 dogs
34 counterweight
35 hydraulic forging press
36 crown
37 cross head
38 upper die block
39 lower die block
40 anvil
41 hydraulic piston
42 pillar guide
43 rollover device
44 burden chain (chain sling)
45 crane hook
46 workpiece
47 gas furnace (gas-fired furnace)
48 gas burner
49 charging opening
50 chain curtain
51 vertical-lift door
52 hot-air duct
53 air preheater
54 gas pipe
55 electric door-lifting mechanism
56 air blast

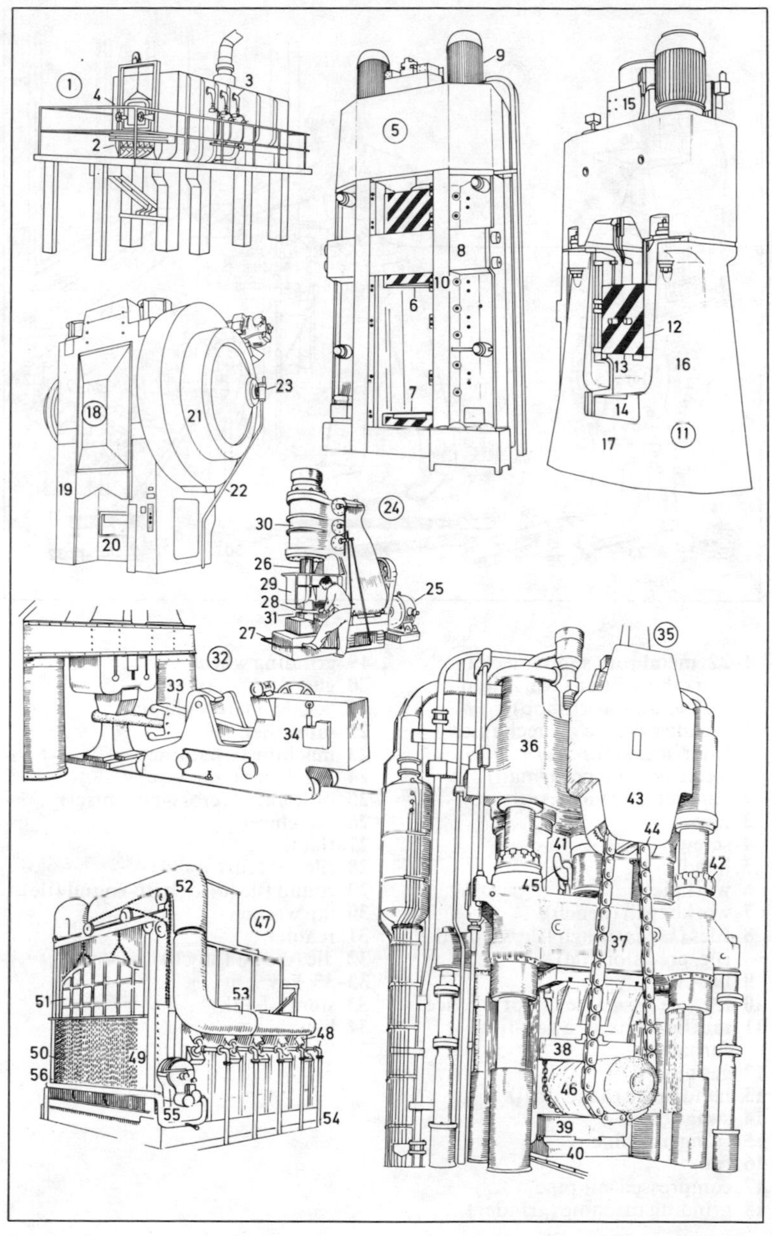
1
4
3
2
5
9
15
8
10
6
12
13
16
14
11
17
7
18
21
23
19
22
20
24
30
26
25
29
28
31
27
32
33
34
35
36
43
44
41
42
45
37
38
46
39
40
47
52
51
53
48
50
49
56
55
54

140 Metalworker

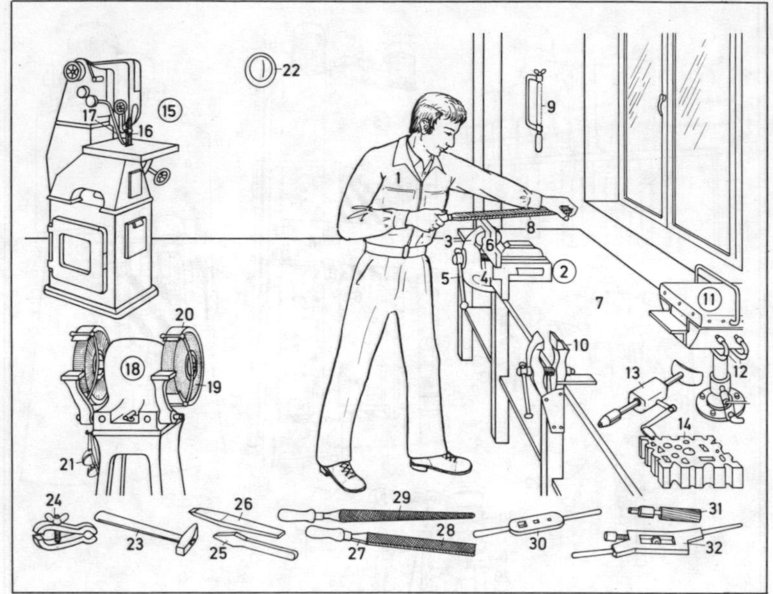

1–22 metalwork shop (mechanic's workshop, fitter's workshop, locksmith's workshop)
1 metalworker (*e.g.* mechanic, fitter, locksmith; *form. also:* wrought-iron craftsman)
2 parallel-jaw vice (*Am.* vise)
3 jaw
4 screw
5 handle
6 workpiece
7 workbench (bench)
8 files (*kinds:* rough file, smooth file, precision file)
9 hacksaw
10 leg vice (*Am.* vise), a spring vice
11 muffle furnace, a gas-fired furnace
12 gas pipe
13 hand brace (hand drill)
14 swage block
15 filing machine
16 file
17 compressed-air pipe
18 grinding machine (grinder)
19 grinding wheel
20 guard
21 goggles (safety glasses)
22 safety helmet
23 machinist's hammer
24 hand vice (*Am.* vise)
25 cape chisel (cross-cut chisel)
26 flat chisel
27 flat file
28 file cut (cut)
29 round file (*also:* half-round file)
30 tap wrench
31 reamer
32 die (die and stock)
33–35 key
33 stem (shank)
34 bow
35 bit

36–43 door lock, a mortise (mortice) lock
36 back plate
37 spring bolt (latch bolt)
38 tumbler
39 bolt
40 keyhole
41 bolt guide pin
42 tumbler spring
43 follower, with square hole
44 cylinder lock (safety lock)
45 cylinder (plug)
46 spring
47 pin
48 safety key, a flat key
49 lift-off hinge
50 hook-and-ride band
51 strap hinge
52 vernier calliper (caliper) gauge (*Am.* gage)
53 feeler gauge (*Am.* gage)
54 vernier depth gauge (*Am.* gage)
55 vernier
56 straightedge
57 square
58 breast drill
59 twist bit (twist drill)
60 screw tap (tap)
61 halves of a screw die
62 screwdriver
63 scraper (*also:* pointed triangle scraper)
64 centre (*Am.* center) punch
65 round punch
66 flat-nose pliers
67 detachable-jaw cut nippers
68 gas pliers
69 pincers

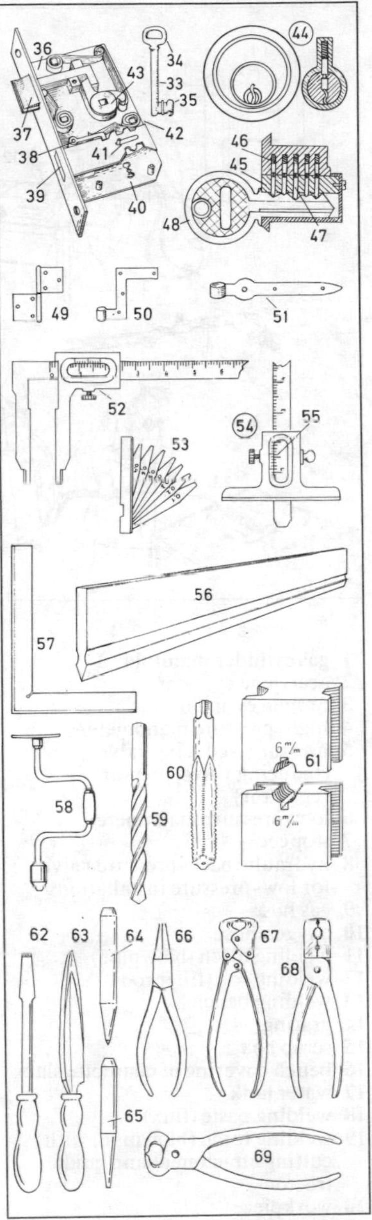

141 Gas Welder

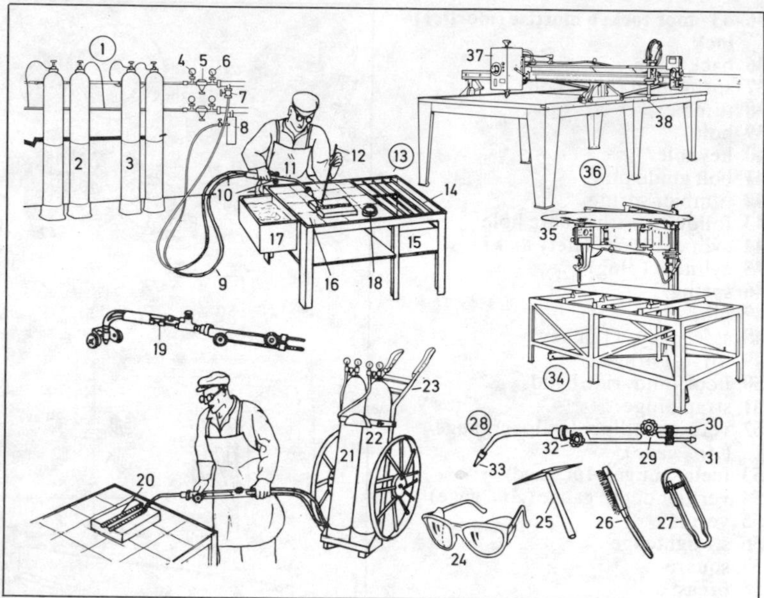

1 gas cylinder manifold
2 acetylene cylinder
3 oxygen cylinder
4 high-pressure manometer
5 pressure-reducing valve (reducing valve, pressure regulator)
6 low-pressure manometer
7 stopcock
8 hydraulic back-pressure valve for low-pressure installations
9 gas hose
10 oxygen hose
11 welding torch (blowpipe)
12 welding rod (filler rod)
13 welding bench
14 grating
15 scrap box
16 bench covering of chamotte slabs
17 water tank
18 welding paste (flux)
19 welding torch (blowpipe) with cutting attachment and guide tractor
20 workpiece
21 oxygen cylinder
22 acetylene cylinder
23 cylinder trolley
24 welding goggles
25 chipping hammer
26 wire brush
27 torch lighter (blowpipe lighter)
28 welding torch (blowpipe)
29 oxygen control
30 oxygen connection
31 gas connection (acetylene connection)
32 gas control (acetylene control)
33 welding nozzle
34 cutting machine
35 circular template
36 universal cutting machine
37 tracing head
38 cutting nozzle

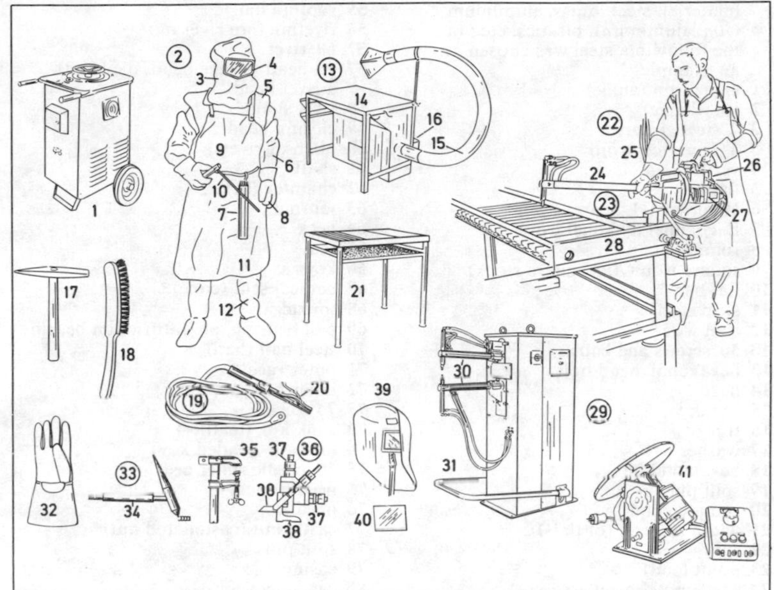

1 welding transformer
2 arc welder
3 arc welding helmet
4 flip-up window
5 shoulder guard
6 protective sleeve
7 electrode case
8 three-fingered welding glove
9 electrode holder
10 electrode
11 leather apron
12 shin guard
13 welding table with fume extraction equipment
14 table top
15 movable extractor duct
16 extractor support
17 chipping hammer
18 wire brush
19 welding lead
20 electrode holder
21 welding bench
22 spot welding
23 spot welding electrode holder
24 electrode arm
25 power supply (lead)
26 electrode-pressure cylinder
27 welding transformer
28 workpiece
29 foot-operated spot welder
30 welder electrode arms
31 foot pedal for welding pressure adjustment
32 five-fingered welding glove
33 inert-gas torch for inert-gas welding (gas-shielded arc welding)
34 inert-gas (shielding-gas) supply
35 work clamp (earthing clamp)
36 fillet gauge (*Am.* gage) (weld gauge) [for measuring throat thickness]
37 micrometer
38 measuring arm
39 arc welding helmet
40 filter lens
41 small turntable

143 Sections, Bolts, and Machine Parts

[material: steel, brass, aluminium (*Am.* aluminum), plastics, etc.; in the following, steel was chosen as an example]

1 angle iron (angle)
2 leg (flange)
3-7 steel girders
3 T-iron (tee-iron)
4 vertical leg
5 flange
6 H-girder (H-beam)
7 E-channel (channel iron)
8 round bar
9 square iron (*Am.* square stock)
10 flat bar
11 strip steel
12 iron wire
13-50 screws and bolts
13 hexagonal-head bolt
14 head
15 shank
16 thread
17 washer
18 hexagonal nut
19 split pin
20 rounded end
21 width of head (of flats)
22 stud
23 point (end)
24 castle nut (castellated nut)
25 hole for the split pin
26 cross-head screw, a sheet-metal screw (self-tapping screw)
27 hexagonal socket head screw
28 countersunk-head bolt
29 catch
30 locknut (locking nut)
31 bolt (pin)
32 collar-head bolt
33 set collar (integral collar)
34 spring washer (washer)
35 round nut, an adjusting nut
36 cheese-head screw, a slotted screw
37 tapered pin
38 screw slot (screw slit, screw groove)
39 square-head bolt
40 grooved pin, a cylindrical pin
41 T-head bolt
42 wing nut (fly nut, butterfly nut)
43 rag bolt
44 barb
45 wood screw
46 countersunk head
47 wood screw thread
48 grub screw
49 pin slot (pin slit, pin groove)
50 round end
51 nail (wire nail)
52 head
53 shank
54 point
55 roofing nail
56 riveting (lap riveting)
57-60 rivet
57 set head (swage head, die head), a rivet head
58 rivet shank
59 closing head
60 pitch of rivets
61 shaft
62 chamfer (bevel)
63 journal
64 neck
65 seat
66 keyway
67 conical seat (cone)
68 thread
69 ball bearing, an antifriction bearing
70 steel ball (ball)
71 outer race
72 inner race
73-74 keys
73 sunk key (feather)
74 gib (gib-headed key)
75-76 needle roller bearing
75 needle cage
76 needle
77 castle nut (castellated nut)
78 split pin
79 casing
80 casing cover
81 grease nipple (lubricating nipple)
82-96 gear wheels, cog wheels
82 stepped gear wheel
83 cog (tooth)
84 space between teeth
85 keyway (key seat, key slot)
86 bore
87 herringbone gear wheel
88 spokes (arms)
89 helical gearing (helical spur wheel)
90 sprocket
91 bevel gear wheel (bevel wheel)
92-93 spiral toothing
92 pinion
93 crown wheel
94 epicyclic gear (planetary gear)
95 internal toothing
96 external toothing
97-107 absorption dynamometer
97 shoe brake (check brake, block brake)
98 brake pulley
99 brake shaft (brake axle)
100 brake block (brake shoe)
101 pull rod
102 brake magnet
103 brake weight
104 band brake
105 brake band
106 brake lining
107 adjusting screw, for even application of the brake

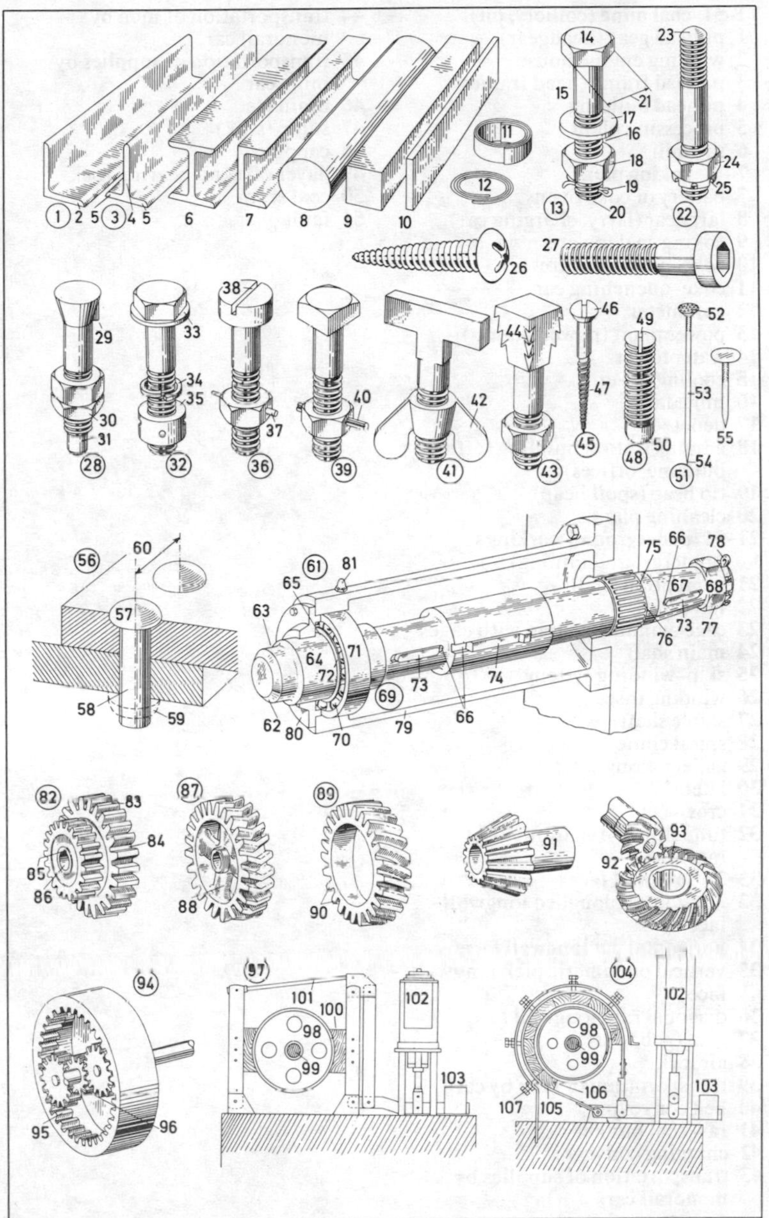
1
2
5
3
4
5
6
7
8
9
10
11
12
13
14
15
16
17
18
19
20
21
22
23
24
25
26
27
28
29
30
31
32
33
34
35
36
37
38
39
40
41
42
43
44
45
46
47
48
49
50
51
52
53
54
55
56
57
58
59
60
61
62
63
64
65
66
67
68
69
70
71
72
73
74
75
76
77
78
79
80
81
82
83
84
85
86
87
88
89
90
91
92
93
94
95
96
97
98
99
100
101
102
103
104
105
106
107

1–51 coal mine (colliery, pit)
1 pithead gear (headgear)
2 winding engine house
3 pithead frame (head frame)
4 pithead building
5 processing plant
6 sawmill
7–11 coking plant
7 battery of coke ovens
8 larry car (larry, charging car)
9 coking coal tower
10 coke-quenching tower
11 coke-quenching car
12 gasometer
13 power plant (power station)
14 water tower
15 cooling tower
16 mine fan
17 depot
18 administration building (office building, offices)
19 tip heap (spoil heap)
20 cleaning plant
21–51 underground workings (underground mining)
21 ventilation shaft
22 fan drift
23 cage-winding system with cages
24 main shaft
25 skip-winding system
26 winding inset
27 staple shaft
28 spiral chute
29 gallery along seam
30 lateral
31 cross-cut
32 tunnelling (*Am.* tunneling) machine
33–37 longwall faces
33 horizontal ploughed longwall face
34 horizontal cut longwall face
35 vertical pneumatic pick longwall face
36 diagonal ram longwall face
37 goaf (gob, waste)
38 air lock
39 transportation of men by cars
40 belt conveying
41 raw coal bunker
42 charging conveyor
43 transportation of supplies by monorail car
44 transportation of men by monorail car
45 transportation of supplies by mine car
46 drainage
47 sump (sink)
48 capping
49 [layer of] coal-bearing rock
50 coal seam
51 fault

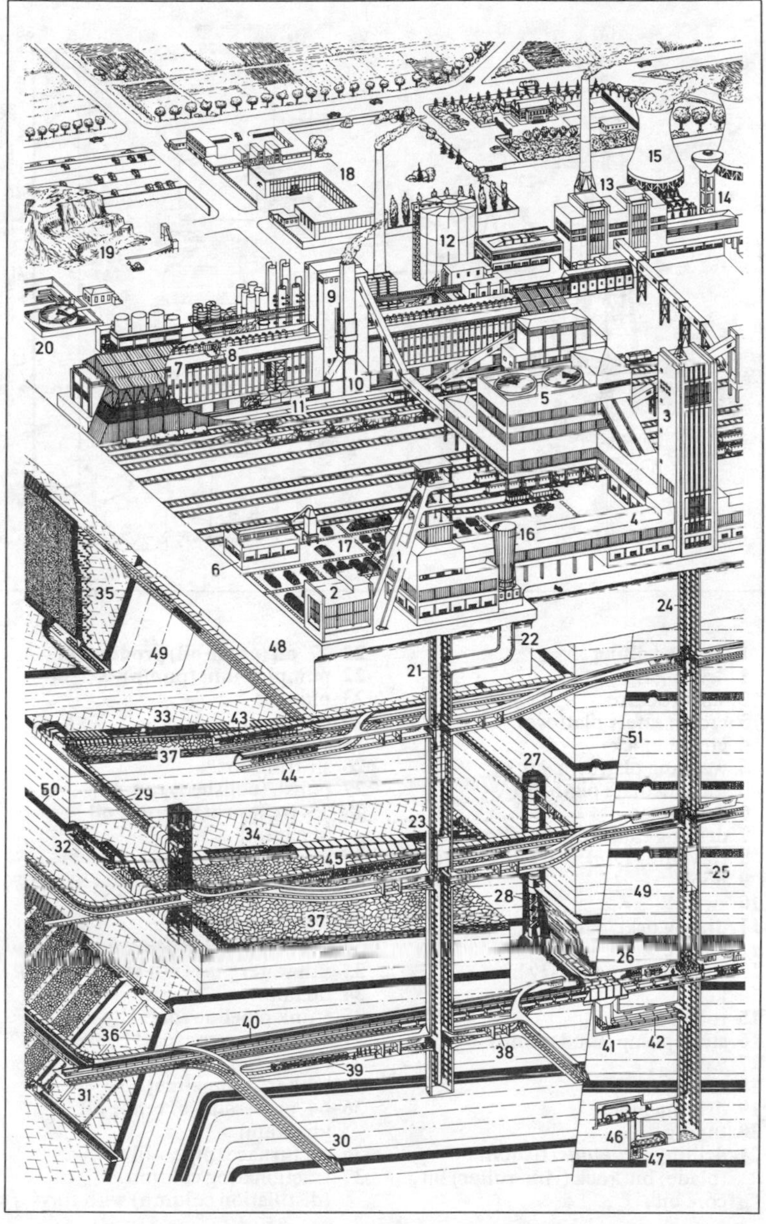
15
18
13
14
12
19
9
20
8
7
10
5
11
3
4
16
17
1
6
35
2
24
48
22
49
21
33
43
51
37
44
27
50
29
23
34
32
45
25
28
49
37
26
40
36
38
41
42
39
31
46
30
47

145 Mineral Oil (Oil, Petroleum)

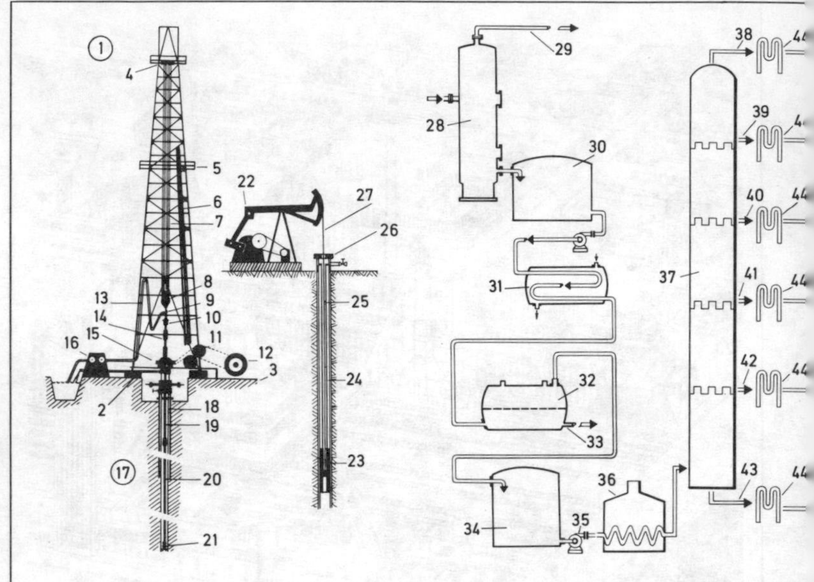

1–21 oil drilling
1 drilling rig
2 substructure
3 crown safety platform
4 crown blocks
5 working platform, an intermediate platform
6 drill pipes
7 drilling cable (drilling line)
8 travelling (*Am.* traveling) block
9 hook
10 swivel
11 draw works, a hoist
12 engine
13 standpipe and rotary hose
14 kelly
15 rotary table
16 slush pump (mud pump)
17 well
18 casing
19 drilling pipe
20 tubing
21 drilling bit; *kinds:* fishtail (blade) bit, rock (*Am.* roller) bit, core bit
22–27 oil (crude oil) production
22 pumping unit (pump)
23 plunger
24 tubing
25 sucker rods (pumping rods)
26 stuffing box
27 polish (polished) rod
28–35 treatment of crude oil [diagram]
28 gas separator
29 gas pipe (gas outlet)
30 wet oil tank (wash tank)
31 water heater
32 water and brine separator
33 salt water pipe (salt water outlet)
34 oil tank
35 trunk pipeline for oil [to the refinery or transport by tanker lorry (*Am.* tank truck), oil tanker, or pipeline]
36–64 processing of crude oil [diagram]
36 oil furnace (pipe still)
37 fractionating column (distillation column) with trays

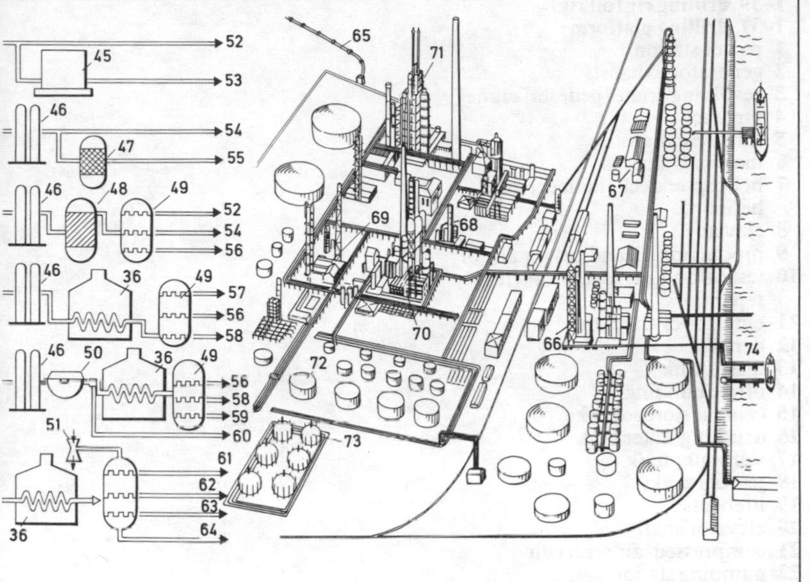

38 top gases (tops)
39 light distillation products
40 heavy distillation products
41 petroleum
42 gas oil component
43 residue
44 condenser (cooler)
45 compressor
46 desulphurizing (desulphurization, *Am.* desulfurizing, desulfurization) plant
47 reformer (hydroformer, platformer)
48 catalytic cracker (cat cracker)
49 distillation column
50 de-waxing (wax separation)
51 vacuum equipment
52–64 oil products
52 fuel gas
53 liquefied petroleum gas (liquid gas)
54 regular grade petrol (*Am.* gasoline)
55 super grade petrol (*Am.* gasoline)
56 diesel oil
57 aviation fuel
58 light fuel oil
59 heavy fuel oil
60 paraffin (paraffin oil, kerosene)
61 spindle oil
62 lubricating oil
63 cylinder oil
64 bitumen
65–74 oil refinery
65 pipeline (oil pipeline)
66 distillation plants
67 lubricating oil refinery
68 desulphurizing (desulphurization, *Am.* desulfurizing, desulfurization) plant
69 gas-separating plant
70 catalytic cracking plant
71 catalytic reformer
72 storage tank
73 spherical tank
74 tanker terminal

1–39 drilling rig (oil rig)
1–37 drilling platform
1 power station
2 generator exhausts
3 revolving crane (pedestal crane)
4 piperack
5 turbine exhausts
6 materials store
7 helicopter deck (heliport deck, heliport)
8 elevator
9 production oil and gas separator
10 test oil and gas separators (test separators)
11 emergency flare stack
12 derrick
13 diesel tank
14 office building
15 cement storage tanks
16 drinking water tank
17 salt water tank
18 jet fuel tanks
19 lifeboats
20 elevator shaft
21 compressed-air reservoir
22 pumping station
23 air compressor
24 air lock
25 seawater desalination plant
26 inlet filters for diesel fuel
27 gas cooler
28 control panel for the separators
29 toilets (lavatories)
30 workshop
31 pig trap [the 'pig' is used to clean the oil pipeline]
32 control room
33 accommodation modules (accommodation)
34 high-pressure cementing pumps
35 lower deck
36 middle deck
37 top deck (main deck)
38 substructure
39 mean sea level

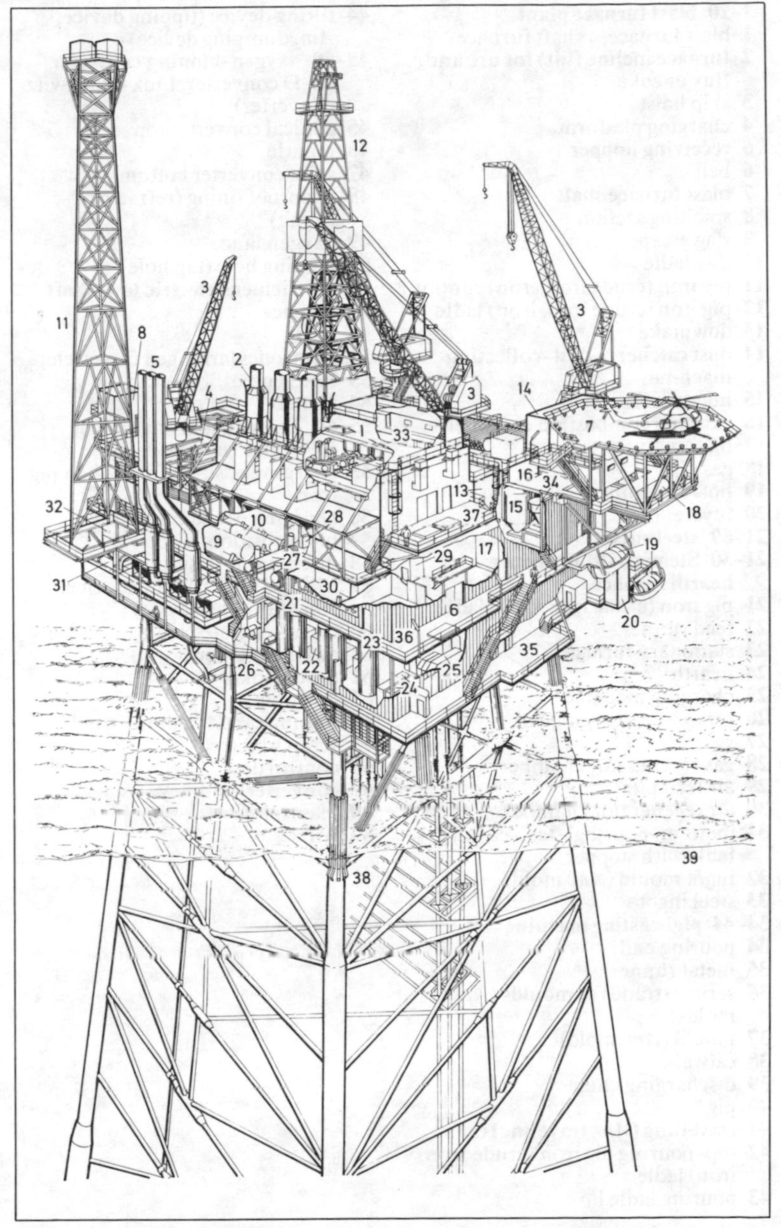
12
3
3
11
8
5
2
4
3
14
1
33
7
16
34
13
32
10
28
37
15
18
9
29
17
27
19
31
30
21
6
20
23
36
35
26
22
25
24
38
39

147 Iron and Steel Works

1–20 blast furnace plant
1 blast furnace, a shaft furnace
2 furnace incline (lift) for ore and flux or coke
3 skip hoist
4 charging platform
5 receiving hopper
6 bell
7 blast furnace shaft
8 smelting section
9 slag escape
10 slag ladle
11 pig iron (crude iron, iron) runout
12 pig iron (crude iron, iron) ladle
13 downtake
14 dust catcher, a dust-collecting machine
15 hot-blast stove
16 external combustion chamber
17 blast main
18 gas pipe
19 hot-blast pipe
20 tuyère
21–69 steelworks
21–30 Siemens-Martin open-hearth furnace
21 pig iron (crude iron, iron) ladle
22 feed runner
23 stationary furnace
24 hearth
25 charging machine
26 scrap iron charging box
27 gas pipe
28 gas regenerator chamber
29 air feed pipe
30 air regenerator chamber
31 [bottom-pouring] steel-casting ladle with stopper
32 ingot mould (*Am.* mold)
33 steel ingot
34–44 pig-casting machine
34 pouring end
35 metal runner
36 series (strand) of moulds (*Am.* molds)
37 mould (*Am.* mold)
38 catwalk
39 discharging chute
40 pig
41 travelling (*Am.* traveling) crane
42 top-pouring pig iron (crude iron, iron) ladle
43 pouring ladle lip
44 tilting device (tipping device, *Am.* dumping device)
45–50 oxygen-blowing converter (L–D converter, Linz–Donawitz converter)
45 conical converter top
46 mantle
47 solid converter bottom
48 fireproof lining (refractory lining)
49 oxygen lance
50 tapping hole (tap hole)
51–54 Siemens electric low-shaft furnace
51 feed
52 electrodes [arranged in a circle]
53 bustle pipe
54 runout
55–69 Thomas converter (basic Bessemer converter)
55 charging position for molten pig iron
56 charging position for lime
57 blow position
58 discharging position
59 tilting device (tipping device, *Am.* dumping device)
60 crane-operated ladle
61 auxiliary crane hoist
62 lime bunker
63 downpipe
64 tipping car (*Am.* dump truck)
65 scrap iron feed
66 control desk
67 converter chimney
68 blast main
69 wind box

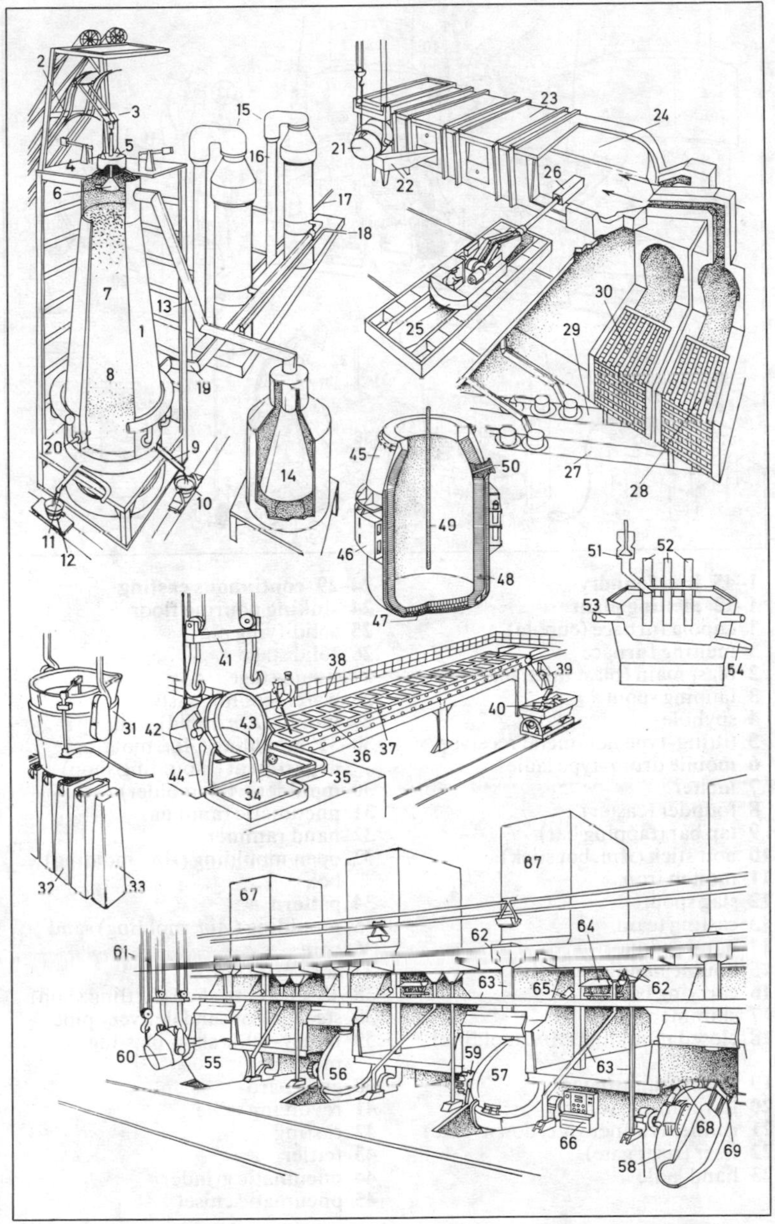
1
2
3
4
5
6
7
8
9
10
11
12
13
14
15
16
17
18
19
20
21
22
23
24
25
26
27
28
29
30
31
32
33
34
35
36
37
38
39
40
41
42
43
44
45
46
47
48
49
50
51
52
53
54
55
56
57
58
59
60
61
62
62
63
63
64
65
66
67
67
68
69

1–45 iron foundry
1–12 melting plant
1 cupola furnace (cupola), a melting furnace
2 blast main (blast inlet, blast pipe)
3 tapping spout
4 spyhole
5 tilting-type hot-metal receiver
6 mobile drum-type ladle
7 melter
8 founder (caster)
9 tap bar (tapping bar)
10 bott stick (*Am.* bot stick)
11 molten iron
12 slag spout
13 casting team
14 hand shank
15 double handle (crutch)
16 carrying bar
17 skimmer rod
18 closed moulding (*Am.* molding) box
19 upper frame (cope)
20 lower frame (drag)
21 runner (runner gate, down-gate)
22 riser (riser gate)
23 hand ladle

24–29 continuous casting
24 sinking pouring floor
25 solidifying pig
26 solid stage
27 liquid stage
28 water-cooling system
29 mould (*Am.* mold) wall
30–37 moulding (*Am.* molding) **department** (moulding shop)
30 moulder (*Am.* molder)
31 pneumatic rammer
32 hand rammer
33 open moulding (*Am.* molding) box
34 pattern
35 moulding (*Am.* molding) sand
36 core
37 core print
38–45 cleaning shop (fettling shop)
38 steel grit or sand delivery pipe
39 rotary-table shot-blasting machine
40 grit guard
41 revolving table
42 casting
43 fettler
44 pneumatic grinder
45 pneumatic chisel

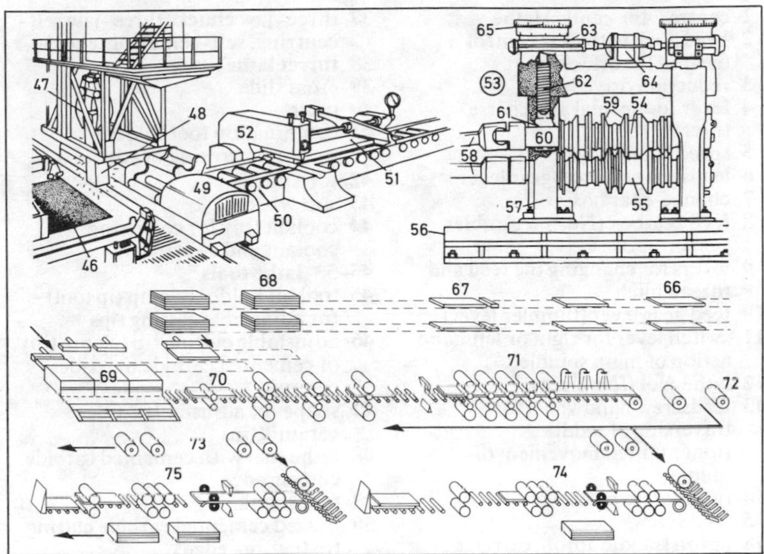

46–75 rolling mill
46 soaking pit
47 soaking pit crane
48 ingot
49 ingot tipper
50 blooming train (roller path)
51 workpiece
52 bloom shears
53 two-high mill
54–55 set of rolls (set of rollers)
54 upper roll (upper roller)
55 lower roll (lower roller)
56–60 roll stand
56 base plate
57 housing (frame)
58 coupling spindle
59 groove
60 roll bearing
61–65 adjusting equipment
61 chock
62 main screw
63 gear
64 motor
65 indicator for rough and fine adjustment

66–75 continuous rolling mill train for the manufacture of strip [diagram]
66–68 processing of semi-finished product
66 semi-finished product
67 gas cutting installation
68 stack of finished steel sheets
69 continuous reheating furnaces
70 blooming train
71 finishing train
72 coiler
73 collar bearing for marketing
74 5 mm shearing train
75 10 mm shearing train

149 Machine Tools I

1 **centre** (*Am.* center) **lathe**
2 headstock with gear control (geared headstock)
3 reduction drive lever
4 lever for normal and coarse threads
5 speed change lever
6 leadscrew reverse-gear lever
7 change-gear box
8 feed gearbox (Norton tumbler gear)
9 levers for changing the feed and thread pitch
10 feed gear lever (tumbler lever)
11 switch lever for right or left hand action of main spindle
12 lathe foot (footpiece)
13 leadscrew handwheel for traversing of saddle (longitudinal movement of saddle)
14 tumbler reverse lever
15 feed screw
16 apron (saddle apron, carriage apron)
17 lever for longitudinal and transverse motion
18 drop (dropping) worm (feed trip, feed tripping device) for engaging feed mechanisms
19 lever for engaging half nut of leadscrew (lever for clasp nut engagement)
20 lathe spindle
21 tool post
22 top slide (tool slide, tool rest)
23 cross slide
24 bed slide
25 coolant supply pipe
26 tailstock centre (*Am.* center)
27 barrel (tailstock barrel)
28 tailstock barrel clamp lever
29 tailstock
30 tailstock barrel adjusting handwheel
31 lathe bed
32 leadscrew
33 feed shaft
34 reverse shaft for right and left hand motion and engaging and disengaging
35 four-jaw chuck (four-jaw independent chuck)
36 gripping jaw
37 three-jaw chuck (three-jaw self-centring, self-centering, chuck)
38 **turret lathe**
39 cross slide
40 turret
41 combination toolholder (multiple turning head)
42 top slide
43 star wheel
44 coolant tray for collecting coolant and swarf
45-53 lathe tools
45 tool bit holder (clamp tip tool) for adjustable cutting tips
46 adjustable cutting tip (clamp tip) of cemented carbide or oxide ceramic
47 shapes of adjustable oxide ceramic tips
48 lathe tool with cemented carbide cutting edge
49 tool shank
50 brazed cemented carbide cutting tip (cutting edge)
51 internal facing tool (boring tool) for corner work
52 general-purpose lathe tool
53 parting (parting-off) tool
54 lathe carrier
55 driving (driver) plate
56-72 measuring instruments
56 plug gauge (*Am.* gage)
57 'GO' gauging (*Am.* gaging) member (end)
58 'NOT GO' gauging (*Am.* gaging) member (end)
59 calliper (caliper, snap) gauge (*Am.* gage)
60 'GO' side
61 'NOT GO' side
62 micrometer
63 measuring scale
64 graduated thimble
65 frame
66 spindle (screwed spindle)
67 vernier calliper (caliper) gauge (*Am.* gage)
68 depth gauge (*Am.* gage) attachment rule
69 vernier scale
70 outside jaws
71 inside jaws
72 vernier depth gauge (*Am.* gage)

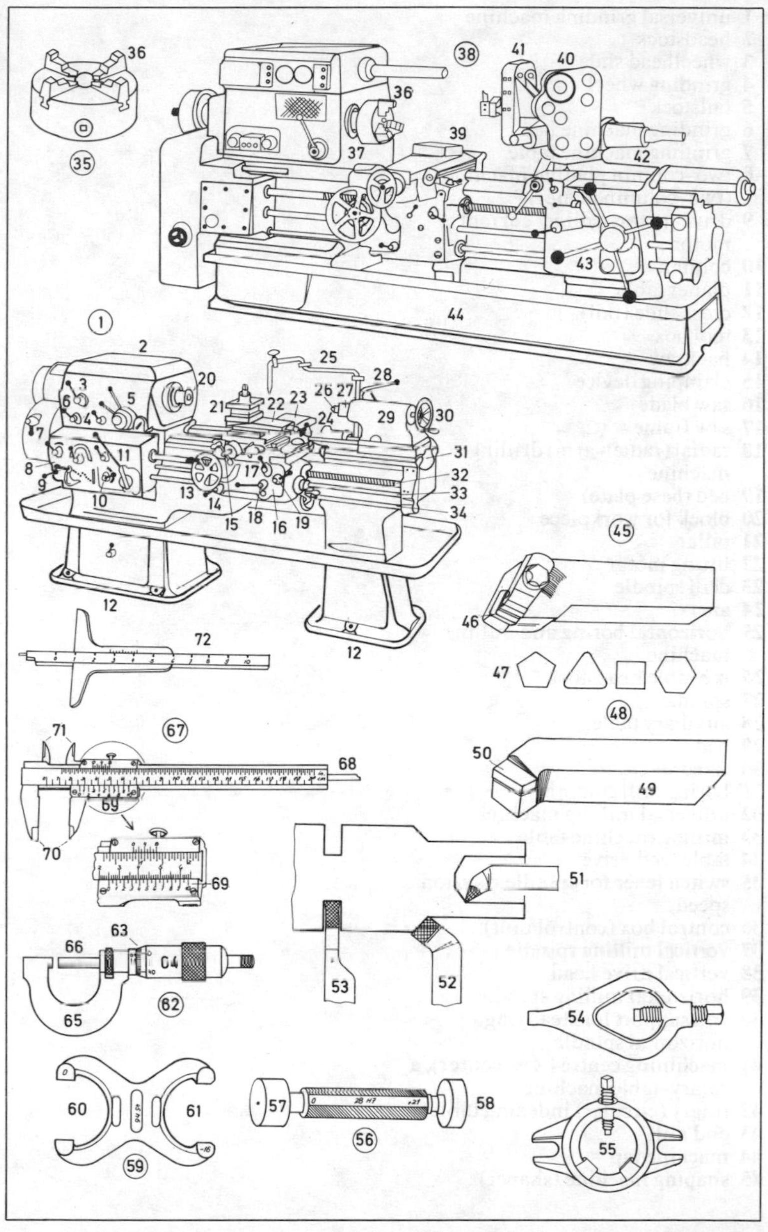

1 universal grinding machine
2 headstock
3 wheelhead slide
4 grinding wheel
5 tailstock
6 grinding machine bed
7 grinding machine table
8 two-column planing machine (two-column planer)
9 drive motor, a direct current motor
10 column
11 planer table
12 cross slide (rail)
13 tool box
14 hacksaw
15 clamping device
16 saw blade
17 saw frame
18 radial (radial-arm) drilling machine
19 bed (base plate)
20 block for workpiece
21 pillar
22 lifting motor
23 drill spindle
24 arm
25 horizontal boring and milling machine
26 movable headstock
27 spindle
28 auxiliary table
29 bed
30 fixed steady
31 boring mill column
32 universal milling machine
33 milling machine table
34 table feed drive
35 switch lever for spindle rotation speed
36 control box (control unit)
37 vertical milling spindle
38 vertical drive head
39 horizontal milling spindle
40 end support for steadying horizontal spindle
41 machining centre (*Am.* center), a rotary-table machine
42 rotary (circular) indexing table
43 end mill
44 machine tap
45 shaping machine (shaper)

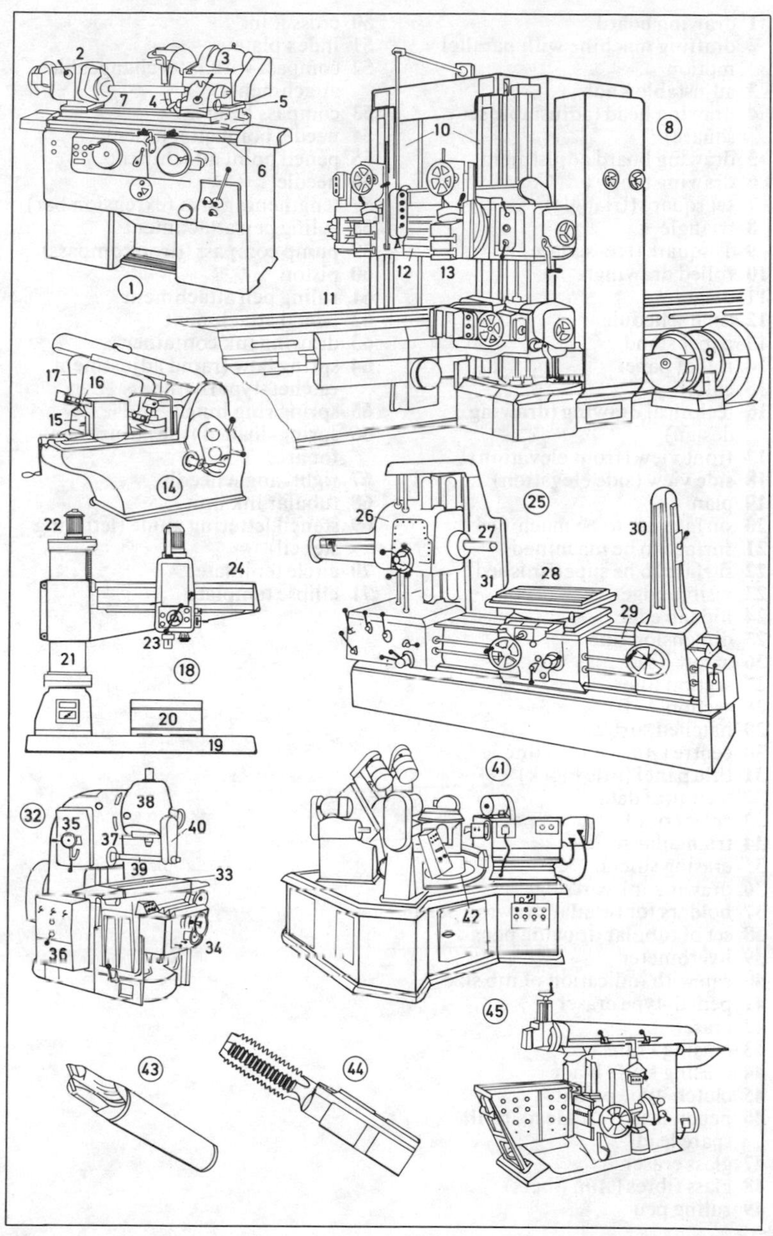
2
3
7
4
5
6
1
10
8
12
13
11
9
17
16
15
14
22
24
23
21
18
20
19
26
27
25
30
28
31
29
32
35
38
37
40
39
33
36
34
41
42
45
43
44

151 Drawing Office

1 drawing board
2 drafting machine with parallel motion
3 adjustable knob
4 drawing head (adjustable set square)
5 drawing board adjustment
6 drawing table
7 set square (triangle)
8 triangle
9 T–square (tee–square)
10 rolled drawing
11 diagram
12 time schedule
13 paper stand
14 roll of paper
15 cutter
16 technical drawing (drawing, design)
17 front view (front elevation)
18 side view (side elevation)
19 plan
20 surface not to be machined
21 surface to be machined
22 surface to be superfinished
23 visible edge
24 hidden edge
25 dimension line
26 arrow head
27 section line
28 section A–B
29 hatched surface
30 centre (*Am.* center) line
31 title panel (title block)
32 technical data
33 ruler (rule)
34 triangular scale
35 erasing shield
36 drawing ink cartridge
37 holders for tubular drawing pens
38 set of tubular drawing pens
39 hygrometer
40 cap with indication of nib size
41 pencil–type eraser
42 eraser
43 erasing knife
44 erasing knife blade
45 clutch–type pencil
46 pencil lead (refill lead, refill, spare lead)
47 glass eraser
48 glass fibres (*Am.* fibers)
49 ruling pen
50 cross joint
51 index plate
52 compass with interchangeable attachments
53 compass head
54 needle point attachment
55 pencil point attachment
56 needle
57 lengthening arm (extension bar)
58 ruling pen attachment
59 pump compass (drop compass)
60 piston
61 ruling pen attachment
62 pencil attachment
63 drawing ink container
64 spring bow (rapid adjustment, ratchet–type) compass
65 spring ring hinge
66 spring–loaded fine adjustment for arcs
67 right–angle needle
68 tubular ink unit
69 stencil lettering guide (lettering stencil)
70 circle template
71 ellipse template

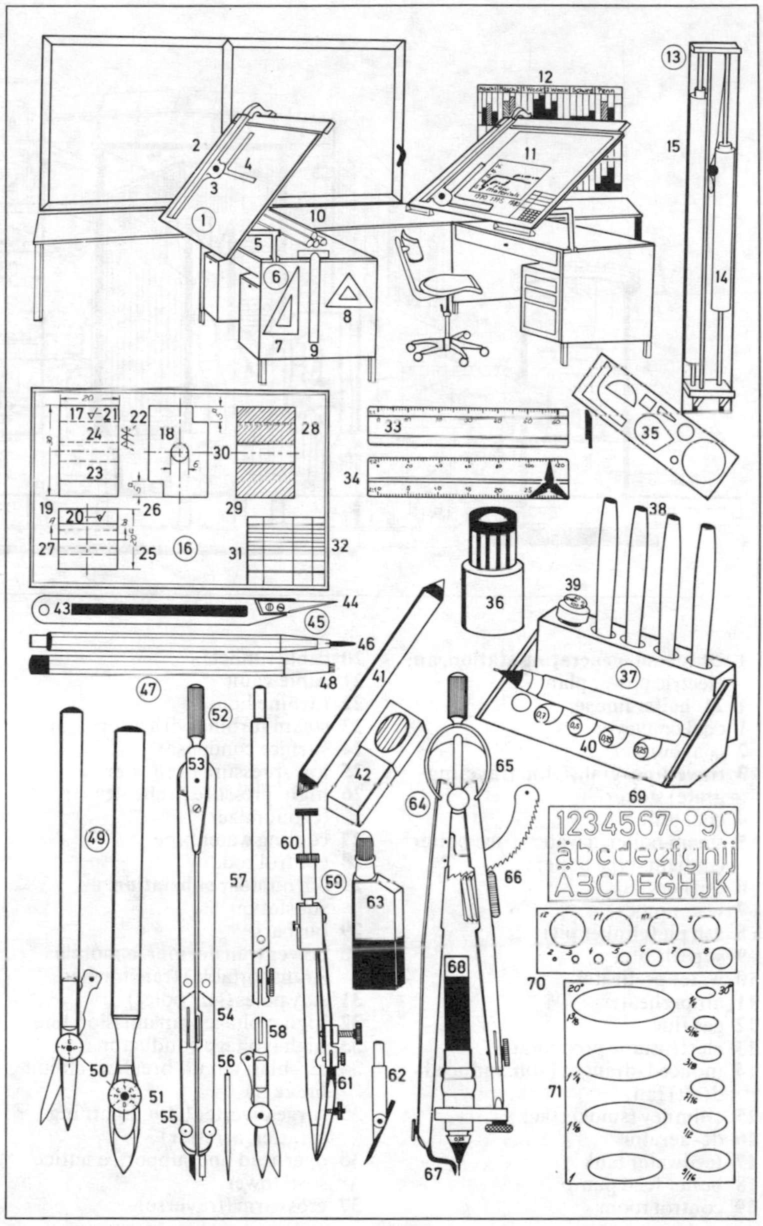
1234567o°90
äbcdeefghij
A3CDEGHJK

152 Power Plant (Power Station) I

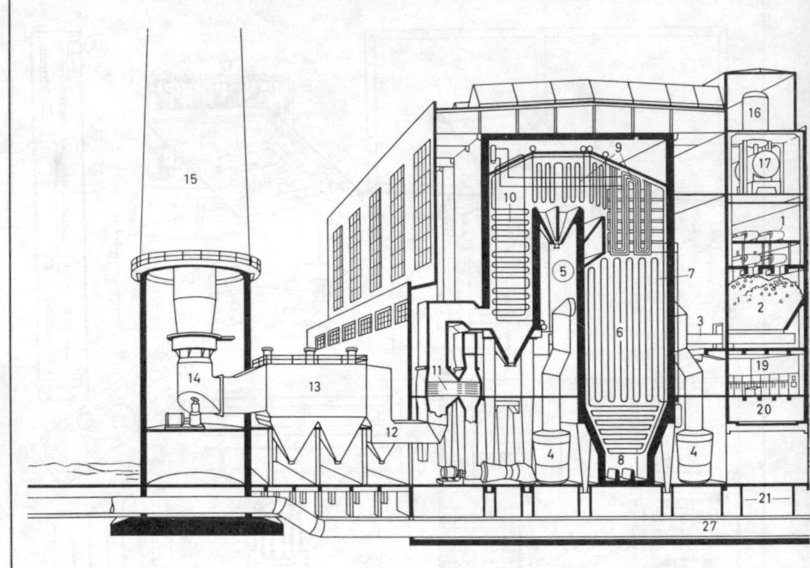

1-28 steam-generating station, an electric power plant
1-21 boiler house
1 coal conveyor
2 coal bunker
3 travelling-grate (*Am.* traveling-grate) stoker
4 coal mill
5 steam boiler, a water-tube boiler (radiant-type boiler)
6 burners
7 water pipes
8 ash pit (clinker pit)
9 superheater
10 water preheater
11 air preheater
12 gas flue
13 electrostatic precipitator
14 induced-draught (*Am.* induced-draft) fan
15 chimney (smokestack)
16 de-aerator
17 feedwater tank
18 boiler feed pump
19 control room
20 cable tunnel
21 cable vault
22 turbine house
23 steam turbine with alternator
24 surface condenser
25 low-pressure preheater
26 high-pressure preheater (economizer)
27 cooling water pipe
28 control room
29-35 outdoor substation, a substation
29 busbars
30 power transformer, a mobile (transportable) transformer
31 stay poles (guy poles)
32 high-voltage transmission line
33 high-voltage conductor
34 air-blast circuit breaker (circuit breaker)
35 surge diverter (*Am.* lightning arrester, arrester)
36 overhead line support, a lattice steel tower
37 cross arm (traverse)

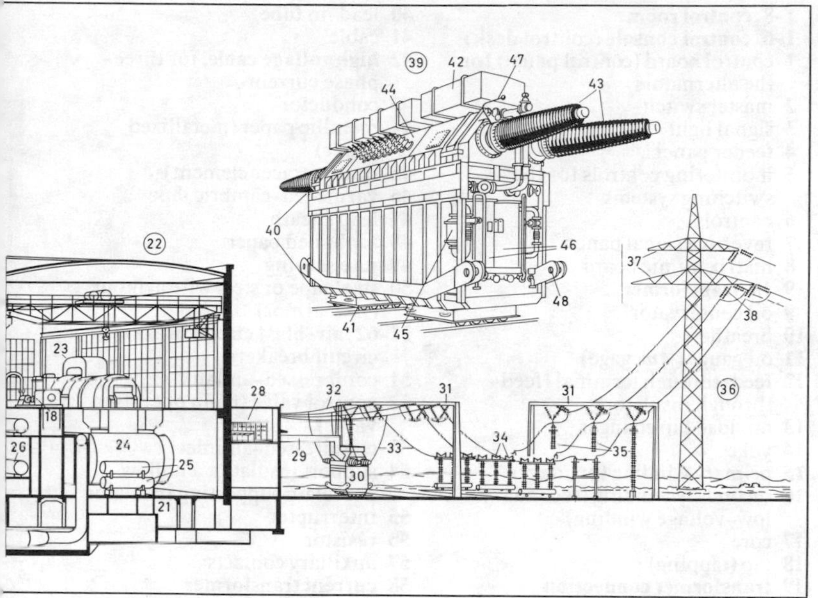

38 strain insulator
39 **mobile (transportable) transformer** (power transformer, transformer)
40 transformer tank
41 bogie (*Am.* truck)
42 oil conservator
43 primary voltage terminal (primary voltage bushing)
44 low-voltage terminals (low-voltage bushings)
45 oil-circulating pump
46 oil cooler
47 arcing horn
48 transport lug

153 Power Plant (Power Station) II

1–8 control room
1–6 control console (control desk)
1 control board (control panel) for the alternators
2 master switch
3 signal light
4 feeder panel
5 monitoring controls for the switching systems
6 controls
7 revertive signal panel
8 matrix mimic board
9–18 transformer
9 oil conservator
10 breather
11 oil gauge (*Am.* gage)
12 feed-through terminal (feed-through insulator)
13 on-load tap changer
14 yoke
15 primary winding (primary)
16 secondary winding (secondary, low-voltage winding)
17 core
18 tap (tapping)
19 transformer connection
20 star connection (star network, Y-connection)
21 delta connection (mesh connection)
22 neutral point
23–30 steam turbine, a turbogenerator unit
23 high-pressure cylinder
24 medium-pressure cylinder
25 low-pressure cylinder
26 three-phase generator (generator)
27 hydrogen cooler
28 leakage steam path
29 jet nozzle
30 turbine monitoring panel with measuring instruments
31 automatic voltage regulator
32 synchro
33 cable box
34 conductor
35 feed-through terminal (feed-through insulator)
36 core
37 casing
38 filling compound (filler)
39 lead sheath
40 lead-in tube
41 cable
42 high voltage cable, for three-phase current
43 conductor
44 metallic paper (metallized paper)
45 tracer (tracer element)
46 varnished-cambric tape
47 lead sheath
48 asphalted paper
49 jute serving
50 steel tape or steel wire armour (*Am.* armor)
51–62 air-blast circuit breaker, a circuit breaker
51 compressed-air tank
52 control valve (main operating valve)
53 compressed-air inlet
54 support insulator, a hollow porcelain supporting insulator
55 interrupter
56 resistor
57 auxiliary contacts
58 current transformer
59 voltage transformer (potential transformer)
60 operating mechanism housing
61 arcing horn
62 spark gap

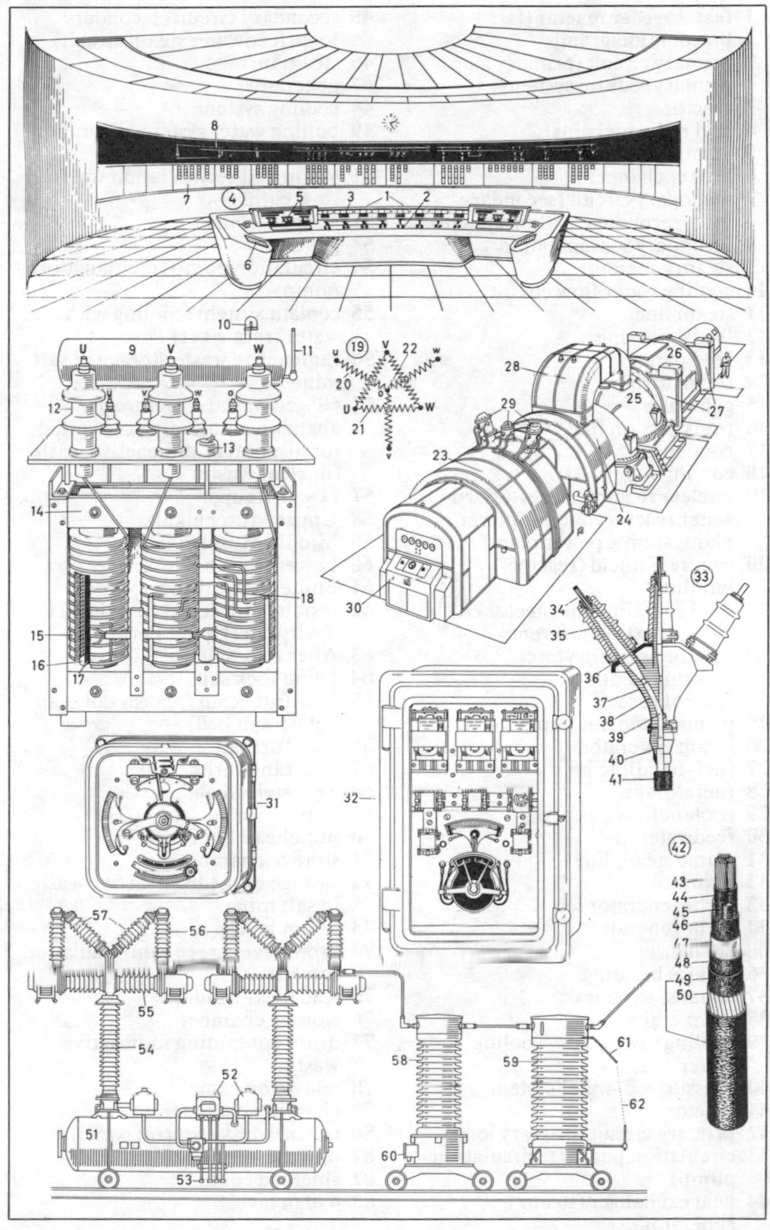
1
2
3
4
5
6
7
8
9
10
11
12
13
14
15
16
17
18
19
20
21
22
23
24
25
26
27
28
29
30
31
32
33
34
35
36
37
38
39
40
41
42
43
44
45
46
47
48
49
50
51
52
53
54
55
56
57
58
59
60
61
62
U
V
W

1 **fast-breeder reactor** (fast breeder) [diagram]
2 primary circuit (primary loop, primary sodium system)
3 reactor
4 fuel rods (fuel pins)
5 primary sodium pump
6 heat exchanger
7 secondary circuit (secondary loop, secondary sodium system)
8 secondary sodium pump
9 steam generator
10 cooling water flow circuit
11 steam line
12 feedwater line
13 feed pump
14 steam turbine
15 generator
16 transmission line
17 condenser
18 cooling water
19 **nuclear reactor,** a pressurized-water reactor (nuclear power plant, atomic power plant)
20 concrete shield (reactor building)
21 steel containment (steel shell) with air extraction vent
22 reactor pressure vessel
23 control rod drive
24 control rods
25 primary coolant pump
26 steam generator
27 fuel-handling hoists
28 fuel storage
29 coolant flow passage
30 feedwater line
31 prime steam line
32 manway
33 turbogenerator set
34 turbogenerator
35 condenser
36 service building
37 exhaust gas stack
38 polar crane
39 cooling tower, a dry cooling tower
40 pressurized-water system
41 reactor
42 primary circuit (primary loop)
43 circulation pump (recirculation pump)
44 heat exchanger (steam generator)
45 secondary circuit (secondary loop, feedwater steam circuit)
46 steam turbine
47 generator
48 cooling system
49 boiling water system [diagram]
50 reactor
51 steam and recirculation water flow paths
52 steam turbine
53 generator
54 circulation pump (recirculation pump)
55 coolant system (cooling with water from river)
56 **radioactive waste storage in salt mine**
57-68 geological structure of abandoned salt mine converted for disposal of radioactive waste (nuclear waste)
57 Lower Keuper
58 Upper Muschelkalk
59 Middle Muschelkalk
60 Lower Muschelkalk
61 Bunter downthrow
62 residue of leached (lixiviated) Zechstein (Upper Permian)
63 Aller rock salt
64 Leine rock salt
65 Stassfurt seam (potash salt seam, potash salt bed)
66 Stassfurt salt
67 grenzanhydrite
68 Zechstein shale
69 shaft
70 minehead buildings
71 storage chamber
72 storage of medium-active waste in salt mine
73 511 m level
74 protective screen (anti-radiation screen)
75 lead glass window
76 storage chamber
77 drum containing radioactive waste
78 television camera
79 charging chamber
80 control desk (control panel)
81 upward ventilator
82 shielded container
83 490 m level

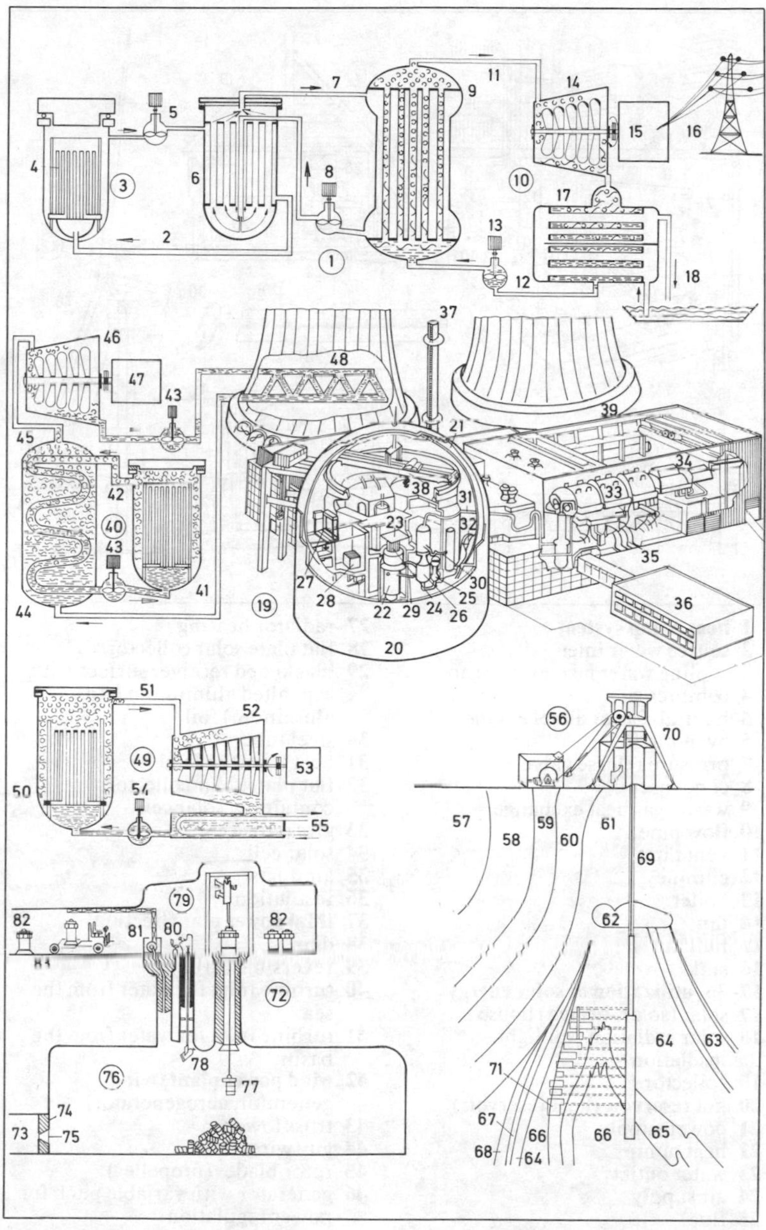
1
2
3
4
5
6
7
8
9
10
11
12
13
14
15
16
17
18
19
20
21
22
23
24
25
26
27
28
29
30
31
32
33
34
35
36
37
38
39
40
41
42
43
44
45
46
47
48
49
50
51
52
53
54
55
56
57
58
59
60
61
62
63
64
65
66
67
68
69
70
71
72
73
74
75
76
77
78
79
80
81
82

155 Modern Sources of Energy

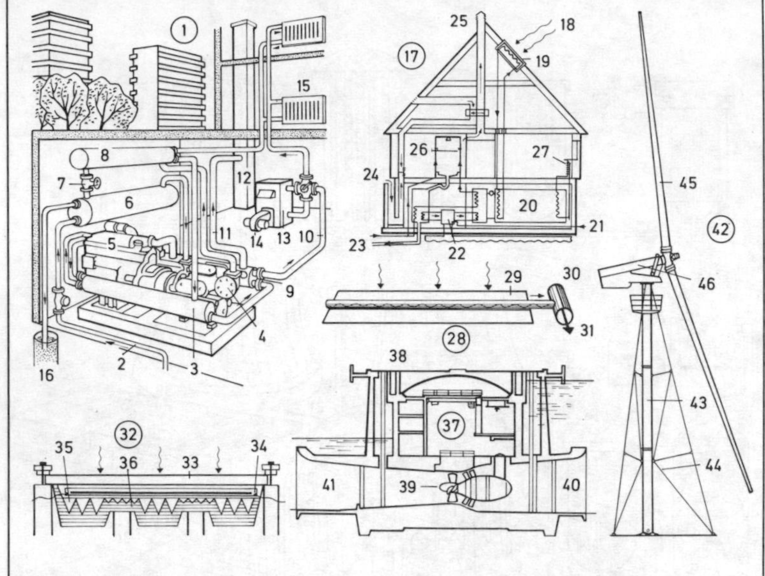

1 heat pump system
2 source water inlet
3 cooling water heat exchanger
4 compressor
5 natural-gas or diesel engine
6 evaporator
7 pressure release valve
8 condenser
9 waste-gas heat exchanger
10 flow pipe
11 vent pipe
12 chimney
13 boiler
14 fan
15 radiator
16 sink
17–36 utilization of solar energy
17 solar (solar-heated) house
18 solar radiation (sunlight, insolation)
19 collector
20 hot reservoir (heat reservoir)
21 power supply
22 heat pump
23 water outlet
24 air supply
25 flue
26 hot water supply
27 radiator heating
28 flat plate solar collector
29 blackened receiver surface with asphalted aluminium (*Am.* aluminum) foil
30 steel tube
31 heat transfer fluid
32 flat plate solar collector, containing solar cell
33 glass cover
34 solar cell
35 air ducts
36 insulation
37 tidal power plant [section]
38 dam
39 reversible turbine
40 turbine inlet for water from the sea
41 turbine inlet for water from the basin
42 wind power plant (wind generator, aerogenerator)
43 truss tower
44 guy wire
45 rotor blades (propeller)
46 generator with variable pitch for power regulation

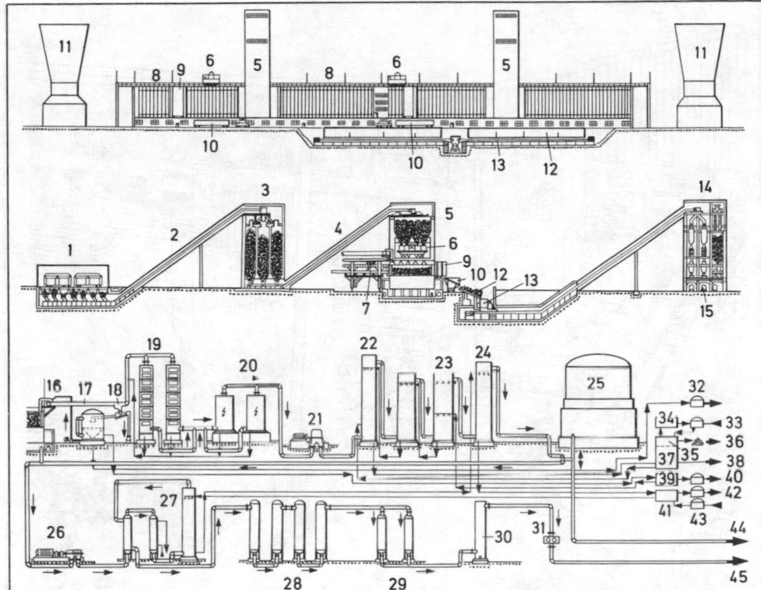

1-15 coking plant
1 dumping of coking coal
2 belt conveyor
3 service bunker
4 coal tower conveyor
5 coal tower
6 larry car (larry, charging car)
7 pusher ram
8 battery of coke ovens
9 coke guide
10 quenching car, with engine
11 quenching tower
12 coke loading bay (coke wharf)
13 coke side bench
14 screening of lump coal and culm
15 coke loading
16-45 coke-oven gas processing
16 discharge (release) of gas from the coke ovens
17 gas-collecting main
18 coal tar extraction
19 gas cooler
20 electrostatic precipitator
21 gas extractor
22 hydrogen sulphide (*Am.* hydrogen sulfide) scrubber (hydrogen sulphide wet collector)
23 ammonia scrubber (ammonia wet collector)
24 benzene (benzol) scrubber
25 gas holder
26 gas compressor
27 debenzoling by cooler and heat exchanger
28 desulphurization (*Am.* desulfurization) of pressure gas
29 gas cooling
30 gas drying
31 gas meter
32 crude tar tank
33 sulphuric acid (*Am.* sulfuric acid) supply
34 production of sulphuric acid (*Am.* sulfuric acid)
35 production of ammonium sulphate (*Am.* ammonium sulfate)
36 ammonium sulphate (*Am.* ammonium sulfate)
37 recovery plant for recovering the scrubbing agents
38 waste water discharge
39 phenol extraction from the gas water
40 crude phenol tank
41 production of crude benzol (crude benzene)
42 crude benzol (crude benzene) tank
43 scrubbing oil tank
44 low-pressure gas main
45 high-pressure gas main

157 Sawmill

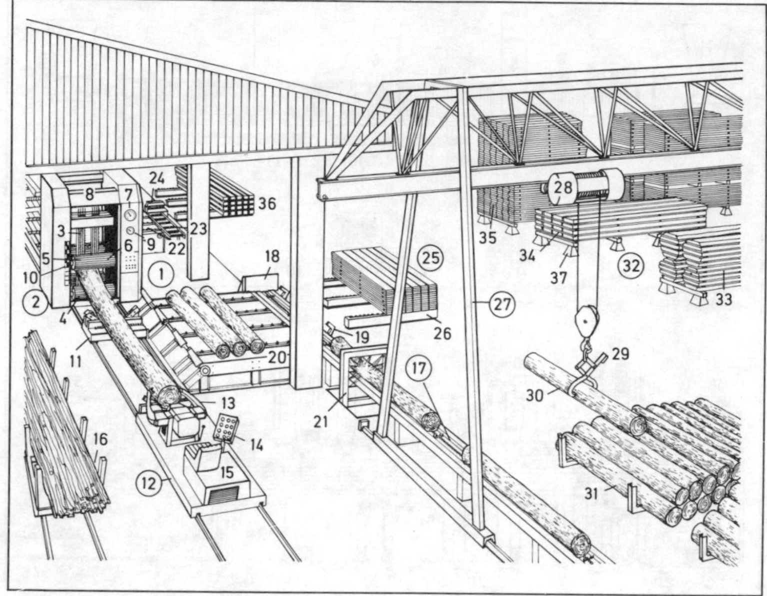

1 sawmill
2 vertical frame saw (*Am.* gang mill)
3 saw blades
4 feed roller
5 guide roller
6 fluting (grooving, grooves)
7 oil pressure gauge (*Am.* gage)
8 saw frame
9 feed indicator
10 log capacity scale
11 auxiliary carriage
12 carriage
13 log grips
14 remote control panel
15 carriage motor
16 truck for splinters (splints)
17 endless log chain (*Am.* jack chain)
18 stop plate
19 log-kicker arms
20 cross conveyor
21 washer (washing machine)
22 cross chain conveyor for sawn timber
23 roller table
24 undercut swing saw
25 piling
26 roller trestles
27 gantry crane
28 crane motor
29 pivoted log grips
30 roundwood (round timber)
31 log dump
32 squared timber store
33 sawn logs
34 planks
35 boards (planks)
36 squared timber
37 stack bearer
38 automatic cross-cut chain saw
39 log grips
40 feed roller
41 chain-tensioning device
42 saw-sharpening machine
43 grinding wheel (teeth grinder)
44 feed pawl
45 depth adjustment for the teeth grinder

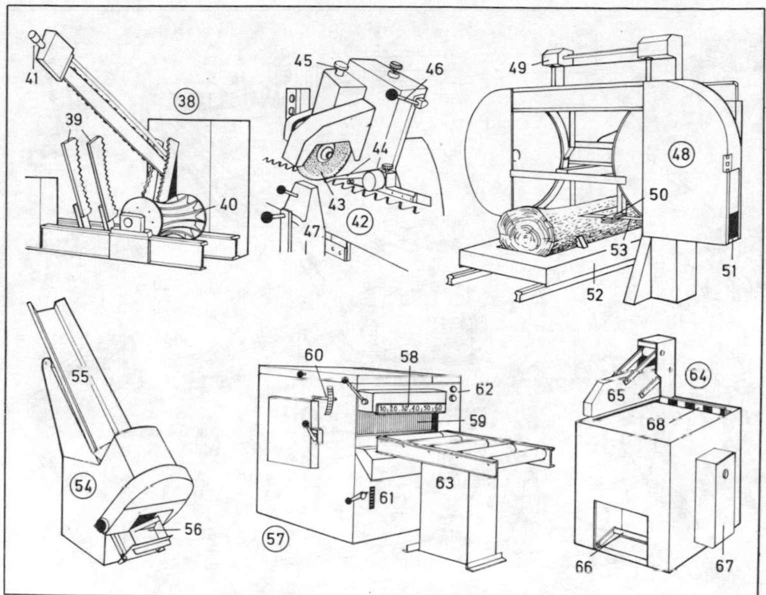

46 lifter (lever) for the grinder chuck
47 holding device for the saw blade
48 horizontal bandsaw for sawing logs
49 height adjustment
50 chip remover
51 chip extractor
52 carriage
53 bandsaw blade
54 automatic blocking saw
55 feed channel
56 discharge opening
57 twin edger (double edger)
58 breadth scale (width scale)
59 kick-back guard
60 height scale
61 in-feed scale
62 indicator lamps
63 feed table
64 undercut swing saw
65 automatic hold-down with protective hood
66 foot switch
67 distribution board (panelboard)
68 length stop

158 Quarry

1 **quarry**, an open-cast working
2 overburden
3 working face
4 loose rock pile (blasted rock)
5 quarryman (quarrier), a quarry worker
6 sledge hammer
7 wedge
8 block of stone
9 driller
10 safety helmet
11 hammer drill (hard-rock drill)
12 borehole
13 universal excavator
14 large-capacity truck
15 rock face
16 inclined hoist
17 primary crusher
18 stone-crushing plant
19 coarse rotary (gyratory) crusher; *sim.:* fine rotary (gyratory) crusher
20 hammer crusher (impact crusher)
21 vibrating screen
22 screenings (fine dust)
23 stone chippings
24 crushed stone
25 shot firer
26 measuring rod
27 blasting cartridge
28 fuse (blasting fuse)
29 plugging sand (stemming sand) bucket
30 dressed stone
31 pick
32 crowbar (pinch bar)
33 fork
34 stonemason
35-38 **stonemason's tools**
35 stonemason's hammer
36 mallet
37 drove chisel (drove, boaster, broad chisel)
38 dressing axe (*Am.* ax)

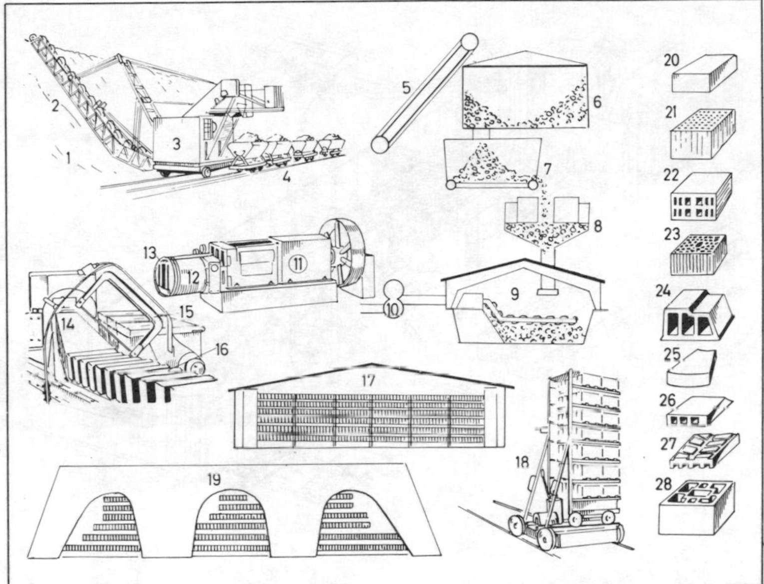

1 clay pit
2 loam, an impure clay (raw clay)
3 overburden excavator, a large-scale excavator
4 narrow-gauge (*Am.* narrow-gage) track system
5 inclined hoist
6 souring chambers
7 box feeder (feeder)
8 edge runner mill (edge mill, pan grinding mill)
9 rolling plant
10 double-shaft trough mixer (mixer)
11 extrusion press (brick-pressing machine)
12 vacuum chamber
13 die
14 clay column
15 cutter (brick cutter)
16 unfired brick (green brick)
17 drying shed
18 mechanical finger car (stacker truck)
19 circular kiln (brick kiln)
20 solid brick (building brick)
21-22 perforated bricks and hollow blocks
21 perforated brick with vertical perforations
22 hollow clay block with horizontal perforations
23 hollow clay block with vertical perforations
24 floor brick
25 compass brick (radial brick, radiating brick)
26 hollow flooring block
27 paving brick
28 cellular brick [for fireplaces] (chimney brick)

160 Cement Works (Cement Factory)

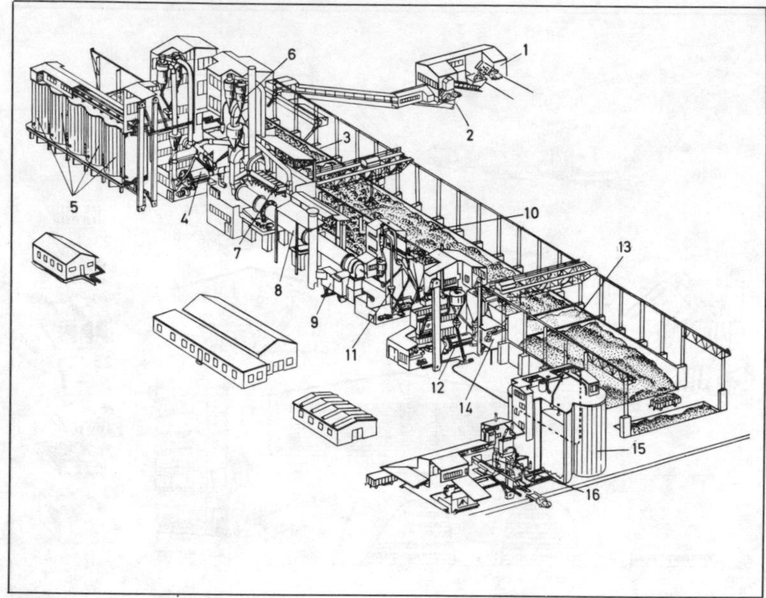

1 raw materials (limestone, clay, and marl)
2 hammer crusher (hammer mill)
3 raw material store
4 raw mill for simultaneously grinding and drying the raw materials with exhaust gas from the heat exchanger
5 raw meal silos
6 heat exchanger (cyclone heat exchanger)
7 dust collector (an electrostatic precipitator) for the heat exchanger exhaust from the raw mill
8 rotary kiln
9 clinker cooler
10 clinker store
11 primary air blower
12 cement-grinding mill
13 gypsum store
14 gypsum crusher
15 cement silo
16 cement-packing plant

1 grinding cylinder (ball mill) for the preparation of the raw material in water
2 sample sagger (saggar, seggar), with aperture for observing the firing process
3 bottle kiln (beehive kiln) [diagram]
4 firing mould (*Am.* mold)
5 tunnel kiln
6 Seger cone (pyrometric cone, *Am.* Orton cone) for measuring high temperatures
7 de-airing pug mill (de-airing pug press), an extrusion press
8 clay column
9 thrower throwing a ball (bat) of clay
10 slug of clay
11 turntable; *sim.:* potter's wheel
12 filter press
13 filter cake
14 jiggering, with a profiling tool; *sim.:* jollying
15 plaster mould (*Am.* mold) for slip casting
16 turntable glazing machine
17 porcelain painter (china painter)
18 hand-painted vase
19 repairer
20 pallet (modelling, *Am.* modoling, tool)
21 shards (sherds, potsherds)

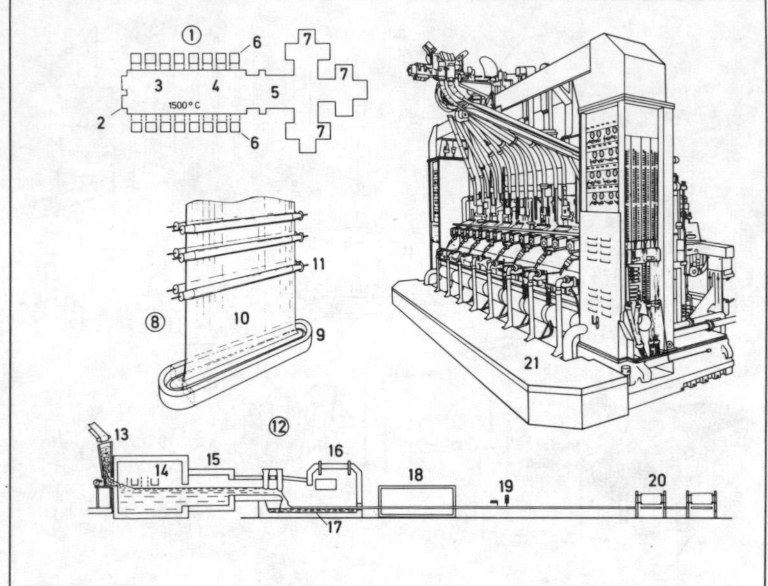

1–20 sheet glass production (flat glass production)
1 glass furnace (tank furnace) for the Fourcault process [diagram]
2 filling end, for feeding in the batch (frit)
3 melting bath
4 refining bath (fining bath)
5 working baths (working area)
6 burners
7 drawing machines
8 Fourcault glass-drawing machine
9 slot
10 glass ribbon (ribbon of glass, sheet of glass) being drawn upwards
11 rollers (drawing rolls)
12 float glass process
13 batch (frit) feeder (funnel)
14 melting bath
15 cooling tank
16 float bath in a protective inert-gas atmosphere
17 molten tin
18 annealing lehr
19 automatic cutter
20 stacking machines
21 IS (individual-section) machine, a bottle-making machine
22–37 blowing processes
22 blow-and-blow process
23 introduction of the gob of molten glass
24 first blowing
25 suction
26 transfer from the parison mould (*Am.* mold) to the blow mould (*Am.* mold)
27 reheating
28 blowing (suction, final shaping)
29 delivery of the completed vessel
30 press-and-blow process
31 introduction of the gob of molten glass
32 plunger
33 pressing
34 transfer from the press mould (*Am.* mold) to the blow mould (*Am.* mold)

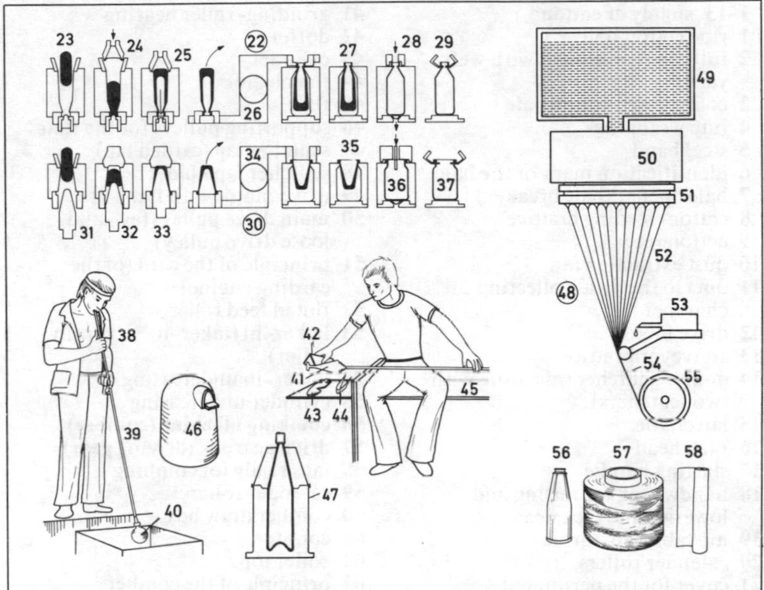

35 reheating
36 blowing (suction, final shaping)
37 delivery of the completed vessel
38–47 glassmaking (glassblowing, glassblowing by hand, glass forming)
38 glassmaker (glassblower)
39 blowing iron
40 gob
41 hand-blown goblet
42 clappers for shaping the base (foot) of the goblet
43 trimming tool
44 tongs
45 glassmaker's chair (gaffer's chair)
46 covered glasshouse pot
47 mould (*Am.* mold), into which the parison is blown
48–55 production of glass fibre (*Am.* glass fiber)
48 continuous filament process
49 glass furnace
50 bushing containing molten glass
51 bushing tips
52 glass filaments
53 sizing
54 strand (thread)
55 spool
56–58 glass fibre (*Am.* glass fiber) products
56 glass yarn (glass thread)
57 sleeved glass yarn (glass thread)
58 glass wool

163 Cotton Spinning I

1–13 supply of cotton
1 ripe cotton boll
2 full cop (cop wound with weft yarn)
3 compressed cotton bale
4 jute wrapping
5 steel band
6 identification mark of the bale
7 bale opener (bale breaker)
8 cotton-feeding brattice
9 cotton feed
10 dust extraction fan
11 duct to the dust-collecting chamber
12 drive motor
13 conveyor brattice
14 **double scutcher** (machine with two scutchers)
15 lap cradle
16 rack head
17 starting handle
18 handwheel, for raising and lowering the rack head
19 movable lap-turner
20 calender rollers
21 cover for the perforated cylinders
22 dust escape flue (dust discharge flue)
23 drive motors (beater drive motors)
24 beater driving shaft
25 three-blade beater (Kirschner beater)
26 grid [for impurities to drop]
27 pedal roller (pedal cylinder)
28 control lever for the pedal roller, a pedal lever
29 variable change-speed gear
30 cone drum box
31 stop and start levers for the hopper
32 wooden hopper delivery roller
33 hopper feeder
34 **carding machine** (card, carding engine)
35 card can (carding can), for receiving the coiled sliver
36 can holder
37 calender rollers
38 carded sliver (card sliver)
39 vibrating doffer comb
40 start-stop lever
41 grinding-roller bearing
42 doffer
43 cylinder
44 flat clearer
45 flats
46 supporting pulleys for the flats
47 scutcher lap (carded lap)
48 scutcher lap holder
49 drive motor with flat belt
50 main drive pulley (fast-and-loose drive pulley)
51 principle of the card (of the carding engine)
52 fluted feed roller
53 licker-in (taker-in, licker-in roller)
54 licker-in undercasing
55 cylinder undercasing
56 **combing machine** (comber)
57 drive gearbox (driving gear)
58 laps ready for combing
59 calender rollers
60 comber draw box
61 counter
62 coiler top
63 principle of the comber
64 lap
65 bottom nipper
66 top nipper
67 top comb
68 combing cylinder
69 plain part of the cylinder
70 needled part of the cylinder
71 detaching rollers
72 carded and combed sliver

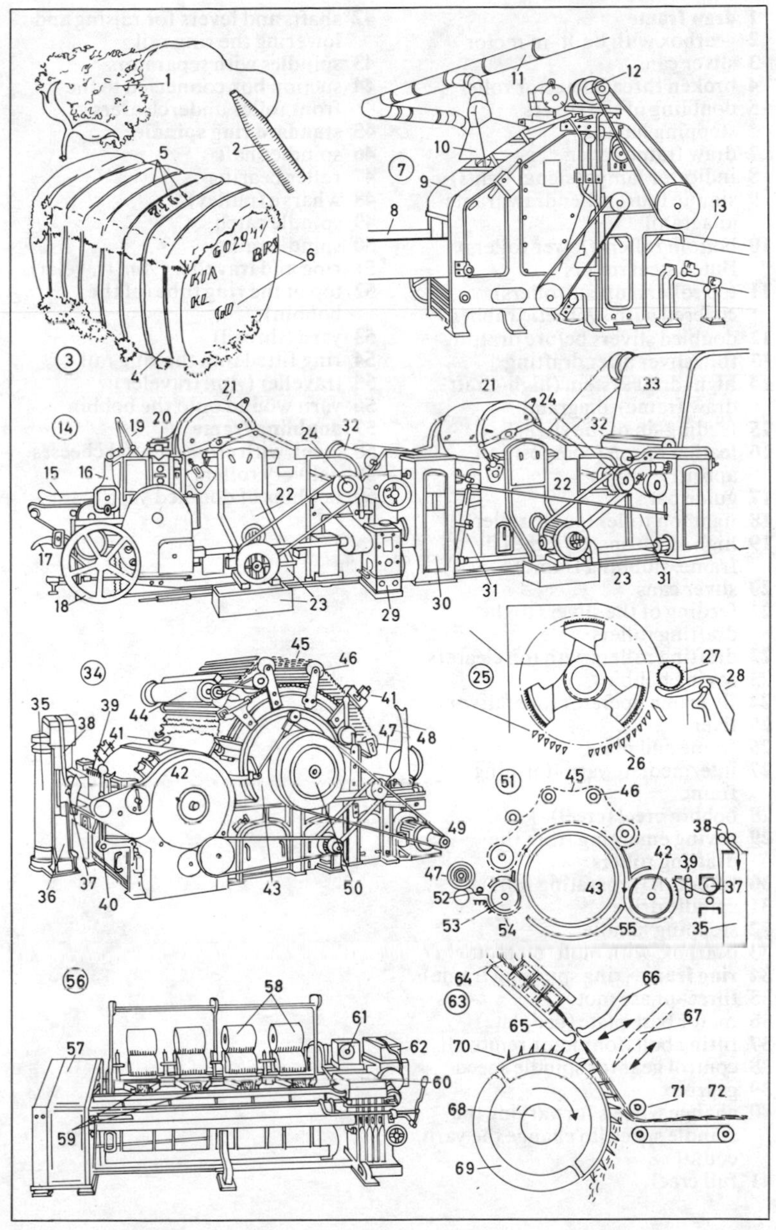
1
2
3
4
5
6
7
8
9
10
11
12
13
14
15
16
17
18
19
20
21
22
23
24
25
26
27
28
29
30
31
32
33
34
35
36
37
38
39
40
41
42
43
44
45
46
47
48
49
50
51
52
53
54
55
56
57
58
59
60
61
62
63
64
65
66
67
68
69
70
71
72

1 **draw frame**
2 gearbox with built-in motor
3 sliver cans
4 broken thread detector roller
5 doubling of the slivers
6 stopping handle
7 draw frame cover
8 indicator lamps (signal lights)
9 simple four-roller draw frame [diagram]
10 bottom rollers (lower rollers), fluted steel rollers
11 top rollers (upper rollers) covered with synthetic rubber
12 doubled slivers before drafting
13 thin sliver after drafting
14 high-draft system (high-draft draw frame) [diagram]
15 feeding-in of the sliver
16 leather apron (composition apron)
17 guide bar
18 light top roller (guide roller)
19 high-draft speed frame (fly frame, slubbing frame)
20 sliver cans
21 feeding of the slivers to the drafting rollers
22 drafting rollers with top clearers
23 roving bobbins
24 fly frame operator (operative)
25 flyer
26 frame end plate
27 intermediate yarn-forming frame
28 bobbin creel (creel)
29 roving emerging from the drafting rollers
30 lifter rail (separating rail)
31 spindle drive
32 stopping handle
33 gearbox, with built-on motor
34 **ring frame** (ring spinning frame)
35 three-phase motor
36 motor base plate (bedplate)
37 lifting bolt [for motor removal]
38 control gear for spindle speed
39 gearbox
40 change wheels for varying the spindle speed [to change the yarn count]
41 full creel
42 shafts and levers for raising and lowering the ring rail
43 spindles with separators
44 suction box connected to the front roller underclearers
45 **standard ring spindle**
46 spindle shaft
47 roller bearing
48 wharve (pulley)
49 spindle catch
50 spindle rail
51 ring and traveller (*Am.* traveler)
52 top of the ring tube (of the bobbin)
53 yarn (thread)
54 ring fitted into the ring rail
55 traveller (*Am.* traveler)
56 yarn wound onto the bobbin
57 **doubling frame**
58 creel, with cross-wound cheeses
59 delivery rollers
60 bobbins of doubled yarn

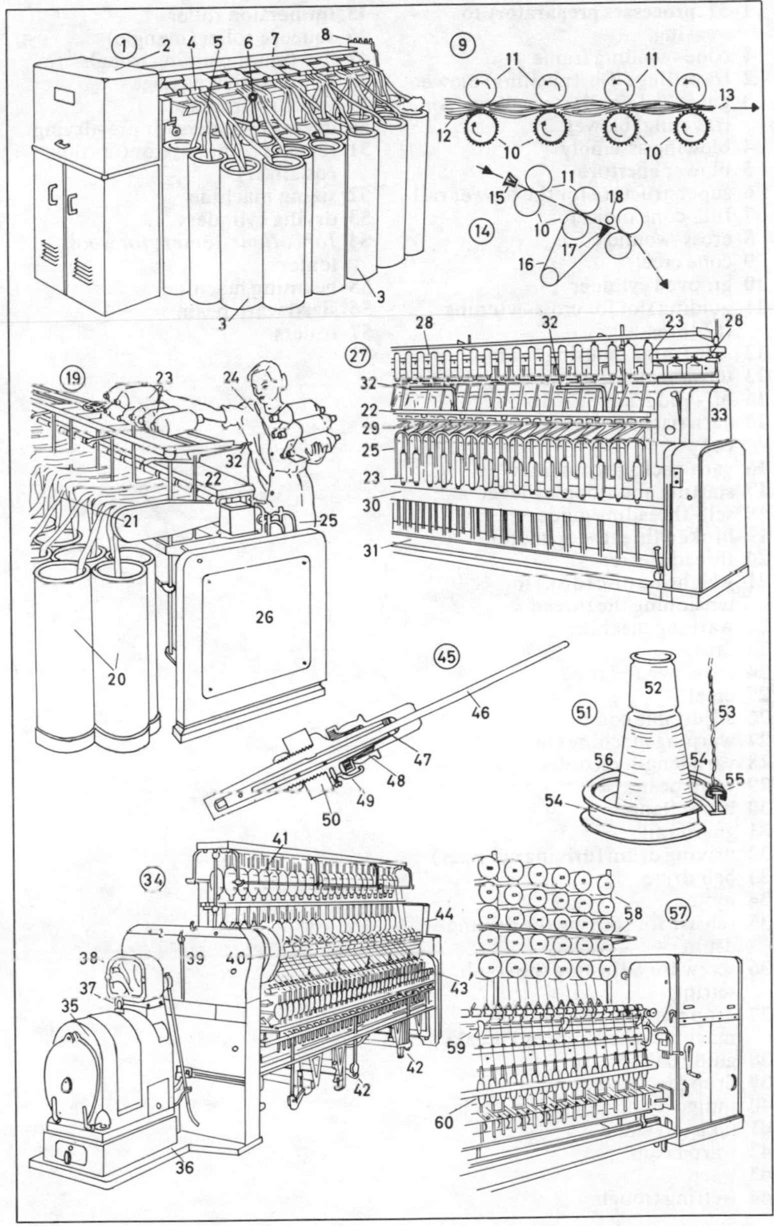
1
2
3
4
5
6
7
8
9
10
11
12
13
14
15
16
17
18
19
20
21
22
23
24
25
26
27
28
29
30
31
32
33
34
35
36
37
38
39
40
41
42
43
44
45
46
47
48
49
50
51
52
53
54
55
56
57
58
59
60

165 Weaving I

1–57 processes preparatory to weaving
1 cone–winding frame
2 travelling (*Am.* traveling) blower
3 guide rail, for the travelling (*Am.* traveling) blower
4 blowing assembly
5 blower aperture
6 superstructure for the blower rail
7 full–cone indicator
8 cross–wound cone
9 cone creel
10 grooved cylinder
11 guiding slot for cross–winding the threads
12 side frame, housing the motor
13 tension and slub–catching device
14 off–end framing with filter
15 yarn package, a ring tube or mule cop
16 yarn package container
17 starting and stopping lever
18 self–threading guide
19 broken thread stop motion
20 thread clearer
21 weighting disc (disk) for tensioning the thread
22 warping machine
23 fan
24 cross–wound cone
25 creel
26 adjustable comb
27 warping machine frame
28 yarn length recorder
29 warp beam
30 beam flange
31 guard rail
32 driving drum (driving cylinder)
33 belt drive
34 motor
35 release for starting the driving drum
36 screw for adjusting the comb setting
37 drop pins, for stopping the machine when a thread breaks
38 guide bar
39 drop pin rollers
40 indigo dying and sizing machine
41 take–off stand
42 warp beam
43 warp
44 wetting trough
45 immersion roller
46 squeeze roller (mangle)
47 dye liquor padding trough
48 air oxidation passage
49 washing trough
50 drying cylinders for pre–drying
51 tension compensator (tension equalizer)
52 sizing machine
53 drying cylinders
54 *for cotton:* stenter; *for wool:* tenter
55 beaming machine
56 sized warp beam
57 rollers

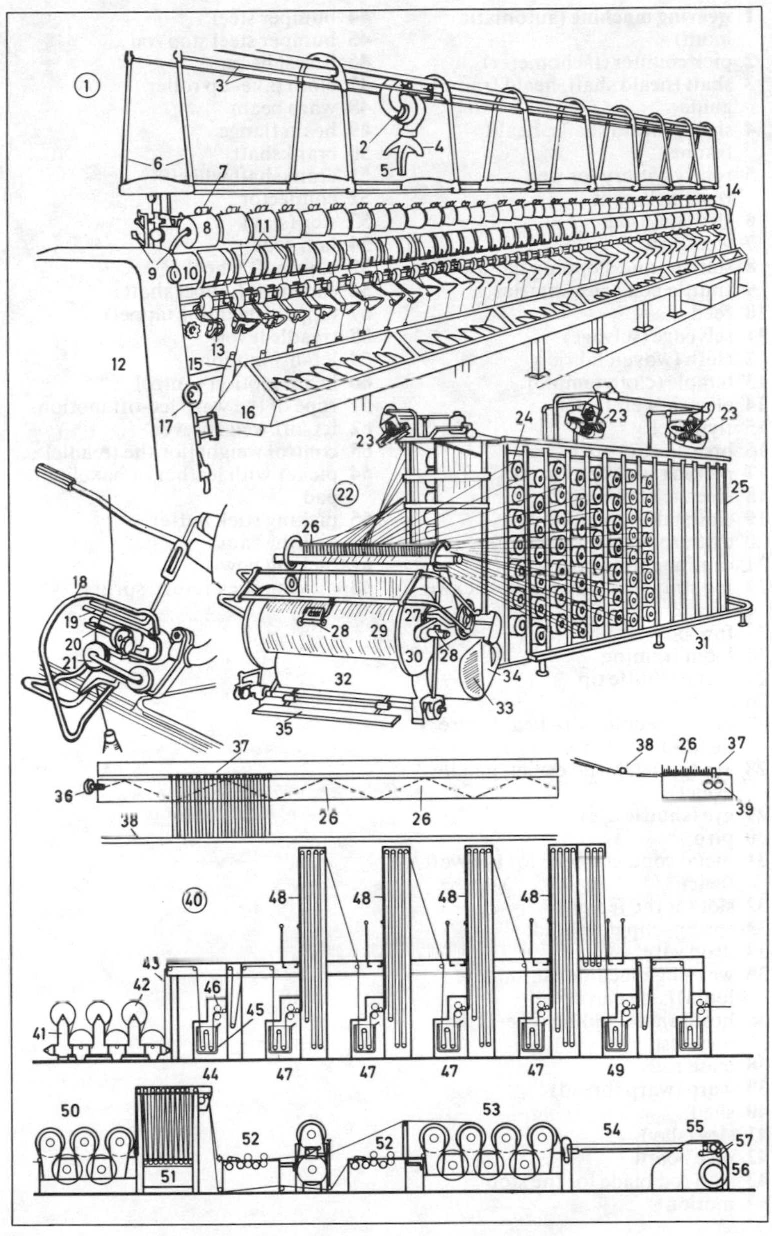
1
2
3
4
5
6
7
8
9
10
11
12
13
14
15
16
17
18
19
20
21
22
23
24
25
26
27
28
29
30
31
32
33
34
35
36
37
38
39
40
41
42
43
44
45
46
47
48
49
50
51
52
53
54
55
56
57

1 **weaving machine** (automatic loom)
2 pick counter (tachometer)
3 shaft (heald shaft, heald frame) guide
4 shafts (heald shafts, heald frames)
5 rotary battery for weft replenishment
6 sley (slay) cap
7 weft pirn
8 starting and stopping handle
9 shuttle box, with shuttles
10 reed
11 selvedge (selvage)
12 cloth (woven fabric)
13 temple (cloth temple)
14 electric weft feeler
15 flywheel
16 breast beam board
17 picking stick (pick stick)
18 electric motor
19 cloth take-up motion
20 cloth roller (fabric roller)
21 can for empty pirns
22 lug strap, for moving the picking stick
23 fuse box
24 loom framing
25 metal shuttle tip
26 shuttle
27 heald (heddle, wire heald, wire heddle)
28 eye (eyelet, heald eyelet, heddle eyelet)
29 eye (shuttle eye)
30 pirn
31 metal contact sleeve for the weft feeler
32 slot for the feeler
33 spring-clip pirn holder
34 drop wire
35 weaving machine (automatic loom) [side elevation]
36 heald shaft guiding wheels
37 backrest
38 lease rods
39 warp (warp thread)
40 shed
41 sley (slay)
42 race board
43 stop rod blade for the stop motion
44 bumper steel
45 bumper steel stop rod
46 breast beam
47 cloth take-up roller
48 warp beam
49 beam flange
50 crankshaft
51 crankshaft wheel
52 connector
53 sley (slay)
54 lam rods
55 camshaft wheel
56 camshaft (tappet shaft)
57 tappet (shedding tappet)
58 treadle lever
59 let-off motion
60 beam motion control
61 rope of the warp let-off motion
62 let-off weight lever
63 control weight [for the treadle]
64 picker with leather or bakelite pad
65 picking stick buffer
66 picking cam
67 picking bowl
68 picking stick return spring

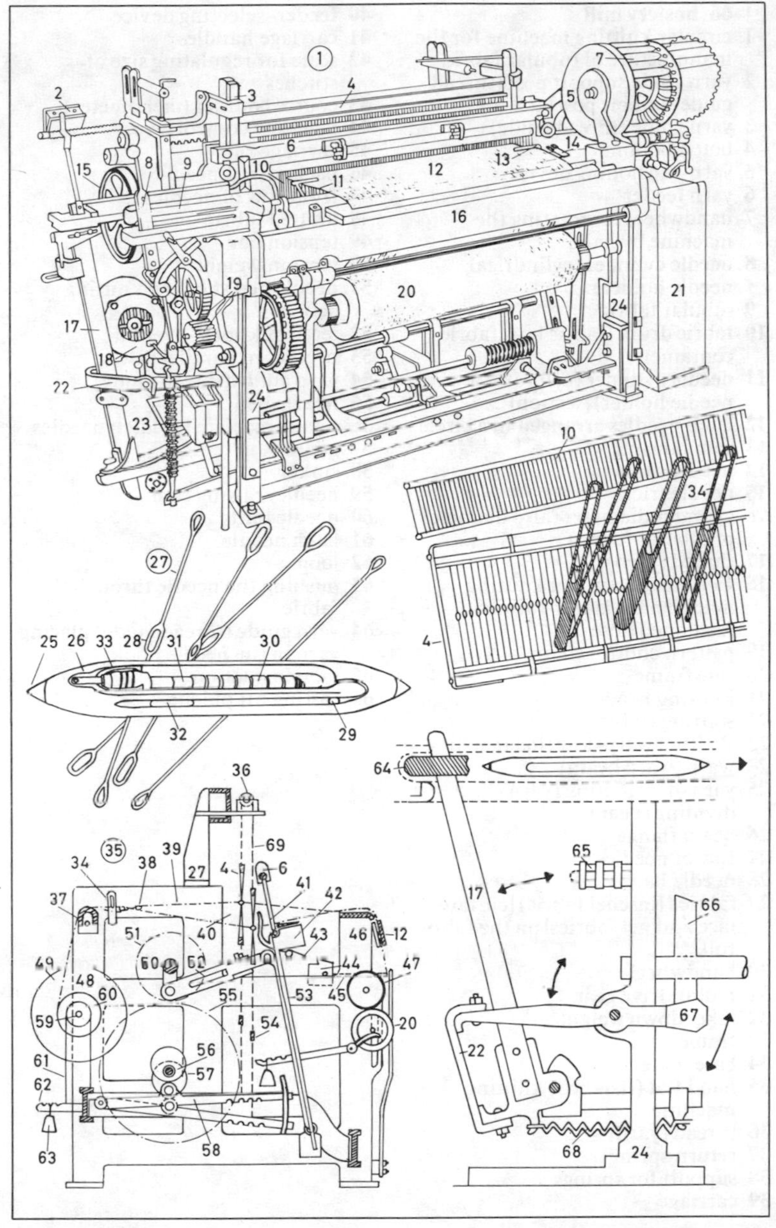
1
2
3
4
5
6
7
8
9
10
11
12
13
14
15
16
17
18
19
20
21
22
23
24
10
34
4
27
25
26
33
28
31
30
32
29
64
36
69
35
34
38
39
27
4
6
37
41
42
51
40
43
49
50
52
46
12
48
60
44
47
55
45
59
53
54
20
61
56
57
62
58
63
65
17
66
67
22
68
24

167 Knitting

1–66 hosiery mill
1 circular knitting machine for the manufacture of tubular fabric
2 yarn guide support post (thread guide support post)
3 yarn guide (thread guide)
4 bottle bobbin
5 yarn-tensioning device
6 yarn feeder
7 handwheel for rotating the machine by hand
8 needle cylinder (cylindrical needle holder)
9 tubular fabric
10 fabric drum (fabric box, fabric container)
11 needle cylinder (cylindrical needle holder) [section]
12 latch needles arranged in a circle
13 cam housing
14 needle cams
15 needle trick
16 cylinder diameter (also diameter of tubular fabric)
17 thread (yarn)
18 Cotton's patent flat knitting machine for ladies' fully-fashioned hose
19 pattern control chain
20 side frame
21 knitting head
22 starting rod
23 Raschel warp-knitting machine
24 warp (warp beam)
25 yarn-distributing (yarn-dividing) beam
26 beam flange
27 row of needles
28 needle bar
29 fabric (Raschel fabric) [curtain lace and net fabrics] on the fabric roll
30 handwheel
31 motor drive gear
32 take-down weight
33 frame
34 base plate
35 hand flat (flat-bed) knitting machine
36 thread (yarn)
37 return spring
38 support for springs
39 carriage
40 feeder-selecting device
41 carriage handles
42 scale for regulating size of stitches
43 course counter (tachometer)
44 machine control lever
45 carriage rail
46 back row of needles
47 front row of needles
48 knitted fabric
49 tension bar
50 tension weight
51 needle bed showing knitting action
52 teeth of knock-over bit
53 needles in parallel rows
54 yarn guide (thread guide)
55 needle bed
56 retaining plate for latch needles
57 guard cam
58 sinker
59 needle-raising cam
60 needle butt
61 latch needle
62 loop
63 pushing the needle through the fabric
64 yarn guide (thread guide) placing yarn in the needle hook
65 loop formation
66 casting off of loop

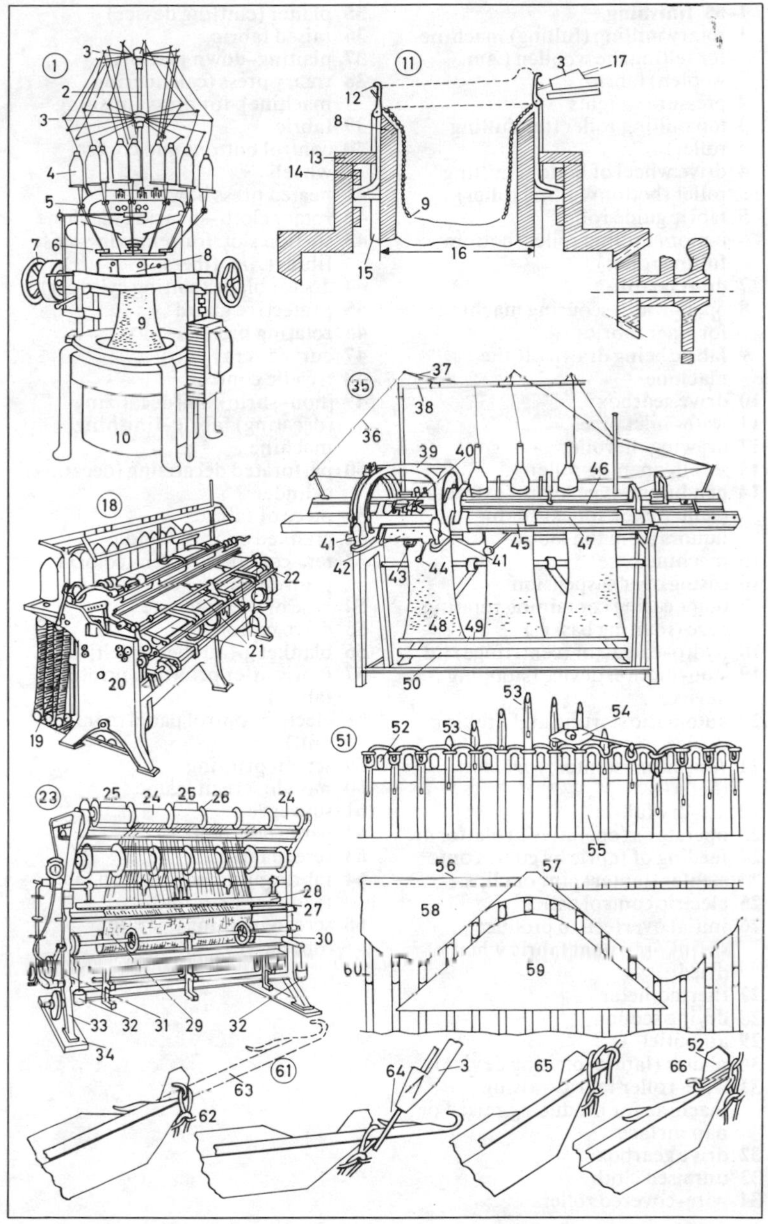
1
2
3
4
5
6
7
8
9
10
11
12
13
14
15
16
17
18
19
20
21
22
23
24
25
26
27
28
29
30
31
32
33
34
35
36
37
38
39
40
41
42
43
44
45
46
47
48
49
50
51
52
53
54
55
56
57
58
59
60
61
62
63
64
65
66

1-65 finishing
1 rotary milling (fulling) machine for felting the woollen (*Am.* woolen) fabric
2 pressure weights
3 top milling roller (top fulling roller)
4 drive wheel of bottom milling roller (bottom fulling roller)
5 fabric guide roller
6 bottom milling roller (bottom fulling roller)
7 draft board
8 open-width scouring machine for finer fabrics
9 fabric being drawn off the machine
10 drive gearbox
11 water inlet pipe
12 drawing-in roller
13 scroll-opening roller
14 pendulum-type hydro-extractor (centrifuge), for extracting liquors from the fabric
15 machine base
16 casing over suspension
17 outer casing containing rotating cage (rotating basket)
18 hydro-extractor (centrifuge) lid
19 stop-motion device (stopping device)
20 automatic starting and braking device
21 *for cotton:* stenter; *for wool:* tenter
22 air-dry fabric
23 operator's (operative's) platform
24 feeding of fabric by guides onto stenter (tenter) pins or clips
25 electric control panel
26 initial overfeed to produce shrink-resistant fabric when dried
27 thermometer
28 drying section
29 air outlet
30 plaiter (fabric-plaiting device)
31 wire-roller fabric-raising machine for producing raised or nap surface
32 drive gearbox
33 unraised cloth
34 wire-covered rollers
35 plaiter (cuttling device)
36 raised fabric
37 plaiting-down platform
38 rotary press (calendering machine), for press finishing
39 fabric
40 control buttons and control wheels
41 heated press bowl
42 rotary cloth-shearing machine
43 suction slot, for removing loose fibres (*Am.* fibers)
44 doctor blade (cutting cylinder)
45 protective guard
46 rotating brush
47 curved scray entry
48 treadle control
49 [non-shrinking] decatizing (decating) fabric-finishing machine
50 perforated decatizing (decating) cylinder
51 piece of fabric
52 cranked control handle
53 ten-colour (*Am.* ten-color) roller printing machine
54 base of the machine
55 drive motor
56 blanket [of rubber or felt]
57 fabric after printing (printed fabric)
58 electric control panel (control unit)
59 screen printing
60 mobile screen frame
61 squeegee
62 pattern stencil
63 screen table
64 fabric gummed down on table ready for printing
65 screen printing operator (operative)

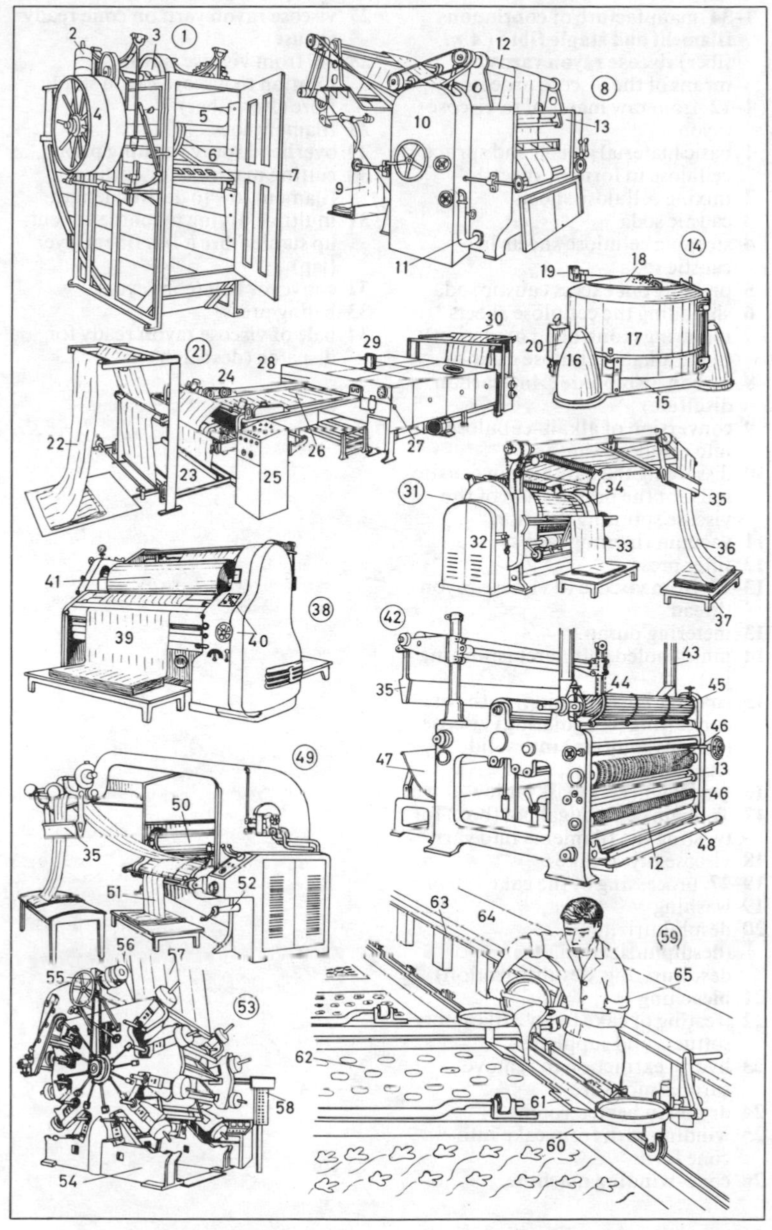
1
2
3
4
5
6
7
8
9
10
11
12
13
14
15
16
17
18
19
20
21
22
23
24
25
26
27
28
29
30
31
32
33
34
35
36
37
38
39
40
41
42
43
44
45
46
47
48
49
50
51
52
53
54
55
56
57
58
59
60
61
62
63
64
65

169 Synthetic (Man-made) Fibres (*Am.* Fibers) I

1-34 manufacture of **continuous filament and staple fibre** (*Am.* fiber) **viscose rayon yarns** by means of the viscose process
1-12 from raw material to viscose rayon
1 basic material [beech and spruce cellulose in form of sheets]
2 mixing cellulose sheets
3 caustic soda
4 steeping cellulose sheets in caustic soda
5 pressing out excess caustic soda
6 shredding the cellulose sheets
7 maturing (controlled oxidation) of the alkali-cellulose crumbs
8 carbon disulphide (*Am.* carbon disulfide)
9 conversion of alkali-cellulose into cellulose xanthate
10 dissolving the xanthate in caustic soda for the preparation of the viscose spinning solution
11 vacuum ripening tanks
12 filter press
13-27 from viscose to viscose rayon thread
13 metering pump
14 multi-holed spinneret (spinning jet)
15 coagulating (spinning) bath for converting (coagulating) viscose (viscous solution) into solid filaments
16 Godet wheel, a glass pulley
17 Topham centrifugal pot (box) for twisting the filaments into yarn
18 viscose rayon cake
19-27 processing of the cake
19 washing
20 desulphurizing (desulphurization, *Am.* desulfurizing, desulfurization)
21 bleaching
22 treating of cake to give filaments softness and suppleness
23 hydro-extraction to remove surplus moisture
24 drying in heated room
25 winding yarn from cake into cone form
26 cone-winding machine
27 viscose rayon yarn on cone ready for use
28-34 from viscose spinning solution to viscose rayon staple fibre (*Am.* fiber)
28 filament tow
29 overhead spray washing plant
30 cutting machine for cutting filament tow to desired length
31 multiple drying machine for cut-up staple fibre (*Am.* fiber) layer (lap)
32 conveyor belt (conveyor)
33 baling press
34 bale of viscose rayon ready for dispatch (despatch)

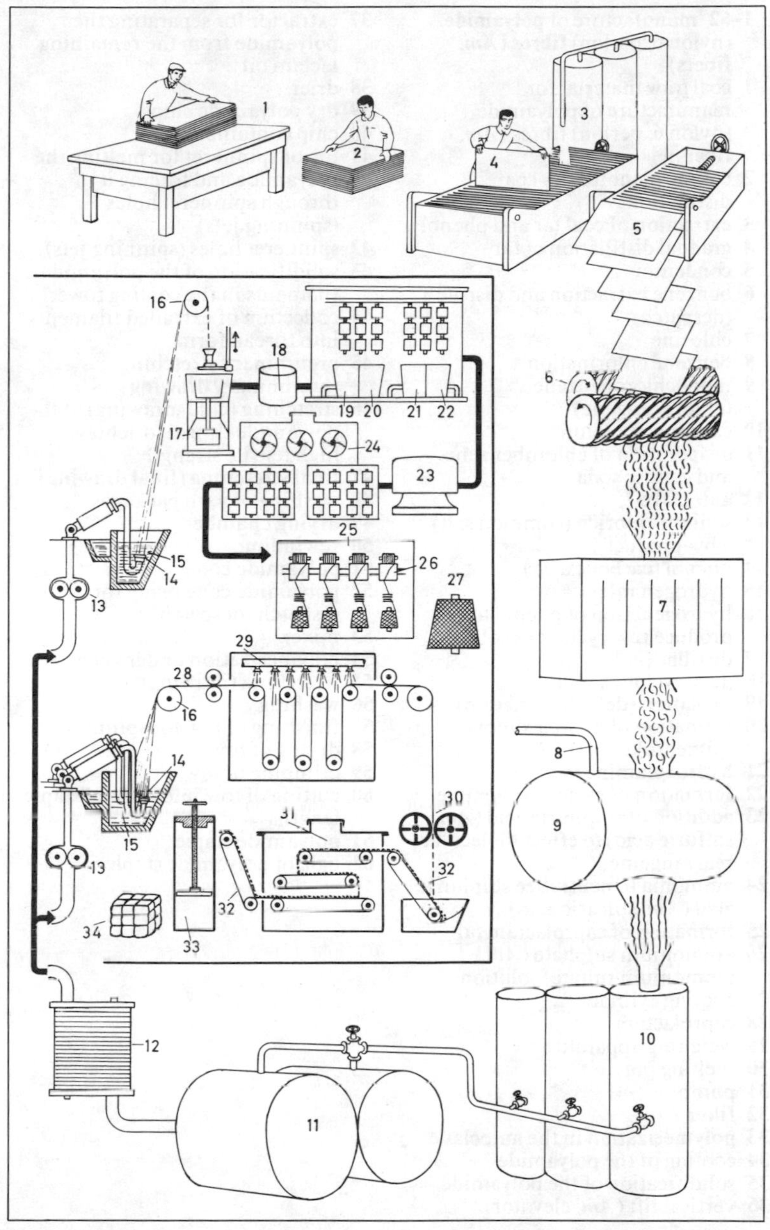
1
2
3
4
5
6
7
8
9
10
11
12
13
14
15
16
17
18
19
20
21
22
23
24
25
26
27
28
29
30
31
32
33
34

170 Synthetic (Man-made) Fibres (*Am.* Fibers) II

1-62 manufacture of **polyamide** (nylon 6, perlon) **fibres** (*Am.* fibers)
1 coal [raw material for manufacture of polyamide (nylon 6, perlon) fibres (*Am.* fibers)]
2 coking plant for dry coal distillation
3 extraction of coal tar and phenol
4 gradual distillation of tar
5 condenser
6 benzene extraction and dispatch (despatch)
7 chlorine
8 benzene chlorination
9 monochlorobenzene (chlorobenzene)
10 caustic soda solution
11 evaporation of chlorobenzene and caustic soda
12 autoclave
13 sodium chloride (common salt), a by-product
14 phenol (carbolic acid)
15 hydrogen inlet
16 hydrogenation of phenol to produce raw cyclohexanol
17 distillation
18 pure cyclohexanol
19 oxidation (dehydrogenation)
20 formation of cyclohexanone (pimehinketone)
21 hydroxylamine inlet
22 formation of cyclohexanoxime
23 addition of sulphuric acid (*Am.* sulfuric acid) to effect molecular rearrangement
24 ammonia to neutralize sulphuric acid (*Am.* sulfuric acid)
25 formation of caprolactam oil
26 ammonium sulphate (*Am.* ammonium sulfate) solution
27 cooling cylinder
28 caprolactam
29 weighing apparatus
30 melting pot
31 pump
32 filter
33 polymerization in the autoclave
34 cooling of the polyamide
35 solidification of the polyamide
36 vertical lift (*Am.* elevator)
37 extractor for separating the polyamide from the remaining lactam oil
38 drier
39 dry polyamide chips
40 chip container
41 top of spinneret for melting the polyamide and forcing it through spinneret holes (spinning jets)
42 spinneret holes (spinning jets)
43 solidification of the polyamide filaments in the cooling tower
44 collection of extruded filaments into thread form
45 preliminary stretching (preliminary drawing)
46 stretching (cold-drawing) of the polyamide thread to achieve high tensile strength
47 final stretching (final drawing)
48 washing of yarn packages
49 drying chamber
50 rewinding
51 polyamide cone
52 polyamide cone ready for dispatch (despatch)
53 mixer
54 polymerization under vacua
55 stretching (drawing)
56 washing
57 finishing of tow for spinning
58 drying of tow
59 crimping of tow
60 cutting of tow into normal staple lengths
61 polyamide staple
62 bale of polyamide staple

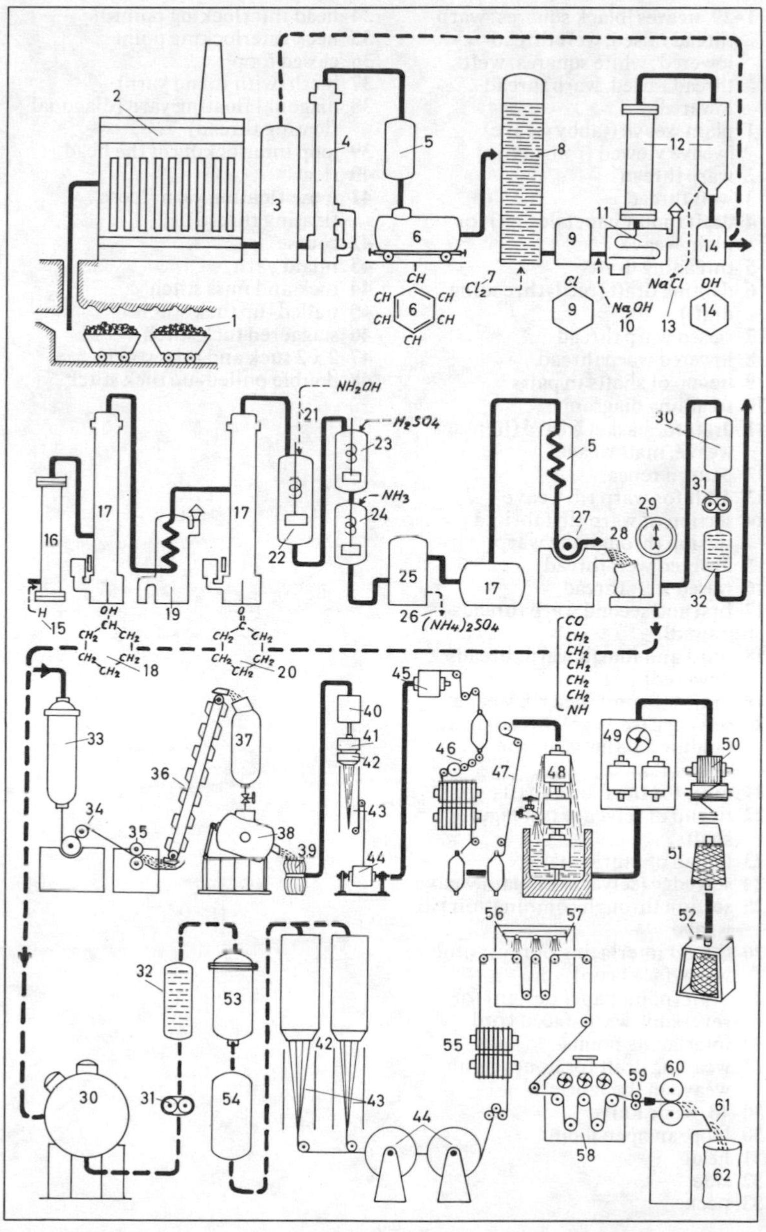
CH
Cl_2
Cl
NaOH
NaCl
OH
NH_2OH
H_2SO_4
NH_3
H
OH
CH_2 CH CH_2
CH_2 CH_2 CH_2
O
CH_2 C CH_2
CH_2 CH_2 CH_2
$(NH_4)_2SO_4$
CO
CH_2
CH_2
CH_2
CH_2
CH_2
NH

171 Weaves and Knits

1–29 weaves [black squares: warp thread raised, weft thread lowered; white squares: weft thread raised, warp thread lowered]

1 plain weave (tabby weave) [weave viewed from above]
2 warp thread
3 weft thread
4 draft (point paper design) for plain weave
5 threading draft
6 denting draft (reed-threading draft)
7 raised warp thread
8 lowered warp thread
9 tie-up of shafts in pairs
10 treadling diagram
11 draft for basket weave (hopsack weave, matt weave)
12 pattern repeat
13 draft for warp rib weave
14 section of warp rib fabric, a section through the warp
15 lowered weft thread
16 raised weft thread
17 first and second warp threads [raised]
18 third and fourth warp threads [lowered]
19 draft for combined rib weave
20 selvedge (selvage) thread draft (additional shafts for the selvedge)
21 draft for the fabric shafts
22 tie-up of selvedge (selvage) shafts
23 tie-up of fabric shafts
24 selvedge (selvage) in plain weave
25 section through combination rib weave
26 thread interlacing of reversible warp-faced cord
27 draft (point paper design) for reversible warp-faced cord
28 interlacing points
29 weaving draft for honeycomb weave in the fabric

30–48 basic knits

30 loop, an open loop
31 head
32 side
33 neck
34 head interlocking point
35 neck interlocking point
36 closed loop
37 mesh [with inlaid yarn]
38 diagonal floating yarn (diagonal floating thread)
39 loop interlocking at the head
40 float
41 loose floating yarn (loose floating thread)
42 course
43 inlaid yarn
44 tuck and miss stitch
45 pulled-up tuck stitch
46 staggered tuck stitch
47 2 x 2 tuck and miss stitch
48 double pulled-up tuck stitch

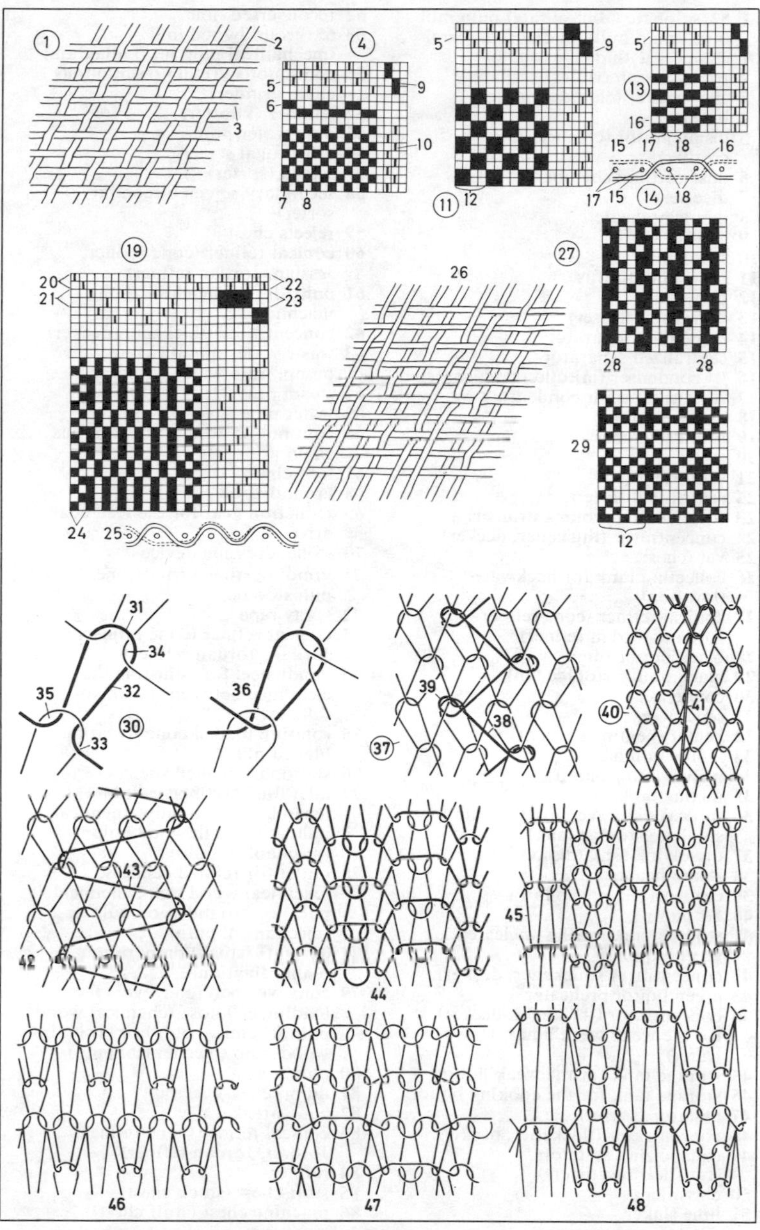
1
2
3
4
5
6
9
10
7
8
5
9
11
12
5
13
16
15
17
18
16
17
15
14
18
19
20
21
22
23
24
25
26
27
28
28
29
12
31
34
35
32
30
33
36
39
38
37
40
41
43
42
44
45
46
47
48

1-52 sulphate (*Am.* sulfate) pulp mill (kraft pulp mill) [in diagram form]
1 chippers with dust extractor
2 rotary screen (riffler)
3 chip packer (chip distributor)
4 blower
5 disintegrator (crusher, chip crusher)
6 dust-settling chamber
7 digester
8 liquor preheater
9 control tap
10 swing pipe
11 blow tank (diffuser)
12 blow valve
13 blow pit (diffuser)
14 turpentine separator
15 centralized separator
16 jet condenser (injection condenser)
17 storage tank for condensate
18 hot water tank
19 heat exchanger
20 filter
21 presorter
22 centrifugal screen
23 rotary sorter (rotary strainer)
24 concentrator (thickener, decker)
25 vat (chest)
26 collecting tank for backwater (low box)
27 conical refiner (cone refiner, Jordan, Jordan refiner)
28 black liquor filter
29 black liquor storage tank
30 condenser
31 separators
32 heater (heating element)
33 liquor pump
34 heavy liquor pump
35 mixing tank
36 salt cake storage tank (sodium sulphate storage tank)
37 dissolving tank (dissolver)
38 steam heater
39 electrostatic precipitator
40 air pump
41 storage tank for the uncleared green liquor
42 concentrator (thickener, decker)
43 green liquor preheater
44 concentrator (thickener, decker) for the weak wash liquor (wash water)
45 storage tank for the weak liquor
46 storage tank for the cooking liquor
47 agitator (stirrer)
48 concentrator (thickener, decker)
49 causticizing agitators (causticizing stirrers)
50 classifier
51 lime slaker
52 reconverted lime
53-65 groundwood mill (mechanical pulp mill) [diagram]
53 continuous grinder (continuous chain grinder)
54 strainer (knotter)
55 pulp water pump
56 centrifugal screen
57 screen (sorter)
58 secondary screen (secondary sorter)
59 rejects chest
60 conical refiner (cone refiner, Jordan, Jordan refiner)
61 pulp-drying machine (pulp machine)
62 concentrator (thickener, decker)
63 waste water pump (white water pump, pulp water pump)
64 steam pipe
65 water pipe
66 continuous grinder (continuous chain grinder)
67 feed chain
68 groundwood
69 reduction gear for the feed chain drive
70 stone-dressing device
71 grinding stone (grindstone, pulpstone)
72 spray pipe
73 conical refiner (cone refiner, Jordan, Jordan refiner)
74 handwheel for adjusting the clearance between the knives (blades)
75 rotating bladed cone (rotating bladed plug)
76 stationary bladed shell
77 inlet for unrefined cellulose (chemical wood pulp, chemical pulp) or groundwood pulp (mechanical pulp)
78 outlet for refined cellulose (chemical wood pulp, chemical pulp) or groundwood pulp (mechanical pulp)
79-86 stuff (stock) preparation plant [diagram]
79 conveyor belt (conveyor) for loading cellulose (chemical wood pulp, chemical pulp) or groundwood pulp (mechanical pulp)
80 pulper
81 dump chest
82 cone breaker
83 conical refiner (cone refiner, Jordan, Jordan refiner)
84 refiner
85 stuff chest (stock chest)
86 machine chest (stuff chest)

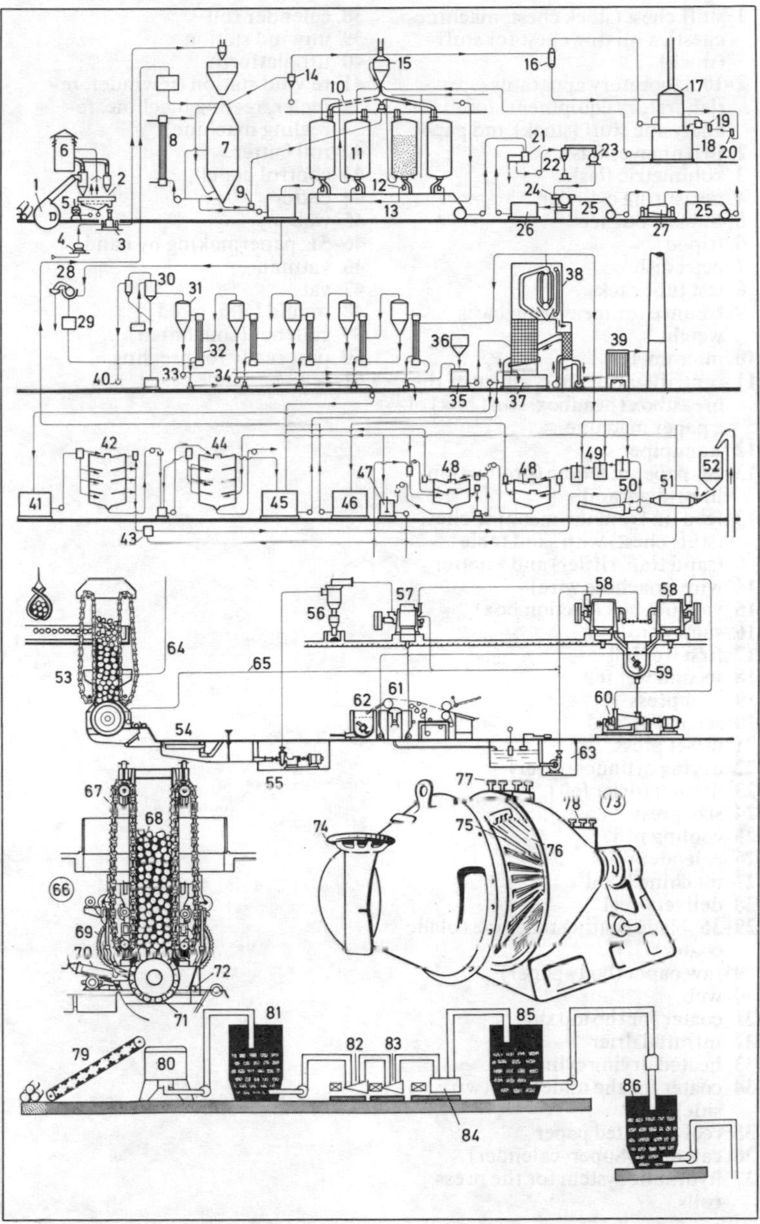
1
2
3
4
5
6
7
8
9
10
11
12
13
14
15
16
17
18
19
20
21
22
23
24
25
26
27
28
29
30
31
32
33
34
35
36
37
38
39
40
41
42
43
44
45
46
47
48
49
50
51
52
53
54
55
56
57
58
59
60
61
62
63
64
65
66
67
68
69
70
71
72
73
74
75
76
77
78
79
80
81
82
83
84
85
86

173 Papermaking II

1 stuff chest (stock chest, machine chest), a mixing chest for stuff (stock)
2–10 laboratory apparatus (laboratory equipment) for analysing stuff (stock) and paper
2 Erlenmeyer flask
3 volumetric flask
4 measuring cylinder
5 Bunsen burner
6 tripod
7 petri dish
8 test tube rack
9 balance for measuring basis weight
10 micrometer
11 centrifugal cleaners ahead of the breastbox (headbox, stuff box) of a paper machine
12 standpipe
13–28 paper machine (production line) [diagram]
13 feed-in from the machine chest (stuff chest) with sand table (sand trap, riffler) and knotter
14 wire (machine wire)
15 vacuum box (suction box)
16 suction roll
17 first wet felt
18 second wet felt
19 first press
20 second press
21 offset press
22 drying cylinder (drier)
23 dry felt (drier felt)
24 size press
25 cooling roll
26 calender rolls
27 machine hood
28 delivery reel
29–35 blade coating machine (blade coater)
29 raw paper (body paper)
30 web
31 coater for the top side
32 infrared drier
33 heated drying cylinder
34 coater for the underside (wire side)
35 reel of coated paper
36 calender (Super-calender)
37 hydraulic system for the press rolls
38 calender roll
39 unwind station
40 lift platform
41 rewind station (rewinder, re-reeler, reeling machine, re-reeling machine)
42 roll cutter
43 control panel
44 cutter
45 web
46–51 papermaking by hand
46 vatman
47 vat
48 mould (*Am.* mold)
49 coucher (couchman)
50 post ready for pressing
51 felt

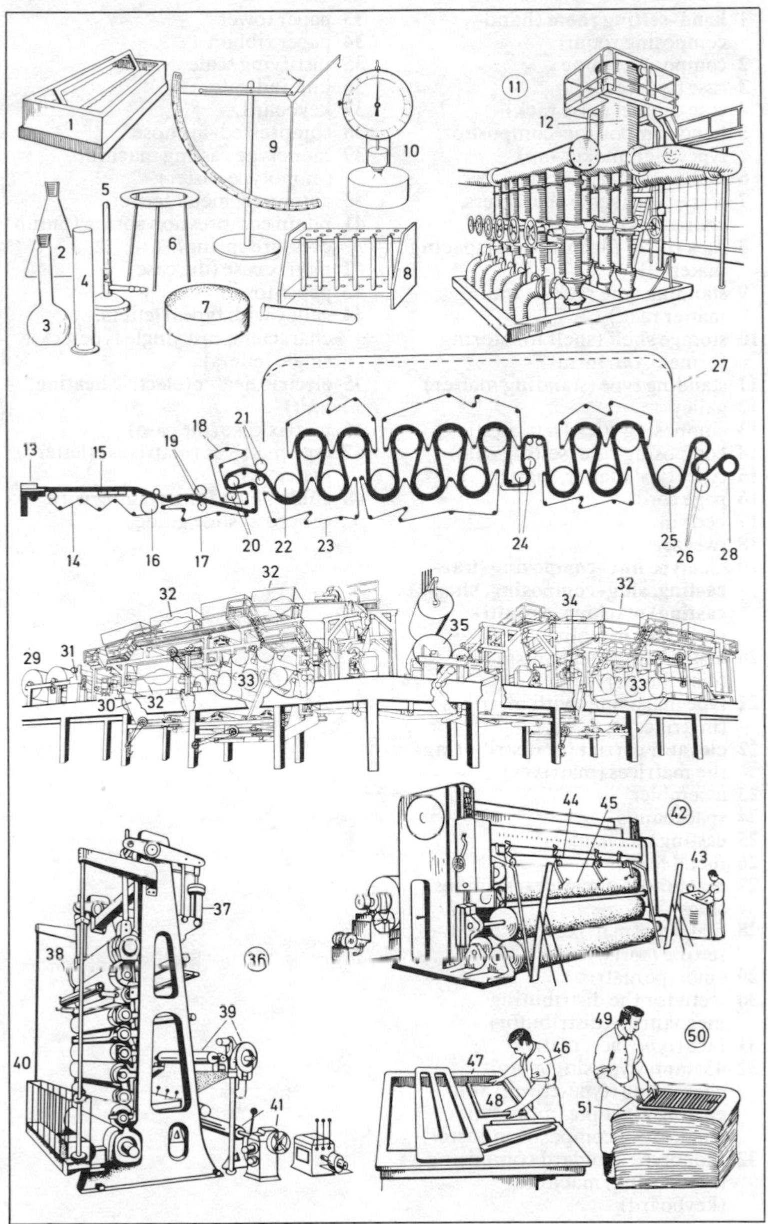
1
2
3
4
5
6
7
8
9
10
11
12
13
14
15
16
17
18
19
20
21
22
23
24
25
26
27
28
29
30
31
32
33
34
35
36
37
38
39
40
41
42
43
44
45
46
47
48
49
50
51

1 **hand-setting room** (hand-composing room)
2 composing frame
3 case (typecase)
4 case cabinet (case rack)
5 hand compositor (compositor, typesetter, maker-up)
6 manuscript (typescript)
7 sorts, types (type characters, characters)
8 rack (case) for furniture (spacing material)
9 standing type rack (standing matter rack)
10 storage shelf (shelf for storing formes, *Am.* forms)
11 standing type (standing matter)
12 galley
13 composing stick (setting stick)
14 composing rule (setting rule)
15 type (type matter, matter)
16 page cord
17 bodkin
18 tweezers
19 **Linotype line-composing (line-casting, slug-composing, slug-casting) machine, a multi-magazine machine**
20 distributing mechanism (distributor)
21 type magazines with matrices (matrixes)
22 elevator carrier for distributing the matrices (matrixes)
23 assembler
24 spacebands
25 casting mechanism
26 metal feeder
27 machine-set matter (cast lines, slugs)
28 matrices (matrixes) for hand-setting (sorts)
29 Linotype matrix
30 teeth for the distributing mechanism (distributor)
31 face (type face, matrix)
32-45 **monotype single-unit composing** (typesetting) **and casting machine** (monotype single-unit composition caster)
32 monotype standard composing (typesetting) machine (keyboard)
33 paper tower
34 paper ribbon
35 justifying scale
36 unit indicator
37 keyboard
38 compressed-air hose
39 monotype casting machine (monotype caster)
40 automatic metal feeder
41 pump compression spring (pump pressure spring)
42 matrix case (die case)
43 paper tower
44 galley with types (letters, characters, cast single types, cast single letters)
45 electric heater (electric heating unit)
46 matrix case (die case)
47 type matrices (matrixes) (letter matrices)
48 guide block for engaging with the cross-slide guide

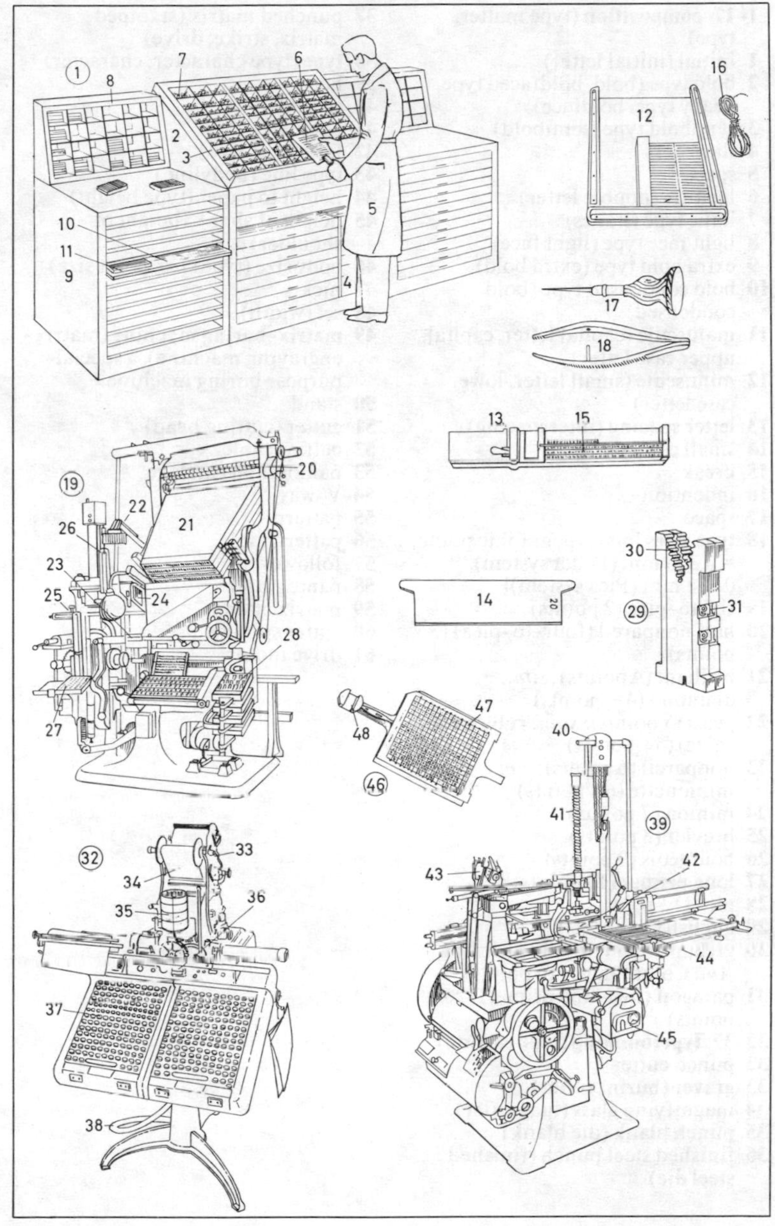
1
2
3
4
5
6
7
8
9
10
11
12
13
14
15
16
17
18
19
20
21
22
23
24
25
26
27
28
29
30
31
32
33
34
35
36
37
38
39
40
41
42
43
44
45
46
47
48

175 Composing Room (Case Room) II

1–17 composition (type matter, type)
1 initial (initial letter)
2 bold type (bold, boldfaced type, heavy type, boldface)
3 semibold type (semibold)
4 line
5 space
6 ligature (double letter)
7 italic type (italics)
8 light face type (light face)
9 extra bold type (extra bold)
10 bold condensed type (bold condensed)
11 majuscule (capital letter, capital, upper case letter)
12 minuscule (small letter, lower case letter)
13 letter spacing (interspacing)
14 small capitals
15 break
16 indention
17 space
18 type sizes [one typographic point = 0.376 mm (Didot system), 0.351 mm (Pica system)]
19 six-to-pica (2 points)
20 half nonpareil (four-to-pica) (3 points)
21 brilliant (4 points); *sim.:* diamond ($4\frac{1}{2}$ points)
22 pearl (5 points); *sim.:* ruby (*Am.* agate) ($5\frac{1}{2}$ points)
23 nonpareil (6 points); *sim.:* minionette ($6\frac{1}{2}$ points)
24 minion (7 points)
25 brevier (8 points)
26 bourgeois (9 points)
27 long primer (10 points)
28 pica (12 points)
29 english (14 points)
30 great primer (two-line brevier, *Am.* Columbian) (16 points)
31 paragon (two-line primer) (20 points)
32–37 typefounding (type casting)
32 punch cutter
33 graver (burin, cutter)
34 magnifying glass (magnifier)
35 punch blank (die blank)
36 finished steel punch (finished steel die)
37 punched matrix (stamped matrix, strike, drive)
38 type (type character, character)
39 head
40 shoulder
41 counter
42 face (type face)
43 type line (bodyline)
44 height to paper (type height)
45 height of shank (height of shoulder)
46 body size (type size, point size)
47 nick
48 set (width)
49 matrix-boring machine (matrix-engraving machine), a special-purpose boring machine
50 stand
51 cutter (cutting head)
52 cutting table
53 pantograph carriage
54 V-way
55 pattern
56 pattern table
57 follower
58 pantograph
59 matrix clamp
60 cutter spindle
61 drive motor

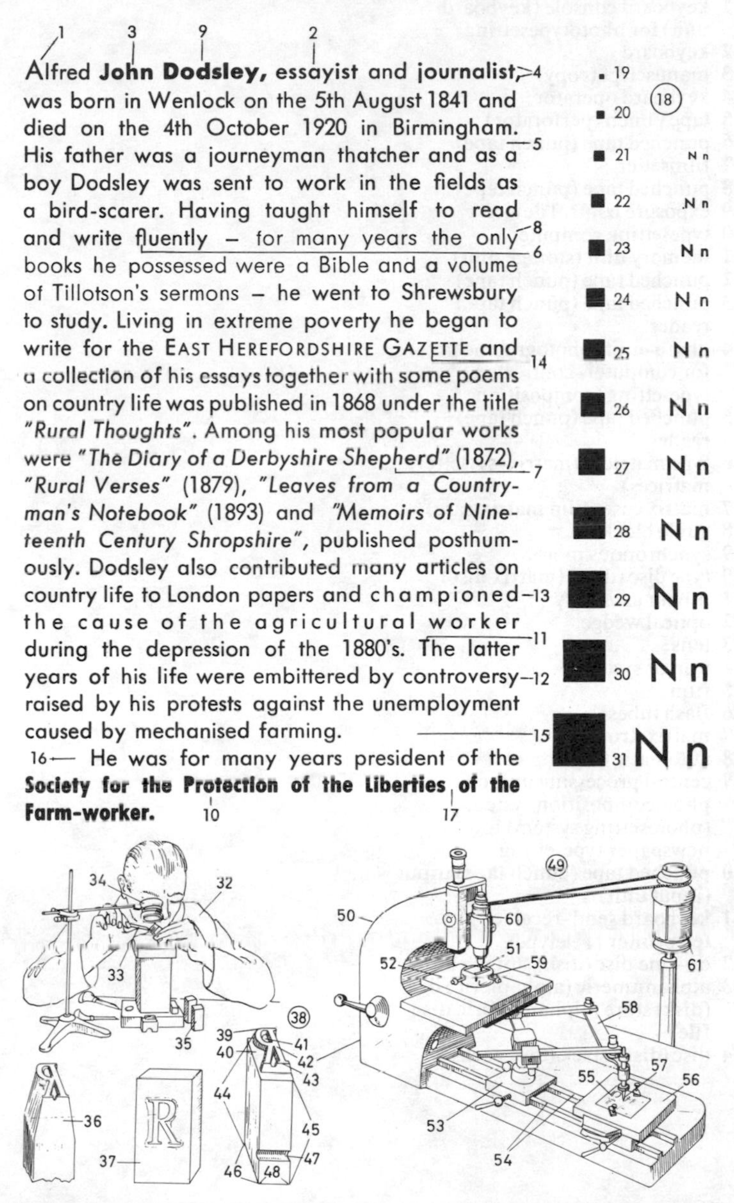
Alfred John Dodsley, essayist and journalist, was born in Wenlock on the 5th August 1841 and died on the 4th October 1920 in Birmingham. His father was a journeyman thatcher and as a boy Dodsley was sent to work in the fields as a bird-scarer. Having taught himself to read and write fluently – for many years the only books he possessed were a Bible and a volume of Tillotson's sermons – he went to Shrewsbury to study. Living in extreme poverty he began to write for the EAST HEREFORDSHIRE GAZETTE and a collection of his essays together with some poems on country life was published in 1868 under the title "Rural Thoughts". Among his most popular works were "The Diary of a Derbyshire Shepherd" (1872), "Rural Verses" (1879), "Leaves from a Countryman's Notebook" (1893) and "Memoirs of Nineteenth Century Shropshire", published posthumously. Dodsley also contributed many articles on country life to London papers and championed the cause of the agricultural worker during the depression of the 1880's. The latter years of his life were embittered by controversy raised by his protests against the unemployment caused by mechanised farming.
He was for many years president of the Society for the Protection of the Liberties of the Farm-worker.
Nn

176 Composing Room (Case Room) III (Phototypesetting, Photocomposition, Photosetting, Filmsetting)

1 keyboard console (keyboard unit) for phototypesetting
2 keyboard
3 manuscript (copy)
4 keyboard operator
5 tape punch (perforator)
6 punched tape (punch tape)
7 filmsetter
8 punched tape (punch tape)
9 exposure control device
10 typesetting computer
11 memory unit (storage unit)
12 punched tape (punch tape)
13 punched tape (punch tape) reader
14 photo-unit (photographic unit) for computer-controlled typesetting (composition)
15 punched tape (punch tape) reader
16 type matrices (matrixes) (letter matrices)
17 matrix case (film matrix case)
18 guide block
19 synchronous motor
20 type disc (disk) (matrix disc)
21 mirror assembly
22 optical wedge
23 lens
24 mirror system
25 film
26 flash tubes
27 matrix drum
28 automatic film copier
29 central processing unit of a photocomposition system (photosetting system) for newspaper typesetting
30 punched tape (punch tape) input (input unit)
31 keyboard send-receive teleprinter (Teletype)
32 on-line disc (disk) storage unit
33 alphanumeric (alphameric) disc (disk) store (alphanumeric disc file)
34 disc (disk) stack (disc pack)

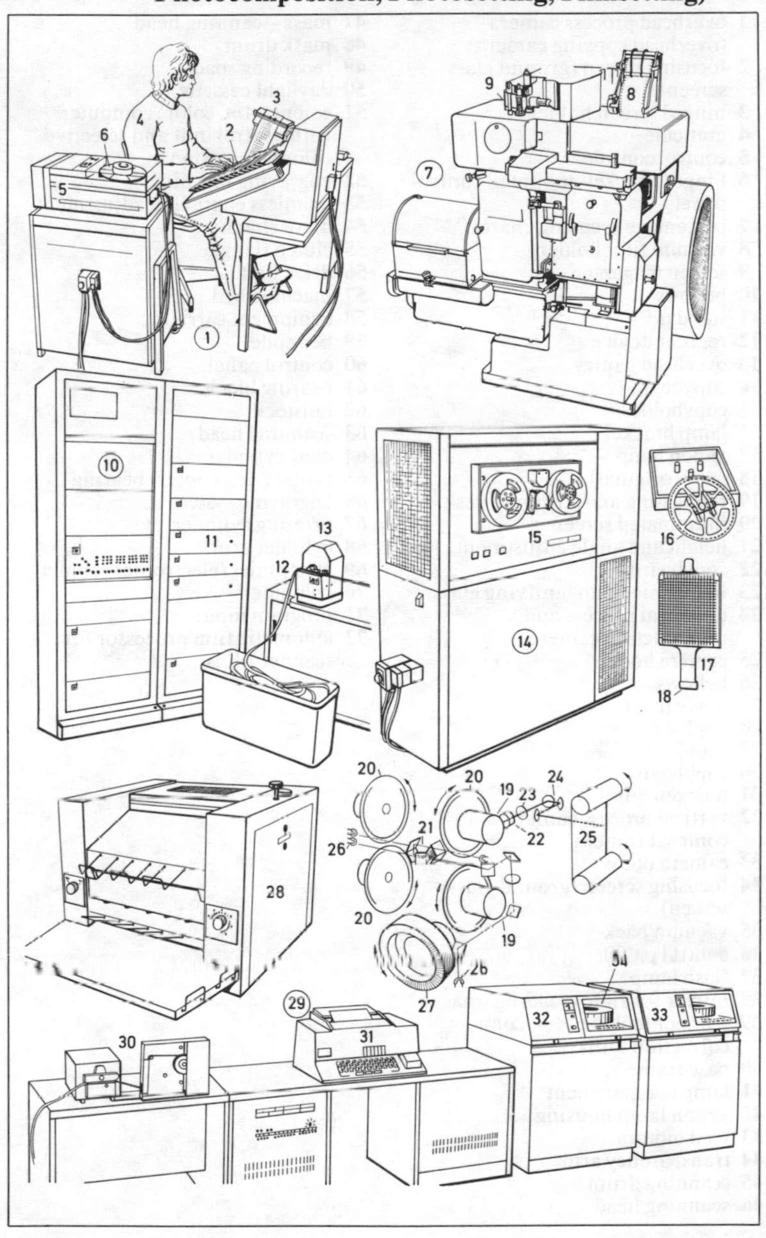
1
2
3
4
5
6
7
8
9
10
11
12
13
14
15
16
17
18
19
20
21
22
23
24
25
26
27
28
29
30
31
32
33
34

177 Photomechanical Reproduction

1 overhead process camera (overhead copying camera)
2 focusing screen (ground glass screen)
3 hinged screen holder
4 graticule
5 control console
6 hinged bracket-mounted control panel
7 percentage focusing charts
8 vacuum film holder
9 screen magazine
10 bellows
11 standard
12 register device
13 overhead gantry
14 copyboard
15 copyholder
16 lamp bracket
17 xenon lamp
18 copy (original)
19 retouching and stripping desk
20 illuminated screen
21 height and angle adjustment
22 copyboard
23 linen tester, a magnifying glass
24 universal process and reproduction camera
25 camera body
26 bellows
27 lens carrier
28 angled mirror
29 stand
30 copyboard
31 halogen lamp
32 vertical process camera, a compact camera
33 camera body
34 focusing screen (ground glass screen)
35 vacuum back
36 control panel
37 flash lamp
38 mirror for right-reading images
39 scanner (colour, *Am.* color, correction unit)
40 base frame
41 lamp compartment
42 xenon lamp housing
43 feed motors
44 transparency arm
45 scanning drum
46 scanning head
47 mask-scanning head
48 mask drum
49 recording spacc
50 daylight cassette
51 colour (*Am.* color) computer with control unit and selective colour correction
52 engraving machine
53 seamless engraving adjustment
54 drive clutch
55 clutch flange
56 drive unit
57 machine bed
58 equipment carrier
59 bed slide
60 control panel
61 bearing block
62 tailstock
63 scanning head
64 copy cylinder
65 centre (*Am.* center) bearing
66 engraving system
67 printing cylinder
68 cylinder arm
69 electronics (electronic) cabinet
70 computers
71 program input
72 automatic film processor for scanner films

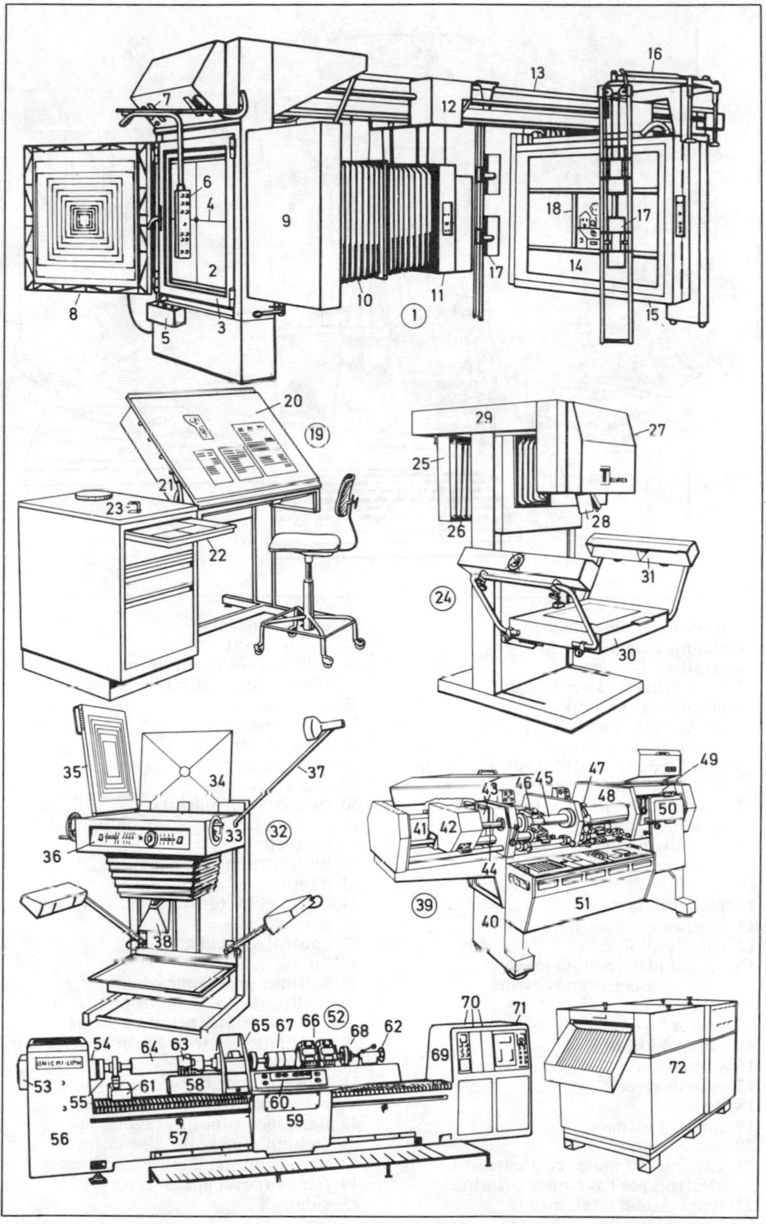
1
2
3
4
5
6
7
8
9
10
11
12
13
14
15
16
17
18
17
19
20
21
22
23
24
25
26
27
28
29
30
31
32
33
34
35
36
37
38
39
40
41
42
43
44
45
46
47
48
49
50
51
52
53
54
55
56
57
58
59
60
61
62
63
64
65
66
67
68
69
70
71
72

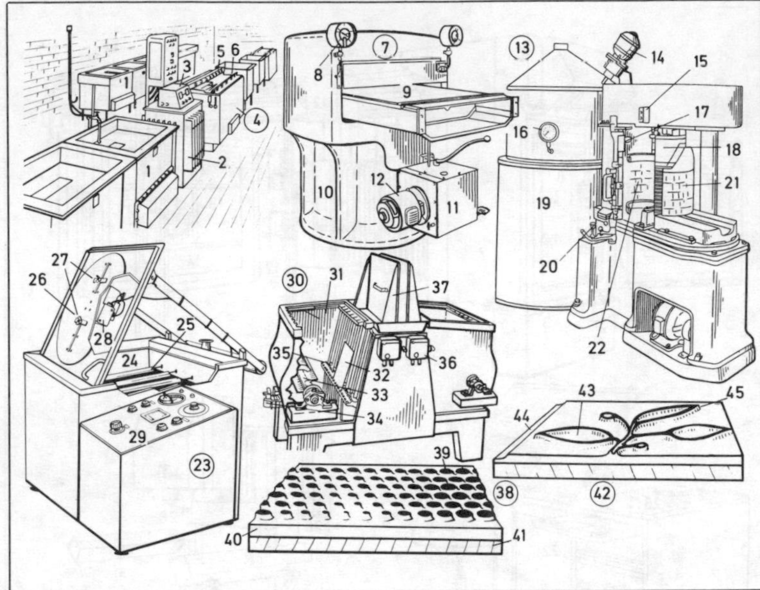

1-6 electrotyping plant
1 cleaning tank
2 rectifier
3 measuring and control unit
4 electroplating tank (electroplating bath, electroplating vat)
5 anode rod (copper anodes)
6 plate rod (cathode)
7 hydraulic moulding (*Am.* molding) press
8 pressure gauge (*Am.* gage) (manometer)
9 apron
10 round base
11 hydraulic pressure pump
12 drive motor
13 curved plate casting machine (curved electrotype casting machine)
14 motor
15 control knobs
16 pyrometer
17 mouth piece
18 core
19 melting furnace
20 starting lever
21 cast curved plate (cast curved electrotype) for rotary printing
22 fixed mould (*Am.* mold)
23 etching machine
24 etching tank with etching solution (etchant, mordant) and filming agent (film former)
25 paddles
26 turntable
27 plate clamp
28 drive motor
29 control unit
30 twin etching machine
31 etching tank (etching bath) [in section]
32 photoprinted zinc plate
33 paddle
34 outlet cock (drain cock, *Am.* faucet)
35 plate rack
36 control switches
37 lid
38 halftone photoengraving (halftone block, halftone plate), a block (plate, printing plate)
39 dot (halftone dot), a printing element
40 etched zinc plate
41 block mount (block mounting, plate mount, plate mounting)
42 line block (line engraving, line etching, line plate, line cut)
43 non-printing, deep-etched areas
44 flange (bevel edge)
45 sidewall

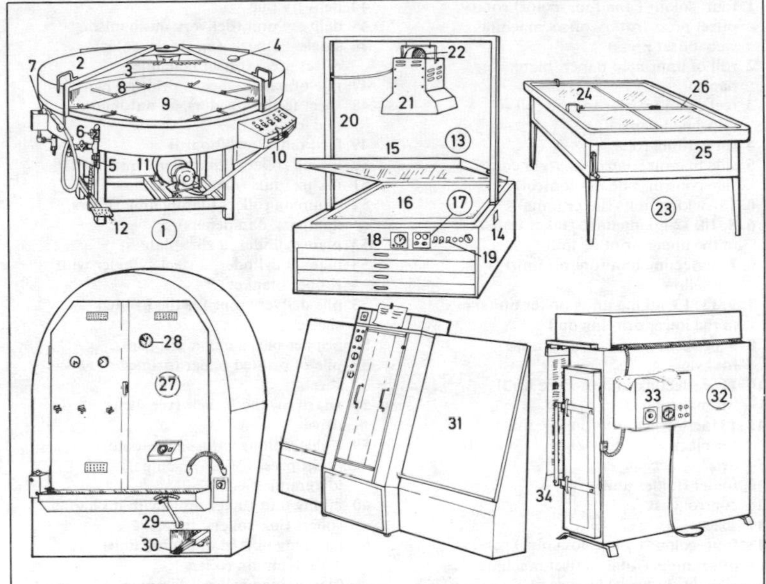

1 plate whirler (whirler, plate-coating machine) for coating offset plates
2 sliding lid
3 electric heater
4 temperature gauge (*Am.* gage)
5 water connection for the spray unit
6 spray unit
7 hand spray
8 plate clamps
9 zinc plate (*also:* magnesium plate, copper plate)
10 control panel
11 drive motor
12 brake pedal
13 vacuum printing frame (vacuum frame, printing-down frame)
14 base of the vacuum printing frame (vacuum frame, printing-down frame)
15 plate glass frame
16 coated offset plate
17 control panel
18 exposure timer
19 vacuum pump switch
20 support
21 point light exposure lamp, a quartz-halogen lamp
22 fan blower
23 stripping table (make-up table) for stripping films
24 crystal glass screen
25 light box
26 straightedge rules
27 vertical plate-drying cabinet
28 hygrometer
29 speed control
30 brake pedal
31 processing machine for presensitized plates
32 burning-in oven for glue-enamel plates (diazo plates)
33 control box (control unit)
34 diazo plate

1 four-colour (*Am.* four-color) rotary offset press (rotary offset machine, web-offset press)
2 roll of unprinted paper (blank paper)
3 reel stand (carrier for the roll of unprinted paper)
4 forwarding rolls
5 side margin control (margin control, side control, side lay control)
6-13 inking units (inker units)
6, 8, 10, 12 inking units (inker units) in the upper printing unit
6-7 perfecting unit (double unit) for yellow
7, 9, 11, 13 inking units (inker units) in the lower printing unit
8-9 perfecting unit (double unit) for cyan
10-11 perfecting unit (double unit) for magenta
12-13 perfecting unit (double unit) for black
14 drier
15 folder (folder unit)
16 control desk
17 sheet
18 four-colour (*Am.* four-color) rotary offset press (rotary offset machine, web-offset press) [diagram]
19 reel stand
20 side margin control (margin control, side control, side lay control)
21 inking rollers (ink rollers, inkers)
22 ink duct (ink fountain)
23 damping rollers (dampening rollers, dampers, dampeners)
24 blanket cylinder
25 plate cylinder
26 route of the paper (of the web)
27 drier
28 chilling rolls (cooling rollers, chill rollers)
29 folder (folder unit)
30 four-colour (*Am.* four-color) sheet-fed offset machine (offset press) [diagram]
31 sheet feeder (feeder)
32 feed table (feed board)
33 route of the sheets through swing-grippers to the feed drum
34 feed drum
35 impression cylinder
36 transfer drums (transfer cylinders)
37 blanket cylinder
38 plate cylinder
39 damping unit (dampening unit)
40 inking units (inker units)
41 printing unit
42 delivery cylinder
43 chain delivery
44 delivery pile
45 delivery unit (delivery mechanism)
46 single-colour (*Am.* single-color) offset press (offset machine)
47 pile of paper (sheets, printing paper)
48 sheet feeder (feeder), an automatic pile feeder
49 feed table (feed board)
50 inking rollers (ink rollers, inkers)
51 inking units (inker units)
52 damping rollers (dampening rollers, dampers, dampeners)
53 plate cylinder, a zinc plate
54 blanket cylinder, a steel cylinder with rubber blanket
55 pile delivery unit for the printed sheets
56 gripper bar, a chain gripper
57 pile of printed paper (printed sheets)
58 guard for the V-belt (vee-belt) drive
59 single-colour (*Am.* single-color) offset press (offset machine) [diagram]
60 inking unit (inker unit) with inking rollers (ink rollers, inkers)
61 damping unit (dampening unit) with damping rollers (dampening rollers, dampers, dampeners)
62 plate cylinder
63 blanket cylinder
64 impression cylinder
65 delivery cylinders with grippers
66 drive wheel
67 feed table (feed board)
68 sheet feeder (feeder)
69 pile of unprinted paper (blank paper, unprinted sheets, blank sheets)
70 small sheet-fed offset press
71 inking unit (inker unit)
72 suction feeder
73 pile feeder
74 instrument panel (control panel) with counter, pressure gauge (*Am.* gage), air regulator, and control switch for the sheet feeder (feeder)
75 flat-bed offset press (offset machine) ('Mailänder' proofing press, proof press)
76 inking unit (inker unit)
77 inking rollers (ink rollers, inkers)
78 bed (press bed, type bed, forme bed, *Am.* form bed)
79 cylinder with rubber blanket
80 starting and stopping lever for the printing unit
81 impression-setting wheel (impression-adjusting wheel)

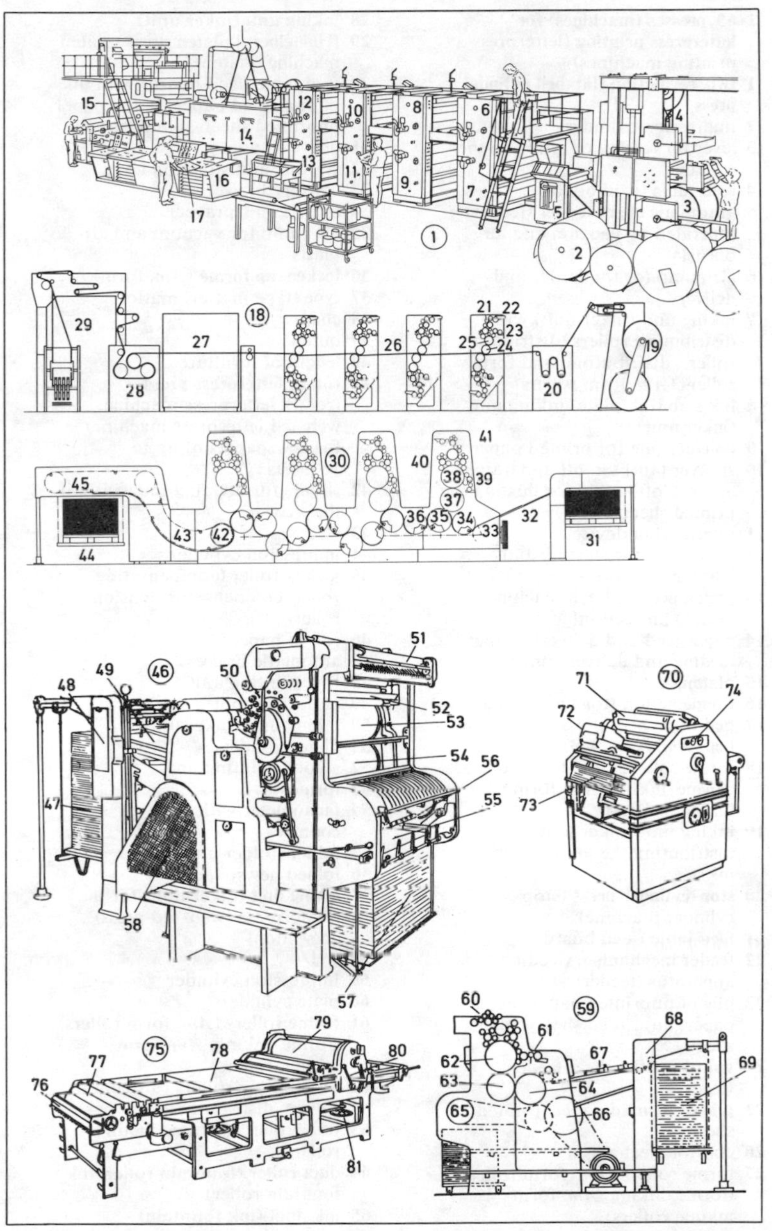
15
12
10
8
6
4
14
13
11
9
7
16
17
5
3
1
2
29
18
21 22
23
27
26
25
24
19
28
20
41
30
40
38
39
45
37
36
35
34
32
33
43
42
31
44
51
49
46
50
48
52
53
54
56
70
71
74
72
47
55
73
58
57
60
59
61
68
79
75
67
77
80
62
69
76
78
63
64
65
66
81

181 Letterpress Printing

1-65 presses (machines) for letterpress printing (letterpress printing machines)
1 **two-revolution flat-bed cylinder press**
2 impression cylinder
3 lever for raising or lowering the cylinder
4 feed table (feed board)
5 automatic sheet feeder (feeder) [operated by vacuum and air blasts]
6 air pump for the feeder and delivery
7 inking unit (inker unit) with distributing rollers (distributor rollers, distributors) and forme rollers (*Am.* form rollers)
8 ink slab (ink plate) inking unit (inker unit)
9 delivery pile for printed paper
10 sprayer (anti set-off apparatus, anti set-off spray) for dusting the printed sheets
11 interleaving device
12 foot pedal for starting and stopping the press
13 **platen press** (platen machine, platen) [in section]
14 paper feed and delivery (paper feeding and delivery unit)
15 platen
16 toggle action (toggle-joint action)
17 bed (type bed, press bed, forme bed, *Am.* form bed)
18 forme rollers (*Am.* form rollers) (forme-inking, *Am.* form-inking, rollers)
19 inking unit (inker unit) for distributing the ink (printing ink)
20 **stop-cylinder press** (stop-cylinder machine)
21 feed table (feed board)
22 feeder mechanism (feeding apparatus, feeder)
23 pile of unprinted paper (blank paper, unprinted sheets, blank sheets)
24 guard for the sheet feeder (feeder)
25 pile of printed paper (printed sheets)
26 control mechanism
27 forme rollers (*Am.* form rollers) (forme-inking, *Am.* form-inking, rollers)
28 inking unit (inker unit)
29 **[Heidelberg] platen press** (platen machine, platen)
30 feed table (feed board) with pile of unprinted paper (blank paper, unprinted sheets, blank sheets)
31 delivery table
32 starting and stopping lever
33 delivery blower
34 spray gun (sprayer)
35 air pump for vacuum and air blasts
36 **locked-up forme** (*Am.* form)
37 type (type matter, matter)
38 chase
39 quoin
40 length of furniture
41 **rotary letterpress press** (rotary letterpress machine, web-fed letterpress machine) for newspapers of up to 16 pages
42 slitters for dividing the width of the web
43 web
44 impression cylinder
45 jockey roller (compensating roller, compensator, tension roller)
46 roll of paper
47 automatic brake
48 first printing unit
49 perfecting unit
50 inking unit (inker unit)
51 plate cylinder
52 second printing unit
53 former
54 tachometer with sheet counter
55 folder (folder unit)
56 folded newspaper
57 **inking unit** (inker unit) for the rotary press (web-fed press) [in section]
58 web
59 impression cylinder
60 plate cylinder
61 forme rollers (*Am.* form rollers) (forme-inking, *Am.* form-inking, rollers)
62 distributing rollers (distributor rollers, distributors)
63 lifter roller (ductor, ductor roller)
64 duct roller (fountain roller, ink fountain roller)
65 ink duct (ink fountain)

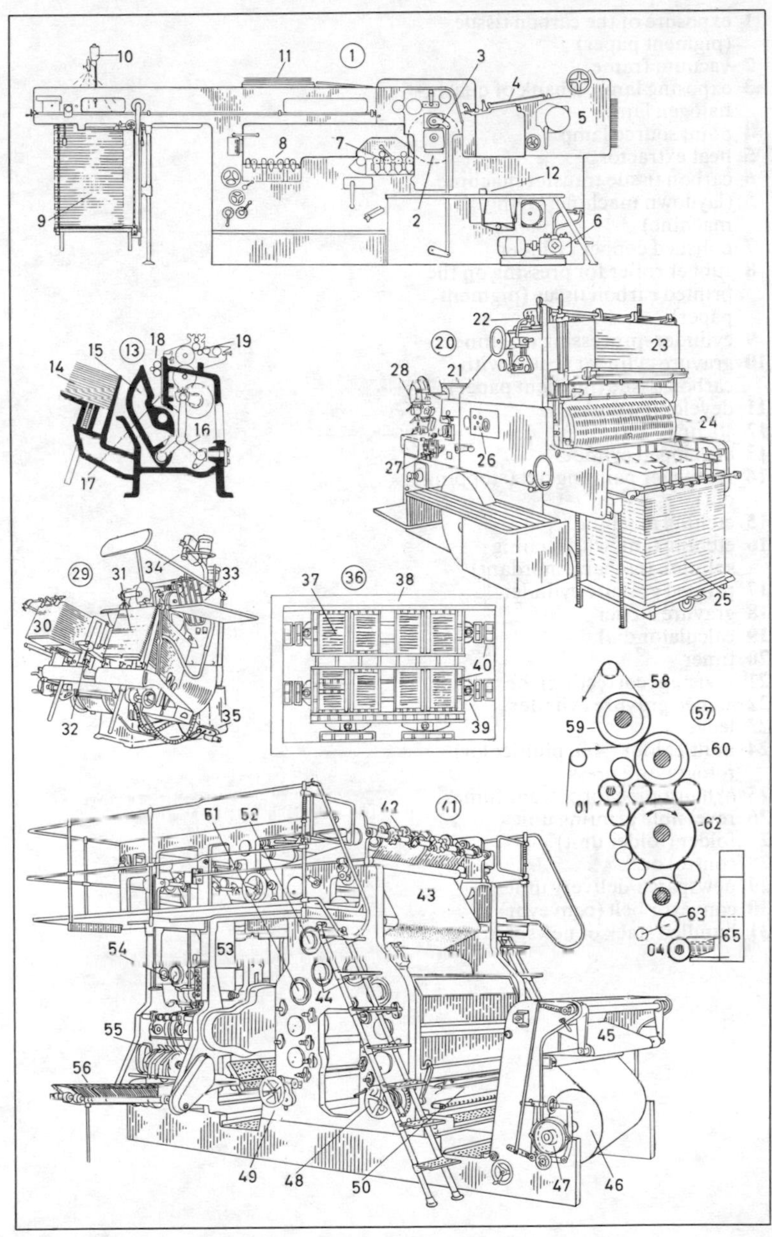

1
2
3
4
5
6
7
8
9
10
11
12
13
14
15
16
17
18
19
20
21
22
23
24
25
26
27
28
29
30
31
32
33
34
35
36
37
38
39
40
41
42
43
44
45
46
47
48
49
50
51
52
53
54
55
56
57
58
59
60
61
62
63
64
65

182 Photogravure (Gravure Printing, Intaglio Printing)

1 exposure of the carbon tissue (pigment paper)
2 vacuum frame
3 exposing lamp, a bank of quartz-halogen lamps
4 point source lamp
5 heat extractor
6 carbon tissue transfer machine (laydown machine, laying machine)
7 polished copper cylinder
8 rubber roller for pressing on the printed carbon tissue (pigment paper)
9 cylinder-processing machine
10 gravure cylinder coated with carbon tissue (pigment paper)
11 developing tank
12 staging
13 developed cylinder
14 retoucher painting out (stopping out)
15 etching machine
16 etching tank with etching solution (etchant, mordant)
17 printed gravure cylinder
18 gravure etcher
19 calculator dial
20 timer
21 revising (correcting) the cylinder
22 etched gravure cylinder
23 ledge
24 multicolour (*Am.* multicolor) rotogravure press
25 exhaust pipe for solvent fumes
26 reversible printing unit
27 folder (folder unit)
28 control desk
29 newspaper delivery unit
30 conveyor belt (conveyor)
31 bundled stack of newspapers

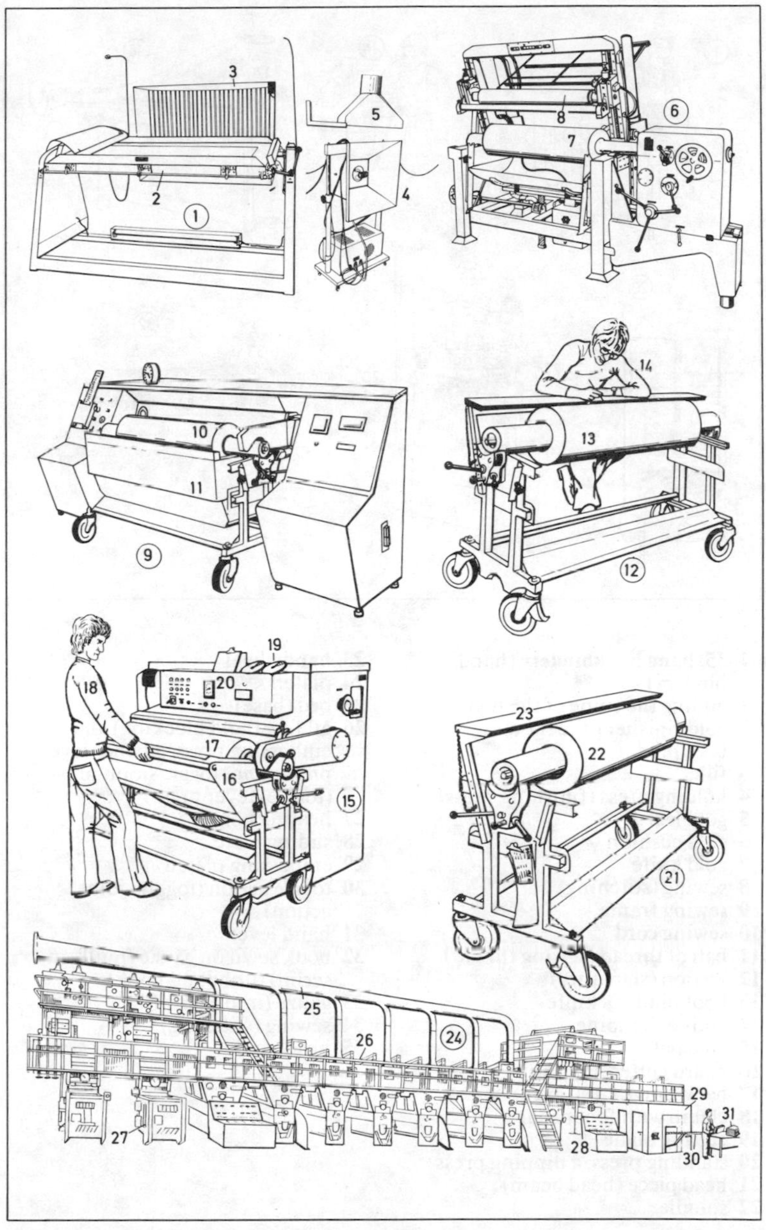
1
2
3
4
5
6
7
8
9
10
11
12
13
14
15
16
17
18
19
20
21
22
23
24
25
26
27
28
29
30
31

183 Bookbinding I

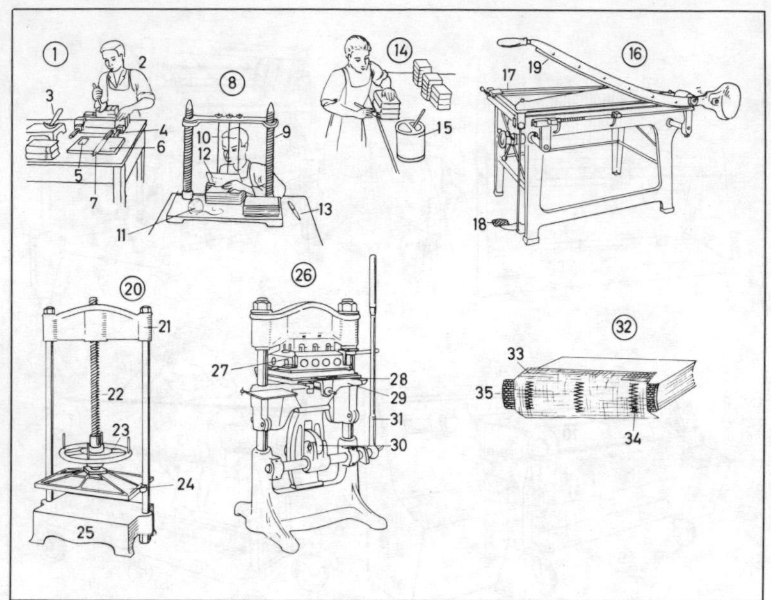

1–35 hand bookbindery (hand bindery)
1 gilding the spine of the book
2 gold finisher (gilder), a bookbinder
3 fillet
4 holding press (finishing press)
5 gold leaf
6 gold cushion
7 gold knife
8 sewing (stitching)
9 sewing frame
10 sewing cord
11 ball of thread (sewing thread)
12 section (signature)
13 bookbinder's knife
14 gluing the spine
15 glue pot
16 board cutter (guillotine)
17 back gauge (*Am.* gage)
18 clamp with foot pedal
19 cutting blade
20 standing press, a nipping press
21 head piece (head beam)
22 spindle
23 handwheel
24 platen
25 bed (base)
26 gilding (gold blocking) and embossing press, a hand-lever press; *sim.:* toggle-joint press (toggle-lever press)
27 heating box
28 sliding plate
29 embossing platen
30 toggle action (toggle-joint action)
31 hand lever
32 book sewn on gauze (mull, scrim) (unbound book)
33 gauze (mull, scrim)
34 sewing (stitching)
35 headband

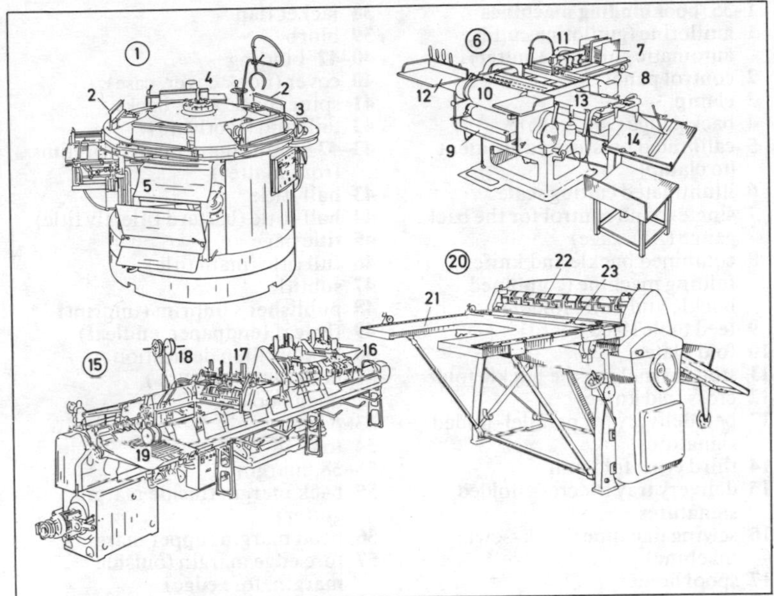

1-23 bookbinding machines
1 **adhesive binder** (perfect binder) for short runs
2 manual feed station
3 cutoff knife and roughing station
4 gluing mechanism
5 delivery (book delivery)
6 **case maker** (case-making machine)
7 board feed hopper
8 pickup sucker
9 glue tank
10 cover cylinder
11 picker head
12 feed table for covering materials [linen, paper, leather]
13 pressing mechanism
14 delivery table
15 **gang stitcher** (gathering and wire-stitching machine, gatherer and wire stitcher)
16 sheet feeder (sheet-feeding station)
17 folder-feeding station
18 stitching wire feed mechanism
19 delivery table
20 **rotary board cutter** (rotary board-cutting machine)
21 feed table with cut-out section
22 rotary cutter
23 feed guide

185 Bookbinding III

1–35 bookbinding machines
1 guillotine (guillotine cutter, automatic guillotine cutter)
2 control panel
3 clamp
4 back gauge (*Am.* gage)
5 calibrated pressure adjustment [to clamp]
6 illuminated cutting scale
7 single-hand control for the back gauge (*Am.* gage)
8 combined buckle and knife folding machine (combined buckle and knife folder)
9 feed table (feed board)
10 fold plates
11 stop for making the buckle fold
12 cross fold knives
13 belt delivery for parallel-folded signatures
14 third cross fold unit
15 delivery tray for cross-folded signatures
16 sewing machine (book-sewing machine)
17 spool holder
18 thread cop (thread spool)
19 gauze roll holder (mull roll holder, scrim roll holder)
20 gauze (mull, scrim)
21 needle cylinder with sewing needles
22 sewn book
23 delivery
24 reciprocating saddle
25 sheet feeder (feeder)
26 feed hopper
27 casing-in machine
28 joint and side pasting attachment
29 blade
30 preheater unit
31 gluing machine for whole-surface, stencil, edge, and strip gluing
32 glue tank
33 glue roller
34 feed table
35 delivery
36 book
37 dust jacket (dust cover, bookjacket, wrapper), a publisher's wrapper
38 jacket flap
39 blurb
40–42 binding
40 cover (book cover, case)
41 spine (backbone, back)
42 tailband (footband)
43–47 preliminary matter (prelims, front matter)
43 half-title
44 half-title (bastard title, fly title)
45 title page
46 full title (main title)
47 subtitle
48 publisher's imprint (imprint)
49 fly leaf (endpaper, endleaf)
50 handwritten dedication
51 bookplate (ex libris)
52 open book
53 page
54 fold
55–58 margin
55 back margin (inside margin, gutter)
56 head margin (upper margin)
57 fore edge margin (outside margin, fore edge)
58 tail margin (foot margin, tail, foot)
59 type area
60 chapter heading
61 asterisk
62 footnote
63 page number
64 double-column page
65 column
66 running title (running head)
67 caption
68 marginal note (side note)
69 signature (signature code)
70 attached bookmark (attached bookmarker)
71 loose bookmark (loose bookmarker)

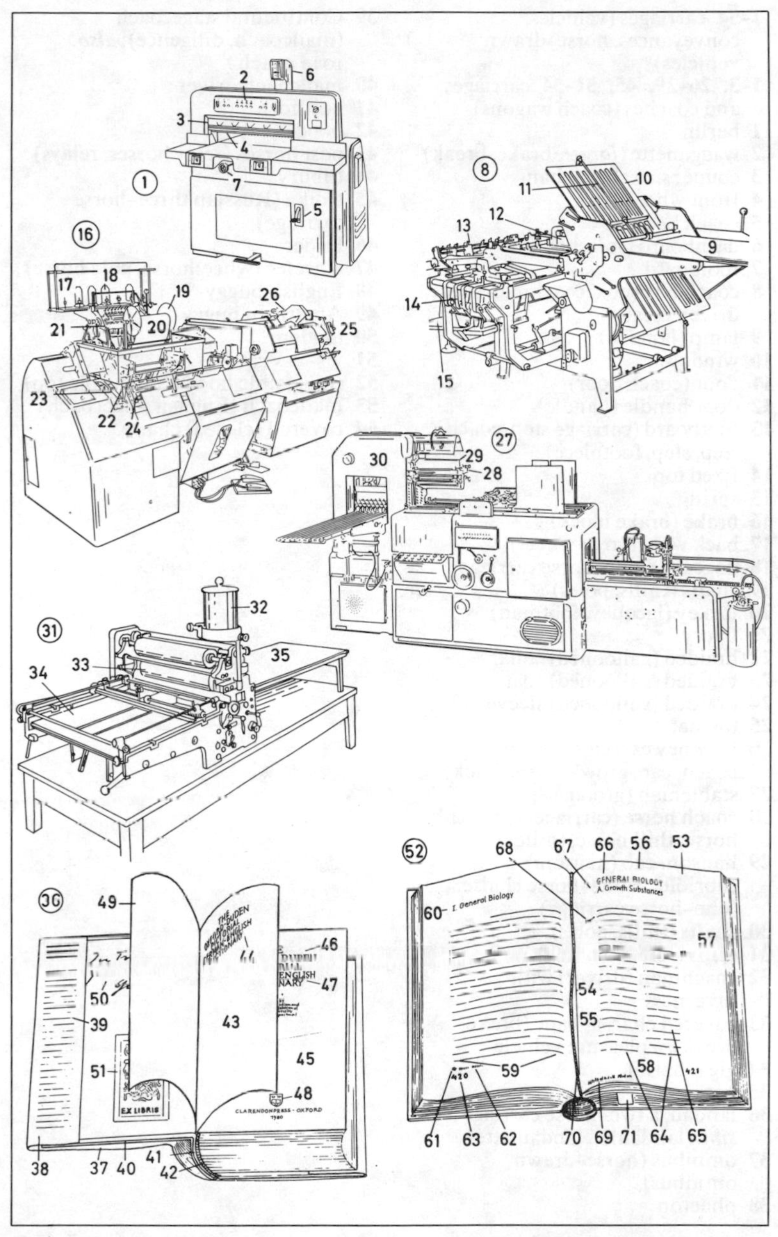
1
2
3
4
5
6
7
8
9
10
11
12
13
14
15
16
17
18
19
20
21
22
23
24
25
26
27
28
29
30
31
32
33
34
35
36
37
38
39
40
41
42
43
44
45
46
47
48
49
50
51
52
53
54
55
56
57
58
59
60
61
62
63
64
65
66
67
68
69
70
71
CLARENDON PRESS · OXFORD
EX LIBRIS
GENERAL BIOLOGY
A. Growth Substances
I. General Biology
420
421

186 Horse-drawn Carriages

1-54 carriages (vehicles, conveyances, horse-drawn vehicles)
1-3, 26-39, 45, 51-54 carriages and coaches (coach wagons)
1 berlin
2 waggonette (*larger:* brake, break)
3 coupé; *sim.:* brougham
4 front wheel
5 coach body
6 dashboard (splashboard)
7 footboard
8 coach box (box, coachman's seat, driver's seat)
9 lamp (lantern)
10 window
11 door (coach door)
12 door handle (handle)
13 footboard (carriage step, coach step, step, footpiece)
14 fixed top
15 spring
16 brake (brake block)
17 back wheel (rear wheel)
18 dogcart, a one-horse carriage
19 shafts (thills, poles)
20 lackey (lacquey, footman)
21 livery
22 braided (gallooned) collar
23 braided (gallooned) coat
24 braided (gallooned) sleeve
25 top hat
26 hackney carriage (hackney coach, cab, growler, *Am.* hack)
27 stableman (groom)
28 coach horse (carriage horse, cab horse, thill horse, thiller)
29 hansom cab (hansom), a cabriolet, a one-horse chaise (one-horse carriage)
30 shafts (thills, poles)
31 reins (rein, *Am.* line)
32 coachman (driver) with inverness
33 covered char-a-banc (brake, break), a pleasure vehicle
34 gig (chaise)
35 barouche
36 landau, a two-horse carriage; *sim.:* landaulet, landaulette
37 omnibus (horse-drawn omnibus)
38 phaeton
39 Continental stagecoach (mailcoach, diligence); *also:* road coach
40 mailcoach driver
41 posthorn
42 hood
43 post horses (relay horses, relays)
44 tilbury
45 troika (Russian three-horse carriage)
46 leader
47 wheeler (wheelhorse, pole horse)
48 English buggy
49 American buggy
50 tandem
51 vis-à-vis
52 collapsible hood (collapsible top)
53 mailcoach (English stagecoach)
54 covered (closed) chaise

1
2
9
10
14
8
6
7
15
5
12
11
4
13
16
3
17
25
22
23
21
19
24
18
20
26
32
31
28
30
27
29
33
34
35
36
37
38
42
41
40
43
44
45
47
46
39
48
49
50
52
51
53
54

187 Bicycle

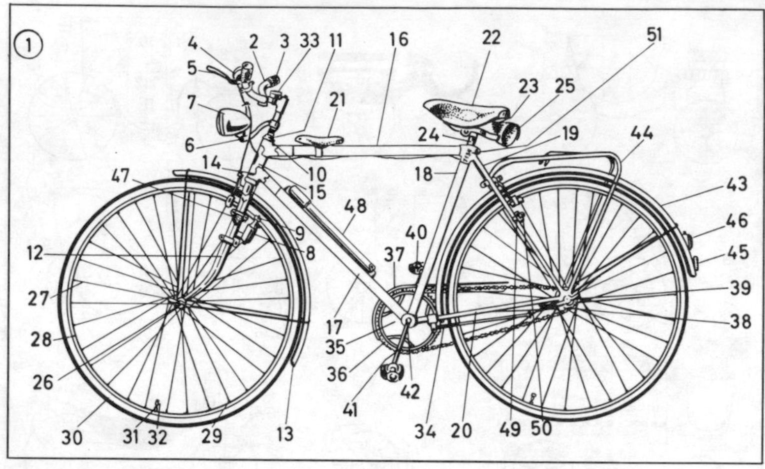

1 bicycle (cycle, *coll.* bike, *Am.* wheel), a gent's bicycle, a touring bicycle (touring cycle, roadster)
2 handlebar (handlebars), a touring cycle handlebar
3 handlebar grip (handgrip, grip)
4 bicycle bell
5 hand brake (front brake), a rim brake
6 lamp bracket
7 headlamp (bicycle lamp)
8 dynamo
9 pulley
10–12 front forks
10 handlebar stem
11 steering head
12 fork blades (fork ends)
13 front mudguard (*Am.* front fender)
14–20 bicycle frame
14 steering tube (fork column)
15 head badge
16 crossbar (top tube)
17 down tube
18 seat tube
19 seat stays
20 chain stays
21 child's seat (child carrier seat)
22 bicycle saddle
23 saddle springs
24 seat pillar
25 saddle bag (tool bag)
26–32 wheel (front wheel)
26 hub
27 spoke
28 rim (wheel rim)
29 spoke nipple (spoke flange, spoke end)
30 tyres (*Am.* tires) (tyre, pneumatic tyre, high-pressure tyre); *inside:* tube (inner tube), *outside:* tyre (outer case, cover)
31 valve, a tube valve with valve tube or a patent valve with ball
32 valve sealing cap
33 bicycle speedometer with milometer
34 kick stand (prop stand)
35–42 bicycle drive (chain drive)
35–39 chain transmission
35 chain wheel
36 chain, a roller chain
37 chain guard
38 sprocket wheel (sprocket)
39 wing nut (fly nut, butterfly nut)
40 pedal

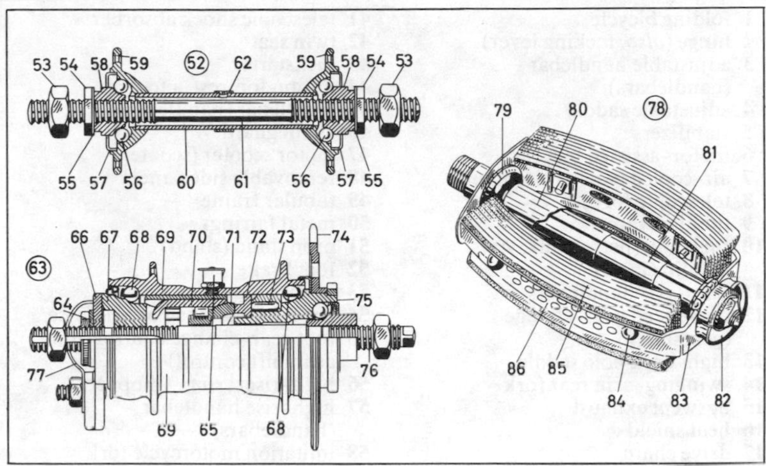

41 crank
42 bottom bracket bearing
43 rear mudguard (*Am.* rear fender)
44 luggage carrier (carrier)
45 reflector
46 rear light (rear lamp)
47 footrest
48 bicycle pump
49 bicycle lock, a wheel lock
50 patent key
51 cycle serial number (factory number, frame number)
52 front hub (front hub assembly)
53 wheel nut
54 locknut (locking nut)
55 washer (slotted cone adjusting washer)
56 ball bearing
57 dust cap
58 cone (adjusting cone)
59 centre (*Am.* center) hub
60 spindle
61 axle
62 clip covering lubrication hole (lubricator)
63 free-wheel hub with back-pedal brake (with coaster brake)
64 safety nut
65 lubricator
66 brake arm
67 brake arm cone
68 bearing cup with ball bearings in ball race
69 hub shell (hub body, hub barrel)
70 brake casing
71 brake cone
72 driver
73 driving barrel
74 sprocket
75 thread head
76 axle
77 bracket
78 bicycle pedal (pedal, reflector pedal)
79 cup
80 spindle
81 axle
82 dust cap
83 pedal frame
84 rubber stud
85 rubber block (rubber tread)
86 glass reflector

188 Motorcycles, Bicycles, Scooters, Mopeds

1 folding bicycle
2 hinge (*also:* locking lever)
3 adjustable handlebar (handlebars)
4 adjustable saddle
5 stabilizers
6 motor-assisted bicycle
7 air-cooled two-stroke engine
8 telescopic forks
9 tubular frame
10 fuel tank (petrol tank, *Am.* gasoline tank)
11 semi-rise handlebars
12 two-speed gear-change (gearshift)
13 high-back polo saddle
14 swinging-arm rear fork
15 upswept exhaust
16 heat shield
17 drive chain
18 crash bar (roll bar)
19 speedometer (*coll.* speedo)
20 battery-powered moped, an electrically-powered vehicle
21 swivel saddle
22 battery compartment
23 wire basket
24 touring moped (moped)
25 pedal crank (pedal drive, starter pedal)
26 single-cylinder two-stroke engine
27 spark-plug cap
28 fuel tank (petrol tank, *Am.* gasoline tank)
29 moped headlamp (front lamp)
30–35 handlebar fittings
30 twist grip throttle control (throttle twist grip)
31 twist grip (gear-change, gearshift)
32 clutch lever
33 hand brake lever
34 speedometer (*coll.* speedo)
35 rear-view mirror (mirror)
36 front wheel drum brake (drum brake)
37 Bowden cables (brake cables)
38 stop and tail light unit
39 light motorcycle with kickstarter
40 housing for instruments with speedometer and electronic rev counter (revolution counter)
41 telescopic shock absorber
42 twin seat
43 kickstarter
44 pillion footrest, a footrest
45 handlebar (handlebars)
46 chain guard
47 motor scooter (scooter)
48 removable side panel
49 tubular frame
50 metal fairings
51 prop stand (stand)
52 foot brake
53 horn (hooter)
54 hook for handbag or briefcase
55 foot gear-change control (foot gearshift control)
56 high-riser; *sim.:* Chopper
57 high-rise handlebar (handlebars)
58 imitation motorcycle fork
59 banana saddle
60 chrome bracket

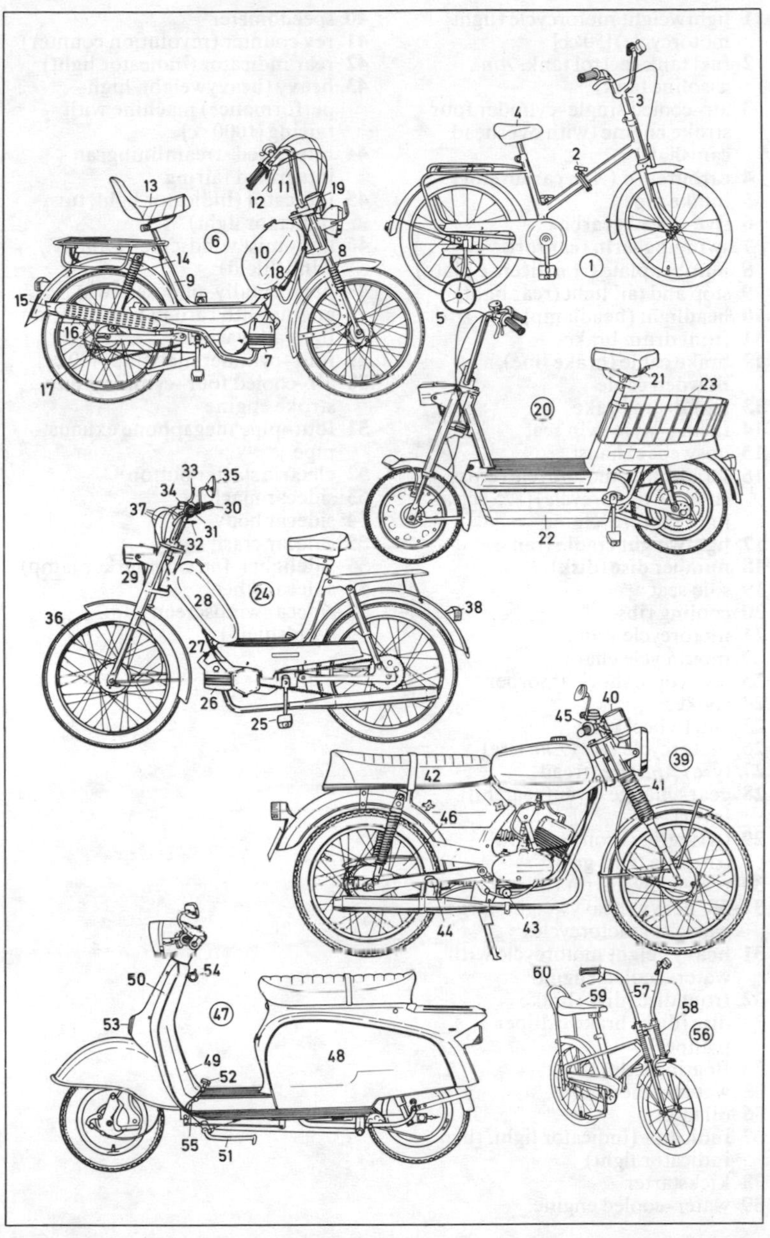
1
2
3
4
5
6
7
8
9
10
11
12
13
14
15
16
17
18
19
20
21
22
23
24
25
26
27
28
29
30
31
32
33
34
35
36
37
38
39
40
41
42
43
44
45
46
47
48
49
50
51
52
53
54
55
56
57
58
59
60

189 Motorcycle

1 lightweight motorcycle (light motorcycle) [50 cc]
2 fuel tank (petrol tank, *Am.* gasoline tank)
3 air-cooled single-cylinder four-stroke engine (with overhead camshaft)
4 carburettor (*Am.* carburetor)
5 intake pipe
6 five-speed gearbox
7 swinging-arm rear fork
8 number plate (*Am.* license plate)
9 stop and tail light (rear light)
10 headlight (headlamp)
11 front drum brake
12 brake cable (brake line), a Bowden cable
13 rear drum brake
14 racing-style twin seat
15 upswept exhaust
16 scrambling motorcycle (cross-country motorcycle) [125 cc], a light motorcycle
17 lightweight cradle frame
18 number disc (disk)
19 solo seat
20 cooling ribs
21 motorcycle stand
22 motorcycle chain
23 telescopic shock absorber
24 spokes
25 rim (wheel rim)
26 motorcycle tyre (*Am.* tire)
27 tyre (*Am.* tire) tread
28 gear-change lever (gearshift lever)
29 twist grip throttle control (throttle twist grip)
30 rear-view mirror (mirror)
31-58 heavy (heavyweight, large-capacity) motorcycles
31 heavyweight motorcycle with water-cooled engine
32 front disc (disk) brake
33 disc (disk) brake calliper (caliper)
34 floating axle
35 water cooler
36 oil tank
37 indicator (indicator light, turn indicator light)
38 kickstarter
39 water-cooled engine
40 speedometer
41 rev counter (revolution counter)
42 rear indicator (indicator light)
43 heavy (heavyweight, high-performance) machine with fairing [1000 cc]
44 integrated streamlining, an integrated fairing
45 indicator (indicator light, turn indicator light)
46 anti-mist windscreen (*Am.* windshield)
47 horizontally-opposed twin engine with cardan transmission
48 light alloy wheel
49 four-cylinder machine [400 cc]
50 air-cooled four-cylinder four-stroke engine
51 four-pipe megaphone exhaust pipe
52 electric starter button
53 sidecar machine
54 sidecar body
55 sidecar crash bar
56 sidelight (*Am.* sidemarker lamp)
57 sidecar wheel
58 sidecar windscreen (*Am.* windshield)

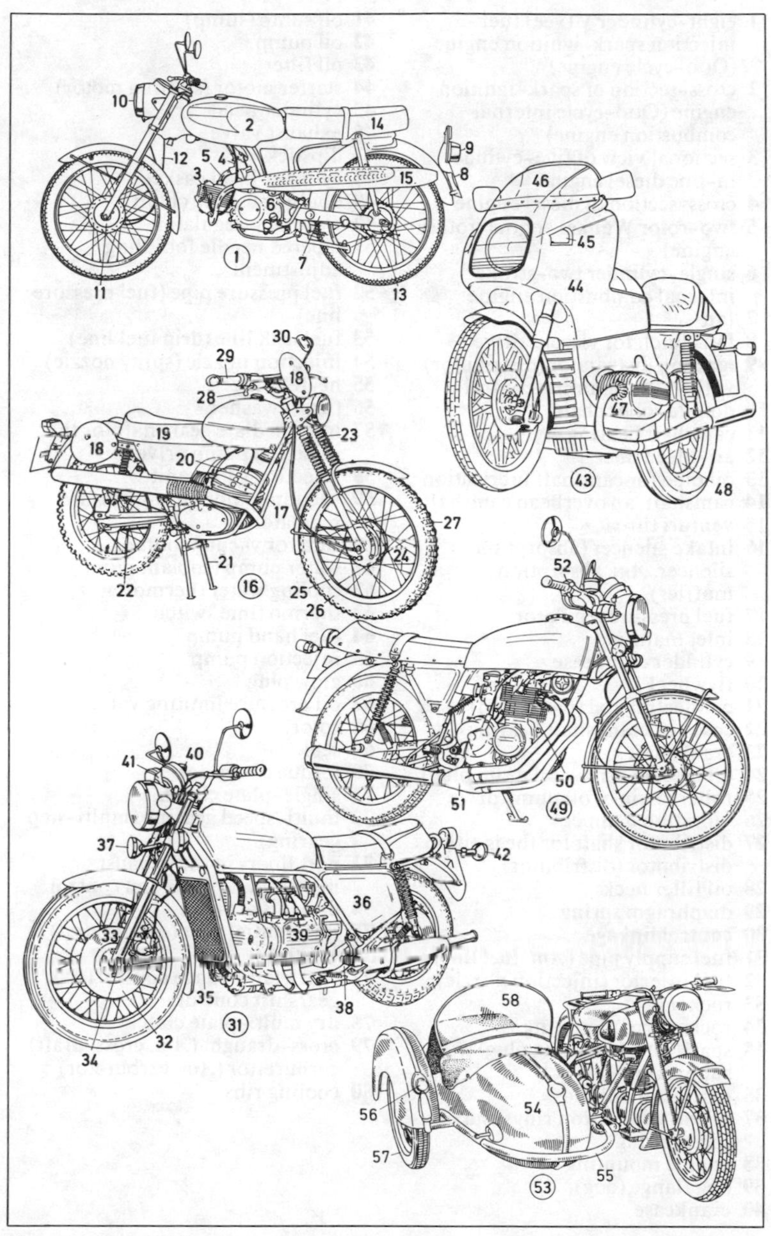
10
2
14
9
12
5
4
3
8
15
6
1
7
11
13
46
45
44
30
29
18
28
19
23
18
20
17
27
24
21
22
16
25
26
47
43
48
52
41
40
50
51
49
37
42
36
33
39
35
38
31
32
34
58
54
56
57
55
53

190 Internal Combustion Engines

1 eight-cylinder V (vee) fuel-injection spark-ignition engine (Otto-cycle engine)
2 cross-section of spark-ignition engine (Otto-cycle internal combustion engine)
3 sectional view of five-cylinder in-line diesel engine
4 cross-section of diesel engine
5 two-rotor Wankel engine (rotary engine)
6 single-cylinder two-stroke internal combustion engine
7 fan
8 fan clutch for viscous drive
9 ignition distributor (distributor) with vacuum timing control
10 double roller chain
11 camshaft bearing
12 air-bleed duct
13 oil pipe for camshaft lubrication
14 camshaft, an overhead camshaft
15 venturi throat
16 intake silencer (absorption silencer, *Am.* absorption muffler)
17 fuel pressure regulator
18 inlet manifold
19 cylinder crankcase
20 flywheel
21 connecting rod (piston rod)
22 cover of crankshaft bearing
23 crankshaft
24 oil bleeder screw (oil drain plug)
25 roller chain of oil pump drive
26 vibration damper
27 distributor shaft for the ignition distributor (distributor)
28 oil filler neck
29 diaphragm spring
30 control linkage
31 fuel supply pipe (*Am.* fuel line)
32 fuel injector (injection nozzle)
33 rocker arm
34 rocker arm mounting
35 spark plug (sparking plug) with suppressor
36 exhaust manifold
37 piston with piston rings and oil scraper ring
38 engine mounting
39 dog flange (dog)
40 crankcase
41 oil sump (sump)
42 oil pump
43 oil filter
44 starter motor (starting motor)
45 cylinder head
46 exhaust valve
47 dipstick
48 cylinder head gasket
49 double bushing chain
50 warm-up regulator
51 tapered needle for idling adjustment
52 fuel pressure pipe (fuel pressure line)
53 fuel leak line (drip fuel line)
54 injection nozzle (spray nozzle)
55 heater plug
56 thrust washer
57 intermediate gear shaft for the injection pump drive
58 injection timer unit
59 vacuum pump (low-pressure regulator)
60 cam for vacuum pump
61 water pump (coolant pump)
62 cooling water thermostat
63 thermo time switch
64 fuel hand pump
65 injection pump
66 glow plug
67 oil pressure limiting valve
68 rotor
69 seal
70 torque converter
71 single-plate clutch
72 multi-speed gearing (multi-step gearing)
73 port liners in the exhaust manifold for emission control
74 disc (disk) brake
75 differential gear (differential)
76 generator
77 foot gear-change control (foot gearshift control)
78 dry multi-plate clutch
79 cross-draught (*Am.* cross-draft) carburettor (*Am.* carburetor)
80 cooling ribs

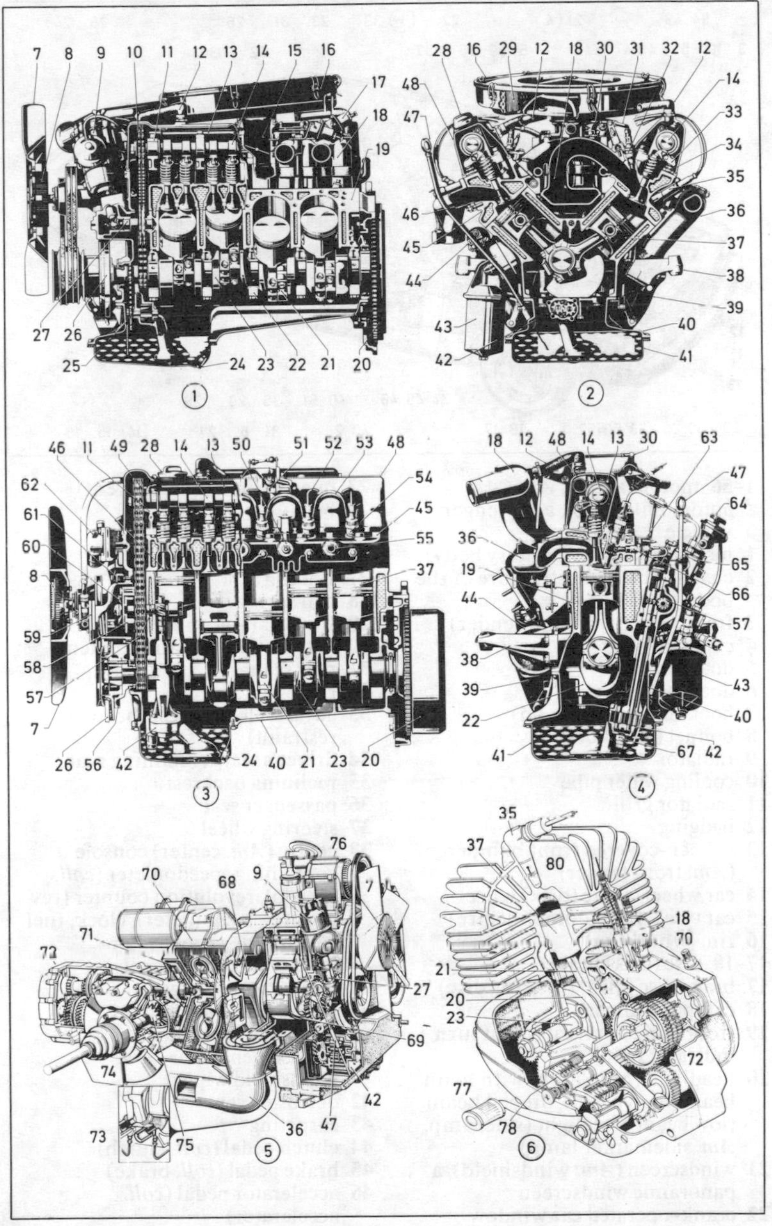
7 8 9 10 11 12 13 14 15 16
17
18
19
27 26
25
24 23 22 21 20
1
28 16 29 12 18 30 31 32 12
48
47
14
33
34
35
46
36
45
37
44
38
39
43
40
42
41
2
46 11 49 28 14 13 50 51 52 53 48
62
54
61
45
60
55
8
37
59
58
57
7
26 56 42 24 40 21 23 20
3
18 12 48 14 13 30 63
47
64
36
65
19
66
44
57
38
43
39
40
22
41 67 42
4
76
70 68 9
7
71
72
27
69
74
42
73 75 36 47
5
35
37 80
18
70
21
20
23
72
77
78
6

191 Motor Car (*Am.* Automobile) I

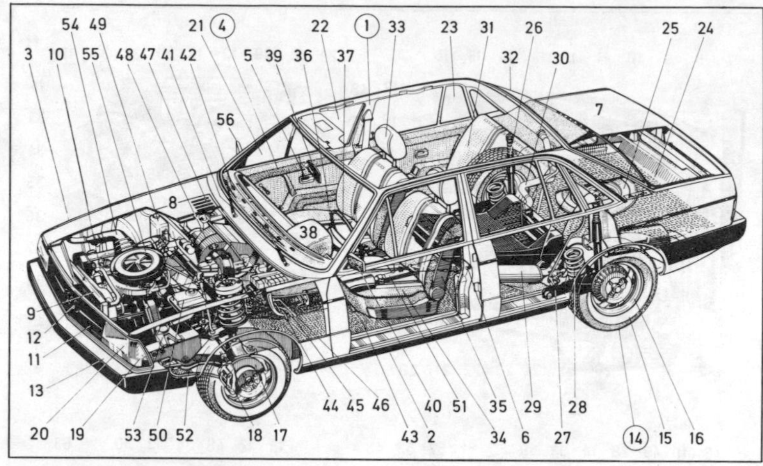

1–56 motor car (car, *Am.* automobile, auto), a passenger vehicle
1 monocoque body (unitary body)
2 chassis, the understructure of the body
3 front wing (*Am.* front fender)
4 car door
5 door handle
6 door lock
7 boot lid (*Am.* trunk lid)
8 bonnet (*Am.* hood)
9 radiator
10 cooling water pipe
11 radiator grill
12 badging
13 rubber-covered front bumper (*Am.* front fender)
14 car wheel, a disc (disk) wheel
15 car tyre (*Am.* automobile tire)
16 rim (wheel rim)
17–18 disc (disk) brake
17 brake disc (disk) (braking disc)
18 calliper (caliper)
19 front indicator light (front turn indicator light)
20 headlight (headlamp) with main beam (high beam), dipped beam (low beam), sidelight (side lamp, *Am.* sidemarker lamp)
21 windscreen (*Am.* windshield), a panoramic windscreen
22 crank-operated car window
23 quarter light (quarter vent)
24 boot (*Am.* trunk)
25 spare wheel
26 damper (shock absorber)
27 trailing arm
28 coil spring
29 silencer (*Am.* muffler)
30 automatic ventilation system
31 rear seats
32 rear window
33 adjustable headrest (head restraint)
34 driver's seat, a reclining seat
35 reclining backrest
36 passenger seat
37 steering wheel
38 centre (*Am.* center) console containing speedometer (*coll.* speedo), revolution counter (rev counter, tachometer), clock, fuel gauge (*Am.* gage), water temperature gauge, oil temperature gauge
39 inside rear-view mirror
40 left-hand wing mirror
41 windscreen wiper (*Am.* windshield wiper)
42 defroster vents
43 carpeting
44 clutch pedal (*coll.* clutch)
45 brake pedal (*coll.* brake)
46 accelerator pedal (*coll.* accelerator)

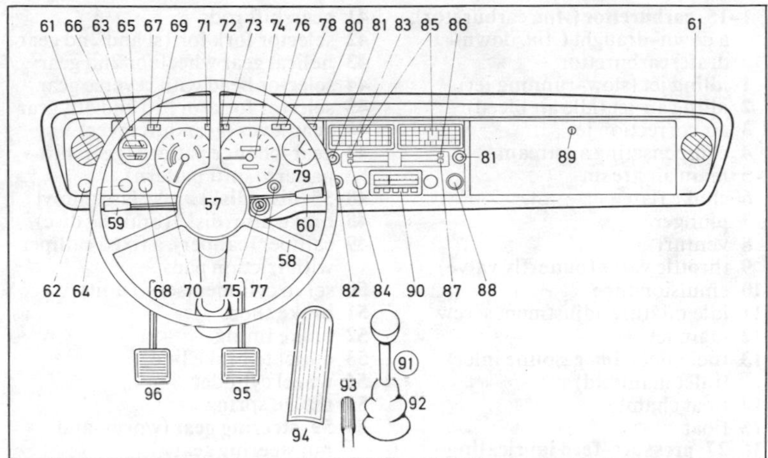

47 inlet vent
48 blower fan
49 brake fluid reservoir
50 battery
51 exhaust pipe
52 front running gear with front wheel drive
53 engine mounting
54 intake silencer (*Am.* intake muffler)
55 air filter (air cleaner)
56 right-hand wing mirror
57–90 dashboard (fascia panel)
57 controlled-collapse steering column
58 steering wheel spoke
59 indicator and dimming switch
60 wiper/washer switch and horn
61 side window blower
62 sidelight, headlight, and parking light switch
63 fog lamp warning light
64 fog headlamp and rear lamp switch
65 fuel gauge (*Am.* gage)
66 water temperature gauge (*Am.* gage)
67 warning light for rear fog lamp
68 hazard flasher switch
69 main beam warning light
70 electric rev counter (revolution counter)
71 fuel warning light
72 warning light for the hand brake and dual-circuit brake system
73 oil pressure warning light
74 speedometer (*coll.* speedo) with trip mileage recorder
75 starter and steering lock
76 warning lights for turn indicators and hazard flashers
77 switch for the courtesy light and reset button for the trip mileage recorder
78 ammeter
79 electric clock
80 warning light for heated rear window
81 switch for the leg space ventilation
82 rear window heating switch
83 ventilation switch
84 temperature regulator
85 fresh-air inlet and control
86 fresh air regulator
87 warm-air regulator
88 cigar lighter
89 glove compartment (glove box) lock
90 car radio
91 gear lever (gearshift lever, floor-type gear-change)
92 leather gaiter
93 hand brake lever
94 accelerator pedal
95 brake pedal
96 clutch pedal

1–15 carburettor (*Am.* carburetor), a down-draught (*Am.* down-draft) carburettor
1 idling jet (slow-running jet)
2 idling air jet (idle air bleed)
3 air correction jet
4 compensating airstream
5 main airstream
6 choke flap
7 plunger
8 venturi
9 throttle valve (butterfly valve)
10 emulsion tube
11 idle mixture adjustment screw
12 main jet
13 fuel inlet (*Am.* gasoline inlet) (inlet manifold)
14 float chamber
15 float
16–27 pressure-feed lubricating system
16 oil pump
17 oil sump
18 sump filter
19 oil cooler
20 oil filter
21 main oil gallery (drilled gallery)
22 crankshaft drilling (crankshaft tributary, crankshaft bleed)
23 crankshaft bearing (main bearing)
24 camshaft bearing
25 connecting-rod bearing
26 gudgeon pin (piston pin)
27 bleed
28–47 four-speed synchromesh gearbox
28 clutch pedal
29 crankshaft
30 drive shaft (propeller shaft)
31 starting gear ring
32 sliding sleeve for 3rd and 4th gear
33 synchronizing cone
34 helical gear wheel for 3rd gear
35 sliding sleeve for 1st and 2nd gear
36 helical gear wheel for 1st gear
37 lay shaft
38 speedometer drive
39 helical gear wheel for speedometer drive
40 main shaft
41 gearshift rods
42 selector fork for 1st and 2nd gear
43 helical gear wheel for 2nd gear
44 selector head with reverse gear
45 selector fork for 3rd and 4th gear
46 gear lever (gearshift lever)
47 gear-change pattern (gearshift pattern, shift pattern)
48–55 disc (disk) brake [assembly]
48 brake disc (disk) (braking disc)
49 calliper (caliper), a fixed calliper with friction pads
50 servo cylinder (servo unit)
51 brake shoes
52 brake lining
53 outlet to brake line
54 wheel cylinder
55 return spring
56–59 steering gear (worm-and-nut steering gear)
56 steering column
57 worm gear sector
58 steering drop arm
59 worm
60–64 water-controlled heater
60 air intake
61 heat exchanger (heater box)
62 blower fan
63 flap valve
64 defroster vent
65–71 live axle (rigid axle)
65 propeller shaft
66 trailing arm
67 rubber bush
68 coil spring
69 damper (shock absorber)
70 Panhard rod
71 stabilizer bar
72–84 MacPherson strut unit
72 body-fixing plate
73 upper bearing
74 suspension spring
75 piston rod
76 suspension damper
77 rim (wheel rim)
78 stub axle
79 steering arm
80 track-rod ball-joint
81 trailing link arm
82 bump rubber (rubber bonding)
83 lower bearing
84 lower suspension arm

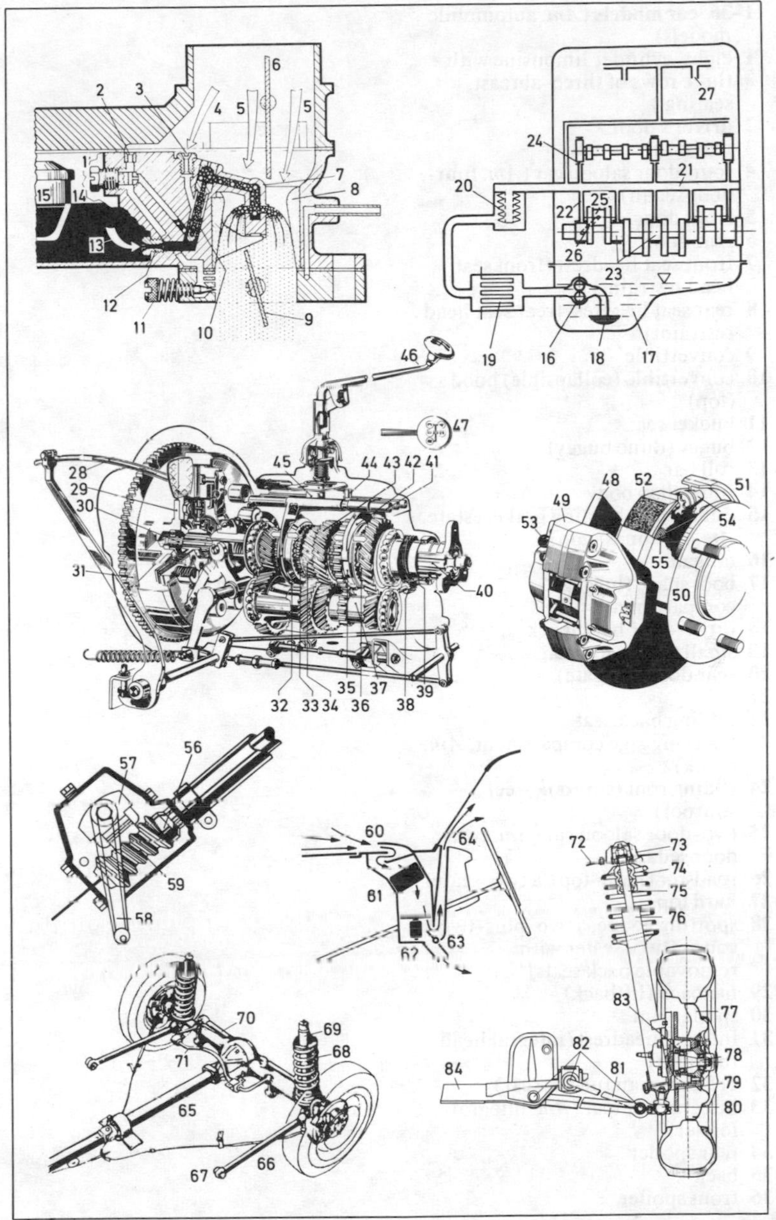
1
2
3
4
5
5
6
7
8
9
10
11
12
13
14
15
16
17
18
19
20
21
22
23
24
25
26
27
28
29
30
31
32
33
34
35
36
37
38
39
40
41
42
43
44
45
46
47
48
49
50
51
52
53
54
55
56
57
58
59
60
61
62
63
64
65
66
67
68
69
70
71
72
73
74
75
76
77
78
79
80
81
82
83
84

1-36 car models (*Am.* automobile models)
1 eight-cylinder limousine with three rows of three-abreast seating
2 driver's door
3 rear door
4 four-door saloon car (*Am.* four-door sedan)
5 front door
6 rear door
7 front seat headrest (front seat head restraint)
8 rear seat headrest (rear seat head restraint)
9 convertible
10 convertible (collapsible) hood (top)
11 bucket seat
12 buggy (dune buggy)
13 roll bar
14 fibre glass body
15 estate car (shooting brake, estate, *Am.* station wagon)
16 tailgate
17 boot space (luggage compartment)
18 three-door hatchback
19 small three-door car
20 rear door (tailgate)
21 sill
22 folding back seat
23 boot (luggage compartment, *Am.* trunk)
24 sliding roof (sunroof, steel sunroof)
25 two-door saloon car (*Am.* two-door sedan)
26 roadster (hard-top), a two-seater
27 hard top
28 sporting coupé, a two-plus-two coupé (two-seater with removable back seats)
29 fastback (liftback)
30 spoiler rim
31 integral headrest (integral head restraint)
32 GT car (gran turismo car)
33 integral bumper (*Am.* integral fender)
34 rear spoiler
35 back
36 front spoiler

1
2
3
4
5
6
7
8
9
10
11
12
13
14
15
16
17
18
19
20
21
22
23
24
25
26
27
28
29
30
31
32
33
34
35
36

1 light cross-country lorry (light truck, pickup truck) with all-wheel drive (four-wheel drive)
2 cab (driver's cab)
3 loading platform (body)
4 spare tyre (*Am.* spare tire), a cross-country tyre
5 light lorry (light truck, pickup truck)
6 platform truck
7 medium van
8 sliding side door [for loading and unloading]
9 minibus
10 folding top (sliding roof)
11 rear door
12 hinged side door
13 luggage compartment
14 passenger seat
15 cab (driver's cab)
16 air inlet
17 motor coach (coach, bus)
18 luggage locker
19 hand luggage (suitcase, case)
20 heavy lorry (heavy truck, heavy motor truck)
21 tractive unit (tractor, towing vehicle)
22 trailer (drawbar trailer)
23 swop platform (body)
24 three-way tipper (three-way dump truck)
25 tipping body (dump body)
26 hydraulic cylinder
27 supported container platform
28 articulated vehicle, a vehicle tanker
29 tractive unit (tractor, towing vehicle)
30–33 semi-trailer (skeletal)
30 tank
31 turntable
32 undercarriage
33 spare wheel
34 midi bus [for short-route town operations]
35 outward-opening doors
36 double-deck bus (double-decker bus)
37 lower deck (lower saloon)
38 upper deck (upper saloon)
39 boarding platform
40 trolley bus
41 current collector
42 trolley (trolley shoe)
43 overhead wires
44 trolley bus trailer
45 pneumatically sprung rubber connection

3
6
2
4
1
5
7
8
11
10
13
16
14
15
9
12
17
18
18
18
19
20
25
24
23
26
21
22
27
30
31
32
28
33
29
38
36
35
34
37
39
43
42
41
45
44
40

195 Garage (*Am.* Shop)

1–55 agent's garage (distributor's garage, *Am.* specialty shop)
1–23 diagnostic test bay
1 computer
2 main computer plug
3 computer harness (computer cable)
4 switch from automatic to manual
5 slot for program cards
6 print-out machine (printer)
7 condition report (data print-out)
8 master selector (hand control)
9 light read-out [green: OK; red: not OK]
10 rack for program cards
11 mains button
12 switch for fast readout
13 firing sequence insert
14 shelf for used cards
15 cable boom
16 oil temperature sensor
17 test equipment for wheel and steering alignment
18 right-hand optic plate
19 actuating transistors
20 projector switch
21 check light for wheel alignment, a row of photocells
22 check light for steering alignment, a row of photocells
23 power screwdriver
24 beam setter
25 hydraulic lift
26 adjustable arm of hydraulic lift
27 hydraulic lift pad
28 excavation
29 pressure gauge (*Am.* gage)
30 grease gun
31 odds-and-ends box
32 wall chart [of spare parts]
33 automatic computer test
34 motor car (car, *Am.* automobile, auto), a passenger vehicle
35 engine compartment
36 bonnet (*Am.* hood)
37 bonnet support (*Am.* hood support)
38 computer harness (computer cable)

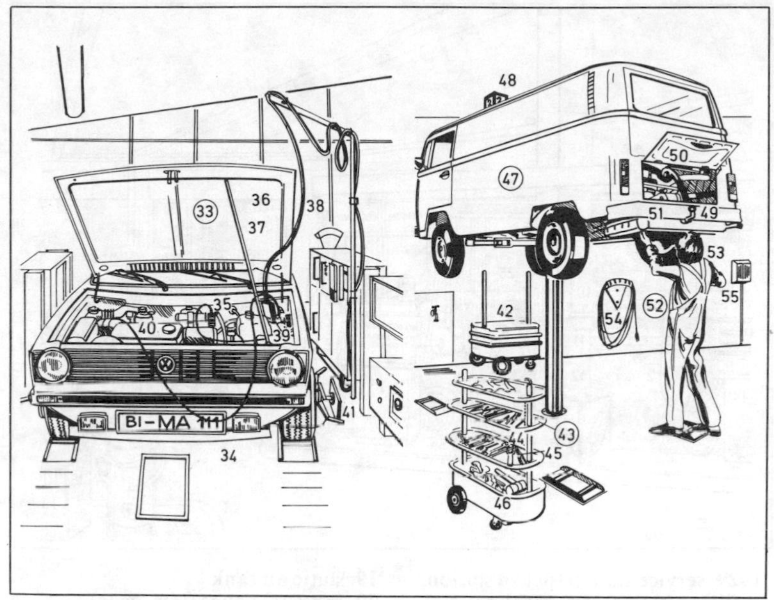

39 main computer socket; *also:* multi-outlet socket
40 oil temperature sensor
41 wheel mirror for visual wheel and steering alignment
42 tool trolley
43 tools
44 impact wrench
45 torque wrench
46 body hammer (roughing-out hammer)
47 vehicle under repair, a minibus
48 car location number
49 rear engine
50 tailgate
51 exhaust system
52 exhaust repair
53 motor car mechanic (motor vehicle mechanic, *Am.* automotive mechanic)
54 air hose
55 intercom

1–29 service station (petrol station, filling station, *Am.* gasoline station, gas station), a self-service station
1 petrol (*Am.* gasoline) pump (blending pump) for regular and premium grade petrol (*Am.* gasoline) (*sim.:* for derv)
2 hose (petrol pump, *Am.* gasoline pump, hose)
3 nozzle
4 cash readout
5 volume read-out
6 price display
7 indicator light
8 driver using self-service petrol pump (*Am.* gasoline pump)
9 fire extinguisher
10 paper-towel dispenser
11 paper towel
12 litter receptacle
13 two-stroke blending pump
14 meter
15 engine oil
16 oil can
17 tyre pressure gauge (*Am.* tire pressure gage)
18 air hose
19 static air tank
20 pressure gauge (*Am.* gage) (manometer)
21 air filler neck
22 repair bay (repair shop)
23 car-wash hose, a hose (hosepipe)
24 accessory shop
25 petrol can (*Am.* gasoline can)
26 rain cape
27 car tyres (*Am.* automobile tires)
28 car accessories
29 cash desk (console)

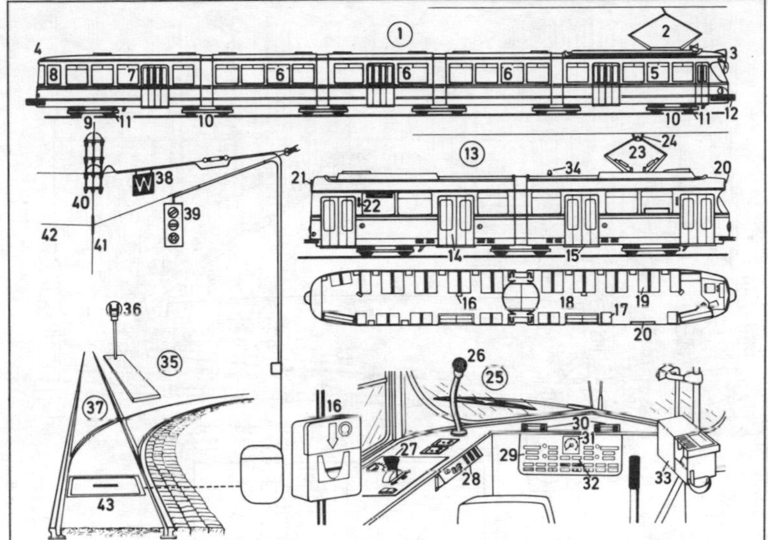

1 twelve-axle articulated railcar for interurban rail service
2 current collector
3 head of the railcar
4 rear of the railcar
5 carriage A containing the motor
6 carriage B (*also:* carriages C and D)
7 carriage E containing the motor
8 rear controller
9 bogie
10 carrying bogie
11 wheel guard
12 bumper (*Am.* fender)
13 six-axle articulated railcar ('Mannheim' type) for tram (*Am.* streetcar, trolley) and urban rail services
14 entrance and exit door, a double folding door
15 step
16 ticket-cancelling machine
17 single seat
18 standing room portion
19 double seat
20 route (number) and destination sign
21 route sign (number sign)
22 indicator (indicator light)
23 pantograph (current collector)
24 carbon or aluminium (*Am.* aluminum) alloy trolley shoes
25 driver's position
26 microphone
27 controller
28 radio equipment (radio communication set)
29 dashboard
30 dashboard lighting
31 speedometer
32 buttons controlling doors, windscreen wipers, internal and external lighting
33 ticket counter with change machine
34 radio antenna
35 tram stop (*Am.* streetcar stop, trolley stop)
36 tram stop sign (*Am.* streetcar stop sign, trolley stop sign)
37 electric change points
38 points signal (switch signal)
39 points change indicator
40 trolley wire contact point
41 trolley wire (overhead contact wire)
42 overhead cross wire
43 electric (*also:* electrohydraulic, electromechanical) points mechanism

198 Cross-section of a Street

1-5 road layers
1 anti-frost layer
2 bituminous sub-base course
3 base course
4 binder course
5 bituminous surface
6 kerb (curb)
7 kerbstone (curbstone)
8 paving (pavement)
9 pavement (*Am.* sidewalk, walkway)
10 gutter
11 pedestrian crossing (zebra crossing, *Am.* crosswalk)
12 street corner
13 street
14 electricity cables
15 telephone cables
16 telephone cable pipeline
17 cable manhole with cover (with manhole cover)
18 lamp post with lamp
19 electricity cables for technical installations
20 subscribers' (*Am.* customers') telephone lines
21 gas main
22 water main
23 drain
24 drain cover
25 drain pipe
26 waste pipe
27 combined sewer
28 district heating main
29 underground tunnel

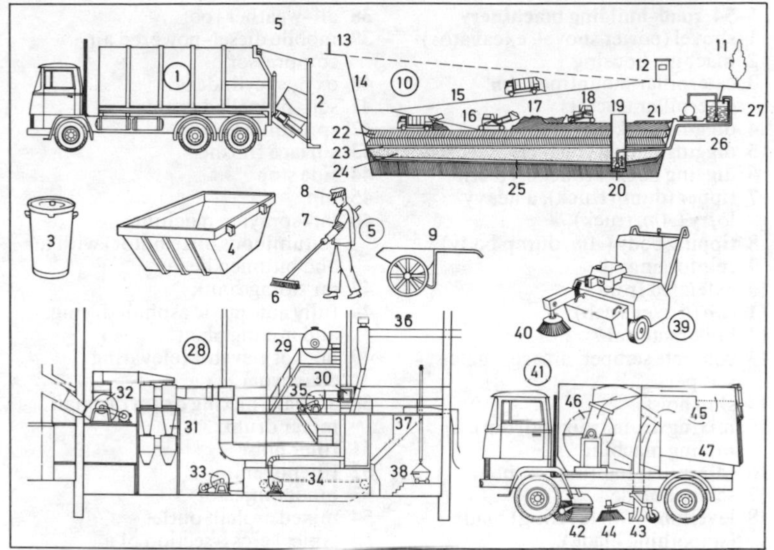

1 refuse collection vehicle (*Am.* garbage truck)
2 dustbin-tipping device (*Am.* garbage can dumping device), a dust-free emptying system
3 dustbin (*Am.* garbage can, trash can)
4 refuse container (*Am.* garbage container)
5 road sweeper (*Am.* street sweeper)
6 broom
7 fluorescent armband
8 cap with fluorescent band
9 road sweeper's (*Am.* street sweeper's) barrow
10 controlled tip (*Am.* sanitary landfill, sanitary fill)
11 screen
12 weigh office
13 fence
14 embankment
15 access ramp
16 bulldozer
17 refuse (*Am.* garbage)
18 bulldozer for dumping and compacting
19 pump shaft
20 waste water pump
21 porous cover
22 compacted and decomposed refuse
23 gravel filter layer
24 morainic filter layer
25 drainage layer
26 drain pipe
27 water tank
28 refuse (*Am.* garbage) incineration unit
29 furnace
30 oil-firing system
31 separation plant
32 extraction fan
33 low-pressure fan for the grate
34 continuous feed grate
35 fan for the oil-firing system
36 conveyor for separately incinerated material
37 coal feed conveyor
38 truck for carrying fuller's earth
39 mechanical sweeper
40 circular broom
41 road-sweeping lorry (street-cleaning lorry, street cleaner)
42 cylinder broom
43 suction port
44 feeder broom
45 air flow
46 fan
47 dust collector

200 Road Construction I (Road Building, Road Making)

1–54 road-building machinery
1 shovel (power shovel, excavator)
2 machine housing
3 caterpillar mounting (*Am.* caterpillar tractor)
4 digging bucket arm (dipper stick)
5 digging bucket (bucket)
6 digging bucket (bucket) teeth
7 tipper (dump truck), a heavy lorry (*Am.* truck)
8 tipping body (*Am.* dump body)
9 reinforcing rib
10 extended front
11 cab (driver's cab)
12 bulk material
13 concrete scraper, an aggregate scraper
14 skip hoist
15 mixing drum (mixer drum), a mixing machine
16 caterpillar hauling scraper
17 scraper blade
18 levelling (*Am.* leveling) blade (smoothing blade)
19 grader (motor grader)
20 scarifier (ripper, road ripper, rooter)
21 grader levelling (*Am.* leveling) blade (grader ploughshare, *Am.* plowshare)
22 blade-slewing gear (slew turntable)
23 light railway (narrow-gauge, *Am.* narrow-gage, railway)
24 light railway (narrow-gauge, *Am.* narrow-gage) diesel locomotive
25 trailer wagon (wagon truck, skip)
26 tamper (rammer); *heavier:* frog
27 guide rods
28 bulldozer
29 bulldozer blade
30 pushing frame
31 road-metal spreading machine (macadam spreader, stone spreader)
32 tamping beam
33 sole-plate
34 side stop
35 side of storage bin
36 three-wheeled roller, a road roller
37 roller
38 all-weather roof
39 mobile diesel-powered air compressor
40 oxygen cylinder
41 self-propelled gritter
42 spreading flap
43 surface finisher
44 side stop
45 bin
46 tar-spraying machine (bituminous distributor) with tar and bitumen heater
47 tar storage tank
48 fully automatic asphalt drying and mixing plant
49 bucket elevator (elevating conveyor)
50 asphalt-mixing drum (asphalt mixer drum)
51 filler hoist
52 filler opening
53 binder injector
54 mixed asphalt outlet
55 typical cross-section of a bituminous road
56 grass verge
57 crossfall
58 asphalt surface (bituminous layer, bituminous coating)
59 base (base course)
60 gravel sub-base course (hardcore sub-base course, Telford base), an anti-frost layer
61 sub-drainage
62 perforated cement pipe
63 drainage ditch
64 soil covering

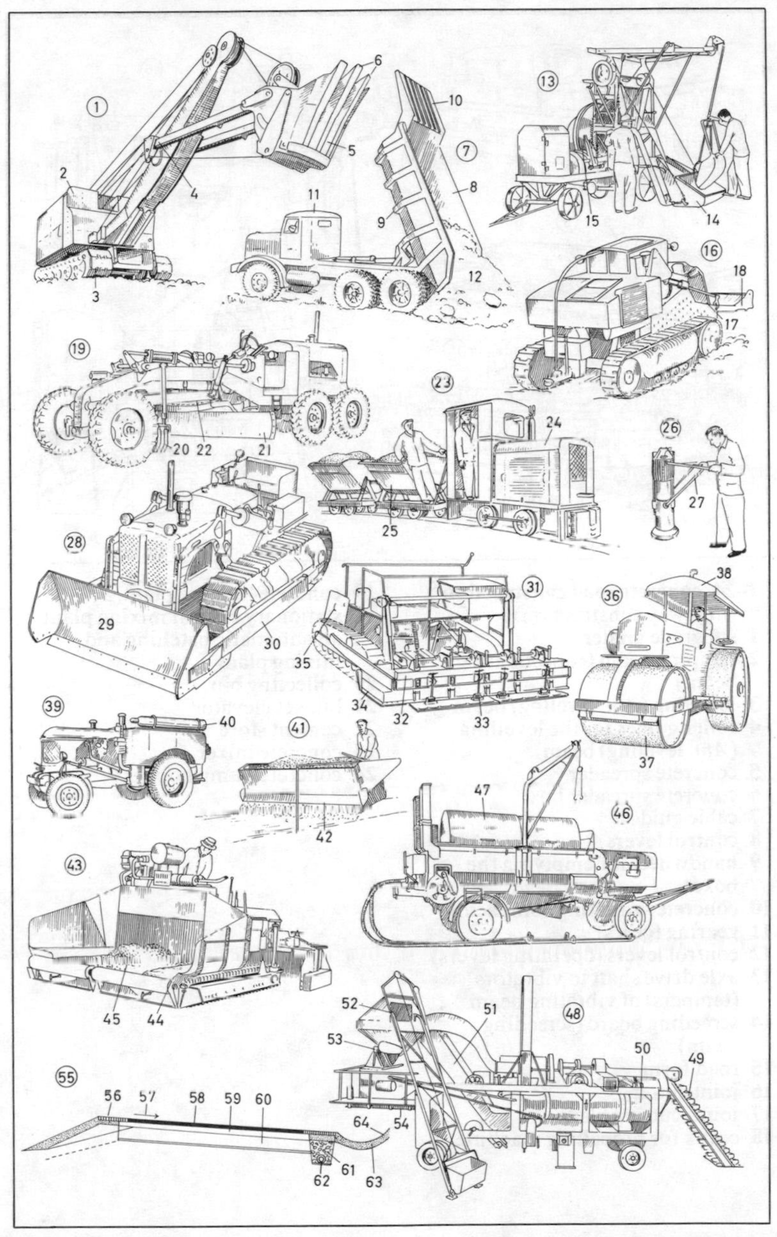
1
2
3
4
5
6
7
8
9
10
11
12
13
14
15
16
17
18
19
20
21
22
23
24
25
26
27
28
29
30
31
32
33
34
35
36
37
38
39
40
41
42
43
44
45
46
47
48
49
50
51
52
53
54
55
56
57
58
59
60
61
62
63
64

201 Road Construction II (Road Building, Road Making)

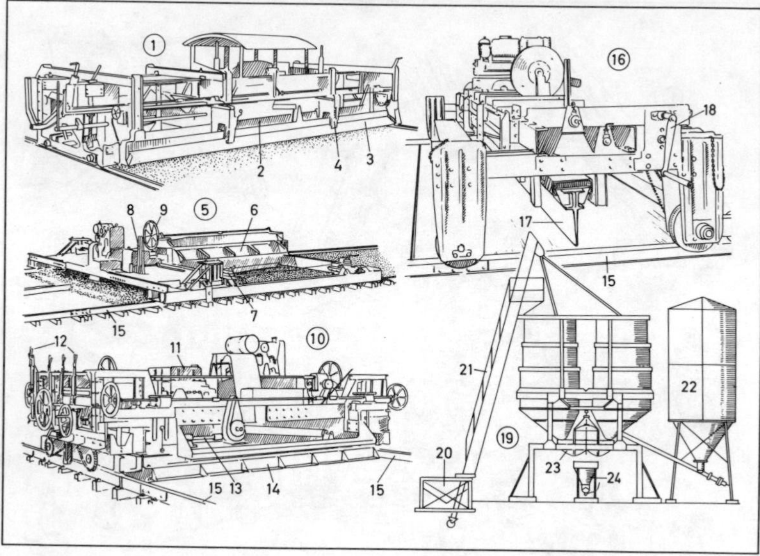

1-24 concrete road construction (highway construction)

1 subgrade grader

2 tamping beam (consolidating beam)

3 levelling (*Am.* leveling) beam

4 roller guides for the levelling (*Am.* leveling) beam

5 concrete spreader

6 concrete spreader box

7 cable guides

8 control levers

9 handwheel for emptying the boxes

10 concrete-vibrating compactor

11 gearing (gears)

12 control levers (operating levers)

13 axle drive shaft to vibrators (tampers) of vibrating beam

14 screeding board (screeding beam)

15 road form

16 joint cutter

17 joint-cutting blade

18 crank for propelling machine

19 concrete-mixing plant, a stationary central mixing plant, an automatic batching and mixing plant

20 collecting bin

21 bucket elevator

22 cement store

23 concrete mixer

24 concrete pump hopper

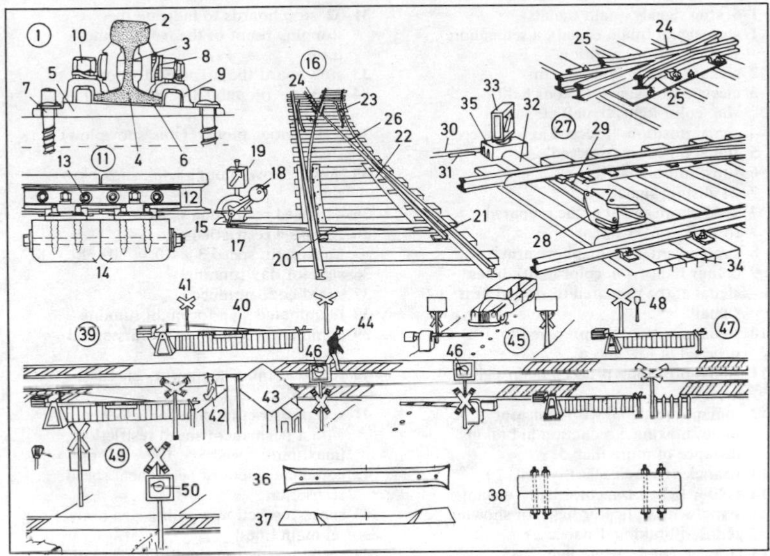

1-38 line (track)
1 rail
2 rail head
3 web (rail web)
4 rail foot (rail bottom)
5 sole-plate (base plate)
6 cushion
7 coach screw (coach bolt)
8 lock washers (spring washers)
9 rail clip (clip)
10 T-head bolt
11 rail joint (joint)
12 fishplate
13 fishbolt
14 coupled sleeper (*Am.* coupled tie, coupled crosstie)
15 coupling bolt
16 manually-operated points (switch)
17 switch stand
18 weight
19 points signal (switch signal, points signal lamp, switch signal lamp)
20 pull rod
21 switch blade (switch tongue)
22 slide chair
23 check rail (guard rail)
24 frog
25 wing rail
26 closure rail
27 remote-controlled points (switch)
28 point lock (switch lock)
29 stretcher bar
30 point wire
31 turnbuckle
32 channel
33 electrically illuminated points signal (switch signal)
34 trough
35 points motor with protective casing
36 steel sleeper (*Am.* steel tie, steel crosstie)
37 concrete sleeper (*Am.* concrete tie, concrete crosstie)
38 coupled sleeper (*Am.* coupled tie, coupled crosstie)
39-50 level crossings (*Am.* grade crossings)
39 protected level crossing (*Am.* protected grade crossing)
40 barrier (gate)
41 warning cross (*Am.* crossbuck)
42 crossing keeper (*Am.* gateman)
43 crossing keeper's box (*Am.* gateman's box)
44 linesman (*Am.* trackwalker)
45 half-barrier crossing
46 warning light
47 intercom controlled crossing; *sim.:* telephone-controlled crossing
48 intercom system
49 unprotected level crossing (*Am.* unprotected grade crossing)
50 warning light

203 Railway Line (*Am.* Railroad Track) II (Signalling Equipment)

1-6 stop signals (main signals)
1 stop signal (main signal), a semaphore signal in 'stop' position
2 signal arm (semaphore arm)
3 electric stop signal (colour light, *Am.* color light, signal) at 'stop'
4 signal position: 'proceed at low speed'
5 signal position: 'proceed'
6 substitute signal
7-24 distant signals
7 semaphore signal at 'be prepared to stop at next signal'
8 supplementary semaphore arm
9 colour light (*Am.* color light) distant signal at 'be prepared to stop at next signal'
10 signal position: 'be prepared to proceed at low speed'
11 signal position: 'proceed main signal ahead'
12 semaphore signal with indicator plate showing a reduction in braking distance of more than 5%
13 triangle (triangle sign)
14 colour light (*Am.* color light) distant signal with indicator light for showing reduced braking distance
15 supplementary white light
16 distant signal indicating 'be prepared to stop at next signal' (yellow light)
17 second distant signal (distant signal with supplementary light, without indicator plate)
18 distant signal with speed indicator
19 distant speed indicator
20 distant signal with route indicator
21 route indicator
22 distant signal without supplementary arm in position: 'be prepared to stop at next signal'
23 distant signal without supplementary arm in 'be prepared to proceed' position
24 distant signal identification plate
25-44 supplementary signals
25 stop board for indicating the stopping point at a control point
26-29 approach signs
26 approach sign 100 m from distant signal
27 approach sign 175 m from distant signal
28 approach sign 250 m from distant signal
29 approach sign at a distance of 5% less than the braking distance on the section
30 chequered sign indicating stop signals (main signals) not positioned immediately to the right of or over the line (track)
31-32 stop boards to indicate the stopping point of the front of the train
33 stop board (be prepared to stop)
34-35 snow plough (*Am.* snowplow) signs
34 'raise snow-plough (*Am.* snowplow)' sign
35 'lower snow-plough (*Am.* snowplow)' sign
36-44 speed restriction signs
36-38 speed restriction sign [maximum speed 3 × 10 = 30 kph]
36 sign for day running
37 speed code number
38 illuminated sign for night running
39 commencement of temporary speed restriction
40 termination of temporary speed restriction
41 speed restriction sign for a section with a permanent speed restriction [maximum speed 5 × 10 = 50 kph]
42 commencement of permanent speed restriction
43 speed restriction warning sign [only on main lines]
44 speed restriction sign [only on main lines]
45-52 points signals (switch signals)
45-48 single points (single switches)
45 route straight ahead (main line)
46 [right] branch
47 [left] branch
48 branch [seen from the frog]
49-52 double crossover
49 route straight ahead from left to right
50 route straight ahead from right to left
51 turnout to the left from the left
52 turnout to the right from the right
53 manually-operated signal box (*Am.* signal tower, switch tower)
54 lever mechanism
55 points lever (switch lever) [blue], a lock lever
56 signal lever [red]
57 catch
58 route lever
59 block instruments
60 block section panel
61 electrically-operated signal box (*Am.* signal tower, switch tower)
62 points (switch) and signal knobs
63 lock indicator panel
64 track and signal indicator
65 track diagram control layout
66 track diagram control panel (domino panel)
67 push buttons
68 routes
69 intercom system

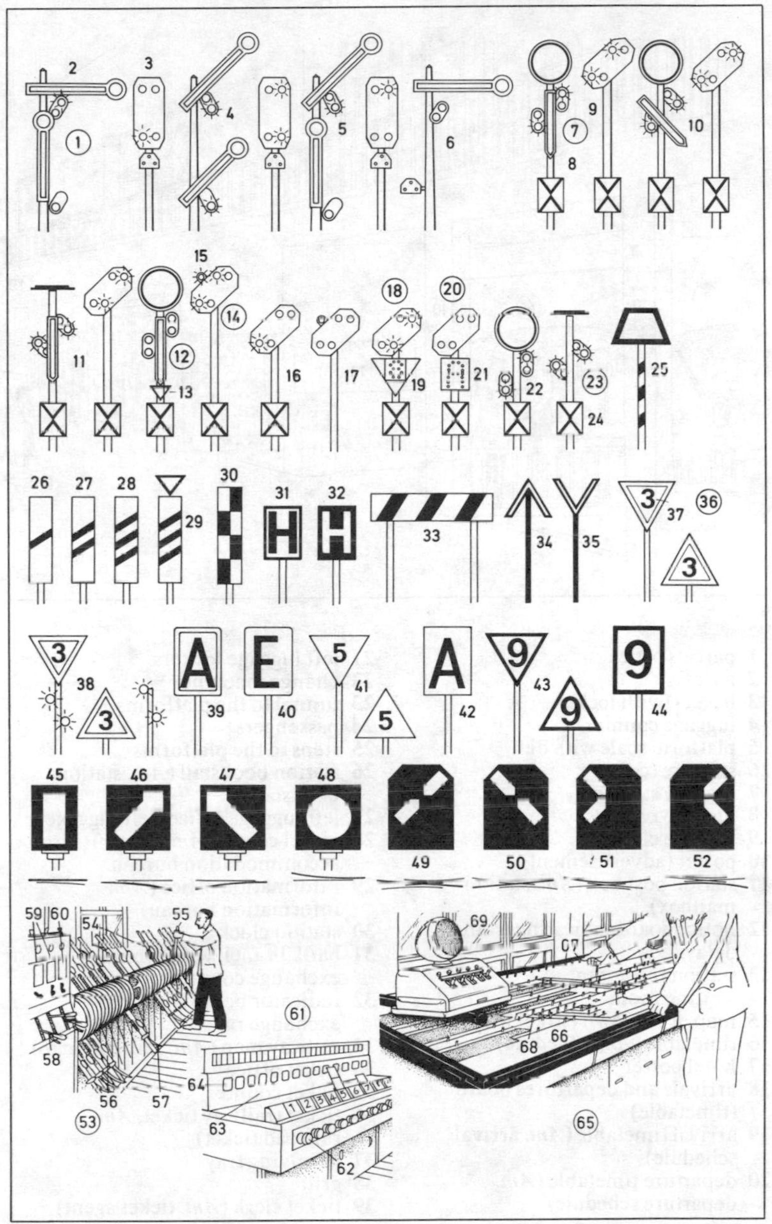
1 2 3 4 5 6 7 8 9 10
11 12 13 14 15 16 17 18 19 20 21 22 23 24 25
26 27 28 29 30 31 32 33 34 35 36 37
H
H
3
3
38 39 40 41 42 43 44
3
3
A
E
5
5
A
9
9
9
45 46 47 48 49 50 51 52
59 60 54 55 58 56 57 53 61 64 63 62
69 67 68 66 65
1 2 3 4 5 6 7

204 Station Hall

1 parcels office
2 parcels
3 basket [with lock]
4 luggage counter
5 platform scale with dial
6 suitcase (case)
7 luggage sticker
8 luggage receipt
9 luggage clerk
10 poster (advertisement)
11 station post box (*Am.* station mailbox)
12 notice board indicating train delays
13 station restaurant
14 waiting room
15 map of the town (street map)
16 timetable (*Am.* schedule)
17 hotel porter
18 arrivals and departures board (timetable)
19 arrival timetable (*Am.* arrival schedule)
20 departure timetable (*Am.* departure schedule)
21 left luggage lockers
22 change machine
23 tunnel to the platforms
24 passengers
25 steps to the platforms
26 station bookstall (*Am.* station bookstand)
27 left luggage office (left luggage)
28 travel centre (*Am.* center); *also:* accommodation bureau
29 information office (*Am.* information bureau)
30 station clock
31 bank branch with foreign exchange counter
32 indicator board showing exchange rates
33 railway map (*Am.* railroad map)
34 ticket office
35 ticket counter
36 ticket (railway ticket, *Am.* railroad ticket)
37 revolving tray
38 grill
39 ticket clerk (*Am.* ticket agent)

40 ticket-printing machine (ticket-stamping machine)
41 hand-operated ticket printer
42 pocket timetable (*Am.* pocket train schedule)
43 luggage rest
44 first aid station
45 Travellers' (*Am.* Travelers') Aid
46 telephone box (telephone booth, telephone kiosk, call box)
47 cigarettes and tobacco kiosk
48 flower stand
49 railway information clerk
50 official timetable (official railway guide, *Am.* train schedule)

205 Station Platform

1 platform
2 steps to the platform
3 bridge to the platforms
4 platform number
5 platform roofing
6 passengers
7–12 luggage
7 suitcase (case)
8 luggage label
9 hotel sticker
10 travelling (*Am.* traveling) bag
11 hat box
12 umbrella, a walking-stick umbrella
13 main building; *also:* offices
14 platform
15 crossing
16 news trolley
17 news vendor (*Am.* news dealer)
18 reading matter for the journey
19 edge of the platform
20 railway policeman (*Am.* railroad policeman)
21 destination board
22 destination indicator
23 departure time indicator
24 delay indicator
25 suburban train, a railcar
26 special compartment
27 platform loudspeaker
28 station sign
29 electric trolley (electric truck)
30 loading foreman
31 porter (*Am.* redcap)
32 barrow
33 drinking fountain
34 electric Trans-Europe Express; *also:* Intercity train
35 electric locomotive, an express locomotive
36 collector bow (sliding bow)
37 secretarial compartment
38 destination board
39 wheel tapper
40 wheel-tapping hammer
41 station foreman
42 signal
43 red cap

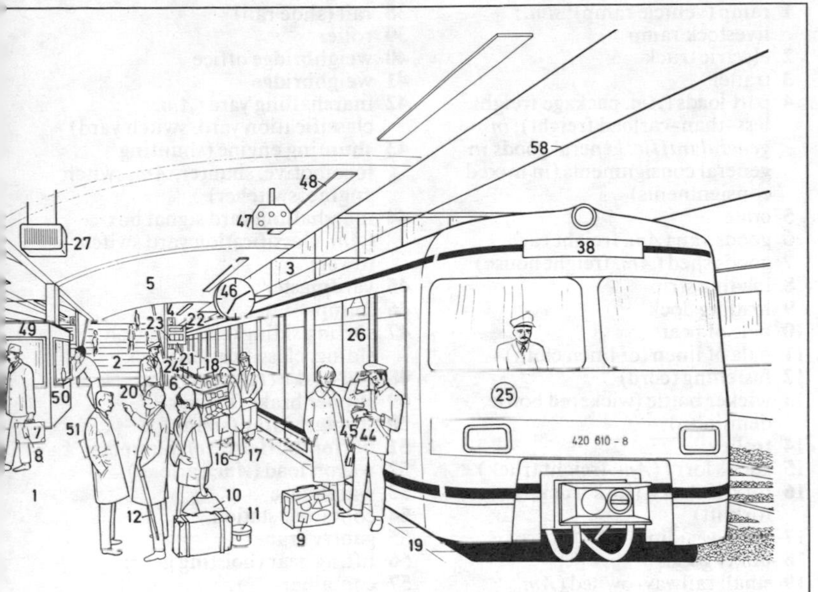

44 inspector
45 pocket timetable (*Am.* pocket train schedule)
46 platform clock
47 starting signal
48 platform lighting
49 refreshment kiosk
50 beer bottle
51 newspaper
52 parting kiss
53 embrace
54 platform seat
55 litter bin (*Am.* litter basket)
56 platform post box (*Am.* platform mailbox)
57 platform telephone
58 trolley wire (overhead contact wire)
59–61 track
59 rail
60 sleeper (*Am.* tie, crosstie)
61 ballast (bed)

206 Goods Station (Freight Depot)

1 ramp (vehicle ramp); *sim.:* livestock ramp
2 electric truck
3 trailer
4 part loads (*Am.* package freight, less-than-carload freight); *in general traffic:* general goods in general consignments (in mixed consignments)
5 crate
6 goods van (*Am.* freight car)
7 goods shed (*Am.* freight house)
8 loading strip
9 loading dock
10 bale of peat
11 bale of linen (of linen cloth)
12 fastening (cord)
13 wicker bottle (wickered bottle, demijohn)
14 trolley
15 goods lorry (*Am.* freight truck)
16 forklift truck (fork truck, forklift)
17 loading siding
18 bulky goods
19 small railway-owned (*Am.* railroad-owned) container
20 showman's caravan (*sim.:* circus caravan)
21 flat wagon (*Am.* flat freight car)
22 loading gauge (*Am.* gage)
23 bale of straw
24 flat wagon (*Am.* flatcar) with side stakes
25 fleet of lorries (*Am.* trucks)
26–39 goods shed (*Am.* freight house)
26 goods office (forwarding office, *Am.* freight office)
27 part-load goods (*Am.* package freight)
28 forwarding agent (*Am.* freight agent, shipper)
29 loading foreman
30 consignment note (waybill)
31 weighing machine
32 pallet
33 porter
34 electric cart (electric truck)
35 trailer
36 loading supervisor
37 goods shed door (*Am.* freight house door)
38 rail (slide rail)
39 roller
40 weighbridge office
41 weighbridge
42 marshalling yard (*Am.* classification yard, switch yard)
43 shunting engine (shunting locomotive, shunter, *Am.* switch engine, switcher)
44 marshalling yard signal box (*Am.* classification yard switch tower)
45 yardmaster
46 hump
47 sorting siding (classification siding, classification track)
48 rail brake (retarder)
49 slipper brake (slipper)
50 storage siding (siding)
51 buffer (buffers, *Am.* bumper)
52 wagon load (*Am.* carload)
53 warehouse
54 container station
55 gantry crane
56 lifting gear (hoisting gear)
57 container
58 container wagon (*Am.* container car)
59 semi-trailer

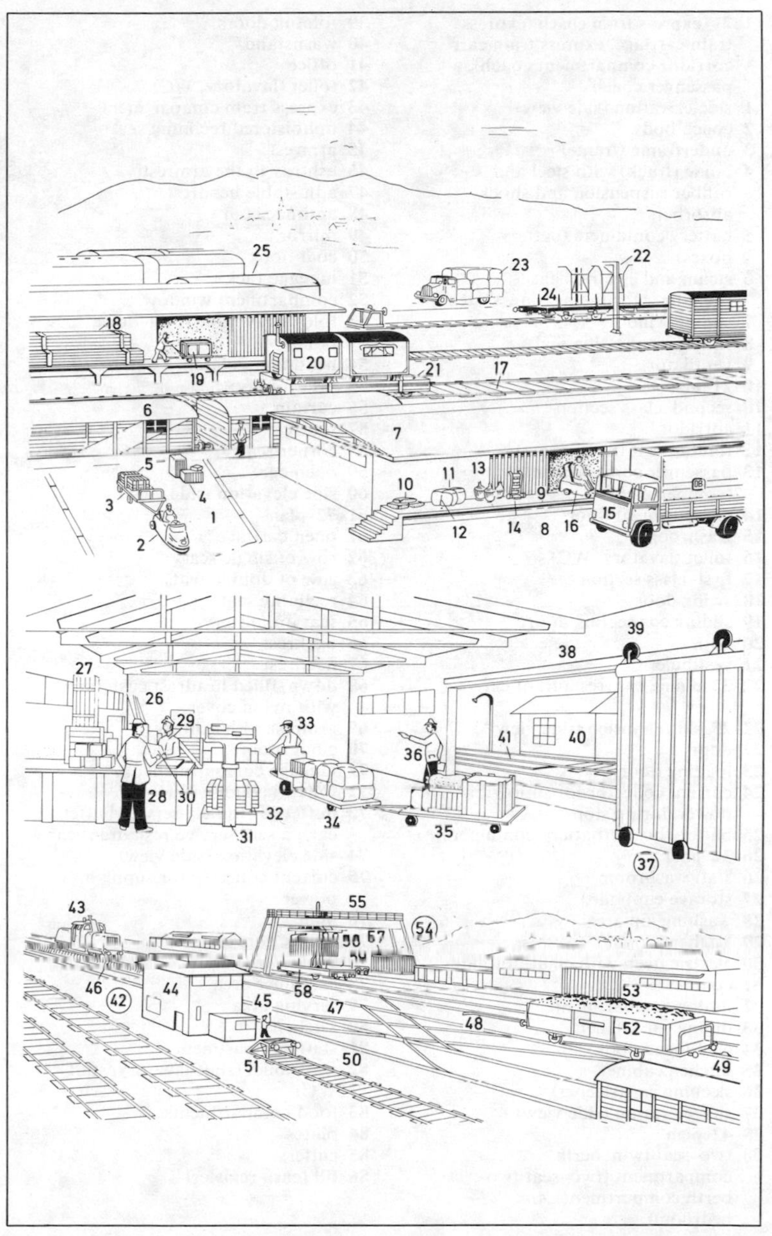
1
2
3
4
5
6
7
8
9
10
11
12
13
14
15
16
17
18
19
20
21
22
23
24
25
26
27
28
29
30
31
32
33
34
35
36
37
38
39
40
41
42
43
44
45
46
47
48
49
50
51
52
53
54
55
56
57
58

207 Railway Vehicles (Rolling Stock) I

1-21 express train coach (express train carriage, express train car, corridor compartment coach), a passenger coach
1 side elevation (side view)
2 coach body
3 underframe (frame)
4 bogie (truck) with steel and rubber suspension and shock absorbers
5 battery containers (battery boxes)
6 steam and electric heat exchanger for the heating system
7 sliding window
8 rubber connecting seal
9 ventilator
10-21 plan
10 second-class section
11 corridor
12 folding seat (tip-up seat)
13 passenger compartment (compartment)
14 compartment door
15 washroom
16 toilet (lavatory, WC)
17 first-class section
18 swing door
19 sliding connecting door
20 door
21 vestibule
22-32 dining car (restaurant car, diner)
22-25 side elevation (side view)
22 door
23 loading door
24 current collector for supplying power during stops
25 battery boxes (battery containers)
26-32 plan
26 staff washroom
27 storage cupboard
28 washing-up area
29 kitchen
30 electric oven with eight hotplates
31 counter
32 dining compartment
33 dining car kitchen
34 chef (head cook)
35 kitchen cabinet
36 sleeping car (sleeper)
37 side elevation (side view)
38-42 plan
38 two-seat twin-berth compartment (two-seat two-berth compartment, *Am.* bedroom)
39 folding doors
40 washstand
41 office
42 toilet (lavatory, WC)
43 express train compartment
44 upholstered reclining seat
45 armrest
46 ashtray in the armrest
47 adjustable headrest
48 antimacassar
49 mirror
50 coat hook
51 luggage rack
52 compartment window
53 fold-away table (pull-down table)
54 heating regulator
55 litter receptacle
56 curtain
57 footrest
58 corner seat
59 open car
60 side elevation (side view)
61-72 plan
61 open carriage
62 row of single seats
63 row of double seats
64 reclining seat
65 seat upholstery
66 backrest
67 headrest
68 down-filled headrest cushion with nylon cover
69 armrest with ashtray
70 cloakroom
71 luggage compartment
72 toilet (lavatory, WC)
73 buffet car (quick-service buffet car), a self-service restaurant car
74 side elevation (side view)
75 current collector for supplying power
76 plan
77 dining compartment
78-79 buffet (buffet compartment)
78 customer area
79 serving area
80 kitchen
81 staff compartment
82 staff toilet (staff lavatory, staff WC)
83 food compartments
84 plates
85 cutlery
86 till (cash register)

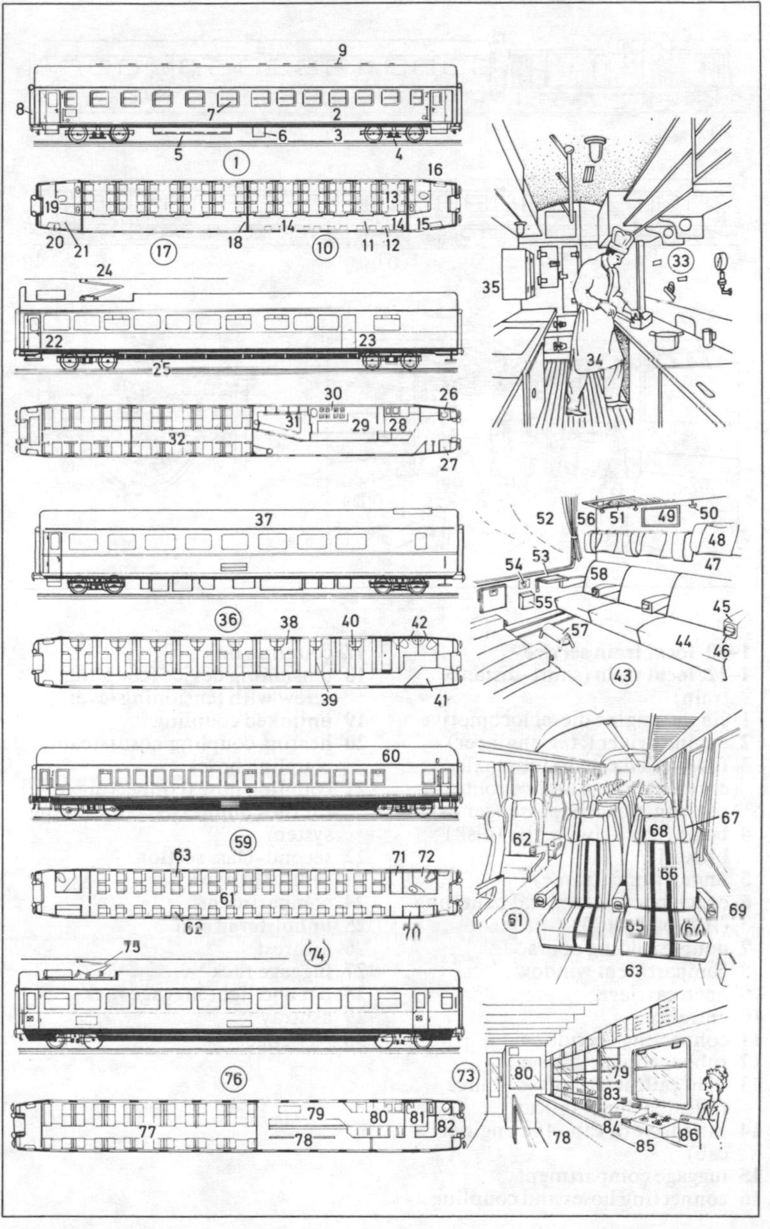
9
8
7
2
6
3
5
4
1
16
19
13
14
14
15
20
21
18
11
12
17
10
24
22
23
25
35
33
34
30
26
31
29
28
32
27
37
52
56
51
49
50
48
47
54
53
58
55
45
36
38
40
42
57
44
46
39
41
43
60
67
68
62
59
63
71
72
66
61
62
70
61
65
64
69
75
74
63
76
73
80
79
83
77
79
80
81
82
78
84
78
85
86

208 Railway Vehicles (Rolling Stock) II

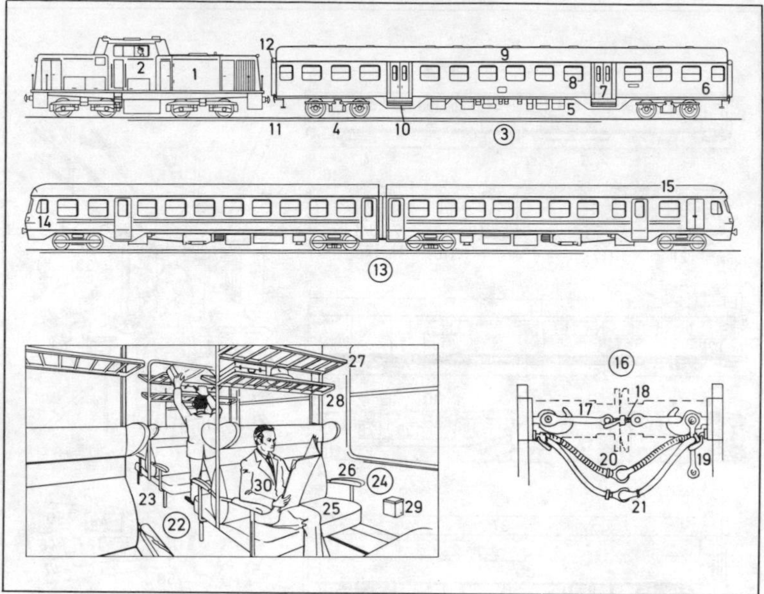

1–30 local train service
1–12 local train (short-distance train)
1 single-engine diesel locomotive
2 engine driver (*Am.* engineer)
3 four-axled coach (four-axled car) for short-distance routes, a passenger coach (passenger car)
4 bogie (truck) [with disc (disk) brakes]
5 underframe (frame)
6 coach body with metal panelling (*Am.* paneling)
7 double folding doors
8 compartment window
9 open carriage
10 entrance
11 connecting corridor
12 rubber connecting seal
13 light railcar, a short-distance railcar, a diesel railcar
14 cab (driver's cab, *Am.* engineer's cab)
15 luggage compartment
16 connecting hoses and coupling
17 coupling link
18 tensioning device (coupling screw with tensioning lever)
19 unlinked coupling
20 heating coupling hose (steam coupling hose)
21 coupling hose (connecting hose) for the compressed-air braking system
22 second-class section
23 central gangway
24 compartment
25 upholstered seat
26 armrest
27 luggage rack
28 hat and light luggage rack
29 ashtray
30 passenger

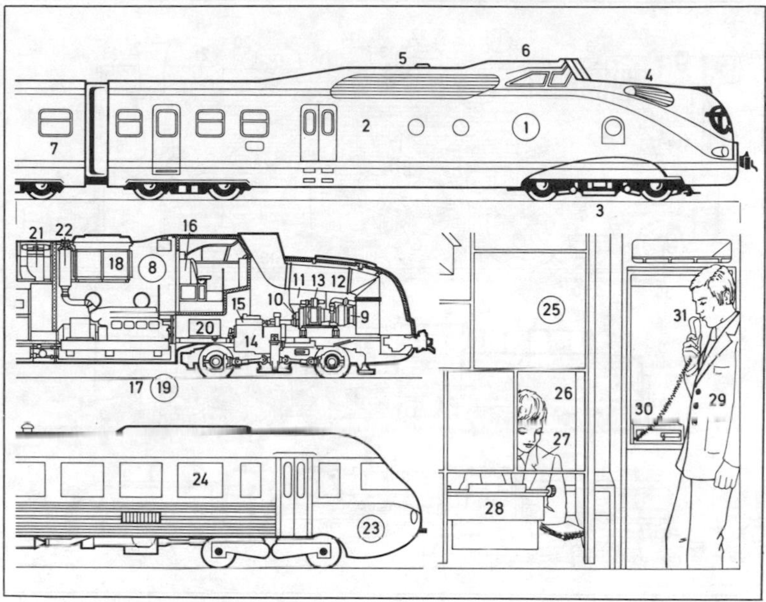

1–22 Trans-Europe Express
1 German Federal Railway trainset, a diesel trainset or gas turbine trainset
2 driving unit
3 drive wheel unit
4 main engine
5 diesel generator unit
6 cab (driver's cab, *Am.* engineer's cab)
7 second coach
8 gas turbine driving unit [diagram]
9 gas turbine
10 turbine transmission
11 air intake
12 exhaust with silencers (*Am.* mufflers)
13 dynastarter
14 Voith transmission
15 heat exchanger for the transmission oil
16 gas turbine controller
17 gas turbine fuel tank
18 oil-to-air cooling unit for transmission and turbine
19 auxiliary diesel engine
20 fuel tank
21 cooling unit
22 exhaust with silencers (*Am.* mufflers)
23 **Société Nationale des Chemins de Fer Français** (SNCF) experimental trainset with six-cylinder underfloor diesel engine and twin-shaft gas turbine
24 turbine unit with silencers (*Am.* mufflers)
25 secretarial compartment
26 typing compartment
27 secretary
28 typewriter
29 travelling (*Am.* traveling) salesman
30 dictating machine
31 microphone

210 Railway Vehicles (Rolling Stock) IV

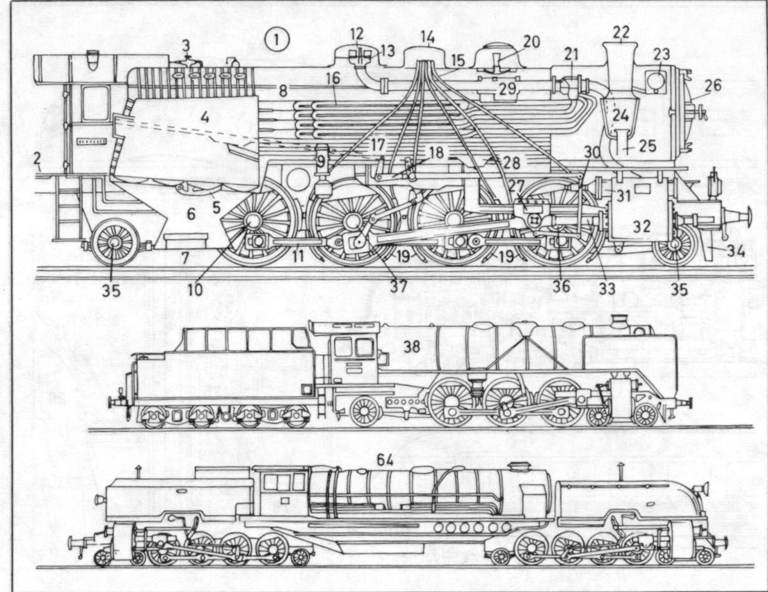

1–69 steam locomotives

2–37 locomotive boiler and driving gear

2 tender platform with coupling
3 safety valve for excess boiler pressure
4 firebox
5 drop grate
6 ashpan with damper doors
7 bottom door of the ashpan
8 smoke tubes (flue tubes)
9 feed pump
10 axle bearing
11 connecting rod
12 steam dome
13 regulator valve (regulator main valve)
14 sand dome
15 sand pipes (sand tubes)
16 boiler (boiler barrel)
17 fire tubes or steam tubes
18 reversing gear (steam reversing gear)
19 sand pipes
20 feed valve
21 steam collector
22 chimney (smokestack, smoke outlet and waste steam exhaust)
23 feedwater preheater (feedwater heater, economizer)
24 spark arrester
25 blast pipe
26 smokebox door
27 cross head
28 mud drum
29 top feedwater tray
30 combination lever
31 steam chest
32 cylinder
33 piston rod with stuffing box (packing box)
34 guard iron (rail guard, *Am.* pilot, cowcatcher)
35 carrying axle (running axle, dead axle)
36 coupled axle
37 driving axle
38 express locomotive with tender

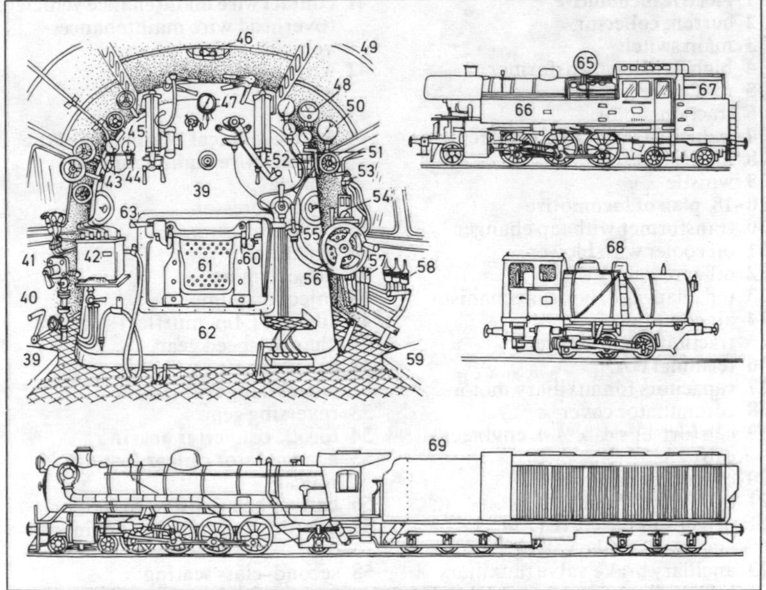

39–63 cab (driver's cab, *Am.* engineer's cab)
39 fireman's seat
40 drop grate lever
41 line steam injector
42 automatic lubricant pump (automatic lubricator)
43 preheater pressure gauge (*Am.* gage)
44 carriage heating pressure gauge (*Am.* gage)
45 water gauge (*Am.* gage)
46 light
47 boiler pressure gauge (*Am.* gage)
48 distant-reading temperature gauge (*Am.* gage)
49 cab (driver's cab, *Am.* engineer's cab)
50 brake pressure gauge (*Am.* gage)
51 whistle valve handle
52 driver's timetable (*Am.* engineer's schedule)
53 driver's brake valve (*Am.* engineer's brake valve)
54 speed recorder (tachograph)
55 sanding valve
56 reversing wheel
57 emergency brake valve
58 release valve
59 driver's seat (*Am.* engineer's seat)
60 firehole shield
61 firehole door
62 vertical boiler
63 firedoor handle handgrip
64 articulated locomotive (Garratt locomotive)
65 tank locomotive
66 water tank
67 fuel tender
68 steam storage locomotive (fireless locomotive)
69 condensing locomotive (locomotive with condensing tender)

1 electric locomotive
2 current collector
3 main switch
4 high-tension transformer
5 roof cable
6 traction motor
7 inductive train control system
8 main air reservoir
9 whistle
10–18 plan of locomotive
10 transformer with tap changer
11 oil cooler with blower
12 oil-circulating pump
13 tap changer driving mechanism
14 air compressor
15 traction motor blower
16 terminal box
17 capacitors for auxiliary motors
18 commutator cover
19 cab (driver's cab, *Am.* engineer's cab)
20 controller handwheel
21 dead man's handle
22 driver's brake valve (*Am.* engineer's brake valve)
23 ancillary brake valve (auxiliary brake valve)
24 pressure gauge (*Am.* gage)
25 bypass switch for the dead man's handle
26 tractive effort indicator
27 train heating voltage indicator
28 contact wire voltage indicator (overhead wire voltage indicator)
29 high-tension voltage indicator
30 on/off switch for the current collector
31 main switch
32 sander switch (sander control)
33 anti-skid brake switch
34 visual display for the ancillary systems
35 speedometer
36 running step indicator
37 clock
38 controls for the inductive train control system
39 cab heating switch
40 whistle lever
41 contact wire maintenance vehicle (overhead wire maintenance vehicle), a diesel railcar
42 work platform (working platform)
43 ladder
44–54 mechanical equipment of the contact wire maintenance vehicle
44 air compressor
45 blower oil pump
46 generator
47 diesel engine
48 injection pump
49 silencer (*Am.* muffler)
50 change-speed gear
51 cardan shaft
52 wheel flange lubricator
53 reversing gear
54 torque converter bearing
55 accumulator railcar (battery railcar)
56 battery box (battery container)
57 cab (driver's cab, *Am.* engineer's cab)
58 second-class seating arrangement
59 toilet (lavatory, WC)
60 fast electric multiple-unit train
61 front railcar
62 driving trailer car

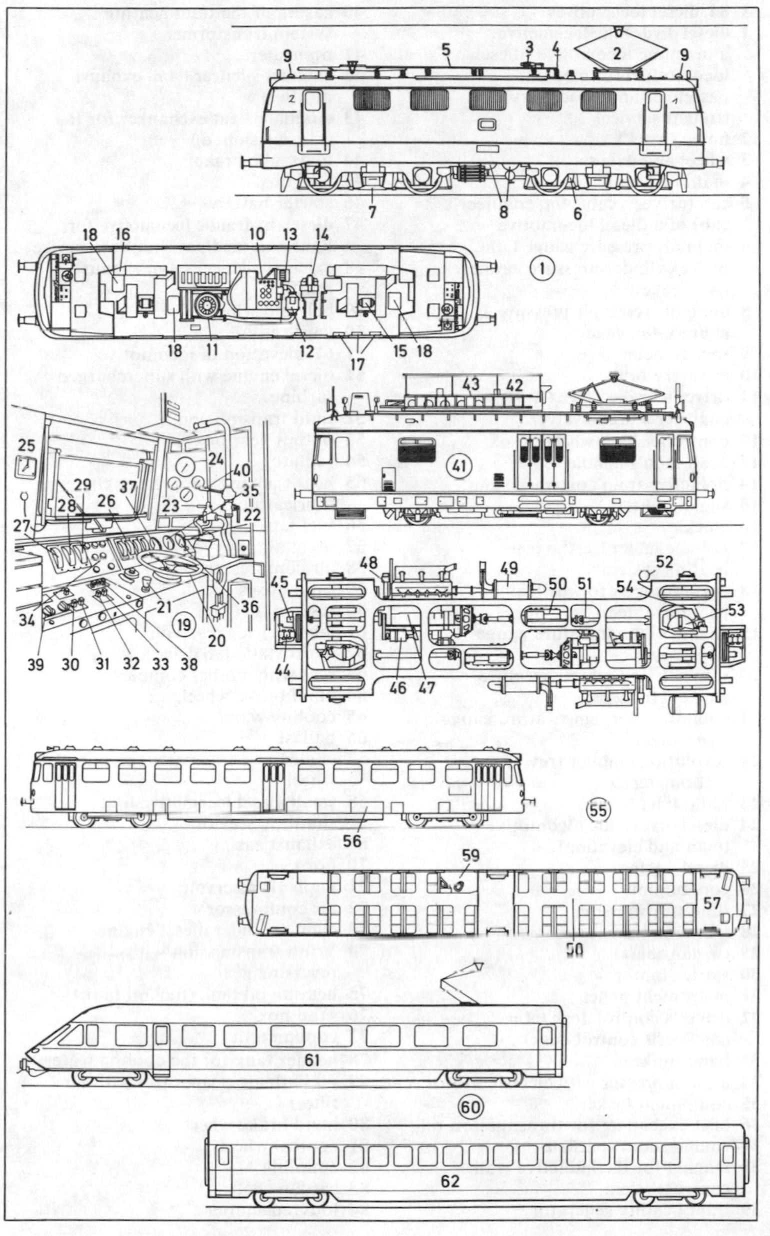
9
5
3
4
2
9
7
8
6
18
16
10
13
14
1
18
11
12
17
15
18
43
42
41
25
29
28
37
26
24
40
35
22
23
27
34
21
36
19
20
39
30
31
32
33
38
48
49
52
45
50
51
54
53
44
46
47
55
56
59
57
61
60
62

1-84 diesel locomotives
1 **diesel-hydraulic locomotive,** a mainline locomotive (diesel locomotive) for medium passenger and goods service (freight service)
2 bogie (truck)
3 wheel and axle set
4 main fuel tank
5 cab (driver's cab, *Am.* engineer's cab) of a diesel locomotive
6 main air pressure gauge (*Am.* gage)
7 brake cylinder pressure gauge (*Am.* gage)
8 main air reservoir pressure gauge (*Am.* gage)
9 speedometer
10 auxiliary brake
11 driver's brake valve (*Am.* engineer's brake valve)
12 controller handwheel
13 dead man's handle
14 inductive train control system
15 signal lights
16 clock
17 voltage meter for the train heating system
18 current meter for the train heating system
19 engine oil temperature gauge (*Am.* gage)
20 transmission oil temperature gauge (*Am.* gage)
21 cooling water temperature gauge (*Am.* gage)
22 revolution counter (rev counter, tachometer)
23 radio telephone
24 diesel-hydraulic locomotive [plan and elevation]
25 diesel engine
26 cooling unit
27 fluid transmission
28 wheel and axle drive
29 cardan shaft
30 starter motor
31 instrument panel
32 driver's control desk (*Am.* engineer's control desk)
33 hand brake
34 air compressor with electric motor
35 equipment locker
36 heat exchanger for transmission oil
37 engine room ventilator
38 magnet for the inductive train control system
39 train heating generator
40 casing of the train heating system transformer
41 preheater
42 exhaust silencer (*Am.* exhaust muffler)
43 auxiliary heat exchanger for the transmission oil
44 hydraulic brake
45 tool box
46 starter battery
47 **diesel-hydraulic locomotive** for light and medium shunting service
48 exhaust silencer (*Am.* exhaust muffler)
49 bell and whistle
50 yard radio
51-67 elevation of locomotive
51 diesel engine with supercharged turbine
52 fluid transmission
53 output gear box
54 radiator
55 heat exchanger for the engine lubricating oil
56 fuel tank
57 main air reservoir
58 air compressor
59 sand boxes
60 reserve fuel tank
61 auxiliary air reservoir
62 hydrostatic fan drive
63 seat with clothes compartment
64 hand brake wheel
65 cooling water
66 ballast
67 engine and transmission control wheel
68 **small diesel locomotive** for shunting service
69 exhaust casing
70 horn
71 main air reservoir
72 air compressor
73 eight–cylinder diesel engine
74 Voith transmission with reversing gear
75 heating oil tank (fuel oil tank)
76 sand box
77 cooling unit
78 header tank for the cooling water
79 oil bath air cleaner (oil bath air filter)
80 hand brake wheel
81 control wheel
82 coupling
83 cardan shaft
84 louvred shutter

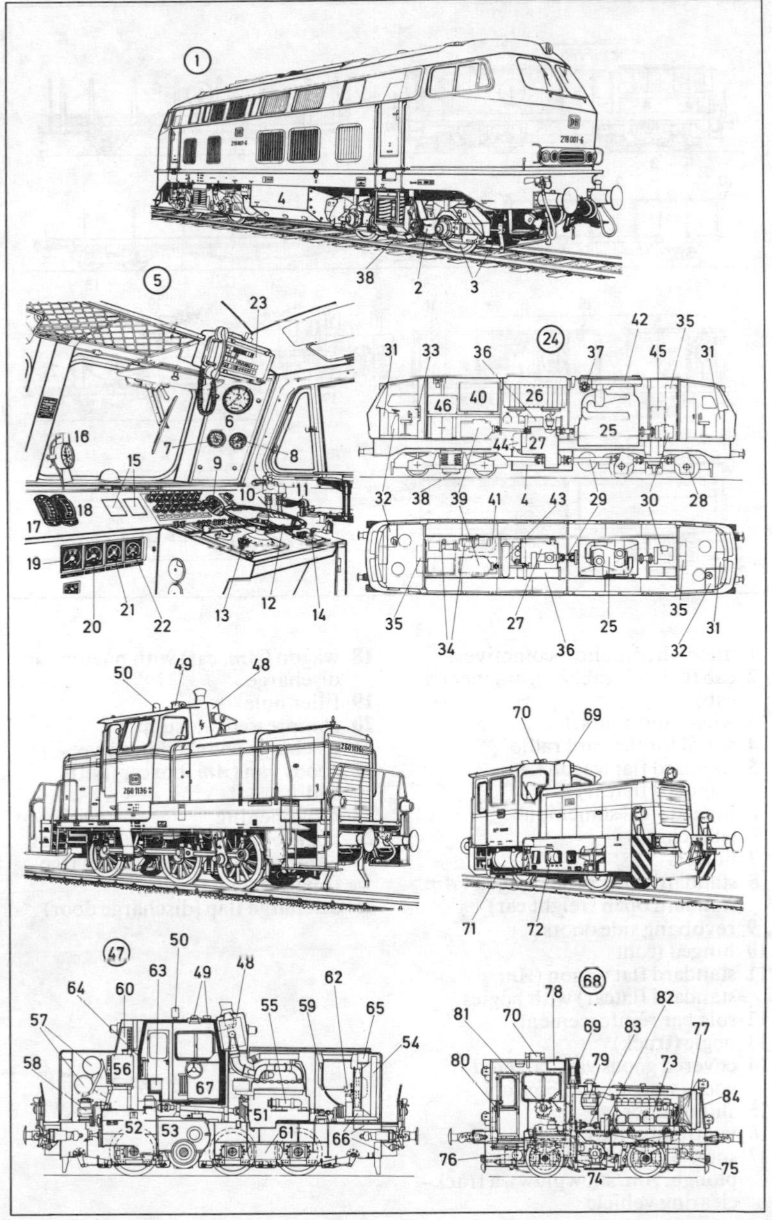
1
4
38
2
3
218 001-6
5
23
16
6
7
8
15
9
10
11
18
17
19
20
21
22
13
12
14
24
31
33
36
37
42
35
45
31
46
40
26
25
44
27
32
38
39
41
4
43
29
30
28
35
34
27
36
25
35
32
31
50
49
48
260 1136
70
69
71
72
47
50
63
49
48
62
64
60
57
55
59
65
54
58
56
67
51
52
53
61
66
68
78
82
81
70
69
83
77
80
79
73
84
76
74
75

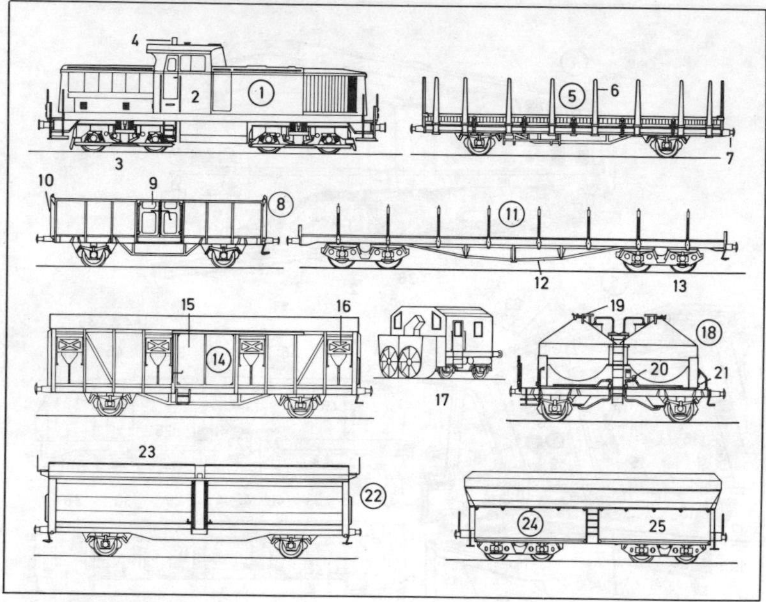

1 diesel-hydraulic locomotive
2 cab (driver's cab, *Am.* engineer's cab)
3 wheel and axle set
4 aerial for the yard radio
5 standard flat wagon (*Am.* standard flatcar)
6 hinged steel stanchion (stanchion)
7 buffers
8 standard open goods wagon (*Am.* standard open freight car)
9 revolving side doors
10 hinged front
11 standard flat wagon (*Am.* standard flatcar) with bogies
12 sole bar reinforcement
13 bogie (truck)
14 covered goods van (covered goods wagon, *Am.* boxcar)
15 sliding door
16 ventilation flap
17 snow blower (rotary snow plough, *Am.* snowplow), a track-clearing vehicle
18 wagon (*Am.* car) with pneumatic discharge
19 filler hole
20 compressed-air supply
21 discharge connection valve
22 goods van (*Am.* boxcar) with sliding roof
23 roof opening
24 bogie open self-discharge wagon (*Am.* bogie open self-discharge freight car)
25 discharge flap (discharge door)

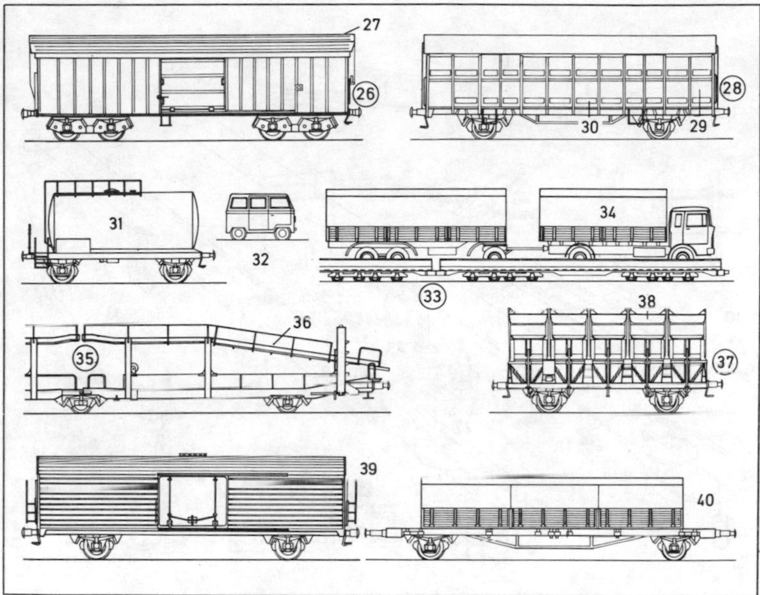

26 bogie wagon with swivelling (*Am.* swiveling) roof
27 swivelling (*Am.* swiveling) roof
28 large-capacity wagon (*Am.* large-capacity car) for small livestock
29 sidewall with ventilation flaps (slatted wall)
30 ventilation flap
31 tank wagon (*Am.* tank car)
32 track inspection railcar
33 open special wagons (*Am.* open special freight cars)
34 lorry (*Am.* truck) with trailer
35 two-tier car carrier (double-deck car carrier)
36 hinged upper deck
37 tipper wagon (*Am.* dump car) with skips
38 skip
39 general-purpose refrigerator wagon (refrigerator van, *Am.* refrigerator car)
40 interchangeable bodies for flat wagons (*Am.* flatcars)

214 Mountain Railways (*Am.* Mountain Railroads) and Cableways

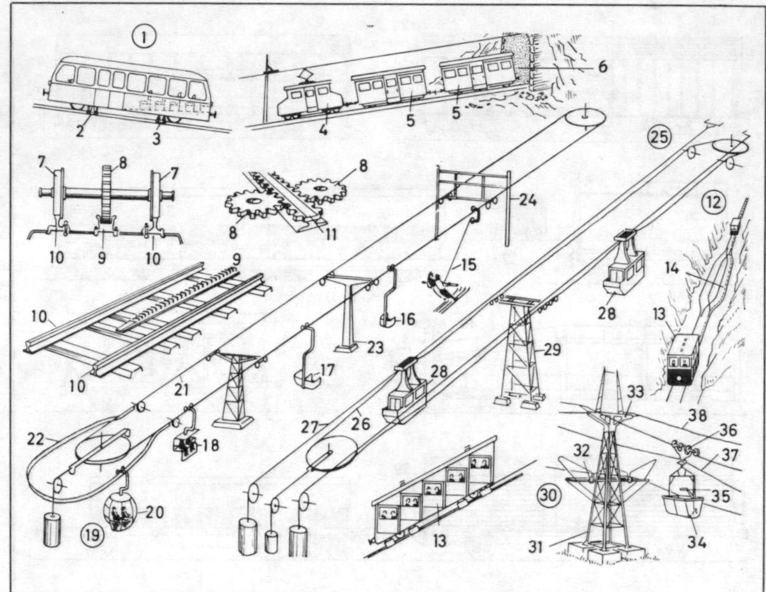

1-14 mountain railways (*Am.* mountain railroads)
1 adhesion railcar
2 drive
3 emergency brake
4-5 rack mountain railway (rack-and-pinion railway, cog railway, *Am.* cog railroad, rack railroad)
4 electric rack railway locomotive (*Am.* electric rack railroad locomotive)
5 rack railway coach (rack railway trailer, *Am.* rack railroad car)
6 tunnel
7-11 rack railways (rack-and-pinion railways, *Am.* rack railroads) [systems]
7 running wheel (carrying wheel)
8 driving pinion
9 rack [with teeth machined on top edge]
10 rail
11 rack [with teeth on both outer edges]
12 funicular railway (funicular, cable railway)
13 funicular railway car
14 haulage cable
15-38 cableways (ropeways, cable suspension lines)
15-24 single-cable ropeways (single-cable suspension lines), endless ropeways
15 drag lift
16-18 chair lift
16 lift chair, a single chair
17 double lift chair, a two-seater chair
18 double chair (two-seater chair) with coupling
19 gondola cableway, an endless cableway
20 gondola (cabin)
21 endless cable, a suspension (supporting) and haulage cable
22 U-rail
23 single-pylon support
24 gantry support
25 double-cable ropeway (double-cable suspension line), a suspension line with balancing cabins
26 haulage cable
27 suspension cable (supporting cable)
28 cabin
29 intermediate support
30 cableway (ropeway, suspension line), a double-cable ropeway (double-cable suspension line)
31 pylon
32 haulage cable roller
33 cable guide rail (suspension cable bearing)
34 skip, a tipping bucket (*Am.* dumping bucket)
35 stop
36 pulley cradle

37 haulage cable
38 suspension cable (supporting cable)
39 **valley station** (lower station)
40 tension weight shaft
41 tension weight for the suspension cable (supporting cable)
42 tension weight for the haulage cable
43 tension cable pulley
44 suspension cable (supporting cable)
45 haulage cable
46 balance cable (lower cable)
47 auxiliary cable (emergency cable)
48 auxiliary-cable tensioning mechanism (emergency-cable tensioning mechanism)
49 haulage cable rollers
50 spring buffer (*Am.* spring bumper)
51 valley station platform (lower station platform)
52 cabin (cableway gondola, ropeway gondola, suspension line gondola), a large-capacity cabin
53 pulley cradle
54 suspension gear
55 stabilizer
56 guide rail
57 **top station** (upper station)
58 suspension cable guide (supporting cable guide)
59 suspension cable anchorage (supporting cable anchorage)
60 haulage cable rollers
61 haulage cable guide wheel
62 haulage cable driving pulley
63 main drive
64 standby drive
65 control room
66 **cabin pulley cradle**
67 main pulley cradle
68 double cradle
69 two-wheel cradle
70 running wheels
71 suspension cable brake (supporting cable brake), an emergency brake in case of haulage cable failure
72 suspension gear bolt
73 haulage cable sleeve
74 balance cable sleeve (lower cable sleeve)
75 derailment guard
76 **cable supports** (ropeway supports, suspension line supports, intermediate supports)
77 pylon, a framework support
78 tubular steel pylon, a tubular steel support
79 suspension cable guide rail (supporting cable guide rail, support guide rail)
80 support truss, a frame for work on the cable
81 base of the support

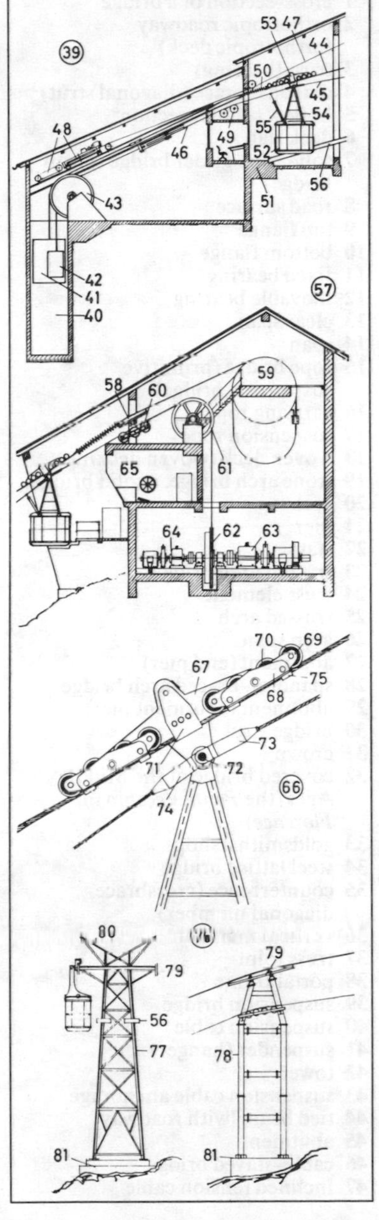

215 Bridges

1 cross-section of a bridge
2 orthotropic roadway (orthotropic deck)
3 truss (bracing)
4 diagonal brace (diagonal strut)
5 hollow tubular section
6 deck slab
7 solid-web girder bridge (beam bridge)
8 road surface
9 top flange
10 bottom flange
11 fixed bearing
12 movable bearing
13 clear span
14 span
15 rope bridge (primitive suspension bridge)
16 carrying rope
17 suspension rope
18 woven deck (woven decking)
19 stone arch bridge, a solid bridge
20 arch
21 pier
22 statue
23 trussed arch bridge
24 truss element
25 trussed arch
26 arch span
27 abutment (end pier)
28 spandrel-braced arch bridge
29 abutment (abutment pier)
30 bridge strut
31 crown
32 covered bridge of the Middle Ages (the *Ponte Vecchio* in *Florence*)
33 goldsmiths' shops
34 steel lattice bridge
35 counterbrace (crossbrace, diagonal member)
36 vertical member
37 truss joint
38 portal frame
39 suspension bridge
40 suspension cable
41 suspender (hanger)
42 tower
43 suspension cable anchorage
44 tied beam [with roadway]
45 abutment
46 cable-stayed bridge
47 inclined tension cable
48 inclined cable anchorage
49 reinforced concrete bridge
50 reinforced concrete arch
51 inclined cable system (multiple cable system)
52 flat bridge, a plate girder bridge
53 stiffener
54 pier
55 bridge bearing
56 cutwater
57 straits bridge, a bridge built of precast elements
58 precast construction unit
59 viaduct
60 valley bottom
61 reinforced concrete pier
62 scaffolding
63 lattice swing bridge
64 turntable
65 pivot pier
66 pivoting half (pivoting section, pivoting span, movable half) of bridge
67 flat swing bridge
68 middle section
69 pivot
70 parapet (handrailing)

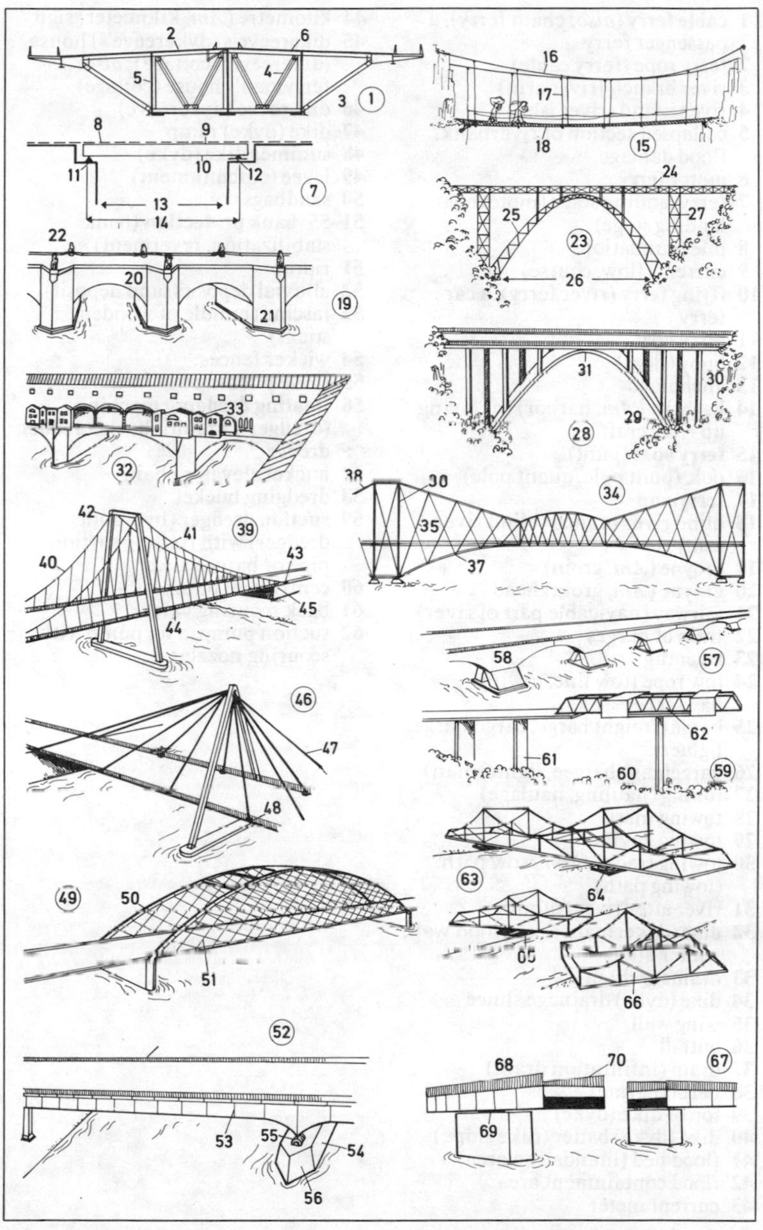
1
2
3
4
5
6
7
8
9
10
11
12
13
14
15
16
17
18
19
20
21
22
23
24
25
26
27
28
29
30
31
32
33
34
35
36
37
38
39
40
41
42
43
44
45
46
47
48
49
50
51
52
53
54
55
56
57
58
59
60
61
62
63
64
65
66
67
68
69
70

1 **cable ferry** (*also:* chain ferry), a passenger ferry
2 ferry rope (ferry cable)
3 river branch (river arm)
4 river island (river islet)
5 collapsed section of riverbank, flood damage
6 **motor ferry**
7 ferry landing stage (motorboat landing stage)
8 pile foundations
9 current (flow, course)
10 **flying ferry** (river ferry), a car ferry
11 ferry boat
12 buoy (float)
13 anchorage
14 harbour (*Am.* harbor) for laying up river craft
15 **ferry boat** (punt)
16 pole (punt pole, quant pole)
17 ferryman
18 blind river branch (blind river arm)
19 groyne (*Am.* groin)
20 groyne (*Am.* groin) head
21 fairway (navigable part of river)
22 **train of barges**
23 river tug
24 tow rope (tow line, towing hawser)
25 barge (freight barge, cargo barge, lighter)
26 bargeman (bargee, lighterman)
27 **towing** (hauling, haulage)
28 towing mast
29 towing engine
30 towing track; *form.:* tow path (towing path)
31 river after river training
32 **dike** (dyke, main dike, flood wall, winter dike)
33 drainage ditch
34 dike (dyke) drainage sluice
35 wing wall
36 outfall
37 drain (infiltration drain)
38 berm (berme)
39 top of dike (dyke)
40 dike (dyke) batter (dike slope)
41 flood bed (inundation area)
42 flood containment area
43 current meter
44 kilometre (*Am.* kilometer) sign
45 dikereeve's (dykereeve's) house (dikereeve's cottage); *also:* ferryman's house (cottage)
46 dikereeve (dykereeve)
47 dike (dyke) ramp
48 summer dike (dyke)
49 levee (embankment)
50 sandbags
51–55 **bank protection** (bank stabilization, revetment)
51 riprap
52 alluvial deposit (sand deposit)
53 fascine (bundle of wooden sticks)
54 wicker fences
55 stone pitching
56 **floating dredging machine** (dredger), a multi-bucket ladder dredge
57 bucket elevator chain
58 dredging bucket
59 **suction dredger** (hydraulic dredger) with trailing suction pipe or barge sucker
60 centrifugal pump
61 back scouring valve
62 suction pump, a jet pump with scouring nozzles

1
3
49
2
5
4
42
9
48
7
6
8
14
10
11
47
15
17
44
44
12
46
18
16
19
20
45
43
13
21
22
23
26
27
24
28
32
25
29
41
31
30
33
39
38
35
34
40
55
37
54
36
53
59
60
61
50
52
51
56
62
57
58

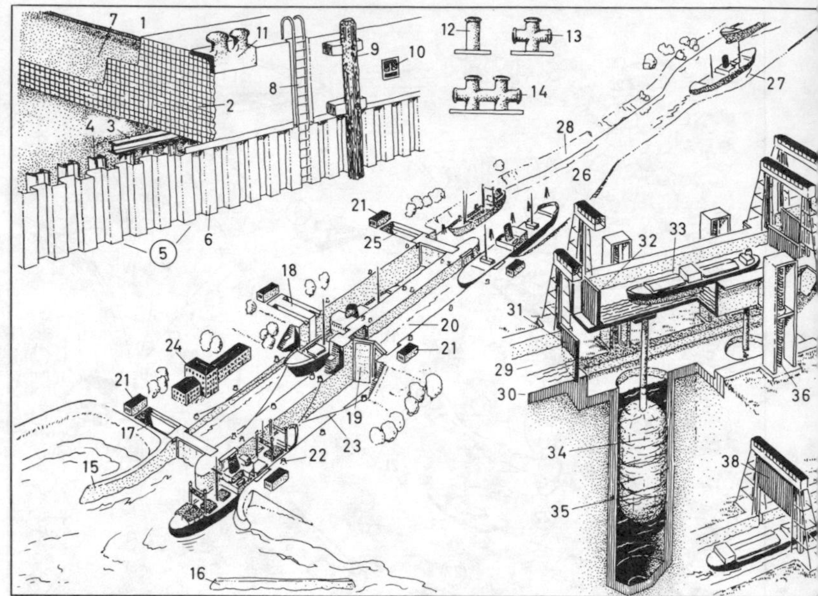

1–14 quay wall
1 road surface
2 body of wall
3 steel sleeper
4 steel pile
5 sheet pile wall (sheet pile bulkhead, sheetpiling)
6 box pile
7 backfilling (filling)
8 ladder
9 fender (fender pile)
10 recessed bollard
11 double bollard
12 bollard
13 cross-shaped bollard (cross-shaped mooring bitt)
14 double cross-shaped bollard (double cross-shaped mooring bitt)
15–28 canal
15–16 canal entrance
15 mole
16 breakwater
17–25 staircase of locks
17 lower level
18 lock gate, a sliding gate
19 mitre (*Am.* miter) gate
20 lock (lock chamber)
21 power house
22 warping capstan (hauling capstan), a capstan
23 warp
24 offices (e.g. canal administration, river police, customs)
25 upper level (head)
26 lock approach
27 lay-by
28 bank slope
29–38 boat lift (*Am.* boat elevator)
29 lower pound (lower reach)
30 canal bed
31 pound lock gate, a vertical gate
32 lock gate
33 boat tank (caisson)
34 float
35 float shaft
36 lifting spindle
37 upper pound (upper reach)
38 vertical gate
39–46 pumping plant and reservoir
39 forebay
40 surge tank
41 pressure pipeline

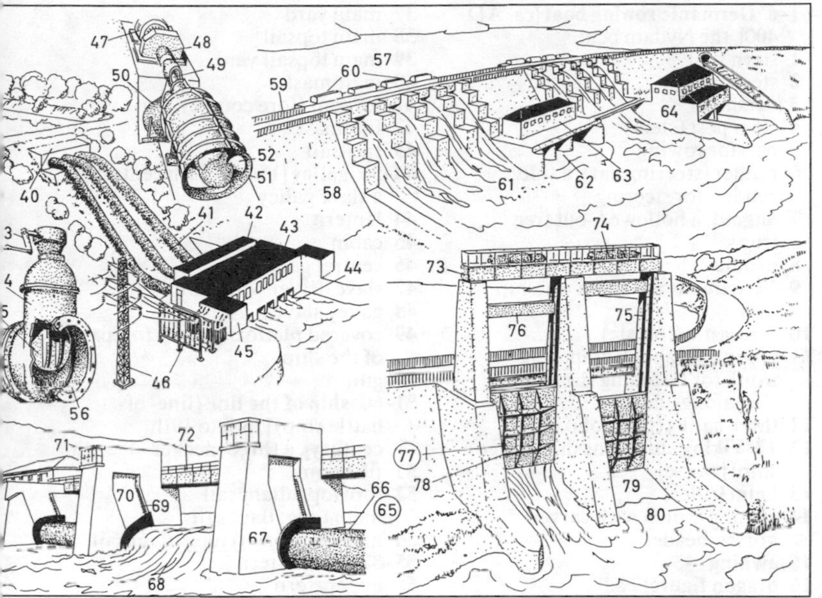

42 valve house (valve control house)
43 turbine house (pumping station)
44 discharge structure (outlet structure)
45 control station
46 transformer station
47–52 axial-flow pump (propeller pump)
47 drive motor
48 gear
49 drive shaft
50 pressure pipe
51 suction head
52 impeller wheel
53–56 sluice valve (sluice gate)
53 crank drive
54 valve housing
55 sliding valve (sliding gate)
56 discharge opening
57–64 dam (barrage)
57 reservoir (storage reservoir, impounding reservoir, impounded reservoir)
58 masonry dam
59 crest of dam
60 spillway (overflow spillway)
61 stilling basin (stilling box, stilling pool)
62 scouring tunnel (outlet tunnel, waste water outlet)
63 valve house (valve control house)
64 power station
65–72 rolling dam (weir), a barrage; *other system:* shutter weir
65 roller, a barrier
66 roller top
67 flange
68 submersible roller
69 rack track
70 recess
71 hoisting gear cabin
72 service bridge (walkway)
73–80 sluice dam
73 hoisting gear bridge
74 hoisting gear (winding gear)
75 guide groove
76 counterweight (counterpoise)
77 sluice gate (floodgate)
78 reinforcing rib
79 dam sill (weir sill)
80 wing wall

218 Types of Historical Ship

1–6 Germanic rowing boat [ca. AD 400], the Nydam boat
1 stern post
2 steersman
3 oarsman
4 stem post (stem)
5 oar, for rowing
6 rudder (steering oar), a side rudder, for steering
7 dugout, a hollowed-out tree trunk
8 paddle
9–12 trireme, a Roman warship
9 ram
10 forecastle (fo'c'sle)
11 grapple (grapnel, grappling iron), for fastening the enemy ship alongside
12 three banks (tiers) of oars
13–17 Viking ship (longship, dragon ship) [Norse]
13 helm (tiller)
14 awning crutch with carved horses' heads
15 awning
16 dragon figurehead
17 shield
18–26 cog (Hansa cog, Hansa ship)
18 anchor cable (anchor rope, anchor hawser)
19 forecastle (fo'c'sle)
20 bowsprit
21 furled (brailed-up) square sail
22 town banner (city banner)
23 aftercastle (sterncastle)
24 rudder, a stem rudder
25 elliptical stern (round stern)
26 wooden fender
27–43 caravel (carvel) ['Santa Maria' 1492]
27 admiral's cabin
28 spanker boom
29 mizzen (mizen, mutton spanker, lateen spanker), a lateen sail
30 lateen yard
31 mizzen (mizen) mast
32 lashing
33 mainsail (main course), a square sail
34 bonnet, a removable strip of canvas
35 bowline
36 bunt line (martinet)
37 main yard
38 main topsail
39 main topsail yard
40 mainmast
41 foresail (fore course)
42 foremast
43 spritsail
44–50 galley [15th to 18th century], a slave galley
44 lantern
45 cabin
46 central gangway
47 slave driver with whip
48 galley slaves
49 covered platform in the forepart of the ship
50 gun
51–60 ship of the line (line-of-battle ship) [18th to 19th century], a three-decker
51 jib boom
52 fore topgallant sail
53 main topgallant sail
54 mizzen (mizen) topgallant sail
55–57 gilded stern
55 upper stern
56 stern gallery
57 quarter gallery, a projecting balcony with ornamental portholes
58 lower stern
59 gunports for broadside fire
60 gunport shutter

1
2
3
4
5
6
7
8
9
10
11
12
13
14
15
16
17
18
19
20
21
22
23
24
25
26
27
28
29
30
31
32
33
34
35
36
37
38
39
40
41
42
43
44
45
46
47
48
49
50
51
52
53
54
55
56
57
58
59
60

219 Sailing Ship I

1–72 rigging (rig, tackle) and sails of a bark (barque)
1–9 masts
1 bowsprit with jib boom
2–4 foremast
2 lower foremast
3 fore topmast
4 fore topgallant mast
5–7 mainmast
5 lower mainmast
6 main topmast
7 main topgallant mast
8–9 mizzen (mizen) mast
8 lower mizzen (lower mizen)
9 mizzen (mizen) topmast
10–19 standing rigging
10 stay
11 topmast stay
12 topgallant stay
13 royal stay
14 jib stay
15 bobstay
16 shrouds
17 fore topmast rigging (main topmast rigging, mizzen (mizen) topmast rigging)
18 fore topgallant rigging (main topgallant rigging)
19 backstays
20–31 fore-and-aft sails
20 fore topmast staysail
21 inner jib
22 outer jib
23 flying jib
24 main topmast staysail
25 main topgallant staysail
26 main royal staysail
27 mizzen (mizen) staysail
28 mizzen (mizen) topmast staysail
29 mizzen (mizen) topgallant staysail
30 mizzen (mizen, spanker, driver)
31 gaff topsail
32–45 spars
32 foreyard
33 lower fore topsail yard
34 upper fore topsail yard
35 lower fore topgallant yard
36 upper fore topgallant yard
37 fore royal yard
38 main yard
39 lower main topsail yard
40 upper main topsail yard
41 lower main topgallant yard
42 upper main topgallant yard
43 main royal yard
44 spanker boom
45 spanker gaff
46 footrope
47 lifts
48 spanker boom topping lift
49 spanker peak halyard
50 foretop
51 fore topmast crosstrees
52 maintop
53 main topmast crosstrees
54 mizzen (mizen) top
55–66 square sails
55 foresail (fore course)
56 lower fore topsail
57 upper fore topsail
58 lower fore topgallant sail
59 upper fore topgallant sail
60 fore royal
61 mainsail (main course)
62 lower main topsail
63 upper main topsail
64 lower main topgallant sail
65 upper main topgallant sail
66 main royal sail
67–71 running rigging
67 braces
68 sheets
69 spanker sheet
70 spanker vangs
71 bunt line
72 reef

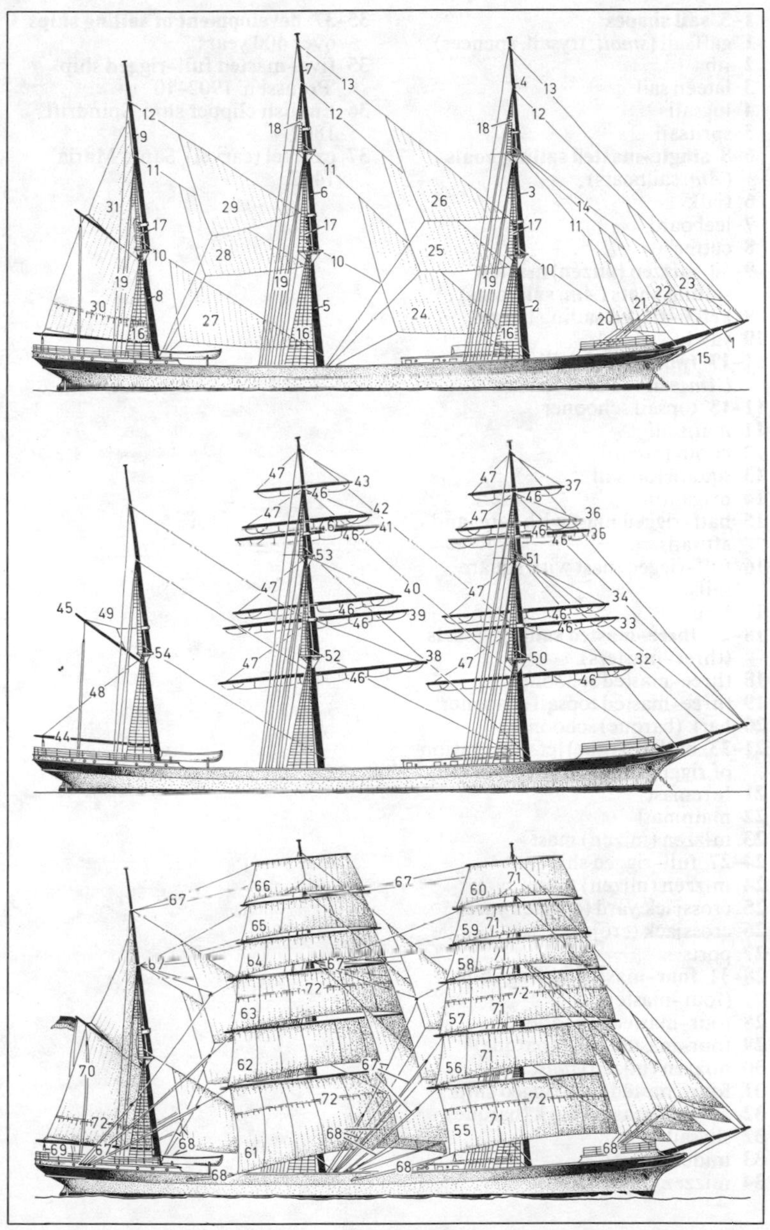
1
2
3
4
5
6
7
8
9
10
11
12
13
14
15
16
17
18
19
20
21
22
23
24
25
26
27
28
29
30
31
32
33
34
35
36
37
38
39
40
41
42
43
44
45
46
47
48
49
50
51
52
53
54
55
56
57
58
59
60
61
62
63
64
65
66
67
68
69
70
71
72

1–5 sail shapes
1 gaffsail (*small:* trysail, spencer)
2 jib
3 lateen sail
4 lugsail
5 spritsail
6–8 single-masted sailing boats (*Am.* sailboats)
6 tjalk
7 leeboard
8 cutter
9–10 mizzen (mizen) masted sailing boats (*Am.* sailboats)
9 ketch-rigged sailing barge
10 yawl
11–17 two-masted sailing boats (*Am.* sailboats)
11–13 topsail schooner
11 mainsail
12 boom foresail
13 square foresail
14 brigantine
15 half-rigged mast with fore-and-aft sails
16 full-rigged mast with square sails
17 brig
18–27 three-masted sailing vessels (three-masters)
18 three-masted schooner
19 three-masted topsail schooner
20 bark (barque) schooner
21–23 bark (barque) [cf. illustration of rigging and sails in plate 219]
21 foremast
22 mainmast
23 mizzen (mizen) mast
24–27 full-rigged ship
24 mizzen (mizen) mast
25 crossjack yard (crojack yard)
26 crossjack (crojack)
27 ports
28–31 four-masted sailing ships (four-masters)
28 four-masted schooner
29 four-masted bark (barque)
30 mizzen (mizen) mast
31 four-masted full-rigged ship
32–34 five-masted bark (barque)
32 skysail
33 middle mast
34 mizzen (mizen) mast
35–37 development of sailing ships over 400 years
35 five-masted full-rigged ship 'Preussen' 1902–10
36 English clipper ship 'Spindrift' 1867
37 caravel (carvel) 'Santa Maria' 1492

1
2
3
4
5
6
7
8
9
10
11
12
13
14
15
16
17
18
19
20
21
22
23
24
25
26
27
28
29
30
31
32
33
34
35
36
37

221 Types of Ship

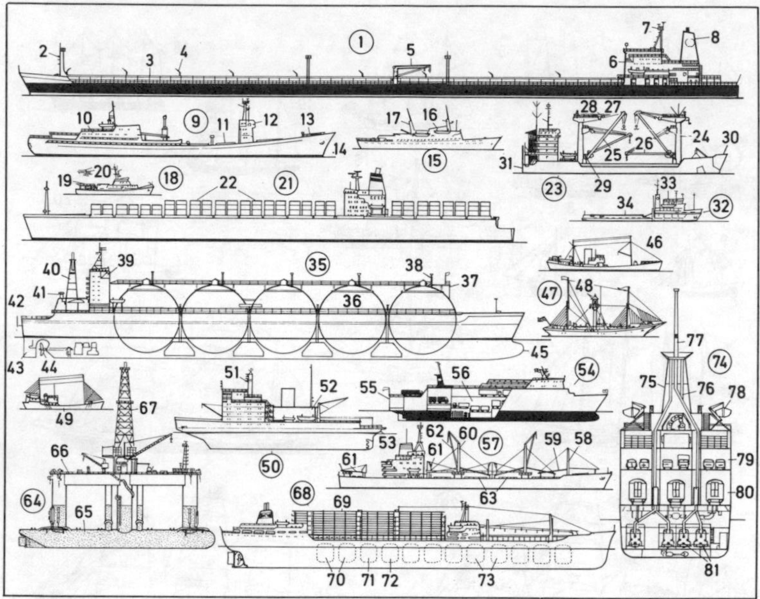

1 **ULCC** (ultra large crude carrier) of the 'all-aft' type
2 foremast
3 catwalk with the pipes
4 fire gun (fire nozzle)
5 deck crane
6 deckhouse with the bridge
7 aft signal (signalling) and radar mast
8 funnel
9 **nuclear research ship** 'Otto Hahn', a bulk carrier
10 aft superstructure (engine room)
11 cargo hatchway for bulk goods (bulk cargoes)
12 bridge
13 forecastle (fo'c'sle)
14 stem
15 **seaside pleasure boat**
16 dummy funnel
17 exhaust mast
18 **rescue cruiser**
19 helicopter platform (working deck)
20 rescue helicopter
21 **all-container ship**
22 containers stowed on deck
23 **cargo ship**
24-29 cargo gear (cargo-handling gear)
24 bipod mast
25 jumbo derrick boom (heavy-lift derrick boom)
26 derrick boom (cargo boom)
27 tackle
28 block
29 thrust bearing
30 bow doors
31 stern loading door
32 **offshore drilling rig supply vessel**
33 compact superstructure
34 loading deck (working deck)
35 **liquefied-gas tanker**
36 spherical tank
37 navigational television receiver mast
38 vent mast
39 deckhouse
40 funnel
41 ventilator
42 transom stern (transom)
43 rudder blade (rudder)
44 ship's propeller (ship's screw)
45 bulbous bow
46 steam trawler
47 **lightship** (light vessel)
48 lantern (characteristic light)
49 smack
50 **ice breaker**
51 steaming light mast
52 helicopter hangar
53 stern towing point, for gripping the bow of ships in tow
54 **roll-on-roll-off (ro-ro) trailer ferry**
55 stern port (stern opening) with ramp
56 heavy vehicle lifts (*Am.* heavy vehicle elevators)
57 **multi-purpose freighter**
58 ventilator-type samson (sampson) post (ventilator-type king post)
59 derrick boom (cargo boom, cargo gear, cargo-handling gear)
60 derrick mast
61 deck crane
62 jumbo derrick boom (heavy-lift derrick boom)
63 cargo hatchway

64 **semisubmersible drilling vessel**
65 floating vessel with machinery
66 drilling platform
67 derrick
68 **cattleship** (cattle vessel)
69 superstructure for transporting livestock
70 fresh water tanks
71 fuel tank
72 dung tank
73 fodder tanks
74 **train ferry** [cross section]
75 funnel
76 exhaust pipes
77 mast
78 ship's lifeboat hanging at the davit
79 car deck
80 main deck (train deck)
81 main engines
82 **passenger liner** (liner, ocean liner)
83 stem
84 funnel with lattice casing
85 flag dressing (rainbow dressing, string of flags extending over mastheads, e.g., on the maiden voyage)
86 **trawler,** a factory ship
87 gallows
88 stern ramp
89 **container ship**
90 loading bridge (loading platform)
91 sea ladder (jacob's ladder, rope ladder)
92 **barge and push tug assembly**
93 push tug
94 tug-pushed dumb barge (tug-pushed lighter)
95 pilot boat
96 **combined cargo and passenger liner**
97 passengers disembarking by boat
98 accommodation ladder
99 coaster (coasting vessel)
100 customs *or* police launch
101-128 **excursion steamer** (pleasure steamer)
101-106 lifeboat launching gear
101 davit
102 wire rope span
103 lifeline
104 tackle
105 block
106 fall
107 ship's lifeboat (ship's boat) covered with tarpaulin
108 stem
109 passenger
110 steward
111 deck-chair
112 deck hand
113 deck bucket
114 boatswain (bo's'n, bo'sun, bosun)
115 tunic
116 awning
117 stanchion
118 ridge rope (jackstay)
119 lashing
120 bulwark
121 guard rail
122 handrail (top rail)
123 companion ladder (companionway)
124 lifebelt (lifebuoy)
125 lifebuoy light (lifebelt light, signal light)
126 officer of the watch (watchkeeper)
127 reefer (*Am.* pea jacket)
128 binoculars

222 Shipbuilding

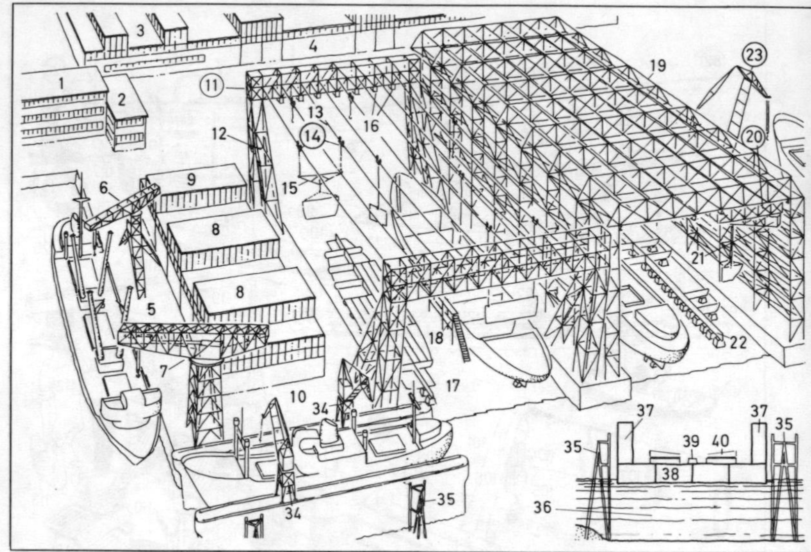

1-43 shipyard (shipbuilding yard, dockyard, *Am.* navy yard)
1 administrative offices
2 ship-drawing office
3-4 shipbuilding sheds
3 mould (*Am.* mold) loft
4 erection shop
5-9 fitting-out quay
5 quay
6 tripod crane
7 hammer-headed crane
8 engineering workshop
9 boiler shop
10 repair quay
11-26 slipways (slips, building berths, building slips, stocks)
11-18 cable crane berth, a slipway (building berth)
11 slipway portal
12 bridge support
13 crane cable
14 crab (jenny)
15 cross piece
16 crane driver's cabin (crane driver's cage)
17 slipway floor
18 staging, a scaffold
19-21 frame slipway
19 slipway frame
20 overhead travelling (*Am.* traveling) crane (gantry crane)
21 slewing crab
22 keel in position
23 luffing jib crane, a slipway crane
24 crane rails (crane track)
25 gantry crane
26 gantry (bridge)
27 trestles (supports)
28 crab (jenny)
29 hull frames in position
30 ship under construction
31-33 dry dock
31 dock floor (dock bottom)
32 dock gates (caisson)
33 pumping station (power house)
34-43 floating dock (pontoon dock)
34 dock crane (dockside crane), a jib crane
35 fender pile
36-43 working of docks
36 dock basin
37-38 dock structure
37 side tank (side wall)
38 bottom tank (bottom pontoon)
39 keel block

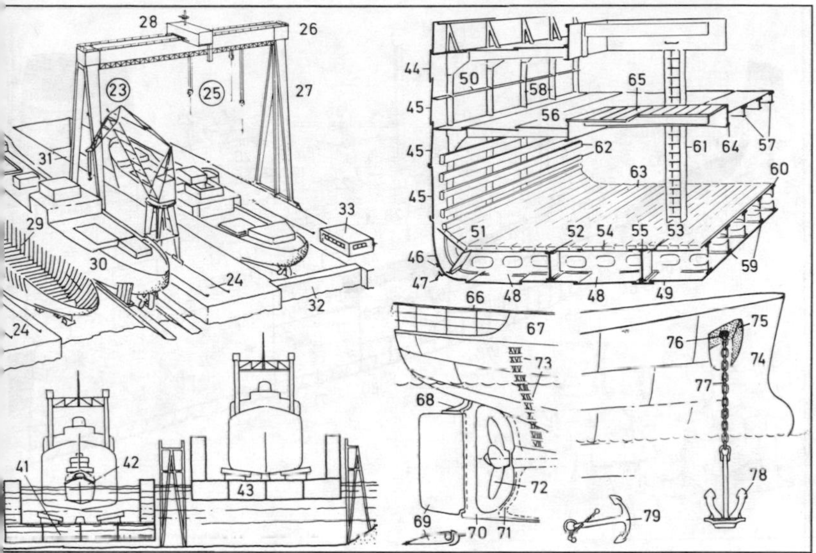

40 bilge block (bilge shore, side support)
41-43 docking a ship
41 flooded floating dock
42 tug towing the ship
43 emptied (pumped-out) dock
44-61 structural parts of the ship
44-56 longitudinal structure
44-49 shell (shell plating, skin)
44 sheer strake
45 side strake
46 bilge strake
47 bilge keel
48 bottom plating
49 flat plate keel (keel plate)
50 stringer (side stringer)
51 tank margin plate
52 longitudinal side girder
53 centre (*Am.* center) plate girder (centre girder, kelson, keelson, vertical keel)
54 tank top plating (tank top, inner bottom plating)
55 centre (*Am.* center) strake
56 deck plating
57 deck beam
58 frame (rib)
59 floor plate
60 cellular double bottom
61 hold pillar (pillar)
61, 63 dunnage
62 side battens (side ceiling, spar ceiling)
63 ceiling (floor ceiling)
64-65 hatchway
64 hatch coaming
65 hatch cover (hatchboard)
66-72 stern
66 guard rail
67 bulwark
68 rudder stock
69-70 Oertz rudder
69 rudder blade (rudder)
70-71 stern frame
70 rudder post
71 propeller post (screw post)
72 ship's propeller (ship's screw)
73 draught (draft) marks
74-79 bow
74 stem, a bulbous stem (bulbous bow)
75 hawse
76 hawse pipe
77 anchor cable (chain cable)
78 stockless anchor (patent anchor)
79 stocked anchor

223 Motor Ship

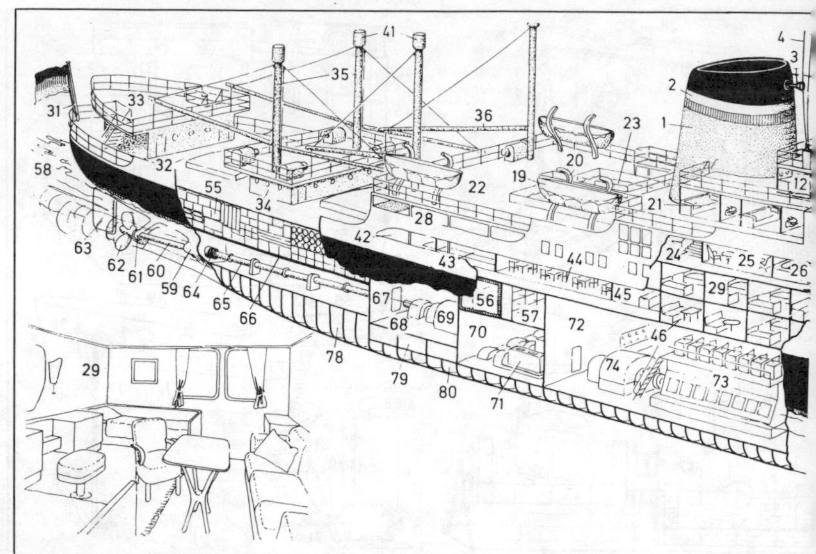

1–71 combined cargo and passenger ship [of the older type]
1 funnel
2 funnel marking
3 siren (fog horn)
4–11 compass platform (compass bridge, compass flat, monkey bridge)
4 antenna lead-in (antenna down-lead)
5 radio direction finder (RDF) antenna (direction finder antenna, rotatable loop antenna, aural null loop antenna)
6 magnetic compass (mariner's compass)
7 morse lamp (signalling, *Am.* signaling, lamp)
8 radar antenna (radar scanner)
9 code flag signal
10 code flag halyards
11 triatic stay (signal stay)
12–18 bridge deck (bridge)
12 radio room
13 captain's cabin
14 navigating bridge
15 starboard sidelight [green; port sidelight red]
16 wing of bridge
17 shelter (weather cloth, dodger)
18 wheelhouse
19–21 boat deck
19 ship's lifeboat
20 davit
21 officer's cabin
22–27 promenade deck
22 sun deck (lido deck)
23 swimming pool
24 companion ladder (companionway)
25 library (ship's library)
26 lounge
27 promenade
28–30 A-deck
28 semi-enclosed deck space
29 double-berth cabin, a cabin
30 de luxe cabin
31 ensign staff
32–42 B-deck (main deck)
32 after deck
33 poop
34 deckhouse
35 samson (sampson) post (king post)
36 derrick boom (cargo boom)

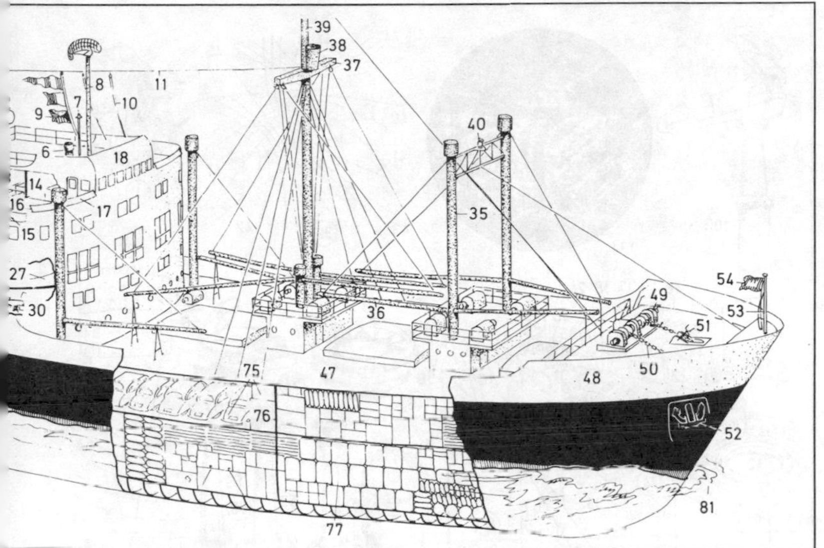

37 crosstrees (spreader)
38 crow's nest
39 topmast
40 forward steaming light
41 ventilator lead
42 galley (caboose, cookroom, ship's kitchen)
43 ship's pantry
44 dining room
45 purser's office
46 single-berth cabin
47 foredeck
48 forecastle (fo'c'sle)
49–51 ground tackle
49 windlass
50 anchor cable (chain cable)
51 compressor (chain compressor)
52 anchor
53 jackstaff
54 jack
55 after holds
56 cold storage room (insulated hold)
57 store room
58 wake
59 shell bossing (shaft bossing)
60 tail shaft (tail end shaft)
61 shaft strut (strut, spectacle frame, propeller strut, propeller bracket)
62 three-blade ship's propeller (ship's screw)
63 rudder blade (rudder)
64 stuffing box
65 propeller shaft
66 shaft alley (shaft tunnel)
67 thrust block
68–74 diesel-electric drive
68 electric engine room
69 electric motor
70 auxiliary engine room
71 auxiliary engines
72 main engine room
73 main engine, a diesel engine
74 generator
75 forward holds
76 tween deck
77 cargo
78 ballast tank (deep tank) for water ballast
79 fresh water tank
80 fuel tank
81 bow wave

224 Navigation

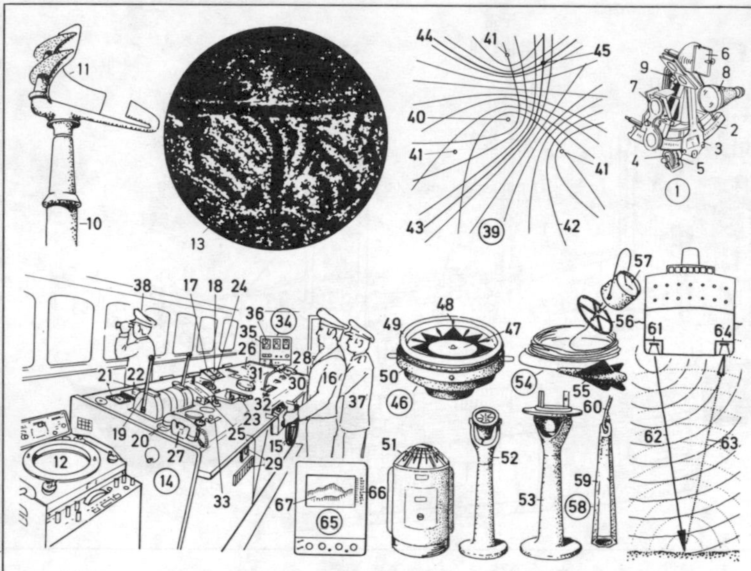

1 sextant
2 graduated arc
3 index bar (index arm)
4 decimal micrometer
5 vernier
6 index mirror
7 horizon glass (horizon mirror)
8 telescope
9 grip (handgrip)
10-13 radar equipment (radar apparatus)
10 radar pedestal
11 revolving radar reflector
12 radar display unit (radar screen)
13 radar image (radar picture)
14-38 wheelhouse
14 steering and control position
15 ship's wheel for controlling the rudder mechanism
16 helmsman (*Am.* wheelsman)
17 rudder angle indicator
18 automatic pilot (autopilot)
19 control lever for the variable-pitch propeller (reversible propeller, feathering propeller, feathering screw)
20 propeller pitch indicator
21 main engine revolution indicator
22 ship's speedometer (log)
23 control switch for bow thruster (bow-manoeuvring, *Am.* maneuvering, propeller)
24 echo recorder (depth recorder, echograph)
25 engine telegraph (engine order telegraph)
26 controls for the anti-rolling system (for the stabilizers)
27 local-battery telephone
28 shipping traffic radio telephone
29 navigation light indicator panel (running light indicator panel)
30 microphone for ship's address system
31 gyro compass (gyroscopic compass), a compass repeater
32 control button for the ship's siren (ship's fog horn)
33 main engine overload indicator
34 detector indicator unit for fixing the ship's position
35 rough focusing indicator
36 fine focusing indicator
37 navigating officer
38 captain
39 Decca navigation system
40 master station
41 slave station
42 null hyperbola
43 hyperbolic position line 1
44 hyperbolic position line 2
45 position (fix, ship fix)
46-53 compasses
46 liquid compass (fluid compass, spirit compass, wet compass), a magnetic compass
47 compass card
48 lubber's line (lubber's mark, lubber's point)
49 compass bowl
50 gimbal ring
51-53 gyro compass (gyroscopic compass, gyro compass unit)
51 master compass (master gyro compass)
52 compass repeater (gyro repeater)
53 compass repeater with pelorus
54 patent log (screw log, mechanical log, towing log, taffrail log, speedometer)

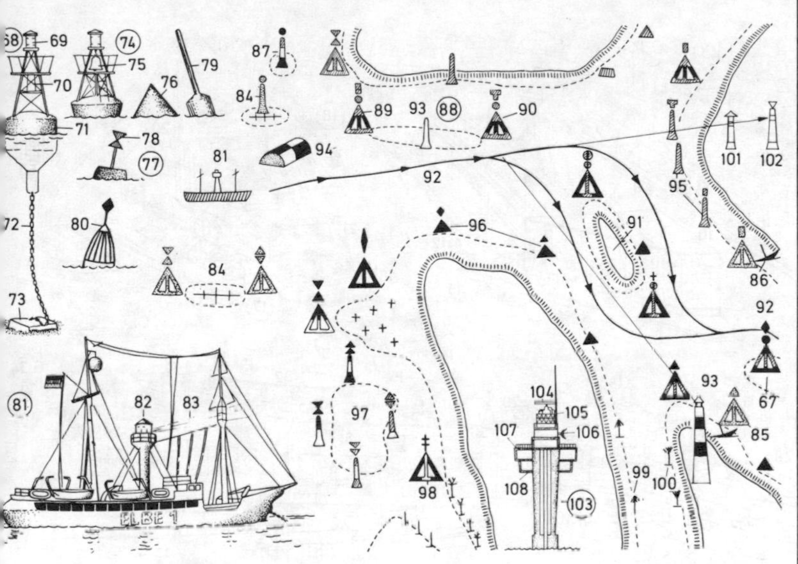

55 rotator
56 governor
57 log clock
58-67 leads
58 hand lead
59 lead (lead sinker)
60 leadline
61-67 echo sounder (echo sounding machine)
61 sound transmitter
62 sound wave (sound impulse)
63 echo (sound echo, echo signal)
64 echo receiver (hydrophone)
65 echograph (echo sounding machine recorder)
66 depth scale
67 echogram (depth recording, depth reading)
68-108 sea marks (floating navigational marks) **for buoyage and lighting systems**
68-83 fairway marks (channel marks)
68 light and whistle buoy
69 light (warning light)
70 whistle
71 buoy
72 mooring chain
73 sinker (mooring sinker)
74 light and bell buoy
75 bell
76 conical buoy
77 can buoy
78 topmark
79 spar buoy
80 topmark buoy
81 lightship (light vessel)
82 lantern mast (lantern tower)
83 beam of light
84-102 fairway markings (channel markings)
84 wreck [green buoys]
85 wreck to starboard
86 wreck to port
87 shoals (shallows, shallow water, *Am.* flats)
88 middle ground to port
89 division (bifurcation) [beginning of the middle ground; topmark: red cylinder above red ball]
90 convergence (confluence) [end of the middle ground; topmark: red St. Antony's cross above red ball]
91 middle ground
92 main fairway (main navigable channel)
93 secondary fairway (secondary navigable channel)
94 can buoy
95 port hand buoys (port hand marks) [red]
96 starboard hand buoys (starboard hand marks) [black]
97 shoals (shallows, shallow water, *Am.* flats) outside the fairway
98 middle of the fairway (mid-channel)
99 starboard markers (inverted broom]
100 port markers [upward-pointing broom]
101-102 range lights (leading lights)
101 lower range light (lower leading light)
102 higher range light (higher leading light)
103 lighthouse
104 radar antenna (radar scanner)
105 lantern (characteristic light)
106 radio direction finder (RDF) antenna
107 machinery and observation platform (machinery and observation deck)
108 living quarters

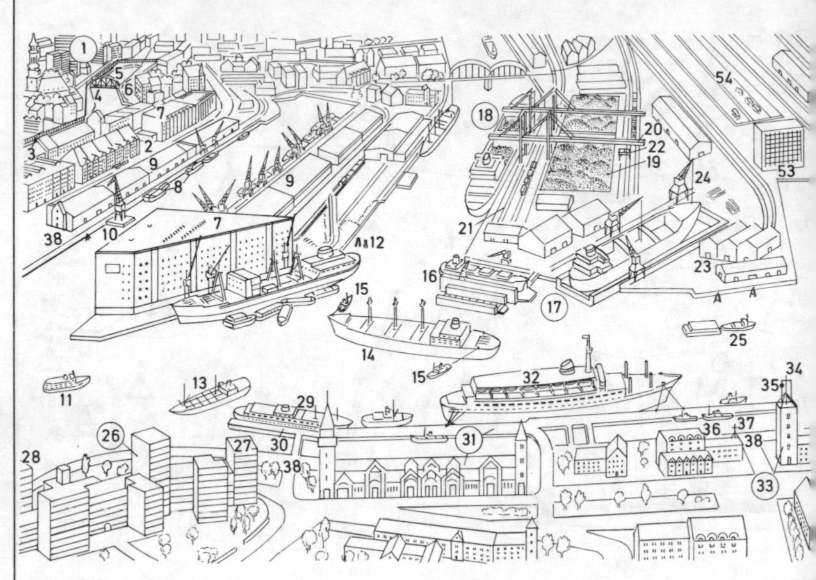

1 dock area
2 free port (foreign trade zone)
3 free zone frontier (free zone enclosure)
4 customs barrier
5 customs entrance
6 port custom house
7 entrepôt
8 barge (dumb barge, lighter)
9 break-bulk cargo transit shed (general cargo transit shed, package cargo transit shed)
10 floating crane
11 harbour (*Am.* harbor) ferry (ferryboat)
12 fender (dolphin)
13 bunkering boat
14 break-bulk carrier (general cargo ship)
15 tug
16 floating dock (pontoon dock)
17 dry dock
18 coal wharf
19 coal bunker
20 transporter loading bridge
21 quayside railway
22 weighing bunker
23 warehouse
24 quayside crane
25 launch and lighter
26 port hospital
27 quarantine wing
28 Institute of Tropical Medicine
29 excursion steamer (pleasure steamer)
30 jetty
31 passenger terminal
32 liner (passenger liner, ocean liner)
33 meteorological office, a weather station
34 signal mast (signalling mast)
35 storm signal
36 port administration offices
37 tide level indicator
38 quayside road (quayside roadway)
39 roll-on roll-off (ro-ro) system (roll-on roll-off operation)
40 gantry

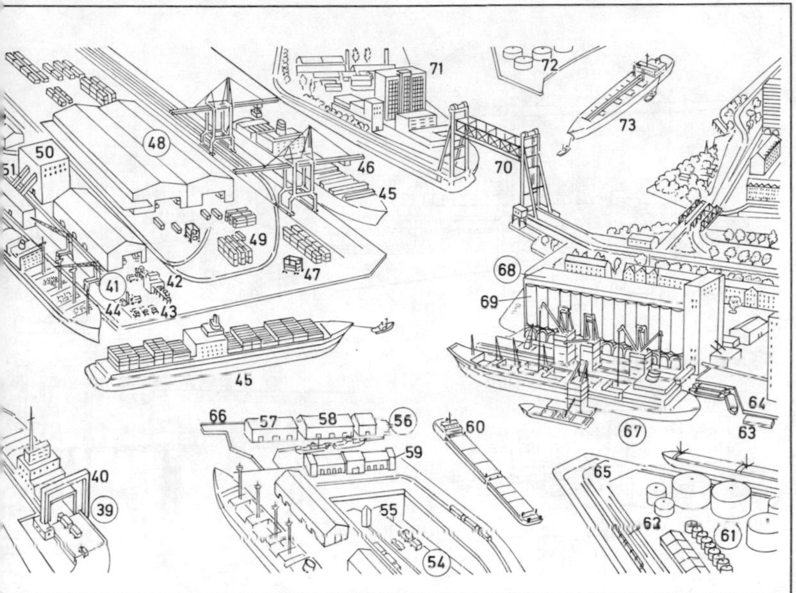

41 truck-to-truck system (truck-to-truck operation)
42 foil-wrapped unit loads
43 pallets
44 forklift truck (fork truck, forklift)
45 container ship
46 transporter container-loading bridge
47 container carrier truck
48 container terminal (container berth)
49 unit load
50 cold store
51 conveyor belt (conveyor)
52 fruit storage shed (fruit warehouse)
53 office building
54 urban motorway (*Am.* freeway)
55 harbour (*Am.* harbor) tunnels
56 fish dock
57 fish market
58 auction room
59 fish-canning factory
60 push tow
61 tank farm
62 railway siding
63 landing pontoon (landing stage)
64 quay
65 breakwater (mole)
66 pier (jetty), a quay extension
67 bulk carrier
68 silo
69 silo cylinder
70 lift bridge
71 industrial plant
72 storage tanks
73 tanker

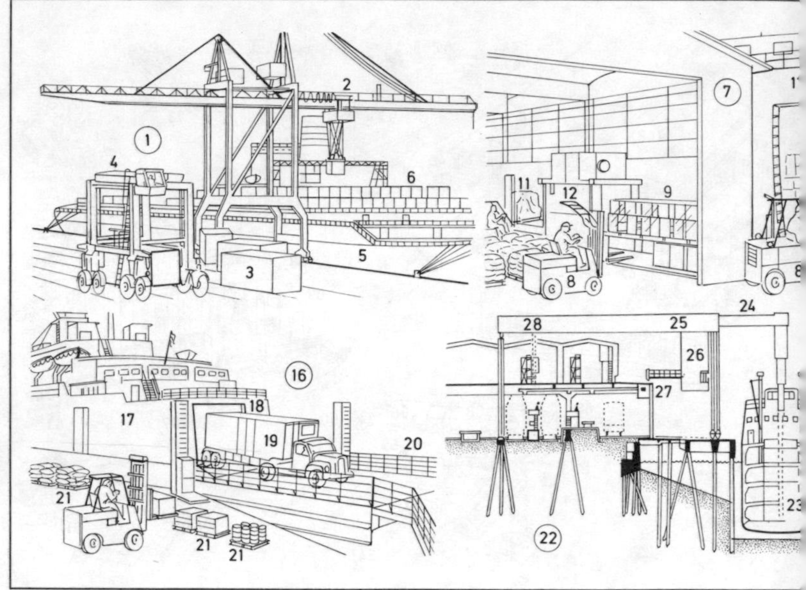

1 container terminal (container berth), a modern cargo-handling berth
2 transporter container-loading bridge (loading bridge); *sim.:* transtainer crane (transtainer)
3 container
4 truck (carrier)
5 all-container ship
6 containers stowed on deck
7 truck-to-truck handling (horizontal cargo handling with pallets)
8 forklift truck (fork truck, forklift)
9 unitized foil-wrapped load (unit load)
10 flat pallet, a standard pallet
11 unitized break-bulk cargo
12 heat sealing machine
13 break-bulk carrier (general cargo ship)
14 cargo hatchway
15 receiving truck on board ship
16 multi-purpose terminal
17 roll-on roll-off ship (ro-ro-ship)
18 stern port (stern opening)
19 driven load, a lorry (*Am.* truck)
20 ro-ro depot
21 unitized load (unitized package)
22 banana-handling terminal [section]
23 seaward tumbler
24 jib
25 elevator bridge
26 chain sling
27 lighting station
28 shore-side tumbler for loading trains and lorries (*Am.* trucks)
29 bulk cargo handling
30 bulk carrier
31 floating bulk-cargo elevator
32 suction pipes
33 receiver
34 delivery pipe
35 bulk transporter barge
36 floating pile driver
37 pile driver frame
38 pile hammer

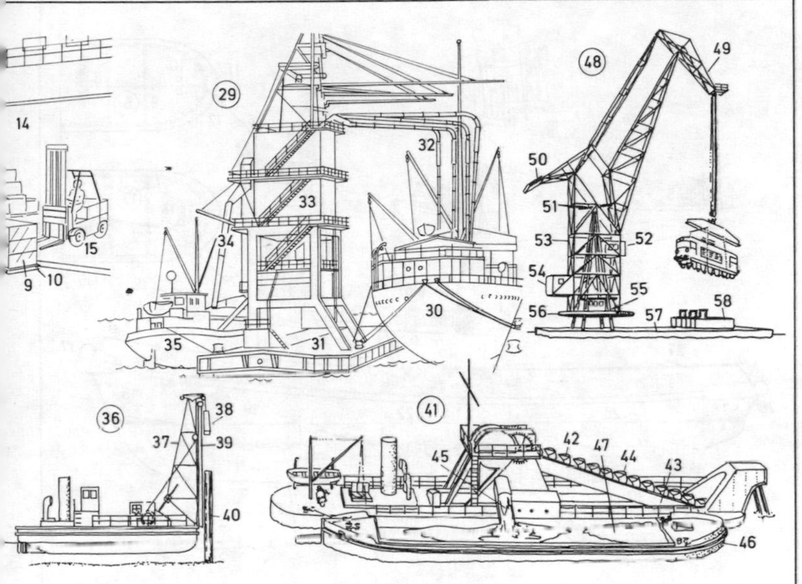

39 driving guide rail
40 pile
41 bucket dredger, a dredger
42 bucket chain
43 bucket ladder
44 dredger bucket
45 chute
46 hopper barge
47 spoil
48 floating crane
49 jib (boom)
50 counterweight (counterpoise)
51 adjusting spindle
52 crane driver's cabin (crane driver's cage)
53 crane framework
54 winch house
55 control platform
56 turntable
57 pontoon, a pram
58 engine superstructure (engine mounting)

227 Salvage (Salving) and Towage

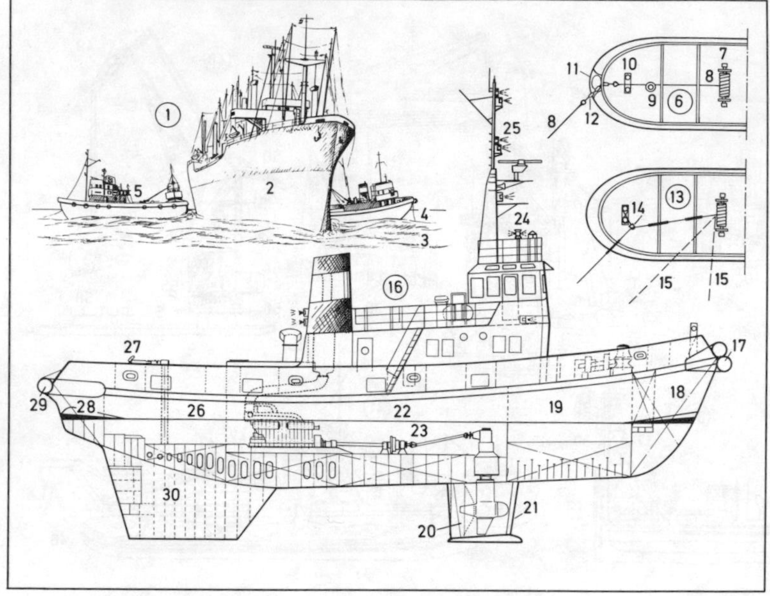

1 salvaging (salving) of a ship run aground
2 ship run aground (damaged vessel)
3 sandbank; *also:* quicksand
4 open sea
5 tug (salvage tug)
6–15 towing gear
6 towing gear for towing at sea
7 towing winch (towing machine, towing engine)
8 tow rope (tow line, towing hawser)
9 tow rope guide
10 cross-shaped bollard
11 hawse hole
12 anchor cable (chain cable)
13 towing gear for work in harbours (*Am.* harbors)
14 guest rope
15 position of the tow rope (tow line, towing hawser)
16 tug (salvage tug) [vertical elevation]
17 bow fender (pudding fender)
18 forepeak
19 living quarters
20 Schottel propeller
21 Kort vent
22 engine and propeller room
23 clutch coupling
24 compass platform (compass bridge, compass flat, monkey bridge)
25 fire-fighting equipment
26 stowage
27 tow hook
28 afterpeak
29 stern fender
30 main manoeuvring (*Am.* maneuvering) keel

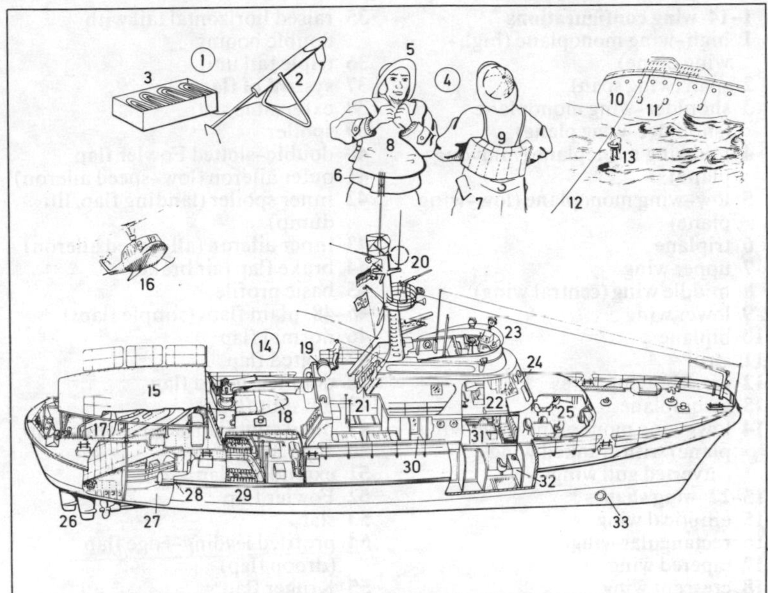

1 rocket apparatus (rocket gun, line-throwing gun)
2 life rocket (rocket)
3 rocket line (whip line)
4 oilskins
5 sou'wester (southwester)
6 oilskin jacket
7 oilskin coat
8 inflatable life jacket
9 cork life jacket (cork life preserver)
10 stranded ship (damaged vessel)
11 oil bag, for trickling oil on the water surface
12 lifeline
13 breeches buoy
14 rescue cruiser
15 helicopter landing deck
16 rescue helicopter
17 daughter boat
18 inflatable boat (inflatable dinghy)
19 life raft
20 fire-fighting equipment for fires at sea
21 hospital unit with operating cabin and exposure bath
22 navigating bridge
23 upper tier of navigating bridge
24 lower tier of navigating bridge
25 messroom
26 rudders and propeller (screw)
27 stowage
28 foam can
29 side engines
30 shower
31 coxswain's cabin
32 crew member's single-berth cabin
33 bow propeller

1–14 wing configurations
1 high-wing monoplane (high-wing plane)
2 span (wing span)
3 shoulder-wing monoplane (shoulder-wing plane)
4 midwing monoplane (midwing plane)
5 low-wing monoplane (low-wing plane)
6 triplane
7 upper wing
8 middle wing (central wing)
9 lower wing
10 biplane
11 strut
12 cross bracing wires
13 sesquiplane
14 low-wing monoplane (low-wing plane) with cranked wings (inverted gull wings)
15–22 wing shapes
15 elliptical wing
16 rectangular wing
17 tapered wing
18 crescent wing
19 delta wing
20 swept-back wing with semi-positive sweepback
21 swept-back wing with positive sweepback
22 ogival wing (ogee wing)
23–36 tail shapes (tail unit shapes, empennage shapes)
23 normal tail (normal tail unit)
24–25 vertical tail (vertical stabilizer and rudder)
24 vertical stabilizer (vertical fin, tail fin)
25 rudder
26–27 horizontal tail
26 tailplane (horizontal stabilizer)
27 elevator
28 cruciform tail (cruciform tail unit)
29 T-tail (T-tail unit)
30 lobe
31 V-tail (vee-tail, butterfly tail)
32 double tail unit (twin tail unit)
33 end plate
34 double tail unit (twin tail unit) of a twin-boom aircraft
35 raised horizontal tail with double booms
36 triple tail unit
37 system of flaps
38 extensible slat
39 spoiler
40 double-slotted Fowler flap
41 outer aileron (low-speed aileron)
42 inner spoiler (landing flap, lift dump)
43 inner aileron (all-speed aileron)
44 brake flap (air brake)
45 basic profile
46–48 plain flaps (simple flaps)
46 normal flap
47 slotted flap
48 double-slotted flap
49–50 split flaps
49 plain split flap (simple split flap)
50 zap flap
51 extending flap
52 Fowler flap
53 slat
54 profiled leading-edge flap (droop flap)
55 Krüger flap

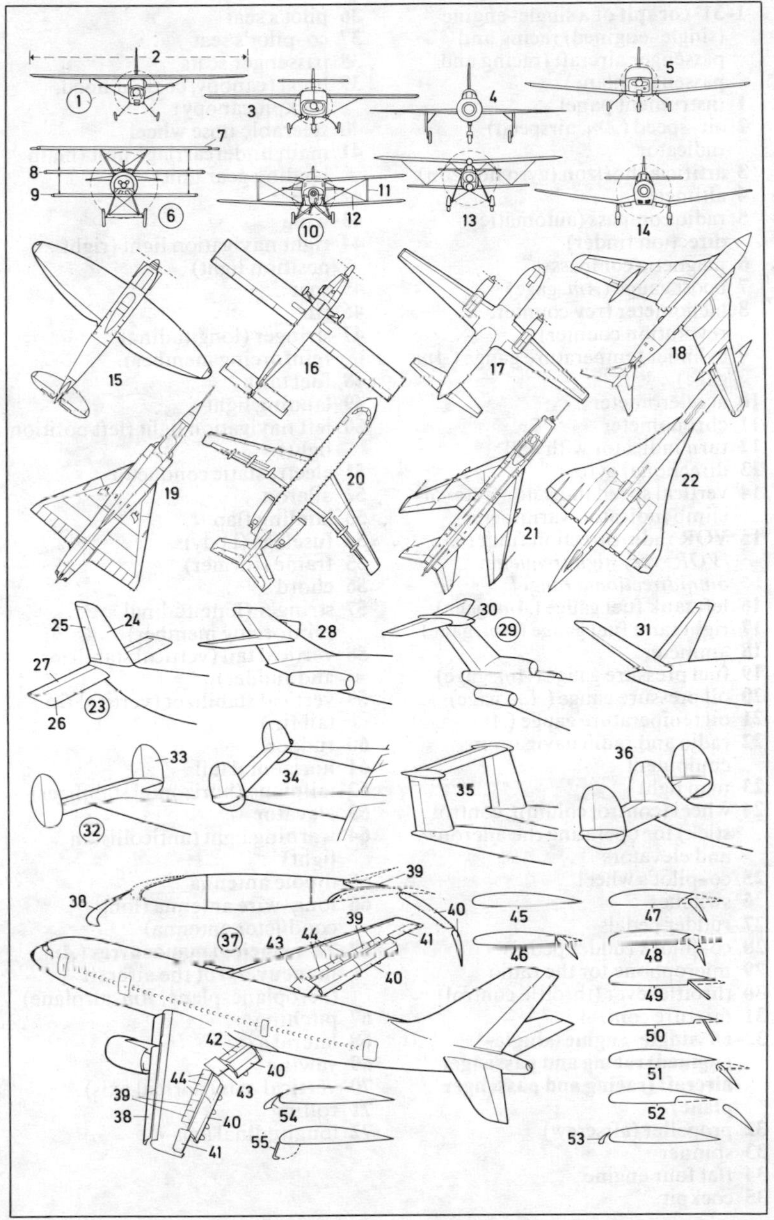
1
2
3
4
5
6
7
8
9
10
11
12
13
14
15
16
17
18
19
20
21
22
23
24
25
26
27
28
29
30
31
32
33
34
35
36
37
38
39
40
41
42
43
44
45
46
47
48
49
50
51
52
53
54
55

1–31 cockpit of a single-engine (single-engined) racing and passenger aircraft (racing and passenger plane)
1 instrument panel
2 air-speed (*Am.* airspeed) indicator
3 artificial horizon (gyro horizon)
4 altimeter
5 radio compass (automatic direction finder)
6 magnetic compass
7 boost gauge (*Am.* gage)
8 tachometer (rev counter, revolution counter)
9 cylinder temperature gauge (*Am.* gage)
10 accelerometer
11 chronometer
12 turn indicator with ball
13 directional gyro
14 vertical speed indicator (rate-of-climb indicator, variometer)
15 VOR radio direction finder *[VOR: very high frequency omnidirectional range]*
16 left tank fuel gauge (*Am.* gage)
17 right tank fuel gauge (*Am.* gage)
18 ammeter
19 fuel pressure gauge (*Am.* gage)
20 oil pressure gauge (*Am.* gage)
21 oil temperature gauge (*Am.* gage)
22 radio and radio navigation equipment
23 map light
24 wheel (control column, control stick) for operating the ailerons and elevators
25 co-pilot's wheel
26 switches
27 rudder pedals
28 co-pilot's rudder pedals
29 microphone for the radio
30 throttle lever (throttle control)
31 mixture control
32–66 single-engine (single-engined) racing and passenger aircraft (racing and passenger plane)
32 propeller (airscrew)
33 spinner
34 flat four engine
35 cockpit
36 pilot's seat
37 co-pilot's seat
38 passenger seats
39 hood (canopy, cockpit hood, cockpit canopy)
40 steerable nose wheel
41 main undercarriage unit (main landing gear unit)
42 step
43 wing
44 right navigation light (right position light)
45 spar
46 rib
47 stringer (longitudinal reinforcing member)
48 fuel tank
49 landing light
50 left navigation light (left position light)
51 electrostatic conductor
52 aileron
53 landing flap
54 fuselage (body)
55 frame (former)
56 chord
57 stringer (longitudinal reinforcing member)
58 vertical tail (vertical stabilizer and rudder)
59 vertical stabilizer (vertical fin, tail fin)
60 rudder
61 horizontal tail
62 tailplane (horizontal stabilizer)
63 elevator
64 warning light (anticollision light)
65 dipole antenna
66 long-wire antenna (long-conductor antenna)
67–72 principal manoeuvres (*Am.* maneuvers) of the aircraft (aeroplane, plane, *Am.* airplane)
67 pitching
68 lateral axis
69 yawing
70 vertical axis (normal axis)
71 rolling
72 longitudinal axis

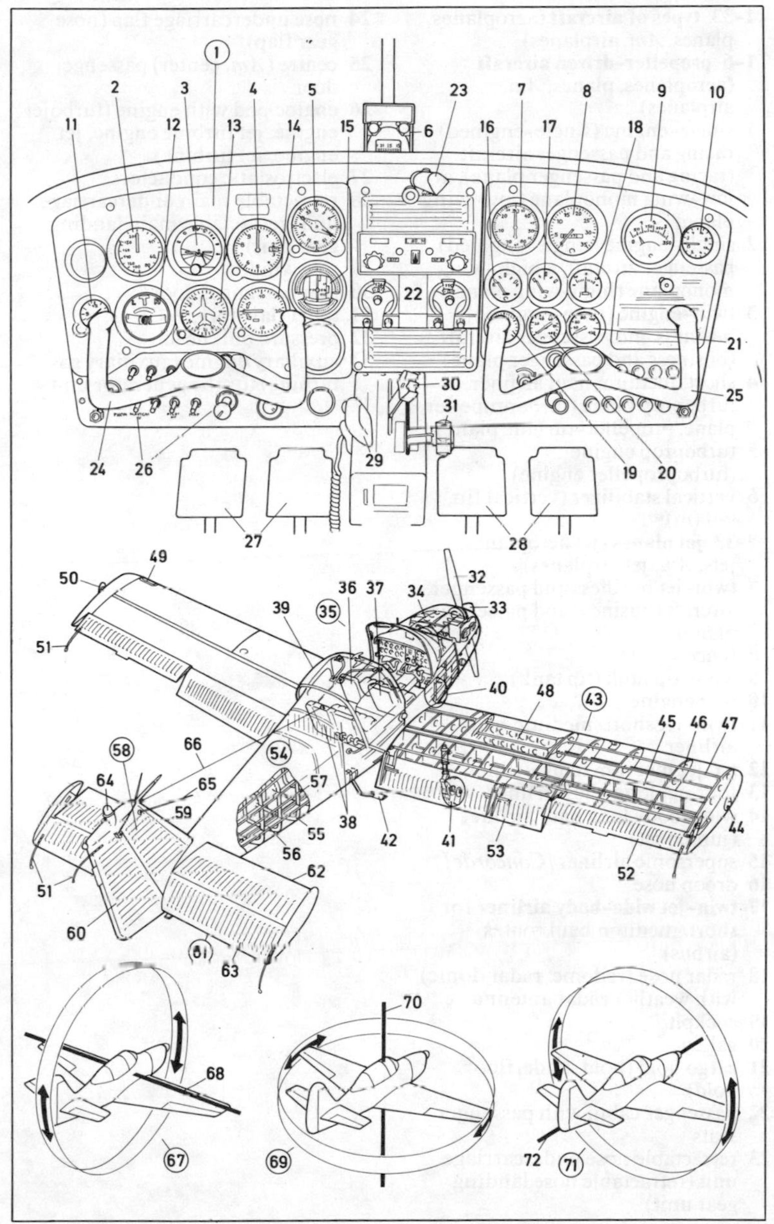
1
2
3
4
5
6
7
8
9
10
11
12
13
14
15
16
17
18
19
20
21
22
23
24
25
26
27
28
29
30
31
32
33
34
35
36
37
38
39
40
41
42
43
44
45
46
47
48
49
50
51
52
53
54
55
56
57
58
59
60
61
62
63
64
65
66
67
68
69
70
71
72

1–33 types of aircraft (aeroplanes, planes, *Am.* airplanes)
1–6 propeller-driven aircraft (aeroplanes, planes, *Am.* airplanes)
1 single-engine (single-engined) racing and passenger aircraft (racing and passenger plane), a low-wing monoplane (low-wing plane)
2 single-engine (single-engined) passenger aircraft, a high-wing monoplane (high-wing plane)
3 twin-engine (twin-engined) business and passenger aircraft (business and passenger plane)
4 short/medium haul airliner, a turboprop plane (turbopropeller plane, propeller-turbine plane)
5 turboprop engine (turbopropeller engine)
6 vertical stabilizer (vertical fin, tail fin)
7–33 jet planes (jet aeroplanes, jets, *Am.* jet airplanes)
7 twin-jet business and passenger aircraft (business and passenger plane)
8 fence
9 wing-tip tank (tip tank)
10 rear engine
11 twin-jet short/medium haul airliner
12 tri-jet medium haul airliner
13 four-jet long haul airliner
14 wide-body long haul airliner (jumbo jet)
15 supersonic airliner *[Concorde]*
16 droop nose
17 **twin-jet wide-body airliner** for short/medium haul routes (airbus)
18 radar nose (radome, radar dome) with weather radar antenna
19 cockpit
20 galley
21 cargo hold (hold, underfloor hold)
22 passenger cabin with passenger seats
23 retractable nose undercarriage unit (retractable nose landing gear unit)
24 nose undercarriage flap (nose gear flap)
25 centre (*Am.* center) passenger door
26 engine pod with engine (turbojet engine, jet turbine engine, jet engine, jet turbine)
27 electrostatic conductors
28 retractable main undercarriage unit (retractable main landing gear unit)
29 side window
30 rear passenger door
31 toilet (lavatory, WC)
32 pressure bulkhead
33 auxiliary engine (auxiliary gas turbine) for the generator unit

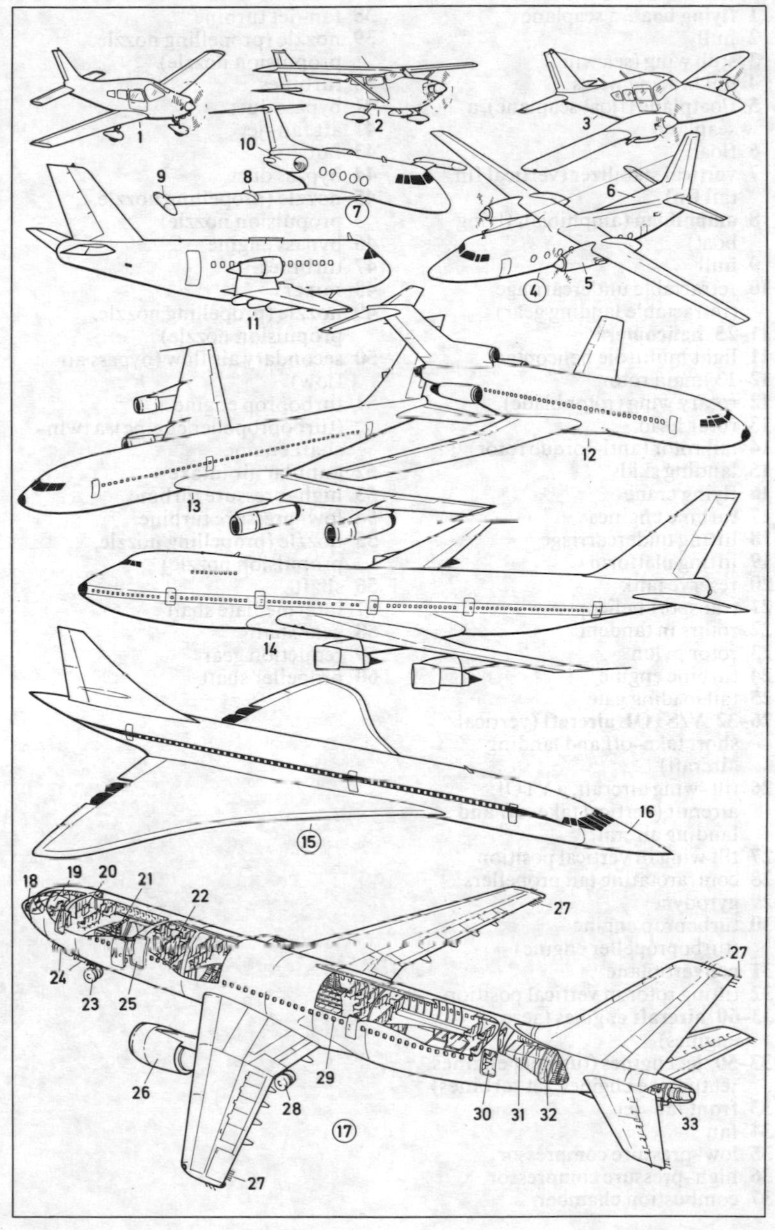
1
2
3
4
5
6
7
8
9
10
11
12
13
14
15
16
17
18
19
20
21
22
23
24
25
26
27
28
29
30
31
32
33

1 **flying boat**, a seaplane
2 hull
3 stub wing (sea wing)
4 tail bracing wires
5 floatplane (float seaplane), a seaplane
6 float
7 vertical stabilizer (vertical fin, tail fin)
8 **amphibian** (amphibian flying boat)
9 hull
10 retractable undercarriage (retractable landing gear)
11–25 **helicopters**
11 light multirole helicopter
12–13 main rotor
12 rotary wing (rotor blade)
13 rotor head
14 tail rotor (anti-torque rotor)
15 landing skids
16 flying crane
17 turbine engines
18 lifting undercarriage
19 lifting platform
20 reserve tank
21 transport helicopter
22 rotors in tandem
23 rotor pylon
24 turbine engine
25 tail loading gate
26–32 **V/STOL aircraft** (vertical/ short take-off and landing aircraft)
26 tilt-wing aircraft, a VTOL aircraft (vertical take-off and landing aircraft)
27 tilt wing in vertical position
28 contrarotating tail propellers
29 gyrodyne
30 turboprop engine (turbopropeller engine)
31 convertiplane
32 tilting rotor in vertical position
33–60 **aircraft engines** (aero engines)
33–50 jet engines (turbojet engines, jet turbine engines, jet turbines)
33 front fan-jet
34 fan
35 low-pressure compressor
36 high-pressure compressor
37 combustion chamber
38 fan-jet turbine
39 nozzle (propelling nozzle, propulsion nozzle)
40 turbines
41 bypass duct
42 aft fan-jet
43 fan
44 bypass duct
45 nozzle (propelling nozzle, propulsion nozzle)
46 bypass engine
47 turbines
48 mixer
49 nozzle (propelling nozzle, propulsion nozzle)
50 secondary air flow (bypass air flow)
51 turboprop engine (turbopropeller engine), a twin-shaft engine
52 annular air intake
53 high-pressure turbine
54 low-pressure turbine
55 nozzle (propelling nozzle, propulsion nozzle)
56 shaft
57 intermediate shaft
58 gear shaft
59 reduction gear
60 propeller shaft

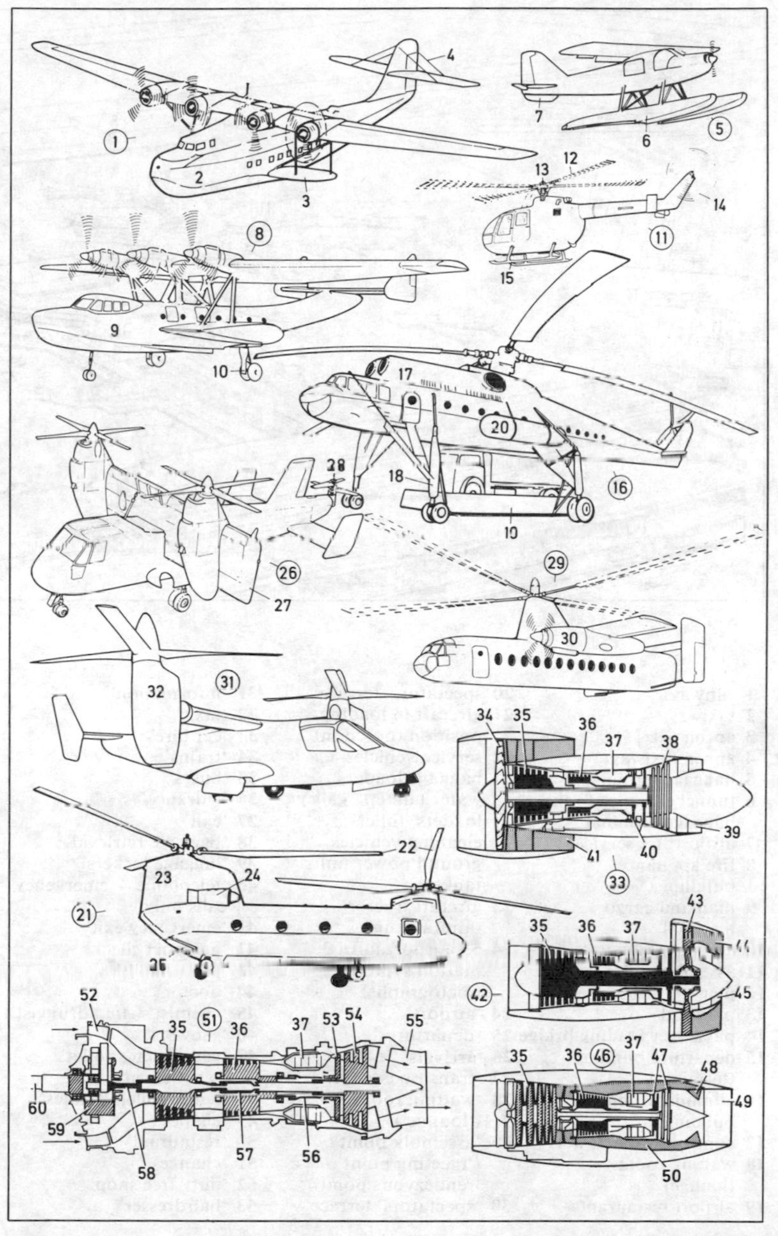
1
2
3
4
5
6
7
8
9
10
11
12
13
14
15
16
17
18
20
10
21
22
23
24
25
26
27
28
29
30
31
32
33
34
35
36
37
38
39
40
41
42
43
44
45
46
47
48
49
50
51
52
53
54
55
56
57
58
59
60

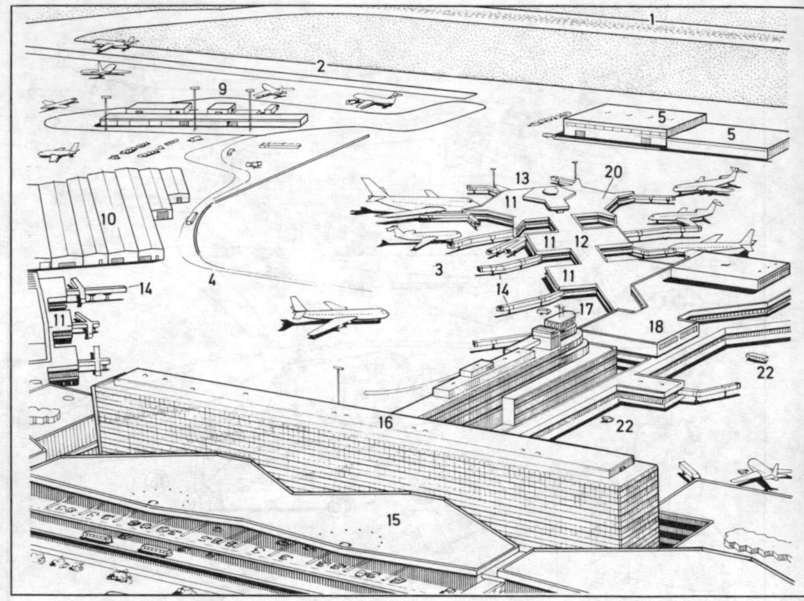

1 runway
2 taxiway
3 apron
4 apron taxiway
5 baggage terminal
6 tunnel entrance to the baggage terminal
7 airport fire service
8 fire appliance building
9 mail and cargo terminal
10 cargo warehouse
11 assembly point
12 pier
13 pierhead
14 passenger loading bridge
15 departure building (terminal)
16 administration building
17 control tower (tower)
18 waiting room (lounge)
19 airport restaurant
20 spectators' terrace
21 aircraft in loading position (nosed in)
22 service vehicles, e.g. baggage loaders, water tankers, galley loaders, toilet-cleaning vehicles, ground power units, tankers
23 aircraft tractor (aircraft tug)
24-53 airport information symbols (pictographs)
24 'airport'
25 'departures'
26 'arrivals'
27 'transit passengers'
28 'waiting room' ('lounge')
29 'assembly point' ('meeting point', 'rendezvous point')
30 'spectators' terrace'
31 'information'
32 'taxis'
33 'car hire'
34 'trains'
35 'buses'
36 'entrance'
37 'exit'
38 'baggage retrieval'
39 'luggage lockers'
40 'telephone – emergency calls only'
41 'emergency exit'
42 'passport check'
43 'press facilities'
44 'doctor'
45 'chemist' (*Am.* 'druggist')
46 'showers'
47 'gentlemen's toilet' ('gentlemen')
48 'ladies toilet' ('ladies')
49 'chapel'
50 'restaurant'
51 'change'
52 'duty free shop'
53 'hairdresser'

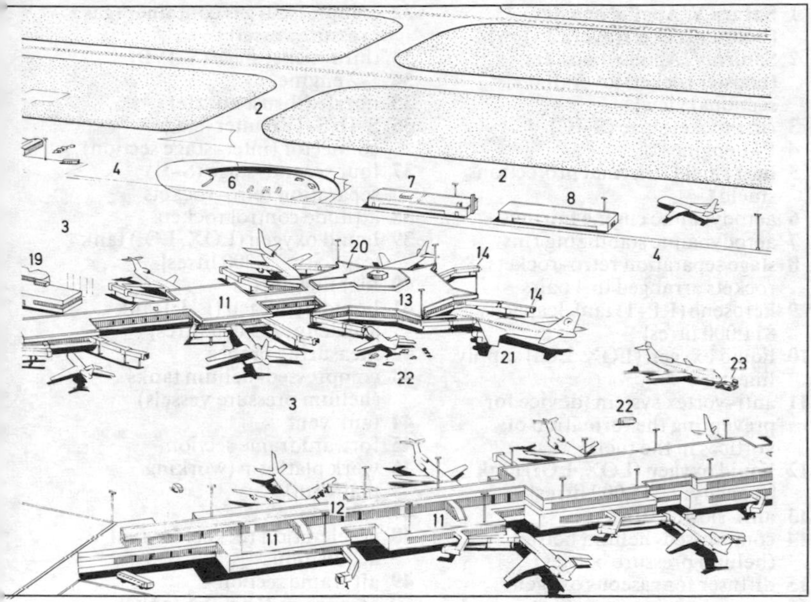

24
25
26
27
28
29
30
31
32
TAXI
33
34
DB
35
BUS
36
37
38
39
40
41
42
43
press
44
45
46
47
48
49
50
51
100
5
2
52
53

1 **Saturn V 'Apollo' booster** (booster rocket) [overall view]
2 Saturn V 'Apollo' booster (booster rocket) [overall sectional view]
3 first rocket stage (S–IC)
4 F–1 engines
5 heat shield (thermal protection shield)
6 aerodynamic engine fairings
7 aerodynamic stabilizing fins
8 stage separation retro–rockets, 8 rockets arranged in 4 pairs
9 kerosene (RP–1) tank [capacity: 811,000 litres]
10 liquid oxygen (LOX, LO_2) supply lines
11 anti–vortex system (device for preventing the formation of vortices in the fuel)
12 liquid oxygen (LOX, LO_2) tank [capacity: 1,315,000 litres]
13 anti–slosh baffles
14 compressed–helium bottles (helium pressure bottles)
15 diffuser for gaseous oxygen
16 inter–tank connector (inter–tank section)
17 instruments and system–monitoring devices
18 second rocket stage (S–II)
19 J–2 engines
20 heat shield (thermal protection shield)
21 engine mounts and thrust structure
22 acceleration rockets for fuel acquisition
23 liquid hydrogen (LH_2) suction line
24 liquid oxygen (LOX, LO_2) tank [capacity: 1,315,000 litres]
25 standpipe
26 liquid hydrogen (LH_2) tank [capacity: 1,020,000 litres]
27 fuel level sensor
28 work platform (working platform)
29 cable duct
30 manhole
31 S–IC/S–II inter–stage connector (inter–stage section)
32 compressed–gas container (gas pressure vessel)
33 third rocket stage (S–IVB)
34 J–2 engine
35 nozzle (thrust nozzle)
36 S–II/S–IVB inter–stage connector (inter–stage section)
37 four second–stage (S–II) separation retro–rockets
38 attitude control rockets
39 liquid oxygen (LOX, LO_2) tank [capacity: 77,200 litres]
40 fuel line duct
41 liquid hydrogen (LH_2) tank [capacity: 253,000 litres]
42 measuring probes
43 compressed–helium tanks (helium pressure vessels)
44 tank vent
45 forward frame section
46 work platform (working platform)
47 cable duct
48 acceleration rockets for fuel acquisition
49 aft frame section
50 compressed–helium tanks (helium pressure vessels)
51 liquid hydrogen (LH_2) line
52 liquid oxygen (LOX, LO_2) line
53 24–panel instrument unit
54 LM hangar (lunar module hangar)
55 LM (lunar module)
56 Apollo SM (service module), containing supplies and equipment
57 SM (service module) main engine
58 fuel tank
59 nitrogen tetroxide tank
60 pressurized gas delivery system
61 oxygen tanks
62 fuel cells
63 manoeuvring (*Am.* maneuvering) rocket assembly
64 directional antenna assembly
65 space capsule (command section)
66 launch phase escape tower

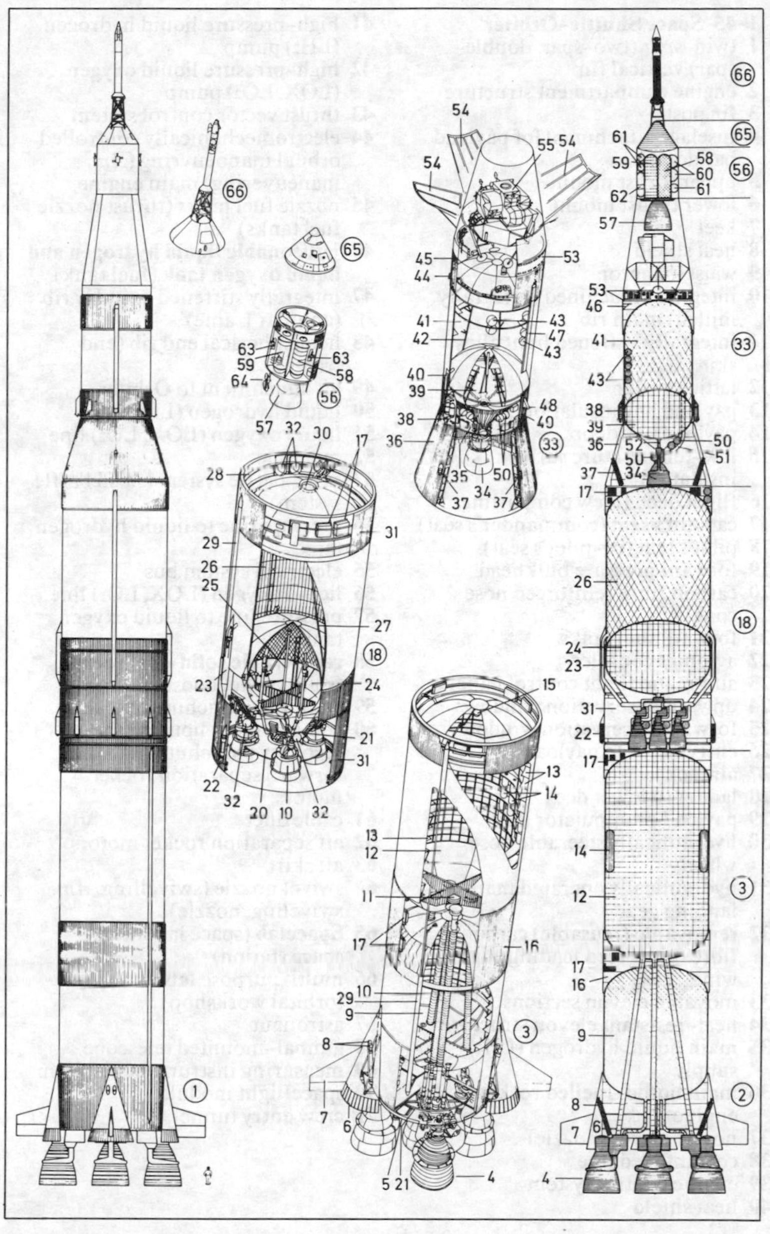
1
66
65
63
59
64
63
58
56
57
32
30
17
28
31
29
26
25
27
18
23
24
21
31
22
32
20
10
32
54
55
54
54
45
44
53
41
42
43
47
43
40
39
38
36
48
49
33
35
34
50
37
37
15
13
14
13
12
11
17
16
10
29
9
8
7
6
5
21
4
3
66
61
59
65
58
60
61
56
62
57
53
46
41
33
43
38
39
36
52
50
51
50
37
34
17
26
18
24
23
31
22
17
14
12
3
17
16
9
8
2
7
6
4

1–45 Space Shuttle–Orbiter
1 twin-spar (two-spar, double-spar) vertical fin
2 engine compartment structure
3 fin post
4 fuselage attachment [of payload bay doors]
5 upper thrust mount
6 lower thrust mount
7 keel
8 heat shield
9 waist longeron
10 integrally machined (integrally milled) main rib
11 integrally stiffened light alloy skin
12 lattice girder
13 payload bay insulation
14 payload bay door
15 low-temperature surface insulation
16 flight deck (crew compartment)
17 captain's seat (commander's seat)
18 pilot's seat (co-pilot's seat)
19 forward pressure bulkhead
20 carbon fibre reinforced nose cone
21 forward fuel tanks
22 avionics consoles
23 automatic flight control panel
24 upward observation windows
25 forward observation windows
26 entry hatch to payload bay
27 air lock
28 ladder to lower deck
29 payload manipulator arm
30 hydraulically steerable nose wheel
31 hydraulically operated main landing gear
32 removable (reusable) carbon fibre reinforced leading edge [of wing]
33 movable elevon sections
34 heat-resistant elevon structure
35 main liquid hydrogen (LH_2) supply
36 main liquid-fuelled rocket engine
37 nozzle (thrust nozzle)
38 coolant feed line
39 engine control system
40 heat shield
41 high-pressure liquid hydrogen (LH_2) pump
42 high-pressure liquid oxygen (LOX, LO_2) pump
43 thrust vector control system
44 electromechanically controlled orbital manoeuvring (*Am.* maneuvering) main engine
45 nozzle fuel tanks (thrust nozzle fuel tanks)
46 **jettisonable liquid hydrogen and liquid oxygen tank** (fuel tank)
47 integrally stiffened annular rib (annular frame)
48 hemispherical end rib (end frame)
49 aft attachment to Orbiter
50 liquid hydrogen (LH_2) line
51 liquid oxygen (LOX, LO_2) line
52 manhole
53 surge baffle system (slosh baffle system)
54 pressure line to liquid hydrogen tank
55 electrical system bus
56 liquid oxygen (LOX, LO_2) line
57 pressure line to liquid oxygen tank
58 **recoverable solid-fuel rocket** (solid rocket booster)
59 auxiliary parachute bay
60 compartment housing the recovery parachutes and the forward separation rocket motors
61 cable duct
62 aft separation rocket motors
63 aft skirt
64 swivel nozzle (swivelling, *Am.* swiveling, nozzle)
65 **Spacelab** (space laboratory, space station)
66 multi-purpose laboratory (orbital workshop)
67 astronaut
68 gimbal-mounted telescope
69 measuring instrument platform
70 spaceflight module
71 crew entry tunnel

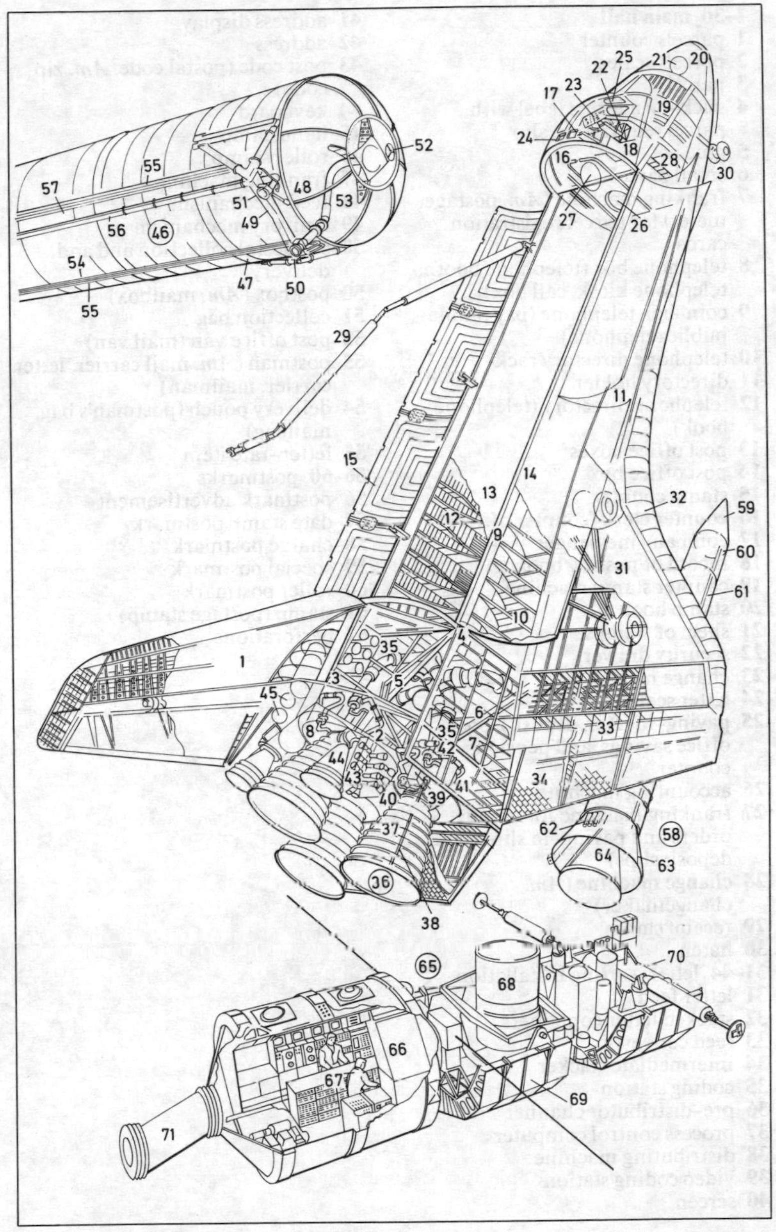
20
21
25
22
23
17
19
24
18
16
28
30
52
55
57
48
51
53
49
56
46
27
26
54
47
50
55
29
11
15
14
13
32
59
12
9
60
31
61
10
35
4
1
3
5
45
6
8
2
35
33
42
7
44
43
34
41
40
39
37
62
58
64
63
36
38
65
70
68
66
67
69
71

236 Post Office I

1-30 main hall
1 parcels counter
2 parcels scales
3 parcel
4 stick-on address label with parcel registration slip
5 glue pot
6 small parcel
7 franking machine (*Am.* postage meter) for parcel registration cards
8 telephone box (telephone booth, telephone kiosk, call box)
9 coin-box telephone (pay phone, public telephone)
10 telephone directory rack
11 directory holder
12 telephone directory (telephone book)
13 post office boxes
14 post office box
15 stamp counter
16 counter clerk (counter officer)
17 company messenger
18 record of posting book
19 counter stamp machine
20 stamp book
21 sheet of stamps
22 security drawer
23 change rack
24 letter scales
25 paying-in (*Am.* deposit), post office savings, and pensions counter
26 accounting machine
27 franking machine for money orders and paying-in slips (*Am.* deposit slips)
28 change machine (*Am.* changemaker)
29 receipt stamp
30 hatch
31-44 letter-sorting installation
31 letter feed
32 stacked letter containers
33 feed conveyor
34 intermediate stacker
35 coding station
36 pre-distributor channel
37 process control computer
38 distributing machine
39 video coding station
40 screen
41 address display
42 address
43 post code (postal code, *Am.* zip code)
44 keyboard
45 handstamp
46 roller stamp
47 franking machine
48 feed mechanism
49 delivery mechanism
50-55 postal collection and and delivery
50 postbox (*Am.* mailbox)
51 collection bag
52 post office van (mail van)
53 postman (*Am.* mail carrier, letter carrier, mailman)
54 delivery pouch (postman's bag, mailbag)
55 letter-rate item
56-60 postmarks
56 postmark advertisement
57 date stamp postmark
58 charge postmark
59 special postmark
60 roller postmark
61 stamp (postage stamp)
62 perforations

OXFORD OX2 6DP
BERLIN ist eine Reise wert
Come and see BERLIN
OXFORD
22.5.79
GREAT BRITAIN
POSTAGE PAID
07
LPBR 208F
50e ANNIVERSAIRE
ROTARY
INTERNATIONAL
LUXEMBOURG
BITTE AUCH IN DER
ABSENDERANGABE
VERGISS
MEIN
NICHT:
DIE POSTLEITZAHL
GUMMERSBACH 1
me
25.2.76-16
5270
DEUTSCHE BUNDESPOST

237 Post Office II (Telephones and Telegraphy)

1 **telephone box** (telephone booth, telephone kiosk, call box), a public telephone
2 telephone user (*with own telephone:* telephone subscriber, telephone customer)
3 coin-box telephone (pay phone, public telephone) for local and long-distance calls (trunk calls)
4 emergency telephone
5 telephone directory (telephone book)
6–26 **telephone instruments** (telephones)
6 standard table telephone
7 telephone receiver (handset)
8 earpiece
9 mouthpiece (microphone)
10 dial (push-button keyboard)
11 finger plate (dial finger plate, dial wind-up plate)
12 finger stop (dial finger stop)
13 cradle (handset cradle, cradle switch)
14 receiver cord (handset cord)
15 telephone casing (telephone cover)
16 subscriber's (customer's) private meter
17 switchboard (exchange) for a system of extensions
18 push button for connecting main exchange lines
19 push buttons for calling extensions
20 push-button telephone
21 earthing button for the extensions
22–26 switchboard with extensions
22 exchange
23 switchboard operator's set
24 main exchange line
25 switching box (automatic switching system, automatic connecting system, switching centre, *Am.* center)
26 extension
27–41 **telephone exchange**
27 fault repair service
28 maintenance technician
29 testing board (testing desk)
30 telegraphy
31 teleprinter (teletypewriter)
32 paper tape
33 directory enquiries
34 information position (operator's position)
35 operator
36 microfilm reader
37 microfilm file
38 microfilm card with telephone numbers
39 date indicator display
40 testing and control station
41 switching centre (*Am.* center) for telephone, telex, and data transmission services
42 **selector**, a motor uniselector made of noble metals; *sim.:* electronic selector
43 contact arc (bank)
44 contact arm (wiper)
45 contact field
46 contact arm tag
47 electromagnet
48 selector motor
49 restoring spring (resetting spring)
50 **communication links**
51–52 satellite radio link
51 earth station with directional antenna
52 communications satellite with directional antenna
53 coastal station
54–55 intercontinental radio link
54 short-wave station
55 ionosphere
56 submarine cable (deep-sea cable)
57 underwater amplifier
58 **data transmission** (data services)
59 input/output device for data carriers
60 data processor
61 teleprinter
62–64 data carriers
62 punched tape (punch tape)
63 magnetic tape
64 punched card (punch card)
65 telex link
66 teleprinter (page printer)
67 dialling (*Am.* dialing) unit
68 telex tape (punched tape, punch tape) for transmitting the text at maximum speed
69 telex message
70 keyboard

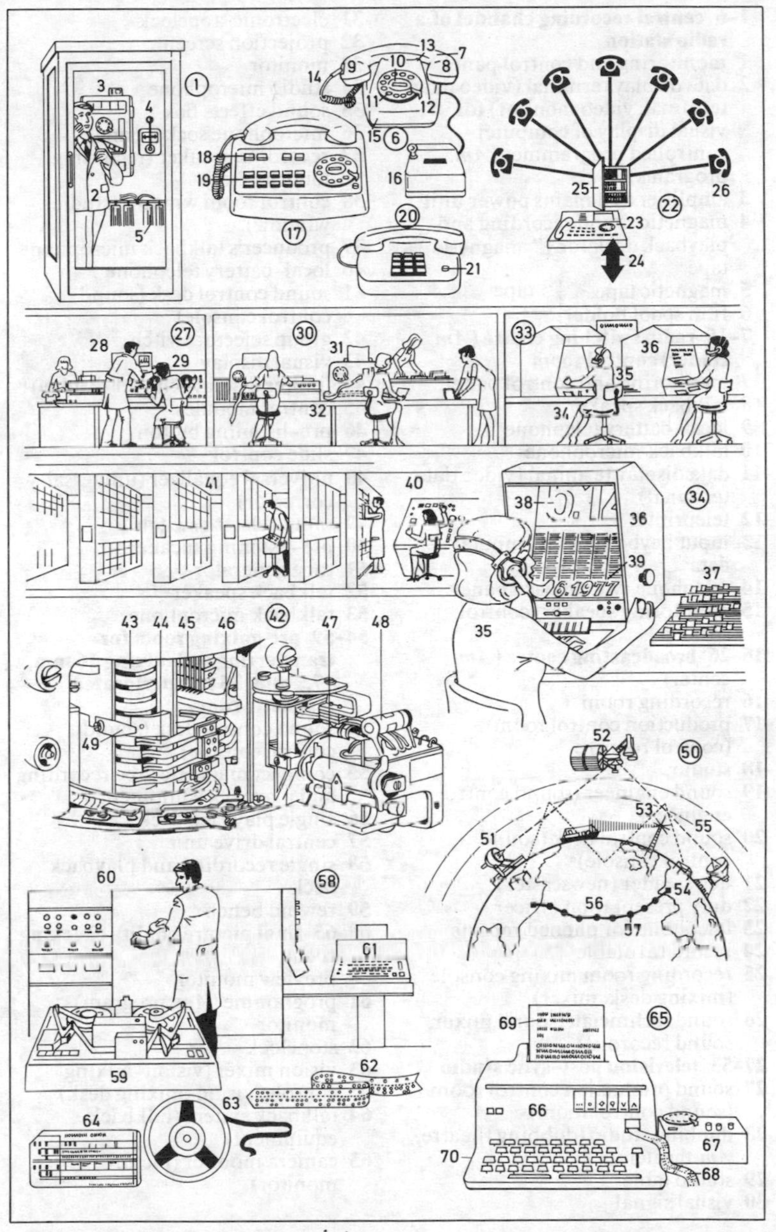

1 2 3 4 5
6 7 8 9 10 11 12 13 14 15 16
17 18 19
20 21
22 23 24 25 26
27 28 29
30 31 32
33 34 35 36
34 35 36 37 38 39
6.1977
40 41
42 43 44 45 46 47 48 49
50 51 52 53 54 55 56 57
58 59 60 61
62 63 64
65 66 67 68 69 70

1–6 central recording channel of a radio station
1 monitoring and control panel
2 data display terminal (video data terminal, video monitor) for visual display of computer-controlled programmes (*Am.* programs)
3 amplifier and mains power unit
4 magnetic sound recording and playback deck for $\frac{1}{4}''$ magnetic tape
5 magnetic tape, a $\frac{1}{4}''$ tape
6 film spool holder
7–15 radio switching centre (*Am.* center) control room
7 monitoring and control panel
8 talkback speaker
9 local-battery telephone
10 talkback microphone
11 data display terminal (video data terminal)
12 teleprinter
13 input keyboard for computer data
14 telephone switchboard panel
15 monitoring speaker (control speaker)
16–26 broadcasting centre (*Am.* center)
16 recording room
17 production control room (control room)
18 studio
19 sound engineer (sound control engineer)
20 sound control desk (sound control console)
21 newsreader (newscaster)
22 duty presentation officer
23 telephone for phoned reports
24 record turntable
25 recording room mixing console (mixing desk, mixer)
26 sound technician (sound mixer, sound recordist)
27–53 television post-sync studio
27 sound production control room (sound control room)
28 dubbing studio (dubbing theatre, *Am* theater)
29 studio table
30 visual signal
31 electronic stopclock
32 projection screen
33 monitor
34 studio microphone
35 sound effects box
36 microphone socket panel
37 recording speaker (recording loudspeaker)
38 control room window (studio window)
39 producer's talkback microphone
40 local-battery telephone
41 sound control desk (sound control console)
42 group selector switch
43 visual display
44 limiter display (clipper display)
45 control modules
46 pre-listening buttons
47 slide control
48 universal equalizer (universal corrector)
49 input selector switch
50 pre-listening speaker
51 tone generator
52 talkback speaker
53 talkback microphone
54–59 pre-mixing room for transferring and mixing 16 mm, 17.5 mm, 35 mm perforated magnetic film
54 sound control desk (sound control console)
55 compact magnetic tape recording and playback equipment
56 single playback deck
57 central drive unit
58 single recording and playback deck
59 rewind bench
60–65 final picture quality checking room
60 preview monitor
61 programme (*Am.* program) monitor
62 stopclock
63 vision mixer (vision-mixing console, vision-mixing desk)
64 talkback system (talkback equipment)
65 camera monitor (picture monitor)

1
2
1
3
4
5
6
7
8
9
10
11
12
13
14
15
16
17
18
19
20
21
22
23
24
25
26
27
28
29
30
31
32
32
33
34
35
36
37
38
39
40
41
42
43
44
45
46
47
48
49
50
51
52
53
54
55
56
56
57
58
59
60
61
62
63
64
65
65
65
65

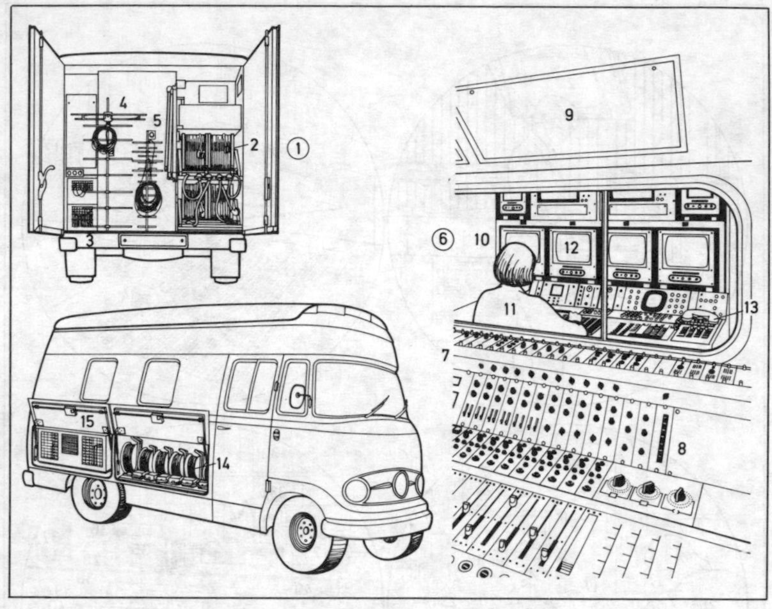

1-15 outside broadcast (OB) vehicle (television OB van; *also:* sound OB van, radio OB van)
1 **rear equipment section of the OB vehicle**
2 camera cable
3 cable connection panel
4 television (TV) reception aerial (receiving aerial) for Channel I
5 television (TV) reception aerial (receiving aerial) for Channel II
6 **interior equipment (on-board equipment) of the OB vehicle**
7 sound production control room (sound control room)
8 sound control desk (sound control console)
9 monitoring loudspeaker
10 vision control room (video control room)
11 video controller (vision controller)
12 camera monitor (picture monitor)
13 on-board telephone (intercommunication telephone)
14 microphone cable
15 air-conditioning equipment

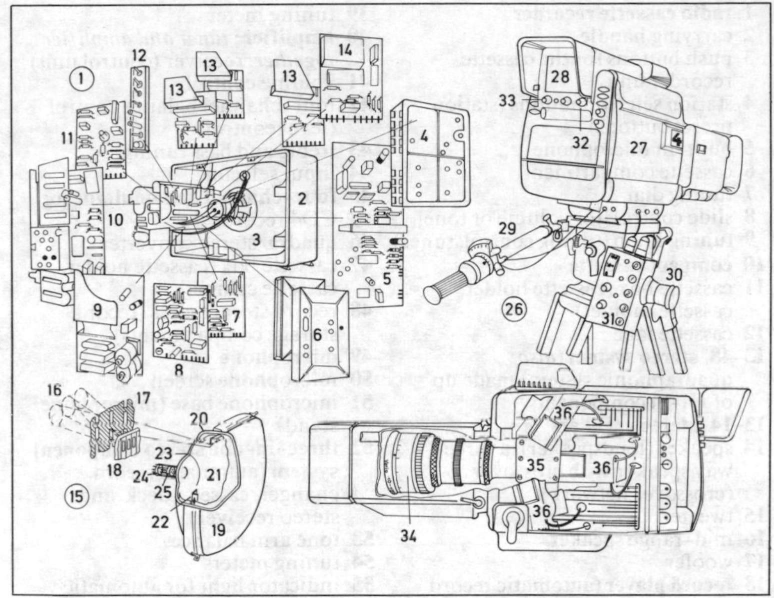

1 colour (*Am.* color) television (TV) receiver (colour television set) of modular design
2 television cabinet
3 television tube (picture tube)
4 IF (intermediate frequency) amplifier module
5 colour (*Am.* color) decoder module
6 VHF and UHF tuner
7 horizontal synchronizing module
8 vertical deflection module
9 horizontal linearity control module
10 horizontal deflection module
11 control module
12 convergence module
13 colour (*Am.* color) output stage module
14 sound module
15 colour (*Am.* color) picture tube
16 electron beams
17 shadow mask with elongated holes
18 strip of fluorescent (luminescent, phosphorescent) material
19 coating (film) of fluorescent material
20 inner magnetic screen (screening)
21 vacuum
22 temperature-compensated shadow mask mount
23 centring (centering) ring for the deflection system
24 electron gun assembly
25 rapid heat-up cathode
26 television (TV) camera
27 camera head
28 camera monitor
29 control arm (control lever)
30 focusing adjustment
31 control panel
32 contrast control
33 brightness control
34 zoom lens
35 beam-splitting prism (beam splitter)
36 pickup unit (colour, *Am.* color, pickup tube)

241 Music Systems (Audio Systems)

1 **radio cassette recorder**
2 carrying handle
3 push buttons for the cassette recorder unit
4 station selector buttons (station preset buttons)
5 built-in microphone
6 cassette compartment
7 tuning dial
8 slide control [for volume or tone]
9 tuning knob (tuning control, tuner)
10 **compact cassette**
11 cassette box (cassette holder, cassette cabinet)
12 cassette tape
13–48 **stereo system** (*also:* quadraphonic system) made up of Hi-Fi components
13–14 **stereo speakers**
14 speaker (loudspeaker), a three-way speaker with crossover (crossover network)
15 tweeter
16 mid-range speaker
17 woofer
18 **record player** (automatic record changer, auto changer)
19 record player housing (record player base)
20 turntable
21 tone arm
22 counterbalance (counterweight)
23 gimbal suspension
24 stylus pressure control (stylus force control)
25 anti-skate control
26 magnetic cartridge with (conical or elliptical) stylus, a diamond
27 tone arm lock
28 tone arm lift
29 speed selector (speed changer)
30 starter switch
31 treble control
32 dust cover
33 **stereo cassette deck**
34 cassette compartment
35–36 recording level meters (volume unit meters, VU meters)
35 left-channel recording level meter
36 right-channel recording level meter
37 **tuner**
38 VHF (FM) station selector buttons
39 tuning meter
40 **amplifier;** *tuner and amplifier together:* receiver (control unit)
41 volume control
42 four-channel balance control (level control)
43 treble and bass tuning
44 input selector
45 **four-channel demodulator** for CD4 records
46 quadra/stereo converter
47 cassette box (cassette holder, cassette cabinet)
48 record storage slots (record storage compartments)
49 **microphone**
50 microphone screen
51 microphone base (microphone stand)
52 **three-in-one stereo component system** (automatic record changer, cassette deck, and stereo receiver)
53 tone arm balance
54 tuning meters
55 indicator light for automatic FeO/CrO_2 tape switch-over
56 **open-reel-type recorder**, a two or four-track unit
57 tape reel (open tape reel)
58 open-reel tape (recording tape, $\frac{1}{4}''$ tape)
59 sound head housing with erasing head (erase head), recording head, and reproducing head (*or:* combined head)
60 tape deflector roller and end switch (limit switch)
61 recording level meter (VU meter)
62 tape speed selector
63 on/off switch
64 tape counter
65 stereo microphone sockets (stereo microphone jacks)
66 **headphones** (headset)
67 padded headband (padded headpiece)
68 membrane
69 earcups (earphones)
70 headphone cable plug, a standard multi-pin plug
71 headphone cable (headphone cord)

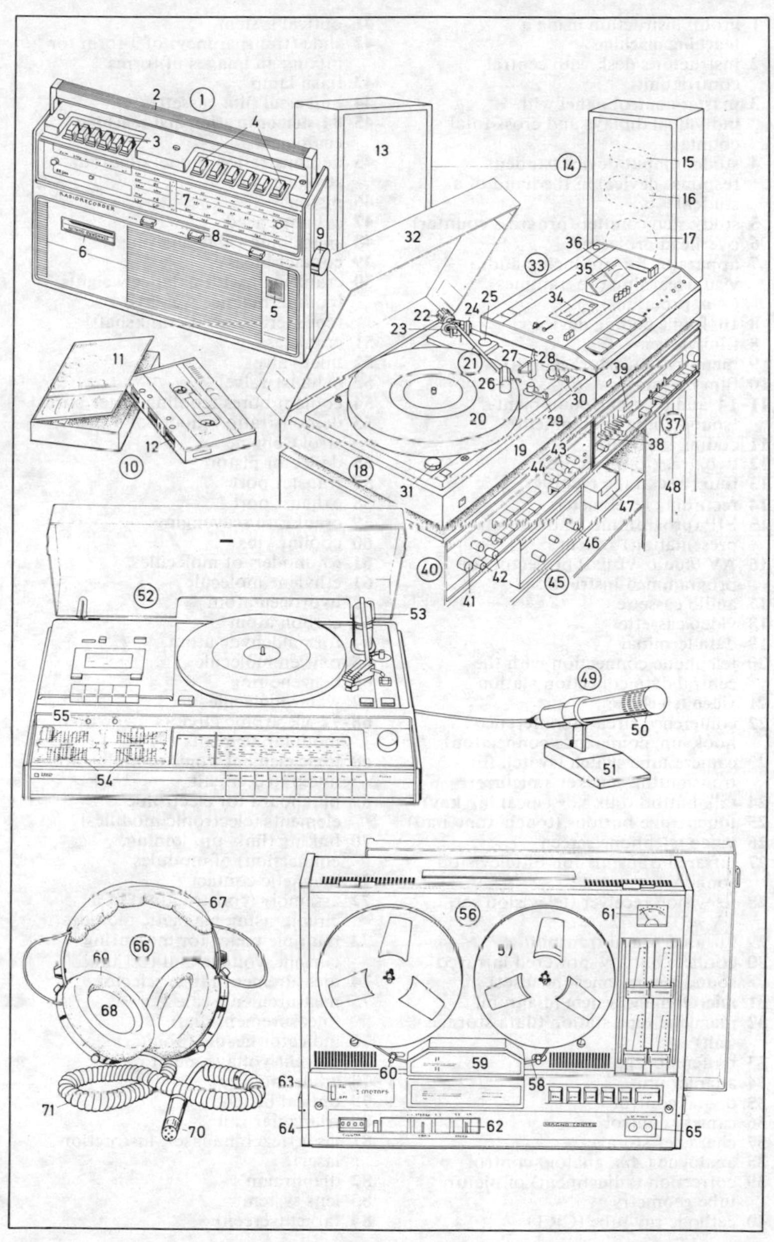
1
2
3
4
5
6
7
8
9
10
11
12
13
14
15
16
17
18
19
20
21
22
23
24
25
26
27
28
29
30
31
32
33
34
35
36
37
38
39
40
41
42
43
44
45
46
47
48
49
50
51
52
53
54
55
56
57
58
59
60
61
62
63
64
65
66
67
68
69
70
71
RADIORECORDER
3 motors

1 group instruction using a **teaching machine**
2 instructor's desk with central control unit
3 master control panel with individual diplays and cross total counters
4 student input device (student response device) in the hand of a student
5 study step counter (progress counter)
6 overhead projector
7 apparatus for producing audio-visual learning programmes (*Am.* programs)
8-10 frame coding device
8 film viewer
9 memory unit (storage unit)
10 film perforator
11-14 audio coding equipment (sound coding equipment)
11 coding keyboard
12 two-track tape recorder
13 four-track tape recorder
14 recording level meter
15 PIP (programmed individual presentation) system
16 AV (audio-visual) projector for programmed instruction
17 audio cassette
18 video cassette
19 data terminal
20 telephone connection with the central data collection station
21 **video telephone**
22 conference circuit (conference hook-up, conference connection)
23 camera tube switch (switch for transmitting speaker's picture)
24 talk button (talk key, speaking key)
25 touch-tone buttons (touch-tone pad)
26 video telephone screen
27 infrared transmission of television sound
28 television receiver (television set, TV set)
29 infrared sound transmitter
30 cordless battery-powered infrared sound headphones (headset)
31 **microfilming system** [diagram]
32 magnetic tape station (data storage unit)
33 buffer storage
34 adapter unit
35 digital control
36 camera control
37 character storage
38 analogue (*Am.* analog) control
39 correction (adjustment) of picture tube geometry
40 cathode ray tube (CRT)
41 optical system
42 slide (transparency) of a form for mixing-in images of forms
43 flash lamp
44 universal film cassettes
45-84 **demonstration and teaching equipment**
45 demonstration model of a four-stroke engine
46 piston
47 cylinder head
48 spark plug (sparking plug)
49 contact breaker
50 crankshaft with balance weights (counterbalance weights) (counterbalanced crankshaft)
51 crankcase
52 inlet valve
53 exhaust valve
54 coolant bores (cooling water bores)
55 demonstration model of a two-stroke engine
56 deflector piston
57 transfer port
58 exhaust port
59 crankcase scavenging
60 cooling ribs
61-67 models of molecules
61 ethylene molecule
62 hydrogen atom
63 carbon atom
64 formaldehyde atom
65 oxygen molecule
66 benzene ring
67 water molecule
68-72 electronic circuits made up of modular elements
68 logic element (logic module), an integrated circuit
69 plugboard for electronic elements (electronic modules)
70 linking (link-up, joining, connection) of modules
71 magnetic contact
72 assembly (construction) of a circuit, using magnetic modules
73 multiple meter for measuring current, voltage and resistance
74 measurement range selector
75 measurement scale (measurement dial)
76 indicator needle (pointer)
77 current/voltage meter
78 adjusting screw
79 optical bench
80 triangular rail
81 laser (teaching laser, instruction laser)
82 diaphragm
83 lens system
84 target (screen)

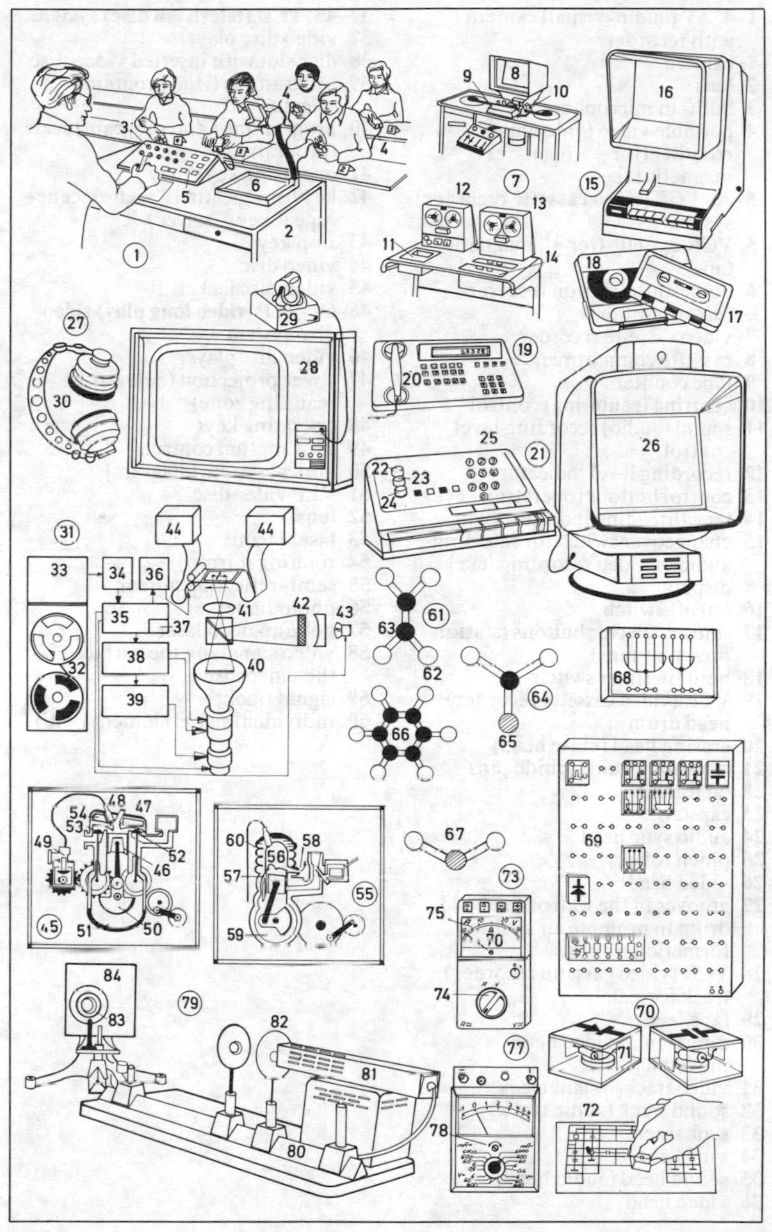
1
2
3
4
5
6
7
8
9
10
11
12
13
14
15
16
17
18
19
20
21
22
23
24
25
26
27
28
29
30
31
32
33
34
35
36
37
38
39
40
41
42
43
44
45
46
47
48
49
50
51
52
53
54
55
56
57
58
59
60
61
62
63
64
65
66
67
68
69
70
71
72
73
74
75
77
78
79
80
81
82
83
84

243 Audiovision (AV)

1-4 AV (audio-visual) camera with recorder
1 camera
2 lens
3 built-in microphone
4 portable video (videotape) recorder (for $\frac{1}{4}$″ open-reel magnetic tape
5-36 VCR (video cassette recorder) system
5 VCR cassette (for $\frac{1}{2}$″ magnetic tape)
6 domestic television receiver (*also:* monitor)
7 video cassette recorder
8 cassette compartment
9 tape counter
10 centring (centering) control
11 sound (audio) recording level control
12 recording level indicator
13 control buttons (operating keys)
14 tape threading indicator light
15 changeover switch for selecting audio or video recording level display
16 on/off switch
17 station selector buttons (station preset buttons)
18 built-in timer switch
19 VCR (video cassette recorder) head drum
20 erasing head (erase head)
21 stationary guide (guide pin)
22 tape guide
23 capstan
24 audio sync head
25 pinch roller
26 video head
27 grooves in the wall of the head drum to promote air cushion formation
28 VCR (video cassette recorder) track format
29 tape feed
30 direction of video head movement
31 video track, a slant track
32 sound track (audio track)
33 sync track
34 sync head
35 sound head (audio head)
36 video head
37-45 TED (television disc) system
37 video disc player
38 disc slot with inserted video disc
39 programme (*Am.* program) selector
40 programme (*Am.* program) scale (programme dial)
41 operating key ('play')
42 key for repeating a scene (scene-repeat key, 'select')
43 stop key
44 video disc
45 video disc jacket
46-60 VLP (video long play) video disc system
46 video disc player
47 cover projection (*below it:* scanning zone)
48 operating keys
49 slow motion control
50 optical system [diagram]
51 VLP video disc
52 lens
53 laser beam
54 rotating mirror
55 semi-reflecting mirror
56 photodiode
57 helium-neon laser
58 video signals on the surface of the video disc
59 signal track
60 individual signal element ('pit')

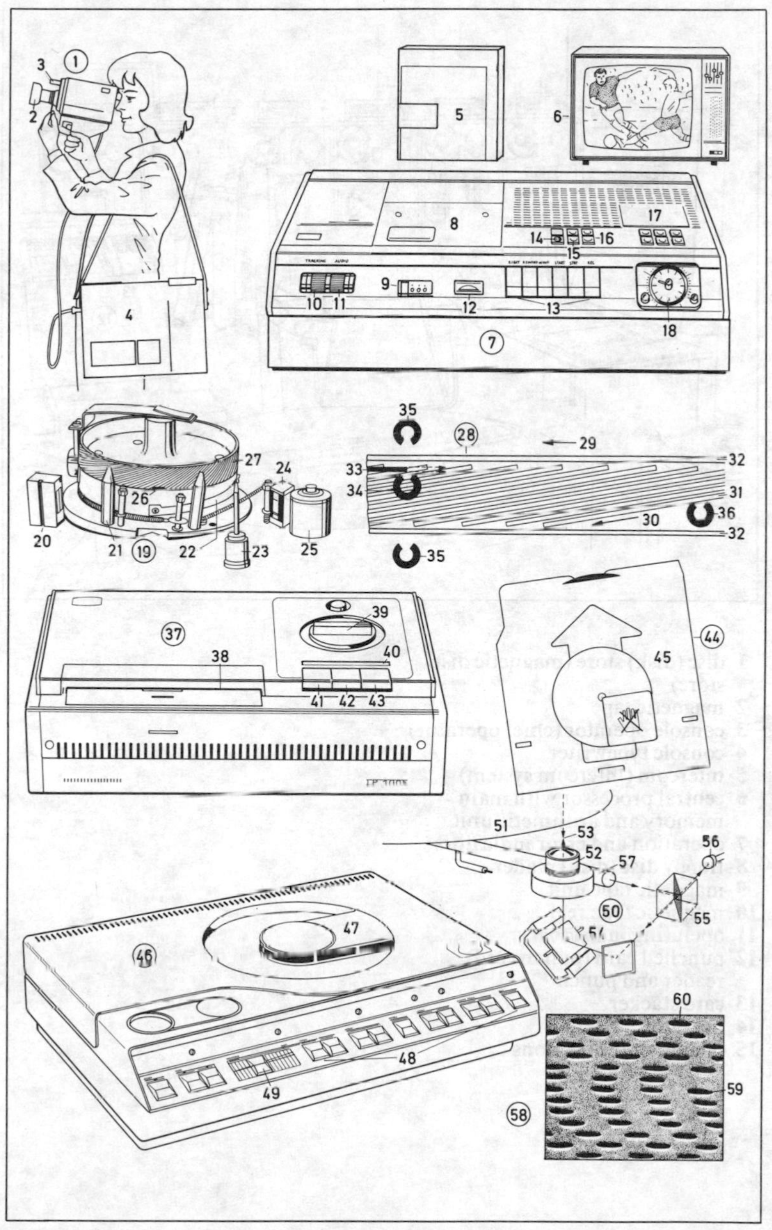

1
2
3
4
5
6
7
8
9
10
11
12
13
14
15
16
17
18
19
20
21
22
23
24
25
26
27
28
29
30
31
32
33
34
35
36
37
38
39
40
41
42
43
44
45
46
47
48
49
50
51
52
53
54
55
56
57
58
59
60

244 Computer Centre (*Am.* Center)

1 disc (disk) store (magnetic disc store)
2 magnetic tape
3 console operator (chief operator)
4 console typewriter
5 intercom (intercom system)
6 central processor with main memory and arithmetic unit
7 operation and error indicators
8 floppy disc (disk) reader
9 magnetic tape unit
10 magnetic tape reel
11 operating indicators
12 punched card (punch card) reader and punch
13 card stacker
14 operator
15 operating instructions

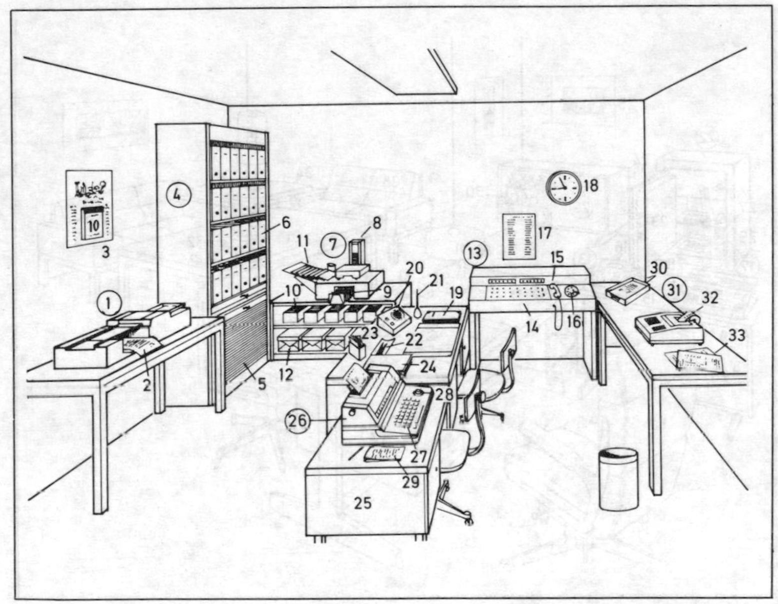

1–33 receptionist's office (secretary's office)
1 facsimile telegraph
2 transmitted copy (received copy)
3 wall calendar
4 filing cabinet
5 tambour door (roll-up door)
6 file (document file)
7 transfer-type addressing machine
8 vertical stencil magazine
9 stencil ejection
10 stencil storage drawer
11 paper feed
12 stock of notepaper
13 switchboard (internal telephone exchange)
14 push-button keyboard for internal connections
15 handset
16 dial
17 internal telephone list
18 master clock (main clock)
19 folder containing documents, correspondence, etc. for signing (to be signed)
20 intercom (office intercom)
21 pen
22 pen and pencil tray
23 card index
24 stack (set) of forms
25 typing desk
26 memory typewriter
27 keyboard
28 rotary switch for the main memory and the magnetic tape loop
29 shorthand pad (*Am.* steno pad)
30 letter tray
31 office calculator
32 printer
33 business letter

1–36 executive's office
1 swivel chair
2 desk
3 writing surface (desk top)
4 desk drawer
5 cupboard (storage area) with door
6 desk mat (blotter)
7 business letter
8 appointments diary
9 desk set
10 intercom (office intercom)
11 desk lamp
12 pocket calculator (electronic calculator)
13 telephone, an executive-secretary system
14 dial; *also:* push-button keyboard
15 call buttons
16 receiver (telephone receiver)
17 dictating machine
18 position indicator
19 control buttons (operating keys)
20 cabinet
21 visitor's chair
22 safe
23 bolts (locking mechanism)
24 armour (*Am.* armor) plating
25 confidential documents
26 patent
27 petty cash
28 picture
29 bar (drinks cabinet)
30 bar set
31–36 conference grouping
31 conference table
32 pocket-sized dictating machine (micro cassette recorder)
33 ashtray
34 corner table
35 table lamp
36 two-seater sofa [part of the conference grouping]

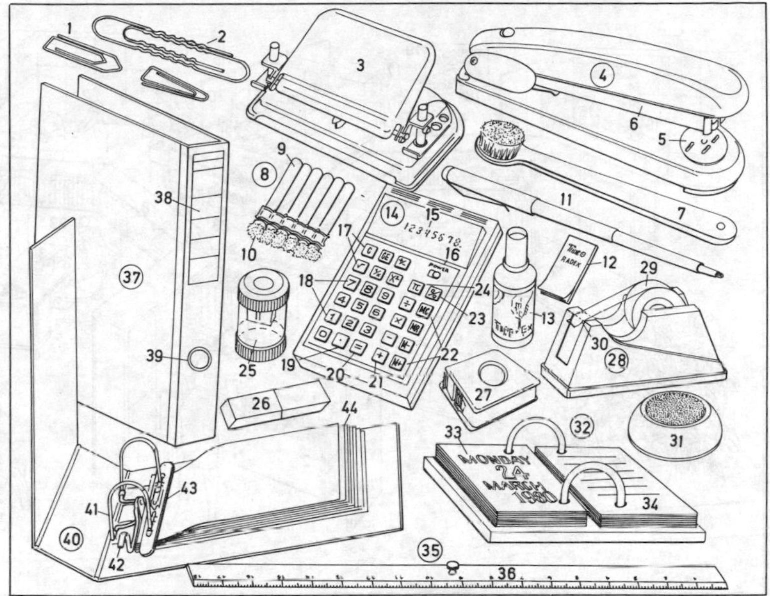

1-44 office equipment (office supplies, office materials)
1, 2 paper clips
3 punch
4 stapler (stapling machine)
5 anvil
6 spring-loaded magazine
7 type-cleaning brush for typewriters
8 type cleaner (type-cleaning kit)
9 fluid container (fluid reservoir)
10 cleaning brush
11 felt tip pen
12 correcting paper [for typing errors]
13 correcting fluid [for typing errors]
14 electronic pocket calculator
15 eight-digit fluorescent display
16 on/off switch
17 function keys
18 number keys
19 decimal key
20 'equals' key
21 instruction keys (command keys)
22 memory keys
23 percent key (percentage key)
24 π-key (pi-key) for mensuration of circles
25 pencil sharpener
26 typewriter rubber
27 adhesive tape dispenser
28 adhesive tape holder (roller-type adhesive tape dispenser)
29 roll of adhesive tape
30 tear-off edge
31 moistener
32 desk diary
33 date sheet (calendar sheet)
34 memo sheet
35 ruler
36 centimetre and millimetre (*Am.* centimeter and millimeter) graduations
37 file (document file)
38 spine label (spine tag)
39 finger hole
40 arch board file
41 arch unit
42 release lever (locking lever, release/lock lever)
43 compressor
44 bank statement (statement of account)

1–48 open plan office
1 partition wall (partition screen)
2 filing drawer with suspension file system
3 suspension file
4 file tab
5 file (document file)
6 filing clerk
7 clerical assistant
8 note for the files
9 telephone
10 filing shelves
11 clerical assistant's desk
12 office cupboard
13 plant stand (planter)
14 indoor plants (houseplants)
15 programmer
16 data display terminal (visual display unit)
17 customer service representative
18 customer
19 computer-generated design (computer-generated art)
20 sound-absorbing partition
21 typist
22 typewriter
23 filing drawer
24 customer card index
25 office chair, a swivel chair
26 typing desk
27 card index box
28 multi-purpose shelving
29 proprietor
30 business letter
31 proprietor's secretary
32 shorthand pad (*Am.* steno pad)
33 audio typist
34 dictating machine
35 earphone
36 statistics chart
37 pedestal containing a cupboard or drawers
38 sliding-door cupboard
39 office furniture arranged in an angular configuration
40 wall-mounted shelf
41 letter tray

42 wall calendar
43 data centre (*Am.* center)
44 calling up information on the data display terminal (visual display unit)
45 waste paper basket
46 sales statistics
47 EDP print-out, a continuous fan-fold sheet
48 connecting element

249 Office V (Office Machinery)

1 **electric typewriter**, a golf ball typewriter
2–6 keyboard
2 space bar
3 shift key
4 line space and carrier return key
5 shift lock
6 margin release key
7 tabulator key
8 tabulator clear key
9 on/off switch
10 striking force control (impression control)
11 ribbon selector
12 margin scale
13 left margin stop
14 right margin stop
15 golf ball (spherical typing element) bearing the types
16 ribbon cassette
17 paper bail with rollers
18 platen
19 typing opening (typing window)
20 paper release lever
21 carrier return lever
22 platen knob
23 line space adjuster
24 variable platen action lever
25 push-in platen variable
26 erasing table
27 transparent cover
28 exchange golf ball (exchange typing element)
29 type
30 golf ball cap (cap of typing element)
31 teeth
32 **web-fed automatic copier**
33 magazine for paper roll
34 paper size selection (format selection)
35 print quantity selection
36 contrast control
37 main switch (on/off switch)
38 start print button
39 document glass
40 transfer blanket
41 toner roll
42 exposure system
43 print delivery (copy delivery)
44 **letter-folding machine**
45 paper feed
46 folding mechanism
47 receiving tray
48 **small offset press**
49 paper feed
50 lever for inking the plate cylinder
51–52 inking unit (inker unit)
51 distributing roller (distributor)
52 ink roller (inking roller, fountain roller)
53 pressure adjustment
54 sheet delivery (receiving table)
55 printing speed adjustment
56 jogger for aligning the piles of sheets
57 pile of paper (pile of sheets)
58 folding machine
59 gathering machine (collating machine, assembling machine) for short runs
60 gathering station (collating station, assembling station)
61 adhesive binder (perfect binder) for hot adhesives
62 **magnetic tape dictating machine**
63 headphones (headset, earphones)
64 on/off switch
65 microphone cradle
66 foot control socket
67 telephone adapter socket
68 headphone socket (earphone socket, headset socket)
69 microphone socket
70 built-in loudspeaker
71 indicator lamp (indicator light)
72 cassette compartment
73 forward wind, rewind, and stop buttons
74 time scale with indexing marks
75 time scale stop

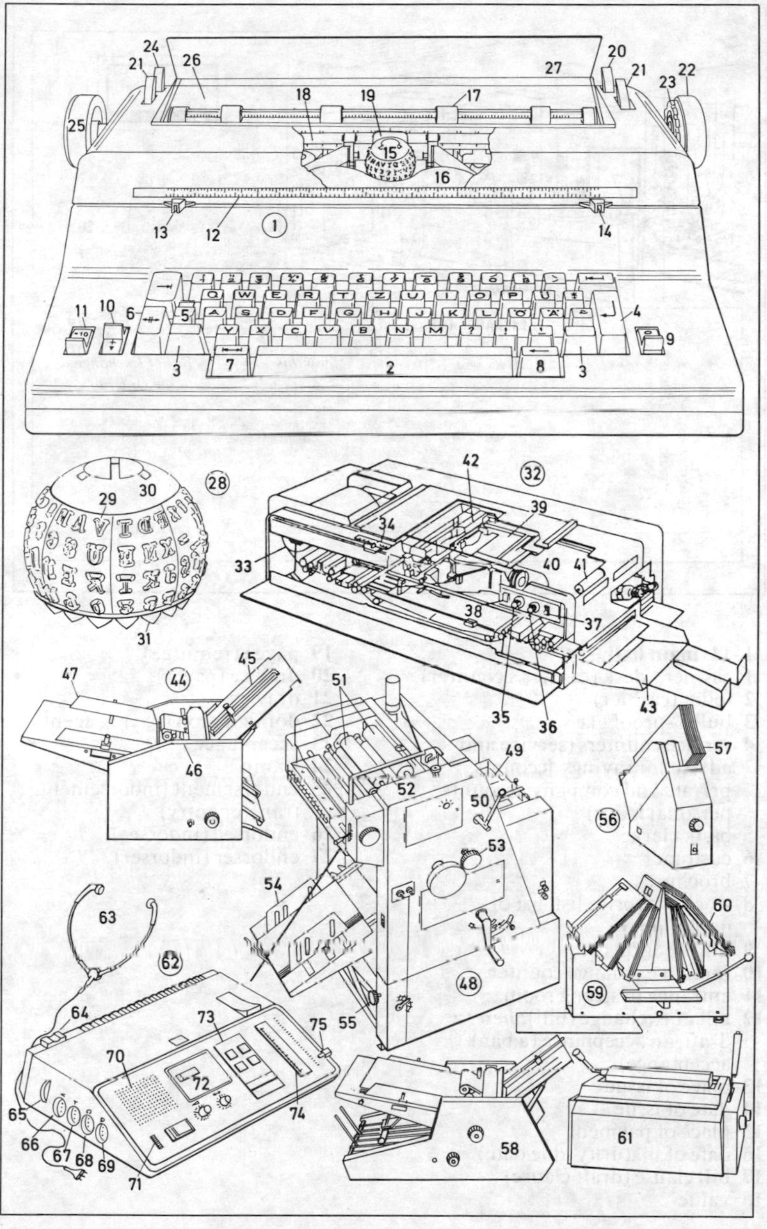
1
2
3
4
5
6
7
8
9
10
11
12
13
14
15
16
17
18
19
20
21
22
23
24
25
26
27
28
29
30
31
32
33
34
35
36
37
38
39
40
41
42
43
44
45
46
47
48
49
50
51
52
53
54
55
56
57
58
59
60
61
62
63
64
65
66
67
68
69
70
71
72
73
74
75

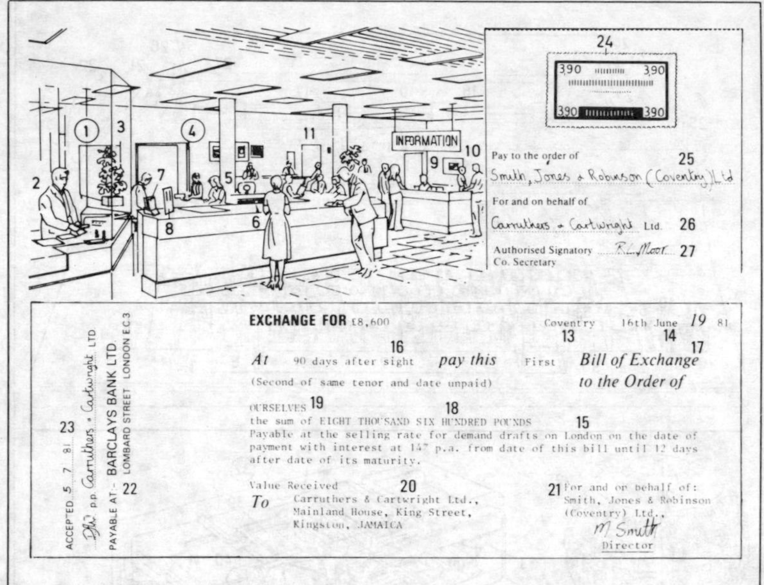

1–11 main hall
1 cashier's desk (cashier's counter)
2 teller (cashier)
3 bullet-proof glass
4 service counters (service and advice for savings accounts, private and company accounts, personal loans)
5 bank clerk
6 customer
7 brochures
8 stock list (price list, list of quotations)
9 information counter
10 foreign exchange counter
11 entrance to strong room
12 **bill of exchange** (bill); *here:* a draft, an acceptance (a bank acceptance)
13 place of issue
14 date of issue
15 place of payment
16 date of maturity (due date)
17 bill clause (draft clause)
18 value
19 payee (remittee)
20 drawee (payer)
21 drawer
22 domicilation (paying agent)
23 acceptance
24 stamp
25 endorsement (indorsement, transfer entry)
26 endorsee (indorsee)
27 endorser (indorser)

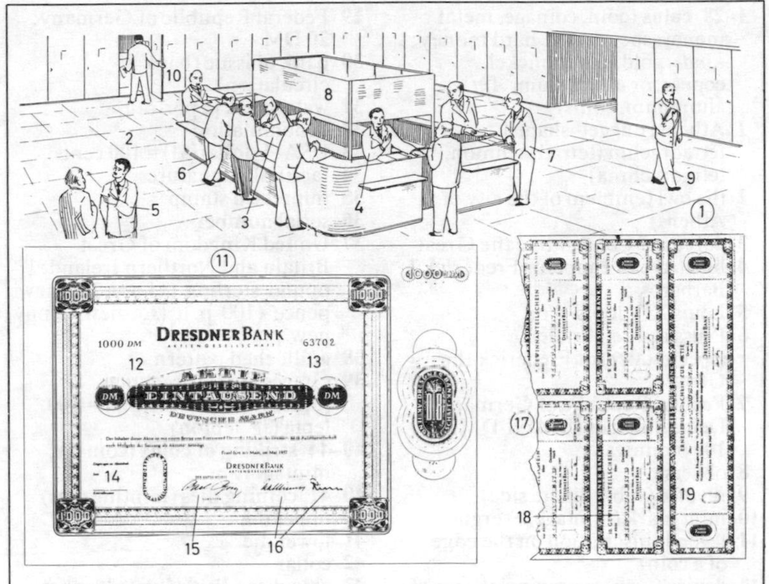

1–10 stock exchange (exchange for the sale of securities, stocks, and bonds)

1 exchange hall (exchange floor)
2 market for securities
3 broker's post
4 sworn stockbroker (exchange broker, stockbroker, *Am.* specialist), an inside broker
5 kerbstone broker (kerbstoner, curbstone broker, curbstoner, outside broker), a commercial broker dealing in unlisted securities
6 member of the stock exchange (stockjobber, *Am.* floor trader, room trader)
7 stock exchange agent (boardman), a bank employee
8 quotation board
9 stock exchange attendant (waiter)
10 telephone box (telephone booth, telephone kiosk, call box)

11–19 securities; *kinds:* share (*Am.* stock), fixed-income security, annuity, bond, debenture bond, municipal bond (corporation stock), industrial bond, convertible bond

11 share certificate (*Am.* stock certificate); *here:* bearer share (share warrant)
12 par (par value, nominal par, face par) of the share
13 serial number
14 page number of entry in bank's share register (bank's stock ledger)
15 signature of the chairman of the board of governors
16 signature of the chairman of the board of directors
17 sheet of coupons (coupon sheet, dividend coupon sheet)
18 dividend warrant (dividend coupon)
19 talon

252 Money (Coins and Notes, *Am.* Coins and Bills)

1-28 coins (coin, coinage, metal money, specie, *Am.* hard money; *kinds:* gold, silver, nickel, copper, or aluminium, *Am.* aluminum, coins)
1 Athens: nugget-shaped tetradrachm (tetradrachmon, tetradrachma)
2 the owl (emblem of the city of Athens)
3 aureus of Constantine the Great
4 bracteate of Emperor Frederick I Barbarossa
5 Louis XIV louis-d'or
6 Prussia: 1 reichstaler (speciestaler) of Frederick the Great
7 Federal Republic of Germany: 5 Deutschmarks (DM); 1 DM = 100 pfennigs
8 obverse
9 reverse (subordinate side)
10 mint mark (mintage, exergue)
11 legend (inscription on the edge of a coin)
12 device (type), a provincial coat of arms
13 Austria: 25 schillings; 1 sch = 100 groschen
14 provincial coats of arms
15 Switzerland: 5 francs; 1 franc = 100 centimes
16 France: 1 franc = 100 centimes
17 Belgium: 100 francs
18 Luxembourg (Luxemburg): 1 franc
19 Netherlands: $2\frac{1}{2}$ guilders; 1 guilder (florin, gulden) = 100 cents
20 Italy: 10 lire (*sg.* lira)
21 Vatican City: 10 lire (*sg.* lira)
22 Spain: 1 peseta = 100 céntimos
23 Portugal: 1 escudo = 100 centavos
24 Denmark: 1 krone = 100 öre
25 Sweden: 1 krona = 100 öre
26 Norway: 1 krone = 100 öre
27 Czechoslovakia: 1 koruna = 100 heller
28 Yugoslavia: 1 dinar = 100 paras
29-39 banknotes (*Am.* bills) (paper money, notes, treasury notes)
29 Federal Republic of Germany: 20 DM
30 bank of issue (bank of circulation)
31 watermark [a portrait]
32 denomination
33 USA: 1 dollar($1)= 100 cents
34 facsimile signatures
35 impressed stamp
36 serial number
37 United Kingdom of Great Britain and Northern Ireland: 1 pound sterling (£1) = 100 new pence (100 p.); (*sg.* new penny, new p.)
38 guilloched pattern
39 Greece: 1,000 drachmas (drachmae); 1 drachma = 100 lepta (*sg.* lepton)
40-44 striking of coins (coinage, mintage)
40-41 coining dies (minting dies)
40 upper die
41 lower die
42 collar
43 coin disc (disk) (flan, planchet, blank)
44 coining press (minting press)

1
2
3
4
5
6
7
8
9
10
11
12
13
14
15
16
17
18
19
20
21
22
23
24
25
26
27
28
29
30
31
32
33
34
35
36
37
38
39
40
41
42
43
44

253 Flags

1-3 flag of the United Nations
1 flagpole (flagstaff) with truck
2 halyard (halliard, haulyard)
3 bunting
4 flag of the Council of Europe
5 Olympic flag
6 flag at half-mast (*Am.* at half-staff) [as a token of mourning]
7-11 flag
7 flagpole (flagstaff)
8 ornamental stud
9 streamer
10 pointed tip of the flagpole
11 bunting
12 banner (gonfalon)
13 cavalry standard (flag of the cavalry)
14 standard of the German Federal President [ensign of head of state]
15-21 national flags
15 the Union Jack (Great Britain)
16 the Tricolour (*Am.* Tricolor) (France)
17 the Danebrog (Dannebrog) (Denmark)
18 the Stars and Stripes (Star-Spangled Banner) (USA)
19 the Crescent (Turkey)
20 the Rising Sun (Japan)
21 the Hammer and Sickle (USSR)
22-34 signal flags, a hoist
22-28 letter flags
22 letter A, a burgee (swallow-tailed flag)
23 G, pilot flag
24 H ('pilot on board')
25 L ('you should stop, I have something important to communicate')
26 P, the Blue Peter ('about to set sail')
27 W ('I require medical assistance')
28 Z, an oblong pennant (oblong pendant)
29 code pennant (code pendant), used in the International Signals Code
30-32 substitute flags (repeaters), triangular flags (pennants, pendants)
33-34 numeral pennants (numeral pendants)
33 number 1
34 number 0
35-38 customs flags
35 customs boat pennant (customs boat pendant)
36 'ship cleared through customs'
37 customs signal flag
38 powder flag ['inflammable (flammable) cargo']

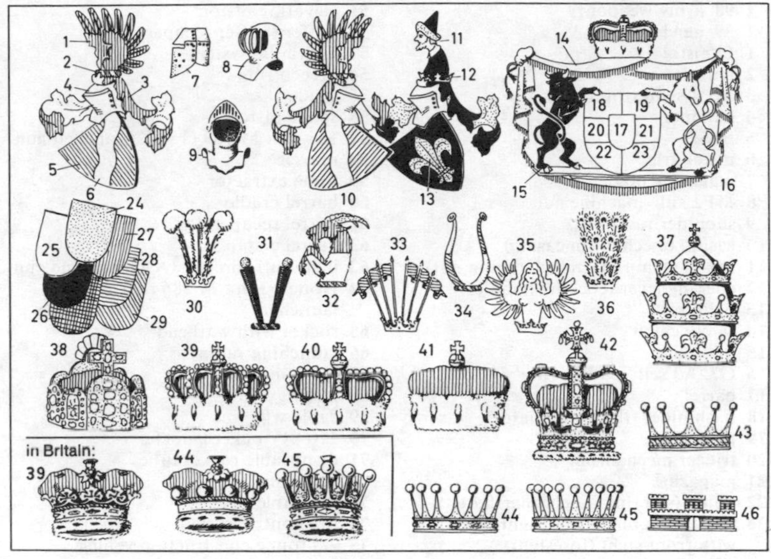

1-36 heraldry (blazonry)
1, 11, 30-36 crests
1-6 coat-of-arms (achievement of arms, hatchment, achievement)
1 crest
2 wreath of the colours (*Am.* colors)
3 mantle (mantling)
4, 7-9 helmets (helms)
4 tilting helmet (jousting helmet)
5 shield
6 bend sinister wavy
7 pot-helmet (pot-helm, heaume)
8 barred helmet (grilled helmet)
9 helmet affronty with visor open
10-13 marital achievement (marshalled, *Am.* marshaled, coat-of-arms)
10 arms of the baron (of the husband)
11-13 arms of the family of the femme (of the wife)
11 demi-man; *also:* demi-woman
12 crest coronet
13 fleur-de-lis
14 mantling
15-16 supporters (heraldic beasts)
15 bull
16 unicorn
17-23 blazon
17 inescutcheon (heart-shield)
18-23 quarterings one to six
18, 20, 22 dexter, right
18-19 chief
19, 21, 23 sinister, left
22-23 base
24-29 tinctures
24-25 metals
24 or (gold) [yellow]
25 argent (silver) [white]
26 sable
27 gules
28 azure
29 vert
30 ostrich feathers (treble plume)
31 truncheon
32 demi-goat
33 tournament pennons
34 buffalo horns
35 harpy
36 plume of peacock's feathers
37-46 crowns and coronets
37 tiara (papal tiara)
38 Imperial Crown [German, until 1806]
39 ducal coronet (duke's coronet)
40 prince's coronet
41 elector's coronet
42 English Royal Crown
43-45 coronets of rank
43 baronet's coronet
44 baron's coronet (baronial coronet)
45 count's coronet
46 mauerkrone (mural crown) of a city crest

255 Armed Forces I (Army)

1-98 army weaponry
1-39 hand weapons
1 P1 pistol
2 barrel
3 front sight (foresight)
4 hammer
5 trigger
6 pistol grip
7 magazine holder
8 MP2 sub-machine gun
9 shoulder rest (butt)
10 casing (mechanism casing)
11 barrel clamp (barrel-clamping nut)
12 cocking lever (cocking handle)
13 palm rest
14 safety catch
15 magazine
16 G3-A3 self-loading rifle
17 barrel
18 flash hider (flash eliminator)
19 palm rest
20 trigger mechanism
21 magazine
22 notch (sighting notch, rearsight)
23 front sight block (foresight block) with front sight (foresight)
24 rifle butt (butt)
25 44 mm anti-tank rocket launcher
26 rocket (projectile)
27 buffer
28 telescopic sight (telescope sight)
29 firing mechanism
30 cheek rest
31 shoulder rest (butt)
32 MG3 machine gun (Spandau)
33 barrel casing
34 gas regulator
35 belt-changing flap
36 rearsight
37 front sight block (foresight block) with front sight (foresight)
38 pistol grip
39 shoulder rest (butt)
40-95 heavy weapons
40 120 mm AM 50 mortar
41 barrel
42 bipod
43 gun carriage
44 buffer (buffer ring)
45 sight (sighting mechanism)
46 base plate
47 striker pad
48 traversing handle
49-74 artillery weapons mounted on self-propelled gun carriages
49 175 mm SFM 107 cannon
50 drive wheel
51 elevating piston
52 buffer (buffer recuperator)
53 hydraulic system
54 breech ring
55 spade
56 spade piston
57 155 mm M 109 G self-propelled gun
58 muzzle
59 fume extractor
60 barrel cradle
61 barrel recuperator
62 barrel clamp
63 light anti-aircraft (AA) machine gun
64 Honest John M 386 rocket launcher
65 rocket with warhead
66 launching ramp
67 elevating gear
68 jack
69 cable winch
70 110 SF rocket launcher
71 disposable rocket tubes
72 tube bins
73 turntable
74 fire control system
75 2.5 tonne construction vehicle
76 lifting arms (lifting device)
77 shovel
78 counterweight (counterpoise)
79-95 armoured (*Am.* armored) vehicles
79 M 113 armoured (*Am.* armored) ambulance
80 Leopard 1 A 3 tank
81 protection device
82 infrared laser rangefinder
83 smoke canisters (smoke dispensers)
84 armoured (*Am.* armored) turret
85 skirt
86 road wheel
87 track
88 anti-tank tank
89 fume extractor
90 protection device
91 armoured (*Am.* armored) personnel carrier
92 cannon
93 armoured (*Am.* armored) recovery vehicle
94 levelling (*Am.* leveling) and support shovel
95 jib
96 25 tonne all-purpose vehicle
97 drop windscreen (*Am.* drop windshield)
98 canvas cover

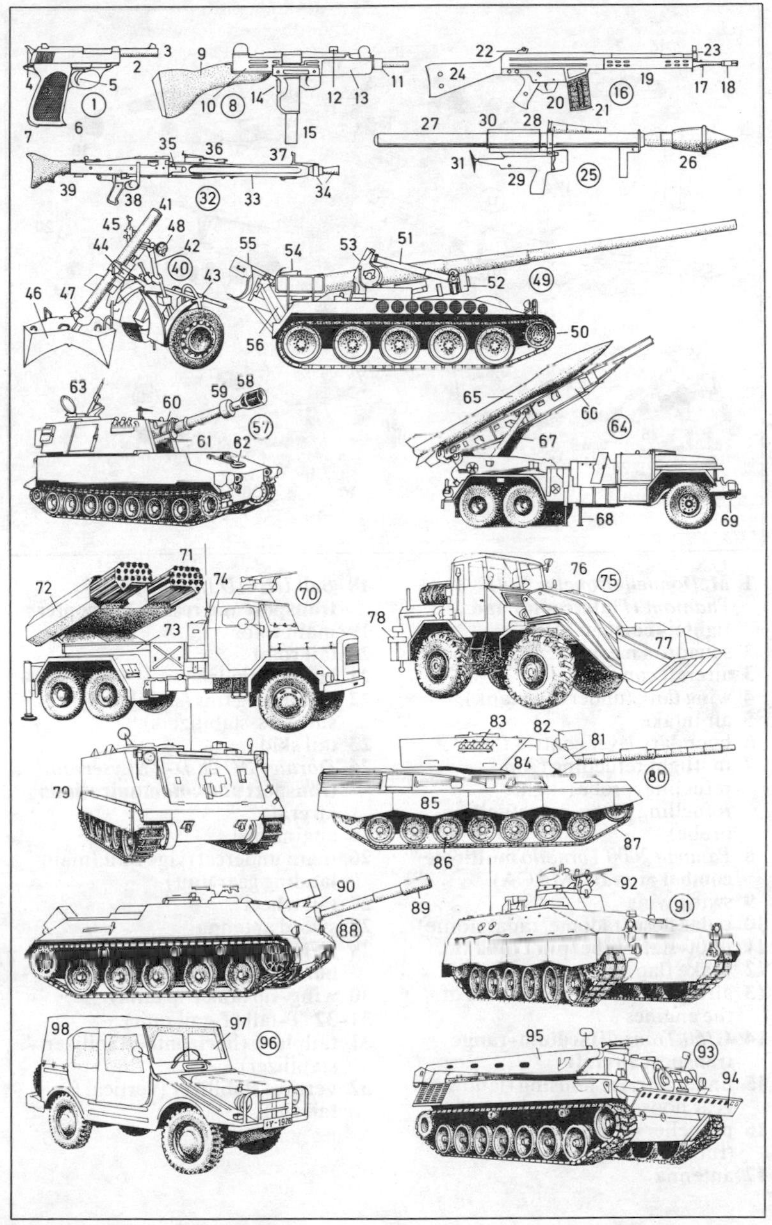
1
2
3
4
5
6
7
8
9
10
11
12
13
14
15
16
17
18
19
20
21
22
23
24
25
26
27
28
29
30
31
32
33
34
35
36
37
38
39
40
41
42
43
44
45
46
47
48
49
50
51
52
53
54
55
56
57
58
59
60
61
62
63
64
65
66
67
68
69
70
71
72
73
74
75
76
77
78
79
80
81
82
83
84
85
86
87
88
89
90
91
92
93
94
95
96
97
98
Y-1926

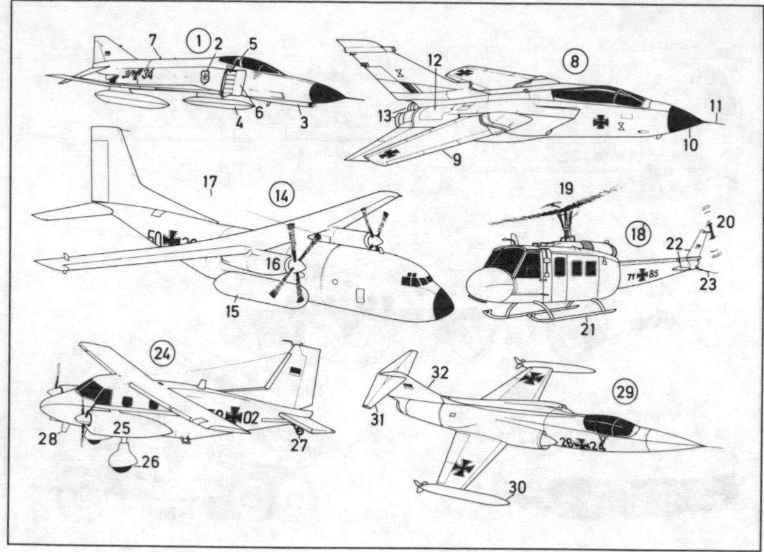

1 *McDonnell-Douglas F-4F Phantom II* **interceptor and fighter-bomber**
2 squadron marking
3 aircraft cannon
4 wing tank (underwing tank)
5 air intake
6 boundary layer control flap
7 in-flight refuelling (*Am.* refueling) probe (flight refuelling probe, air refuelling probe)
8 *Panavia 2000 Tornado* **multirole combat aircraft** (MRCA)
9 swing wing
10 radar nose (radome, radar dome)
11 pitot-static tube (pitot tube)
12 brake flap (air brake)
13 afterburner exhaust nozzles of the engines
14 *C160 Transall* **medium-range transport aircraft**
15 undercarriage housing (landing gear housing)
16 propeller-turbine engine (turboprop engine)
17 antenna
18 *Bell UH-ID Iroquois* **light transport and rescue helicopter**
19 main rotor
20 tail rotor
21 landing skids
22 stabilizing fins (stabilizing surfaces, stabilizers)
23 tail skid
24 *Dornier DO 28 D-2 Skyservant* **transport and communications aircraft**
25 engine pod
26 main undercarriage unit (main landing gear unit)
27 tail wheel
28 sword antenna
29 *F-104 G Starfighter* **fighter-bomber**
30 wing-tip tank (tip tank)
31-32 T-tail (T-tail unit)
31 tailplane (horizontal stabilizer, stabilizer)
32 vertical stabilizer (vertical fin, tail fin)

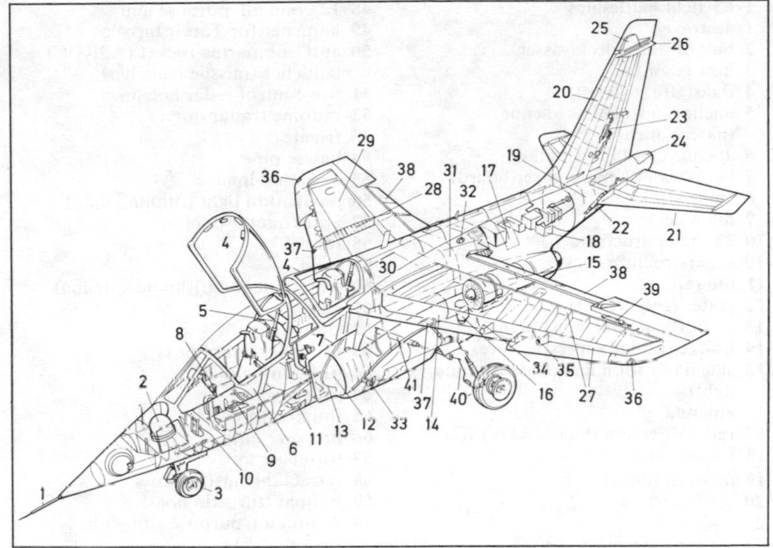

1–41 *Dornier–Dassault–Breguet Alpha Jet* Franco-German jet trainer
1 pitot-static tube (pitot tube)
2 oxygen tank
3 forward-retracting nose wheel
4 cockpit canopy (cockpit hood)
5 canopy jack
6 pilot's seat (student pilot's seat), an ejector seat (ejection seat)
7 observer's seat (instructor's seat), an ejector seat (ejection seat)
8 control column (control stick)
9 thrust lever
10 rudder pedals with brakes
11 front avionics bay
12 air intake to the engine
13 boundary layer control flap
14 air intake duct
15 turbine engine
16 reservoir for the hydraulic system
17 battery housing
18 rear avionics bay
19 baggage compartment
20 triple-spar tail construction
21 horizontal tail
22 servo-actuating mechanism for the elevator
23 servo-actuating mechanism for the rudder
24 brake chute housing (drag chute housing)
25 VHF (very high frequency) antenna (UHF antenna)
26 VOR (very high frequency omnidirectional range) antenna
27 twin-spar wing construction
28 former with integral spars
29 integral wing tanks
30 centre-section (*Am.* center-section) fuel tank
31 fuselage tanks
32 gravity fuelling (*Am.* fueling) point
33 pressure fuelling (*Am.* fueling) point
34 inner wing suspension
35 outer wing suspension
36 navigation lights (position lights)
37 landing lights
38 landing flap
39 aileron actuator
40 forward-retracting main undercarriage unit (main landing gear unit)
41 undercarriage hydraulic cylinder (landing gear hydraulic cylinder)

1-63 light battleships
1 destroyer
2 hull of flush-deck vessel
3 bow (stem)
4 flagstaff (jackstaff)
5 anchor, a stockless anchor (patent anchor)
6 anchor capstan (windlass)
7 breakwater (*Am.* manger board)
8 chine strake
9 main deck
10-28 superstructures
10 superstructure deck
11 life rafts
12 cutter (ship's boat)
13 davit (boat-launching crane)
14 bridge (bridge superstructure)
15 side navigation light (side running light)
16 antenna
17 radio direction finder (RDF) frame
18 lattice mast
19 forward funnel
20 aft funnel
21 cowl
22 aft superstructure (poop)
23 capstan
24 companion ladder (companionway, companion hatch)
25 ensign staff
26 stern, a transom stern
27 waterline
28 searchlight
29-37 armament
29 100 mm gun turret
30 four-barrel anti-submarine rocket launcher (missile launcher)
31 40 mm twin anti-aircraft (AA) gun
32 MM 38 anti-aircraft (AA) rocket launcher (missile launcher) in launching container
33 anti-submarine torpedo tube
34 depth-charge thrower
35 weapon system radar
36 radar antenna (radar scanner)
37 optical rangefinder
38 destroyer
39 bower anchor
40 propeller guard
41 tripod lattice mast
42 pole mast
43 ventilator openings (ventilator grill)
44 exhaust pipe
45 ship's boat
46 antenna
47 radar-controlled 127 mm all-purpose gun in turret
48 127 mm all-purpose gun
49 launcher for Tartar missiles
50 anti-submarine rocket (ASROC) launcher (missile launcher)
51 fire control radar antennas
52 radome (radar dome)
53 frigate
54 hawse pipe
55 steaming light
56 navigation light (running light)
57 air extractor duct
58 funnel
59 cowl
60 whip antenna (fishpole antenna)
61 cutter
62 stern light
63 propeller guard boss
64-91 fighting ships
64 submarine
65 flooded foredeck
66 pressure hull
67 turret
68 retractable instruments
69 E-boat (torpedo boat)
70 76 mm all-purpose gun with turret
71 missile-launching housing
72 deckhouse
73 40 mm anti-aircraft (AA) gun
74 propeller guard moulding (*Am.* molding)
75 143 class E-boat (143 class torpedo boat)
76 breakwater (*Am.* manger board)
77 radome (radar dome)
78 torpedo tube
79 exhaust escape flue
80 mine hunter
81 reinforced rubbing strake
82 inflatable boat (inflatable dinghy)
83 davit
84 minesweeper
85 cable winch
86 towing winch (towing machine, towing engine)
87 mine-sweeping gear (paravanes)
88 crane (davit)
89 landing craft
90 bow ramp
91 stern ramp
92-97 auxiliaries
92 tender
93 servicing craft
94 minelayer
95 training ship
96 deep-sea salvage tug
97 fuel tanker (replenishing ship)

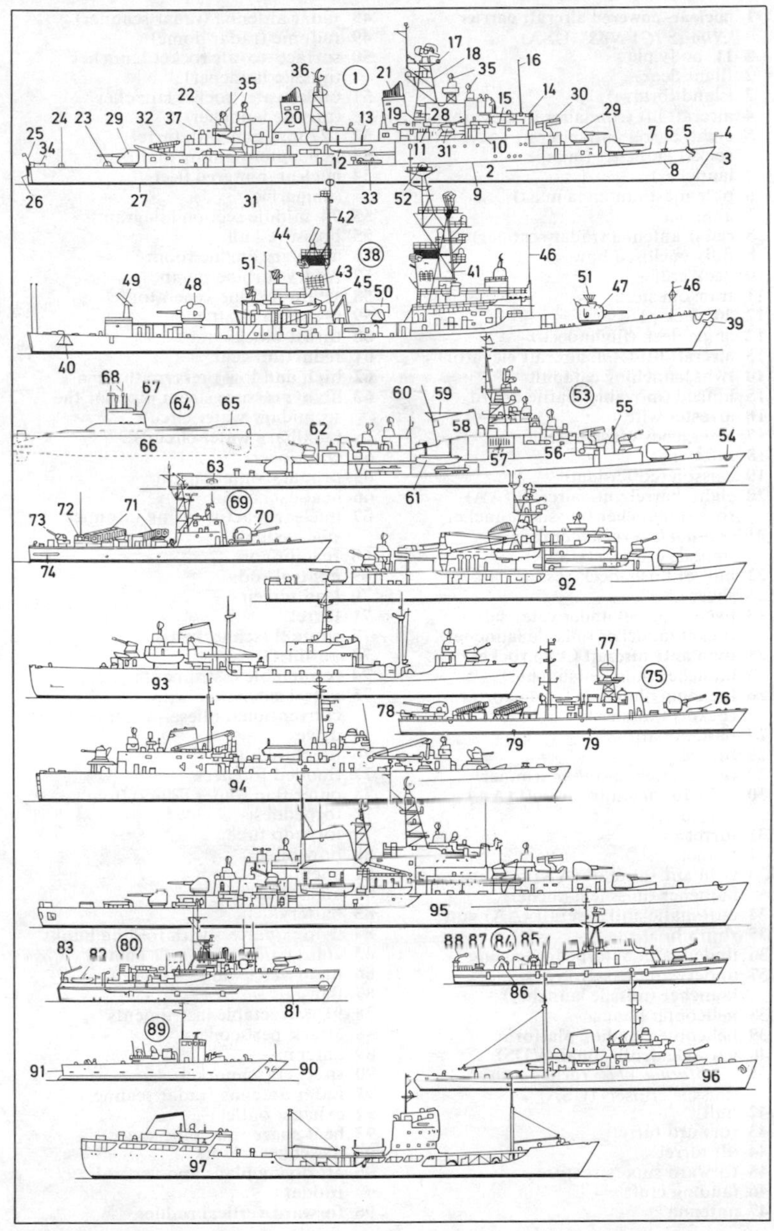
1
2
3
4
5
6
7
8
9
10
11
12
13
14
15
16
17
18
19
20
21
22
23
24
25
26
27
28
29
30
31
32
33
34
35
36
37
38
39
40
41
42
43
44
45
46
47
48
49
50
51
52
53
54
55
56
57
58
59
60
61
62
63
64
65
66
67
68
69
70
71
72
73
74
75
76
77
78
79
80
81
82
83
84
85
86
87
88
89
90
91
92
93
94
95
96
97

259 Warships II (Modern Fighting Ships)

1 **nuclear-powered aircraft carrier** '*Nimitz ICVN68*' (USA)
2-11 body plan
2 flight deck
3 island (bridge)
4 aircraft lift (*Am.* aircraft elevator)
5 eight-barrel anti-aircraft (AA) rocket launcher (missile launcher)
6 pole mast (antenna mast)
7 antenna
8 radar antenna (radar scanner)
8 fully enclosed bow
10 deck crane
11 transom stern
12-20 deck plan
12 angle deck (flight deck)
13 aircraft lift (*Am.* aircraft elevator)
14 twin launching catapult
15 hinged (movable) baffle board
16 arrester wire
17 emergency crash barrier
18 safety net
19 caisson (cofferdam)
20 eight-barrel anti-aircraft (AA) rocket launcher (missile launcher)
21 '*Kara*' *class* **rocket cruiser** (missile cruiser) (USSR)
22 hull of flush–deck vessel
23 sheer
24 twelve-barrel underwater salvo rocket launcher (missile launcher)
25 twin anti-aircraft (AA) rocket launcher (missile launcher)
26 launching housing for 4 short-range rockets (missiles)
27 baffle board
28 bridge
29 radar antenna (radar scanner)
30 twin 76 mm anti-aircraft (AA) gun turret
31 turret
32 funnel
33 twin anti-aircraft (AA) rocket launcher (missile launcher)
34 automatic anti-aircraft (AA) gun
35 ship's boat
36 underwater 5-torpedo housing
37 underwater 6-salvo rocket launcher (missile launcher)
38 helicopter hangar
39 helicopter landing platform
40 variable depth sonar (VDS)
41 '*California*' *class* **rocket cruiser** (missile cruiser) (USA)
42 hull
43 forward turret
44 aft turret
45 forward superstructure
46 landing craft
47 antenna
48 radar antenna (radar scanner)
49 radome (radar dome)
50 surface-to-air rocket launcher (missile launcher)
51 underwater rocket launcher (missile launcher)
52 127 mm gun with turret
53 helicopter landing platform
54 **nuclear-powered fleet submarine**
55-74 middle section [diagram]
55 pressure hull
56 auxiliary engine room
57 rotary turbine pump
58 steam turbine generator
59 propeller shaft
60 thrust block
61 reduction gear
62 high and low pressure turbine
63 high-pressure steam pipe for the secondary water circuit (auxiliary water circuit)
64 condenser
65 primary water circuit
66 heat exchanger
67 nuclear reactor casing (atomic pile casing)
68 reactor core
69 control rods
70 lead screen
71 turret
72 snorkel (schnorkel)
73 air inlet
74 retractable instruments
75 **patrol submarine** with conventional (diesel-electric) drive
76 pressure hull
77 flooded foredeck
78 outer flap (outer doors) [for torpedoes]
79 torpedo tube
80 bow bilge
81 anchor
82 anchor winch
83 battery
84 living quarters with folding bunks
85 commanding officer's cabin
86 main hatchway
87 flagstaff
88-91 retractable instruments
88 attack periscope
89 antenna
90 snorkel (schnorkel)
91 radar antenna (radar scanner)
92 exhaust outlet
93 heat space (hot-pipe space)
94 diesel generators
95 aft diving plane and vertical rudder
96 forward vertical rudder

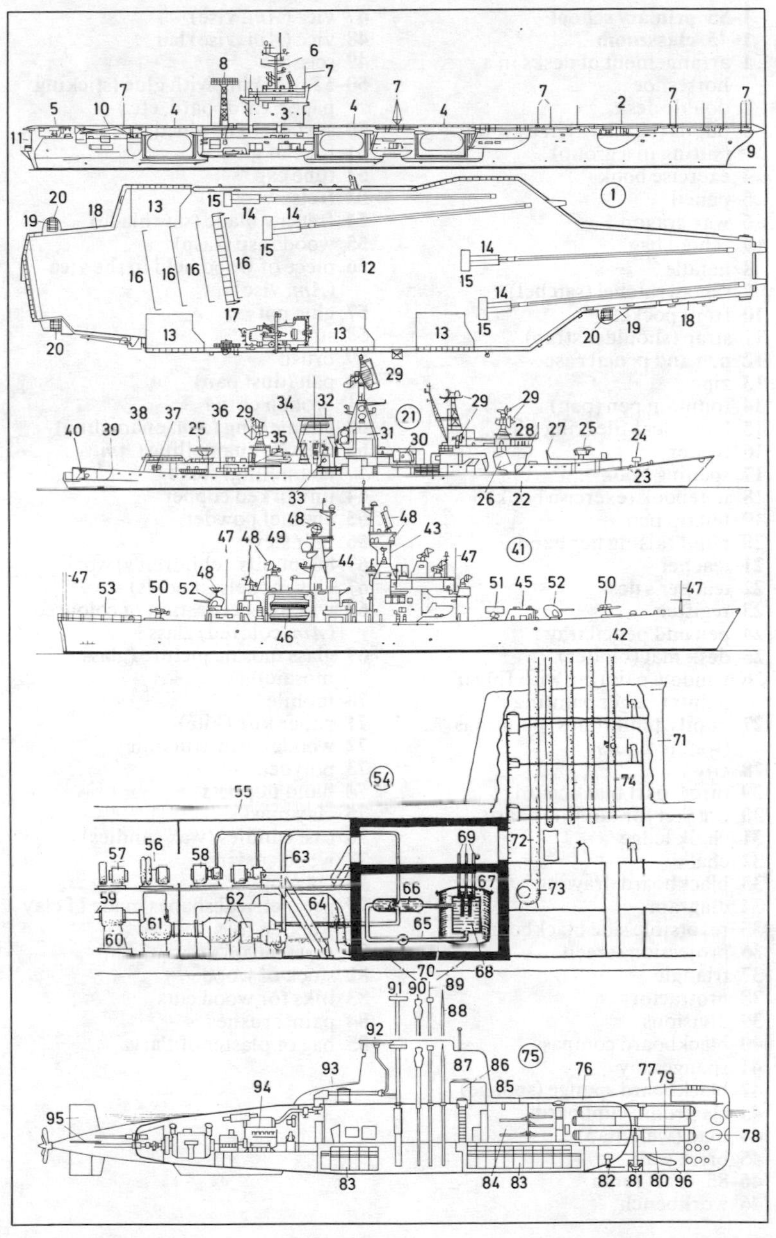

1
2
3
4
5
6
7
8
9
10
11
12
13
14
15
16
17
18
19
20
21
22
23
24
25
26
27
28
29
30
31
32
33
34
35
36
37
38
39
40
41
42
43
44
45
46
47
48
49
50
51
52
53
54
55
56
57
58
59
60
61
62
63
64
65
66
67
68
69
70
71
72
73
74
75
76
77
78
79
80
81
82
83
84
85
86
87
88
89
90
91
92
93
94
95
96

1-85 primary school
1-45 classroom
1 arrangement of desks in a horseshoe
2 double desk
3 pupils (children) in a group (sitting in a group)
4 exercise book
5 pencil
6 wax crayon
7 school bag
8 handle
9 school satchel (satchel)
10 front pocket
11 strap (shoulder strap)
12 pen and pencil case
13 zip
14 fountain pen (pen)
15 loose-leaf file (ring file)
16 reader
17 spelling book
18 notebook (exercise book)
19 felt tip pen
20 pupil raising her hand
21 teacher
22 teacher's desk
23 register
24 pen and pencil tray
25 desk mat (blotter)
26 window painting with finger paints (finger painting)
27 pupils' (children's) paintings (watercolours)
28 cross
29 three-part blackboard
30 bracket for holding charts
31 chalk ledge
32 chalk
33 blackboard drawing
34 diagram
35 reversible side blackboard
36 projection screen
37 triangle
38 protractor
39 divisions
40 blackboard compass
41 sponge tray
42 blackboard sponge (sponge)
43 classroom cupboard
44 map (wall map)
45 brick wall
46-85 craft room
46 workbench
47 vice (*Am.* vise)
48 vice (*Am.* vise) bar
49 scissors
50-52 working with glue (sticking paper, cardboard, etc.)
50 surface to be glued
51 tube of glue
52 tube cap
53 fretsaw
54 fretsaw blade (saw blade)
55 wood rasp (rasp)
56 piece of wood held in the vice (*Am.* vise)
57 glue pot
58 stool
59 brush
60 pan (dust pan)
61 broken china
62 enamelling (*Am.* enameling)
63 electric enamelling (*Am.* enameling) stove
64 unworked copper
65 enamel powder
66 hair sieve
67-80 pupils' (children's) work
67 clay models (models)
68 window decoration of coloured (*Am.* colored) glass
69 glass mosaic picture (glass mosaic)
70 mobile
71 paper kite (kite)
72 wooden construction
73 polyhedron
74 hand puppets
75 clay masks
76 cast candles (wax candles)
77 wood carving
78 clay jug
79 geometrical shapes made of clay
80 wooden toys
81 materials
82 stock of wood
83 inks for wood cuts
84 paintbrushes
85 bag of plaster of Paris

water cycle.
condensation
beaker
ice cubes
drops of water
steam
water
READER
GLUE
GYPSUM POWDER

261 School II (Secondary School, High School)

1–45 grammar school; *also:* upper band of a comprehensive school (*Am.* alternative school)
1–13 chemistry
1 chemistry lab (chemistry laboratory) with tiered rows of seats
2 chemistry teacher
3 demonstration bench (teacher's bench)
4 water pipe
5 tiled working surface
6 sink
7 television monitor, a screen for educational programmes (*Am.* programs)
8 overhead projector
9 projector top for skins
10 projection lens with right-angle mirror
11 pupils' (*Am.* students') bench with experimental apparatus
12 electrical point (socket)
13 projection table
14–34 biology preparation room (biology prep room)
14 skeleton
15 casts of skulls
16 calvarium of Pithecanthropus Erectus
17 skull of Steinheim man
18 calvarium of Peking man (of Sinanthropus)
19 skull of Neanderthal man, a skull of primitive man
20 Australopithecine skull (skull of Australopithecus)
21 skull of present-day man
22 dissecting bench
23 chemical bottles
24 gas tap
25 petri dish
26 measuring cylinder
27 work folder (teaching material)
28 textbook
29 bacteriological cultures
30 incubator
31 test tube rack
32 washing bottle
33 water tank
34 sink
35 language laboratory
36 blackboard
37 console
38 headphones (headset)
39 microphone
40 earcups
41 padded headband (padded headpiece)
42 programme (*Am.* program) recorder, a cassette recorder
43 pupil's (*Am.* student's) volume control
44 master volume control
45 control buttons (operating keys)

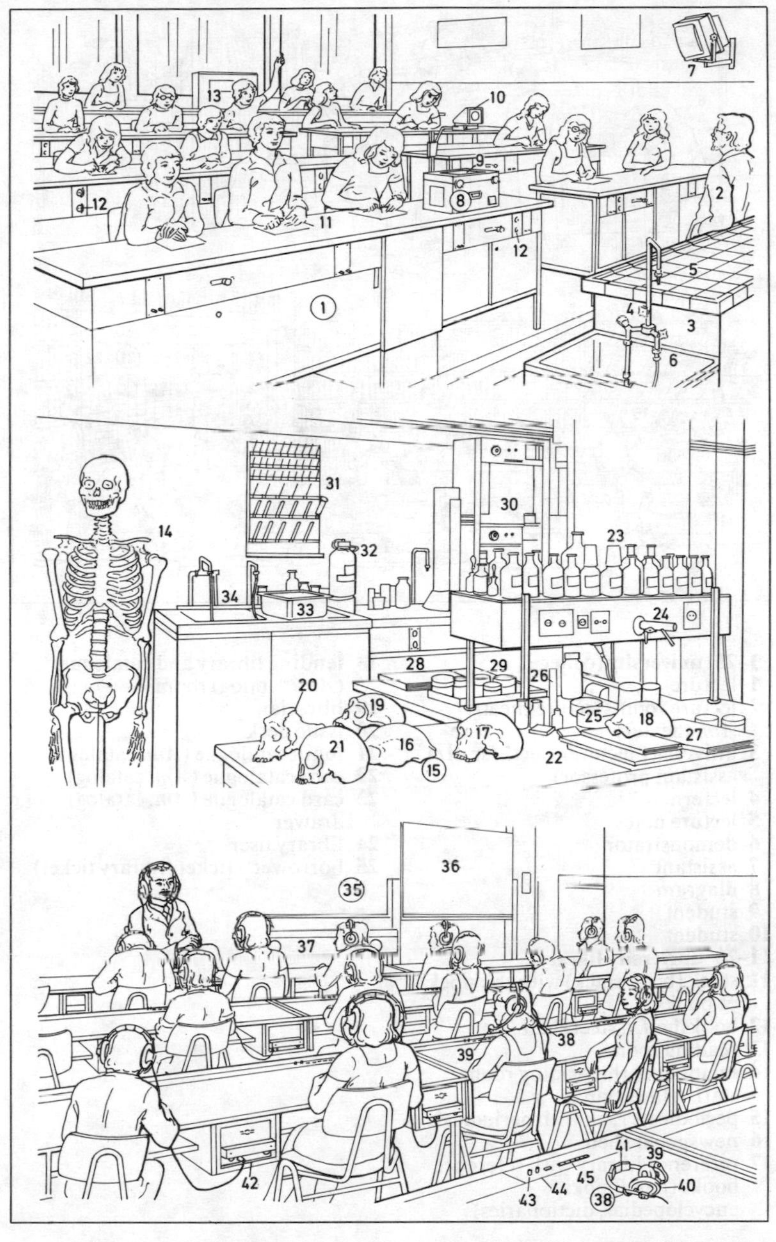

1–25 university (college)
1 lecture
2 lecture room (lecture theatre, *Am.* theater)
3 university lecturer (lecturer, *Am.* assistant professor)
4 lectern
5 lecture notes
6 demonstrator
7 assistant
8 diagram
9 student
10 student
11–25 university library
11 stack (book stack) with the stock of books
12 bookshelf, a steel shelf
13 reading room
14 member of the reading room staff, a librarian
15 periodicals rack with periodicals
16 newspaper shelf
17 reference library with reference books (handbooks, encyclopedias, dictionaries)
18 lending library and catalogue (*Am.* catalog) room
19 librarian
20 issue desk
21 main catalogue (*Am.* catalog)
22 card catalogue (*Am.* catalog)
23 card catalogue (*Am.* catalog) drawer
24 library user
25 borrower's ticket (library ticket)

1–15 election meeting, a public meeting
1–2 committee
1 chairman
2 committee member
3 committee table
4 bell
5 election speaker (speaker)
6 rostrum
7 microphone
8 meeting (audience)
9 man distributing leaflets
10 stewards
11 armband (armlet)
12 banner
13 placard
14 proclamation
15 heckler
16–30 election
16 polling station (polling place)
17 election officer
18 electoral register
19 polling card with registration number (polling number)
20 ballot paper with the names of the parties and candidates
21 ballot envelope
22 voter
23 polling booth
24 elector (qualified voter)
25 election regulations
26 clerk
27 clerk with the duplicate list
28 election supervisor
29 ballot box
30 slot

264 Police

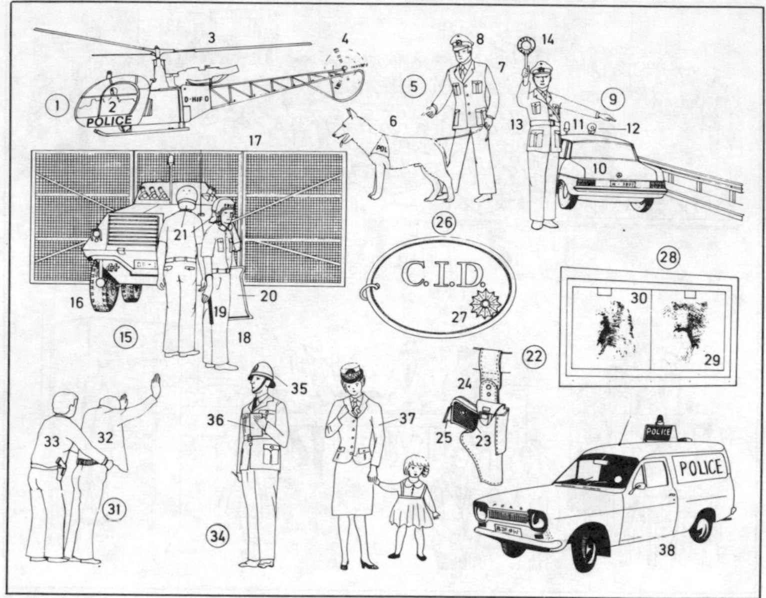

1–33 police duties
1 police helicopter (traffic helicopter) for controlling (*Am.* controling) traffic from the air
2 cockpit
3 rotor (main rotor)
4 tail rotor
5 police dog and handler
6 police dog
7 uniform
8 uniform cap, a peaked cap with cockade
9 traffic control by a mobile traffic patrol
10 patrol car
11 blue light
12 loud hailer (loudspeaker)
13 patrolman (police patrolman)
14 police signalling (*Am.* signaling) disc (disk)
15 riot duty
16 special armoured (*Am.* armored) car
17 barricade
18 policeman (police officer) in riot gear
19 truncheon (baton)
20 riot shield
21 protective helmet (helmet)
22 service pistol
23 pistol grip
24 quick-draw holster
25 magazine
26 police identification disc (disk)
27 police badge
28 fingerprint identification (dactyloscopy)
29 fingerprint
30 illuminated screen
31 search
32 suspect
33 detective (plainclothes policeman)
34 English policeman
35 helmet
36 pocket book
37 policewoman
38 police van

1–26 café, *sim.:* espresso bar, tea room
1 counter (cake counter)
2 coffee urn
3 tray for the money
4 gateau
5 meringue with whipped cream
6 trainee pastry cook
7 counter assistant
8 newspaper shelves (newspaper rack)
9 wall lamp
10 corner seat, an upholstered seat
11 café table
12 marble top
13 waitress
14 tray
15 bottle of lemonade
16 lemonade glass
17 chess players playing a game of chess
18 coffee set
19 cup of coffee
20 small sugar bowl
21 cream jug (*Am.* creamer)
22–24 café customers
22 gentleman
23 lady
24 man reading a newspaper
25 newspaper
26 newspaper holder

1–29 restaurant
1–11 bar (counter)
1 beer pump (beerpull)
2 drip tray
3 beer glass
4 froth (head)
5 spherical ashtray for cigarette and cigar ash
6 beer glass (beer mug)
7 beer warmer
8 bartender (barman, *Am.* barkeeper, barkeep)
9 shelf for glasses
10 shelf for bottles
11 stack of plates
12 coat stand
13 hat peg
14 coat hook
15 wall ventilator
16 bottle
17 complete meal
18 waitress
19 tray
20 lottery ticket seller
21 menu (menu card)
22 cruet stand
23 toothpick holder
24 matchbox holder
25 customer
26 beer mat
27 meal of the day
28 flower seller (flower girl)
29 flower basket
30–44 wine restaurant (wine bar)
30 wine waiter, a head waiter
31 wine list
32 wine carafe
33 wineglass
34 tiled stove
35 stove tile
36 stove bench
37 wooden panelling (*Am.* paneling)
38 corner seat
39 corner table
40 regular customer
41 cutlery chest
42 wine cooler
43 bottle of wine
44 ice cubes (ice, lumps of ice)

45–78 self-service restaurant
45 stack of trays
46 drinking straws (straws)
47 serviettes (napkins)
48 cutlery holders
49 cool shelf
50 slice of honeydew melon
51 plate of salad
52 plate of cheeses
53 fish dish
54 filled roll
55 meat dish with trimmings
56 half chicken
57 basket of fruit
58 fruit juice
59 drinks shelf
60 bottle of milk
61 bottle of mineral water
62 vegetarian meal (diet meal)
63 tray
64 tray counter
65 food price list
66 serving hatch
67 hot meal
68 beer pump (beerpull)
69 cash desk
70 cashier
71 proprietor
72 rail
73 dining area
74 table
75 open sandwich
76 ice-cream sundae
77 salt cellar and pepper pot
78 table decoration (flower arrangement)

267 Hotel

1–26 vestibule (foyer, reception hall)
1 doorman (commissionaire)
2 letter rack with pigeon holes
3 key rack
4 globe lamp, a frosted glass globe
5 indicator board (drop board)
6 indicator light
7 chief receptionist
8 register (hotel register)
9 room key
10 number tag (number tab) showing room number
11 hotel bill
12 block of registration forms
13 passport
14 hotel guest
15 lightweight suitcase, a light suitcase for air travel
16 wall desk
17 porter (*Am.* baggage man)
18–26 lobby (hotel lobby)
18 page (pageboy, *Am.* bell boy)
19 hotel manager
20 dining room (hotel restaurant)
21 chandelier
22 fireside
23 fireplace
24 mantelpiece (mantelshelf)
25 fire (open fire)
26 armchair
27–38 hotel room, a double room with bath
27 double door
28 service bell panel
29 wardrobe trunk
30 clothes compartment
31 linen compartment
32 double washbasin
33 room waiter
34 room telephone
35 velour (velours) carpet
36 flower stand
37 flower arrangement
38 double bed
39 banquet room
40–43 private party
40 speaker proposing a toast
41 42's neighbour (*Am.* neighbor)
42 43's partner

43 42's partner
44–46 **thé dansant** (tea dance) in the foyer
44 bar trio
45 violinist
46 couple dancing (dancing couple)
47 waiter
48 napkin
49 cigar and cigarette boy
50 cigarette tray
51 **hotel bar**
52 foot rail
53 bar stool
54 bar
55 bar customer
56 cocktail glass (*Am.* highball glass)
57 whisky (whiskey) glass
58 champagne cork
59 champagne bucket (champagne cooler)
60 measuring beaker (measure)
61 cocktail shaker
62 bartender (barman, *Am.* barkeeper, barkeep)
63 barmaid
64 shelf for bottles
65 shelf for glasses
66 mirrored panel
67 ice bucket

268 Town (Town Centre, *Am.* Downtown)

1 parking meter
2 map of the town (street map)
3 illuminated board
4 key
5 litter bin (*Am.* litter basket)
6 street lamp (street light)
7 street sign showing the name of the street
8 drain
9 clothes shop (fashion house)
10 shop window
11 window display (shop window display)
12 window decoration (shop window decoration)
13 entrance
14 window
15 window box
16 neon sign
17 tailor's workroom
18 pedestrian
19 shopping bag
20 road sweeper (*Am.* street sweeper)
21 broom
22 rubbish (litter)
23 tramlines (*Am.* streetcar tracks)
24 pedestrian crossing (zebra crossing, *Am.* crosswalk)
25 tram stop (*Am.* streetcar stop, trolley stop)
26 tram stop sign (*Am.* streetcar stop sign, trolley stop sign)
27 tram timetable (*Am.* streetcar schedule)
28 ticket machine
29 'pedestrian crossing' sign
30 traffic policeman on traffic duty (point duty)
31 traffic control cuff
32 white cap
33 hand signal
34 motorcyclist
35 motorcycle
36 pillion passenger (pillion rider)
37 bookshop
38 hat shop (hatter's shop); *for ladies' hats:* milliner's shop
39 shop sign
40 insurance company office

41 department store
42 shop front
43 advertisement
44 flags
45 illuminated letters
46 tram (*Am.* streetcar, trolley)
47 furniture lorry (*Am.* furniture truck)
48 flyover
49 suspended street lamp
50 stop line
51 pedestrian crossing (*Am.* crosswalk)
52 traffic lights
53 traffic light post
54 set of lights
55 pedestrian lights
56 telephone box (telephone booth, telephone kiosk, call box)
57 cinema advertisement (film poster)
58 pedestrian precinct (paved zone)
59 street café
60 group seated (sitting) at a table
61 sunshade
62 steps to the public lavatories (public conveniences)
63 taxi rank (taxi stand)
64 taxi (taxicab, cab)
65 taxi sign
66 traffic sign showing 'taxi rank' ('taxi stand')
67 taxi telephone
68 post office
69 cigarette machine
70 advertising pillar
71 poster (advertisement)
72 white line
73 lane arrow for turning left
74 lane arrow for going straight ahead
75 news vendor (*Am.* news dealer)

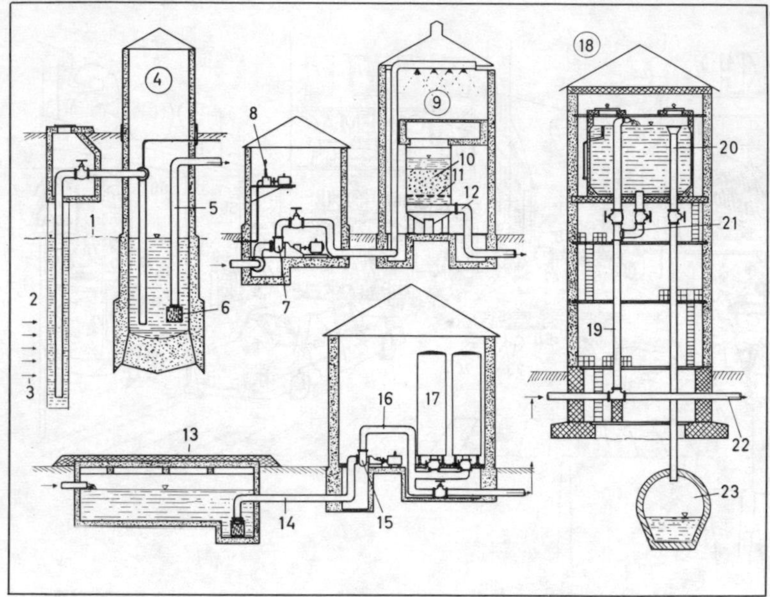

1–66 drinking water supply
1 water table (groundwater level)
2 water-bearing stratum (aquifer, aquafer)
3 groundwater stream (underground stream)
4 collector well for raw water
5 suction pipe
6 pump strainer (with foot valve)
7 bucket pump with motor
8 vacuum pump with motor
9 rapid-filter plant
10 filter gravel (filter bed)
11 filter bottom, a grid
12 filtered water outlet
13 purified water tank
14 suction pipe with pump strainer and foot valve
15 main pump with motor
16 delivery pipe
17 compressed-air vessel (air vessel, air receiver)
18 water tower
19 riser pipe (riser)
20 overflow pipe
21 outlet
22 distribution main
23 excess water conduit
24–39 tapping a spring
24 chamber
25 chamber wall
26 manhole
27 ventilator
28 step irons
29 filling (backing)
30 outlet control valve
31 outlet valve
32 strainer
33 overflow pipe (overflow)
34 bottom outlet
35 earthenware pipes
36 impervious stratum (impermeable stratum)
37 rough rubble
38 water-bearing stratum (aquifer, aquafer)
39 loam seal (clay seal)
40–52 individual water supply
40 well
41 suction pipe

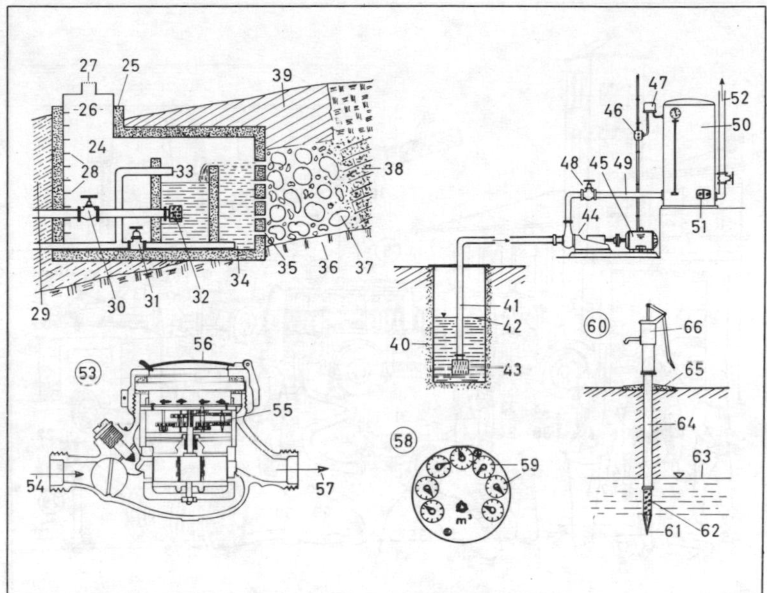

42 water table (groundwater level)
43 pump strainer with foot valve
44 centrifugal pump
45 motor
46 motor safety switch
47 manostat, a switching device
48 stopcock
49 delivery pipe
50 compressed-air vessel (air vessel, air receiver)
51 manhole
52 delivery pipe
53 water meter, a rotary meter
54 water inlet
55 counter gear assembly
56 cover with glass lid
57 water outlet
58 water-meter dial
59 counters
60 driven well (tube well, drive well)
61 pile shoe
62 filter
63 water table (groundwater level)
64 well casing
65 well head
66 hand pump

270 Fire Service (*Am.* Fire Department)

1–46 fire service drill (extinguishing, climbing, ladder, and rescue work)
1–3 fire station
1 engine and appliance room
2 firemen's quarters
3 drill tower
4 fire alarm (fire alarm siren, fire siren)
5 fire engine
6 blue light (warning light), a flashing light (*Am.* flashlight)
7 horn (hooter)
8 motor pump, a centrifugal pump
9 motor turntable ladder (*Am.* aerial ladder)
10 ladder, a steel ladder (automatic extending ladder)
11 ladder mechanism
12 jack
13 ladder operator
14 extension ladder
15 ceiling hook (*Am.* preventer)
16 hook ladder (*Am.* pompier ladder)
17 holding squad
18 jumping sheet (sheet)
19 ambulance car (ambulance)
20 resuscitator (resuscitation equipment), oxygen apparatus
21 ambulance attendant (ambulance man)
22 armband (armlet, brassard)
23 stretcher
24 unconscious man
25 pit hydrant
26 standpipe (riser, vertical pipe)
27 hydrant key
28 hose reel (*Am.* hose cart, hose wagon, hose truck, hose carriage)
29 hose coupling
30 soft suction hose
31 delivery hose
32 dividing breeching
33 branch
34 branchmen
35 surface hydrant (fire plug)
36 officer in charge
37 fireman (*Am.* firefighter)

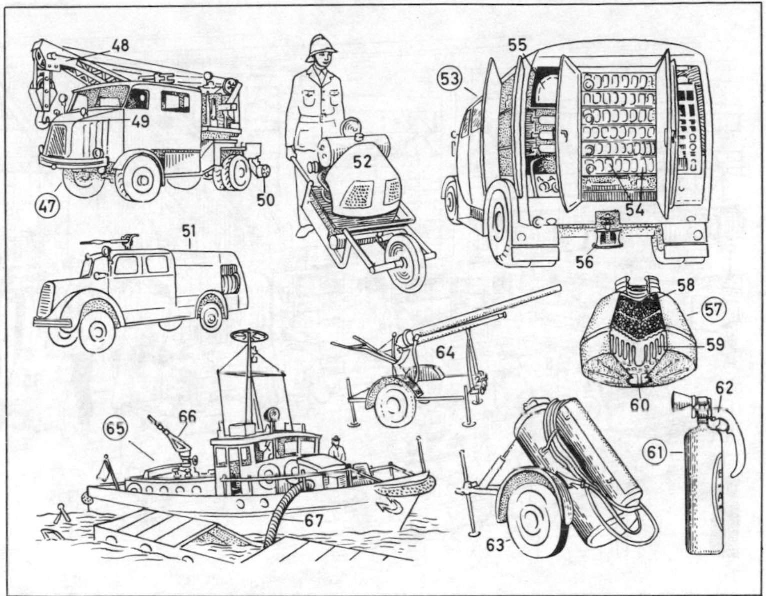

38 helmet (fireman's helmet, *Am.* fire hat)
39 breathing apparatus
40 face mask
41 walkie-talkie set
42 hand lamp
43 small axe (*Am.* ax, pompier hatchet)
44 hook belt
45 beltline
46 protective clothing of asbestos (asbestos suit) or of metallic fabric
47 breakdown lorry (*Am.* crane truck, wrecking crane)
48 lifting crane
49 load hook (draw hook, *Am.* drag hook)
50 support roll
51 water tender
52 portable pump
53 hose layer
54 flaked lengths of hose
55 cable drum
56 winch
57 face mask filter
58 active carbon (activated carbon, activated charcoal)
59 dust filter
60 air inlet
61 portable fire extinguisher
62 trigger valve
63 large mobile extinguisher (wheeled fire extinguisher)
64 foam-making branch (*Am.* foam gun)
65 fireboat
66 monitor (water cannon)
67 suction hose

271 Department Store

1 cashier
2 electric cash register (till)
3 number keys
4 cancellation button
5 cash drawer (till)
6 compartments (money compartments) for coins and notes (*Am.* bills)
7 receipt (sales check)
8 cash total
9 adding mechanism
10 goods
11 glass-roofed well
12 men's wear department
13 showcase (display case, indoor display window)
14 wrapping counter
15 tray for purchases
16 customer
17 hosiery department
18 shop assistant (*Am.* salesgirl, saleslady)
19 price card
20 glove stand
21 duffle coat, a three-quarter length coat
22 escalator
23 fluorescent light (fluorescent lamp)
24 office (e.g. customer accounts office, travel agency, manager's office)
25 poster (advertisement)
26 theatre (*Am.* theater) and concert booking office (advance booking office)
27 shelves
28 ladies' wear department
29 ready-made dress (ready-to-wear dress, *coll.* off-the-peg dress)
30 dust cover
31 clothes rack
32 changing booth (fitting booth)
33 shop walker (*Am.* floorwalker, floor manager)
34 dummy
35 seat (chair)

36 fashion journal (fashion magazine)
37 tailor marking a hemline
38 measuring tape (tape measure)
39 tailor's chalk (French chalk)
40 hemline marker
41 loose-fitting coat
42 sales counter
43 warm-air curtain
44 doorman (commissionaire)
45 lift (*Am.* elevator)
46 lift cage (lift car, *Am.* elevator car)
47 lift operator (*Am.* elevator operator)
48 controls (lift controls, *Am.* elevator controls)
49 floor indicator
50 sliding door
51 lift shaft (*Am.* elevator shaft)
52 bearer cable
53 control cable
54 guide rail
55 customer
56 hosiery
57 linen goods (table linen and bed linen)
58 fabric department
59 roll of fabric (roll of material, roll of cloth)
60 head of department (department manager)
61 sales counter
62 jewellery (*Am.* jewelry) department
63 assistant (*Am.* salesgirl, saleslady), selling new lines (new products)
64 special counter (extra counter)
65 placard advertising special offers
66 curtain department
67 display on top of the shelves

272 Park

1–40 formal garden (French Baroque garden), palace gardens
1 grotto (cavern)
2 stone statue, a river nymph
3 orangery (orangerie)
4 boscage (boskage)
5 maze (labyrinth of paths and hedges)
6 open-air theatre (*Am.* theater)
7 Baroque palace
8 fountains
9 cascade (broken artificial waterfall, artificial falls)
10 statue, a monument
11 pedestal (base of statue)
12 globe-shaped tree
13 conical tree
14 ornamental shrub
15 wall fountain
16 park bench
17 pergola (bower, arbour, *Am.* arbor)
18 gravel path (gravel walk)
19 pyramid tree (pyramidal tree)
20 cupid (cherub, amoretto, amorino)
21 fountain
22 fountain
23 overflow basin
24 basin
25 kerb (curb)
26 man out for a walk
27 tourist guide
28 group of tourists
29 park by-laws (bye-laws)
30 park keeper
31 garden gates, wrought iron gates
32 park entrance
33 park railings
34 railing (bar)
35 stone vase
36 lawn
37 border, a trimmed (clipped) hedge
38 park path
39 parterre
40 birch (birch tree)

41–72 landscaped park (jardin anglais)
41 flower bed
42 park bench (garden seat)
43 litter bin (*Am.* litter basket)
44 play area
45 stream
46 jetty
47 bridge
48 park chair
49 animal enclosure
50 pond
51–54 waterfowl
51 wild duck with young
52 goose
53 flamingo
54 swan
55 island
56 water lily
57 open-air café
58 sunshade
59 tree
60 treetop (crown)
61 group of trees
62 fountain
63 weeping willow
64 modern sculpture
65 hothouse
66 park gardener
67 broom
68 minigolf course
69 minigolf player
70 minigolf hole
71 mother with pram (baby carriage)
72 courting couple (young couple)

273 Children's Playground

1 table tennis
2 table
3 table tennis net
4 table tennis racket (raquet) (table tennis bat)
5 table tennis ball
6 badminton game (shuttlecock game)
7 shuttlecock
8 maypole swing
9 child's bicycle
10 football (soccer)
11 goal (goalposts)
12 football
13 goal scorer
14 goalkeeper
15 skipping (*Am.* jumping rope)
16 skipping rope (*Am.* skip rope, jump rope, jumping rope)
17 climbing tower
18 rubber tyre (*Am.* tire) swing
19 lorry tyre (*Am.* truck tire)
20 bouncing ball
21 adventure playground
22 log ladder
23 lookout platform
24 slide
25 litter bin (*Am.* litter basket)
26 teddy bear
27 wooden train set
28 paddling pool
29 sailing boat (yacht, *Am.* sailboat)
30 toy duck
31 pram (baby carriage)
32 high bar (bar)
33 go–cart (soap box)
34 starter's flag
35 seesaw
36 robot
37 flying model aeroplanes (*Am.* airplanes)
38 model aeroplane (*Am.* airplane)
39 double swing
40 swing seat
41 flying kites
42 kite
43 tail of the kite
44 kite string
45 revolving drum
46 spider's web

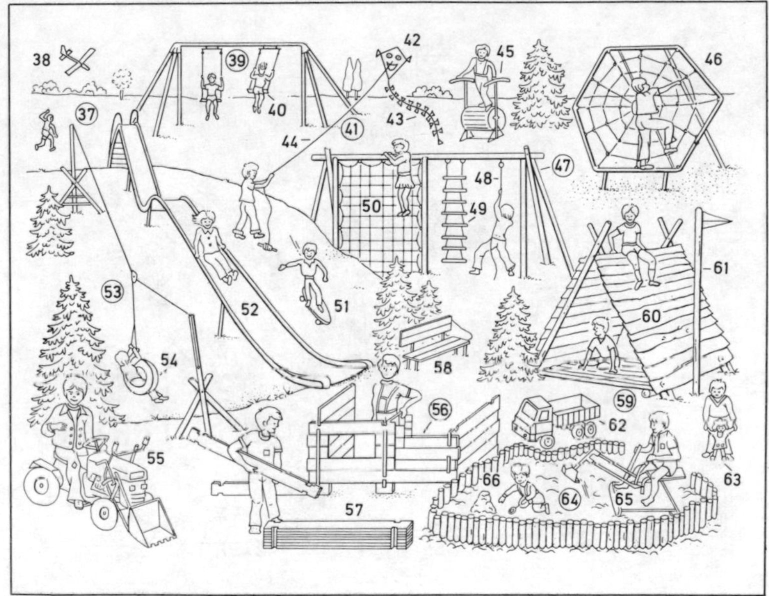

47 climbing frame
48 climbing rope
49 rope ladder
50 climbing net
51 skateboard
52 up-and-down slide
53 rubber tyre (*Am.* tire) cable car
54 rubber tyre (*Am.* tire)
55 tractor, a pedal car
56 den
57 presawn boards
58 seat (bench)
59 Indian hut
60 climbing roof
61 flagpole (flagstaff)
62 toy lorry (*Am.* toy truck)
63 walking doll
64 sandpit (*Am.* sandbox)
65 toy excavator (toy digger)
66 sandhill

1–21 spa gardens
1–7 salina (salt works)
1 thorn house (graduation house)
2 thorns (brushwood)
3 brine channels
4 brine pipe from the pumping station
5 salt works attendant
6–7 inhalational therapy
6 open-air inhalatorium (outdoor inhalatorium)
7 patient inhaling (taking an inhalation)
8 hydropathic (pump room) with kursaal (casino)
9 colonnade
10 spa promenade
11 avenue leading to the mineral spring
12–14 rest cure
12 sunbathing area (lawn)
13 deck-chair
14 sun canopy
15 pump room
16 rack for glasses
17 tap
18 patient taking the waters
19 bandstand
20 spa orchestra giving a concert
21 conductor

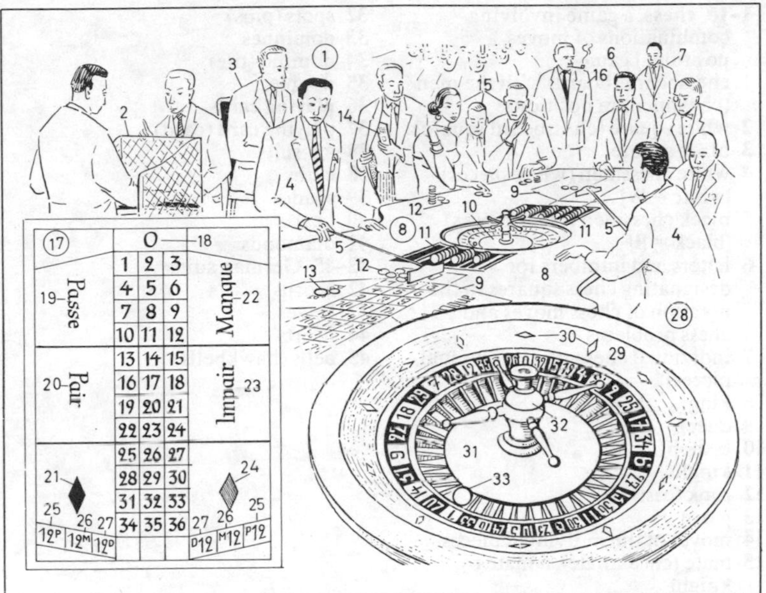

1-33 roulette, a game of chance (gambling game)
1 gaming room in a casino (gambling casino)
2 cash desk
3 tourneur (dealer)
4 croupier
5 rake
6 head croupier
7 hall manager
8 roulette table (gaming table, gambling table)
9 roulette layout
10 roulette wheel
11 bank
12 chip (check, plaque)
13 stake
14 membership card
15 roulette player
16 private detective (house detective)
17 roulette layout
18 zero (nought, O)
19 passe (high) [numbers 19 to 36]
20 pair (even numbers)
21 noir (black)
22 manque (low) [numbers 1 to 18]
23 impair [odd numbers]
24 rouge (red)
25 douze premier (first dozen) [numbers 1 to 12]
26 douze milieu (second dozen) [numbers 13 to 24]
27 douze dernier (third dozen) [numbers 25 to 36]
28 roulette wheel (roulette)
29 roulette bowl
30 fret (separator)
31 revolving disc (disk) showing numbers 0 to 36
32 spin
33 roulette ball

1–16 chess, a game involving combinations of moves, a positional game
1 chessboard (board) with the men (chessmen) in position
2 white square (chessboard square)
3 black square
4 white chessmen (white pieces) [white = W]
5 black chessmen (black pieces) [black = B]
6 letters and numbers for designating chess squares in the notation of chess moves and chess problems
7 individual chessmen (individual pieces)
8 king
9 queen
10 bishop
11 knight
12 rook (castle)
13 pawn
14 moves of the individual pieces
15 mate (checkmate), a mate by knight
16 chess clock, a double clock for chess matches (chess championships)
17–19 draughts (*Am.* checkers)
17 draughtboard (*Am.* checkerboard)
18 white draughtsman (*Am.* checker, checkerman); *also:* piece for backgammon and nine men's morris
19 black draughtsman (*Am.* checker, checkerman)
20 **salta**
21 salta piece
22 backgammon board
23–25 nine men's morris
23 nine men's morris board
24 mill
25 double mill
26–28 halma
26 halma board
27 yard (camp, corner)
28 halma pieces (halma men) of various colours (*Am.* colors)
29 **dice** (dicing)
30 dice cup
31 dice
32 spots (pips)
33 **dominoes**
34 domino (tile)
35 double
36 **playing cards**
37 playing card (card)
38–45 suits
38 clubs
39 spades
40 hearts
41 diamonds
42–45 German suits
42 acorns
43 leaves
44 hearts
45 bells (hawkbells)

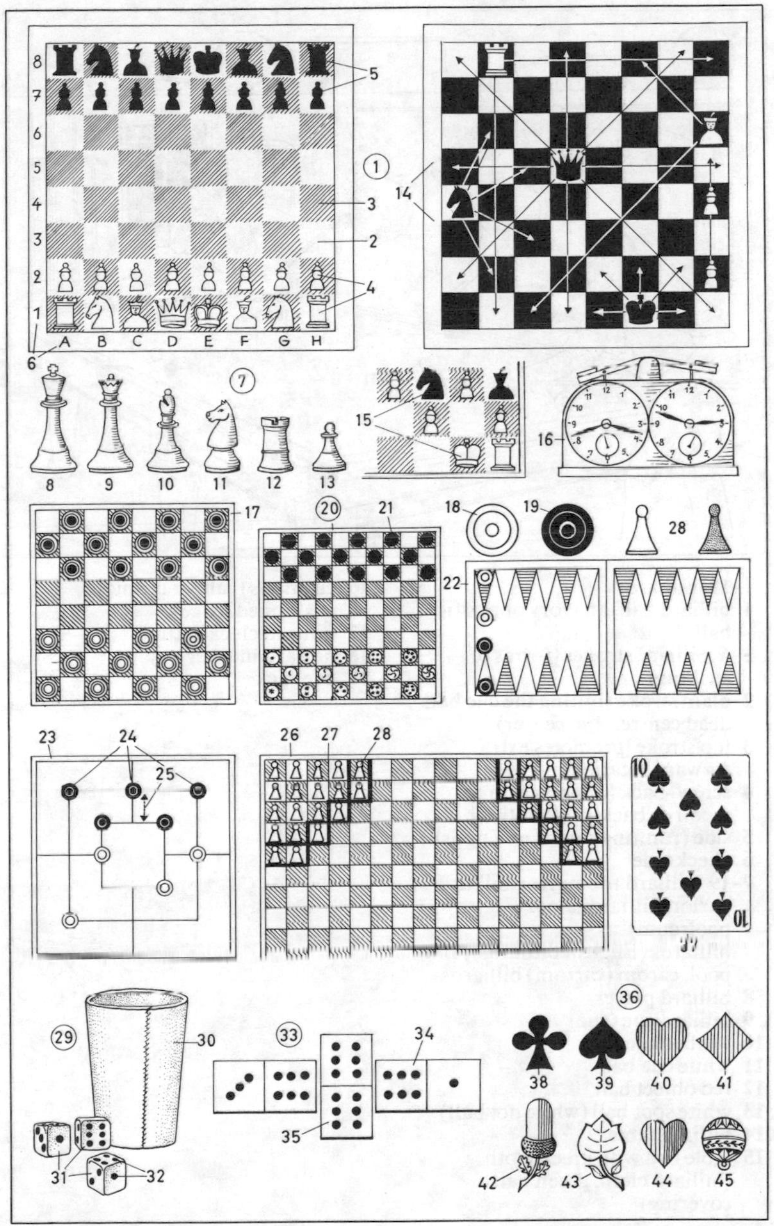
8
7
6
5
4
3
2
1
A
B
C
D
E
F
G
H
1
2
3
4
5
6
7
8
9
10
11
12
13
14
15
16
17
18
19
20
21
22
23
24
25
26
27
28
29
30
31
32
33
34
35
36
38
39
40
41
42
43
44
45

277 Billiards

1–19 billiards

1 billiard ball, an ivory or plastic ball

2–6 billiard strokes (forms of striking)

2 plain stroke (hitting the cue ball dead centre, *Am.* center)

3 top stroke [promotes extra forward rotation]

4 screw-back [imparts a direct recoil or backward motion]

5 side (running side, *Am.* English)

6 check side

7–19 billiard room (*Am.* billiard parlor, billiard saloon, poolroom)

7 billiards (English billiards); *sim.:* pool, carom (carrom) billiards

8 billiard player

9 billiard cue (cue)

10 leather cue tip

11 white cue ball

12 red object ball

13 white spot ball (white dot ball)

14 billiard table

15 table bed with green cloth (billiard cloth, green baize covering)

16 cushions (rubber cushions, cushioned ledge)

17 billiard clock, a timer

18 billiard marker

19 cue rack

Camping and Caravanning (*Am.* Trailering) 278

1-59 camp site (camping site, *Am.* campground)

1 reception (office)

2 camp site attendant

3 folding trailer (collapsible caravan, collapsible trailer)

4 hammock

5-6 washing and toilet facilities

5 toilets and washrooms (*Am.* lavatories)

6 washbasins and sinks

7 bungalow (chalet)

8-11 scout camp

8 bell tent

9 pennon

10 camp fire

11 boy scout (scout)

12 sailing boat (yacht, *Am.* sailboat)

13 landing stage (jetty)

14 inflatable boat (inflatable dinghy)

15 outboard motor (outboard)

16 trimaran

17 thwart (oarsman's bench)

18 rowlock (oarlock)

19 oar

20 boat trailer (boat carriage)

21 ridge tent

22 flysheet

23 guy line (guy)

24 tent peg (peg)

25 mallet

26 groundsheet ring

27 bell end

28 erected awning

29 storm lantern, a paraffin lamp

30 sleeping bag

31 air mattress (inflatable air-bed)

32 water carrier (drinking water carrier)

33 double-burner gas cooker for propane gas or butane gas

34 propane or butane gas bottle

35 pressure cooker

36 frame tent

37 awning

38 tent pole

39 wheelarch doorway

40 mesh ventilator

41 transparent window

42 pitch number

43 folding camp chair

44 folding camp table

45 camping tableware

46 camper

47 charcoal grill (barbecue)

48 charcoal

49 bellows

50 roof rack

51 roof lashing

52 caravan (*Am.* trailer)

53 box for gas bottle

54 jockey wheel

55 drawbar coupling

56 roof ventilator

57 caravan awning

58 inflatable igloo tent

59 camp bed (*Am.* camp cot)

279 Surf Riding (Surfing), Skin Diving (Underwater Swimming)

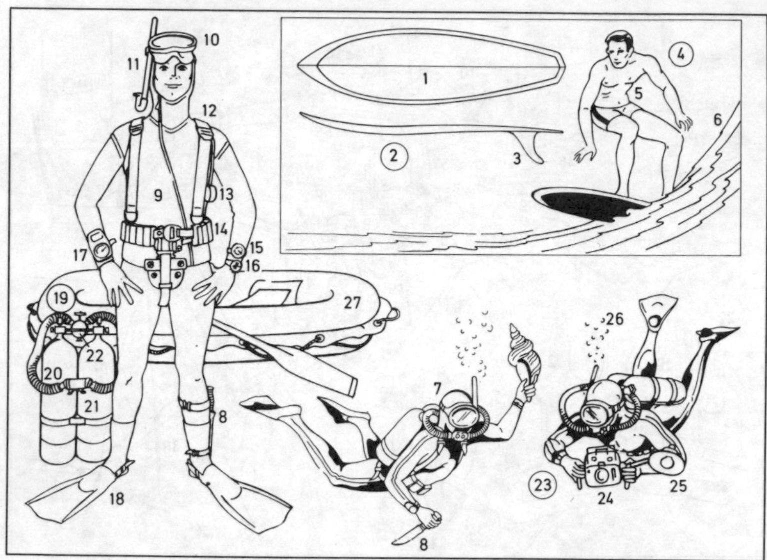

1–6 surf riding (surfing)
1 plan view of surfboard
2 section of surfboard
3 skeg (stabilizing fin)
4 big wave riding
5 surfboarder (surfer)
6 breaker
7–27 skin diving (underwater swimming)
7 skin diver (underwater swimmer)
8–22 underwater swimming set
8 knife
9 neoprene wetsuit
10 diving mask (face mask, mask), a pressure-equalizing mask
11 snorkel (schnorkel)
12 harness of diving apparatus
13 compressed-air pressure gauge (*Am.* gage)
14 weight belt
15 depth gauge (*Am.* gage)
16 waterproof watch for checking duration of dive
17 decometer for measuring stages of ascent
18 fin (flipper)
19 diving apparatus (*also:* aqualung, scuba), with two cylinders (bottles)
20 two-tube demand regulator
21 compressed-air cylinder (compressed-air bottle)
22 on/off valve
23 underwater photography
24 underwater camera
25 underwater flashlight
26 exhaust bubbles
27 inflatable boat (inflatable dinghy)

1 lifesaver (lifeguard)
2 lifeline
3 lifebelt (lifebuoy)
4 storm signal
5 time ball
6 warning sign
7 tide table, a notice board showing times of low tide and high tide
8 board showing water and air temperature
9 bathing platform
10 pennon staff
11 pennon
12 paddle boat (peddle boat)
13 surf riding (surfing) behind motorboat
14 surfboarder (surfer)
15 surfboard
16 water ski
17 inflatable beach mattress
18 beach ball
19–23 beachwear
19 beach suit
20 beach hat
21 beach jacket
22 beach trousers
23 beach shoe (bathing shoe)
24 beach bag
25 bathing gown (bathing wrap)
26 bikini (ladies' two-piece bathing suit)
27 bikini bottom
28 bikini top
29 bathing cap (swimming cap)
30 bather
31 deck tennis (quoits)
32 rubber ring (quoit)
33 inflatable rubber animal
34 beach attendant
35 sandcastle
36 roofed wicker beach chair
37 underwater swimmer
38 diving goggles
39 snorkel (schnorkel)
40 hand harpoon (fish spear, fish lance)
41 fin (flipper) for diving (for underwater swimming)
42 bathing suit (swimsuit)
43 bathing trunks (swimming trunks)
44 bathing cap (swimming cap)
45 beach tent, a ridge tent
46 lifeguard station

281 Swimming Bath (Leisure Centre, *Am.* Center)

1-9 swimming pool with artificial waves, an indoor pool
1 artificial waves
2 beach area
3 edge of the pool
4 swimming pool attendant (pool attendant, swimming bath attendant)
5 sun bed
6 lifebelt
7 water wings
8 bathing cap
9 channel to outdoor mineral bath
10 solarium
11 sunbathing area
12 sun bather
13 sun ray lamp
14 bathing towel
15 nudist sunbathing area
16 nudist (naturist)
17 screen (fence)
18 sauna (mixed sauna)
19 wood panelling (*Am.* paneling)
20 tiered benches
21 sauna stove
22 stones
23 hygrometer
24 thermometer
25 towel
26 water tub for moistening the stones in the stove
27 birch rods (birches) for beating the skin
28 cooling room for cooling off (cooling down) after the sauna
29 lukewarm shower
30 cold bath
31 hot whirlpool (underwater massage bath)
32 step into the bath
33 massage bath
34 jet blower
35 hot whirlpool [diagram]
36 section of the bath
37 step
38 circular seat
39 water extractor
40 water jet pipe
41 air jet pipe

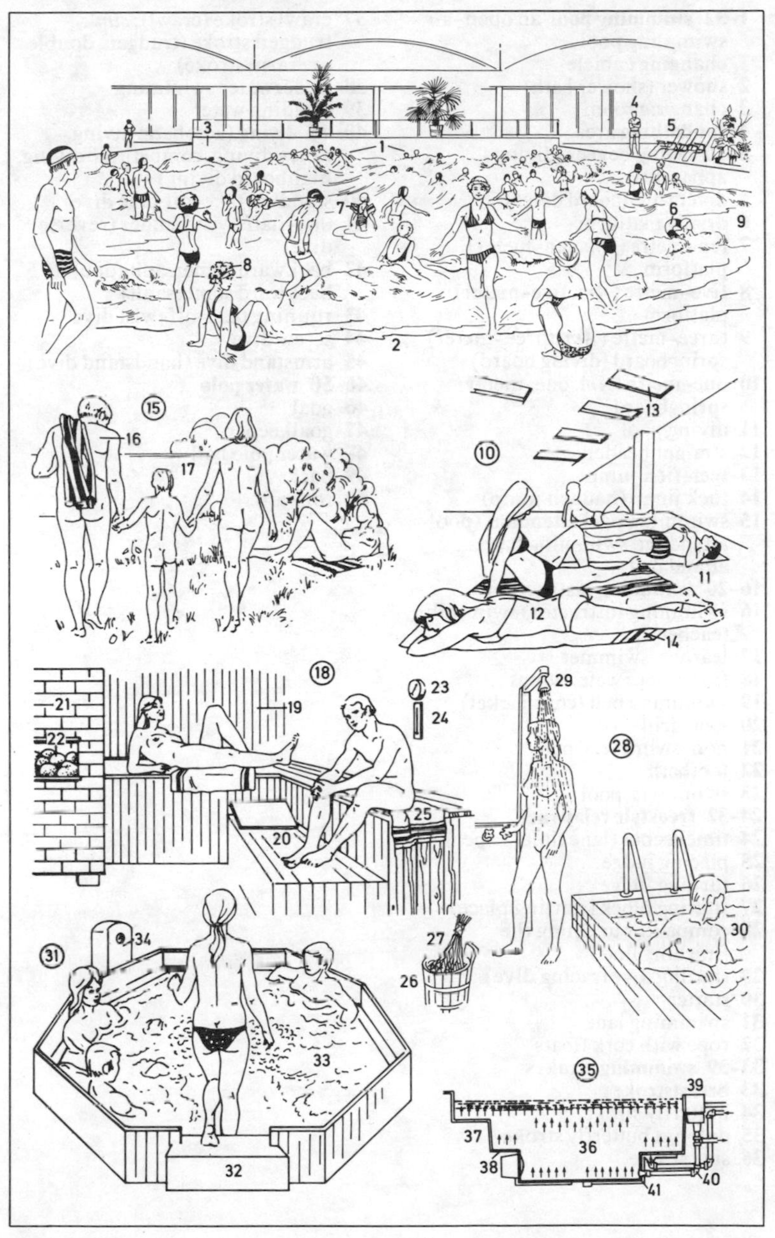
1
2
3
4
5
6
7
8
9
10
11
12
13
14
15
16
17
18
19
20
21
22
23
24
25
26
27
28
29
30
31
32
33
34
35
36
37
38
39
40
41

1–32 swimming pool, an open-air swimming pool
1 changing cubicle
2 shower (shower bath)
3 changing room
4 sunbathing area
5–10 diving boards (diving apparatus)
5 diver (highboard diver)
6 diving platform
7 ten-metre (*Am.* ten-meter) platform
8 five-metre (*Am.* five-meter) platform
9 three-metre (*Am.* three-meter) springboard (diving board)
10 one-metre (*Am.* one-meter) springboard
11 diving pool
12 straight header
13 feet-first jump
14 tuck jump (haunch jump)
15 swimming pool attendant (pool attendant, swimming bath attendant)
16–20 swimming instruction
16 swimming instructor (swimming teacher)
17 learner-swimmer
18 float; *sim.:* water wings
19 swimming belt (cork jacket)
20 land drill
21 non-swimmers' pool
22 footbath
23 swimmers' pool
24–32 freestyle relay race
24 timekeeper (lane timekeeper)
25 placing judge
26 turning judge
27 starting block (starting place)
28 competitor touching the finishing line
29 starting dive (racing dive)
30 starter
31 swimming lane
32 rope with cork floats
33–39 swimming strokes
33 breaststroke
34 butterfly stroke
35 dolphin butterfly stroke
36 side stroke
37 crawl stroke (crawl); *sim.:* trudgen stroke (trudgen, double overarm stroke)
38 underwater swimming
39 treading water
40–45 diving (acrobatic diving, fancy diving, competitive diving, highboard diving)
40 standing take-off pike dive
41 one-half twist isander (reverse dive)
42 backward somersault (double backward somersault)
43 running take-off twist dive
44 screw dive
45 armstand dive (handstand dive)
46–50 water polo
46 goal
47 goalkeeper
48 water polo ball
49 back
50 forward

1
2
3
4
5
6
7
8
9
10
11
12
13
14
15
16
17
18
19
20
21
22
23
24
25
26
27
28
29
30
31
32
33
34
35
36
37
38
39
40
41
42
43
44
45
46
47
48
49
50

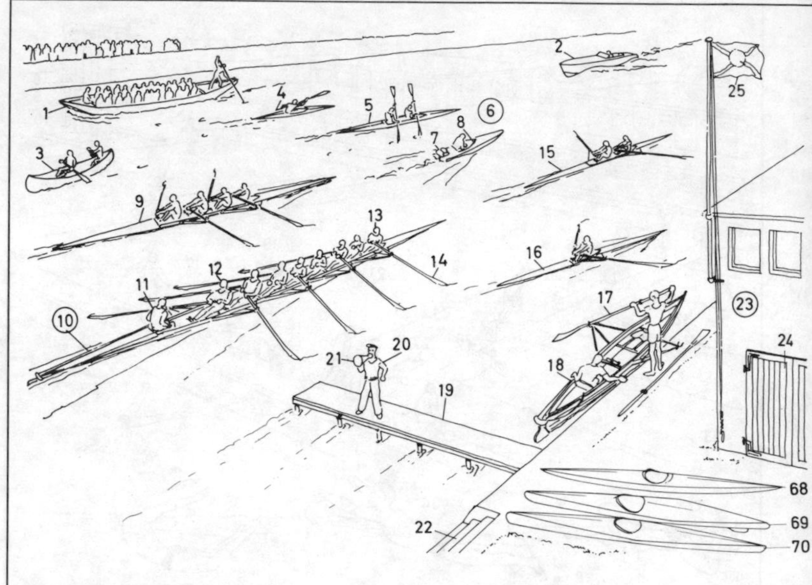

1–18 taking up positions for the regatta
1 punt, a pleasure boat
2 motorboat
3 Canadian canoe
4 kayak (Alaskan canoe, slalom canoe), a canoe
5 tandem kayak
6 outboard motorboat (outboard speedboat, outboard)
7 outboard motor (outboard)
8 cockpit
9–16 racing boats (sportsboats)
9–15 shells (rowing boats, *Am.* rowboats)
9 coxless four, a carvel-built boat
10 eight (eight-oared racing shell)
11 cox
12 stroke, an oarsman
13 bow ('number one')
14 oar
15 coxless pair
16 single sculler (single skuller, racing sculler, racing skuller, skiff)
17 scull (skull)
18 coxed single, a clinker-built single
19 jetty (landing stage, mooring)
20 rowing coach
21 megaphone
22 quayside steps
23 clubhouse (club)
24 boathouse
25 club's flag
26–33 four-oared gig, a touring boat
26 oar
27 cox's seat
28 thwart (seat)
29 rowlock (oarlock)
30 gunwale (gunnel)
31 rising
32 keel
33 skin (shell, outer skin) [clinker-built]
34 single-bladed paddle (paddle)
35–38 oar (scull, skull)
35 grip
36 leather sheath
37 shaft (neck)

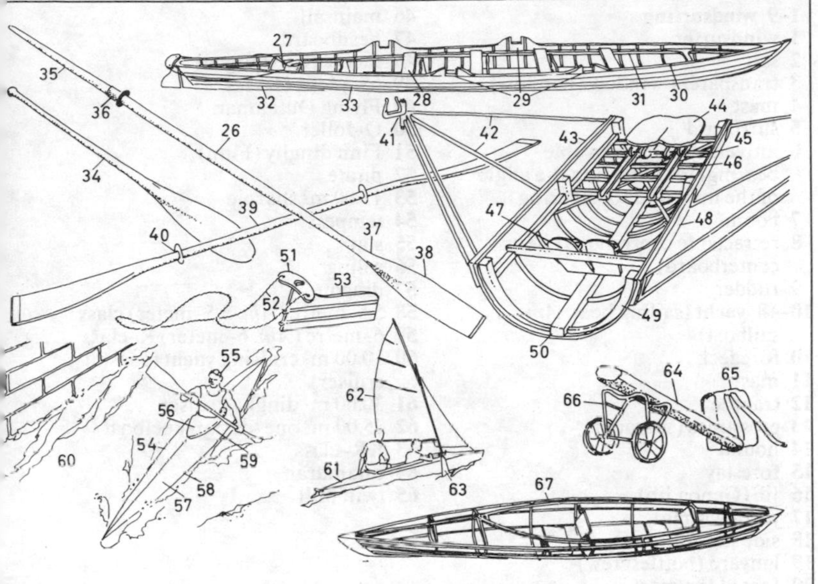

38 blade
39 double-bladed paddle (double-ended paddle)
40 drip ring
41–50 sliding seat
41 rowlock (oarlock)
42 outrigger
43 saxboard
44 sliding seat
45 runner
46 strut
47 stretcher
48 skin (shell, outer skin)
49 frame (rib)
50 kelson (keelson)
51–53 rudder (steering rudder)
51 yoke
52 lines (steering lines)
53 blade (rudder blade, rudder)
54–66 folding boats (foldboats, canoes)
54 one-man kayak
55 canoeist
56 spraydeck
57 deck
58 rubber-covered canvas hull
59 cockpit coaming (coaming)
60 channel for rafts alongside weir
61 two-seater folding kayak, a touring kayak
62 sail of folding kayak
63 leeboard
64 bag for the rods
65 rucksack
66 boat trailer (boat carriage)
67 frame of folding kayak
68–70 kayaks
68 Eskimo kayak
69 wild-water racing kayak
70 touring kayak

1-9 windsurfing
1 windsurfer
2 sail
3 transparent window (window)
4 mast
5 surfboard
6 universal joint (movable bearing) for adjusting the angle of the mast and for steering
7 boom
8 retractable centreboard (*Am.* centerboard)
9 rudder
10-48 yacht (sailing boat, *Am.* sailboat)
10 foredeck
11 mast
12 trapeze
13 crosstrees (spreader)
14 hound
15 forestay
16 jib (Genoa jib)
17 jib downhaul
18 side stay (shroud)
19 lanyard (bottlescrew)
20 foot of the mast
21 kicking strap (vang)
22 jam cleat
23 foresheet (jib sheet)
24 centreboard (*Am.* centerboard) case
25 bitt
26 centreboard (*Am.* centerboard)
27 traveller (*Am.* traveler)
28 mainsheet
29 fairlead
30 toestraps (hiking straps)
31 tiller extension (hiking stick)
32 tiller
33 rudderhead (rudder stock)
34 rudder blade (rudder)
35 transom
36 drain plug
37 gooseneck
38 window
39 boom
40 foot
41 clew
42 luff (leading edge)
43 leech pocket (batten cleat, batten pocket)
44 batten
45 leech (trailing edge)
46 mainsail
47 headboard
48 racing flag (burgee)
49-65 yacht classes
49 Flying Dutchman
50 O-Joller
51 Finn dinghy (Finn)
52 pirate
53 12.00 m^2 sharpie
54 tempest
55 star
56 soling
57 dragon
58 5.5-metre (*Am.* 5.5-meter) class
59 6-metre (*Am.* 6-meter) R-class
60 30.00 m^2 cruising yacht (coastal cruiser)
61 30.00 m^2 dinghy cruiser
62 25.00 m^2 one-design keelboat
63 KR-class
64 catamaran
65 twin hull

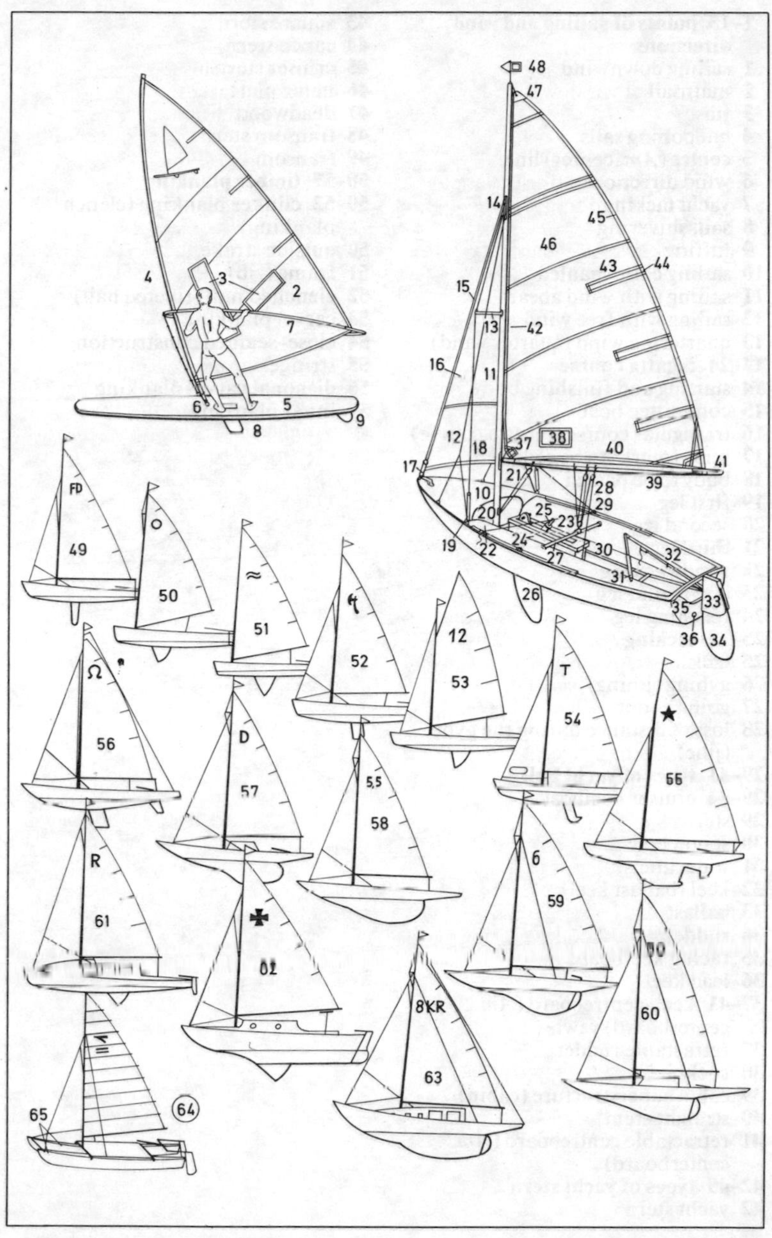
48
47
14
45
46
43
44
4
3
2
1
7
15
13
42
16
11
6
5
9
8
12
18
37
38
40
41
17
21
39
10
28
20
25
29
23
19
22
24
27
30
32
31
26
35
33
36
34
FD
49
O
50
≈
51
52
12
53
Ω
56
D
57
5,5
58
T
54
★
66
R
61
62
6
59
60
8KR
63
65
64

1–13 points of sailing and wind directions
1 sailing downwind
2 mainsail
3 jib
4 ballooning sails
5 centre (*Am.* center) line
6 wind direction
7 yacht tacking
8 sail, shivering
9 luffing
10 sailing close-hauled
11 sailing with wind abeam
12 sailing with free wind
13 quartering wind (quarter wind)
14–24 regatta course
14 starting and finishing buoy
15 committee boat
16 triangular course (regatta course)
17 buoy (mark) to be rounded
18 buoy to be passed
19 first leg
20 second leg
21 third leg
22 windward leg
23 downwind leg
24 reaching leg
25–28 tacking
25 tack
26 gybing (jibing)
27 going about
28 loss of distance during the gybe (jibe)
29–41 types of yacht hull
29–34 cruiser keelboat
29 stern
30 spoon bow
31 waterline
32 keel (ballast keel)
33 ballast
34 rudder
35 racing keelboat
36 lead keel
37–41 keel-centreboard (*Am.* centerboard) yawl
37 retractable rudder
38 cockpit
39 cabin superstructure (cabin)
40 straight stem
41 retractable centreboard (*Am.* centerboard)
42–49 types of yacht stern
42 yacht stern
43 square stern
44 canoe stern
45 cruiser stern
46 name plate
47 deadwood
48 transom stern
49 transom
50–57 timber planking
50–52 clinker planking (clench planking)
50 outside strake
51 frame (rib)
52 clenched nail (riveted nail)
53 carvel planking
54 close-seamed construction
55 stringer
56 diagonal carvel planking
57 inner planking

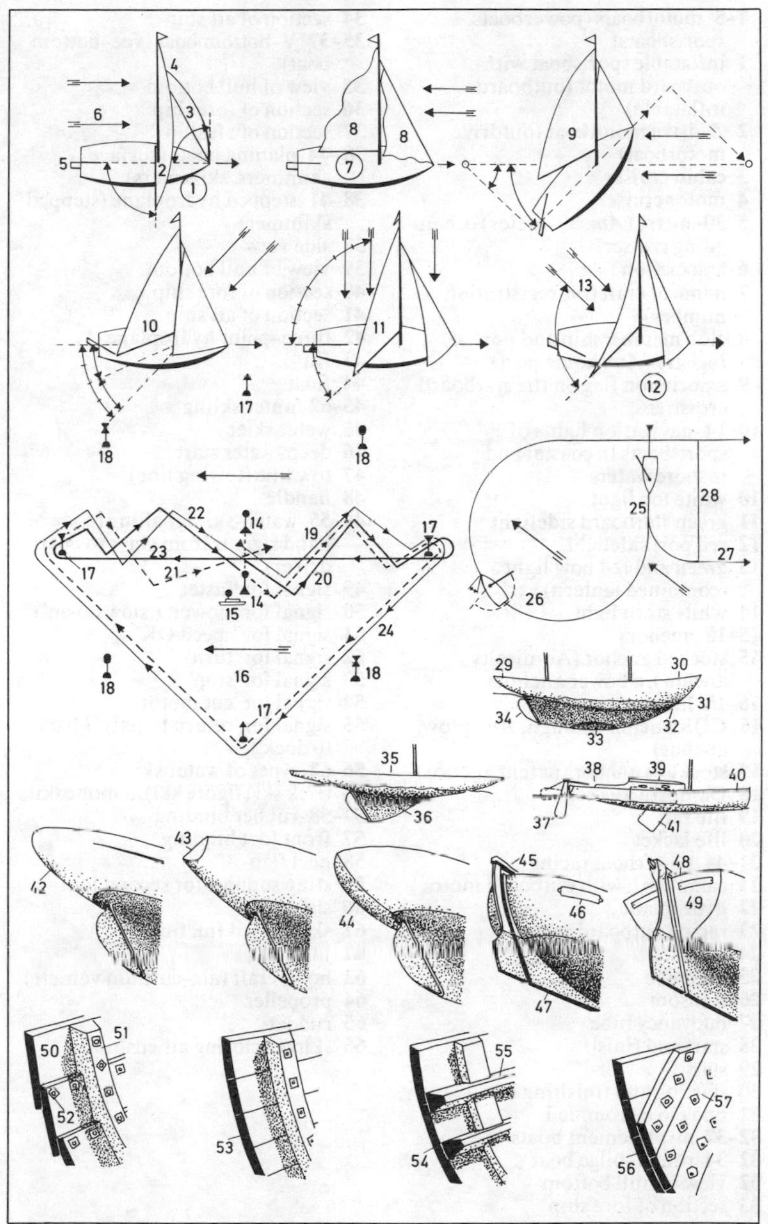

1–5 motorboats (powerboats, sportsboats)
1 inflatable sportsboat with outboard motor (outboard inflatable)
2 Z-drive motorboat (outdrive motorboat)
3 cabin cruiser
4 motor cruiser
5 30-metre (*Am.* 30-meter) ocean-going cruiser
6 association flag
7 name of craft (*or:* registration number)
8 club membership and port of registry (*Am.* home port)
9 association flag on the starboard crosstrees
10–14 navigation lights of sportsboats in coastal and inshore waters
10 white top light
11 green starboard sidelight
12 red port sidelight
13 green and red bow light (combined lantern)
14 white stern light
15–18 anchors
15 stocked anchor (Admiralty anchor), a bower anchor
16–18 lightweight anchor
16 CQR anchor (plough, *Am.* plow, anchor)
17 stockless anchor (patent anchor)
18 Danforth anchor
19 life raft
20 life jacket
21–44 powerboat racing
21 catamaran with outboard motor
22 hydroplane
23 racing outboard motor
24 tiller
25 fuel pipe
26 transom
27 buoyancy tube
28 start and finish
29 start
30 starting and finishing line
31 buoy to be rounded
32–37 displacement boats
32–34 round-bilge boat
32 view of hull bottom
33 section of fore ship
34 section of aft ship
35–37 V-bottom boat (vee-bottom boat)
35 view of hull bottom
36 section of fore ship
37 section of aft ship
38–44 planing boats (surface skimmers, skimmers)
38–41 stepped hydroplane (stepped skimmer)
38 side view
39 view of hull bottom
40 section of fore ship
41 section of aft ship
42 three-point hydroplane
43 fin
44 float
45–62 water skiing
45 water skier
46 deep-water start
47 tow line (towing line)
48 handle
49–55 water-ski signalling (code of hand signals from skier to boat driver)
49 signal for 'faster'
50 signal for 'slower' ('slow down')
51 signal for 'speed OK'
52 signal for 'turn'
53 signal for 'stop'
54 signal for 'cut motor'
55 signal for 'return to jetty' ('back to dock')
56–62 types of water ski
56 trick ski (figure ski), a monoski
57–58 rubber binding
57 front foot binding
58 heel flap
59 strap support for second foot
60 slalom ski
61 skeg (fixed fin, fin)
62 jump ski
63 hovercraft (air-cushion vehicle)
64 propeller
65 rudder
66 skirt enclosing air cushion

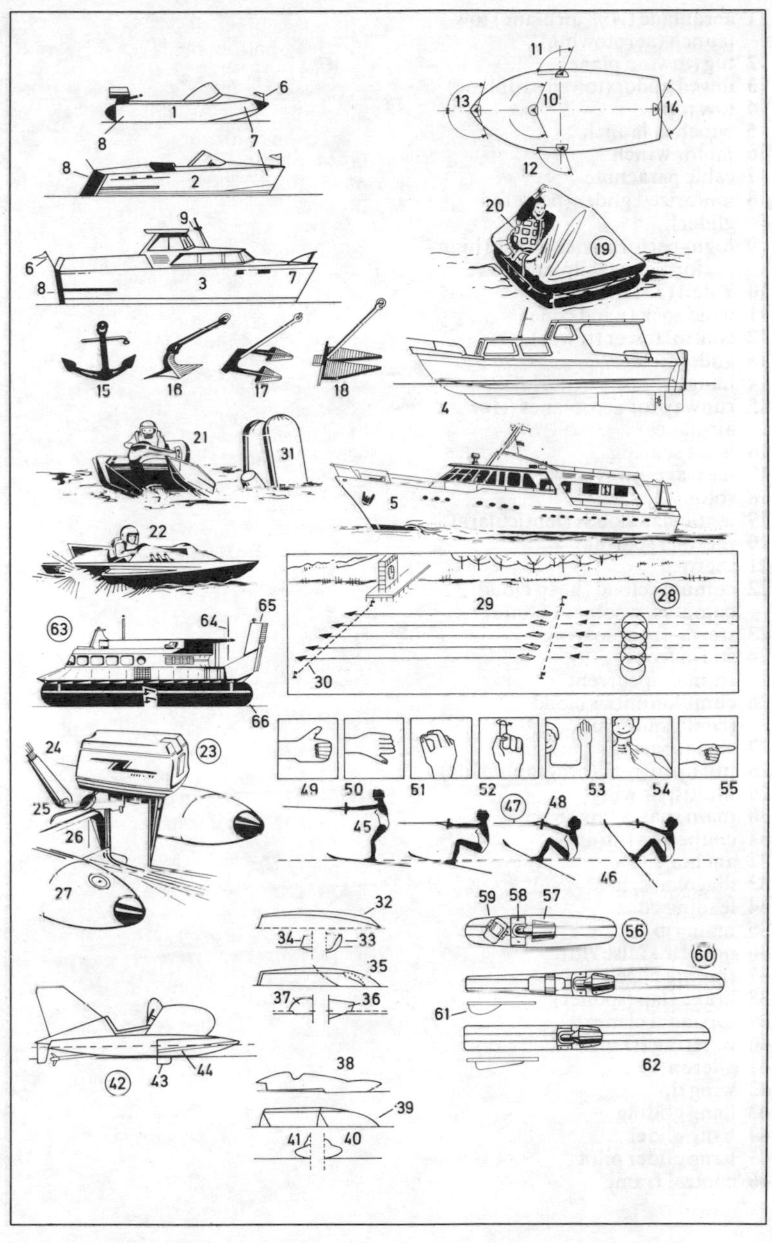
1
2
3
4
5
6
7
8
9
10
11
12
13
14
15
16
17
18
19
20
21
22
23
24
25
26
27
28
29
30
31
32
33
34
35
36
37
38
39
40
41
42
43
44
45
46
47
48
49
50
51
52
53
54
55
56
57
58
59
60
61
62
63
64
65
66

287 Gliding (Soaring)

1 aeroplane (*Am.* airplane) tow launch (aerotowing)
2 tug (towing plane)
3 towed glider (towed sailplane)
4 tow rope
5 winched launch
6 motor winch
7 cable parachute
8 motorized glider (powered glider)
9 high-performance glider (high-performance sailplane)
10 T-tail (T-tail unit)
11 wind sock (wind cone)
12 control tower (tower)
13 glider field
14 hangar
15 runway for aeroplanes (*Am.* airplanes)
16 wave soaring
17 lee waves (waves, wave system)
18 rotor
19 lenticular clouds (lenticulars)
20 thermal soaring
21 thermal
22 cumulus cloud (heap cloud, cumulus, woolpack cloud)
23 storm-front soaring
24 storm front
25 frontal upcurrent
26 cumulonimbus cloud (cumulonimbus)
27 slope soaring
28 hill upcurrent (orographic lift)
29 multispar wing
30 main spar, a box spar
31 connector fitting
32 anchor rib
33 diagonal spar
34 leading edge
35 main rib
36 nose rib (false rib)
37 trailing edge
38 brake flap (spoiler)
39 torsional clamp
40 covering (skin)
41 aileron
42 wing tip
43 hang gliding
44 hang glider
45 hang glider pilot
46 control frame

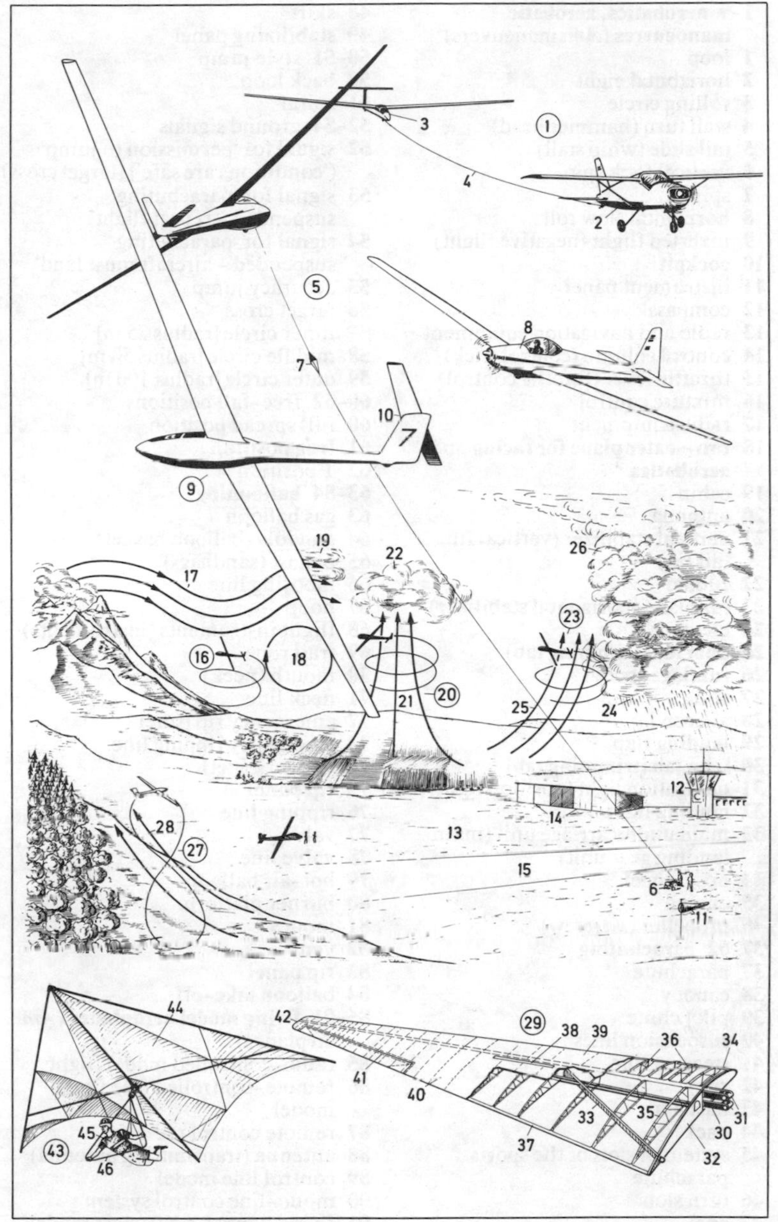
1
2
3
4
5
6
7
8
9
10
11
12
13
14
15
16
17
18
19
20
21
22
23
24
25
26
27
28
29
30
31
32
33
34
35
36
37
38
39
40
41
42
43
44
45
46

1–9 aerobatics, aerobatic manoeuvres (*Am.* maneuvers)
1 loop
2 horizontal eight
3 rolling circle
4 stall turn (hammer head)
5 tail slide (whip stall)
6 vertical flick spin
7 spin
8 horizontal slow roll
9 inverted flight (negative flight)
10 cockpit
11 instrument panel
12 compass
13 radio and navigation equipment
14 control column (control stick)
15 throttle lever (throttle control)
16 mixture control
17 radio equipment
18 two-seater plane for racing and aerobatics
19 cabin
20 antenna
21 vertical stabilizer (vertical fin, tail fin)
22 rudder
23 tailplane (horizontal stabilizer)
24 elevator
25 trim tab (trimming tab)
26 fuselage (body)
27 wing
28 aileron
29 landing flap
30 trim tab (trimming tab)
31 navigation light (position light) [red]
32 landing light
33 main undercarriage unit (main landing gear unit)
34 nose wheel
35 engine
36 propeller (airscrew)
37–62 parachuting
37 parachute
38 canopy
39 pilot chute
40 suspension lines
41 steering line
42 riser
43 harness
44 pack
45 system of slots of the sports parachute
46 turn slots
47 apex
48 skirt
49 stabilizing panel
50–51 style jump
50 back loop
51 spiral
52–54 ground signals
52 signal for 'permission to jump' ('conditions are safe') (target cross)
53 signal for 'parachuting suspended – repeat flight'
54 signal for 'parachuting suspended – aircraft must land'
55 accuracy jump
56 target cross
57 inner circle [radius 25 m]
58 middle circle [radius 50 m]
59 outer circle [radius 100 m]
60–62 free-fall positions
60 full spread position
61 frog position
62 T position
63–84 ballooning
63 gas balloon
64 gondola (balloon basket)
65 ballast (sandbags)
66 mooring line
67 hoop
68 flight instruments (instruments)
69 trail rope
70 mouth (neck)
71 neck line
72 emergency rip panel
73 emergency ripping line
74 network (net)
75 rip panel
76 ripping line
77 valve
78 valve line
79 hot-air balloon
80 burner platform
81 mouth
82 vent
83 rip panel
84 balloon take-off
85–91 flying model aeroplanes (*Am.* airplanes)
85 radio-controlled model flight
86 remote-controlled free flight model
87 remote control radio
88 antenna (transmitting antenna)
89 control line model
90 mono-line control system
91 flying kennel, a K9-class model

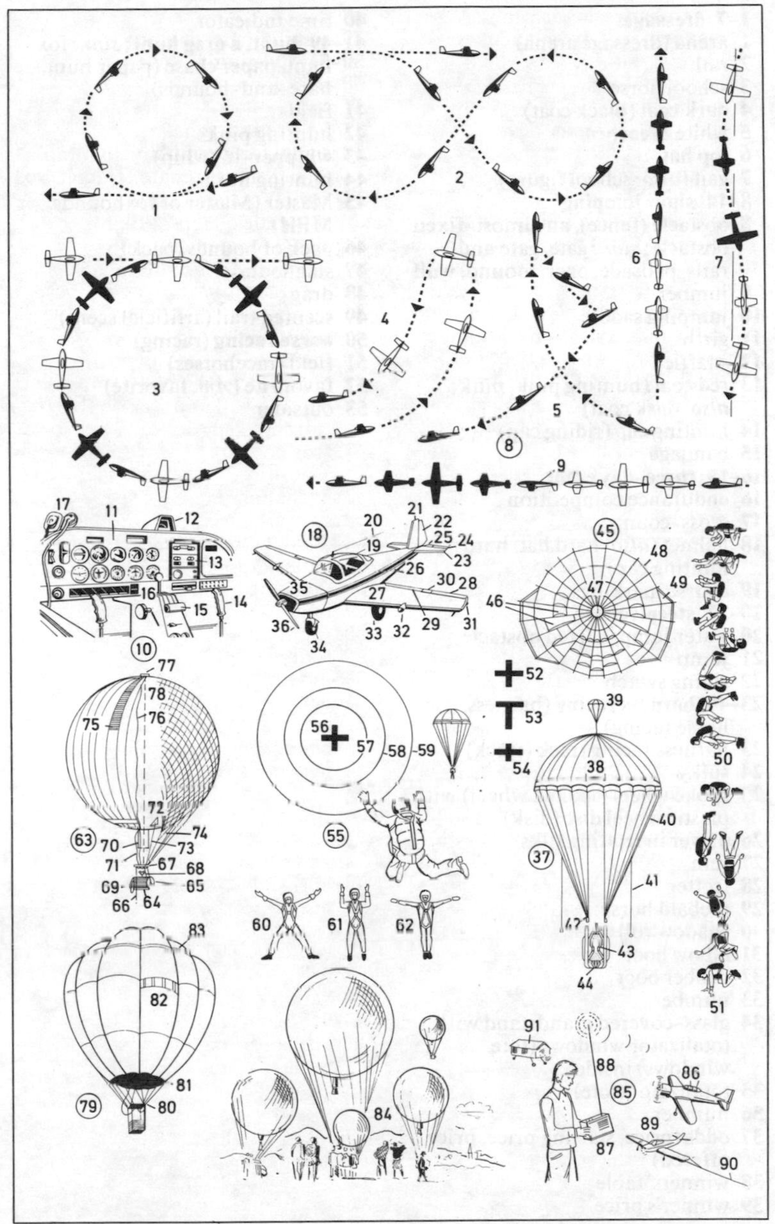
1
2
3
4
5
6
7
8
9
10
11
12
13
14
15
16
17
18
19
20
21
22
23
24
25
26
27
28
29
30
31
32
33
34
35
36
37
38
39
40
41
42
43
44
45
46
47
48
49
50
51
52
53
54
55
56
57
58
59
60
61
62
63
64
65
66
67
68
69
70
71
72
73
74
75
76
77
78
79
80
81
82
83
84
85
86
87
88
89
90
91

289 Horsemanship, Equestrian Sport

1–7 dressage
1 arena (dressage arena)
2 rail
3 school horse
4 dark coat (black coat)
5 white breeches
6 top hat
7 gait (*also:* school figure)
8–14 show jumping
8 obstacle (fence), an almost-fixed obstacle; *sim.:* gate, gate and rails, palisade, oxer, mound, wall
9 jumper
10 jumping saddle
11 girth
12 snaffle
13 red coat (hunting pink, pink; *also:* dark coat)
14 hunting cap (riding cap)
15 bandage
16–19 three-day event
16 endurance competition
17 cross-country
18 helmet (*also:* hard hat, hard hunting cap)
19 course markings
20–22 steeplechase
20 water jump, a fixed obstacle
21 jump
22 riding switch
23–40 harness racing (harness horse racing)
23 harness racing track (track)
24 sulky
25 spoke wheel (spoked wheel) with plastic wheel disc (disk)
26 driver in trotting silks
27 rein
28 trotter
29 piebald horse
30 shadow roll
31 elbow boot
32 rubber boot
33 number
34 glass-covered grandstand with totalizator windows (tote windows) inside
35 totalizator (tote)
36 number
37 odds (price, starting price, price offered)
38 winners' table
39 winner's price
40 time indicator
41–49 hunt, a drag hunt; *sim.:* fox hunt, paper chase (paper hunt, hare-and-hounds)
41 field
42 hunting pink
43 whipper-in (whip)
44 hunting horn
45 Master (Master of foxhounds, MFH)
46 pack of hounds (pack)
47 staghound
48 drag
49 scented trail (artificial scent)
50 horse racing (racing)
51 field (racehorses)
52 favourite (*Am.* favorite)
53 outsider

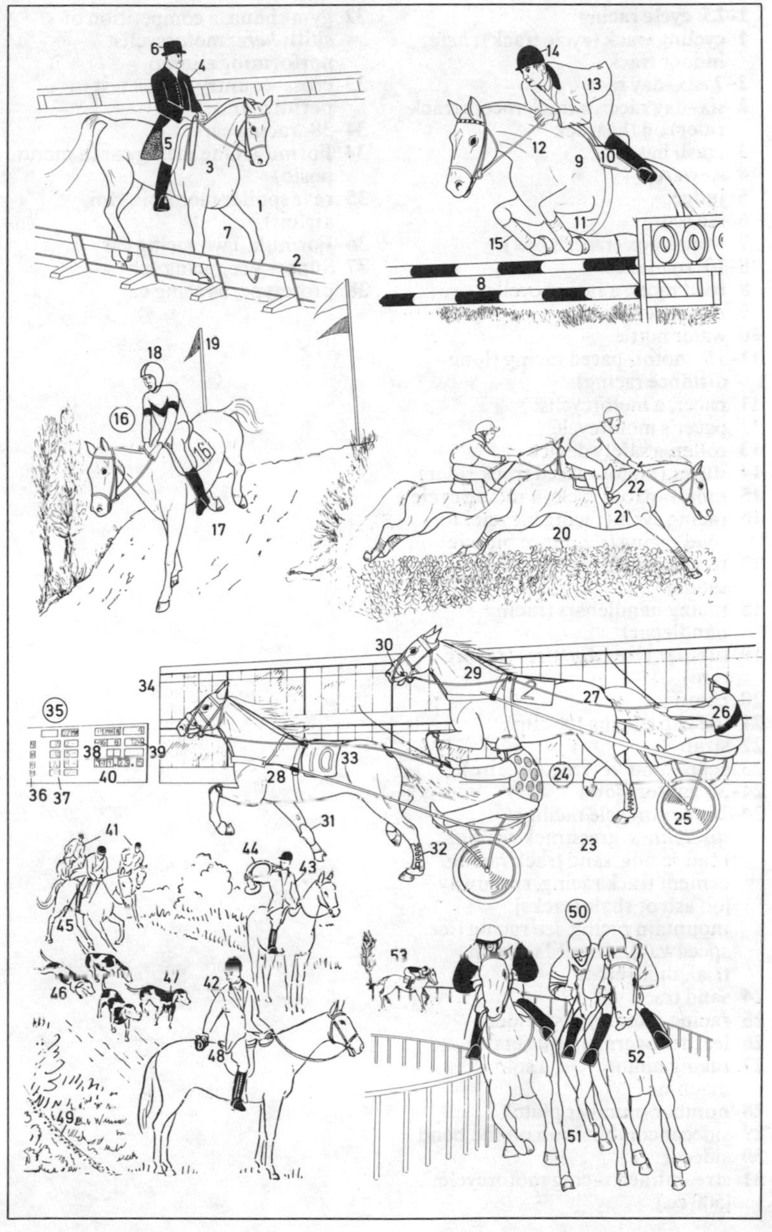
1
2
3
4
5
6
7
8
9
10
11
12
13
14
15
16
17
18
19
20
21
22
23
24
25
26
27
28
29
30
31
32
33
34
35
36
37
38
39
40
41
42
43
44
45
46
47
48
49
50
51
52
53

1–23 cycle racing
1 cycling track (cycle track); *here:* indoor track
2–7 six-day race
2 six-day racer, a track racer (track rider) on the track
3 crash hat
4 stewards
5 judge
6 lap scorer
7 rider's box (racer's box)
8–10 road race
8 road racer, a racing cyclist
9 racing jersey
10 water bottle
11–15 motor-paced racing (long-distance racing)
11 pacer, a motorcyclist
12 pacer's motorcycle
13 roller, a safety device
14 stayer (motor-paced track rider)
15 motor-paced cycle, a racing cycle
16 racing cycle (racing bicycle) for road racing (road race bicycle)
17 racing saddle, an unsprung saddle
18 racing handlebars (racing handlebar)
19 tubular tyre (*Am.* tire) (racing tyre)
20 chain
21 toe clip (racing toe clip)
22 strap
23 spare tubular tyre (*Am.* tire)
24–38 motorsports
24–28 motorcycle racing; *disciplines:* grasstrack racing, road racing, sand track racing, cement track racing, speedway [on ash or shale tracks], mountain racing, ice racing (ice speedway), scramble racing, trial, moto cross
24 sand track
25 racing motorcyclist (rider)
26 leather overalls (leathers)
27 racing motorcycle, a solo machine
28 number (number plate)
29 sidecar combination on the bend
30 sidecar
31 streamlined racing motorcycle [500 cc.]
32 gymkhana, a competition of skill; *here:* motorcyclist performing a jump
33 cross-country race, a test in performance
34–38 racing cars
34 Formula One racing car (a mono posto)
35 rear spoiler (aerofoil, *Am.* airfoil)
36 Formula Two racing car
37 Super-Vee racing car
38 prototype, a racing car

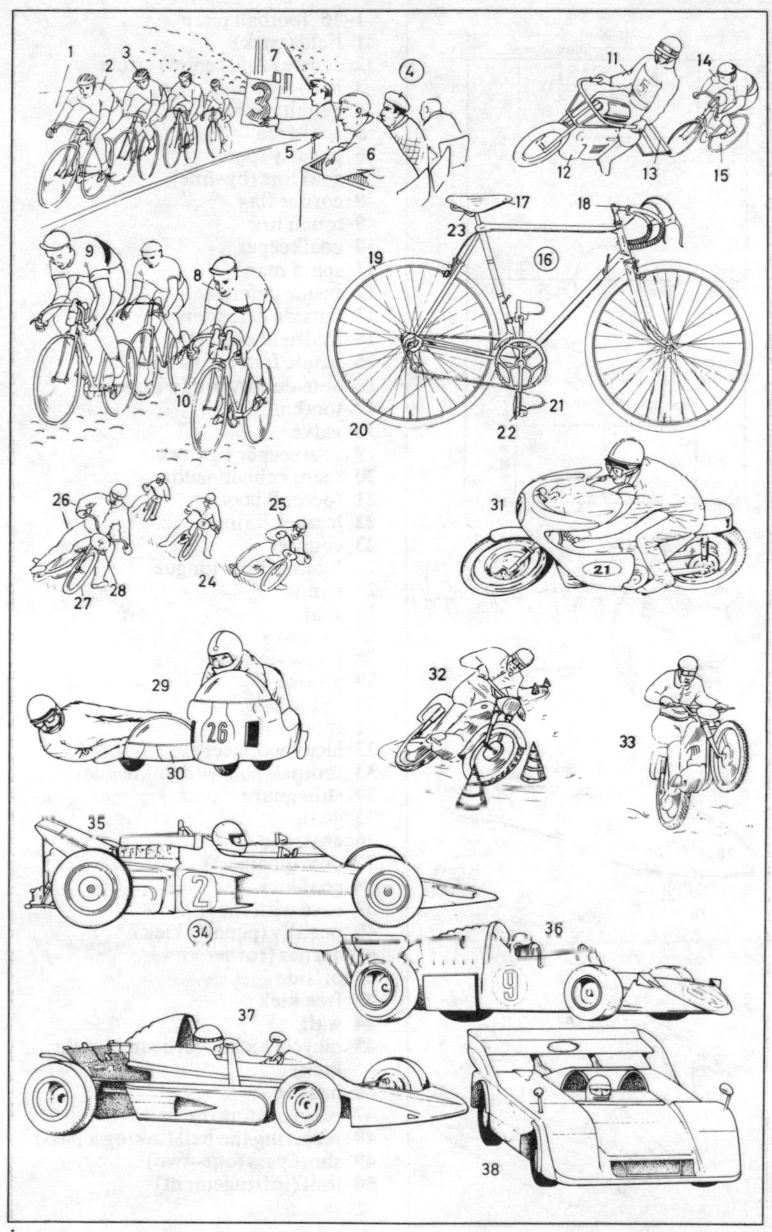
1
2
3
7
4
11
14
5
6
12
13
15
17
18
23
19
16
9
8
10
20
22
21
26
25
31
28
24
27
29
32
30
33
35
34
36
37
38

291 Ball Games I (Football, Association Football, Soccer)

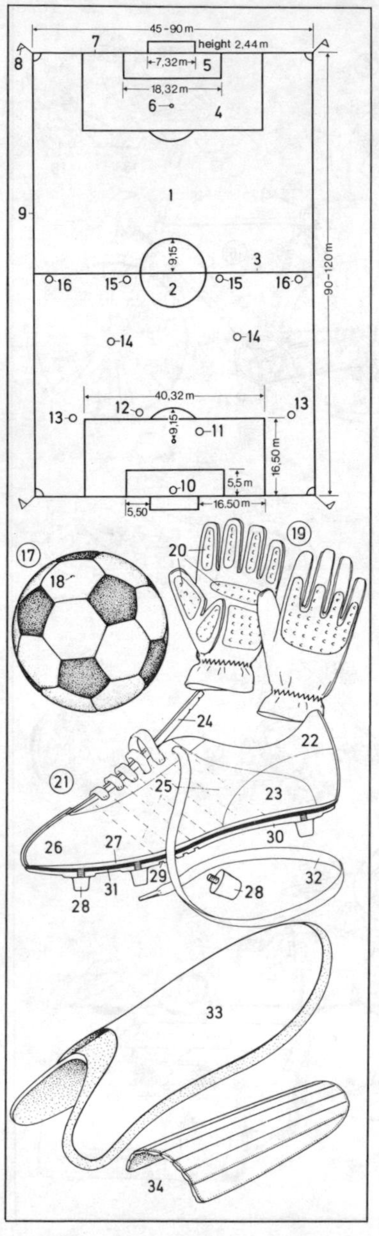

1-16 football pitch
1 field (park)
2 centre (*Am.* center) circle
3 half-way line
4 penalty area
5 goal area
6 penalty spot
7 goal line (by-line)
8 corner flag
9 touch line
10 goalkeeper
11 spare man
12 inside defender
13 outside defender
14 midfield players
15 inside forward (striker)
16 outside forward (winger)
17 football
18 valve
19 goalkeeper's gloves
20 foam rubber padding
21 football boot
22 leather lining
23 counter
24 foam rubber tongue
25 bands
26 shaft
27 insole
28 screw-in stud
29 groove
30 nylon sole
31 inner sole
32 lace (bootlace)
33 football pad with ankle guard
34 shin guard
35 goal
36 crossbar
37 post (goalpost)
38 goal kick
39 save with the fists
40 penalty (penalty kick)
41 corner (corner kick)
42 offside
43 free kick
44 wall
45 bicycle kick (overhead bicycle kick)
46 header
47 pass (passing the ball)
48 receiving the ball (taking a pass)
49 short pass (one-two)
50 foul (infringement)

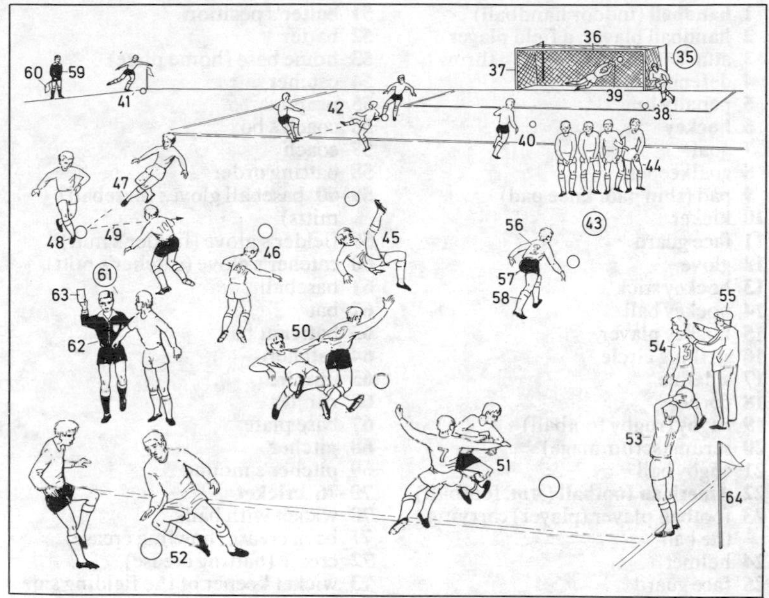

51 obstruction
52 dribble
53 throw-in
54 substitute
55 coach
56 shirt (jersey)
57 shorts
58 sock (football sock)
59 linesman
60 linesman's flag
61 sending-off
62 referee
63 red card; *also:* yellow card
64 centre (*Am.* center) flag

1 **handball** (indoor handball)
2 handball player, a field player
3 attacker, making a jump throw
4 defender
5 penalty line
6 **hockey**
7 goal
8 goalkeeper
9 pad (shin pad, knee pad)
10 kicker
11 face guard
12 glove
13 hockey stick
14 hockey ball
15 hockey player
16 striking circle
17 sideline
18 corner
19 **rugby** (rugby football)
20 scrum (scrummage)
21 rugby ball
22 **American football** (*Am.* football)
23 football player (player) carrying the ball
24 helmet
25 face guard
26 padded jersey
27 ball (pigskin)
28 **basketball**
29 basketball
30 backboard
31 basket posts
32 basket
33 basket ring
34 target rectangle
35 basketball player shooting
36 end line
37 restricted area
38 free-throw line
39 substitute
40–69 **baseball**
40–58 field (park)
40 spectator barrier
41 outfielder
42 short stop
43 second base
44 baseman
45 runner
46 first base
47 third base
48 foul line (base line)
49 pitcher's mound
50 pitcher
51 batter's position
52 batter
53 home base (home plate)
54 catcher
55 umpire
56 coach's box
57 coach
58 batting order
59–60 baseball gloves (baseball mitts)
59 fielder's glove (fielder's mitt)
60 catcher's glove (catcher's mitt)
61 baseball
62 bat
63 batter at bat
64 catcher
65 umpire
66 runner
67 base plate
68 pitcher
69 pitcher's mound
70–76 **cricket**
70 wicket with bails
71 back crease (bowling crease)
72 crease (batting crease)
73 wicket keeper of the fielding side
74 batsman
75 bat (cricket bat)
76 fielder (bowler)
77–82 **croquet**
77 winning peg
78 hoop
79 corner peg
80 croquet player
81 croquet mallet
82 croquet ball

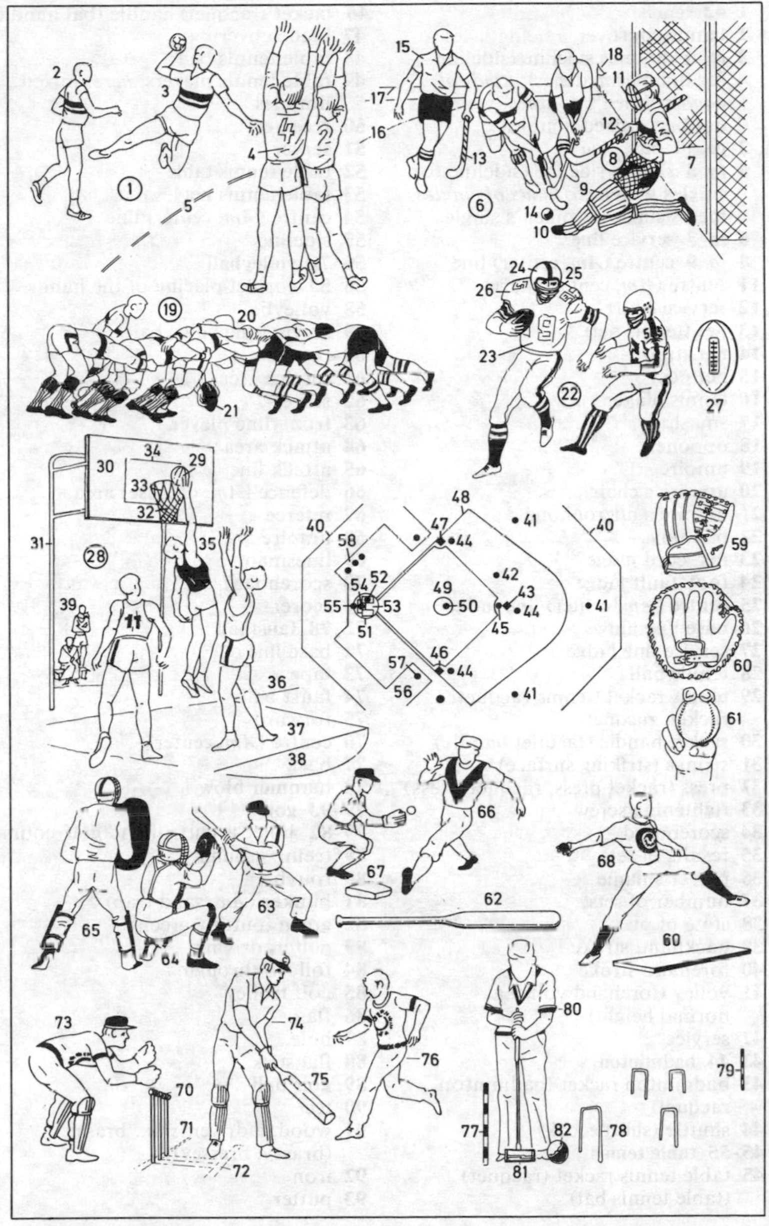

293 Ball Games III

1-42 tennis
1 tennis court
2 *to* **3** doubles sideline (sideline for doubles matches); *kinds of doubles:* men's doubles, women's doubles, mixed doubles
3 *to* **10** base line
4 *to* **5** singles sideline (sideline for singles matches); *kinds of singles:* men's singles, women's singles
6 *to* **7** service line
8 *to* **9** centre (*Am.* center) line
11 centre (*Am.* center) mark
12 service court
13 net (tennis net)
14 net strap
15 net post
16 tennis player
17 smash
18 opponent
19 umpire
20 umpire's chair
21 umpire's microphone
22 ball boy
23 net-cord judge
24 foot-fault judge
25 centre (*Am.* center) line judge
26 base line judge
27 service line judge
28 tennis ball
29 tennis racket (tennis racquet, racket, racquet)
30 racket handle (racquet handle)
31 strings (striking surface)
32 press (racket press, racquet press)
33 tightening screw
34 scoreboard
35 results of sets
36 player's name
37 number of sets
38 state of play
39 backhand stroke
40 forehand stroke
41 volley (forehand volley at normal height)
42 service
43-44 badminton
43 badminton racket (badminton racquet)
44 shuttle (shuttlecock)
45-55 table tennis
45 table tennis racket (racquet) (table tennis bat)
46 racket (racquet) handle (bat handle)
47 blade covering
48 table tennis ball
49 table tennis players; *here:* mixed doubles
50 receiver
51 server
52 table tennis table
53 table tennis net
54 centre (*Am.* center) line
55 sideline
56-71 volleyball
56-57 correct placing of the hands
58 volleyball
59 serving the volleyball
60 blocker
61 service area
62 server
63 front-line player
64 attack area
65 attack line
66 defence (*Am.* defense) area
67 referee
68 umpire
69 linesman
70 scoreboard
71 scorer
72-78 faustball
72 base line
73 tape
74 faust ball
75 forward
76 centre (*Am.* center)
77 back
78 hammer blow
79-93 golf
79-82 hole, a part of the golf course
79 teeing ground
80 rough
81 bunker (*Am.* sand trap)
82 green (putting green)
83 golfer, driving
84 follow-through
85 golf trolley
86 flag
87 hole
88 flagstick
89 golf ball
90 tee
91 wood, a driver; *sim.:* brassie (brassy, brassey)
92 iron
93 putter

SCORES
SETS GAMES
BORG
ASHE
6 3
4 6
2 6
7 5
2 4
2 1

1-33 fencing (modern fencing)
1-18 foil
1 fencing master (fencing instructor)
2 piste
3 on guard line
4 centre (*Am.* center) line
5-6 fencers (foil fencers, foilsmen, foilists) in a bout
5 attacker (attacking fencer) in lunging position (lunging)
6 defender (defending fencer), parrying
7 straight thrust, a fencing movement
8 parry of the tierce
9 line of fencing
10 the three fencing measures [short, medium, and long measure]
11 foil, a thrust weapon
12 fencing glove
13 fencing mask (foil mask)
14 neck flap (neck guard) on the fencing mask
15 metallic jacket
16 fencing jacket
17 heelless fencing shoes
18 first position for fencer's salute (initial position, on guard position)
19-24 sabre (*Am.* saber) fencing
19 sabreurs (sabre fencers, *Am.* saber fencers)
20 (light) sabre (*Am.* saber)
21 sabre (*Am.* saber) glove (sabre gauntlet)
22 sabre (*Am.* saber) mask
23 cut at head
24 parry of the fifth (quinte)
25-33 épée, with electrical scoring equipment
25 épéeist
26 electric épée; *also:* electric foil
27 épée point
28 scoring lights
29 spring-loaded wire spool
30 indicator light
31 wire
32 electronic scoring equipment
33 on guard position

34-45 fencing weapons
34 light sabre (*Am.* saber), a cut and thrust weapon
35 guard
36 épée, a thrust weapon
37 French foil, a thrust weapon
38 guard (coquille)
39 Italian foil
40 foil pommel
41 handle
42 cross piece (quillons)
43 guard (coquille)
44 blade
45 button
46 engagements
47 quarte (carte) engagement
48 tierce engagement (*also:* sixte engagement)
49 circling engagement
50 seconde engagement (*also:* octave engagement)
51-53 target areas
51 the whole body in épée fencing (men)
52 head and upper body down to the groin in sabre (*Am.* saber) fencing (men)
53 trunk from the neck to the groin in foil fencing (ladies and men)

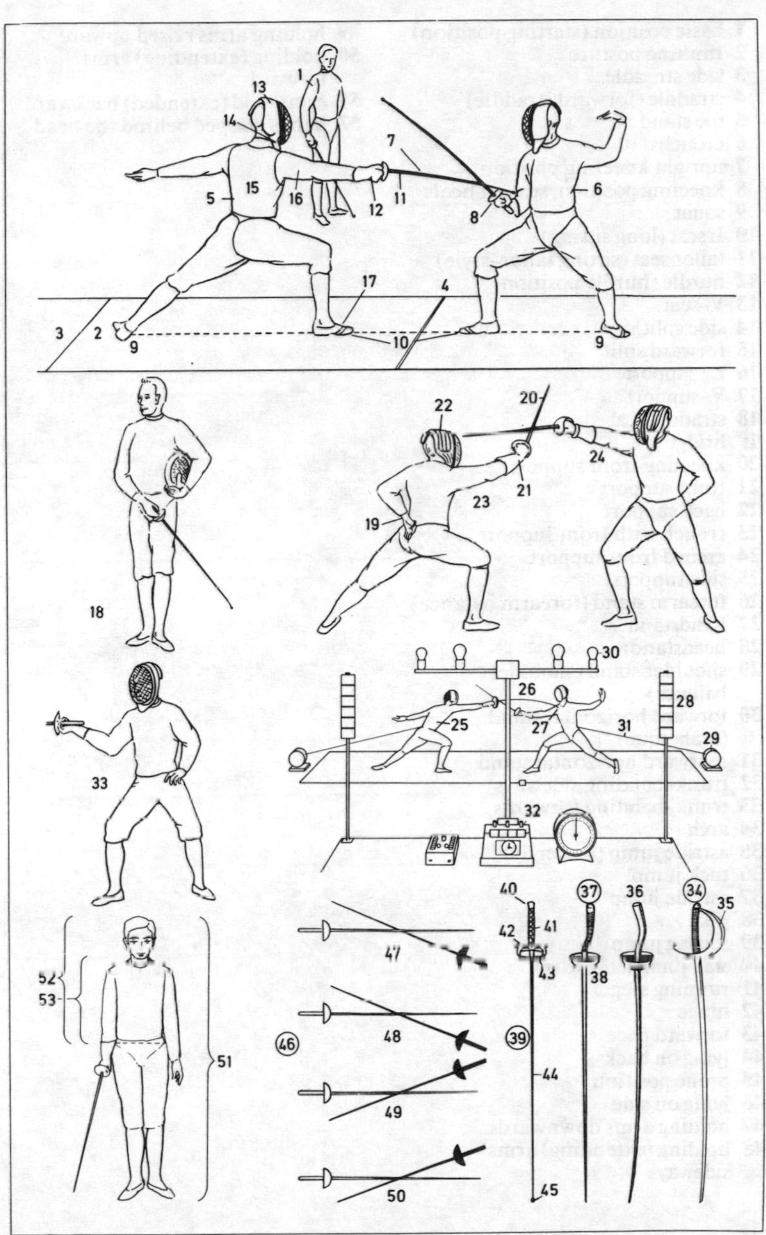
1
2
3
4
5
6
7
8
9
10
11
12
13
14
15
16
17
18
19
20
21
22
23
24
25
26
27
28
29
30
31
32
33
34
35
36
37
38
39
40
41
42
43
44
45
46
47
48
49
50
51
52
53

295 Free Exercise

1 basic position (starting position)
2 running posture
3 side straddle
4 straddle (forward straddle)
5 toe stand
6 crouch
7 upright kneeling position
8 kneeling position, seat on heels
9 squat
10 L seat (long sitting)
11 tailor seat (sitting tailor-style)
12 hurdle (hurdle position)
13 V-seat
14 side split
15 forward split
16 L-support
17 V-support
18 straddle seat
19 bridge
20 kneeling front support
21 front support
22 back support
23 crouch with front support
24 arched front support
25 side support
26 forearm stand (forearm balance)
27 handstand
28 headstand
29 shoulder stand (shoulder balance)
30 forward horizontal stand (arabesque)
31 rearward horizontal stand
32 trunk-bending sideways
33 trunk-bending forwards
34 arch
35 astride jump (butterfly)
36 tuck jump
37 astride jump
38 pike
39 scissor jump
40 stag jump (stag leap)
41 running step
42 lunge
43 forward pace
44 lying on back
45 prone position
46 lying on side
47 holding arms downwards
48 holding (extending) arms sideways
49 holding arms raised upward
50 holding (extending) arms forward
51 arms held (extended) backward
52 hands clasped behind the head

47
48
49
50
51
1
2
3
4
6
7
8
9
5
52
20
10
11
12
13
21
14
15
22
23
24
16
17
18
19
25
30
31
26
27
28
29
32
33
34
35
36
37
38
41
42
39
40
43
44
45
46

1–11 gymnastics apparatus in men's Olympic gymnastics
1 long horse (horse, vaulting horse)
2 parallel bars
3 bar
4 rings (stationary rings)
5 pommel horse (side horse)
6 pommel
7 horizontal bar (high bar)
8 bar
9 upright
10 stay wires
11 floor (12 m x 12 m floor area)
12–21 auxiliary apparatus and apparatus for school and club gymnastics
12 springboard (Reuther board)
13 landing mat
14 bench
15 box
16 small box
17 buck
18 mattress
19 climbing rope (rope)
20 wall bars
21 window ladder
22–39 positions in relation to the apparatus
22 side, facing
23 side, facing away
24 end, facing
25 end, facing away
26 outside, facing
27 inside, facing
28 front support
29 back support
30 straddle position
31 seated position outside
32 riding seat outside
33 hang
34 reverse hang
35 hang with elbows bent
36 piked reverse hang
37 straight inverted hang
38 straight hang
39 bent hang
40–46 grasps (kinds of grasp)
40 overgrasp on the horizontal bar
41 undergrasp on the horizontal bar
42 combined grasp on the horizontal bar
43 cross grasp on the horizontal bar
44 rotated grasp on the horizontal bar
45 outside grip on the parallel bars
46 rotated grasp on the parallel bars
47 leather handstrap
48–60 exercises
48 long-fly on the horse
49 rise to straddle on the parallel bars
50 crucifix on the rings
51 scissors (scissors movement) on the pommel horse
52 legs raising into a handstand on the floor
53 squat vault on the horse
54 double leg circle on the pommel horse
55 hip circle backwards on the rings
56 lever hang on the rings
57 rearward swing on the parallel bars
58 forward kip into upper arm hang on the parallel bars
59 backward underswing on the horizontal bar
60 backward grand circle on the horizontal bar
61–63 gymnastics kit
61 singlet (vest, *Am.* undershirt)
62 gym trousers
63 gym shoes
64 wristband

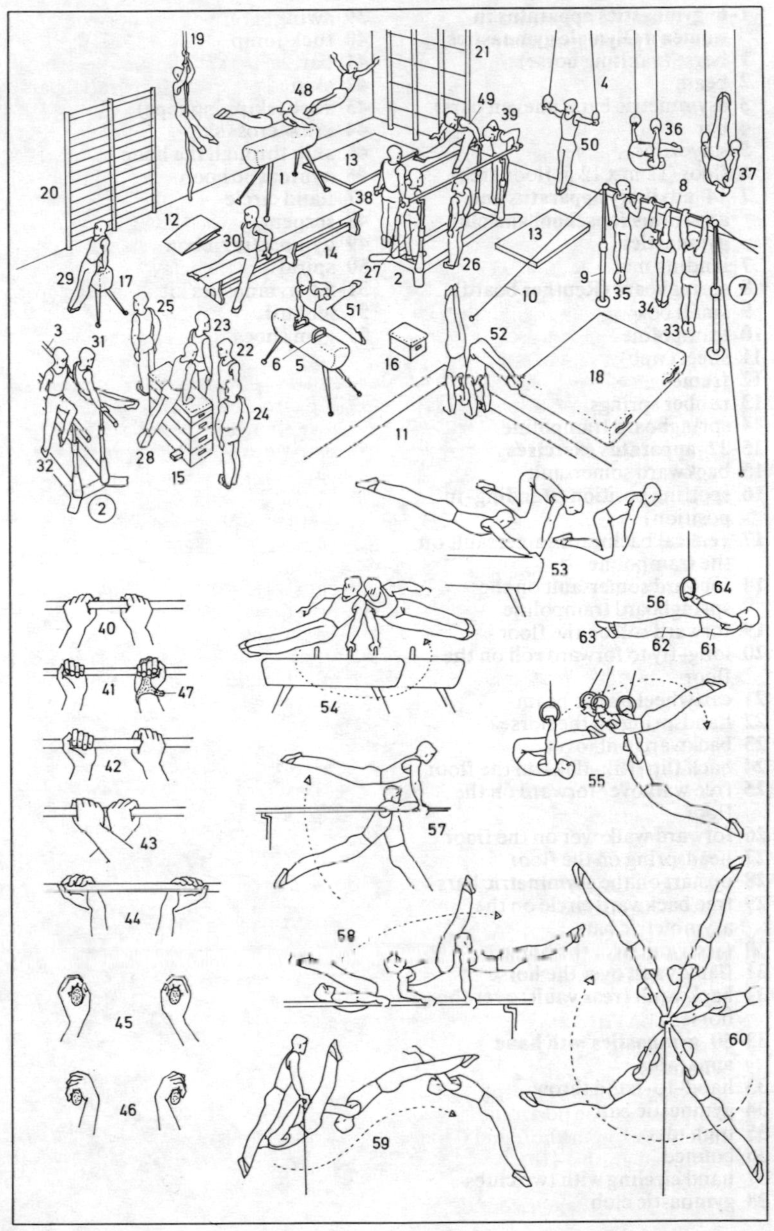
19
21
48
4
49
39
36
37
50
13
1
38
20
8
12
30
14
27
2
26
13
9
29
17
25
7
35
34
10
51
52
33
3
31
23
22
6
5
16
18
24
28
11
32
15
2
53
64
56
40
63
62
61
41
47
54
42
55
57
43
44
58
45
60
46
59

297 Apparatus Gymnastics II (Women's Gymnastics)

1–6 gymnastics apparatus in women's Olympic gymnastics
1 horse (vaulting horse)
2 beam
3 asymmetric bars (uneven bars)
4 bar
5 stay wires
6 floor (12 m x 12 m floor area)
7–14 auxiliary apparatus and apparatus for school and club gymnastics
7 landing mat
8 springboard (Reuther board)
9 small box
10 trampoline
11 sheet (web)
12 frame
13 rubber springs
14 springboard trampoline
15–32 apparatus exercises
15 backward somersault
16 spotting position (standing-in position)
17 vertical backward somersault on the trampoline
18 forward somersault on the springboard trampoline
19 forward roll on the floor
20 long-fly to forward roll on the floor
21 cartwheel on the beam
22 handspring on the horse
23 backward walkover
24 back flip (flik-flak) on the floor
25 free walkover forward on the floor
26 forward walkover on the floor
27 headspring on the floor
28 upstart on the asymmetric bars
29 free backward circle on the asymmetric bars
30 face vault over the horse
31 flank vault over the horse
32 back vault (rear vault) over the horse
33–50 gymnastics with hand apparatus
33 hand-to-hand throw
34 gymnastic ball
35 high toss
36 bounce
37 hand circling with two clubs
38 gymnastic club
39 swing
40 tuck jump
41 bar
42 skip
43 rope (skipping rope)
44 criss-cross skip
45 skip through the hoop
46 gymnastic hoop
47 hand circle
48 serpent
49 gymnastic ribbon
50 spiral
51–52 gymnastics kit
51 leotard
52 gym shoes

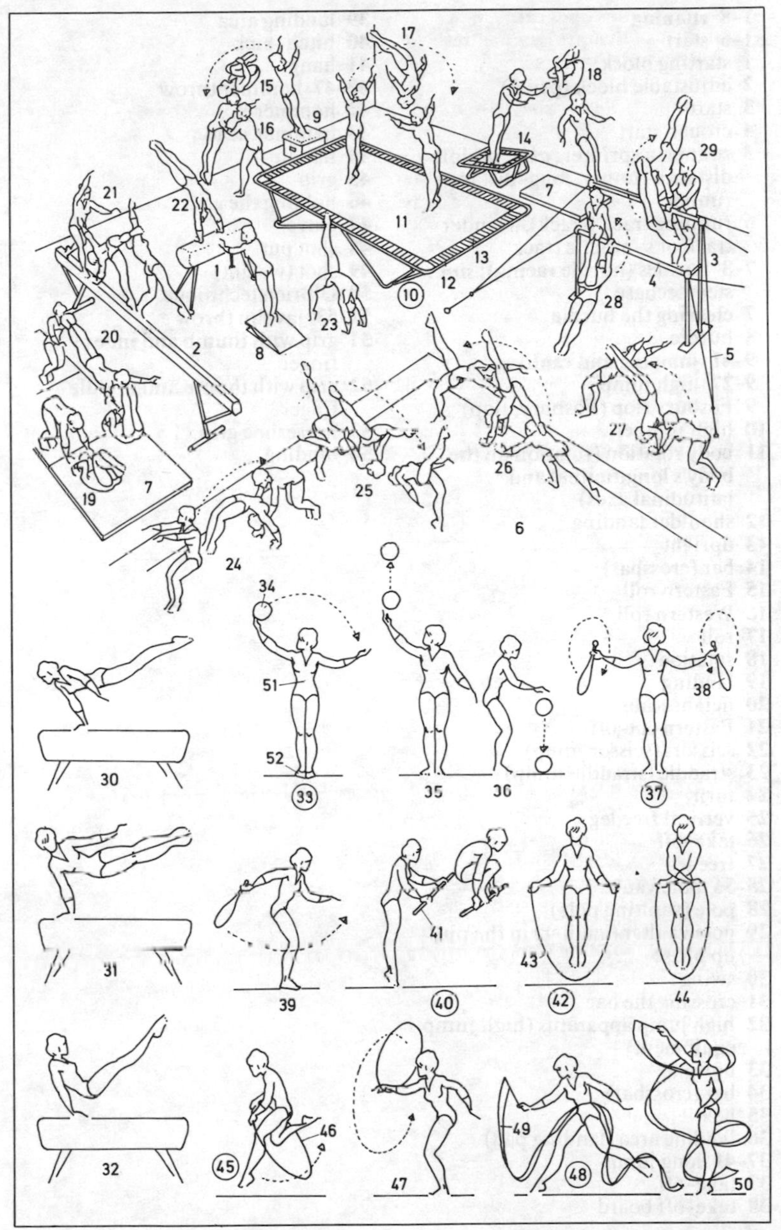
17
15
18
9
16
14
29
21
22
7
11
3
1
13
12
10
4
28
20
2
23
8
5
27
26
25
19
7
6
24
34
51
38
52
30
33
35
36
37
41
43
31
39
40
42
44
49
46
45
47
48
50

1-8 running
1-6 start
1 starting block
2 adjustable block (pedal)
3 start
4 crouch start
5 runner, a sprinter; *also:* middle-distance runner, long-distance runner
6 running track (track), a cinder track or synthetic track
7-8 hurdles (hurdle racing); *sim.:* steeplechase
7 clearing the hurdle
8 hurdle
9-41 jumping and vaulting
9-27 high jump
9 Fosbury flop (Fosbury, flop)
10 high jumper
11 body rotation (rotation on the body's longitudinal and latitudinal axes)
12 shoulder landing
13 upright
14 bar (crossbar)
15 Eastern roll
16 Western roll
17 roll
18 rotation
19 landing
20 height scale
21 Eastern cut-off
22 scissors (scissor jump)
23 straddle (straddle jump)
24 turn
25 vertical free leg
26 take-off
27 free leg
28-36 pole vault
28 pole (vaulting pole)
29 pole vaulter (vaulter) in the pull-up phase
30 swing
31 crossing the bar
32 high jump apparatus (high jump equipment)
33 upright
34 bar (crossbar)
35 box
36 landing area (landing pad)
37-41 long jump
37 take-off
38 take-off board
39 landing area
40 hitch-kick
41 hang
42-47 hammer throw
42 hammer
43 hammer head
44 handle
45 grip
46 holding the grip
47 glove
48 shot put
49 shot (weight)
50 O'Brien technique
51-53 javelin throw
51 grip with thumb and index finger
52 grip with thumb and middle finger
53 horseshoe grip
54 binding

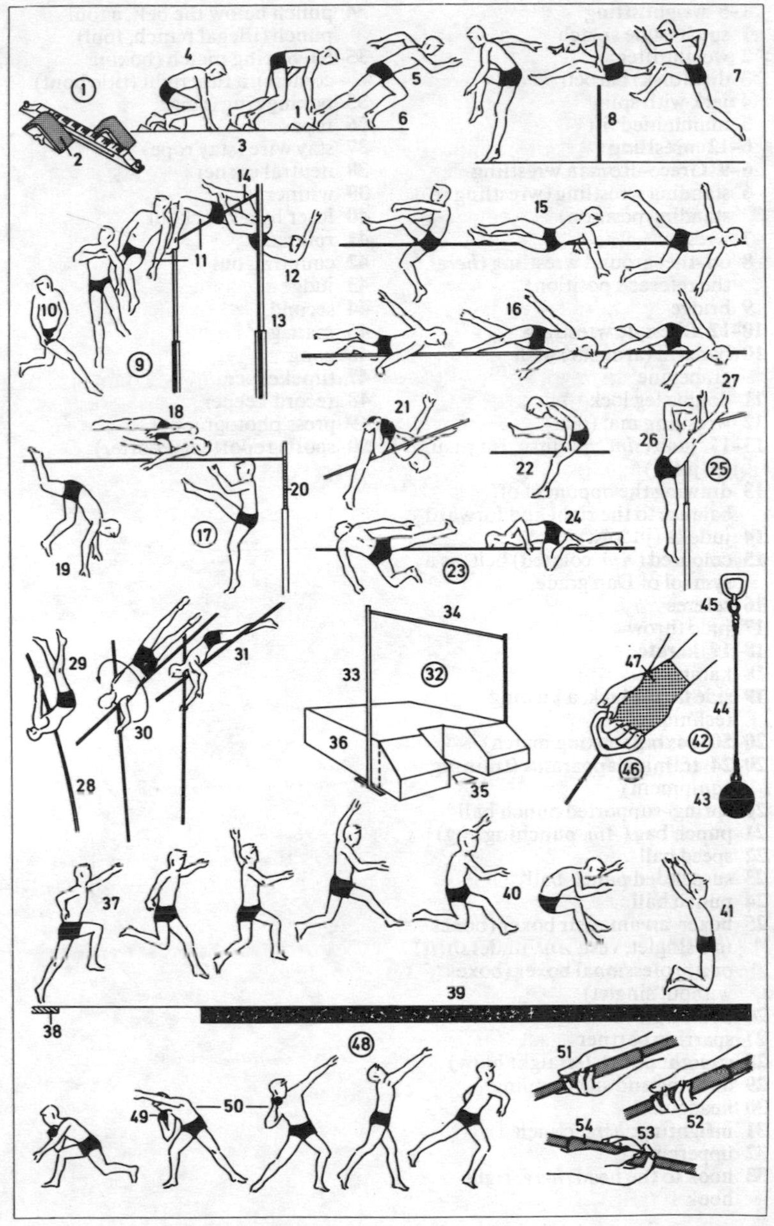
1
2
3
4
1
5
6
8
7
14
11
12
10
9
13
15
16
18
27
21
26
22
25
20
19
17
24
23
45
34
29
31
33
32
47
44
30
36
42
28
46
35
43
37
40
41
39
38
48
51
50
49
52
54
53

299 Weightlifting and Combat Sports

1–5 weightlifting
1 squat–style snatch
2 weightlifter
3 disc (disk) barbell
4 jerk with split
5 maintained lift
6–12 wrestling
6–9 Greco–Roman wrestling
6 standing wrestling (wrestling in standing position)
7 wrestler
8 on–the–ground wrestling (*here:* the referee's position)
9 bridge
10–12 freestyle wrestling
10 bar arm (arm bar) with grapevine
11 double leg lock
12 wrestling mat (mat)
13–17 judo (*sim.:* ju–jitsu, jiu jitsu, ju–jutsu)
13 drawing the opponent off balance to the right and forward
14 judoka (judoist)
15 coloured (*Am.* colored) belt, as a symbol of Dan grade
16 referee
17 judo throw
18–19 karate
18 karateka
19 side thrust kick, a kicking technique
20–50 boxing (boxing match)
20–24 training apparatus (training equipment)
20 spring–supported punch ball
21 punch bag (*Am.* punching bag)
22 speed ball
23 suspended punch ball
24 punch ball
25 boxer, an amateur boxer (boxes in a singlet, vest, *Am.* undershirt) or a professional boxer (boxes without singlet)
26 boxing glove
27 sparring partner
28 straight punch (straight blow)
29 ducking and sidestepping
30 headguard
31 infighting; *here:* clinch
32 uppercut
33 hook to the head; *here:* right hook
34 punch below the belt, a foul punch (illegal punch, foul)
35–50 boxing match (boxing contest), a title fight (title bout)
35 boxing ring (ring)
36 ropes
37 stay wire (stay rope)
38 neutral corner
39 winner
40 loser by a knockout
41 referee
42 counting out
43 judge
44 second
45 manager
46 gong
47 timekeeper
48 record keeper
49 press photographer
50 sports reporter (reporter)

1
2
3
4
5
6
7
8
9
10
11
12
13
14
15
16
17
18
19
20
21
22
23
24
25
26
27
28
29
30
31
32
33
34
35
36
37
38
39
40
41
42
43
44
45
46
47
48
49
50

1–57 mountaineering (mountain climbing, Alpinism)
1 hut (Alpine Club hut, mountain hut, base)
2–13 climbing (rock climbing) [rock climbing technique]
2 rock face (rock wall)
3 fissure (vertical, horizontal, or diagonal fissure)
4 ledge (rock ledge, grass ledge, scree ledge, snow ledge, ice ledge)
5 mountaineer (climber, mountain climber, Alpinist)
6 anorak (high-altitude anorak, snowshirt, padded jacket)
7 breeches (climbing breeches)
8 chimney
9 belay (spike, rock spike)
10 belay
11 rope sling (sling)
12 rope
13 spur
14–21 snow and ice climbing [snow and ice climbing technique]
14 ice slope (firn slope)
15 snow and ice climber
16 ice axe (*Am.* ax)
17 step (ice step)
18 snow goggles
19 hood (anorak hood)
20 cornice (snow cornice)
21 ridge (ice ridge)
22–27 rope (roped party)
22 glacier
23 crevasse
24 snow bridge
25 leader
26 second man (belayer)
27 third man (non-belayer)
28–30 roping down (abseiling, rapelling)
28 abseil sling
29 sling seat
30 Dülfer seat
31–57 mountaineering equipment (climbing equipment, snow and ice climbing equipment)
31 ice axe (*Am.* ax)
32 wrist sling
33 pick
34 adze (*Am.* adz)
35 karabiner hole
36 short-shafted ice axe (*Am.* ax)
37 hammer axe (*Am.* ax)
38 general-purpose piton
39 abseil piton (ringed piton)
40 ice piton (semi-tubular screw ice piton, corkscrew piton)
41 drive-in ice piton
42 mountaineering boot
43 corrugated sole
44 climbing boot
45 roughened stiff rubber upper
46 karabiner
47 screwgate
48 crampons (lightweight crampons, twelve-point crampons, ten-point crampons)
49 front points
50 point guards
51 crampon strap
52 crampon cable fastener
53 safety helmet (protective helmet)
54 helmet lamp
55 snow gaiters
56 climbing harness
57 sit harness

20
21
12
8
13
10
9
11
28
30
6
19
18
5
14
7
2
2
15
4
16
29
3
17
1
27
22
26
25
56
24
53
49
54
57
23
48
40
46
51
33
35
34
38
47
50
32
42
43
55
31
41
36
39
31
44
52
37
45

301 Winter Sports I (Skiing)

1–72 skiing
1 compact ski
2 safety binding (release binding)
3 strap
4 steel edge
5 ski stick (ski pole)
6 grip
7 loop
8 basket
9 ladies' one-piece ski suit
10 skiing cap (ski cap)
11 skiing goggles
12 cemented sole skiing boot
13 crash helmet
14–20 cross-country equipment
14 cross-country ski
15 cross-country rat trap binding
16 cross-country boot
17 cross-country gear
18 peaked cap
19 sunglasses
20 cross-country poles made of bamboo
21–24 ski-waxing equipment
21 ski wax
22 waxing iron (blowlamp, blowtorch)
23 waxing cork
24 wax scraper
25 downhill racing pole
26 herringbone, for climbing a slope
27 sidestep, for climbing a slope
28 ski bag
29 slalom
30 gate pole
31 racing suit
32 downhill racing
33 'egg' position, the ideal downhill racing position
34 downhill ski
35 ski jumping
36 lean forward
37 number
38 ski jumping ski
39 grooves (3 to 5 grooves)
40 cable binding
41 ski jumping boots
42 cross-country
43 cross-country stretch-suit
44 course
45 course-marking flag
46 layers of a modern ski
47 special core
48 laminates
49 stabilizing layer (stabilizer)
50 steel edge
51 aluminium (*Am.* aluminum) upper edge
52 synthetic bottom (artificial bottom)
53 safety jet
54–56 parts of the binding
54 automatic heel unit
55 toe unit
56 ski stop
57–63 ski lift
57 double chair lift
58 safety bar with footrest
59 ski lift
60 track
61 hook
62 automatic cable pulley
63 haulage cable
64 slalom
65 open gate
66 closed vertical gate
67 open vertical gate
68 transversal chicane
69 hairpin
70 elbow
71 corridor
72 Allais chicane

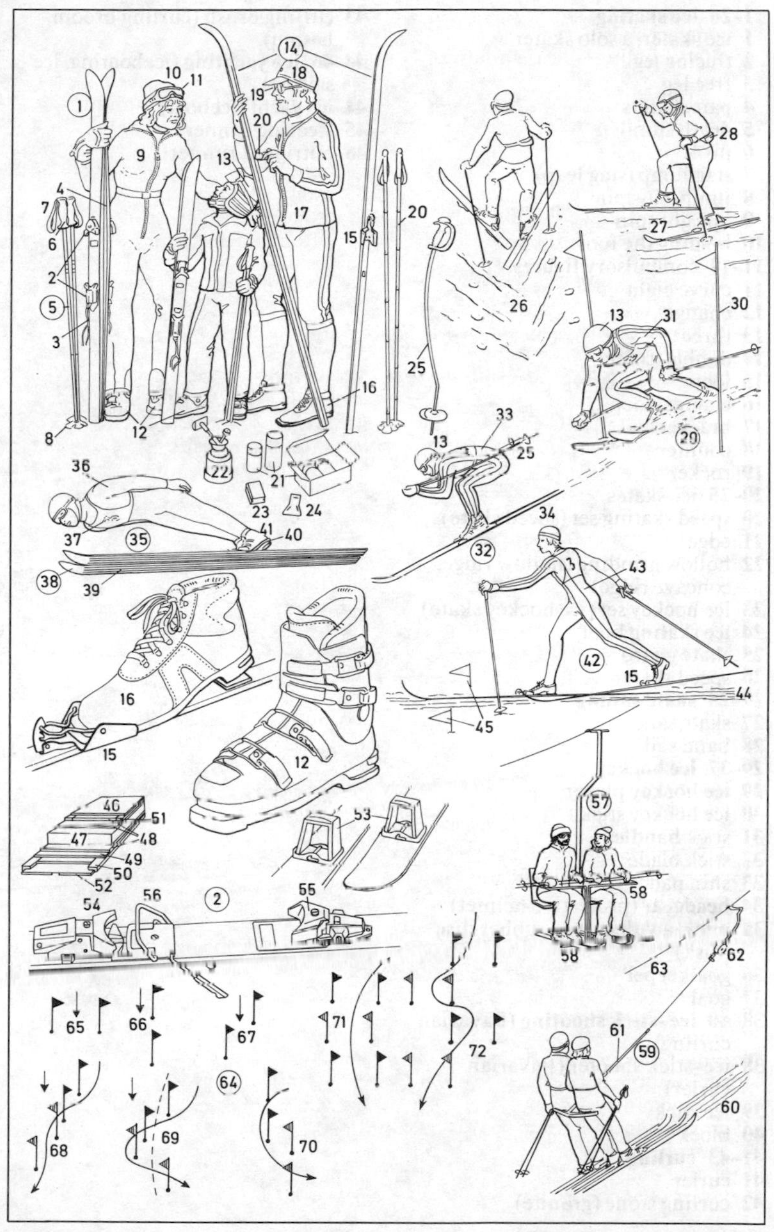

302 Winter Sports II

1–26 ice skating
1 ice skater, a solo skater
2 tracing leg
3 free leg
4 pair skaters
5 death spiral
6 pivot
7 stag jump (stag leap)
8 jump–sit–spin
9 upright spin
10 holding the foot
11–19 compulsory figures
11 curve eight
12 change
13 three
14 double–three
15 loop
16 change–loop
17 bracket
18 counter
19 rocker
20–25 ice skates
20 speed skating set (speed skate)
21 edge
22 hollow grinding (hollow ridge, concave ridge)
23 ice hockey set (ice hockey skate)
24 ice skating boot
25 skate guard
26 speed skater
27–28 skate sailing
27 skate sailor
28 hand sail
29–37 ice hockey
29 ice hockey player
30 ice hockey stick
31 stick handle
32 stick blade
33 shin pad
34 headgear (protective helmet)
35 puck, a vulcanized rubber disc (disk)
36 goalkeeper
37 goal
38–40 ice–stick shooting (Bavarian curling)
38 ice–stick shooter (Bavarian curler)
39 ice stick
40 block
41–43 curling
41 curler
42 curling stone (granite)
43 curling brush (curling broom, besom)
44–46 ice yachting (iceboating, ice sailing)
44 ice yacht (iceboat)
45 steering runner
46 outrigged runner

1
2
3
4
5
6
7
8
9
10
11
12
13
14
15
16
17
18
19
20
21
22
23
24
25
26
27
28
29
30
31
32
33
34
35
36
37
38
39
40
41
42
43
44
45
46

303 Winter Sports III

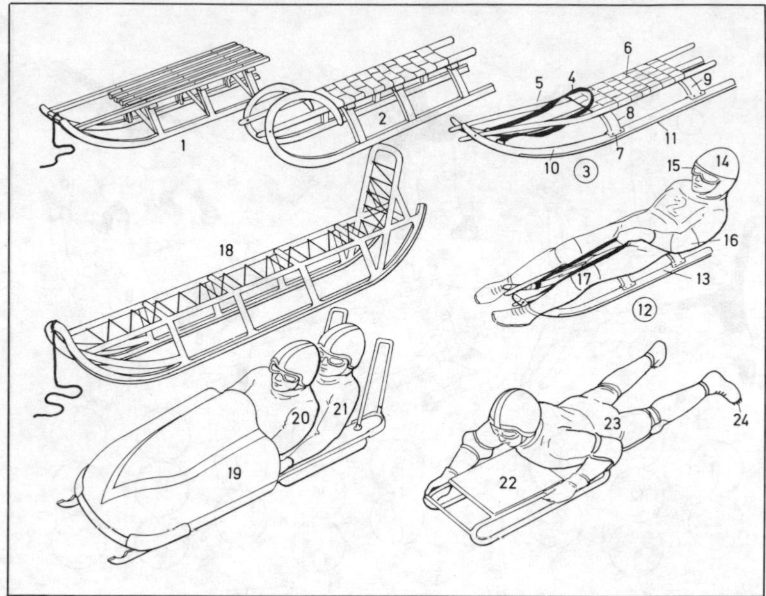

1 toboggan (sledge, *Am.* sled)
2 toboggan (sledge, *Am.* sled) with seat of plaid straps
3 junior luge toboggan (junior luge, junior toboggan)
4 rein
5 bar (strut)
6 seat
7 bracket
8 front prop
9 rear prop
10 movable runner
11 metal face
12 luge tobogganer
13 luge toboggan (luge, toboggan)
14 crash helmet
15 goggles
16 elbow pad
17 knee pad
18 Nansen sledge, a polar sledge
19–21 bobsleigh (bobsledding)
19 bobsleigh (bobsled), a two-man bobsleigh (a boblet)
20 steersman
21 brakeman
22–24 skeleton tobogganing (Cresta tobogganing)
22 skeleton (skeleton toboggan)
23 skeleton rider
24 rake, for braking and steering

1 avalanche (snow avalanche, *Am.* snowslide); *kinds:* wind avalanche, ground avalanche
2 avalanche wall, a deflecting wall (diverting wall); *sim.:* avalanche wedge
3 avalanche gallery
4 snowfall
5 snowdrift
6 snow fence
7 avalanche forest [planted as protection against avalanches]
8 street-cleaning lorry (street cleaner)
9 snow plough (*Am.* snowplow) attachment
10 snow chain (skid chain, tyre chain, *Am.* tire chain)
11 radiator bonnet (*Am.* radiator hood)
12 radiator shutter and shutter opening (louvre shutter)
13 snowman
14 snowball fight
15 snowball
16 ski bob
17 slide
18 boy, sliding
19 icy surface (icy ground)
20 snow-covered roof
21 icicle
22 man clearing snow
23 snow push (snow shovel)
24 heap of snow
25 horse-drawn sleigh (horse sleigh)
26 sleigh bells (bells, set of bells)
27 foot muff (*Am.* foot bag)
28 earmuff
29 handsledge (tread sledge); *sim.:* push sledge
30 slush

1-13 skittles
1-11 skittle frame
1 front pin (front)
2 left front second pin (left front second)
3 running three [left]
4 right front second pin (right front second)
5 running three [right]
6 left corner pin (left corner), a corner (copper)
7 landlord
8 right corner pin (right corner), a corner (copper)
9 back left second pin (back left second)
10 back right second pin (back right second)
11 back pin (back)
12 pin
13 landlord
14-20 tenpin bowling
14 frame
15 bowling ball (ball with finger holes)
16 finger hole
17-20 deliveries
17 straight ball
18 hook ball (hook)
19 curve
20 back-up ball (back-up)
21 boules; *sim.:* Italian game of boccie, green bowls (bowls)
22 boules player
23 jack (target jack)
24 grooved boule
25 group of players
26 rifle shooting
27-29 shooting positions
27 standing position
28 kneeling position
29 prone position
30-33 targets
30 target for 50 m events (50 m target)
31 circle
32 target for 100 m events (100 m target)
33 bobbing target (turning target, running-boar target)
34-39 ammunition
34 air rifle cartridge
35 rimfire cartridge for zimmerstutzen (indoor target rifle), a smallbore German single-shot rifle
36 case head
37 caseless round
38 .22 long rifle cartridge
39 .222 Remington cartridge
40-49 sporting rifles
40 air rifle
41 optical sight
42 front sight (foresight)
43 smallbore standard rifle
44 international smallbore free rifle
45 palm rest for standing position
46 butt plate with hook
47 butt with thumb hole
48 smallbore rifle for bobbing target (turning target)
49 telescopic sight (riflescope, telescope sight)
50 optical ring sight
51 optical ring and bead sight
52-66 archery (target archery)
52 shot
53 archer
54 competition bow
55 riser
56 point-of-aim mark
57 grip (handle)
58 stabilizer
59 bow string (string)
60 arrow
61 pile (point) of the arrow
62 fletching
63 nock
64 shaft
65 cresting
66 target
67 Basque game of pelota (jai alai)
68 pelota player
69 wicker basket (cesta)
70-78 skeet (skeet shooting), a kind of clay pigeon shooting
70 skeet over-and-under shotgun
71 muzzle with skeet choke
72 ready position on call
73 firing position
74 shooting range
75 high house
76 low house
77 target's path
78 shooting station (shooting box)
79 aero wheel
80 handle
81 footrest
82 go-karting (karting)
83 go-kart (kart)
84 number plate (number)
85 pedals
86 pneumatic tyre (*Am.* tire)
87 petrol tank (*Am.* gasoline tank)
88 frame
89 steering wheel
90 bucket seat
91 protective bulkhead
92 two-stroke engine
93 silencer (*Am.* muffler)

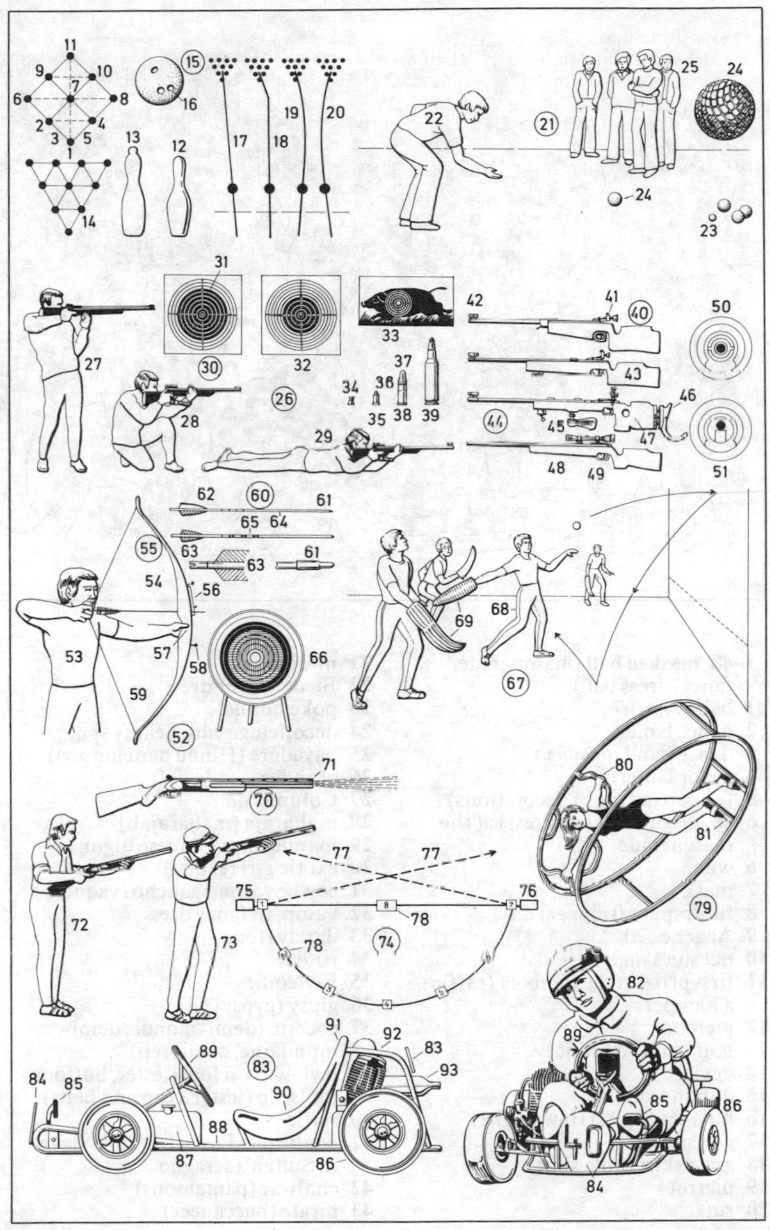

1–48 masked ball (masquerade, fancy-dress ball)
1 ballroom
2 dance band
3 dance band musician
4 paper lantern
5 festoon (string of decorations)
6–48 disguise (fancy dress) at the masquerade
6 witch
7 mask
8 fur trapper (trapper)
9 Apache girl
10 net stocking
11 first prize in the tombola (raffle), a hamper
12 pierette
13 half mask (domino)
14 devil
15 domino
16 hula-hula girl (Hawaii girl)
17 garland
18 grass skirt (hula skirt)
19 pierrot
20 ruff
21 midinette
22 Biedermeier dress
23 poke bonnet
24 décolletage with beauty spot
25 bayadère (Hindu dancing girl)
26 grandee
27 Columbine
28 maharaja (maharajah)
29 mandarin, a Chinese dignitary
30 exotic girl (exotic)
31 cowboy; *sim.:* gaucho (vaquero)
32 vamp, in fancy dress
33 dandy (fop)
34 rosette
35 harlequin
36 gipsy (gypsy) girl
37 cocotte (demi-monde, demi-mondaine, demi-rep)
38 owl-glass, a fool (jester, buffoon)
39 foolscap (jester's cap and bells)
40 rattle
41 odalisque, Eastern female slave in Sultan's seraglio
42 chalwar (pantaloons)
43 pirate (buccaneer)

44 tattoo
45 paper hat
46 false nose
47 clapper (rattle)
48 slapstick
49–54 fireworks
49 percussion cap
50 cracker
51 banger
52 jumping jack
53 cannon cracker (maroon, marroon)
54 rocket
55 paper ball
56 jack-in-the-box
57–70 carnival procession
57 carnival float (carnival truck)
58 King Carnival
59 bauble (fool's sceptre, *Am.* scepter)
60 fool's badge
61 Queen Carnival
62 confetti
63 giant
64 beauty queen
65 fairy-tale figure
66 paper streamer
67 majorette
68 king's guard
69 buffoon, a clown
70 lansquenet's drum

307 Circus

1–63 travelling (*Am.* traveling) circus
1 circus tent (big top), a four-pole tent
2 tent pole
3 spotlight
4 lighting technician
5 trapeze platform
6 trapeze
7 trapeze artist
8 rope ladder
9 bandstand
10 circus band
11 ring entrance (arena entrance)
12 wings
13 tent prop (prop)
14 safety net
15 seats for the spectators
16 circus box
17 circus manager
18 agent
19 entrance and exit
20 steps
21 ring (arena)
22 ring fence
23 musical clown (clown)
24 clown
25 comic turn (clown act), a circus act
26 circus riders (bareback riders)
27 ring attendant, a circus attendant
28 pyramid
29 support
30–31 performance by liberty horses
30 circus horse, performing the levade (pesade)
31 ringmaster
32 vaulter
33 emergency exit
34 caravan (circus caravan, *Am.* trailer)
35 springboard acrobat (springboard artist)
36 springboard
37 knife thrower
38 circus marksman
39 assistant
40 tightrope dancer
41 tightrope

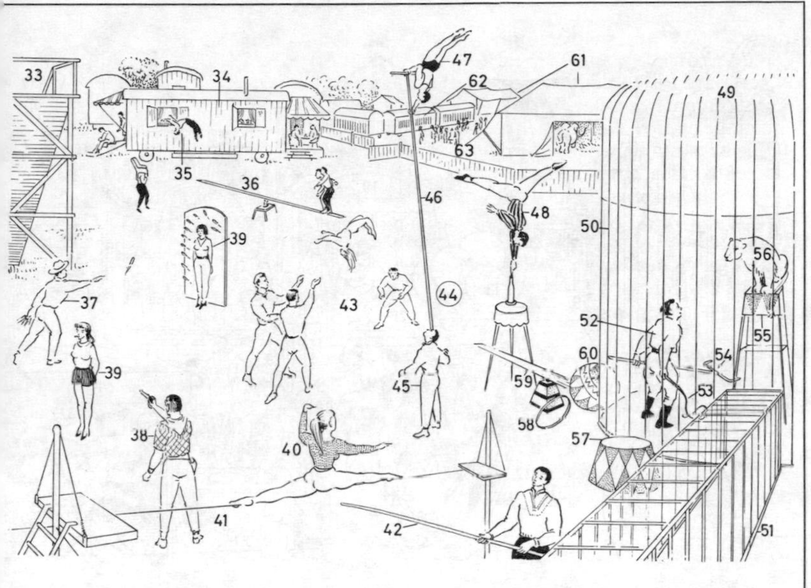

42 balancing pole
43 throwing act
44 balancing act
45 support
46 pole (bamboo pole)
47 acrobat
48 equilibrist (balancer)
49 wild animal cage, a round cage
50 bars of the cage
51 passage (barred passage, passage for the wild animals)
52 tamer (wild animal tamer)
53 whip
54 fork
55 pedestal
56 wild animal (tiger, lion)
57 stand
58 hoop (jumping hoop)
59 seesaw
60 ball
61 camp
62 cage caravan
63 menagerie

308 Fair, Fairground

1–69 fair (annual fair)
1 fairground
2 children's merry-go-round, (whirligig), a roundabout (*Am.* carousel)
3 refreshment stall (drinks stall)
4 chairoplane
5 up-and-down roundabout
6 show booth (booth)
7 box (box office)
8 barker
9 medium
10 showman
11 try-your-strength machine
12 hawker
13 balloon
14 paper serpent
15 windmill
16 pickpocket (thief)
17 vendor
18 Turkish delight
19 freak show
20 giant
21 fat lady
22 dwarfs (midgets)
23 beer marquee
24 sideshow
25–28 travelling (*Am.* traveling) artistes (travelling show people)
25 fire eater
26 sword swallower
27 strong man
28 escapologist
29 spectators
30 ice-cream vendor (ice-cream man)
31 ice-cream cornet
32 hot-dog stand
33 grill (*Am.* broiler)
34 hot dog
35 sausage tongs
36 fortune teller
37 big wheel (Ferris wheel)
38 orchestrion (automatic organ)
39 scenic railway (switchback)
40 toboggan slide (chute)
41 swing boats
42 swing boat, turning full circle
43 full circle
44 lottery booth (tombola booth)

45 wheel of fortune
46 devil's wheel (typhoon wheel)
47 throwing ring (quoit)
48 prizes
49 sandwich man on stilts
50 sandwich board (placard)
51 cigarette seller, an itinerant trader (a hawker)
52 tray
53 fruit stall
54 wall-of-death rider
55 hall of mirrors
56 concave mirror
57 convex mirror
58 shooting gallery
59 hippodrome
60 junk stalls (second-hand stalls)
61 first aid tent (first aid post)
62 dodgems (bumper cars)
63 dodgem car (bumper car)
64–66 pottery stand
64 barker
65 market woman
66 pottery
67 visitors to the fair
68 waxworks
69 wax figure

309 Flea Market

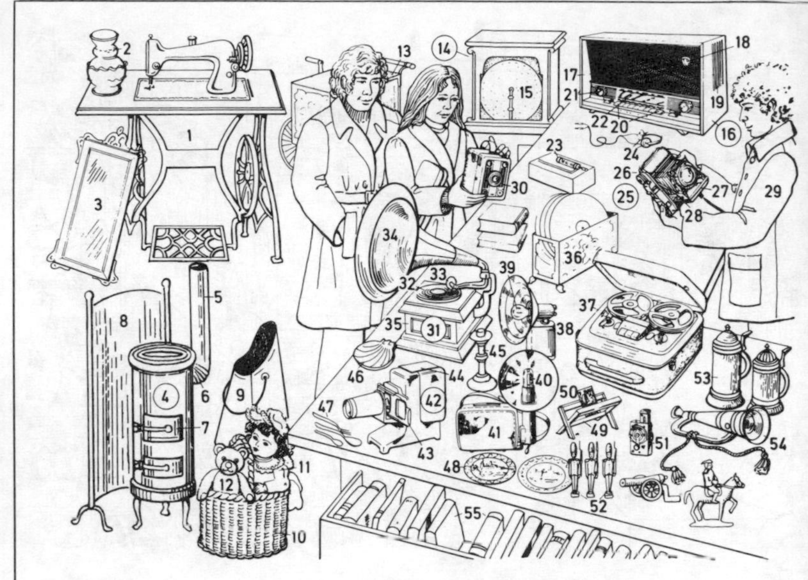

1 treadle sewing machine
2 flower vase
3 wall mirror
4 cylindrical stove
5 stovepipe
6 stovepipe elbow
7 stove door
8 stove screen
9 coal scuttle
10 firewood basket
11 doll
12 teddy bear
13 barrel organ
14 orchestrion
15 metal disc (disk)
16 radio (radio set, *joc.:* 'steam radio'), a superheterodyne (superhet)
17 baffle board
18 'magic eye', a tuning indicator valve
19 loudspeaker aperture
20 station selector buttons (station preset buttons)
21 tuning knob
22 frequency bands
23 crystal detector (crystal set)
24 headphones (headset)
25 folding camera
26 bellows
27 hinged cover
28 spring extension
29 salesman
30 box camera
31 gramophone
32 record (gramophone record)
33 needle head with gramophone needle
34 horn
35 gramophone box
36 record rack
37 portable tape recorder
38 flashgun
39 flash bulb
40–41 electronic flash (electronic flashgun)
40 flash head
41 accumulator
42 slide projector
43 slide holder

44 lamphouse
45 candlestick
46 scallop shell
47 cutlery
48 souvenir plate
49 drying rack for photographic plates
50 photographic plate
51 delayed-action release
52 tin soldiers (*sim.*: lead soldiers)
53 beer mug (stein)
54 bugle
55 second-hand books
56 grandfather clock
57 clock case
58 pendulum
59 time weight
60 striking weight
61 rocking chair
62 sailor suit
63 sailor's hat
64 washing set
65 washing basin
66 water jug
67 washstand
68 dolly
69 washtub
70 washboard
71 humming top
72 slate
73 pencil box
74 adding machine
75 paper roll
76 number keys
77 abacus
78 inkwell, with lid
79 typewriter
80 [hand-operated] calculating machine (calculator)
81 operating handle
82 result register (product register)
83 rotary counting mechanism (rotary counter)
84 kitchen scales
85 waist slip (underskirt)
86 wooden handcart
87 wall clock
88 bed warmer
89 milk churn

1-13 film studios (studio complex, *Am.* movie studios)
1 lot (studio lot)
2 processing laboratories (film laboratories, motion picture laboratories)
3 cutting rooms
4 administration building (office building, offices)
5 film (motion picture) storage vault (film library, motion picture library)
6 workshop
7 film set (*Am.* movie set)
8 power house
9 technical and research laboratories
10 groups of stages
11 concrete tank for marine sequences
12 cyclorama
13 hill
14-60 shooting (filming)
14 music recording studio (music recording theatre, *Am.* theater)
15 'acoustic' wall lining
16 screen (projection screen)
17 film orchestra
18 exterior shooting (outdoor shooting, exterior filming, outdoor filming)
19 camera with crystal-controlled drive
20 cameraman
21 assistant director
22 boom operator (boom swinger)
23 recording engineer (sound recordist)
24 portable sound recorder with crystal-controlled drive
25 microphone boom
26-60 shooting (filming) in the studio (on the sound stage, on the stage, in the filming hall)
26 production manager
27 leading lady (film actress, film star, star)
28 leading man (film actor, film star, star)
29 film extra (extra)
30 arrangement of microphones for stereo and sound effects

31 studio microphone
32 microphone cable
33 side flats and background
34 clapper boy
35 clapper board (clapper) with slates (boards) for the film title, shot number (scene number), and take number
36 make-up artist (hairstylist)
37 lighting electrician (studio electrician, lighting man, *Am.* gaffer)
38 diffusing screen
39 continuity girl (script girl)
40 film director (director)
41 cameraman (first cameraman)
42 camera operator, an assistant cameraman (camera assistant)
43 set designer (art director)
44 director of photography
45 filmscript (script, shooting script, *Am.* movie script)
46 assistant director
47 soundproof film camera (soundproof motion picture camera), a wide screen camera (cinemascope camera)
48 soundproof housing (soundproof cover, blimp)
49 camera crane (dolly)
50 hydraulic stand
51 mask (screen) for protection from spill light (gobo, nigger)
52 tripod spotlight (fill-in light, filler light, fill light, filler)
53 spotlight catwalk
54 recording room
55 recording engineer (sound recordist)
56 mixing console (mixing desk)
57 sound assistant (assistant sound engineer)
58 magnetic sound recording equipment (magnetic sound recorder)
59 amplifier and special effects equipment, e.g. for echo and sound effects
60 sound recording camera (optical sound recorder)

311 Films (Motion Pictures) II

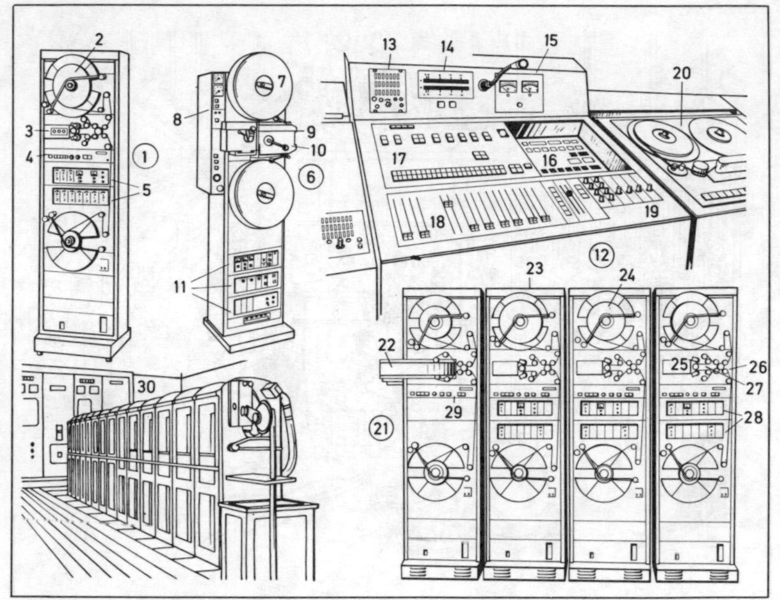

1–46 sound recording and re-recording (dubbing)
1 magnetic sound recording equipment (magnetic sound recorder)
2 magnetic film spool
3 magnetic head support assembly
4 control panel
5 magnetic sound recording and playback amplifier
6 optical sound recorder (sound recording camera, optical sound recording equipment)
7 daylight film magazine
8 control and monitoring panel
9 eyepiece for visual control of optical sound recording
10 deck
11 recording amplifier and mains power unit
12 control desk (control console)
13 monitoring loudspeaker (control loudspeaker)
14 recording level indicators
15 monitoring instruments
16 jack panel
17 control panel
18 sliding control
19 equalizer
20 magnetic sound deck
21 mixer for magnetic film
22 film projector
23 recording and playback equipment
24 film reel (film spool)
25 head support assembly for the recording head, playback head, and erasing head (erase head)
26 film transport mechanism
27 synchronizing filter
28 magnetic sound amplifier
29 control panel
30 film-processing machines (film-developing machines) in the processing laboratory (film laboratory, motion picture laboratory)
31 echo chamber
32 echo chamber loudspeaker
33 echo chamber microphone

34–36 sound mixing (sound dubbing, mixing of several sound tracks)
34 mixing room (dubbing room)
35 mixing console (mixing desk) for mono or stereo sound
36 dubbing mixers (recording engineers, sound recordists) dubbing (mixing)
37–41 synchronization (syncing, dubbing, post-synchronization, post-syncing)
37 dubbing studio (dubbing theatre, *Am.* theater)
38 dubbing director
39 dubbing speaker (dubbing actress)
40 boom microphone
41 microphone cable

42–46 cutting (editing)
42 cutting table (editing table, cutting bench)
43 film editor (cutter)
44 film turntable, for picture and sound tracks
45 projection of the picture
46 loudspeaker

1–23 film projection (motion picture projection)
1 cinema (picture house, *Am.* movie theater, movie house)
2 cinema box office (*Am.* movie theater box office)
3 cinema ticket (*Am.* movie theater ticket)
4 usherette
5 cinemagoers (filmgoers, cinema audience, *Am.* moviegoers, movie audience)
6 safety lighting (emergency lighting)
7 emergency exit
8 stage
9 rows of seats (rows)
10 stage curtain (screen curtain)
11 screen (projection screen)
12 projection room (projection booth)
13 lefthand projector
14 righthand projector
15 projection room window with projection window and observation port
16 reel drum (spool box)
17 house light dimmers (auditorium lighting control)
18 rectifier, a selenium or mercury vapour rectifier for the projection lamps
19 amplifier
20 projectionist
21 rewind bench for rewinding the film
22 film cement (splicing cement)
23 slide projector for advertisements
24–52 film projectors
24 sound projector (film projector, cinema projector, theatre projector, *Am.* movie projector)
25–38 projector mechanism
25 fireproof reel drums (spool boxes) with circulating oil cooling system
26 feed sprocket (supply sprocket)
27 take-up sprocket
28 magnetic head cluster
29 guide roller (guiding roller) with framing control

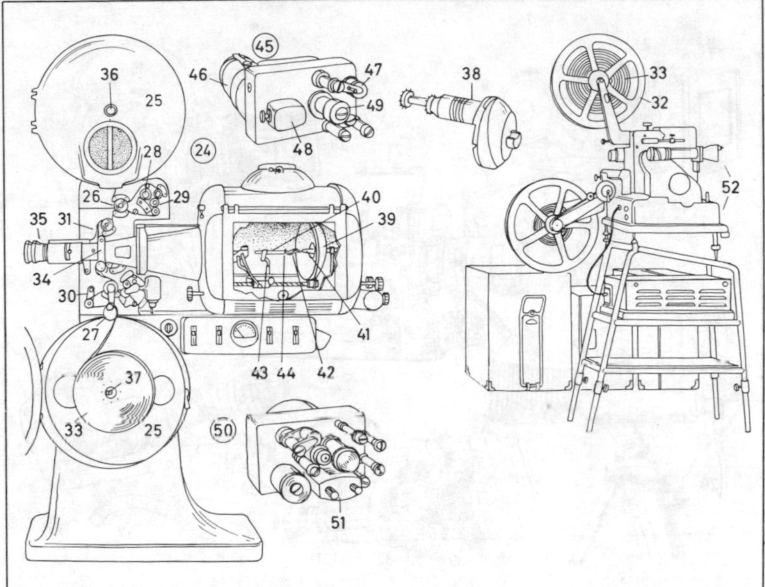

30 loop former for smoothing out the intermittent movement; *also:* film break detector
31 film path
32 film reel (film spool)
33 reel of film
34 film gate (picture gate, projector gate) with cooling fan
35 projection lens (projector lens)
36 feed spindle
37 take-up spindle with friction drive
38 maltese cross mechanism (maltese cross movement, Geneva movement)
39-44 lamphouse
39 mirror arc lamp, with aspherical (non-spherical) concave mirror and blowout magnet for stabilizing the arc (*also:* high-pressure xenon arc lamp)
40 positive carbon (positive carbon rod)
41 negative carbon (negative carbon rod)
42 arc
43 carbon rod holder
44 crater (carbon crater)
45 optical sound unit [also designed for multi-channel optical stereophonic sound and for push-pull sound tracks]
46 sound optics
47 sound head
48 exciter lamp in housing
49 photocell in hollow drum
50 attachable four-track magnetic sound unit (penthouse head, magnetic sound head)
51 four-track magnetic head
52 narrow gauge (*Am.* narrow-gage) cinema projector for mobile cinema

313 Films (Motion Pictures) IV

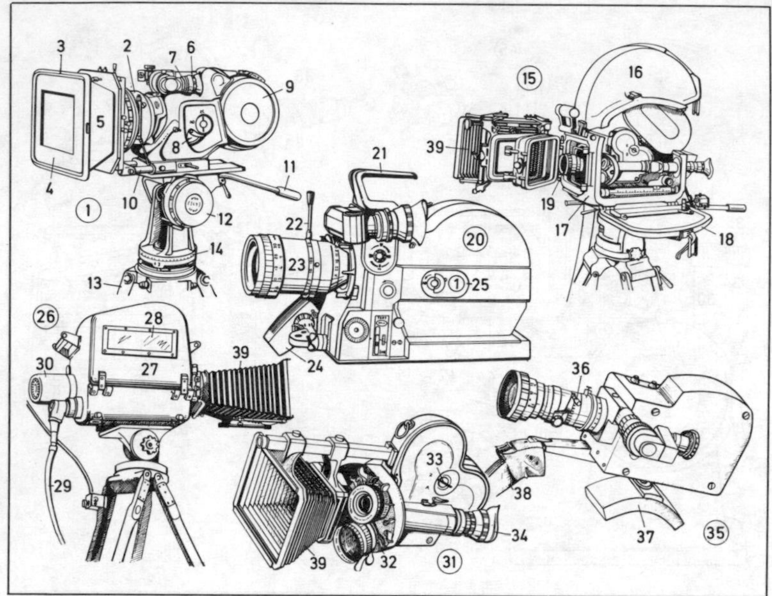

1-39 motion picture cameras (film cameras)
1 standard-gauge (*Am.* standard-gage) motion picture camera (standard-gauge, *Am.* standard-gage, 35 mm camera)
2 lens (object lens, taking lens)
3 lens hood (sunshade) with matte box
4 matte (mask)
5 lens hood barrel
6 viewfinder eyepiece
7 eyepiece control ring
8 opening control for the segment disc (disk) shutter
9 magazine housing
10 slide bar for the lens hood
11 control arm (control lever)
12 pan and tilt head
13 wooden tripod
14 degree scale
15 soundproof (blimped) motion picture camera (film camera)
16-18 soundproof housing (blimp)
16 upper section of the soundproof housing
17 lower section of the soundproof housing
18 open sidewall of the soundproof housing
19 camera lens
20 lightweight professional motion picture camera
21 grip (handgrip)
22 zooming lever
23 zoom lens (variable focus lens, varifocal lens) with infinitely variable focus
24 handgrip with shutter release
25 camera door
26 sound camera (newsreel camera) for recording sound and picture
27 soundproof housing (blimp)
28 window for the frame counters and indicator scales
29 pilot tone cable (sync pulse cable)
30 pilot tone generator (signal generator, pulse generator)
31 professional narrow-gauge (*Am.* narrow-gage) motion picture camera, a 16 mm camera
32 lens turret (turret head)
33 housing lock
34 eyecup
35 high-speed camera, a special narrow-gauge (*Am.* narrow-gage) camera
36 zooming lever
37 rifle grip
38 handgrip with shutter release
39 lens hood bellows

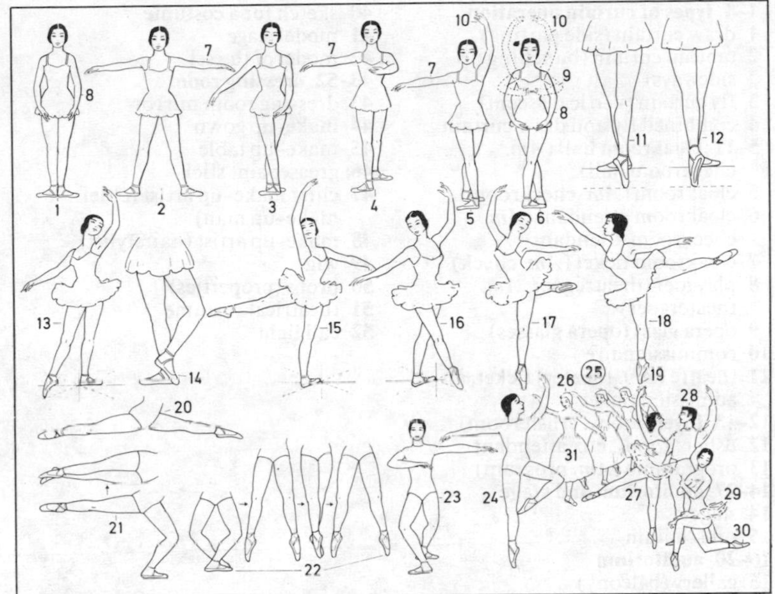

1–6 the five positions (ballet positions)
1 first position
2 second position
3 third position
4 fourth position [open]
5 fourth position [crossed; extended fifth position]
6 fifth position
7–10 ports de bras (arm positions)
7 port de bras à coté
8 port de bras en bas
9 port de bras en avant
10 port de bras en haut
11 dégagé à la quatrième devant
12 dégagé à la quatrième derrière
13 effacé
14 sur le cou-de-pied
15 écarté
16 croisé
17 attitude
18 arabesque
19 à pointe (on full point)
20 splits
21 cabriole (capriole)
22 entrechat (entrechat quatre)
23 préparation [e.g. for a pirouette]
24 pirouette
25 corps de ballet
26 ballet dancer (ballerina)
27–28 pas de trois
27 prima ballerina
28 principal male dancer (leading soloist)
29 tutu
30 point shoe, a ballet shoe (ballet slipper)
31 ballet skirt

315 Theatre (*Am.* Theater) I

1–4 types of curtain operation
1 draw curtain (side parting)
2 tableau curtain (bunching up sideways)
3 fly curtain (vertical ascent)
4 combined fly and draw curtain
5–11 cloakroom hall (*Am.* checkroom hall)
5 cloakroom (*Am.* checkroom)
6 cloakroom attendant (*Am.* checkroom attendant)
7 cloakroom ticket (*Am.* check)
8 playgoer (theatregoer, *Am.* theatergoer)
9 opera glass (opera glasses)
10 commissionaire
11 theatre (*Am.* theater) ticket, an admission ticket
12–13 foyer (lobby, crush room)
12 usher; *form.*: box attendant
13 programme (*Am.* program)
14–27 auditorium and stage
14 stage
15 proscenium
16–20 auditorium
16 gallery (balcony)
17 upper circle
18 dress circle (*Am.* balcony, mezzanine)
19 front stalls
20 seat (theatre seat, *Am.* theater seat)
21–27 rehearsal (stage rehearsal)
21 chorus
22 singer
23 singer
24 orchestra pit
25 orchestra
26 conductor
27 baton (conductor's baton)
28–42 paint room, a workshop
28 stagehand (scene shifter)
29 catwalk (bridge)
30 set piece
31 reinforcing struts
32 built piece (built unit)
33 backcloth (backdrop)
34 portable box for paint containers
35 scene painter
36 paint trolley
37 stage designer (set designer)
38 costume designer
39 design for a costume
40 sketch for a costume
41 model stage
42 model of the set
43–52 dressing room
43 dressing room mirror
44 make-up gown
45 make-up table
46 greasepaint stick
47 chief make-up artist (chief make-up man)
48 make-up artist (hairstylist)
49 wig
50 props (properties)
51 theatrical costume
52 call light

1
2
3
4
5
A
6
7
8
9
10
11
12
13
14
15
16
17
18
19
20
21
22
23
24
25
26
27
28
29
30
31
32
33
34
35
36
37
38
39
40
41
42
43
44
45
46
47
48
49
50
51
52

1–60 stagehouse with machinery (machinery in the flies and below stage)
1 control room
2 control console (lighting console, lighting control console) with preset control for presetting lighting effects
3 lighting plot (light plot)
4 grid (gridiron)
5 fly floor (fly gallery)
6 sprinkler system for fire prevention (for fire protection)
7 fly man
8 fly lines (lines)
9 cyclorama
10 backcloth (backdrop, background)
11 arch, a drop cloth
12 border
13 compartment (compartment-type, compartmentalized) batten (*Am.* border light)
14 stage lighting units (stage lights)
15 horizon lights (backdrop lights)
16 adjustable acting area lights (acting area spotlights)
17 scenery projectors (projectors)
18 monitor (water cannon) (a piece of safety equipment)
19 travelling (*Am.* traveling) lighting bridge (travelling lighting gallery)
20 lighting operator (lighting man)
21 portal spotlight (tower spotlight)
22 adjustable proscenium
23 curtain (theatrical curtain)
24 iron curtain (safety curtain, fire curtain)
25 forestage (apron)
26 footlight (footlights, floats)
27 prompt box
28 prompter
29 stage manager's desk
30 stage director (stage manager)
31 revolving stage
32 trap opening
33 lift (*Am.* elevator)
34 bridge (*Am.* elevator), a rostrum
35 pieces of scenery
36 scene
37 actor
38 actress
39 extras (supers, supernumeraries)
40 director (producer)
41 prompt book (prompt script)
42 director's table (producer's table)
43 assistant director (assistant producer)
44 director's script (producer's script)
45 stage carpenter
46 stagehand (scene shifter)
47 set piece
48 mirror spot (mirror spotlight)
49 automatic filter change (with colour filters, colour mediums, gelatines)
50 hydraulic plant room
51 water tank
52 suction pipe
53 hydraulic pump
54 pressure pipe
55 pressure tank (accumulator)
56 pressure gauge (*Am.* gage)
57 level indicator (liquid level indicator)
58 control lever
59 operator
60 rams

1
2
3
4
5
6
7
8
9
10
11
12
13
14
15
16
17
18
19
20
21
22
23
24
25
26
27
28
29
30
31
32
33
34
35
36
37
38
39
40
41
42
43
44
45
46
47
48
49
50
51
52
53
54
55
56
57
58
59
60

317 Discotheque

1 bar
2 barmaid
3 bar stool
4 shelf for bottles
5 shelf for glasses
6 beer glass
7 wine and liqueur glasses
8 beer tap (tap)
9 bar
10 refrigerator (fridge, *Am.* icebox)
11 bar lamps
12 indirect lighting
13 colour (*Am.* color) organ (clavilux)
14 dance floor lighting
15 speaker (loudspeaker)
16 dance floor
17–18 dancing couple
17 dancer
18 dancer
19 record player
20 microphone
21 tape recorder
22–23 stereo system (stereo equipment)
22 tuner
23 amplifier
24 records (discs)
25 disc jockey
26 mixing console (mixing desk, mixer)
27 tambourine
28 mirrored wall
29 ceiling tiles
30 ventilators
31 toilets (lavatories, WC)
32 long drink
33 cocktail (*Am.* highball)

1–33 nightclub (night spot)
1 cloakroom (*Am.* checkroom)
2 cloakroom attendant (*Am.* checkroom attendant)
3 band
4 clarinet
5 clarinettist (*Am.* clarinetist)
6 trumpet
7 trumpeter
8 guitar
9 guitarist (guitar player)
10 drums
11 drummer
12 speaker (loudspeaker)
13 bar
14 barmaid
15 bar
16 bar stool
17 tape recorder
18 receiver
19 spirits
20 cine projector for porno films (sex films, blue movies)
21 box containing screen
22 stage
23 stage lighting
24 spotlight
25 festoon lighting
26 festoon lamp (lamp, light bulb)
27–32 striptease act (striptease number)
27 striptease artist (stripper)
28 suspender (*Am.* garter)
29 brassière (bra)
30 fur stole
31 gloves
32 stocking
33 hostess

319 Bullfighting, Rodeo

1–33 bullfight (corrida, corrida de toros)
1 mock bullfight
2 novillero
3 mock bull (dummy bull)
4 novice banderillero (apprentice banderillero)
5 bullring (plaza de toros) [diagram]
6 main entrance
7 boxes
8 stands
9 arena (ring)
10 bullfighters' entrance
11 torril door
12 exit gate for killed bulls
13 slaughterhouse
14 bull pens (corrals)
15 paddock
16 lancer on horseback (picador)
17 lance (pike pole, javelin)
18 armoured (*Am.* armored) horse
19 leg armour (*Am.* armor)
20 picador's round hat
21 banderillero, a torero
22 banderillas (barbed darts)
23 shirtwaist
24 bullfight
25 matador (swordsman), a torero
26 queue, a distinguishing mark of the matador
27 red cloak (capa)
28 fighting bull
29 montera [hat made of tiny black silk chenille balls]
30 killing the bull (kill)
31 matador in charity performances [without professional uniform]
32 estoque (sword)
33 muleta
34 **rodeo**
35 young bull
36 cowboy
37 stetson (stetson hat)
38 scarf (necktie)
39 rodeo rider
40 lasso

1
2
3
4
5
6
7
8
9
10
11
12
13
14
15
16
17
18
19
20
21
22
23
24
25
26
27
28
29
30
31
32
33
34
35
36
37
38
39
40

320 Musical Notation I

1–2 medieval (mediaeval) notes
1 plainsong notation (neumes, neums, pneumes, square notation)
2 mensural notation
3–7 musical note (note)
3 note head
4 note stem (note tail)
5 hook
6 stroke
7 dot indicating augmentation of note's value
8–11 clefs
8 treble clef (G-clef, violin clef)
9 bass clef (F-clef)
10 alto clef (C-clef)
11 tenor clef
12–19 note values
12 breve (brevis, *Am.* double-whole note)
13 semibreve (*Am.* whole note)
14 minim (*Am.* half note)
15 crotchet (*Am.* quarter note)
16 quaver (*Am.* eighth note)
17 semiquaver (*Am.* sixteenth note)
18 demisemiquaver (*Am.* thirty-second note)
19 hemidemisemiquaver (*Am.* sixty-fourth note)
20–27 rests
20 breve rest
21 semibreve rest (*Am.* whole rest)
22 minim rest (*Am.* half rest)
23 crotchet rest (*Am.* quarter rest)
24 quaver rest (*Am.* eighth rest)
25 semiquaver rest (*Am.* sixteenth rest)
26 demisemiquaver rest (*Am.* thirty-second rest)
27 hemidemisemiquaver rest (*Am.* sixty-fourth rest)
28–42 time (time signatures, measure, *Am.* meter)
28 two-eight time
29 two-four time
30 two-two time
31 four-eight time
32 four-four time (common time)
33 four-two time
34 six-eight time
35 six-four time
36 three-eight time
37 three-four time
38 three-two time
39 nine-eight time
40 nine-four time
41 five-four time
42 bar (bar line, measure line)
43–44 staff (stave)
43 line of the staff
44 space
45–49 scales
45 C major scale naturals: c, d, e, f, g, a, b, c
46 A minor scale [natural] naturals: a, b, c, d, e, f, g, a
47 A minor scale [harmonic]
48 A minor scale [melodic]
49 chromatic scale
50–54 accidentals (inflections, key signatures)
50–51 signs indicating the raising of a note
50 sharp (raising the note a semitone or half-step)
51 double sharp (raising the note a tone or full-step)
52–53 signs indicating the lowering of a note
52 flat (lowering the note a semitone or half-step)
53 double flat (lowering the note a tone or full-step)
54 natural
55–68 keys (major keys and the related minor keys having the same signature)
55 C major (A minor)
56 G major (E minor)
57 D major (B minor)
58 A major (F sharp minor)
59 E major (C sharp minor)
60 B major (G sharp minor)
61 F sharp major (D sharp minor)
62 C major (A minor)
63 F major (D minor)
64 B flat major (G minor)
65 E flat major (C minor)
66 A flat major (F minor)
67 D flat major (B flat minor)
68 G flat major (E flat minor)

1
Magni - fí-cat
2
Nu kom der heidē Heiland,
3 4 5 6 7
8 9 10 11 12 13 14 15 16 17 18 19 20 21 22 23 24 25 26 27
28 29 30 31 32 33 34 35 36 37 38 39 40 41 42 43 44
45 46 47
48
49
50 51 52 53 54
55 56 57 58 59 60 61
62 63 64 65 66 67 68

321 Musical Notation II

1–5 chord
1–4 triad
1 major triad
2 minor triad
3 diminished triad
4 augmented triad
5 chord of four notes, a chord of the seventh (seventh chord, dominant seventh chord)
6–13 intervals
6 unison (unison interval)
7 major second
8 major third
9 perfect fourth
10 perfect fifth
11 major sixth
12 major seventh
13 perfect octave
14–22 ornaments (graces, grace notes)
14 long appoggiatura
15 acciaccatura (short appoggiatura)
16 slide
17 trill (shake) without turn
18 trill (shake) with turn
19 upper mordent (inverted mordent, pralltriller)
20 lower mordent (mordent)
21 turn
22 arpeggio
23–26 other signs in musical notation
23 triplet; *corresponding groupings:* duplet (couplet), quadruplet, quintuplet, sextolet (sextuplet), septolet (septuplet, septimole)
24 tie (bind)
25 pause (pause sign)
26 repeat mark
27–41 expression marks (signs of relative intensity)
27 marcato (marcando, markiert, attack, strong accent)
28 presto (quick, fast)
29 portato (lourer, mezzo staccato, carried)
30 tenuto (held)
31 crescendo (increasing gradually in power)
32 decrescendo (diminuendo, decreasing or diminishing gradually in power)
33 legato (bound)
34 staccato (detached)
35 piano (soft)
36 pianissimo (very soft)
37 pianissimo piano (as soft as possible)
38 forte (loud)
39 fortissimo (very loud)
40 forte fortissimo (double fortissimo, as loud as possible)
41 forte piano (loud and immediately soft again)
42–50 divisions of the compass
42 subcontra octave (double contra octave)
43 contra octave
44 great octave
45 small octave
46 one-line octave
47 two-line octave
48 three-line octave
49 four-line octave
50 five-line octave

1 2 3 4 5 6 7 8 9 10 11 12 13
14 15 16 17 18 19 20 21
22 23 27 24 25 26
28 Presto
29 30 ten. 33
cresc. decresc.
cresc. decresc.
31 32 34
p pp ppp f ff fff fp
35 36 37 38 39 40 41
8va sopra
42 43 44 45 46 47 48 49 50
8va bassa
$_2A\ _2B\ _2H\ _1C$ usw
in Britain:
$A_2\ B\flat_2 B_2 C_1$ etc.
$_1H$ C H c h c^1 $h^1 c^2 h^2 c^3 h^3 c^4 h^4 c^5$
B_1 C B c b c′ b′ c″ b″ c‴ b‴ c⁗ b⁗ c⁗′

1 lur, a bronze trumpet
2 panpipes (Pandean pipes, syrinx)
3 aulos, a double shawm
4 aulos pipe
5 phorbeia (peristomion, capistrum, mouth band)
6 crumhorn (crummhorn, cromorne, krumbhorn, krummhorn)
7 recorder (fipple flute)
8 bagpipe; *sim.:* musette
9 bag
10 chanter (melody pipe)
11 drone (drone pipe)
12 curved cornett (zink)
13 serpent
14 shawm (schalmeyes); *larger:* bombard (bombarde, pommer)
15 cythara (cithara); *sim. and smaller:* lyre
16 arm
17 bridge
18 sound box (resonating chamber, resonator)
19 plectrum, a plucking device
20 kit (pochette), a miniature violin
21 cittern (cithern, cither, cister, citole), a plucked instrument; *sim.:* pandora (bandora, bandore)
22 sound hole
23 viol (descant viol, treble viol), a viola da gamba; *larger:* tenor viol, bass viol (viola da gamba, gamba), violone (double bass viol)
24 viol bow
25 hurdy-gurdy (vielle à roue, symphonia, armonie, organistrum)
26 friction wheel
27 wheel cover (wheel guard)
28 keyboard (keys)
29 resonating body (resonator, sound box)
30 melody strings
31 drone strings (drones, bourdons)
32 dulcimer
33 rib (resonator wall)
34 beater for the Valasian dulcimer
35 hammer (stick) for the Appenzell dulcimer
36 clavichord; *kinds:* fretted or unfretted clavichord
37 clavichord mechanism
38 key (key lever)
39 balance rail
40 guiding blade
41 guiding slot
42 resting rail
43 tangent
44 string
45 harpsichord (clavicembalo, cembalo), a wing-shaped stringed keyboard instrument; *sim.:* spinet (virginal)
46 upper keyboard (upper manual)
47 lower keyboard (lower manual)
48 harpsichord mechanism
49 key (key lever)
50 jack
51 slide (register)
52 tongue
53 quill plectrum
54 damper
55 string
56 portative organ, a portable organ; *larger:* positive organ (positive)
57 pipe (flue pipe)
58 bellows

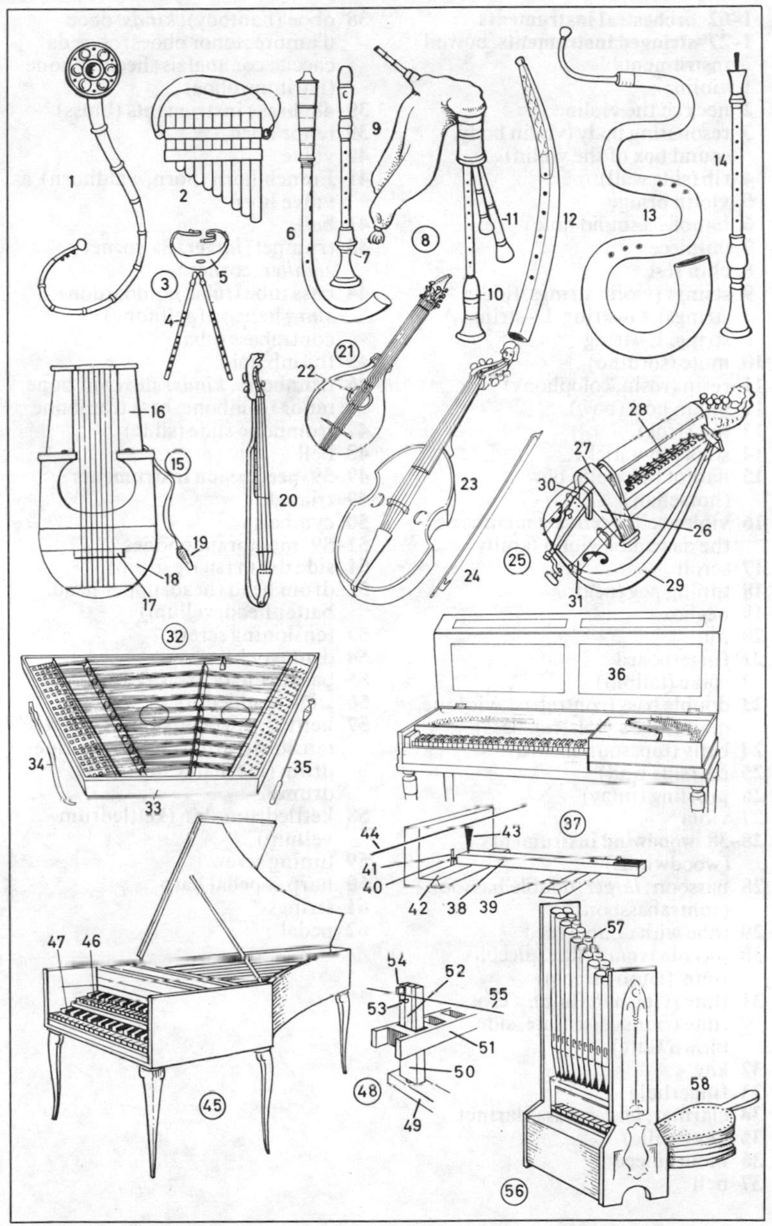
1
2
3
4
5
6
7
8
9
10
11
12
13
14
15
16
17
18
19
20
21
22
23
24
25
26
27
28
29
30
31
32
33
34
35
36
37
38
39
40
41
42
43
44
45
46
47
48
49
50
51
52
53
54
55
56
57
58

323 Musical Instruments II

1–62 orchestral instruments
1–27 stringed instruments, bowed instruments
1 violin
2 neck of the violin
3 resonating body (violin body, sound box of the violin)
4 rib (side wall)
5 violin bridge
6 F–hole, a sound hole
7 tailpiece
8 chin rest
9 strings (violin strings, fiddle strings): G–string, D–string, A–string, E–string
10 mute (sordino)
11 resin (rosin, colophony)
12 violin bow (bow)
13 nut (frog)
14 stick (bow stick)
15 hair of the violin bow (horsehair)
16 violoncello (cello), a member of the da gamba violin family
17 scroll
18 tuning peg (peg)
19 pegbox
20 nut
21 fingerboard
22 spike (tailpin)
23 double bass (contrabass, violone, double bass viol, *Am.* bass)
24 belly (top, soundboard)
25 rib (side wall)
26 purfling (inlay)
27 viola
28–38 woodwind instruments (woodwinds)
28 bassoon; *larger:* double bassoon (contrabassoon)
29 tube with double reed
30 piccolo (small flute, piccolo flute, flauto piccolo)
31 flute (German flute), a cross flute (transverse flute, side-blown flute)
32 key
33 fingerhole
34 clarinet; *larger:* bass clarinet
35 key (brille)
36 mouthpiece
37 bell
38 oboe (hautboy); *kinds:* oboe d'amore; tenor oboes: oboe da caccia, cor anglais; heckelphone (baritone oboe)
39–48 brass instruments (brass)
39 tenor horn
40 valve
41 French horn (horn, waldhorn), a valve horn
42 bell
43 trumpet; *larger:* B♭ cornet; *smaller:* cornet
44 bass tuba (tuba, bombardon); *sim.:* helicon (pellitone), contrabass tuba
45 thumb hold
46 trombone; *kinds:* alto trombone, tenor trombone, bass trombone
47 trombone slide (slide)
48 bell
49–59 percussion instruments
49 triangle
50 cymbals
51–59 membranophones
51 side drum (snare drum)
52 drum head (head, upper head, batter head, vellum)
53 tensioning screw
54 drumstick
55 bass drum (Turkish drum)
56 stick (padded stick)
57 kettledrum (timpano), a screw-tensioned drum; *sim.:* machine drum (mechanically tuned drum)
58 kettledrum skin (kettledrum vellum)
59 tuning screw
60 harp, a pedal harp
61 strings
62 pedal

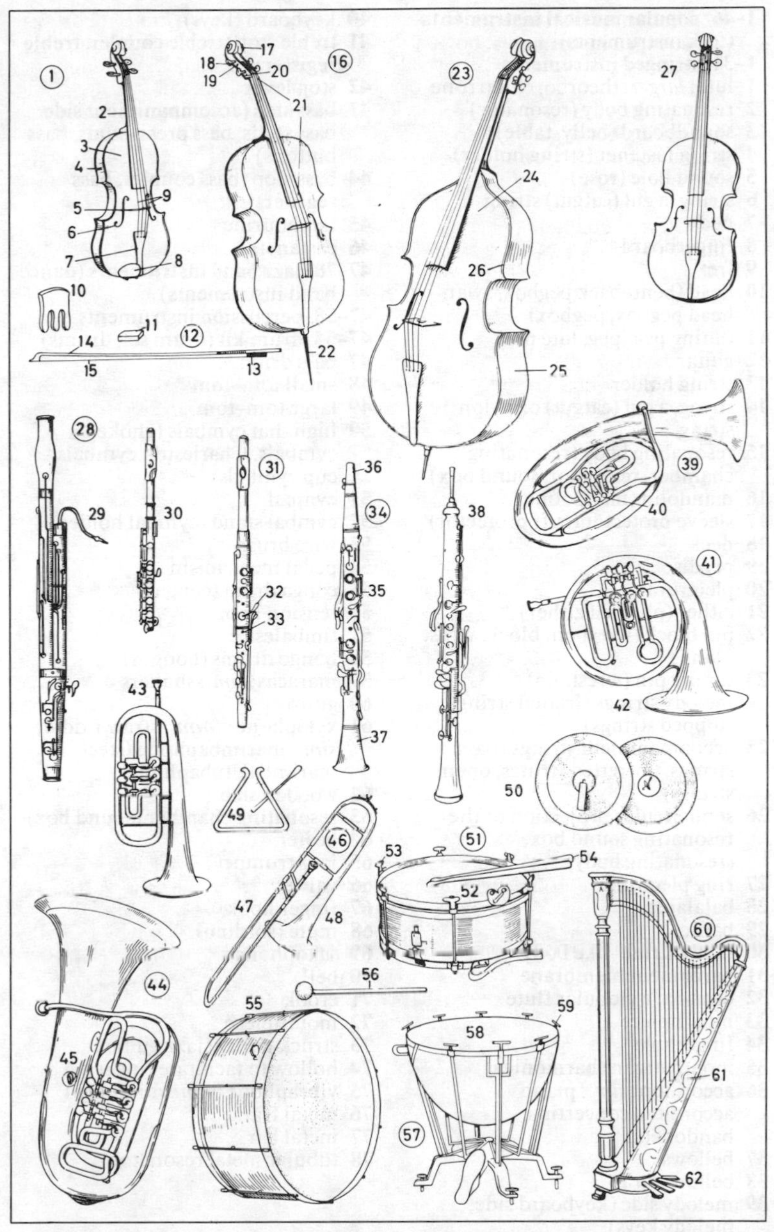
1
2
3
4
5
6
7
8
9
10
11
12
13
14
15
16
17
18
19
20
21
22
23
24
25
26
27
28
29
30
31
32
33
34
35
36
37
38
39
40
41
42
43
44
45
46
47
48
49
50
51
52
53
54
55
56
57
58
59
60
61
62

1–46 popular musical instruments (folk instruments)
1–31 stringed instruments
1 lute; *larger:* theorbo, chitarrone
2 resonating body (resonator)
3 soundboard (belly, table)
4 string fastener (string holder)
5 sound hole (rose)
6 string, a gut (catgut) string
7 neck
8 fingerboard
9 fret
10 head (bent-back pegbox, swan-head pegbox, pegbox)
11 tuning peg (peg, lute pin)
12 guitar
13 string holder
14 string, a gut (catgut) or nylon string
15 resonating body (resonating chamber, resonator, sound box)
16 mandolin (mandoline)
17 sleeve protector (cuff protector)
18 neck
19 pegdisc
20 plectrum
21 zither (plucked zither)
22 pin block (wrest pin block, wrest plank)
23 tuning pin (wrest pin)
24 melody strings (fretted strings, stopped strings)
25 accompaniment strings (bass strings, unfretted strings, open strings)
26 semicircular projection of the resonating sound box (resonating body)
27 ring plectrum
28 balalaika
29 banjo
30 tambourine-like body
31 parchment membrane
32 ocarina, a globular flute
33 mouthpiece
34 fingerhole
35 mouth organ (harmonica)
36 accordion; *sim.:* piano accordion, concertina, bandoneon
37 bellows
38 bellows strap
39 melody side (keyboard side, melody keys)
40 keyboard (keys)
41 treble stop (treble coupler, treble register)
42 stop lever
43 bass side (accompaniment side, bass studs, bass press-studs, bass buttons)
44 bass stop (bass coupler, bass register)
45 tambourine
46 castanets
47–78 jazz band instruments (dance band instruments)
47–58 percussion instruments
47–54 drum kit (drum set, drums)
47 bass drum
48 small tom-tom
49 large tom-tom
50 high-hat cymbals (choke cymbals, Charleston cymbals, cup cymbals)
51 cymbal
52 cymbal stand (cymbal holder)
53 wire brush
54 pedal mechanism
55 conga drum (conga)
56 tension hoop
57 timbales
58 bongo drums (bongos)
59 maracas; *sim.:* shakers
60 guiro
61 xylophone; *form.:* straw fiddle; *sim.:* marimbaphone (steel marimba), tubaphone
62 wooden slab
63 resonating chamber (sound box)
64 beater
65 jazz trumpet
66 valve
67 finger hook
68 mute (sordino)
69 saxophone
70 bell
71 crook
72 mouthpiece
73 struck guitar (jazz guitar)
74 hollow to facilitate fingering
75 vibraphone (*Am.* vibraharp)
76 metal frame
77 metal bar
78 tubular metal resonator

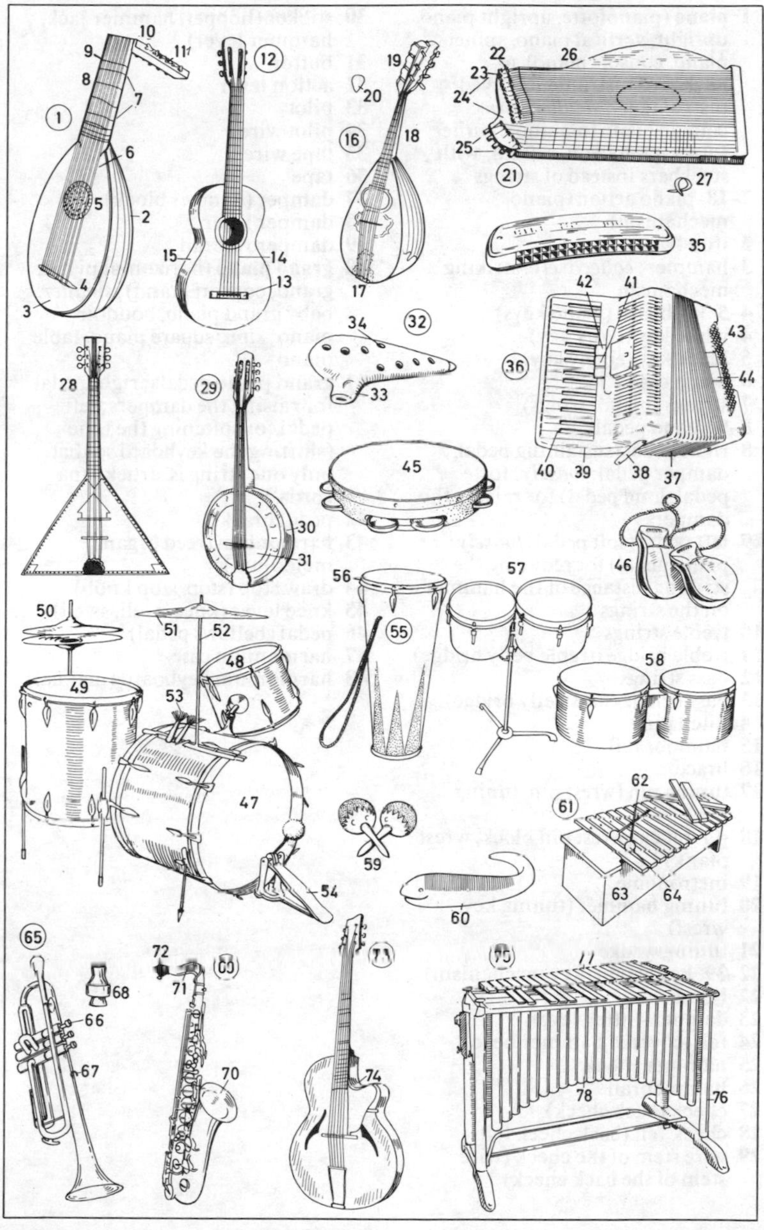
1
2
3
4
5
6
7
8
9
10
11
12
13
14
15
16
17
18
19
20
21
22
23
24
25
26
27
28
29
30
31
32
33
34
35
36
37
38
39
40
41
42
43
44
45
46
47
48
49
50
51
52
53
54
55
56
57
58
59
60
61
62
63
64
65
66
67
68
70
71
72
74
76
78

325 Musical Instruments IV

1 **piano** (pianoforte, upright piano, upright, vertical piano, spinet piano, console piano), a keyboard instrument (keyed instrument); *smaller form:* cottage piano (pianino); *earlier forms:* pantaleon, celesta, with steel bars instead of strings
2–18 piano action (piano mechanism)
2 iron frame
3 hammer; *collectively:* striking mechanism
4–5 keyboard (piano keys)
4 white key (ivory key)
5 black key (ebony key)
6 piano case
7 strings (piano strings)
8–9 piano pedals
8 right pedal (sustaining pedal, damper pedal; *loosely:* forte pedal, loud pedal) for raising the dampers
9 left pedal (soft pedal; *loosely:* piano pedal) for reducing the striking distance of the hammers on the strings
10 treble strings
11 treble bridge (treble belly bridge)
12 bass strings
13 bass bridge (bass belly bridge)
14 hitch pin
15 hammer rail
16 brace
17 tuning pin (wrest pin, tuning peg)
18 pin block (wrest pin block, wrest plank)
19 metronome
20 tuning hammer (tuning key, wrest)
21 tuning wedge
22–39 key action (key mechanism)
22 beam
23 damper-lifting lever
24 felt-covered hammer head
25 hammer shank
26 hammer rail
27 check (back check)
28 check felt (back check felt)
29 wire stem of the check (wire stem of the back check)
30 sticker (hopper, hammer jack, hammer lever)
31 button
32 action lever
33 pilot
34 pilot wire
35 tape wire
36 tape
37 damper (damper block)
38 damper lifter
39 damper rest rail
40 **grand piano** (horizontal piano, grand, concert grand); *smaller:* baby grand piano, boudoir piano; *sim.:* square piano, table piano
41 grand piano pedals; right pedal for raising the dampers; left pedal for softening the tone (shifting the keyboard so that only one string is struck 'una corda')
42 pedal bracket
43 **harmonium** (reed organ, melodium)
44 draw stop (stop, stop knob)
45 knee lever (knee swell, swell)
46 pedal (bellows pedal)
47 harmonium case
48 harmonium keyboard (manual)

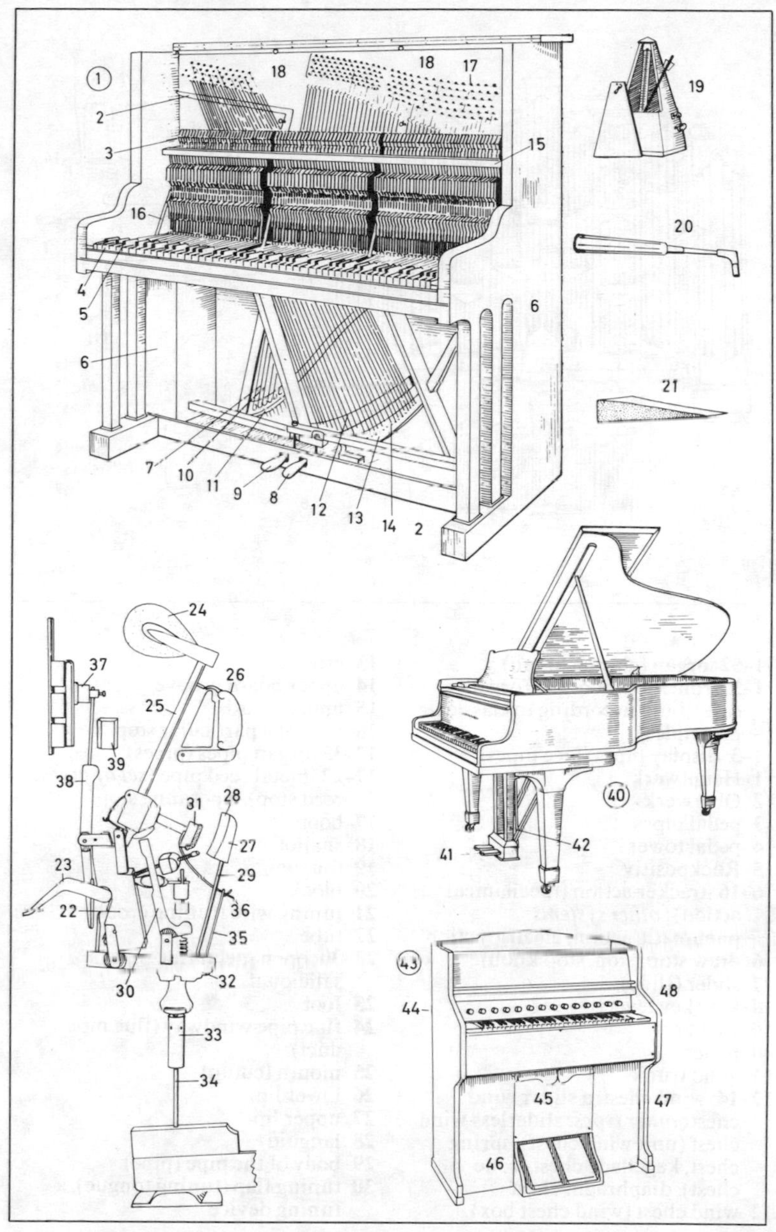
1
18
18
17
19
2
3
15
16
20
4
5
6
6
21
7
10
11
9
8
12
13
14
2
24
37
26
25
39
38
28
31
27
40
23
29
42
41
22
36
35
43
30
32
48
44
33
34
45
47
46

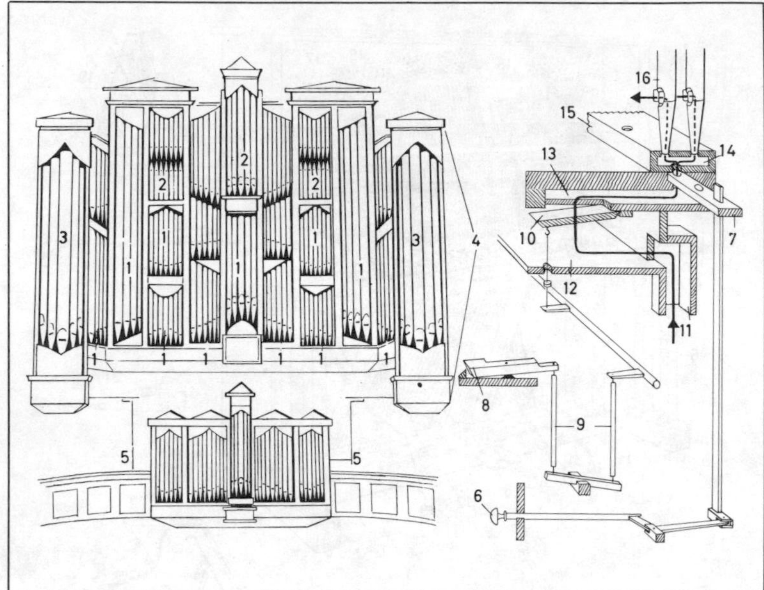

1-52 organ (church organ)
1-5 front view of organ (organ case) [built according to classical principles]
1-3 display pipes (face pipes)
1 Hauptwerk
2 Oberwerk
3 pedal pipes
4 pedal tower
5 Rückpositiv
6-16 tracker action (mechanical action); *other systems:* pneumatic action, electric action
6 draw stop (stop, stop knob)
7 slider (slide)
8 key (key lever)
9 sticker
10 pallet
11 wind trunk
12-14 wind chest, a slider wind chest; *other types:* sliderless wind chest (unit wind chest), spring chest, kegellade chest (cone chest), diaphragm chest
12 wind chest (wind chest box)
13 groove
14 upper board groove
15 upper board
16 pipe of a particular stop
17-35 organ pipes (pipes)
17-22 metal reed pipe (*set of pipes:* reed stop), a posaune stop
17 boot
18 shallot
19 tongue
20 block
21 tuning wire (tuning crook)
22 tube
23-30 open metal flue pipe, a salicional
23 foot
24 flue pipe windway (flue pipe duct)
25 mouth (cutup)
26 lower lip
27 upper lip
28 languid
29 body of the pipe (pipe)
30 tuning flap (tuning tongue), a tuning device

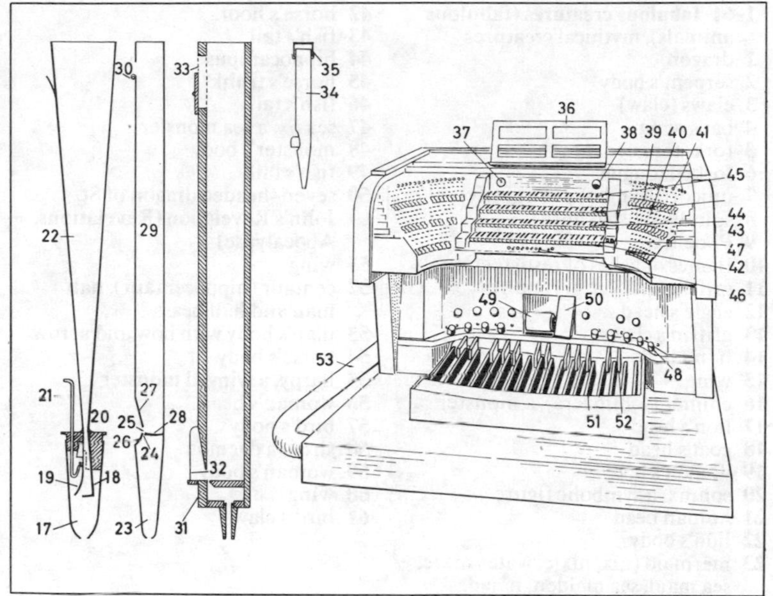

31–33 open wooden flue pipe (open wood), principal (diapason)
31 cap
32 ear
33 tuning hole (tuning slot), with slide
34 stopped flue pipe
35 stopper
36–52 organ console (console) of an electric action organ
36 music rest (music stand)
37 crescendo roller indicator
38 voltmeter
39 stop tab (rocker)
40 free combination stud (free combination knob)
41 cancel buttons for reeds, couplers etc.
42 manual I, for the Rückpositiv
43 manual II, for the Hauptwerk
44 manual III, for the Oberwerk
45 manual IV, for the Schwellwerk
46 thumb pistons controlling the manual stops (free or fixed combinations) and buttons for setting the combinations
47 switches for current to blower and action
48 toe piston, for the coupler
49 crescendo roller (general crescendo roller)
50 balanced swell pedal
51 pedal key [natural]
52 pedal key [sharp or flat]
53 cable (transmission cable)

327 Fabulous Creatures (Fabled Beings)

1–61 fabulous creatures (fabulous animals), mythical creatures
1 dragon
2 serpent's body
3 claws (claw)
4 bat's wing
5 fork-tongued mouth
6 forked tongue
7 unicorn [symbol of virginity]
8 spirally twisted horn
9 Phoenix
10 flames or ashes of resurrection
11 griffin (griffon, gryphon)
12 eagle's head
13 griffin's claws
14 lion's body
15 wing
16 chimera (chimaera), a monster
17 lion's head
18 goat's head
19 dragon's body
20 sphinx, a symbolic figure
21 human head
22 lion's body
23 mermaid (nix, nixie, water nixie, sea maid, sea maiden, naiad, water nymph, water elf, ocean nymph, sea nymph, river nymph); *sim.:* Nereids, Oceanids (sea divinities, sea deities, sea goddesses); *male:* nix (merman, seaman)
24 woman's trunk
25 fish's tail (dolphin's tail)
26 Pegasus (favourite, *Am.* favorite, steed of the Muses, winged horse); *sim.:* hippogryph
27 horse's body
28 wings
29 Cerberus (hellhound)
30 three-headed dog's body
31 serpent's tail
32 Lernaean (Lernean) Hydra
33 nine-headed serpent's body
34 basilisk (cockatrice)
35 cock's head
36 dragon's body
37 giant (titan)
38 rock
39 serpent's foot
40 triton, a merman (demigod of the sea)
41 conch shell trumpet
42 horse's hoof
43 fish's tail
44 hippocampus
45 horse's trunk
46 fish's tail
47 sea ox, a sea monster
48 monster's body
49 fish's tail
50 seven-headed dragon of St. John's Revelation (Revelations, Apocalypse)
51 wing
52 centaur (hippocentaur), half man and half beast
53 man's body with bow and arrow
54 horse's body
55 harpy, a winged monster
56 woman's head
57 bird's body
58 siren, a daemon
59 woman's body
60 wing
61 bird's claw

1
2
3
4
5
6
7
8
9
10
11
12
13
14
15
16
17
18
19
20
21
22
23
24
25
26
27
28
29
30
31
32
33
34
35
36
37
38
39
40
41
42
43
44
45
46
47
48
49
50
51
52
53
54
55
56
57
58
59
60
61

1–40 prehistoric finds
1–9 **Old Stone Age** (Palaeolithic, Paleolithic, period) and **Mesolithic period**
1 hand axe (*Am.* ax) (fist hatchet), a stone tool
2 head of throwing spear, made of bone
3 bone harpoon
4 head
5 harpoon thrower, made of reindeer antler
6 painted pebble
7 head of a wild horse, a carving
8 Stone Age idol, an ivory statuette
9 bison, a cave painting (rock painting) [cave art, cave painting]
10–20 **New Stone Age** (Neolithic period)
10 amphora [corded ware]
11 bowl [menhir group]
12 collared flask [Funnel-Beaker culture]
13 vessel with spiral pattern [spiral design pottery]
14 bell beaker [beaker pottery]
15 pile dwelling (lake dwelling, lacustrine dwelling)
16 dolmen (cromlech), a megalithic tomb (*coll.:* giant's tomb); *other kinds:* passage grave, gallery grave (long cist); *when covered with earth:* tumulus (barrow, mound)
17 stone cist, a contracted burial
18 menhir (standing stone), a monolith
19 boat axe (*Am.* ax), a stone battle axe
20 clay figurine (an idol)
21–40 **Bronze Age** and **Iron Age;** *epochs:* Hallstatt period, La Tène period
21 bronze spear head
22 hafted bronze dagger
23 socketed axe (*Am.* ax) with haft fastened to rings, a bronze axe
24 girdle clasp
25 necklace (lunula)
26 gold neck ring
27 violin-bow fibula (safety pin)
28 serpentine fibula; *other kinds:* boat fibula, arc fibula
29 bulb-head pin, a bronze pin
30 two-piece spiral fibula; *sim.:* disc (disk) fibula
31 hafted bronze knife
32 iron key
33 ploughshare (*Am.* plowshare)
34 sheet-bronze situla, a funerary vessel
35 pitcher [chip-carved pottery]
36 miniature ritual cart (miniature ritual chariot)
37 Celtic silver coin
38 face urn, a cinerary urn; *other kinds:* domestic urn, embossed urn
39 urn grave in stone chamber
40 urn with cylindrical neck

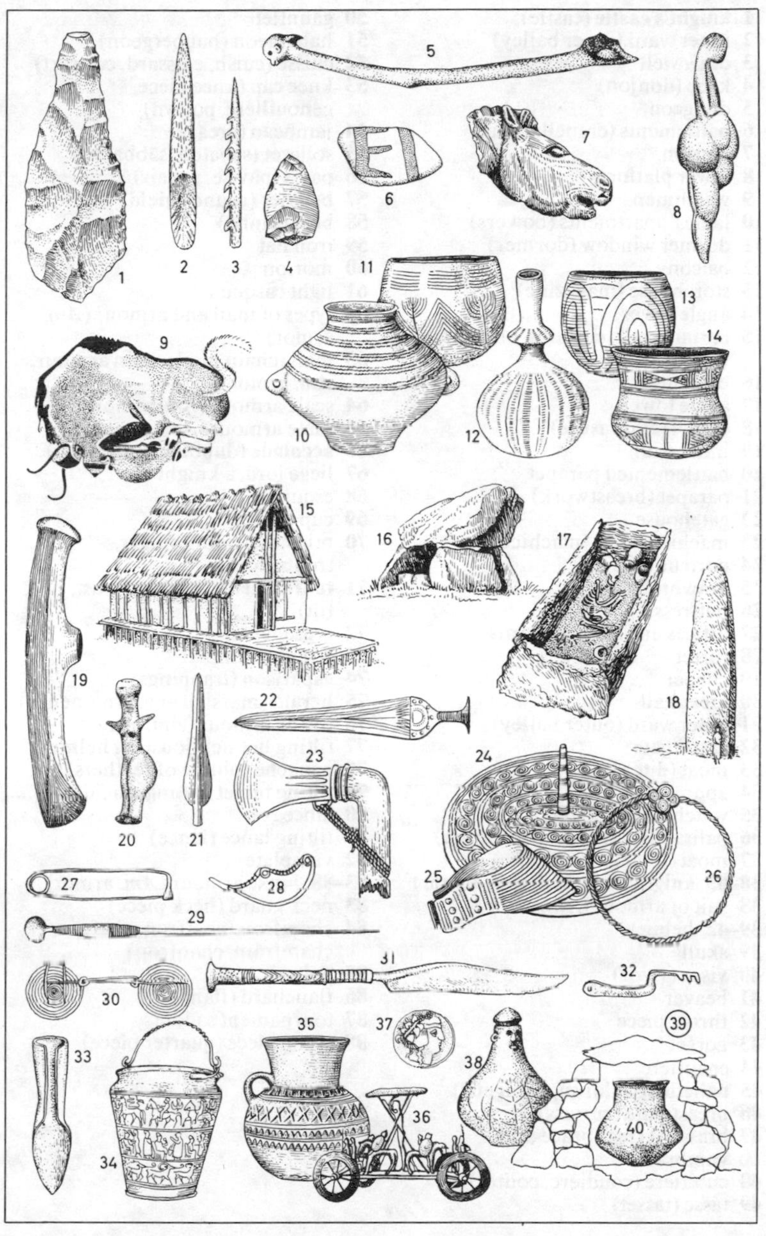
1
2
3
4
5
6
7
8
9
10
11
12
13
14
15
16
17
18
19
20
21
22
23
24
25
26
27
28
29
30
31
32
33
34
35
36
37
38
39
40

329 Chivalry

1 **knight's castle** (castle)
2 inner ward (inner bailey)
3 draw well
4 keep (donjon)
5 dungeon
6 battlements (crenellation)
7 merlon
8 tower platform
9 watchman
10 ladies' apartments (bowers)
11 dormer window (dormer)
12 balcony
13 storehouse (magazine)
14 angle tower
15 curtain wall (curtains, enclosure wall)
16 bastion
17 angle tower
18 crenel (embrasure)
19 inner wall
20 battlemented parapet
21 parapet (breastwork)
22 gatehouse
23 machicolation (machicoulis)
24 portcullis
25 drawbridge
26 buttress
27 offices and service rooms
28 turret
29 chapel
30 great hall
31 outer ward (outer bailey)
32 castle gate
33 moat (ditch)
34 approach
35 watchtower (turret)
36 palisade (pallisade, palisading)
37 moat (ditch, fosse)
38–65 **knight's armour** (*Am.* armor)
38 suit of armour (*Am.* armor)
39–42 helmet
39 skull
40 visor (vizor)
41 beaver
42 throat piece
43 gorget
44 epaulière
45 pallette (pauldron, besageur)
46 breastplate (cuirass)
47 brassard (rear brace and vambrace)
48 cubitière (coudière, couter)
49 tasse (tasset)
50 gauntlet
51 habergeon (haubergeon)
52 cuisse (cuish, cuissard, cuissart)
53 knee cap (knee piece, genouillère, poleyn)
54 jambeau (greave)
55 solleret (sabaton, sabbaton)
56 pavis (pavise, pavais)
57 buckler (round shield)
58 boss (umbo)
59 iron hat
60 morion
61 light casque
62 types of mail and armour (*Am.* armor)
63 mail (chain mail, chain armour, *Am.* armor)
64 scale armour (*Am.* armor)
65 plate armour (*Am.* armor)
66 **accolade** (dubbing, knighting)
67 liege lord, a knight
68 esquire
69 cup bearer
70 minstrel (minnesinger, troubadour)
71 **tournament** (tourney, joust, just, tilt)
72 crusader
73 Knight Templar
74 caparison (trappings)
75 herald (marshal at tournament)
76 tilting armour (*Am.* armor)
77 tilting helmet (jousting helmet)
78 panache (plume of feathers)
79 tilting target (tilting shield)
80 lance rest
81 tilting lance (lance)
82 vamplate
83–88 horse armour (*Am.* armor)
83 neck guard (neck piece)
84 chamfron (chaffron, chafron, chamfrain, chanfron)
85 poitrel
86 flanchard (flancard)
87 tournament saddle
88 rump piece (quarter piece)

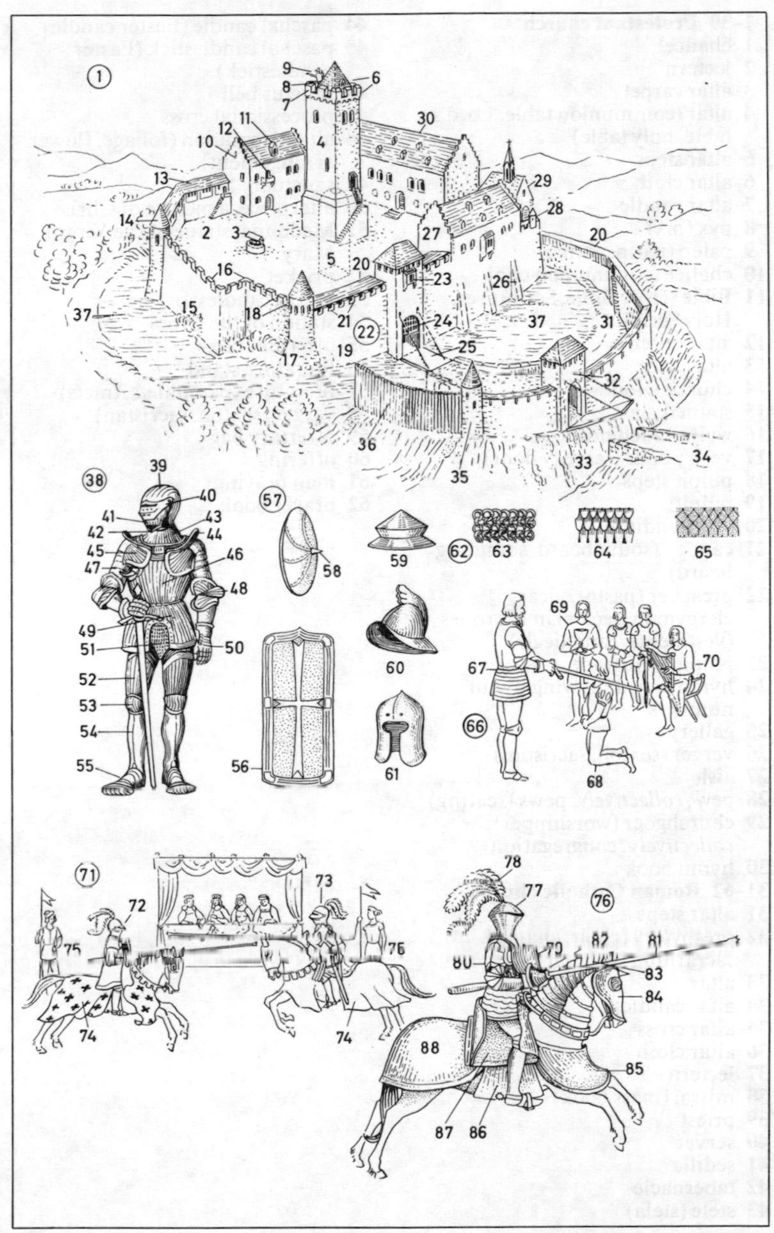

1
2
3
4
5
6
7
8
9
10
11
12
13
14
15
16
17
18
19
20
21
22
23
24
25
26
27
28
29
30
31
32
33
34
35
36
37
38
39
40
41
42
43
44
45
46
47
48
49
50
51
52
53
54
55
56
57
58
59
60
61
62
63
64
65
66
67
68
69
70
71
72
73
74
75
76
77
78
79
80
81
82
83
84
85
86
87
88

1–30 Protestant church
1 chancel
2 lectern
3 altar carpet
4 altar (communion table, Lord's table, holy table)
5 altar steps
6 altar cloth
7 altar candle
8 pyx (pix)
9 paten (patin, patine)
10 chalice (communion cup)
11 Bible (Holy Bible, Scriptures, Holy Scripture)
12 altar crucifix
13 altarpiece
14 church window
15 stained glass
16 wall candelabrum
17 vestry door (sacristy door)
18 pulpit steps
19 pulpit
20 antependium
21 canopy (soundboard, sounding board)
22 preacher (pastor, vicar, clergyman, rector) in his robes (vestments, canonicals)
23 pulpit balustrade
24 hymn board showing hymn numbers
25 gallery
26 verger (sexton, sacristan)
27 aisle
28 pew; *collectively:* pews (seating)
29 churchgoer (worshipper); *collectively:* congregation
30 hymn book
31–62 Roman Catholic church
31 altar steps
32 presbytery (choir, chancel, sacrarium, sanctuary)
33 altar
34 altar candles
35 altar cross
36 altar cloth
37 lectern
38 missal (mass book)
39 priest
40 server
41 sedilia
42 tabernacle
43 stele (stela)
44 paschal candle (Easter candle)
45 paschal candlestick (Easter candlestick)
46 sanctus bell
47 processional cross
48 altar decoration (foliage, flower arrangement)
49 sanctuary lamp
50 altarpiece, a picture of Christ
51 Madonna, statue of the Virgin Mary
52 pricket
53 votive candles
54 station of the Cross
55 offertory box
56 literature stand
57 literature (pamphlets, tracts)
58 verger (sexton, sacristan)
59 offertory bag
60 offering
61 man praying
62 prayer book

14
21
13
15
24
26
123
1-4
26
22
23
12
17
16
18
4
8
9
11
10
7
6
17
19
25
20
5
2
3
1
28
30
29
27
50
49
42
43
51
53
44
48
54
46
45
47
52
41
39
36
34
38
40
33
35
37
32
31
62
56
57
55
61
59
60
58

331 Church II

1 church
2 steeple
3 weathercock
4 weather vane (wind vane)
5 apex
6 church spire (spire)
7 church clock (tower clock)
8 belfry window
9 electrically operated bell
10 ridge cross
11 church roof
12 memorial chapel
13 vestry (sacristy), an annexe (annex)
14 memorial tablet (memorial plate, wall memorial, wall stone)
15 side entrance
16 church door (main door, portal)
17 churchgoer
18 graveyard wall (churchyard wall)
19 graveyard gate (churchyard gate, lichgate, lychgate)
20 vicarage (parsonage, rectory)
21–41 graveyard (churchyard, God's acre, *Am.* burying ground)
21 mortuary
22 grave digger
23 grave (tomb)
24 grave mound
25 cross
26 gravestone (headstone, tombstone)
27 family grave (family tomb)
28 graveyard chapel
29 child's grave
30 urn grave
31 urn
32 soldier's grave
33–41 funeral (burial)
33 mourners
34 grave
35 coffin (*Am.* casket)
36 spade
37 clergyman
38 the bereaved
39 widow's veil, a mourning veil
40 pallbearers
41 bier
42–50 procession (religious procession)
42 processional crucifix
43 cross bearer (crucifer)
44 processional banner, a church banner
45 acolyte
46 canopy bearer
47 priest
48 monstrance with the Blessed Sacrament (consecrated Host)
49 canopy (baldachin, baldaquin)
50 nuns
51 participants in the procession
52–58 monastery
52 cloister
53 monastery garden
54 monk, a Benedictine monk
55 habit (monk's habit)
56 cowl (hood)
57 tonsure
58 breviary
59 catacomb, an early Christian underground burial place
60 niche (tomb recess, arcosolium)
61 stone slab

1
2
3
4
5
6
7
8
9
10
11
12
13
14
15
15
16
17
18
19
20
21
22
23
24
25
26
27
28
29
30
31
32
33
34
35
36
37
38
39
40
41
42
43
44
45
46
47
48
49
50
51
52
53
54
55
56
57
58
59
60
61

1 Christian baptism (christening)
2 baptistery (baptistry)
3 Protestant clergyman
4 robes (vestments, canonicals)
5 bands
6 collar
7 child to be baptized (christened)
8 christening robe (christening dress)
9 christening shawl
10 font
11 font basin
12 baptismal water
13 godparents
14 church wedding (wedding ceremony, marriage ceremony)
15–16 bridal couple
15 bride
16 bridegroom (groom)
17 ring (wedding ring)
18 bride's bouquet (bridal bouquet)
19 bridal wreath
20 veil (bridal veil)
21 buttonhole
22 clergyman
23 witnesses [to the marriage]
24 bridesmaid
25 kneeler
26 Holy Communion
27 communicants
28 Host (wafer)
29 communion cup
30 rosary
31 paternoster
32 Ave Maria; *set of 10:* decade
33 crucifix
34–54 liturgical vessels (ecclesiastical vessels)
34 monstrance
35 Host (consecrated Host, Blessed Sacrament)
36 lunula (lunule)
37 rays
38 censer (thurible), for offering incense (for incensing)
39 thurible chain
40 thurible cover
41 thurible bowl
42 incense boat
43 incense spoon
44 cruet set
45 water cruet
46 wine cruet
47 holy water basin
48 ciborium containing the sacred wafers
49 chalice
50 dish for communion wafers
51 paten (patin, patine)
52 altar bells
53 pyx (pix)
54 aspergillum
55–72 forms of Christian crosses
55 Latin cross (cross of the Passion)
56 Greek cross
57 Russian cross
58 St. Peter's cross
59 St. Anthony's cross (tau cross)
60 St. Andrew's cross (saltire cross)
61 Y-cross
62 cross of Lorraine
63 ansate cross
64 patriarchal cross
65 cardinal's cross
66 Papal cross
67 Constantinian cross, a monogram of Christ (CHR)
68 crosslet
69 cross moline
70 cross of Jerusalem
71 cross botonnée (cross treflée)
72 fivefold cross (quintuple cross)

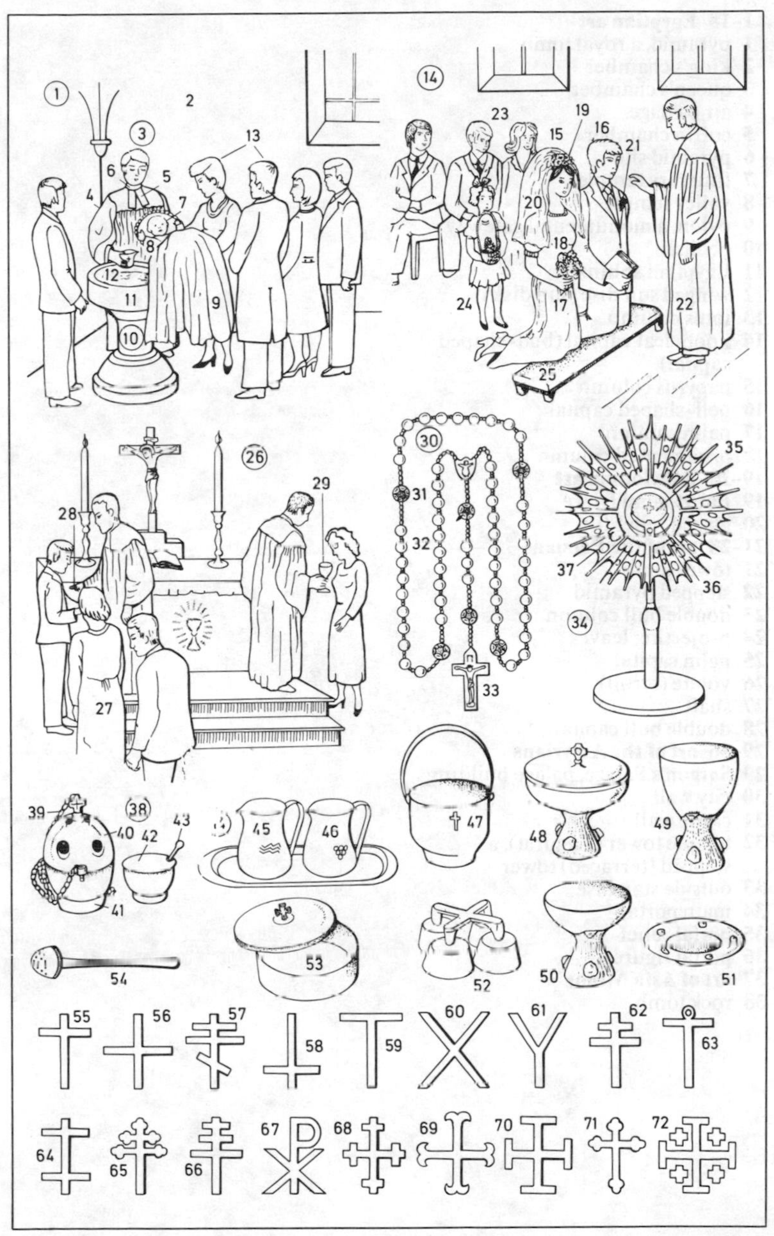
1
2
3
4
5
6
7
8
9
10
11
12
13
14
15
16
17
18
19
20
21
22
23
24
25
26
27
28
29
30
31
32
33
34
35
36
37
38
39
40
41
42
43
45
46
47
48
49
50
51
52
53
54
55
56
57
58
59
60
61
62
63
64
65
66
67
68
69
70
71
72

1–18 Egyptian art
1 pyramid, a royal tomb
2 king's chamber
3 queen's chamber
4 air passage
5 coffin chamber
6 pyramid site
7 funerary temple
8 valley temple
9 pylon, a monumental gateway
10 obelisks
11 Egyptian sphinx
12 winged sun disc (sun disk)
13 lotus column
14 knob-leaf capital (bud-shaped capital)
15 papyrus column
16 bell-shaped capital
17 palm column
18 ornamented column
19–20 Babylonian art
19 Babylonian frieze
20 glazed relief tile
21–28 art of the Persians
21 tower tomb
22 stepped pyramid
23 double bull column
24 projecting leaves
25 palm capital
26 volute (scroll)
27 shaft
28 double bull capital
29–36 art of the Assyrians
29 Sargon's Palace, palace buildings
30 city wall
31 castle wall
32 temple tower (ziggurat), a stepped (terraced) tower
33 outside staircase
34 main portal
35 portal relief
36 portal figure
37 art of Asia Minor
38 rock tomb

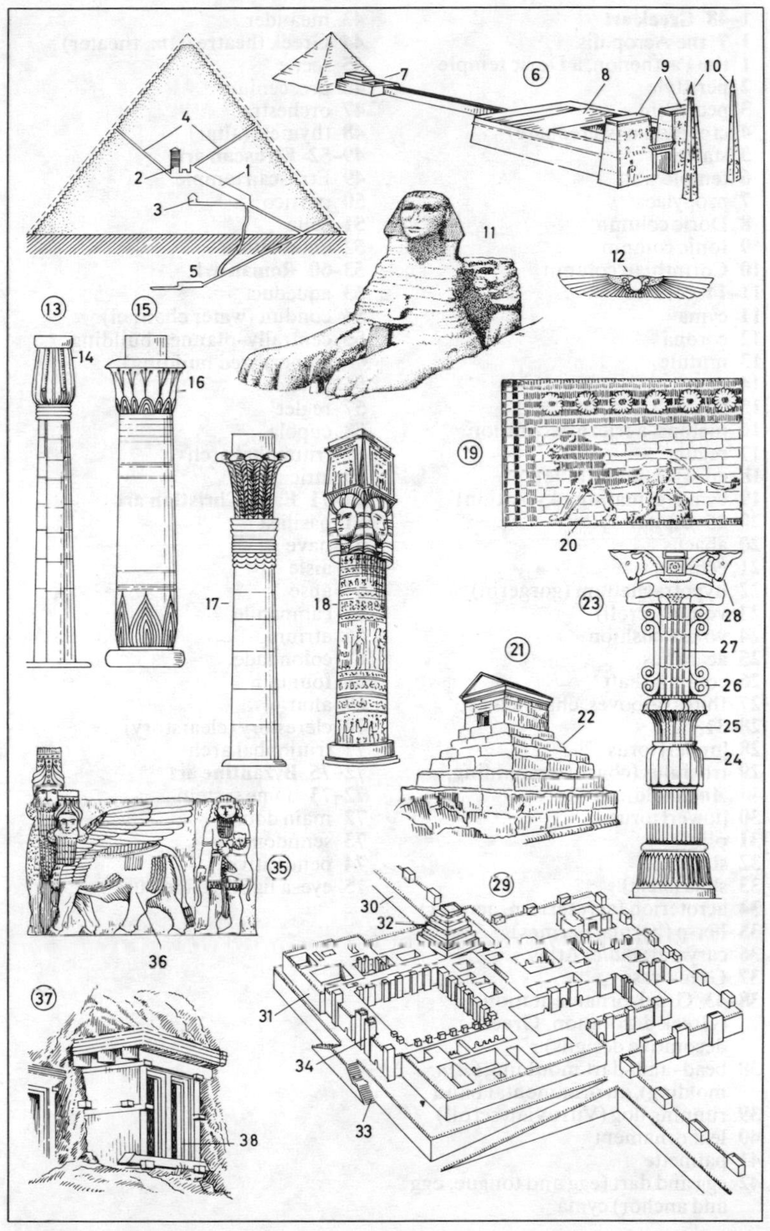
1
2
3
4
5
6
7
8
9
10
11
12
13
14
15
16
17
18
19
20
21
22
23
24
25
26
27
28
29
30
31
32
33
34
35
36
37
38

1–48 Greek art
1–7 the Acropolis
1 the Parthenon, a Doric temple
2 peristyle
3 pediment
4 crepidoma (stereobate)
5 statue
6 temple wall
7 propylaea
8 Doric column
9 Ionic column
10 Corinthian column
11–14 cornice
11 cyma
12 corona
13 mutule
14 dentils
15 triglyph
16 metope, a frieze decoration
17 regula
18 epistyle (architrave)
19 cyma (cymatium, kymation)
20–25 capital
20 abacus
21 echinus
22 hypotrachelium (gorgerin)
23 volute (scroll)
24 volute cushion
25 acanthus
26 column shaft
27 flutes (grooves, channels)
28–31 base
28 [upper] torus
29 trochilus (concave moulding, *Am.* molding)
30 [lower] torus
31 plinth
32 stylobate
33 stele (stela)
34 acroterion (acroterium, acroter)
35 herm (herma, hermes)
36 caryatid; *male:* Atlas
37 Greek vase
38–43 Greek ornamentation (Greek decoration, Greek decorative designs)
38 bead-and-dart moulding (*Am.* molding), an ornamental band
39 running dog (Vitruvian scroll)
40 leaf ornament
41 palmette
42 egg and dart (egg and tongue, egg and anchor) cyma
43 meander
44 Greek theatre (*Am.* theater)
45 scene
46 proscenium
47 orchestra
48 thymele (altar)
49–52 Etruscan art
49 Etruscan temple
50 portico
51 cella
52 entablature
53–60 Roman art
53 aqueduct
54 conduit (water channel)
55 centrally-planned building (centralized building)
56 portico
57 reglet
58 cupola
59 triumphal arch
60 attic
61–71 Early Christian art
61 basilica
62 nave
63 aisle
64 apse
65 campanile
66 atrium
67 colonnade
68 fountain
69 altar
70 clerestory (clearstory)
71 triumphal arch
72–75 Byzantine art
72–73 dome system
72 main dome
73 semidome
74 pendentive
75 eye, a lighting aperture

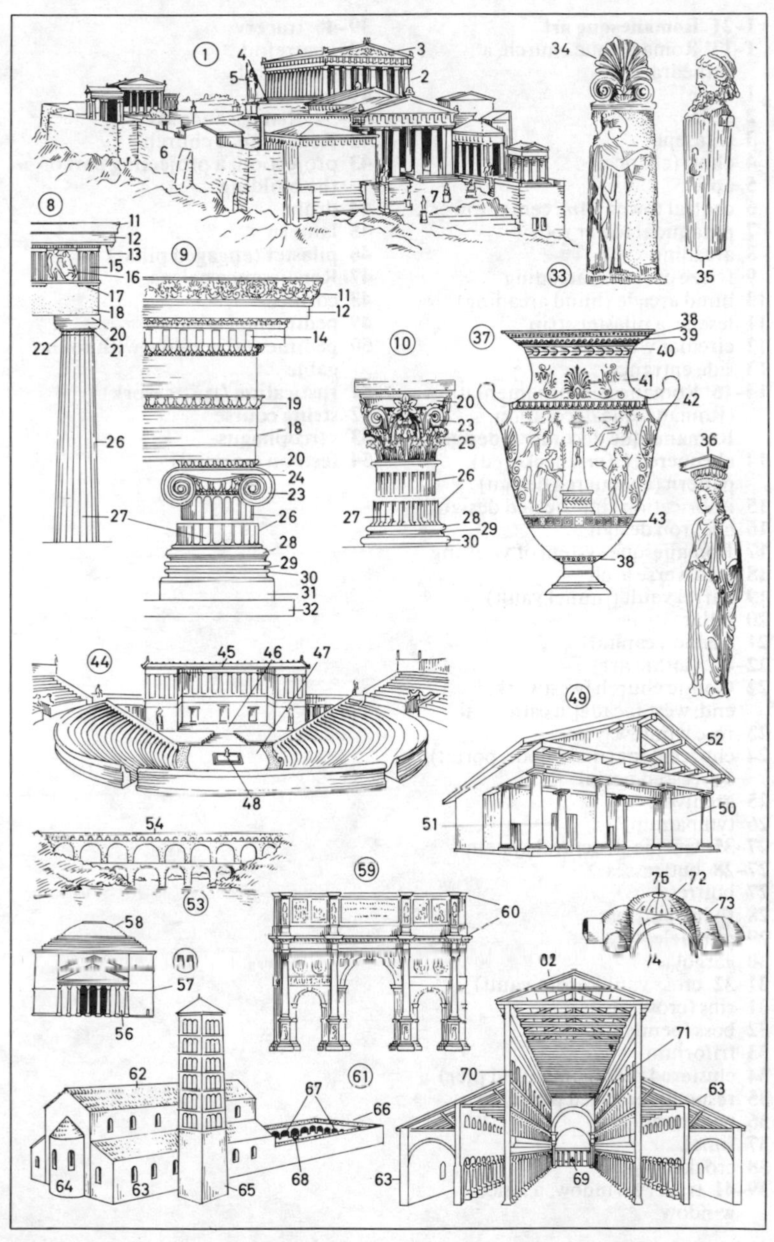
1
2
3
4
5
6
7
8
9
10
11
12
13
14
15
16
17
18
19
20
21
22
23
24
25
26
27
28
29
30
31
32
33
34
35
36
37
38
39
40
41
42
43
44
45
46
47
48
49
50
51
52
53
54
56
57
58
59
60
61
62
63
64
65
66
67
68
69
70
71
72
73
75

1–21 Romanesque art
1–13 Romanesque church, a cathedral
1 nave
2 aisle
3 transept
4 choir (chancel)
5 apse
6 central tower (*Am.* center tower)
7 pyramidal tower roof
8 arcading
9 frieze of round arcading
10 blind arcade (blind arcading)
11 lesene, a pilaster strip
12 circular window
13 side entrance
14–16 Romanesque ornamentation (Romanesque decoration, Romanesque decorative designs)
14 chequered (*Am.* checkered) pattern (chequered design)
15 imbrication (imbricated design)
16 chevron design
17 Romanesque system of vaulting
18 transverse arch
19 barrel vault (tunnel vault)
20 pillar
21 cushion capital
22–41 Gothic art
22 Gothic church [westwork, west end, west façade], a cathedral
23 rose window
24 church door (main door, portal), a recessed portal
25 archivolt
26 tympanum
27–35 Gothic structural system
27–28 buttresses
27 buttress
28 flying buttress
29 pinnacle
30 gargoyle
31–32 cross vault (groin vault)
31 ribs (cross ribs)
32 boss (pendant)
33 triforium
34 clustered pier (compound pier)
35 respond (engaged pillar)
36 pediment
37 finial
38 crocket
39–41 tracery window, a lancet window
39–40 tracery
39 quatrefoil
40 cinquefoil
41 mullions
42–54 Renaissance art
42 Renaissance church
43 projection, a projecting part of the building
44 drum
45 lantern
46 pilaster (engaged pillar)
47 Renaissance palace
48 cornice
49 pedimental window
50 pedimental window with round gable
51 rustication (rustic work)
52 string course
53 sarcophagus
54 festoon (garland)

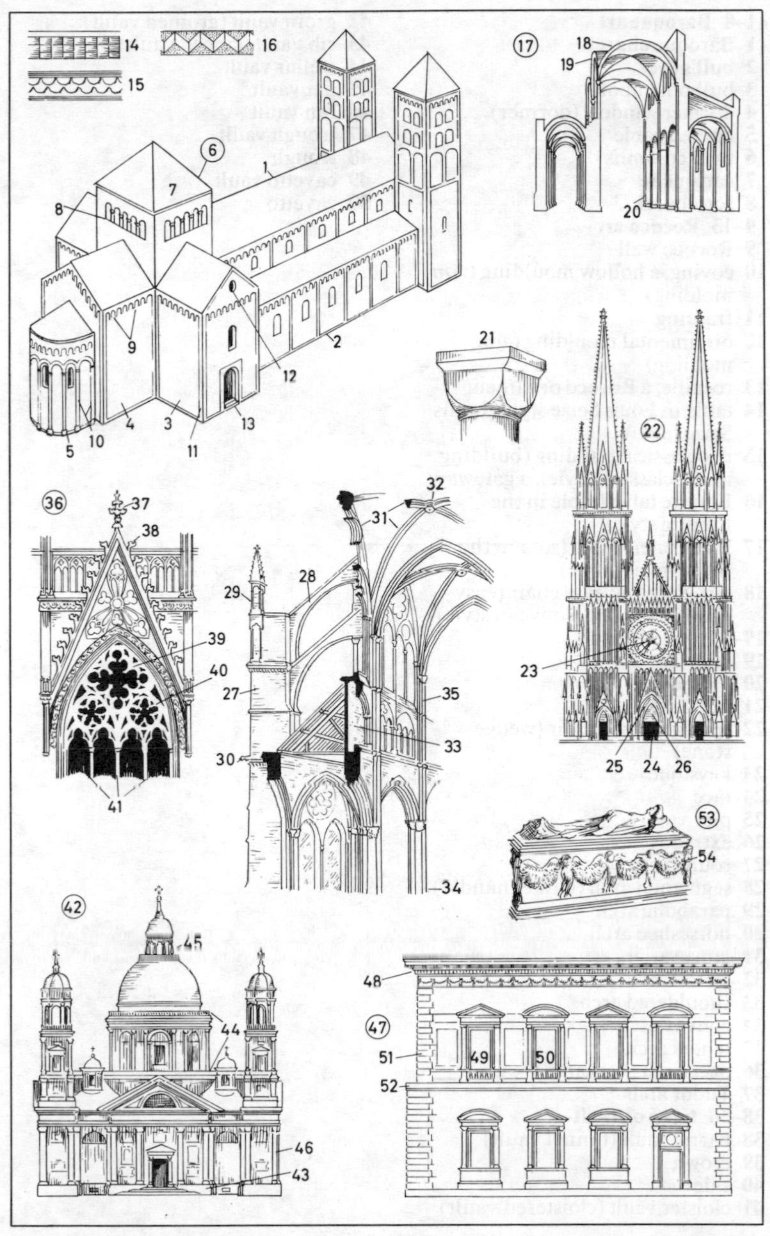
14
15
16
17
18
19
20
6
1
7
8
9
12
2
10
5
4
3
11
13
21
22
36
37
38
39
40
41
32
31
28
29
27
35
33
30
34
23
25
24
26
53
54
42
45
44
46
43
48
47
51
49
50
52

1–8 Baroque art
1 Baroque church
2 bull's eye
3 bulbous cupola
4 dormer window (dormer)
5 curved gable
6 twin columns
7 cartouche
8 scrollwork
9–13 Rococo art
9 Rococo wall
10 coving, a hollow moulding (*Am.* molding)
11 framing
12 ornamental moulding (*Am.* molding)
13 rocaille, a Rococo ornament
14 table in Louis Seize style (Louis Seize table)
15 neoclassical building (building in neoclassical style), a gateway
16 Empire table (table in the Empire style)
17 Biedermeier sofa (sofa in the Biedermeier style)
18 Art Nouveau easy chair (easy chair in the Art Nouveau style)
19–37 types of arch
19 arch
20 abutment
21 impost
22 springer, a voussoir (wedge stone)
23 keystone
24 face
25 pier
26 extrados
27 round arch
28 segmental arch (basket handle)
29 parabolic arch
30 horseshoe arch
31 lancet arch
32 trefoil arch
33 shouldered arch
34 convex arch
35 tented arch
36 ogee arch (keel arch)
37 Tudor arch
38–50 types of vault
38 barrel vault (tunnel vault)
39 crown
40 side
41 cloister vault (cloistered vault)
42 groin vault (groined vault)
43 rib vault (ribbed vault)
44 stellar vault
45 net vault
46 fan vault
47 trough vault
48 trough
49 cavetto vault
50 cavetto

1
2
3
4
5
6
7
8
9
10
11
12
13
14
15
16
17
18
19
20
21
22
23
24
25
26
27
28
29
30
31
32
33
34
35
36
37
38
39
40
41
42
43
44
45
46
47
48
49
50

1-6 Chinese art
1 pagoda (multi-storey, multistory, pagoda), a temple tower
2 storey (story) roof (roof of storey)
3 pailou (pailoo), a memorial archway
4 archway
5 porcelain vase
6 incised lacquered work
7-11 Japanese art
7 temple
8 bell tower
9 supporting structure
10 bodhisattva (boddhisattva), a Buddhist saint
11 torii, a gateway
12-18 Islamic art
12 mosque
13 minaret, a prayer tower
14 mihrab
15 minbar (mimbar, pulpit)
16 mausoleum, a tomb
17 stalactite vault (stalactitic vault)
18 Arabian capital
19-28 Indian art
19 dancing Siva (Shiva), an Indian god
20 statue of Buddha
21 stupa (Indian pagoda), a mound (dome), a Buddhist shrine
22 umbrella
23 stone wall (*Am.* stone fence)
24 gate
25 temple buildings
26 shikara (sikar, sikhara, temple tower)
27 chaitya hall
28 chaitya, a small stupa

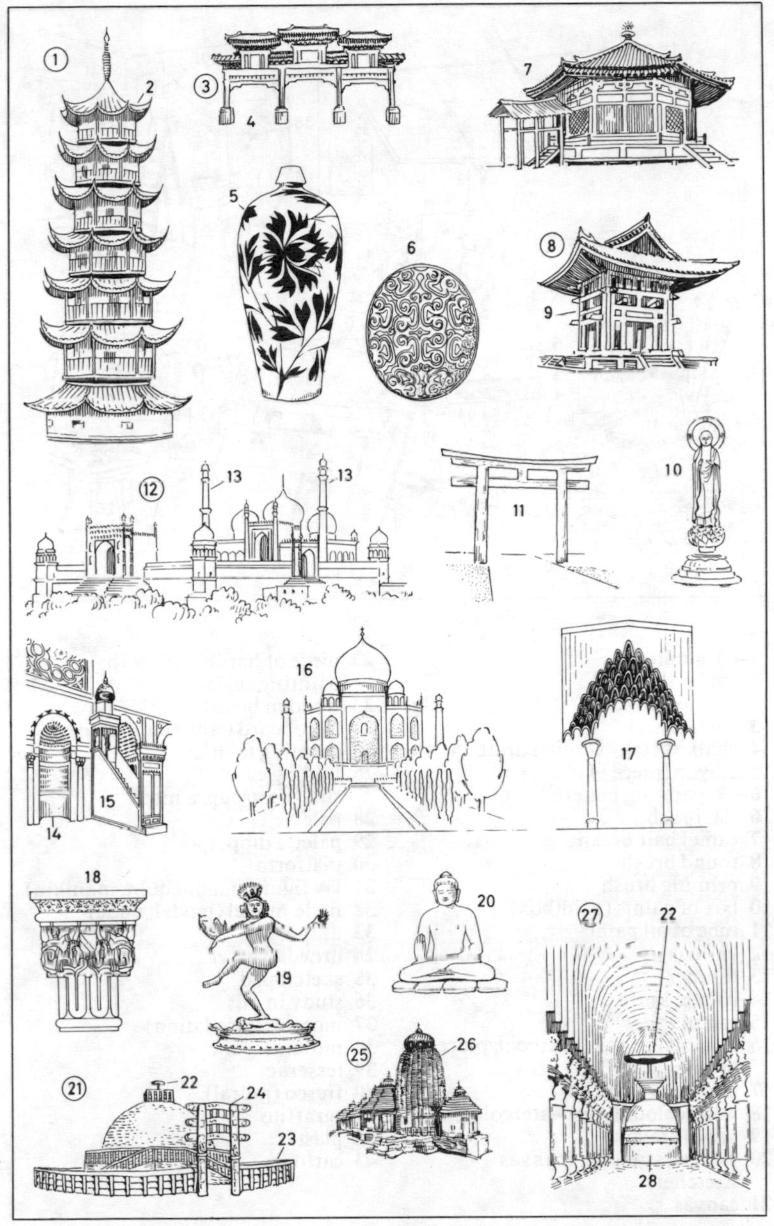
1
2
3
4
5
6
7
8
9
10
11
12
13
13
14
15
16
17
18
19
20
21
22
23
24
25
26
27
22
28

338 Artist's Studio

1–43 studio
1 studio skylight
2 painter, an artist
3 studio easel
4 chalk sketch, a rough draft
5 crayon (piece of chalk)
6–19 painting materials
6 flat brush
7 camel hair brush
8 round brush
9 priming brush
10 box of paints (paintbox)
11 tube of oil paint
12 varnish
13 thinner
14 palette knife
15 spatula
16 charcoal pencil (charcoal, piece of charcoal)
17 tempera (gouache)
18 watercolour (*Am.* watercolor)
19 pastel crayon
20 wedged stretcher (canvas stretcher)
21 canvas
22 piece of hardboard, with painting surface
23 wooden board
24 fibreboard (*Am.* fiberboard)
25 painting table
26 folding easel
27 still life group, a motif
28 palette
29 palette dipper
30 platform
31 lay figure (mannequin, manikin)
32 nude model (model, nude)
33 drapery
34 drawing easel
35 sketch pad
36 study in oils
37 mosaic (tessellation)
38 mosaic figure
39 tesserae
40 fresco (mural)
41 sgraffito
42 plaster
43 cartoon

1 sculptor
2 proportional dividers
3 calliper (caliper)
4 plaster model, a plaster cast
5 block of stone (stone block)
6 modeller (*Am.* modeler)
7 clay figure, a torso
8 roll of clay, a modelling (*Am.* modeling) substance
9 modelling (*Am.* modeling) stand
10 wooden modelling (*Am.* modeling) tool
11 wire modelling (*Am.* modeling) tool
12 beating wood
13 claw chisel (toothed chisel, tooth chisel)
14 flat chisel
15 point (punch)
16 iron-headed hammer
17 gouge (hollow chisel)
18 spoon chisel
19 wood chisel, a bevelled-edge chisel
20 V-shaped gouge
21 mallet
22 framework
23 baseboard
24 armature support (metal rod)
25 armature
26 wax model
27 block of wood
28 wood carver (wood sculptor)
29 sack of gypsum powder (gypsum)
30 clay box
31 modelling (*Am.* modeling) clay (clay)
32 statue, a sculpture
33 low relief (bas-relief)
34 modelling (*Am.* modeling) board
35 wire frame, wire netting
36 circular medallion (tondo)
37 mask
38 plaque

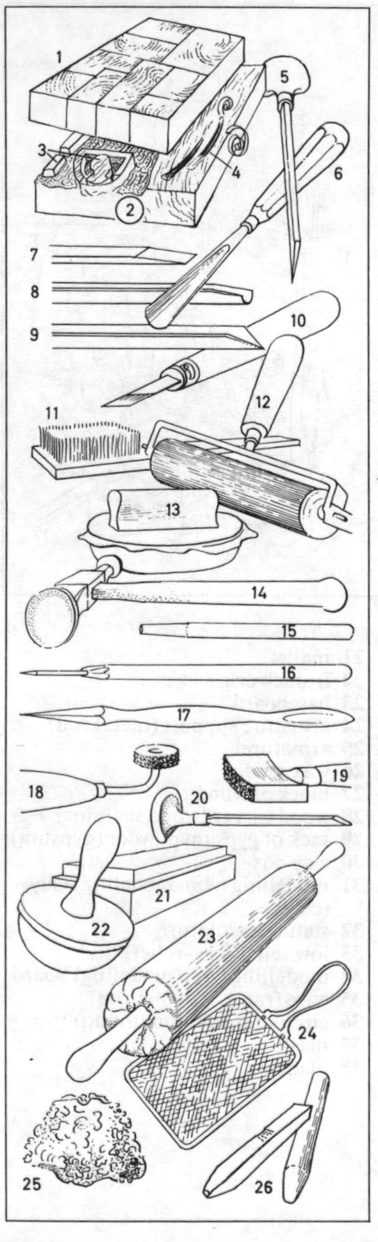

1-13 wood engraving (xylography), a relief printing method (a letterpress printing method)
1 end-grain block for wood engravings, a wooden block
2 wooden plank for woodcutting, a relief image carrier
3 positive cut
4 plank cut
5 burin (graver)
6 U-shaped gouge
7 scorper (scauper, scalper)
8 scoop
9 V-shaped gouge
10 contour knife
11 brush
12 roller (brayer)
13 pad (wiper)
14-24 copperplate engraving (chalcography), an intaglio process; *kinds:* etching, mezzotint, aquatint, crayon engraving
14 hammer
15 burin
16 etching needle (engraver)
17 scraper and burnisher
18 roulette
19 rocking tool (rocker)
20 round-headed graver, a graver (burin)
21 oilstone
22 dabber (inking ball, ink ball)
23 leather roller
24 sieve
25-26 lithography (stone lithography), a planographic printing method
25 sponge for moistening the lithographic stone
26 lithographic crayons (greasy chalk)
27-64 graphic art studio, a printing office (*Am.* printery)
27 broadside (broadsheet, single sheet)
28 full-colour (*Am.* full-color) print (colour print, chromolithograph)
29 platen press, a hand press
30 toggle
31 platen
32 type forme (*Am.* form)

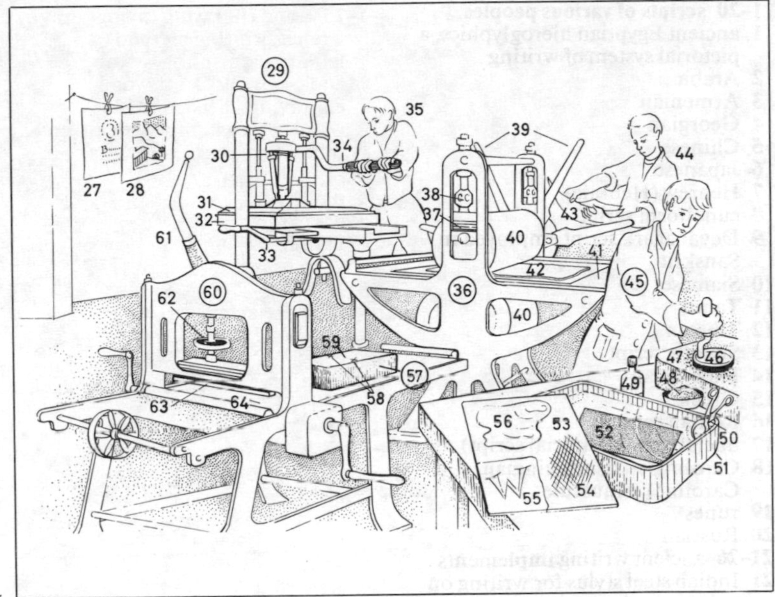

33 feed mechanism
34 bar (devil's tail)
35 pressman
36 copperplate press
37 tympan
38 pressure regulator
39 star wheel
40 cylinder
41 bed
42 felt cloth
43 proof (pull)
44 copperplate engraver
45 lithographer (litho artist), grinding the stone
46 grinding disc (disk)
47 grain (granular texture)
48 pulverized glass
49 rubber solution
50 tongs
51 etching bath for etching
52 zinc plate
53 polished copperplate
54 cross hatch
55 etching ground
56 non-printing area
57 lithographic stone
58 register marks
59 printing surface (printing image carrier)
60 lithographic press
61 lever
62 scraper adjustment
63 scraper
64 bed

341 Script I

1–20 scripts of various peoples
1 ancient Egyptian hieroglyphics, a pictorial system of writing
2 Arabic
3 Armenian
4 Georgian
5 Chinese
6 Japanese
7 Hebrew (Hebraic)
8 cuneiform script
9 Devanagari, script employed in Sanskrit
10 Siamese
11 Tamil
12 Tibetan
13 Sinaitic script
14 Phoenician
15 Greek
16 Roman capitals
17 uncial (uncials, uncial script)
18 Carolingian (Carlovingian, Caroline) minuscule
19 runes
20 Russian
21–26 ancient writing implements
21 Indian steel stylus for writing on palm leaves
22 ancient Egyptian reed pen
23 writing cane
24 brush
25 Roman metal pen (stylus)
26 quill (quill pen)
27 Korean

1

3

圖書館
图书馆 5

اتصف بالشجاعة اما

2

მამინ პიროვ

4

新しい 6

7

8

9

ยัง ไร เกือน เก่า ลบ

10

11

12

13

14

Τῆς παρελθούσης νυκτὸ

15

IMPCAESARI·

16

MINISUENJE

17

addiem festum

18

19

Кожух генератора и

20

책입니다 27

21

22

23

24

25

26

1-15 types (type faces)
1 Gothic type (German black-letter type)
2 Schwabacher type (German black-letter type)
3 Fraktur (German black-letter type)
4 Humanist (Mediaeval)
5 Transitional
6 Didone
7 Sanserif (Sanserif type, Grotesque)
8 Egyptian
9 typescript (typewriting)
10 English hand (English handwriting, English writing)
11 German hand (German handwriting, German writing)
12 Latin script
13 shorthand (shorthand writing, stenography)
14 phonetics (phonetic transcription)
15 Braille
16-29 punctuation marks (stops)
16 full stop (period, full point)
17 colon
18 comma
19 semicolon
20 question mark (interrogation point, interrogation mark)
21 exclamation mark (*Am.* exclamation point)
22 apostrophe
23 dash (em rule)
24 parentheses (round brackets)
25 square brackets
26 quotation mark (double quotation marks, paired quotation marks, inverted commas)
27 guillemet (French quotation mark)
28 hyphen
29 marks of omission (ellipsis)
30-35 accents and diacritical marks (diacritics)
30 acute accent (acute)
31 grave accent (grave)
32 circumflex accent (circumflex)
33 cedilla [under c]
34 diaeresis (*Am.* dieresis) [over e]
35 tilde [over n]
36 section mark
37-70 newspaper, a national daily newspaper
37 newspaper page
38 front page
39 newspaper heading
40 contents
41 price
42 date of publication
43 place of publication
44 headline
45 column
46 column heading
47 column rule
48 leading article (leader, editorial)
49 reference to related article
50 brief news item
51 political section
52 page heading
53 cartoon
54 report by newspaper's own correspondent
55 news agency's sign
56 advertisement (*coll.* ad)
57 sports section
58 press photo
59 caption
60 sports report
61 sports news item
62 home and overseas news section
63 news in brief (miscellaneous news)
64 television programmes (*Am.* programs)
65 weather report
66 weather chart (weather map)
67 arts section (feuilleton)
68 death notice
69 advertisements (classified advertising)
70 job advertisement, a vacancy (a situation offered)

Oxford 1
Oxford 2
Oxford 3
Oxford 4
Oxford 5
Oxford 6
Oxford 7
Oxford 8
Oxford 9
Oxford 10
Oxford 11
Oxford 12
13
ˈɔksfəd 14
15
. 16
: 17
, 18
; 19
? 20
! 21
’ 22
— 23
() 24
[] 25
„ “ 26
» « 27
- 28
... 29
é 30
è 31
ê 32
ç 33
ë 34
ñ 35
§ 36
37
69
GUARDIAN PERSONAL
HOMEFINDER
A houseproud nation?
APPOINTMENTS
68
70
THE GUARDIAN
SPORTS GUARDIAN
PARLIAMENT 52
51
57
Unions will have to pay to strike soon, says PM
Walker plan to cut
McKenzie—just one of the lads
60
48
ARTS GUARDIAN 67
54
OVERSEAS NEWS 62
of its own
Fulham win a round in pay inquiry
TELEVISION/RADIO
64
39 THE GUARDIAN
43
42
41
NEWS IN BRIEF
Kidnap shooting widow's despair
58
61
BBC-1
46
Steelmen cheer rejection of 14pc offer
44
Thatcher will cut strikers' benefit
63
Mugabe banned from campaign in two areas
GEC loses takeover battle
BBC-2
59
ITV—LONDON
45
47
FAKENHAM
Anxiety over Tito
ENTERTAINMENTS
40
50
56
Plan to dock state pay revived
38
53
Colin will be 8 years old for the rest of his life.
55
65
INSIDE
40
Iran 'hostage solution' on Carter's desk
66

343 Colour (*Am.* Color)

1 red
2 yellow
3 blue
4 pink
5 brown
6 azure (sky blue)
7 orange
8 green
9 violet
10 additive mixture of colours (*Am.* colors)
11 white
12 subtractive mixture of colours (*Am.* colors)
13 black
14 solar spectrum (colours, *Am.* colors, of the rainbow)
15 grey (*Am.* gray) scale
16 heat colours (*Am.* colors)

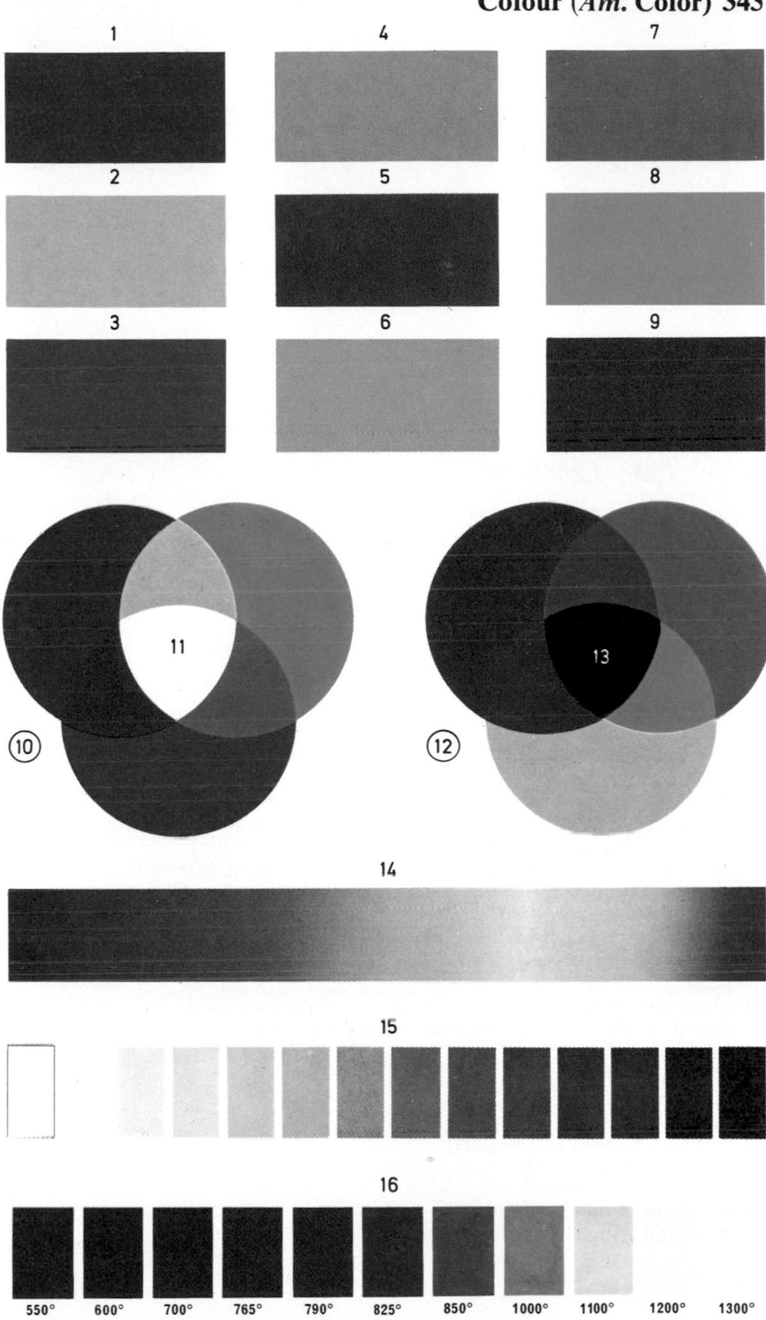
1
4
7
2
5
8
3
6
9
11
13
10
12
14
15
16
550°
600°
700°
765°
790°
825°
850°
1000°
1100°
1200°
1300°

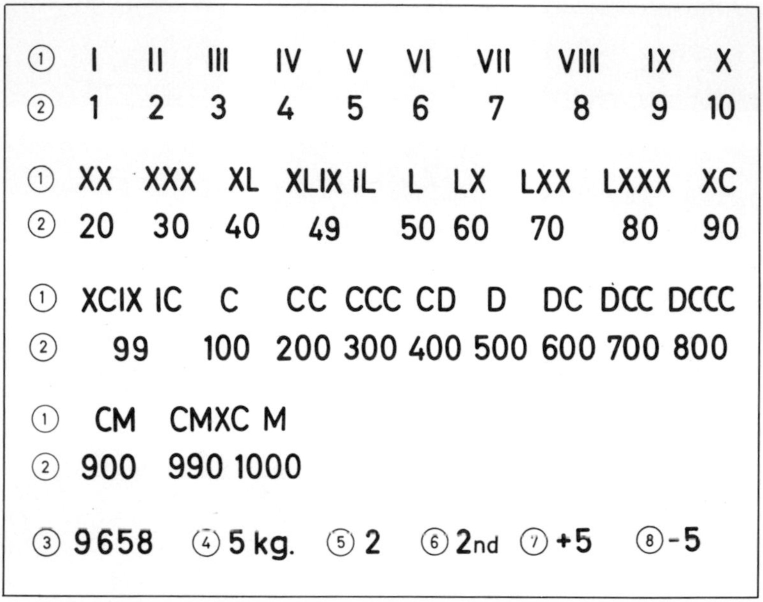

① I II III IV V VI VII VIII IX X
② 1 2 3 4 5 6 7 8 9 10

① XX XXX XL XLIX IL L LX LXX LXXX XC
② 20 30 40 49 50 60 70 80 90

① XCIX IC C CC CCC CD D DC DCC DCCC
② 99 100 200 300 400 500 600 700 800

① CM CMXC M
② 900 990 1000

③ 9658 ④ 5 kg. ⑤ 2 ⑥ 2nd ⑦ +5 ⑧ -5

1–26 arithmetic
1–22 numbers
1 Roman numerals
2 Arabic numerals
3 abstract number, a four-figure number [8: units; 5: tens; 6: hundreds; 9: thousands]
4 concrete number
5 cardinal number (cardinal)
6 ordinal number (ordinal)
7 positive number [with plus sign]
8 negative number [with minus sign]
9 algebraic symbols
10 mixed number [3: whole number (integer); $\frac{1}{3}$: fraction]
11 even numbers
12 odd numbers
13 prime numbers
14 complex number [3: real part; $2\sqrt{-1}$: imaginary part]
15–16 vulgar fractions
15 proper fraction [2: numerator, horizontal line; 3: denominator]
16 improper fraction, also the reciprocal of item 15
17 compound fraction (complex fraction)
18 improper fraction [when cancelled down produces a whole number]
19 fractions of different denominations [35: common denominator]
20 proper decimal fraction with decimal point and decimal places [3: tenths; 5: hundredths; 7: thousandths]
21 recurring decimal
22 recurring decimal

(9) a, b, c ... (10) $3\frac{1}{3}$ (11) 2, 4, 6, 8 (12) 1, 3, 5, 7

(13) 3, 5, 7, 11 (14) $3+2\sqrt{-1}$ (15) $\frac{2}{3}$ (16) $\frac{3}{2}$

(17) $\frac{\frac{5}{6}}{\frac{3}{4}}$ (18) $\frac{12}{4}$ (19) $\frac{4}{5}+\frac{2}{7}=\frac{38}{35}$ (20) 0·357

(21) 0·6666.... = $0\cdot\bar{6}$ (22) (23) 3 + 2 = 5

(24) 3 - 2 = 1 (25) 3 · 2 = 6
3 × 2 = 6 (26) 6 ÷ 2 = 3

23–26 fundamental arithmetical operations

23 addition (adding) [3 and 2: the terms of the sum; +: plus sign; =: equals sign; 5: the sum]

24 subtraction (subtracting); [3: the minuend; – : minus sign; 2: the subtrahend; 1: the remainder (difference)]

25 multiplication (multiplying); [3: the multiplicand; × : multiplication sign; 2: the multiplier; 2 and 3: factors; 6: the product]

26 division (dividing); [6: the dividend; ÷: division sign; 2: the divisor; 3: the quotient]

① $3^2 = 9$ ② $\sqrt[3]{8} = 2$ ③ $\sqrt{4} = 2$

④ $3x + 2 = 12$

⑤ $4a + 6ab - 2ac = 2a(2 + 3b - c)$ ⑥ $\log_{10} 3 = 0{\cdot}4771$

⑦ $\frac{P[£1000] \times R[5\%] \times T[2\,years]}{100} = I[£100]$

1–24 arithmetic

1–10 advanced arithmetical operations

1 raising to a power [three squared (3^2): the power; 3: the base; 2: the exponent (index); 9: value of the power]

2 evolution (extracting a root); [cube-root of 8: cube root; 8: the radical; 3: the index (degree) of the root; $\sqrt{\ }$: radical sign; 2: value of the root]

3 square root

4–5 algebra

4 simple equation [3, 2: the coefficients; x: the unknown quantity]

5 identical equation; [a, b, c: algebraic symbols]

6 logarithmic calculation (taking the logarithm, log); [log: logarithm sign; 3: number whose logarithm is required; 10: the base; 0: the characteristic; 4771: the mantissa; 0.4771: the logarithm]

7 simple interest formula; [P: the principal; R: rate of interest; T: time; I: interest (profit); %: percentage sign]

8–10 rule of three (rule-of-three sum, simple proportion)

8 statement with the unknown quantity x

9 equation (conditional equation)

10 solution

11–14 higher mathematics

11 arithmetical series with the elements 2, 4, 6, 8

12 geometrical series

13–14 infinitesimal calculus

13 derivative [dx, dy: the differentials; d: differential sign]

14 integral (integration); [x: the variable; C: constant of integration; S: the integral sign; dx: the differential]

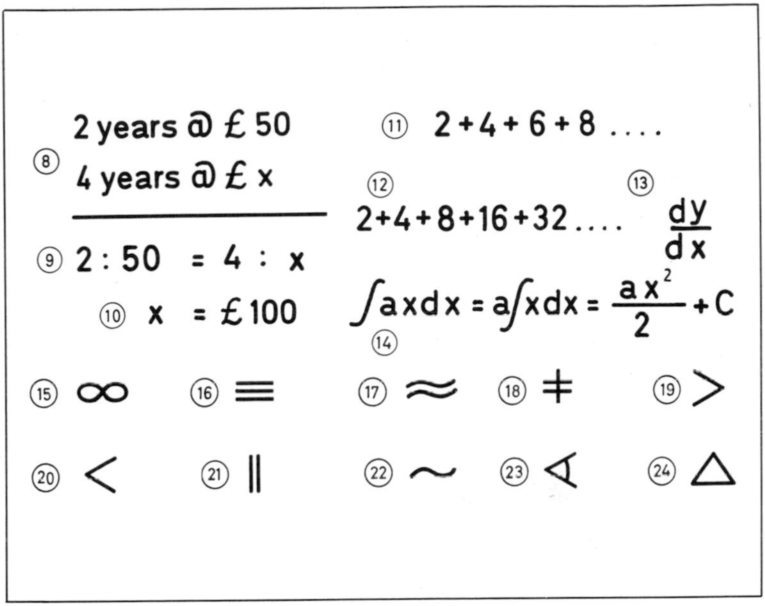

(8) 2 years @ £ 50

4 years @ £ x

(9) 2 : 50 = 4 : x

(10) x = £ 100

(11) $2 + 4 + 6 + 8 \ldots$

(12) $2 + 4 + 8 + 16 + 32 \ldots$

(13) $\frac{dy}{dx}$

(14) $\int ax\,dx = a\int x\,dx = \frac{ax^2}{2} + C$

(15) ∞ (16) $\equiv$ (17) $\approx$ (18) $\neq$ (19) $>$

(20) $<$ (21) $\parallel$ (22) $\sim$ (23) $\sphericalangle$ (24) $\triangle$

15–24 mathematical symbols
15 infinity
16 identically equal to (the sign of identity)
17 approximately equal to
18 unequal to
19 greater than
20 less than
21–24 geometrical symbols
21 parallel (sign of parallelism)
22 similar to (sign of similarity)
23 angle symbol
24 triangle symbol

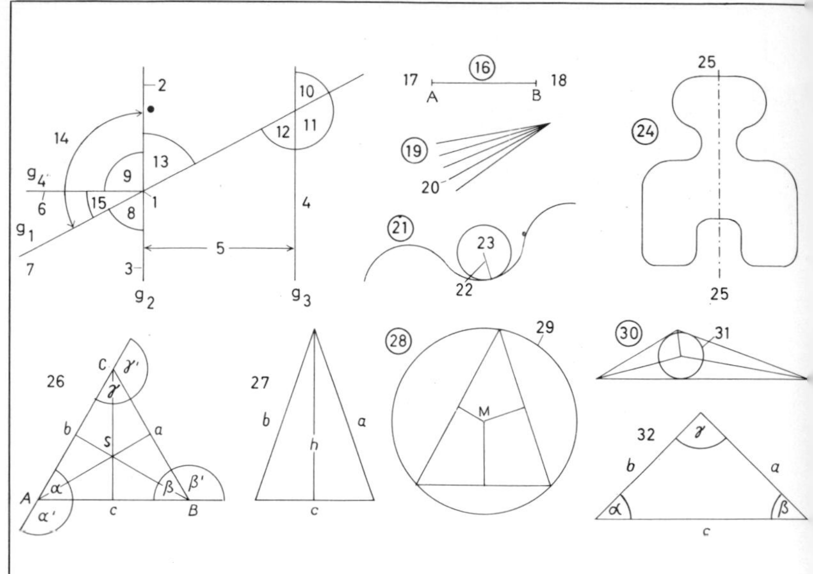

1–58 plane geometry (elementary geometry, Euclidian geometry)

1–23 point, line, angle

1 point [point of intersection of g_1 and g_2], the angular point of 8

2, 3 straight line g_2

4 the parallel to g_2

5 distance between the straight lines g_2 and g_3

6 perpendicular (g_4) on g_2

7, 3 the arms of 8

8, 13 vertically opposite angles

8 angle

9 right angle [90°]

10, 11, 12 reflex angle

10 acute angle, also the alternate angle to 8

11 obtuse angle

12 corresponding angle to 8

13, 9, 15 straight angle [180°]

14 adjacent angle; *here:* supplementary angle to 13

15 complementary angle to 8

16 straight line AB

17 end A

18 end B

19 pencil of rays

20 ray

21 curved line

22 radius of curvature

23 centre (*Am.* center) of curvature

24–58 plane surfaces

24 symmetrical figure

25 axis of symmetry

26–32 plane triangles

26 equilateral triangle; [A, B, C: the vertices; a, b, c: the sides; α (alpha), β (beta), γ (gamma): the interior angles; α′, β′, γ′: the exterior angles; S: the centre (*Am.* center)]

27 isoceles triangle [a, b: the sides (legs); c: the base; h: the perpendicular, an altitude]

28 acute-angled triangle with perpendicular bisectors of the sides

29 circumcircle (circumscribed circle)

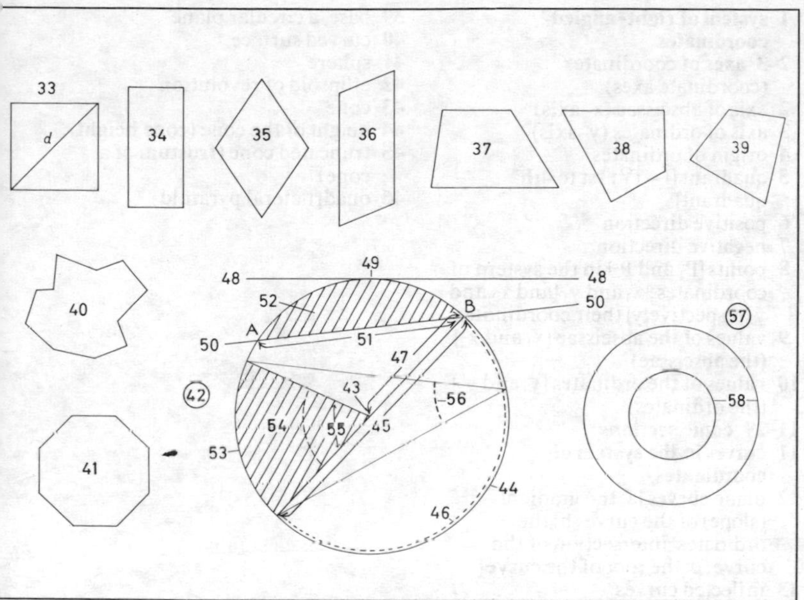

30 obtuse-angled triangle with bisectors of the angles
31 inscribed circle
32 right-angled triangle and the trigonometrical functions of angles; [a, b: the catheti; c: the hypotenuse; γ: the right angle; $\frac{a}{c}$ = sin α (sine); $\frac{b}{c}$ = cos α (cosine); $\frac{a}{b}$ = tan α (tangent); $\frac{b}{a}$ = cot α (cotangent)]
33–39 **quadrilaterals**
33–36 **parallelograms**
33 square [d: a diagonal]
34 rectangle
35 rhombus (rhomb, lozenge)
36 rhomboid
37 trapezium
38 deltoid (kite)
39 irregular quadrilateral
40 polygon
41 regular polygon
42 **circle**
43 centre (*Am.* center)
44 circumference (periphery)
45 diameter
46 semicircle
47 radius (r)
48 tangent
49 point of contact (P)
50 secant
51 the chord AB
52 segment
53 arc
54 sector
55 angle subtended by the arc at the centre (*Am.* center) (centre, *Am.* center, angle)
56 circumferential angle
57 ring (annulus)
58 concentric circles

347 Mathematics IV (Geometry II)

1 system of right-angled coordinates
2–3 axes of coordinates (coordinate axes)
2 axis of abscissae (x–axis)
3 axis of ordinates (y–axis)
4 origin of ordinates
5 quadrant [I – IV: 1st to 4th quadrant]
6 positive direction
7 negative direction
8 points [P_1 and P_2] in the system of coordinates; x_1 and y_1 [and x_2 and y_2 respectively] their coordinates
9 values of the abscissae [x_1 and x_2] (the abscissae)
10 values of the ordinates [y_1 and y_2] (the ordinates)
11–29 conic sections
11 curves in the system of coordinates
12 plane curves [a: the gradient (slope) of the curve; b: the ordinates' intersection of the curve; c: the root of the curve]
13 inflected curves
14 parabola, a curve of the second degree
15 branches of the parabola
16 vertex of the parabola
17 axis of the parabola
18 a curve of the third degree
19 maximum of the curve
20 minimum of the curve
21 point of inflexion (of inflection)
22 ellipse
23 transverse axis (major axis)
24 conjugate axis (minor axis)
25 foci of the ellipse [F_1 and F_2]
26 hyperbola
27 foci [F_1 and F_2]
28 vertices [S_1 and S_2]
29 asymptotes [a and b]
30–46 solids
30 cube
31 square, a plane (plane surface)
32 edge
33 corner
34 quadratic prism
35 base
36 parallelepiped
37 triangular prism
38 cylinder, a right cylinder
39 base, a circular plane
40 curved surface
41 sphere
42 ellipsoid of revolution
43 cone
44 height of the cone (cone height)
45 truncated cone (frustum of a cone)
46 quadrilateral pyramid

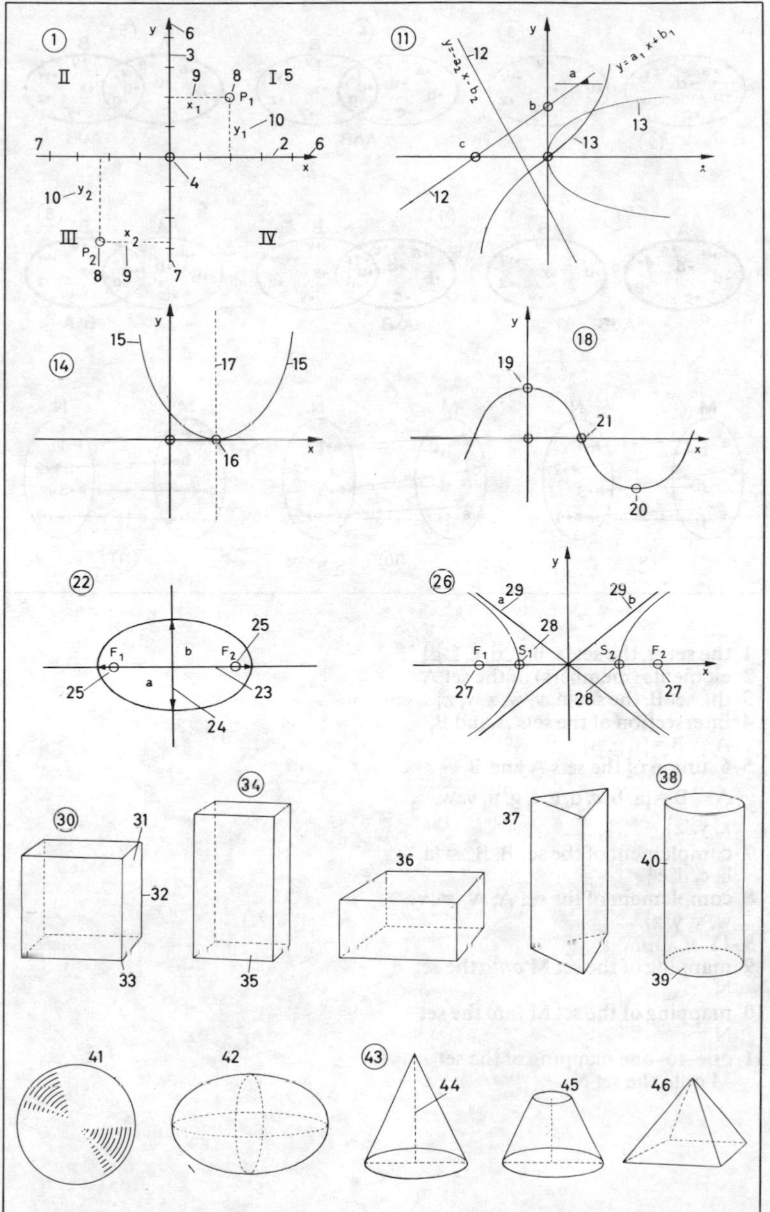
1
y
6
3
II
9
8
I 5
x_1
P_1
y_1
10
7
2
6
x
4
10
y_2
III
x_2
IV
P_2
8
9
7
11
$y=a_2x+b_2$
12
y
$y=a_1x+b_1$
a
b
13
c
13
x
12
14
y
15
17
15
16
x
18
y
19
21
x
20
22
25
F_1
b
F_2
25
a
23
24
26
y
a
29
29
b
28
F_1
S_1
S_2
F_2
x
27
28
27
34
38
30
31
37
32
36
40
33
35
39
41
42
43
44
45
46

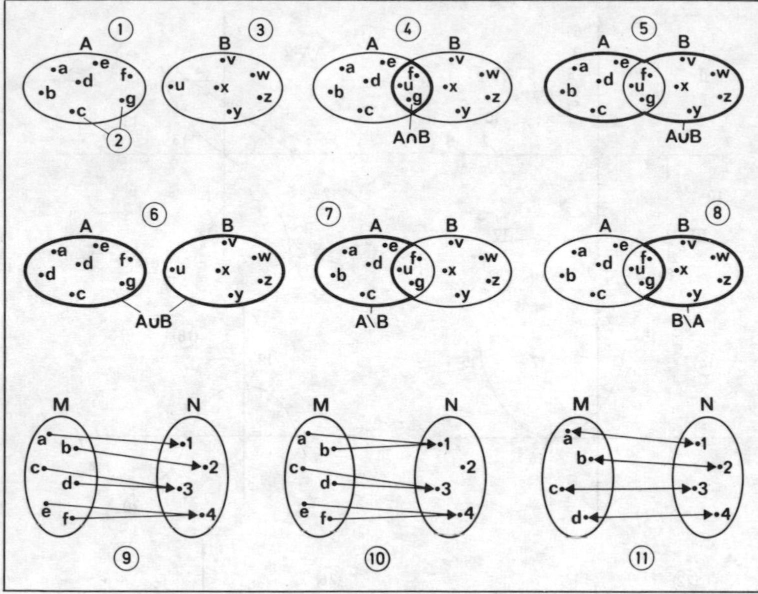

1 the set A, the set {a, b, c, d, e, f, g}
2 elements (members) of the set A
3 the set B, the set {u, v, w, x, y, z}
4 intersection of the sets A and B, $A \cap B = \{f, g, u\}$
5–6 union of the sets A and B,

$A \cup B = \{a, b, c, d, e, f, g, u, v, w, x, y, z\}$

7 complement of the set B, $B' = \{a, b, c, d, e\}$
8 complement of the set A, $A' = \{v, w, x, y, z\}$
9–11 mappings
9 mapping of the set M *onto* the set N
10 mapping of the set M *into* the set N
11 one-to-one mapping of the set M onto the set N

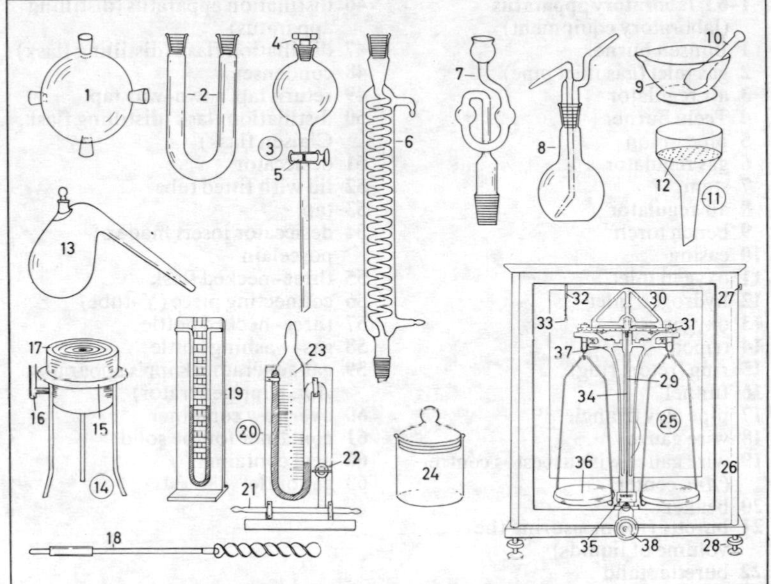

1–38 laboratory apparatus (laboratory equipment)
1 Scheidt globe
2 U-tube
3 separating funnel
4 octagonal ground-glass stopper
5 tap (*Am.* faucet)
6 coiled condenser
7 air lock
8 wash-bottle
9 mortar
10 pestle
11 filter funnel (Büchner funnel)
12 filter (filter plate)
13 retort
14 water bath
15 tripod
16 water gauge (*Am.* gage)
17 insertion rings
18 stirrer
19 manometer for measuring positive and negative pressures
20 mirror manometer for measuring small pressures
21 inlet
22 tap (*Am.* faucet)
23 sliding scale
24 weighing bottle
25 analytical balance
26 case
27 sliding front panel
28 three-point support
29 column (balance column)
30 balance beam (beam)
31 rider bar
32 rider holder
33 rider
34 pointer
35 scale
36 scale pan
37 stop
38 stop knob

1–63 laboratory apparatus (laboratory equipment)
1 Bunsen burner
2 gas inlet (gas inlet pipe)
3 air regulator
4 Teclu burner
5 pipe union
6 gas regulator
7 stem
8 air regulator
9 bench torch
10 casing
11 oxygen inlet
12 hydrogen inlet
13 oxygen jet
14 tripod
15 ring (retort ring)
16 funnel
17 pipe clay triangle
18 wire gauze
19 wire gauze with asbestos centre (*Am.* center)
20 beaker
21 burette (for measuring the volume of liquids)
22 burette stand
23 burette clamp
24 graduated pipette
25 pipette
26 measuring cylinder (measuring glass)
27 measuring flask
28 volumetric flask
29 evaporating dish (evaporating basin), made of porcelain
30 tube clamp (tube clip, pinchcock)
31 clay crucible with lid
32 crucible tongs
33 clamp
34 test tube
35 test tube rack
36 flat-bottomed flask
37 ground glass neck
38 long-necked round-bottomed flask
39 Erlenmeyer flask (conical flask)
40 filter flask
41 fluted filter
42 one-way tap
43 calcium chloride tube
44 stopper with tap
45 cylinder
46 distillation apparatus (distilling apparatus)
47 distillation flask (distilling flask)
48 condenser
49 return tap, a two-way tap
50 distillation flask (distilling flask, Claisen flask)
51 desiccator
52 lid with fitted tube
53 tap
54 desiccator insert made of porcelain
55 three-necked flask
56 connecting piece (Y-tube)
57 three-necked bottle
58 gas-washing bottle
59 gas generator (Kipp's apparatus, *Am.* Kipp generator)
60 overflow container
61 container for the solid
62 acid container
63 gas outlet

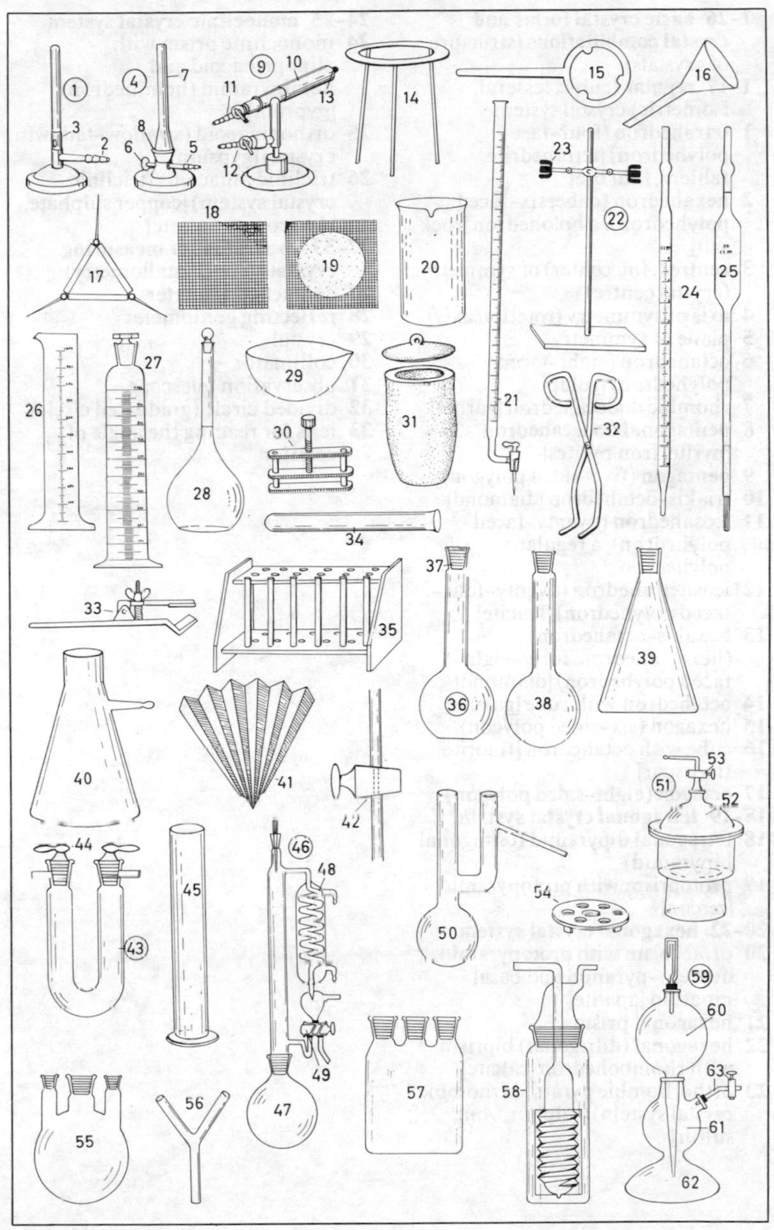
1
2
3
4
5
6
7
8
9
10
11
12
13
14
15
16
17
18
19
20
21
22
23
24
25
26
27
28
29
30
31
32
33
34
35
36
37
38
39
40
41
42
43
44
45
46
47
48
49
50
51
52
53
54
55
56
57
58
59
60
61
62
63

351 Crystals, Crystallography

1–26 basic crystal forms and crystal combinations (structure of crystals)
1–17 regular (cubic, tesseral, isometric) crystal system
1 tetrahedron (four-faced polyhedron) [tetrahedrite, fahlerz, fahl ore]
2 hexahedron (cube, six-faced polyhedron), a holohedron [rock salt]
3 centre (*Am.* center) of symmetry (crystal centre)
4 axis of symmetry (rotation axis)
5 plane of symmetry
6 octahedron (eight-faced polyhedron) [gold]
7 rhombic dodecahedron [garnet]
8 pentagonal dodecahedron [pyrite, iron pyrites]
9 pentagon (five-sided polygon)
10 triakis-octahedron [diamond]
11 icosahedron (twenty-faced polyhedron), a regular polyhedron
12 icositetrahedron (twenty-four-faced polyhedron) [leucite]
13 hexakis-octahedron (hexoctahedron, forty-eight-faced polyhedron) [diamond]
14 octahedron with cube [galena]
15 hexagon (six-sided polygon)
16 cube with octahedron [fluorite, fluorspar]
17 octagon (eight-sided polygon)
18–19 tetragonal crystal system
18 tetragonal dipyramid (tetragonal bipyramid)
19 protoprism with protopyramid [zircon]
20–22 hexagonal crystal system
20 protoprism with protopyramid, deutero-pyramid and basal pinacoid [apatite]
21 hexagonal prism
22 hexagonal (ditrigonal) biprism with rhombohedron [calcite]
23 orthorhombic pyramid (rhombic crystal system) [sulphur, *Am.* sulfur]
24–25 monoclinic crystal system
24 monoclinic prism with clinoprinacoid and hemipyramid (hemihedron) [gypsum]
25 orthopinacoid (swallow-tail twin crystal) [gypsum]
26 triclinic pinacoids (triclinic crystal system) [copper sulphate, *Am.* copper sulfate]
27–33 apparatus for measuring crystals (for crystallometry)
27 contact goniometer
28 reflecting goniometer
29 crystal
30 collimator
31 observation telescope
32 divided circle (graduated circle)
33 lens for reading the angle of rotation

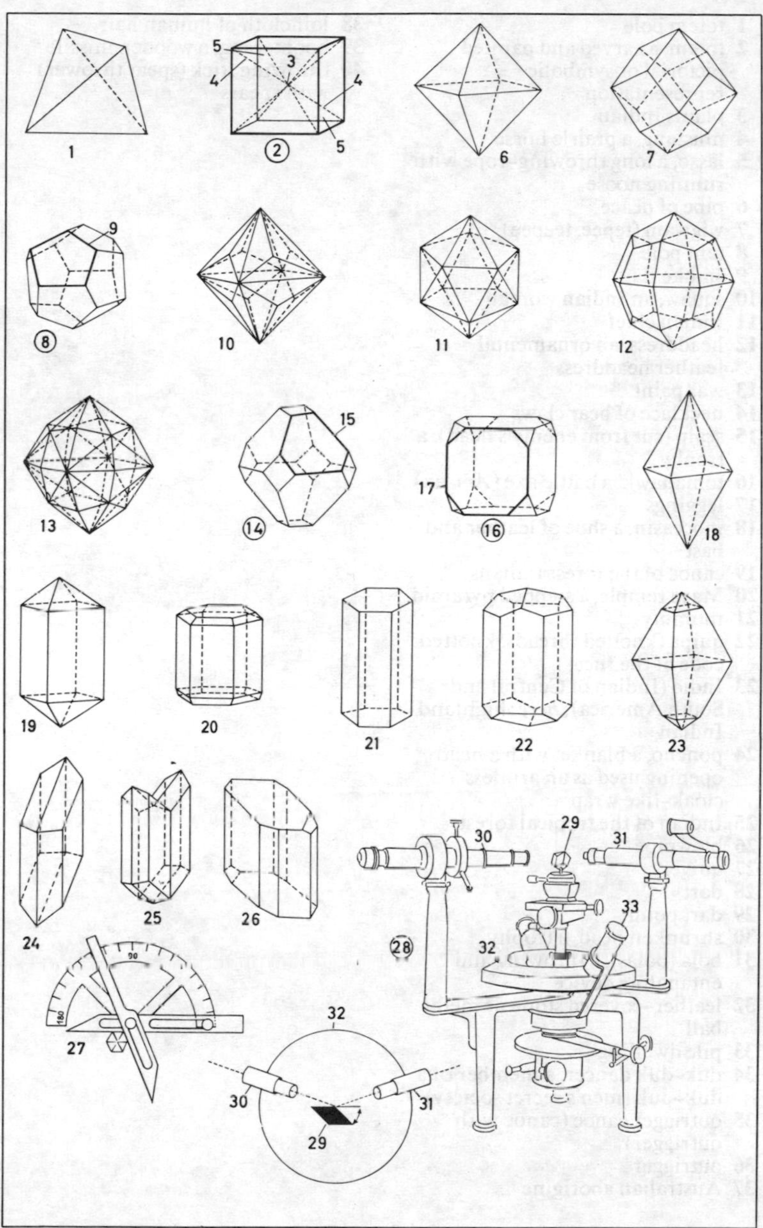
1
5
3
4
4
5
2
5
6
7
9
8
10
11
12
13
15
14
17
16
18
19
20
21
22
23
24
25
26
90
180
27
28
29
30
31
33
32
32
30
31
29

1 totem pole
2 totem, a carved and painted pictorial or symbolic representation
3 plains Indian
4 mustang, a prairie horse
5 lasso, a long throwing-rope with running noose
6 pipe of peace
7 wigwam (tepee, teepee)
8 tent pole
9 smoke flap
10 squaw, an Indian woman
11 Indian chief
12 headdress, an ornamental feather headdress
13 war paint
14 necklace of bear claws
15 scalp (cut from enemy's head), a trophy
16 tomahawk, a battle axe (*Am.* ax)
17 leggings
18 moccasin, a shoe of leather and bast
19 canoe of the forest Indians
20 Maya temple, a stepped pyramid
21 mummy
22 quipa (knotted threads, knotted code of the Incas)
23 Indio (Indian of Central and South America); *here:* highland Indian
24 poncho, a blanket with a head opening used as an armless cloak-like wrap
25 Indian of the tropical forest
26 blowpipe
27 quiver
28 dart
29 dart point
30 shrunken head, a trophy
31 bola (bolas), a throwing and entangling device
32 leather-covered stone or metal ball
33 pile dwelling
34 duk-duk dancer, a member of a duk-duk (men's secret society)
35 outrigger canoe (canoe with outrigger)
36 outrigger
37 Australian aborigine
38 loincloth of human hair
39 boomerang, a wooden missile
40 throwing stick (spear thrower) with spears

1
2
3
4
5
6
7
8
9
10
11
12
13
14
15
16
17
18
19
20
21
22
23
24
25
26
27
28
29
30
31
32
33
34
35
36
37
38
39
40

353 Ethnology II

1 Eskimo
2 sledge dog (sled dog), a husky
3 dog sledge (dog sled)
4 igloo, a dome-shaped snow hut
5 block of snow
6 entrance tunnel
7 blubber-oil lamp
8 wooden missile
9 lance
10 harpoon
11 skin float
12 kayak, a light one-man canoe
13 skin-covered wooden or bone frame
14 paddle
15 reindeer harness
16 reindeer
17 Ostyak (Ostiak)
18 passenger sledge
19 yurt (yurta), a dwelling tent of the western and central Asiatic nomads
20 felt covering
21 smoke outlet
22 Kirghiz
23 sheepskin cap
24 shaman
25 decorative fringe
26 frame drum
27 Tibetan
28 flintlock with bayonets
29 prayer wheel
30 felt boot
31 houseboat (sampan)
32 junk
33 mat sail
34 rickshaw (ricksha)
35 rickshaw coolie (cooly)
36 Chinese lantern
37 samurai
38 padded armour (*Am.* armor)
39 geisha
40 kimono
41 obi
42 fan
43 coolie (cooly)
44 kris (creese, crease), a Malayan dagger
45 snake charmer
46 turban
47 flute
48 dancing snake

1
2
3
4
5
6
7
8
9
10
11
12
13
14
15
16
17
18
19
20
21
22
23
24
25
26
27
28
29
30
31
32
33
34
35
37
38
39
40
41
42
43
44
45
46
47
48

1 camel caravan
2 riding animal
3 pack animal
4 oasis
5 grove of palm trees
6 bedouin (beduin)
7 burnous
8 Masai warrior
9 headdress (hairdress)
10 shield
11 painted ox hide
12 long-bladed spear
13 negro
14 dance drum
15 throwing knife
16 wooden mask
17 figure of an ancestor
18 slit gong
19 drumstick
20 dugout, a boat hollowed out of a tree trunk
21 negro hut
22 negress
23 lip plug (labret)
24 grinding stone
25 Herero woman
26 leather cap
27 calabash (gourd)
28 beehive-shaped hut
29 bushman
30 earplug
31 loincloth
32 bow
33 knobkerry (knobkerrie), a club with round, knobbed end
34 bushman woman making a fire by twirling a stick
35 windbreak
36 Zulu in dance costume
37 dancing stick
38 bangle
39 ivory war horn
40 string of amulets and bones
41 pigmy
42 magic pipe for exorcising evil spirits
43 fetish

1
2
3
4
5
6
7
8
9
10
11
12
13
14
15
16
17
18
19
20
21
22
23
24
25
26
27
28
29
30
31
32
33
34
35
36
37
38
39
40
41
42
43

355 Historical Costumes

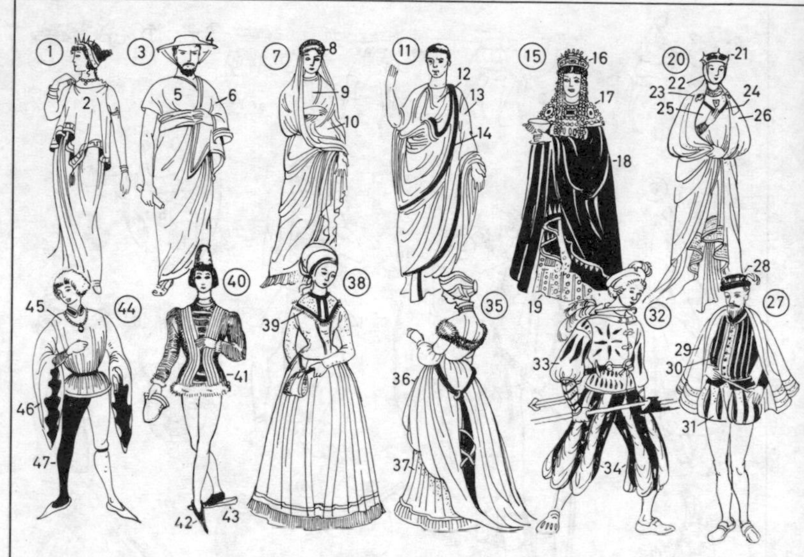

1 Greek woman
2 peplos
3 Greek
4 petasus (Thessalonian hat)
5 chiton, a linen gown worn as a basic garment
6 himation, woollen (*Am.* woolen) cloak
7 Roman woman
8 toupee wig (partial wig)
9 stola
10 palla, a coloured (*Am.* colored) wrap
11 Roman
12 tunica (tunic)
13 toga
14 purple border (purple band)
15 Byzantine empress
16 pearl diadem
17 jewels
18 purple cloak
19 long tunic
20 German princess [13th cent.]
21 crown (diadem)
22 chinband
23 tassel
24 cloak cord
25 girt-up gown (girt-up surcoat, girt-up tunic)
26 cloak
27 German dressed in the Spanish style [ca. 1575]
28 wide-brimmed cap
29 short cloak (Spanish cloak, short cape)
30 padded doublet (stuffed doublet, peasecod)
31 stuffed trunk-hose
32 lansquenet (German mercenary soldier) [ca. 1530]
33 slashed doublet (paned doublet)
34 Pluderhose (loose breeches, paned trunk-hose, slops)
35 woman of Basle [ca. 1525]
36 overgown (gown)
37 undergown (petticoat)
38 woman of Nuremberg [ca. 1500]
39 shoulder cape
40 Burgundian [15th cent.]
41 short doublet
42 piked shoes (peaked shoes, copped shoes, crackowes, poulaines)
43 pattens (clogs)

44 young nobleman [ca. 1400]
45 short, padded doublet (short, quilted doublet, jerkin)
46 dagged sleeves (petal-scalloped sleeves)
47 hose
48 Augsburg patrician lady [ca. 1575]
49 puffed sleeve
50 overgown (gown, open gown, sleeveless gown)
51 French lady [ca. 1600]
52 millstone ruff (cartwheel ruff, ruff)
53 corseted waist (wasp waist)
54 gentleman [ca. 1650]
55 wide-brimmed felt hat (cavalier hat)
56 falling collar (wide-falling collar) of linen
57 white lining
58 jack boots (bucket-top boots)
59 lady [ca. 1650]
60 full puffed sleeves (puffed sleeves)
61 gentleman [ca. 1700]
62 three-cornered hat
63 dress sword
64 lady [ca. 1700]
65 lace fontange (high headdress of lace)
66 lace-trimmed loose-hanging gown (loose-fitting housecoat, robe de chambre, negligée, contouche)
67 band of embroidery
68 lady [ca. 1880]
69 bustle
70 lady [ca. 1858]
71 poke bonnet
72 crinoline
73 gentleman of the Biedermeier period
74 high collar (choker collar)
75 embroidered waistcoat (vest)
76 frock coat
77 pigtail wig
78 ribbon (bow)
79 ladies in court dress [ca. 1780]
80 train
81 upswept Rococo coiffure
82 hair decoration
83 panniered overskirt

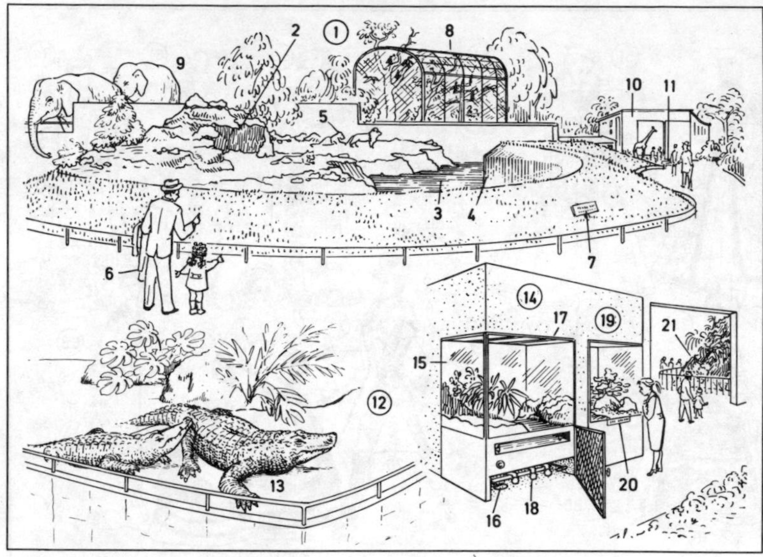

1 outdoor enclosure (enclosure)
2 rocks
3 moat
4 enclosing wall
5 animals on show; *here:* a pride of lions
6 visitor to the zoo
7 notice
8 aviary
9 elephant enclosure
10 animal house (e.g. carnivore house, giraffe house, elephant house, monkey house)
11 outside cage, animals' summer quarters
12 reptile enclosure
13 Nile crocodile
14 terrarium and aquarium
15 glass case
16 fresh-air inlet
17 ventilator
18 underfloor heating
19 aquarium
20 information plate
21 flora in artificially maintained climate

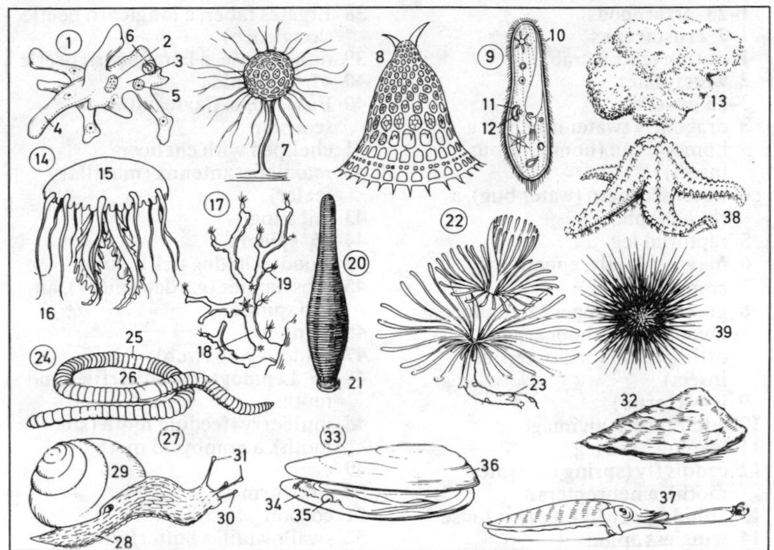

1–12 unicellular (one-celled, single-celled) animals (protozoans)
1 amoeba, a rhizopod
2 cell nucleus
3 protoplasm
4 pseudopod
5 excretory vacuole (contractile vacuole, an organelle)
6 food vacuole
7 Actinophrys, a heliozoan
8 radiolarian; *here:* siliceous skeleton
9 slipper animalcule, a Paramecium
10 cilium
11 macronucleus (meganucleus)
12 micronucleus
13–39 multicellular animals (metazoans)
13 bath sponge, a porifer (sponge)
14 medusa, a discomedusa (jellyfish), a coelenterate
15 umbrella
16 tentacle
17 red coral (precious coral), a coral animal (anthozoan, reef-building animal)
18 coral colony
19 coral polyp
20–26 worms (Vermes)
20 leech, an annelid
21 sucker
22 Spirographis, a bristle worm
23 tube
24 earthworm
25 segment
26 clitellum [accessory reproductive organ]
27–36 molluscs (*Am.* mollusks)
27 edible snail, a snail
28 creeping foot
29 shell (snail shell)
30 stalked eye
31 tentacle (horn, feeler)
32 oyster
33 freshwater pearl mussel
34 mother-of-pearl (nacre)
35 pearl
36 mussel shell
37 cuttlefish, a cephalopod
38–39 echinoderms
38 starfish (sea star)
39 sea urchin (sea hedgehog)

1–23 arthropods
1–2 crustaceans
1 mitten crab, a crab
2 water slater
3–23 insects
3 dragonfly (water nymph), a homopteran (homopterous insect)
4 water scorpion (water bug), a rhynchophore
5 raptorial leg
6 mayfly (dayfly, ephemerid)
7 compound eye
8 green grasshopper (green locust, meadow grasshopper), an orthopteron (orthopterous insect)
9 larva (grub)
10 adult insect, an imago
11 leaping hind leg
12 caddis fly (spring fly, water moth), a neuropteran
13 aphid (greenfly), a plant louse
14 wingless aphid
15 winged aphid
16–20 dipterous insects (dipterans)
16 gnat (mosquito, midge), a culicid
17 proboscis (sucking organ)
18 bluebottle (blowfly), a fly
19 maggot (larva)
20 chrysalis (pupa)
21–23 Hymenoptera
21–22 ant
21 winged female
22 worker
23 bumblebee (humblebee)
24–39 beetles (Coleoptera)
24 stag beetle, a lamellicorn beetle
25 mandibles
26 trophi
27 antenna (feeler)
28 head
29–30 thorax
29 thoracic shield (prothorax)
30 scutellum
31 tergites
32 stigma
33 wing (hind wing)
34 nervure
35 point at which the wing folds
36 elytron (forewing)
37 ladybird (ladybug), a coccinellid
38 Ergates faber, a longicorn beetle (longicorn)
39 dung beetle, a lamellicorn beetle
40–47 arachnids
40 Euscorpius flavicandus, a scorpion
41 cheliped with chelicer
42 maxillary antenna (maxillary feeler)
43 tail sting
44–46 spiders
44 wood tick (dog tick), a tick
45 cross spider (garden spider), an orb spinner
46 spinneret
47 spider's web (web)
48–56 Lepidoptera (butterflies and moths)
48 mulberry-feeding moth (silk moth), a bombycid moth
49 eggs
50 silkworm
51 cocoon
52 swallowtail, a butterfly
53 antenna (feeler)
54 eyespot
55 privet hawkmoth, a hawkmoth (sphinx)
56 proboscis

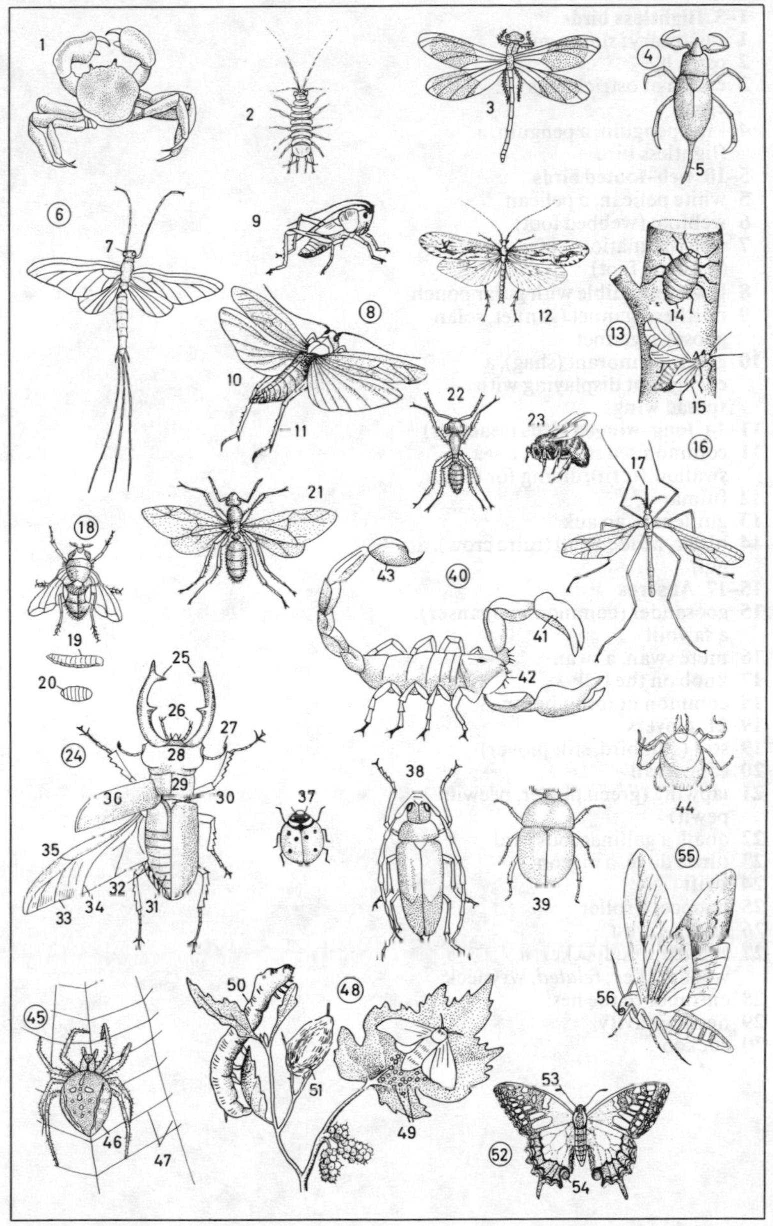
1
2
3
4
5
6
7
8
9
10
11
12
13
14
15
16
17
18
19
20
21
22
23
24
25
26
27
28
29
30
30
31
32
33
34
35
36
37
38
39
40
41
42
43
44
45
46
47
48
49
50
51
52
53
54
55
56

1-3 flightless birds
1 cassowary; *sim.:* emu
2 ostrich
3 clutch of ostrich eggs [12 - 14 eggs]
4 king penguin, a penguin, a flightless bird
5-10 web-footed birds
5 white pelican, a pelican
6 webfoot (webbed foot)
7 web (palmations) of webbed foot (palmate foot)
8 lower mandible with gular pouch
9 northern gannet (gannet, solan goose), a gannet
10 green cormorant (shag), a cormorant displaying with spread wings
11-14 long-winged birds (seabirds)
11 common sea swallow, a sea swallow (tern), diving for food
12 fulmar
13 guillemot, an auk
14 black-headed gull (mire crow), a gull
15-17 Anseres
15 goosander (common merganser), a sawbill
16 mute swan, a swan
17 knob on the bill
18 common heron, a heron
19-21 plovers
19 stilt (stilt bird, stilt plover)
20 coot, a rail
21 lapwing (green plover, peewit, pewit)
22 quail, a gallinaceous bird
23 turtle dove, a pigeon
24 swift
25 hoopoe, a roller
26 erectile crest
27 spotted woodpecker, a woodpecker; *related:* wryneck
28 entrance to the nest
29 nesting cavity
30 cuckoo

1
2
3
4
5
6
7
8
9
10
11
12
13
14
15
16
17
18
19
20
21
22
23
24
25
26
27
28
29
30

1, 3, 4, 5, 7, 9, 10 songbirds
1 goldfinch, a finch
2 bee eater
3 redstart (star finch), a thrush
4 bluetit, a tit (titmouse), a resident bird (non-migratory bird)
5 bullfinch
6 common roller (roller)
7 golden oriole, a migratory bird
8 kingfisher
9 white wagtail, a wagtail
10 chaffinch

1
2
3
4
5
6
7
8
9
10
S. Vogel

1-20 songbirds
1-3 Corvidae (corvine birds, crows)
1 jay (nutcracker)
2 rook, a crow
3 magpie
4 starling (pastor, shepherd bird)
5 house sparrow
6-8 finches
6-7 buntings
6 yellowhammer (yellow bunting)
7 ortolan (ortolan bunting)
8 siskin (aberdevine)
9 great titmouse (great tit, ox eye), a titmouse (tit)
10 golden-crested wren (goldcrest); *sim.:* firecrest, one of the Regulidae
11 nuthatch
12 wren
13-17 thrushes
13 blackbird
14 nightingale (*poet.:* philomel, philomela)
15 robin (redbreast, robin redbreast)
16 song thrush (throstle, mavis)
17 thrush nightingale
18-19 larks
18 woodlark
19 crested lark (tufted lark)
20 common swallow (barn swallow, chimney swallow), a swallow

1-13 diurnal birds of prey
1-4 falcons
1 merlin
2 peregrine falcon
3 leg feathers
4 tarsus
5-9 eagles
5 white-tailed sea eagle (white-tailed eagle, grey sea eagle, erne)
6 hooked beak
7 claw (talon)
8 tail
9 common buzzard
10-13 accipiters
10 goshawk
11 common European kite (glede, kite)
12 sparrow hawk (spar-hawk)
13 marsh harrier (moor buzzard, moor harrier, moor hawk)
14-19 owls (nocturnal birds of prey)
14 long-eared owl (horned owl)
15 eagle-owl (great horned owl)
16 plumicorn (feathered ear, ear tuft, ear, horn)
17 barn owl (white owl, silver owl, yellow owl, church owl, screech owl)
18 facial disc (disk)
19 little owl (sparrow owl)

363 Birds V (Exotic Birds)

1 sulphur-crested cockatoo, a parrot
2 blue-and-yellow macaw
3 blue bird of paradise
4 sappho
5 cardinal (cardinal bird)
6 toucan (red-billed toucan), one of the Piciformes

1
2
3
4
5
6
S. Vogel

1–18 fishes
1 man-eater (blue shark, requin), a shark
2 nose (snout)
3 gill slit (gill cleft)
4 mirror carp, a carp
5 gill cover (operculum)
6 dorsal fin
7 pectoral fin
8 pelvic fin (abdominal fin, ventral fin)
9 anal fin
10 caudal fin (tail fin)
11 scale
12 catfish (sheatfish, sheathfish, wels)
13 barbel
14 herring
15 brown trout, a trout
16 pike (northern pike)
17 freshwater eel (eel)
18 sea horse (Hippocampus, horsefish)
19 tufted gills
20–26 Amphibia (amphibians)
20–22 salamanders
20 greater water newt (crested newt), a water newt
21 dorsal crest
22 fire salamander, a salamander
23–26 salientians (anurans, batrachians)
23 European toad, a toad
24 tree frog (tree toad)
25 vocal sac (vocal pouch, croaking sac)
26 adhesive disc (disk)
27–41 reptiles
27, 30–37 lizards
27 sand lizard
28 hawksbill turtle (hawksbill)
29 carapace (shell)
30 basilisk
31 desert monitor, a monitor lizard (monitor)
32 common iguana, an iguana
33 chameleon, one of the Chamaeleontidae (Rhiptoglossa)
34 prehensile foot
35 prehensile tail
36 wall gecko, a gecko
37 slowworm (blindworm), one of the Anguidae

38–41 snakes
38 ringed snake (ring snake, water snake, grass snake), a colubrid
39 collar
40–41 vipers (adders)
40 common viper, a poisonous (venomous) snake
41 asp (asp viper)

1
2
3
4
5
6
7
8
9
10
11
12
13
14
15
16
17
18
19
20
21
22
23
24
25
26
27
28
29
30
31
32
33
34
35
36
37
38
39
40
41

365 Lepidoptera (Butterflies and Moths)

1–6 butterflies
1 red admiral
2 peacock butterfly
3 orange tip (orange tip butterfly)
4 brimstone (brimstone butterfly)
5 Camberwell beauty (mourning cloak, mourning cloak butterfly)
6 blue (lycaenid butterfly, lycaenid)
7–11 moths (Heterocera)
7 garden tiger
8 red underwing
9 death's-head moth (death's-head hawkmoth), a hawkmoth (sphinx)
10 caterpillar
11 chrysalis (pupa)

Lepidoptera (Butterflies and Moths) 365

1 platypus (duck-bill, duck-mole), a monotreme (oviparous mammal)
2–3 marsupial mammals (marsupials)
2 New World opossum, a didelphid
3 red kangaroo (red flyer), a kangaroo
4–7 insectivores (insect-eating mammals)
4 mole
5 hedgehog
6 spine
7 shrew (shrew mouse), one of the Soricidae
8 nine-banded armadillo (peba)
9 long-eared bat (flitter-mouse), a flying mammal (chiropter, chiropteran)
10 pangolin (scaly ant-eater), a scaly mammal
11 two-toed sloth (unau)
12–19 rodents
12 guinea pig (cavy)
13 porcupine
14 beaver
15 jerboa
16 hamster
17 water vole
18 marmot
19 squirrel
20 African elephant, a proboscidean (proboscidian)
21 trunk (proboscis)
22 tusk
23 manatee (manati, lamantin), a sirenian
24 South African dassie (das, coney, hyrax), a procaviid
25–31 ungulates
25–27 odd-toed ungulates
25 African black rhino, a rhinoceros (nasicorn)
26 Brazilian tapir, a tapir
27 zebra
28–31 even-toed ungulates
28–30 ruminants
28 llama
29 Bactrian camel (two-humped camel)
30 guanaco
31 hippopotamus

1
2
3
4
5
6
7
8
9
10
11
12
13
14
15
16
17
18
19
20
21
22
23
24
25
26
27
28
29
30
31

367 Mammals II

1–10 ungulates, ruminants
1–10
1 elk (moose)
2 wapiti (*Am.* elk)
3 chamois
4 giraffe
5 black buck, an antelope
6 mouflon (moufflon)
7 ibex (rock goat, bouquetin, steinbock)
8 water buffalo (Indian buffalo, water ox)
9 bison
10 musk ox
11–22 carnivores (beasts of prey)
11–13 Canidae
11 black-backed jackal (jackal)
12 red fox
13 wolf
14–17 martens
14 stone marten (beach marten)
15 sable
16 weasel
17 sea otter, an otter
18–22 seals (pinnipeds)
18 fur seal (sea bear, ursine seal)
19 common seal (sea calf, sea dog)
20 walrus (morse)
21 whiskers
22 tusk
23–29 whales
23 bottle-nosed dolphin (bottle-nose dolphin)
24 common dolphin
25 sperm whale (cachalot)
26 blowhole (spout hole)
27 dorsal fin
28 flipper
29 tail flukes (tail)

1
2
3
4
5
6
7
8
9
10
11
12
13
14
15
16
17
18
19
20
21
22
23
24
25
26
27
28
29

1-11 carnivores (beasts of prey)
1 striped hyena, a hyena
2-8 felines (cats)
2 lion
3 mane (lion's mane)
4 paw
5 tiger
6 leopard
7 cheetah (hunting leopard)
8 lynx
9-11 bears
9 raccoon (racoon, *Am.* coon)
10 brown bear
11 polar bear (white bear)
12-16 primates
12-13 monkeys
12 rhesus monkey (rhesus, rhesus macaque)
13 baboon
14-16 anthropoids (anthropoid apes, great apes)
14 chimpanzee
15 orang-utan (orang-outan)
16 gorilla

1
3
2
4
5
6
7
8
9
10
11
14
12
15
16
13

1
2
3
4
5
6
7
8
9
10
11
12
13
14
15
16
17
18
19
20
S. Vogel

1 Gigantocypris agassizi
2 Macropharynx longicaudatus (pelican eel)
3 Pentacrinus (feather star), a sea lily, an echinoderm
4 Thaumatolampas diadema, a cuttlefish [luminescent]
5 Atolla, a deep-sea medusa, a coelenterate
6 Melanocetes, a pediculate [luminescent]
7 Lophocalyx philippensis, a glass sponge
8 Mopsea, a sea fan [colony]
9 Hydrallmania, a hydroid polyp, a coelenterate [colony]
10 Malacosteus indicus, a stomiatid [luminescent]
11 Brisinga endecacnemos, a sand star (brittle star), an echinoderm [luminescent only when stimulated]
12 Pasiphaea, a shrimp, a crustacean
13 Echiostoma, a stomiatid, a fish [luminescent]
14 Umbellula encrinus, a sea pen (sea feather), a coelenterate [colony, luminescent]
15 Polycheles, a crustacean
16 Lithodes, a crustacean, a crab
17 Archaster, a starfish (sea star), an echinoderm
18 Oneirophanta, a sea cucumber, an echinoderm
19 Palaeopneustes niasicus, a sea urchin (sea hedgehog), an echinoderm
20 Chitonactis, a sea anemone (actinia), a coelenterate

1 tree
2 bole (tree trunk, trunk, stem)
3 crown of tree (crown)
4 top of tree (treetop)
5 bough (limb, branch)
6 twig (branch)
7 bole (tree trunk) [cross section]
8 bark (rind)
9 phloem (bast sieve tissue, inner fibrous bark)
10 cambium (cambium ring)
11 medullary rays (vascular rays, pith rays)
12 sapwood (sap, alburnum)
13 heartwood (duramen)
14 pith
15 **plant**
16-18 root
16 primary root
17 secondary root
18 root hair
19-25 shoot (sprout)
19 leaf
20 stalk
21 side shoot (offshoot)
22 terminal bud
23 flower
24 flower bud
25 leaf axil with axillary bud
26 **leaf**
27 leaf stalk (petiole)
28 leaf blade (blade, lamina)
29 venation (veins, nervures, ribs)
30 midrib (nerve)
31-38 leaf shapes
31 linear
32 lanceolate
33 orbicular (orbiculate)
34 acerose (acerous, acerate, acicular, needle-shaped)
35 cordate
36 ovate
37 sagittate
38 reniform
39-42 compound leaves
39 digitate (digitated, palmate, quinquefoliolate)
40 pinnatifid
41 abruptly pinnate
42 odd-pinnate
43-50 leaf margin shapes
43 entire
44 serrate (serrulate, saw-toothed)
45 doubly toothed
46 crenate
47 dentate
48 sinuate
49 ciliate (ciliated)
50 cilium
51 **flower**
52 flower stalk (flower stem, scape)
53 receptacle (floral axis, thalamus, torus)
54 ovary
55 style
56 stigma
57 stamen
58 sepal
59 petal
60 ovary and stamen [section]
61 ovary wall
62 ovary cavity
63 ovule
64 embryo sac
65 pollen
66 pollen tube
67-77 inflorescences
67 spike (racemose spike)
68 raceme (simple raceme)
69 panicle
70 cyme
71 spadix (fleshy spike)
72 umbel (simple umbel)
73 capitulum
74 composite head (discoid flower head)
75 hollow flower head
76 bostryx (helicoid cyme)
77 cincinnus (scorpioid cyme, curled cyme)
78-82 roots
78 adventitious roots
79 tuber (tuberous root, swollen taproot)
80 adventitious roots (aerial roots)
81 root thorns
82 pneumatophores
83-85 blade of grass
83 leaf sheath
84 ligule (ligula)
85 leaf blade (lamina)
86 embryo (seed, germ)
87 cotyledon (seed leaf, seed lobe)
88 radicle
89 hypocotyl
90 plumule (leaf bud)
91-102 fruits
91-96 dehiscent fruits
91 follicle
92 legume (pod)
93 siliqua (pod)
94 schizocarp
95 pyxidium (circumscissile seed vessel)
96 poricidal capsule (porose capsule)
97-102 indehiscent fruits
97 berry
98 nut
99 drupe (stone fruit) (cherry)
100 aggregate fruit (compound fruit) (rose hip)
101 aggregate fruit (compound fruit) (raspberry)
102 pome (apple)

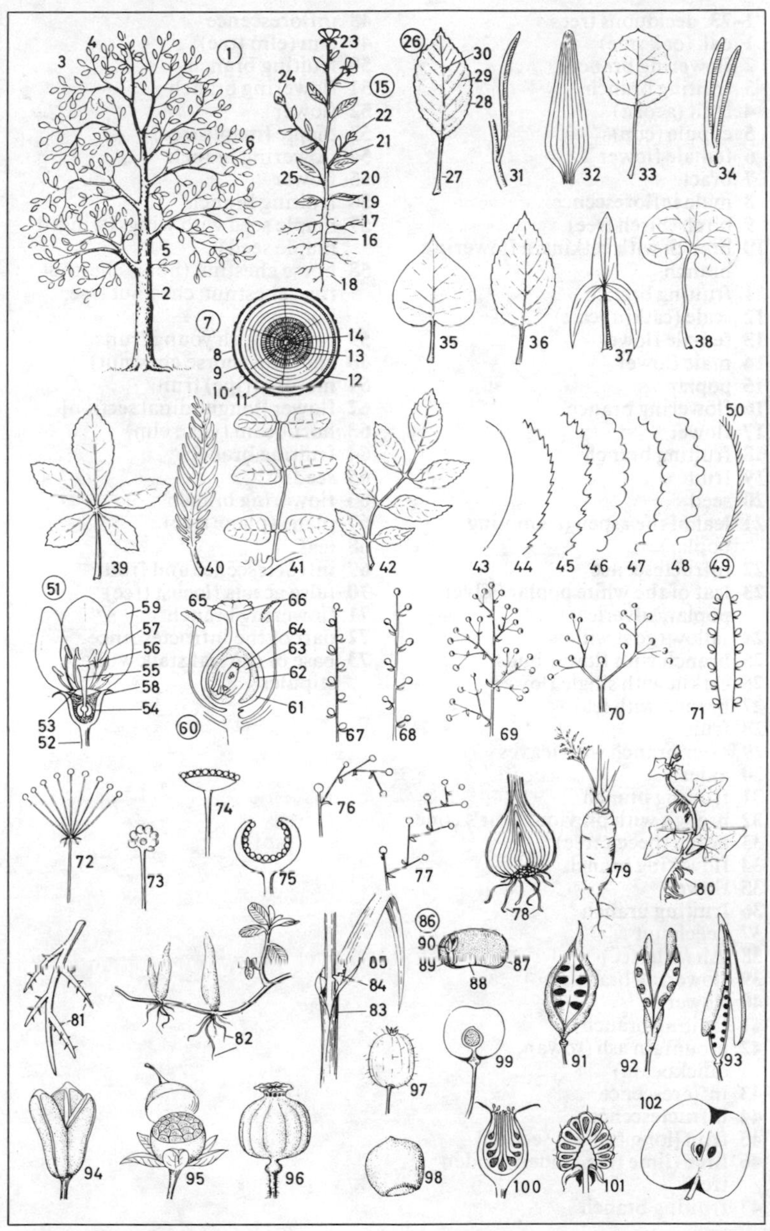
1
2
3
4
5
6
7
8
9
10
11
12
13
14
15
16
17
18
19
20
21
22
23
24
25
26
27
28
29
30
31
32
33
34
35
36
37
38
39
40
41
42
43
44
45
46
47
48
49
50
51
52
53
54
55
56
57
58
59
60
61
62
63
64
65
66
67
68
69
70
71
72
73
74
75
76
77
78
79
80
81
82
83
84
85
86
87
88
89
90
91
92
93
94
95
96
97
98
99
100
101
102

371 Deciduous Trees

1–73 deciduous trees
1 oak (oak tree)
2 flowering branch
3 fruiting branch
4 fruit (acorn)
5 cupule (cup)
6 female flower
7 bract
8 male inflorescence
9 birch (birch tree)
10 branch with catkins, a flowering branch
11 fruiting branch
12 scale (catkin scale)
13 female flower
14 male flower
15 poplar
16 flowering branch
17 flower
18 fruiting branch
19 fruit
20 seed
21 leaf of the aspen (trembling poplar)
22 infructescence
23 leaf of the white poplar (silver poplar, silverleaf)
24 sallow (goat willow)
25 branch with flower buds
26 catkin with single flower
27 branch with leaves
28 fruit
29 osier branch with leaves
30 alder
31 fruiting branch
32 branch with previous year's cone
33 beech (beech tree)
34 flowering branch
35 flower
36 fruiting branch
37 beech nut
38 ash (ash tree)
39 flowering branch
40 flower
41 fruiting branch
42 mountain ash (rowan, quickbeam)
43 inflorescence
44 infructescence
45 fruit [longitudinal section]
46 lime (lime tree, linden, linden tree)
47 fruiting branch
48 inflorescence
49 elm (elm tree)
50 fruiting branch
51 flowering branch
52 flower
53 maple (maple tree)
54 flowering branch
55 flower
56 fruiting branch
57 maple seed with wings (winged maple seed)
58 horse chestnut (horse chestnut tree, chestnut, chestnut tree, buckeye)
59 branch with young fruits
60 chestnut (horse chestnut)
61 mature (ripe) fruit
62 flower [longitudinal section]
63 hornbeam (yoke elm)
64 fruiting branch
65 seed
66 flowering branch
67 plane (plane tree)
68 leaf
69 infructescence and fruit
70 false acacia (locust tree)
71 flowering branch
72 part of the infructescence
73 base of the leaf stalk with stipules

1–71 coniferous trees (conifers)
1 silver fir (European silver fir, common silver fir)
2 fir cone, a fruit cone
3 cone axis
4 female flower cone
5 bract scale (bract)
6 male flower shoot
7 stamen
8 cone scale
9 seed with wing (winged seed)
10 seed [longitudinal section]
11 fir needle (needle)
12 spruce (spruce fir)
13 spruce cone
14 cone scale
15 seed
16 female flower cone
17 male inflorescence
18 stamen
19 spruce needle
20 pine (Scots pine)
21 dwarf pine
22 female flower cone
23 short shoot with bundle of two leaves
24 male inflorescences
25 annual growth
26 pine cone
27 cone scale
28 seed
29 fruit cone of the arolla pine (Swiss stone pine)
30 fruit cone of the Weymouth pine (white pine)
31 short shoot [cross section]
32 larch
33 flowering branch
34 scale of the female flower cone
35 anther
36 branch with larch cones (fruit cones)
37 seed
38 cone scale
39 arbor vitae (tree of life, thuja)
40 fruiting branch
41 fruit cone
42 scale
43 branch with male and female flowers
44 male shoot
45 scale with pollen sacs
46 female shoot
47 juniper (juniper tree)
48 female shoot [longitudinal section]
49 male shoot
50 scale with pollen sacs
51 fruiting branch
52 juniper berry
53 fruit [cross section]
54 seed
55 stone pine
56 male shoot
57 fruit cone with seeds [longitudinal section]
58 cypress
59 fruiting branch
60 seed
61 yew (yew tree)
62 male flower shoot and female flower cone
63 fruiting branch
64 fruit
65 cedar (cedar tree)
66 fruiting branch
67 fruit scale
68 male flower shoot and female flower cone
69 mammoth tree (Wellingtonia, sequoia)
70 fruiting branch.
71 seed

1
2
3
5
4
8
9
10
6
11
7
6
12
13
19
14
15
16
17
18
20
26
31
25
23
24
30
♀
♂
33
35
34
36
38
27
28
22
29
21
32
37
37
55
57
56
60
47
42
41
40
51
52
53
58
59
54
52
39
45
44
♂
♀
43
48
49
50
46
64
61
70
66
67
69
63
64
♂
62
♀
65
70
♀
♂
68
71

373 Ornamental Shrubs and Trees I

1 forsythia
2 ovary and stamen
3 leaf
4 yellow-flowered jasmine (jasmin, jessamine)
5 flower [longitudinal section] with styles, ovaries and stamens
6 privet (common privet)
7 flower
8 infructescence
9 mock orange (sweet syringa)
10 snowball (snowball bush, guelder rose)
11 flower
12 fruits
13 oleander (rosebay, rose laurel)
14 flower [longitudinal section]
15 red magnolia
16 leaf
17 japonica (japanese quince)
18 fruit
19 common box (box, box tree)
20 female flower
21 male flower
22 fruit [longitudinal section]
23 weigela (weigelia)
24 yucca [part of the inflorescence]
25 leaf
26 dog rose (briar rose, wild briar)
27 fruit
28 kerria
29 fruit
30 cornelian cherry
31 flower
32 fruit (cornelian cherry)
33 sweet gale (gale)

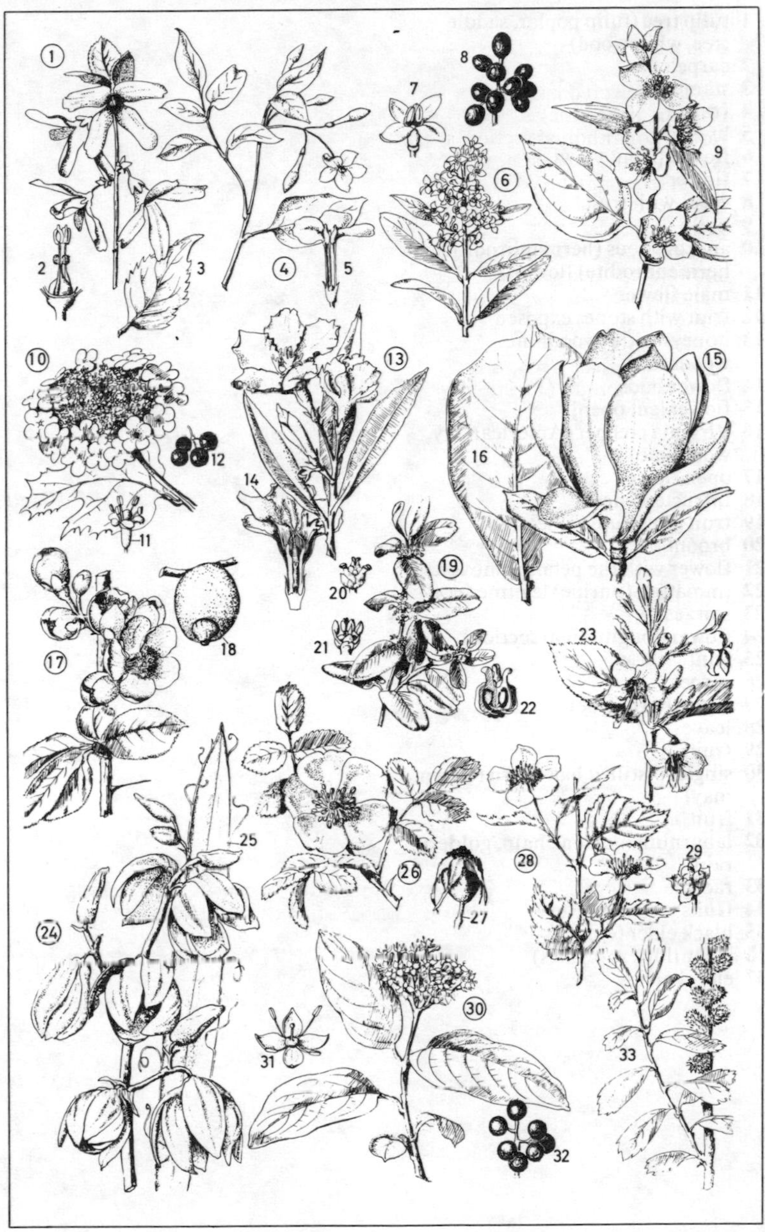
1
2
3
4
5
6
7
8
9
10
11
12
13
14
15
16
17
18
19
20
21
22
23
24
25
26
27
28
29
30
31
32
33

374 Ornamental Shrubs and Trees II

1 tulip tree (tulip poplar, saddle tree, whitewood)
2 carpels
3 stamen
4 fruit
5 hyssop
6 flower [front view]
7 flower
8 calyx with fruit
9 holly
10 androgynous (hermaphroditic, hermaphrodite) flower
11 male flower
12 fruit with stones exposed
13 honeysuckle (woodbine, woodbind)
14 flower buds
15 flower [cut open]
16 Virginia creeper (American ivy, woodbine)
17 open flower
18 infructescence
19 fruit [longitudinal section]
20 broom
21 flower with the petals removed
22 immature (unripe) legume (pod)
23 spiraea
24 flower [longitudinal section]
25 fruit
26 carpel
27 blackthorn (sloe)
28 leaves
29 fruits
30 single-pistilled hawthorn (thorn, may)
31 fruit
32 laburnum (golden chain, golden rain)
33 raceme
34 fruits
35 black elder (elder)
36 elder flowers (cymes)
37 elderberries

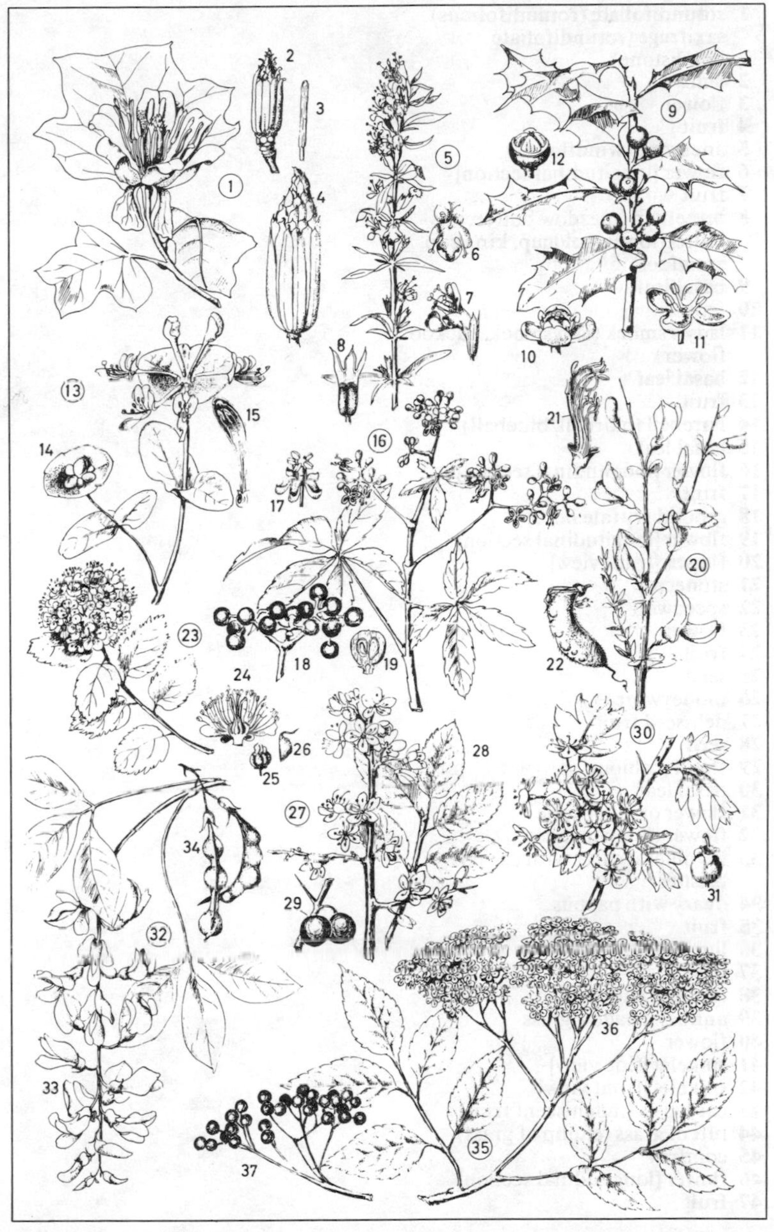

1
2
3
4
5
6
7
8
9
10
11
12
13
14
15
16
17
18
19
20
21
22
23
24
25
26
27
28
29
30
31
32
33
34
35
36
37

375 Meadow Flowers and Wayside Flowers (Wild Flowers) I

1 rotundifoliate (rotundifolious) saxifrage (rotundifoliate breakstone)
2 leaf
3 flower
4 fruit
5 anemone (windflower)
6 flower [longitudinal section]
7 fruit
8 buttercup (meadow buttercup, butterflower, goldcup, king cup, crowfoot)
9 basal leaf
10 fruit
11 lady's smock (ladysmock, cuckoo flower)
12 basal leaf
13 fruit
14 harebell (hairbell, bluebell)
15 basal leaf
16 flower [longitudinal section]
17 fruit
18 ground ivy (ale hoof)
19 flower [longitudinal section]
20 flower [front view]
21 stonecrop
22 speedwell
23 flower
24 fruit
25 seed
26 moneywort
27 dehisced fruit
28 seed
29 small scabious
30 basal leaf
31 flower of outer series
32 flower of inner series
33 involucral calyx with pappus bristles
34 ovary with pappus
35 fruit
36 lesser celandine
37 fruit
38 leaf axil with bulbil
39 annual meadow grass
40 flower
41 spikelet [side view]
42 spikelet [front view]
43 caryopsis (indehiscent fruit)
44 tuft of grass (clump of grass)
45 comfrey
46 flower [longitudinal section]
47 fruit

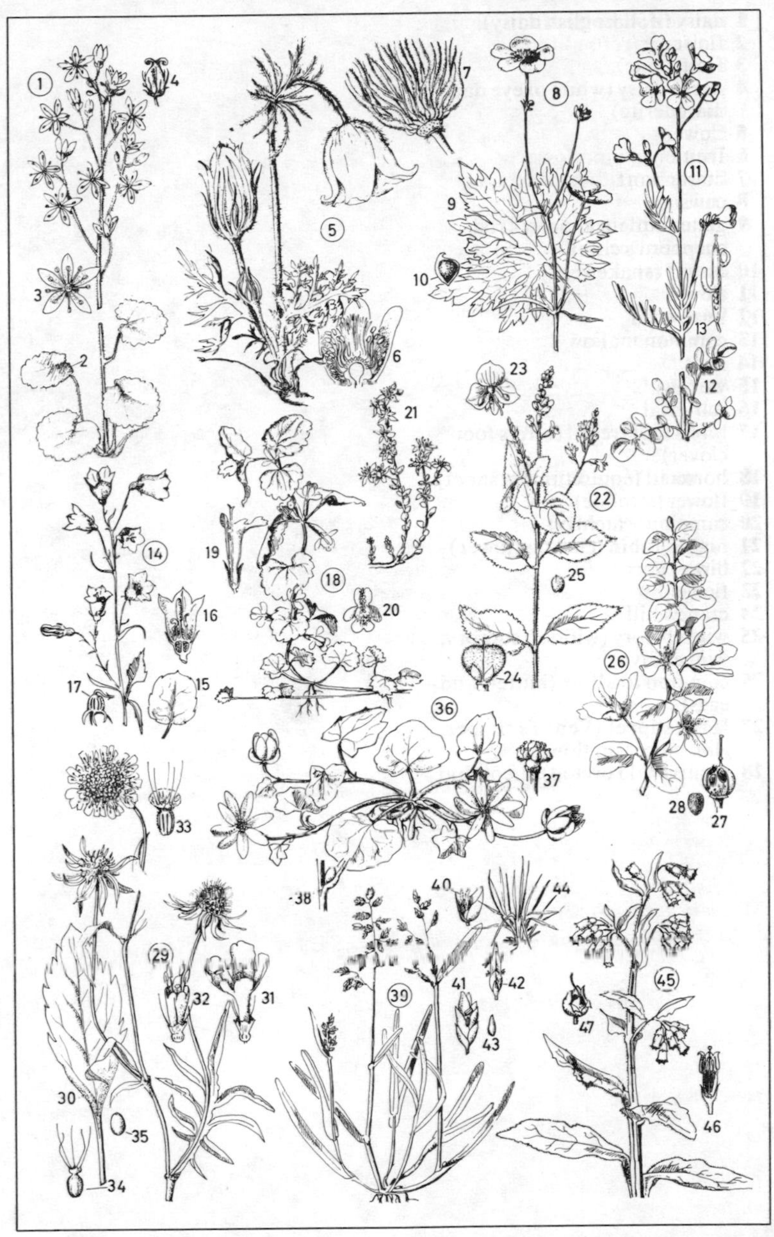

1
2
3
4
5
6
7
8
9
10
11
12
13
14
15
16
17
18
19
20
21
22
23
24
25
26
27
28
29
30
31
32
33
34
35
36
37
38
39
40
41
42
43
44
45
46
47

1 daisy (*Am.* English daisy)
2 flower
3 fruit
4 oxeye daisy (white oxeye daisy, marguerite)
5 flower
6 fruit
7 masterwort
8 cowslip
9 great mullein (Aaron's rod, shepherd's club)
10 bistort (snakeweed)
11 flower
12 knapweed
13 common mallow
14 fruit
15 yarrow
16 self-heal
17 bird's foot trefoil (bird's foot clover)
18 horsetail (equisetum) [a shoot]
19 flower (strobile)
20 campion (catchfly)
21 ragged robin (cuckoo flower)
22 birth-wort
23 flower
24 crane's bill
25 wild chicory (witloof, succory, wild endive)
26 common toadflax (butter-and-eggs)
27 lady's slipper (Venus's slipper, *Am.* moccasin flower)
28 orchis (wild orchid), an orchid

1
2
3
4
5
6
7
8
9
10
11
12
13
14
15
16
17
18
19
20
21
22
23
24
25
26
27
28

377 Plants of Forest, Marsh, and Heathland

1 wood anemone (anemone, windflower)
2 lily of the valley
3 cat's foot (milkwort); *sim.:* sandflower (everlasting)
4 turk's cap (turk's cap lily)
5 goatsbeard (goat's beard)
6 ramson
7 lungwort
8 corydalis
9 orpine (livelong)
10 daphne
11 touch-me-not
12 staghorn (stag horn moss, stag's horn, stag's horn moss, coral evergreen)
13 butterwort, an insectivorous plant
14 sundew; *sim.:* Venus's flytrap
15 bearberry
16 polypody (polypod), a fern; *sim.:* male fern, brake (bracken, eagle fern), royal fern (royal osmund, king's fern, ditch fern)
17 haircap moss (hair moss, golden maidenhair), a moss
18 cotton grass (cotton rush)
19 heather (heath, ling); *sim.:* bell heather (cross-leaved heather)
20 rock rose (sun rose)
21 marsh tea
22 sweet flag (sweet calamus, sweet sedge)
23 bilberry (whortleberry, huckleberry, blueberry); *sim.:* cowberry (red whortleberry), bog bilberry (bog whortleberry), crowberry (crakeberry)

1
2
3
4
5
6
7
8
9
10
11
12
13
14
15
16
17
18
19
20
21
22
23

378 Alpine Plants, Aquatic Plants (Water Plants), and Marsh Plants

1-13 alpine plants
1 alpine rose (alpine rhododendron)
2 flowering shoot
3 alpine soldanella (soldanella)
4 corolla opened out
5 seed vessel with the style
6 alpine wormwood
7 inflorescence
8 auricula
9 edelweiss
10 flower shapes
11 fruit with pappus tuft
12 part of flower head (of capitulum)
13 stemless alpine gentian

14-57 aquatic plants (water plants) and marsh plants
14 white water lily
15 leaf
16 flower
17 Queen Victoria water lily (Victoria regia water lily, royal water lily, Amazon water lily)
18 leaf
19 underside of the leaf
20 flower
21 reed mace bulrush (cattail, cat's tail, cattail flag, club rush)
22 male part of the spadix
23 male flower
24 female part
25 female flower
26 forget-me-not
27 flowering shoot
28 flower [section]
29 frog's bit
30 watercress
31 stalk with flowers and immature (unripe) fruits
32 flower
33 siliqua (pod) with seeds
34 two seeds
35 duckweed (duck's meat)
36 plant in flower
37 flower
38 fruit
39 flowering rush
40 flower umbel
41 leaves
42 fruit
43 green alga
44 water plantain
45 leaf
46 panicle
47 flower
48 honey wrack, a brown alga
49 thallus (plant body, frond)
50 holdfast
51 arrow head
52 leaf shapes
53 inflorescence with male flowers [above] and female flowers [below]
54 sea grass
55 inflorescence
56 Canadian waterweed (Canadian pondweed)
57 flower

1
2
3
4
5
6
7
8
9
10
11
12
13
14
15
16
17
18
19
20
21
22
23
24
25
26
27
28
29
30
31
32
33
34
35
36
37
38
39
40
41
42
43
44
45
46
47
48
49
50
51
52
53
54
55
56
57

379 Poisonous Plants

1 aconite (monkshood, wolfsbane, helmet flower)
2 foxglove (Digitalis)
3 meadow saffron (naked lady, naked boys)
4 hemlock (Conium)
5 black nightshade (common nightshade, petty morel)
6 henbane
7 deadly nightshade (belladonna, banewort, dwale), a solanaceous herb
8 thorn apple (stramonium, stramony, *Am.* jimson weed, jimpson weed, Jamestown weed, stinkweed)
9 cuckoo pint (lords-and-ladies, wild arum, wake-robin)
10-13 poisonous fungi (poisonous mushrooms, toadstools)
10 fly agaric (fly amanita, fly fungus), an agaric
11 amanita
12 Satan's mushroom
13 woolly milk cap

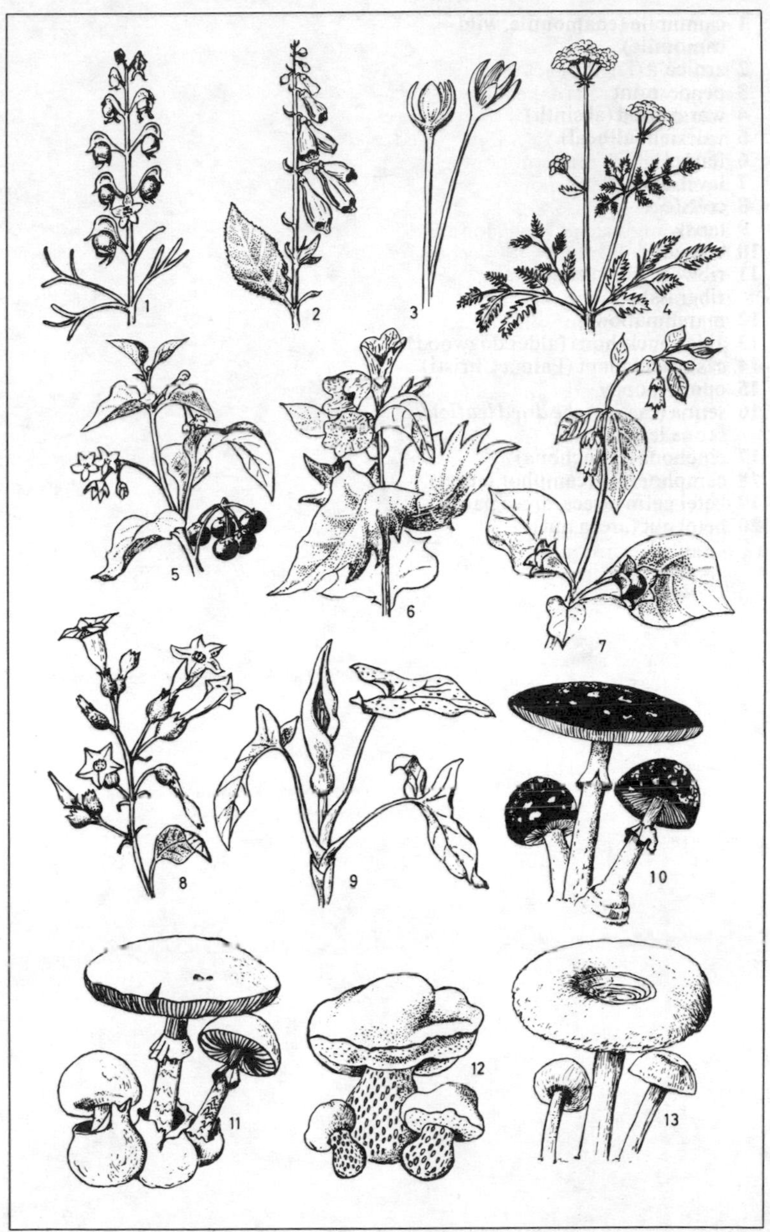
1
2
3
4
5
6
7
8
9
10
11
12
13

1 camomile (chamomile, wild camomile)
2 arnica
3 peppermint
4 wormwood (absinth)
5 valerian (allheal)
6 fennel
7 lavender
8 coltsfoot
9 tansy
10 centaury
11 ribwort (ribwort plantain, ribgrass)
12 marshmallow
13 alder buckthorn (alder dogwood)
14 castor-oil plant (Palma Christi)
15 opium poppy
16 senna (cassia); *the dried leaflets:* senna leaves
17 cinchona (chinchona)
18 camphor tree (camphor laurel)
19 betel palm (areca, areca palm)
20 betel nut (areca nut)

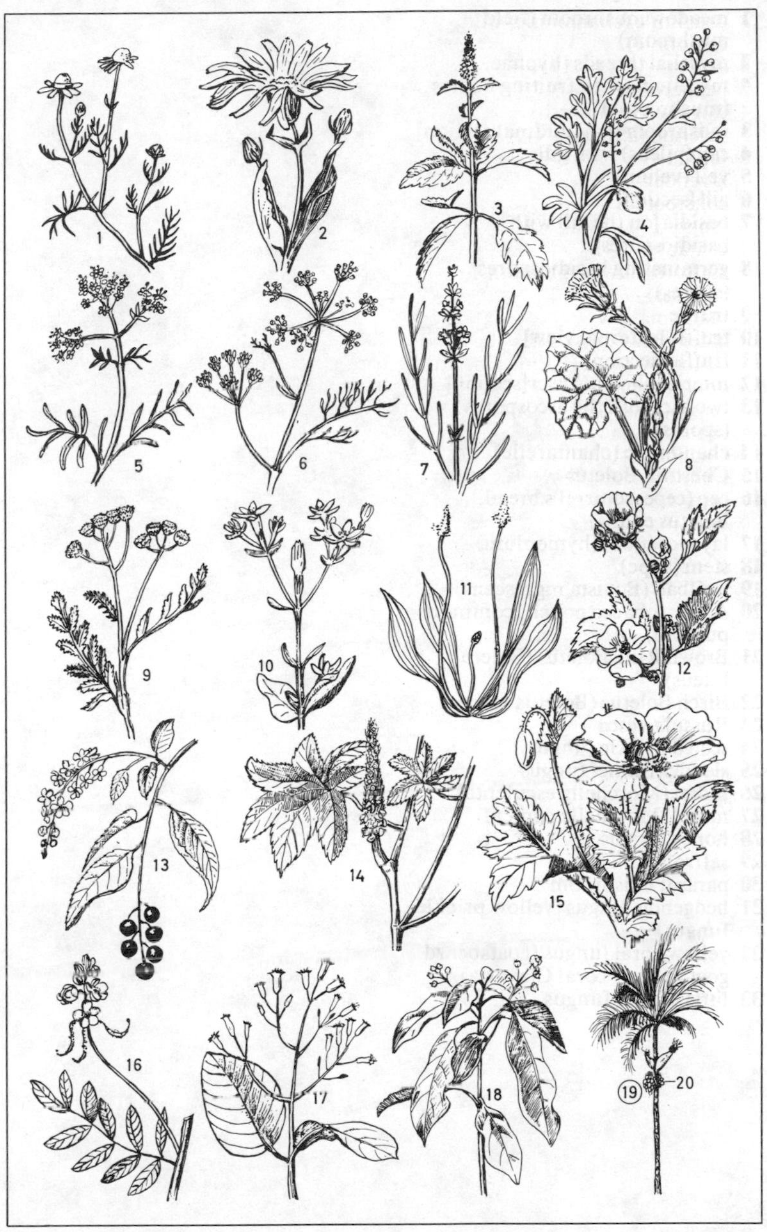
1
2
3
4
5
6
7
8
9
10
11
12
13
14
15
16
17
18
19
20

381 Edible Fungi (Esculent Fungi)

1 meadow mushroom (field mushroom)
2 mycelial threads (hyphae, mycelium) with fruiting bodies (mushrooms)
3 mushroom [longitudinal section]
4 cap (pileus) with gills
5 veil (velum)
6 gill [section]
7 basidia [on the gill with basidiospores]
8 germinating basidiospores (spores)
9 truffle
10 truffle [external view]
11 truffle [section]
12 interior showing asci [section]
13 two asci with the ascospores (spores)
14 chanterelle (chantarelle)
15 Chestnut Boletus
16 cep (cepe, squirrel's bread, Boletus edulis)
17 layer of tubes (hymenium)
18 stem (stipe)
19 puffball (Bovista nigrescens)
20 devil's tobacco pouch (common puffball)
21 Brown Ring Boletus (Boletus luteus)
22 Birch Boletus (Boletus scaber)
23 Russula vesca
24 scaled prickle fungus
25 slender funnel fungus
26 morel (Morchella esculenta)
27 morel (Morchella conica)
28 honey fungus
29 saffron milk cap
30 parasol mushroom
31 hedgehog fungus (yellow prickle fungus)
32 yellow coral fungus (goatsbeard, goat's beard, coral Clavaria)
33 little cluster fungus

1
2
3
4
5
6
7
8
9
10
11
12
13
14
15
16
17
18
19
20
21
22
23
24
25
26
27
28
29
30
31
32
33

382 Tropical Plants used as Stimulants, Spices, and Flavourings (*Am.* Flavorings)

1 coffee tree (coffee plant)
2 fruiting branch
3 flowering branch
4 flower
5 fruit with two beans [longitudinal section]
6 coffee bean; *when processed:* coffee
7 tea plant (tea tree)
8 flowering branch
9 tea leaf; *when processed:* tea
10 fruit
11 maté shrub (maté, yerba maté, Paraguay tea)
12 flowering branch with androgynous (hermaphroditic, hermaphrodite) flowers
13 male flower
14 androgynous (hermaphroditic, hermaphrodite) flower
15 fruit
16 cacao tree (cacao)
17 branch with flowers and fruits
18 flower [longitudinal section]
19 cacao beans (cocoa beans); *when processed:* cocoa, cocoa powder
20 seed [longitudinal section]
21 embryo
22 cinnamon tree (cinnamon)
23 flowering branch
24 fruit
25 cinnamon bark; *when crushed:* cinnamon
26 clove tree
27 flowering branch
28 flower bud; *when dried:* clove
29 flower
30 nutmeg tree
31 flowering branch
32 female flower [longitudinal section]
33 mature (ripe) fruit
34 nutmeg with mace, a seed with laciniate aril
35 seed [cross section]; *when dried:* nutmeg
36 pepper plant
37 fruiting branch
38 inflorescence
39 fruit [longitudinal section] with seed (peppercorn); *when ground:* pepper
40 Virginia tobacco plant
41 flowering shoot
42 flower
43 tobacco leaf; *when cured:* tobacco
44 mature (ripe) fruit capsule
45 seed
46 vanilla plant
47 flowering shoot
48 vanilla pod; *when cured:* stick of vanilla
49 pistachio tree
50 flowering branch with female flowers
51 drupe (pistachio, pistachio nut)
52 sugar cane
53 plant in bloom
54 panicle
55 flower

Tropical Plants used as Stimulants, Spices, and Flavourings (*Am.* Flavorings) 382

383 Plants used in Industry

1 rape (cole, coleseed)
2 basal leaf
3 flower [longitudinal section]
4 mature (ripe) siliqua (pod)
5 oleiferous seed
6 flax
7 peduncle (pedicel, flower stalk)
8 seed vessel (boll)
9 hemp
10 fruiting female (pistillate) plant
11 female inflorescence
12 flower
13 male inflorescence
14 fruit
15 seed
16 cotton
17 flower
18 fruit
19 lint [cotton wool]
20 silk-cotton tree (kapok tree, capoc tree, ceiba tree)
21 fruit
22 flowering branch
23 seed
24 seed [longitudinal section]
25 jute
26 flowering branch
27 flower
28 fruit
29 olive tree (olive)
30 flowering branch
31 flower
32 fruit
33 rubber tree (rubber plant)
34 fruiting branch
35 fig
36 flower
37 gutta-percha tree
38 flowering branch
39 flower
40 fruit
41 peanut (ground nut, monkey nut)
42 flowering shoot
43 root with fruits
44 nut (kernel) [longitudinal section]
45 sesame plant (simsim, benniseed)
46 flowers and fruiting branch
47 flower [longitudinal section]
48 coconut palm (coconut tree, coco palm, cocoa palm)
49 inflorescence
50 female flower
51 male flower [longitudinal section]
52 fruit [longitudinal section]
53 coconut (cokernut)
54 oil palm
55 male spadix
56 infructescence with fruit
57 seed with micropyles (foramina) (foraminate seed)
58 sago palm
59 fruit
60 bamboo stem (bamboo culm)
61 branch with leaves
62 spike
63 part of bamboo stem with joints
64 papyrus plant (paper reed, paper rush)
65 umbel
66 spike

1
2
3
4
5
6
7
8
9
10
11
12
13
14
15
16
17
18
19
20
21
22
23
24
25
26
27
28
29
30
31
32
33
34
35
36
♀
♂
37
38
39
40
41
42
43
44
45
46
47
48
49
50
51
52
53
54
55
56
57
58
59
60
61
62
63
64
65
66

384 Southern Fruits (Tropical, Subtropical, and Mediterranean Fruits)

1 date palm (date)
2 fruiting palm
3 palm frond
4 male spadix
5 male flower
6 female spadix
7 female flower
8 stand of fruit
9 date
10 date kernel (seed)
11 fig
12 branch with pseudocarps
13 fig with flowers [longitudinal section]
14 female flower
15 male flower
16 pomegranate
17 flowering branch
18 flower [longitudinal section, corolla removed]
19 fruit
20 seed [longitudinal section]
21 seed [cross section]
22 embryo
23 lemon; *sim.:* tangerine (mandarin), orange, grapefruit
24 flowering branch
25 orange flower [longitudinal section]
26 fruit
27 orange [cross section]
28 banana plant (banana tree)
29 crown
30 herbaceous stalk with overlapping leaf sheaths
31 inflorescence with young fruits
32 infructescence (bunch of fruit)
33 banana
34 banana flower
35 banana leaf [diagram]
36 almond
37 flowering branch
38 fruiting branch
39 fruit
40 drupe containing seed [almond]
41 carob
42 branch with female flowers
43 female flower
44 male flower
45 fruit
46 siliqua (pod) [cross section]
47 seed
48 sweet chestnut (Spanish chestnut)
49 flowering branch
50 female inflorescence
51 male flower
52 cupule containing seeds (nuts, chestnuts)
53 Brazil nut
54 flowering branch
55 leaf
56 flower [from above]
57 flower [longitudinal section]
58 opened capsule, containing seeds (nuts)
59 Brazil nut [cross section]
60 nut [longitudinal section]
61 pineapple plant (pineapple)
62 pseudocarp with crown of leaves
63 syncarp
64 pineapple flower
65 flower [longitudinal section]

1
2
3
4
5
6
7
8
9
10
11
12
13
14
15
16
17
18
19
20
21
22
23
24
25
26
27
28
29
30
31
32
33
34
35
36
37
38
39
40
41
42
43
44
45
46
47
48
49
50
51
52
53
54
55
56
57
58
59
60
61
62
63
64
65

Ordering of Entries

In the index the entries are ordered as follows:

1. Entries consisting of single words, e.g.: 'hair'.
2. Entries consisting of noun + adjective. Within this category the adjectives are entered alphabetically, e.g. 'hair, bobbed' is followed by 'hair, closely-cropped'.

   Where adjective and noun are regarded as elements of a single lexical item, they are not inverted, e.g.: 'blue spruce', not 'spruce, blue'.
3. Entries consisting of other phrases, e.g. 'hair curler', 'ham on the bone', are alphabetized as headwords.

Where a whole phrase makes the meaning or use of a headword highly specific, the whole phrase is entered alphabetically. For example 'ham on the bone' follows 'hammock'.

Index

References
The numbers in bold type refer to the sections in which the word may be found, and those in normal type refer to the items named in the pictures. Homonyms, and in some cases uses of the same word in different fields, are distinguished by section headings (in italics), some of which are abbreviated, to help to identify at a glance the field required. In most cases the full form referred to by the abbreviations will be obvious. Those which are not are explained in the following list:

Agr.	Agriculture/Agricultural	*Hydr. Eng.*	Hydraulic Engineering
Alp. Plants	Alpine Plants	*Impl.*	Implements
Art. Studio	Artist's Studio	*Inf. Tech.*	Information Technology
Bldg.	Building	*Intern. Combust. Eng.*	Internal Combustion Engine
Carp.	Carpenter	*Moon L.*	Moon Landing
Cement Wks.	Cement Works	*Music Not.*	Musical Notation
Cost.	Costumes	*Overh. Irrign.*	Overhead Irrigation
Cyc.	Cycle	*Platem.*	Platemaking
Decid.	Deciduous	*Plant. Propagn.*	Propagation of Plants
D.I.Y.	Do-it-yourself	*Rm.*	Room
Dom. Anim.	Domestic Animals	*Sp.*	Sports
Equest.	Equestrian Sport	*Text.*	Textile[s]
Gdn.	Garden	*Veg.*	Vegetable[s]

A

Aaron's rod **376** 9
abacus **309** 77
abacus *Art* **334** 20
abattoir **94**
abdomen *Man* **16** 35-37, 36
abdomen *Bees* **77** 10-19
abdomen *Forest Pests* **82** 9
abdomen, lower ~ **16** 37
abdomen, upper ~ **16** 35
abductor hallucis **18** 49
abductor of the hallux **18** 49
aberdevine **361** 8
aborigine, Australian ~ **352** 37
abrasion platform **13** 31
abrasive wheel combination **111** 28, 35
abscissa **347** 9
abseiling **300** 28-30
abseil piton **300** 39
abseil sling **300** 28
absinth **380** 4
absorber attachment **27** 44
absorption dynamometer **143** 97-107
absorption muffler **190** 16
absorption silencer **190** 16
abutment *Bridges* **215** 27, 29, 45
abutment *Art* **336** 20
abutment pier **215** 29
acanthus **334** 25
acceleration rocket **234** 22, 48
accelerator **191** 46
accelerator lock **85** 17
accelerator pedal **191** 46, 94
accelerometer **230** 10
accent, acute ~ **342** 30
accent, circumflex ~ **342** 32
accent, grave ~ **342** 31
accent, strong ~ **321** 27
accents **342** 30-35
acceptance **250** 12, 23
access balcony **37** 72-76
access flap **6** 21, 25
accessories **115** 43-105
accessory shoe **114** 4; **115** 20
accessory shop **196** 24
access ramp **199** 15
acciaccatura **321** 15
accipiters **362** 10-13
accolade **329** 66
accommodation **146** 33
accommodation bureau **204** 28
accommodation ladder **221** 98
accomodation module **146** 33
accompaniment side **324** 43
accompaniment string **324** 25
accordion **324** 36
account, private ~ **250** 4
accounting machine **236** 26
accumulator **309** 41
accumulator *Theatre* **316** 55
accumulator railcar **211** 55
accuracy jump **288** 55
acerate **370** 34
acerose **370** 34
acerous **370** 34
acetylene connection **141** 31
acetylene control **141** 32
acetylene cylinder **141** 2, 22
achene **58** 23
achievement **254** 1-6
achievement, marital ~ **254** 10-13
achievement of arms **254** 1-6
Achilles' tendon **18** 48
acicular **370** 34
acid container **350** 62
Ackermann steering system **85** 31, 37
acolyte **331** 45
aconite **379** 1
acorn **371** 4
acorns **276** 42
acrobat **307** 47
Acropolis **334** 1-7
acroter **334** 34
acroterion **334** 34
acroterium **334** 34
acting area light **316** 16
acting area spotlight **316** 16
actinia **369** 20
Actinophrys **357** 7
action **326** 6-16
action lever **325** 32
activated blade attachment **84** 33
actor **316** 37
actress **316** 38
actuating transistor **195** 19
acuity projector **111** 47
acute **342** 30
ad **342** 56
Adam's apple **19** 13
adapter **112** 55
adapter, four-socket ~ **127** 8
adapter, four-way ~ **127** 8
adapter ring **115** 82
adapter unit **242** 34
adders **364** 40-41
adding **344** 23
adding machine **309** 74
adding mechanism **271** 9
addition **344** 23
address **236** 42
address display **236** 41
addressing machine, transfer-type ~ **245** 7
address label **236** 4
address system, ship's ~ **224** 30
A-deck **223** 28-30
adhesion railcar **214** 1
adhesive, hot ~ **249** 61
adhesive binder *Bookbind.* **184** 1
adhesive binder *Office* **249** 61
adhesive tape dispenser **247** 27
adhesive tape dispenser, roller-type ~ **247** 28
adhesive tape holder **247** 28
adjusting cone **187** 58
adjusting equipment **148** 61-65
adjusting knob **116** 54
adjusting nut **143** 35
adjusting screw *Bldg. Site* **119** 79

adjusting screw *Mach. Parts etc.* **143** 107
adjusting screw *Inf. Tech.* **242** 78
adjusting spindle **226** 51
adjusting washer **187** 55
adjustment, circular ~ **14** 62
adjustment, coarse ~ **112** 4
adjustment, fine ~ *Optic. Instr.* **112** 5
adjustment, fine ~ *Photog.* **116** 33
adjustment, fine ~ *Joiner* **133** 36
adjustment, fine ~ *Drawing Off.* **151** 66
adjustment knob **11** 41
administration area **5** 17
administration building *Coal* **144** 18
administration building *Airport* **233** 16
administration building *Films* **310** 4
Admiralty anchor **286** 15
admission ticket **315** 11
adult insect **358** 10
advance booking office **271** 26
adventure playground **273** 21
advertisement **98** 2; **204** 10; **268** 43, 71; **271** 25; **312** 23; **342** 56, 69
advertising, classified ~ **342** 69
advertising calendar **22** 10
advertising pillar **268** 70
adze **300** 34
aerator **56** 15
aerial **213** 4
aerial ladder **270** 9
aerial sports **288**
aerobatic manoeuvres **288** 1-9
aerobatics **288** 1-9
aero engines **232** 33-60
aerofoil, rear ~ **290** 35
aerogenerator **55** 34; **155** 42
aeroplane **230** 67-72
aeroplane, propeller-driven ~ **231** 1-6
aeroplane, types of ~ **231** 1-33
aeroplane tow launch **287** 1
aerotowing **287** 1
aero wheel **305** 79
Afghan **70** 23
Afghan hound **70** 23
A flat major **320** 66
Africa **14** 14
African hemp **53** 9
African marigold **60** 20
Afro look **34** 26
afterburner exhaust nozzle **256** 13
aftercastle **218** 23
after deck **223** 32
afterpeak **227** 28
aftershave lotion **49** 38
aft fan-jet **232** 42
aft ship **286** 34, 37, 41
agaric **379** 10
agate **175** 22
agent **307** 18
aggregate scraper **200** 13
agitator *Agr. Mach.* **64** 70
agitator *Paperm.* **172** 47
agricultural implements **66**
agricultural machinery **64; 65**
agricultural worker **63** 5
agriculture **63**
Agulhas Current **14** 37
aileron **230** 52; **287** 41; **288** 28
aileron, inner ~ **229** 43
aileron, outer ~ **229** 41
aileron actuator **257** 39
aiming position **86** 34
air-bed, inflatable ~ **278** 31
air blast **139** 56
air-blast circuit breaker **152** 34; **153** 51-62
air-bleed duct *Roof & Boilerr.* **38** 51
air-bleed duct *Intern. Combust. Eng.* **190** 12
air blower, primary ~ **160** 11
air brake **229** 44; **256** 12
airbus **231** 17
air cleaner **191** 55
air compressor *Painter* **129** 33
air compressor *Offshore Drill.* **146** 23
air compressor *Railw.* **211** 14, 44; **212** 34, 58, 72
air compressor, diesel-powered ~ **200** 39
air compressor, mobile ~ **200** 39
air-conditioning **26** 20
air-conditioning equipment **239** 15
air correction jet **192** 3
aircraft **229; 230; 231; 232**
aircraft, propeller-driven ~ **231** 1-6
aircraft, single-engine ~ **230** 1-31, 32-66; **231** 1, 2
aircraft, tilt-wing ~ **232** 26
aircraft, twin-boom ~ **229** 34
aircraft, twin-engine ~ **231** 3
aircraft, twin-jet ~ **231** 7
aircraft, types of ~ **231** 1-33
aircraft cannon **256** 3
aircraft carrier, nuclear-powered ~ **259** 1
aircraft elevator **259** 4, 13
aircraft engines **232** 33-60
aircraft lift **259** 4, 13
aircraft tractor **233** 23
aircraft tug **233** 23
air currents **9** 25-29
air cushion **286** 66
air-cushion vehicle **286** 63
air duct **155** 35
airer **50** 32
airer, extending ~ **50** 34
air extraction vent **154** 21
air extractor duct **258** 57
air extractor pipe **133** 40
air feed pipe **147** 29
air filler neck **196** 21
air filter **191** 55
air flow **199** 45
air flow, secondary ~ **232** 50
air force **256; 257**
air hose *Garage* **195** 54
air hose *Serv. Stat.* **196** 18
air inlet *Lorries etc.* **194** 16
air inlet *Warships* **259** 73
air inlet *Fire Brig.* **270** 60
air inlet and outlet **92** 14
air intake *Car* **192** 60
air intake *Railw.* **209** 11
air intake *Air Force* **256** 5; **257** 12
air intake, annular ~ **232** 52
air intake duct **257** 14
air jet pipe **281** 41
air line **75** 28
airliner, four-jet ~ **231** 13
airliner, supersonic ~ **231** 15
airliner, tri-jet ~ **231** 12
airliner, twin-jet ~ **231** 11, 17
airliner, wide-body ~ **231** 14, 17
air lock *Coal* **144** 38
air lock *Offshore Drill.* **146** 24
air lock *Space* **235** 27
air lock *Chem.* **349** 7
air masses, homogeneous ~ **8** 1-4
air mattress **278** 31
air outlet **168** 29
air oxidation passage **165** 48
air passage **333** 4
airplane *see* aeroplane
airport **233**
'airport' **233** 24
airport fire service **233** 7
airport information symbols **233** 24-53
airport restaurant **233** 19
air preheater *Forging* **139** 53
air preheater *Power Plant* **152** 11
air pump *Paperm.* **172** 40
air pump *Letterpress* **181** 6, 35
air receiver **269** 17, 50
air refuelling probe **256** 7
air regenerator chamber **147** 30
air regulator *Offset Print.* **180** 74
air regulator *Chem.* **350** 3, 8
air reservoir, auxiliary ~ **212** 61
air reservoir, main ~ **211** 8; **212** 57, 71
air rifle **305** 40
air rifle cartridge **305** 34
airscrew **230** 32; **288** 36
air space **74** 61
air-speed indicator **230** 2
airsports **288**
airstream, cold ~ **9** 29
airstream, main ~ **192** 5
airstream, warm ~ **9** 28
air supply **155** 24
air survey camera **14** 63
air temperature **280** 8
air vent cap **38** 52
air vessel **269** 17, 50
aisle *Map* **15** 112
aisle *Forestry* **84** 1

aisle *Church* **330** 27
aisle *Art* **334** 63; **335** 2
alarm clock **110** 19
alarm clock, electric ~ **43** 16
albumen **74** 62
alburnum *Carp.* **120** 85
alburnum *Bot.* **370** 12
Alcor **3** 29
Aldebaran **3** 25
alder **371** 30
alder buckthorn **380** 13
alder dogwood **380** 13
alder-swamp peat **13** 18
ale **93** 26
ale hoof **375** 18
Alençon lace **102** 30
alfalfa grass **136** 26
alga, brown ~ **378** 48
alga, green ~ **378** 43
algebra **345** 4-5
alighting board **77** 49
alkali-cellulose **169** 9
alkali-cellulose crumbs **169** 7
Allais chicane **301** 72
all-container ship **221** 21; **226** 5
Aller rock salt **154** 63
allheal **380** 5
allonge periwig **34** 2
allotment **52** 1-32
allotment holder **52** 24
all-purpose gun **258** 70
all-purpose gun, radar-controlled ~ **258** 47, 48
all-purpose trailer **62** 40
all-purpose vehicle **255** 96
all-speed aileron **229** 43
alluvial deposit **216** 52
all-weather roof **200** 38
all-wheel drive **194** 1
almond *Tablew. etc.* **45** 41
almond *South. Fruits* **384** 36
aloe **53** 13
alphanumeric disc store **176** 33
alpha particle **1** -31; **227**
alpha radiation **1** 30-31
Alpine Club hut **300** 1
alpine rhododendron **378** 1
alpine rose **378** 1
alpine soldanella **378** 3
alpine strawberry **58** 16
alpine wormwood **378** 6
Alpinism **300** 1-57
Alpinist **300** 5
Alsatian **70** 25
alsike **69** 3
alsike clover **69** 3
Altair **3** 9
altar **330** 4, 33; **334** 48, 69
altar bell **332** 52
altar candle **330** 7, 34
altar carpet **330** 3
altar cloth **330** 6, 36
altar cross **330** 35
altar crucifix **330** 12
altar decoration **330** 48
altarpiece **330** 13, 50
altar steps **330** 5, 31
alternative school **261** 1-45
alternator **152** 23; **153** 1
altimeter **230** 4
altitude **346** 27
altitude scale **7** 35
alto clef **320** 10
altocumulus **8** 15
altocumulus castellanus **8** 16
altocumulus floccus **8** 16
altostratus **8** 8
altostratus praecipitans **8** 9
alto trombone **323** 46
aluminium foil, asphalted ~ **155** 29
aluminum *see* aluminium
A major **320** 58
amanita **379** 11
amaryllis **53** 8
Amazon water lily **378** 17
ambulance **270** 19
ambulance, armoured ~ **255** 79
ambulance attendant **270** 21
ambulance car **270** 19
ambulance man **270** 21
America **14** 12-13
American blight **80** 32
American football **292** 22
American ivy **51** 5; **374** 16
A minor **320** 55, 62
A minor scale **320** 46, 47, 48
ammeter *Car* **191** 78
ammeter *Aircraft* **230** 18
ammonia **170** 24
ammonia scrubber **156** 23
ammonia wet collector **156** 23
ammonium sulphate **156** 36
ammonium sulphate, production of ~ **156** 35
ammonium sulphate solution **170** 26
ammunition **87** 19; **305** 34-49
amoeba **357** 1
amoretto **272** 20
amorino **272** 20
Amphibia **364**; **364** 20-26
amphibian **232** 8
amphibians **364** 20-26
amplifier **241** 40; **312** 19; **317** 23
amplifier, underwater ~ **237** 57
amplifier and mains power unit **238** 3
amplifier equipment **310** 59
amplitude adjustment **10** 11
amulet **354** 40
anaesthesia and breathing apparatus **26** 1
anaesthesia and respiratory apparatus **26** 24
anaesthetic, local ~ **24** 53
analog *see* analogue
analogue control **242** 38
analogue output **112** 45
analyser **23** 53
analysis, automatic ~ **25** 48
analytical balance **349** 25
anchor **223** 52; **259** 81
anchor, lightweight ~ **286** 16-18
anchor, stocked ~ **222** 79; **286** 15
anchor, stockless ~ **222** 78; **258** 5; **286** 17
anchorage **216** 13
anchor cable **218** 18; **222** 77; **223** 50; **227** 12
anchor capstan **258** 6
anchor hawser **218** 18
anchor rib **287** 32
anchor rope **218** 18
anchors **286** 15-18
anchor winch **259** 82
ancillary brake valve **211** 23
Andromeda **3** 24
anemometer **10** 28
anemone **375** 5; **377** 1
aneroid barometer **10** 4
aneroid box **10** 6
aneroid capsule **10** 6
angiographic examination table **27** 26
angiography room **27** 12
angle *Mach. Parts etc.* **143** 1
angle *Maths.* **346** 1-23; **346** 8-13, 8, 55
angle, acute ~ **346** 10
angle, adjacent ~ **346** 14
angle, alternate ~ **346** 10
angle, circumferential ~ **346** 56
angle, exterior ~ **346** 26
angle, interior ~ **346** 26
angle, obtuse ~ **346** 11
angle, straight ~ **346** 13,9-15
angle brace **118** 25; **119** 63; **121** 57
angle deck **259** 12
angle iron **143** 1
angle of departure **87** 75
angle of descent **87** 78
angle of dip **12** 3
angle of elevation **87** 76
angle of rotation **351** 33
angle of the mouth **16** 14; **19** 19
angle shears **125** 2
angle symbol **345** 23
angle tie **118** 25; **121** 57
angle tongs **137** 37
angle tower **329** 14, 17
angling **89** 20-94
angling fence **133** 19
Angora cat **73** 17
Angoumois grain moth **81** 29
Angoumois grain moth caterpillar **81** 30
Angoumois moth **81** 29
Anguidae **364** 37
animal, cloven-hoofed ~ **73** 9
animal, inflatable ~ **280** 33
animal, rubber ~ **280** 33
animal, toy ~ **46** 13; **47** 6
animal, wild ~ **307** 56
animal enclosure **272** 49
animal house **356** 10
animals, domestic ~ **73** 18-36
animals, fabulous ~ **327** 1-61
animals, multicellular ~ **357** 13-39
animals, one-celled ~ **357** 1-12

animals, single-celled ~ **357** 1-12
animals, unicellular ~ **357** 1-12
ankle guard **291** 33
ankle sock, children's ~ **29** 30
annealing lehr **162** 18
annelid **357** 20
annexe **331** 13
annuity **251** 11-19
annulus **346** 57
Annunciation lily **60** 12
anode, copper ~ **178** 5
anode rod **178** 5
anorak *Child. Clothes* **29** 62
anorak *Mountain.* **300** 6
anorak hood **300** 19
Anseres **359** 15-17
ant **358** 21-22
Antarctica **14** 18
Antarctic Circumpolar Drift **14** 44
Antarctic Continent **14** 18
Antarctic Ocean **14** 22
antelope **367** 5
antenna *Meteorol. Instr.* **10** 59, 68
antenna *Forest Pests* **82** 3
antenna *Air Force* **256** 17
antenna *Warships* **258** 16, 46; **259** 7, 47, 89
antenna *Airsports* **288** 20, 88
antenna *Articulates* **358** 27, 53
antenna, maxillary ~ **358** 42
antenna, trichotomous ~ **81** 5
antenna down-lead **223** 4
antenna lead-in **223** 4
antenna mast **259** 6
antependium **330** 20
anther *Soft Fruit* **58** 45
anther *Drupes & Nuts* **59** 10
anther *Conifers* **372** 35
anthozoan **357** 17
anthropoid apes **368** 14-16
anthropoids **368** 14-16
anti-aircraft gun **258** 73
anti-aircraft gun, automatic ~ **259** 34
anti-aircraft machine gun **255** 63
anti-aircraft missile launcher **258** 32; **259** 5, 20
anti-aircraft rocket launcher **258** 32; **259** 5, 20
anticline **12** 16, 27
anticlinorium **12** 20
anticollision light **230** 64
anticyclone **9** 6
antifriction bearing **143** 69
anti-frost layer **198** 1; **200** 60
antimacassar **207** 48
anti-mist windscreen **189** 46
anti-mist windshield **189** 46
anti-radiation screen **154** 74
anti-rolling system **224** 26
antirrhinum **51** 32
anti set-off apparatus **181** 10
anti set-off spray **181** 10
anti-skate control **241** 25
anti-skid brake switch **211** 33
anti-slosh baffle **234** 13
anti-submarine missile launcher **258** 30, 50
anti-submarine rocket launcher **258** 30, 50
anti-submarine torpedo tube **258** 33
anti-syphon trap *Bathrm. etc.* **49** 27
anti-syphon trap *Plumb. etc.* **126** 26
anti-tank rocket launcher **255** 25
anti-tank tank **255** 88
anti-torque rotor **232** 14
anti-vortex system **234** 11
antler, palmate ~ **88** 40
antler, royal ~ **88** 8
antler, surroyal ~ **88** 9
antlers **88** 5-11, 29-31
anurans **364** 23-26
anus **20** 62
anvil *Plumb.* **125** 22
anvil *Blacksm.* **137** 11, 11-16; **138** 33
anvil *Forging* **139** 17, 31, 40
anvil *Office* **247** 5
anvil, clockmaker's ~ **109** 7
aorta **18** 10; **20** 54
aorta, abdominal ~ **18** 16
Apache girl **306** 9
apartment **37** 64-68, 69-71; **46**
apartment, ladies' ~ **329** 10
apartment building **37** 72-76
apartment building, high-rise ~ **37** 82
apartment building, multistory ~ **37** 77-81
apartment house **37** 72-76
apartment house, high-rise ~ **37** 82
apartment house, multistory ~ **37** 77-81
apatite **351** 20
aperture **115** 62, 63
aperture control, automatic ~ **117** 20
aperture control ring **115** 5; **117** 4
aperture ring **115** 5; **117** 4
aperture scale **115** 56
aperture setting **117** 4
aperture-setting control **114** 34
aperture-setting ring **115** 5; **117** 4
aperture-stop slide **112** 16
apex *Hunt.* **87** 77
apex *Airsports* **288** 47
apex *Church* **331** 5
aphid **80** 32; **358** 13
aphid, winged ~ **82** 39; **358** 15
aphid, wingless ~ **358** 14
apiarist **77** 57
apiary **77** 56
apiculture **77**
à pointe **314** 19
Apollo booster **234** 1, 2
Apollo service module **234** 56
Apollo space capsule **6** 9
Apollo spacecraft **6** 1
apostrophe **342** 22
apparatus, auxiliary ~ **296** 12-21; **297** 7-14
apparatus exercises **297** 15-32
apparatus gymnastics **296**; **297**
appendix **20** 18
appendix, vermiform ~ **20** 18
Appenzell dulcimer **322** 35
apple **58** 56; **99** 86; **370** 102
apple blossom **58** 54
appleblossom weevil **80** 10
apple core **58** 59
apple pip **58** 60
apple skin **58** 57
apple stalk **58** 61
apple tree **58** 51, 52
appliance room **270** 1
appliqué **29** 20
appoggiatura **321** 14, 15
appointments book **22** 11
appointments diary **246** 8
approach **329** 34
approach sign **203** 26, 27, 28, 29
approach signs **203** 26-29
apricot **59** 35
apricot blossom **59** 34
apricot branch, flowering ~ **59** 33
apricot flower **59** 34
apricot leaf **59** 36
apricot tree **59** 33-36
apron *Mach. Tools* **149** 16
apron *Electrotyp. etc.* **178** 9
apron *Airport* **233** 3
apron *Theatre* **316** 25
apron, butcher's ~ **96** 39
apron, composition ~ **164** 16
apron, frilled ~ **31** 33
apron, leather ~ *Arc Weld.* **142** 11
apron, leather ~ *Cotton Spin.* **164** 16
apron taxiway **233** 4
apse **334** 64; **335** 5
aquafer **12** 22; **269** 2, 38
aqualung **279** 19
aquarium **356** 14, 19
Aquarius **4** 63
aquatint **340** 14-24
aqueduct **334** 53
aquifer **12** 22; **269** 2, 38
Aquila **3** 9
aquilegia **60** 10
arabesque *Free Exerc.* **295** 30
arabesque *Ballet* **314** 18
arachnids **358** 40-47
araucaria **53** 16
arbor **272** 17
arbor vitae **372** 39
arbour **272** 17
arc *Films* **312** 42
arc *Maths.* **346** 53, 55
arc, graduated ~ **224** 2
arcade, blind ~ **335** 10
arcading **335** 8
arcading, blind ~ **335** 10
arcading, round ~ **335** 9
arc fibula **328** 28
arch *Bldg. Site* **119** 6

arch *Bridges* **215** 20
arch *Free Exerc.* **295** 34
arch *Theatre* **316** 11
arch *Art* **336** 19
arch, convex ~ **336** 34
arch, longitudinal ~ **19** 61
arch, parabolic ~ **336** 29
arch, reinforced concrete ~ **215** 50
arch, round ~ **336** 27
arch, segmental ~ **336** 28
arch, shouldered ~ **336** 33
arch, superciliary ~ **16** 5
arch, tented ~ **336** 35
arch, transverse ~ **335** 18
arch, trellis ~ **52** 12
arch, triumphal ~ **334** 59, 71
arch, trussed ~ **215** 25
arch, Tudor ~ **336** 37
arch, types of ~ **336** 19-37
Archaster **369** 17
arch board file **247** 40
arch bridge, spandrel-braced ~ **215** 28
arch bridge, stone ~ **215** 19
arched front support **295** 24
Archer *Astron.* **3** 37; **4** 61
archer *Sports* **305** 53
archery **305** 52-66
archimedes drill **108** 4
architrave **334** 18
archivolt **335** 25
arch span **215** 26
arch unit **247** 41
archway **337** 4
archway, memorial ~ **337** 3
arcing horn **152** 47; **153** 61
arcosolium **331** 60
Arctic Ocean **14** 21
arc welder **142** 2
arc welding, gas-shielded ~ **142** 33
arc welding helmet **142** 3, 39
area, epicentral ~ **11** 38
area spraying **83** 1
areca **380** 19
areca nut **380** 20
areca palm **380** 19
arena *Equest.* **289** 1
arena *Circus* **307** 21
arena *Bullfight. etc.* **319** 9
arena entrance **307** 11
areola **16** 29
argent **254** 25
Argo **3** 45
Aries **4** 53
aril, laciniate ~ **382** 34
arista **68** 12
arithmetic **344** 1-26; **345** 1-24
arithmetic unit **244** 6
arm *Man* **16** 43-48; **17** 12-14
arm *Living Rm.* **42** 22
arm *Flat* **46** 28
arm *Shoem.* **100** 25
arm *Photog.* **115** 93
arm *Joiner* **132** 63
arm *Mach. Parts etc.* **143** 88
arm *Mach. Tools* **150** 24
arm *Music. Instr.* **322** 16
arm *Maths.* **346** 7-3
arm, adjustable ~ **195** 26
arm, hydraulic ~ **85** 21
arm, supplementary ~ **203** 22, 23
arm, upper ~ **16** 43
armadillo **366** 8
armament **258** 29-37
armature **339** 25
armature support **339** 24
armband **263** 11; **270** 22
armband, fluorescent ~ **199** 7
arm bandage **21** 1
arm bar **299** 10
armchair **42** 21; **267** 26
armed forces **255; 256; 257**
armlet **263** 11; **270** 22
armonie **322** 25
armor *see* armour
armour **329** 38, 62
armour, knight's ~ **329** 38-65
armour, padded ~ **353** 38
armour, steel tape ~ **153** 50
armour, steel wire ~ **153** 50
armoured car **264** 16
armoured vehicles **255** 79-95
armour plating **246** 24
armpit **16** 26
armpit hair **16** 27
arm positions **314** 7-10
armrest **106** 18; **109** 3; **207** 45, 69; **208** 26
arm sling **21** 2
arms of the baron **254** 10
arms of the family of the femme **254** 11-13
arms of the family of the wife **254** 11-13
arms of the husband **254** 10
armstand dive **282** 45
army **255**
army weaponry **255** 1-98
arnica **380** 2
A road **15** 83
arolla pine **372** 29
arpeggio **321** 22
arrangement of desks **260** 1
arrester **152** 35
arrester wire **259** 16
arris **121** 12
arris fillet **121** 31
'arrivals' **233** 26
arrivals and departures board **204** 18
arrival schedule **204** 19
arrival timetable **204** 19
arrow **305** 60
arrow head *Drawing Off.* **151** 26
arrow head *Alp. Plants etc.* **378** 51
art **333; 334; 335; 336; 337**
art, Babylonian ~ **333** 19-20
art, Baroque ~ **336** 1-8
art, Byzantine ~ **334** 72-75
art, Chinese ~ **337** 1-6
art, computer-generated ~ **248** 19
art, Early Christian ~ **334** 61-71
art, Egyptian ~ **333** 1-18
art, Etruscan ~ **334** 49-52
art, Gothic ~ **335** 22-41
art, Greek ~ **334** 1-48
art, Indian ~ **337** 19-28
art, Islamic ~ **337** 12-18
art, Japanese ~ **337** 7-11
art, Renaissance ~ **335** 42-54
art, Rococo ~ **336** 9-13
art, Roman ~ **334** 53-60
art, Romanesque ~ **335** 1-21
art director **310** 43
artery, carotid ~ **18** 1
artery, femoral ~ **18** 19
artery, frontal ~ **18** 5
artery, iliac ~ **18** 17
artery, pulmonary ~ **18** 11; **20** 55
artery, radial ~ **18** 21
artery, subclavian ~ **18** 7
artery, temporal ~ **18** 3
artery, tibial ~ **18** 20
artery forceps **26** 49
arthropods **358** 1-23
articulates **358**
artillery weapons **255** 49-74
artist **338** 2
artistes, travelling ~ **308** 25-28
Art Nouveau easy chair **336** 18
art of Asia Minor **333** 37
art of the Assyrians **333** 29-36
art of the Persians **333** 21-28
arts section **342** 67
ascent, vertical ~ **315** 3
ascent stage **6** 37-47
ascospore **381** 13
ascus **381** 12, 13
ash box door **38** 39
ashpan **210** 6, 7
ash pit **152** 8
ashtray **42** 29; **104** 5; **207** 46, 69; **208** 29; **246** 33
ashtray, spherical ~ **266** 5
ash tree **371** 38
Asia **14** 16
asp **364** 41
asparagus **57** 14
asparagus bed **52** 25
asparagus cutter **56** 10
asparagus knife **56** 10
asparagus patch **52** 25
asparagus server **45** 77
asparagus slice **45** 77
aspen **371** 21
aspergillum **332** 54
asphalt drying and mixing plant **200** 48
asphalt mixer drum **200** 50
asphalt-mixing drum **200** 50
aspiration psychrometer **10** 33
asp viper **364** 41
assay balance **108** 35
assembler **174** 23
assembling machine **249** 59
assembling station **249** 60
assembly of a circuit **242** 72
assembly point *Airport* **233** 11
'assembly point' *Airport* **233** 29
assistant *Univ.* **262** 7
assistant *Store* **271** 63
assistant *Circus* **307** 39

assistant, cellarer's ~ **79** 12
assistant, dentist's ~ **24** 18
assistant, doctor's ~ **22** 19
assistant cameraman **310** 42
assistant director *Films* **310** 21, 46
assistant director *Theatre* **316** 43
assistant producer **316** 43
assistant professor **262** 3
assistant sound engineer **310** 57
association flag **286** 6, 9
association football **291**
asterisk **185** 61
asteroids **4** 47
astride jump **295** 35, 37
astronaut **6** 11; **235** 67
astronomy **3; 4; 5**
asymmetric bars **297** 3
asymptote **347** 29
athletics **298**
Atlantic Ocean **14** 20
Atlas **334** 36
atmosphere **7**
atoll **13** 32
Atolla **369** 5
atom **1; 2**
atomic pile casing **259** 67
atomic power plant **154** 19
atom layer **7** 32
atom models **1** 1-8
atrium *Man* **20** 45
atrium *Art* **334** 66
attachment to Orbiter **235** 49
attack **321** 27
attack area **293** 64
attacker *Ball Games* **292** 3
attacker *Fencing* **294** 5
attacking fencer **294** 5
attack line **293** 65
attack periscope **259** 88
attic **38** 1-29, 18; **334** 60
attitude **314** 17
attitude control rocket **234** 38
aubretia **51** 7
auction room **225** 58
audience **263** 8
audio cassette **242** 17
audio coding equipment **242** 11-14
audio head **243** 35
audio level control **117** 16
audio recording level control **243** 11
audio sync head **243** 24
audio systems **241**
audio track **243** 32
audio typist **248** 33
audiovision **243**
audio-visual camera **243** 1-4
audio-visual projector **242** 16
auditorium **315** 14-27, 16-20
auditorium lighting control **312** 17
auger *Agr. Mach.* **64** 6, 25
auger *Carp.* **120** 65
augmented triad **321** 4
auk **359** 13
aulos **322** 3
aulos pipe **322** 4
aural syringe **22** 74
aureus **252** 3
auricle **17** 56; **20** 24
auricula **378** 8
Auriga **3** 27
auriscope **22** 74
aurora **7** 30
Australia **14** 17
Australopithecus **261** 20
auto **191** 1-56; **195** 34
autoclave **170** 12, 33
autofocus override switch **117** 11
automatic flight control panel **235** 23
automatic-threading button **117** 83
automobile **191** 1-56; **192; 193; 195** 34
automobile models **193** 1-36
automobile tire **191** 15; **196** 27
automotive mechanic **195** 53
autopilot **224** 18
auto-soling machine **100** 2
auxiliaries **258** 92-97
auxiliary brake valve **211** 23
auxiliary-cable tensioning mechanism **214** 48
auxiliary engine room **223** 70; **259** 56
auxiliary parachute bay **235** 59
AV **243**
avalanche **304** 1
avalanche forest **304** 7
avalanche gallery **304** 3
avalanche wall **304** 2
avalanche wedge **304** 2
Ave Maria **332** 32
avenue **274** 11
aviary **356** 8
aviation fuel **145** 57
avionics bay, front ~ **257** 11
avionics bay, rear ~ **257** 18
avionics console **235** 22
awn **68** 12
awner **64** 10
awning *Dwellings* **37** 71
awning *Ship* **218** 15; **221** 116
awning *Camping* **278** 28, 37
awning crutch **218** 14
ax *see* axe
axe **85** 1; **120** 73; **270** 43
axe, bronze ~ **328** 23
axe, socketed ~ **328** 23
axial-flow pump **217** 47-52
axis *Astron.* **4** 22
axis *Maths.* **347** 17
axis, anticlinal ~ **12** 17
axis, celestial ~ **4** 10
axis, conjugate ~ **347** 24
axis, coordinate ~ **347** 2-3
axis, earth's ~ **4** 22-28
axis, floral ~ **370** 53
axis, lateral ~ **230** 68
axis, longitudinal ~ **230** 72
axis, major ~ **347** 23
axis, minor ~ **347** 24
axis, normal ~ **230** 70
axis, polar ~ **113** 15, 18
axis, synclinal ~ **12** 19
axis, transverse ~ **347** 23
axis, vertical ~ **230** 70
axis mount, English-type ~ **113** 22
axis mounting, English-type ~ **113** 22
axis of abscissae **347** 2
axis of ordinates **347** 3
axis of rotation, instantaneous ~ **4** 25
axis of rotation, mean ~ **4** 27
axis of symmetry *Maths.* **346** 25
axis of symmetry *Crystals* **351** 4
axle **187** 61, 76, 81
axle, coupled ~ **210** 36
axle, floating ~ *Agr. Mach.* **65** 33
axle, floating ~ *Motorcycle* **189** 34
axle, live ~ **192** 65-71
axle, rigid ~ **192** 65-71
axle bearing **210** 10
axle drive shaft **201** 13
azalea **53** 12
azimuth **87** 74
azure *Heraldry* **254** 28
azure *Colour* **343** 6

B

baboon **368** 13
baby **28** 5
baby bath **28** 3
baby carriage **28** 34; **272** 71; **273** 31
baby clothes **29** 1-12
baby doll **48** 25
baby grand piano **325** 40
baby pants **28** 22
baby pants, rubber ~ **29** 10
baby powder **28** 14
baby scales **22** 42
back *Man* **16** 22-25
back *Tablew. etc.* **45** 56
back *Horse* **72** 29
back *Mills* **91** 2
back *Roof* **122** 86
back *Bookbind.* **185** 41
back *Car* **193** 35
back *Swim.* **282** 49
back *Ball Games* **293** 77
back *Sports* **305** 11
backband **71** 19
backboard **292** 30
backbone *Man* **17** 2-5
backbone *Bookbind.* **185** 41
back check **325** 27
back check felt **325** 28
backcloth **315** 33; **316** 10
back comb **105** 6
back crease **292** 71
back cushion **42** 25
back cut **84** 29
backdrop **315** 33; **316** 10
backdrop light **316** 15
back fat **95** 40
backfilling **217** 7

back flip **297** 24
backgammon **276** 18
backgammon board **276** 22
back gauge **183** 17; **185** 4, 7
background *Films* **310** 33
background *Theatre* **316** 10
backhand stroke **293** 39
backing **269** 29
backing disc, rubber ~ **134** 22
backing paper *Photog.* **114** 21
backing paper *Paperhanger* **128** 5
back left second pin **305** 9
back loop **288** 50
back of the hand **19** 83
backpack unit **6** 20
back-pedal brake **187** 63
back pin **305** 11
back plate **140** 36
back-pressure valve, hydraulic ~ **141** 8
backrest *Weaving* **166** 37
backrest *Railw.* **207** 66
backrest, reclining ~ **191** 35
back right second pin **305** 10
back scouring valve **216** 61
backside **16** 40
back sight leaf **87** 67
back sight slide **87** 69
back standard adjustment **114** 55
backstay **219** 19
backstitch seam **102** 1
back support **295** 22; **296** 29
back-up ball **305** 20
back vault **297** 32
backward grand circle **296** 60
backward somersault *Swim.* **282** 42
backward somersault *Gymn.* **297** 15
backward underswing **296** 59
backward walkover **297** 23
backwater **172** 26
bacon **96** 2
Bactrian camel **366** 29
badge, fool's ~ **306** 60
badger **88** 48
badging **191** 12
badminton **293** 43-44
badminton game **273** 6
badminton racket **293** 43
badminton racquet **293** 43
baffle board *Warships* **259** 27
baffle board **309** 17
baffle board, hinged **259** 15
baffle board, movable ~ **259** 15
bag *Doc.* **22** 33
bag *Hunt.* **86** 38
bag *Music. Instr.* **322** 9
bag, girl's ~ **29** 56
bag, heat-sealed ~ **76** 29
bag, paper ~ **98** 48
bag, postman's ~ **236** 54
bag filter **83** 54
bag-full indicator **50** 61, 73
baggage compartment **257** 19
baggage loader **233** 22
baggage man **267** 17
'baggage retrieval' **233** 38
baggage terminal **233** 5, 16
bagging nozzle **83** 55
bag net **77** 54
bagpipe **322** 8
bag sealer **40** 47
baguette **97** 12
bag wig **34** 4
bail **292** 70
bailey, inner ~ **329** 2
bailey, outer ~ **329** 31
bait **86** 21
bait, poisoned ~ **83** 31
bait, weighted ~ **89** 36
bait needle **89** 41
baits **89** 65-76
bait tin **89** 24
bakehouse **97** 55-74
baker's shop **97** 1-54
bakery **97** 55-74
baking ingredient **99** 62
baking ingredients **98** 8-11
balalaika **324** 28
Balance *Astron.* **3** 19; **4** 59
balance *Paperm.* **173** 9
balance beam **349** 30
balance cable **214** 46
balance cable sleeve **214** 74
balance column **349** 29
balancer **307** 48
balance rail **322** 39
balance weight **242** 50
balance wheel **110** 39
balancing act **307** 44
balancing cabins **214** 25
balancing knob **116** 39
balancing pole **307** 42
balcony *Dwellings* **37** 18, 69, 73
balcony *Theatre* **315** 16; **315** 18
balcony *Chivalry* **329** 12
balcony, projecting ~ **218** 57
baldachin **331** 49
baldaquin **331** 49
bald patch **34** 21
bale **55** 31; **63** 34; **75** 7; **83** 13; **169** 34; **170** 62; **206** 10, 11, 23
bale arm **89** 62
bale breaker **163** 7
bale loader, hydraulic ~ **63** 37
bale opener **163** 7
baler, high-pressure ~ **63** 35
baling press **169** 33
balk **63** 3
ball *Infant Care etc.* **28** 16
ball *Bicycle* **187** 31
ball *Aircraft* **230** 12
ball *Ball Games* **292** 27
ball *Circus* **307** 60
ball, ivory ~ **277** 1
ball, metal ~ **352** 32
ball, paper ~ **306** 55
ball, plastic ~ **277** 1
ball, steel ~ **143** 70
ball, stone ~ **352** 32
ball and socket head **114** 47
ballast *Station* **205** 61
ballast *Railw.* **212** 66
ballast *Sailing* **285** 33
ballast *Airsports* **288** 65
ballast keel **285** 32
ballast tank **223** 78
ball bearing **143** 69; **187** 56, 68
ball boy **293** 22
ballerina **314** 26
ballet **314**
ballet dancer **314** 26
ballet positions **314** 1-6
ballet shoe **314** 30
ballet skirt **314** 31
ballet slipper **314** 30
ball games **291**; **292**; **293**
ballistics **87** 73
ball mill **161** 1
ball of clay **161** 9
ball of the foot **19** 58
ball of the thumb **19** 75
balloon **308** 13
balloon, gas ~ **288** 63
balloon, hot-air ~ **288** 79
balloon, manned ~ **7** 16
balloon basket **288** 64
ballooning **288** 63-84
ballot box **263** 29
ballot envelope **263** 21
ballot paper **263** 20
ball race **187** 68
ballroom **306** 1
Balmer series **1** 21
baluster **38** 29; **123** 51
balustrade **38** 25; **123** 22, 50
bamboo cane **136** 31
bamboo culm **383** 60
bamboo stem **383** 60, 63
banana **99** 90; **384** 33
banana flower **384** 34
banana-handling terminal **226** 22
banana leaf **384** 35
banana plant **384** 28
banana saddle **188** 59
banana tree **384** 28
band *Ball Games* **291** 25
band *Nightclub* **318** 3
band *Church* **332** 5
band, fluorescent ~ **199** 8
band, iron ~ **130** 16
band, ornamental ~ **334** 38
band, steel ~ **163** 5
bandage *First Aid* **21** 9
bandage *Equest.* **289** 15
bandages, emergency ~ **21** 1-13
band brake **143** 104
banderilla **319** 22
banderillero **319** 4, 21
band of barrel **130** 8
bandoneon **324** 36
bandora **322** 21
bandsaw **134** 50; **157** 48
bandsaw, horizontal ~ **157** 48
bandsaw blade **157** 53
bandstand **274** 19; **307** 9
band wheel **104** 15
bandwheel cover **133** 32
banewort **379** 7
banger **306** 51
bangle *Jewell.* **36** 17
bangle *Ethnol.* **354** 38
bangle, asymmetrical ~ **36** 26

bangs **34** 36
banjo **324** 29
bank *Phys. Geog.* **13** 4
bank *Post* **237** 43
bank *Bank* **250**
bank *Roulette* **275** 11
bank acceptance **250** 12
bank branch **204** 31
bank clerk **250** 5
bank employee **251** 7
banknotes **252** 29-39
bank of circulation **252** 30
bank of issue **252** 30
bank of oars **218** 12
bank protection **216** 51-55
bank slope **217** 28
bank stabilization **216** 51-55
bank statement **247** 44
banner *Flags* **253** 12
banner *Election* **263** 12
banner, processional ~ **331** 44
banquet room **267** 39
bantam **74** 56
baptism, Christian ~ **332** 1
baptistery **332** 2
bar *Horse* **71** 41
bar *Office* **246** 29
bar *Restaurant* **266** 1-11
bar *Hotel* **267** 54
bar *Park* **272** 34
bar *Playground* **273** 32
bar *Gymn.* **296** 3, 8; **297** 4, 41
bar *Athletics* **298** 14, 34
bar *Winter Sp.* **303** 5
bar *Circus* **307** 50
bar *Disco* **317** 1, 9
bar *Nightclub* **318** 13, 15
bar *Music. Not.* **320** 42
bar *Graphic Art* **340** 34
bar, flat ~ **143** 10
bar, metal ~ **324** 77
bar, round ~ **143** 8
bar, sliding ~ **75** 21
bar arm **299** 10
barb *Bees* **77** 10
barb *Fish Farm.* **89** 80
barb *Mach. Parts etc.* **143** 44
barbecue **278** 47
barbel **364** 13
bar bender **119** 21
barber **106** 1
barber's shop **106** 1-42
barchan **13** 40
barchane **13** 40
bar customer **267** 55
bareback rider **307** 26
barge **216** 22, 25; **225** 8
barge and push tug assembly **221** 92
bargeboard **37** 8
bargee **216** 26
bargeman **216** 26
barge sucker **216** 59
bark *Carp.* **120** 86
bark *Ship* **219** 1-72; **220** 21-23
bark *Bot.* **370** 8
bark, five-masted ~ **220** 32-34
bark, four-masted ~ **220** 29
bark beetle **82** 22
bark brush **56** 23
barkeep **266** 8; **267** 62
barkeeper **266** 8; **267** 62
barker **308** 8, 64
barkhan **13** 40
barking **85** 23
barking iron **85** 8
bark schooner **220** 20
bark scraper **56** 14
bark spud **85** 8
bark stripping **85** 23
bar lamp **317** 11
barley **68** 1, 26
barley, germinated ~ **92** 23
barley elevator **92** 33
barley hopper **92** 2
barley reception **92** 41
barley silo **92** 31
bar line **320** 42
barmaid **267** 63; **317** 2; **318** 14
barman **266** 8; **267** 62
barn owl **362** 17
barn swallow **361** 20
barograph **10** 4
barouche **186** 35
barque **219** 1-72; **220** 21-23
barque, five-masted ~ **220** 32-34
barque, four-masted ~ **220** 29
barque schooner **220** 20
barrage **217** 57-64, 65-72
barrel *Cooper* **130** 5
barrel *Mach. Tools* **149** 27
barrel *Army* **255** 2, 17, 41
barrel, aluminium ~ **93** 17
barrel, rifled ~ **87** 26
barrel, semi-oval ~ **89** 3
barrel, smooth-bore ~ **87** 27
barrel casing **87** 35; **255** 33
barrel clamp **255** 11, 62
barrel-clamping nut **255** 11
barrel cradle **255** 60
barrelhead **130** 10
barrel organ **309** 13
barrel recuperator **255** 61
barrel-shape **36** 75
barrel-shape, standard ~ **36** 56
barrel stave **130** 9
barrel store **93** 16
barrel vault **335** 19; **336** 38
barricade **264** 17
barrier *Supermkt.* **99** 5
barrier *Railw.* **202** 40
barrier *Hydr. Eng.* **217** 65
barrow *Station* **205** 32
barrow *Prehist.* **328** 16
barrow, road sweeper's ~ **199** 9
barrow, street sweeper's ~ **199** 9
bars **75** 5
bar set **246** 30
bar stool **267** 53; **317** 3; **318** 16
bartender **266** 8; **267** 62
bar trio **267** 44
barysphere **11** 5
basal pinacoid **351** 20
base *Dining Rm.* **44** 23
base *Mills* **91** 33
base *Optic. Instr.* **112** 3; **113** 2
base *Floor etc. Constr.* **123** 21, 63
base *Bookbind.* **183** 25
base *Road Constr.* **200** 59
base *Heraldry* **254** 22-23
base *Mountain.* **300** 1
base *Art* **334** 28-31
base *Maths.* **345** 1, 6; **346** 27; **347** 35, 39
base, horizontal ~ **112** 72
base, round ~ *Hairdresser* **105** 27
base, round ~ *Basketm.* **136** 19
base, round ~ *Electrotyp. etc.* **178** 10
base, woven ~ **136** 20
baseball **292** 40-69, 61
baseball glove **292** 59-60
baseball mitt **292** 59-60
baseboard *Photog.* **116** 27
baseboard *Sculpt. Studio* **339** 23
base course *Dwellings* **37** 17
base course *Carp.* **120** 28
base course *Street Sect.* **198** 3
base course *Road Constr.* **200** 59
base course, concrete ~ **118** 2
base course, natural stone ~ **37** 85
base frame **177** 40
base line **292** 48; **293** 3-10, 72
base line judge **293** 26
baseman **292** 44
basement **37** 1; **118** 1
basement stairs **123** 16
basement wall **123** 1
basement window **37** 27; **118** 3
base of goblet **162** 42
base of machine **168** 54
base of statue **272** 11
base of support **214** 81
base plate *Optic. Instr.* **112** 27
base plate *Iron Foundry etc.* **148** 56
base plate *Mach. Tools* **150** 19
base plate *Knitting* **167** 34
base plate *Railw.* **202** 5
base plate *Army* **255** 46
base plate *Ball Games* **292** 67
base unit **39** 9
basic knits **171** 30-48
basic position **295** 1
basidia **381** 7
basidiospore **381** 8
basilica **334** 61
basilisk *Fabul. Creat.* **327** 34
basilisk *Fish etc.* **364** 30
basin *Doc.* **23** 25
basin *Dent.* **24** 12
basin *Park* **272** 24
basis weight **173** 9
basket *Kitch. Utensils* **40** 42
basket *Butch.* **96** 18
basket *Supermkt.* **99** 8
basket *Basketm.* **136** 16
basket *Station* **204** 3

basket *Ball Games* **292** 32
basket *Winter Sp.* **301** 8
basket, rotating ~ **168** 17
basket, wicker ~ **305** 69
basket, wire ~ **55** 50; **66** 25; **188** 23
basketball **292** 28, 29
basketball player **292** 35
basket handle **336** 28
basket maker **136** 33
basket making **136** 1-40
basket post **292** 31
basket ring **292** 33
basketry **136** 1-40
basket weave **171** 11
basketwork **136** 1-40, 16
bas-relief **339** 33
bass **323** 23
bass belly bridge **325** 13
bass bridge **325** 13
bass button **324** 43
bass clarinet **323** 34
bass clef **320** 9
bass coupler **324** 44
bass drum **323** 55; **324** 47
bassinet **28** 30
bassinet covers **28** 31
bassoon **323** 28
bass press-stud **324** 43
bass register **324** 44
bass side **324** 43
bass stop **324** 44
bass string **324** 25; **325** 12
bass stud **324** 43
bass trombone **323** 46
bass tuba **323** 44
bass tuning **241** 43
bass viol **322** 23
bast **136** 29
bastard title **185** 44
bastion **329** 16
bat **292** 62, 75
batch **162** 2
batch feeder **162** 13
batch funnel **162** 13
batching and mixing plant, automatic ~ **201** 19
batch of eggs **80** 2, 30
bath *Bathrm. etc.* **49** 1
bath *Hotel* **267** 27-38
bath *Swim.* **281** 36
bath, cold ~ **281** 30
bat handle **293** 46
bather **280** 30
bathing beach **280**
bathing cap **280** 29, 44; **281** 8
bathing gown **280** 25
bathing platform **280** 9
bathing shoe **280** 23
bathing suit **280** 42
bathing suit, two-piece ~ **280** 26
bathing towel **281** 14
bathing trunks **280** 43
bathing wrap **280** 25
bath mat **49** 48
batholite **11** 29
bath robe **29** 24
bathroom **49**
bathroom cabinet, mirrored ~ **49** 31
bathroom mule **49** 46
bathroom scales **49** 47
bathroom tissue **49** 11
bathroom tissue holder **49** 10
bath salts **49** 5; **99** 34
bath sponge *Bathrm. etc.* **49** 6
bath sponge *Invertebr.* **357** 13
bat of clay **161** 9
baton **264** 19
baton, conductor's ~ **315** 27
batrachians **364** 23-26
batsman **292** 74
batten *Roof* **122** 17
batten *Sailing* **284** 44
batten, compartmentalized ~ **316** 13
batten, compartment-type ~ **316** 13
batten cleat **284** 43
batten door **37** 34
batten gauge **122** 18
batten pocket **284** 43
batter **292** 52, 63
batterboard **118** 69
batter's position **292** 51
battery *Agr. Mach.* **65** 53
battery *Poultry Farm* **74** 19
battery *Photog.* **114** 66
battery *Car* **191** 50
battery *Warships* **259** 83
battery, rotary ~ **166** 5
battery box **207** 5, 25; **211** 56
battery cage **74** 20
battery cell **110** 7
battery chamber *Photog.* **115** 10
battery chamber *Cine Film* **117** 5
battery compartment **188** 22
battery container **207** 5, 25; **211** 56
battery feeding **74** 23
battery holder **115** 76
battery housing **257** 17
battery railcar **211** 55
battery switch **115** 13
battery system **74** 18
battery tester **25** 52
battery unit **115** 75
batting crease **292** 72
batting order **292** 58
battle axe **352** 16
battle axe, stone ~ **328** 19
battlement **329** 6
battleships, light ~ **258** 1-63
bauble **306** 59
baulk *Agr.* **63** 3
baulk *Carp.* **120** 87
baumkuchen **97** 46
Bavarian curler **302** 38
Bavarian curling **302** 38-40
bay *Phys. Geog.* **13** 7
bay *Game* **88** 7
bay *Carp.* **120** 59
bayadère **306** 25
bay antler **88** 7
bayonet **353** 28
bayonet fitting **127** 65, 69
B-deck **223** 32-42
beach **13** 35-44
beach, raised ~ **11** 54
beach area **281** 2
beach attendant **280** 34
beach bag **280** 24
beach ball **280** 18
beach chair, roofed ~ **280** 36
beach chair, wicker ~ **280** 36
beach grass **15** 7
beach hat **280** 20
beach jacket **280** 21
beach marten **367** 14
beach mattress, inflatable ~ **280** 17
beach shoe **280** 23
beach suit **33** 24; **280** 19
beach tent **280** 45
beach trousers **280** 22
beachwear **280** 19-23
beacon **15** 10, 49
bead **87** 72
bead-and-dart moulding **334** 38
beading **123** 64
beading hammer **125** 15
beading iron **125** 8
beading pin **128** 30
beading swage **125** 15
beak **88** 84
beak, flat ~ **137** 12
beak, hooked ~ **362** 6
beak, round ~ **137** 13
beaker **350** 20
beaker pottery **328** 14
beam *Agr. Mach.* **65** 9, 71
beam *Game* **88** 11, 30
beam *Carp.* **120** 19, 24
beam *Gymn.* **297** 2
beam *Music. Instr.* **325** 22
beam *Chem.* **349** 30
beam, central ~ **27** 3
beam, dipped ~ **191** 20
beam, high ~ **191** 20
beam, low ~ **191** 20
beam, main ~ *Carp.* **120** 38
beam, main ~ *Roof* **121** 66
beam, main ~ *Car* **191** 20
beam, tied ~ **215** 44
beam bridge **215** 7
beam compass **125** 11
beam compass, glazier's ~ **124** 22
beam entry point **1** 64
beam flange **165** 30; **166** 49; **167** 26
beam head **121** 33
beaming machine **165** 55
beam motion control **166** 60
beam of light **224** 83
beam setter **195** 24
beam splitter **240** 35
beam-splitting prism *Optic. Instr.* **112** 13
beam-splitting prism *Broadcast.* **240** 35
beam trammel **125** 11
bean **57** 8, 11
bean, bush ~ **57** 8
bean, climbing ~ **57** 8
bean flower **57** 9
bean plant **52** 28; **57** 8
bean pole **52** 28
beanstalk **57** 10

bearberry **377** 15
beard *Arable Crops* **68** 12
beard *Dom. Anim.* **73** 15
beard *Game* **88** 73
beard, circular ~ **34** 15
beard, full ~ **34** 15
beard, round ~ **34** 15
bearded couch grass **61** 30
beards **34** 1-25
bearer cable **119** 37; **271** 52
bearer share **251** 11
bearing, axial-radial ~ **113** 3
bearing, centre ~ **177** 65
bearing, fixed ~ **215** 11
bearing, hydrostatic ~ **5** 10
bearing, jewelled ~ **110** 33
bearing, lower ~ **192** 83
bearing, main ~ **192** 23
bearing, movable ~ *Bridges* **215** 12
bearing, movable ~ *Sailing* **284** 6
bearing, upper ~ **192** 73
bearing block **177** 61
bearing cup **187** 68
bears **368** 9-11
beasts of prey **367** 11-22; **368** 1-11
beater *Hunt.* **86** 37
beater *Bakery* **97** 70
beater *Music. Instr.* **322** 34; **324** 64
beater, revolving ~ **64** 13
beater, three-blade ~ **163** 25
beater drive motor **163** 23
beater driving shaft **163** 24
beating **86** 34-39
beating machine **131** 4
beating wood **339** 12
beauty parlor **105** 1-39
beauty queen **306** 64
beauty salon **105** 1-39
beauty shop **105** 1-39
beauty spot **306** 24
beaver *Chivalry* **329** 41
beaver *Mammals* **366** 14
beck, flat ~ **137** 12
beck, round ~ **137** 13
bed *Phys. Geog.* **13** 49
bed *Hosp.* **25** 10
bed *Joiner* **133** 50
bed *Mach. Tools* **150** 19, 29
bed *Offset Print.* **180** 78
bed *Letterpress* **181** 17
bed *Bookbind.* **183** 25
bed *Station* **205** 61
bed *Graphic Art* **340** 41, 64
bed, children's ~ **47** 1
bed, double ~ **43** 4-13; **267** 38
bed, rear ~ **85** 49
bed bug **81** 39
bedder **91** 23
bed frame **43** 5
bed linen **271** 57
Bedlington terrier **70** 18
bed monitor **25** 19
bedouin **354** 6
bedrock **13** 70
bedroom **43**
bedroom, twin-berth **207** 38
bedroom, two-berth ~ **207** 38
bedroom, two-seat ~ **207** 38
bedroom lamp **43** 19
bedside cabinet **43** 17
bedside rug **43** 22
bed slide **149** 24
bedspread **43** 7
bedstead **43** 4-6
bed stone **91** 23
beduin **354** 6
bed unit **46** 16
bed unit drawer **46** 18
bed unit shelf **46** 19
bed warmer **309** 88
bee **77** 1-25
bee, male ~ **77** 5
beech cellulose **169** 1
beech gall **82** 37
beech nut **371** 37
beech tree **371** 33
bee eater **360** 2
beef **95** 14-37
beehive **77** 45-50
beehive kiln **161** 3
bee house **77** 56
beekeeper **77** 57
beekeeping **77**
beeman **77** 57
beer **99** 72
beer, bottled ~ **93** 26
beer, canned ~ **99** 73
beer barrel **93** 17
beer bottle **93** 26; **205** 50
beer can **93** 25
beer crate **93** 24
beer filter **93** 15
beer glass **45** 91; **93** 30; **266** 3, 6; **317** 6
beer marquee **308** 23
beer mat **266** 26
beer mug **266** 6; **309** 53
beerpull **266** 1, 68
beer pump **266** 1, 68
beer tap **317** 8
beer warmer **266** 7
bees **77**
bee shed **77** 51
bee smoker **77** 59
bee sting ointment **77** 68
beeswax **77** 67
beet **68** 44, 45
beet carrion beetle **80** 45
beet cleaner **64** 89
beet elevator **64** 94
beet elevator belt **64** 95
beet harvester **64** 85-96
beet hopper **64** 96
beetle **82** 26, 42
beet leaf **68** 47
beetles **358** 24-39
beet top **68** 46
bee veil **77** 58
begonia **53** 10
begonia, tuberous ~ **51** 19
belay **300** 9, 10
belayer **300** 26
belfry window **331** 8
bell *Plumb. etc.* **126** 16
bell *Iron & Steel* **147** 6
bell *Railw.* **212** 49
bell *Navig.* **224** 75
bell *Election* **263** 4
bell *Winter Countr.* **304** 26
bell *Music. Instr.* **323** 37, 42, 48; **324** 70
bell, electric ~ **127** 15
bell, electrically operated ~ **331** 9
belladonna **379** 7
Bellatrix **3** 13
bell beaker **328** 14
bell boy **267** 18
bell end **278** 27
bellows *Photog.* **114** 53; **116** 31
bellows *Photomech. Reprod.* **177** 10, 26
bellows *Camping* **278** 49
bellows *Flea Market* **309** 26
bellows *Music. Instr.* **322** 58; **324** 37
bellows pedal **325** 46
bellows strap **324** 38
bellows unit **115** 85
bell push **127** 2
bells **276** 45
bell sleeve, pleated ~ **30** 54
bell tent **278** 8
bell tower **337** 8
belly *Sea Fish.* **90** 20
belly *Meat* **95** 39, 41
belly *Music. Instr.* **323** 24; **324** 3
belly-band **71** 36
belt **30** 11; **31** 10; **32** 39
belt, coloured ~ **299** 15
belt, flat ~ **163** 49
belt, stretch ~ **31** 63
belt buckle **31** 12
belt-changing flap **255** 35
belt conveying **144** 40
belt conveyor **156** 2
belt delivery **185** 13
belt drive **165** 33
belt guard **133** 31
beltline **270** 45
belt roller **133** 18
belt-tensioning lever **133** 16
bench *Goldsm. etc.* **108** 20
bench *Plumb.* **125** 10
bench *Blacksm.* **137** 21
bench *Metalwkr.* **140** 7
bench *Playground* **273** 58
bench *Gymn.* **296** 14
bench, collapsible ~ **134** 41
bench, oarsman's ~ **278** 17
bench, paperhanger's ~ **128** 31
bench, pupil's ~ **261** 11
bench, student's ~ **261** 11
bench, teacher's ~ **261** 3
bench, tiered ~ **281** 20
bench, woodworker's ~ **132** 29-37
bench apron **108** 21
bench brush **108** 33
bench covering **141** 16
bench holdfast **132** 36
bench stop **132** 36
bench top **132** 34
bench torch **350** 9
bend **126** 46
bending iron *Bldg. Site* **119** 77

bending iron *Blacksm.* **137** 39
bending machine **125** 28, 30
bending table **119** 20
bending tool **136** 34
bend of hook **89** 81
bend sinister wavy **254** 6
Benguela Current **14** 43
benniseed **383** 45
bent hang **296** 39
benzene chlorination **170** 8
benzene extraction **170** 6
benzene ring **242** 66
benzene scrubber **156** 24
benzol scrubber **156** 24
beret **35** 27
berlin **186** 1
berm **216** 38
Bermuda shorts **31** 44
berry **58** 9, 11; **370** 97
berry bush **52** 19
berry bushes **58** 1-30
berry tree, standard ~ **52** 11
besageur **329** 45
besom *Roof & Boilerr.* **38** 36
besom *Winter Sp.* **302** 43
Bessemer converter **147** 55-69
best end of loin **95** 7
beta particle **1** 32
beta radiation **1** 32
Betelgeuse **3** 13
betel nut **380** 20
betel palm **380** 19
bevel *Carp.* **120** 81
bevel *Mach. Parts etc.* **143** 62
bevel edge **178** 44
bevel gear **91** 25
bevel gearing **91** 25
bevel gear wheel **143** 91
bevel wheel **143** 91
bez antler **88** 7
bez tine **88** 7
B flat major **320** 64
B flat minor **320** 67
bib *Infant Care etc.* **28** 43
bib *Ladies' Wear* **30** 24
bib and brace *Child. Clothes* **29** 40
bib and brace *Ladies' Wear* **30** 21
bib and brace overalls **33** 44
Bible **330** 11
bib skirt **29** 41
biceps brachii **18** 37
biceps femoris **18** 61
bick, flat ~ **137** 12
bick, round ~ **137** 13
bicycle **187**
bicycle, child's ~ **273** 9
bicycle, folding ~ **188** 1
bicycle, gent's ~ **187** 1
bicycle, motor-assisted ~ **188** 6
bicycle bell **187** 4
bicycle drive **187** 35-42
bicycle frame **187** 14-20
bicycle kick **291** 45
bicycle lamp **187** 7
bicycle lock **187** 49
bicycle pedal **187** 78
bicycle pump **187** 48
bicycles **188**
bicycle saddle **187** 22
bicycle speedometer **187** 33
bidet **49** 7
Biedermeier dress **306** 22
Biedermeier sofa **336** 17
bier **331** 41
bifurcation **224** 89
Big Dipper **3** 29
big top **307** 1
big wave riding **279** 4
big wheel **308** 37
bike **187** 1
bikini **280** 26
bikini bottom **280** 27
bikini briefs **32** 15
bikini top **280** 28
bilberry **377** 23
bile duct, common ~ **20** 37-38
bilge block **222** 40
bilge keel **222** 47
bilge shore **222** 40
bilge strake **222** 46
bill *Game* **88** 84
bill *Bank* **250** 12
bill *Birds* **359** 17
billboard **118** 45
bill clause **250** 17
billhook **56** 9; **85** 11
billiard ball **277** 1
billiard clock **277** 17
billiard cloth **277** 15
billiard cue **277** 9
billiard marker **277** 18
billiard parlor **277** 7-19
billiard player **277** 8
billiard room **277** 7-19
billiards **277** 1-19
billiards, English ~ **277** 7
billiards, French ~ **277** 7
billiards, German ~ **277** 7
billiard saloon **277** 7-19
billiard strokes **277** 2-6
billiard table **277** 14
bill of exchange **250** 12
bills **252** 29-39
bin **200** 45
bind **321** 24
binder **107** 6
binder course **198** 4
binder injector **200** 53
binding *Bookbind.* **185** 40-42
binding *Athletics* **298** 54
binding, parts of ~ **301** 54-56
binding, rubber ~ **286** 57-58
bindweed **61** 26
binoculars **86** 6; **111** 17; **221** 128
biology preparation room **261** 14-34
biopsy forceps **23** 17
biplane **229** 10
bipod **255** 42
bipod mast **221** 24
biprism, ditrigonal ~ **351** 22
biprism, hexagonal ~ **351** 22
bipyramid, tetragonal ~ **351** 18
birch **51** 13; **272** 40; **281** 27
Birch Boletus **381** 22
birch rod **281** 27
birch tree **51** 13; **272** 40; **371** 9
bird **86** 50
bird, flightless ~ **359** 4
bird, gallinaceous ~ **359** 22
bird, migratory ~ **360** 7
bird, non-migratory ~ **360** 4
bird, resident ~ **360** 4
bird cherry **59** 5
bird-foot **69** 11
birds **359; 360; 361; 362; 363**
birds, corvine ~ **361** 1-3
birds, European ~ **360**
birds, exotic ~ **363**
birds, flightless ~ **359** 1-3
birds, long-winged ~ **359** 11-14
birds, web-footed ~ **359** 5-10
bird's foot **69** 11
bird's foot clover **376** 17
bird's foot trefoil **69** 11; **376** 17
birdsmouth **84** 28
birds of prey **362**
birds of prey, diurnal ~ **362** 1-13
birds of prey, nocturnal ~ **362** 14-19
birth-wort **376** 22
biscuit tin, decorative ~ **46** 12
bisector **346** 28, 30
bishop **276** 10
bismarck **97** 29
bison **328** 9; **367** 9
bistort **376** 10
bit **140** 35
bitch **73** 16
biting housefly **81** 4
bitt **284** 25
bitter **93** 26
bitumen **145** 64
bituminous distributor **200** 46
black **343** 13
black arches moth **82** 17
black-backed jackal **367** 11
black beetle **81** 17
blackberry **58** 29
blackbird **361** 13
blackboard **47** 13; **48** 16; **261** 36
blackboard, three-part ~ **260** 29
blackboard chalk **48** 15
blackboard compass **260** 40
blackboard drawing **260** 33
blackboard sponge **260** 42
black buck **367** 5
blackcock **86** 11; **88** 66
black elder **374** 35
Black Forest clock **109** 31
Black Forest gateau **97** 24
black-headed gull **359** 14
black liquor filter **172** 28
black liquor storage tank **172** 29
black nightshade **379** 5
black rhino **366** 25
black salsify **57** 35
blacksmith **137; 138**
blacksmith's tools **137** 22-39
blackthorn **374** 27
bladder **20** 33, 78

blade *Kitch. Utensils* **40** 40
blade *Tablew. etc.* **45** 54
blade *Gdn. Tools* **56** 36
blade *Arable Crops* **68** 20
blade *Paperm.* **172** 74
blade *Bookbind.* **185** 29
blade *Rowing* **283** 38, 53
blade *Fencing* **294** 44
blade *Bot.* **370** 28
blade, flexible ~ **85** 20
blade, front ~ **85** 35
blade, lower ~ **23** 14
blade, rear ~ **85** 40
blade, rotating ~ **39** 24
blade bit **145** 21
bladebone **95** 22, 30, 32, 42
blade coater **173** 29-35
blade coating machine **173** 29-35
blade covering **293** 47
bladed cone, rotating ~ **172** 75
bladed plug, rotating ~ **172** 75
bladed shell, stationary ~ **172** 76
blade of grass **370** 83-85
blade-slewing gear **200** 22
blancmange powder **98** 50
blank **252** 43
blanket **71** 44; **168** 56
blanket, rubber ~ **180** 54, 79
blanket cylinder **180** 24, 37, 54, 63
blast burner **108** 16
blast furnace **147** 1
blast furnace plant **147** 1-20
blast furnace shaft **147** 7
blasting cartridge **158** 27
blasting fuse **158** 28
blast inlet **148** 2
blast lamp **108** 16
blast main **147** 17, 68; **148** 2
blastodisc **74** 65
blast pipe *Blacksm.* **137** 6
blast pipe *Iron Foundry etc.* **148** 2
blast pipe *Railw.* **210** 25
blazer **33** 54
blazing star **51** 31
blazon **254** 17-23
blazonry **254** 1-36
bleach **105** 1
bleach-hardener **116** 10
bleaching **169** 21
bleach tube **105** 3
bleed **192** 27
bleeder **38** 65
bleeding heart **60** 5
blender **40** 46
blending pump **196** 1
Blessed Sacrament **331** 48; **332** 35
blimp **310** 48; **313** 16-18, 27
blind *Hosp.* **25** 9
blind *Hunt.* **86** 9
blinder **71** 26
blind spot **19** 50
blindworm **364** 37
blinker **71** 26
blob marker **83** 9
blob marking **83** 6
block *Headgear* **35** 3
block *Plumb.* **125** 21
block *Mach. Tools* **150** 20
block *Ship* **221** 28, 105
block *Winter Sp.* **302** 40
block *Music. Instr.* **326** 20
block, adjustable ~ **298** 2
block, charcoal ~ **108** 37
block, clay ~ **159** 22, 23
block, halftone ~ **178** 38
block, hollow ~ **119** 24; **159** 21-22, 22, 23
block, pumice concrete ~ **119** 24
block, rubber ~ **187** 85
block, tongued and grooved ~ **123** 74
block, travelling ~ **145** 8
block, wooden ~ **340** 1
block and tackle **137** 20
block board **132** 73
block brake **143** 97
blocker **293** 60
blocking saw **157** 54
block instruments **203** 59
block making **178**
block mount **178** 41
block mountain **12** 4-11
block mounting **178** 41
block of flats **37** 72-76
block of flats, high-rise ~ **37** 82
block of flats, multi-storey ~ **37** 77-81
block section panel **203** 60
block step **123** 17
blood, arterial ~ **18** 12
blood, venous ~ **18** 11
blood circulation **18** 1-21
blood pressure **23** 32; **25** 1
blood sausage **99** 56
blood sedimentation **23** 42
blood smear **23** 50
bloodstone **108** 48
blood vessel **19** 33
bloomer **97** 8
blooming train **148** 50, 70
bloom shears **148** 52
blossom **59** 9; **69** 14; **80** 11
blotter **46** 23; **246** 6; **260** 25
blouse **30** 9
blouse, girl's ~ **29** 58
blow, straight ~ **299** 28
blow-and-blow process **162** 22
blower *Furrier* **131** 10
blower *Paperm.* **172** 4
blower *Railw.* **211** 11
blower, travelling ~ **165** 2, 3
blower aperture **165** 5
blower fan **191** 48; **192** 62
blower oil pump **211** 45
blower rail **165** 6
blowfly **358** 18
blowhole **367** 26
blowing **162** 28, 36
blowing, first ~ **162** 24
blowing assembly **165** 4
blowing iron **162** 39
blowing processes **162** 22-37
blowlamp **126** 74; **301** 22
blow mould **162** 26, 34
blowout magnet **312** 39
blowpipe *Gas Weld.* **141** 11, 19; **141** 28
blowpipe *Ethnol.* **352** 26
blowpipe lighter **141** 27
blow pit **172** 13
blow position **147** 57
blow tank **172** 11
blowtorch **126** 74; **301** 22
blow valve **172** 12
blubber-oil lamp **353** 7
blue *Colour* **343** 3
blue *Lepidopt.* **365** 6
blue-and-yellow macaw **363** 2
bluebell **375** 14
blueberry **377** 23
blue bird of paradise **363** 3
bluebottle **61** 1; **358** 18
blue light **264** 11; **270** 6
Blue Peter **253** 26
blue shark **364** 1
blue spruce **51** 10
bluetit **360** 4
blurb **185** 39
B minor **320** 57, 60
boar *Dom. Anim.* **73** 9
boar *Game* **88** 51
boar, young ~ **88** 51
board *Bldg. Site* **118** 22, 87; **119** 16
board *Carp.* **120** 1, 91
board *Sawmill* **157** 35
board *Games* **276** 1
board, illuminated ~ **268** 3
board, presawn ~ **273** 57
board, squared ~ **120** 95
board, unsquared ~ **120** 94
board, wooden ~ **338** 23
board cutter **183** 16
board cutter, rotary ~ **184** 20
board-cutting machine, rotary ~ **184** 20
board feed hopper **184** 7
board games **276**
boarding **121** 75
boarding, horizontal ~ **37** 84
boarding platform **194** 39
boardman **251** 7
board platform **118** 28
board-sawing machine **132** 68
board support **132** 70
boarhound **86** 33
boar hunt **86** 31
boaster **158** 37
boat, carvel-built ~ **283** 9
boat, inflatable ~ **228** 18; **258** 82; **278** 14; **279** 27
boat, ship's ~ **221** 107; **258** 12, 45; **259** 35
boat, V-bottom ~ **286** 35-37
boat, vee-bottom ~ **286** 35-37
boat axe **328** 19
boat carriage **278** 20; **283** 66
boat deck **223** 19-21
boat elevator **217** 29-38
boater **35** 35
boat fibula **328** 28
boathouse **283** 24
boat-launching crane **258** 13

boat lift **217** 29-38
boat neck **30** 34
boats, folding ~ **283** 54-66
boatswain **221** 114
boat tank **217** 33
boat trailer **278** 20; **283** 66
bobbin *Shoem.* **100** 29
bobbin *Dressm.* **103** 12
bobbin *Cotton Spin.* **164** 52, 56, 60
bobbin creel **164** 28
bobbin lace **102** 18
bobbin thread **104** 16
bobble **29** 4
boblet **303** 19
bobsled **303** 19
bobsledding **303** 19-21
bobsleigh **303** 19-21
bobsleigh, two-man ~ **303** 19
bobstay **219** 15
bob wig **34** 2
boccie **305** 21
bock beer **93** 26
bodhisattva **337** 10
bodice **31** 30
bodkin *Basketm.* **136** 35
bodkin *Composing Rm.* **174** 17
bodkin beard **34** 13
body *Flat* **46** 3
body *Joiner* **132** 24
body *Lorries etc.* **194** 3, 23
body *Aircraft* **230** 54
body *Airsports* **288** 26
body, bird's ~ **327** 57
body, dog's ~ **327** 30
body, dragon's ~ **327** 19, 36
body, fibre glass ~ **193** 14
body, horse's ~ **327** 27, 54
body, human ~ **16** 1-54
body, interchangeable ~ **213** 40
body, lion's ~ **327** 14, 22
body, man's ~ **327** 53
body, monocoque ~ **191** 1
body, monster's ~ **327** 48
body, pituitary ~ **17** 43
body, serpent's ~ **327** 2, 33
body, tambourine-like ~ **324** 30
body, unitary ~ **191** 1
body, woman's ~ **327** 59
body brush **71** 55
body-fixing plate **192** 72
body hammer **195** 46
bodyline **175** 43
body louse **81** 41
body of barrel **130** 6
body of wall **217** 2
body paper **173** 29
body plan **259** 2-11
body rotation **298** 11
body size **175** 46
body temperature **23** 3
body tube **113** 8, 31-39
bog **13** 14-24
bog bilberry **377** 23
bogie *Bldg. Site* **119** 32
bogie *Power Plant* **152** 41
bogie *Tram* **197** 9
bogie *Railw.* **207** 4; **208** 4; **212** 2; **213** 11, 13
bogie open freight car **213** 24
bogie open wagon **213** 24
bogie wagon **213** 26
bog pool **13** 23
bog whortleberry **377** 23
Bohr-Sommerfeld model **1** 26
boiler *Roof & Boilerr.* **38** 24, 68
boiler *Bakery* **97** 69
boiler *Energy Sources* **155** 13
boiler *Railw.* **210** 16
boiler, radiant-type ~ **152** 5
boiler, vertical ~ **210** 62
boiler barrel **210** 16
boiler feed pump **152** 18
boiler house *Market Gdn.* **55** 7
boiler house *Power Plant* **152** 1-21
boiler pressure **210** 3
boiler pressure gauge **210** 47
boiler room *Roof & Boilerr.* **38** 38-43
boiler room *Market Gdn.* **55** 7
boiler shop **222** 9
boiler suit **30** 21
boiling fowl **99** 60
boiling water system **154** 49
bola **352** 31
bolas **352** 31
bold **175** 2
bold condensed **175** 10
boldface **175** 2
bole **84** 19, 22; **85** 23, 41; **370** 2, 7
Boletus edulis **381** 16
Boletus luteus **381** 21
Boletus scaber **381** 22
boll **383** 8
bollard **217** 12
bollard, cross-shaped ~ **217** 13, 14; **227** 10
bollard, double ~ **217** 11, 14
bollard, recessed ~ **217** 10
bolster *Bedrm.* **43** 11
bolster *Tablew. etc.* **45** 55
bolster plate **85** 48
bolt *Slaughterho.* **94** 4
bolt *Roof* **121** 98
bolt *Metalwkr.* **140** 39
bolt *Mach. Parts etc.* **143** 31
bolt *Office* **246** 23
bolt, collar-head ~ **143** 32
bolt, countersunk-head ~ **143** 28
bolt, hexagonal-head ~ **143** 13
bolt, square-head ~ **143** 39
bolt, T-head ~ **143** 41
bolter **91** 26
bolt guide pin **140** 41
bolt handle **87** 22
bolt lever **87** 22
bolts **143** 13-50
bombard **322** 14
bombardon **323** 44
bomber jacket **31** 42
bombycid moth **358** 48
bond *Bldg. Site* **118** 30
bond *Stock Exch.* **251** 1-10, 11-19
bond, convertible ~ **251** 11-19
bond, English ~ **118** 62
bond, industrial ~ **251** 11-19
bond, municipal ~ **251** 11-19
bonding, rubber ~ **192** 82
bone **70** 33; **354** 40
bone, ethmoid ~ **17** 39
bone, frontal ~ **17** 30
bone, hyoid ~ **20** 2
bone, jugal ~ **16** 8
bone, lachrimal ~ **17** 40
bone, malar ~ **16** 8
bone, metacarpal ~ **17** 16
bone, nasal ~ **17** 41
bone, occipital ~ **17** 32
bone, parietal ~ **17** 31
bone, sphenoid ~ **17** 38
bone, tarsal ~ **17** 26
bone, temporal ~ **17** 33
bone, zygomatic ~ **16** 8; **17** 37
bone chisel **24** 49
bone-cutting forceps **26** 51
bone lace **102** 18
bone nippers **26** 51
bones **17** 1-29
bone saw *Slaughterho.* **94** 19
bone saw *Butch.* **96** 56
bongo drum **324** 58
boning knife **96** 36
bonnet *Car* **191** 8
bonnet *Garage* **195** 36
bonnet *Ship* **218** 34
bonnet support **195** 37
book **42** 4; **46** 8; **185** 36, 52
book, children's ~ **47** 17; **48** 23
book, second-hand ~ **309** 55
book, sewn ~ **185** 22
book, unbound ~ **183** 32
bookbinder **183** 2
bookbinding **183**; **184**; **185**
bookbinding machines **184** 1-23; **185** 1-35
bookcase unit **46** 7
book cover **185** 40
book delivery **184** 5
bookjacket **185** 37
bookmark, attached ~ **185** 70
bookmark, loose ~ **185** 71
bookmarker, attached ~ **185** 70
bookmarker, loose ~ **185** 71
bookplate **185** 51
book-sewing machine **185** 16
bookshelf **42** 3; **43** 14; **262** 12
bookshelf unit **46** 7
bookshop **268** 37
book stack **262** 11
boom *Bldg. Site* **119** 36
boom *Docks* **226** 49
boom *Sailing* **284** 7, 39
boom, double ~ **229** 35
boomerang **352** 39
boom foresail **220** 12
boom microphone **311** 40
boom operator **310** 22
boom swinger **310** 22
booster rocket **234** 1, 2

boost gauge **230** 7
boot *Shoem.* **100** 57
boot *Car* **191** 24; **193** 23
boot *Music. Instr.* **326** 17
boot, baby's ~ **101** 56
boot, felt ~ **353** 30
boot, ladies' ~ **101** 12
boot, men's ~ **101** 5
boot, pony-skin ~ **101** 10
boot, rubber ~ **289** 32
boot, Western ~ **101** 9
bootee **28** 45; **29** 5
Boötes **3** 30
booth **308** 6
bootlace **100** 64; **291** 32
boot lid **191** 7
bootmaker **100**
boot space **193** 17
borage family **69** 13
Boraginaceae **69** 13
border *Fruit & Veg. Gdn.* **52** 18, 22
border *Basketm.* **136** 17
border *Park* **272** 37
border *Theatre* **316** 12
border light **316** 13
bore **143** 86
bore axis **87** 38
bore diameter **87** 40
borehole **158** 12
borer **80** 18
boring machine **175** 49
boring mill **138** 22
boring mill column **150** 31
boring motor **133** 7
boring tool **149** 51
borrower's ticket **262** 25
boscage **272** 4
bosh **137** 8
bo's'n **221** 114
bosom **16** 30
boss *Chivalry* **329** 58
boss *Art* **335** 32
bostryx **370** 76
bo'sun **221** 114
botany **370**
bottle *Brew.* **93** 21
bottle *Restaurant* **266** 16
bottle *Swim.* **279** 19
bottle, collapsible ~ **116** 9
bottle, non-returnable ~ **93** 29
bottle, three-necked ~ **350** 57
bottle, wicker ~ **206** 13
bottle, wickered ~ **206** 13
bottle basket **79** 13
bottle bobbin **167** 4
bottle-capping machine **76** 46
bottle kiln **161** 3
bottle-making machine **162** 21
bottle-nosed dolphin **367** 23
bottle-opener **45** 47
bottle rack *Kitch.* **39** 6
bottle rack *Wine Cell.* **79** 11
bottlescrew **284** 19
bottle warmer **28** 21
bottle washer **93** 19
bottle-washing machine **93** 19
bottle-washing plant **93** 18
bottling **93** 22
bottling machine, circular ~ **79** 9
bottling machine, semi-automatic ~ **79** 9
bottom **16** 40
bottom, artificial ~ **301** 52
bottom, cellular ~ **222** 60
bottom, cut-in ~ **119** 56
bottom, double ~ **222** 60
bottom, synthetic ~ **301** 52
bottom bracket bearing **187** 42
bottom outlet **269** 34
bottom plating **222** 48
bottom plating, inner ~ **222** 54
bott stick **148** 10
boudoir piano **325** 40
bough **370** 5
bouillon cube **98** 27
boule, grooved ~ **305** 24
boules **305** 21
boules player **305** 22
bounce **297** 36
bouncing ball **273** 20
boundary layer control flap **256** 6; **257** 13
boundary ridge **63** 3
boundary stone **63** 2
bouquet, bridal ~ **332** 18
bouquetin **367** 7
bourgeois **175** 26
bout **294** 5-6
Bovista nigrescens **381** 19
bow *Ladies' Wear* **30** 46
bow *Hairst. etc.* **34** 7
bow *Metalwkr.* **140** 34
bow *Shipbuild.* **222** 74-79
bow *Warships* **258** 3
bow *Rowing* **283** 13
bow *Music. Instr.* **323** 12
bow *Ethnol.* **354** 32
bow *Hist. Cost.* **355** 78
bow, bulbous ~ **221** 45; **222** 74
bow, fully enclosed ~ **259** 9
bow, sliding ~ **205** 36
bow and arrow **327** 53
bow bilge **259** 80
Bowden cable **188** 37; **189** 12
bow door **221** 30
bowed instruments **323** 1-27
bowels **20** 14-22
bower **272** 17
bower, ladies' ~ **329** 10
bower anchor **258** 39; **286** 15
bow fender **227** 17
bow gin **87** 48
bowl **40** 6; **45** 63; **105** 1; **107** 36
bowler **292** 76
bowler hat **35** 28
bow light, green and red ~ **286** 13
bowline **218** 35
bowling ball **305** 15
bowling crease **292** 71
bowl lid **107** 37
bowls **305** 21
bow-manoeuvring propeller **224** 23
bow propeller **228** 33
bow ramp **258** 90
bowsprit **218** 20; **219** 1
bow stick **323** 14
bow string **305** 59
bow thruster **224** 23
bow-tie **32** 47; **33** 11, 16
bow trap **87** 48
bow wave **223** 81
box *Livestock* **75** 2
box *Carriages* **186** 8
box *Gymn.* **296** 15
box *Athletics* **298** 35
box *Fair* **308** 7
box *Bullfight. etc.* **319** 7
box, centrifugal ~ **169** 17
box, coach's ~ **292** 56
box, crossing keeper's ~ **202** 43
box, gateman's ~ **202** 43
box, racer's ~ **290** 7
box, rider's ~ **290** 7
box, small ~ **296** 16; **297** 9
box attendant **315** 12
box camera **309** 30
boxcar **213** 14, 22
boxer *Dog* **70** 10
boxer *Sports* **299** 25
box feeder **159** 7
box gutter **122** 83
boxing **299** 20-50
boxing contest **299** 35-50
boxing glove **299** 26
boxing match **299** 20-50, 35-50
boxing ring **299** 35
box office **308** 7
box pile **217** 6
boxroom door **38** 20
box spar **287** 30
box spur **71** 50
box trap **86** 20
box tree **373** 19
boy scout **278** 11
bra **32** 1; **318** 29
bra, longline ~ **32** 4
brace *Bldg. Site* **119** 63
brace *Carp.* **120** 27, 54
brace *Roof* **121** 41, 58, 69, 82
brace *Ship* **219** 67
brace *Music. Instr.* **325** 16
brace, diagonal ~ *Bldg. Site* **118** 88; **119** 51
brace, diagonal ~ *Bridges* **215** 4
bracelet **36** 3
bracelet, cultured pearl ~ **36** 9
bracelet, gemstone ~ **36** 25
bracelet watch **36** 33
braces **29** 26, 34; **32** 30
braces, adjustable ~ **33** 45
braces clip **32** 31
brachioradialis **18** 39
bracing **215** 3
bracing, diagonal ~ **119** 14
bracken **15** 5; **377** 16
bracket *Doc.* **23** 10
bracket *Plumb. etc.* **126** 6
bracket *Bicycle* **187** 77

bracket *School* **260** 30
bracket *Winter Sp.* **302** 17; **303** 7
bracket, chrome ~ **188** 60
bracket, round ~ **342** 24
bracket, square ~ **342** 25
Brackett series **1** 23
bract **371** 7; **372** 5
bracteate **252** 4
bract scale **372** 5
braid, floral ~ **30** 28
braid embroidery **102** 31
braid work **102** 31
Braille **342** 15
brain-stem **17** 47; **18** 24
brake *Mills* **91** 8
brake *Carriages* **186** 2, 16
brake *Car* **191** 45
brake *Air Force* **257** 10
brake *Forest Plants etc.* **377** 16
brake, automatic ~ **181** 47
brake, auxiliary ~ **212** 10
brake, covered ~ **186** 33
brake, front ~ **187** 5
brake, hydraulic ~ **212** 44
brake arm **187** 66
brake arm cone **187** 67
brake axle **143** 99
brake band **143** 105
brake block *Mach. Parts etc.* **143** 100
brake block *Carriages* **186** 16
brake cable **188** 37; **189** 12
brake casing **187** 70
brake chute housing **257** 24
brake cone **187** 71
brake cylinder pressure gauge **212** 7
brake disc **191** 17; **192** 48
brake drum **138** 11, 20
brake flap *Aircraft* **229** 44
brake flap *Air Force* **256** 12
brake flap *Gliding* **287** 38
brake fluid reservoir **191** 49
brake line *Motorcycle* **189** 12
brake line *Car* **192** 53
brake lining *Blacksm.* **138** 13
brake lining *Mach. Parts etc.* **143** 106
brake lining *Car* **192** 52
brake lock **56** 38
brake magnet **143** 102
brakeman **303** 21
brake pedal *Gdn. Tools* **56** 40
brake pedal *Offset Platem.* **179** 12, 30
brake pedal *Car* **191** 45, 95
brake pressure gauge **210** 50
brake pulley **143** 98
brake shaft **143** 99
brake shoe *Blacksm.* **138** 12
brake shoe *Mach. Parts etc.* **143** 100
brake shoe *Car* **192** 51
brake system, dual-circuit ~ **191** 72
brake-testing equipment **138** 16
brake weight **143** 103
brake wheel **91** 7
braking disc **191** 17; **192** 48
braking distance **203** 29
braking roller **138** 18
branch *Railw.* **203** 48
branch *Fire Brig.* **270** 33
branch *Maths.* **347** 15
branch *Bot.* **370** 5, 6
branch *Decid. Trees* **371** 10, 25, 27, 32, 59
branch *Conifers* **372** 36, 43
branch *Trop. Plants* **382** 17
branch *Industr. Plants* **383** 61
branch *South. Fruits* **384** 12, 42
branch, flowering ~ **58** 32, 52; **59** 1, 26, 37
branch, fruit-bearing ~ **59** 19, 48
branch, fruiting ~ **59** 30
branch, left ~ **203** 47
branch, right ~ **203** 46
branch line **15** 23
branchman **270** 34
brandy **98** 59
brandy glass **45** 88
brashing **84** 12
brass **323** 39-48
brassard *Fire Brig.* **270** 22
brassard *Chivalry* **329** 47
brassica **57** 32
brassicas **57** 28-34
brassie **293** 91
brassière **32** 1; **318** 29
brassière, longline ~ **32** 4
brass instruments **323** 39-48
brayer **340** 12
Brazil Current **14** 35
Brazil nut **384** 53, 59
breach **13** 34
bread **45** 22; **97** 2
bread, kinds of ~ **97** 6-12; **99** 11
bread, wrapped ~ **97** 48-50
bread basket **45** 20
bread-corn **68** 1-37
bread counter **99** 9
bread crust **97** 4
breadth scale **157** 58
bread unit **97** 56-57
break *Brew.* **93** 2
break *Composing Rm.* **175** 15
break *Carriages* **186** 2
break, covered ~ **186** 33
break-bulk cargo, unitized ~ **226** 11
break-bulk cargo elevator, floating ~ **226** 31
break-bulk cargo transit shed **225** 9
break-bulk carrier **225** 14; **226** 13
breakdown lorry **270** 47
breaker *Overh. Irrign.* **67** 34
breaker *Swim.* **279** 6
breaker spring **67** 35
break removal **93** 1-5
breakstone, rotundifoliate ~ **375** 1
breakwater *Hydr. Eng.* **217** 16
breakwater *Docks* **225** 65
breakwater *Warships* **258** 7, 76
breast *Man* **16** 28-29
breast *Horse* **72** 19
breast beam **166** 46
breast beam board **166** 16
breastbone *Man* **17** 8
breastbone *Meat* **95** 27
breastbox **173** 11
breast collar **71** 28
breast collar ring **71** 27
breast drill **140** 58
breast harness **71** 26-36
breast of veal **95** 4
breastplate **329** 46
breast pocket **33** 9
breasts **16** 28-29
breaststroke **282** 33
breastwork **329** 21
breather **153** 10
breathing apparatus **26** 1; **270** 39
breathing tube **27** 37
breccia **11** 27
breeches **300** 7
breeches, loose ~ **355** 34
breeches, white ~ **289** 5
breeches buoy **228** 13
brooch ring **36** 21
breeding comb **77** 46
breeds of dog **70**
breeze **120** 44
breve **320** 12
breve rest **320** 20
breviary **331** 58
brevier **175** 25
brevis **320** 12
brewer **92** 49
brewery **93** 1-31
brewhouse **93** 1-31
brewing **92; 93**
briar grain **107** 41
briar rose **373** 26
brick **118** 40
brick, cellular ~ **159** 28
brick, green ~ **159** 16
brick, perforated ~ **159** 21-22, 21
brick, radial ~ **159** 25
brick, radiating ~ **159** 25
brick, solid ~ **159** 20
brick, standard ~ **118** 58
brick, unfired ~ **159** 16
brick cutter **159** 15
brickfield **159**
brick hammer **118** 53
brick kiln **159** 19
bricklayer **118** 18
bricklayer's tools **118** 50-57
brickmason **118** 18
brickmason's tools **118** 50-57
brick-pressing machine **159** 11
brickwork, frost-resistant ~ **122** 39
brickwork base **123** 15
brickworks *Map* **15** 89
brickworks **159**
brickyard **159**
bride **332** 15
bridegroom **332** 16
bridesmaid **332** 24
bridge *Map* **15** 44

bridge *Opticn.* **111** 11
bridge *Station* **205** 3
bridge *Ship* **221** 6, 12; **223** 12-18
bridge *Shipbuild.* **222** 26
bridgc *Warships* **258** 14; **259** 3, 28
bridge *Park* **272** 47
bridge *Free Exerc.* **295** 19
bridge *Sports* **299** 9
bridge *Theatre* **315** 29; **316** 34
bridge *Music. Instr.* **322** 17
bridge, cable-stayed ~ **215** 46
bridge, covered ~ **215** 32
bridge, cross-section of ~ **215** 1
bridge, dental ~ **24** 26
bridge, flat ~ **215** 52
bridge, iron ~ **15** 56
bridge, reinforced concrete ~ **215** 49
bridge, rope ~ **215** 15
bridge, solid ~ **215** 19
bridge, stone ~ **15** 50
bridge bearing **215** 55
bridge deck **223** 12-18
bridge over railway **15** 40
bridge ring **89** 58
bridges **215**
bridge strut **215** 30
bridge superstructure **258** 14
bridge support **222** 12
bridge under railway **15** 42
bridle **71** 7-13
bridle path **12** 46
briefcase **41** 17
briefs **32** 26
brig **220** 17
brigantine **220** 14
brightness control **240** 33
brille **323** 35
brilliant **175** 21
brilliant cut **36** 44
brimstone butterfly **365** 4
brine channel **274** 3
brine pipe **274** 4
briolette, faceted ~ **36** 86
Brisinga endecacnemos **369** 11
brisket, hind ~ **95** 25
brisket, middle ~ **95** 26
brisket of beef **95** 23
bristle **88** 52
bristles *Hairst. etc.* **34** 23
bristles *Household* **50** 47
bristletail **81** 14
bristle worm **357** 22
broach **109** 8
broaching tap **93** 14
broach roof **121** 22
broach roof, conical ~ **121** 24
B road **15** 36
broad axe **120** 70
broad bean *Veg.* **57** 8
broad bean *Fodder Plants* **69** 15
broadcasting **238**; **239**; **240**
broadcasting centre **238** 16-26
broadcasting station **15** 33
broadsheet **340** 27
broadside **340** 27
broadside fire **218** 59
broadtail *Ladies' Wear* **30** 60
broadtail *Furrier* **131** 21
brochure **250** 7
broderie anglaise **102** 11
broiler **98** 6; **308** 33
broiler chicken **74** 12
broiler rearing **74** 11-17
broken thread detector roller **164** 4
broken thread stop motion **165** 19
broker, commercial ~ **251** 5
broker, inside ~ **251** 4
broker, outside ~ **251** 5
bronchus **20** 5
Bronze Age **328** 21-40
brooch, ivory ~ **36** 30
brooch, modern-style ~ **36** 19
brooch, pearl ~ **36** 7
brood bud bulblet **54** 27, 29
brood cell **77** 31
brood chamber **77** 46
brooder **74** 3
brook **13** 8; **15** 80
broom **38** 36; **50** 46; **62** 5; **199** 6; **268** 21; **272** 67
broom *Shrubs etc.* **374** 20
broom, circular ~ **199** 40
broom, cylinder ~ **199** 42
broom, inverted ~ **224** 99
broom, upward-pointing ~ **224** 100
broom handle **38** 37; **50** 49
broom head **50** 48
broomstick **38** 37; **50** 49
brougham **186** 3
brow antler **88** 6
browband **71** 9
brown **343** 5
brown ale **93** 26
brown bear **368** 10
brown leaf-eating weevil **80** 49
Brown Ring Boletus **381** 21
brown-tail moth **80** 28
brown trout **364** 15
brow point **88** 6
brow snag **88** 6
brow tine **88** 6
brush *Roof & Boilerr.* **38** 32
brush *Household* **50** 42, 53
brush *Bees* **77** 7
brush *Forestry* **84** 5
brush *Game* **88** 47
brush *School* **260** 59
brush *Graphic Art* **340** 11
brush *Script* **341** 24
brush, camel hair ~ **338** 7
brush, dry ~ **128** 49
brush, flat ~ *Painter* **129** 17
brush, flat ~ *Art. Studio* **338** 6
brush, rotating ~ **168** 46
brush, round ~ **338** 8
brush, stiff-bristle ~ **105** 16
brush, wire ~ *Gas Weld.* **141** 26
brush, wire ~ *Arc Weld.* **142** 18
brush, wire ~ *Music. Instr.* **324** 53
brush head **50** 79
brush head, detachable ~ **49** 30
brushwood *Map* **15** 15
brushwood *Forestry* **84** 5
brushwood *Spa* **274** 2
Brussels lace **102** 18
Brussels sprout **57** 30
bubble bath **49** 3
bubble chamber **1** 58
bubble float, oval ~ **89** 47
buccaneer **306** 43
Büchner funnel **349** 11
buck *Dom. Anim.* **73** 18
buck *Game* **88** 28, 40, 59
buck *Gymn.* **296** 17
buck, young ~ **88** 39
bucket *Household* **50** 54
bucket *Mills* **91** 36
bucket *Bldg. Site* **118** 82
bucket *Road Constr.* **200** 5
bucket chain **226** 42
bucket dredger **226** 41
bucket elevator **200** 49; **201** 21
bucket elevator chain **216** 57
bucket ladder **226** 43
bucket pump **269** 7
bucket seat *Car* **193** 11
bucket seat *Sports* **305** 90
bucket teeth **200** 6
bucket-top boot **355** 58
buckeye **371** 58
buckle **101** 52
buckle and knife folder **185** 8
buckle and knife folding machine **185** 8
buckle fold **185** 11
buckler **329** 57
bucksaw **120** 61
bud **54** 23, 26; **58** 27; **59** 22; **60** 16; **61** 3
bud, axillary ~ **370** 25
bud, terminal ~ **370** 22
bud cutting **54** 22
Buddha **337** 20
budding **54** 30
budding knife **54** 31
buffalo **367** 8
buffalo horn **254** 34
buffer *Station* **206** 51
buffer *Railw.* **213** 7
buffer *Army* **255** 27, 44, 52
buffer recuperator **255** 52
buffer ring **255** 44
buffer storage **242** 33
buffet **207** 78-79
buffet car, quick-service ~ **207** 73
buffet compartment **207** 78-79
buffing machine **108** 46
buffing wheel **100** 10
buffoon **306** 38, 69
bug **81** 39
buggy **193** 12
buggy, American ~ **186** 49
buggy, English ~ **186** 48
bugle **309** 54
building, centralized ~ **334** 55

building, centrally-planned ~ **334** 55
building, model ~ **48** 28
building, neoclassical ~ **336** 15
building, public ~ **15** 54
building berth **222** 11-18
building berths **222** 11-26
building block **28** 41; **48** 27
building board, lightweight ~ **123** 58
building brick *Infant Care etc.* **28** 41
building brick *Kindergart.* **48** 27
building brick *Brickwks.* **159** 20
building glazier **124** 8
building site **118; 119**
building slips **222** 11-26
building timber **120** 10, 83-96
built piece **315** 32
built unit **315** 32
bulb, glass ~ **127** 57
bulb, old ~ **54** 28
bulb-head pin **328** 29
bulbil **54** 27, 29; **375** 38
bulk cargo **221** 11
bulk cargo handling **226** 29
bulk carrier *Ship* **221** 9
bulk carrier *Docks* **225** 67; **226** 30
bulk goods **221** 11
bulkhead, protective ~ **305** 91
bulk material **200** 12
bulk transporter barge **226** 35
Bull *Astron.* **3** 25; **4** 54
bull *Dom. Anim.* **73** 1
bull *Heraldry* **254** 15
bull, mock ~ **319** 3
bull, young ~ **319** 35
bulldog **70** 1
bulldozer **199** 16; **200** 28
bulldozer blade **200** 29
bulldozer for dumping and compacting **199** 18
bullfight **319** 1-33, 24
bullfight, mock ~ **319** 1
bullfighting **319**
bullfinch **360** 5
bull pen **319** 14
bullring **319** 5
bull's eye **336** 2
bull's-eye glass **124** 6
bull terrier **70** 16
bulrush **136** 27
bulwark **221** 120; **222** 67
bumblebee **358** 23
bumper *Tram* **197** 12
bumper *Station* **206** 51
bumper, front ~ **191** 13
bumper, integral ~ **193** 33
bumper car **308** 62, 63
bumper steel **166** 44
bumper steel stop rod **166** 45
bump rubber **192** 82
bun **34** 29
bun, iced ~ **97** 39
bun, plaited ~ **97** 41
bunches **34** 30
bunch of fruit **384** 32
bunch of grapes **78** 5; **99** 89
bunch pink **60** 6
bungalow **278** 7
bunghole **130** 7
bunk, folding ~ **259** 84
bunk, rear ~ **85** 49
bunk-bed **47** 1
bunker **293** 81
bunkering boat **225** 13
Bunsen burner **173** 5; **350** 1
Bunter downthrow **154** 61
bunting **253** 3, 11
buntings **361** 6-7
bunt line **218** 36; **219** 71
buoy **90** 2; **216** 12; **224** 71; **285** 17, 18; **286** 31
buoy, conical ~ **224** 76
buoy, green ~ **224** 84
buoy, port hand ~ **224** 95
buoy, starboard hand ~ **224** 96
buoyancy tube **286** 27
buoy rope **90** 3
bur **24** 37
burden chain **139** 44
burette **350** 21
burette clamp **350** 23
burette stand **350** 22
burgee **253** 22; **284** 48
Burgundian **355** 40
burial **331** 33-41
burial place, underground ~ **331** 59
burin **175** 33; **340** 5, 15, 20
burner *Power Plant* **152** 6
burner *Glass Prod.* **162** 6
burner, gas ~ **139** 3, 48
burner platform **288** 80
burner ventilator **92** 17
burning-in oven **179** 32
burnisher *Goldsm. etc.* **108** 51
burnisher *Watchm.* **109** 17
burnishing **109** 17
burnous **354** 7
burr **88** 5, 29
burrow *Soft Fruit* **58** 63
burrow *Hunt.* **86** 26
burying ground **331** 21-41
bus **194** 17
bus, double-deck ~ **194** 36
bus, double-decker ~ **194** 36
bus, electrical system ~ **235** 55
busbar **152** 29
buses *Lorries etc.* **194**
'buses' *Airport* **233** 35
bush, rubber ~ **192** 67
bushing **162** 50
bushing chain, double ~ **190** 49
bushing tip **162** 51
bushman **354** 29
bushman woman **354** 34
business and passenger aircraft **231** 3, 7
business letter **245** 33; **246** 7; **248** 30
business trip **209** 29
bust **42** 17
bustle **355** 69
bustle pipe **147** 53
butane gas **278** 33
butane gas bottle **278** 34
butcher **96** 38, 58
butcher knife **94** 15; **96** 37
butcher's shop **96** 1-30
butt *Hunt.* **86** 47-52, 51; **87** 3, 7
butt *Meat* **95** 50
butt *Army* **255** 9, 24, 31, 39
butt *Sports* **305** 47
butt, bound ~ **89** 55
butt, cork ~ **89** 50
butt end **85** 41
butter **98** 22; **99** 47
butter, branded ~ **76** 37
butter-and-eggs **376** 26
butter churn **76** 33
butter-cream cake **97** 24
buttercup **375** 8
butter dish **45** 36
butterflies **358** 48-56; **365** 1-6
butterflower **375** 8
butterfly *Free Exerc.* **295** 35
butterfly *Articulates* **358** 52
butterfly nut **143** 42; **187** 39
butterfly stroke **282** 34
butterfly tail **229** 31
butterfly valve **192** 9
butter knife **45** 73
butter-making, continuous ~ **76** 33
buttermilk tank **76** 18
butter shaping and packing machine **76** 32
butter supply pipe **76** 34
butterwort **377** 13
button *Tram* **197** 32
button *Fencing* **294** 45
button *Music. Instr.* **325** 31
button, staghorn ~ **29** 33
button box **103** 15
buttonhole **332** 21
buttonhole stitch **102** 6
button stitch **102** 6
butt plate *Hunt.* **87** 14
butt plate *Sports* **305** 46
buttress *Chivalry* **329** 26
buttress *Art* **335** 27
buttresses **335** 27-28
butt ring **89** 58
buzzer, electric ~ **127** 15
buzz saw **119** 19; **125** 24; **134** 50
buzz saw blade **132** 59
by-line **291** 7
bypass air flow **232** 50
bypass duct **232** 41, 44
bypass engine **232** 46
bypass switch **211** 25

C

cab *Carriages* **186** 26, 28
cab *Lorries etc.* **194** 2
cab *Town* **268** 64
cab, driver's ~ **64** 36; **194** 2, 15; **200** 11; **208** 14; **209** 6; **210** 39-63, 49; **211** 19, 57; **212** 5; **213** 2
cab, engineer's ~ **208** 14; **209** 6; **210** 39-63, 49; **211** 19, 57; **212** 5; **213** 2

cabbage, green ~ **57** 32
cabbage, red ~ **57** 32
cabbage, round ~ **57** 32
cabbage lettuce **57** 36
cabbage white butterfly **80** 47, 48
cab frame **65** 21
cab heating switch **211** 39
cab horse **186** 28
cabin *Railw.* **214** 20, 28
cabin *Ship* **218** 45
cabin *Sailing* **285** 39
cabin *Airsports* **288** 19
cabin, admiral's ~ **218** 27
cabin, captain's ~ **223** 13
cabin, commanding officer's ~ **259** 85
cabin, coxswain's ~ **228** 31
cabin, crane driver's ~ **119** 35; **222** 16; **226** 52
cabin, de luxe ~ **223** 30
cabin, double-berth ~ **223** 29
cabin, large-capacity ~ **214** 52
cabin, officer's ~ **223** 21
cabin, single-berth ~ **223** 46; **228** 32
cabin cruiser **286** 3
cabinet **22** 40; **246** 20
cabinet maker **132** 38
cabin pulley cradle **214** 66
cabin superstructure **285** 39
cable *Sea Fish.* **90** 26
cable *Power Plant* **153** 41
cable *Music. Instr.* **326** 53
cable, auxiliary ~ **214** 47
cable, electric ~ **56** 32
cable, endless ~ **214** 21
cable, high-voltage ~ **153** 42
cable, lower ~ **214** 46
cable, moisture-proof ~ **127** 42
cable, submarine ~ **237** 56
cable, thermoplastic ~ **127** 42
cable, three-core ~ **127** 44
cable binding **301** 40
cable boom **195** 15
cable box **153** 33
cable clip **127** 40
cable connection **6** 26
cable connection panel **239** 3
cable crane berth **222** 11-18
cable drum **85** 39; **270** 55
cable duct **234** 29, 47; **235** 61
cable ferry **216** 1
cable guide **201** 7
cable guide rail **214** 33
cable manhole **198** 17
cable parachute **287** 7
cable pattern **30** 39
cable pulley, automatic ~ **301** 62
cable railway **214** 12
cable release **23** 9; **114** 38; **115** 101
cable release, double ~ **115** 102
cable release socket **117** 6
cable support **214** 76
cable suspension lines **214** 15-38
cable tunnel **152** 20
cable vault **152** 21
cableway **214** 30
cableway, endless ~ **214** 19
cableway gondola **214** 52
cableways **214** 15-38
cable winch **85** 38, 46; **255** 69; **258** 85
cabochon, high ~ **36** 79
cabochon, octagonal ~ **36** 81
cabochon, oval ~ **36** 80
cabochon, round ~ **36** 78
cabochon, simple ~ **36** 78
cabochons **36** 78-81
caboose **223** 42
cabriole **314** 21
cabriolet **186** 29
cacao bean **382** 19
cacao tree **382** 16
cachalot **367** 25
caddis fly **358** 12
caecum **20** 17
café **265** 1-26
café, open-air ~ **272** 57
café customers **265** 22-24
café table **265** 11
cage *Fish Farm.* **89** 1
cage *Coal* **144** 23
cage *Circus* **307** 50
cage, crane driver's ~ **119** 35; **222** 16; **226** 52
cage, outside ~ **356** 11
cage, rotating ~ **168** 17
cage, round ~ **307** 49
cage, stepped ~ **74** 20
cage, tiered ~ **74** 20
cage caravan **307** 62
cage system **74** 18
cage-winding system **144** 23
caisson **217** 33; **222** 32; **259** 19
cake **169** 19-27, 22
cake counter **99** 9; **265** 1
cake plate **97** 25
cakes **97** 17-47
cake tin **40** 28, 29
calabash **354** 27
calcaneum **17** 27
calcite **351** 22
calcium chloride tube **350** 43
calculating machine **309** 80
calculation, logarithmic ~ **345** 6
calculator **309** 80
calculator, electronic ~ **246** 12
calculator dial *Photog.* **114** 57
calculator dial *Photograv.* **182** 19
calculus, infinitesimal ~ **345** 13-14
calendar **22** 10
calendar clock **110** 19
calendar sheet **247** 33
calender **173** 36
calendering machine **168** 38
calender roll **173** 26, 38
calender roller **163** 20, 37, 59
calf *Man* **16** 53
calf *Farm Bldgs.* **62** 33
calf *Dom. Anim.* **73** 1
calf *Game* **88** 1
calf *Meat* **95** 1-13
caliber **87** 40
calibre **87** 40
California Current **14** 39
caliper *see* calliper
call, local ~ **237** 3
call, long-distance ~ **237** 3
call box **204** 46; **236** 8; **237** 1; **251** 10; **268** 56
call button **25** 6; **127** 3; **246** 15
calliper *Car* **191** 18
calliper *Sculpt. Studio* **339** 3
calliper, fixed ~ **192** 49
calliper, inside ~ **135** 23
calliper, outside ~ **135** 18
calliper gauge **149** 59
calliper square **85** 10
call light **315** 52
callosity **72** 27
calls for luring game **87** 43-47
calm **9** 11
calm belts **9** 46-47
calms, equatorial ~ **9** 46
calvarium **261** 16, 18
calyx **58** 8; **374** 8
calyx, involucral ~ **375** 33
calyx, renal ~ **20** 30
cam **190** 60
Camberwell beauty **365** 5
cambium ring **370** 10
came **124** 13
camel **366** 29
camel caravan **354** 1
camera *Atom* **1** 60
camera *Optic. Instr.* **112** 14, 20
camera *Cine Film* **117** 28
camera *Audiovis.* **243** 1
camera *Films* **310** 19
camera, cartridge-loading ~ **114** 11
camera, compact ~ *Cine Film* **117** 51
camera, compact ~ *Photomech. Reprod.* **177** 32
camera, folding ~ **114** 49; **309** 25
camera, high-speed ~ **313** 35
camera, large-format ~ *Optic. Instr.* **112** 25, 36
camera, large-format ~ *Photog.* **114** 49, 61
camera, miniature ~ *Doc.* **23** 7
camera, miniature ~ *Optic. Instr.* **112** 26
camera, miniature ~ *Photog.* **114** 1; **115** 1
camera, 35 mm ~ *Photog.* **114** 1
camera, 16 mm ~ *Cine Film* **117** 43
camera, 35 mm ~ *Films* **313** 1
camera, 16 mm ~ *Films* **313** 31
camera, narrow-gauge ~ **313** 35
camera, photogrammetric ~ **112** 68
camera, professional press-type ~ **117** 66
camera, rapid-sequence ~ **115** 77

camera, single-lens reflex ~ **115** 1
camera, spectrographic ~ **5** 6
camera, stereometric ~ **112** 71
camera, subminiature ~ **114** 16
camera, Super-8 ~ **117** 51
camera, underwater ~ **279** 24
camera assistant **117** 68; **310** 42
camera back **114** 54; **115** 23
camera body *Photog.* **115** 2
camera body *Photomech. Reprod.* **177** 25, 33
camera cable **239** 2
camera case **115** 103
camera control **242** 36
camera crane **310** 49
camera door **313** 25
camera head **240** 27
camera lens **313** 19
cameraman **117** 67; **310** 20
cameraman, first ~ **310** 41
camera monitor **238** 65; **239** 12; **240** 28
camera operator **310** 42
camera tube switch **242** 23
cam housing **167** 13
camomile *Weeds* **61** 8
camomile *Med. Plants* **380** 1
camp *Games* **276** 27
camp *Circus* **307** 61
campanile **334** 65
camp bed **278** 59
camp chair, folding ~ **278** vp
camp cot **278** 59
camper **278** 46
camp fire **278** 10
campground **278** 1-59
camphor laurel **380** 18
camphor tree **380** 18
camping **278**
camping site **278** 1-59
camping tableware **278** 45
campion **376** 20
camp site **278** 1-59
camp site attendant **278** 2
camp table, folding ~ **278** 44
camshaft **166** 56; **190** 11, 14
camshaft bearing **192** 24
camshaft lubrication **190** 13
camshaft wheel **166** 55
can *Butch.* **96** 26
can *Supermkt.* **99** 91
can *Painter* **129** 7
can *Weaving* **166** 21
Canadian pondweed **378** 56
Canadian waterweed **378** 56
canal *Map* **15** 57
canal *Hydr. Eng.* **217** 15-28
canal, auditory ~ **17** 34, 58
canal, stomachic-intestinal ~ **77** 15-19
canal administration **217** 24
canal bed **217** 30
canal entrance **217** 15-16
Canary Current **14** 41
can buoy **224** 77, 94
cancel button **326** 41
cancellation button **271** 4
Cancer **4** 56
candelabra **45** 16
candidate **263** 20
candies **47** 31, 32
candies *Grocer* **98** 75-86
candle, cast ~ **260** 76
candle, paschal ~ **330** 44
candle, wax ~ **77** 66; **260** 76
candlestick **309** 45
candlestick, paschal ~ **330** 45
candlewick yarn **35** 9
candy **98** 75
cane, flowering ~ **58** 14
can holder **163** 36
Canidae **367** 11-13
canine **19** 17
Canis Major **3** 14
Canis Minor **3** 15
canister **84** 35; **129** 16
canned vegetables **98** 17
cannon *Horse* **72** 23
cannon *Army* **255** 49, 92
cannon cracker **306** 53
canoe **352** 19
canoe, Alaskan ~ **283** 4
canoe, Canadian ~ **283** 3
canoeing **283**
canoeist **283** 55
canoes **283** 54-66
canoe stern **285** 44
canoe with outrigger **352** 35
cañon **13** 45
canonicals *Church* **330** 22; **332** 4
canopy *Infant Care etc.* **28** 32
canopy *Dwellings* **37** 67
canopy *Child. Rm.* **47** 12
canopy *Kindergart.* **48** 26
canopy *Supermkt.* **99** 24
canopy *Aircraft* **230** 39
canopy *Airsports* **288** 38
canopy *Church* **330** 21; **331** 49
canopy bearer **331** 46
canopy jack **257** 5
cant chisel **132** 11
canteen **119** 45
canter **72** 42
cant hook **85** 7
canting table **133** 17
cantle **71** 39, 46
canvas **338** 21
canvas hull, rubber-covered ~ **283** 58
canvas stretcher **338** 20
canyon **13** 45
canyon river **13** 51
cap *Bees* **77** 30
cap *Drawing Off.* **151** 40
cap *Refuse Coll.* **199** 8
cap *Music. Instr.* **326** 31
cap *Edib. Fungi* **381** 4
cap, astrakhan ~ **35** 34
cap, corduroy ~ **35** 25
cap, fox ~ **35** 31
cap, leather ~ **35** 32; **354** 26
cap, linen ~ **35** 8
cap, mink ~ **35** 17, 20
cap, musquash ~ **35** 33
cap, peaked ~ **35** 17, 29; **264** 8; **301** 18
cap, sheepskin ~ **353** 23
cap, white ~ **268** 32
cap, wide-brimmed ~ **355** 28
cap, workman's ~ **35** 40
capa **319** 27
capacitor **211** 17
cap and bells **306** 39
caparison **329** 74
cape **30** 65; **105** 34; **106** 4
cape, short ~ **355** 29
cape chisel **140** 25
capeline **21** 3
Capella **3** 27
caper **98** 42
capercaillie **88** 72
capillary tube stand **23** 42
capistrum **322** 5
capital *Composing Rm.* **175** 11
capital *Art* **334** 20-25
capital, Arabian ~ **337** 18
capital, bell-shaped ~ **333** 16
capital, bud-shaped ~ **333** 14
capital, Roman ~ **341** 16
capital, small ~ **175** 14
capitulum **61** 14; **370** 73; **378** 12
capoc tree **383** 20
cap of typing element **249** 30
capon **73** 21
capper **76** 46
capping *Bees* **77** 39
capping *Coal* **144** 48
Capricorn **3** 36; **4** 62
capriole **71** 5
caprolactam **170** 28
caprolactam oil **170** 25
caps, ladies' ~ **35** 1-21
caps, men's ~ **35** 22-40
capstan *Cine Film* **117** 34
capstan *Hydr. Eng.* **217** 22
capstan *Audiovis.* **243** 23
capstan *Warships* **258** 23
capstan idler **117** 35
capsule **384** 58
capsule, poricidal ~ **370** 96
capsule, porose ~ **370** 96
captain **224** 38
caption **185** 67; **342** 59
car *Car* **191** 1-56
car *Garage* **195** 34
car *Railw.* **213** 18
car, four-axled ~ **208** 3
car, large-capacity ~ **213** 28
car, open ~ **207** 59
car accessory **196** 28
carapace **364** 29
caravan **270** 52; **307** 34
caravan, collapsible ~ **278** 3
caravan, showman's ~ **206** 20
caravan awning **278** 57
caravanning **278**
caravel **218** 27-43; **220** 37
caraway roll **97** 31
caraway stick **97** 31
carbide, cemented ~ **149** 46
carbine **86** 30
carbolic acid **170** 14
carbon, active ~ **270** 58
carbon, negative ~ **312** 41
carbon, positive ~ **312** 40
carbon atom **242** 63
carbon crater **312** 44

carbon disulfide **169** 8
carbon disulphide **169** 8
carbon disulphide injector **83** 33
carbon rod, negative ~ **312** 41
carbon rod, positive ~ **312** 40
carbon rod holder **312** 43
carbon tissue **182** 1, 10
carbon tissue, printed ~ **182** 8
carbon tissue transfer machine **182** 6
carburetor *see* carburettor
carburettor **189** 4; **192** 1-15
carburettor, cross-draught ~ **190** 79
car carrier, double-deck ~ **213** 35
car carrier, two-tier ~ **213** 35
carcase **118** 1-49
carcass **118** 1-49
carcassing **118** 1-49
car coat **33** 63
card *Cotton Spin.* **163** 34, 51
card *Games* **276** 37
card, patient's ~ **25** 5
card, used ~ **195** 14
cardan coupling **67** 6
cardan joint **67** 6, 28
cardan mount **6** 36
cardan shaft **64** 40, 48; **67** 16; **211** 51; **212** 29, 83
cardan shaft connection **64** 63
cardan transmission **189** 47
cardboard **260** 50-52
card can **163** 35
card catalogue **262** 22
card catalogue drawer **262** 23
car deck **221** 79
cardiac rhythm **25** 1
cardiac sulcus, longitudinal ~ **20** 25
cardigan **31** 50; **33** 30
cardinal *Maths.* **344** 5
cardinal *Birds* **363** 5
cardinal bird **363** 5
card index **245** 23
card index box **46** 10; **248** 27
carding can **163** 35
carding engine **163** 34, 51
carding machine **163** 34
car door **191** 4
card sliver **163** 38
card stacker **244** 13
car ferry **216** 10
cargo **223** 77
cargo and passenger liner **221** 96
cargo and passenger ship **223** 1-71
cargo barge **216** 25
cargo boom **221** 26, 59; **223** 36
cargo gear **221** 24-29, 59
cargo handling, horizontal ~ **226** 7
cargo-handling berth **226** 1
cargo-handling gear **221** 24-29, 59
cargo hatchway **221** 11, 63; **226** 14
cargo hold **231** 21
cargo ship **221** 23
cargo warehouse **233** 10
'car hire' **233** 33
Carina **3** 46
carload **206** 52
car location number **195** 48
car models **193** 1-36
carnation **60** 6
carnival **306**
carnival float **306** 57
carnival procession **306** 57-70
carnival truck **306** 57
carnivore house **356** 10
carnivores **367** 11-22; **368** 1-11
carob **384** 41
carom billiards **277** 7
carousel **308** 2
carp **89** 26; **364** 4
carpel **58** 36, 59; **59** 13; **374** 2, 26
carpenter **120** 12
carpenter's tools **120** 60-82
carpenter's yard **120** 1-59
carpet **44** 16
carpet, fitted ~ **41** 18; **43** 23
carpet, oriental ~ **46** 36
carpet, velour ~ **267** 35
carpet beater head **50** 79
carpet beater nozzle **50** 71
carpet brush **50** 45
carpet cleaning **50** 53-86
carpeting **191** 43
carpet sweeper **50** 57
carpet sweeper and shampooer, combined ~ **50** 76
carp hook **89** 86
carp pond **89** 6
carpus *Man* **17** 15; **19** 76
carpus *Horse* **72** 22
car radio **191** 90
carriage *Hosp.* **26** 36
carriage *Sawmill* **157** 12, 52
carriage *Knitting* **167** 39
carriage *Tram* **197** 5, 6, 7
carriage, auxiliary ~ **157** 11
carriage, one-horse ~ **186** 18, 29
carriage, open ~ **207** 61; **208** 9
carriage, three-horse ~ **186** 45
carriage, two-horse ~ **186** 36
carriage apron **149** 16
carriage handle **167** 41
carriage heating pressure gauge **210** 44
carriage horse **186** 28
carriage motor **157** 15
carriage rail **167** 45
carriages **186** 1-54, 1-3,26-39,45,51-54
carriages, horse-drawn ~ **186**
carriage sprayer **83** 38
carriage step **186** 13
carrier *Bicycle* **187** 44
carrier *Docks* **226** 4
carrier return lever **249** 21
carrion flower **53** 15
carrot **57** 17
carrot, stump-rooted ~ **57** 18
carrycot **28** 48
carry-home pack **93** 28
carrying axle **210** 35
carrying bar **148** 16
carrying bogie **197** 10
carrying cart **56** 26
carrying grip **21** 22
carrying handle **241** 2
carrying rope **215** 16
carrying saddle **73** 4
carrying strap **115** 9
carrying wheel **214** 7
cart **86** 39
cart, electric ~ **206** 34
carte engagement **294** 47
cartilage, costal ~ **17** 11
cartilage, thyroid ~ **20** 3
cartoon *Art. Studio* **338** 43
cartoon *Script* **342** 53
cartouche **336** 7
cartridge *Hunt.* **87** 19, 54
cartridge *Cine Film* **117** 30
cartridge *Slaughterho.* **94** 5
cartridge, full-jacketed ~ **87** 55
cartridge, instamatic ~ **114** 15
cartridge, magnetic ~ **241** 26
cartridge, subminiature ~ **114** 17
cartridge chamber **87** 15
cartwheel **297** 21
cartwheel ruff **355** 52
car tyre **191** 15; **196** 27
carvel **218** 27-43; **220** 37
carvel planking **285** 53
carvel planking, diagonal ~ **285** 56
carver **96** 35
carving knife **45** 69; **96** 35
carving set **45** 69-70
car-wash hose **196** 23
car wheel **191** 14
car window, crank-operated ~ **191** 22
caryatid **334** 36
caryopsis **375** 43
cascade **272** 9
case *Meteorol. Instr.* **10** 18
case *Doc.* **22** 33
case *Composing Rm.* **174** 3, 8
case *Bookbind.* **185** 40
case *Lorries etc.* **194** 19
case *Station* **204** 6; **205** 7
case *Chem.* **349** 26
case, cardboard ~ **87** 50
case cabinet **174** 4
case head **305** 36
case maker **184** 6
case-making machine **184** 6
case rack **174** 4
case room **174; 175; 176**
cash desk **196** 29; **266** 69; **275** 2
cash drawer **271** 5
cashier **99** 94; **250** 2; **266** 70; **271** 1
cash readout **196** 4
cash register **47** 34; **99** 93; **207** 86
cash register, electric ~ **271** 2
cash total **271** 8
casing *Mach. Parts etc.* **143** 79
casing *Oil, Petr.* **145** 18

casing *Power Plant* **153** 37
casing *Text. Finish.* **168** 16
casing *Army* **255** 10
casing *Chem.* **350** 10
casing, outer ~ **168** 17
casing, protective ~ *Meteorol. Instr.* **10** 39
casing, protective ~ *Railw.* **202** 35
casing cover **143** 80
casing-in machine **185** 27
casino **274** 8; **275** 1
cask **130** 5
casket **331** 35
casque, light ~ **329** 61
Cassegrain cage **5** 4
casserole dish **40** 14
cassette, compact ~ **241** 10
cassette, daylight ~ **177** 50
cassette, 35 mm ~ **114** 7
cassette, single-8 ~ **117** 39
cassette box **241** 11, 47
cassette cabinet **241** 11, 47
cassette compartment **241** 6, 34; **243** 8; **249** 72
cassette deck **241** 52
cassette exit slot **114** 10
cassette holder **241** 11, 47
cassette recorder **117** 73; **261** 42
cassette recorder unit **241** 3
cassette slit **114** 10
cassette tape **241** 12
cassia **380** 16
Cassiopeia **3** 33
cassowary **359** 1
cast **89** 64, 78
cast, long ~ **89** 58
castanets **324** 46
caster **148** 8
castes of bees **77** 1,4,5
cast glass **124** 6
casting **148** 42
casting, continuous ~ **148** 24-29
casting mechanism **174** 25
casting net **89** 31
casting off **167** 66
casting team **148** 13
castle *Games* **276** 12
castle, knight's ~ **329** 1
castle gate **329** 32
castle nut **143** 77
castle wall **333** 31
cast line **174** 27
cast of skull **261** 15
castor *Household* **50** 81
castor *Horse* **72** 27
castor *Pest Contr.* **83** 61
Castor and Pollux **3** 28
castor-oil plant **380** 14
casual **101** 34
casualty **21** 20
cat **62** 3; **73** 17
catacomb **331** 59
catalogue, main ~ **262** 21
catalogue room **262** 18
catalytic cracking plant **145** 70
catamaran **284** 64; **286** 21
cataract **11** 45
catch *Mach. Parts etc.* **143** 29
catch *Railw.* **203** 57
catcher **292** 54, 64
catchfly **376** 20
catchment area **12** 24
catchup **45** 43
cat cracker **145** 48
caterpillar **58** 64; **82** 16, 20, 31, 44, 47; **365** 10; **80** 3, 8, 14, 17, 29, 44, 48
caterpillar hauling scraper **200** 16
caterpillar mounting **200** 3
caterpillar tractor **200** 3
catfish **364** 12
cathedral **335** 1-13, 22
catheter **26** 31
catheter, cardiac ~ **25** 53
catheter gauge unit **27** 30
catheter holder **26** 30
catheterization **27** 30
cathetus **346** 32
cathode **178** 6
cathode ray tube **242** 40
catkin **59** 39; **371** 10, 26
catkin, male ~ **59** 45
catkin scale **371** 12
cat ladder **38** 4; **122** 63
cat litter **99** 38
cats **368** 2-8
cat's foot **377** 3
cat's tail **378** 21
catsuit **29** 19
catsup **45** 43
cattail **378** 21
cattail flag **378** 21
cattle **62** 45; **73** 1-2
cattleship **221** 68
cattle vessel **221** 68
catwalk *Iron & Steel* **147** 38
catwalk *Ship* **221** 3
catwalk *Theatre* **315** 29
cauliflower **57** 31; **99** 84
causticizing agitator **172** 49
causticizing stirrer **172** 49
caustic soda **169** 3, 4, 5, 10; **170** 11
caustic soda solution **170** 10
cautery **24** 43
cavalier hat **355** 55
cavalry saddle **71** 45-49
cavalry standard **253** 13
cave *Phys. Geog.* **13** 76
cave *Map* **15** 85
cave, dripstone ~ **13** 79
cave, limestone ~ **13** 79
cave art **328** 9
cave formations **13** 80-81
cave painting **328** 9
cavern *Phys. Geog.* **13** 76
cavern *Park* **272** 1
cavetto **336** 50
cavetto vault **336** 49
caviare knife **45** 81
cavity **91** 36
cavity, nasal ~ **17** 53
cavity, tympanic ~ **17** 60
cavity of the uterus **20** 80
cavy **366** 12
C-clef **320** 10
cecum **20** 17
cedar tree **372** 65
cedilla **342** 33
ceiba tree **383** 20
ceiling **222** 63
ceiling, concrete ~ **123** 28
ceiling, false ~ **123** 61, 68-69
ceiling beam **120** 38
ceiling construction **123**
ceiling hook **270** 15
ceiling joint **126** 48
ceiling joist **119** 5; **120** 38; **121** 54
ceiling light **24** 20; **75** 8
ceiling paper **128** 53
ceiling paperhanger **128** 50
ceiling plaster **123** 59, 72
ceiling tile **317** 29
celeriac **57** 27
celesta **325** 1
Celestial River **3** 12
Celestial Ship **3** 45
cell **77** 26-30, 27
cell, sealed ~ **77** 32, 33
cella **334** 51
cellarman **79** 18
cellar steps, outside ~ **118** 4
cellar window **37** 27; **118** 3
cell nucleus **357** 2
cello **323** 16
cellulose, refined ~ **172** 78
cellulose, unrefined ~ **172** 77
cellulose sheet **169** 2, 4, 6
cellulose xanthate **169** 9
cembalo **322** 45
cement *Man* **19** 29
cement *Bldg. Site* **118** 43
cement factory **160**
cement-grinding mill **160** 12
cementing pump, high-pressure ~ **146** 34
cement-packing plant **160** 16
cement screed **123** 14
cement silo **119** 30; **160** 15
cement storage tank **146** 15
cement store **201** 22
cement track racing **290** 24-28
cementum, dental ~ **19** 29
cement works **160**
cemetery **15** 106
censer **332** 38
cent **252** 19, 33
Centaur *Astron.* **3** 39
centaur *Fabul. Creat.* **327** 52
Centaurus **3** 39
centaury **61** 1; **380** 10
centavo **252** 23
center *see* centre
centerboard *see* centreboard
centering *see* centring
centime **252** 15, 16
centimeter *see* centimetre
centimetre graduation **247** 36
céntimo **252** 22
central heating, full ~ **38** 38-81
central heating furnace **38** 57
central heating system, coke-fired ~ **38** 38
central heating system, oil-fired ~ **38** 44-60

centre *Turner* **135** 8
centre *Ball Games* **293** 76
centre *Maths.* **346** 26, 43, 55
centre, asbestos ~ **350** 19
centre, live ~ **135** 11
centre angle **346** 55
centreboard **284** 26
centreboard, retractable ~ **284** 8; **285** 41
centreboard case **284** 24
centre circle **291** 2
centre console **191** 38
centre flag **291** 64
centre girder **222** 53
centre lathe **149** 1
centre line *Drawing Off.* **151** 30
centre line *Sailing* **285** 5
centre line *Ball Games* **293** 8-9, 54
centre line *Fencing* **294** 4
centre line judge **293** 25
centre mark **293** 11
centre of curvature **346** 23
centre of symmetry **351** 3
centre plate girder **222** 53
centre punch **134** 31; **140** 64
centre-section fuel tank **257** 30
centre strake **222** 55
centrifuge **23** 59
centrifuge, pendulum-type ~ **168** 14
centrifuge lid **168** 18
centring apparatus, universal ~ **111** 21
centring control **243** 10
centring ring **240** 23
centring suction holder **111** 22
centrosphere **11** 5
cep **381** 16
cepe **381** 16
cephalopod **357** 37
Cerberus **327** 29
cereal **68** 1
cereal product **99** 62
cereal products **98** 35-39
cereals **68** 1-37
cerebellum **17** 45; **18** 23
cerebrum **17** 42; **18** 22
cesta **305** 69
Cetus **3** 11
chaffinch **360** 10
chaffron **329** 84
chafron **329** 84
chain **74** 14; **75** 15; **99** 95; **118** 30
chain *Bicycle* **187** 36
chain *Cyc. Racing* **290** 20
chain armour **329** 63
chain cable **222** 77; **223** 50; **227** 12
chain compressor **223** 51
chain curtain **139** 50
chain cutter **120** 17
chain delivery **180** 43
chain drive **187** 35-42
chain feeder **74** 25
chain ferry **216** 1
chain grinder, continuous ~ **172** 53, 66
chain gripper **180** 56
chain guard **187** 37; **188** 46
chain guide **120** 15
chain mail **329** 63
chain mortiser **132** 49
chain mortising machine **132** 49
chain reaction **1** 41, 48
chain saw **120** 14
chain sling *Forging* **139** 44
chain sling *Docks* **226** 26
chain stay **187** 20
chain stitch **102** 2
chain-tensioning device **157** 41
chain transmission **187** 35-39
chain wheel **187** 35
chair **42** 34; **271** 35
chair, adjustable ~ **105** 17; **106** 16
chair, barber's ~ **106** 16
chair, cane ~ **43** 3
chair, dentist's ~ **24** 3
chair, double ~ **214** 18
chair, folding ~ **28** 33
chair, gaffer's ~ **162** 45
chair, glassmaker's ~ **162** 45
chair, hairdresser's ~ **105** 17; **106** 16
chair, single ~ **214** 16
chair, steel ~ **67** 2
chair, tubular steel ~ **41** 21
chair, two-seater ~ **214** 17, 18
chair, umpire's ~ **293** 20
chair, visitor's ~ **246** 21
chair grip **21** 21
chair lift **214** 16-18
chair lift, double ~ **301** 57
chairman **263** 1
chairman of board of directors **251** 16
chairman of board of governors **251** 15
chairoplane **308** 4
chaise **186** 34
chaise, closed ~ **186** 54
chaise, covered ~ **186** 54
chaise, one-horse ~ **186** 29
chaitya **337** 28
chaitya hall **337** 27
chalaza **74** 63
chalcography **340** 14-24
chalet **278** 7
chalice **330** 10; **332** 49
chalk **48** 15; **260** 32; **338** 5
chalk, French ~ **104** 24
chalk, tailor's ~ **104** 24
chalk ledge **260** 31
chalk sketch **338** 4
chalwar **306** 42
Chamaeleontidae **364** 33
chamber *Atom* **1** 66
chamber *Forest Pests* **82** 36
chamber *Hunt.* **87** 20
chamber *Water* **269** 24
chamber, king's ~ **333** 2
chamber, photographic ~ **113** 40
chamber, queen's ~ **333** 3
chamber, stone ~ **328** 39
chamber wall **269** 25
chameleon **364** 33
chamfer **143** 62
chamfering hammer **125** 14
chamfrain **329** 84
chamfron **329** 84
chamois **367** 3
chamomile **61** 8; **380** 1
chamotte slab **141** 16
champagne **99** 78
champagne bucket **267** 59
champagne cooler **267** 59
champagne cork **267** 58
champagne glass **45** 86
champagne glasses **45** 85-86
chancel **330** 1, 32; **335** 4
chandelier **267** 21
chanfron **329** 84
'change' *Airport* **233** 51
change *Winter Sp.* **302** 12
change-gear box **149** 7
change-gear handle **132** 56
change gears **10** 14
change-loop **302** 16
change machine **197** 33; **204** 22; **236** 28
changemaker **236** 28
changeover switch **50** 59; **243** 15
change points, electric ~ **197** 37
change rack **236** 23
change-speed gear **163** 29; **211** 50
change wheel **164** 40
changing booth **271** 32
changing cubicle **282** 1
changing room **282** 3
changing top **28** 4
changing unit **28** 11
channel *Overh. Irrign.* **67** 13
channel *Railw.* **202** 32
channel *Swim.* **281** 9
channel *Rowing* **283** 60
channel *Art* **334** 27
channel, distributary ~ **13** 2
channel, navigable ~ **224** 92, 93
channel iron **143** 7
channel markings **224** 84-102
channel marks **224** 68-83
chantarelle **381** 14
chanter **322** 10
chanterelle **381** 14
chapel *Map* **15** 61, 107
'chapel' *Airport* **233** 49
chapel *Chivalry* **329** 29
chaplet **34** 32
chaplet hairstyle **34** 31
chaps **70** 26
chapter heading **185** 60
char-a-banc, covered ~ **186** 33
character **174** 7, 44; **175** 38
characteristic **345** 6
characteristic light **221** 48; **224** 105
character storage **242** 37
charcoal **278** 48
charcoal, activated ~ **270** 58

charcoal grill **278** 47
charcoal pencil **338** 16
chard **57** 28
charge postmark **236** 58
charger **25** 51
charging car **144** 8; **156** 6
charging chamber **154** 79
charging conveyor **144** 42
charging door **38** 61; **139** 4
charging machine **147** 25
charging opening **139** 49
charging platform **147** 4
charging position **147** 55, 56
Charioteer **3** 27
charity performance **319** 31
Charles's Wain **3** 29
Charleston cymbals **324** 50
charlock **61** 18
charm **36** 35
chart **22** 32; **76** 8; **260** 30
chart, illustrated ~ **22** 16
chase **181** 38
chasing **87** 28
chasing hammer **108** 41
chassis *Overh. Irrign.* **67** 14
chassis *Blacksm.* **138** 28
chassis *Car* **191** 2
check *Roulette* **275** 12
check *Theatre* **315** 7
check *Music. Instr.* **325** 27
check brake **143** 97
checker **276** 18, 19
checkerboard **276** 17
checkerman **276** 18, 19
checkers **276** 17-19
check felt **325** 28
check light **195** 21, 22
checkmate **276** 15
checkout **99** 92
check rail **202** 23
checkroom **315** 5; **318** 1
checkroom attendant **315** 6; **318** 2
checkroom hall **315** 5-11
check side **277** 6
cheek *Man* **16** 9
cheek *Hunt.* **87** 4
cheekbone **16** 8; **17** 37
cheek piece **71** 8
cheek rest **255** 30
cheek strap **71** 8
cheese **98** 5; **99** 49; **266** 52
cheese, cross-wound ~ **164** 58
cheese, round ~ **99** 42
cheese, whole ~ **99** 40
cheeseboard **45** 35
cheesecake **97** 23
cheese counter **99** 39
cheese dish **40** 7
cheesefly **81** 15
cheese knife **45** 72
cheese machine **76** 47
cheetah **368** 7
chef **207** 34
chelicer **358** 41
cheliped **358** 41
chemical bottle **116** 10; **261** 23
'chemist' **233** 45
chemistry **261** 1-13
chemistry laboratory **261** 1; **349**; **350**
chemistry teacher **261** 2
chequer-board cut **36** 66
cheroot **107** 4
cherry *Drupes & Nuts* **59** 5, 6-8
cherry *Goldsm. etc.* **108** 7
cherry *Bot.* **370** 99
cherry blossom **59** 3
cherry flan **97** 22
cherry flower **59** 3
cherry fruit **59** 6-8
cherry fruit fly **80** 18
cherry leaf **59** 2
cherry stone **59** 7
cherry tree **59** 1, 11-18
cherub **272** 20
chess **265** 17; **276** 1-16
chessboard **47** 20; **276** 1
chessboard square **276** 2
chess championship **276** 16
chess clock **276** 16
chessman **276** 1, 4, 5, 7
chess match **276** 16
chess move **276** 6
chess player **265** 17
chess problem **276** 6
chess square **276** 6
chest *Man* **16** 28-30; **17** 8-11
chest *Paperm.* **172** 25
chest grip **21** 37
chestnut *Horse* **72** 27
chestnut *Decid. Trees* **371** 60
chestnut *South. Fruits* **384** 52
Chestnut Boletus **381** 15
chestnut tree **371** 58
chest of drawers **41** 8
chevron design **335** 16
chew **107** 19
chewing tobacco **107** 19
Chianti **98** 61; **99** 77
chibonk **107** 32
chibonque **107** 32
chick **74** 2
chicken **62** 36; **73** 19-26; **96** 24
chicken run **74** 11
chick-pea **69** 19
chick unit **74** 1
chicory **57** 40
chief **254** 18-19
chignon **34** 29
child **260** 3
child, small ~ **28** 42
child carrier seat **187** 21
children's room **47**
chilling roll **100** 20
chill roller **180** 28
chimera **327** 16
chimney *Map* **15** 38
chimney *Dwellings* **37** 10
chimney *Roof & Boilerr.* **38** 5
chimney *Bldg. Site* **118** 21
chimney *Carp.* **120** 47
chimney *Roof* **122** 13
chimney *Blacksm.* **137** 7
chimney *Power Plant* **152** 15
chimney *Energy Sources* **155** 12
chimney *Railw.* **210** 22
chimney *Mountain.* **300** 8
chimney bond **118** 66
chimney brick **159** 28
chimney flashing **122** 14
chimney swallow **361** 20
chimney sweep **38** 31
chimney sweeper **38** 31
chimpanzee **368** 14
chin **16** 15
china, broken ~ **260** 61
china cabinet **44** 26
china manufacture **161**
china painter **161** 17
China rose **60** 15
chinband **355** 22
chinch **81** 39
chinchona **380** 17
Chinese lantern **52** 15
chine strake **258** 8
chin rest **323** 8
chintuft **34** 10
chip *Basketm.* **136** 12
chip *Roulette* **275** 12
chip basket **136** 11
chip container **170** 40
chip crusher **172** 5
chip distributor **172** 3
chip extractor **157** 51
chip-extractor opening **132** 48
chip packer **172** 3
chip pan **40** 41
chipper **172** 1
chipping hammer *Blacksm.* **137** 38
chipping hammer *Gas Weld.* **141** 25
chipping hammer *Arc Weld.* **142** 17
chip remover **157** 50
chiropter **366** 9
chiropteran **366** 9
chisel **120** 71
chisel, bevelled-edge ~ **132** 7; **339** 19
chisel, blacksmith's ~ **137** 38
chisel, broad ~ **158** 37
chisel, flat ~ **140** 26; **339** 14
chisel, hollow ~ **339** 17
chisel, pneumatic ~ **148** 45
chisel, toothed ~ **339** 13
chisels **132** 7-11
chitarrone **324** 1
chiton **355** 5
Chitonactis **369** 20
chivalry **329**
chive **57** 22
chlorine **170** 7
chlorine ion **1** 10
chlorobenzene **170** 9, 11
chock *Bldg. Site* **119** 40
chock *Iron Foundry etc.* **148** 61
chocolate **98** 80
chocolate, bar of ~ **98** 78
chocolate box **98** 79
chocolate liqueur **98** 83
choir **330** 32; **335** 4
choke cymbals **324** 50
choke flap **192** 6
choker **36** 16
choker collar **355** 74
cholecystography **27** 4

Chopper **188** 56
chopper drum **64** 34
chopping board **96** 57
chord *Aircraft* **230** 56
chord *Music. Not.* **321** 1-5, 5
chord *Maths.* **346** 51
chord, lower ~ **121** 73, 79
chord, upper ~ **121** 74, 80
chorus **315** 21
chow **70** 21
christening **332** 1
christening dress **332** 8
christening robe **332** 8
christening shawl **332** 9
chromatic scale **320** 49
chromolithograph **340** 28
chronometer **230** 11
chrysalis **77** 30, 32; **80** 4, 25, 43; **81** 3, 21, 24; **82** 13, 21, 32; **358** 20; **365** 11
chrysanthemum **51** 29; **61** 7
chuck *Meat* **95** 19
chuck *D.I.Y.* **134** 48
chuck *Turner* **135** 6
chuck, four-jaw ~ **149** 35
chuck, independent ~ **149** 35
chuck, quick-action ~ **132** 54
chuck, self-centring ~ **149** 37
chuck, three-jaw ~ **149** 37
chuck, two-jaw ~ **135** 10
church **15** 53, 61, 107; **330; 331** 1; **332**
church, Baroque ~ **336** 1
church, Gothic ~ **335** 22
church, Protestant ~ **330** 1-30
church, Renaissance ~ **335** 42
church, Roman Catholic ~ **330** 31-62
church, Romanesque ~ **335** 1-13
church banner **331** 44
church clock **331** 7
church door *Church* **331** 16
church door *Art* **335** 24
churchgoer **330** 29; **331** 17
church landmark **15** 64
church organ **326** 1-52
church owl **362** 17
church roof **331** 11
church spire **331** 6
church wedding **332** 14
church window **330** 14
churchyard **331** 21-41
churchyard gate **331** 19
churchyard wall **331** 18
chute *Docks* **226** 45
chute *Fair* **308** 40
chute, spiral ~ **144** 28
chute, three-way ~ **92** 34
ciborium **332** 48
cigar, Brazilian ~ **107** 2
cigar and cigarette boy **267** 49
cigar box **107** 1
cigar case **107** 8
cigar cutter **107** 9
cigarette, filter-tipped ~ **107** 12
cigarette, Russian ~ **107** 14
cigarette beetle **81** 25
cigarette case **107** 10
cigarette holder **107** 16
cigarette lighter **107** 27, 30
cigarette machine **268** 69
cigarette packet **107** 11
cigarette paper **107** 17
cigarette roller **107** 15
cigarettes and tobacco kiosk **204** 47
cigarette seller **308** 51
cigarette tip **107** 13
cigarette tray **267** 50
cigarillo **107** 3
cigar lighter **191** 88
ciliate **370** 49
cilium *Man* **19** 41
cilium *Invertebr.* **357** 10
cilium *Bot.* **370** 50
cinchona **380** 17
cincinnus **370** 77
cine camera **117** 1
cine film **117**
cinema **312** 1
cinema, mobile ~ **312** 52
cinema advertisement **268** 57
cinema audience **312** 5
cinema box office **312** 2
cinemagoer **312** 5
cinema projector **312** 24
cinema projector, narrow-gauge ~ **312** 52
cinemascope camera **310** 47
cinema ticket **312** 3
cine projector **117** 78; **318** 20
cinnamon **382** 25
cinnamon bark **382** 25
cinnamon tree **382** 22
cinquefoil **335** 40
circle *Sports* **305** 31
circle *Maths.* **346** 42
circle, circumscribed ~ **346** 29
circle, divided ~ *Optic. Instr.* **113** 27
circle, divided ~ *Crystals* **351** 32
circle, graduated ~ *Optic. Instr.* **113** 27
circle, graduated ~ *Crystals* **351** 32
circle, inner ~ **288** 57
circle, inscribed ~ **346** 31
circle, middle ~ **288** 58
circle, outer ~ **288** 59
circle, upper ~ **315** 17
circles, concentric ~ **346** 58
circles, polar ~ **14** 11
circle template **151** 70
circling engagement **294** 49
circuit, integrated ~ *Clocks* **110** 16
circuit, integrated ~ *Inf. Tech.* **242** 68
circuit, primary ~ **154** 2, 42
circuit, secondary ~ **154** 7, 45
circuit breaker **127** 19, 33, 36; **152** 34; **153** 51-62
circuit breaker, miniature ~ **41** 20
circuit breaker consumer unit **127** 33
circular broom **199** 40
circular saw attachment **84** 33; **134** 52
circular saw blade **132** 59
circulation, atmospheric ~ **9** 46-52
circulation pump **154** 43, 54
circulatory system **18** 1-21
circumcircle **346** 29
circumference *Cooper* **130** 23
circumference *Maths.* **346** 44
circumference, staved ~ **130** 2
circumflex **342** 32
circus **307**
circus, travelling ~ **307** 1-63
circus act **307** 25
circus attendant **307** 27
circus band **307** 10
circus box **307** 16
circus caravan **206** 20; **307** 34
circus horse **307** 30
circus manager **307** 17
circus marksman **307** 38
circus rider **307** 26
circus tent **307** 1
circus trailer **307** 34
cirrocumulus **8** 14
cirrostratus **8** 7
cirrus **8** 6
cist, long ~ **328** 16
cist, stone ~ **328** 17
cistern **49** 16
cithara **322** 15
cittern **322** 21
city **15** 51
city banner **218** 22
city wall **333** 30
Claisen flask **350** 50
clamp *Atom* **2** 43
clamp *Overh. Irrign.* **67** 30
clamp *Goldsm. etc.* **108** 34
clamp *Joiner* **132** 51; **133** 9
clamp *Bookbind.* **183** 18; **185** 3
clamp *Chem.* **350** 33
clamp, horizontal ~ **14** 57
clamp, vertical ~ **14** 55
clamp handle **133** 8
clamping device *Atom* **2** 43
clamping device *Mach. Tools* **150** 15
clamping plate, hinged ~ **117** 90
clamping screw **133** 23
clamping shoe **133** 10
clamp lever **132** 67
clamp tip **149** 46
clamp tip tool **149** 45
clapper *Carnival* **306** 47
clapper *Films* **310** 35
clapper board **310** 35
clapper boy **310** 34
clappers **162** 42
clarinet **318** 4; **323** 34
clarinettist **318** 5
clasp, white gold ~ **36** 10
clasp nut **149** 19
classes, social ~of bees **77** 1,4,5
classification siding **206** 47
classification track **206** 47
classification yard **206** 42
classification yard switch tower **206** 44

classifier **172** 50
classroom **260** 1-45
classroom cupboard **260** 43
clavicembalo **322** 45
clavichord **322** 36
clavichord mechanism **322** 37
clavicle **17** 6
clavilux **317** 13
claw **327** 3; **362** 7
claw, bird's ~ **327** 61
claw, double ~ **77** 8
claw chisel **339** 13
claw head **120** 75
claws, griffin's ~ **327** 13
clay **160** 1; **260** 79; **339** 8, 31
clay, impure ~ **159** 2
clay, raw ~ **159** 2
clay box **339** 30
clay column *Brickwks.* **159** 14
clay column *Porcelain Manuf.* **161** 8
clay pigeon shooting **305** 70-78
clay pit *Map* **15** 88
clay pit *Brickwks.* **159** 1
cleaner, centrifugal ~ **173** 11
cleaner, ultrasonic ~ **109** 23
cleaning brush *Hunt.* **87** 62
cleaning brush *Office* **247** 10
cleaning fluid **111** 32
cleaning machine *Brew.* **92** 36
cleaning machine *Watchm.* **109** 30
cleaning plant **144** 20
cleaning rag **50** 55
cleaning rod **87** 61
cleaning shop **148** 38-45
cleaning tank **178** 1
cleaning tow **87** 63
cleanout door **38** 39
cleansing pond **89** 6
clear-felling system **84** 4-14
clearing *Map* **15** 2
clearing *Forestry* **84** 13
clearstory **334** 70
cleat *Carp.* **120** 45
cleat *Floor etc. Constr.* **123** 67
cleaver, butcher's ~ **94** 18
cleaving hammer **85** 5
clefs **320** 8-11
cleft, anal ~ **16** 41
clench planking **285** 50-52
clerestory **334** 70
clergyman **330** 22; **331** 37; **332** 22
clergyman, Protestant ~ **332** 3
clerical assistant **248** 7
clerk **263** 26, 27
clew **284** 41
click **110** 34
click beetle **80** 37, 38
click wheel **110** 35
cliff **13** 28
cliff face **13** 28
cliffline **13** 25-31
cliffs **13** 25-31
climate, artificially maintained ~ **356** 21
climate, boreal ~ **9** 56
climate, equatorial ~ **9** 53
climates **9** 53-58
climates, polar ~ **9** 57-58
climatic map **9** 40-58
climatology **9**
climber *Flower Gdn.* **51** 5
climber *Fruit & Veg. Gdn.* **52** 5
climber *Indoor Plants* **53** 2
climber *Veg.* **57** 8
climber *Mountain.* **300** 5
climbing **300** 2-13
climbing boot **300** 44
climbing breeches **300** 7
climbing equipment **300** 31-57
climbing frame **273** 47
climbing harness **300** 56
climbing net **273** 50
climbing plant **53** 2
climbing roof **273** 60
climbing rope **273** 48; **296** 19
climbing tower **273** 17
clinch **299** 31
clinker cooler **160** 9
clinker pit **152** 8
clinker planking **285** 50-52
clinker store **160** 10
clinoprinacoid **351** 24
clip *Atom* **2** 18
clip *Bicycle* **187** 62
clip *Railw.* **202** 9
clipper display **238** 44
clippers, electric ~ **105** 21; **106** 32
clipper ship, English ~ **220** 36
clitellum **357** 26
clitoris **20** 88
Clivia minata **53** 8
cloak **355** 18, 26
cloak, red ~ **319** 27
cloak, short ~ **355** 29
cloak, Spanish ~ **355** 29
cloak, woollen ~ **355** 6
cloak cord **355** 24
cloakroom **48** 34; **207** 70; **315** 5; **318** 1
cloakroom attendant **315** 6, **318** 2
cloakroom hall **315** 5-11
cloakroom ticket **315** 7
cloche **35** 12
clock **191** 38; **211** 37; **212** 16
clock, double ~ **276** 16
clock, electric ~ **191** 79
clock, main ~ **245** 18
clock case **110** 26; **309** 57
clockmaker **109** 1
clocks **110**
clockwork **110** 36
clockwork drive **10** 14
clockwork mechanism **110** 36
clod **63** 7
clog **101** 44; **355** 43
cloister **331** 52
cloister vault **336** 41
closed vertical gate **301** 66
close-up bellows attachment **115** 85
close-up equipment **115** 81-98
close-up lens **117** 55
closing gear **90** 27
closing head **143** 59
closure rail **202** 26
cloth **166** 12; **271** 59
cloth, damask ~ **45** 2
cloth, felt ~ **340** 42
cloth, flannel ~ **128** 48
cloth, linen ~ **206** 11
cloth, sterile ~ **26** 38
cloth, unraised ~ **168** 33
clothes, children's ~ **29**
clothes, teenagers' ~ **29** 48-68
clothes brush **50** 44; **104** 31
clothes closet **43** 1
clothes closet door **46** 2
clothes compartment **212** 63; **267** 30
clothes line **38** 23; **50** 33
clothes louse **81** 41
clothes moth **81** 13
clothes rack **271** 31
clothes rack, movable ~ **103** 17
clothes shop **268** 9
clothing, protective ~ **84** 26; **270** 46
cloth roller **166** 20
cloth-shearing machine, rotary ~ **168** 42
cloth take-up motion **166** 19
cloth take-up roller **166** 47
cloth temple **166** 13
cloud, lenticular ~ **287** 19
cloud chamber photograph **2** 26
cloud chamber track **2** 27
cloud cover **9** 20-24
clouds **8** 1-19, 1-4, 5-12, 13-17
clouds, luminous ~ **7** 22
clouds, noctilucent ~ **7** 22
clout **121** 94
clout nail **121** 94; **122** 96
clove **382** 28
clove carnation **60** 7
clove pink **60** 7
clover, four-leaf ~ **69** 5
clover broadcaster **66** 26
clove tree **382** 26
clown **306** 69; **307** 24
clown, musical ~ **307** 23
clown act **307** 25
club **283** 23
club hammer **126** 77
clubhouse **283** 23
club membership **286** 8
club rush **378** 21
clubs **276** 38
clump of grass **375** 44
cluster of eggs **80** 2, 30
cluster of grapes **78** 5
cluster of stars **3** 26
clutch **191** 44
clutch, dry ~ **190** 78
clutch, fluid ~ **65** 37
clutch, main ~ **65** 39
clutch, multi-plate ~ **190** 78
clutch, single-plate ~ **190** 71
clutch coupling **227** 23
clutch flange **177** 55
clutch lever **188** 32
clutch pedal **191** 44, 96; **192** 28

C major **320** 55, 62
C major scale **320** 45
C minor **320** 59, 65
coach *Lorries etc.* **194** 17
coach *Ball Games* **291** 55; **292** 57
coach, four-axled ~ **208** 3
coach, second ~ **209** 7
coach body **186** 5; **207** 2; **208** 6
coach bolt **202** 7
coach box **186** 8
coach door **186** 11
coaches **186** 1-3,26-39,45,51-54
coach horse **186** 28
coachman **186** 32
coach screw **202** 7
coach step **186** 13
coach wagons **186** 1-3,26-39,45,51-54
coagulating bath **169** 15
coal **170** 1
coal bunker **152** 2; **225** 19
coal conveyor **152** 1
coal distillation, dry ~ **170** 2
coal feed conveyor **199** 37
coal mill **152** 4
coal mine **144** 1-51
coal scuttle **309** 9
coal seam **144** 50
coal shovel **38** 43
coal tar **170** 3
coal tar extraction **156** 18
coal tower **156** 5
coal tower conveyor **156** 4
coal wharf **225** 18
coaming **283** 59
coarse dirt hose **50** 84
coarse fishing **89** 20-31
coastal cruiser **284** 60
coastal lake **13** 44
coaster **221** 99
coaster brake **187** 63
coasting vessel **221** 99
coat **29** 54; **30** 60
coat, black ~ **289** 4
coat, braided ~ **186** 23
coat, cloth ~ **30** 61; **33** 66
coat, dark ~ **289** 4, 13
coat, fur ~ **30** 60
coat, gallooned ~ **186** 23
coat, loden ~ **29** 31; **30** 64
coat, loose-fitting ~ **271** 41
coat, mink ~ **131** 24
coat, ocelot ~ **131** 25
coat, oilskin ~ **228** 7
coat, poncho-style ~ **30** 68
coat, poplin ~ **33** 60
coat, red ~ **289** 13
coat, three-quarter length ~ **271** 21
coat belt **33** 59
coat button **33** 64
coat collar **33** 58
coater **173** 31, 34
coat hanger **41** 3
coat hook **41** 2; **207** 50; **266** 14
coating, bituminous ~ **200** 58
coating of fluorescent material **240** 19
coat-of-arms **254** 1-6
coat-of-arms, marshalled ~ **254** 10-13
coat-of-arms, provincial ~ **252** 12, 14
coat pocket **33** 61
coat rack **41** 1
coat stand **266** 12
coat-tail **33** 14
cob **59** 49
cobalt bomb **2** 28
cobnut **59** 49
coccinellid **358** 37
coccyx **17** 5; **20** 60
cochlea **17** 63
cock *Farm Bldgs.* **62** 37
cock *Dom. Anim.* **73** 21
cockade **264** 8
cockatrice **327** 34
cockchafer **82** 1
cockchafer grub **82** 12
cocker spaniel **70** 38
cocking handle **255** 12
cocking lever **255** 12
cocking piece **121** 30
cock pheasant **88** 77
cock pigeon **73** 33
cockpit *Aircraft* **230** 1-31, 35; **231** 19
cockpit *Police* **264** 2
cockpit *Rowing* **283** 8
cockpit *Sailing* **285** 38
cockpit *Airsports* **288** 10
cockpit canopy **230** 39; **257** 4
cockpit coaming **283** 59
cockpit hood **230** 39; **257** 4
cockroach **81** 17
cockscomb **73** 22
cock's foot **69** 25
cock's head **69** 10
cock's tread **74** 65
cocktail **317** 33
cocktail fork **45** 76
cocktail glass **267** 56
cocktail shaker **267** 61
cocoa *Grocer* **98** 66
cocoa *Trop. Plants* **382** 19
cocoa bean **382** 19
cocoa palm **383** 48
cocoa powder **382** 19
coconut **383** 53
coconut oil **98** 23
coconut palm **383** 48
coconut tree **383** 48
cocoon *Forest Pests* **82** 21
cocoon *Articulates* **358** 51
coco palm **383** 48
cocotte **306** 37
cod **90** 22
code flag halyard **223** 10
code flag signal **223** 9
cod end **90** 22
code pendant **253** 29
code pennant **253** 29
coding keyboard **242** 11
coding station **236** 35
cod line **90** 23
codling moth **58** 62
codlin moth **58** 62
coefficient **345** 4
coelenterate **357** 14; **369** 5, 9, 14, 20
coffee **98** 65-68, 67; **99** 68-70, 68; **265** 19
coffee *Trop. Plants* **382** 6
coffee, instant ~ **99** 70
coffee, pure ~ **98** 65
coffee bean **382** 6
coffee cup **44** 29
coffee grinder, electric ~ **39** 24; **98** 69
coffee maker **39** 38
coffee plant **382** 1
coffee pot **44** 28
coffee roaster **98** 70
coffee service **44** 27
coffee set **44** 27; **265** 18
coffee table **42** 28
coffee tree **382** 1
coffee urn **265** 2
cofferdam **259** 19
coffin **331** 35
coffin chamber **333** 5
cog *Mach. Parts etc.* **143** 83
cog *Ship* **218** 18-26
cog, wooden ~ **91** 9
cognac **98** 59
cog railroad **214** 4-5
cog railway **214** 4-5
cog wheels **143** 82-96
coiffure, upswept ~ **355** 81
coiffures **34** 27-38
coil **89** 21
coiled-coil filament **127** 58
coiler **148** 72
coiler top **163** 62
coil spring **191** 28; **192** 68
coin **252** 1-28
coin, Celtic ~ **328** 37
coin, gold ~ **36** 37
coin, silver ~ **328** 37
coinage **252** 1-28, 40-44
coin-box telephone **236** 9; **237** 3
coin bracelet **36** 36
coin disc **252** 43
coining dies **252** 40-41
coining press **252** 44
coins **252** 1-28
coins, aluminium ~ **252** 1-28
coins, copper ~ **252** 1-28
coins, gold ~ **252** 1-28
coins, nickel ~ **252** 1-28
coins, silver ~ **252** 1-28
coin setting **36** 38
coke **147** 2
coke guide **156** 9
coke loading **156** 15
coke loading bay **156** 12
coke oven **144** 7; **156** 8, 16
coke-oven gas processing **156** 16-45
coke-quenching car **144** 11
coke-quenching tower **144** 10
cokernut **383** 53
coke side bench **156** 13
coke wharf **156** 12
coking coal **156** 1
coking coal tower **144** 9
coking plant *Coal* **144** 7-11

coking plant *Coking* **156** 1-15
coking plant *Synth. Fibres* **170** 2
col **12** 47
cold-drawing **170** 46
cold house **55** 33
cold light source **23** 8
cold room **94** 21-24
cold shelf **96** 12; **98** 3
cold storage room **223** 56
cold store **94** 21-24; **225** 50
cold tap **126** 29
cold water tank **92** 9
cole **383** 1
Coleoptera **358** 24-39
coleseed **383** 1
collar *Jewell.* **36** 16
collar *Dog* **70** 13
collar *Game* **88** 27
collar *Roof* **121** 35, 70
collar *Money* **252** 42
collar *Church* **332** 6
collar *Fish etc.* **364** 39
collar, braided ~ **186** 22
collar, cowl ~ **30** 3
collar, Dutch ~ **71** 28
collar, fur ~ **30** 63
collar, fur-trimmed ~ **30** 63
collar, gallooned ~ **186** 22
collar, ground glass ~ **115** 53, 64
collar, high ~ **355** 74
collar, integral ~ **143** 33
collar, knitted ~ **33** 31
collar, matt ~ **115** 53, 64
collar, padded ~ **101** 20
collar, pointed ~ **71** 15
collar, stand-up ~ **30** 43
collar, turndown ~ **30** 5; **31** 69
collar, wide-falling ~ **355** 56
collar beam **121** 35, 38, 70
collar beam roof **121** 34
collar beam roof structure **121** 37
collar bearing **148** 73
collarbone **17** 6
collating machine **249** 59
collating station **249** 60
collecting bin **201** 20
collecting hopper **92** 20
collecting tank **172** 26
collecting vessel **10** 40, 45
collection **74** 36
collection bag **236** 51
collector **155** 19
collector bow **205** 36
collector well **269** 4
college **262** 1-25
colliery **144** 1-51
collimator **111** 46; **351** 30
colon **342** 17
colon, ascending ~ **20** 19
colon, descending ~ **20** 21
colon, transverse ~ **20** 20
colonnade **274** 9; **334** 67
colophony **323** 11
color *see* colour
Colorado beetle **80** 52
colour **343**
colour analyser **116** 36
colour analyser lamp **116** 37
colour chemicals **116** 52
colour computer **177** 51
colour conversion filter step **117** 38
colour correction, selective ~ **177** 51
colour correction unit **177** 39
colour decoder module **240** 5
colour developer **116** 10
colour enlarger **116** 40
colour filter **316** 49
colour indicator **127** 37
colour light distant signal **203** 9, 14
colour light signal **203** 3
colour medium **316** 49
colour-mixing knob **116** 43-45
colour organ **317** 13
colour output stage module **240** 13
colour pickup tube **240** 36
colour picture tube **240** 15
colour print **340** 28
colour printing paper **116** 51
colour processing chemicals **116** 52
colours of the rainbow **343** 14
colour television receiver **240** 1
colour television set **240** 1
colposcope **23** 5
coltsfoot **380** 8
colubrid **364** 38
Columbian **175** 30
columbine *Gdn. Flowers* **60** 10
Columbine *Carnival* **306** 27
column *Photog.* **116** 42
column *Forging* **139** 10
column *Mach. Tools* **150** 10
column *Bookbind.* **185** 65
column *Script* **342** 45
column *Chem.* **349** 29
column, angled ~ **116** 28
column, bent ~ **113** 21
column, central ~ **114** 46
column, Corinthian ~ **334** 10
column, Doric ~ **334** 8
column, Ionic ~ **334** 9
column, ornamented ~ **333** 18
column, spinal ~ **17** 2-5
column, vertebral ~ **17** 2-5
column box **119** 11, 73
column heading **342** 46
column rule **342** 47
column shaft **334** 26
coma position **21** 24
comb *Infant Care etc.* **28** 8
comb *Dom. Anim.* **73** 22
comb *Hairdresser* **105** 6
comb, adjustable ~ **165** 26
comb, top ~ **163** 67
combat sports **299**
comber **163** 56, 63
comber draw box **163** 60
comb foundation **77** 43
combination, two-piece ~ **30** 45
combination cutting pliers **126** 60; **127** 53
combination lever **210** 30
combination rib weave **171** 25
combination toolholder **149** 41
combine **64** 1-33
combined grasp **296** 42
combine harvester **63** 31; **64** 1-33
combing cylinder **163** 68
combing machine **163** 56
comb setting **165** 36
combustion chamber **232** 37
combustion chamber, external ~ **147** 16
comfrey **375** 45
comic turn **307** 25
comma **342** 18
command key **247** 21
command module **6** 9
command section **234** 65
commencement of speed restriction **203** 39, 42
commissionaire **267** 1; **271** 44; **315** 10
commissure, labial ~ **16** 14; **19** 19
committee **263** 1-2
committee boat **285** 15
committee member **263** 2
committee table **263** 3
common box **373** 19
common buzzard **362** 9
common comfrey **69** 13
common denominator **344** 19
common dolphin **367** 24
common European kite **362** 11
common flea **81** 42
common groundsel **61** 12
common heron **359** 18
common housefly **81** 2
common iguana **364** 32
common mallow **376** 13
common merganser **359** 15
common myrtle **53** 11
common nightshade **379** 5
common orache **61** 24
common pheasant **88** 77
common privet **373** 6
common puffball **381** 20
common roller **360** 6
common salt **170** 13
common seal **367** 19
common sea-swallow **359** 11
common silver fir **372** 1
common swallow **361** 20
common time **320** 32
common toadflax **376** 26
common vetch **69** 18
common viper **364** 40
communicant **332** 27
communication line **127** 23
communication link **237** 50
communications satellite **237** 52
communion cup **330** 10; **332** 29
communion table **330** 4
communion wafer **332** 50
commutator cover **211** 18
companion hatch **258** 24

companion ladder **221** 123; **223** 24; **258** 24
companionway **221** 123; **222** 23; **223** 24; **258** 24
company account **250** 4
company messenger **236** 17
compartment *Forestry* **84** 2
compartment *Railw.* **207** 13; **208** 24
compartment *Store* **271** 6
compartment, secretarial ~ **205** 37; **209** 25
compartment, special ~ **205** 26
compartment, twin-berth ~ **207** 38
compartment, two-berth ~ **207** 38
compartment, two-seat ~ **207** 38
compartment batten **316** 13
compartment door **207** 14
compartment window **207** 52; **208** 8
compass *Drawing Off.* **151** 52
compass *Airsports* **288** 12
compass, divisions of ~ **321** 42-50
compass, fluid ~ **224** 46
compass, gyroscopic ~ **224** 31, 51-53
compass, liquid ~ **224** 46
compass, magnetic ~ **223** 6; **224** 46; **230** 6
compass, mariner's ~ **223** 6
compass, ratchet-type ~ **151** 64
compass, spirit ~ **224** 46
compass, wet ~ **224** 46
compass bowl **224** 49
compass brick **159** 25
compass bridge **223** 4-11; **227** 24
compass card **224** 47
compasses **224** 46-53
compass flat **223** 4-11; **227** 24
compass head **151** 53
compass plane **132** 28
compass platform **223** 4-11; **227** 24
compass repeater **224** 31, 52, 53
compass saw **120** 63; **126** 70; **132** 3
compendium of games **47** 18
compensating airstream **192** 4
compensating roller **181** 45
compensation pendulum **109** 33
compensator **181** 45
compensator level **112** 69
competition bow **305** 54
competitor **282** 28
complementary angle **346** 15
complement of set **348** 7, 8
composing frame **174** 2
composing room **174**; **175**; **176**
composing rule **174** 14
composing stick **174** 13
composition **175** 1-17
composition, computer-controlled ~ **176** 14
compositor **174** 5
compost heap **52** 6
comprehensive school **261** 1-45
compress **27** 4
compressed-air bottle **279** 21
compressed-air braking system **208** 21
compressed-air cylinder **279** 21
compressed-air hose **174** 38
compressed-air inlet **153** 53
compressed-air line *Joiner* **133** 45
compressed-air line *Blacksm.* **138** 5
compressed-air pipe *Forging* **139** 22
compressed-air pipe *Metalwkr.* **140** 17
compressed-air pressure gauge **279** 13
compressed-air reservoir *Agr. Mach.* **64** 92
compressed-air reservoir *Offshore Drill.* **146** 21
compressed-air supply **213** 20
compressed-air system **138** 1
compressed-air tank *Blacksm.* **138** 4
compressed-air tank *Power Plant* **153** 51
compressed-air vessel **269** 17, 50
compressed-gas container **234** 32
compressed-helium bottle **234** 14
compressed-helium tank **234** 43, 50
compression bandage **21** 17
compression plate **2** 25
compressor *Painter* **129** 33
compressor *Blacksm.* **138** 3
compressor *Oil, Petr.* **145** 45
compressor *Energy Sources* **155** 4
compressor *Ship* **223** 51
compressor *Office* **247** 43
compressor, high-pressure ~ **232** 36
compressor, low-pressure ~ **232** 35
computer **23** 53; **177** 70; **195** 1
computer cable **195** 3, 38
computer centre **244**
computer data **238** 13
computer harness **195** 3, 38
computer plug, main ~ **195** 2
computer socket, main ~ **195** 39
computer test, automatic ~ **195** 33
computing scale **98** 12
concave **64** 11
concave ridge **302** 22
concentrator **172** 24, 42, 44, 48, 62
concert grand **325** 40
concertina **324** 36
conch shell trumpet **327** 41
concrete, heavy ~ **119** 72
concrete, rammed ~ **118** 1
concrete, tamped ~ **118** 1
concrete aggregate **118** 36; **119** 26
concrete bucket **119** 38
concrete mixer **47** 40; **118** 33; **119** 29; **201** 23
concrete-mixing plant **201** 19
concrete pump hopper **201** 24
concreter **119** 9
concrete road construction **201** 1-24
concrete scraper **200** 13
concrete spreader **201** 5
concrete spreader box **201** 6
concrete tamper **119** 83
concrete test cube **119** 84
concrete-vibrating compactor **201** 10
concrete vibrator **119** 88
condensate **172** 17
condenser *Brew.* **92** 6
condenser *Optic. Instr.* **112** 8; **113** 32
condenser *Oil, Petr.* **145** 44
condenser *Nucl. Energy* **154** 17, 35
condenser *Energy Sources* **155** 8
condenser *Synth. Fibres* **170** 5
condenser *Paperm.* **172** 30
condenser *Warships* **259** 64
condenser *Chem.* **350** 48
condenser, coiled ~ **349** 6
condenser, universal ~ **112** 66
condensing locomotive **210** 69
condensing tender **210** 69
condition report **195** 7
conductor *Power Plant* **153** 34, 43
conductor *Spa* **274** 21
conductor *Theatre* **315** 26
conductor, copper ~ **127** 43
conductor, electrostatic ~ **230** 51; **231** 27
conductor, high-voltage ~ **152** 33
conduit **334** 54
cone *Phys. Geog.* **11** 24
cone *Mach. Parts etc.* **143** 67
cone *Synth. Fibres* **169** 27
cone *Bicycle* **187** 58
cone *Maths.* **347** 43
cone *Decid. Trees* **371** 32
cone, cross-wound ~ **165** 8, 24
cone, pyrometric ~ **161** 6
cone, truncated ~ **347** 45
cone axis **372** 3
cone breaker **172** 82
cone chest **326** 12-14
cone creel **165** 9
cone drum box **163** 30
cone height **347** 44
cone nozzle **83** 23
cone refiner **172** 27, 60, 73, 83
cone scale **372** 8, 14, 27, 38
cone-winding frame **165** 1

cone-winding machine **169** 26
coney **366** 24
confectionery **97** 17-47; **98** 75-86
confectionery unit **97** 67-70
conference circuit **242** 22
conference connection **242** 22
conference grouping **246** 31-36
conference hook-up **242** 22
conference table **246** 31
confetti **306** 62
configuration, angular ~ **248** 39
confluence **224** 90
conga drum **324** 55
congregation **330** 29
conifers **372** 1-71
Conium **379** 4
connecting corridor **208** 11
connecting door, sliding ~ **207** 19
connecting element **248** 48
connecting hose **208** 16, 21
connecting lead **25** 20, 56
connecting piece **350** 56
connecting rod *Agr.* **63** 20
connecting rod *Intern. Combust. Eng.* **190** 21
connecting rod *Railw.* **210** 11
connecting-rod bearing **192** 25
connecting seal, rubber ~ **207** 8; **208** 12
connecting shaft **63** 20
connecting system, automatic ~ **237** 25
connection, internal ~ **245** 14
connection, pneumatically sprung ~ **194** 45
connection, rubber ~ **194** 45
connection of modules **242** 70
connection rebar **119** 10, 71
connector *Moon L.* **6** 28
connector *Weaving* **166** 52
connector, thermoplastic ~ **127** 29
connector fitting **287** 31
consignment, general ~ **206** 4
consignment, mixed ~ **206** 4
consignment note **206** 30
console *Joiner* **133** 24
console *Serv. Stat.* **196** 29
console *School* **261** 37
console *Music. Instr.* **326** 36-52
console operator **244** 3
console piano **325** 1
console typewriter **244** 4
consolidating beam **201** 2
constant of integration **345** 14
constellations **3** 9-48
construction, close-seamed ~ **285** 54
construction, wooden ~ **260** 72
construction of circuit **242** 72
construction set **48** 22
construction site **118; 119**
construction unit, precast ~ **215** 58
construction vehicle **255** 75
consulting room **23** 1
contact, auxiliary ~ **153** 57
contact, magnetic ~ **242** 71
contact arc **237** 43
contact arm **237** 44
contact arm tag **237** 46
contact breaker **242** 49
contact field **237** 45
contact goniometer **351** 27
contact maker **127** 38-39
contact sleeve, metal ~ **166** 31
contact spring **127** 28
contact wire maintenance vehicle **211** 41, 44-54
contact wire voltage indicator **211** 28
container **206** 57; **221** 22; **226** 3, 6
container *Chem.* **350** 61
container, plastic ~ **83** 25
container, railroad-owned ~ **206** 19
container, railway-owned ~ **206** 19
container, shielded ~ **154** 82
container berth **225** 48; **226** 1
container car **206** 58
container carrier truck **225** 47
container for vegetables **96** 51
container platform **194** 27
container ship **221** 89; **225** 45
container station **206** 54
container terminal **225** 48; **226** 1
container wagon **206** 58
containment, steel ~ **154** 21
contents **342** 40
continents **14** 12-18
continuity girl **310** 39
continuity tester **127** 55
continuous feed grate **199** 34
continuous filament process **162** 48
continuous reheating furnace **148** 69
continuous rolling mill train **148** 66-75
contouche **355** 66
contour **15** 62
contour, submarine ~ **15** 11
contour knife **340** 10
contrabass **323** 23
contrabassoon **323** 28
contrabass tuba **323** 44
contracted burial **328** 17
contractile vacuole **357** 5
contra octave **321** 43
contrast control **240** 32; **249** 36
contrast medium injector **27** 15
control, digital ~ **242** 35
control, manual ~ **115** 52
control, sliding ~ **311** 18
control and monitoring panel **311** 8
control arm **240** 29; **313** 11
control board **153** 1
control box *Moon L.* **6** 23
control box *Mach. Tools* **150** 36
control box *Offset Platem.* **179** 33
control button *Hosp.* **25** 30
control button *Cine Film* **117** 98
control button *Text. Finish.* **168** 40
control button *Navig.* **224** 32
control button *Audiovis.* **243** 13
control button *Office* **246** 19
control button *School* **261** 45
control cable **271** 53
control column **230** 24; **257** 8; **288** 14
control console *Power Plant* **153** 1-6
control console *Photomech. Reprod.* **177** 5
control console *Films* **311** 12
control console *Theatre* **316** 2
control desk *Hosp.* **27** 10
control desk *Brew.* **93** 1
control desk *Iron & Steel* **147** 66
control desk *Power Plant* **153** 1-6
control desk *Nucl. Energy* **154** 80
control desk *Offset Print.* **180** 16
control desk *Photograv.* **182** 28
control desk *Films* **311** 12
control desk, driver's ~ **212** 32
control desk, engineer's ~ **212** 32
control device **26** 7
control frame **287** 46
control gear **164** 38
control grip *Pest Contr.* **83** 19
control grip *Photog.* **115** 76
control handle, cranked ~ **168** 52
control knob *Hosp.* **25** 49; **27** 41
control knob *Electrotyp. etc.* **178** 15
controller **197** 27
controller, rear ~ **197** 8
controller handwheel **211** 20; **212** 12
control lever *Agr. Mach.* **64** 59
control lever *Pest Contr.* **83** 21
control lever *Cine Film* **117** 63
control lever *Cotton Spin.* **163** 28
control lever *Road Constr.* **201** 8, 12
control lever *Navig.* **224** 19
control lever *Broadcast.* **240** 29
control lever *Films* **313** 11
control lever *Theatre* **316** 58
control line model **288** 89
control linkage **190** 30
control loudspeaker **311** 13

control mechanism **181** 26
control module **238** 45; **240** 11
control panel *Hosp.* **26** 20; **27** 10
control panel *Roof & Boilerr.* **38** 67
control panel *Dairy.* **76** 11
control panel *Brew.* **93** 1, 20
control panel *Offshore Drill.* **146** 28
control panel *Power Plant* **153** 1
control panel *Nucl. Energy* **154** 80
control panel *Paperm.* **173** 43
control panel *Photomech. Reprod.* **177** 36, 60
control panel *Offset Platem.* **179** 10, 17
control panel *Offset Print.* **180** 74
control panel *Bookbind.* **185** 2
control panel *Broadcast.* **240** 31
control panel *Films* **311** 4, 17, 29
control panel, bracket-mounted ~ **177** 6
control panel, electric ~ **168** 25, 58
control panel, hinged ~ **177** 6
control platform **226** 55
control point **203** 25
control rod *Nucl. Energy* **154** 24
control rod *Warships* **259** 69
control rod drive **154** 23
control room *Hosp.* **25** 1-9
control room *Offshore Drill.* **146** 32
control room *Power Plant* **152** 19, 28; **153** 1-8
control room *Railw.* **214** 65
control room *Broadcast.* **238** 17
control room *Theatre* **316** 1
control room, central ~ *Dairy.* **76** 7
control room, central ~ *Brew.* **92** 25
control room window **238** 38
controls **25** 29; **153** 6; **271** 48
control speaker **238** 15
control station **217** 45
control stick **230** 24; **257** 8; **288** 14
control switch *Hosp.* **25** 29
control switch *Electrotyp. etc.* **178** 36
control switch *Offset Print.* **180** 74
control switch *Navig.* **224** 23
control tap **172** 9
control tower **233** 17; **287** 12
control unit *Hosp.* **26** 7
control unit *Opticn.* **111** 29
control unit *Blacksm.* **138** 31
control unit *Mach. Tools* **150** 36
control unit *Photomech. Reprod.* **177** 51
control unit *Electrotyp. etc.* **178** 29
control unit *Offset Platem.* **179** 33
control unit *Audio* **241** 40
control unit, central ~ *Hosp.* **25** 1, 20
control unit, central ~ *Inf. Tech.* **242** 2
control unit, electric ~ **168** 58
control valve **153** 52
control weight **166** 63
control well **117** 98
control wheel *Text. Finish.* **168** 40
control wheel *Railw.* **212** 81
convenience outlet **127** 5
convenience outlet, double ~ **127** 6
convent **15** 63
convergence **224** 90
convergence module **240** 12
conversion filter step **117** 38
converter **92** 42
converter bottom, solid ~ **147** 47
converter chimney **147** 67
converter top, conical ~ **147** 45
converter tube **27** 19
convertible **193** 9
convertiplane **232** 31
conveyances **186** 1-54
conveyor *Poultry Farm* **74** 22
conveyor *Dairy.* **76** 23
conveyor *Bldg. Site* **118** 77
conveyor *Synth. Fibres* **169** 32
conveyor *Paperm.* **172** 79
conveyor *Photograv.* **182** 30
conveyor *Refuse Coll.* **199** 36
conveyor *Docks* **225** 51
conveyor belt *Dairy.* **76** 23
conveyor belt *Bldg. Site* **118** 77
conveyor belt *Synth. Fibres* **169** 32
conveyor belt *Paperm.* **172** 79
conveyor belt *Photograv.* **182** 30
conveyor belt *Docks* **225** 51
conveyor brattice **163** 13
conveyor trolley **74** 39
conveyor unit **83** 59
cook, head ~ **207** 34
cooker **96** 47
cooker, calor gas ~ **278** 33
cooker, double-burner ~ **278** 33
cooker, electric ~ **39** 12; **46** 32
cooker, gas ~ **39** 12; **278** 33
cooker hood **39** 17; **46** 31
cooker unit **39** 12-17
cooking liquor **172** 46
cooking pot **39** 29; **40** 12
cookroom **223** 42
coolant **149** 44
coolant bore **242** 54
coolant-collecting plant **92** 7
coolant feed line **235** 38
coolant flow passage **154** 29
coolant pump **190** 61
coolant pump, primary ~ **154** 25
coolant supply pipe **138** 26; **149** 25
coolant system **154** 55
coolant tray **149** 44
cooler *Oil, Petr.* **145** 44
cooler *Coking* **156** 27
coolie **353** 43
cooling **170** 34
cooling compressor **92** 22
cooling cylinder **170** 27
cooling fan **312** 34
cooling rib **189** 20; **190** 80; **242** 60
cooling roll **173** 25
cooling roller **180** 28
cooling room **281** 28
cooling system **154** 48
cooling table **97** 67
cooling tank **162** 15
cooling tower *Coal* **144** 15
cooling tower *Nucl. Energy* **154** 39
cooling tower *Synth. Fibres* **170** 43
cooling unit **209** 21; **212** 26, 77
cooling water *Nucl. Energy* **154** 18
cooling water *Railw.* **212** 65, 78
cooling water bore **242** 54
cooling water flow circuit **154** 10
cooling water heat exchanger **155** 3
cooling water pipe *Opticn.* **111** 31
cooling water pipe *Power Plant* **152** 27
cooling water pipe *Car* **191** 10
cooling water temperature gauge **212** 21
cooling water thermostat **190** 62
cool shelf **266** 49
coon **368** 9
cooper **130** 11
coordinate **347** 2-3, 8
coordinate, right-angled ~ **347** 1
coot **359** 20
cop, full ~ **163** 2
cope **148** 19
copier, automatic ~ **249** 32
copier, web-fed ~ **249** 32
coping stone **37** 37
copper **305** 6, 18
copper, unworked ~ **260** 64
copper cylinder, polished ~ **182** 7
copper plate **179** 9
copperplate, polished ~ **340** 53
copperplate engraver **340** 44
copperplate engraving **340** 14-24
copperplate press **340** 36
copper sulphate **351** 26
copy **176** 3; **177** 18
copy, received ~ **245** 2

copy, transmitted ~ **245** 2
copyboard **177** 14, 22, 30
copy cylinder **177** 64
copy delivery **249** 43
copyholder **177** 15
copying camera, overhead ~ **177** 1
copying stand **115** 90, 92, 93
copypod **115** 90
copy stand **115** 90, 92, 93
coquille **294** 38, 43
coral, precious ~ **357** 17
coral, red ~ **357** 17
coral animal **357** 17
coral Clavaria **381** 32
coral colony **357** 18
coral evergreen **377** 12
coral polyp **357** 19
coral reef **13** 32
cor anglais **323** 38
cord **206** 12
cord, warp-faced ~ **171** 26, 27
cordate **370** 35
corded ware **328** 10
cordon, horizontal ~ **52** 17, 29
cordon, quadruple ~ **52** 1
cordon, vertical ~ **52** 2
core *Phys. Geog.* **11** 5
core *Soft Fruit* **58** 36, 59
core *Iron Foundry etc.* **148** 36
core *Power Plant* **153** 17, 36
core *Electrotyp. etc.* **178** 18
core, soft-lead ~ **87** 56
core, special ~ **301** 47
core bit **145** 21
core print **148** 37
corking machine, semi-automatic ~ **79** 10
corkscrew **40** 18; **45** 46
corkscrew piton **300** 40
cormorant **359** 10
corn **68** 1, 31
corn camomile **61** 8
corn campion **61** 6
corn cob **68** 36
corn cockle **61** 6
cornea **19** 47
cornelian cherry **373** 30, 32
corner *Games* **276** 27
corner *Ball Games* **291** 41; **292** 18
corner *Sports* **305** 6; **305** 8
corner *Maths.* **347** 33
corner bottom slate **122** 77
corner brace **120** 26
corner flag **291** 8
corner kick **291** 41
corner peg **292** 79
corner seat **207** 58; **265** 10; **266** 38
corner section **42** 26
corner stile **120** 52
corner strut **120** 52
corner stud **120** 52
corner table **246** 34; **266** 39
corner unit **39** 27
corner work **149** 51
cornet **323** 43
cornett, curved ~ **322** 12
cornfield **63** 32
corn flower **61** 1
corn head **64** 35
cornice *Carp.* **120** 34
cornice *Mountain.* **300** 20
cornice *Art* **334** 11-14; **335** 48
corn marigold **61** 7
corn poppy **61** 2
corn removal **92** 38
corn salad **57** 38
corn spurrey **69** 12
corn stem **68** 5
corn weevil **81** 26
corolla **59** 11; **378** 4
corolla, papilionaceous ~ **57** 1
corona **334** 12
corona, solar ~ **4** 39
Corona Borealis **3** 31
coronet, baronet's ~ **254** 43
coronet, baronial ~ **254** 44
coronet, count's ~ **254** 45
coronet, ducal ~ **254** 39
coronet, elector's ~ **254** 41
coronet, prince's ~ **254** 40
coronets **254** 37-46
coronets of rank **254** 43-45
corporation stock **251** 11-19
corps de ballet **314** 25
corpus callosum **17** 44
corpus cavernosum and spongiosum **20** 67
corral **319** 14
correcting fluid **247** 13
correcting lens **115** 22
correcting paper **247** 12
correction lens **115** 72
corrector, universal ~ **238** 48
corrector plate **113** 11
correspondence **245** 19
correspondence file **22** 12
correspondent **342** 54
corresponding angle **346** 12
corrida **319** 1-33
corridor *Railw.* **207** 11
corridor *Winter Sp.* **301** 71
corridor compartment coach **207** 1-21
Corvidae **361** 1-3
corydalis **377** 8
cosine **346** 32
cosmetics **99** 27-35
cosmetics gondola **99** 23
cossack trousers **30** 44
costume, theatrical ~ **315** 51
costume designer **315** 38
costumes, historical ~ **355**
cot, collapsible ~ **28** 1
cotangent **346** 32
cottage, dikereeve's ~ **216** 45
cottage, ferryman's ~ **216** 45
cottage piano **325** 1
cotter punch **137** 31
cotton *Cotton Spin.* **163** 1-13
cotton *Industr. Plants* **383** 16
cotton bale, compressed ~ **163** 3
cotton bobbin **100** 29
cotton boll, ripe ~ **163** 1
cotton feed **163** 9
cotton-feeding brattice **163** 8
cotton grass **377** 18
cotton reel **104** 9
cotton rush **377** 18
cotton spinning **163; 164**
cotton wool **99** 28
cotton wool ball **99** 30
cotyledon **370** 87
couch *Doc.* **22** 43
couch *Weeds* **61** 30
coucher **173** 49
couch grass **61** 30
couchman **173** 49
coudé ray path **5** 3
coudière **329** 48
coulee **13** 45
coulter **65** 10
coulter, disc ~ **64** 66; **65** 69
coulter, drill ~ **65** 76
coulter, rolling ~ **64** 66; **65** 69
coulter, skim ~ **65** 68
counter *Child. Rm.* **47** 28
counter *Shoem.* **100** 59
counter *Shoes* **101** 37
counter *Cotton Spin.* **163** 61
counter *Composing Rm.* **175** 41
counter *Offset Print.* **180** 74
counter *Railw.* **207** 31
counter *Café* **265** 1
counter *Restaurant* **266** 1-11
counter *Water* **269** 59
counter *Ball Games* **291** 23
counter *Winter Sp.* **302** 18
counter *Flea Market* **309** 83
counter, cashier's ~ **250** 1
counter, extra ~ **271** 64
counter, special ~ **271** 64
counter assistant **265** 7
counterbalance **241** 22
counterbalance weight **242** 50
counterblow hammer **139** 5
counterbrace **215** 35
counter clerk **236** 16
counter gear assembly **269** 55
counter officer **236** 16
counterpoise *Optic. Instr.* **113** 19
counterpoise *Hydr. Eng.* **217** 76
counterpoise *Docks* **226** 50
counterpoise *Army* **255** 78
counter stamp machine **236** 19
counter tube **2** 21
counter tube casing **2** 20
counterweight *Overh. Irrign.* **67** 37
counterweight *Optic. Instr.* **113** 10
counterweight *Bldg. Site* **119** 33
counterweight *Forging* **139** 34
counterweight *Hydr. Eng.* **217** 76
counterweight *Docks* **226** 50
counterweight *Audio* **241** 22
counterweight *Army* **255** 78
counting, automatic ~ **74** 52
counting beads **47** 14
counting blocks **48** 17
counting mechanism **309** 83
counting out **299** 42
country estate **15** 94
countryside in winter **304**

coupé *Carriages* **186** 3
coupé *Car* **193** 28
couple **267** 46; **272** 72; **317** 17-18
couple, bridal ~ **332** 15-16
coupler *Bldg. Site* **119** 53
coupler *Plumb. etc.* **126** 43
coupler *Music. Instr.* **326** 41
couplet **321** 23
coupling *Agr. Mach.* **65** 61
coupling *Bldg. Site* **119** 53
coupling *Railw.* **208** 16; **210** 2; **212** 82; **214** 18
coupling, front ~ **65** 50
coupling, unlinked ~ **208** 19
coupling bolt **202** 15
coupling hook **122** 64
coupling hose **208** 21
coupling link **208** 17
coupling screw **208** 18
coupling spindle **148** 58
coupon **251** 17
coupon sheet **251** 17
courbette **71** 6
course *Weaves* **171** 42
course *Rivers* **216** 9
course *Winter Sp.* **301** 44
course, damp-proof ~ **123** 4
course, first ~ **118** 67
course, second ~ **118** 68
course, triangular ~ **285** 16
course counter **167** 43
course-marking flag **301** 45
course markings **289** 19
courser **70** 24
court dress **355** 79
courtesy light **191** 77
court shoe **101** 29
court shoe, fabric ~ **101** 54
court shoe, sling-back ~ **101** 53
couter **329** 48
cove **13** 7
cover *Atom* **2** 14
cover *Dining Rm.* **44** 5
cover *Tablew. etc.* **45** 3-12
cover *Optic. Instr.* **113** 13
cover *Photog.* **115** 11
cover *Bldg. Site* **118** 22
cover *Bookbind.* **185** 40
cover *Bicycle* **187** 30
cover *Water* **269** 56
cover, canvas ~ **255** 98
cover, glass ~ *Kitch. Utensils* **40** 7
cover, glass ~ *Energy Sources* **155** 33
cover, hinged ~ **309** 27
cover, nylon ~ **207** 68
cover, porous ~ **199** 21
cover, screw-in ~ **115** 11
cover, screw-on ~ **83** 40
cover, soundproof ~ **310** 48
cover, terry ~ **49** 14
cover, transparent ~ **249** 27
coverall **29** 23
cover cylinder **184** 10
covering **287** 40
covering, felt ~ **353** 20
covering, green baize ~ **277** 15
covering material **184** 12
cover projection **243** 47
coving **336** 10
cow **73** 1
cowberry **377** 23
cowboy **306** 31; **319** 36
cowboy boot **101** 9
cowcatcher **210** 34
cow corn **68** 31
cowl *Blacksm.* **137** 7
cowl *Warships* **258** 21, 59
cowl *Church* **331** 56
cowl collar **30** 3
cowl neck jumper **30** 2
Cowper's gland **20** 75
cowshed **62** 7
cowslip **376** 8
cox **283** 11
coxed single **283** 18
coxless four **283** 9
coxless pair **283** 15
CQR anchor **286** 16
Crab *Astron.* **4** 56
crab *Shipbuild.* **222** 14, 28
crab *Articulates* **358** 1
crab *Deep Sea Fauna* **369** 16
crab apple tree **58** 51
crab louse **81** 40
cracker **306** 50
cracker, catalytic ~ **145** 48
crackowe **355** 42
cradle **237** 13
cradle, bouncing ~ **28** 2
cradle, double ~ **214** 68
cradle, two-wheel ~ **214** 69
cradle frame, lightweight ~ **189** 17
cradle switch **237** 13
craft room **260** 46-85
crakeberry **377** 23
cramp **119** 58; **120** 66
cramp iron **119** 58; **121** 97
crampon **300** 48
crampon cable fastener **300** 52
crampon strap **300** 51
Crane *Astron.* **3** 42
crane *Warships* **258** 88
crane, floating ~ **225** 10; **226** 48
crane, flying ~ **232** 16
crane, hammer-headed ~ **222** 7
crane, overhead ~ **222** 20
crane, polar ~ **154** 38
crane, revolving ~ **146** 3
crane, travelling ~ **147** 41; **222** 20
crane cable **222** 13
crane framework **226** 53
crane hoist, auxiliary ~ **147** 61
crane hook **139** 45
crane motor **157** 28
crane's bill **53** 1; **376** 24
crane track **119** 27
crane truck **270** 47
crank *Agr. Mach.* **64** 43
crank *Bicycle* **187** 41
crank *Road Constr.* **201** 18
crankcase **190** 40; **242** 51
crankcase scavenging **242** 59
crank drive **217** 53
crankshaft **166** 50; **190** 23; **192** 29
crankshaft, counterbalanced ~ **242** 50
crankshaft bearing **190** 22; **192** 23
crankshaft bleed **192** 22
crankshaft drilling **192** 22
crankshaft tributary **192** 22
crankshaft wheel **166** 51
crash bar **188** 18
crash barrier **259** 17
crash hat **290** 3
crash helmet **301** 13; **303** 14
crate **76** 30; **206** 5
crater **312** 44
crater, volcanic ~ **11** 16
cravat **32** 40
craw **73** 20
crawl **282** 37
crawl stroke **282** 37
crayon **47** 26; **338** 5
crayon, wax ~ **48** 11; **260** 6
crayon engraving **340** 14-24
cream **99** 27, 46
cream, whipped ~ **97** 28; **265** 5
cream cake **97** 21, 24
creamer **265** 21
creamery butter machine **76** 33
cream heater **76** 13
cream jar **28** 13
cream jug **265** 21
cream maturing vat **76** 31
cream pie **97** 24
cream puff **97** 27
cream roll **97** 17
cream separator **76** 14
cream supply pump **76** 40
cream tank **76** 19
crease *Men's Wear* **33** 6
crease *Ball Games* **292** 72
crease *Ethnol.* **353** 44
creatures, fabulous ~ **327** 1-61
creatures, mythical ~ **327** 1-61
creek *Phys. Geog.* **13** 8
creek *Map* **15** 80
creel *Fish Farm.* **89** 25
creel *Cotton Spin.* **164** 28, 58
creel *Weaving* **165** 25
creel, full ~ **164** 41
creeper **51** 5; **52** 5; **53** 2; **57** 8
creeping foot **357** 28
creese **353** 44
crenate **370** 46
crenel **329** 18
crenellation **329** 6
crepe paper **49** 11
crepidoma **334** 4
crescendo **321** 31
crescendo roller **326** 49
crescendo roller indicator **326** 37
crescent *Astron.* **4** 3, 7
crescent *Bakery* **97** 32
crescent *Supermkt.* **99** 13
Crescent *Flags* **253** 19

crescent-forming machine **97** 64
crescent moon **4** 3, 7
crescent roll **97** 32; **99** 13
crescent wing **229** 18
crest *Horse* **72** 12, 14
crest *Dom. Anim.* **73** 22
crest *Heraldry* **254** 1
crest, dorsal ~ **364** 21
crest, erectile ~ **359** 26
Cresta tobogganing **303** 22-24
crest coronet **254** 12
crested lark **361** 19
crested newt **364** 20
cresting **305** 65
crest of dam **217** 59
crests **254** 1,11,30-36
crevasse **12** 50; **300** 23
crew compartment **6** 41; **235** 16
crew cut **34** 11
crew entry tunnel **235** 71
cricket **292** 70-76
cricket bat **292** 75
crimping **170** 59
crimping iron **106** 26
crimson clover **69** 4
crinoline **355** 72
crispbread **97** 50
criss-cross skip **297** 44
cristobalite **1** 12
croaking sac **364** 25
crocket **335** 38
croisé **314** 16
croissant **97** 32; **99** 13
crojack **220** 26
crojack yard **220** 25
cromlech **328** 16
crook **324** 71
crook of the arm **16** 44
crop **73** 20
crops, arable ~ **68**
croquant **98** 85
croquet **292** 77-82
croquet ball **292** 82
croquet mallet **292** 81
croquet player **292** 80
Cross *Astron.* **3** 44
cross *Plumb. etc.* **126** 50
cross *School* **260** 28
cross *Church* **331** 25
cross, ansate ~ **332** 63
cross, cardinal's ~ **332** 65
cross, Constantinian ~ **332** 67
cross, fivefold ~ **332** 72
cross, Greek ~ **332** 56
cross, Latin ~ **332** 33
cross, Papal ~ **332** 66
cross, patriarchal ~ **332** 64
cross, processional ~ **330** 47
cross, quintuple ~ **332** 72
cross, Russian ~ **332** 57
cross, saltire ~ **332** 60
cross, St. Andrew's ~ **332** 60
cross, St. Anthony's ~ **332** 59
cross, St. Peter's ~ **332** 58
cross arm **152** 37
cross arms **10** 30
crossbar *Goldsm. etc.* **108** 5
crossbar *Bicycle* **187** 16
crossbar *Ball Games* **291** 36
crossbar *Athletics* **298** 14, 34
cross beam **119** 57
cross bearer **331** 43
cross bond, English ~ **118** 65
cross botonnée **332** 71
crossbrace **215** 35
cross bracing wire **229** 12
crossbuck **202** 41
cross chain conveyor **157** 22
cross conveyor **157** 20
cross-country *Equest.* **289** 17
cross-country *Winter Sp.* **301** 42
cross-country binding **301** 15
cross-country boot **301** 16
cross-country equipment **301** 14-20
cross-country gear **301** 17
cross-country lorry **194** 1
cross-country motorcycle **189** 16
cross-country pole **301** 20
cross-country race **290** 33
cross-country ski **301** 14
cross-country stretch-suit **301** 43
cross-country tyre **194** 4
cross-cut **144** 31
cross-cut, octagonal ~ **36** 53
cross-cut, oval hexagonal ~ **36** 63
cross-cut, round hexagonal ~ **36** 65
cross-cut, trapezium ~ **36** 58
cross-cut chain saw **157** 38
cross-cut chisel **140** 25
cross-cut saw **120** 14
crosses, Christian ~ **332** 55-72
crossfall **200** 57
cross fold knife **185** 12
cross fold unit, third ~ **185** 14
cross grasp **296** 43
cross hairs **87** 32
cross hairs, double ~ **115** 66
cross hatch **340** 54
cross head *Forging* **139** 37
cross head *Railw.* **210** 27
crossing **205** 15
crossing, intercom-controlled ~ **202** 47
crossing, telephone-controlled ~ **202** 47
crossing keeper **202** 42
crossing the bar **298** 31
crossjack **220** 26
crossjack yard **220** 25
cross joint **151** 50
cross lacing **29** 37
crosslet **332** 68
cross moline **332** 69
cross of Jerusalem **332** 70
cross of Lorraine **332** 62
cross of the Passion **332** 55
crossover **241** 14
crossover, double ~ **203** 49-52
crossover network **241** 14
cross piece *Bldg. Site* **119** 61
cross piece *Shipbuild.* **222** 15
cross piece *Fencing* **294** 42
cross rib **335** 31
cross slide **149** 23, 39; **150** 12
cross-slide guide **174** 48
cross spider **358** 45
cross stitch **102** 5
cross stitch, Russian ~ **102** 9
cross strut **119** 67
cross tie *Roof* **121** 30
crosstie *Station* **205** 60
crosstie, concrete ~ **202** 37
crosstie, coupled ~ **202** 14, 38
crosstie, steel ~ **202** 36
cross total counter **242** 3
crosstrees **223** 37; **284** 13
crosstrees, starboard ~ **286** 9
cross treflée **332** 71
cross vault **335** 31-32
crosswalk **198** 11; **268** 24, 51
cross-winding the threads **165** 11
cross wire, overhead ~ **197** 42
cross wires **87** 32
crotchet **320** 15
crotchet rest **320** 23
crouch **295** 6, 23
crouch start **298** 4
croup **72** 31
croupier **275** 4
croupier, head ~ **275** 6
crow **86** 50, 51; **361** 2
crowbar **158** 32
crowberry **377** 23
crowfoot **375** 8
crown *Man* **16** 1; **19** 37
crown *Dent.* **24** 28
crown *Forging* **139** 36
crown *Bridges* **215** 31
crown *Park* **272** 60
crown *Art* **336** 39
crown *Hist. Cost.* **355** 21
crown *South. Fruits* **384** 29
crown, gold ~ **24** 28
crown, mural ~ **254** 46
crown block **145** 4
crown cork **93** 27
crown cork bottle-opener **45** 47
crown cork closure **93** 27
crown cork opener **45** 47
crown of hooks **81** 38
crown-of-the-field **61** 6
crown of tree **370** 3
crownpiece **71** 10
crowns **254** 37-46
crown safety platform **145** 3
crown wheel *Clocks* **110** 41
crown wheel *Mach. Parts etc.* **143** 93
crows **361** 1-3
crow's nest **223** 38
crucible, clay ~ **350** 31
crucible, graphite ~ **108** 10
crucible tongs **108** 11; **350** 32
crucifer **331** 43
crucifix *Gymn.* **296** 50
crucifix *Church* **332** 33
crucifix, processional ~ **331** 42
crude benzene, production of ~ **156** 41
crude benzene tank **156** 42
crude benzol, production of ~ **156** 41

crude benzol tank **156** 42
crude oil production **145** 22-27
crude phenol tank **156** 40
crude tar tank **156** 32
cruet set **332** 44
cruet stand **266** 22
cruiser **286** 5
cruiser keelboat **285** 29-34
cruiser stern **285** 45
cruising yacht **284** 60
crumb **97** 3
crumhorn **322** 6
crupper **71** 34; **72** 31
crupper-strap **71** 34
crusader **329** 72
crushed grape transporter **78** 16
crusher **172** 5
crusher, coarse ~ **158** 19
crusher, fine ~ **158** 19
crusher, gyratory ~ **158** 19
crusher, primary ~ **158** 17
crusher, rotary ~ **158** 19
crush hat **35** 36
crush room **315** 12-13
crust **97** 4, 5
crust, earth's ~ **11** 1
crust, outer ~ **11** 1
crustacean **369** 12, 15, 16
crustaceans **358** 1-2
crusta petrosa **19** 29
crutch **148** 15
Crux **3** 44
cryosurgery **22** 63
Cryptolestes **81** 27
crystal **351** 29
crystal centre **351** 3
crystal combinations **351** 1-26
crystal cone **77** 21
crystal detector **309** 23
crystal forms **351** 1-26
crystallography **351**
crystallometry **351** 27-33
crystal plate glass **124** 5
crystals **351** 1-26
crystal set **309** 23
crystal system **351** 1-17
cub **88** 42
cube *Kindergart.* **48** 21
cube *Maths.* **347** 30
cube *Crystals* **351** 2, 14, 16
cube root **345** 2
cube sugar **98** 53
cubic crystal system **351** 1-17
cubitière **329** 48
cuckoo **359** 30
cuckoo clock **109** 31
cuckoo flower **375** 11; **376** 21
cuckoo pint **379** 9
cucumber **57** 13; **99** 83
cue **277** 9
cue ball, white ~ **277** 11
cue rack **277** 19
cue tip, leather ~ **277** 10
cuff **25** 16; **30** 14; **32** 45
cuff, fur ~ **30** 62
cuff, fur-trimmed ~ **30** 62
cuff, inflatable ~ **23** 34
cuff, ribbed ~ **30** 30
cuff link **32** 46; **36** 21
cuff protector **324** 17
cuff slit **30** 48
cuirass **329** 46
cuish **329** 52
cuissard **329** 52
cuisse **329** 52
culicid **358** 16
culm *Arable Crops* **68** 6
culm *Coking* **156** 14
culotte **31** 48; **29** 59
cultivator *Market Gdn.* **55** 21
cultivator *Agr. Mach.* **65** 55
cultivator, three-pronged ~ **56** 13
cultivator attachment **56** 21
culture, bacteriological ~ **261** 29
cumulonimbus **8** 17; **287** 26
cumulonimbus cloud **287** 26
cumulus **8** 1; **287** 22
cumulus cloud **287** 22
cumulus congestus **8** 2
cumulus humilis **8** 1
cup *Bicycle* **187** 79
cup *Decid. Trees* **371** 5
cup, baby's ~ **28** 27
cup, hemispherical ~ **10** 30
cup, rust-proof ~ **122** 102
cup, zinc ~ **122** 102
cup bearer **329** 69
cupboard **246** 5
cupboard, children's ~ **47** 21
cupboard, sliding-door ~ **248** 38
cupboard base unit **42** 6
cupboard unit **42** 7
cupboard unit, two-door ~ **46** 6
cup cymbals **324** 50
cupid **272** 20
cupola *Iron Foundry etc.* **148** 1
cupola *Art* **334** 58
cupola, bulbous ~ **336** 3
cupola furnace **148** 1
cupule **59** 42; **371** 5; **384** 52
curb **198** 6; **272** 25
curb bit **71** 13, 52
curb chain **71** 12
curbstone **198** 7
curbstone broker **251** 5
curbstoner **251** 5
curd cheese **76** 38
curd cheese, packeted ~ **76** 45
curd cheese machine **76** 38
curd cheese packing machine **76** 44
curd cheese pump **76** 39
curds separator **76** 41
curettage **26** 52
curette **22** 50; **26** 52
curing floor **92** 18
curing kiln **92** 30
curl **34** 3
curl brush **105** 13
curl clip **105** 14
curler *Hairdresser* **105** 4
curler *Winter Sp.* **302** 41
curling **302** 41-43
curling broom **302** 43
curling brush **302** 43
curling iron **105** 5; **106** 31
curling stone **302** 42
curling tongs **105** 5; **106** 31
curly kale **57** 34
currant **58** 12, 14; **98** 9
currant bush **52** 19; **58** 10
current **216** 9
current, cold ~ **9** 29
current, three-phase ~ **153** 42
current, warm ~ **9** 28
current collector *Lorries etc.* **194** 41
current collector *Tram* **197** 2, 23
current collector *Railw.* **207** 24, 75; **211** 2, 30
current meter *Railw.* **212** 18
current meter *Rivers* **216** 43
current rating **127** 37
currents, oceanic ~ **14** 30-45
current transformer **153** 58
current/voltage meter **242** 77
currycomb **71** 54
curtail step **123** 18, 42
curtain *Dining Rm.* **44** 13
curtain *Railw.* **207** 56
curtain *Chivalry* **329** 15
curtain, iron ~ **316** 24
curtain, theatrical **316** 23
curtain department **271** 66
curtain lace **167** 29
curtain operation, types of ~ **315** 1-4
curtain rail **44** 15
curtain wall **329** 15
curvature **346** 22
curve *Sports* **305** 19
curve *Maths.* **347** 11, 18
curve, ballistic ~ **87** 79
curve, hypsographic ~ **11** 6-12
curve, inflected ~ **347** 13
curve, plane ~ **347** 12
curved electrotype casting machine **178** 13
curved plate casting machine **178** 13
curve eight **302** 11
curvet **71** 6
cushion **42** 23; **47** 8; **202** 6
cushion, gilder's ~ **129** 50
cushion, rubber ~ **277** 16
cushion capital **335** 21
cusp **20** 48
customer **98** 43; **99** 2, 18; **111** 2; **248** 18; **250** 6; **266** 25; **271** 16, 55
customer accounts office **271** 24
customer area **207** 78
customer card index **248** 24
customer service representative **248** 17
customs **217** 24
customs barrier **225** 4
customs boat pendant **253** 35
customs boat pennant **253** 35
customs entrance **225** 5
customs flags **253** 35-38

customs launch **221** 100
customs signal flag **253** 37
cut *Metalwkr.* **140** 28
cut *Fencing* **294** 23
cut, antique ~ **36** 49
cut, cold ~ **96** 14
cut, positive ~ **340** 3
cut, round ~ **36** 42-43
cut, standard ~ **36** 48
cut and thrust weapon **294** 34
cutlery **45; 309** 47
cutlery chest **266** 41
cutlery drawer **39** 10; **44** 21
cutlery holder **266** 48
cutlet **95** 12
cut nippers, detachable-jaw ~ **140** 67
cutoff knife and roughing station **184** 3
cuts **36** 42-86
cuts, fancy ~ **36** 68-71
cutter *Paperhanger* **128** 42
cutter *Joiner* **132** 20
cutter *Drawing Off.* **151** 15
cutter *Brickwks.* **159** 15
cutter *Paperm.* **173** 44
cutter *Composing Rm.* **175** 33, 51
cutter *Ship* **220** 8
cutter *Warships* **258** 12, 61
cutter *Films* **311** 43
cutter, automatic ~ **162** 19
cutter, fine ~ **133** 37
cutter, rotary ~ *Forestry* **85** 26
cutter, rotary ~ *Bookbind.* **184** 22
cutter, spherical ~ **108** 7
cutter, universal ~ **134** 28
cutter bar **64** 3
cutter for metal watch straps **109** 19
cutter spindle **175** 60
cutting *Map* **15** 84
cutting *Plant Propagn.* **54** 19, 20
cutting *Synth. Fibres* **170** 60
cutting *Films* **311** 42, 46
cutting, shooting ~ **54** 24
cutting, sprouting ~ **54** 24
cutting attachment **141** 19
cutting bench **117** 96; **311** 42
cutting blade **183** 19
cutting cylinder *Gdn. Tools* **56** 35
cutting cylinder *Text. Finish.* **168** 44
cutting drum **64** 34
cutting edge **45** 57, **66** 14; **85** 2
cutting edge, cemented carbide ~ **149** 48, 50
cutting edge, razor's ~ **106** 40
cutting head **175** 51
cutting-in brush **129** 20
cutting machine *Furrier* **131** 5
cutting machine *Gas Weld.* **141** 34
cutting machine *Synth. Fibres* **169** 30
cutting machine, universal ~ **141** 36
cutting nozzle **141** 38
cutting-off machine **125** 16
cutting pliers **127** 51
cutting point **136** 35
cutting room **310** 3
cutting scale, illuminated ~ **185** 6
cutting shears **103** 3
cutting table *Dressm.* **103** 4
cutting table *Cine Film* **117** 96
cutting table *Composing Rm.* **175** 52
cutting table *Films* **311** 42
cutting template **103** 13
cutting tip, adjustable ~ **149** 45, 46
cutting tip, cemented carbide ~ **149** 50
cutting unit *Gdn. Tools* **56** 33, 41
cutting unit *Agr. Mach.* **64** 8
cuttlefish **357** 37; **369** 4
cuttling device **168** 35
cutup **326** 25
cutwater **215** 56
cutworm **80** 44
cyan filter adjustment **116** 45
cyclamen **53** 5
cycle **187** 1
cycle, motor-paced ~ **290** 15
cycle racing **290** 1-23
cycle serial number **187** 51
cycle track **290** 1
cycling track **290** 1
cyclohexanol, pure ~ **170** 18
cyclohexanol, raw ~ **170** 16
cyclohexanone **170** 20
cyclohexanoxime **170** 22
cyclone **4** 38; **9** 5
cyclone heat exchanger **160** 6
cyclorama **310** 12; **316** 9
cyclotron **2** 49
Cygnus **3** 23
cylinder *Cooper* **130** 27
cylinder *Metalwkr.* **140** 45
cylinder *Cotton Spin.* **163** 43
cylinder *Offset Print.* **180** 79
cylinder *Railw.* **210** 32
cylinder *Swim.* **279** 19
cylinder *Graphic Art* **340** 40
cylinder *Chem.* **350** 45
cylinder, developed ~ **182** 13
cylinder, grooved ~ **165** 10
cylinder, high-pressure ~ **153** 23
cylinder, hydraulic ~ **64** 8; **194** 26
cylinder, low-pressure ~ **153** 25
cylinder, medium-pressure ~ **153** 24
cylinder, perforated ~ **163** 21
cylinder, right ~ **347** 38
cylinder, steel ~ **180** 54
cylinder arm **177** 68
cylinder crankcase **190** 19
cylinder diameter **167** 16
cylinder head **190** 45; **242** 47
cylinder head gasket **190** 48
cylinder lock **140** 44
cylinder oil **145** 63
cylinder-processing machine **182** 9
cylinder temperature gauge **230** 9
cylinder trimmer **85** 25
cylinder trolley **141** 23
cylinder undercasing **163** 55
cyma **334** 11, 19
cymatium **334** 19
cymbal **324** 51
cymbal holder **324** 52
cymbals **323** 50
cymbal stand **324** 52
cyme **370** 70; **374** 36
cyme, curled ~ **370** 77
cyme, helicoid ~ **370** 76
cyme, scorpioid ~ **370** 77
cypress **372** 58
cythara **322** 15

D

dabber **340** 22
dachshund **70** 39
dactyloscopy **264** 28
dado, oil-painted ~ **129** 15
daemon **327** 58
da gamba violin **323** 16
dagger, bronze ~ **328** 22
dagger, hafted ~ **328** 22
dagger, Malayan ~ **353** 44
dahlia **51** 20; **60** 23
dairy **76** 1-48
dairy cow **62** 34; **75** 17
dairy cow shed **75** 14
dairy plant **76** 1-48
dairy product **99** 43
daisy **376** 1
dam *Map* **15** 69
dam *Game* **88** 1
dam *Energy Sources* **155** 38
dam *Hydr. Eng.* **217** 57-64
damp course **123** 4
dampener **180** 23, 52, 61
dampening roller **180** 23, 52, 61
dampening unit **180** 39, 61
damper *Offset Print.* **180** 23, 52, 61
damper *Car* **191** 26; **192** 69
damper *Music. Instr.* **322** 54; **325** 37
damper, electromagnetic ~ **11** 40
damper block **325** 37
damper door **210** 6
damper lifter **325** 38
damper-lifting lever **325** 23
damper pedal **325** 8
damper rest rail **325** 39
damping roller **180** 23, 52, 61
damping unit **180** 39, 61
dam sill **217** 79
dance band **306** 2
dance band instruments **324** 47-78
dance band musician **306** 3
dance costume **354** 36
dance drum **354** 14
dance floor **317** 16

dance floor lighting **317** 14
dancer **317** 17, 18
dancer, principal ~ **314** 28
dancing girl, Hindu ~ **306** 25
dancing snake **353** 48
dancing stick **354** 37
dandelion **51** 34; **61** 13
dandy **306** 33
dandy brush **71** 55
Danebrog **253** 17
Danforth anchor **286** 18
danger zone **2** 50
Dan grade **299** 15
Danish pastry **97** 30
Dannebrog **253** 17
daphne **377** 10
dark beer **93** 26
darkroom equipment **116** 1-60
darkroom lamp **116** 21
dark slide **114** 64
darning stitch **102** 17
dart **352** 28
dart, barbed ~ **319** 22
dart point **352** 29
das **366** 24
dash **342** 23
dashboard *Carriages* **186** 6
dashboard *Car* **191** 57-90
dashboard *Tram* **197** 29
dashboard lighting **197** 30
dassie **366** 24
data, technical ~ **151** 32
data carrier **237** 59, 62-64
data centre **248** 43
data collection station, central ~ **242** 20
data display terminal **238** 2, 11; **248** 16, 44
data output **112** 44
data print-out **195** 7
data processor **237** 60
data recording back **115** 67
data service **237** 58
data storage unit **242** 32
data terminal **242** 19
data transmission **237** 58
data transmission service **237** 41
date **384** 9
date and second button **110** 4
date indicator display **237** 39
date kernel **384** 10
date of issue **250** 14
date of maturity **250** 16
date of publication **342** 42
date palm **384** 1
date sheet **247** 33
date stamp postmark **236** 57
daughter boat **228** 17
davit **221** 78, 101; **223** 20; **258** 13, 83, 88
day cream **99** 27
dayfly **358** 6
daylight film magazine **311** 7
daylight-loading tank **116** 5
day nursery **48**
dead axle **210** 35
deadly nightshade **379** 7
dead man's handle **211** 21; **212** 13
deadwood **285** 47
de-aerator **152** 16
de-airing pug mill **161** 7
de-airing pug press **161** 7
dealer **275** 3
death notice **342** 68
death's-head hawkmoth **365** 9
death's-head moth **365** 9
death spiral **302** 5
debarking **85** 23
debenture bond **251** 11-19
debenzoling **156** 27
decade **332** 32
decatizing cylinder, perforated ~ **168** 50
decay, spontaneous ~ **1** 28
Decca navigation system **224** 39
decimal, recurring ~ **344** 21, 22
decimal fraction, proper ~ **344** 20
decimal key **247** 19
decimal place **344** 20
decimal point **344** 20
deck *Rowing* **283** 57
deck *Films* **311** 10
deck, lower ~ *Offshore Drill.* **146** 35
deck, lower ~ *Lorries etc.* **194** 37
deck, lower ~ *Space* **235** 28
deck, main ~ *Offshore Drill.* **146** 37
deck, main ~ *Ship* **221** 80; **223** 32-42
deck, main ~ *Warships* **258** 9
deck, middle ~ **146** 36
deck, orthotropic ~ **215** 2
deck, top ~ **146** 37
deck, upper ~ *Lorries etc.* **194** 38
deck, upper ~ *Railw.* **213** 36
deck, woven ~ **215** 18
deck beam **222** 57
deck bucket **221** 113
deck-chair **37** 47; **51** 2; **221** 111; **274** 13
deck crane **221** 5, 61
deck crane *Warships* **259** 10
decker **172** 24, 42, 44, 48, 62
deck hand **221** 112
deckhouse **221** 6, 39; **223** 34; **258** 72
decking, woven ~ **215** 18
deck plan **259** 12-20
deck plating **222** 56
deck slab **215** 6
deck space **223** 28
deck tennis **280** 31
declination axis **113** 5, 17
declination bearing **113** 6
declination gear **113** 4
decoder **110** 18
décolletage **306** 24
decometer **279** 17
decoration, Greek ~ **334** 38-43
decoration, Romanesque ~ **335** 14-16
decorative glass worker **124** 8
decorative pieces **35** 4
decoy bird **86** 48
decrescendo **321** 32
dedication, handwritten ~ **185** 50
dedusting fan **83** 53
dedusting screen **83** 56
deep-sea cable **237** 56
deep-sea fauna **369**
deep-sea fishing **90** 1-23
deep-sea floor **11** 10
deep-sea medusa **369** 5
deep-sea salvage tug **258** 96
deep-sea trench **11** 12
deep tank **223** 78
deep-water start **286** 46
deer, antlerless ~ **88** 1
deer fence **84** 7
deer stalking **86** 1-8
defence area **293** 66
defender *Ball Games* **292** 4
defender *Fencing* **294** 6
defending fencer **294** 6
deflection system **240** 23
deflector piston **242** 56
defroster vent **191** 42; **192** 64
dégagé **314** 11, 12
degree **345** 2
degree scale **313** 14
dehydrogenation **170** 19
delayed-action release **115** 15
delay indicator **205** 24
delicatessen shop **98** 1-87
deliveries **305** 17-20
delivery **184** 5; **185** 23, 35
delivery blower **181** 33
delivery cylinder **180** 42, 65
delivery hose **270** 31
delivery mechanism *Offset Print.* **180** 45
delivery mechanism *Post* **236** 49
delivery pile **180** 44; **181** 9
delivery pipe *Docks* **226** 34
delivery pipe *Water* **269** 16, 49, 52
delivery pouch **236** 54
delivery reel **173** 28
delivery roller **164** 59
delivery table **181** 31; **184** 14, 19
delivery tray **185** 15
delivery tube **65** 77
delivery unit **180** 45
delivery valve **67** 9
delphinium **60** 13
delta **13** 1
delta connection **153** 21
delta wing **229** 19
deltoid **346** 38
demand regulator, two-tube ~ **279** 20
demesne **15** 94
demi-goat **254** 32
demigod **327** 40
demijohn **206** 13
demi-man **254** 11
demi-mondaine **306** 37
demi-monde **306** 37
demi-rep **306** 37

demisemiquaver **320** 18
demisemiquaver rest **320** 26
demi-woman **254** 11
demonstration bench **261** 3
demonstration equipment **242** 45-84
demonstration model **242** 45, 55
demonstrator **262** 6
den **273** 56
Deneb **3** 23
denims **31** 60; **33** 22
denomination *Money* **252** 32
denomination *Maths.* **344** 19
denominator **344** 15
dental surgeon **24** 1
dentate **370** 47
dent corn **68** 31
dentil **334** 14
dentine **19** 31
denting draft **171** 6
dentist **24** 1
denture **24** 25
department manager **271** 60
department store **268** 41; **271**
departure building **233** 15
'departures' **233** 25
departure schedule **204** 20
departure time indicator **205** 23
departure timetable **204** 20
deposit counter **236** 25
deposit slip **236** 27
depot **144** 17
depression **9** 5
depth adjustment **64** 88; **65** 60; **157** 45
depth-charge thrower **258** 34
depth gauge *D.I.Y.* **134** 47
depth gauge *Swim.* **279** 15
depth gauge attachment rule **149** 68
depth of focus **11** 34
depth reading **224** 67
depth recorder **224** 24
depth recording **224** 67
depth scale **224** 66
depth wheel **65** 59, 63
derailment guard **214** 75
derivative **345** 13
derrick *Phys. Geog.* **12** 33
derrick *Offshore Drill.* **146** 12
derrick *Ship* **221** 67
derrick boom **221** 26, 59; **223** 36
derrick boom, heavy-lift ~ **221** 25, 62
derrick mast **221** 60
descant viol **322** 23
descent stage **6** 28-36
desert monitor **364** 31
desert zone **9** 54
desiccator **350** 51
desiccator insert **350** 54
design **151** 16
design, chequered ~ **335** 14
design, computer-generated ~ **248** 19
design, imbricated ~ **335** 15
design, knitted ~ **30** 37
design, modular ~ **240** 1
design, quilted ~ **30** 31
design for costume **315** 39
designs, decorative ~ **334** 38-43; **335** 14-16
desk **46** 22; **246** 2
desk, cashier's ~ **250** 1
desk, clerical assistant's ~ **248** 11
desk, double ~ **260** 2
desk, instructor's ~ **242** 2
desk, stage manager's ~ **316** 29
desk, teacher's ~ **260** 22
desk chair **46** 27
desk diary **247** 32
desk drawer **46** 26; **246** 4
desk lamp **246** 11
desk mat **46** 23; **246** 6; **260** 25
desk set **246** 9
desk top **246** 3
desk unit **46** 21
dessert bowl **45** 6
dessert plate **45** 6
dessert spoon **45** 61, 66
destination board **205** 21, 38
destination indicator **205** 22
destination sign **197** 20
destroyer **258** 1, 38
desulfurization *see* desulphurization
desulfurizing *see* desulphurizing
desulphurization **156** 28
desulphurizing **169** 20
desulphurizing plant **145** 46, 68
detaching roller **163** 71
detangling brush **105** 2
detective **264** 33
detector indicator unit **224** 34
detonator cap **87** 58
detritus **12** 45
deutero-pyramid **351** 20
Deutschmark **252** 7
Devanagari **341** 9
developer **27** 33
developer, first ~ **116** 10
developing dish **116** 25
developing dish, semi-automatic ~ **116** 56
developing dish, thermostatically controlled ~ **116** 56
developing solution **116** 9
developing spiral **116** 2
developing tank *Photog.* **116** 1, 20
developing tank *Photograv.* **182** 11
developing tank, multi-unit ~ **116** 3
developing tank thermometer **116** 8
developing tray **116** 25
deviation mirror **113** 11
device **252** 12
devil **306** 14
devil's tail **340** 34
devil's tobacco pouch **381** 20
devil's wheel **308** 46
de-waxing **145** 50
dew claw **88** 23, 57
dewlap **73** 24
dexter **254** 18,20,22
D flat major **320** 67
diabetics file **22** 26
diacritics **342** 30-35
diadem **355** 21
diadem, pearl ~ **355** 16
diaeresis **342** 34
diagnostic test bay **195** 1-23
diagonal **346** 33
diagram *Drawing Off.* **151** 11
diagram *School* **260** 34
diagram *Univ.* **262** 8
dial **204** 5; **237** 10; **245** 16
dial finger plate **237** 11
dial finger stop **237** 12
dialling unit **237** 67
dial wind-up plate **237** 11
diameter **346** 45
diamond *Composing Rm.* **175** 21
diamond *Audio* **241** 26
diamond *Crystals* **351** 10, 13
diamonds **276** 41
diaper, disposable ~ **28** 22
diaphragm *Meteorol. Instr.* **10** 27
diaphragm *Man* **20** 9, 26
diaphragm *Dent.* **24** 33
diaphragm *Inf. Tech.* **242** 82
diaphragm, bladed ~ **2** 33
diaphragm chest **326** 12-14
diaphragm spring **190** 29
diathermy unit **23** 22
diazo plate **179** 32, 34
dibber **54** 7; **56** 1
dibble **54** 7; **56** 1
dice **276** 29, 31
dice cup **47** 42; **276** 30
dicing **276** 29
dictating machine **22** 27; **209** 30; **246** 17; **248** 34
dictating machine, pocket-sized ~ **246** 32
dictionary **262** 17
dictionary, medical ~ **22** 22
didelphid **366** 2
Didone **342** 6
die *Metalwkr.* **140** 32
die *Brickwks.* **159** 13
die, lower ~ **252** 41
die, steel ~ **175** 36
die, upper ~ **252** 40
die and stock **140** 32
die blank **175** 35
die block, lower ~ **139** 14, 39
die block, upper ~ **139** 13, 38
die case **174** 42, 46
die head **143** 57
diesel-electric drive **223** 68-74; **259** 75
diesel engine *Energy Sources* **155** 5
diesel engine *Intern. Combust. Eng.* **190** 4
diesel engine *Railw.* **211** 47; **212** 25, 51
diesel engine *Ship* **223** 73
diesel engine, auxiliary ~ **209** 19

diesel engine, eight-cylinder ~ **212** 73
diesel engine, five-cylinder in-line ~ **190** 3
diesel engine, four-cylinder ~ **65** 44
diesel engine, six-cylinder ~ *Agr. Mach.* **64** 28
diesel engine, six-cylinder ~ *Railw.* **209** 23
diesel engine, underfloor ~ **209** 23
diesel fuel **146** 26
diesel generator **259** 94
diesel generator unit **209** 5
diesel-hydraulic locomotive **212** 1, 24, 47; **213** 1
diesel locomotive **212** 1, 68
diesel locomotive, single-engine ~ **208** 1
diesel locomotives **212** 1-84
diesel oil **145** 56
diesel railcar **208** 13; **211** 41
diesel tank **146** 13
diesel trainset **209** 1
die stock **125** 27
diet meal **266** 62
difference **344** 24
differential *Agr. Mach.* **65** 32
differential *Intern. Combust. Eng.* **190** 75
differential *Maths.* **345** 13, 14
differential gear **65** 32; **190** 75
differential sign **345** 13
diffuser *Photog.* **114** 60
diffuser *Paperm.* **172** 11, 13
diffuser *Space* **234** 15
diffusing screen **310** 38
digester **172** 7
digger **64** 59
digger, toy ~ **273** 65
digging bucket **200** 5
digging bucket arm **200** 4
digging bucket teeth **200** 6
digging fork **66** 22
Digitalis **379** 2
digital readout *Clocks* **110** 2
digital readout *Optic. Instr.* **112** 47
digitate **370** 39
digitated **370** 39
digitus I **19** 52, 64
digitus II **19** 53, 65
digitus III **19** 54, 66
digitus IV **19** 55, 67
digitus V **19** 56, 68
digitus anularis **19** 67
digitus medius **19** 66
digitus minimus **19** 56, 68
dike **216** 34, 39
dike, main ~ **216** 32
dike batter **216** 40
dike ramp **216** 47
dikereeve **216** 46
dike slope **216** 40
diligence **186** 39
dimension line **151** 25
diminished triad **321** 3
diminuendo **321** 32
dimmer switch **127** 17
dimple **16** 16
dinar **252** 28
diner **207** 22-32
dinghy, inflatable ~ **228** 18; **258** 82; **278** 14; **279** 27
dinghy cruiser **284** 61
dining area **266** 73
dining car **207** 22-32
dining car kitchen **207** 33
dining chair **44** 10
dining compartment **207** 32, 77
dining room **44; 223** 44; **267** 20
dining set **42** 33-34; **44** 1-11
dining table **42** 33; **44** 1; **45** 1; **46** 34
dinner dress **33** 7
dinner plate **39** 42; **44** 7; **45** 4
dinner service **44** 33
dinner set **44** 33
diopter control ring **117** 15
dioptric adjustment ring **117** 15
dip, true ~ **12** 3
diploma **106** 42
dipole antenna **230** 65
dipper stick **200** 4
dipstick **190** 47
dipterans **358** 16-20
dipyramid, tetragonal ~ **351** 18
direct current motor **150** 9
direction, negative ~ **347** 7
direction, positive ~ **347** 6
directional antenna *Moon L.* **6** 4, 44
directional antenna *Post* **237** 51, 52
directional antenna assembly **234** 64
directional gyro **230** 13
direction finder, automatic ~ **230** 5
direction finder antenna **223** 5
director **310** 40; **316** 40
director of photography **310** 44
directory enquiries **237** 33
directory holder **236** 11
direct-vision frame finder **117** 58
dirndl **31** 26
dirndl, girl's ~ **29** 36
dirndl apron **31** 31
dirndl blouse **31** 29
dirndl dress **31** 26
dirndl necklace **31** 28
disc *Flat* **46** 15
disc *Agr. Mach.* **65** 83
disc *Disco* **317** 24
disc, adhesive ~ **364** 26
disc, carborundum ~ **24** 35
disc, facial ~ **362** 18
disc, germinal ~ **74** 65
disc, insertable ~ **115** 96
disc, metal ~ **309** 15
disc, plain ~ **65** 84
disc, revolving ~ **275** 31
disc, serrated-edge ~ **65** 85
disc, silver ~ **10** 24
disc, solar ~ **4** 36
disc barbell **299** 3
disc brake *Intern. Combust. Eng.* **190** 74
disc brake *Car* **191** 17-18; **192** 48-55
disc brake *Railw.* **208** 4
disc brake, front ~ **189** 32
disc brake calliper **189** 33
disc clutch **139** 21
disc coulter drive **64** 68
disc fibula **328** 30
discharge, pneumatic ~ **213** 18
discharge connection valve **213** 21
discharge conveyor **64** 83
discharge door **139** 2; **213** 25
discharge flap **213** 25
discharge flume **91** 41
discharge opening *Forging* **139** 2
discharge opening *Sawmill* **157** 56
discharge opening *Hydr. Eng.* **217** 56
discharge pipe **64** 37
discharge structure **217** 44
discharging chute **147** 39
discharging position **147** 58
disc jockey **317** 25
discomedusa **357** 14
discotheque **317**
disc pack **176** 34
disc slot **243** 38
disc stack **176** 34
disc store **244** 1
discussion tube arrangement **112** 22
disc wheel **191** 14
disgorger **89** 40
disguise **306** 6-48
dish **332** 50
dish, three-compartment ~ **40** 8
dish drainer **39** 33
dish rack **39** 41
dish thermometer **116** 13
dishwasher **39** 40
dishwashing machine **39** 40
disinfectant powder **83** 60
disintegrator **172** 5
disk *see* disc
dislocation **11** 50
dispenser **22** 64
displacement **11** 50
displacement boats **286** 32-37
display **47** 30; **271** 67
display, digital ~ *Clocks* **110** 20
display, digital ~ *Optic. Instr.* **112** 47
display, individual ~ **242** 3
display, visual ~ *Railw.* **211** 34
display, visual ~ *Broadcast.* **238** 2, 43
display cabinet **44** 26; **46** 9
display cabinet unit **42** 5
display case **271** 13

display counter **99** 10
display pipes **326** 1-3
display window, indoor ~ **271** 13
dissecting bench **261** 22
dissolver **172** 37
dissolving tank **172** 37
distance **346** 5
distance-measuring instrument **112** 70
distance piece *Bees* **77** 41
distance piece *Bldg. Site* **119** 81
distance scale **115** 4
distance setting **114** 28; **117** 3
distance-setting ring **114** 39; **115** 8
distant signal identification plate **203** 24
distillation **170** 17
distillation, gradual ~ **170** 4
distillation apparatus **350** 46
distillation column **145** 37, 49
distillation flask **350** 47, 50
distillation plant **145** 66
distillation product, heavy ~ **145** 40
distillation product, light ~ **145** 39
distilling apparatus **350** 46
distilling flask **350** 47, 50
distributary **13** 2
distributing machine **236** 38
distributing mechanism **174** 20
distributing pipe **126** 8
distributing roller **181** 7, 62; **249** 51
distribution board **157** 67
distribution main **269** 22
distribution pipe, main ~ **38** 71
distribution steel **119** 69
distributor *Composing Rm.* **174** 20
distributor *Letterpress* **181** 7, 62
distributor *Intern. Combust. Eng.* **190** 9, 27
distributor *Office* **249** 51
distributor cylinder **62** 23
distributor roller **181** 7, 62
distributor shaft **190** 27
distributor unit **62** 22
district boundary **15** 103
district heating main **198** 28
ditch **329** 33, 37
ditch fern **377** 16
divan, double ~ **43** 4-13
diver **282** 5
dividend **344** 26
dividend coupon **251** 18
dividend coupon sheet **251** 17
dividend warrant **251** 18
divider *Agr. Mach.* **64** 1
divider *Bakery* **97** 56
divider and rounder **97** 63
dividing **344** 26
dividing breeching **270** 32
diving, acrobatic ~ **282** 40-45
diving, competitive ~ **282** 40-45
diving, fancy ~ **282** 40-45
diving apparatus **279** 12, 19; **282** 5-10
diving board **282** 9
diving boards **282** 5-10
diving goggles **280** 38
diving mask **279** 10
diving plane, aft ~ **259** 95
diving platform **282** 6
diving pool **282** 11
division *Navig.* **224** 89
division *School* **260** 39
division *Maths.* **344** 26
division sign **344** 26
divisor **344** 26
D major **320** 57
D minor **320** 63
Dobermann terrier **70** 27
dock *Horse* **72** 34
dock *Shipbuild.* **222** 36-43
dock, emptied ~ **222** 43
dock, floating ~ *Shipbuild.* **222** 34-43, 41
dock, floating ~ *Docks* **225** 16
dock area **225** 1
dock basin **222** 36
dock bottom **222** 31
dock crane **222** 34
dock floor **222** 31
dock gate **222** 32
docking a ship **222** 41-43
docking hatch **6** 45
docking target recess **6** 47
docks **225**; **226**
dockside crane **222** 34
dock structure **222** 37-38
dockyard **222** 1-43
doctor **22**; **23**
'doctor' *Airport* **233** 44
doctor blade **168** 44
document **245** 19
document, confidential ~ **246** 25
document file **245** 6; **247** 37; **248** 5
document glass **249** 39
dodecahedron, pentagonal ~ **351** 8
dodecahedron, rhombic ~ **351** 7
dodgem **308** 62
dodgem car **308** 63
dodger **223** 17
doe *Dom. Anim.* **73** 18
doe *Game* **88** 40, 59
doe, barren ~ **88** 34
doe, young ~ **88** 39
doffer **163** 42
doffer comb, vibrating ~ **163** 39
dog *Dom. Anim.* **73** 16
dog *Game* **88** 42
dog *Bldg. Site* **119** 58
dog *Roof* **121** 97
dog *Intern. Combust. Eng.* **190** 39
dog, three-headed ~ **327** 30
dog, toy ~ **47** 7, 41
dog biscuit **99** 37
dog bowl **70** 32
dog brush **70** 28
dogcart **186** 18
dog comb **70** 29
dog flange **190** 39
dog food **99** 36
dog lead **70** 30
dog rose **373** 26
dogs *Dog* **70**
dogs *Forging* **139** 33
dog sled **353** 3
dog sledge **353** 3
Dog Star **3** 14
dog tick **358** 44
do-it-yourself **134**
do-it-yourself enthusiast **134** 61
do-it-yourself work **134** 1-34
doldrums **9** 46
dolina **13** 71
doll **309** 11
doll, sleeping ~ **47** 11
doll, walking ~ **273** 63
dollar **252** 33
doll's pram **47** 10; **48** 24
dolly *Flea Market* **309** 68
dolly *Films* **310** 49
dolmen **328** 16
dolphin **225** 12
dolphin butterfly stroke **282** 35
dome *Brew.* **92** 45
dome *Art* **337** 21
dome, high ~ **36** 79
dome, imperial ~ **121** 25
dome, main ~ **334** 72
dome, revolving ~ **5** 12
dome cover **38** 48
dome shutter **5** 14
dome system **334** 72-73
domicilation **250** 22
dominant seventh chord **321** 5
domino *Games* **276** 34
domino *Carnival* **306** 13, 15
dominoes **276** 33
domino panel **203** 66
donjon **329** 4
donkey **73** 3
door *Farm Bldgs.* **62** 17
door *Carriages* **186** 11
door *Tram* **197** 32
door *Railw.* **207** 20, 22
door, bottom ~ **210** 7
door, double ~ *Tram* **197** 14
door, double ~ *Railw.* **208** 7
door, double ~ *Hotel* **267** 27
door, driver's ~ **193** 2
door, folding ~ *Tram* **197** 14
door, folding ~ *Railw.* **207** 39; **208** 7
door, front ~ *Dwellings* **37** 65
door, front ~ *Hall* **41** 25
door, front ~ *Household* **50** 30
door, front ~ *Floor etc. Constr.* **123** 24
door, front ~ *Car* **193** 5
door, glass ~ **44** 18
door, hinged ~ **194** 12
door, ledged ~ **37** 34
door, main ~ *Church* **331** 16

door, main ~ *Art* **335** 24
door, outer ~ **259** 78
door, outward-opening ~ **194** 35
door, rear ~ *Car* **193** 3, 6, 20
door, rear ~ *Lorries etc.* **194** 11
door, revolving ~ **213** 9
door, side ~ *Lorries etc.* **194** 8, 12
door, side ~ *Railw.* **213** 9
door, sliding ~ *Farm Bldgs.* **62** 16
door, sliding ~ *Brew.* **92** 47
door, sliding ~ *Lorries etc.* **194** 8
door, sliding ~ *Railw.* **213** 15
door, vertical-lift ~ **139** 51
doorbell **127** 2
door frame **41** 26
door handle *Hall* **41** 28
door handle *Carriages* **186** 12
door handle *Car* **191** 5
door-lifting mechanism **139** 55
door lock *Hall* **41** 27
door lock *Metalwkr.* **140** 36-43
door lock *Car* **191** 6
doorman **267** 1; **271** 44
dormer **37** 56; **38** 7; **121** 6; **329** 11; **336** 4
dormer window **37** 56; **38** 7; **121** 6; **329** 11; **336** 4
dormer window, hipped ~ **121** 13
dorsum manus **19** 83
dorsum of the foot **19** 61
dorsum of the hand **19** 83
dorsum pedis **19** 61
dosimeter **2** 8-23
dosing mechanism **83** 60
dosser **78** 15
dosser carrier **78** 14
dot **178** 39
dot, French ~ **102** 13
dot ball, white ~ **277** 13
double **276** 35
double backward somersault **282** 42
double bass **323** 23
double bassoon **323** 28
double bass viol **322** 23; **323** 23
double bull capital **333** 28
double bull column **333** 23
double edger **157** 57
double flat **320** 53
double-lap roofing **122** 2
double leg circle **296** 54
double leg lock **299** 11
double mill **276** 25
double overarm stroke **282** 37
doubles **293** 2-3
doubles, mixed ~ **293** 49
double sharp **320** 51
doubles match **293** 2-3
doubles sideline **293** 2-3
doublet, padded ~ **355** 30, 45
doublet, paned ~ **355** 33
doublet, quilted ~ **355** 45
doublet, short ~ **355** 41, 45
doublet, slashed ~ **355** 33
doublet, stuffed ~ **355** 30
double-three **302** 14
double unit for black **180** 12-13
double unit for cyan **180** 8-9
double unit for magenta **180** 10-11
double unit for yellow **180** 6-7
double-whole note **320** 12
doubling frame **164** 57
doubling of slivers **164** 5
dough mixer **97** 55, 59
doughnut **97** 29
douze dernier **275** 27
douze milieu **275** 26
douze premier **275** 25
dovetail halving **121** 89
dowel hole **120** 22, 23
dowel hole borer **133** 6
dowel hole boring machine **133** 6
down-draught carburettor **192** 1-15
down-gate **148** 21
downhill racing **301** 32
downhill racing pole **301** 25
downhill racing position **301** 33
downhill ski **301** 34
downpipe **37** 13; **38** 10; **122** 29; **147** 63
downspout **37** 13; **38** 10
downtake **147** 13
down-town **268**
down tube **187** 17
downy mildew **80** 20, 21
drachma **252** 39
Draco **3** 32
draff **92** 50
draft *see* draught
draft *Weaves* **171** 4, 11, 13, 19, 21, 27
draft *Bank* **250** 12
draft, rough ~ **338** 4
draft board **168** 7
draft clause **250** 17
drafting **164** 12, 13
drafting machine **151** 2
drafting roller **164** 21, 22, 29
draft mark **222** 73
drag *Iron Foundry etc.* **148** 20
drag *Equest.* **289** 48
drag chute housing **257** 24
drag hook *Horse* **71** 14
drag hook *Fire Brig.* **270** 49
drag hunt **289** 41-49
drag lift **214** 15
Dragon *Astron.* **3** 32
dragon *Sailing* **284** 57
dragon *Fabul. Creat.* **327** 1, 50
dragon, seven-headed ~ **327** 50
dragon beam **120** 42
dragon figurehead **218** 16
dragonfly **358** 3
dragon piece **120** 42
dragon ship **218** 13-17
drain *Street Sect.* **198** 23
drain *Rivers* **216** 37
drain *Town* **268** 8
drainage **144** 46
drainage basin **12** 24
drainage ditch *Road Constr.* **200** 63
drainage ditch *Rivers* **216** 33
drainage layer **199** 25
drainage sluice **216** 34
drainage tube **26** 47
drain cock **178** 34
drain cover **198** 24
drain pipe **198** 25; **199** 26
drain plug **284** 36
drake **73** 35
drapery **338** 33
draught beam **65** 18
draughtboard **276** 17
draught mark **222** 73
draughts **276** 17-19
draughtsman **276** 18, 19
drawbar **64** 47, 61; **65** 18
drawbar coupling *Agr. Mach.* **65** 30
drawbar coupling *Camping* **278** 55
drawbar frame **65** 26
drawbar support **64** 62
drawbar trailer **194** 22
drawbench **108** 2
drawbridge **329** 25
draw cord **29** 67
draw curtain **315** 1
drawee **250** 20
drawer *Dent.* **24** 17
drawer *Hall* **41** 9
drawer *Bedrm.* **43** 18
drawer *Flat* **46** 11
drawer *Bathrm. etc.* **49** 34
drawer *Bank* **250** 21
draw frame **164** 1
draw frame, four-roller ~ **164** 9
draw frame, simple ~ **164** 9
draw frame cover **164** 7
draw hoe **66** 1
draw hook **270** 49
drawing *Drawing Off.* **151** 16
drawing *Synth. Fibres* **170** 55
drawing, final ~ **170** 47
drawing, preliminary ~ **170** 45
drawing, rolled ~ **151** 10
drawing bench **108** 2
drawing board **151** 1
drawing board adjustment **151** 5
drawing easel **338** 34
drawing floor **120** 11
drawing head **151** 4
drawing ink cartridge **151** 36
drawing ink container **151** 63
drawing-in roller **168** 12
drawing knife **120** 79
drawing machine **162** 7
drawing office **151**
drawing pen, tubular ~ **151** 37, 38
drawing roll **162** 11
drawing table **151** 6
draw-in wire **127** 30

drawknife **120** 79
draw-off tap **126** 34
drawshave **120** 79
draw stop **325** 44; **326** 6
drawstring **29** 64, 67
drawstring waist **31** 66
draw well **329** 3
draw wire **127** 30
draw works **145** 11
dredger **216** 56; **226** 41
dredger, hydraulic ~ **216** 59
dredger bucket **226** 44
dredging bucket **216** 58
dredging machine, floating ~ **216** 56
dress **31** 9
dress, button-through ~ **30** 10
dress, jersey ~ **29** 28
dress, knitted ~ **29** 28; **30** 33
dress, off-the-peg ~ **271** 29
dress, peasant-style ~ **30** 27
dress, ready-made ~ **271** 29
dress, ready-to-wear ~ **271** 29
dress, shirt-waister ~ **30** 10
dress, two-piece ~ **30** 33; **31** 11
dress, wrap-around ~ **30** 25
dress, wrapover ~ **30** 25
dressage **289** 1-7
dressage arena **289** 1
dress and jacket combination **31** 6
dress circle **315** 18
dress form **103** 6
dress guard **104** 14
dressing, sterile gauze ~ **21** 6
dressing axe **158** 38
dressing comb **105** 15; **106** 28
dressing floor **92** 8
dressing gown **29** 24; **32** 35
dressing machine **83** 52
dressing material **26** 34
dressing room **315** 43-52
dressing room mirror **315** 43
dressing stool **43** 24
dressing table **43** 25; **105** 19
dressing-table mirror **43** 29
dressmaker **103** 1
dress shirt **32** 43
dress sword **355** 63
dribble **291** 52
drier *Synth. Fibres* **170** 38
drier *Paperm.* **173** 22
drier *Offset Print.* **180** 14, 27
drier, swivel-mounted ~ **105** 25
drier felt **173** 23
driers **50** 23-34
drift net fishing **90** 1-10
drill *Dent.* **24** 6, 17
drill *Agr. Mach.* **65** 74
drill *Goldsm. etc.* **108** 4
drill *Turner* **135** 22
drill, electric ~ **56** 19; **120** 21; **134** 16, 50-55
driller **158** 9
drilling bit **145** 21
drilling cable **145** 7
drilling line **145** 7
drilling machine, electric ~ **108** 6
drilling machine, radial-arm ~ **150** 18
drilling machine, suspended ~ **108** 6
drilling pipe **145** 19
drilling platform **146** 1-37; **221** 66
drilling rig **145** 1; **146** 1-39
drilling vessel, semisubmersible ~ **221** 64
drill pipe **145** 6
drill spindle **150** 23
drill stand **134** 54
drill tower **270** 3
drink, soft ~ **96** 30; **99** 72
drinker, mechanical ~ **74** 16
drinking bowl, mechanical ~ **74** 16
drinking fountain **205** 33
drinking straw **266** 46
drinking trough **74** 6
drinking water carrier **278** 32
drinking water supply **269** 1-66
drinking water tank **146** 16
drinks cabinet **246** 29
drinks cupboard **42** 20
drinks gondola **99** 71
drinks shelf **266** 59
drinks stall **308** 3
drip, intravenous ~ **25** 13; **26** 9
drip fuel line **190** 53
drip ring **283** 40
dripstone **13** 80
drip tray **266** 2
drive *Composing Rm.* **175** 37
drive *Railw.* **214** 2
drive, clockwork ~ **10** 14
drive, conventional ~ **259** 75
drive, crystal-controlled ~ **310** 19, 24
drive, fluid ~ **65** 37
drive, hydraulic ~ **139** 9, 15
drive, main ~ **214** 63
drive belt **103** 10
drive-belt gear **109** 21
drive chain **188** 17
drive clutch **177** 54
drive connection **67** 19
drive gearbox **163** 57; **168** 10, 32
drive mechanism **110** 43
drive motor *Poultry Farm* **74** 37
drive motor *Dressm.* **103** 9
drive motor *Forging* **139** 25
drive motor *Mach. Tools* **150** 9
drive motor *Cotton Spin.* **163** 12, 23, 49
drive motor *Text. Finish.* **168** 55
drive motor *Composing Rm.* **175** 61
drive motor *Electrotyp. etc.* **178** 12, 28
drive motor *Offset Platem.* **179** 11
drive motor *Hydr. Eng.* **217** 47
drive pulley, fast-and-loose ~ **163** 50
drive pulley, main ~ **163** 50
driver *Carriages* **186** 32
driver *Bicycle* **187** 72
driver *Serv. Stat.* **196** 8
driver *Ship* **219** 30
driver *Equest.* **289** 26
driver *Ball Games* **293** 91
driver plate **149** 55
driver's brake valve **210** 53; **211** 22; **212** 11
driver's position *Agr. Mach.* **64** 33
driver's position *Tram* **197** 25
drive shaft *Car* **192** 30
drive shaft *Hydr. Eng.* **217** 49
drive unit *Shoem.* **100** 8
drive unit *Photomech. Reprod.* **177** 56
drive unit, central ~ **238** 57
drive well **269** 60
drive wheel *Agr. Mach.* **65** 80
drive wheel *Shoem.* **100** 8
drive wheel *Text. Finish.* **168** 4
drive wheel *Offset Print.* **180** 66
drive wheel *Army* **255** 50
drive wheel unit **209** 3
driving **86** 34-39
driving axle **210** 37
driving axle gearing **64** 30
driving barrel **187** 73
driving cylinder **165** 32
driving drum **165** 32, 35
driving gear *Cotton Spin.* **163** 57
driving gear *Railw.* **210** 2-37
driving guide rail **226** 39
driving pinion **214** 8
driving plate *Turner* **135** 9
driving plate *Mach. Tools* **149** 55
driving shaft **163** 24
driving trailer car **211** 62
driving unit **209** 2
driving wheel tyre **64** 31
drizzle **9** 33
drone *Bees* **77** 5
drone *Music. Instr.* **322** 11
drone cell **77** 36
drone pipe **322** 11
drone string **322** 31
droop flap **229** 54
droop nose **229** 16
drop **98** 76
drop, plain ~ **36** 85
drop board **267** 5
drop cloth **316** 11
drop compass **151** 59
drop forging **139**
drop grate **210** 5
drop grate lever **210** 40
drop hammer, air-lift ~ **139** 24
drop hammer, short-stroke ~ **139** 11
drop net **89** 29
drop pin **165** 37
droppings removal **74** 23-27

dropping worm **149** 18
drop pin roller **165** 39
drop windscreen **255** 97
drop windshield **255** 97
drop wire **166** 34
drop worm **149** 18
drove **158** 37
drove chisel **158** 37
'druggist' **233** 45
drum *Meteorol. Instr.* **10** 5, 16, 20
drum *Household* **50** 29
drum *Agr. Mach.* **64** 12
drum *Painter* **129** 9
drum *Cooper* **130** 13
drum *Nucl. Energy* **154** 77
drum *Nightclub* **318** 10
drum *Music. Instr.* **323** 57
drum *Art* **335** 44
drum, hollow ~ **312** 49
drum, lansquenet's ~ **306** 70
drum, revolving ~ **273** 45
drum brake **188** 36
drum brake, front ~ **189** 11
drum brake, rear ~ **189** 13
drum head **323** 52
drum kit **324** 47-54
drummer **318** 11
drum of paint **129** 9
drums **324** 47-54
drum set **324** 47-54
drumstick *Supermkt.* **99** 59
drumstick *Music. Instr.* **323** 54
drumstick *Ethnol.* **354** 19
drupe **59** 41, 43, 49; **370** 99; **382** 51; **384** 40
drupes **59** 59, 1-36
dryas **51** 7
dry bulb thermometer **10** 34
dry cell battery **127** 27
dry cooling tower **154** 39
dry dock **222** 31-33; **225** 17
drying **169** 24; **170** 58
drying cabinet **116** 23
drying chamber **170** 49
drying cylinder **165** 50, 53; **173** 22
drying cylinder, heated ~ **173** 33
drying floor **92** 16
drying kiln **92** 29
drying machine **169** 31
drying rack *Agr.* **63** 28, 29
drying rack *Flea Market* **309** 49
drying section **168** 28
drying shed **159** 17
dry-seed dressing **83** 52
dry zone, equatorial ~ **9** 54
D sharp minor **320** 61
dual film-tape recording **117** 70
dual film-tape reproduction **117** 75
dual film-tape system **117** 7
dubbing *Films* **311** 1-46, 37-41
dubbing *Chivalry* **329** 66
dubbing actress **311** 39
dubbing director **311** 38
dubbing mixer **311** 36
dubbing room **311** 34
dubbing speaker **311** 39
dubbing studio *Broadcast.* **238** 28
dubbing studio *Films* **311** 37
dubbing theatre *Broadcast.* **238** 28
dubbing theatre *Films* **311** 37
duck **73** 35
duck, toy ~ **49** 4; **273** 30
duck, wild ~ **86** 41; **272** 51
duck-bill **366** 1
duck hunting **86** 40
ducking **299** 29
duckling **73** 35
duck-mole **366** 1
duck shooting **86** 40
duck's meat **378** 35
duckweed **378** 35
duct **163** 11
duct, cystic ~ **20** 38
duct, hepatic ~ **20** 37
duct, spermatic ~ **20** 74
ductor **181** 63
ductor roller **181** 63
duct roller **181** 64
due date **250** 16
duffle coat **271** 21
dugout **218** 7; **354** 20
duk-duk dancer **352** 34
dulcimer **322** 32
Dülfer seat **300** 30
dumb barge **225** 8
dumb barge, tug-pushed ~ **221** 94
dummy *Infant Care etc.* **28** 15
dummy *Store* **271** 34
dummy, dressmaker's ~ **103** 6
dummy bull **319** 3
dummy funnel **221** 16
dump body **194** 25; **200** 8
dump car **213** 37
dump chest **172** 81
dumping bucket **214** 34
dumping device **147** 44, 59
dump truck **47** 38; **147** 64; **200** 7
dump truck, three-way ~ **194** 24
dune, crescentic ~ **13** 40
dune, migratory ~ **13** 39
dune, travelling ~ **13** 39
dune, wandering ~ **13** 39
dune buggy **193** 12
dung **63** 15
dungarees **29** 40; **30** 21
dung beetle **358** 39
dungeon **329** 5
dunging, mechanical ~ **74** 23-27
dunging chain **74** 27
dunging conveyor **74** 27
dung tank **221** 72
dunnage **222** 62u.63
duodenum **20** 14, 43
duplet **321** 23
duplicate list **263** 27
duramen **120** 84; **370** 13
dust, fine ~ **158** 22
dust, lunar ~ **6** 14
dust bag container **50** 62
dustbin **199** 3
dustbin-tipping device **199** 2
dust brush **109** 18
dust cap **187** 57, 82
dust catcher *Goldsm. etc.* **108** 45
dust catcher *Iron & Steel* **147** 14
dust-collecting chamber **163** 11
dust-collecting machine **147** 14
dust collector *Goldsm. etc.* **108** 45
dust collector *Cement Wks.* **160** 7
dust collector *Refuse Coll.* **199** 47
dust container **50** 86
dust counter **112** 42
dust cover *Bookbind.* **185** 37
dust cover *Audio* **241** 32
dust cover *Store* **271** 30
dust discharge flue **163** 22
dust escape flue **163** 22
dust exhauster **108** 43
dust extraction fan **163** 10
dust extractor **92** 40; **172** 1
dust filter **270** 59
dust hood **133** 20
dust jacket **185** 37
dust pan **50** 52; **260** 60
dust removal fan **83** 53
dust removal screen **83** 56
dust-settling chamber **172** 6
dust shield **2** 48
Dutch clover **69** 2
'duty free shop' **233** 52
duty presentation officer **238** 22
duvet, quilted ~ **43** 8
dwale **379** 7
dwarf **308** 22
dwarf French bean **57** 8
dwarf pine **372** 21
dwelling **37**
dwelling, lacustrine ~ **328** 15
dye liquor padding trough **165** 47
dye spray **100** 35
dyke *see* dike
dynamo **187** 8
dynastarter **209** 13

E

Eagle **3** 9
eagle fern **377** 16
eagle owl *Hunt.* **86** 48, 51
eagle owl *Birds* **362** 15
eagles **362** 5-9
ear *Man* **16** 18
ear *Arable Crops* **68** 2
ear *Dog* **70** 2
ear *Horse* **72** 1
ear *Dom. Anim.* **73** 11
ear *Game* **88** 16, 32, 44, 61
ear *Music. Instr.* **326** 32
ear *Birds* **362** 16

ear, external ~ **17** 56-58
ear, feathered ~ *Game* **88** 78
ear, feathered ~ *Birds* **362** 16
ear, internal ~ **17** 62-64
ear, middle ~ **17** 59-61
earcup **241** 69; **261** 40
earflap **35** 31
ear lobe **17** 57
earmuff **304** 28
earphone *Hairst. etc.* **34** 38
earphone *Audio* **241** 69
earphone *Office* **248** 35; **249** 63
earphones **34** 37
earphone socket *Cine Film* **117** 10
earphone socket *Office* **249** 68
ear piece *Forestry* **84** 23
earpiece *Post* **237** 8
earplug **354** 30
earrings **36** 13
earrings, drop ~ **36** 11
earrings, pendant ~ **36** 11
earth **4** 8, 30
Earth **4** 45
earth **6** 17
earth, composted ~ **55** 15
earth, excavated ~ **118** 78
earth, prepared ~ **55** 15
earth core **11** 5
earthing button **237** 21
earthing clamp **142** 35
earth moth **80** 42
earthquake **11** 32-38
earthquake, submarine ~ **11** 53
earthquake focus **11** 32
earth station **237** 51
earthworm **357** 24
earthworm, artificial ~ **89** 67
ear tuft **362** 16
earwig **81** 11
easel **116** 35
easel, folding ~ **338** 26
East Australian Current **14** 38
Easter candle **330** 44
Easter candlestick **330** 45
easterlies **9** 48, 49
Eastern cut-off **298** 21
Eastern roll **298** 15
east point **4** 14
easy chair **336** 18
eaves **38** 11; **121** 4; **122** 36
eaves, rafter-supported ~ **37** 9
eaves course **122** 49, 76
eaves fascia **122** 42
eaves joint **122** 76
E-boat **258** 69, 75
écarté **314** 15
ECG **23** 28
ECG amplitude **25** 49
ECG analyser **25** 45
ECG analysis **25** 50
ECG impulse **25** 46
ECG lead **25** 43
ECG machine, portable ~ **23** 46
ECG monitor **25** 2, 21, 28, 47
ECG recorder **25** 41
ECG recording unit **25** 27
ECG rhythm **25** 48
E-channel **143** 7
echinoderm **369** 3, 11, 17, 18, 19
echinoderms **357** 38-39
Echinops **53** 14
echinus **334** 21
Echiostoma **369** 13
echo **224** 63
echo chamber **311** 31
echo chamber loudspeaker **311** 32
echo chamber microphone **311** 33
echogram **224** 67
echograph **224** 24, 65
echo receiver **224** 64
echo recorder **224** 24
echo signal **224** 63
echo sounder **224** 61-67
echo sounding machine **224** 61-67
echo sounding machine recorder **224** 65
eclipse **4** 33
eclipse, lunar ~ **4** 29-35, 34-35
eclipse, solar ~ **4** 29-35, 32, 39, 41
ecliptic **3** 2; **4** 22
economizer *Power Plant* **152** 26
economizer *Railw.* **210** 23
Edam cheese **99** 42
edelweiss **378** 9
edge *Tablew. etc.* **45** 57
edge *Forestry* **85** 2
edge *Winter Sp.* **302** 21
edge *Maths.* **347** 32
edge, aluminium ~ **301** 51
edge, front ~ **122** 88
edge, hidden ~ **151** 24
edge, matching ~ **128** 21
edge, non-matching ~ **128** 22
edge, razor's ~ **106** 40
edge, steel ~ **301** 4, 50
edge, upper ~ **301** 51
edge, visible ~ **151** 23
edge board, lower ~ **118** 74
edge board, upper ~ **118** 73
edge mill **159** 8
edge of platform **205** 19
edge of pool **281** 3
edge runner mill **159** 8
edge sander **133** 12
edge-sanding machine **133** 12
edge-veneering machine **133** 26
edging *Flower Gdn.* **51** 15
edging *Opticn.* **111** 35
edging, concrete ~ **52** 20
edging, hoop ~ **55** 38
edging machine **111** 24
editing **311** 42-46
editing table **117** 96; **311** 42
editorial **342** 48
EDP print-out **248** 47
education, nursery ~ **48** 1-20
education, pre-school ~ **48** 1-20
eel **364** 17
eel hook **89** 87
effacé **314** 13
efflux viscometer **129** 38
E flat major **320** 65
E flat minor **320** 68
egg *Man* **20** 84
egg *Poultry Farm* **74** 58
egg *Bees* **77** 26, 27
egg *Gdn. Pests* **80** 15, 55
egg *Forest Pests* **82** 19
egg *Supermkt.* **99** 50
egg *Articulates* **358** 49
egg and anchor cyma **334** 42
egg and dart cyma **334** 42
egg and tongue cyma **334** 42
egg box **74** 42, 45
egg collection **74** 22, 34
egg collection system **74** 34
egg-counting board **89** 19
egg gallery **82** 23
egg integument **74** 59
egg-packing machine, fully automatic ~ **74** 46
egg position **301** 33
egg production **74** 34-53
eggshell **74** 59
egg timer **110** 31
egg weigher **74** 43
Egyptian **342** 8
eight **283** 10
eighth note **320** 16
eighth rest **320** 24
ejection seat **257** 6, 7
ejector seat **257** 6, 7
E-layer **7** 27
elbow *Man* **16** 45
elbow *Overh. Irrign.* **67** 6
elbow *Horse* **72** 20
elbow *Winter Sp.* **301** 70
elbow boot **289** 31
elbow coupling **126** 40
elbow joint **126** 51, 52
elbow pad **303** 16
elbow screw joint **126** 40, 45
elbow snips **125** 2
elder **374** 35
elderberry **374** 37
elder flower **374** 36
election **263** 16-30
election meeting **263** 1-15
election officer **263** 17
election regulations **263** 25
election speaker **263** 5
election supervisor **263** 28
elector **263** 24
electoral register **263** 18
electric action organ **326** 36-52
electrical fitter **127** 1
electrical point **261** 12
electrical socket **261** 12
electrical system bus **235** 55
electric engine room **223** 68
electrician **127** 1
electricity cable **198** 14, 19
electricity meter **127** 32
electricity meter cupboard **127** 31
electricity transmission line **15** 113
electric light bulb **127** 56

electric power plant **152** 1-28
electrocardiogram monitor **25** 2, 21, 28
electrocardiograph **23** 28; **25** 41
electrode *Hosp.* **25** 26, 35, 38
electrode *Slaughterho.* **94** 8
electrode *Arc Weld.* **142** 10
electrode *Iron & Steel* **147** 52
electrode, central ~ **2** 3
electrode, platinum-iridium ~ **24** 44
electrode, strap-on ~ **23** 30
electrode arm **142** 24
electrode case **142** 7
electrode exit point **25** 34
electrode holder **142** 9, 20
electrode lead **25** 25
electrode-pressure cylinder **142** 26
electromagnet **237** 47
electron **1** 3, 17, 27, 32
electron, free ~ **1** 25
electron beam **240** 16
electron gun **113** 31
electron gun assembly **240** 24
electronic circuits **242** 68-72
electronics, remote ~ **112** 53
electronics cabinet **177** 69
electron microscope **113** 30
electron shell **1** 6, 8
electron spin **1** 4
electroplating bath **178** 4
electroplating tank **178** 4
electroplating vat **178** 4
electrotome **22** 38
electrotype, curved ~ **178** 21
electrotyping **178**
electrotyping plant **178** 1-6
element, electronic ~ **242** 69
element, fissionable ~ **1** 49
element, front ~ **115** 7
element, fusible ~ **127** 36
element, oscillating ~ **110** 9
element of set **348** 2
elephant **366** 20
elephant, toy ~ **47** 6
elephant enclosure **356** 9
elephant house **356** 10
elevating conveyor **200** 49
elevating drum, rotary ~ **64** 74
elevating gear **255** 67
elevating piston **255** 51
elevation, front ~ **151** 17
elevation, side ~ **151** 18
elevator *Offshore Drill.* **146** 8
elevator *Synth. Fibres* **170** 36
elevator *Aircraft* **229** 27; **230** 63
elevator *Air Force* **257** 22
elevator *Store* **271** 45
elevator *Airsports* **288** 24
elevator *Theatre* **316** 33, 34
elevator, chain and slat ~ **64** 7
elevator, open-web ~ **64** 69
elevator bridge **226** 25
elevator car **271** 46
elevator carrier **174** 22
elevator controls **271** 48
elevator operator **271** 47
elevator shaft *Offshore Drill.* **146** 20
elevator shaft *Store* **271** 51
elevon section, movable ~ **235** 33
elevon structure, heat-resistant ~ **235** 34
elk **367** 1, 2
ellipse **347** 22
ellipse template **151** 71
ellipsis **342** 29
ellipsoid of revolution **347** 42
elm tree **371** 49
elytron **82** 10; **358** 36
E major **320** 59
embankment *Map* **15** 104
embankment *Refuse Coll.* **199** 14
embankment *Rivers* **216** 49
embossing platen **183** 29
embrace **205** 53
embrasure **329** 18
embroidery **29** 29; **30** 42; **355** 67
embryo *Arable Crops* **68** 16
embryo *Bot.* **370** 86
embryo *Trop. Plants* **382** 21
embryo *South. Fruits* **384** 22
embryo plant **68** 14
embryo sac **370** 64
emergency brake **214** 3, 71
emergency brake valve **210** 57
emergency cable **214** 47
emergency-cable tensioning mechanism **214** 48
emergency crash barrier **259** 17
'emergency exit' *Airport* **233** 41
emergency exit **307** 33; **312** 7
emergency flare stack **146** 11
emergency lighting **312** 6
emergency telephone **237** 4
emery paper **135** 25
eminence, frontal ~ **16** 4
eminence, thenar ~ **19** 75
E minor **320** 56
emission control **190** 73
Emmental cheese **99** 41
empennage shapes **229** 23-36
Empire table **336** 16
empress, Byzantine ~ **355** 15
emptying system, dust-free ~ **199** 2
em rule **342** 23
emu **359** 1
emulsion **129** 4
emulsion paint **129** 4
emulsion paste **128** 28
emulsion tube **192** 10
enamel **19** 30
enamelling **260** 62
enamelling stove, electric ~ **260** 63
enamel powder **260** 65
enchasing hammer **108** 41
enclosing wall **356** 4
enclosure, outdoor ~ **356** 1
enclosure wall **329** 15
encyclopaedia **42** 18; **262** 17
end *Basketm.* **136** 23
end *Mach. Parts etc.* **143** 23
end, hipped ~ **122** 10
end, partial-hipped ~ **121** 17
end, round ~ **143** 50
end, rounded ~ **143** 20
end, west ~ **335** 22
end frame, hemispherical ~ **235** 48
end-grain block **340** 1
endive **57** 39
endive leaf **57** 39
endleaf **185** 49
end line **292** 36
end mill **150** 43
end moraine **12** 55
endorsee **250** 26
endorsement **250** 25
endorser **250** 27
endpaper **185** 49
end pier **215** 27
end plate **229** 33
end rib, hemispherical ~ **235** 48
end ring **89** 52
end support **150** 40
end switch **241** 60
endurance competition **289** 16
energy **1** 55
energy, solar ~ **155** 17-36
energy level **1** 15, 27
energy sources **155**
energy system **6** 6, 8
engagement **294** 46
engine *Moon L.* **6** 30
engine *Oil, Petr.* **145** 12
engine *Aircraft* **231** 26
engine *Airsports* **288** 35
engine, air-cooled ~ **188** 7; **189** 3, 50
engine, auxiliary ~ *Ship* **223** 71
engine, auxiliary ~ *Aircraft* **231** 33
engine, eight-cylinder ~ **190** 1
engine, four-cylinder ~ **189** 50
engine, four-stroke ~ **189** 3, 50
engine, main ~ *Railw.* **209** 4
engine, main ~ *Ship* **221** 81; **223** 73
engine, rear ~ *Garage* **195** 49
engine, rear ~ *Aircraft* **231** 10
engine, side ~ **228** 29
engine, single-cylinder ~ **188** 26; **189** 3
engine, twin-shaft ~ **232** 51
engine, two-stroke ~ **188** 7, 26; **242** 55; **305** 92
engine, water-cooled ~ **189** 31, 39
engine and propeller room **227** 22
engine and transmission control wheel **212** 67
engine compartment **195** 35
engine compartment structure **235** 2
engine control system **235** 39
engine driver **208** 2

engineer **208** 2
engineering workshop **222** 8
engineer's brake valve **210** 53; **211** 22; **212** 11
engine fairing, aerodynamic ~ **234** 6
engine mount **234** 21
engine mounting **190** 38; **191** 53; **226** 58
engine oil **196** 15
engine oil temperature gauge **212** 19
engine order telegraph **224** 25
engine pod **231** 26; **256** 25
engine room *Ship* **221** 10
engine room *Fire Brig.* **270** 1
engine room ventilator **212** 37
engine superstructure **226** 58
engine telegraph **224** 25
english *Composing Rm.* **175** 29
English *Billiards* **277** 5
English daisy **376** 1
English hand **342** 10
English ryegrass **69** 26
English setter **70** 41
engraver **340** 16
engraving **36** 41
engraving ball **108** 34
engraving machine **177** 52
engraving system **177** 66
enlarger **116** 26
enlarger head **116** 41
enlarging meter **116** 53
enlarging photometer **116** 53
ensign of head of state **253** 14
ensign staff **223** 31; **258** 25
entablature **334** 52
entire **370** 43
entrance **77** 48; **99** 4; **208** 10; **307** 19
'entrance' *Airport* **233** 36
entrance, bullfighters' ~ **319** 10
entrance, main ~ **319** 6
entrance, side ~ **331** 15; **335** 13
entrance and exit door **197** 14
entrance hall **41** 1-29
entrance tunnel **353** 6
entrechat **314** 22
entrepôt **225** 7
entry/exit hatch **6** 38
entry hatch **6** 10; **235** 26
epaulière **329** 44
épée **294** 25-33, 36
épée, electric ~ **294** 26
épéeist **294** 25
épée point **294** 27
ephemerid **358** 6
epicalyx **58** 22
epicenter **11** 33
epicentre **11** 33
epididymis **20** 73
epiglottis **17** 51
epistyle **334** 18
equalizer **311** 19
equalizer, universal ~ **238** 48
'equals' key **247** 20
equals sign **344** 23
equation, conditional ~ **345** 9
equation, identical ~ **345** 5
equation, simple ~ **345** 4
equator **14** 1
equator, celestial ~ **3** 3
Equatorial Countercurrent **14** 33
equestrian sport **289**
equilibrist **307** 48
equinoxes **3** 6-7
equipment carrier **177** 58
equipment locker **212** 35
equipment section **239** 1
equisetum **376** 18
equitation **71** 1-6
erase head **241** 59; **243** 20; **311** 25
eraser **151** 42
eraser, glass ~ **151** 47
eraser, pencil-type ~ **151** 41
erasing head **241** 59; **243** 20; **311** 25
erasing knife **151** 43
erasing knife blade **151** 44
erasing shield **151** 35
erasing table **249** 26
erasion **26** 52
erection shop **222** 4
Ergates faber **358** 38
ergometer, bicycle ~ **23** 26
ergometry **23** 26-31
ergot **68** 4
Eridamus **3** 12
Erlenmeyer flask **173** 2; **350** 39
ermine moth **80** 5
erne **362** 5
error indicator **244** 7
eruption **7** 21
escalator **271** 22
escape wheel **110** 40
escapologist **308** 28
escarpment **13** 57
escudo **252** 23
Eskimo **353** 1
Eskimo kayak **283** 68
esophagus **17** 49
espalier **37** 33; **52** 1,2,16,17,29
espalier, free-standing ~ **52** 16
espalier fruit tree **52** 1,2,16,17,29
esparto grass **136** 26
espresso bar **265** 1-26
esquire **329** 68
estate **193** 15
estate car **193** 15
estoque **319** 32
etchant **178** 24; **182** 16
etching **340** 14-24
etching bath **178** 31; **340** 51
etching ground **340** 55
etching machine *Electrotyp. etc.* **178** 23
etching machine *Photograv.* **182** 15
etching needle **340** 16
etching solution **178** 24; **182** 16
etching tank **178** 24, 31; **182** 16
ethmoid **17** 39
ethnology **352; 353; 354**
ethylene molecule **242** 61
Eurobottle **93** 26
Europe **14** 15
European silver fir **372** 1
European Southern Observatory **5** 1-16
European toad **364** 23
Euscorpius flavicandus **358** 40
evacuating pump, centrifugal ~ **67** 11, 23
evaporating basin **350** 29
evaporating dish **350** 29
evaporator **155** 6
evening dress **33** 13
evening gown **30** 53
evening sandal **101** 27
evening suit **33** 7
everlasting **377** 3
ever-ready case **115** 103
evolution **345** 2
ewe **73** 13; **75** 10
examination couch **22** 43; **23** 4
examination table **27** 1, 26
excavation *Bldg. Site* **118** 69-82
excavation *Garage* **195** 28
excavation side **118** 72
excavator **118** 76, 81; **200** 1
excavator, large-scale ~ **159** 3
excavator, toy ~ **273** 65
excavator, universal ~ **158** 13
excess water conduit **269** 23
exchange *Post* **237** 17, 22
exchange *Stock Exch.* **251** 1-10
exchange broker **251** 4
exchange floor **251** 1
exchange golf ball **249** 28
exchange hall **251** 1
exchange rate **204** 32
exchange typing element **249** 28
excited state **1** 19
exciter lamp **312** 48
exclamation mark **342** 21
exclamation point **342** 21
exclusion principle **1** 7
excretory vacuole **357** 5
excursion steamer **221** 101-128; **225** 29
executive-secretary system **246** 13
exercise book **47** 24; **260** 4, 18
exercises **296** 48-60
exergue **252** 10
exhaust *Agr. Mach.* **64** 38
exhaust *Railw.* **209** 12, 22
exhaust, upswept ~ **188** 15; **189** 15
exhaust bubbles **279** 26
exhaust casing **212** 69
exhaust escape flue **258** 79
exhaust fan *Brew.* **92** 15
exhaust fan *Joiner* **133** 33
exhaust gas **160** 4
exhaust gas stack **154** 37
exhaust manifold **190** 36, 73
exhaust mast **221** 17

exhaust muffler **212** 42, 48
exhaust outlet **259** 92
exhaust pipe *Photograv.* **182** 25
exhaust pipe *Car* **191** 51
exhaust pipe *Ship* **221** 76
exhaust pipe *Warships* **258** 44
exhaust pipe, four-pipe ~ **189** 51
exhaust port **242** 58
exhaust repair **195** 52
exhaust silencer **212** 42, 48
exhaust system **195** 51
exhaust valve **190** 46; **242** 53
'exit' *Airport* **233** 37
exit **307** 19
exit, emergency ~ **99** 79
exit gate **319** 12
ex libris **185** 51
exosphere **7** 31
exotic **306** 30
expansion line **1** 61
expansion tank **38** 24
experimental apparatus **261** 11
explosion, atomic ~ **7** 11
exponent **345** 1
exposing lamp **182** 3
exposure bath **228** 21
exposure control device **176** 9
exposure control switch **117** 17
exposure counter **115** 17
exposure meter **114** 29
exposure meter, hand-held ~ **114** 56
exposure meter control step **117** 37
exposure meter needle **115** 57
exposure system **249** 42
exposure time balancing knob **116** 39
exposure timer **116** 24; **179** 18
expression marks **321** 27-41
express locomotive **205** 35
express train car **207** 1-21
express train carriage **207** 1-21
express train coach **207** 1-21
express train compartment **207** 43
extension *Joiner* **133** 13
extension *Post* **237** 17, 19, 21, 22-26, 26
extension arm **132** 63
extension bar **151** 57
extension bellows **115** 85
extension cord **127** 10
extension ladder **270** 14
extension lead **127** 10
extension plug **127** 11
extension socket **127** 12
extension tube *Household* **50** 70
extension tube *Photog.* **115** 81
extensor, common ~ **18** 57, 63
extensor, radial ~ **18** 56
extensor carpi radialis longus **18** 56
extensor communis digitorum **18** 57, 63
extinguisher, mobile ~ **270** 63
extra **310** 29; **316** 39
extra bold **175** 9
extracting a root **345** 2
extraction fan **199** 32
extraction forceps **24** 47
extraction of phenol **170** 3
extraction vent **49** 20
extractor **170** 37
extractor duct, movable ~ **142** 15
extractor fan **133** 33
extractor grid **100** 13
extractor support **142** 16
extrados **336** 26
extremity, fimbriated ~ **20** 82
extrusion press **159** 11; **161** 7
eye *Man* **16** 7; **19** 38-51
eye *Horse* **72** 4
eye *Dom. Anim.* **73** 32
eye *Game* **88** 15, 33, 43, 60
eye *Fish Farm.* **89** 82
eye *Mills* **91** 19
eye *Blacksm.* **137** 29
eye *Weaving* **166** 28, 29
eye *Art* **334** 75
eye, compound ~ *Bees* **77** 20-24
eye, compound ~ *Articulates* **358** 7
eye, simple ~ **77** 2
eye, stalked ~ **357** 30
eyeball **19** 45
eye-bright **61** 27
eyebrow *Man* **19** 38
eyebrow *Roof* **121** 23
eyecup **115** 73; **117** 14; **313** 34
eyeground **22** 32
eyelash **19** 41
eyelet *Shoem.* **100** 63
eyelet *Glaz.* **124** 23
eyelet *Weaving* **166** 28
eyelet, hook, and press-stud setter **100** 53
eyelet embroidery **102** 11
eyelid, lower ~ **19** 40
eyelid, upper ~ **19** 39
eye muscles **19** 44
eyepiece **113** 20; **115** 42; **117** 14; **311** 9
eyepiece, binocular ~ **23** 6
eyepiece control ring **313** 7
eyepiece focusing knob **112** 56
eyespot **358** 54

F

fabled beings **327**
fabric *Bldg. Site* **118** 1-49
fabric *Knitting* **167** 29, 48
fabric *Text. Finish.* **168** 39, 51, 64
fabric *Weaves* **171** 29
fabric *Store* **271** 59
fabric, air-dry ~ **168** 22
fabric, metallic ~ **270** 46
fabric, non-woven ~ **103** 27
fabric, printed ~ **168** 57
fabric, raised ~ **168** 36
fabric, shrink-resistant ~ **168** 26
fabric, tubular ~ **167** 1, 9
fabric, woollen ~ *Dressm.* **103** 27
fabric, woollen ~ *Text. Finish.* **168** 1
fabric, woven ~ **166** 12
fabric box **167** 10
fabric container **167** 10
fabric department **271** 58
fabric drum **167** 10
fabric-finishing machine, decatizing ~ **168** 49
fabric for upholstery **134** 60
fabric guide roller **168** 5
fabric-plaiting device **168** 30
fabric-raising machine **168** 31
fabric roll **167** 29
fabric roller **166** 20
fabric shaft **171** 21, 23
fabric wallhanging **128** 18
fabulous creatures **327**
façade, west ~ **335** 22
face *Man* **16** 4-17
face *Horse* **72** 5
face *Clocks* **110** 25
face *Blacksm.* **137** 28
face *Composing Rm.* **174** 31; **175** 42
face *Art* **336** 24
face, metal ~ **303** 11
face compress **106** 25
face guard **292** 11, 25
face mask *Fire Brig.* **270** 40
face mask *Swim.* **279** 10
face mask filter **270** 57
face par **251** 12
face pipes **326** 1-3
facet **77** 20
face urn **328** 38
face vault **297** 30
facing **24** 32
facing, decorative ~ **30** 47
facsimile signature **252** 34
facsimile telegraph **245** 1
factor **344** 25
factory number **187** 51
factory ship *Sea Fish.* **90** 11
factory ship *Ship* **221** 86
fahlerz **351** 1
fahl ore **351** 1
fair **308**
fair, annual ~ **308** 1-69
fairground **308** 1
fairing **189** 43
fairing, integrated ~ **189** 44
fairing, metal ~ **188** 50
fairlead **284** 29
fairway **216** 21
fairway, main ~ **224** 92
fairway, secondary ~ **224** 93
fairway markings **224** 84-102
fairway marks **224** 68-83
fair-weather cumulus **8** 1
fairy-tale figure **306** 65
falcon **86** 46
falconer **86** 42

falconry **86** 42-46
falcons **362** 1-4
fall **221** 106
falling wedge **85** 4
fallow **63** 1
fallow buck **88** 40
fallow deer **88** 40-41
falls **11** 45
falls, artificial ~ **272** 9
false acacia **371** 70
false oat **69** 22
family grave **331** 27
family tomb **331** 27
fan *Roof & Boilerr.* **38** 58
fan *Agr. Mach.* **64** 15; **65** 52
fan *Pest Contr.* **83** 49
fan *Game* **88** 75
fan *Energy Sources* **155** 14
fan *Weaving* **165** 23
fan *Intern. Combust. Eng.* **190** 7
fan *Refuse Coll.* **199** 35, 46
fan *Aircraft* **232** 34, 43
fan *Ethnol.* **353** 42
fan, low-pressure ~ **199** 33
fan blower **179** 22
fan clutch **190** 8
fancy appliqué **35** 7
fancy dress **306** 6-48, 32
fancy-dress ball **306** 1-48
fan drift **144** 22
fan drive, hydrostatic ~ **212** 62
fan fold sheet, continuous ~ **248** 47
fang **19** 36
fan-jet turbine **232** 38
fanlight **37** 35
fan nozzle **83** 4
fan tail **73** 29
fan vault **336** 46
faradization unit **23** 37
farm **15** 101
farm buildings **62**
farmer **62** 6
farmhand **63** 5
farming **63**
farm labourer **63** 5
farmland **63** 17
farm produce **68** 1-47
farm road **63** 18
farmstead **62**
farm track **63** 18
farm vehicle engineering **138**
farmworker **63** 5
farmyard **62** 31
farmyard hedge **62** 35
farmyard manure **63** 15
farrowing and store pen **75** 40
farrowing rails **75** 43
fascia panel **191** 57-90
fascine **216** 53
fashion catalogue **104** 6
fashion doll **47** 9; **48** 32
fashion house **268** 9
fashion journal **104** 4; **271** 36
fashion magazine **104** 4; **271** 36
fast and slow motion switch **117** 87
fastback **193** 29
fast breeder **154** 1
fast-breeder reactor **154** 1
fastening *Plant Propagn.* **54** 13
fastening *Station* **206** 12
fat end **95** 53
fat lady **308** 21
fattening pond **89** 6
faucet *Kitch.* **39** 36
faucet *Plumb. etc.* **126** 34
faucet *Electrotyp. etc.* **178** 34
faucet *Chem.* **349** 5, 22
faucet, outside ~ **37** 41
fault *Phys. Geog.* **12** 4
fault *Coal* **144** 51
fault, distributive ~ **12** 8
fault, multiple ~ **12** 8
fault, normal ~ **12** 7
fault-block mountain **12** 4-11
faulting **12** 4-20
fault line **12** 5
fault repair service **237** 27
faults, complex ~ **12** 8-11
fault throw **12** 6
fault trace **12** 5
faustball **293** 72-78, 74
favorite **289** 52
favourite **289** 52
fawn **88** 39
fawn, female ~ **88** 34
F-clef **320** 9
F contact **115** 14
feather *Headgear* **35** 6, 12
feather *Dom. Anim.* **73** 31
feather *Mach. Parts etc.* **143** 73
feather *Chivalry* **329** 78
feather, falcate ~ **88** 68
feather, peacock's ~ **254** 36
feather star **369** 3
feed *Iron & Steel* **147** 51
feed *Mach. Tools* **149** 9
feed adjustment **100** 28
feed board **180** 32, 49, 67; **181** 4, 21, 30; **185** 9
feed chain **172** 67
feed chain drive **172** 69
feed channel **157** 55
feed conveyor **236** 33
feed conveyor, endless-chain ~ **74** 25
feed dispenser **74** 13
feed drum **180** 33, 34
feeder *Agr. Mach.* **64** 72
feeder *Poultry Farm* **74** 49-51
feeder *Brickw.* **159** 7
feeder *Offset Print.* **180** 31, 48, 68, 74
feeder *Letterpress* **181** 22, 24
feeder *Bookbind.* **185** 25
feeder, automatic ~ **181** 5
feeder, mechanical ~ **74** 13, 23
feeder broom **199** 44
feeder mechanism **181** 22
feeder panel **153** 4
feeder-selecting device **167** 40
feeder skip **118** 35
feed gearbox **149** 8
feed gear lever **149** 10
feed guide **184** 23
feed hopper *Poultry Farm* **74** 24
feed hopper *Bookbind.* **185** 26
feed-in **173** 13
feed indicator **157** 9
feeding, mechanical ~ **74** 23-27
feeding apparatus **181** 22
feeding bottle **28** 19
feeding bowl **70** 32
feeding-in **164** 15
feeding passage **75** 3
feeding place **86** 28
feeding site **80** 50
feeding trough *Poultry Farm* **74** 21
feeding trough *Livestock* **75** 37
feeding trough, adjustable ~ **74** 4
feed mechanism *Agr. Mach.* **65** 78
feed mechanism *Mach. Tools* **149** 18
feed mechanism *Post* **236** 48
feed mechanism *Graphic Art* **340** 33
feed motor **177** 43
feed pawl **157** 44
feed pipe **96** 50
feed pump *Nucl. Energy* **154** 13
feed pump *Railw.* **210** 9
feed roll **85** 19
feed roller **85** 24; **157** 4, 40
feed roller, fluted ~ **163** 52
feed runner **147** 22
feed screw **149** 15
feed setting **100** 28
feed shaft **149** 33
feed spindle **312** 36
feed spool **117** 31
feed sprocket **312** 26
feed supply pipe **74** 15
feed table *Sawmill* **157** 63
feed table *Offset Print.* **180** 32, 49, 67
feed table *Letterpress* **181** 4, 21, 30
feed table *Bookbind.* **184** 12, 21; **185** 9, 34
feed-through insulator **153** 12, 35
feed-through terminal **153** 12, 35
feed trip **149** 18
feed tripping device **149** 18
feed valve **210** 20
feedwater heater **210** 23
feedwater line **154** 12, 30
feedwater preheater **210** 23
feedwater steam circuit **154** 45
feedwater tank **152** 17
feedwater tray, top ~ **210** 29
feeler *Agr. Mach.* **64** 86
feeler *Forest Pests* **82** 3
feeler *Weaving* **166** 32
feeler *Invertebr.* **357** 31
feeler *Articulates* **358** 27, 53
feeler, maxillary ~ **358** 42

feeler gauge **140** 53
feeler support wheel **64** 88
feet-first jump **282** 13
felines **368** 2-8
feller **84** 20
felling **84** 27
felling wedge **84** 4, 30
felling wedge, hydraulic ~ **84** 25
felt **173** 51
felt, dry ~ **173** 23
felt nail **122** 96
felt pen **48** 18
felt tip pen **247** 11; **260** 19
female, winged ~ **358** 21
femur **17** 22
fence *Joiner* **132** 65
fence *Refuse Coll.* **199** 13
fence *Aircraft* **231** 8
fence *Swim.* **281** 17
fence *Equest.* **289** 8
fence, electrified ~ **62** 46
fence, paling ~ **52** 10
fence, protective ~ **84** 7
fence, stone ~ **337** 23
fence, timber ~ **118** 44
fence, wicker ~ **216** 54
fence, wire ~ **15** 39
fence, wire netting ~ **84** 7
fence, wooden ~ **37** 53
fence adjustment handle **132** 66
fence rack **63** 28
fencers **294** 5-6
fencer's salute **294** 18
fencing **294**
fencing, modern ~ **294** 1-33
fencing glove **294** 12
fencing instructor **294** 1
fencing jacket **294** 16
fencing mask **294** 13, 14
fencing master **294** 1
fencing measure **294** 10
fencing movement **294** 7
fencing shoe, heelless ~ **294** 17
fencing weapons **294** 34-45
fender *Horse* **71** 40
fender *Tram* **197** 12
fender *Hydr. Eng.* **217** 9
fender *Docks* **225** 12
fender, front ~ *Bicycle* **187** 13
fender, front ~ *Car* **191** 3; **191** 3, 13
fender, integral ~ **193** 33
fender, wooden ~ **218** 26
fender pile *Hydr. Eng.* **217** 9
fender pile *Shipbuild.* **222** 35
F-1 engine **234** 4
fennel **380** 6
fen peat **13** 17
fermentation room **97** 72
fermentation thermometer **93** 9
fermentation trolley **97** 73
fermentation vessel **93** 8
fermenter **93** 8
fermenting cellar **93** 7
fern **377** 16
ferret **86** 24
ferreter **86** 25
ferreting **86** 23
ferries **221**
Ferris wheel **308** 37
ferroconcrete construction **119** 1-89
ferrule **45** 53
ferry, flying ~ **216** 10
ferryboat **216** 11, 15; **225** 11
ferry cable **216** 2
ferry landing stage **216** 7
ferryman **216** 17
ferry rope **216** 2
fertilizer, artificial ~ **63** 14
fertilizer, chemical ~ **63** 14
fertilizer, lime ~ **63** 14
fertilizer, nitrogen ~ **63** 14
fertilizer, phosphoric acid ~ **63** 14
fertilizer, potash ~ **63** 14
fertilizer spreader **62** 21
fescue **69** 24
festoon *Carnival* **306** 5
festoon *Art* **335** 54
festoon lamp **318** 26
festoon lighting **318** 25
fetish **354** 43
fetlock **72** 24
fettler **148** 43
fettling shop **148** 38-45
feuilleton **342** 67
F-hole **323** 6
fiber *see* fibre
fibre **77** 23
fibre, glass ~ **151** 48
fibre, loose ~ **168** 43
fibreboard **338** 24
fibula **17** 24
fibula, serpentine ~ **328** 28
fibula, spiral ~ **328** 30
fibula, two-piece ~ **328** 30
fiddle string **323** 9
field *Agr.* **63** 4, 17
field *Equest.* **289** 41, 51
field *Ball Games* **291** 1; **292** 40-58
field, fallow ~ **63** 1
field bean **69** 15
field bindweed **61** 26
field camomile **61** 8
field chopper, self-propelled ~ **64** 34-39
fielder **292** 76
field eryngo **61** 32
field glasses **86** 6
field guard **63** 13
field illumination **112** 33
fielding side **292** 73
field lens **115** 40
field mangel **69** 21
field marigold **61** 7
field mushroom **381** 1
field pests **80** 37-55
field player **292** 2
field poppy **61** 2
field sprinkler **67** 32
fig **383** 35; **384** 11, 13
fighter-bomber **256** 1, 29
fighting bull **319** 28
fighting ships **258** 64-91
fighting ships, modern ~ **259**
figure, clay ~ **48** 13; **339** 7
figure, plasticine ~ **48** 13
figure, symbolic ~ **327** 20
figure, symmetrical ~ **346** 24
figure, wax ~ **308** 69
figurehead **218** 16
figures, compulsory ~ **302** 11-19
figure ski **286** 56
figurine, clay ~ **328** 20
filament **169** 17, 22; **170** 44
filament, continuous ~ **169** 1-34
filament, solid ~ **169** 15
filament lamp **127** 56
filament tow **169** 28, 30
file *Doc.* **22** 12, 26
file *Metalwkr.* **140** 16
file *Office* **245** 6; **247** 37; **248** 5
file, flat ~ **108** 49; **140** 27
file, half-round ~ **140** 29
file, rough ~ **140** 8
file, round ~ **108** 47; **140** 29
file, smooth ~ **140** 8
file handle **108** 50
filet **102** 22
file tab **248** 4
filigree work **102** 30
filing cabinet **245** 4
filing clerk **248** 6
filing drawer **248** 2, 23
filing machine **140** 15
filing shelf **248** 10
fill, sanitary ~ **199** 10
filler *Tobacc. etc.* **107** 7
filler *Paperhanger* **128** 3
filler *Power Plant* **153** 38
filler *Films* **310** 52
filler hoist **200** 51
filler hole **213** 19
filler light **310** 52
filler opening **200** 52
filler rod **141** 12
fillet *Meat* **95** 13
fillet *Carp.* **120** 45
fillet *Floor etc. Constr.* **123** 57, 67
fillet *Bookbind.* **183** 3
fillet, tilting ~ **121** 31
fillet gauge **142** 36
filleting knife **89** 38
fillet of beef **95** 24
fillet of pork **95** 44
filling *Dent.* **24** 30
filling *Tablew. etc.* **45** 38
filling *Hydr. Eng.* **217** 7
filling *Water* **269** 29
filling compound **153** 38
filling end **162** 2
filling inlet **50** 12
filling knife **128** 35
filling machine **76** 21, 26
filling material **24** 51
filling station **196** 1-29
fill-in light **310** 52
fill light **310** 52
film *Atom* **2** 10, 13
film *Photog.* **114** 9
film *Composing Rm.* **176** 25
film, cine ~ **117**
film, exposed ~ **117** 42

film, unexposed ~ **117** 41
film actor **310** 28
film actress **310** 27
film advance **114** 32
film advance lever, single-stroke ~ **115** 16
film agitator, automatic ~ **116** 19
film and sound cutting table **117** 96
film and tape synchronizing head **117** 102
film back **115** 80
film break detector **312** 30
film camera **27** 20
film camera, soundproof ~ **310** 47; **313** 15
film cameras **313** 1-39
film cassette **112** 65
film cassette, miniature ~ **114** 7
film cassette, universal ~ **242** 44
film cement **312** 22
film clip **116** 14
film copier, automatic ~ **176** 28
film-developing machine **311** 30
film director **310** 40
film dosimeter **2** 8
film drier **116** 23
film editor **311** 43
film extra **310** 29
film feed spool **117** 79
film former **178** 24
film gate **117** 30; **312** 34
film gate opening **117** 40
filmgoer **312** 5
filming **310** 14-60, 26-60
filming, exterior ~ **310** 18
filming, outdoor ~ **310** 18
filming agent **178** 24
filming speed selector **117** 12
film laboratory **310** 2, 30
film library **310** 5
film magazine **113** 40
film marker **117** 95
film matrix case **176** 17
film of fluorescent material **240** 19
film orchestra **310** 17
film path **312** 31
film perforator **117** 95; **242** 10
film poster **268** 57
film-processing machine **311** 30
film processor, automatic ~ **177** 72
film projection **312** 1-23
film projector **311** 22; **312** 24
film projectors **312** 24-52
film reel **311** 24; **312** 32
film-ring dosimeter **2** 11
films **310**; **311**; **312**; **313**
filmscript **310** 45
film set **310** 7
filmsetter **176** 7
filmsetting **176**
film speed setting **117** 18
film spool **114** 8; **311** 24; **312** 32
film spool holder **238** 6
film star **310** 27, 28
film storage vault **310** 5
film studios **310** 1-13
film title **310** 35
film transport **114** 32
film transport handle **116** 7
film transport mechanism **311** 26
film turntable **117** 99; **311** 44
film viewer **117** 91; **242** 8
film wind **114** 32
film window **114** 18; **115** 28, 34
filter *Atom* **2** 9, 12, 14
filter *Weaving* **165** 14
filter *Synth. Fibres* **170** 32
filter *Paperm.* **172** 20
filter *Water* **269** 62
filter *Chem.* **349** 12
filter, fluted ~ **350** 41
filter adjustment **116** 43, 44, 45
filter bed **269** 10
filter bottom **269** 11
filter cake **161** 13
filter change, automatic ~ **316** 49
filtered water outlet **269** 12
filter flask **350** 40
filter funnel **349** 11
filter gravel **269** 10
filter lens **142** 40
filter mount **115** 6
filter pick-up **112** 57
filter plate **349** 12
filter press *Porcelain Manuf.* **161** 12
filter press *Synth. Fibres* **169** 12
filter screen **116** 22
fimbria **20** 82
fin *Swim.* **279** 18
fin *Bathing* **280** 41
fin *Motorboats etc.* **286** 43
fin, abdominal ~ **364** 8
fin, anal ~ **364** 9
fin, caudal ~ **364** 10
fin, dorsal ~ *Fish etc.* **364** 6
fin, dorsal ~ *Mammals* **367** 27
fin, fixed ~ **286** 61
fin, pectoral ~ **364** 7
fin, pelvic ~ **364** 8
fin, ventral ~ **364** 8
fin, vertical ~ *Aircraft* **229** 24; **230** 59; **231** 6; **232** 7
fin, vertical ~ *Space* **235** 1
fin, vertical ~ *Air Force* **256** 32
fin, vertical ~ *Airsports* **288** 21
final image tube **113** 39
final picture quality checking room **238** 60-65
finch **360** 1
finches **361** 6-8
finds, prehistoric ~ **328** 1-40
fine cut **107** 25
fine focusing indicator **224** 36
finger, fifth ~ **19** 68
finger, fourth ~ **19** 67
finger, little ~ **19** 68
finger, middle ~ **19** 66
finger, pivoted ~ **74** 36
finger, second ~ **19** 65
finger, third ~ **19** 66
fingerboard **323** 21; **324** 8
finger guard **83** 20; **85** 15
finger hole *Office* **247** 39
finger hole *Sports* **305** 16
fingerhole *Music. Instr.* **323** 33; **324** 34
finger hook **324** 67
fingernail **19** 80
finger pad **19** 78
finger paint **260** 26
finger painting **260** 26
finger plate **237** 11
fingerprint **264** 29
fingerprint identification **264** 28
finger roll **97** 15
finger stop **237** 12
fingertip **19** 79
finial **335** 37
fining bath **162** 4
fining lap **111** 37, 38
finish **286** 28
finish, gloss ~ **128** 32
finished malt collecting hopper **92** 20
finishing **168** 1-65; **170** 57
finishing bur **24** 38
finishing layer **123** 40
finishing line **282** 28; **286** 30
finishing machine **100** 3
finishing of textile fabrics **168**
finishing press **183** 4
finishing train **148** 71
Finn **284** 51
Finn dinghy **284** 51
fin post **235** 3
fipple flute **322** 7
fir cone **372** 2
fire, blacksmith's ~ **137** 1-8; **138** 34
fire, open ~ **267** 25
fire alarm **270** 4
fire alarm siren **270** 4
fire appliance building **233** 8
fire-arm **87** 2
fireboat **270** 65
firebox **210** 4
fire control radar antenna **258** 51
fire control system **255** 74
firecrest **361** 10
fire curtain **316** 24
fire department **270**
firedoor handle handgrip **210** 63
fire eater **308** 25
fire engine **270** 5
fire extinguisher **196** 9
fire extinguisher, portable ~ **270** 61
fire extinguisher, wheeled ~ **270** 63
firefighter **270** 37
fire-fighting equipment **227** 25; **228** 20
fire gable **121** 9

fire gun **221** 4
fire hat **270** 38
firehole door **210** 61
firehole shield **210** 60
fireman **270** 37
fire nozzle **221** 4
fireplace **267** 23
fire plug **270** 35
fire prevention **316** 6
fire protection **316** 6
fire salamander **364** 22
fire service **270**
fire service drill **270** 1-46
fireside **267** 22
fire siren **270** 4
fire station **270** 1-3
fire tube **210** 17
firewood basket **309** 10
fireworks **306** 49-54
firing mechanism **255** 29
firing mould **161** 4
firing pin **87** 21
firing position **305** 73
firing process **161** 2
firing sequence insert **195** 13
firing trigger **87** 11
firmer chisel **134** 30
firn basin **12** 48
fir needle **372** 11
firn field **12** 48
firn slope **300** 14
first aid **21**
first aid dressing **21** 5
first aid kit **21** 4
first aid post **308** 61
first aid station **204** 44
first aid tent **308** 61
first base **292** 46
first-class section **207** 17
first floor **37** 2; **118** 7
first-floor landing **123** 23
first position **294** 18
Fish *Astron.* **4** 64
fish *Grocer* **98** 19
fish *Fish etc.* **364**
fish, canned ~ **96** 28
fish, female ~ **89** 13
fish basket **89** 25
fishbolt **202** 13
fishbone stitch **102** 7
fish-canning factory **225** 59
fish culture **89** 1-19
fish dish **266** 53
fish dock **225** 56
fish egg **89** 12
fishes **364** 1-18
fisheye **115** 44
fish farming **89** 1-19
fish fork **45** 8, 65
fish hook **89** 79
fishing **89** 26
fishing boat **89** 27; **90** 24
fishing line **89** 63
fishing lugger **90** 1
fishing pliers **89** 37
fishing tackle **89** 37-94
fishing tackle, suspended ~ **90** 29
fish knife *Tablew. etc.* **45** 8, 64
fish knife *Fish Farm.* **89** 39
fish ladder **89** 93
fish lance **280** 40
fish market **225** 57
fish pass **89** 93
fishplate **202** 12
fishpole antenna **258** 60
fish spawn **89** 12
fish spear **280** 40
fishtail bit **145** 21
fish way **89** 93
fission **1** 43, 46
fission, nuclear ~ **1** 34
fission fragment **1** 44, 47, 51
fission fragments **1** 37-38
fissure **11** 52
fissure, diagonal ~ **300** 3
fissure, horizontal ~ **300** 3
fissure, vertical ~ **300** 3
fissure bur **24** 39
fist **16** 48
fist hatchet **328** 1
fitch **129** 19
fitter **140** 1
fitting booth **271** 32
fitting of the frame **111** 10
fitting-out quay **222** 5-9
fittings **126** 38-52
five-four time **320** 41
fix **224** 45
flag *Flags* **253** 7-11
flag *Town* **268** 44
flag *Ball Games* **293** 86
flag, club's ~ **283** 25
flag, linesman's ~ **291** 60
flag, Olympic ~ **253** 5
flag, swallow-tailed ~ **253** 22
flag at half-mast **253** 6
flag at half-staff **253** 6
flag dressing **221** 85
flag of the Council of Europe **253** 4
flag of the United Nations **253** 1-3
flagpole **253** 1, 7; **273** 61
flags **253**
flags, national ~ **253** 15-21
flags, triangular ~ **253** 30-32
flagstaff **253** 1, 7; **258** 4; **259** 87; **273** 61
flagstick **293** 88
flagstone **51** 17
flail rotor **64** 73
flame regulator **107** 31
flamingo **272** 53
flan **252** 43
flancard **329** 86
flan case **97** 47
flanchard **329** 86
flange *Cooper* **130** 28
flange *Mach. Parts etc.* **143** 2, 5
flange *Electrotyp. etc.* **178** 44
flange *Hydr. Eng.* **217** 67
flange, bottom ~ **215** 10
flange, top ~ **215** 9
flange mount **130** 20
flanging, swaging, and wiring machine **125** 25
flank *Man* **16** 32
flank *Game* **88** 26
flank *Meat* **95** 2, 15-16
flank *Bldg. Site* **119** 6
flank, thick ~ **95** 15, 36
flank, thin ~ **95** 16
flank vault **297** 31
flans **97** 22-24
flap *Child. Clothes* **29** 35
flap *Horse* **71** 40, 47
flap *Aircraft* **229** 37
flap, double-slotted ~ **229** 48
flap, extending ~ **229** 51
flap, fur ~ **35** 32
flap, normal ~ **229** 46
flap, outer ~ **259** 78
flap, slotted ~ **229** 47
flap, split ~ **229** 49
flap extension **78** 19
flaps, plain ~ **229** 46-48
flaps, simple ~ **229** 46-48
flaps, split ~ **229** 49-50
flap valve **192** 63
flare, pork ~ **95** 45
flash, battery-portable ~ **114** 65
flash, electronic ~ **114** 65, 68; **309** 40-41
flash, single-unit ~ **114** 68
flash bar **114** 75
flash bulb **309** 39
flash contact **114** 30
flash cube **114** 74
flash cube contact **114** 13
flash cube unit **114** 73
flash eliminator **255** 18
flashgun **114** 68; **309** 38
flashgun, electronic ~ **309** 40-41
flash head **114** 67; **309** 40
flash hider **255** 18
flash lamp *Photomech. Reprod.* **177** 37
flash lamp *Inf. Tech.* **242** 43
flashlight *Electr.* **127** 26
flashlight *Fire Brig.* **270** 6
flashlight, underwater ~ **279** 25
flash socket **115** 14
flash switch **114** 33
flash tube **176** 26
flask, collared ~ **328** 12
flask, conical ~ **350** 39
flask, flat-bottomed ~ **350** 36
flask, long-necked ~ **350** 38
flask, round-bottomed ~ **350** 38
flask, three-necked ~ **350** 55
flask, volumetric ~ **173** 3
flat *Dwellings* **37** 64-68, 69-71
flat *Flat* **46**
flat *Music. Not.* **320** 52
flat-bed cylinder press, two-revolution ~ **181** 1
flat-bed knitting machine **167** 35
flat-bed offset machine **180** 75
flat-bed offset press **180** 75
flatcar **206** 24; **213** 5, 11, 40
flat clearer **163** 44
flat four engine **230** 34
flat glass production **162** 1-20
flat plate keel **222** 49
flats *Cotton Spin.* **163** 45, 46
flats *Navig.* **224** 87, 97

flatter **137** 35
flatworm **81** 35
flauto piccolo **323** 30
flavourings **382**
flax **383** 6
flay brush **129** 21
flaying knife **94** 13
flea **81** 42
flea beetle **80** 39
flea market **309**
fleet of lorries **206** 25
fleet submarine, nuclear-powered ~ **259** 54
flesh *Soft Fruit* **58** 24, 35, 58
flesh *Drupes & Nuts* **59** 6
fletching **305** 62
fleur-de-lis **254** 13
flews **70** 26
flex **50** 66, 77
flex hook **50** 65
flexor, radial ~ **18** 40
flexor, ulnar ~ **18** 58
flexor carpi radialis **18** 40
flexor carpi ulnaris **18** 58
flies **316** 1-60
flight, negative ~ **288** 9
flight board **77** 49
flight deck *Space* **235** 16
flight deck *Warships* **259** 2, 12
flight instrument **288** 68
flight of wild ducks **86** 41
flight refuelling probe **256** 7
flik-flak **297** 24
flint **107** 28
flint corn **68** 31
flintlock **353** 28
flint maize **68** 31
flip-over numeral **110** 20
flipper *Swim.* **279** 18
flipper *Bathing* **280** 41
flipper *Mammals* **367** 28
flip-up window **142** 4
flitch of bacon **96** 2
flitter-mouse **366** 9
float *Bldg. Site* **118** 57
float *Plumb. etc.* **126** 15
float *Weaves* **171** 40
float *Car* **192** 15
float *Rivers* **216** 12
float *Hydr. Eng.* **217** 34
float *Aircraft* **232** 6
float *Swim.* **282** 18
float *Motorboats etc.* **286** 44
float *Theatre* **316** 26
float, cork ~ *Fish Farm.* **89** 43
float, cork ~ *Swim.* **282** 32
float, lead-weighted ~ **89** 48
float, plastic ~ **89** 44
float, polystyrene ~ **89** 46
float, quill ~ **89** 45
float, skin ~ **353** 11
float, sliding ~ **89** 43, 48
float, spherical ~ **90** 19
float, wooden ~ **90** 6
float bath **162** 16
float chamber **192** 14
float glass process **162** 12
floating thread, diagonal ~ **171** 38
floating thread, loose ~ **171** 41
floating vessel **221** 65
floating yarn, diagonal ~ **171** 38
floating yarn, loose ~ **171** 41
float lever **65** 43
float line **90** 4
floatplane **232** 5
floats **89** 43-48
float seaplane **232** 5
float shaft **217** 35
flood bed **216** 41
flood containment area **216** 42
flood damage **216** 5
floodgate **217** 77
flood plain **13** 62
flood wall **216** 32
floor **296** 11; **297** 6
floor, blind ~ **123** 38, 73
floor, concrete ~ **118** 16
floor, false ~ **120** 43; **123** 68
floor, ferroconcrete ~ **119** 8
floor, first ~ **37** 2, 3; **118** 7, 14
floor, inserted ~ **120** 43; **123** 68
floor, reinforced concrete ~ **119** 8; **123** 35
floor, ribbed ~ **123** 35
floor, second ~ **37** 3; **118** 14
floor, upper ~ **37** 3; **118** 14
floor and carpet cleaning **50** 53-86
floorboard **120** 36
floor brick **159** 24
floor brush **129** 27
floor ceiling **222** 63
floor cleaning **50** 53-86
floor cloth **50** 55
floor construction **123**
floor filling **120** 44; **123** 69
floor grinding machine **138** 7
floor indicator **271** 49
flooring block, hollow ~ **159** 26
floor manager **271** 33
floor nozzle **50** 71
floor plate **222** 59
floor socket **127** 23
floor socket, sunken ~ **127** 24
floor trader **251** 6
floorwalker **271** 33
flop **298** 9
floppy disc reader **244** 8
flora **356** 21
florin **252** 19
flour **91** 28; **97** 52
flour beetle **81** 18
flour corn **68** 31
flour silo **97** 74
flow **216** 9
flow chart **76** 9
flow coating machine **129** 34
flow diagram **76** 9; **92** 25
flower *Soft Fruit* **58** 4
flower *Drupes & Nuts* **59** 9
flower *Weeds* **61** 10, 19, 22
flower *Arable Crops* **68** 42
flower *Fodder Plants* **69** 7, 14
flower *Gdn. Pests* **80** 11
flower *Bot.* **370** 23, 51
flower *Decid. Trees* **371** 17, 26, 35, 40, 52, 55, 62
flower *Shrubs etc.* **373** 5, 7, 11, 14, 31; **374** 6, 7, 15, 21, 24
flower *Flowers etc.* **375** 3, 6, 16, 19, 20, 23, 40, 46; **376** 2, 5, 11, 19, 23
flower *Alp. Plants etc.* **378** 16, 20, 28, 31, 32, 37, 47, 57
flower *Trop. Plants* **382** 4, 17, 18, 29, 42, 55
flower *Industr. Plants* **383** 12, 17, 27, 31, 36, 39, 46, 47
flower *South. Fruits* **384** 13, 18, 56, 57, 65
flower, amaranthine ~ **60** 21
flower, androgynous ~ *Shrubs etc.* **374** 10
flower, androgynous ~ *Trop. Plants* **382** 12, 14
flower, female ~ *Drupes & Nuts* **59** 38
flower, female ~ *Decid. Trees* **371** 6, 13
flower, female ~ *Conifers* **372** 43
flower, female ~ *Shrubs etc.* **373** 20
flower, female ~ *Alp. Plants etc.* **378** 25; **378** 53
flower, female ~ *Trop. Plants* **382** 32, 50
flower, female ~ *Industr. Plants* **383** 50
flower, female ~ *South. Fruits* **384** 7, 14, 42, 43
flower, forced ~ **55** 24
flower, fumariaceous ~ **60** 5
flower, hermaphroditic ~ *Shrubs etc.* **374** 10
flower, hermaphroditic ~ *Trop. Plants* **382** 12, 14
flower, male ~ *Drupes & Nuts* **59** 39
flower, male ~ *Decid. Trees* **371** 14
flower, male ~ *Conifers* **372** 43
flower, male ~ *Shrubs etc.* **373** 21; **374** 11
flower, male ~ *Alp. Plants etc.* **378** 23, 53
flower, male ~ *Trop. Plants* **382** 13
flower, male ~ *Industr. Plants* **383** 51
flower, male ~ *South. Fruits* **384** 5, 15, 44, 51
flower, open ~ **374** 17
flower, withered ~ **58** 55
flower arrangement **266** 78; **267** 37; **330** 48
flower basket **266** 29
flower bed *Fruit & Veg. Gdn.* **52** 18
flower bed *Market Gdn.* **55** 37
flower bed *Park* **272** 41
flower box **37** 20
flower bud *Soft Fruit* **58** 27
flower bud *Bot.* **370** 24
flower bud *Decid. Trees* **371** 25
flower bud *Shrubs etc.* **374** 14

flower bud *Trop. Plants* **382** 28
flower cone, female ~ **372** 4, 16, 22, 34, 62, 68
flower garden **51** 1-35
flower girl **266** 28
flower head *Weeds* **61** 14
flower head *Alp. Plants etc.* **378** 12
flower head, discoid ~ **370** 74
flower head, hollow ~ **370** 75
flowering branch *Decid. Trees* **371** 2, 10, 16, 34, 39, 51, 54, 66, 71
flowering branch *Conifers* **372** 33
flowering branch *Trop. Plants* **382** 8, 12, 23, 27, 31, 50
flowering branch *Industr. Plants* **383** 22, 26, 30, 38
flowering branch *South. Fruits* **384** 17, 24, 37, 49, 54
flowering rush **378** 39
flowering shoot *Alp. Plants etc.* **378** 2, 27
flowering shoot *Trop. Plants* **382** 41, 47
flowering shoot *Industr. Plants* **383** 42
flower of inner series **375** 32
flower of outer series **375** 31
flower pot **54** 8
flowers, wild ~ **375; 376**
flower seller **266** 28
flower shoot **59** 28
flower shoot, male ~ **372** 6, 62, 68
flower stalk *Drupes & Nuts* **59** 4
flower stalk *Bot.* **370** 52
flower stalk *Industr. Plants* **383** 7
flower stand **204** 48; **267** 36
flower stem **370** 52
flower umbel **378** 40
flower vase **309** 2
flower window **37** 68
flowmeter *Hosp.* **26** 3
flowmeter *Dairy.* **76** 4
flow path **154** 51
flow pipe *Roof & Boilerr.* **38** 74
flow pipe *Plumb. etc.* **126** 23
flow pipe *Energy Sources* **155** 10
fluate **128** 7
flue **155** 25
flueblock **38** 40
flue brush **38** 35
flue pipe **322** 57
flue pipe, metal ~ **326** 23-30
flue pipe, open ~ **326** 23-30, 31-33
flue pipe, stopped ~ **326** 34
flue pipe, wooden ~ **326** 31-33
flue pipe duct **326** 24
flue pipe windway **326** 24
flue tube **210** 8
fluid container **247** 9
fluid reservoir **247** 9
fluid transmission **212** 27, 52
fluorescent display, eight-digit ~ **247** 15
fluorescent material **240** 18
fluorescent tube **127** 61, 62
fluorite **351** 16
fluoroscope, mobile ~ **26** 14
fluorspar **351** 16
fluothane container **26** 26
flush-deck vessel **258** 2; **259** 22
flushing lever *Bathrm. etc.* **49** 17
flushing lever *Plumb. etc.* **126** 19
flushing valve **126** 37
flush pipe **126** 17
flute *Mills* **91** 17
flute *Music. Instr.* **323** 31
flute *Art* **334** 27
flute *Ethnol.* **353** 47
flute, globular ~ **324** 32
flute, small ~ **323** 30
fluting **157** 6
flux *Goldsm. etc.* **108** 36
flux *Plumb.* **125** 7
flux *Gas Weld.* **141** 18
flux *Iron & Steel* **147** 2
fly *Men's Wear* **33** 48
fly *Fish Farm.* **89** 65
fly *Articulates* **358** 18
fly agaric **379** 10
fly amanita **379** 10
fly and draw curtain **315** 4
fly curtain **315** 3
flyer **164** 25
fly floor **316** 5
fly frame **164** 19
fly frame operative **164** 24
fly frame operator **164** 24
fly front **33** 62
fly fungus **379** 10
fly gallery **316** 5
flying boat **232** 1
flying boat, amphibian ~ **232** 8
flying buttress **335** 28
Flying Dutchman **284** 49
fly leaf **185** 49
fly line **316** 8
fly man **316** 7
fly nut *Mach. Parts etc.* **143** 42
fly nut *Bicycle* **187** 39
flyover **268** 48
flysheet **278** 22
fly swat **83** 32
fly title **185** 44
flywheel *Weaving* **166** 15
flywheel *Intern. Combust. Eng.* **190** 20
F major **320** 63
F minor **320** 66
foal **73** 2
foam bath **49** 3
foam can **228** 28
foam canister **83** 6
foam feed pipe **83** 10
foam gun **270** 64
foam-making branch **270** 64
focal length setting **117** 3
focimeter **111** 33
fo'c'sle **218** 10, 19; **221** 13; **223** 48
focus **347** 25, 27
focus, seismic ~ **11** 32
focusing adjustment **240** 30
focusing aid **115** 60
focusing device **5** 11
focusing hood **114** 23; **115** 68
focusing ring **114** 39; **115** 8
focusing screen *Optic. Instr.* **112** 21
focusing screen *Photog.* **115** 39
focusing screen *Photomech. Reprod.* **177** 2, 34
focusing screens, interchangeable ~ **115** 58-66
focusing stage **115** 86
focusing telescope **115** 74
focusing wedge **115** 55
focus setting **114** 28; **117** 3
fodder plants **69** 1-28
fodder silo **62** 11, 43
fodder tank **221** 73
fog **9** 31
fog, high ~ **8** 4
fog headlamp and rear lamp switch **191** 64
fog horn **223** 3
fog horn, ship's ~ **224** 32
fog lamp, rear ~ **191** 67
fog lamp warning light **191** 63
foil **294** 1-18, 11
foil, electric ~ **294** 26
foil, French ~ **294** 37
foil, Italian ~ **294** 39
foil fencers **294** 5-6
foilists **294** 5-6
foil mask **294** 13
foil pommel **294** 40
foilsmen **294** 5-6
fold **185** 54
fold, asymmetrical ~ **12** 13
fold, gluteal ~ **16** 42
fold, nasolabial ~ **16** 11
fold, normal ~ **12** 12
fold, reclined ~ **12** 15
fold, recumbent ~ **12** 15
fold, symmetrical ~ **12** 12
fold-away table **207** 53
foldboats **283** 54-66
folder *Offset Print.* **180** 15, 29
folder *Letterpress* **181** 55
folder *Photograv.* **182** 27
folder *Office* **245** 19
folder-feeding station **184** 17
folder unit *Offset Print.* **180** 15, 29
folder unit *Letterpress* **181** 55
folder unit *Photograv.* **182** 27
folding **12** 4-20
folding machine **249** 58
folding mechanism **249** 46
fold mountains **12** 12-20
fold plate **185** 10
fold unit **74** 1
foliage **330** 48
foliage plant **39** 37
folk instruments **324** 1-46
follicle *Man* **20** 84

follicle *Bot.* **370** 91
follower *Metalwkr.* **140** 43
follower *Composing Rm.* **175** 57
follow-through **293** 84
font **332** 10
fontange, lace ~ **355** 65
font basin **332** 11
food, canned ~ **96** 25; **98** 15-20
food, frozen ~ **99** 58-61
food compartment **207** 83
food pests **81** 15-30
food price list **266** 65
food slicer **40** 38
food store, self-service ~ **99** 1-96
food vacuole **357** 6
fool **306** 38
foolscap **306** 39
foot *Man* **16** 54; **17** 26-29; **19** 52-63
foot *Shoem.* **100** 23
foot *Photog.* **114** 71
foot *Joiner* **132** 29
foot *Blacksm.* **137** 15
foot *Bookbind.* **185** 58
foot *Sailing* **284** 40
foot *Music. Instr.* **326** 23
foot, palmate ~ **73** 36; **359** 7
foot, prehensile ~ **364** 34
foot, rubber ~ **114** 45
foot, second ~ **286** 59
foot, serpent's ~ **327** 39
foot, webbed ~ **73** 36; **359** 6, 7
footage counter **117** 52
foot bag *Infant Care etc.* **28** 38
foot bag *Winter Countr.* **304** 27
football **273** 10,12; **291** 17; **292** 22
football boot **291** 21
football pad **291** 33
football pitch **291** 1-16
football player **292** 23
football sock **291** 58
footband **185** 42
foot bar lever **100** 27
footbath **282** 22
footbed, surgical ~ **101** 50
foot binding, front ~ **286** 57
footboard **186** 7, 13
foot brake **188** 52
footbridge **15** 78
foot control **139** 27
foot control socket **219** 66
foot-fault judge **293** 24
foot ferry **15** 60
foot gear-change control **188** 55; **190** 77
foot gearshift control **188** 55; **190** 77
footing **123** 2
foot lever **83** 34
footlight **316** 26
footman **186** 20
foot margin **185** 58
foot muff *Infant Care etc.* **28** 38
foot muff *Winter Countr.* **304** 27
foot muscle **18** 49
footnote **185** 62
foot of bed **43** 4
foot of goblet **162** 42
foot of machine **133** 25
foot of mast **284** 20
foot passenger ferry **15** 60
footpath **15** 43
footpath under railway **15** 44
foot pedal *Pest Contr.* **83** 34
foot pedal *Forging* **139** 27
foot pedal *Arc Weld.* **142** 31
foot pedal *Letterpress* **181** 12
foot pedal *Bookbind.* **183** 18
footpiece *Mach. Tools* **149** 12
footpiece *Carriages* **186** 13
footprints **126** 59
foot rail **267** 52
footrest *Hairdresser* **105** 18; **106** 19
footrest *Bicycle* **187** 47
footrest *Motorcycles etc.* **188** 44
footrest *Railw.* **207** 57
footrest *Winter Sp.* **301** 58
footrest *Sports* **305** 81
footrope *Sea Fish.* **90** 9, 18
footrope *Ship* **219** 46
foot scraper **123** 25
foot switch *Hosp.* **27** 21
foot switch *Dressm.* **103** 26
foot switch *Sawmill* **157** 66
foot switch, electric ~ **50** 2
foot treadle **83** 34
foot valve **269** 6, 14, 43
footwear **101**
fop **306** 33
forage harvester, self-propelled ~ **64** 34-39
forage plants *Fodder Plants* **69** 1-28
foramen **383** 57
forceps **22** 52
forceps, obstetrical ~ **26** 53
forcing **55** 24
forcing bed **55** 16
forcing house **55** 4
forearm *Man* **16** 46
forearm *Horse* **72** 21
forearm balance **295** 26
forearm stand **295** 26
forebay **217** 39
forecarriage **65** 14-19
forecastle **218** 10, 19; **221** 13; **223** 48
forecourse **218** 41; **219** 55
foredeck **223** 47; **284** 10
foredeck, flooded ~ **258** 65; **259** 77
fore edge **185** 57
fore edge margin **185** 57
fore end **95** 51
forefinger **19** 65
forefoot **72** 22-26
foregrip **87** 13
forehand **72** 18-27
forehand stroke **293** 40
forehand volley **293** 41
forehead *Man* **16** 4-5
forehead *Horse* **72** 3
foreign counter **204** 31
foreign exchange counter **204** 31; **250** 10
foreign trade zone **225** 2
foreleg **70** 5; **88** 25, 64
forelock **72** 2
foremast **218** 42; **219** 2-4; **220** 21; **221** 2
foremast, lower ~ **219** 2
forepart **218** 49
forepaw **70** 6
forepeak **227** 18
fore royal **219** 60
fore royal yard **219** 37
foresail **218** 41; **219** 55
foresail, square ~ **220** 13
foresheet **284** 23
fore ship **286** 33, 36, 40
foresight **255** 3, 23, 37; **305** 42
foresight block **255** 23, 37
foreskin **20** 70
forest **84** 1-34
forestage **316** 25
forestay **284** 15
forest Indian **352** 19
forest labourer **84** 18
forest pests **82**
forestry **84; 85**
forestry office **15** 3
forest track **84** 3
foretop **219** 50
fore topgallant mast **219** 4
fore topgallant rigging **219** 18
fore topgallant sail **218** 52
fore topmast **219** 3
fore topmast crosstrees **219** 51
fore topmast rigging **219** 17
fore topmast staysail **219** 20
forewing **358** 36
foreyard **219** 32
forge **137** 1-8, 1, 34
forget-me-not **378** 26
forging and sizing press **139** 18
forging press, hydraulic ~ **139** 35
fork *Tablew. etc.* **45** 7, 58
fork *Agr. Impl.* **66** 3, 7, 22
fork *Horse* **71** 29
fork *Optic. Instr.* **113** 12
fork *Quarry* **158** 33
fork *Circus* **307** 54
fork, rear ~ **188** 14; **189** 7
fork, swinging-arm ~ **188** 14; **189** 7
fork blade **187** 12
fork column **187** 14
fork end **187** 12
forklift **93** 23; **206** 16; **225** 44; **226** 8
forklift truck **93** 23; **206** 16; **225** 44; **226** 8
fork mount **113** 24
fork mounting **113** 12, 24
forks, front ~ **187** 10-12
forks, telescopic ~ **188** 8
fork spanner **134** 2
fork truck **93** 23; **206** 16; **225** 44; **226** 8
fork wrench **134** 2
form *see* forme
form *Office* **245** 24

formaldehyde atom **242** 64
format selection **249** 34
forme **174** 10
forme, locked up ~ **181** 36
forme bed **180** 78; **181** 17
forme-inking roller **181** 18, 27, 61
former *Opticn.* **111** 25, 26
former *Plumb. etc.* **126** 83
former *Letterpress* **181** 53
former *Aircraft* **230** 55
former *Air Force* **257** 28
forme roller **181** 7, 18, 27
forms **36** 42-86
Formula One racing car **290** 34
Formula Two racing car **290** 36
formwork **119** 54-76
forsythia **373** 1
forte **321** 38
forte fortissimo **321** 40
forte pedal **325** 8
forte piano **321** 41
fortissimo **321** 39
fortress **15** 74
fortune teller **308** 36
forward *Swim.* **282** 50
forward *Ball Games* **293** 75
forward, reverse and still projection switch **117** 88
forward horizontal stand **295** 30
forwarding agent **206** 28
forwarding office **206** 26
forwarding roll **180** 4
forward kip **296** 58
forward pace **295** 43
forward roll **297** 19, 20
forward somersault **297** 18
forward split **295** 15
forward straddle **295** 4
forward walkover **297** 26
forward wind button **249** 73
Fosbury flop **298** 9
fosse **329** 37
fossette **16** 16
foul **291** 50; **299** 34
foul line **292** 48
foundation *Bees* **77** 43
foundation *Floor etc. Constr.* **123** 2
foundation base **123** 3
foundation pile **5** 28
foundation trench **118** 75
founder **148** 8
fountain **272** 8, 21, 22, 62; **334** 68
fountain pen **260** 14
fountain roller **181** 64; **249** 52
Fourcault glass-drawing machine **162** 8
Fourcault process **162** 1
four-channel balance control **241** 42
four-channel demodulator **241** 45
four-channel level control **241** 42
four-eight time **320** 31
four-four time **320** 32
four-masters **220** 28-31
four-to-pica **175** 20
four-two time **320** 33
four-wheel drive **194** 1
fowl, domestic ~ **73** 19-36
Fowler flap **229** 52
Fowler flap, double-slotted ~ **229** 40
fowl run **74** 11
foxglove **379** 2
fox hunt **289** 41-49
fox terrier, wire-haired ~ **70** 15
foyer **5** 25; **267** 1-26, 44-46; **315** 12-13
fraction **344** 10, 19
fraction, complex ~ **344** 17
fraction, compound ~ **344** 17
fraction, improper ~ **344** 16, 18
fraction, proper ~ **344** 15
fractionating column **145** 37
fractions, vulgar **344** 15-16
fractocumulus **8** 12
fractostratus **8** 11
Fraktur **342** 3
frame *Agr. Mach.* **65** 8, 90
frame *Bees* **77** 40
frame *Mills* **91** 3
frame *Opticn.* **111** 5
frame *Basketm.* **136** 22
frame *Forging* **139** 16
frame *Iron Foundry etc.* **148** 57
frame *Mach. Tools* **149** 65
frame *Knitting* **167** 33
frame *Railw.* **207** 3; **208** 5
frame *Shipbuild.* **222** 58
frame *Aircraft* **230** 55
frame *Rowing* **283** 49, 67
frame *Sailing* **285** 51
frame *Gymn.* **297** 12
frame *Sports* **305** 14, 88
frame, aluminium ~ **50** 19
frame, annular ~ **235** 47
frame, bone ~ **353** 13
frame, C-shaped ~ **26** 19; **27** 17
frame, ferroconcrete ~ **119** 2
frame, heated ~ **55** 16
frame, iron ~ **325** 2
frame, lower ~ **148** 20
frame, metal ~ *Opticn.* **111** 7
frame, metal ~ *Music. Instr.* **324** 76
frame, plate glass ~ **179** 15
frame, reinforced concrete ~ **119** 2
frame, sectional ~ **65** 56
frame, shell ~ **111** 8
frame, tortoiseshell ~ **111** 8
frame, tubular ~ **188** 9, 49
frame, upper ~ **148** 19
frame, wire ~ **339** 35
frame, wooden ~ **353** 13
frame bar **64** 51
frame-clamping machine **133** 42
frame-coding device **242** 8-10
frame counter **115** 17; **313** 28
frame-cramping machine **133** 42
frame drum **353** 26
frame end plate **164** 26
frame hive **77** 45-50
frame-mounting device **133** 48
frame number **187** 51
frame sample **124** 2
frame-sanding pad **133** 34
frame saw, vertical ~ **157** 2
frame section, aft ~ **234** 49
frame section, forward ~ **234** 45
frame slipway **222** 19-21
frame stand **133** 43
frame tent **278** 36
frame timber **119** 64
frame timber, bolted ~ **119** 74
frame vent **55** 17
frame wood **124** 3
frame wood sample **124** 2
framework **339** 22
framework support **214** 77
framing **336** 11
framing chisel **132** 11
framing control **312** 29
framing table **132** 62
franc **252** 15, 16, 17, 18
Frankfurter **96** 8
Frankfurter garland cake **97** 42
Frankfurter sausage **96** 8
franking machine **22** 24; **236** 7, 27, 47
freak show **308** 19
free backward circle **297** 29
free combination knob **326** 40
free combination stud **326** 40
free exercise **295**
free-fall positions **288** 60-62
free flight model, remote-controlled ~ **288** 86
free kick **291** 43
free leg *Athletics* **298** 27
free leg *Winter Sp.* **302** 3
free leg, vertical ~ **298** 25
free port **225** 2
freestyle relay race **282** 24-32
freestyle wrestling **299** 10-12
free-throw line **292** 38
free walkover forward **297** 25
freeway *Map* **15** 16
freeway *Docks* **225** 54
free-wheel hub **187** 63
freezer **22** 63; **96** 21; **97** 65; **98** 74
freezer, upright ~ **39** 7
free zone enclosure **225** 3
free zone frontier **225** 3
freight agent **206** 28
freight barge **216** 25
freight car **206** 6
freight car, flat ~ **206** 21
freight car, open ~ **213** 8, 33
freight car, special ~ **213** 33
freight depot *Map* **15** 91
freight depot *Station* **206**
freighter **221** 57
freight house **206** 7, 26-39
freight house door **206** 37

freight office **206** 26
freight truck **206** 15
French chalk **271** 39
French horn **323** 41
French lady **355** 51
French toast **97** 54
French window **37** 21
frequency band **309** 22
fresco **338** 40
fresh-air inlet **356** 16
fresh-air inlet and control **191** 85
fresh-air regulator **191** 86
fresh meat counter **99** 51
fresh milk filling and packing plant **76** 20
fresh milk tank **76** 15
fresh oil tank **65** 46
freshwater eel **364** 17
freshwater pearl mussel **357** 33
fresh water tank **221** 70; **223** 79
Fresnel lens **115** 64
fret *Roulette* **275** 30
fret *Music. Instr.* **324** 9
fretsaw **135** 12; **260** 53
fretsaw blade **135** 13; **260** 54
friction drive **116** 33; **312** 37
friction pad **192** 49
friction tape **127** 34
friction wheel **322** 26
fridge *Kitch.* **39** 2
fridge *Flat* **46** 33
fridge *Disco* **317** 10
frieze **335** 9
frieze, Babylonian ~ **333** 19
frieze decoration **334** 16
frigate **258** 53
frill **31** 34; **32** 44
frill collar **31** 46
frill front **32** 44
fringe **34** 36
fringe, decorative ~ **353** 25
fringe region **7** 34
frit **162** 2
frit feeder **162** 13
frit funnel **162** 13
frock coat **355** 76
frog *Agr. Mach.* **65** 8
frog *Road Constr.* **200** 26
frog *Railw.* **202** 24
frog *Music. Instr.* **323** 13
frog position **288** 61
frog's bit **378** 29
frond **378** 19
front **305** 1
front, cold ~ **8** 13; **9** 27
front, extended ~ **200** 10
front, hinged ~ **213** 10
front, occluded ~ **9** 25
front, warm ~ **8** 5; **9** 26
frontalis **19** 4
front axle pivot pin **65** 48
front axle suspension **65** 49
front band **71** 9
front element mount **115** 6
front fan-jet **232** 33
front-line player **293** 63
front panel, sliding ~ **349** 27
front roller underclearer **164** 44
fronts **9** 25-29
fronts, cold ~ **8** 13-17
fronts, warm ~ **8** 5-12
front seat headrest **193** 7
front seat head restraint **193** 7
front sight block **255** 23, 37
front support *Free Exerc.* **295** 21, 23
front support *Gymn.* **296** 28
front wheel drive **191** 52
front wheel drum brake **188** 36
froth **266** 4
frozen food compartment **39** 5
fruit *Weeds* **61** 11, 20, 23
fruit *Restaurant* **266** 57
fruit *Decid. Trees* **371** 4, 19, 28, 45, 69
fruit *Conifers* **372** 53, 64
fruit *Shrubs etc.* **373** 12, 18, 22, 27, 29, 32; **374** 4, 8, 12, 19, 25, 29, 31, 34
fruit *Flowers etc.* **375** 4, 7, 10, 13, 17, 24, 35, 37, 47; **376** 3, 6, 14
fruit *Alp. Plants etc.* **378** 11, 38, 42
fruit *Trop. Plants* **382** 3, 5, 10, 15, 17, 24, 39
fruit *Industr. Plants* **383** 14, 18, 21, 28, 32, 40, 43, 52, 56, 59
fruit *South. Fruits* **384** 19, 26, 39, 45
fruit, aggregate ~ *Soft Fruit* **58** 28
fruit, aggregate ~ *Bot.* **370** 100, 101
fruit, canned ~ **98** 16
fruit, compound ~ *Soft Fruit* **58** 28
fruit, compound ~ *Bot.* **370** 100, 101
fruit, dehisced ~ **375** 27
fruit, immature ~ **378** 31
fruit, indehiscent ~ **375** 43
fruit, mature ~ *Decid. Trees* **371** 61
fruit, mature ~ *Trop. Plants* **382** 33
fruit, ripe ~ *Decid. Trees* **371** 61
fruit, ripe ~ *Trop. Plants* **382** 33
fruit, soft ~ **58** 1-30
fruit, stewed ~ **45** 30
fruit, unripe ~ **378** 31
fruit, young ~ *Decid. Trees* **371** 59
fruit, young ~ *South. Fruits* **384** 31
fruit and vegetable counter **99** 80
fruit and vegetable garden **52** 1-32
fruit bowl **45** 29, 40
fruit capsule, mature ~ **382** 44
fruit capsule, ripe ~ **382** 44
fruit cone **372** 2, 29, 30, 36, 41, 57
fruit dish **45** 28
fruit flan **97** 22; **99** 20
fruit garden **52**
fruiting body **381** 2
fruiting branch *Decid. Trees* **371** 3, 11, 18, 31, 36, 41, 47, 50, 56, 64
fruiting branch *Conifers* **372** 40, 51, 59, 63, 66, 70
fruiting branch *Trop. Plants* **382** 2, 37
fruiting branch *Industr. Plants* **383** 34, 46
fruiting branch *South. Fruits* **384** 38
fruiting palm **384** 2
fruit juice **98** 18; **266** 58
fruit juice, bottled ~ **99** 74
fruit juice, canned ~ **99** 75
fruit knife **45** 71
fruit pests **80** 1-19
fruit picker **56** 22
fruit pip **58** 37, 60
fruit preserver **40** 23
fruits **370** 91-102
fruits, dehiscent ~ **370** 91-96
fruits, indehiscent ~ **370** 97-102
fruits, Mediterranean ~ **384**
fruits, southern ~ **384**
fruits, subtropical ~ **384**
fruits, tropical ~ **384**
fruit scale **372** 67
fruit spoon **45** 66
fruit stall **308** 53
fruit storage shed **225** 52
fruit tree, standard ~ **52** 30
fruit trees, dwarf ~ **52** 1,2,16,17,29
fruit warehouse **225** 52
frustum of a cone **347** 45
frying pan **40** 4
fry pond **89** 6
F sharp major **320** 61
F sharp minor **320** 58
fuchsia **53** 3
fuel cell **234** 62
fuel gas **145** 52
fuel gauge **191** 38, 65
fuel-handling hoist **154** 27
fuel hand pump **190** 64
fuel-injection engine **190** 1
fuel injector **190** 32
fuel inlet **192** 13
fuel leak line **190** 53
fuel level sensor **234** 27
fuel line **190** 31
fuel line duct **234** 40
fuel oil **38** 50
fuel oil, heavy ~ **145** 59
fuel oil, light ~ **145** 58
fuel oil tank **212** 75
fuel pin **154** 4
fuel pipe **286** 25
fuel pressure gauge **230** 19
fuel pressure line **190** 52
fuel pressure pipe **190** 52
fuel pressure regulator **190** 17
fuel rod **154** 4

fuel storage **154** 28
fuel supply pipe **190** 31
fuel tank *Moon L.* **6** 7, 29, 37
fuel tank *Agr. Mach.* **65** 42
fuel tank *Motorcycles etc.* **188** 10, 28
fuel tank *Motorcycle* **189** 2
fuel tank *Railw.* **209** 20; **212** 56
fuel tank *Ship* **221** 71; **223** 80
fuel tank *Aircraft* **230** 48
fuel tank *Space* **234** 58
fuel tank, forward ~ **235** 21
fuel tank, jettisonable ~ **235** 46
fuel tank, main ~ **212** 4
fuel tanker **258** 97
fuel tender **210** 67
fuel warning light **191** 71
full circle **308** 43
full-colour print **340** 28
full-cone indicator **165** 7
fuller's earth **199** 38
fulling machine, rotary ~ **168** 1
fulling roller, bottom ~ **168** 6
fulling roller, top ~ **168** 3
full point **342** 16
full spread position **288** 60
full-step **320** 51, 53
full stop **342** 16
full title **185** 46
fulmar **359** 12
fume extraction equipment **142** 13
fume extractor **255** 59, 89
fumigation chamber, mobile ~ **83** 15
fumigation plant, vacuum ~ **83** 11
fumigator, vacuum ~ **83** 11
function, trigonometrical ~ **346** 32
function key **247** 17
funeral **331** 33-41
fungi, edible ~ **381**
fungi, esculent ~ **381**
fungi, poisonous ~ **379** 10-13
funicular **214** 12
funicular railway car **214** 13
funnel *Photog.* **116** 12
funnel *Ship* **221** 8, 40, 75, 84; **223** 1
funnel *Warships* **258** 58; **259** 32
funnel *Chem.* **350** 16
funnel, aft ~ **258** 20
funnel, forward ~ **258** 19
Funnel-Beaker culture **328** 12
funnel marking **223** 2
fur marker **131** 22
furnace **199** 29
furnace, continuous ~ **139** 1
furnace, electric ~ **147** 51-54
furnace, gas ~ **139** 47
furnace, gas-fired ~ **139** 47; **140** 11
furnace, low-shaft ~ **147** 51-54
furnace, stationary ~ **147** 23
furnace bed **38** 66
furnace incline **147** 2
furnace lift **147** 2
furnace thermometer **38** 64
furniture **174** 8; **181** 40
furniture lorry **268** 47
furniture truck **268** 47
furrier **131** 1
furrow *Agr.* **63** 8
furrow *Mills* **91** 17
furrow, gluteal ~ **16** 42
furrow wheel **65** 16
fur seal **367** 18
fur-sewing machine **131** 9
fur side **131** 12, 17
furskin **131** 5
furskin, cut ~ **131** 14
furskin, uncut ~ **131** 6
furskins **131** 11-21
fur trapper **306** 8
fur worker **131** 8, 23
fuse *Electr.* **127** 19, 36
fuse *Quarry* **158** 28
fuse box *Hall* **41** 19
fuse box *Weaving* **166** 23
fuse carrier **127** 68
fuse cartridge **127** 36
fuse holder **127** 35
fuselage **230** 54; **288** 26
fuselage attachment **235** 4
fuselage tank **257** 31
fuse wire **127** 68

G

gable **37** 15; **121** 5; **122** 25
gable, curved ~ **336** 5
gable, round ~ **335** 50
gable end **37** 15; **122** 25
gable roof **37** 5; **121** 1
gable slate **122** 80
gaffer **310** 37
gaffsail **220** 1
gaff topsail **219** 31
gag *Horse* **71** 53
gag *Fish Farm.* **89** 42
gag bit **71** 53
gage *see* gauge
gaillardia **60** 19
gait **289** 7
gaiter, leather ~ **191** 92
gaits of the horse **72** 39-44
Galaxy **3** 35
gale **373** 33
galena **351** 14
galingale **53** 17
gall *Gdn. Pests* **80** 33
gall *Forest Pests* **82** 34
gallant soldier **61** 31
gall bladder **20** 11, 36
galleries under bark **82** 23-24
gallery *Forest Pests* **82** 24
gallery *Coal* **144** 29
gallery *Theatre* **315** 16
gallery *Church* **330** 25
gallery, drilled ~ **192** 21
gallery grave **328** 16
galley *Composing Rm.* **174** 12, 44
galley *Ship* **218** 44-50; **223** 42
galley *Aircraft* **231** 20
galley loader **233** 22
galley slave **218** 48
gall gnat **80** 40
gall midge **80** 40
gallop, full ~ **72** 43-44, 43, 44
gallows **221** 87
gall wasp **82** 33
galvanometer **11** 44
gamba **322** 23
gambling casino **275** 1
gambling game **275** 1-33
gambling table **275** 8
gambrel **94** 21
gambrel roof **121** 18
gambrel stick **94** 21
game **86** 28; **88**
game, furred ~ **86** 35
game, positional ~ **276** 1-16
game, winged ~ **86** 41
game of chance **275** 1-33
game path **86** 16
game preserve **86** 1-8
gaming room **275** 1
gaming table **275** 8
gamma radiation **1** 33, 40
gammon steak **95** 54
gander **73** 34
gang mill **157** 2
gang stitcher **184** 15
gangway **38** 3
gangway, central ~ *Railw.* **208** 23
gangway, central ~ *Ship* **218** 46
gannet **359** 9
gantry *Photomech. Reprod.* **177** 13
gantry *Shipbuild.* **222** 26
gantry *Docks* **225** 40
gantry crane **157** 27; **206** 55; **222** 20, 25
gantry support **214** 24
garage *Dwellings* **37** 32, 79
garage *Garage* **195**
garage, agent's ~ **195** 1-55
garage, distributor's ~ **195** 1-55
garage driveway **37** 52
garbage **199** 17
garbage can **199** 3
garbage can dumping device **199** 2
garbage container **199** 4
garbage disposition **199**
garbage incineration unit **199** 28
garbage truck **199** 1
garden **37** 57
garden, Baroque ~ **272** 1-40
garden, formal ~ **272** 1-40
garden, front ~ **37** 58
garden chair **37** 49
gardener **55** 20
garden fence **52** 10
garden flowers **60**
garden gate **272** 31
garden hedge **51** 9
garden hoe **66** 1
garden hose **37** 42; **56** 27
garden house **52** 14

garden ladder **52** 8
garden light **37** 38
garden mould **55** 15
garden pansy **60** 2
garden parasol **37** 48
garden path **51** 14; **52** 23
garden pests **80**
garden pond **51** 16
garden rake **51** 4
garden rose **60** 15
garden seat **272** 42
garden shed **52** 3
garden shovel **55** 14
garden sieve **55** 13
garden spider **358** 45
garden strawberry **58** 16
garden table **37** 50
garden tiger **365** 7
garden tools **56**
garden wall **37** 37
gargoyle **335** 30
garland **306** 17; **335** 54
garnet **351** 7
Garratt locomotive **210** 64
garter **318** 28
gas, liquid ~ **145** 53
gas, natural ~ **12** 30
gas appliances **126** 12-25
gas bottle **278** 53
gas cap **12** 30
gas circulation unit **83** 16
gas-collecting main **156** 17
gas compressor **156** 26
gas connection **141** 31
gas control **141** 32
gas cooler *Offshore Drill.* **146** 27
gas cooler *Coking* **156** 19
gas cooling **156** 29
gas cutting installation **148** 67
gas cylinder **138** 35
gas cylinder manifold **141** 1
gas drying **156** 30
gas extractor **156** 21
gas fitter **126** 1
gas fitter's tools **126** 58-86
gas flue **152** 12
gas generator **350** 59
gas holder **156** 25
gas hose **141** 9
gas inlet **350** 2
gas inlet pipe **350** 2
gaskin **72** 36
gas lighter **107** 30
gas main **198** 21
gas main, high-pressure ~ **156** 45
gas main, low-pressure ~ **156** 44
gas meter *Plumb. etc.* **126** 5
gas meter *Coking* **156** 31
gas oil component **145** 42
gasoline can **196** 25
gasoline canister **84** 36
gasoline inlet **192** 13
gasoline pump **196** 1
gasoline pump, self-service ~ **196** 8
gasoline pump hose **196** 2
gasoline station **196** 1-29
gasoline tank **188** 10, 28; **189** 2; **305** 87
gasometer **144** 12
gas outlet *Oil, Petr.* **145** 29
gas outlet *Chem.* **350** 63
gas pipe *Pest Contr.* **83** 14
gas pipe *Forging* **139** 54
gas pipe *Metalwkr.* **140** 12
gas pipe *Oil, Petr.* **145** 29
gas pipe *Iron & Steel* **147** 18, 27
gas pliers *Plumb. etc.* **126** 58
gas pliers *Metalwkr.* **140** 68
gas pressure vessel **234** 32
gas regenerator chamber **147** 28
gas regulator **255** 34; **350** 6
gas-separating plant **145** 69
gas separator **145** 28
gas station **196** 1-29
gas supply **27** 41
gas tap **261** 24
gastrocnemius **18** 62
gas tube **83** 35
gas turbine **209** 9
gas turbine, auxiliary ~ **231** 33
gas turbine, twin-shaft ~ **209** 23
gas turbine controller **209** 16
gas turbine driving unit **209** 8
gas turbine fuel tank **209** 17
gas turbine trainset **209** 1
gas-washing bottle **350** 58
gas water **156** 39
gas welder **141**
gas welding torch **130** 14
gate **202** 40; **289** 8; **337** 24
gate, removable ~ **118** 46
gate, sliding ~ **217** 18, 55
gate, vertical ~ **217** 31, 38
gate, wrought iron ~ **272** 31
gate and rails **289** 8
gateau **99** 15; **265** 4
gateaux **97** 22-24
gatehouse **329** 22
gateman **202** 42
gate pole **301** 30
gateway **336** 15; **337** 11
gateway, monumental ~ **333** 9
gatherer and wire stitcher **184** 15
gathering and wire-stitching machine **184** 15
gathering machine **249** 59
gathering station **249** 60
gaucho **306** 31
gauge **76** 6
gauntlet **329** 50
gauze **183** 33; **185** 20
gauze, sterile ~ **22** 58
gauze, wire ~ **350** 18, 19
gauze roll holder **185** 19
G-clef **320** 8
gear *Gdn. Tools* **56** 20
gear *Iron Foundry etc.* **148** 63
gear *Road Constr.* **201** 11
gear *Hydr. Eng.* **217** 48
gear, epicyclic ~ **143** 94
gear, planetary ~ **143** 94
gearbox *Agr. Mach.* **65** 79
gearbox *Turner* **135** 4
gearbox *Cotton Spin.* **164** 2, 33, 39
gearbox, five-speed ~ **189** 6
gear-change *Agr. Mach.* **65** 35
gear-change *Motorcycles etc.* **188** 31
gear-change, floor-type ~ **191** 91
gear-change, two-speed ~ **188** 12
gear-change lever **189** 28
gear-change pattern **192** 47
gear control **149** 2
gearing *Agr. Mach.* **64** 50, 65
gearing *Overh. Irrign.* **67** 21
gearing *Road Constr.* **201** 11
gearing, helical ~ **143** 89
gearing, multi-speed ~ **190** 72
gearing, multi-step ~ **190** 72
gear lever **191** 91; **192** 46
gear meter **76** 4
gears *Agr. Mach.* **64** 50, 65
gears *Overh. Irrign.* **67** 21
gear shaft **232** 58
gear shaft, intermediate ~ **190** 57
gearshift **65** 23, 35; **188** 31
gearshift, two-speed ~ **188** 12
gearshift lever *Motorcycle* **189** 28
gearshift lever *Car* **191** 91; **192** 46
gearshift pattern **192** 47
gearshift rod **192** 41
gearshift switch **134** 46
gear wheel, helical ~ **192** 34, 36, 39, 43
gear wheel, herringbone ~ **143** 87
gear wheel, stepped ~ **143** 82
gear wheels **143** 82-96
gecko **364** 36
Geiger counter **2** 19
Geiger-Müller counter **2** 19
geisha **353** 39
gelatine **316** 49
gelding **73** 2
Gemini **3** 28; **4** 55
general cargo ship **225** 14; **226** 13
general cargo transit shed **225** 9
general practice **22** 1-74
general practitioner **23** 2
general service lamp **127** 56
generator *Nucl. Energy* **154** 15, 47, 53
generator *Energy Sources* **155** 46
generator *Intern. Combust. Eng.* **190** 76
generator *Railw.* **211** 46
generator *Ship* **223** 74
generator exhaust **146** 2
generator unit **231** 33
Geneva movement **312** 38
Genoa jib **284** 16
genouillère **329** 53
gentleman *Café* **265** 22

gentleman *Hist. Cost.* **355** 54, 61, 73
'gentlemen' **233** 47
'gentlemen's toilet' **233** 47
geodesy **14** 46-62
geography, physical ~ **11; 12; 13**
geology **12** 1-33
geometrical shape **260** 79
geometrid **80** 16; **82** 28
geometry **346; 347**
geometry, elementary ~ **346** 1-58
geometry, Euclidian ~ **346** 1-58
geranium **53** 1
gerbera **51** 26
germ **370** 86
German hand **342** 11
German pointer **70** 40
German sheepdog **70** 25
German shepherd **70** 25
geyser *Phys. Geog.* **11** 21
geyser *Plumb. etc.* **126** 12-13
G flat major **320** 68
gherkin, pickled ~ **98** 29
giant **306** 63; **308** 20; **327** 37
gib *Plumb.* **125** 3
gib *Mach. Parts etc.* **143** 74
gig **186** 34
gig, four-oared ~ **283** 26-33
Gigantocypris agassizi **369** 1
gilder **183** 2
gilding *Painter* **129** 40
gilding *Bookbind.* **183** 1
gilding and embossing press **183** 26
gill *Dom. Anim.* **73** 24
gill *Edib. Fungi* **381** 4, 6
gill, tufted ~ **364** 19
gill cleft **364** 3
gill cover **364** 5
gill slit **364** 3
gillyflower **60** 7
gimbal ring **224** 50
gimbal suspension **241** 23
gimlet **120** 65
gimping **102** 28
gimping needle **102** 29
gingerbread **97** 51
gipsy girl **306** 36
gipsy moth **80** 1
giraffe **367** 4
giraffe house **356** 10
girder, steel ~ **143** 3-7
girdle **32** 5
girdle clasp **328** 24
girl, exotic ~ **306** 30
girt **120** 50
girth **71** 18, 36; **289** 11
girth, emergency ~ **71** 23
girth, second ~ **71** 23
glacier *Phys. Geog.* **12** 49
glacier *Mountain.* **300** 22
glacier snout **12** 51
glacier table **12** 56
gladiolus **51** 28; **60** 11
gland, bulbourethral ~ **20** 75
gland, parotid ~ **19** 9
gland, pituitary ~ **17** 43
gland, prostate ~ **20** 76
gland, submandibular ~ **19** 11
gland, submaxillary ~ **19** 11
gland, suprarenal ~ **20** 29
gland, thyroid ~ **20** 1
glans penis **20** 69
glass **54** 9
glass, armoured ~ **109** 29
glass, bullet-proof ~ **250** 3
glass, coloured ~ **260** 68
glass, crystal ~ **45** 86
glass, frosted ~ **124** 5
glass, laminated ~ **124** 5
glass, lined ~ **124** 6
glass, molten ~ **162** 23, 31, 50
glass, ornamental ~ **124** 6
glass, patterned ~ **124** 5
glass, pulverized ~ **340** 48
glass, raw ~ **124** 6
glass, shatterproof ~ **124** 5
glass, stained ~ **124** 6; **330** 15
glass, tapered ~ **45** 85
glass, thick ~ **124** 5
glass, wired ~ **124** 6
glassblower **162** 38
glassblowing **162** 38-47
glass case **356** 15
glass cloth **130** 29
glass cutter, diamond ~ **124** 25
glass cutter, steel ~ **124** 26
glass cutters **124** 25-26
glass-drawing machine **162** 8
glasses **111** 9
glass fibre, production of ~ **162** 48-55
glass fibre products **162** 56-58
glass filament **162** 52
glass forming **162** 38-47
glass furnace **162** 1, 49
glass holder **124** 9
glasshouse pot, covered ~ **162** 46
glassmaker **162** 38
glassmaking **162** 38-47
glass mosaic picture **260** 69
glass paper **135** 25
glass pliers **124** 19
glass ribbon **162** 10
glass sponge **369** 7
glass wool **162** 58
glassworker **124** 8
glazier **124; 124** 8
glazing sheet **116** 58
glazing sprig **124** 24
glede **362** 11
glider **287** 3
glider, high-performance ~ **287** 9
glider, motorized ~ **287** 8
glider, powered ~ **287** 8
glider field **287** 13
gliding **287**
globe **42** 13
globe, frosted glass ~ **267** 4
globe, solar ~ **4** 36
globe, terrestrial ~ **4** 8
globe artichoke **57** 41
globe lamp **267** 4
globe thistle **53** 14
glove **33** 67; **292** 12; **298** 47; **318** 31
glove, catcher's ~ **292** 60
glove, fielder's ~ **292** 59
glove, goalkeeper's ~ **291** 19
glove box lock **191** 89
glove compartment lock **191** 89
glove stand **271** 20
glow plug **190** 66
gloxinia **53** 7
glue **48** 4; **260** 50-52, 51
glue, joiner's ~ **132** 13
glue-enamel plate **179** 32
glue pot **132** 12, 13; **183** 15; **236** 5; **260** 57
glue roller **185** 33
glue size **128** 4
glue tank **184** 9; **185** 32
glue well **132** 13
gluing **183** 14
gluing machine **185** 31
gluing mechanism **184** 4
glume **68** 11
gluteus maximus **18** 60
G major **320** 56
G minor **320** 64
gnat **358** 16
goaf **144** 37
goal *Playground* **273** 11
goal *Swim.* **282** 46
goal *Ball Games* **291** 35; **292** 7
goal *Winter Sp.* **302** 37
goal area **291** 5
goalkeeper *Playground* **273** 14
goalkeeper *Swim.* **282** 47
goalkeeper *Ball Games* **291** 10; **292** 8
goalkeeper *Winter Sp.* **302** 36
goal kick **291** 38
goal line **291** 7
goalpost **273** 11; **291** 37
goal scorer **273** 13
Goat *Astron.* **3** 36; **4** 62
goat *Dom. Anim.* **73** 14
goatee beard **34** 10
goat's beard *Forest Plants etc.* **377** 5
goatsbeard *Forest Plants etc.* **377** 5
goat's beard *Edib. Fungi* **381** 32
goatsbeard *Edib. Fungi* **381** 32
goat willow **371** 24
gob *Coal* **144** 37
gob *Glass Prod.* **162** 40
gobbler **73** 28
goblet, hand-blown ~ **162** 41
gobo **310** 51
gob of molten glass **162** 23, 31
go-cart **273** 33
god, Indian ~ **337** 19
godet **30** 52
Godet wheel **169** 16
godparent **332** 13
God's acre **331** 21-41
'GO' gauging member **149** 57
goggles **140** 21; **303** 15
going about **285** 27
go-kart **305** 83
go-karting **305** 82
gold *Heraldry* **254** 24
gold *Crystals* **351** 6
gold and silver balance **108** 35

goldcrest **361** 10
goldcup **375** 8
gold cushion **183** 6
golden chain **374** 32
golden crested wren **361** 10
golden maidenhair **377** 17
golden oriole **360** 7
golden rain **374** 32
goldfinch **360** 1
gold finisher **183** 2
gold knife **183** 7
gold leaf **129** 45, 52; **183** 5
gold size **129** 44
goldsmith **108** 17
golf **293** 79-93
golf ball *Office* **249** 15
golf ball *Ball Games* **293** 89
golf ball cap **249** 30
golf ball typewriter **249** 1
golf course **293** 79-82
golfer **293** 83
golf trolley **293** 85
gondola *Supermkt.* **99** 23, 43, 62
gondola *Railw.* **214** 20
gondola *Airsports* **288** 64
gondola cableway **214** 19
gonfalon **253** 12
gong **299** 46
goods **271** 10
goods, bulky ~ **206** 18
goods, general ~ **206** 4
goods depot **15** 91
goods lorry **206** 15
goods office **206** 26
goods shed **206** 7, 26-39
goods shed door **206** 37
goods shelf **47** 36; **98** 14
goods station **206**
goods van **206** 6; **213** 22
goods van, covered ~ **213** 14
goods wagon, covered ~ **213** 14
goods wagon, open ~ **213** 8
goosander **359** 15
goose **73** 34; **272** 52
gooseberry **58** 9
gooseberry bush **52** 19; **58** 1
gooseberry cane, flowering ~ **58** 2
gooseberry flan **97** 22
gooseberry flower **58** 6
goosefoot **61** 25
gooseneck **284** 37
gorge **13** 52
gorgerin **334** 22
gorget **329** 43
gorilla **368** 16
goshawk **362** 10
'GO' side **149** 60
gosling **73** 34
gouache **338** 17
gouge **132** 9; **135** 15; **339** 17
gouge, U-shaped ~ **340** 6
gouge, V-shaped ~ **339** 20; **340** 9
gourd **354** 27
governor **224** 56
gown **105** 34; **106** 4; **355** 25, 36, 66
gown, linen ~ **355** 5
gown, open ~ **355** 50
gown, sleeveless ~ **355** 50
graben **12** 11
grace notes **321** 14-22
graces **321** 14-22
grade crossing, protected ~ **202** 39
grade crossing, unprotected ~ **202** 49
grade crossings **202** 39-50
grader **200** 19
grader levelling blade **200** 21
grader ploughshare **200** 21
gradient **347** 12
grading **74** 44
grading, automatic ~ **74** 52
graduated measuring rod **14** 47
graduation house *Map* **15** 32
graduation house *Spa* **274** 1
graftage **54** 30-39
grafting **54** 30-39
grain *Arable Crops* **68** 1-37, 4, 37
grain *Brew.* **92** 50
grain *Graphic Art* **340** 47
grain, farinaceous ~ **68** 13
grain auger **64** 20
grain harvest **63** 31-41
grain leaf **68** 8, 19
grain lifter **64** 2
grain pest **81** 27
grain tank **64** 23
grain tank auger **64** 24
grain tank unloader **64** 25
grain unloader spout **64** 26
grain weevil **81** 16
grammar school **261** 1-45
gramophone **309** 31
gramophone box **309** 35
gramophone needle **309** 33
gramophone record **309** 32
granary weevil **81** 16
grand **325** 40
grandee **306** 26
grandfather clock **110** 24; **309** 56
grand piano **325** 40
grand piano pedal **325** 41
grandstand, glass-covered ~ **289** 34
granite **302** 42
gran turismo car **193** 32
granular texture **340** 47
grape **80** 21; **99** 89
grape berry moth **80** 22, 23, 24
grape crusher **78** 17
grapefruit **384** 23
grape gatherer **78** 11
grape phylloxera **80** 26
grapevine *Wine Grow.* **78** 2-9
grapevine *Sports* **299** 10
grape worm **80** 23, 24
graphic art **340**
graphic art studio **340** 27-64
graphite **1** 54
grapnel **218** 11
grapple **218** 11
grappling iron **218** 11
grasp, kinds of ~ **296** 40-46
grasping arm **2** 47
grass **136** 26
grass, paniculate ~ **69** 27
grassbox **56** 29
grasshopper, artificial ~ **89** 68
grassland **15** 18
grassland, marshy ~ **15** 19
grassland, rough ~ **15** 5
grass ledge **300** 4
grass shears **56** 48
grass snake **364** 38
grasstrack racing **290** 24-28
grass verge **200** 56
grate **199** 33
graticule *Map* **14** 1-7
graticule *Hunt.* **87** 31-32
graticule *Photomech. Reprod.* **177** 4
graticule adjuster screw **87** 30
graticule system **87** 31
grating **141** 14
grating spectrograph **5** 5
graupel **9** 35
grave *Church* **331** 23, 34
grave *Script* **342** 31
grave, child's ~ **331** 29
grave, soldier's ~ **331** 32
grave digger **331** 22
gravel **118** 36; **119** 26
gravel filter layer **199** 23
grave mound **331** 24
graver **175** 33; **340** 5
graver, round-headed ~ **340** 20
gravestone **331** 26
graveyard **331** 21-41
graveyard chapel **331** 28
graveyard gate **331** 19
graveyard wall **331** 18
gravity fault **12** 7
gravity fuelling point **257** 32
gravity hammer, air-lift ~ **139** 24
gravity mixer **118** 33
gravure cylinder **182** 10
gravure cylinder, etched ~ **182** 22
gravure cylinder, printed ~ **182** 17
gravure etcher **182** 18
gravure printing **182**
gravy boat **45** 17
gravy ladle **45** 18
gray *see* grey
grayhound **70** 24
grease gun **195** 30
grease nipple **143** 81
greasepaint stick **315** 46
greasy chalk **340** 26
great apes **368** 14-16
Great Bear **3** 29
great brain **17** 42; **18** 22
Great Dane **70** 14
Great Dog **3** 14
Greater Bear **3** 29
greater burnet saxifrage **69** 28
Greater Dog **3** 14
greater water newt **364** 20
great hall **329** 30
great horned owl **362** 15
great mullein **376** 9

great primer **175** 30
great tit **361** 9
great titmouse **361** 9
greave **329** 54
Greek **355** 3
Greek woman **355** 1
green *Ball Games* **293** 82
green *Colour* **343** 8
green bowls **305** 21
green cloth **277** 15
green cormorant **359** 10
greenfly **358** 13
greengage **59** 24
green grasshopper **358** 8
greenhouse, heated ~ **55** 32
greenhouse, polythene ~ **55** 40
greenhouse, unheated ~ **55** 33
green liquor, uncleared ~ **172** 41
green liquor preheater **172** 43
green locust **358** 8
green oak roller moth **82** 43
green oak tortrix **82** 43
green plover **359** 21
Greenwich meridian **14** 5
grenzanhydrite **154** 67
Gretchen style **34** 31
greyhound **70** 24
grey scale **343** 15
grey sea eagle **362** 5
grid *Cotton Spin.* **163** 26
grid *Water* **269** 11
grid *Theatre* **316** 4
grid hearth **139** 1
gridiron **316** 4
griffin **327** 11
grill *Painter* **129** 12
grill *Station* **204** 38
grill *Fair* **308** 33
grinder *Painter* **129** 29
grinder *Metalwkr.* **140** 18
grinder, continuous ~ **172** 53, 66
grinder, pneumatic ~ **148** 44
grinder chuck **157** 46
grinding, hollow ~ **302** 22
grinding cylinder **161** 1
grinding disc **340** 46
grinding machine **140** 18
grinding machine, universal ~ **150** 1
grinding machine bed **150** 6
grinding machine table **150** 7
grinding-roller bearing **163** 41
grinding stone *Paperm.* **172** 71
grinding stone *Ethnol.* **354** 24
grinding wheel *Dent.* **24** 36
grinding wheel *D.I.Y.* **134** 23
grinding wheel *Blacksm.* **137** 19; **138** 8
grinding wheel *Metalwkr.* **140** 19
grinding wheel *Mach. Tools* **150** 4
grinding wheel *Sawmill* **157** 43
grindstone **172** 71
grip *Photog.* **114** 37
grip *Cine Film* **117** 61
grip *Bicycle* **187** 3
grip *Navig.* **224** 9
grip *Rowing* **283** 35
grip *Athletics* **298** 45
grip *Winter Sp.* **301** 6
grip *Sports* **305** 57
grip *Films* **313** 21
gripper **180** 65
gripper bar **180** 56
gripping jaw **149** 36
grip sole **101** 19
grist **92** 42
grit guard **148** 40
gritter, self-propelled ~ **200** 41
grocer **98** 41
grocer's shop **98** 1-87
groceryman **98** 41
grocery store **98** 1-87
groin *Man* **16** 38
groin *see* groyne
groin vault **335** 31-32; **336** 42
groom *Carriages* **186** 27
groom *Church* **332** 16
groove *Iron Foundry etc.* **148** 59
groove *Sawmill* **157** 6
groove *Ball Games* **291** 29
groove *Winter Sp.* **301** 39
groove *Music. Instr.* **326** 13
groove *Art* **334** 27
groove, anal ~ **16** 41
grooving **157** 6
groschen **252** 13
Grotesque **342** 7
grotto **272** 1
ground **123** 9
ground, fallow ~ **63** 1
ground, icy ~ **304** 19
ground avalanche **304** 1
ground control **6** 44
ground floor **37** 2; **118** 7
ground-floor landing **123** 23
ground game **86** 35
ground ivy **375** 18
ground layer **7** 7
ground nut **383** 41
ground-nut oil **98** 24
ground power unit **233** 22
groundsheet ring **278** 26
ground signals **288** 52-54
ground state level **1** 18
ground tackle **223** 49-51
groundwater **12** 21
groundwater level **269** 1, 42, 63
groundwater stream **269** 3
groundwood **172** 68
groundwood mill **172** 53-65
groundwood pulp **172** 77, 78
group **260** 3; **268** 60
group instruction **242** 1
group selector switch **238** 42
grove **354** 5
grower **55** 20
grower, commercial ~ **55** 20
growing stock **74** 1
growler **186** 26
growth, annual ~ **372** 25
groyne *Phys. Geog.* **13** 37
groyne *Rivers* **216** 19
groyne head *Phys. Geog.* **13** 38
groyne head *Rivers* **216** 20
grub **58** 64; **77** 29; **81** 20; **358** 9; **80** 6, 19, 36, 41, 46, 53, 54; **82** 25, 36
grubber **55** 21; **65** 55
grub screw **143** 48
Grus **3** 42
G sharp minor **320** 60
GT car **193** 32
guanaco **366** 30
guard *Blacksm.* **138** 9
guard *Metalwkr.* **140** 20
guard *Fencing* **294** 35, 38, 43
guard, king's ~ **306** 68
guard, protective ~ **168** 45
guard board **118** 29
guard cam **167** 57
guard for V-belt drive **180** 58
guard iron **210** 34
guard netting **118** 90
guard rail *Roof & Boilerr.* **38** 28
guard rail *Agr. Mach.* **64** 55
guard rail *Forestry* **84** 8
guard rail *Floor etc. Constr.* **123** 53
guard rail *Weaving* **165** 31
guard rail *Railw.* **202** 23
guard rail *Ship* **221** 121
guard rail *Shipbuild.* **222** 66
gudgeon pin **192** 26
guelder rose **373** 10
guest rope **227** 14
gugelhupf **97** 33
guide **23** 21
guide, stationary ~ **243** 21
guide bar *Cotton Spin.* **164** 17
guide bar *Weaving* **165** 38
guide bearing **113** 14
guide block **174** 48; **176** 18
guide chain **65** 13
guide-chain crossbar **65** 12
guide dog **70** 25
guide groove **217** 75
guide notch **117** 36
guide pin **243** 21
guide post **15** 110
guide rail *Weaving* **165** 3
guide rail *Railw.* **214** 56
guide rail *Store* **271** 54
guide rod **200** 27
guide roller *Sawmill* **157** 5
guide roller *Cotton Spin.* **164** 18
guide roller *Films* **312** 29
guide step **117** 36
guide tractor **141** 19
guiding blade **322** 40
guiding roller **312** 29
guiding slot *Weaving* **165** 11
guiding slot *Music. Instr.* **322** 41
guilder **252** 19
guillemet **342** 27
guillemot **359** 13
guillotine *Plumb.* **125** 26
guillotine *Bookbind.* **183** 16; **185** 1

guillotine cutter, automatic ~ **185** 1
guinea fowl **73** 27
guinea pig **366** 12
guiro **324** 60
guitar **318** 8; **324** 12, 73
guitarist **318** 9
guitar player **318** 9
gulden **252** 19
gules **254** 27
Gulf Stream **14** 30
gull **359** 14
gullet *Man* **17** 49; **20** 23, 40
gullet *Bees* **77** 19
gullet *Forestry* **84** 28
gull wing, inverted ~ **229** 14
gully **12** 44
gum **19** 15
gun **218** 50
gun, pneumatic ~ **94** 3
gun, self-cocking ~ **87** 23
gun, self-propelled ~ **255** 57
gun barrel, rifled ~ **87** 34
gun carriage **255** 43
gun carriage, self-propelled ~ **255** 49-74
gun dog **86** 7
gunnel **283** 30
gunport **218** 59
gunport shutter **218** 60
gun slit **86** 52
gun turret **258** 29
gunwale **283** 30
gutta-percha tree **383** 37
gutter *Dwellings* **37** 6, 11
gutter *Roof & Boilerr.* **38** 9
gutter *Roof* **122** 28, 92
gutter *Bookbind.* **185** 55
gutter *Street Sect.* **198** 10
gutter, parallel ~ **122** 83
gutter bracket **122** 32
guy *Wine Grow.* **78** 8
guy *Camping* **278** 23
guy line **278** 23
guy pole **152** 31
guy wire *Wine Grow.* **78** 8
guy wire *Energy Sources* **155** 44
gybe **285** 28
gybing **285** 26
gymkhana **290** 32
gymnastic ball **297** 34
gymnastic club **297** 38
gymnastic hoop **297** 46
gymnastic ribbon **297** 49
gymnastics **297** 33-50
gymnastics, men's ~ **296** 1-11
gymnastics, Olympic ~ **296** 1-11; **297** 1-6
gymnastics, women's ~ **297**
gymnastics apparatus **296** 1-11; **297** 1-6
gymnastics kit **296** 61-63; **297** 51-52
gym shoe **296** 63; **297** 52
gym trousers **296** 62
gypsum *Sculpt. Studio* **339** 29
gypsum *Crystals* **351** 24, 25
gypsum crusher **160** 14
gypsum powder **339** 29
gypsum store **160** 13
gyro compass **224** 31, 51-53
gyro compass unit **224** 51-53
gyrodyne **232** 29
gyro horizon **230** 3
gyro repeater **224** 52

H

habergeon **329** 51
habit, monk's ~ **331** 55
hack **186** 26
hacking knife **128** 37
hackney carriage **186** 26
hackney coach **186** 26
hacksaw **134** 3, 17; **136** 40; **138** 23; **140** 9; **150** 14
hacksaw frame **126** 71
haematite **108** 48
haft **137** 30
hail **9** 36
hail, soft ~ **9** 35
hair **16** 3
hair, bobbed ~ **34** 34
hair, closely-cropped ~ **34** 11
hair, curled ~ **34** 33
hair, curly ~ **34** 18
hair, long ~ **34** 1
hair, pinned-up ~ **34** 28
hair, shingled ~ **34** 34
hair, swept-back ~ **34** 28
hair, swept-up ~ **34** 28
hairbell **375** 14
hairbrush **28** 7; **105** 10
haircap moss **377** 17
hair clip **105** 11
hair curler **106** 31
haircut **106** 3
haircuts **34** 1-25
haircutting scissors **105** 7; **106** 34
hair decoration **355** 82
hairdress **354** 9
hairdresser **105** 35; **106** 1
'hairdresser' *Airport* **233** 53
hairdresser, ladies' ~ **105**
hairdresser, men's ~ **106**
hairdresser's tools **105** 1-16
hairdressing salon, ladies' ~ **105** 1-39
hairdressing salon, men's ~ **106** 1-42
hair drier, hand-held ~ **105** 33; **106** 22
hair element **10** 9
hair-fixing spray **105** 24
hair moss **377** 17
hairpin *Needlewk.* **102** 29
hairpin *Winter Sp.* **301** 69
hairpin work **102** 28
hair sieve **260** 66
hair spray **105** 24
hairstyle **106** 3
hairstyles **34** 1-25
hairstyles, girls' ~ **34** 27-38
hairstyles, ladies' ~ **34** 27-38
hairstylist **310** 36; **315** 48
hair tonic **106** 10
hair trigger **87** 12
hairworm **80** 51
hake **65** 19
hake chain **65** 17
half-barrier crossing **202** 45
half chicken **266** 56
half mask **306** 13
half-moon **4** 4, 6
half nonpareil **175** 20
half note **320** 14
half nut **149** 19
half rest **320** 22
half-step **320** 50, 52
half-title **185** 43, 44
halftone dot **178** 39
half-way line **291** 3
hall **41** 1-29
hall, main ~ **236** 1-30; **250** 1-11
halliard **253** 2
hall manager **275** 7
hall mirror **41** 6
hall of mirrors **308** 55
Hallstatt period **328** 21-40
hallux **19** 52
halma **276** 26-28
halma board **276** 26
halma man **276** 28
halma piece **276** 28
halogen lamp **177** 31
halothane container **26** 26
halt **15** 27
halter **71** 7-11
halter top **31** 64
halved joint **121** 86
halving joint **121** 86
halyard **253** 2
ham **95** 51
hame **71** 14
hammer **85** 5; **126** 78; **134** 7; **137** 26; **139** 26
hammer *Army* **255** 4
hammer *Athletics* **298** 42
hammer *Music. Instr.* **322** 35; **325** 3
hammer *Graphic Art* **340** 14
hammer, anvil and stirrup **17** 61
hammer, bricklayer's ~ **118** 53
hammer, brickmason's ~ **118** 53
hammer, carpenter's ~ **120** 74
hammer, flat-face ~ **137** 35
hammer, glazier's ~ **124** 18
hammer, iron-headed ~ **339** 16
hammer, machinist's ~ *D.I.Y.* **134** 40
hammer, machinist's ~ *Metalwkr.* **140** 23
hammer, shoemaker's ~ **100** 37
hammer, stonemason's ~ **158** 35
Hammer and Sickle **253** 21
hammer axe **300** 37
hammer blow **293** 78
hammer crusher *Quarry* **158** 20
hammer crusher *Cement Wks.* **160** 2
hammer cylinder **139** 30
hammer drill **158** 11

hammer drill, electric ~ **134** 43
hammer forging **139**
hammer guide **139** 29
hammer head *Airsports* **288** 4
hammer head *Athletics* **298** 43
hammer head, felt-covered ~ **325** 24
hammer jack **325** 30
hammer lever **325** 30
hammer mill **160** 2
hammer rail **325** 15, 26
hammer shank **325** 25
hammer throw **298** 42-47
hammock **278** 4
ham on the bone **96** 1; **99** 52
hamper **306** 11
hamster **366** 16
hand **16** 47, 48; **17** 15-17; **19** 64-83
hand apparatus **297** 33-50
hand axe **328** 1
handball **292** 1
handball player **292** 2
hand bindery **183** 1-38
handbook **262** 17
hand bookbindery **183** 1-38
hand brace **140** 13
hand brake **187** 5; **191** 72; **212** 33
hand brake lever **188** 33; **191** 93
hand brake wheel **212** 64, 80
hand camera, large-format ~ **114** 36
handcart **120** 6
handcart, wooden ~ **309** 86
hand circle **297** 47
hand circling **297** 37
handclap **117** 69
hand-composing room **174** 1
hand compositor **174** 5
hand control **195** 8
hand cream **99** 27
hand cultivator **55** 21
hand die **126** 85
hand die, electric ~ **125** 12
hand drill **140** 13
hand flat knitting machine **167** 35
hand gallop **72** 42
hand glass *Hairdresser* **105** 23; **106** 7
hand glass *Opticn.* **111** 16
handgrip *Photog.* **114** 37
handgrip *Cine Film* **117** 5, 61
handgrip *Bicycle* **187** 3
handgrip *Navig.* **224** 9
handgrip *Films* **313** 21, 24, 38
hand guard **94** 10
hand hair drier **105** 33; **106** 22
hand hammer, blacksmith's **137** 23
hand harpoon **280** 40
handicraft **48** 3
hand-ironing pad **104** 30
hand-iron press **103** 18
handkerchief **33** 10
hand ladle **148** 23
hand lamp **270** 42
hand lance **83** 46
handle *Atom* **2** 39
handle *Hosp.* **26** 12
handle *Infant Care etc.* **28** 50
handle *Tablew. etc.* **45** 51, 59, 62
handle *Household* **50** 9, 63
handle *Market Gdn.* **55** 27
handle *Agr. Mach.* **65** 2
handle *Agr. Impl.* **66** 17
handle *Pest Contr.* **83** 19
handle *Forestry* **85** 3
handle *Hairdresser* **106** 37
handle *Joiner* **132** 10, 18
handle *D.I.Y.* **134** 47
handle *Metalwkr.* **140** 5
handle *Carriages* **186** 12
handle *School* **260** 8
handle *Motorboats etc.* **286** 48
handle *Fencing* **294** 41
handle *Athletics* **298** 44
handle *Sports* **305** 57, 80
handle, bound ~ **89** 55
handle, cork ~ **89** 50
handle, double ~ **148** 15
handle, fixed ~ **129** 7
handle, insulated ~ **127** 54
handle, tubular ~ **50** 64
hand lead **224** 58
handlebar **187** 2; **188** 45
handlebar, adjustable ~ **188** 3
handlebar, semi-rise ~ **188** 11
handlebar fittings **188** 30-35
handlebar grip **187** 3
handlebar moustache **34** 8
handlebars **34** 8
handlebar stem **187** 10
handler **264** 5
hand lever *Joiner* **132** 55
hand lever *Bookbind.* **183** 31
hand-lever press **183** 26
hand luggage **194** 19
hand mirror *Hairdresser* **105** 23; **106** 7
hand mirror *Opticn.* **111** 16
hand net **89** 2
handpiece **24** 6
hand press **340** 29
hand pump **83** 26; **269** 66
hand puppet **260** 74
handrail *Roof & Boilerr.* **38** 28
handrail *Hall* **41** 23
handrail *Floor etc. Constr.* **123** 53, 79
handrail *Ship* **221** 122
handrailing **215** 70
hand rammer **148** 32
hand-removing tool **109** 10
handrest **112** 58
hand sail **302** 28
hand saw **120** 60; **126** 72; **134** 27
handscrew **132** 14
handset **237** 7; **245** 15
handset cord **237** 14
handset cradle **237** 13
hand-setting room **174** 1
hand shank **148** 14
hand shears *Tailor* **104** 11
hand shears *Bldg. Site* **119** 87
hand signal **268** 33
handsledge **304** 29
hand spray *Pest Contr.* **83** 24
hand spray *Hairdresser* **105** 30; **106** 13
hand spray *Painter* **129** 35
hand spray *Offset Platem.* **179** 7
handspring **297** 22
handstamp **236** 45
handstand **295** 27; **296** 52
handstand dive **282** 45
hand steel shears **119** 22
handstrap, leather ~ **296** 47
hand-to-hand throw **297** 33
hand towel **28** 9; **49** 23; **106** 24
hand vice **140** 24
hand weapons **255** 1-39
handwheel *Shoem.* **100** 24
handwheel *Cooper* **130** 19
handwheel *Cotton Spin.* **163** 18
handwheel *Knitting* **167** 7, 30
handwheel *Paperm.* **172** 74
handwheel *Bookbind.* **183** 23
handwheel *Road Constr.* **201** 9
handwriting, English ~ **342** 10
handwriting, German ~ **342** 11
hang **296** 33, 35; **298** 41
hangar **287** 14
hanger **215** 41
hang glider **287** 44
hang glider pilot **287** 45
hang gliding **287** 43
Hansa cog **218** 18-26
Hansa ship **218** 18-26
hansom **186** 29
hansom cab **186** 29
harbour **216** 14; **225**; **226**
harbour ferry **225** 11
harbour tunnel **225** 55
hardboard **338** 22
hardcore **123** 12
hardener **130** 33
hardie **137** 32
hard-rock drill **158** 11
hard-top **193** 26
hardwood cutting **54** 25
hardy **137** 32
hare **86** 35; **88** 59
hare-and-hounds **289** 41-49
harebell **375** 14
hare call **87** 44
hare hunting **86** 34-39
harlequin **306** 35
harmonica **324** 35
harmonium **325** 43
harmonium case **325** 47
harmonium keyboard **325** 48
harness *Horse* **71** 7-25
harness *Airsports* **288** 43
harness horse racing **289** 23-40
harness of diving apparatus **279** 12
harness racing **289** 23-40
harness racing track **289** 23
harp **323** 60

harpoon **353** 10
harpoon, bone ~ **328** 3
harpoon thrower **328** 5
harpsichord **322** 45
harpsichord mechanism **322** 48
harpy **254** 35; **327** 55
harrow, disc ~ **65** 82
harrow, rotary ~ **65** 89
harrow, spike-tooth ~ **65** 88
harrow, three-section ~ **65** 88, 89
hasp **71** 14
hat **35** 9
hat, Alpine ~ **35** 23
hat, felt ~ **35** 15, 24; **355** 55
hat, fox ~ **35** 19
hat, hard ~ **289** 18
hat, huntsman's ~ **86** 5
hat, iron ~ **329** 59
hat, knitted ~ **35** 10
hat, ladies' ~ **41** 11
hat, lightweight ~ **35** 37
hat, loden ~ **35** 23
hat, men's ~ **35** 13
hat, mink ~ **35** 18
hat, mohair ~ **35** 6, 11
hat, paper ~ **306** 45
hat, picador's ~ **319** 20
hat, sailor's ~ **309** 63
hat, Thessalonian ~ **355** 4
hat, three-cornered ~ **355** 62
hat, trilby-style ~ **35** 14
hat, Tyrolean ~ **35** 24
hat, wide-brimmed ~ **35** 38; **355** 55
hat, woollen ~ **29** 57; **35** 10, 26
hat and light luggage rack **208** 28
hat box **205** 11
hatch *Roof & Boilerr.* **38** 14
hatch *Roof* **122** 24
hatch *Post* **236** 30
hatchback **193** 18
hatchboard **222** 65
hatch coaming **222** 64
hatch cover **222** 65
hatcher **74** 30
hatchery **89** 11-19
hatchet **270** 43
hatchet iron **125** 5
hatching compartment **74** 30
hatching jar **89** 17
hatching tray **74** 31, 32
hatchment **254** 1-6
hatch platform **6** 34
hatchway **222** 64-65
hatchway, main ~ **259** 86
H atom **1** 26
hat peg **266** 13
hats, ladies' ~ **35** 1-21
hats, men's ~ **35** 22-40
hat shop **268** 38
hatter's shop **268** 38
haubergeon **329** 51
haulage *Forestry* **85** 42
haulage *Rivers* **216** 27
haulage cable *Railw.* **214** 14, 26, 37, 42, 45
haulage cable *Winter Sp.* **301** 63
haulage cable driving pulley **214** 62
haulage cable guide wheel **214** 61
haulage cable roller **214** 32, 49, 60
haulage cable sleeve **214** 73
hauling **216** 27
hauling capstan **217** 22
haulm conveyor **64** 76
haulm conveyor agitator **64** 77
haulm conveyor drive **64** 78
haulm elevator **64** 90
haulm stripper **64** 73
haulm stripper, flexible ~ **64** 76
haulyard **253** 2
haunch *Horse* **72** 35
haunch *Game* **88** 21, 37
haunch jump **282** 14
Hauptwerk **326** 1, 43
hautboy **323** 38
haute école **71** 1-6
Havana cigar **107** 2
Hawaii girl **306** 16
hawk, male ~ **86** 46
hawkbells **276** 45
hawker **308** 12, 51
hawking **86** 42-46
hawkmoth **82** 27; **358** 55; **365** 9
hawksbill turtle **364** 28
hawse **222** 75
hawse hole **227** 11
hawse pipe **222** 76; **258** 54
hawthorn **374** 30
hay **75** 13
hay, tedded ~ **63** 25
hay fork, three-pronged ~ **66** 3
hay harvest **63** 19-30
haymaking **63** 19-30
hay rack, double ~ **75** 12
hayrake **66** 23
hay tripod **63** 30
hazard flasher **191** 76
hazard flasher switch **191** 68
hazel **59** 49
hazel branch, flowering ~ **59** 44
hazel bush **59** 44-51
hazel grouse **88** 69
hazel hen **88** 69
hazel leaf **59** 51
hazelnut **59** 49
hazel tree **59** 44-51
H-beam **143** 6
head *Man* **16** 1-18; **17** 42-55
head *Arable Crops* **68** 2
head *Horse* **72** 1-11
head *House Insects etc.* **81** 33, 36
head *Forest Pests* **82** 2
head *Game* **88** 12
head *Brew.* **93** 31
head *Tobacc. etc.* **107** 23
head *Carp.* **120** 58
head *Roof* **122** 87
head *Mach. Parts etc.* **143** 14, 52
head *Weaves* **171** 31
head *Composing Rm.* **175** 39
head *Hydr. Eng.* **217** 25
head *Restaurant* **266** 4
head *Music. Instr.* **323** 52; **324** 10
head *Prehist.* **328** 4
head *Articulates* **358** 28
head, bald ~ **34** 22
head, binocular ~ **112** 12
head, cock's ~ **327** 35
head, combined ~ **241** 59
head, composite ~ **370** 74
head, countersunk ~ **143** 46
head, eagle's ~ **327** 12
head, goat's ~ **327** 18
head, human ~ **327** 21
head, lion's ~ **327** 17
head, partly bald ~ **34** 20
head, pig's ~ **95** 43
head, rotating ~ **64** 52
head, shrunken ~ **352** 30
head, woman's ~ **327** 56
head and neck **19** 1-13
head badge **187** 15
headband **183** 35
headband, padded ~ **241** 67; **261** 41
head bandage **21** 3
head beam **183** 21
headboard *Bedrm.* **43** 6
headboard *Sailing* **284** 47
headbox **173** 11
head cellarman **79** 17
headcheese **96** 9
headdress **354** 9; **355** 65
headdress, feather ~ **352** 12
headdress, ornamental ~ **352** 12
head drum **243** 19, 27
header *Carp.* **120** 41
header *Roof* **121** 71
header *Ball Games* **291** 46
header joist **120** 41
header tank **212** 78
head frame **144** 3
headgear **35**; **144** 1; **302** 34
headguard **299** 30
heading **130** 10
heading bond **118** 60
heading course **118** 64
head interlocking point **171** 34
headlamp **187** 7; **189** 10; **191** 20
headlight **189** 10; **191** 20
head line *Man* **19** 73
headline *Sea Fish.* **90** 7
headline *Script* **342** 44
head margin **185** 56
head of department **271** 60
head of railcar **197** 3
headphone cable **241** 71
headphone cable plug **241** 70
headphone cord **241** 71
headphones **241** 66; **249** 63; **261** 38; **309** 24
headphone socket **117** 10; **249** 68

headpiece **71** 7-11
head piece **183** 21
headpiece, padded ~ **241** 67; **261** 41
head post **123** 54
headrace **91** 41
head rail **120** 58
headrest *First Aid* **21** 13
headrest *Railw.* **207** 67
headrest, adjustable ~ **191** 33; **207** 47
headrest, integral ~ **193** 31
headrest cushion, down-filled ~ **207** 68
head restraint, adjustable ~ **191** 33
head restraint, integral ~ **193** 31
headset **241** 66; **249** 63; **261** 38; **309** 24
headset socket **249** 68
headspring **297** 27
headstall **71** 7-11
headstand **295** 28
headstock **150** 2
headstock, geared ~ **149** 2
headstock, movable ~ **150** 26
headstone **331** 26
head support assembly **311** 25
heald, wire ~ **166** 27
heald eyelet **166** 28
heald frame **166** 4
heald frame guide **166** 3
heald shaft **166** 4
heald shaft guide **166** 3
heald shaft guiding wheel **166** 36
health insurance certificate **22** 9
heap cloud **8** 1, 2, 17; **287** 22
heart **18** 14; **20** 8, 24-25, 45-57
heart cherry **59** 5
hearth *Blacksm.* **137** 1-8, 1; **138** 34
hearth *Iron & Steel* **147** 24
heart line **19** 74
heart plank **120** 93
heart rhythm **25** 1
hearts **276** 40, 44
heartsease pansy **60** 2
heart-shield **254** 17
heartwood *Carp.* **120** 84
heartwood *Bot.* **370** 13
heartwood plank **120** 93
heat **1** 55
heat colour **343** 16
heater **172** 32
heater, electric ~ **174** 45; **179** 3
heater, gas ~ **126** 25
heater, water-controlled ~ **192** 60-64
heater box **192** 61
heater plug **190** 55
heat exchanger *Nucl. Energy* **154** 6, 44
heat exchanger *Coking* **156** 27
heat exchanger *Cement Wks.* **160** 4, 6
heat exchanger *Paperm.* **172** 19
heat exchanger *Car* **192** 61
heat exchanger *Railw.* **207** 6; **209** 15; **212** 36, 55
heat exchanger *Warships* **259** 66
heat exchanger, auxiliary ~ **212** 43
heat exchanger exhaust **160** 7
heat extractor **182** 5
heath **15** 5
heath and moor **15** 5
heather **377** 19
heating, underfloor ~ **356** 18
heating box **183** 27
heating coupling hose **208** 20
heating element **172** 32
heating engineer **126**
heating oil **38** 50
heating oil tank **212** 75
heating pipe **55** 8
heating regulator **207** 54
heating system **207** 6
heating system, hot-water ~ **38** 38-81
heating unit, electric ~ **174** 45
heat pump **155** 22
heat pump system **155** 1
heat reservoir **155** 20
heat-sealing machine **76** 27; **226** 12
heat shield *Motorcycles etc.* **188** 16
heat shield *Space* **234** 5, 20; **235** 8, 40
heat space **259** 93
heat transfer fluid **155** 31
heaume **254** 7
Heaviside-Kennelly Layer **7** 27
heavy-duty boot **101** 39
heavy liquor pump **172** 34
heavy vehicle elevator **221** 56
heavy vehicle lift **221** 56
heckelphone **323** 38
heckler **263** 15
heddle, wire ~ **166** 27
heddle eyelet **166** 28
hedge *Map* **15** 98
hedge *Dwellings* **37** 59
hedge *Fruit & Veg. Gdn.* **52** 32
hedge, trimmed ~ **272** 37
hedgehog **366** 5
hedgehog fungus **381** 31
hedge mustard **61** 16
hedge shears **56** 49
hedge trimmer **134** 55
hedge trimmer, battery-operated ~ **56** 17
hedge-trimming attachment **134** 55
heel *Man* **19** 63
heel *Agr. Impl.* **66** 15
heel *Bakery* **97** 5
heel *Shoem.* **100** 67
heel, high ~ **101** 28
heel, raised ~ **101** 33
heelbone **17** 27
heel flap **286** 58
heel trimmer **100** 4
heel unit, automatic ~ **301** 54
height adjuster **106** 17
height-adjuster bar **106** 17
height adjustment *Hosp.* **27** 3
height adjustment *Photog.* **116** 34
height adjustment *Sawmill* **157** 49
height adjustment crank **64** 57
height adjustment wheel **132** 60
height and angle adjustment **177** 21
height gauge **22** 69
height of shank **175** 45
height of shoulder **175** 45
height scale *Sawmill* **157** 60
height scale *Athletics* **298** 20
height to paper **175** 44
helicon **323** 44
helicopter deck **146** 7
helicopter hangar **221** 52; **259** 38
helicopter landing deck **228** 15
helicopter landing platform **259** 39, 53
helicopter platform **221** 19
helicopters **232** 11-25
heliostat **5** 29
heliozoan **357** 7
heliport **146** 7
heliport deck **146** 7
helium atom (model) **1** 5
helium-neon laser **243** 57
helium nucleus **1** 30-31
helium pressure bottle **234** 14
helium pressure vessel **234** 43, 50
heller **252** 27
hellhound **327** 29
helm **218** 13
helmet *Police* **264** 35
helmet *Equest.* **289** 18
helmet *Ball Games* **292** 24
helmet *Chivalry* **329** 39-42
helmet, barred ~ **254** 8
helmet, fireman's ~ **270** 38
helmet, grilled ~ **254** 8
helmet, protective ~ *Police* **264** 21
helmet, protective ~ *Mountain.* **300** 53
helmet, protective ~ *Winter Sp.* **302** 34
helmet affronty **254** 9
helmet flower **379** 1
helmet lamp **300** 54
helmets **254** 4,7-9
helms **254** 4,7-9
helmsman **224** 16
helper **21** 19
helve **85** 3
hemidemisemiquaver **320** 19
hemidemisemiquaver rest **320** 27
hemihedron **351** 24
hemipyramid **351** 24
hemisphere, northern ~ **3** 1-35

hemline marker **271** 40
hemlock **379** 4
hemp **383** 9
hem stitch work **102** 14
hen **62** 36; **73** 19
hen, fattened ~ **98** 7
henbane **379** 6
hen pheasant **88** 77
herald **329** 75
heraldic beasts **254** 15-16
heraldry **254** 1-36
herb, primulaceous ~ **53** 5
herb, solanaceous ~ **53** 6; **379** 7
Hercules **3** 21
herd **86** 15
Herdsman **3** 30
Herero woman **354** 25
herm **334** 35
herma **334** 35
hermes **334** 35
heron **86** 46; **359** 18
herring **364** 14
herringbone **301** 26
herringbone stitch **102** 9
herring drift net **90** 2-10
herring lugger **90** 1
Hessian fly **80** 40
Heterocera **365** 7-11
hexagon **351** 15
hexagonal crystal system **351** 20-22
hexahedron **351** 2
hexakis-octahedron **351** 13
hexoctahedron **351** 13
H-girder **143** 6
hibernation cocoon **80** 31
hide **88** 56
hide, raised ~ **86** 14-17, 14
hide beetle **81** 22
hieroglyphics, ancient Egyptian ~ **341** 1
Hi-Fi component **241** 13-48
high **9** 6
high-altitude anorak **300** 6
highball **317** 33
highball glass **267** 56
high bar *Playground* **273** 32
high bar *Gymn.* **296** 7
highboard diver **282** 5
highboard diving **282** 40-45
high chair, baby's ~ **28** 33
high-draft draw frame **164** 14
high-draft speed frame **164** 19
high-draft system **164** 14
high frequency **7** 26
high-hat cymbals **324** 50
high house **305** 75
high jump **298** 9-27
high jump apparatus **298** 32
high jump equipment **298** 32
high jumper **298** 10
highland Indian **352** 23
high-moor bog **13** 19
high-mountain region **12** 39-47
high performance sailplane **287** 9
high-pile lining **101** 3
high-pressure area **9** 6
high-pressure belt **9** 47
high-pressure manometer **141** 4
high-pressure xenon arc lamp **312** 39
high-rise handlebar **188** 57
high-riser **188** 56
high school **261**
high school riding **71** 1-6
high seat **86** 14
high-speed plate, automatic ~ **39** 15
high-tension voltage indicator **211** 29
high tide **280** 7
high toss **297** 35
high-water line **13** 35
high-water mark **13** 35
highway construction **201** 1-24
hiking boot **101** 18
hiking stick **284** 31
hiking strap **284** 30
hill *Phys. Geog.* **13** 66
hill *Films* **310** 13
hillside spring **12** 38
hill upcurrent **287** 28
himation **355** 6
hind **86** 13
hind, young ~ **88** 1
hinge **188** 2
hip *Man* **16** 33
hip *Horse* **72** 32
hip *Roof* **121** 12
hip bone **17** 18
hip circle backwards **296** 55
hip dormer window **121** 13
hip end **121** 11
hip grip **21** 38
hipped-gable roof **121** 16
hippocampus *Fabul. Creat.* **327** 44
Hippocampus *Fish etc.* **364** 18
hippocentaur **327** 52
hippodrome **308** 59
hippogryph **327** 26
hippopotamus **366** 31
hip rafter **121** 62
hip roof **37** 64; **121** 10, 60
hip tile **122** 9
historical ship, types of ~ **218**
hitch **65** 61
hitch, adjustable ~ **64** 60
hitch, front ~ **65** 50
hitch-kick **298** 40
hitch pin **325** 14
hive **77** 52
hive-bee **77** 1-25
hock **72** 37
hockey **292** 6
hockey ball **292** 14
hockey player **292** 15
hockey stick **292** 13
hod **122** 22
hod hook **122** 23
hoe **66** 24
hoe and fork, combined ~ **56** 7
hoe handle **66** 2
hog **94** 11
hogpen **62** 8; **75** 35
hoist *Oil, Petr.* **145** 11
hoist *Flags* **253** 22-34
hoist, builder's ~ **118** 31
hoist, inclined ~ **158** 16; **159** 5
hoisting gear **206** 56; **217** 74
hoisting gear bridge **217** 73
hoisting gear cabin **217** 71
hoisting rope **120** 37
hold **223** 55, 75
hold, insulated ~ **223** 56
hold, underfloor ~ **231** 21
hold-down, automatic ~ **157** 65
holdfast *Carp.* **120** 66
holdfast *Alp. Plants etc.* **378** 50
holding device **157** 47
holding forceps **23** 12
holding press **183** 4
holding squad **270** 17
hold pillar **222** 61
hole *Phys. Geog.* **13** 34
hole *Ball Games* **293** 79-82, 87
hole, elongated ~ **240** 17
hole, square ~ **140** 43
hollowing tool **135** 17
hollow of the throat **16** 20
hollow-shaft boring bit **133** 7
holly **374** 9
holohedron **351** 2
holster **264** 24
Holy Bible **330** 11
Holy Communion **332** 26
Holy Scripture **330** 11
holy table **330** 4
holy water basin **332** 47
home and overseas news section **342** 62
home base **292** 53
home plate **292** 53
home port **286** 8
homogenizer **76** 12
homopteran **358** 3
honey **77** 33
honey, strained ~ **77** 62-63
honey bag **77** 18
honey-bee **77** 1-25
honey cell **77** 33
honeycomb **77** 31-43, 45
honeycomb, artificial ~ **77** 42
honeycomb, natural ~ **77** 60
honeycomb weave **171** 29
honeydew melon **266** 50
honey extractor **77** 61
honey fungus **381** 28
honey gland **59** 18
honey in the comb **77** 64
honey jar **77** 63
honey pail **77** 62
honey sac **77** 18
honey separator **77** 61
honeysuckle **374** 13
honey super **77** 45
honey wrack **378** 48
hood *Infant Care etc.* **28** 26
hood *Child. Clothes* **29** 2
hood *Ladies' Wear* **30** 69
hood *Headgear* **35** 2
hood *Blacksm.* **137** 7

hood *Carriages* **186** 42
hood *Car* **191** 8
hood *Garage* **195** 36
hood *Aircraft* **230** 39
hood *Mountain.* **300** 19
hood *Church* **331** 56
hood, collapsible ~ **186** 52; **193** 10
hood, convertible ~ **193** 10
hood, detachable ~ **31** 21
hood, falcon's ~ **86** 44
hood, folding ~ **28** 35
hood, protective ~ **157** 65
hood drawstring **29** 64
hood support **195** 37
hoof *Horse* **72** 26
hoof *Game* **88** 24
hoof, horse's ~ **327** 42
hoofprints **86** 8
hook *Roof & Boilerr.* **38** 22
hook *Horse* **71** 14
hook *Shoem.* **100** 62
hook *Oil, Petr.* **145** 9
hook *Sports* **299** 33
hook *Winter Sp.* **301** 61
hook *Sports* **305** 18, 46
hook *Music. Not.* **320** 5
hook, blunt ~ **26** 50
hook, butcher's ~ **96** 55
hook, closed ~ **89** 85
hook, concealed ~ **89** 75
hook, double ~ **89** 83
hook, open ~ **89** 83
hook, treble ~ **89** 85
hookah **107** 42
hook-and-ride band **140** 50
hook ball **305** 18
hook belt **270** 44
hook disgorger **89** 40
hook ladder **270** 16
hooks **89** 79-87
hoop *Airsports* **288** 67
hoop *Ball Games* **292** 78
hoop *Circus* **307** 58
hoopoe **359** 25
hoop of barrel **130** 8
hooter *Motorcycles etc.* **188** 53
hooter *Fire Brig.* **270** 7
hop boiler **92** 52
hop garden **15** 114
hop growing **83** 27
hopper *Agr. Mach.* **64** 59
hopper *Wine Grow.* **78** 18
hopper *Mills* **91** 13
hopper *Cotton Spin.* **163** 31
hopper *Music. Instr.* **325** 30
hopper, endless-floor ~ **64** 84
hopper barge **226** 46
hopper delivery roller, wooden ~ **163** 32
hopper feeder **163** 33
hopsack weave **171** 11
horizon **13** 21
horizon, artificial ~ **230** 3
horizon glass **224** 7
horizon light **316** 15
horizon mirror **224** 7
horizontal bar **296** 7
horizontal boring and milling machine **150** 25
horizontal deflection module **240** 10
horizontal eight **288** 2
horizontal linearity control module **240** 9
horizontally-opposed twin engine **189** 47
horizontal milling spindle **150** 39
horizontal piano **325** 40
horizontal slow roll **288** 8
horizontal synchronizing module **240** 7
horn *Horse* **71** 38
horn *Motorcycles etc.* **188** 53
horn *Car* **191** 60
horn *Railw.* **212** 70
horn *Fire Brig.* **270** 7
horn *Flea Market* **309** 34
horn *Music. Instr.* **323** 41
horn *Invertebr.* **357** 31
horn *Birds* **362** 16
horn, spirally twisted ~ **327** 8
hornbeam **371** 63
horned owl **362** 14
horns **88** 29-31
horse *Horse* **71; 72**
horse *Dom. Anim.* **73** 2
horse *Carp.* **120** 18
horse *Gymn.* **296** 1; **297** 1
horse, armoured ~ **319** 18
horse, piebald ~ **289** 29
horse, toy ~ **47** 15
horse, wild ~ **328** 7
horse, winged ~ **327** 26
horse armour **329** 83-88
horse bean **69** 15
horse box **75** 2
horse brush **71** 55
horse chestnut **371** 60
horse chestnut tree **371** 58
horsefish **364** 18
horsehair **323** 15
horsehair brush **100** 12
horse latitudes **9** 47
horsemanship **289**
horse racing **289** 50
horse-radish **57** 20
horse's head **72** 1-11
horseshoe *Game* **88** 71
horseshoe *School* **260** 1
horseshoe arch **336** 30
horseshoe grip **298** 53
horseshoe marking **88** 71
horseshoe mount **113** 25
horseshoe mounting *Astron.* **5** 9
horseshoe mounting *Optic. Instr.* **113** 25
horse sleigh **304** 25
horse stall **75** 2
horsetail **376** 18
horst **12** 10
hose *Household* **50** 75
hose *Bldg. Site* **118** 38
hose *Serv. Stat.* **196** 2; **196** 23
hose *Fire Brig.* **270** 54
hose *Hist. Cost.* **355** 47
hose, rotary ~ **145** 13
hose carriage **270** 28
hose cart **270** 28
hose connection **83** 30
hose connector **56** 45
hose coupling **270** 29
hose layer **270** 53
hosepipe **118** 38; **196** 23
hose reel **56** 26; **270** 28
hose truck **270** 28
hose wagon **270** 28
hosiery **271** 56
hosiery department **271** 17
hosiery mill **167** 1-66
hosiery shelf **99** 25
hospital **25; 26; 27**
hospital bed **25** 10
hospital unit **228** 21
Host **331** 48; **332** 28, 35
hostess **318** 33
hot-air duct **139** 52
hot-air gun **130** 25
hot-air sterilizer **22** 71
hotbed **55** 16
hotbed vent **55** 17
hot-blast pipe **147** 19
hot-blast stove **147** 15
hot dog **308** 34
hot-dog stand **308** 32
hotel **267**
hotel bar **267** 51
hotel bill **267** 11
hotel guest **267** 14
hotel lobby **267** 18-26
hotel manager **267** 19
hotel porter **204** 17
hotel register **267** 8
hotel restaurant **267** 20
hotel room **267** 27-38
hotel sticker **205** 9
hothouse **55** 4; **272** 65
hot-metal receiver, tilting-type ~ **148** 5
hot-pipe space **259** 93
hotplate **39** 15; **207** 30
hotplate, electric ~ **45** 45
hot reservoir **155** 20
hot-shoe contact **114** 72
hot-shoe flash contact **115** 21
hot tap **126** 28
hot water supply **155** 26
hot water tank **38** 68
hot water tank *Brew.* **92** 10
hot water tank *Paperm.* **172** 18
hound *Hunt.* **86** 33
hound *Sailing* **284** 14
hour and minute button **110** 3
hour axis **5** 8
hour axis drive **5** 7
hourglass **110** 31
hour hand **110** 13
house *Dwellings* **37** 54
house *Farm Bldgs.* **62** 1
house *Bldg. Site* **118** 1-49
house, detached ~ **37** 1-53
house, dikereeve's ~ **216** 45
house, duplex ~ **37** 64-68
house, ferryman's ~ **216** 45
house, semi-detached ~ **37** 69-71
house, solar ~ **155** 17
house, solar-heated ~ **155** 17
house, terraced ~ **37** 58-63

house, timber ~ **37** 84-86
houseboat **353** 31
house cat **62** 3
housecoat *Underwear etc.* **32** 20
housecoat *Hist. Cost.* **355** 66
house cricket **81** 7
house detective **275** 16
house dress **31** 36
housefly **81** 1, 2
house frock **31** 36
household appliances **50**
household utensils **50**
house insects **81** 1-14
houseleek **51** 7
house light dimmer **312** 17
houseplant **42** 36; **248** 14
houseplants **53**
house sparrow **361** 5
house spider **81** 9
house telephone **127** 3
house wall **120** 29
housewife **39** 1
housing *Meteorol. Instr.* **10** 18
housing *Iron Foundry etc.* **148** 57
housing *Films* **312** 48
housing, protective ~ **10** 39
housing, soundproof ~ **310** 48; **313** 16-18, 27
housing development **37** 54-57
housing estate **37** 54-57
housing lock **313** 33
hover **74** 3
hovercraft **286** 63
hub **187** 26
hub, centre ~ **187** 59
hub, front ~ **187** 52
hub assembly, front ~ **187** 52
hub barrel **187** 69
hub body **187** 69
hub shell **187** 69
huckleberry **377** 23
hula-hula girl **306** 16
hula skirt **306** 18
hull *Aircraft* **232** 2, 9
hull *Warships* **258** 2; **259** 22, 42
hull bottom **286** 32, 35, 39
hull frame **222** 29
human flea **81** 42
Humanist **342** 4
human louse **81** 40, 41
humblebee **358** 23
humerus **17** 12
humidifier **79** 22
hummock **13** 42
hump **206** 46
hundreds **344** 3
hunt **289** 41-49
Hunter *Astron.* **3** 13
hunter **86** 1
hunting **86** 1-52, 9-12, 14-17
hunting cap **289** 14
hunting cap, hard ~ **289** 18
hunting clothes **86** 2
hunting dog **86** 33
hunting equipment **87** 41-48
hunting horn **87** 60; **289** 44
hunting knife **87** 42
hunting knife, double-edged ~ **87** 41
hunting leopard **368** 7
hunting pink **289** 13, 42
hunting rifle **86** 4
hunting rifles **87** 1-40
hunting screen **86** 9
hunting weapons **87**
huntsman **86** 1
hurdle *Free Exerc.* **295** 12
hurdle *Athletics* **298** 8
hurdle position **295** 12
hurdle racing **298** 7-8
hurdles **298** 7-8
hurdy-gurdy **322** 25
hurst **91** 20
husk **59** 50; **68** 33
husk corn **68** 31
husky **70** 22; **353** 2
hut **300** 1
hut, beehive-shaped ~ **354** 28
hut, Indian ~ **273** 59
Hydra **3** 16
Hydra, Lernaean ~ **327** 32
Hydrallmania **369** 9
hydrangea **51** 11
hydrant key **270** 27
hydraulic engineering **217**
hydraulic lift pad **195** 27
hydraulic plant **92** 13
hydraulic plant room **316** 50
hydraulic system *Agr. Mach.* **64** 65
hydraulic system *Paperm.* **173** 37
hydraulic system *Army* **255** 53
hydraulic system *Air Force* **257** 16
hydrocyanic acid **83** 15
hydro-extraction **169** 23
hydro-extractor, pendulum-type ~ **168** 14
hydro-extractor lid **168** 18
hydroformer **145** 47
hydrogenation **170** 16
hydrogen atom **1** 15; **242** 62
hydrogen atom (model) **1** 1
hydrogen balloon **10** 56
hydrogen bomb explosion **7** 12
hydrogen cooler **153** 27
hydrogen inlet *Synth. Fibres* **170** 15
hydrogen inlet *Chem.* **350** 12
hydrogen sulphide scrubber **156** 22
hydrogen sulphide wet collector **156** 22
hydrogen tank **6** 6
hydropathic **274** 8
hydrophone **224** 64
hydroplane **286** 22
hydroplane, stepped ~ **286** 38-41
hydroplane, three-point ~ **286** 42
hydrosphere **11** 2
hydroxylamine inlet **170** 21
hyena **368** 1
hygrograph **10** 8, 50
hygrometer *Drawing Off.* **151** 39
hygrometer *Offset Platem.* **179** 28
hygrometer *Swim.* **281** 23
hygrometer element **10** 9
hymenium **381** 17
Hymenoptera **358** 21-23
hymn board **330** 24
hymn book **330** 30
hymn number **330** 24
hyoid **20** 2
hyperbola **347** 26
hyperbolic position line **224** 43, 44
hyphae **381** 2
hyphen **342** 28
hypocentre **11** 32
hypocotyl **370** 89
hypophysis cerebri **17** 43
hypotenuse **346** 32
hypotrachelium **334** 22
hyrax **366** 24
hyssop **374** 5

I

ibex **367** 7
ice **266** 44
ice, glacial ~ **12** 48-56
ice accident **21** 28-33
ice axe **300** 16, 31
ice axe, short-shafted ~ **300** 36
iceboat **302** 44
iceboating **302** 44-46
icebox **39** 2; **46** 33; **317** 10
ice breaker **221** 50
ice bucket **267** 67
ice-cream cornet **308** 31
ice-cream man **308** 30
ice-cream sundae **266** 76
ice-cream vendor **308** 30
ice-crystal cloud **8** 6
ice-crystal cloud veil **8** 7
ice cube **266** 44
ice hockey **302** 29-37
ice hockey player **302** 29
ice hockey set **302** 23
ice hockey skate **302** 23
ice hockey stick **302** 30
ice ledge **300** 4
ice pellets **9** 35
ice piton **300** 40, 41
ice racing **290** 24-28
ice ridge **300** 21
ice sailing **302** 44-46
ice skater **302** 1
ice skates **302** 20-25
ice skating **302** 1-26
ice skating boot **302** 24
ice slope **300** 14
ice speedway **290** 24-28
ice step **300** 17
ice stick **302** 39
ice-stick shooter **302** 38
ice-stick shooting **302** 38-40
ice yacht **302** 44
ice yachting **302** 44-46
icicle **304** 21

icing, chocolate ~ **97** 34
icing sugar **98** 54
icosahedron **351** 11
icositetrahedron **351** 12
identification mark **163** 6
identification number **85** 33
identification tally **74** 55
idle air bleed **192** 2
idle mixture adjustment screw **192** 11
idling adjustment **190** 51
idling air jet **192** 2
idling jet **192** 1
idol **328** 20
igloo **353** 4
igloo tent, inflatable ~ **278** 58
ignition distributor **190** 9, 27
iguana **364** 32
ileum **20** 16
ilium **17** 18
illumination, incident ~ **112** 59, 63
illumination, vertical ~ **112** 59, 63
illumination beam path **112** 6
illumination optics **112** 7
illumination path **112** 6
image beam **115** 35
image converter **26** 15, 18; **27** 19
imago **358** 10
imbrication **335** 15
imitation motorcycle fork **188** 58
immersion heater **40** 17
immersion roller **165** 45
immersion vibrator **119** 88
impact crusher **158** 20
impact wrench **195** 44
impair **275** 23
impeller wheel **217** 52
Imperial Crown **254** 38
impost **336** 21
impounding reservoir **217** 57
impregnating spray **50** 40
impression-adjusting wheel **180** 81
impression control **249** 10
impression cylinder **180** 35, 64; **181** 2, 44, 59
impression-setting wheel **180** 81
impression tray **24** 56
imprint, publisher's ~ **185** 48
impulse generator, programmed ~ **25** 33
impulse meter, automatic ~ **25** 42
incense boat **332** 42
incense spoon **332** 43
incident light measurement **114** 60
incident neutron **1** 42
incisor **19** 16, 34
inclined cable anchorage **215** 48
inclined cable system **215** 51
incubation tank, long ~ **89** 18
incubator **261** 30
incubator, Californian ~ **89** 15
incus and stapes **17** 61
indention **175** 16
index **345** 1, 2
index arm **224** 3
index bar **224** 3
index cards **22** 7
index finger **19** 65
indexing mark **249** 74
indexing table, rotary ~ **150** 42
index mirror **224** 6
index plate **151** 51
Indian **352** 25
Indian chief **352** 11
Indian corn **68** 31
Indian cress **53** 4
Indian meal moth **81** 28
Indian Ocean **14** 23
indicator *Hosp.* **26** 28
indicator *Motorcycle* **189** 37, 45
indicator *Tram* **197** 22
indicator, rear ~ **189** 42
indicator and dimming switch **191** 59
indicator board *Station* **204** 32
indicator board *Hotel* **267** 5
indicator for rough and fine adjustment **148** 65
indicator lamp *Sawmill* **157** 62
indicator lamp *Cotton Spin.* **164** 8
indicator lamp *Office* **249** 71
indicator light *Hosp.* **25** 6
indicator light *Motorcycle* **189** 37, 45
indicator light *Serv. Stat.* **196** 7
indicator light *Tram* **197** 22
indicator light *Railw.* **203** 14
indicator light *Audio* **241** 55
indicator light *Office* **249** 71
indicator light *Hotel* **267** 6
indicator light *Fencing* **294** 30
indicator light, front ~ **191** 19
indicator light, rear ~ **189** 42
indicator needle *Photog.* **114** 58
indicator needle *Inf. Tech.* **242** 76
indicator plate **203** 12
indicator scale **114** 58; **313** 28
indigo dying and sizing machine **165** 40
Indio **352** 23
individual-section machine **162** 21
indoor target rifle **305** 35
indorsee **250** 26
indorsement **250** 25
indorser **250** 27
induced-draught fan **152** 14
induction coil **11** 44
industrial plant **225** 71
inert-gas atmosphere **162** 16
inert-gas supply **142** 34
inert-gas torch **142** 33
inert-gas welding **142** 33
inert-gas welding equipment **138** 29
inertial measurement unit **6** 43
inescutcheon **254** 17
infant care **28**
infants' wear **29** 13-30
in-feed scale **157** 61
infighting **299** 31
infiltration drain **216** 37
infinity **345** 15
inflating bulb **25** 17
inflator **22** 37
inflections **320** 50-54
inflight antenna **6** 46
inflight refuelling probe **256** 7
inflorescence **371** 43, 48; **378** 7, 53, 55; **382** 38; **383** 49; **384** 31
inflorescence, female ~ **59** 46; **68** 32; **383** 11; **384** 50
inflorescence, male ~ **59** 39; **68** 35; **371** 8; **372** 17, 24; **383** 13
inflorescences **370** 67-77
'information' **233** 31
information bureau **204** 29
information clerk **204** 49
information counter **250** 9
information office **204** 29
information plate **356** 20
information position **237** 34
information technology **242**
infrared drier **173** 32
infrared laser rangefinder **255** 82
infrared sound headphones **242** 30
infrared sound transmitter **242** 29
infrared transmission **242** 27
infraspinatus **18** 53
infringement **291** 50
infructescence **61** 15; **371** 22, 44, 69, 72; **373** 8; **374** 18; **383** 56; **384** 32
infusion apparatus **25** 11
infusion bottle **25** 12
infusion device **25** 14
ingot **148** 48
ingot mould **147** 32
ingot tipper **148** 49
ingress/egress hatch **6** 38
ingress/egress platform **6** 34
inhalation **274** 7
inhalational therapy **274** 6-7
inhalator **23** 24
inhalatorium **274** 6
inhaler **26** 2, 29
inhaling apparatus **23** 24
inhaling tube **26** 2, 29
initial **175** 1
initial position *Fish Farm.* **89** 33
initial position *Fencing* **294** 18
injection condenser **172** 16
injection nozzle **190** 32, 54
injection pump *Intern. Combust. Eng.* **190** 65
injection pump *Railw.* **211** 48

injection pump drive **190** 57
injection timer unit **190** 58
ink **260** 83
ink ball **340** 22
ink duct **180** 22; **181** 65
inker **180** 21, 50, 60, 77
inker unit **180** 6-13, 40, 51, 60, 71, 76; **181** 7, 8, 19, 28, 50, 57; **249** 51-52
ink fountain **180** 22; **181** 65
ink fountain roller **181** 64
inking ball **340** 22
inking roller **180** 21, 50, 60, 77; **249** 52
inking unit **180** 6-13, 40, 51, 60, 71, 76; **181** 7, 8, 19, 28, 50, 57; **249** 51-52
ink pad **22** 30
ink plate **181** 8
ink roller **180** 21, 50, 60, 77; **249** 52
ink slab **181** 8
ink unit, tubular ~ **151** 68
inkwell **309** 78
inlay **323** 26
inlet *Paperm.* **172** 77
inlet *Chem.* **349** 21
inlet filter **146** 26
inlet manifold **190** 18; **192** 13
inlet valve **242** 52
inlet vent **191** 47
inner tube **187** 30
input **117** 27
input keyboard **238** 13
input/output device **237** 59
input selector **241** 44
input selector switch **238** 49
input unit **176** 30
inscription **252** 11
insect, homopterous ~ **358** 3
insect, orthopterous ~ **358** 8
insectivores **366** 4-7
insects **358** 3-23
insects, dipterous ~ **358** 16-20
insert, wood ~ **85** 4
insertion ring **349** 17
inshore fishing **90** 24-29
inside defender **291** 12
inside forward **291** 15
insolation **155** 18
insole **291** 27
inspection apparatus **79** 20
inspection window **38** 62
inspector **205** 44
instep **19** 61
instruction, programmed ~ **242** 16
instruction key **247** 21
instruction laser **242** 81
instrument, keyed ~ **325** 1
instrument, plucked ~ **322** 21
instrument basin **27** 5
instrument cabinet **24** 16
instrument housing *Atom* **2** 5, 22
instrument housing *Meteorol. Instr.* **10** 59
instrument panel *Offset Print.* **180** 74
instrument panel *Railw.* **212** 31
instrument panel *Aircraft* **230** 1
instrument panel *Airsports* **288** 11
instruments, dental ~ **24** 4
instruments, orchestral ~ **323** 1-62
instruments, retractable ~ **258** 68; **259** 74, 88-91
instruments for gynecological and proctological examinations **23** 3-21
instruments for minor surgery **22** 48-50
instrument table **22** 45
instrument table, mobile ~ **26** 37
instrument tray **24** 5; **26** 39
instrument unit **234** 53
insufflator **23** 18
insulating board **122** 44
insulating casing **10** 26
insulating tape **127** 34
insulation *Slaughterho.* **94** 10
insulation *Energy Sources* **155** 36
insurance company office **268** 40
intaglio printing **182**
intaglio process **340** 14-24
intake muffler **191** 54
intake pipe **189** 5
intake silencer **190** 16; **191** 54
integer **344** 10
integral **345** 14
integral sign **345** 14
integration **345** 14
intensive care unit **25** 1-30
interceptor **256** 1
Intercity train **205** 34
intercom *Doc.* **22** 34
intercom *Garage* **195** 55
intercom *Computer* **244** 5
intercom *Office* **245** 20; **246** 10
intercommunication telephone **239** 13
intercom system *Railw.* **202** 48; **203** 69
intercom system *Computer* **244** 5
interest **345** 7
interior equipment **239** 6
interlacing point **171** 28
interleaving device **181** 11
intermediate frequency amplifier module **240** 4
intermediate image screen **113** 37
internal combustion engine, single-cylinder ~ **190** 6
internal combustion engine, two-stroke ~ **190** 6
internal combustion engines **190**
internal facing tool **149** 51
International Signals Code **253** 29
interrogation mark **342** 20
interrogation point **342** 20
interrupter **153** 55
intersection **347** 12
intersection of sets **348** 4
interspacing **175** 13
inter-stage connector **234** 31, 36
inter-stage section **234** 31, 36
inter-tank connector **234** 16
inter-tank section **234** 16
intervals **321** 6-13
intestine **77** 15
intestine, large ~ **20** 17-22
intestine, small ~ **20** 14-16
intestines **20** 14-22
intestinum crassum **20** 17-22
intestinum tenue **20** 14-16
intrusion **11** 30
inundation area **216** 41
inverness **186** 32
invertebrates **357**
inverted comma **342** 26
inverted flight **288** 9
involucre **59** 50
ion chamber **2** 2, 17
ionization chamber **2** 2, 17
ionizing particle **1** 58
ionosphere *Atmos.* **7** 23
ionosphere *Post* **237** 55
iris *Man* **19** 42
iris *Flower Gdn.* **51** 27
iris *Gdn. Flowers* **60** 8
iron *Shoem.* **100** 9
iron *Tailor* **104** 29
iron *Ball Games* **293** 92
iron, electric ~ **50** 6
iron, lightweight ~ **50** 6
iron, molten ~ **148** 11
iron, slater's ~ **122** 84
iron, square ~ **143** 9
Iron Age **328** 21-40
iron and steel works **147**
ironer **103** 19
iron foundry **148** 1-45
iron handle **50** 9
ironing board **50** 16
ironing-board cover **50** 17
ironing head **50** 4
ironing machine, electric ~ **50** 1
ironing surface *Household* **50** 16
ironing surface *Dressm.* **103** 23
ironing table **50** 15
iron ladle **147** 12, 21, 42
iron pyrites **351** 8
iron runout **147** 11
irons **50** 1-20
iron well **50** 18
irradiation table **2** 36
irrigation, overhead ~ **67**
irrigation system, portable ~ **67** 3
irrigation unit, long-range ~ **67** 18
ischium **17** 19
island *Phys. Geog.* **13** 6
island *Warships* **259** 3
island *Park* **272** 55
isobar **9** 1
isocheim **9** 42
isohel **9** 44

isohyet **9** 45
isometric crystal system **351** 1-17
isosceles triangle **346** 27
isoseismal **11** 37
isothere **9** 43
isotherm **9** 40
issue desk **262** 20
Italian ryegrass **69** 26
italics **175** 7
ITOS satellite **10** 64
ivory carver **135**

J

jack *Ship* **223** 54
jack *Army* **255** 68
jack *Fire Brig.* **270** 12
jack *Sports* **305** 23
jack *Music. Instr.* **322** 50
jack, hydraulic ~ **85** 45
jackal **367** 11
jack boot **355** 58
jack chain, endless ~ **157** 17
jacket **29** 51; **31** 2; **33** 2
jacket, baby's ~ **28** 25; **29** 9
jacket, casual ~ **33** 39
jacket, cork ~ **282** 19
jacket, denim ~ **33** 21
jacket, leather ~ **33** 43
jacket, metallic ~ **294** 15
jacket, mink ~ **30** 1
jacket, oilskin ~ **228** 6
jacket, padded ~ **300** 6
jacket, pile ~ **29** 44
jacket, poplin ~ **31** 37
jacket, short-sleeved ~ **33** 26
jacket, suede ~ **30** 58
jacket button **33** 55
jacket crown **24** 28
jacket flap **185** 38
jack-in-the-box **306** 56
jack panel **311** 16
jack plane **132** 16
jack rafter **121** 61, 63
jack spur, screwed ~ **71** 50
jack spur, strapped ~ **71** 51
jackstaff **223** 53; **258** 4
jackstay **221** 118
jacob's ladder **221** 91
jai alai **305** 67
jam **98** 52
jam, whole-fruit ~ **98** 51
jamb **118** 11; **120** 32, 51
jambeau **329** 54
jam cleat **284** 22
Jamestown weed **379** 8
Japan Current **14** 31
Japanese quince **373** 17
japonica **373** 17
jardin anglais **272** 41-72
javelin **319** 17
javelin throw **298** 51-53
jaw *Man* **16** 17
jaw *Hosp.* **26** 46
jaw *Joiner* **132** 33
jaw *Metalwkr.* **140** 3
jaw, lower ~ *Man* **17** 35
jaw, lower ~ *Horse* **72** 11
jaw, upper ~ **17** 36; **19** 27
jawbone, lower ~ **17** 35
jawbone, upper ~ **17** 36
jaws, inside ~ **149** 71
jaws, outside ~ **149** 70
jaw trap **87** 48
jay **361** 1
jazz band instruments **324** 47-78
jazz guitar **324** 73
jazz trumpet **324** 65
jeans **31** 60; **33** 22
jejunum **20** 15
jellyfish **357** 14
jelly roll **97** 19
J-2 engine **234** 19, 34
jenny **222** 14, 28
jerboa **366** 15
jerkin **355** 45
jerkin head roof **121** 16
jerk with split **299** 4
jersey **291** 56
jersey, padded ~ **292** 26
jess **86** 45
jester **306** 38
jet **83** 19
jet, main ~ **192** 12
jet aeroplanes **231** 7-33
jet airplanes **231** 7-33
jet blower **281** 34
jet condenser **172** 16
jet engine **231** 26
jet engines **232** 33-50
jet fuel tank **146** 18
jet nozzle **153** 29
jet planes **231** 7-33
jet pump **216** 62
jets **231** 7-33
jet stream level **7** 5
jet trainer **257** 1-41
jet turbine **231** 26
jet turbine engine **231** 26
jet turbine engines **232** 33-50
jet turbines **232** 33-50
jetty *Map* **15** 59
jetty *Docks* **225** 30, 66
jetty *Park* **272** 46
jetty *Camping* **278** 13
jetty *Rowing* **283** 19
jewel **110** 33; **355** 17
jewel box **36** 31
jewel case **36** 31
jewellery **36**; **36** 1
jewellery department **271** 62
jewelry *see* jewellery
jib *Bldg. Site* **119** 36
jib *Ship* **220** 2
jib *Docks* **226** 24, 49
jib *Army* **255** 95
jib *Sailing* **284** 16; **285** 3
jib, flying ~ **219** 23
jib, inner ~ **219** 21
jib, outer ~ **219** 22
jib boom **218** 51; **219** 1
jib crane **222** 34
jib downhaul **284** 17
jibe **285** 28
jibing **285** 26
jib sheet **284** 23
jib stay **219** 14
jig **134** 42
jiggering **161** 14
jig saw **108** 12
jigsaw puzzle **48** 9
jigsaw puzzle piece **48** 10
jimpson weed **379** 8
jimson weed **379** 8
job advertisement **342** 70
jockey **22** 68
jockey cap **35** 8
jockey roller **181** 45
jockey wheel **278** 54
jogger **249** 56
join **122** 94
joiner **132** 38; **133**
joiner's tools **132** 1-28
joining of modules **242** 70
joint *Phys. Geog.* **13** 50
joint *Plumb. etc.* **126** 38
joint *Railw.* **202** 11
joint *Industr. Plants* **383** 63
joint, pre-packed ~ **96** 22
joint, universal ~ **284** 6
joint and side pasting attachment **185** 28
joint cutter **201** 16
joint-cutting blade **201** 17
jointed charlock **61** 21
jointer **133** 37
joint vice **108** 34
joist **121** 54
joist shuttering **119** 12
jollying **161** 14
Jordan **172** 27, 60, 73, 83
Jordan refiner **172** 27, 60, 73, 83
journal **143** 63
joust **329** 71
jousting helmet *Heraldry* **254** 4
jousting helmet *Chivalry* **329** 77
judge *Cyc. Racing* **290** 5
judge *Sports* **299** 43
judo **299** 13-17
judoist **299** 14
judoka **299** 14
judo throw **299** 17
jug **39** 30
jug, clay ~ **260** 78
juice extractor **40** 19
ju-jitsu **299** 13-17
jumbo derrick boom **221** 25, 62
jumbo jet **231** 14
jump **289** 21
jumper *Child. Clothes* **29** 43
jumper *Equest.* **289** 9
jumper, child's ~ **29** 47
jumper, cowl neck ~ **30** 2
jumper, polo neck ~ **30** 7
jumper, short-sleeved ~ **31** 67
jumping **298** 9-41
jumping hoop **307** 58
jumping jack **306** 52
jumping rope **273** 15, 16
jumping saddle **289** 10
jumping sheet **270** 18
jump rope **273** 16
jump-sit-spin **302** 8
jump ski **286** 62
jumpsuit **31** 53
jump throw **292** 3

junior hacksaw **127** 52
juniper berry **372** 52
juniper tree **372** 47
junk **353** 32
junk stall **308** 60
Jupiter **4** 48
just **329** 71
justifying scale **174** 35
jute **383** 25

K

kail **57** 34
kale **57** 34
kangaroo **366** 3
kapok tree **383** 20
karabiner **300** 46
karabiner hole **300** 35
karate **299** 18-19
karateka **299** 18
karst formation **13** 71-83
karst spring **13** 74
kart **305** 83
karting **305** 82
kayak **283** 4; **353** 12
kayak, folding ~ **283** 61, 62, 67
kayak, one-man ~ **283** 54
kayak, two-seater ~ **283** 61
kayaks **283** 68-70
Keel *Astron.* **3** 46
keel *Shipbuild.* **222** 22
keel *Space* **235** 7
keel *Rowing* **283** 32
keel *Sailing* **285** 32
keel, lead ~ **285** 36
keel, vertical ~ **222** 53
keel arch **336** 36
keel block **222** 39
keel-centreboard yawl **285** 37-41
keel plate **222** 49
keelson **222** 53; **283** 50
keep **329** 4
keep net **89** 28
kegellade chest **326** 12-14
kelly **145** 14
kelson **222** 53; **283** 50
kerb **198** 6; **272** 25
kerbstone **198** 7
kerbstone broker **251** 5
kerbstoner **251** 5
kerf **84** 28
kernel **68** 13; **383** 44
kerosene **145** 60
kerosene tank **234** 9
kerria **373** 28
ketchup **45** 43
kettle, brass ~ **42** 14
kettle, whistling ~ **39** 16; **40** 10
kettledrum **323** 57
Keuper **154** 57
key *Map* **14** 27-29
key *Metalwkr.* **140** 33-35
key *Town* **268** 4
key *Music. Instr.* **322** 28, 38, 49; **323** 32, 35; **324** 40; **326** 8
key, black ~ **325** 5
key, ebony ~ **325** 5
key, flat ~ **140** 48
key, gib-headed ~ **143** 74
key, iron ~ **328** 32
key, ivory ~ **325** 4
key, sunk ~ **143** 73
key, white ~ **325** 4
key action **325** 22-39
keyboard *Composing Rm.* **174** 32, 37; **176** 2
keyboard *Post* **236** 44; **237** 70
keyboard *Office* **245** 27; **249** 2-6
keyboard *Music. Instr.* **322** 28; **324** 40; **325** 4-5
keyboard, lower ~ **322** 47
keyboard, upper ~ **322** 46
keyboard console **176** 1
keyboard instrument **325** 1
keyboard operator **176** 4
keyboard send-receive teleprinter **176** 31
keyboard side **324** 39
keyboard unit **176** 1
keyhole **140** 40
keyhole saw **120** 63; **126** 70; **132** 3
key lever **322** 38, 49; **326** 8
key mechanism **325** 22-39
key rack **267** 3
keys *Mach. Parts etc.* **143** 73-74
keys *Music. Not.* **320** 55-68
key seat **143** 85
key signatures **320** 50-54
key slot **143** 85
keystone **336** 23
keyway **143** 66, 85
kick-back guard **132** 47; **157** 59
kicker **292** 10
kicking strap **284** 21
kick stand **187** 34
kickstarter **188** 39, 43; **189** 38
kidney, left ~ **20** 30-31
kidney, right ~ **20** 28
kidney dish **23** 45
kidney vetch **69** 6
kieselguhr **93** 3
kieselguhr filter **93** 4
kill *Hunt.* **86** 38
kill *Bullfight. etc.* **319** 30
killer **94** 1
kiln **92** 19
kiln, circular ~ **159** 19
kiln, rotary ~ **160** 8
kilning floor **92** 16-18
kilns **161**
kilometer *see* kilometre
kilometre sign **216** 44
kimono **353** 40
kindergarten **48**
king **276** 8
King Carnival **306** 58
king cup **375** 8
kingfisher **360** 8
king penguin **359** 4
king pin roof structure **121** 42
king post **223** 35
king post, ventilator-type ~ **221** 58
king's fern **377** 16
Kipp generator **350** 59
Kipp's apparatus **350** 59
Kirghiz **353** 22
Kirschner beater **163** 25
kit **322** 20
kitchen **39, 207** 29, 80
kitchen, ship's ~ **223** 42
kitchen appliances **40**
kitchen cabinet **207** 35
kitchen chair **39** 43
kitchen clock **39** 20; **109** 34
kitchen cupboard **39** 8
kitchen lamp **39** 39
kitchen roll **40** 1
kitchen scales **309** 84
kitchen table **39** 44
kitchen unit **46** 29
kitchen utensils **40**
kite *Playground* **273** 41, 42
kite *Maths.* **346** 38
kite *Birds* **362** 11
kite, paper ~ **260** 71
kite string **273** 44
knapsack **86** 3
knapsack sprayer, plunger-type ~ **83** 43
knapweed **376** 12
kneading machine **97** 55
knee *Man* **16** 50
knee *Horse* **72** 22
knee-breeches **33** 40
kneecap *Man* **17** 23
knee cap *Chivalry* **329** 53
kneeler **332** 25
knee lever **325** 45
kneeling front support **295** 20
kneeling position *Free Exerc.* **295** 8
kneeling position *Sports* **305** 28
knee mounting **113** 21
knee pad *Ball Games* **292** 9
knee pad *Winter Sp.* **303** 17
knee piece **329** 53
knee roll **71** 48
knee strap **33** 41
knee swell **325** 45
knife *Tablew. etc.* **45** 7, 50
knife *Forestry* **85** 11
knife *Paperhanger* **128** 38
knife *Paperm.* **172** 74
knife *Swim.* **279** 8
knife, bookbinder's ~ **183** 13
knife, bronze ~ **328** 31
knife, butcher's ~ *Slaughterho.* **94** 15
knife, butcher's ~ *Butch.* **96** 37
knife, cobbler's ~ **100** 50
knife, electrician's ~ **127** 63
knife, gardener's ~ **56** 9
knife, gilder's ~ **129** 51
knife, hafted ~ **328** 31
knife, shoemaker's ~ **100** 50
knife, surgical ~ **26** 43
knife blade **96** 32
knife case **94** 12
knife coulter **65** 10
knife handle **96** 34
knife rest **45** 11
knife thrower **307** 37

knight *Games* **276** 11
knight *Chivalry* **329** 67
knighting **329** 66
Knight Templar **329** 73
knit **101** 43
knits **171**
knits, basic ~ **171** 30-48
knit stitch **101** 43
knitting **167**
knitting head **167** 21
knitting machine, circular ~ **167** 1
knitting machine, flat ~ **167** 18
knives, butcher's ~ **96** 31-37
knob **359** 17
knob, adjustable ~ **151** 3
knobkerrie **354** 33
knobkerry **354** 33
knob-leaf capital **333** 14
knockout **299** 40
knock-over bit **167** 52
knot *Meteorol. etc.* **9** 12
knot *Ladies' Wear* **31** 47
knot *Underwear etc.* **32** 42
knot *Roof* **122** 68
knot, French ~ **102** 13
knot hole cutter **132** 53
knot hole moulding machine **132** 52
knot stitch, twisted ~ **102** 13
knotted work **102** 21
knotter **172** 54; **173** 13
knotting machine **85** 18
knuckle *Man* **19** 82
knuckle *Meat* **95** 38, 42, 49
knuckle, fore ~ **95** 5, 8
knuckle, hind ~ **95** 1, 10
knuckle of pork **96** 17
Kocher's forceps **22** 49
kohlrabi **57** 26
Korean **341** 27
Kort vent **227** 21
koruna **252** 27
kraft pulp mill **172** 1-52
KR-class **284** 63
kris **353** 44
krona **252** 25
krone **252** 24, 26
Krüger flap **229** 55
krummhorn **322** 6
Kuroshio **14** 31
Kuro Siwo **14** 31
kursaal **274** 8
kymation **334** 19

L

label **54** 4
laboratory **23** 41-59
laboratory, multi-purpose ~ **235** 66
laboratory and research microscope **112** 1
laboratory apparatus *Doc.* **23** 57
laboratory apparatus *Paperm.* **173** 2-10
laboratory apparatus *Chem.* **349** 1-38; **350** 1-63
laboratory equipment *Doc.* **23** 57
laboratory equipment *Paperm.* **173** 2-10
laboratory equipment *Chem.* **349** 1-38; **350** 1-63
laboratory microscope **112** 1
laboratory technician **23** 41
laboratory timer **116** 18
laborer *see* labourer
labourer, bricklayer's ~ **118** 19
labourer, builder's ~ **118** 19
Labrador Current **14** 40
labret **354** 23
laburnum **374** 32
labyrinth **17** 62
lace **100** 64; **291** 32
lace, cotton ~ **31** 32
lace, Venetian ~ **102** 30
lace fastening **101** 21
lackey **186** 20
lackey moth **80** 13
lacolith **11** 30
lacquered work, incised ~ **337** 6
lacquey **186** 20
lactam oil **170** 37
ladder *Moon L.* **6** 35
ladder *Roof & Boilerr.* **38** 15
ladder *Child. Rm.* **47** 5
ladder *Fruit & Veg. Gdn.* **52** 8
ladder *Bldg. Site* **118** 42
ladder *Railw.* **211** 43
ladder *Hydr. Eng.* **217** 8
ladder *Space* **235** 28
ladder, aluminium ~ **50** 35
ladder, arched ~ **5** 20
ladder, extending ~ **270** 10
ladder, standard ~ **118** 86
ladder, steel ~ **270** 10
ladder dredge, multi-bucket ~ **216** 56
ladder hook **122** 15, 69
ladder mechanism **270** 11
ladder operator **270** 13
ladder scaffold **118** 86-89
'ladies' **233** 48
'ladies' toilet' **233** 48
ladies' wear **30; 31**
ladies' wear department **271** 28
ladle **130** 32
ladle, crane-operated ~ **147** 60
ladle, drum-type ~ **148** 6
ladle, mobile ~ **148** 6
lady *Café* **265** 23
lady *Hist. Cost.* **355** 59, 64, 68, 70, 79
ladybird **358** 37
ladybug **358** 37
lady-finger **69** 6
lady's finger **69** 6
ladysmock **375** 11
lady's slipper **376** 27
lady's smock **375** 11
lager **93** 26
lager cellar **93** 12
lagging **38** 72
lagoon **13** 33
lake **13** 3
lake, coastal ~ **13** 44
lake, ox-bow ~ **15** 75
lake dwelling **328** 15
lamantin **366** 23
lamb **73** 13; **75** 11
lamb's lettuce **57** 38
lamellicorn **82** 1
lamellicorn beetle **358** 24, 39
lamina **68** 20; **370** 28, 85
laminate **301** 48
lamp *Dent.* **24** 19
lamp *Dining Rm.* **44** 12
lamp *Watchm.* **109** 12
lamp *Carriages* **186** 9
lamp *Street Sect.* **198** 18
lamp *Nightclub* **318** 26
lamp, directional ~ **22** 44
lamp, fluorescent ~ **49** 32; **271** 23
lamp, front ~ **188** 29
lamp, individual ~ **26** 11
lamp, pendant ~ **44** 12
lamp, rear ~ **187** 46
lamp, side ~ **191** 20
lamp bracket *Photomech. Reprod.* **177** 16
lamp bracket *Bicycle* **187** 6
lamp compartment **177** 41
lampholder **127** 60
lamphouse **112** 28, 59; **116** 29; **309** 44; **312** 39-44
lamphouse connector **112** 60
lamp housing **116** 29
lamp post **198** 18
lam rod **166** 54
lance *Gdn. Tools* **56** 25
lance *Bullfight. etc.* **319** 17
lance *Chivalry* **329** 81
lance *Ethnol.* **353** 9
lanceolate **370** 32
lancer **319** 16
lance rest **329** 80
lancet arch **336** 31
lancet window **335** 39-41
land **87** 39
landau **186** 36
landaulette **186** 36
land drill **282** 20
landfill, sanitary ~ **199** 10
landing *Floor etc. Constr.* **123** 34-41
landing *Athletics* **298** 19
landing, intermediate ~ **123** 52-62
landing area **298** 36, 39
landing beam **123** 34, 55
landing beam, main ~ **123** 66
landing craft **258** 89; **259** 46
landing flap **229** 42; **230** 53; **257** 38; **288** 29
landing gear, hydraulically operated ~ **235** 31
landing gear, main ~ **235** 31
landing gear, retractable ~ **232** 10
landing gear housing **256** 15
landing gear hydraulic cylinder **257** 41
landing gear unit, forward-retracting ~ **257** 40

landing gear unit, main ~ **230** 41; **231** 28; **257** 40; **288** 33
landing gear unit, retractable ~ **231** 28
landing light **230** 49; **257** 37; **288** 32
landing mat **296** 13; **297** 7
landing net **89** 2
landing pad *Moon L.* **6** 33
landing pad *Athletics* **298** 36
landing pontoon **225** 63
landing skid **232** 15; **256** 21
landing stage **225** 63; **278** 13; **283** 19
landing unit, main ~ **256** 26
landlord **305** 7, 13
landside **65** 5, 67
landslide **11** 46
landslip **11** 46
land surveying **14** 46-62
land wheel **65** 15
lane *Map* **15** 112
lane *Forestry* **84** 1
lane arrow **268** 73, 74
lane timekeeper **282** 24
language laboratory **261** 35
languid **326** 28
lansquenet **355** 32
lantern *Carriages* **186** 9
lantern *Ship* **218** 44; **221** 48
lantern *Navig.* **224** 105
lantern *Art* **335** 45
lantern, Chinese ~ **353** 36
lantern, combined ~ **286** 13
lantern, paper ~ **52** 15; **306** 4
lantern mast **224** 82
lantern tower **224** 82
lanyard **284** 19
lap *Dom. Anim.* **73** 23
lap *Roof* **122** 100
lap *Cotton Spin.* **163** 58, 64
lap, carded ~ **163** 47
lapboard **136** 7
lap cradle **163** 15
lapel **31** 23; **33** 5
lapel, silk ~ **33** 8
lapping plate **125** 4
lap riveting **143** 56
lap scorer **290** 6
lap-turner, movable ~ **163** 19
lapwing **359** 21
larch **372** 32
larch cone **372** 36
lard **96** 5
large cabbage white butterfly **80** 47
larks **361** 10-19
larkspur **60** 13
larmier **88** 14
larry **144** 8; **156** 6
larry car **144** 8; **156** 6
larva **58** 64; **77** 29; **80** 6, 19, 36, 38, 41, 46; **81** 20; **358** 9, 19; **82** 12, 25, 36
larva, first-generation ~ **80** 23
larva, mature ~ **80** 53
larva, second-generation ~ **80** 24
larva, young ~ **77** 28; **80** 54
larynx **20** 2-3
laser **242** 81
laser beam **243** 53
lashing *Bldg. Site* **118** 30
lashing *Ship* **218** 32; **221** 119
lasso **319** 40; **352** 5
last **100** 34
last, iron ~ **100** 54
last, wooden ~ **100** 32
latch bolt **140** 37
latch needle **167** 12, 56, 61
lateen sail **218** 29; **220** 3
lateen spanker **218** 29
lateen yard **218** 30
La Tène period **328** 21-40
lateral **144** 30
lath **123** 70
lath, double ~ **122** 43
lath, tilting ~ **122** 43
lath, toothed ~ **122** 26
lath axe **122** 21
lathe **135** 1
lathe, watchmaker's ~ **109** 20
lathe bed **135** 2; **149** 31
lathe carrier **149** 54
lathe foot **149** 12
lathe spindle **149** 20
lathe tool **149** 48, 52
lathe tools **149** 45-53
lathing **123** 71
latissimus dorsi **18** 59
latitude **14** 6
latrine **118** 49
lattice casing **221** 84
lattice girder **235** 12
lattice mast **258** 18
lattice structures **1** 9-14
lattice swing bridge **215** 63
launch **225** 25
launcher **258** 49
launching container **258** 32
launching housing **259** 26
launching ramp **255** 66
launch phase escape tower **234** 66
lauter battery **92** 51
lauter tun **92** 50
lava plateau **11** 14
lava stream **11** 18
lavatories **317** 31
lavatory **49** 12; **146** 29; **207** 16, 42, 72; **211** 59; **231** 31; **278** 5
lavatory, public ~ **268** 62
lavender **380** 7
lawn **37** 46; **51** 33; **272** 36; **274** 12
lawn aerator **56** 15
lawn mower, electric ~ **56** 31
lawn mower, motor ~ **56** 28
lawn rake **51** 3; **56** 3
lawn sprinkler **37** 43; **56** 43
lay-by **217** 27
layer **54** 11, 12
layer, bast ~ **54** 35
layer, bituminous ~ **200** 58
layer, level ~ **123** 39
layer, raffia ~ **54** 35
layer, top ~ **123** 41
layer cloud **8** 3, 4, 8, 9, 10
layering **54** 10
layette **28**
layette box **28** 18
lay figure **338** 31
laying battery **74** 19
laying hen **74** 57
laying-on trowel **118** 56
laying up **216** 14
lay shaft **192** 37
L-D converter **147** 45-50
lead *Kitch.* **39** 25
lead *Dog* **70** 30
lead *Slaughterho.* **94** 9
lead *Arc Weld.* **142** 25
lead *Navig.* **224** 59
lead, electric ~ *Household* **50** 77
lead, electric ~ *Gdn. Tools* **56** 32
lead, oval ~ **89** 88
lead, pear-shaped ~ **89** 90
lead, spare ~ **151** 46
lead came **124** 13
leader *Dwellings* **37** 13
leader *Roof & Boilerr.* **38** 10
leader *Fish Farm.* **89** 78
leader *Photog.* **114** 9
leader *Carriages* **186** 46
leader *Mountain.* **300** 25
leader *Script* **342** 48
lead hammer **124** 11
leading article **342** 48
leading edge *Sailing* **284** 42
leading edge *Gliding* **287** 34
leading edge, carbon fibre reinforced ~ **235** 32
leading edge flap, profiled ~ **229** 54
leading lady **310** 27
leading light, higher ~ **224** 102
leading light, lower ~ **224** 101
leading lights **224** 101-102
leading man **310** 28
leading soloist **314** 28
lead-in tube **153** 40
lead knife **124** 12
leadline **224** 60
leads **89** 88-92; **224** 58-67
leadscrew **149** 19, 32
leadscrew handwheel **149** 13
leadscrew reverse-gear lever **149** 6
lead shot **89** 89
lead sinker **224** 59
leaf **58** 3, 53; **59** 17; **68** 8; **333** 24; **370** 19, 26; **371** 21, 23, 27, 29, 68; **372** 23; **373** 3, 16, 25; **374** 28; **375** 2; **378** 15, 18, 19, 41, 45; **384** 55, 62
leaf, alternate pinnate ~ **59** 40
leaf, basal ~ **375** 9, 12, 15, 30; **383** 2
leaf, pinnate ~ **57** 3
leaf, sprouting ~ **59** 29
leaf, ternate ~ **58** 19
leaf, trifoliate ~ **58** 19
leaf, young ~ **59** 29
leaf axil **370** 25; **375** 38
leaf blade **68** 20; **370** 28, 85
leaf bud **59** 47; **370** 90
leaf cluster, rooted ~ **54** 17
leaf drop **80** 20
leaf fat **95** 45

leaflet **263** 9
leaf margin shapes **370** 43-50
leaf ornament **334** 40
leaf roller **82** 43
leaf shapes **370** 31-38
leaf sheath **68** 9, 21; **370** 83; **384** 30
leaf stalk **370** 27; **371** 73
leaf tendril **57** 4
leaf vegetables **57** 28-34
leakage steam path **153** 28
lean forward **301** 36
lean-to roof **37** 78; **121** 7
leaping hind leg **358** 11
learner-swimmer **282** 17
learning programme, audio-visual ~ **242** 7
lease rod **166** 38
leash **70** 30
leather beetle **81** 22
leathers **290** 26
leather side **131** 13, 18
leaves **276** 43
leaves, compound ~ **370** 39-42
lebkuchen **97** 51
lectern **262** 4; **330** 2, 37
lecture **262** 1
lecture notes **262** 5
lecturer **262** 3
lecture room **262** 2
lecture theatre **262** 2
lederhosen **29** 32
ledge *Photograv.* **182** 23
ledge *Mountain.* **300** 4
ledge, cushioned ~ **277** 16
ledger **118** 26
ledger tube **119** 48
leeboard **220** 7; **283** 63
leech *Sailing* **284** 45
leech *Invertebr.* **357** 20
leech pocket **284** 43
leek **57** 21
lee waves **287** 17
left **254** 19,21,23
left corner pin **305** 6
left front second pin **305** 2
left luggage locker **204** 21
left luggage office **204** 27
left tank fuel gauge **230** 16
leg *Man* **16** 49-54; **17** 22-25
leg *Game* **88** 21, 37, 81
leg *Meat* **95** 1, 38
leg *Mach. Parts etc.* **143** 2
leg *Maths.* **346** 27
leg, back ~ **82** 8
leg, broken ~ **21** 11
leg, downwind ~ **285** 23
leg, first ~ **285** 19
leg, fractured ~ **21** 11
leg, front ~ **82** 6
leg, hind ~ *Dog* **70** 7
leg, hind ~ *Horse* **72** 33-37
leg, hind ~ *Bees* **77** 3, 6-9
leg, hind ~ *Game* **88** 22, 63
leg, middle ~ **82** 7
leg, second ~ **285** 20
leg, third ~ **285** 21
leg, tubular ~ **114** 44
leg, vertical ~ **143** 4
leg, windward ~ **285** 22
leg armour **319** 19
legato **321** 33
leg boot, high ~ **101** 7, 13
leg boot, men's ~ **101** 7, 13
legend **252** 11
leg feather **362** 3
leggings **28** 24; **29** 45; **352** 17
leg holder **23** 11
leg of mutton piece **95** 22, 29
leg ring **74** 54
legs **82** 6-8
leg space ventilation **191** 81
leg support **23** 10, 11
legume **57** 6; **370** 92
legume, immature ~ **374** 22
legume, unripe ~ **374** 22
Leguminosae **57** 1-11
leg vice **140** 10
Leine rock salt **154** 64
leisure centre **281**
lemon **384** 23
lemonade **265** 15
lemonade glass **265** 16
lemon peel, candied ~ **98** 10
lemon squeezer **40** 9
lending library **262** 18
length adjustment **100** 20
lengthening arm **151** 57
lengths of material **104** 2
length stop **157** 68
lens *Man* **19** 48
lens *Photog.* **115** 32, 84; **116** 32
lens *Composing Rm.* **176** 23
lens *Audiovis.* **243** 2, 52
lens *Films* **313** 2
lens *Crystals* **351** 33
lens, bifocal ~ **111** 15
lens, concave and convex ~ **111** 41
lens, convex and concave ~ **111** 42
lens, fisheye ~ **115** 44
lens, flat ~ **111** 38
lens, flush ~ **114** 5
lens, interchangeable ~ **112** 62; **115** 43
lens, long focal length ~ **115** 48
lens, long-focus ~ **115** 49
lens, medium focal length ~ **115** 47
lens, negative ~ **111** 37
lens, normal ~ **115** 3-8, 46; **117** 49
lens, plano-concave ~ **111** 39, 40
lens, positive ~ **111** 37
lens, short focal length ~ **115** 45
lens, special ~ **111** 38
lens, standard ~ **115** 3-8, 46; **117** 49
lens, telephoto ~ **115** 48
lens, variable focus ~ **117** 2
lens, varifocal ~ **117** 2
lens, wide-angle ~ **115** 45; **117** 48
lens barrel **115** 3
lens carrier **177** 27
lens case **115** 104
lens head **117** 46-49
lens hood **313** 3, 10
lens hood barrel **313** 5
lens hood bellows **313** 39
lens panel **112** 18
lens pouch, soft-leather ~ **115** 105
lens standard **114** 52
lens surface **111** 37
lens system **242** 83
lens turret **117** 46; **313** 32
lenticular **287** 19
Lent lily **60** 3, 12
Leo **3** 17; **4** 57
Leonberger **73** 16
leopard **368** 6
leotard **297** 51
Lepidoptera **358** 48-56; **365**
lepton **252** 39
lesene **335** 11
Lesser Bear **3** 34
lesser celandine **375** 36
Lesser Dog **3** 15
lesser housefly **81** 1
less-than-carload freight **206** 4
let-off motion **166** 59
let-off weight lever **166** 62
let-out section **131** 7
let-out strip **131** 7
letter **174** 44
letter, capital ~ **175** 11
letter, double ~ **175** 6
letter, initial ~ **175** 1
letter, lower case ~ **175** 12
letter, small ~ **175** 12
letter, upper case ~ **175** 11
letter carrier **236** 53
letter container **236** 32
letter feed **236** 31
letter flags **253** 22-28
letter-folding machine **249** 44
lettering **129** 40
lettering brush **129** 41
lettering stencil **151** 69
letter matrix **174** 47; **176** 16
letterpress machine, rotary ~ **181** 41
letterpress machine, web-fed ~ **181** 41
letterpress press, rotary ~ **181** 41
letterpress printing **181**
letterpress printing machines **181** 1-65
letterpress printing method **340** 1-13
letter rack **267** 2
letter-rate item **236** 55
letters, illuminated ~ **268** 45
letter scales **236** 24
letter-sorting installation **236** 31-44
letter spacing **175** 13
letter tray **245** 30; **248** 41
lettuce **57** 36
lettuce leaf **57** 37
leucite **351** 12
levade *Horse* **71** 4
levade *Circus* **307** 30
levee **13** 9; **216** 49

level **14** 48
level, lower ~ **217** 17
level, motor-driven ~ **112** 69
level, upper ~ **217** 25
level crossing **15** 26
level crossing, protected ~ **202** 39
level crossing, unprotected ~ **202** 49
level crossings **202** 39-50
level indicator **316** 57
leveling *see* levelling
levelling **14** 46
levelling and support shovel **255** 94
levelling beam **201** 3, 4
levelling blade **200** 18
levelling staff **14** 47
lever *Plumb. etc.* **126** 19
lever *Sawmill* **157** 46
lever *Cotton Spin.* **164** 42
lever *Office* **249** 50
lever *Graphic Art* **340** 61
lever for normal and coarse threads **149** 4
lever hang **296** 56
lever mechanism **203** 54
liberty horses **307** 30-31
Libra **3** 19; **4** 59
librarian **262** 14, 19
library, ship's ~ **223** 25
library ticket **262** 25
library user **262** 24
license plate **189** 8
lichgate **331** 19
licker-in **163** 53
licker-in roller **163** 53
licker-in undercasing **163** 54
lid *Kitch. Utensils* **40** 13
lid *Electrotyp. etc.* **178** 37
lid *Chem.* **350** 52
lid, glass ~ **269** 56
lid, hinged ~ **127** 24
lid, sliding ~ **179** 2
lid clip **50** 83
lido deck **223** 22
Lieberkühn reflector **115** 97
liege lord **329** 67
lifebelt **221** 124; **222** 24; **280** 3; **281** 6
lifebelt light **221** 125
lifeboat *Offshore Drill.* **146** 19
lifeboat **221** 78, 107; **223** 19
lifeboat launching gear **221** 101-106
lifebuoy *Ship* **221** 124
lifebuoy *Shipbuild.* **222** 24
lifebuoy *Bathing* **280** 3
lifebuoy light **221** 125
lifeguard **280** 1
lifeguard station **280** 46
life jacket **286** 20
life jacket, cork ~ **228** 9
life jacket, inflatable ~ **228** 8
life line **19** 72
lifeline **221** 103; **228** 12; **280** 2
life preserver, cork ~ **228** 9
life raft **228** 19; **258** 11; **286** 19
life rocket **228** 2
lifesaver **21** 36; **280** 1
life saving **228**
life support pack **6** 20
life support system **6** 20
lift *Ship* **219** 47
lift *Store* **271** 45
lift *Theatre* **316** 33
lift, hydraulic ~ **195** 25, 26
lift, vertical ~ **170** 36
liftback **193** 29
lift bridge **225** 70
lift cage **271** 46
lift car **271** 46
lift chair **214** 16
lift chair, double ~ **214** 17
lift controls **271** 48
lift device **103** 24
lift dump **229** 42
lifter *Agr. Mach.* **64** 59
lifter *Sawmill* **157** 46
lifter rail **164** 30
lifter roller **181** 63
lifting arm **255** 76
lifting bolt **164** 37
lifting crane **270** 48
lifting device **255** 76
lifting gear **206** 56
lifting hook **85** 6
lifting motor **150** 22
lifting platform **232** 19
lifting rod **65** 29
lifting rod adjustment **65** 25
lifting spindle **217** 36
lifting undercarriage **232** 18
lift-off hinge **140** 49
lift operator **271** 47
lift platform **173** 40
lift shaft **271** 51
ligament, falciform ~ **20** 34
ligature *First Aid* **21** 14-17
ligature *Composing Rm.* **175** 6
ligature-holding forceps **26** 44
light **106** 8; **210** 46; **224** 69
light, flashing ~ **270** 6
light, fluorescent ~ **271** 23
light, leaded ~ **124** 14
light, polar ~ **7** 30
light, rear ~ **187** 46; **189** 9
light, supplementary ~ **203** 17
light ale **93** 26
light and bell buoy **224** 74
light and whistle buoy **224** 68
light beer **93** 26
light box **179** 25
light bulb **127** 60; **318** 26
light-emitting diode readout **110** 2
lighter **216** 25; **225** 8, 25
lighter, disposable ~ **107** 30
lighter, tug-pushed ~ **221** 94
lighterman **216** 26
light face **175** 8
lighthouse *Map* **15** 8
lighthouse *Navig.* **224** 103
lighting, external ~ **197** 32
lighting, indirect ~ **317** 12
lighting, internal ~ **197** 32
lighting aperture **334** 75
lighting bridge, travelling ~ **316** 19
lighting console **316** 2
lighting control console **316** 2
lighting effects **316** 2
lighting electrician **310** 37
lighting gallery, travelling ~ **316** 19
lighting man **310** 37; **316** 20
lighting operator **316** 20
lighting plot **316** 3
lighting station **226** 27
lighting technician **307** 4
lightning **9** 39
lightning arrester **152** 35
lightning conductor **38** 30
lightning rod **38** 30
light plot **316** 3
light railway diesel locomotive **200** 24
light rays **1** 62
light readout **195** 9
lights, set of ~ **268** 54
light section tube **112** 38
light-sensitive section **77** 22
lightship *Map* **15** 13
lightship *Ship* **221** 47
lightship *Navig.* **224** 81
light source *Atom* **1** 59
light source *Optic. Instr.* **112** 52
light source, photometric ~ **112** 50
light stop **5** 22
light vessel **221** 47; **224** 81
ligula **68** 22; **370** 84
ligule **68** 22; **370** 84
lily **60** 12
lily of the valley **377** 2
limb **370** 5
limb, fractured ~ **21** 10
limb, moon's ~ **4** 41
limbing machine **85** 18
limbs **16** 43-54
lime **147** 56
lime, reconverted ~ **172** 52
lime bunker **147** 62
lime kiln **15** 86
limerick **89** 84
lime slaker **172** 51
limestone **160** 1
lime tree **371** 46
limiter display **238** 44
limit switch **241** 60
limousine **193** 1
linden plant **53** 9
linden tree **371** 46
line *Horse* **71** 33
line *Composing Rm.* **175** 4
line *Carriages* **186** 31
line *Railw.* **202** 1-38
line *Theatre* **316** 8
line *Maths.* **346** 1-23
line, curved ~ **346** 21
line, equinoctial ~ **3** 3
line, horizontal ~ **344** 15
line, local ~ **15** 25
line, straight ~ **346** 2-3, 5, 16
linear **370** 31
line block **178** 42
line-casting machine **174** 19
line cut **178** 42
line engraving **178** 42

line etching **178** 42
line glass **124** 6
line guide **89** 60
linen **206** 11
linen, dirty ~ **50** 22
linen bin **50** 21
linen compartment **267** 31
linen drawer **44** 22; **47** 22
linen goods **271** 57
linen shelf **43** 2
linen tester **177** 23
line-of-battle ship **218** 51-60
line of fencing **294** 9
line of latitude **14** 2
line of life **19** 72
line of longitude **14** 4
line of the head **19** 73
line of the heart **19** 74
line of the staff **320** 43
line plate **178** 42
liner **221** 82; **225** 32
lines *Horse* **71** 25
lines *Rowing* **283** 52
line shooting **89** 20
linesman *Railw.* **202** 44
linesman *Ball Games* **291** 59; **293** 69
lines of the hand **19** 72-74
line space adjuster **249** 23
line space and carrier return key **249** 4
line steam injector **210** 41
line-throwing gun **228** 1
lingerie **32** 1-15
lining *Bldg. Site* **119** 54
lining *Hist. Cost.* **355** 57
lining, fireproof ~ **147** 48
lining, knitwear ~ **101** 17
lining, leather ~ **291** 22
lining, refractory ~ **147** 48
lining, tricot ~ **101** 17
lining board *Bldg. Site* **118** 41; **119** 18
lining board *Floor etc. Constr.* **123** 56
lining paper **128** 5
lining paper, shredded ~ **128** 8
link **36** 39
link, lower ~ **65** 28
link, top ~ **65** 27
linkage, three-point ~ **64** 45; **65** 72
linking of modules **242** 70
link-up of modules **242** 70
Linotype line-composing machine **174** 19
Linotype matrix **174** 29
lint **383** 19
lintel **37** 25; **118** 9
lintel, reinforced concrete ~ **118** 13
Linz-Donawitz converter **147** 45-50
Lion *Astron.* **3** 17; **4** 57
lion **307** 56; **356** 5; **368** 2
lip, lower ~ *Man* **19** 26
lip, lower ~ *Horse* **72** 10
lip, lower ~ *Music. Instr.* **326** 26
lip, upper ~ *Man* **19** 14
lip, upper ~ *Horse* **72** 8
lip, upper ~ *Music. Instr.* **326** 27
lip of the pudendum **20** 87
lip of the vulva **20** 87
lip plug **354** 23
liquefied-gas tanker **221** 35
liqueur **98** 58
liqueur decanter **45** 48
liqueur glass **45** 89; **317** 7
liquid-column barometer **10** 1
liquid crystal readout **110** 2
liquid feed pipe **74** 26
liquid hydrogen and liquid oxygen tank, jettisonable ~ **235** 46
liquid hydrogen line **234** 51; **235** 50
liquid hydrogen pump, high-pressure ~ **235** 41
liquid hydrogen suction line **234** 23
liquid hydrogen supply, main ~ **235** 35
liquid hydrogen tank **234** 26, 41
liquid level indicator **316** 57
liquid manure channel **75** 44
liquid manure silo **62** 13
liquid oxygen line **234** 52; **235** 51, 56
liquid oxygen pump, high-pressure ~ **235** 42
liquid oxygen supply line **234** 10
liquid oxygen tank **234** 12, 24, 39
liquid stage **148** 27
liquor **168** 14
liquor, weak ~ **172** 45
liquor preheater **172** 8
liquor pump **172** 33
liquor supply pipe **92** 48
lira **252** 20, 21
literature **330** 57
literature stand **330** 56
litho artist **340** 45
Lithodes **369** 16
lithographer **340** 45
lithographic crayon **340** 26
lithographic press **340** 60
lithographic stone **340** 25, 57
lithography **340** 25-26
lithosphere **11** 1
litter *Poultry Farm* **74** 8
litter *Livestock* **75** 6
litter *Town* **268** 22
litter basket **37** 63; **205** 55; **272** 43; **273** 25
litter bin **37** 63; **205** 55; **268** 5; **272** 43; **273** 25
litter receptacle **196** 12; **207** 55
Little Bear **3** 34
little brain **17** 45; **18** 23
little cluster fungus **381** 33
Little Dipper **3** 34
Little Dog **3** 15
little owl **362** 19
livelong **377** 9
live power take-off **65** 31
live power take-off shaft **65** 31
liver **20** 10, 34-35
livery **186** 21
live sound **117** 100
livestock, small **213** 28
livestock ramp **206** 1
living quarters **224** 108; **227** 19; **259** 84
living room **42**
lizards **364** 27,30-37
llama **366** 28
load **73** 5
load, driven ~ **226** 19
load, foil-wrapped ~ **226** 9
load, unitized ~ **226** 9, 21
load hook **270** 49
loading bridge **221** 90; **226** 2
loading chamber **116** 6
loading crane **85** 28, 44
loading deck **221** 34
loading dock **206** 9
loading door **207** 23
loading foreman **205** 30; **206** 29
loading gauge **206** 22
loading platform *Lorries etc.* **194** 3
loading platform *Ship* **221** 90
loading siding **206** 17
loading strip **206** 8
loading supervisor **206** 36
loaf, French ~ **97** 12
loaf, long ~ **97** 8
loaf, round ~ **97** 6, 7; **99** 14
loaf, small ~ **97** 7
loaf, white ~ **97** 9
loaf of bread **97** 2
loam **120** 44; **159** 2
loan, personal ~ **250** 4
lobby **267** 18-26; **315** 12-13
lobe **229** 30
lobe, pulmonary ~ **20** 7
lobe, upper ~ **20** 7
lobe of the liver **20** 35
lobster fork **45** 79
local-battery telephone **224** 27; **238** 9, 40
lock *Map* **15** 58
lock *Hunt.* **87** 9
lock *Hydr. Eng.* **217** 20
lock approach **217** 26
lock chamber **217** 20
lock gate **217** 18, 32
lock indicator panel **203** 63
locking bolt **117** 62
locking lever *Atom* **2** 40
locking lever *Motorcycles etc.* **188** 2
locking lever *Office* **247** 42
locking mechanism **246** 23
locking nut **143** 30; **187** 54
lock lever **203** 55
locknut **143** 30; **187** 54
locksmith **140** 1
lock washer **202** 8
locomotive, articulated ~ **210** 64
locomotive, electric ~ **205** 35; **211** 1

locomotive, elevation of ~ **212** 51-67
locomotive, fireless ~ **210** 68
locomotive, mainline ~ **212** 1
locomotive boiler **210** 2-37
locust tree **371** 70
loft **37** 4; **38** 18
log *Forestry* **84** 20, 31
log *Maths.* **345** 6
log, mechanical ~ **224** 54
log, sawn ~ **157** 33
log, ship's ~ **224** 22
logarithm **345** 6
logarithm sign **345** 6
log capacity scale **157** 10
log chain, endless ~ **157** 17
log clock **224** 57
log dump **85** 32; **157** 31
log grips **85** 29; **157** 13, 39
log grips, pivoted ~ **157** 29
logic element **242** 68
logic module **242** 68
log-kicker arm **157** 19
log ladder **273** 22
loin *Game* **88** 18, 35
loin *Meat* **95** 3
loin *Butch.* **96** 4
loin, pork ~ **95** 46
loincloth **352** 38; **354** 31
loins *Man* **16** 24
loins *Horse* **72** 30
loin strap **71** 32
long-conductor antenna **230** 66
long-distance racing **290** 11-15
long-distance runner **298** 5
long drink **317** 32
long-eared bat **366** 9
long-eared owl **362** 14
long-fly **296** 48; **297** 20
long haul airliner **231** 13, 14
long horse **296** 1
longicorn **358** 38
longicorn beetle **358** 38
longitude **14** 7
long johns **32** 29
long jump **298** 37-41
long line **90** 28
long-line fishing **90** 28-29
long-lining **90** 28-29
long measure **294** 10
long primer **175** 27
long rifle cartridge **305** 38
longship **218** 13-17
long sitting **295** 10
longwall face, cut ~ **144** 34
longwall face, ploughed ~ **144** 33
longwall faces **144** 33-37
long-wire antenna **230** 66
lookout platform **273** 23
loom, automatic ~ **166** 1, 35
loom framing **166** 24
loop *Knitting* **167** 62, 66
loop *Weaves* **171** 39
loop *Airsports* **288** 1
loop *Winter Sp.* **301** 7; **302** 15
loop, closed ~ **171** 36
loop, open ~ **171** 30
loop, platinum ~ **23** 15
loop, primary ~ **154** 2, 42
loop, secondary ~ **154** 7, 45
loop antenna **223** 5
loo paper **49** 11
loop fastening **30** 41
loop formation **167** 65
loop former **312** 30
loose-leaf file **260** 15
Lophocalyx philippensis **369** 7
lopping **85** 11
lords-and-ladies **379** 9
Lord's table **330** 4
lorries **194**
lorry **226** 19
lorry, heavy ~ **194** 20; **200** 7
lorry, light ~ **194** 1, 5
lorry, toy ~ **47** 38; **273** 62
lorry tyre **273** 19
lorry wheel **138** 21
lorry with trailer **213** 34
loser **299** 40
lot **310** 1
lottery booth **308** 44
lottery ticket seller **266** 20
lotus column **333** 13
loud hailer **264** 12
loud pedal **325** 8
loudspeaker **42** 10; **241** 14; **264** 12; **311** 46; **317** 15; **318** 12
loudspeaker, built-in ~ **249** 70
loudspeaker aperture **309** 19
louis-d'or **252** 5
Louis Seize table **336** 14
lounge *Living Rm.* **42**
lounge *Ship* **223** 26
lounge *Airport* **233** 18
'lounge' *Airport* **233** 28
lourer **321** 29
louvre shutter **304** 12
love-lies-bleeding **60** 21
low **9** 5
low box **172** 26
lower cable sleeve **214** 74
lower fore topgallant sail **219** 58
lower fore topgallant yard **219** 35
lower fore topsail **219** 56
lower fore topsail yard **219** 33
Lower Keuper **154** 57
lower main topgallant sail **219** 64
lower main topgallant yard **219** 41
lower main topsail **219** 62
lower main topsail yard **219** 39
Lower Muschelkalk **154** 60
lower station platform **214** 51
low house **305** 76
low-moor bog **13** 14
low-pressure area **9** 5
low-pressure manometer **141** 6
low-pressure regulator **190** 59
low relief **339** 33
low-speed aileron **229** 41
low-temperature surface insulation **235** 15
low tide **280** 7
low-voltage bushing **152** 44
low-voltage terminal **152** 44
lozenge **346** 35
L-seat **295** 10
L-support **295** 16
lubber's line **224** 48
lubber's mark **224** 48
lubber's point **224** 48
lubricant pump, automatic ~ **210** 42
lubricating nipple **143** 81
lubricating oil **145** 62
lubricating oil refinery **145** 67
lubricating system, pressure-feed ~ **192** 16-27
lubrication hole **187** 62
lubrication system **65** 45
lubricator **187** 62, 65
lubricator, automatic ~ **210** 42
lucerne **69** 9
ludo **47** 19
luff **284** 42
luffing **285** 9
luffing jib crane **222** 23
luge **303** 13
luge, junior ~ **303** 3
luge toboggan **303** 13
luge toboggan, junior ~ **303** 3
luge tobogganer **303** 12
luggage **205** 7-12
luggage carrier **187** 44
luggage clerk **204** 9
luggage compartment *Car* **193** 17, 23
luggage compartment *Lorries etc.* **194** 13
luggage compartment *Railw.* **207** 71; **208** 15
luggage counter **204** 4
luggage label **205** 8
luggage locker **194** 18
'luggage lockers' **233** 39
luggage rack **207** 51; **208** 27
luggage receipt **204** 8
luggage rest **204** 43
luggage sticker **204** 7
lugger **90** 1
lugsail **220** 4
lug strap **166** 22
lumbar region **72** 30
lumber **120** 2
lumber, rough ~ **120** 83
lumberer **84** 18
lumbering **84** 15-37
lumberjack **84** 18
lumber-jacket **30** 38
lumberman **84** 18
lumber room door **38** 20
luminescent **369** 14
luminescent material **240** 18
lump coal **156** 14
lunar module **234** 55
lunar module hangar **234** 54
lunation **4** 2-7
lung **18** 13; **20** 6-7
lung, right ~ **20** 6
lunge **295** 42
lunging **294** 5

lunging position **294** 5
lungwort **377** 7
lunula *Man* **19** 81
lunula *Prehist.* **328** 25
lunula *Church* **332** 36
lunule **19** 81
lupin **51** 23
lur **322** 1
lute **324** 1
lute pin **324** 11
lycaenid butterfly **365** 6
lychgate **331** 19
Lyman series **1** 20
lymph gland, submandibular ~ **19** 10
lynx **368** 8
lynx fur **131** 20
lynx skin **131** 15
lynx skin, let-out ~ **131** 16
Lyoner sausage **96** 10
Lyra **3** 22
Lyre *Astron.* **3** 22
lyre *Music. Instr.* **322** 15
lyre flower **60** 5

M

maar **11** 25
macadam spreader **200** 31
macaroni **98** 33
macaroon, coconut ~ **97** 37
mace **382** 34
machicolation **329** 23
machicoulis **329** 23
machine, four-cylinder ~ **189** 49
machine, heavy ~ **189** 43
machine, heavy-weight ~ **189** 43
machine, high-performance ~ **189** 43
machine, multi-magazine ~ **174** 19
machine base **168** 15
machine bed **177** 57
machine chest **172** 86; **173** 1, 13
machine control lever **167** 44
machine drum **323** 57
machine gun **255** 32
machine hood **173** 27
machine housing **200** 2
machine part **111** 30
machine parts **143**
machine processor **116** 60
machinery and observation deck **224** 107
machinery and observation platform **224** 107
machinery shed **62** 15
machine tap **150** 44
machine tools **149**; **150**
machine wire **173** 14
machining centre **150** 41
mackerel sky **8** 14
MacPherson strut unit **192** 72-84
macramé **102** 21
macro equipment **115** 81-98
macro frame **117** 56
macro lens attachment **117** 55
macronucleus **357** 11
Macropharynx longicaudatus **369** 2
macrophoto stand **115** 94
macro zoom lens **117** 53
madeira glass **45** 84
Madonna **330** 51
Madonna lily **60** 12
magazine *Doc.* **22** 4
magazine *Flat* **46** 20
magazine *Hunt.* **87** 17
magazine *Cine Film* **117** 45
magazine *Office* **249** 33
magazine *Army* **255** 15, 21
magazine *Police* **264** 25
magazine *Chivalry* **329** 13
magazine, rotary ~ **114** 77
magazine, spring-loaded ~ **247** 6
magazine back **115** 80
magazine holder **255** 7
magazine housing **313** 9
magazine repeater **87** 2
magazine rifle **87** 2
magazine spring **87** 18
magenta filter adjustment **116** 43
maggot *Gdn. Pests* **80** 19
maggot *Articulates* **358** 19
'magic eye' **309** 18
magmatism, plutonic ~ **11** 29-31
magnesium plate **179** 9
magnet **1** 63; **2** 51; **108** 32; **212** 38
magnetic disc store **244** 1
magnetic film **311** 21
magnetic film spool **311** 2
magnetic head, four-track ~ **312** 51
magnetic head cluster **312** 28
magnetic head support assembly **311** 3
magnetic sound amplifier **311** 28
magnetic sound deck **311** 20
magnetic sound head **312** 50
magnetic sound recorder **310** 58; **311** 1
magnetic sound recording and playback deck **238** 4
magnetic sound recording and playback amplifier **311** 5
magnetic sound recording equipment **310** 58; **311** 1
magnetic sound unit, attachable ~ **312** 50
magnetic sound unit, four-track ~ **312** 50
magnetic tape **237** 63; **238** 4, 5; **244** 2
magnetic tape dictating machine **249** 62
magnetic tape loop **245** 28
magnetic tape recording and playback equipment **238** 55
magnetic tape reel **244** 10
magnetic tape station **242** 32
magnetic tape unit **244** 9
magnifier **175** 34
magnifying glass **175** 34; **177** 23
magnitude **3** 14
magpie **361** 3
magpie moth larva **58** 5
maharaja **306** 28
mahlstick **129** 47
mail **329** 62, 63
mail and cargo terminal **233** 9
mailbag **236** 54
mailbox **236** 50
mail carrier **236** 53
mailcoach **186** 39, 53
mailcoach driver **186** 40
mailman **236** 53
mail van **236** 52
main air pressure gauge **212** 6
main air reservoir pressure gauge **212** 8
main beam warning light **191** 69
main course **218** 33; **219** 61
main drive unit **113** 15
main engine revolution indicator **224** 21
main engine room **223** 72
main exchange line **237** 18, 24
main line **203** 45
mainmast **218** 40; **219** 5-7; **220** 22
mainmast, lower ~ **219** 5
main royal sail **219** 66
main royal staysail **219** 26
main royal yard **219** 43
mainsail **218** 33; **219** 61; **220** 11; **284** 46; **285** 2
mains button **195** 11
mainsheet **284** 28
mains power unit **311** 11
maintained lift **299** 5
maintenance technician **237** 28
main title **185** 46
maintop **219** 52
main topgallant mast **219** 7
main topgallant rigging **219** 18
main topgallant sail **218** 53
main topgallant staysail **219** 25
main topmast **219** 6
main topmast crosstrees **219** 53
main topmast rigging **219** 17
main topmast staysail **219** 24
main topsail **218** 38
main topsail yard **218** 39
main yard **218** 37; **219** 38
maize **68** 1, 31
maize billbug **81** 26
maize cob **68** 36
maize kernel **68** 37
majorette **306** 67
major keys **320** 55-68
major second **321** 7
major seventh **321** 12
major sixth **321** 11
major third **321** 8
major triad **321** 1
majuscule **175** 11

maker-up **174** 5
make-up artist **310** 36; **315** 48
make-up artist, chief ~ **315** 47
make-up gown **315** 44
make-up man, chief ~ **315** 47
make-up table *Offset Platem.* **179** 23
make-up table *Theatre* **315** 45
Malacosteus indicus **369** 10
malaria mosquito **81** 44
malleolus, external ~ **19** 59
malleolus, inner ~ **19** 60
malleolus, internal ~ **19** 60
malleolus, lateral ~ **19** 59
malleolus, medial ~ **19** 60
malleolus, outer ~ **19** 59
malleolus fibulae **19** 59
malleolus medialis **19** 60
malleolus tibulae **19** 60
mallet **118** 54; **120** 67; **125** 18; **132** 5; **158** 36; **278** 25; **339** 21
malleus **17** 61
malt **92** 1-41
malt, green ~ **92** 23
malt beer **93** 26
malt elevator **92** 35
maltese cross mechanism **312** 38
maltese cross movement **312** 38
malting **92** 1-41
maltings **92** 1
malting tower **92** 1
malt silo **92** 37
mamma **16** 28-29
mammal, flying ~ **366** 9
mammal, oviparous ~ **366** 1
mammal, scaly ~ **366** 10
mammals **366**; **367**; **368**
mammals, insect-eating ~ **366** 4-7
mammals, marsupial ~ **366** 2-3
mammoth tree **372** 69
Man **16**; **17**; **18**; **19**; **20**
manager **299** 45
manatee **366** 23
manati **366** 23
mandarin *Carnival* **306** 29
mandarin *South. Fruits* **384** 23
mandible *Man* **17** 35
mandible *Articulates* **358** 25
mandible, lower ~ **359** 8
mandolin **324** 16
mandrel **125** 19
mane **72** 13
mane, lion's ~ **368** 3
man-eater **364** 1
maneuver *see* manoeuvre
maneuvering *see* manoeuvring
mangelwurzel **69** 21
manger board **258** 7, 76
mangle **165** 46
mangold **69** 21
mangoldwurzel **69** 21
manhole *Roof & Boilerr.* **38** 45
manhole *Brew.* **93** 13
manhole *Cooper* **130** 18
manhole *Space* **234** 30; **235** 52
manhole *Water* **269** 26, 51
manhole cover *Roof & Boilerr.* **38** 46
manhole cover *Cooper* **130** 19
manhole cover *Street Sect.* **198** 17
manikin **338** 31
manipulator **2** 38
manipulator, mechanical ~ **139** 32
manipulators **2** 47
man-made fibres **169**; **170**
mannequin **338** 31
manoeuvres, principal, of aircraft **230** 67-72
manoeuvring keel **227** 30
manoeuvring rocket assembly **234** 63
manoeuvring rockets **6** 5, 39
manometer **25** 22; **67** 10; **83** 42; **178** 8; **196** 20; **349** 19
manostat **269** 47
manque **275** 22
mansard dormer window **121** 19
mansard roof **121** 18
mantelpiece **267** 24
mantelshelf **267** 24
mantissa **345** 6
mantle *Phys. Geog.* **11** 3
mantle *Iron & Steel* **147** 46
mantle *Heraldry* **254** 3
mantle clock **42** 16
mantling **254** 3, 14
manual **325** 48; **326** 42, 43, 44, 45
manual, lower ~ **322** 47
manual, upper ~ **322** 46
manual feed station **184** 2
manure **63** 15
manure distributor **62** 21
manure fork, four-pronged ~ **66** 7
manure gutter **75** 20
manure hoe **66** 8
manure removal **74** 23-27; **75** 21
manure spreader **62** 21; **63** 39
manuscript **174** 6; **176** 3
manway **154** 32
map *Map* **14**; **15**
map **204** 15; **260** 44; **268** 2
maple seed **371** 57
maple tree **371** 53
map light **230** 23
map of the world **14** 10-45
mapping **348** 9, 10
mapping, one-to-one ~ **348** 11
mappings **348** 9-11
map projections **14** 8-9
map signs **15** 1-114
map symbols **14** 27-29; **15** 1-114
maraca **324** 59
marcando **321** 27
marcato **321** 27
mare **73** 2
margarine **98** 21; **99** 48
margin **185** 55-58
margin, back ~ **185** 55
margin, inside ~ **185** 55
margin, outside ~ **185** 57
margin, upper ~ **185** 56
margin control **180** 5, 20
margin release key **249** 6
margin scale **249** 12
margin stop, left ~ **249** 13
margin stop, right ~ **249** 14
marguerite **51** 24; **376** 4
marimba, steel ~ **324** 61
marimbaphone **324** 61
marine sequence **310** 11
mark **285** 17
mark, port hand ~ **224** 95
mark, starboard hand ~ **224** 96
marker **85** 12
marker, port ~ **224** 100
marker, starboard ~ **224** 99
market for securities **251** 2
market garden **55** 1-51, 3
market place **15** 52
market square **15** 52
market woman **308** 65
markiert **321** 27
marking, axillary ~ **88** 74
marking hammer **85** 12
marking iron **85** 12
marking out **104** 21
markings, graduated ~ **115** 65
mark of omission **342** 29
marks, diacritical ~ **342** 30-35
marl **160** 1
marmot **366** 18
maroon **306** 53
marquise **36** 55
marriage ceremony **332** 14
Mars **4** 46
marsh *Phys. Geog.* **13** 14-24
marsh *Map* **15** 20
marshal **329** 75
marshaling *see* marshalling
marshalling yard **206** 42
marshalling yard signal box **206** 44
marsh harrier **362** 13
marshmallow *Bakery* **97** 36
marshmallow *Med. Plants* **380** 12
marsh plants **378** 14-57
marsh tea **377** 21
marsupials **366** 2-3
marten **86** 22
martens **367** 14-17
martinet **218** 36
marzipan **98** 82
Masai warrior **354** 8
mash **93** 10
mash copper **92** 44
masher **92** 49
mashhouse **92** 42-53
mashing process **92** 42-53
mash kettle **92** 44
mash thermometer **93** 9
mash tub **92** 43
mash tun **92** 43, 44
mask *Hosp.* **27** 48
mask *Swim.* **279** 10

mask *Carnival* **306** 7
mask *Films* **310** 51; **313** 4
mask *Sculpt. Studio* **339** 37
mask, clay ~ **260** 75
mask, pressure-equalizing ~ **279** 10
mask, wooden ~ **354** 16
mask drum **177** 48
masked ball **306** 1-48
masking frame **116** 35
masking tape **128** 16
mask-scanning head **177** 47
masonry bonds **118** 58-68
masonry dam **217** 58
masquerade **306** 1-48, 6-48
mass **11** 43
mass, continental ~ **11** 7
massage bath **281** 33
mass book **330** 38
masseter **19** 7
massif **12** 39
mast **219** 1-9; **221** 77; **284** 4, 11
mast, full-rigged ~ **220** 16
mast, half-rigged ~ **220** 15
Master **289** 45
master arm **2** 42
master brewer **92** 49
master butcher **96** 38
master clock **245** 18
master compass **224** 51
master control panel **242** 3
master furrow **91** 18
master gyro compass **224** 51
Master of foxhounds **289** 45
master selector **195** 8
master/slave manipulator **2** 47
master station **224** 40
master switch **153** 2
master turner **135** 20
master volume control **261** 44
masterwort **376** 7
mat **299** 12
matador **319** 25, 31
match **107** 22
matchbox **107** 21
matchbox holder **266** 24
match head **107** 23
mate **276** 15
maté **382** 11
material *School* **260** 81
material *Store* **271** 59
material, basic ~ **169** 1
material, radioactive ~ **1** 28
materials store **146** 6
maté shrub **382** 11
mathematics **344; 345; 346; 347; 348**
mathematics, higher ~ **345** 11-14
matinée coat **29** 3
matrix *Man* **20** 79
matrix *Composing Rm.* **174** 21, 31
matrix, punched ~ **175** 37
matrix, stamped ~ **175** 37
matrix-boring machine **175** 49
matrix case **174** 42, 46; **176** 17
matrix clamp **175** 59
matrix disc **176** 20
matrix drum **176** 27
matrix-engraving machine **175** 49
matrix for hand-setting **174** 28
matrix holder **24** 55
matrix mimic board **153** 8
mat sail **353** 33
matte **313** 4
matte box **313** 3
matter **174** 15; **181** 37
matter, front ~ **185** 43-47
matter, machine-set ~ **174** 27
matter, preliminary ~ **185** 43-47
matting, reed ~ **55** 6
matting, straw ~ **55** 6
mattress **47** 3; **296** 18
mattress, foam ~ **43** 10
matt weave **171** 11
maturing **169** 7
mauerkrone **254** 46
mausoleum **337** 16
mavis **361** 16
maw worm **81** 31
maxilla **17** 36; **19** 27
maximum **347** 19
maximum thermometer **10** 53
may **374** 30
Maya temple **352** 20
May bug **82** 1
mayfly **358** 6
maypole swing **273** 8
maze **272** 5
M-cardan **67** 29
meadow **13** 13; **62** 44; **63** 22
meadow buttercup **375** 8
meadow fescue grass **69** 24
meadow flowers **375; 376**
meadow foxtail **69** 27
meadow grass **375** 39
meadow grasshopper **358** 8
meadow mushroom **381** 1
meadow saffron **379** 3
meal, complete ~ **266** 17
meal, deepfreeze ~ **96** 23
meal, deep-frozen ~ **96** 23
meal, hot ~ **266** 67
meal, ready-to-eat ~ **96** 23
meal beetle **81** 18
meal of the day **266** 27
meal worm beetle **81** 18
meander *Phys. Geog.* **13** 11
meander *Art* **334** 43
meander core **13** 12
mean low water **15** 9
mean sea level **146** 39
measure *Hotel* **267** 60
measure *Music. Not.* **320** 28-42
measure line **320** 42
measurement chamber **112** 43
measurement dial **242** 75
measurement range selector *Atom* **2** 4, 23
measurement range selector *Optic. Instr.* **112** 46
measurement range selector *Inf. Tech.* **242** 74
measurement scale **242** 75
measuring and control unit **178** 3
measuring arm **142** 38
measuring beaker **267** 60
measuring cylinder *Doc.* **23** 43
measuring cylinder *Photog.* **116** 11
measuring cylinder *Paperm.* **173** 4
measuring cylinder *School* **261** 26
measuring cylinder *Chem.* **350** 26
measuring device **112** 51
measuring flask **350** 27
measuring glass **10** 47; **350** 26
measuring instrument **153** 30
measuring instrument platform **235** 69
measuring instruments **149** 56-72
measuring machine, universal-type ~ **112** 67
measuring probe **234** 42
measuring rod *Map* **14** 47
measuring rod *Cine Film* **117** 59
measuring rod *Quarry* **158** 26
measuring scale **149** 63
measuring tank **130** 22
measuring tape **103** 2; **271** 38
measuring vessel **93** 3; **130** 33
meat **96** 1-4, 59; **99** 53
meat, canned ~ **98** 20
meat, cold ~ **96** 14
meat, minced ~ **96** 16
meat, roast ~ **45** 27
meat, smoked ~ **96** 3
meat axe **94** 18
meat chopper **40** 39
meat counter **99** 51
meat dish **266** 55
meat grinder **96** 53
meathook **96** 55
meat inspector **94** 24
meat joints **95**
meat mincer **96** 53
meat-mixing trough **96** 40
meat plate **45** 26
meat platter **45** 26
meat product **99** 53
meat salad **96** 13
meat saw **94** 20
mechanic **140** 1
mechanical finger car **159** 18
mechanical pulp mill **172** 53-65
mechanism casing **255** 10
medallion **339** 36
Mediaeval **342** 4
medical card **22** 8
medical laboratory technician **23** 41
medical record **22** 8
medicament, water-soluble ~ **25** 14
medicine **22** 23

medicine cabinet **49** 49
medicine case **24** 7
medicine cupboard **22** 35
medicine sample **22** 41
Mediterranean **14** 25
medium **308** 9
medium haul airliner **231** 12
medium measure **294** 10
medulla oblongata **17** 47; **18** 24
medusa **357** 14
meeting **263** 8
meeting, public ~ **263** 1-15
'meeting point' **233** 29
meganucleus **357** 11
megaphone **283** 21
megaphone exhaust pipe **189** 51
meiobar **9** 3
Melanocetes **369** 6
melodium **325** 43
melody key **324** 39
melody pipe **322** 10
melody side **324** 39
melody string **322** 30; **324** 24
melon **57** 23
melter **148** 7
melting bath **162** 3, 14
melting furnace *Iron Foundry etc.* **148** 1
melting furnace *Electrotyp. etc.* **178** 19
melting plant **148** 1-12
melting pot *Goldsm. etc.* **108** 8
melting pot *Synth. Fibres* **170** 30
member, diagonal ~ **215** 35
member, upright ~ **119** 59
member, vertical ~ **215** 36
member of set **348** 2
membership card **275** 14
membrane **241** 68
membrane, parchment ~ **324** 31
membrane, periodontal ~ **19** 28
membrane, tympanic ~ **17** 59
membrane, vitelline ~ **74** 64
membranophones **323** 51-59
memorial chapel **331** 12
memorial plate **331** 14
memorial tablet **331** 14
memory, main ~ **244** 6; **245** 28
memory key **247** 22
memory typewriter **245** 26
memory unit **176** 11; **242** 9
memo sheet **247** 34
menagerie **307** 63
menhir **328** 18
menhir group **328** 11
men's wear **33**
men's wear department **271** 12
menu **266** 21
menu card **266** 21
Mercator projection **14** 9
Mercury **4** 43
mercury barometer **10** 1
mercury battery **25** 32
mercury column **10** 2
mercury manometer **25** 18
meridian **14** 4
meridian circle **113** 26
meridian of Greenwich **14** 5
meridian of longitude **14** 4
meridians **14** 1-7
meridian telescope **113** 29
meringue **97** 26; **265** 5
merlin **362** 1
merlon **329** 7
mermaid **327** 23
merman **327** 23, 40
merry-go-round **308** 2
mesa **13** 59
mesh **171** 37
mesh connection **153** 21
mesh gauge **102** 25
mesh pin **102** 25
mesh ventilator **278** 40
Mesolithic period **328** 1-9
messroom **228** 25
metacarpal **17** 16
metal, noble ~ **237** 42
metal-blocking device **111** 34
metal feeder **174** 26
metal feeder, automatic ~ **174** 40
metal runner **147** 35
metals **254** 24-25
metal shears **108** 23; **125** 1
metalworker **140** 1
metalwork shop **140** 1-22
metatarsus **17** 28
metazoans **357** 13-39
meteor **7** 18
meteorite crater **6** 16
meteorological instruments **10**
meteorological office **225** 33
meteorological watch office **9** 7
meteorology **8; 9**
meter *Atom* **2** 6
meter *Photog.* **114** 62
meter *Blacksm.* **138** 19
meter *Serv. Stat.* **196** 14
meter *Music. Not.* **320** 28-42
meter, customer's ~ **237** 16
meter, multiple ~ **242** 73
meter, private ~ **237** 16
meter, rotary ~ **269** 53
meter, subscriber's ~ **237** 16
meter cell **114** 3, 24; **115** 37
metering pump **169** 13
metope **334** 16
metre tape measure **103** 2
metronome **325** 19
mezzanine **315** 18
mezzo staccato **321** 29
mezzotint **340** 14-24
micro attachment **115** 89
micro cassette recorder **246** 32
microfilm card **237** 38
microfilm file **237** 37
microfilming system **242** 31
microfilm reader **237** 36
micrometer **142** 37; **149** 62; **173** 10; **224** 4
micrometer eyepiece **14** 53
micrometer head **14** 52
micronucleus **357** 12
microphone **22** 15; **117** 8, 24, 74; **197** 26; **209** 31; **224** 30; **230** 29; **237** 9; **241** 49; **261** 39; **263** 7; **310** 30; **317** 20
microphone, built-in ~ **241** 5; **243** 3
microphone, umpire's ~ **293** 21
microphone base **241** 51
microphone boom **310** 25
microphone boom, telescopic ~ **117** 23
microphone cable **239** 14; **310** 32; **311** 41
microphone connecting cord **117** 25
microphone connecting lead **117** 25
microphone cradle **249** 65
microphone screen **241** 50
microphone socket **249** 69
microphone socket panel **238** 36
microphone stand **241** 51
microprism collar **115** 54
microprism spot **115** 58, 59, 62, 63
micropyle **383** 57
microscope **111** 19; **112** 1
microscope, metallurgical ~ **112** 23
microscope, surgical ~ **112** 31
microscope, universal ~ **112** 54
microscope, wide-field ~ **112** 23, 54
microscope body **113** 31-39
microscope camera, fully automatic ~ **112** 64
microscope for reflected light **112** 23
microscope stage **112** 9
microscope tube **113** 31-39
microwave treatment unit **23** 36; **24** 23
mid-channel **224** 98
middle-distance runner **298** 5
middle ground **224** 91
middle ground to port **224** 88
middle mast **220** 33
Middle Muschelkalk **154** 59
middle of the fairway **224** 98
middle section **259** 55-71
middling **91** 2
midfield player **291** 14
midge **358** 16
midget **308** 22
midi bus **194** 34
midinette **306** 21
mid-range speaker **241** 16
midrib **370** 30
mihrab **337** 14
milch-cow **62** 34; **75** 17
mild **93** 26
mildew **80** 20
milestone **15** 109
milk **99** 45; **266** 60
milk, canned ~ **98** 15
milk, homogenized ~ **99** 44

milk, long-life ~ **99** 44
milk, pasteurized ~ **99** 44
milk, sterilized ~ **76** 16
milk carton **76** 22
milk churn **309** 89
milker **62** 34; **75** 17, 25
milk glass **124** 5
milk heater **76** 13
milking parlour **75** 23
milk jug **44** 31
milkman **75** 25
milk pipe **75** 27
milk pot **40** 15
milk processing area **76** 12-48
milk reception **76** 1
milk tanker **76** 2
milk tub filler **76** 21
milkwort **377** 3
Milky Way **3** 35
mill **276** 24
miller **91** 15
millet **68** 28
millibar scale **10** 3
millimeter graduation **247** 36
millimetre scale **10** 3
milliner **35** 1
milliner's shop **268** 38
milling machine, rotary ~ **168** 1
milling machine, universal ~ **150** 32
milling machine table **150** 33
milling roller, bottom ~ **168** 4, 6
milling roller, top ~ **168** 3
millrace **91** 44
mills **91**
mill spindle **91** 12
millstone **91** 16, 21
millstone, upper ~ **91** 22
millstone casing **91** 20
millstone ruff **355** 52
millstream **91** 44
mill weir **91** 42
mill wheel, breast ~ **91** 37
mill wheel, middleshot ~ **91** 37
mill wheel, overshot ~ **91** 35
mill wheel, undershot ~ **91** 39
milometer **187** 33
mimbar **337** 15
minaret **337** 13
minbar **337** 15
mince **96** 16
mincemeat **96** 16
mincer **40** 39; **96** 53
mincing machine **96** 52, 53
mine **15** 34
mine, disused ~ **15** 35
mine car **144** 45
mine fan **144** 16
minehead buildings **154** 70
mine hunter **258** 80
minelayer **258** 94
mineral bath, outdoor ~ **281** 9
mineral spring **274** 11
mineral water **266** 61
minesweeper **258** 84
mine-sweeping gear **258** 87
miniature film cassette **112** 35
minibus **194** 9; **195** 47
minigolf course **272** 68
minigolf hole **272** 70
minigolf player **272** 69
minim **320** 14
minim rest **320** 22
minimum **347** 20
minimum thermometer **10** 54
mining, underground ~ **144** 21-51
minion **175** 24
minionette **175** 23
mink **30** 60
mink skin **131** 11
mink skin, let-out ~ **131** 19
minnesinger **329** 70
minor keys **320** 55-68
minor planets **4** 47
minor triad **321** 2
minstrel **329** 70
mintage **252** 10, 40-44
minting dies **252** 40-41
minting press **252** 44
mint mark **252** 10
minuend **344** 24
minus blue filter adjustment **116** 44
minuscule **175** 12
minuscule, Carolingian ~ **341** 18
minus green filter adjustment **116** 43
minus red filter adjustment **116** 45
minus sign **344** 8, 24
minute hand **110** 12
Mira **3** 11
mirabelle **59** 25
mire crow **359** 14
mirror **43** 29; **49** 33; **105** 20; **106** 6; **111** 4; **177** 38; **188** 35; **189** 30; **207** 49
mirror, angled ~ **177** 28
mirror, auxiliary ~ **115** 38
mirror, concave ~ **5** 32; **308** 56; **312** 39
mirror, convex ~ **308** 57
mirror, flat ~ **5** 3
mirror, illuminating ~ **14** 59
mirror, main ~ **5** 1; **113** 10
mirror, primary ~ **5** 1; **113** 10
mirror, right-angle ~ **261** 10
mirror, rotating ~ **243** 54
mirror, secondary ~ **5** 2; **113** 11
mirror, semi-reflecting ~ **243** 55
mirror, triple ~ **104** 1
mirror arc lamp **312** 39
mirror assembly **176** 21
mirror carp **364** 4
mirror lens **115** 50
mirror manometer **349** 20
mirror reflex system **115** 31
mirror spot **316** 48
mirror spotlight **316** 48
mirror system **176** 24
missal **330** 38
missile **258** 49
missile, short-range ~ **259** 26
missile, wooden ~ **352** 39; **353** 8
missile cruiser **259** 21, 41
missile launcher, underwater ~ **259** 37, 51
missile-launching housing **258** 71
miter *see* mitre
miter angle **120** 82
mitre **124** 4
mitre block **124** 30
mitre board **124** 31
mitre box *Glaz.* **124** 30
mitre box *Joiner* **132** 43
mitre gate **217** 19
mitre joint **124** 4
mitre shoot **124** 31
mitre square **120** 82
mitring machine **124** 7
mitt, catcher's ~ **292** 60
mitt, fielder's ~ **292** 59
mitten crab **358** 1
mixed asphalt outlet **200** 54
mixer *Dent.* **24** 51
mixer *Kitch. Utensils* **40** 45
mixer *Cine Film* **117** 26
mixer *Synth. Fibres* **170** 53
mixer *Aircraft* **232** 48
mixer *Broadcast.* **238** 25
mixer *Films* **311** 21
mixer *Disco* **317** 26
mixer, double shaft ~ **159** 10
mixer, hand ~ **39** 22
mixer, high-speed ~ **79** 5
mixer, propeller-type ~ **79** 5
mixer drum **200** 15
mixer operator **118** 32
mixer tap **39** 36; **49** 2; **106** 14; **126** 27
mixing **169** 2
mixing chamber **83** 62
mixing chest **173** 1
mixing console *Cine Film* **117** 26
mixing console *Broadcast.* **238** 25
mixing console *Films* **310** 56; **311** 35
mixing console *Disco* **317** 26
mixing desk *Cine Film* **117** 26
mixing desk *Broadcast.* **238** 25
mixing desk *Films* **310** 56; **311** 35
mixing desk *Disco* **317** 26
mixing drum **118** 34; **200** 15
mixing faucet **39** 36; **49** 2; **106** 14; **126** 27
mixing machine **200** 15
mixing plant, central ~ **201** 19
mixing plant, stationary ~ **201** 19
mixing room **311** 34
mixing screw **83** 59
mixing spoon **40** 3
mixing tank **172** 35
mixture, additive ~ **343** 10
mixture, subtractive ~ **343** 12
mixture control **230** 31; **288** 16
Mizar **3** 29
mizen *see* mizzen
mizzen **218** 29; **219** 30

mizzen, lower ~ **219** 8
mizzen mast **218** 31; **219** 8-9; **220** 23, 24, 30, 34
mizzen staysail **219** 27
mizzen top **219** 54
mizzen topgallant sail **218** 54
mizzen topgallant staysail **219** 29
mizzen topmast **219** 9
mizzen topmast rigging **219** 17
mizzen topmast staysail **219** 28
moat **329** 33, 37; **356** 3
mobile **260** 70
moccasin **101** 30; **352** 18
moccasin flower **376** 27
mock orange **373** 9
model, clay ~ **260** 67
model, dressmaker's ~ **103** 6
model, nude ~ **338** 32
model, plaster ~ **339** 4
model, wax ~ **339** 26
model aeroplane **273** 37, 38
model aeroplanes **288** 85-91
model coat **103** 7
model dress **103** 5
model flight, radio-controlled ~ **288** 85
model hat **35** 7
modeling *see* modelling
modeller **339** 6
modelling board **48** 14; **339** 34
modelling clay **48** 12; **339** 31
modelling stand **339** 9
modelling substance **339** 8
modelling tool **161** 20
modelling tool, wire ~ **339** 11
modelling tool, wooden ~ **339** 10
model of set **315** 42
models of molecules **242** 61-67
model stage **315** 41
moderator **1** 54
modular elements **242** 68-72
module, electronic ~ **242** 69
module, lunar ~ **6** 12
module, magnetic ~ **242** 72
moistener **247** 31
moisturising cream **99** 27
molar **19** 18, 35
mold *see* mould
molder **97** 57
mole *Map* **15** 18
mole *Hydr. Eng.* **217** 15
mole *Docks* **225** 65
mole *Mammals* **366** 4
molecular rearrangement **170** 23
molluscs **357** 27-36
monastery *Map* **15** 63
monastery *Church* **331** 52-58
monastery garden **331** 53
money **252**; **265** 3
money, hard ~ **252** 1-28
money, metal ~ **252** 1-28
money, paper ~ **252** 29-39
money compartment **271** 6
money order **236** 27
moneywort **375** 26
monitor **23** 27; **26** 15, 16, 33; **27** 23
monitor *Cine Film* **117** 97
monitor *Broadcast.* **238** 33
monitor *Audiovis.* **243** 6
monitor *Fire Brig.* **270** 66
monitor *Theatre* **316** 18
monitor *Fish etc.* **364** 31
monitor, six-channel ~ **27** 31
monitoring and control panel **238** 1, 7
monitoring controls **153** 5
monitoring instrument **311** 15
monitoring loudspeaker **239** 9; **311** 13
monitoring speaker **238** 15
monitoring unit, mobile ~ **25** 24
monitor lizard **364** 31
monitor support, swivel-mounted ~ **27** 24
monitor unit **25** 44
monk **89** 9
monk, Benedictine ~ **331** 54
monkey bridge **223** 4-11; **227** 24
monkey house **356** 10
monkey nut **383** 41
monkeys **368** 12-13
monkshood **379** 1
monochlorobenzene **170** 9
monoclinic crystal system **351** 24-25
monogram **36** 41
mono-line control system **288** 90
monolith **328** 18
monoplane, high-wing ~ **229** 1; **231** 2
monoplane, low-wing ~ **229** 5, 14; **231** 1
monoplane, midwing ~ **229** 4
monoplane, shoulder-wing ~ **229** 3
mono posto **290** 34
monorail car **144** 43, 44
monoski **286** 56
mono sound **311** 35
monotreme *Mammals* **366** 1
monotype caster **174** 39
monotype casting machine **174** 39
monotype composing and casting machine **174** 32-45
monotype composing machine **174** 32
monsoon **9** 52
monster **327** 16
monster, winged ~ **327** 55
monstrance **331** 48; **332** 34
montera **319** 29
monument *Map* **15** 92
monument *Park* **272** 10
moon **4** 1-9, 31, 45
moon, full ~ **4** 5
moon, new ~ **4** 2
moon, waning ~ **4** 7
moon, waxing ~ **4** 3
moon landing **6**
moor buzzard **362** 13
moor harrier **362** 13
moor hawk **362** 13
mooring **283** 19
mooring bitt, cross-shaped ~ **217** 13, 14
mooring bitt, double ~ **217** 14
mooring chain **224** 72
mooring line **288** 66
mooring sinker **224** 73
moose **367** 1
mop, gilder's ~ **129** 54
mopboard **123** 21, 63
moped **188** 24
moped, battery-powered ~ **188** 20
moped headlamp **188** 29
mopeds **188**
Mopsea **369** 8
moraine, lateral ~ **12** 53
moraine, medial ~ **12** 54
morainic filter layer **199** 24
Morchella conica **381** 27
Morchella esculenta **381** 26
mordant **178** 24; **182** 16
mordent, inverted ~ **321** 19
mordent, lower ~ **321** 20
mordent, upper ~ **321** 19
morel **381** 26, 27
morello **59** 5
morello cherry **59** 5
morion **329** 60
morse **367** 20
morse lamp **223** 7
mortadella **96** 7
mortar *Army* **255** 40
mortar *Chem.* **349** 9
mortar bed **123** 27
mortar pan **118** 39
mortar trough **118** 20, 39, 84
mortar tub **118** 39
mortice *see* mortise
mortise, forked ~ **121** 85
mortise and tenon joint **121** 84, 85
mortise axe **120** 72
mortise chisel **132** 8
mortise lock **140** 36-43
mortiser **120** 17
mortising chain, endless ~ **132** 50
mortuary **331** 21
mosaic **338** 37
mosaic figure **338** 38
mosque **337** 12
mosquito **358** 16
moss **377** 17
moss phlox **60** 14
moss pink **60** 14
moth **58** 64; **81** 13; **82** 15, 18, 45, 48
moth, female ~ **82** 30
moth, male ~ **82** 29
moth, night-flying ~ **82** 14
moth, nocturnal ~ **82** 14
mother **28** 6; **272** 71
mother-of-pearl **357** 34
mother sheep **75** 10
moths **358** 48-56; **365** 7-11
motif *Child. Clothes* **29** 20
motif *Art. Studio* **338** 27

motion, longitudinal ~ **149** 17
motion picture camera, lightweight ~ **313** 20
motion picture camera, narrow-gauge ~ **313** 31
motion picture camera, professional ~ **313** 20, 31
motion picture camera, soundproof ~ **310** 47; **313** 15
motion picture camera, standard-gauge ~ **313** 1
motion picture cameras **313** 1-39
motion picture laboratory **310** 2; **311** 30
motion picture library **310** 5
motion picture projection **312** 1-23
motion pictures **310; 311; 312; 313**
motion picture storage vault **310** 5
motions, rotary ~ **4** 22-28
moto cross **290** 24-28
motor *Forestry* **84** 34
motor *Watchm.* **109** 13
motor *Iron Foundry etc.* **148** 64
motor *Weaving* **165** 12, 34
motor *Electrotyp. etc.* **178** 14
motor *Tram* **197** 5, 7
motor *Water* **269** 45
motor, auxiliary ~ **211** 17
motor, built-in ~ **164** 2
motor, built-on ~ **164** 33
motor, electric ~ *Roof & Boilerr.* **38** 59
motor, electric ~ *Pest Contr.* **83** 53
motor, electric ~ *Blacksm.* **138** 2
motor, electric ~ *Weaving* **166** 18
motor, electric ~ *Railw.* **212** 34
motor, electric ~ *Ship* **223** 69
motor, synchronous ~ **176** 19
motor, three-phase ~ **164** 35
motor, two-stroke ~ **56** 30
motor base plate **164** 36
motor bedplate **164** 36
motorboat **283** 2
motorboat landing stage **216** 7
motorboats **286** 1-5
motor car **191** 1-56; **192; 193; 195** 34
motor car mechanic **195** 53
motor coach **194** 17
motor cruiser **286** 4
motor cultivator **56** 18
motorcycle **189; 268** 35
motorcycle, heavyweight ~ **189** 31
motorcycle, light ~ **188** 39; **189** 1, 16
motorcycle, lightweight ~ **189** 1
motorcycle, pacer's ~ **290** 12
motorcycle chain **189** 22
motorcycle racing **290** 24-28
motorcycles **188**
motorcycles, heavy ~ **189** 31-58
motorcycles, heavyweight ~ **189** 31-58
motorcycles, large-capacity ~ **189** 31-58
motorcycle stand **189** 21
motorcycle tyre **189** 26
motorcyclist **268** 34; **290** 11
motor drive **115** 76
motor drive, attachable ~ **115** 78
motor drive gear **167** 31
motor ferry **216** 6
motor grader **200** 19
motor pump **270** 8
motor safety switch **269** 46
motor saw **84** 22, 27; **85** 13
motor scooter **188** 47
motor ship **223**
motorsports **290** 24-38
motor truck, heavy ~ **194** 20
motor turntable ladder **270** 9
motor uniselector **237** 42
motor unit **50** 82
motor vehicle mechanic **195** 53
motorway *Map* **15** 16
motorway *Docks* **225** 54
motor winch **287** 6
moufflon **367** 6
mouflon **367** 6
mould *Bldg. Site* **119** 84
mould *Iron & Steel* **147** 37
mould *Glass Prod.* **162** 47
mould *Paperm.* **173** 48
mould, fixed ~ **178** 22
mouldboard **65** 4, 64
moulder *Bakery* **97** 57
moulder *Iron Foundry etc.* **148** 30
moulding, concave ~ **334** 29
moulding, hollow ~ **336** 10
moulding, ornamental ~ **336** 12
moulding box, closed ~ **148** 18
moulding box, open ~ **148** 33
moulding department **148** 30-37
moulding press, hydraulic ~ **178** 7
moulding sand **148** 35
moulding shop **148** 30-37
mould loft **222** 3
mould wall **148** 29
mound *Equest.* **289** 8
mound *Prehist.* **328** 16
mound *Art* **337** 21
mountain ash **371** 42
mountain climber **300** 5
mountain climbing **300** 1-57
mountaineer **300** 5
mountaineering **300** 1-57
mountaineering boot **300** 42
mountaineering equipment **300** 31-57
mountain hut **300** 1
mountain racing **290** 24-28
mountain railroads **214** 1-14
mountain railways **214** 1-14
mountain range **12** 39
mountain ridge **12** 36
mountains, folded ~ **12** 12-20
mountain slope **12** 37
mountain top **12** 35
mounting, German type ~ **113** 16
mounting, mobile ~ **27** 22
mounting, underfloor ~ **127** 22
mount of the frame **111** 10
mourner **331** 33
mourning cloak butterfly **365** 5
mourning veil **331** 39
mousetrap **83** 36
moustache, English-style ~ **34** 19
moustache, military ~ **34** 19
moustache, waxed ~ **34** 13
mouth *Man* **16** 13; **19** 14-37
mouth *Horse* **72** 9
mouth *Forestry* **84** 28
mouth *Game* **88** 13, 45
mouth *Joiner* **132** 21
mouth *Airsports* **288** 70, 81
mouth *Music. Instr.* **326** 25
mouth, fork-tongued ~ **327** 5
mouth band **322** 5
mouth gag **22** 48
mouth lamp **24** 42
mouth mirror **24** 41
mouth organ **324** 35
mouthpiece *Hosp.* **27** 38
mouthpiece *Tobacc. etc.* **107** 40
mouth piece *Electrotyp. etc.* **178** 17
mouthpiece *Post* **237** 9
mouthpiece *Music. Instr.* **323** 36; **324** 33, 72
mouthwash **49** 36
movable-comb hive **77** 45-50
movable-frame hive **77** 45-50
movable half **215** 66
move **276** 14
movie audience **312** 5
moviegoer **312** 5
movie house **312** 1
movie projector **312** 24
movie script **310** 45
movie set **310** 7
movie studios **310** 1-13
movie theater **312** 1
movie theater box office **312** 2
movie theater ticket **312** 3
moving iron **137** 39
mower, electric ~ **56** 31
mower, hand ~ **56** 34
mower, motor ~ **56** 28
mower, riding ~ **56** 37
mower, rotary ~ **63** 19
mud drum **210** 28
mudguard, front ~ **187** 13
mudguard, rear ~ **187** 43
mud pump **145** 16
muffle furnace **140** 11
muffler *Car* **191** 29

muffler *Railw.* **209** 12, 22, 24; **211** 49
muffler *Sports* **305** 93
mulberry-feeding moth **358** 48
mule *Dom. Anim.* **73** 8
mule *Shoes* **101** 25
mule, open-toe ~ **101** 22
mule cop **165** 15
muleta **319** 33
mull **183** 33; **185** 20
mullion *Dwellings* **37** 35
mullion *Art* **335** 41
mull roll holder **185** 19
multiple cable system **215** 51
multiple drying machine **169** 31
multiple-frame viewfinder **114** 41
multiple meter **127** 41
multiple-unit train **211** 60
multiplicand **344** 25
multiplication **344** 25
multiplication sign **344** 25
multiplier **344** 25
multiplier phototube **112** 51
multiplier reel **89** 59
multiplying **344** 25
multirole combat aircraft **256** 8
multirole helicopter, light ~ **232** 11
multi-tier transport **74** 35
mummy **352** 21
Munich beer **93** 26
mural **338** 40
Muschelkalk **154** 58, 59, 60
muscle, contractile ~ **77** 17
muscle, deltoid ~ **18** 35
muscle, pectoralis ~ **18** 36
muscle, sternocleidomastoid ~ **18** 34; **19** 1
muscle, sternomastoid ~ **18** 34; **19** 1
muscle, temporal ~ **19** 3
muscle, thenar ~ **18** 41
muscles, ocular ~ **19** 44
muscles of facial expression **19** 6
muscles of the neck **19** 12
muscular system **18** 34-64
musculature **18** 34-64
musette **322** 8
mushroom **381** 2, 3
mushrooms, poisonous ~ **379** 10-13
musical instruments **322; 323; 324; 325; 326**
musical instruments, popular ~ **324** 1-46
musical notation **320; 321**
music recording studio **310** 14
music recording theatre **310** 14
music rest **326** 36
music stand **326** 36
music systems **241**
musk ox **367** 10
mussel shell **357** 36
mustang **352** 4
mustard *Weeds* **61** 16
mustard *Grocer* **98** 28
mute **323** 10; **324** 68
mute swan **359** 16
mutton spanker **218** 29
mutule **334** 13
muzzle *Dog* **70** 3, 31
muzzle *Game* **88** 45
muzzle *Army* **255** 58
muzzle *Sports* **305** 71
mycelium **68** 4; **381** 2
myrtle **53** 11
Myrtus **53** 11

N

Na atom **1** 8
nacre **357** 34
nadir **4** 13
naiad **327** 23
nail **19** 80
nail, clenched ~ **285** 52
nail, galvanized ~ **122** 74
nail, riveted ~ **285** 52
nail, wire ~ **121** 95; **122** 74; **143** 51
nail, wooden ~ **121** 92
nail bag **122** 72
nail claw **120** 75
nail grip **100** 56
nail polish **99** 32
nail puller **100** 47
nail punch **134** 32
nail varnish **99** 32
naked boys **379** 3
naked lady **379** 3
name plate **118** 47; **285** 46
Nansen sledge **303** 18
nape of the neck **16** 21
napkin **45** 9; **266** 47; **267** 48
napkin ring **45** 10
nappy, disposable ~ **28** 22
narcissus **53** 8; **60** 3
narghile **107** 42
narghileh **107** 42
narrow-gauge diesel locomotive **200** 24
narrow-gauge track system **159** 4
nasicorn **366** 25
nasturtium **53** 4
natural **320** 45, 46, 54
natural-gas engine **155** 5
naturist **281** 16
naum keag **100** 7
nave **334** 62; **335** 1
navel **16** 34
navette **36** 55
navigating bridge **223** 14; **228** 22, 23, 24
navigating officer **224** 37
navigation **224**
navigational marks, floating ~ **224** 68-108
navigational television receiver mast **221** 37
navigation equipment **288** 13
navigation light *Air Force* **257** 36
navigation light *Warships* **258** 56
navigation light *Airsports* **288** 31
navigation light, left ~ **230** 50
navigation light, right ~ **230** 44
navigation light, side ~ **258** 15
navigation light indicator panel **224** 29
navigation lights **286** 10-14
navvy **118** 76
navy **258**
navy plug **107** 25
navy yard **222** 1-43
Neanderthal man **261** 19
neck *Man* **16** 19-21
neck *Horse* **72** 12, 15
neck *Game* **88** 3
neck *Meat* **95** 6, 20
neck *Mach. Parts etc.* **143** 64
neck *Weaves* **171** 33
neck *Rowing* **283** 37
neck *Airsports* **288** 70
neck *Music. Instr.* **324** 7, 18
neck, cylindrical ~ **328** 40
neck, ground glass ~ **350** 37
neckband **36** 16
neck brush **106** 27
neckerchief **31** 57
neck flap *Fencing* **294** 14
neck guard *Fencing* **294** 14
neck guard *Chivalry* **329** 83
neck interlocking point **171** 35
necklace **36** 2; **328** 25; **352** 14
necklace, coral ~ **36** 34
necklace, cultured pearl ~ **36** 12
necklace, ivory ~ **36** 28
necklace, pearl ~ **36** 32
neckline *Ladies' Wear* **30** 34
neck line *Airsports* **288** 71
neck of violin **323** 2
neck piece **329** 83
neck ring, gold ~ **328** 26
neck strap **71** 30
necktie **319** 38
nectary **59** 18
needle *Mach. Parts etc.* **143** 76
needle *Drawing Off.* **151** 56
needle *Conifers* **372** 11
needle, hypodermic ~ **22** 65; **24** 54
needle, right-angle ~ **151** 67
needle, surgical ~ **22** 57
needle, tapered ~ **190** 51
needle bar **167** 28
needle bed **167** 51, 55
needle butt **167** 60
needle cage **143** 75
needle cam **167** 14
needle cylinder *Knitting* **167** 8, 11
needle cylinder *Bookbind.* **185** 21
needled part of the cylinder **163** 70
needle file **108** 22
needle head **309** 33
needle holder **22** 59

needle holder, cylindrical ~ **167** 8, 11
needle hook **167** 64
needle-matching system **114** 29
needlepoint **102** 30
needle point attachment **151** 54
needlepoint lace **102** 30
needle-raising cam **167** 59
needle roller bearing **143** 75-76
needles in parallel rows **167** 53
needle trick **167** 15
needlework **102**
negative carrier **116** 30
negative flight **288** 9
negligée **355** 66
negress **354** 22
negro **354** 13
negro hut **354** 21
nematode **80** 51
Neolithic period **328** 10-20
neon sign **268** 16
Neptune **4** 51
Nereid **327** 23
nerve **370** 30
nerve, auditory ~ **17** 64
nerve, femoral ~ **18** 31
nerve, optic ~ *Man* **19** 51
nerve, optic ~ *Bees* **77** 23, 24
nerve, peroneal ~ **18** 33
nerve, radial ~ **18** 28
nerve, sciatic ~ **18** 30
nerve, thoracic ~ **18** 26
nerve, tibial ~ **18** 32
nerve, ulnar ~ **18** 29
nerves **19** 33
nervous system **18** 22-33
nervure *Articulates* **358** 34
nervure *Bot.* **370** 29
nest **359** 28
nesting cavity **359** 29
Net *Astron.* **3** 48
net *Hunt.* **86** 27
net *Sea Fish.* **90** 8
net *Airsports* **288** 74
net *Ball Games* **293** 13
net background **102** 16
net-cord judge **293** 23
net curtain **42** 35; **44** 14
net fabric **167** 29
net post **293** 15
net sonar cable **90** 14
net sonar device **90** 17
net stocking **306** 10
net strap **293** 14
netting **102** 22
netting, wire ~ **339** 35
netting loop **102** 23
netting needle **102** 26
netting thread **102** 24
nettle **61** 33
net vault **336** 45
network **288** 74
neume **320** 1
neuropteran **358** 12
neutral conductor **127** 13
neutral corner **299** 38
neutral point **153** 22
neutron **1** 30, 39, 45, 52, 53
neutron bombardment **1** 36, 50
nevé **12** 48
new-born baby **28** 5
newel **123** 43
newel, open ~ **123** 76
newel, solid ~ **123** 77, 78
newel post **123** 43
Newfoundland dog **70** 34
new penny **252** 37
news, miscellaneous ~ **342** 63
newscaster **238** 21
news dealer **205** 17; **268** 75
news in brief **342** 63
news item **342** 50
newspaper **182** 31; **205** 51; **265** 25; **342** 37-70
newspaper, folded ~ **181** 56
newspaper delivery unit **182** 29
newspaper heading **342** 39
newspaper holder **265** 26
newspaper page **342** 37
newspaper rack **265** 8
newspaper shelf **262** 16; **265** 8
newspaper typesetting **176** 29
newsreader **238** 21
newsreel camera **313** 26
New Stone Age **328** 10-20
news trolley **205** 16
news vendor **205** 17; **268** 75
New World opossum **366** 2
nib **122** 51
nib size **151** 40
niche **331** 60
nick **175** 47
nigger **310** 51
night-care cream **99** 27
nightclub **318** 1-33
nightdress **32** 16
nightgown **32** 16
nightie **32** 16
nightingale **361** 14
nightshirt **32** 37
night spot **318** 1-33
nightwear **32**
nightwear, ladies' ~ **32** 16-21
nightwear, men's ~ **32** 35-37
Nile crocodile **356** 13
nimbostratus **8** 10
nine-eight time **320** 39
nine-four time **320** 40
nine men's morris **276** 18, 23-25
nine men's morris board **276** 23
nipper, bottom ~ **163** 65
nipper, top ~ **163** 66
nippers **100** 40, 41
nipping press **183** 20
nipple **16** 28
nipple key **126** 63
nitrogen tetroxide tank **234** 59
nitrous oxide **26** 3
nix **327** 23
nixie **327** 23
nobleman **355** 44
nock **305** 63
node **68** 7
node, lymph ~ **19** 10
nodosity **80** 27
nogging piece **120** 55
noir **275** 21
nominal par **251** 12
non-belayer **300** 27
nonpareil **175** 23
non-printing area **340** 56
noodle **98** 34; **99** 65
Norfolk Island pine **53** 16
North America **14** 12
North Atlantic Drift **14** 30
North Equatorial Current **14** 32
Northern Cross **3** 23
Northern Crown **3** 31
northern gannet **359** 9
northern pike **364** 16
north light **121** 21
north point **4** 16
North Pole **14** 3
North Sea **14** 26
North Star **3** 1, 34
Norton tumbler gear **149** 8
nose *Man* **16** 10
nose *Dog* **70** 4
nose *Horse* **72** 6
nose *Fish etc.* **364** 2
nose, false ~ **306** 46
noseband **71** 7
nose cone, carbon fibre reinforced ~ **235** 20
nose gear flap **231** 24
nose landing gear unit, retractable ~ **231** 23
nosepiece, revolving ~ **112** 11, 30
nose rib **287** 36
nose undercarriage flap **231** 24
nose undercarriage unit, retractable ~ **231** 23
nose wheel **288** 34
nose wheel, forward-retracting ~ **257** 3
nose wheel, hydraulically steerable ~ **235** 30
nose wheel, steerable ~ **230** 40
nosing **123** 20
nostril **72** 7
notation, mensural ~ **320** 2
notation, square ~ **320** 1
notch *Phys. Geog.* **13** 30
notch *Forestry* **84** 28
notch *Hunt.* **87** 66, 70
notch *Army* **255** 22
notch, wedge-shaped ~ **54** 38
note, marginal ~ **185** 68
note, musical ~ **320** 3-7
notebook **47** 24; **260** 18
note head **320** 3
notepaper **245** 12
notes **252** 29-39
notes, medieval ~ **320** 1-2
note stem **320** 4
note tail **320** 4
note values **320** 12-19
'NOT GO' gauging member **149** 58
'NOT GO' side **149** 61
notice **356** 7

notice board **204** 12
nougat **98** 81
novillero **319** 2
nozzle *Moon L.* **6** 3
nozzle *Household* **50** 67
nozzle *Overh. Irrign.* **67** 33
nozzle *Pest Contr.* **83** 46
nozzle *Serv. Stat.* **196** 3
nozzle *Aircraft* **232** 39, 45, 49, 55
nozzle *Space* **234** 35; **235** 37
nozzle, pistol-type ~ **83** 28
nozzle, revolving ~ **56** 44
nozzle, swivelling ~ **235** 64
nozzle fuel tank **235** 45
nuclear energy **154**
nuclear power plant **154** 19
nuclear reactor casing **259** 67
nuclear research ship **221** 9
nucleus **1** 43
nucleus, atomic ~ **1** 2, 16, 29, 35, 49, 51
nude **338** 32
nudist **281** 16
nudist sunbathing area **281** 15
null hyperbola **224** 42
number *Equest.* **289** 33, 36
number *Cyc. Racing* **290** 28
number *Winter Sp.* **301** 37
number *Sports* **305** 84
number, abstract ~ **344** 3
number, cardinal ~ **344** 5
number, complex ~ **344** 14
number, concrete ~ **344** 4
number, even ~ **344** 11
number, four-figure ~ **344** 3
number, mixed ~ **344** 10
number, negative ~ **344** 8
number, odd ~ **344** 12
number, ordinal ~ **344** 6
number, positive ~ **344** 7
number, prime ~ **344** 13
number, whole ~ **344** 10, 18
number disc **189** 18
number key *Office* **247** 18
number key *Store* **271** 3
number key *Flea Market* **309** 76
'number one' **283** 13
number plate **189** 8; **290** 28; **305** 84
numbers **344** 1-22
number sign **197** 21
number tab **267** 10
number tag **267** 10
numeral, Arabic ~ **344** 2
numeral, Roman ~ **344** 1
numeral pendants **253** 33-34
numeral pennants **253** 33-34
numerator **344** 15
nun **331** 50
nun moth **82** 17
nursery **47**
nursery child **48** 2
nursery education **48** 1-20
nursery gardener **55** 20
nursery hand **55** 45, 46
nursery sapling **83** 15
nursery teacher **48** 1
nut *Bldg. Site* **119** 75
nut *Music. Instr.* **323** 13, 20
nut *Bot.* **370** 98
nut *Industr. Plants* **383** 44
nut *South. Fruits* **384** 52, 58, 60
nut, castellated ~ **143** 24, 77
nut, castle ~ **143** 24
nut, hexagonal ~ **143** 18
nut, round ~ **143** 35
nutation **4** 24
nutcracker **361** 1
nutcrackers **45** 49
nuthatch **361** 11
nutmeg **382** 34, 35
nutmeg tree **382** 30
nuts **59** 59, 37-51
Nydam boat **218** 1-6
nylon **101** 4
nylon 6 fibres **170** 1-62
nylons **99** 26
nylon-thread cop **133** 4
nymph, artificial ~ **89** 66

O

oak **51** 12
oak apple **82** 34
oak gall **82** 34
oak-gall wasp **82** 33
oak tree **51** 12; **371** 1
oar **218** 5; **278** 19; **283** 14, 26, 35-38
oarlock **278** 18; **283** 29, 41
oarsman **218** 3; **283** 12
oasis **354** 4
oat-grass **69** 22
oat panicle **68** 27
oats **68** 1
oats, rolled ~ **98** 37
obelisk **333** 10
Oberwerk **326** 2, 44
obi **353** 41
object ball, red ~ **277** 12
objective, interchangeable ~ **112** 62
objective aperture **113** 35
objective lens **113** 36
objective turret **112** 11, 30
object lens **114** 26; **313** 2
object stage **112** 9
oblique, external ~ **18** 43
obliquus externus abdominis **18** 43
oboe **323** 38
O'Brien technique **298** 50
observation opening **5** 13
observation port *Agr. Mach.* **64** 27
observation port *Films* **312** 15
observation room **5** 33
observation shaft **5** 30
observation telescope **351** 31
observation window **25** 8
observation window, forward ~ **235** 25
observation window, upward ~ **235** 24
observatory **5** 1-16; **9** 7
observatory, solar ~ **5** 29-33
observatory dome **5** 12
obstacle, almost-fixed ~ **289** 8
obstacle, fixed ~ **289** 20
obstruction **291** 51
obverse **252** 8
ocarina **324** 32
occipitalis **18** 50; **19** 2
occipito frontalis **19** 4
occiput **16** 2
occlusion **9** 25
ocean *Phys. Geog.* **13** 26
ocean *Map* **14** 19-26
ocean current, cold ~ **14** 27
ocean current, warm ~ **14** 28
ocean currents **14** 30-45
ocean drifts **14** 30-45
Oceanid **327** 23
ocean liner **221** 82; **225** 32
ocean nymph **327** 23
ocean station vessel **9** 7
ocellus *Dom. Anim.* **73** 32
ocellus *Bees* **77** 2
octagon **351** 17
octahedron **351** 6, 14, 16
Octans **3** 43
Octant **3** 43
octave, five-line ~ **321** 50
octave, four-line ~ **321** 49
octave, great ~ **321** 44
octave, one-line ~ **321** 46
octave, small ~ **321** 45
octave, three-line ~ **321** 48
octave, two-line ~ **321** 47
octave engagement **294** 50
odalisque **306** 41
odd-pinnate **370** 42
odds **289** 37
odds-and-ends box **195** 31
Oertz rudder **222** 69-70
oesophagus *Man* **17** 49; **20** 23, 40
oesophagus *Bees* **77** 19
offcut **120** 96
off-end framing **165** 14
offering **330** 60
offertory bag **330** 59
offertory box **330** 55
office *Coal* **144** 18
office *Railw.* **207** 41
office *Office* **245**; **246**; **247**; **248**; **249**
office *Camping* **278** 1
office *Chivalry* **329** 27
office, executive's ~ **246** 1-36
office, manager's ~ **271** 24
office, open plan ~ **248** 1-48
office, physician's ~ **22** 1-74
office, purser's ~ **223** 45
office, receptionist's ~ **245** 1-33
office, secretary's ~ **245** 1-33
office building *Coal* **144** 18
office building *Offshore Drill.* **146** 14
office building *Docks* **225** 53
office building *Films* **310** 4
office calculator **245** 31
office chair **248** 25
office cupboard **248** 12
office equipment **247** 1-44
office furniture **248** 39
office intercom **245** 20; **246** 10
office machinery **249**

office materials **247** 1-44
officer in charge **270** 36
officer of the watch **221** 126
offices **205** 13; **217** 24; **310** 4
offices, administrative ~ **222** 1
office supplies **247** 1-44
offset machine, four-colour ~ **180** 30
offset machine, rotary ~ **180** 1, 18
offset machine, sheet-fed ~ **180** 30
offset machine, single-colour ~ **180** 46, 59
offset plate **179** 1
offset plate, coated ~ **179** 16
offset platemaking **179**
offset press *Paperm.* **173** 21
offset press *Office* **249** 48
offset press, four-colour ~ **180** 1, 18, 30
offset press, rotary ~ **180** 1, 18
offset press, sheet-fed ~ **180** 30, 70
offset press, single-colour ~ **180** 46, 59
offset printing **180**
offshoot **370** 21
offshore drilling **146**
offshore drilling rig supply vessel **221** 32
offside **291** 42
off switch **10** 15
ogee arch **336** 36
ogee wing **229** 22
oil **98** 24
oil, crude ~ *Phys. Geog.* **12** 31
oil, crude ~ *Oil, Petr.* **145** 28-35, 36-64
oil, mineral ~ **145**
oil, viscous ~ **84** 35
oil and vinegar bottle **45** 42
oil bag **228** 11
oil bath air cleaner *Agr. Mach.* **65** 54
oil bath air cleaner *Railw.* **212** 79
oil bath air filter *Agr. Mach.* **65** 54
oil bath air filter *Railw.* **212** 79
oil bleeder screw **190** 24
oil burner **38** 58-60
oil can **196** 16
oil-circulating pump *Power Plant* **152** 45
oil-circulating pump *Railw.* **211** 12
oil conservator **152** 42; **153** 9
oil cooler *Power Plant* **152** 46
oil cooler *Car* **192** 19
oil cooler *Railw.* **211** 11
oil drain plug **190** 24
oil drilling **145** 1-21
oiler **109** 4
oil filler neck **190** 28
oil filter **190** 43; **192** 20
oil-firing system **199** 30, 35
oil furnace **145** 36
oil gallery, main ~ **192** 21
oil gauge *Roof & Boilerr.* **38** 54
oil gauge *Power Plant* **153** 11
oil heating furnace **38** 57
oil level pipe **38** 53
oil paint **338** 11
oil palm **383** 54
oil pipe **190** 13
oil pipeline **145** 65
oil pressure gauge *Sawmill* **157** 7
oil pressure gauge *Aircraft* **230** 20
oil pressure limiting valve **190** 67
oil pressure warning light **191** 73
oil production **145** 22-27
oil products **145** 52-64
oil pump **190** 42; **192** 16
oil pump drive **190** 25
oil refinery **145** 65-74
oil reservoir **64** 29, 93
oil rig **146** 1-39
oil scraper ring **190** 37
oilskins **228** 4
oil stand **109** 5
oilstone **340** 21
oil sump *Agr. Mach.* **65** 45
oil sump *Intern. Combust. Eng.* **190** 41
oil sump *Car* **192** 17
oil tank *Roof & Boilerr.* **38** 44
oil tank *Agr. Mach.* **64** 93
oil tank *Oil, Petr.* **145** 34
oil tank *Motorcycle* **189** 36
oil temperature gauge *Car* **191** 38
oil temperature gauge *Aircraft* **230** 21
oil temperature sensor **195** 16, 40
oil-to-air cooling unit **209** 18
ointment, tube of ~ **22** 47
O-Joller **284** 50
Old Stone Age **328** 1-9
old woman's tooth **132** 26
oleander **373** 13
olive oil **98** 24
olive tree **383** 29
omnibus, horse-drawn ~ **186** 37
on-board equipment **239** 6
on-board telephone **239** 13
one-design keelboat **284** 62
one-half twist isander **282** 41
Oneirophanta **369** 18
one-second theodolite **112** 73
one-two **291** 49
one-way tap **350** 42
on full point **314** 19
on guard line **294** 3
on guard position **294** 18, 33
onion **57** 24
onion skin **57** 25
on-line disc storage unit **176** 32
on-load tap changer **153** 13
on/off switch *Railw.* **211** 30
on/off switch *Audio* **241** 63
on/off switch *Audiovis.* **243** 16
on/off switch *Office* **247** 16; **249** 9, 37, 64
on/off valve **279** 22
on-ramp **15** 16
on-the-ground wrestling **299** 8
open gate **301** 65
open-hearth furnace **147** 21-30
opening **122** 24
opening, pharyngeal ~ **19** 24
opening control **313** 8
open-newel staircase **123** 76
open-reel tape **241** 58
open vertical gate **301** 67
open work **102** 27
opera glass **315** 9
opera hat **35** 36
operating cabin **228** 21
operating handle **309** 81
operating indicator **244** 11
operating instructions **244** 15
operating key **243** 13, 41, 48; **246** 19; **261** 45
operating lamp **27** 25
operating lamp, shadow-free ~ **26** 10
operating lamp, swivel-mounted ~ **26** 10
operating lever *Pest Contr.* **83** 21
operating lever *Cine Film* **117** 63
operating lever *Road Constr.* **201** 12
operating mechanism housing **153** 60
operating table **26** 8, 36
operating table, pedestal ~ **26** 5
operating theatre **26** 1-33
operating valve **153** 52
operation indicator **244** 7
operations, arithmetical ~ **344** 23-26; **345** 1-10
operator *Post* **237** 35
operator *Computer* **244** 14
operator *Theatre* **316** 59
operator, chief ~ **244** 3
operator's position **237** 34
operator's set **237** 23
operculum **364** 5
ophthalmic test stand **111** 43
ophthalmometer **111** 44
ophthalmoscope **22** 62
opium poppy **380** 15
opponent **293** 18
optical bench **114** 50; **242** 79
optical instruments **112**; **113**
optical sound recorder **310** 60; **311** 6
optical sound recording **311** 9
optical sound recording equipment **311** 6
optical sound unit **312** 45
optical system **242** 41; **243** 50
optician **111** 1
optic plate, right-hand ~ **195** 18

oxygen flow meter **26** 4
oxygen hose **141** 10
oxygen inlet **350** 11
oxygen jet **350** 13
oxygen lance **147** 49
oxygen molecule **242** 65
oxygen supply **25** 22
oxygen tank *Moon L.* **6** 6
oxygen tank *Space* **234** 61
oxygen tank *Air Force* **257** 2
oxygen treatment **25** 23
oxymeter **27** 13
oxysphere **11** 1
oyster **357** 32
oyster fork **45** 80
oyster round **95** 11
ozone layer **7** 13, 19

P

pace **72** 40
pacemaker **25** 36
pacemaker, cardiac ~ **25** 31, 37
pacemaker, internal ~ **25** 37
pacemaker, short-term ~ **25** 25
pacemaker battery **25** 51
pacemaker control unit **25** 40
pacemaker impulse **25** 44
pacemaker unit **25** 30
pacer **290** 11
Pacific Ocean **14** 19
pack *Dom. Anim.* **73** 5
pack *Hunt.* **86** 33
pack *Airsports* **288** 44
pack, disposable ~ **93** 28
package, unitized ~ **226** 21
package cargo transit shed **225** 9
package freight **206** 4, 27
pack animal **354** 3
packing, sterile ~ **26** 31
packing box **210** 33
packing box dispenser **74** 53
packing machine **76** 36
pack of hounds **86** 33; **289** 46
pack saddle **73** 4
pad *Horse* **71** 49
pad *Game* **88** 46
pad *Shoem.* **100** 16
pad *Ball Games* **292** 9
pad *Graphic Art* **340** 13
pad, bakelite ~ **166** 64
pad, leather ~ *Goldsm. etc.* **108** 29
pad, leather ~ *Weaving* **166** 64
pad, suctorial ~ **77** 9
pad, unsterile ~ **26** 23
pad bridge **111** 12
padding, foam rubber ~ **291** 20
paddle *Brew.* **92** 46
paddle *Electrotyp. etc.* **178** 25, 33
paddle *Ship* **218** 8
paddle *Ethnol.* **353** 14
paddle, double-bladed ~ **283** 39
paddle, double-ended ~ **283** 39
paddle, single-bladed ~ **283** 34
paddle boat **280** 12
paddling pool **37** 44; **273** 28
paddock **319** 15
padlock **38** 21
page *Bookbind.* **185** 53
page *Hotel* **267** 18
page, double-column ~ **185** 64
page, front ~ **342** 38
pageboy **267** 18
pageboy style **34** 35
page cord **174** 16
page heading **342** 52
page number **185** 63; **251** 14
page printer **237** 66
pagoda, Indian ~ **337** 21
pagoda, multi-storey ~ **337** 1
pail **50** 54
pailoo **337** 3
pailou **337** 3
paint **129** 6, 7-8, 9; **338** 10
paintbox **48** 6; **338** 10
paintbrush **48** 7; **129** 3; **260** 84
paint bucket **129** 10
paint container **315** 34
Painter *Astron.* **3** 47
painter *Painter* **129** 2
painter *Art. Studio* **338** 2
painting **129** 1; **260** 27
painting, watercolour ~ **48** 5
painting materials **338** 6-19
painting surface **338** 22
painting table **338** 25
paint kettle **129** 8
paint roller **129** 11
paint room **315** 28-42
paint scraper **129** 22
paint trolley **315** 36
pair **275** 20
pairing season **86** 9-12
pair skater **302** 4
pajamas **32** 17, 36
palace, Baroque ~ **272** 7
palace, Renaissance ~ **335** 47
palace buildings **333** 29
palace gardens **272** 1-40
Palaeolithic period **328** 1-9
Palaeopneustes niasicus **369** 19
palate, hard ~ **19** 20
palate, soft ~ **19** 21
pale ale **93** 26
palette **338** 28
palette dipper **338** 29
palette knife **338** 14
paling **52** 10
palisade *Equest.* **289** 8
palisade *Chivalry* **329** 36
palisading **329** 36
palla **355** 10
pallbearer **331** 40
pallet *Porcelain Manuf.* **161** 20
pallet *Station* **206** 32
pallet *Docks* **225** 43; **226** 7
pallet *Music. Instr.* **326** 10
pallet, flat ~ **226** 10
pallet, standard ~ **226** 10
pallette **329** 45
palm **88** 41
Palma Christi **380** 14
palma manus **19** 71
palmate **370** 39
palmation **73** 36; **359** 7
palm capital **333** 25
palm column **333** 17
palmette **334** 41
palm frond **384** 3
palm of the hand **19** 71
palm rest **255** 13, 19; **305** 45
palm tree **354** 5
palpebra, lower ~ **19** 40
palpebra, upper ~ **19** 39
pampas grass **51** 8
pamphlet **330** 57
pan *Household* **50** 52
pan *Carp.* **120** 59
pan *School* **260** 60
panache **329** 78
Panama hat **35** 16
pan and tilt head **114** 48; **313** 12
pancreas **20** 44
Pandean pipes **322** 2
pandora **322** 21
pane **66** 10; **137** 27
panel **120** 59
panel, front ~ **32** 24
panel, mirrored ~ **267** 66
panelboard **157** 67
panelling, metal ~ **208** 6
panelling, wood ~ **281** 19, **266** 37
panel pin **124** 29
pane of glass **124** 16
pangolin **366** 10
pan grinding mill **159** 8
Panhard rod **192** 70
panicle **68** 27; **370** 69; **378** 46; **382** 54
pan loaf **97** 10
pannier **78** 15
panpipes **322** 2
pan set **40** 12-16
pansy **60** 2
pantaleon **325** 1
pantaloons **306** 42
pantie briefs **32** 8
pantie-corselette **32** 3
pantie-girdle **32** 2
pantie-hose **32** 12
panties, long-legged ~ **32** 10
pantile **122** 54
pantograph *Map* **14** 65
pantograph *Composing Rm.* **175** 58
pantograph *Tram* **197** 23
pantograph carriage **175** 53
pantry, ship's ~ **223** 43
pants, long ~ **32** 11
paper *Photog.* **116** 50
paper *Drawing Off.* **151** 14
paper *Paperm.* **173** 2-10
paper *Offset Print.* **180** 47
paper *Letterpress* **181** 46
paper *Office* **249** 57
paper, asphalted ~ **153** 48

paper, blank ~ **180** 2, 69; **181** 23, 30
paper, coated ~ **173** 35
paper, cork ~ **128** 18
paper, metallic ~ *Paperhanger* **128** 18
paper, metallic ~ *Power Plant* **153** 44
paper, metallized ~ **153** 44
paper, natural ~ **128** 18
paper, printed ~ **180** 57; **181** 9, 25
paper, raw ~ **173** 29
paper, unprinted ~ **180** 2, 69; **181** 23, 30
paper, wood ~ **128** 18
paper bag, cone-shaped ~ **98** 49
paper bail **249** 17
paper chase **289** 41-49
paper clip **247** 1, 2
paper edge, butted ~ **128** 20
paper feed **245** 11; **249** 45, 49
paper feed and delivery **181** 14
paper feeding and delivery unit **181** 14
paperhanger **128**
paper hanging **128** 18-53
paperhanging brush **128** 40
paperhanging kit **128** 33
paper hunt **289** 41-49
paper machine **173** 11, 13-28
papermaking **172**; **173**
papermaking by hand **173** 46-51
paper punch **22** 28
paper recorder **25** 56, 57
paper recorder unit **27** 33
paper reed **383** 64
paper release lever **249** 20
paper ribbon **174** 34
paper roll **249** 33; **309** 75
paper roller **128** 47
paper rush **383** 64
paper size selection **249** 34
paper speed scale **116** 54
paper stand **151** 13
paper tape **237** 32
paper towel **196** 11
paper towel dispenser **196** 10
paper tower **174** 33, 43
pappus **375** 34
pappus bristle **375** 33
pappus tuft **378** 11
paprika **57** 42
papyrus column **333** 15
papyrus plant **383** 64
par **251** 12
para **252** 28
parabola **347** 14
parachute *Meteorol. Instr.* **10** 57
parachute *Airsports* **288** 37
parachuting **288** 37-62
paraffin **145** 60
paraffin lamp **278** 29
paraffin oil **145** 60
paragon **175** 31
Paraguay tea **382** 11
parallel **346** 4
parallel bars **296** 2
parallelepiped **347** 36
parallel of latitude **14** 2
parallelograms **346** 33-36
parallels **14** 1-7
Paramecium **357** 9
parapet *Dwellings* **37** 19
parapet *Bridges* **215** 70
parapet *Chivalry* **329** 21
parapet, battlemented ~ **329** 20
parasites **81**
parasites of man **81** 31-42
parasol mushroom **381** 30
paravane **258** 87
parcel *Station* **204** 2
parcel *Post* **236** 3, 6
parcel registration card **236** 7
parcel registration slip **236** 4
parcels counter **236** 1
parcels office **204** 1
parcels scales **236** 2
parent **54** 15
parentheses **342** 24
parent plant **54** 15
paring knife **100** 51
parison **162** 47
parison mould **162** 26
park *Map* **15** 97
park *Park* **272**
park *Ball Games* **291** 1; **292** 40-58
park, landscaped ~ **272** 41-72
parka **29** 66
parka coat **29** 66
park bench **272** 16, 42
park by-law **272** 29
park chair **272** 48
park entrance **272** 32
park gardener **272** 66
parking meter **268** 1
park keeper **272** 30
park path **272** 38
park railing **272** 33
parlour, herringbone ~ **75** 23
parquet floor **123** 74
parquet strip **123** 62
parrot **363** 1
parrying **294** 6
parry of the fifth **294** 24
parry of the quinte **294** 24
parry of the tierce **294** 8
parsley **57** 19
parsonage **331** 20
part, imaginary ~ **344** 14
part, real ~ **344** 14
parterre **272** 39
Parthenon **334** 1
partial-hip end **121** 17
parting, centre ~ **34** 9
parting, side ~ **34** 14
parting kiss **205** 52
parting-off tool **149** 53
parting tool *Turner* **135** 24
parting tool *Mach. Tools* **149** 53
partition **75** 38
partition, framed ~ **120** 48
partition, glass ~ **25** 8
partition, sound-absorbing ~ **248** 20
partition, wooden ~ **38** 19
partition screen **248** 1
partition wall *Bldg. Site* **119** 25
partition wall *Office* **248** 1
part load **206** 4
part-load goods **206** 27
partridge **88** 70
partridge call **87** 47
party **263** 20
party, private ~ **267** 40-43
party blouse **30** 55
party games **276**
party skirt **30** 56
par value **251** 12
Paschen series **1** 22
pas de trois **314** 27-28
Pasiphaea **369** 12
pass *Phys. Geog.* **12** 47
pass *Ball Games* **291** 47
pass, short ~ **291** 49
passage **71** 3
passage, barred ~ **307** 51
passage grave **328** 16
passe **275** 19
passenger **204** 24; **205** 6; **208** 30; **221** 97, 109
passenger aircraft **231** 2
passenger cabin **231** 22
passenger car **208** 3
passenger coach **207** 1-21; **208** 3
passenger compartment **207** 13
passenger door, centre ~ **231** 25
passenger door, rear ~ **231** 30
passenger ferry **216** 1
passenger liner **221** 82; **225** 32
passenger loading bridge **233** 14
passenger seat *Car* **191** 36
passenger seat *Lorries etc.* **194** 14
passenger seat *Aircraft* **230** 38; **231** 22
passenger sledge **353** 18
passenger terminal **225** 31
passenger vehicle **191** 1-56; **195** 34
passerines **361**
Passiflora **53** 2
passion flower **53** 2
passport **267** 13
passport check **233** 42
pastas **98** 32-34
paste **128** 26
paste, heavy-duty ~ **128** 24
pasteboard **128** 31
paste brush **128** 27
pastel crayon **338** 19
pastern **72** 25
pasting machine **128** 25
pastor *Church* **330** 22
pastor *Birds* **361** 4
pastry whirl **97** 38
pasture, rough ~ **15** 5
patch pocket **29** 68; **30** 22; **31** 56; **33** 38; **35** 37
pâté **96** 15

patella **17** 23
paten **330** 9; **332** 51
patent **246** 26
patent anchor **222** 78; **258** 5; **286** 17
patent key **187** 50
patent log **224** 54
patent valve **187** 31
paternoster **332** 31
path, central ~ **55** 42
path, gravel ~ **272** 18
path, unfenced ~ **15** 102
patient **22** 2, 3; **24** 2; **274** 7, 18
patients file **22** 6
patin **330** 9; **332** 51
patine **330** 9; **332** 51
patrician lady **355** 48
patrol car **264** 10
patrolman **264** 13
patrol submarine **259** 75
patten **355** 43
pattern *Iron Foundry etc.* **148** 34
pattern *Composing Rm.* **175** 55
pattern, chequered ~ **335** 14
pattern control chain **167** 19
pattern repeat **171** 12
pattern stencil **168** 62
pattern table **175** 56
pauldron **329** 45
Pauli exclusion principle **1** 7
Pauli principle **1** 7
pause **321** 25
pause sign **321** 25
pavais **329** 56
pavement **37** 60; **198** 8, 9
paving **198** 8
paving, brick ~ **123** 7
paving, flagstone ~ **123** 26
paving brick **159** 27
pavis **329** 56
Pavo **3** 41
paw **88** 46, 50; **368** 4
paw, hind ~ **70** 8
pawn **276** 13
payee **250** 19
payer **250** 20
paying agent **250** 22
paying-in counter **236** 25
paying-in slip **236** 27
payload bay **235** 26
payload bay door **235** 14
payload bay insulation **235** 13
payload manipulator arm **235** 29
pay phone **236** 9; **237** 3
pea **57** 1, 7
peach **59** 31
peach blossom **59** 27
peach flan **97** 22
peach flower **59** 27
peach leaf **59** 32
peach tree **59** 26-32
Peacock *Astron.* **3** 41
peacock *Dom. Anim.* **73** 30
peacock butterfly **365** 2
pea flower **57** 2
pea jacket **221** 127
peak **11** 6; **12** 40
peanut **45** 41; **383** 41
pear **58** 33
pear blossom **58** 38
pearl *Jewell.* **36** 8
pearl *Game* **88** 30
pearl *Composing Rm.* **175** 22
pearl *Invertebr.* **357** 35
pearl barley **98** 35
pear pip **58** 37
pears **99** 87
pear-shape, faceted ~ **36** 84
pear-shape, plain ~ **36** 83
pear-shape, standard ~ **36** 54
pear-shapes **36** 82-86
pear stalk **58** 34
pear tree **58** 31, 32
peasecod **355** 30
peat **55** 31; **206** 10
pea tendril **57** 4
peavy **85** 9
peba **366** 8
pebble, painted ~ **328** 6
pectoralis, greater ~ **18** 36
pectoralis major **18** 36
pedal *Joiner* **132** 72
pedal *Bicycle* **187** 40, 78
pedal *Sports* **305** 85
pedal *Music. Instr.* **323** 62; **325** 41, 46
pedal, adjustable ~ **298** 2
pedal, left ~ **325** 9
pedal, right ~ **325** 8
pedal bracket **325** 42
pedal car **273** 55
pedal crank **188** 25
pedal cylinder **163** 27
pedal drive **188** 25
pedal frame **187** 83
pedal harp **323** 60
pedal key **326** 51, 52
pedal lever **163** 28
pedal mechanism **324** 54
pedal pipe **326** 3
pedal roller **163** 27, 28
pedal tower **326** 4
peddle boat **280** 12
pedestal *Optic. Instr.* **113** 2
pedestal *Office* **248** 37
pedestal *Park* **272** 11
pedestal *Circus* **307** 55
pedestal crane **146** 3
pedestal grinding machine **138** 7
pedestal mat **49** 18
pedestrian **268** 18
pedestrian crossing **198** 11; **268** 24, 51
'pedestrian crossing' sign **268** 29
pedestrian lights **268** 55
pedestrian precinct **268** 58
pedicel **59** 4; **383** 7
pediculate **369** 6
pediment *Phys. Geog.* **13** 65
pediment *Art* **334** 3; **335** 36
peduncle **59** 4; **383** 7
peeler **133** 1
peeling machine **133** 1
peen **66** 10; **137** 27
peewit **359** 21
peg *Floor etc. Constr.* **123** 11
peg *Camping* **278** 24
peg *Music. Instr.* **323** 18; **324** 11
Pegasus *Astron.* **3** 10
Pegasus *Fabul. Creat.* **327** 26
pegbox **323** 19
pegbox, bent-back ~ **324** 10
pegbox, swan-head ~ **324** 10
pegdisc **324** 19
pein **137** 27
Pekinese dog **70** 19
Peking man **261** 18
pelargonium **53** 1
pelican **359** 5
pelican eel **369** 2
pellitone **323** 44
pelorus **224** 53
pelota **305** 67
pelota player **305** 68
pelvis **17** 18-21
pelvis, renal ~ **20** 31
pen *Livestock* **75** 36
pen *Office* **245** 21
pen *School* **260** 14
pen, ballpoint ~ **47** 26
pen, felt tip ~ **47** 26; **48** 18
pen, metal ~ **341** 25
penalty **291** 40
penalty area **291** 4
penalty kick **291** 40
penalty line **292** 5
penalty spot **291** 6
pen and pencil case **260** 12
pen and pencil tray **245** 22; **260** 24
pencil **47** 26; **129** 41; **260** 5
pencil, carpenter's ~ **120** 77
pencil, clutch-type ~ **151** 45
pencil, coloured ~ **48** 11
pencil, lead ~ **118** 51
pencil attachment **151** 62
pencil box **309** 73
pencil holder **22** 31
pencil lead **151** 46
pencil of rays **346** 19
pencil point attachment **151** 55
pencil sharpener **247** 25
pencil silhouette **31** 14
pen clip **2** 18
pendant **335** 32
pendant, gemstone ~ **36** 14
pendant, oblong ~ **253** 28
pendants **253** 30-32
pendeloque **36** 54
pendentive **334** 74
pendulum *Atom* **2** 35
pendulum **110** 27; **309** 58
pendulum device **2** 35
pendulum spray **83** 27
penguin **359** 4
peninsula **13** 5
penis **20** 66
penlight pocket **6** 24
pen meter **2** 15
pennant, oblong ~ **253** 28
pennants **253** 30-32
pennon **278** 9; **280** 11
pennon staff **280** 10
pensions counter **236** 25
Pentacrinus **369** 3
pentagon **351** 9

pentaprism **115** 41, 70
pentaprism viewfinder, interchangeable ~ **115** 69
penthouse **37** 83
penthouse head **312** 50
penthouse roof **37** 55
pent roof **37** 55, 78; **121** 7
penumbra **4** 34
peplos **355** 2
pepper **382** 39
peppercorn **382** 39
peppermint **380** 3
pepper plant **382** 36
pepper pot **266** 77
percentage focusing chart **177** 7
percentage key **247** 23
percentage sign **345** 7
percent key **247** 23
perch **86** 49
percolation of a river **13** 73
percussion cap *Hunt.* **87** 59
percussion cap *Carnival* **306** 49
percussion drill, electric ~ **134** 43
percussion instruments **323** 49-59; **324** 47-58
percussion screwdriver **138** 6
percussor **22** 73
peregrine falcon **362** 2
perennial **52** 22
perennial, flowering ~ **52** 9
perfect binder **184** 1; **249** 61
perfect fifth **321** 10
perfect fourth **321** 9
perfecting unit **181** 49
perfecting unit for black **180** 12-13
perfecting unit for cyan **180** 8-9
perfecting unit for magenta **180** 10-11
perfecting unit for yellow **180** 6-7
perfect octave **321** 13
perforated brick **159** 21
perforation **236** 62
perforator *Paperhanger* **128** 12
perforator *Composing Rm.* **176** 5
perfume bottle **43** 27; **105** 36
perfume spray **43** 26; **106** 21
pergola **37** 80; **51** 1; **272** 17
pericarp **57** 6
pericementum **19** 28
perineum **20** 64
period **342** 16
periodical **262** 15
periodicals rack **262** 15
periodontium **19** 28
periphery **346** 44
peristomion **322** 5
peristyle **334** 2
peritoneum **20** 58
perlon fibres **170** 1-62
Permian **154** 62
peroneus longus **18** 64
perpendicular **346** 6, 27, 28
perpetual frost climate **9** 58
Persian cat **73** 17
Persian lamb **30** 60
personnel carrier, armoured ~ **255** 91
Peru Current **14** 42
pesade **71** 4; **307** 30
peseta **252** 22
pest control **83**
pestle **349** 10
petal **58** 43; **59** 11; **370** 59
petasus **355** 4
pet foods **99** 36-37
petiole **370** 27
petri dish **173** 7; **261** 25
petrol can **196** 25
petrol canister **84** 36
petroleum *Phys. Geog.* **12** 31
petroleum *Oil, Petr.* **145** 41
petroleum gas, liquefied ~ **145** 53
petroleum reservoir **12** 27
petrol lighter **107** 27
petrol motor **83** 41
petrol pump **196** 1
petrol pump, self service ~ **196** 8
petrol pump hose **196** 2
petrol station **196** 1-29
petrol tank **188** 10, 28; **189** 2; **305** 87
petticoat **355** 37
petty cash **246** 27
petty morel **379** 5
petunia **53** 6
pew **330** 28
pewit **359** 21
Pfund series **1** 24
phaeton **86** 18; **186** 38
phalange **17** 17, 29; **19** 77
phalanx **17** 17; **19** 77
pharmacopoeia **22** 23
pharynx **19** 24
phases, lunar ~ **4** 2-7
pheasant **88** 77
pheasant cock **88** 77
pheasant hen **88** 77
pheasant's eye **60** 4
phenol **170** 3, 14, 16
phenol extraction **156** 39
philomel **361** 14
philomela **361** 14
philtrum **16** 12
phloem **370** 9
phlox **60** 14
Phoenix **327** 9
phonation **312** 11
phonetic transcription **342** 14
phorbeia **322** 5
phoropter **111** 44
phosphorescent material **240** 18
photocell *Garage* **195** 21,22
photocell *Films* **312** 49
photocomposition **176**
photocomposition system **176** 29
photodiode **114** 70; **243** 56
photoengraving, halftone ~ **178** 38
photogrammetry **14** 63-66; **112** 67
photographic plate **309** 49, 50
photographic unit **176** 14
photography **114; 115; 116**
photography, underwater ~ **279** 23
photogravure **182**
photomechanical reproduction **177**
photometer **23** 54
photometer, microscopic ~ **112** 49
photometry **23** 52, 53
photomicrographic camera attachment **112** 36
photomicro mount adapter **112** 64
photomicroscope **112** 34
photomicroscope adapter **115** 89
photomultiplier **112** 51
photosetting **176**
photosetting system **176** 29
phototheodolite **112** 67
phototopography **14** 63-66
phototypesetting **176** 1
photo-unit **176** 14
piaffe **71** 1
pianino **325** 1
pianissimo **321** 36
pianissimo piano **321** 37
piano *Music. Not.* **321** 35
piano *Music. Instr.* **325** 1, 40
piano accordion **324** 36
piano action **325** 2-18
piano case **325** 6
pianoforte **325** 1
piano keys **325** 4-5
piano mechanism **325** 2-18
piano pedal **325** 9
piano pedals **325** 8-9
piano string **325** 7
pica **175** 28
picador **319** 16
piccolo **323** 30
Piciformes **363** 6
pick **158** 31; **300** 33
pick counter **166** 2
picker **166** 64
picker head **184** 11
picking bowl **166** 67
picking cam **166** 66
picking knife **136** 38
picking stick **166** 17, 22
picking stick buffer **166** 65
picking stick return spring **166** 68
pickpocket **308** 16
pick stick **166** 17
pickup attachment **62** 41; **63** 27
pickup reel **64** 4
pickup sucker **184** 8
pickup truck **194** 1, 5
pickup unit **240** 36
pictographs **233** 24-53
Pictor **3** 47
picture **43** 20; **246** 28
picture, panoramic ~ **24** 21
picture frame **43** 21
picture gate **312** 34
picture house **312** 1

picture monitor **238** 65; **239** 12
picture rail **128** 29
picture tube **240** 3
picture tube geometry **242** 39
pier *Bridges* **215** 21, 54
pier *Docks* **225** 66
pier *Airport* **233** 12
pier *Art* **336** 25
pier, clustered ~ **335** 34
pier, compound ~ **335** 34
pier, reinforced concrete ~ **215** 61
piercing saw **108** 12
piercing saw blade **108** 13
pierette **306** 12
pierhead **233** 13
pierrot **306** 19
pies **97** 22-24
pig *Farm Bldgs.* **62** 10
pig *Dom. Anim.* **73** 9
pig *Livestock* **75** 39
pig *Slaughterho.* **94** 11
pig *Meat* **95** 38-54
pig *Iron & Steel* **147** 40
pig, solidifying ~ **148** 25
pig-casting machine **147** 34-44
pigeon **73** 33; **359** 23
pigeon hole **267** 2
pig iron, molten ~ **147** 55
pig iron ladle **147** 12, 21, 42
pig iron runout **147** 11
piglet **73** 9; **75** 42
pigment paper **182** 1, 8, 10
pigmy **354** 41
pigpen **62** 8; **75** 35
pigskin **292** 27
pigsty **62** 8; **75** 35
pigtail *Hairst. etc.* **34** 6
pigtail *Tobacc. etc.* **107** 18
pigtail wig **34** 5; **355** 77
pig trap **146** 31
pike *Fish Farm.* **89** 17
pike *Free Exerc.* **295** 38
pike *Fish etc.* **364** 16
pike, spawning ~ **89** 11
piked reverse hang **296** 36
pike pole **319** 17
pi-key **247** 24
pilaster **335** 46
pilaster strip **335** 11
pile **226** 40
pile, steel ~ **217** 4
pile delivery unit **180** 55
pile driver, floating ~ **226** 36
pile driver frame **226** 37
pile dwelling **328** 15; **352** 33
pile feeder **180** 73
pile feeder, automatic ~ **180** 48
pile foundation **216** 8
pile hammer **226** 38
pile of arrow **305** 61
pile shoe **269** 61
pileus **381** 4
piling **157** 25
pillar *Mach. Tools* **150** 21
pillar *Shipbuild.* **222** 61
pillar *Art* **335** 20
pillar, engaged ~ **335** 35, 46
pillar guide **139** 42
pillar stand *Atom* **2** 29
pillar stand *Optic. Instr.* **112** 32
pillar tap **126** 31
pillion footrest **188** 44
pillion passenger **268** 36
pillion rider **268** 36
pillow **27** 27; **43** 12-13; **47** 4
pillowcase **43** 12
pillow lace **102** 18
pillowslip **43** 12
pilot *Railw.* **210** 34
pilot *Music. Instr.* **325** 33
pilot, automatic ~ **224** 18
pilot boat **221** 95
pilot chute **288** 39
pilot flag **253** 23
pilot light **50** 10
pilot light, covered ~ **38** 60
'pilot on board' **253** 24
pilot tone cable **313** 29
pilot tone generator **313** 30
pilot tone socket **117** 7
pilot wire **325** 34
Pilsener beer **93** 26
pimehinketone **170** 20
pin *Roof* **121** 93
pin *Turner* **135** 9
pin *Metalwkr.* **140** 47
pin *Mach. Parts etc.* **143** 31
pin *Sports* **305** 12
pin, bronze ~ **328** 29
pin, cylindrical ~ **143** 40
pin, diamond ~ **36** 18
pin, front ~ **305** 1
pin, grooved ~ **143** 40
pin, split ~ **143** 19, 25, 78
pin, tapered ~ **143** 37
pinacoid, triclinic ~ **351** 26
pinafore, bib top ~ **29** 41
pinafore dress **29** 13; **30** 8; **31** 8
pin block **324** 22; **325** 18
pincers *Shoem.* **100** 40, 41
pincers *Plumb. etc.* **126** 65
pincers *D.I.Y.* **134** 13
pincers *Basketm.* **136** 37
pincers *Metalwkr.* **140** 69
pincers, caudal ~ **81** 12
pinch bar **158** 32
pinchcock **350** 30
pinch roller **243** 25
pinch roller, rubber ~ **117** 35
pincushion **104** 20
pine **372** 20
pineapple **99** 85
pineapple flower **384** 64
pineapple gall **82** 40
pineapple plant **384** 61
pine beauty **82** 46
pine cone **372** 26
pine hawkmoth **82** 27
pine moth **82** 28
pine weevil **82** 41
pin groove **143** 49
pin holder **109** 16
pinion *Game* **88** 76
pinion *Mach. Parts etc.* **143** 92
pink *Equest.* **289** 13
pink *Colour* **343** 4
pinnacle **335** 29
pinnate **370** 41
pinnatifid **370** 40
pinnipeds **367** 18-22
pin slit **143** 49
pin slot **143** 49
pin vice **109** 16
pin wire **124** 28
pip **276** 32
pipe *Living Rm.* **42** 12
pipe *Ship* **221** 3
pipe *Music. Instr.* **322** 57; **326** 16, 29
pipe, briar ~ **107** 39
pipe, cast-iron ~ **37** 14
pipe, cement ~ **200** 62
pipe, clay ~ **107** 34
pipe, Dutch ~ **107** 34
pipe, earthenware ~ **269** 35
pipe, long ~ **107** 35
pipe, magic ~ **354** 42
pipe, perforated ~ **200** 62
pipe, polyester ~ **67** 26
pipe, short ~ **107** 33
pipe, vertical ~ *Dwellings* **37** 14
pipe, vertical ~ *Fire Brig.* **270** 26
pipe bender **125** 28
pipe-bending machine *Plumb.* **125** 28
pipe-bending machine *Plumb. etc.* **126** 82
pipe bowl **107** 36
pipe cleaner **107** 46, 48
pipe clip *Roof* **122** 31
pipe clip *Plumb. etc.* **126** 56
pipe connection, quick-fitting ~ **67** 28
pipe cutter **126** 84
pipe-cutting machine **126** 10
pipeline **145** 65
pipe of peace **352** 6
pipe rack *Living Rm.* **42** 11
piperack *Offshore Drill.* **146** 4
pipe repair stand **126** 11
pipes **326** 17-35
pipe scraper **107** 45
pipe stem **107** 38
pipe still **145** 36
pipe support **67** 7, 25
pipe supports **126** 53-57
pipette **22** 72; **350** 25
pipette, automatic ~ **23** 44
pipette, graduated ~ **350** 24
pipette stand **23** 52
pipetting device, automatic ~ **23** 47
pipe union **350** 5
pipe vice **126** 81
pipe wrench **126** 61; **127** 47; **134** 11
piping **30** 13; **31** 7
pirate *Sailing* **284** 52
pirate *Carnival* **306** 43
pirn **166** 30
pirn, empty ~ **166** 21
pirn holder, spring-clip ~ **166** 33
pirouette **314** 24
Pisces **4** 64

pisciculture **89** 1-19
pistachio **382** 51
pistachio nut **382** 51
pistachio tree **382** 49
piste **294** 2
pistil **59** 13
pistol **255** 1
pistol, captive-bolt ~ **94** 3
pistol grip *Hunt.* **87** 6
pistol grip *D.I.Y.* **134** 44
pistol grip *Army* **255** 6, 38
pistol grip *Police* **264** 23
piston *Drawing Off.* **151** 60
piston *Intern. Combust. Eng.* **190** 37
piston *Inf. Tech.* **242** 46
piston, hydraulic ~ **139** 41
piston pin **192** 26
piston pump lever **83** 45
piston ring **190** 37
piston rod *Intern. Combust. Eng.* **190** 21
piston rod *Car* **192** 75
piston rod *Railw.* **210** 33
pit *Blacksm.* **138** 17
pit *Coal* **144** 1-51
pitcher *Ball Games* **292** 50, 68
pitcher *Prehist.* **328** 35
pitcher's mound **292** 49, 69
pitching **230** 67
pitching, stone ~ **216** 55
pitch number **278** 42
pitch of rivets **143** 60
pith **370** 14
pithead building **144** 4
pithead frame **144** 3
pithead gear **144** 1
Pithecanthropus erectus **261** 16
pith ray **370** 11
pit hydrant **270** 25
piton **300** 38
piton, ringed ~ **300** 39
pitot-static tube **256** 11; **257** 1
pitot tube **256** 11; **257** 1
pivot *Hairdresser* **106** 36
pivot *Bridges* **215** 69
pivot *Winter Sp.* **302** 6
pivot bearing **91** 10
pivoting half **215** 66
pivoting section **215** 66
pivoting span **215** 66
pivot pier **215** 65
pix **330** 8, **332** 53
placard **263** 13; **271** 65; **308** 50
place **44** 5, **45** 3-12
place card **45** 13
place mat **44** 4
place of issue **250** 13
place of payment **250** 15
place of publication **324** 43
place setting **44** 5; **45** 3-12
placing judge **282** 25
plaid strap **303** 2
plain, alluvial ~ **13** 10
plainclothes policeman **264** 33
plain part of the cylinder **163** 69
plains Indian **352** 3
plainsong notation **320** 1
plain-tile roofing **122** 2
plait **97** 41
plait, coiled ~ **34** 38
plaiter **168** 30, 35
plaiting-down platform **168** 37
plaits **34** 30
plaits, coiled ~ **34** 32
plan *Drawing Off.* **151** 19
plan *Railw.* **207** 10-21, 26-32, 38-42, 61-72, 76
planchet **252** 43
plane *Carp.* **120** 64
plane *Aircraft* **230** 67-72
plane *Maths.* **347** 31
plane, abyssal ~ **11** 10
plane, circular ~ **347** 39
plane, high-wing ~ **229** 1; **231** 2
plane, horizontal ~ **4** 12
plane, low-wing ~ **229** 5, 14; **231** 1
plane, midwing ~ **229** 4
plane, propeller-driven ~ **231** 1-6
plane, shoulder-wing ~ **229** 3
plane, two-seater ~ **288** 18
plane, types of ~ **231** 1-33
plane geometry **346** 1-58
plane iron **132** 20
plane of symmetry **351** 5
planer, two-column ~ **150** 8
planer table **150** 11
planes **132** 15-28
planetarium **5** 17-28
plane tree **371** 67
plane triangles **346** 26-32
planets **4** 42-52
planing boats **286** 38-44
planing machine, two-column ~ **150** 8
plank **55** 22; **118** 87; **120** 1, 91; **157** 34, 35
plank, unsquared ~ **120** 94
plank, wooden ~ **340** 2
plank cut **340** 4
planking **119** 52
planking, inner ~ **285** 57
plank platform **118** 28
plank roadway **118** 79
plan of locomotive **211** 10-18
planographic printing method **340** 25-26
plant **370** 15; **382** 50
plant, anagraceous ~ **53** 3
plant, asclepiadaceous ~ **53** 15
plant, climbing ~ **51** 5; **52** 5; **57** 8
plant, cyperacious ~ **53** 17
plant, ericaceous ~ **53** 12
plant, female ~ **383** 10
plant, flowering ~ **58** 17
plant, fruit-bearing ~ **58** 17
plant, gesneriaceous ~ **53** 7
plant, indoor ~ **42** 36; **248** 14
plant, insectivorous ~ **377** 13
plant, liliaceous ~ **53** 13
plant, pistillate ~ **383** 10
plant, pneumatic ~ **92** 12
plant, potted ~ **55** 25
plant, ranunculaceous ~ **60** 13
plant, tiliaceous ~ **53** 9
plant, tuberous ~ **68** 38
plantation, young ~ **84** 11, 12
plant body **378** 49
planter **248** 13
plant in bloom **382** 53
plant in flower **378** 36
plant louse **358** 13
plants, alpine ~ **378** 1-13
plants, aquatic ~ **378** 14-57
plants, drupaceous ~ **59** 1-36
plants, farinaceous ~ **68** 1-37
plants, indoor ~ **53**
plants, leguminous ~ **57** 1-11
plants, medicinal ~ **380**
plants, poisonous ~ **379**
plants, pomiferous ~ **58** 31-61
plants, propagation of ~ **54**
plants, tropical ~ **382**
plants of forest, marsh, and heathland **377**
plant stand **248** 13
plants used in industry **383**
plaque *Roulette* **275** 12
plaque *Sculpt. Studio* **339** 38
plaster *Hosp.* **26** 54
plaster *Paperhanger* **128** 2
plaster *Art. Studio* **338** 42
plaster, adhesive ~ **21** 7; **22** 55
plaster cast **339** 4
plaster cup **134** 18
plasterer **118** 83
plastering **118** 83-91
plaster mould **161** 15
plaster of Paris **128** 2; **260** 85
plasticine **48** 12
plate **266** 11
plate, baby's ~ **28** 28
plate, bottom ~ **45** 3
plate, curved ~ **178** 21
plate, deep ~ **44** 6; **45** 5
plate, front ~ **85** 35
plate, halftone ~ **178** 38
plate, presensitized ~ **179** 31
plate, rear ~ **85** 40
plate, sliding ~ **183** 28
plate, steel ~ **96** 54
plate armour **329** 65
plateau **13** 46
plate clamp *Electrotyp. etc.* **178** 27
plate clamp *Offset Platem.* **179** 8
plate-making machine **179** 1
plate cylinder *Offset Print.* **180** 25, 38, 53, 62
plate cylinder *Letterpress* **181** 51, 60
plate cylinder *Office* **249** 50
plate-drying cabinet, vertical ~ **179** 27
plate girder bridge **215** 52
plate magazine **113** 40
plate mount **178** 41
plate mounting **178** 41
platen *Letterpress* **181** 13, 15, 29
platen *Bookbind.* **183** 24
platen *Office* **249** 18

platen *Graphic Art* **340** 31
platen knob **249** 22
platen machine **181** 13, 29
platen press **181** 13, 29; **340** 29
platen variable **249** 25
plate rack **178** 35
plate rod **178** 6
plate whirler **179** 1
platform *Wine Grow.* **78** 20
platform *Shoes* **101** 8
platform *Bldg. Site* **118** 87; **119** 52
platform *Station* **205** 1, 14
platform *Swim.* **282** 7, 8
platform *Art. Studio* **338** 30
platform, continental ~ **11** 8
platform, covered ~ **218** 49
platform, intermediate ~ **145** 5
platform, operator's ~ **168** 23
platform, wave-cut ~ **13** 31
platform clock **205** 46
platformer **145** 47
platform lighting **205** 48
platform loudspeaker **205** 27
platform mailbox **205** 56
platform number **205** 4
platform post box **205** 56
platform railing **118** 24
platform roofing **205** 5
platform scale **204** 5
platform seat **205** 54
platform sole **101** 8
platform telephone **205** 57
platform truck **194** 6
platypus **366** 1
play area **272** 44
playback deck **238** 4
playback deck, single ~ **238** 56
playback head **311** 25
player **48** 20
player's name **293** 36
playgoer **315** 8
playground, children's ~ **273**
playing card **276** 36, 37
play pen **28** 39
playsuit **29** 11, 19, 22
plaza de toros **319** 5
pleasure boat **283** 1
pleasure steamer **221** 101-128; **225** 29
pleasure vehicle **186** 33
pleat, front ~ **31** 25
plectrum **322** 19; **324** 20
Pleiades **3** 26
Pleiads **3** 26
pleiobar **9** 2
plexus, brachial ~ **18** 27
pliers, flat-nose ~ **126** 62; **140** 66
pliers, multiple ~ **134** 12
pliers, round-nose ~ **126** 64; **127** 50
pliers, shoemaker's ~ **100** 38
plinth *Dwellings* **37** 17
plinth *Carp.* **120** 28
plinth *Art* **334** 31
plinth, natural stone ~ **37** 85
Plough *Astron.* **3** 29
plough *Agr.* **63** 6
plough *Brew.* **92** 24
plough, four-furrow ~ **63** 40
plough, mounted ~ **65** 62
plough, reversible ~ **65** 62
plough, single-bottom ~ **65** 1
plough anchor **286** 16
plough beam **65** 9, 71
plough bottom **65** 4-8, 64-67
plough frame **65** 70
plough handle **65** 3
ploughshare **65** 7, 65; **328** 33
plough stilt **65** 3
plovers **359** 19-21
plow **63** 6
plow *see* plough
plowshare **328** 33
plucking device **322** 19
Pluderhose **355** 34
plug *Tobacc. etc.* **107** 19
plug *Plumb. etc.* **126** 55
plug *Metalwkr.* **140** 45
plug, double-jointed ~ **89** 70
plug, earthed ~ **127** 9
plug, multi-pin ~ **241** 70
plug, single-jointed ~ **89** 69
plug, three-pin ~ **127** 67
plugboard **242** 69
plug gauge **149** 56
plugging **123** 69
plugging sand bucket **158** 29
plug point **127** 5
plug point, double ~ **127** 6
plug socket **50** 78
plum **59** 25
plum, black-skinned ~ **59** 20
plum, oval ~ **59** 20
plumb bob **118** 50, 71
plumber **125; 125** 17; **126; 126** 1
plumber's tools **126** 58-86
plumbing fixtures **126** 26-37
plume *Heraldry* **254** 36
plume *Chivalry* **329** 78
plumicorn **88** 78; **362** 16
plum leaf **59** 21
plummet *Fish Farm.* **89** 91
plummet *Bldg. Site* **118** 50, 71
plum slice **97** 43
plum stone **59** 23
plum tree **59** 19-23
plumule **370** 90
plunger *Oil, Petr.* **145** 23
plunger *Glass Prod.* **162** 32
plunger *Car* **192** 7
plus sign **344** 7, 23
Pluto **4** 52
pneumatic pick longwall face **144** 35
pneumatophore **370** 82
pneume **320** 1
poacher **86** 29
pochette **322** 20
pocket, front ~ **30** 23; **33** 46; **260** 10
pocket, inset ~ **29** 63; **31** 4
pocket billiards **277** 7
pocket book **264** 36
pocket calculator **246** 12
pocket calculator, electronic ~ **247** 14
pocket camera **114** 16
pocket chamber **2** 15
pocket flap **33** 18
pocket meter **2** 15
pocket timetable **204** 42; **205** 45
pocket torch **127** 26
pocket train schedule **204** 42; **205** 45
pod **57** 6; **61** 20, 23; **69** 8, 16; **370** 92, 93; **378** 33; **384** 46
pod, immature ~ **374** 22
pod, mature ~ **383** 4
pod, pouch-shaped ~ **61** 11
pod, ripe ~ **383** 4
pod, unripe ~ **374** 22
pod corn **68** 31
poet's daffodil **60** 4
poet's narcissus **60** 4
point *Game* **88** 10, 31
point *Mach. Parts etc.* **143** 23, 54
point *Sculpt. Studio* **339** 15
point *Maths.* **346** 1-23
point, angular ~ **346** 1
point, diamond ~ **24** 40
point, equinoctial ~ **3** 6, 7
point, front ~ **300** 49
point, typographic ~ **175** 18
pointer *Hosp.* **26** 28
pointer *Dog* **70** 40, 43
pointer *Photog.* **114** 58
pointer *Inf. Tech.* **242** 76
pointer *Chem.* **349** 34
point guard **300** 50
pointing **122** 55
pointing sill **121** 47
point lace **102** 30
point light exposure lamp **179** 21
point lock **202** 28
point-of-aim mark **305** 56
point of Aries **3** 6
point of arrow **305** 61
point of contact **346** 49
point of hook **89** 80
point of inflexion **347** 21
point of intersection **346** 1
point of release **89** 34
point paper design **171** 4, 27
points, equinoctial ~ **3** 6-7
points, manually-operated ~ **202** 16
points, remote-controlled ~ **202** 27
points, single ~ **203** 45-48
points change indicator **197** 39
point shoe **314** 30
point size **175** 46
points knob **203** 62
points lever **203** 55
points mechanism, electric ~ **197** 43
points mechanism, electrohydraulic ~ **197** 43
points mechanism, electromechanical ~ **197** 43
points motor **202** 35
points of sailing **285** 1-13
points of the horse **72** 1-38
point source lamp **182** 4

points signal **197** 38; **202** 19
points signal, electrically illuminated ~ **202** 33
points signal lamp **202** 19
points signals **203** 45-52
point wire **202** 30
poison gland **77** 14
poison sac **77** 13
poitrel **329** 85
poke bonnet **306** 23; **355** 71
poker **38** 41; **137** 5
polar bear **368** 11
Polaris **3** 1, 34
polarizer **112** 14
polarizing filter **112** 19
polar sledge **303** 18
polar wind zone **9** 51
pole *Fruit & Veg. Gdn.* **52** 28
pole *Horse* **71** 21
pole *Fish Farm.* **89** 30
pole *Mills* **91** 32
pole *Carriages* **186** 19, 30
pole *Rivers* **216** 16
pole *Athletics* **298** 28
pole, bamboo ~ **307** 46
pole, celestial ~ **3** 1; **4** 24, 26
pole, geographical ~ **14** 3
pole, hooked ~ **77** 55
pole, terrestrial ~ **14** 3
pole chain **71** 20
pole horse **186** 47
pole mast **258** 42; **259** 6
Pole Star **3** 1, 34
pole vault **298** 28-36
pole vaulter **298** 29
poleyn **329** 53
polhode **4** 28
police **264**
police badge **264** 27
police dog **70** 25; **264** 5, 6
police duties **264** 1-33
police helicopter **264** 1
police identification disc **264** 26
police launch **221** 100
policeman **264** 18, 34
police officer **264** 18
police patrolman **264** 13
police signalling disc **264** 14
police van **264** 38
policewoman **264** 37
polishing **109** 17
polishing and burnishing machine **108** 42
polishing bonnet, lamb's wool ~ **134** 21
polishing brush **100** 11
polishing iron **108** 51
polishing machine attachment **109** 15
polishing wheel **108** 44
polish rod **145** 27
political section **342** 51
Politzer bag **22** 37
polje **13** 72
pollen **77** 3, 35; **370** 65
pollen basket **77** 6
pollen comb **77** 7
pollen sac **372** 45, 50
pollen tube **370** 66
pollex **19** 64
polling booth **263** 23
polling card **263** 19
polling number **263** 19
polling place **263** 16
polling station **263** 16
polo jumper, striped ~ **30** 20
polo neck jumper **30** 7
polo outsole **101** 24
polo saddle, high-back ~ **188** 13
polyamide **170** 34, 35, 37, 41
polyamide chip, dry ~ **170** 39
polyamide cone **170** 51, 52
polyamide fibres **170** 1-62
polyamide filament **170** 43
polyamide staple **170** 61, 62
polyamide thread **170** 46
polyanthus narcissus **60** 4
Polycheles **369** 15
polyester resin **130** 17
polygon **346** 40
polygon, eight-sided ~ **351** 17
polygon, five-sided ~ **351** 9
polygon, regular ~ **346** 41
polygon, six-sided ~ **351** 15
polyhedron **260** 73
polyhedron, eight-faced ~ **351** 6
polyhedron, forty-eight-faced ~ **351** 13
polyhedron, four-faced ~ **351** 1
polyhedron, regular ~ **351** 11
polyhedron, six-faced ~ **351** 2
polyhedron, twenty-faced ~ **351** 11
polyhedron, twenty-four-faced ~ **351** 12
polymerization **170** 33, 54
polyp, hydroid ~ **369** 9
polypod **377** 16
polypody **377** 16
pome **370** 102
pomegranate **384** 16
Pomeranian **70** 20
pomes **58**
pommel **296** 6
pommel horn **71** 38
pommel horse **296** 5
pommer **322** 14
pompier **270** 43
pompier ladder **270** 16
pompon **29** 4
pompon dahlia **60** 23
poncho **352** 24
pond *Map* **15** 79
pond *Park* **272** 50
pons **17** 46
pons cerebelli **17** 46
pons cerebri **17** 46
pontic, porcelain ~ **24** 29
pontoon **226** 57
pontoon, bottom ~ **222** 38
pontoon bridge **15** 46
pontoon dock **222** 34-43; **225** 16
pony **75** 4
ponytail **34** 27
poodle **70** 36
pool, indoor ~ **281** 1-9
pool, non-swimmers' ~ **282** 21
pool, swimmers' ~ **282** 23
pool attendant **281** 4; **282** 15
pool billiards **277** 7
poolroom **277** 7-19
poop **223** 33; **258** 22
poor man's weatherglass **61** 27
popcorn **68** 31
poplar **371** 15
poppy **51** 30; **61** 2
poppy flower **61** 4
poppy seed **61** 5
porcelain manufacture **161**
porcelain painter **161** 17
porcupine **366** 13
porifer **357** 13
pork **95** 38-54
pork, collared ~ **96** 9
porridge oats **98** 37
port *Ship* **220** 27
port *Docks* **225**; **226**
port administration offices **225** 36
portal **331** 16
portal, main ~ **333** 34
portal, recessed ~ **335** 24
portal figure **333** 36
portal frame **215** 38
portal relief **333** 35
portal spotlight **316** 21
portato **321** 29
portcullis **329** 24
port custom house **225** 6
port de bras à coté **314** 7
port de bras en avant **314** 9
port de bras en bas **314** 8
port de bras en haut **314** 10
porter *Brew.* **93** 26
porter *Station* **205** 31; **206** 33
porter *Hotel* **267** 17
porthole **117** 64
porthole, ornamental ~ **218** 57
port hospital **225** 26
portico **334** 50, 56
port liner **190** 73
port of registry **286** 8
ports de bras **314** 7-10
posaune stop **326** 17-22
position **224** 45
position indicator **246** 18
position light **257** 36; **288** 31
position light, left ~ **230** 50
position light, right ~ **230** 44
positions **314** 1-6
positions, arm ~ **314** 7-10
positive **322** 56
post *Dent.* **24** 34
post *Wine Grow.* **78** 7
post *Forestry* **84** 17; **85** 30, 47
post *Mills* **91** 34
post *Carp.* **120** 25
post *Roof* **121** 40, 81
post *Paperm.* **173** 50
post *Ball Games* **291** 37
post, broker's ~ **251** 3
post, principal ~ **120** 53
postage meter **22** 24; **236** 7
postage stamp **236** 61

postal code **236** 43
postal collection **236** 50-55
postal delivery **236** 50-55
postbox **236** 50
post code **236** 43
post crown **24** 31
poster **98** 2; **204** 10; **268** 71; **271** 25
posthorn **186** 41
post horse **186** 43
postman **236** 53
postmark, special ~ **236** 59
postmark advertisement **236** 56
postmarks **236** 56-60
post office **236; 237; 268** 68
post office box **236** 13, 14
post office savings counter **236** 25
post office van **236** 52
post-synchronization **311** 37-41
post-syncing **311** 37-41
post-sync sound **117** 101
post windmill **91** 31
pot *Kitch.* **39** 29
pot *Kitch. Utensils* **40** 12
pot *Plant Propagn.* **54** 8
pot, baby's ~ **28** 47
pot, centrifugal ~ **169** 17
potash salt bed **154** 65
potash salt seam **154** 65
potato **68** 38, 40
potato, flat-oval ~ **68** 38
potato, Irish ~ **68** 38
potato, kidney-shaped ~ **68** 38
potato, long ~ **68** 38
potato, pear-shaped ~ **68** 38
potato, purple ~ **68** 38
potato, red ~ **68** 38
potato, round ~ **68** 38
potato, round-oval ~ **68** 38
potato, white ~ **68** 38
potato, yellow ~ **68** 38
potato apple **68** 43
potato basket **66** 25
potato beetle **80** 52
potato berry **68** 43
potato chipper **40** 43
potato crisp **45** 41
potato dish **45** 31
potato fork **66** 5
potato harvester **64** 59-84
potato haulm **68** 41
potato hoe **66** 24
potato hook **66** 6
potato plant **68** 38
potato planter **66** 21
potato rake **66** 20
potato server **45** 75
potato top **68** 41
potato tuber **68** 40
potential transformer **153** 59
pot-helm **254** 7
pot-helmet **254** 7
pot holder **39** 18
pot holder rack **39** 19
pot plant **39** 37; **44** 25; **55** 25
potsherd **161** 21
potter's wheel **161** 11
pottery **308** 66
pottery, chip-carved ~ **328** 35
pottery stand **308** 64-66
potting bench **55** 12
potting table **55** 12
potty **28** 47
pouch, gular ~ **359** 8
poulaine **355** 42
poulard **98** 7; **99** 58
poultry **73** 19-36
poultry farming **74** 1-27
poultry keeping **74**
poultry management, intensive ~ **74** 1-27
pounce bag **129** 49
pouncing **129** 48
pound, lower ~ **217** 29
pound, upper ~ **217** 37
pound lock gate **217** 31
pound sterling **252** 37
pouring end **147** 34
pouring floor, sinking ~ **148** 24
pouring ladle lip **147** 43
powder, black ~ **87** 53
powder, smokeless ~ **87** 53
powder box **43** 28; **49** 35
powder charge **87** 57
powder flag **253** 38
power **345** 1
powerboat racing **286** 21-44
powerboats **286** 1-5
power control **100** 22
power hacksaw **138** 23
power hammer **137** 9
power house *Hydr. Eng.* **217** 21
power house *Shipbuild.* **222** 33
power house *Films* **310** 8
power lift **65** 24-29
power line **127** 23
powerpack unit **114** 66
power plant *Coal* **144** 13
power plant *Power Plant* **152; 153**
power plant *Glass Prod.* **162**
power regulator **100** 22
power saw *Forestry* **84** 22, 27; **85** 13
power saw *Blacksm.* **138** 23
power screwdriver **195** 23
power shovel **200** 1
power source **110** 7
power station *Coal* **144** 13
power station *Offshore Drill.* **146** 1
power station *Power Plant* **152; 153**
power station *Glass Prod.* **162**
power station *Hydr. Eng.* **217** 64
power supply *Arc Weld.* **142** 25
power supply *Energy Sources* **155** 21
power supply, external **115** 79
power take-off **63** 21; **64** 49
power take-off clutch **65** 40
power take-off gear **65** 38
power take-off gear-change **65** 23, 40
power take-off shaft **63** 21; **64** 49
power transformer **152** 30, 39
power unit **84** 34
power zooming arrangement **117** 19
prairie horse **352** 4
pralltriller **321** 19
pram *Infant Care etc.* **28** 34
pram *Docks* **226** 57
pram *Park* **272** 71
pram *Playground* **273** 31
pram, wicker ~ **28** 30; **48** 24
pram jacket **29** 3
pram suit **29** 1
prayer book **330** 62
prayer tower **337** 13
prayer wheel **353** 29
preacher **330** 22
precession **4** 24
precipitation **8** 18
precipitation, scattered ~ **8** 19
precipitation, types of ~ **8** 18-19
precipitation area **9** 30
precipitation gauge **10** 44
precipitator, electrostatic ~ *Power Plant* **152** 13
precipitator, electrostatic ~ *Coking* **156** 20
precipitator, electrostatic ~ *Cement Wks.* **160** 7
precipitator, electrostatic ~ *Paperm.* **172** 39
precision balance **108** 35
precision bench lathe **109** 20
precision file **140** 8
precision lathe **138** 20
predator, small ~ **86** 19, 20, 22
pre-distributor channel **236** 36
pre-drying **165** 50
preheater **212** 41
preheater, high-pressure ~ **152** 26
preheater, low-pressure ~ **152** 25
preheater pressure gauge **210** 43
preheater unit **185** 30
prehistory **328**
prelims **185** 43-47
pre-listening button **238** 46
pre-listening speaker **238** 50
premasher **92** 42
premixer **97** 58
pre-mixing room **238** 54-59
premolar **19** 18
préparation **314** 23
preparation and sterilization room **26** 34-54
preparation level **64** 16
preparation of surfaces **128** 1-17
preparation room **26** 34-54
prepuce **20** 70
presbytery **330** 32
prescription **22** 3, 20
present-day man **261** 21

preserve **98** 51
preserving jar **40** 25
preset control **316** 2
presorter **172** 21
presorting **64** 82
press *Joiner* **133** 51
press *Ball Games* **293** 32
press, first ~ **173** 19
press, rotary ~ *Text. Finish.* **168** 38
press, rotary ~ *Letterpress* **181** 57
press, second ~ **173** 20
press, web-fed ~ **181** 57
press-and-blow process **162** 30
press attachment **100** 15
press bar **100** 17
press bed **180** 78; **181** 17
press bowl, heated ~ **168** 41
press camera **114** 36
presser **103** 19
'press facilities' **233** 43
press finishing **168** 38
pressing *Glass Prod.* **162** 33
pressing *Paperm.* **173** 50
pressing cloth **104** 32
pressing cushion **104** 28
pressing mechanism **184** 13
pressing pad **104** 28
pressman **340** 35
press mould **162** 34
press photo **342** 58
press photographer **299** 49
press roll **173** 37
press roller **64** 64
pressure, atmospheric ~ **9** 4
pressure, barometric ~ **9** 4
pressure adjustment **249** 53
pressure adjustment, calibrated ~ **185** 5
pressure bulkhead **231** 32
pressure bulkhead, forward ~ **235** 19
pressure chamber **83** 44
pressure cloth **116** 59
pressure cooker *Kitch. Utensils* **40** 21
pressure cooker *Camping* **278** 35
pressure cylinder **133** 46
pressure foot **133** 47
pressure fuelling point **257** 33
pressure gas **156** 28
pressure gauge *Hosp.* **25** 53; **26** 29
pressure gauge *Overh. Irrign.* **67** 10
pressure gauge *Pest Contr.* **83** 42
pressure gauge *Blacksm.* **138** 15
pressure gauge *Electrotyp. etc.* **178** 8
pressure gauge *Offset Print.* **180** 74
pressure gauge *Garage* **195** 29
pressure gauge *Serv. Stat.* **196** 20
pressure gauge *Railw.* **211** 24
pressure gauge *Theatre* **316** 56
pressure graph **27** 31
pressure hull **258** 66; **259** 55, 76
pressure indicator **25** 55
pressure line **235** 54, 57
pressure pipe *Market Gdn.* **55** 8
pressure pipe *Hydr. Eng.* **217** 50
pressure pipe *Theatre* **316** 54
pressure pipeline **217** 41
pressure piston **133** 52
pressure plate **115** 24
pressure point **21** 14
pressure pot **129** 31
pressure pump, hydraulic ~ **178** 11
pressure-reducing valve **141** 5
pressure regulator *Gas Weld.* **141** 5
pressure regulator *Graphic Art* **340** 38
pressure release valve **155** 7
pressure tank **316** 55
pressure trace **25** 57
pressure transducer **27** 32
pressure valve **40** 22
pressure weight **168** 2
pressurized gas delivery system **234** 60
pressurized-water reactor **154** 19
pressurized-water system **154** 40
presto **321** 28
pretzel *Bakery* **97** 44
pretzel *Supermkt.* **99** 16
preventer **270** 15
preview monitor **238** 60
price *Equest.* **289** 37
price *Script.* **342** 41
price card **271** 19
price display **196** 6
price label **96** 6
price list *Butch.* **96** 19
price list *Grocer* **98** 73
price list *Bank* **250** 8
price offered **289** 37
pricket **330** 52
pricking off **54** 5
pricking out **54** 5
priest **330** 39; **331** 47
prima ballerina **314** 27
primary **153** 15
primary school **260** 1 85
primary voltage bushing **152** 43
primary voltage terminal **152** 43
primates **368** 12-16
prime focus cage **5** 2
Prime meridian **14** 5
primer **128** 6
prime steam line **154** 31
priming brush **338** 9
primitive man **261** 19
princess, German ~ **355** 20
principal **345** 7
principal diapason **326** 31-33
print delivery **249** 43
print drier, heated ~ **116** 57
print drier, rapid ~ **116** 57
printer *Garage* **195** 6
printer *Office* **245** 32
printer, rotating ~ **111** 27
printery **340** 27-64
printing, rotary ~ **178** 21
printing cylinder **177** 67
printing-down frame **179** 13
printing element **178** 39
printing image carrier **340** 59
printing office **340** 27-64
printing paper **180** 47
printing paper, photographic ~ **116** 51
printing plate **178** 38
printing speed adjustment **249** 55
printing surface **340** 59
printing unit **180** 41, 80
printing unit, first ~ **181** 48
printing unit, lower ~ **180** 7,9,11,13
printing unit, reversible ~ **182** 26
printing unit, second ~ **181** 52
printing unit, upper ~ **180** 6,8,10,12
print-out machine **195** 6
print quantity selection **249** 35
print tongs **116** 47
prism, hexagonal ~ **351** 21
prism, monoclinic ~ **351** 24
prism, quadratic ~ **347** 34
prism, triangular ~ **347** 37
private detective **275** 16
privet **373** 6
privet hawkmoth **358** 55
prize **306** 11; **308** 48
probe *Dent.* **24** 46
probe *Photog.* **114** 63; **116** 55
probe, bulb-headed ~ **22** 53; **26** 40
probe, hollow ~ **26** 41
probe, olive-pointed ~ **22** 53; **26** 40
probe exposure meter **114** 61
probe lead **116** 38
proboscidean **366** 20
proboscidian **366** 20
proboscis *Articulates* **358** 17, 56
proboscis *Mammals* **366** 21
procaviid **366** 24
process and reproduction camera, universal ~ **177** 24
process camera, overhead ~ **177** 1
process camera, vertical ~ **177** 32
process control computer **236** 37
processing drum **116** 48
processing laboratory **310** 2; **311** 30
processing machine **179** 31
processing plant **144** 5
processing unit, central ~ **176** 29

procession, religious ~ **331** 42-50
processionary moth **82** 14
processor, automatic ~ **116** 60
processor, central ~ **244** 6
proclamation **263** 14
proctoscope **23** 17, 19, 21
proctoscopy **23** 18
Procyon **3** 15
produce, agricultural ~ **68** 1-47
producer **316** 40
product **344** 25
production control room **238** 17
production line **173** 13-28
production manager **310** 26
production oil and gas separator **146** 9
product register **309** 82
profile **118** 69
profile, basic ~ **229** 45
profiling tool **161** 14
profit **345** 7
program *see* programme
program card **195** 5, 10
program input **177** 71
programme **315** 13
programme, computer-controlled ~ **238** 2
programme, educational ~ **261** 7
programme dial **243** 40
programmed individual presentation system **242** 15
programme monitor **238** 61
programmer **248** 15
programme recorder **261** 42
programme scale **243** 40
programme selector **243** 39
program selector control **50** 26
program selector switch **25** 50
progress counter **242** 5
projectile **255** 26
projection *Films* **311** 45
projection *Art* **335** 43
projection, conical ~ **14** 8
projection, cylindrical ~ **14** 9
projection booth **5** 27; **312** 12
projection dome **5** 21
projectionist **312** 20
projection lamp **312** 18
projection lens **261** 10; **312** 35
projection room **312** 12
projection room window **312** 15
projection screen *Optic. Instr.* **112** 24
projection screen *Broadcast.* **238** 32
projection screen *School* **260** 36
projection screen *Films* **310** 16; **312** 11
projection table **261** 13
projection window **312** 15
projector **5** 23; **316** 17
projector, lefthand ~ **312** 13
projector, overhead ~ **242** 6
projector, righthand ~ **312** 14
projector attachment **112** 55
projector gate **312** 34
projector lens **312** 35
projector mechanism **312** 25-38
projector switch **195** 20
projector top **261** 9
promenade **223** 27
promenade deck **223** 22-27
prominence, laryngeal ~ **19** 13
prominence, solar ~ **4** 40
prompt book **316** 41
prompt box **316** 27
prompter **316** 28
prompt script **316** 41
prone position *Free Exerc.* **295** 45
prone position *Sports* **305** 29
prong *Tablew. etc.* **45** 60
prong *Agr. Impl.* **66** 4
proof **340** 43
proofing press **180** 75
proof press **180** 75
prop *Household* **50** 37
prop *Circus* **307** 13
prop *Theatre* **315** 50
prop, front ~ **303** 8
prop, rear ~ **303** 9
propagation **54** 10, 14, 27
propagation of plants **54**
propane gas **278** 33
propane gas bottle **278** 34
propeller *Brew.* **92** 46
propeller *Energy Sources* **155** 45
propeller *Life-Sav.* **228** 26
propeller *Aircraft* **230** 32
propeller *Motorboats etc.* **286** 64
propeller *Airsports* **288** 36
propeller, feathering ~ **224** 19
propeller, reversible ~ **224** 19
propeller, ship's ~ **221** 44; **222** 72; **223** 62
propeller, three-blade ~ **223** 62
propeller, variable-pitch ~ **224** 19
propeller bracket **223** 61
propeller guard **258** 40
propeller guard boss **258** 63
propeller guard moulding **258** 74
propeller mixer **79** 6
propeller pitch indicator **224** 20
propeller post **222** 71
propeller pump **217** 47-52
propeller shaft *Car* **192** 30, 65
propeller shaft *Ship* **223** 65
propeller shaft *Aircraft* **232** 60
propeller shaft *Warships* **259** 59
propeller strut **223** 61
propeller-turbine engine **256** 16
propeller-turbine plane **231** 4
propelling nozzle **232** 39, 45, 49, 55
property **315** 50
proportion, simple ~ **345** 8-10
proportional dividers **339** 2
proprietor **248** 29; **266** 71
prop stand **187** 34; **188** 51
propulsion nozzle **232** 39, 45, 49, 55
propylaea **334** 7
proscenium **315** 15; **334** 46
proscenium, adjustable ~ **316** 22
prostate **20** 76
protection device **255** 81, 90
prothorax **82** 4; **358** 29
proton **1** 2, 16, 31
protoplasm **357** 3
protoprism **351** 19, 20
protopyramid **351** 19, 20
prototype **290** 38
protozoans **357** 1-12
protractor **260** 38
protrusion, massive ~ **11** 29
protuberance, frontal ~ **16** 4
pruner **56** 11
pruning knife **56** 9
pruning saw **56** 16
pruning shears **56** 50
prussic acid **83** 15
pseudocarp **58** 21; **384** 12, 62
pseudopod **357** 4
psychrometer **10** 52
pubis **17** 20
public conveniences **268** 62
publicity calendar **22** 10
puck **302** 35
pudding fender **227** 17
pudenda **16** 39
puffball **381** 19
puff paste **97** 18
puff pastry **97** 18
pug **70** 9; **123** 69
pug dog **70** 9
pull **340** 43
pull-down table **207** 53
pullet **74** 9
pullet fold unit **74** 5
pulley *Cotton Spin.* **164** 48
pulley *Bicycle* **187** 9
pulley, glass ~ **169** 16
pulley cradle **214** 36, 53
pulley cradle, main ~ **214** 67
pullover, heavy ~ **33** 52
pullover, men's ~ **33** 51
pullover, short-sleeved ~ **33** 32
pull rod *Mach. Parts etc.* **143** 101
pull rod *Railw.* **202** 20
pull-switch **127** 16
pull-through **87** 64
pull-up phase **298** 29
pulmonary function test **27** 36
pulp **58** 24, 35, 58; **59** 6
pulp, chemical ~ **172** 77, 78
pulp, dental ~ **19** 32
pulp, mechanical ~ **172** 77, 78
pulp-drying machine **172** 61
pulper **172** 80
pulpit **330** 19; **337** 15
pulpit balustrade **330** 23
pulpit steps **330** 18

pulp machine **172** 61
pulpstone **172** 71
pulp water pump **172** 55, 63
pulsator **75** 32
pulse cable **117** 72
pulse-generating camera **117** 71
pulse generator **313** 30
pulse generator socket **117** 7
pulse rate **23** 27
pulse shape **23** 37
pump *Agr. Mach.* **65** 45
pump *Shoes* **101** 29
pump *Oil, Petr.* **145** 22
pump *Synth. Fibres* **170** 31
pump, centrifugal ~ *Wine Cell.* **79** 7
pump, centrifugal ~ *Rivers* **216** 60
pump, centrifugal ~ *Water* **269** 44
pump, centrifugal ~ *Fire Brig.* **270** 8
pump, direct-connected ~ **83** 41
pump, hydraulic ~ *Agr. Mach.* **64** 29, 91
pump, hydraulic ~ *Theatre* **316** 53
pump, main ~ **269** 15
pump, motor-driven ~ **83** 41
pump, portable ~ **270** 52
pump, power take-off-driven ~ **67** 14, 15
pump compass **151** 59
pump compression spring **174** 41
pump connection **67** 8
pumpernickel **97** 49
pumping plant **217** 39-46
pumping rod **145** 25
pumping station *Offshore Drill.* **146** 22
pumping station *Hydr. Eng.* **217** 43
pumping station *Shipbuild.* **222** 33
pumping station *Spa* **274** 4
pumping unit **145** 22
pumpkin **57** 23
pump pressure spring **174** 41
pump room *Brew.* **92** 11
pump room *Spa* **274** 8, 15
pumps **2** 52
pump shaft **199** 19
pump strainer **269** 6, 14, 43
punch *Shoem.* **100** 45, 46
punch *Goldsm. etc.* **108** 19, 30, 31
punch *Office* **247** 3
punch *Sculpt. Studio* **339** 15
punch, foul ~ **299** 34
punch, hollow ~ **125** 13
punch, illegal ~ **299** 34
punch, revolving ~ **100** 44
punch, rotary ~ **100** 44
punch, round ~ **137** 36; **140** 65
punch, steel ~ **175** 36
punch, straight ~ **299** 28
punch bag **299** 21
punch ball **299** 24
punch ball, spring-supported ~ **299** 20
punch ball, suspended ~ **299** 23
punch blank **175** 35
punch card **237** 64
punch card reader **244** 12
punch cutter **175** 32
punched card **237** 64
punched card reader **244** 12
punched tape **176** 6, 8, 12; **237** 62, 68
punched tape input **176** 30
punched tape reader **176** 13, 15
punching bag **299** 21
punch tape **176** 6, 8, 12; **237** 62, 68
punch tape input **176** 30
punch tape reader **176** 13, 15
punctuation marks **342** 16-29
punt **216** 15; **283** 1
punt pole **89** 30; **216** 16
pup **73** 16
pupa **77** 30, 32; **80** 4, 25, 43; **81** 21, 24; **82** 13, 21, 32; **358** 20; **365** 11
pupa, coarctate ~ **81** 3
pupil *Man* **19** 43
pupil *School* **260** 3, 20
puppy **73** 16
pure culture plant **93** 6
purfling **323** 26
purge valve **6** 25
purified water tank **269** 13
purlin **119** 55; **121** 39, 51, 76
purlin, concrete ~ **119** 4
purlin, inferior ~ **119** 3; **121** 44; **122** 40
purlin roof **121** 46
purlin roof structure **121** 52, 60
purple clover **69** 1
purple medick **69** 9
purse wig **34** 4
push button **203** 67; **237** 18, 19; **241** 3
push-button keyboard **237** 10; **245** 14; **246** 14
push-button telephone **237** 20
pushchair **28** 37
pushchair, doll's ~ **48** 31
pusher ram **156** 7
pushing frame **200** 30
push sledge **304** 29
push tow **225** 60
push tug **221** 93
putlock **118** 27
putlog **118** 27
putter **293** 93
putting green **293** 82
putty **124** 17
putty knife **124** 27; **129** 24
puzzle **48** 9
pyelogram **27** 6
pyelogram cassettes **27** 14
pyelography **27** 4
pygmy poodle **70** 36
pyjamas **32** 17, 36
pyjama top **32** 18
pyjama trousers **32** 19
pylon *Railw.* **214** 31, 77
pylon *Art* **333** 9
pylon, tubular steel ~ **214** 78
pylorus **20** 42
pyramid *Fruit & Veg. Gdn.* **52** 16
pyramid *Circus* **307** 28
pyramid *Art* **333** 1
pyramid, glass ~ **5** 19
pyramid, orthorhombic ~ **351** 23
pyramid, quadrilateral ~ **347** 46
pyramid, stepped ~ **333** 22; **352** 20
pyramid site **333** 6
pyramid tree **52** 16; **272** 19
pyrheliometer **10** 23
pyrite **351** 8
pyrometer **178** 16
pyx **330** 8; **332** 53
pyxidium **370** 95

Q

quack grass **61** 30
quadrant **347** 5
quadraphonic system **241** 13-48
quadra/stereo converter **241** 46
quadrilateral, irregular ~ **346** 39
quadrilaterals **346** 33-39
quadruplet **321** 23
quail **359** 22
quail call **87** 45
quake, tectonic ~ **11** 32-38
quake, volcanic ~ **11** 32-38
quantity, unknown ~ **345** 4, 8
quant pole **89** 30; **216** 16
quantum jump **1** 15
quantum jumps **1** 20-25
quantum transitions **1** 20-25
quarantine wing **225** 27
quarrier **158** 5
quarry *Map* **15** 87
quarry *Quarry* **158** 1
quarryman **158** 5
quarry worker **158** 5
quarte engagement **294** 47
quarter *Shoem.* **100** 61
quarter *Carp.* **120** 25
quarter, first ~ **4** 4
quarter, last ~ **4** 6
quarter, third ~ **4** 6
quarter baulk **120** 90
quarter gallery **218** 57
quarterings **254** 18-23
quartering wind **285** 13
quarter light **191** 23
quarter note **320** 15
quarter of beef **94** 22
quarter piece **329** 88
quarter rest **320** 23
quarters, firemen's ~ **270** 2
quarter vent **191** 23

quarter wind **285** 13
quartz **110** 15
quartz-halogen lamp **179** 21; **182** 3
quartz watch, electronic ~ **110** 14
quatrefoil **335** 39
quaver **320** 16
quaver rest **320** 24
quay **222** 5; **225** 64
quayside crane **225** 24
quayside railway **225** 21
quayside road **225** 38
quayside roadway **225** 38
quayside steps **283** 22
quay wall **217** 1-14
queen *Bees* **77** 4, 38
queen *Games* **276** 9
queen bee **77** 4
Queen Carnival **306** 61
queen cell **77** 37
queen-excluder **77** 47
queen post **121** 46, 52, 68
queen truss **121** 65
Queen Victoria water lily **378** 17
quenching car **156** 10
quenching tower **156** 11
quenching trough **137** 8
question mark **342** 20
queue **34** 6; **319** 26
quickbeam **371** 42
quick grass **61** 30
quick hitch **65** 86
quicksand **227** 3
quid **107** 19
quill **341** 26
quillons **294** 42
quill pen **341** 26
quill plectrum **322** 53
quilting **29** 39; **30** 17
quilt stitching **29** 39; **30** 17
quince, apple-shaped ~ **58** 49
quince, pear-shaped ~ **58** 50
quince leaf **58** 47
quince tree **58** 46
quinquefoliolate **370** 39
quintuplet **321** 23
quipa **352** 22
quitch grass **61** 30
quiver **352** 27
quoin **181** 39
quoit **280** 32; **308** 47
quoits **280** 31
quotation **250** 8
quotation board **251** 8
quotation mark, double ~ **342** 26
quotation mark, French ~ **342** 27
quotient **344** 26

R

rabbet plane **132** 25
rabbit **73** 18; **86** 23; **88** 65
rabbit burrow **86** 26
rabbit fence **84** 7
rabbit hole **86** 26
rabbit net **86** 27
raccoon **368** 9
race, inner ~ **143** 72
race, outer ~ **143** 71
race board **166** 42
racehorse **289** 51
raceme **58** 15; **374** 33
raceme, simple ~ **370** 68
raceway **91** 44
racing **289** 50
racing, motor-paced ~ **290** 11-15
racing and passenger aircraft **230** 1-31, 32-66; **231** 1
racing bicycle **290** 16
racing boats **283** 9-16
racing car **290** 38
racing cars **290** 34-38
racing cycle **290** 15, 16
racing cyclist **290** 8
racing dive **282** 29
racing flag **284** 48
racing handlebar **290** 18
racing jersey **290** 9
racing keelboat **285** 35
racing motorcycle **290** 27
racing motorcycle, streamlined ~ **290** 31
racing motorcyclist **290** 25
racing outboard motor **286** 23
racing saddle **290** 17
racing sculler **283** 16
racing shell, eight-oared ~ **283** 10
racing suit **301** 31
racing toe clip **290** 21
racing tyre **290** 19
rack *Kitch. Utensils* **40** 31
rack *Composing Rm.* **174** 8
rack *Garage* **195** 10
rack *Railw.* **214** 9, 11
rack, removable ~ **40** 24
rack and pinion **112** 39
rack-and-pinion railway **214** 4-5
rack-and-pinion railways **214** 7-11
racket **293** 29
racket handle **293** 30, 46
racket press **293** 32
rack for glasses **274** 16
rack head **163** 16, 18
racking back **118** 61
rack mountain railway **214** 4-5
rack railroad **214** 4-5
rack railroad car **214** 5
rack railroad locomotive, electric ~ **214** 4
rack railway coach **214** 5
rack railway locomotive, electric ~ **214** 4
rack railways **214** 7-11
rack railway trailer **214** 5
rack track **217** 69
racoon **368** 9
racquet *see* racket
radar antenna **223** 8; **224** 104; **258** 36; **259** 8, 29, 48, 91
radar apparatus **224** 10-13
radar display unit **224** 12
radar dome *Aircraft* **231** 18
radar dome *Air Force* **256** 10
radar dome *Warships* **258** 52, 77; **259** 49
radar equipment **224** 10-13
radar image **224** 13
radar nose **231** 18; **256** 10
radar pedestal **224** 10
radar picture **224** 13
radar reflector **10** 58
radar reflector, revolving ~ **224** 11
radar scanner **223** 8; **224** 104; **258** 36; **259** 8, 29, 48, 91
radar screen **224** 12
radial side of the hand **19** 69
radiant energy **10** 23
radiation, solar ~ **155** 18
radiation detectors **2** 1-23
radiation meters **2** 1-23
radiation monitor **2** 1
radiation shield **2** 31, 46
radiation shielding **2** 31
radiation unit **24** 23
radiator *Doc.* **23** 23
radiator *Roof & Boilerr.* **38** 76
radiator *Agr. Mach.* **65** 51
radiator *Plumb. etc.* **126** 20
radiator *Energy Sources* **155** 15
radiator *Car* **191** 9
radiator *Railw.* **212** 54
radiator bonnet **304** 11
radiator brush **129** 21
radiator grill **191** 11
radiator heating **155** 27
radiator hood **304** 11
radiator rib **38** 77; **126** 21
radiators **6** 8
radiator shutter **304** 12
radical **345** 2
radicle **370** 88
radio **238**; **239**
radioactive waste storage **154** 56
radio antenna **197** 34
radio cassette recorder **241** 1
radio communication set **197** 28
radio compass **230** 5
radio direction finder antenna **223** 5; **224** 106
radio direction finder frame **258** 17
radio equipment **197** 28; **230** 22; **288** 13, 17
radiographer **27** 11
radiolarian **357** 8
radio link, intercontinental ~ **237** 54-55
radiometer **10** 71
radio navigation equipment **230** 22
radio OB van **239** 1-15
radiophone **22** 14
radio room **223** 12
radioscope box **74** 47
radioscope table **74** 48
radiosonde **10** 59
radiosonde assembly **10** 55
radio station **238** 1-6

radio switching centre control room **238** 7-15
radio system **6** 26
radio telephone **212** 23
radish **57** 15
radish, white ~ **57** 16
radius *Man* **17** 13
radius *Mills* **91** 2
radius *Maths.* **346** 47
radius of curvature **346** 22
radome *Aircraft* **231** 18
radome *Air Force* **256** 10
radome *Warships* **258** 52, 77; **259** 49
raffia **136** 29
raffle **306** 11
raft **283** 60
rafter **121** 28, 36; **122** 19
rafter, common ~ **121** 56
rafter, principal ~ **121** 55
rafter end **121** 45; **122** 41
rafter head **121** 45; **122** 41
rafter roof **121** 27
rag bolt **143** 43
rag felt **122** 62
ragged robin **376** 21
rail *Atom* **2** 37
rail *Livestock* **75** 16
rail *Joiner* **133** 41
rail *Mach. Tools* **150** 12
rail *Railw.* **202** 1
rail *Station* **205** 59; **206** 38
rail *Railw.* **214** 10
rail *Restaurant* **266** 72
rail *Equest.* **289** 2
rail *Birds* **359** 20
rail, triangular ~ **242** 80
rail bottom **202** 4
rail brake **206** 48
railcar **205** 25
railcar, articulated ~ **197** 1, 13
railcar, front ~ **211** 61
railcar, light ~ **208** 13
railcar, short-distance ~ **208** 13
railcar, six-axle ~ **197** 13
railcar, twelve-axle ~ **197** 1
rail clip **202** 9
rail foot **202** 4
rail guard **210** 34
rail head **202** 2
railing *Bldg. Site* **118** 89
railing *Park* **272** 34
rail joint **202** 11
railroad *see* railway
railroad map **204** 33
railroad policeman **205** 20
railroad station **15** 41
railroad ticket **204** 36
railroad track **202; 203**
rail service, interurban ~ **197** 1
rail service, urban ~ **197** 13
railway, funicular ~ **214** 12
railway, light ~ **200** 23
railway, main line ~ **15** 21
railway, narrow-gauge ~ *Map* **15** 90
railway, narrow-gauge ~ *Road Constr.* **200** 23
railway guide, official ~ **204** 50
railway information clerk **204** 49
railway line **202; 203**
railway map **204** 33
railway policeman **205** 20
railway siding **225** 62
railway station **15** 41
railway ticket **204** 36
railway vehicles **207; 208; 209; 210; 211; 212; 213**
rail web **202** 3
rain **8** 18; **9** 32
rainbow **7** 4
rainbow, colours of the ~ **343** 14
rainbow dressing **221** 85
rain cape **41** 4; **196** 26
rain cloud **8** 10
raincoat **29** 31
rain cover **10** 41
rain gauge **10** 38, 44
rainwater pipe **37** 13; **38** 10; **122** 29
rain zone, temperate ~ **9** 55
rain zone, tropical ~ **9** 53
raisin **98** 8
raising of livestock **75**
raising to a power **345** 1
rake *Roof & Boilerr.* **38** 42
rake *Gdn. Tools* **56** 4
rake *Blacksm.* **137** 4
rake *Roulette* **275** 5
rake *Winter Sp.* **303** 24
rake, wire-tooth ~ **51** 3; **56** 3
rake, wooden ~ **66** 23
raking back **118** 61
Ram *Astron.* **4** 53
ram *Dom. Anim.* **73** 13
ram *Blacksm.* **137** 10
ram *Forging* **139** 12
ram *Ship* **218** 9
ram *Theatre* **316** 60
ram, lower ~ **139** 7
ram, upper ~ **139** 6
rambler **52** 5
ram guide **139** 8
ram longwall face **144** 36
rammer **200** 26
rammer, pneumatic ~ **148** 31
ramp *Bldg. Site* **119** 41
ramp *Floor etc. Constr.* **123** 30
ramp *Station* **206** 1
ramp *Ship* **221** 55
ram piston **65** 21
ramson **377** 6
randing **136** 1, 4
randing, oblique ~ **136** 3
rangefinder **255** 82
rangefinder, optical ~ **258** 37
rangefinder window **114** 40
range light, higher ~ **224** 102
range light, lower ~ **224** 101
range lights **224** 101-102
range selector **114** 59
range switch **114** 59
rape **383** 1
rapelling **300** 28-30
rapid adjustment compass **151** 64
rapid feeding system **74** 23
rapid-filter plant **269** 9
rapid heat-up cathode **240** 25
rapid-loading system **115** 25
rapid scale **98** 12
rapid-veneer press **133** 49
rapping iron **136** 36
raptorial leg **358** 5
Raschel fabric **167** 29
rasp **260** 55
rasp, shoemaker's ~ **100** 49
raspberry **58** 28; **370** 101
raspberry bush **58** 25
raspberry flower **58** 26
ratan chair cane **136** 32
rate-of-climb indicator **230** 14
rate of interest **345** 7
rattan chair cane **136** 32
rattle *Infant Care etc.* **28** 44
rattle *Carnival* **306** 40, 47
rattle, baby's ~ **28** 44
rat trap binding **301** 15
Rautek grip **21** 18
ravine **13** 52
raw coal bunker **144** 41
raw material *Cement Wks.* **160** 1, 4
raw material *Synth. Fibres* **169** 1-12
raw material store **160** 3
raw meal silo **160** 5
raw milk pump **76** 3
raw milk storage tank **76** 5
raw mill **160** 4, 7
ray *Church* **332** 37
ray *Maths.* **346** 20
ray, medullary ~ **370** 11
ray, vascular ~ **370** 11
rays, sun's ~ **4** 9
razor, open ~ **106** 38
razor, straight ~ **106** 38
razor handle **106** 39
R-class **284** 59
reach, lower ~ **217** 29
reach, upper ~ **217** 37
reaching leg **285** 24
reactor **154** 3, 41, 50
reactor, nuclear ~ **1** 48; **154** 19
reactor building **154** 20
reactor core **259** 68
reactor pressure vessel **154** 22
reader **260** 16
reading adjustment **10** 10
reading lamp **43** 15
reading microscope **113** 28
reading room **262** 13
reading room staff **262** 14
readout, digital ~ **110** 2; **112** 47
readout, fast ~ **195** 12
ready position **305** 72
reamer **109** 8; **140** 31
reamer, angled ~ **125** 9
rear brace **329** 47
rearing of livestock **75**
rear of the railcar **197** 4
rear seat headrest **193** 8
rear seat head restraint **193** 8
rearsight **255** 22, 36

rear vault **297** 32
rear-view mirror **188** 35; **189** 30
rear-view mirror, inside ~ **191** 39
rearward horizontal stand **295** 31
rearward swing **296** 57
rear window heating switch **191** 82
rebate plane **132** 25
receipt **98** 44; **271** 7
receipt stamp **236** 29
receiver *Meteorol. Instr.* **10** 63
receiver *Hunt.* **87** 16
receiver *Docks* **226** 33
receiver *Audio* **241** 40
receiver *Office* **246** 16
receiver *Ball Games* **293** 50
receiver *Nightclub* **318** 18
receiver cord **237** 14
receiver surface, blackened ~ **155** 29
receiving hopper **147** 5
receiving table **249** 54
receiving tray **249** 47
receiving truck **226** 15
receptacle **370** 53
reception *Doc.* **22** 5
reception *Camping* **278** 1
reception hall **267** 1-26
receptionist, chief ~ **267** 7
recess **217** 70
reciprocal **344** 16
recirculation pump **154** 43, 54
record **46** 15; **309** 32; **317** 24
record changer, automatic ~ **241** 52
recorder *Meteorol. Instr.* **10** 61
recorder *Hosp.* **25** 3
recorder *Music. Instr.* **322** 7
recorder, eight-channel ~ **27** 28
recorder, open-reel-type ~ **241** 56
recorder, potentiometric ~ **23** 55
recording, photographic ~ **27** 33
recording amplifier **311** 11
recording and playback deck, single ~ **238** 58
recording and playback equipment **311** 23
recording arm **10** 7, 12, 15, 21
recording channel, central ~ **238** 1-6
recording drum **10** 5, 16, 20
recording engineer **310** 23, 55; **311** 36
recording head *Cine Film* **117** 33
recording head *Audio* **241** 59
recording head *Films* **311** 25
recording instrument **10** 61
recording level control **117** 16
recording level display **243** 15
recording level indicator **243** 12; **311** 14
recording level meter **241** 35, 36, 61; **242** 14
recording level meters **241** 35-36
recording loudspeaker **238** 37
recording mechanism **10** 42
recording meter **138** 19
recording paper **25** 4; **27** 29, 34, 40
recording pen **10** 13
recording rain gauge **10** 38
recording room **238** 16; **310** 54
recording room mixing console **238** 25
recording sensitivity selector **117** 16
recording space **177** 49
recording speaker **238** 37
recording tape **241** 58
record keeper **299** 48
record of posting book **236** 18
record player **241** 18; **317** 19
record player base **241** 19
record player housing **241** 19
record rack **309** 36
record storage compartment **241** 48
record storage slot **241** 48
record turntable **238** 24
recovery parachute **235** 60
recovery vehicle, armoured ~ **255** 93
rectangle **346** 34
rectifier *Blacksm.* **138** 30
rectifier *Electrotyp. etc.* **178** 2
rectifier *Films* **312** 18
rector **330** 22
rectory **331** 20
rectoscope **23** 16, 17
rectoscopy **23** 18
rectum **20** 22, 61
rectus abdominis **18** 44
red **343** 1
red admiral **365** 1
red-billed toucan **363** 6
redbreast **361** 15
redcap **205** 31
red card **291** 63
red clover **69** 1
red deer **88** 1, 1-27
red flyer **366** 3
red fox **88** 42; **367** 12
red kangaroo **366** 3
red magnolia **373** 15
redstart **360** 3
red swing filter **116** 46
reducing coupler **126** 39, 41
reducing elbow **126** 49
reducing socket **126** 39, 41
reducing valve **141** 5
reduction drive lever **149** 3
reduction gear *Paperm.* **172** 69
reduction gear *Aircraft* **232** 59
reduction gear *Warships* **259** 61
reduction gearing, multi-step ~ **64** 71
red underwing **365** 8
red whortleberry **377** 23
red wine glass **45** 83
reed *Basketm.* **136** 28
reed *Weaving* **166** 10
reed *Music. Instr.* **326** 41
reed, double ~ **323** 29
reed mace **136** 27
reed mace bulrush **378** 21
reed organ **325** 43
reed pen **341** 22
reed pipe, metal ~ **326** 17-22
reed stop **326** 17-22
reed-threading draft **171** 6
reef **219** 72
reefer **221** 127
reel, fixed-spool ~ **89** 32, 61
reel, multiplying ~ **89** 59
reel, spring-tine ~ **64** 4
reel, stationary-drum ~ **89** 61
reel arm, foldaway ~ **117** 92
reel drum **312** 16
reel drum, fireproof ~ **312** 25
reel gearing **64** 5
reeling machine **173** 41
reel of film **312** 33
reel oven **97** 71
reels **89** 59-64
reel stand **180** 3, 19
referee **291** 62; **293** 67; **299** 16, 41
referee's position **299** 8
reference book **262** 17
reference library **262** 17
refill **151** 46
refill lead **151** 46
refiner **172** 84
refiner, conical ~ **172** 27, 60, 73, 83
refining bath **162** 4
reflected-light microscope **112** 23
reflecting goniometer **351** 28
reflector *Atom* **1** 65
reflector *Optic. Instr.* **113** 1
reflector *Bicycle* **187** 45
reflector, glass ~ **187** 86
reflector, swivel-mounted ~ **114** 69
reflector pedal **187** 78
reflex angle **346** 10,11-12
reflex camera, twin-lens ~ **114** 22
reflex finder **117** 44
reflex mirror **115** 33
reflex system **115** 31
reformer **145** 47
reformer, catalytic ~ **145** 71
refractometer **111** 44
refractometer, dipping ~ **112** 48
refractor **113** 16
refreshment kiosk **205** 49
refreshment stall **308** 3
refrigeration system **93** 11
refrigerator **39** 2; **46** 33; **317** 10
refrigerator car **213** 39
refrigerator shelf **39** 3
refrigerator van **213** 39
refrigerator wagon **213** 39
refuse **199** 17

refuse, compacted and decomposed ~ **199** 22
refuse collection vehicle **199** 1
refuse container **199** 4
refuse disposal **199**
refuse incineration unit **199** 28
regatta **283** 1-18
regatta course **285** 14-24, 16
register *School* **260** 23
register *Hotel* **267** 8
register *Music. Instr.* **322** 51
register device **177** 12
register mark **340** 58
registration form **267** 12
registration number *Election* **263** 19
registration number *Motorboats etc.* **286** 7
reglet **334** 57
regula **334** 17
regular crystal system **351** 1-17
regular customer **266** 40
regular grade gasoline **145** 54
regular grade petrol **145** 54
regulating handle **133** 14
regulating valve **38** 75
regulator **109** 32
regulator main valve **210** 13
regulator valve **210** 13
Regulidae **361** 10
rehearsal **315** 21-27
reheating **162** 27, 35
reichstaler **252** 6
rein **71** 33; **186** 31; **289** 27; **303** 4
reindeer **353** 16
reindeer harness **353** 15
reinforced concrete construction **119** 1-89
reinforcement **119** 54-76, 68
reinforcement, projecting ~ **119** 10, 71
reinforcement, steel-bar ~ **123** 37
reinforcement beading **125** 8
reinforcement binding **119** 66
reinforcement rod **119** 23
reinforcing member, longitudinal ~ **230** 47, 57
reinforcing rib *Road Constr.* **200** 9
reinforcing rib *Hydr. Eng.* **217** 78
reinforcing steel **119** 23
reinforcing strut **315** 31
reins **71** 25, 33
rejects chest **172** 59
relay **186** 43
relay horse **186** 43
release *First Aid* **21** 34
release *Weaving* **165** 35
release, delayed-action ~ **309** 51
release binding **301** 2
release grip **21** 34
release lever *Slaughterho.* **94** 6
release lever *Office* **247** 42
release/lock lever **247** 42
release phase **75** 33
release valve **210** 58
relief image carrier **340** 2
relief printing method **340** 1-13
relief tile, glazed ~ **333** 20
remainder **344** 24
remains **15** 72
Remington cartridge **305** 39
remittee **250** 19
remnant **103** 16
remote control jack **117** 9
remote control panel **157** 14
remote control radio **288** 87
remote control socket **117** 9
rendering, exterior ~ **122** 38
rendering coat **123** 6
'rendezvous point' **233** 29
rendezvous radar antenna **6** 42
reniform **370** 38
rennet vat **76** 48
repair bay **196** 22
repairer **161** 19
repair quay **222** 10
repair shop **196** 22
repeater **87** 2
repeaters **253** 30-32
repeating rifle **87** 2
repeat mark **321** 26
replenishing ship **258** 97
report **342** 54
reproducing head **241** 59
reptile enclosure **356** 12
reptiles **364** 27-41
requin **364** 1
re-recording **311** 1-46
re-reeler **173** 41
re-reeling machine **173** 41
rescue **21** 18-23, 28-33, 34-38
rescue cruiser **221** 18; **228** 14
rescue helicopter **221** 20; **228** 16
rescuer **21** 29, 34
research laboratory **310** 9
research microscope **112** 1, 66
research microscope, binocular ~ **23** 51
research rocket **7** 24
reserve fuel tank **212** 60
reserve tank **232** 20
reservoir *Hydr. Eng.* **217** 39-46
reservoir *Air Force* **257** 16
reservoir, impounded ~ **217** 57
reservoir rock **12** 29
reset button *Cine Film* **117** 86
reset button *Car* **191** 77
resetting button **127** 20
resetting spring **237** 49
residential area **15** 28
residue **145** 43
resin **323** 11
resin, synthetic ~ **130** 26
resistor **153** 56
resonating body **322** 29; **323** 3; **324** 2, 15, 26
resonating chamber **322** 18; **324** 15, 63
resonating sound box **324** 26
resonator **322** 18, 29; **324** 2, 15
resonator, tubular metal ~ **324** 78
resonator wall **322** 33
respiration, artificial ~ **21** 24-27
respirator **21** 27; **26** 25
respiratory apparatus **21** 27; **26** 24
respiratory functions **23** 31
respiratory machine **26** 1
respiratory rate **23** 27
respond **335** 35
'restaurant' *Airport* **233** 50
restaurant **266** 1-29
restaurant car **207** 22-32
restaurant car, self-service ~ **207** 73
rest cure **274** 12-14
resting rail **322** 42
restoring spring **237** 49
restricted area **292** 37
rests **320** 20-27
result register **309** 82
results of sets **293** 35
resuscitation **21** 24-27
resuscitation, mouth-to-mouth ~ **21** 26
resuscitation, mouth-to-nose ~ **21** 26
resuscitation apparatus **21** 27
resuscitation equipment **270** 20
resuscitator **21** 27; **270** 20
retailer **98** 41
retail shop **98** 1-87
retail store **98** 1-87
retaining plate **167** 56
retarder **206** 48
reticella lace **102** 30
reticule **115** 61
Reticulum **3** 48
retina **19** 49
retort **349** 13
retort ring **350** 15
retoucher **182** 14
retouching and stripping desk **177** 19
retrieving **86** 36
retrofocus position **115** 84
return **38** 79
return pipe **38** 56, 79, 80; **126** 24
return spring *Knitting* **167** 37
return spring *Car* **192** 55
return [illegible] **330** 49
Reuther board **296** 12; **297** 8
rev counter **189** 41; **191** 38; **212** 22; **230** 8
rev counter, electric ~ **191** 70
rev counter, electronic ~ **188** 40
reveal **37** 26; **118** 10; **120** 31
revenue stamp **107** 26
revers collar **30** 9
reverse **252** 9
reverse dive **282** 41
reverse gear **192** 44
reverse hang **296** 34
reverse shaft **149** 34
reversing catch **87** 24

reversing clutch **115** 27
reversing gear **210** 18; **211** 53; **212** 74
reversing gears **65** 41
reversing ring **115** 83
reversing wheel **210** 56
revertive signal panel **153** 7
revetment **216** 51-55
revolution counter **189** 41; **191** 38; **212** 22; **230** 8
revolution counter, electric ~ **191** 70
revolution counter, electronic ~ **188** 40
revolving die hammer **85** 12
reward **86** 43
rewind **114** 6; **115** 12
rewind bench **238** 59; **312** 21
rewind button **249** 73
rewind cam **115** 29
rewind crank **114** 6; **115** 12
rewinder *Cine Film* **117** 93
rewinder *Paperm.* **173** 41
rewind handle *Photog.* **114** 6; **115** 12
rewind handle *Cine Film* **117** 93
rewinding **170** 50
rewind release button **115** 27
rewind station **173** 41
rhesus macaque **368** 12
rhesus monkey **368** 12
rhinoceros **366** 25
Rhiptoglossa **364** 33
rhizome **58** 18
rhizopod **357** 1
rhomb **346** 35
rhombic crystal system **351** 23
rhombohedron **351** 22
rhomboid **346** 36
rhombus **346** 35
rhubarb flan **97** 22
rhynchophore **358** 4
rib *Meat* **95** 3
rib *Floor etc. Constr.* **123** 36
rib *Basketm.* **136** 24
rib *Shipbuild.* **222** 58
rib *Aircraft* **230** 46
rib *Rowing* **283** 49
rib *Sailing* **285** 51
rib *Music. Instr.* **322** 33; **323** 4, 25
rib *Art* **335** 31
rib *Bot.* **370** 29
rib, annular ~ **235** 47
rib, false ~ **287** 36
rib, flat ~ **95** 21
rib, fore ~ **95** 18
rib, main ~ *Space* **235** 10
rib, main ~ *Gliding* **287** 35
rib, middle ~ **95** 19
rib, prime ~ **95** 18
rib, top ~ **95** 31
ribbon **34** 7; **355** 78
ribbon, corded ~ **35** 13
ribbon, fancy ~ **35** 14
ribbon cassette **249** 16
ribbon of glass **162** 10
ribbon selector **249** 11
ribbon window **37** 86
Ribes **58** 1-15
ribgrass **380** 11
rib randing **136** 2
ribs, false ~ **17** 10
ribs, true ~ **17** 9
rib vault **336** 43
rib weave, combined ~ **171** 19
ribwort **380** 11
ribwort plantain **380** 11
rice *Arable Crops* **68** 1; **68** 29
rice *Grocer* **98** 38
rice grain **68** 30
rickshaw **353** 34
rickshaw coolie **353** 35
rickstand **63** 28, 29
riddle **55** 13
ride *Map* **15** 112
ride *Forestry* **84** 1
rider *Cyc. Racing* **290** 25
rider *Chem.* **349** 33
rider bar **349** 31
rider holder **349** 32
ridge *Phys. Geog.* **12** 36; **13** 60
ridge *Dwellings* **37** 7
ridge *Roof* **121** 2; **122** 93
ridge *Mountain.* **300** 21
ridge, concave ~ **302** 22
ridge, hollow ~ **302** 22
ridge beam **121** 48
ridge board **121** 48
ridge capping piece **122** 99
ridge course **122** 47, 79
ridge course tile **122** 4
ridge cross **331** 10
ridge hook **122** 65
ridge joint **122** 79
ridge purlin **121** 43
ridge rope **221** 118
ridge tent **278** 21; **280** 45
ridge tile **122** 3, 8, 52
ridge turret **121** 14
ridge vent **55** 11
ridging hoe **56** 5
riding animal **354** 2
riding cap **289** 14
riding seat **296** 32
riding switch **289** 22
riffler **172** 2; **173** 13
rifle, self-loading ~ **255** 16
rifle, short ~ **86** 30
rifle, single-loading ~ **87** 1
rifle, triple-barrelled ~ **87** 23
rifle barrel **87** 26
rifle butt **255** 24
rifle cleaning kit **87** 61-64
rifle grip *Photog.* **115** 100
rifle grip *Films* **313** 37
riflescope **87** 29; **305** 49
rifle shooting **305** 26
rifling **87** 36
rifling calibre **87** 37
rig **219** 1-72
Rigel **3** 13
rigging **219** 1-72
rigging, running ~ **219** 67-71
rigging, standing ~ **219** 10-19
right **254** 18,20,22
right angle **346** 9, 32
right corner pin **305** 8
right front second pin **305** 4
right hook **299** 33
right tank fuel gauge **230** 17
rim *Bicycle* **187** 28
rim *Motorcycle* **189** 25
rim *Car* **191** 16; **192** 77
rim brake **187** 5
rimfire cartridge **305** 35
rind **120** 86; **370** 8
ring *Jewell.* **36** 4
ring *Forestry* **85** 4
ring *Fish Farm.* **89** 56
ring *Cotton Spin.* **164** 51, 54
ring *Sports* **299** 35
ring *Circus* **307** 21
ring *Bullfight. etc.* **319** 9
ring *Church* **332** 17
ring *Maths.* **346** 57
ring *Chem.* **350** 15
ring, all-round ~ **89** 58
ring, annual ~ **84** 24
ring, asymmetrical ~ **36** 27
ring, diamond ~ **36** 23, 24
ring, front ~ **113** 7
ring, gemstone ~ **36** 15
ring, man's ~ **36** 20
ring, rubber ~ *Kitch. Utensils* **40** 26
ring, rubber ~ *Bathing* **280** 32
ring, spring-steel ~ **89** 51
ring and bead sight, optical ~ **305** 51
ring attendant **307** 27
ring cake **97** 33; **99** 22
ringed snake **364** 38
ring entrance **307** 11
ring fence **307** 22
ring file **260** 15
ring finger **19** 67
ring frame **164** 34
ring gauge **108** 25, 27
ring gemstones **36** 72-77
ringmaster **307** 31
ring net **90** 25
ring plectrum **324** 27
ring rail **164** 42, 54
ring-rounding tool **108** 26
rings **296** 4
ring sight, optical ~ **305** 50
ring snake **364** 38
ring spindle, standard ~ **164** 45
ring spinning frame **164** 34
ring tube *Cotton Spin.* **164** 52
ring tube *Weaving* **165** 15
riot duty **264** 15
riot gear **264** 18
riot shield **264** 20
rip panel **288** 75, 83
rip panel, emergency ~ **288** 72
ripper **200** 20
ripping line **288** 76
ripping line, emergency ~ **288** 73
ripple marks **13** 41
riprap **216** 51
rise adjustment **133** 21
rise adjustment wheel **133** 22
rise and fall adjustment wheel **132** 60
riser *Floor etc. Constr.* **123** 33, 48
riser *Iron Foundry etc.* **148** 22
riser *Water* **269** 19

riser *Fire Brig.* **270** 26
riser *Airsports* **288** 42
riser *Sports* **305** 55
riser gate **148** 22
riser pipe **269** 19
rise to straddle **296** 49
rising **283** 31
Rising Sun **253** 20
ritual cart, miniature ~ **328** 36
ritual chariot, miniature ~ **328** 36
river *Phys. Geog.* **13** 61
river *Map* **15** 76
river *Rivers* **216** 31
river, navigable ~ **15** 45
river, subterranean ~ **13** 83
river arm **13** 2; **216** 3
river arm, blind ~ **216** 18
riverbank **216** 5
riverbed **13** 68
river bend **13** 11
river branch **13** 2; **216** 3
river branch, blind ~ **216** 18
river engineering **216**
river ferry **216** 10
river island **216** 4
river islet **216** 4
river mouth **13** 1
river nymph **272** 2; **327** 23
river police **217** 24
rivers **216**
river terrace **13** 49, 63
river tug **216** 23
river valley **13** 57-70
rivet **143** 57-60
rivet head **143** 57
riveting **143** 56
riveting machine **138** 27
rivet shank **143** 58
riving hammer **85** 5
rivulet *Phys. Geog.* **13** 8
rivulet *Map* **15** 80
road **37** 61
road, bituminous ~ **200** 55
road, good ~ **15** 30
road, main ~ **15** 83
road, metalled ~ **15** 30
road, poor ~ **15** 99
road, secondary ~ **15** 36
road, unmetalled ~ **15** 99
road bridge **15** 55
road building **200**; **201**
road-building machinery **200** 1-54
road coach **186** 39
road construction **200**, **201**
road form **201** 15
road layers **198** 1-5
road making **200**; **201**
road-metal spreading machine **200** 31
road over railway **15** 22
road race **290** 8-10
road race bicycle **290** 16
road racer **290** 8
road racing **290** 16, 24-28
road ripper **200** 20
road roller **200** 36
roadster *Bicycle* **187** 1
roadster *Car* **193** 26
road surface **215** 8; **217** 1
road sweeper **199** 5; **268** 20
road-sweeping lorry **199** 41
roadway, orthotropic ~ **215** 2
road wheel **255** 86
roast **45** 27
roasting chicken **98** 6
roasting drum **98** 71
roasting round **95** 11
robe de chambre **355** 66
robes **330** 22; **332** 4
robin **361** 15
robin redbreast **361** 15
robot **273** 36
rocaille **336** 13
rock **13** 25; **327** 38; **356** 2
rock, blasted ~ **158** 4
rock, coal-bearing ~ **144** 49
rock, impermeable ~ **12** 23; **13** 78
rock, impervious ~ **12** 23; **13** 78
rock, loose ~ **158** 4
rock, piece of ~ **6** 15
rock, sedimentary ~ **12** 1; **13** 48
rock, stratified ~ **13** 48
rock bit **145** 21
rock climbing **300** 2-13
rocker *Child. Rm.* **47** 16
rocker *Winter Sp.* **302** 19
rocker *Music. Instr.* **326** 39
rocker *Graphic Art* **340** 19
rocker arm **190** 33
rocker arm mounting **190** 34
rocker switch **127** 4
rockery **37** 40; **51** 6
rocket *Life-Sav.* **228** 2
rocket *Army* **255** 26, 65
rocket *Carnival* **306** 54
rocket, short-range ~ **259** 26
rocket apparatus **228** 1
rocket cruiser **259** 21, 41
rocket engine **6** 3
rocket engine, liquid-fuelled ~ **235** 36
rocket engine, main ~ **235** 36
rocket gun **228** 1
rocket launcher **255** 64, 70
rocket launcher, underwater ~ **259** 37, 51
rocket line **228** 3
rocket stage, first ~ **234** 3
rocket stage, second ~ **234** 18
rocket stage, third ~ **234** 33
rocket tube **255** 71
rock face *Phys. Geog.* **12** 43; **13** 28
rock face *Quarry* **158** 15
rock face *Mountain.* **300** 2
rock garden **37** 40; **51** 6
rock goat **367** 7
rocking chair **309** 61
rocking tool **340** 19
rock island **13** 12
rock ledge **300** 4
rock painting **328** 9
rock plant **51** 7
rock rose **377** 20
rock salt **351** 2
rockslide **11** 46
rock slip **11** 46
rock spike **300** 9
rock terrace **13** 47
rock tomb **333** 38
rock wall **300** 2
rod, carbon-fibre ~ **89** 57
rod, glass ~ **89** 49, 57
rod, iron ~ **130** 3
rod, metal ~ **339** 24
rod, polished ~ **145** 27
rod, telescopic ~ **89** 53
rodents **366** 12-19
rodeo **319** 34
rodeo rider **319** 39
rod rest **89** 23
rods **89** 49-58
rod section **89** 54
rod tip **89** 35
roe *Game* **88** 28-39
roe *Fish Farm.* **89** 12
roe, female ~ **88** 34
roebuck **86** 17; **88** 28
roe call **87** 43
roe deer **88** 28-39
roll *Kitch. Utensils* **40** 31
roll *Tablew. etc.* **45** 21
roll *Horse* **71** 48
roll *Supermkt.* **99** 12
roll *Athletics* **298** 17
roll, brown ~ **97** 13
roll, filled ~ **266** 54
roll, lower ~ **148** 55
roll, upper ~ **148** 54
roll, white ~ **97** 14
roll bar *Agr. Mach.* **65** 21
roll bar *Motorcycles etc.* **188** 18
roll bar *Car* **193** 13
roll bearing **148** 60
roll cutter **173** 42
roller *Hairdresser* **105** 12
roller *Cooper* **130** 26
roller *Glass Prod.* **162** 11
roller *Weaving* **165** 57
roller *Road Constr.* **200** 37
roller *Station* **206** 39
roller *Hydr. Eng.* **217** 65
roller *Office* **249** 17
roller *Cyc. Racing* **290** 13
roller *Graphic Art* **340** 12
roller *Birds* **359** 25; **360** 6
roller, bottom ~ **164** 10
roller, fluted ~ **164** 10
roller, grooved ~ **130** 30
roller, lambskin ~ **130** 31
roller, leather ~ **340** 23
roller, lower ~ *Iron Foundry etc.* **148** 55
roller, lower ~ *Cotton Spin.* **164** 10
roller, rubber ~ **182** 8
roller, rubber-disc ~ **64** 82
roller, steel ~ **164** 10
roller, submersible ~ **217** 68
roller, three-wheeled ~ **200** 36
roller, top ~ **164** 11
roller, upper ~ *Iron Foundry etc.* **148** 54
roller, upper ~ *Cotton Spin.* **164** 11
roller, wire-covered ~ **168** 34

roller bearing **164** 47
roller bit **145** 21
roller chain *Bicycle* **187** 36
roller chain *Intern. Combust. Eng.* **190** 25
roller chain, double ~ **190** 10
roller covering **50** 3
roller guide **201** 4
roller path **148** 50
roller postmark **236** 60
roller printing machine, ten-colour ~ **168** 53
rollers **148** 54-55
roller stamp **236** 46
roller table **157** 23
roller top **217** 66
roller trestle **157** 26
rollfilm **114** 19
rollfilm spool **114** 20
roll holder **40** 1
rolling **230** 71
rolling circle **288** 3
rolling dam **217** 65-72
rolling mill **148** 46-75
rolling plant **159** 9
rolling road **138** 16
rolling shutter frame **37** 29
rolling stock **207; 208; 209; 210; 211; 212; 213**
roll-on roll-off operation **225** 39
roll-on roll-off ship **226** 17
roll-on roll-off system **225** 39
roll-on roll-off trailer ferry **221** 54
rollover device **139** 43
rolls *Bakery* **97** 13-16
rolls *Iron Foundry etc.* **148** 54-55
roll stand **148** 56-60
roll unit **97** 61
roll-up door **245** 5
Roman **355** 11
Roman woman **355** 7
romper **29** 21
romper suit **29** 22
roof **37** 5; **38; 121; 122; 337** 2
roof, cement ~ **122** 97
roof, flat ~ **37** 77
roof, glass ~ **55** 5
roof, hipped ~ **37** 64; **121** 10, 60
roof, imperial ~ **121** 25
roof, mission-tiled ~ **122** 56
roof, pantiled ~ **122** 53
roof, paper ~ **122** 90
roof, pitched ~ **38** 12
roof, plain-tiled ~ **122** 50
roof, sliding ~ **193** 24; **194** 10; **213** 22
roof, snow-covered ~ **304** 20
roof, Spanish-tiled ~ **122** 56
roof, split-tiled ~ **122** 45
roof, swivelling ~ **213** 26, 27
roof, tiled ~ **122** 1
roof beam **121** 29
roof board **122** 61
roof boarding **122** 61
roof cable **211** 5
roof cladding **38** 1
roof course **122** 78
roof covering **38** 1
roofer **122**
roof guard **38** 8
roof hook **38** 6
roofing, cement ~ **122** 90-103
roofing, paper ~ **122** 90-103
roofing felt **122** 62
roofing nail **143** 55
roofing paper **122** 62
roof ladder **38** 4; **122** 63
roof lashing **278** 51
roof opening **213** 23
roof rack **278** 50
roofs, styles and parts of ~ **121** 1-26
roof sheathing **122** 61
roof structures of timber **121** 27-83
roof trestle **122** 66
roof truss **120** 7; **121** 78
roof valley **121** 15; **122** 11, 82
roof ventilator **278** 56
rook *Games* **276** 12
rook *Birds* **361** 2
room, double ~ **267** 27-38
room, heated ~ **169** 24
room divider **42** 19
room key **267** 9
room number **267** 10
room telephone **267** 34
room thermostat **38** 78
room trader **251** 6
room waiter **267** 33
rooster **62** 37; **73** 21
root *Man* **19** 36
root *Plant Propagn.* **54** 21
root *Arable Crops* **68** 17, 45
root *Horse* **72** 34
root *Maths.* **347** 12
root *Bot.* **370** 16-18
root *Industr. Plants* **383** 43
root, adventitious ~ **370** 78, 80
root, aerial ~ **370** 80
root, primary ~ **370** 16
root, secondary ~ **370** 17
root, tuberous ~ **370** 79
root crops **68** 38-45
rooter **200** 20
root gall **80** 27
root hair **68** 18; **370** 18
root louse **80** 26
roots **54** 12; **370** 78-82
rootstock **54** 33
root thorn **370** 81
rope *First Aid* **21** 30
rope *Weaving* **166** 61
rope *Swim.* **282** 32
rope *Gymn.* **296** 19; **297** 43
rope *Mountain.* **300** 12, 22-27
roped party **300** 22-27
rope ladder **221** 91; **273** 49; **307** 8
rope-pulley hoist **118** 91
ropes **299** 36
rope sling **300** 11
ropeway, aerial ~ **15** 67
ropeway, double-cable ~ **214** 25, 30
ropeway gondola **214** 52
ropeways **214** 15-38
ropeways, endless ~ **214** 15-24
ropeways, single-cable ~ **214** 15-24
ropeway support **214** 76
roping down **300** 28-30
ro-ro depot **226** 20
ro-ro-ship **226** 17
ro-ro system **225** 39
ro-ro trailer ferry **221** 54
rosary **332** 30
rose *Market Gdn.* **55** 28
rose *Game* **88** 5, 29
rose *Music. Instr.* **324** 5
rose, bush ~ **52** 13
rose, climbing ~ **52** 12
rose, double ~ **60** 17
rose, ivory ~ **36** 29
rose, rambling ~ **52** 12
rose, standard ~ **51** 25; **52** 21
rosebay **373** 13
rosebud **60** 16
rose cut **36** 45
rose-ear **70** 2
rose hip **370** 100
rose laurel **373** 13
rose thorn **60** 18
rose tree, standard ~ **52** 13, 21
rosette **306** 34
rose window **335** 23
rosin **323** 11
rostrum **263** 6; **316** 34
rotary engine, two-rotor ~ **190** 5
rotary-table machine **150** 41
rotary-table shot-blasting machine **148** 39
rotary turbine pump **259** 57
rotated grasp **296** 44, 46
rotation **298** 18
rotation axis **351** 4
rotator **224** 55
rotisserie **40** 32
rotogravure press, multicolour ~ *Photograv.* **182** 24
rotor *Clocks* **110** 32
rotor *Intern. Combust. Eng.* **190** 68
rotor *Aircraft* **232** 22
rotor *Gliding* **287** 18
rotor, main ~ **232** 12-13; **256** 19; **264** 3
rotor, tail ~ **256** 20
rotor, tilting ~ **232** 32
rotor blade *Energy Sources* **155** 45
rotor blade *Aircraft* **232** 12
rotor head **232** 13
rotor pylon **232** 23
rouge **275** 24
rough **293** 80
rough focusing indicator **224** 35
roughing file **134** 9
roughing-out hammer **195** 46
roughing wheel **111** 36
roulette *Roulette* **275** 1-33, 28
roulette *Graphic Art* **340** 18
roulette ball **275** 33
roulette bowl **275** 29

roulette layout **275** 9, 17
roulette player **275** 15
roulette table **275** 8
roulette wheel **275** 10, 28
round **95** 14
round, caseless ~ **305** 37
roundabout **308** 2
round bar reinforcement **119** 80
round-bilge boat **286** 32-34
round end **95** 52
rounding machine *Bakery* **97** 63
rounding machine *Plumb.* **125** 30
roundwood **120** 35; **157** 30
round worm **81** 31
route **203** 68
route indicator **203** 20, 21
route lever **203** 58
route of the paper **180** 26
route of the sheets **180** 33
route of the web **180** 26
router plane **132** 26
route sign **197** 21
route straight ahead **203** 45, 49, 50
roving **164** 29
roving bobbin **164** 23
row **312** 9
rowan **371** 42
rowboats **283** 9-15
rowing **283**
rowing boat **89** 27
rowing boat, Germanic ~ **218** 1-6
rowing boats **283** 9-15
rowing coach **283** 20
rowlock **278** 18; **283** 29, 41
row of needles **167** 27
row of needles, back ~ **167** 46
row of needles, front ~ **167** 47
row of seats, tiered ~ **261** 1
royal **88** 8
Royal Crown, English ~ **254** 42
royal fern **377** 16
royal osmund **377** 16
royal stay **219** 13
royal water lily **378** 17
rubber, synthetic ~ **164** 11
rubber belt, studded ~ **64** 79
rubber plant **383** 33
rubber solution **340** 49
rubber tree **383** 33
rubber tyre cable car **273** 53
rubber tyre swing **273** 18
rubbing strake, reinforced ~ **258** 81
rubbish **268** 22
rubble **11** 47
rubble, rough ~ **269** 37
ruby **175** 22
ruby, synthetic ~ **110** 33
Rückpositiv **326** 5, 42
rucksack **283** 65
rudder *Ship* **218** 6, 24; **221** 43
rudder *Shipbuild.* **222** 69
rudder *Ship* **223** 63
rudder *Life-Sav.* **228** 26
rudder *Aircraft* **229** 25; **230** 60
rudder *Air Force* **257** 23
rudder *Rowing* **283** 51-53, 53
rudder *Sailing* **284** 9, 34; **285** 34
rudder *Motorboats etc.* **286** 65
rudder *Airsports* **288** 22
rudder, retractable ~ **285** 37
rudder, vertical ~ **259** 95, 96
rudder angle indicator **224** 17
rudder blade **221** 43; **222** 69; **223** 63; **283** 53; **284** 34
rudderhead **284** 33
rudder pedal **230** 27; **257** 10
rudder pedal, co-pilot's ~ **230** 28
rudder post **222** 70
rudder stock **222** 68; **284** 33
ruff *Carnival* **306** 20
ruff *Hist. Cost.* **355** 52
rugby **292** 19
rugby ball **292** 21
rugby football **292** 19
rule **151** 33
rule, folding ~ **120** 76; **134** 33
rule, glazier's ~ **124** 21
rule of three sum **345** 8-10
rule pocket **33** 49
ruler **151** 33; **247** 35
ruling pen **151** 49
ruling pen attachment **151** 58, 61
rum **98** 57
ruminant **73** 1
ruminants **366** 28-30; **367** 1-10
rummer **45** 87
rump *Horse* **72** 31
rump *Game* **88** 20, 36
rump *Meat* **95** 14, 35
rump piece **329** 88
runch **61** 18
rune **341** 19
rung **38** 17; **50** 38
runner *Plant Propagn.* **54** 14, 16
runner *Soft Fruit* **58** 20
runner *Mills* **91** 22
runner *Iron Foundry etc.* **148** 21
runner *Rowing* **283** 45
runner *Ball Games* **292** 45, 66
runner *Athletics* **298** 5
runner, movable ~ **303** 10
runner, outrigged ~ **302** 46
runner bean **52** 28; **57** 8
runner gate **148** 21
running **298** 1-8
running axle **210** 35
running-boar target **305** 33
running dog **334** 39
running gear, front ~ **191** 52
running head **185** 66
running light **258** 56
running light, side ~ **258** 15
running light indicator panel **224** 29
running posture **295** 2
running side **277** 5
running step **295** 41
running step indicator **211** 36
running take-off twist dive **282** 43
running three **305** 3, 5
running title **185** 66
running track **298** 6
running wheel **64** 41, 56; **214** 7, 70
runout **147** 54
runway *Hunt.* **86** 16
runway *Airport* **233** 1
runway *Gliding* **287** 15
rush *Phys. Geog.* **13** 17
rush *Basketm.* **136** 27
rusk **97** 54
Russula vesca **381** 23
rustication **335** 51
rustic work **335** 51
rutting mane **88** 27
rutting season **86** 9-12
rye **68** 1, 2
rye bread **97** 10, 49
rye-bread roll **97** 16
rye flour **97** 52
ryegrass, perennial ~ **69** 26

S

sabaton **329** 55
saber *see* sabre
sable *Ladies' Wear* **30** 60
sable *Heraldry* **254** 26
sable *Mammals* **367** 15
sabot **101** 47
sabre, light ~ **294** 20, 34
sabre fencer **294** 19
sabre fencing **294** 19-24
sabre gauntlet **294** 21
sabre glove **294** 21
sabre mask **294** 22
sabreur **294** 19
sack **38** 34
sacker **92** 39
Sacrament **331** 48
sacrarium **330** 32
sacristan **330** 26, 58
sacristy **331** 13
sacristy door **330** 17
sacrum **17** 21; **20** 59
saddle *Phys. Geog.* **12** 16, 42
saddle *Mach. Tools* **149** 13
saddle, adjustable ~ **188** 4
saddle, English ~ **71** 45-49
saddle, reciprocating ~ **185** 24
saddle, unsprung ~ **290** 17
saddle, western ~ **71** 37-44
saddle apron **149** 16
saddleback roof **37** 5; **121** 1
saddle bag **187** 25
saddle clip **126** 53
saddle-pad **71** 17, 31
saddle roof **37** 5; **121** 1
saddles **71** 37-49
saddle seat **71** 37
saddle spring **187** 23
saddle stitching **31** 45
saddle tree **374** 1
safe **246** 22
safelight **116** 21
safety bar **301** 58
safety binding **301** 2

safety bonnet **85** 36
safety brake **85** 15
safety catch *Atom* **2** 40
safety catch *Household* **50** 25
safety catch *Hunt.* **87** 8, 24
safety catch *Army* **255** 14
safety catch, sliding ~ **87** 25
safety chain **126** 3
safety current **127** 2
safety curtain **316** 24
safety device **290** 13
safety equipment **316** 18
safety glass **124** 5
safety glasses **140** 21
safety helmet **84** 23; **120** 13; **140** 22; **158** 10; **300** 53
safety helmet, shock-resisting ~ **127** 48
safety hood **85** 36
safety jet **301** 53
safety key **140** 48
safety latch **50** 25
safety lighting **312** 6
safety lock **140** 44
safety net *Warships* **259** 18
safety net *Circus* **307** 14
safety nut **187** 64
safety pin **328** 27
safety rail **119** 43
safety valve *Roof & Boilerr.* **38** 70
safety valve *Railw.* **210** 3
safety wall **122** 35
saffron milk cap **381** 29
saggar **161** 2
sagger **161** 2
Sagittarius **3** 37; **4** 61
sagittate **370** 37
sago **98** 39
sago palm **383** 58
sail **219** 1-72; **283** 62; **284** 2; **285** 8
sail, ballooning ~ **285** 4
sail, brailed-up ~ **218** 21
sail, fore-and-aft ~ **220** 15
sail, furled ~ **218** 21
sail, square ~ **218** 21, 33; **219** 55-66; **220** 16
sail axle **91** 5
sailboat *Playground* **273** 29
sailboat *Camping* **278** 12
sailboat *Sailing* **284** 10-48
sailboat, single-masted ~ **220** 6-8
sailboats, mizzen-masted ~ **220** 9-10
sailboats, two-masted ~ **220** 11-17
sailing **284; 285**
sailing barge, ketch-rigged ~ **220** 9
sailing boat *Playground* **273** 29
sailing boat *Camping* **278** 12
sailing boat *Sailing* **284** 10-48
sailing boat, single-masted ~ **220** 6-8
sailing boats, mizzen-masted ~ **220** 9-10
sailing boats, two-masted ~ **220** 11-17
sailing close-hauled **285** 10
sailing downwind **285** 1
sailing ship **219; 220**
sailing ships, development of ~ **220** 35-37
sailing ships, four-masted ~ **220** 28-31
sailing vessels, three-masted ~ **220** 18-27
sailing with free wind **285** 12
sailing with wind abeam **285** 11
sailor suit **309** 62
sailplane **287** 3
sailplane, high-performance ~ **287** 9
sails, fore-and-aft ~ **219** 20-31
sail shapes **220** 1-5
sail top **91** 6
sainfoin **69** 10
saint, Buddhist ~ **337** 10
Saint Andrew's cross bond **118** 65
salad **266** 51
salad bowl **45** 23
salad chicory **57** 40
salad cream **96** 29
salad drawer **39** 4
salad fork **45** 68
salad oil **98** 24; **99** 66
salad plants **57** 36-40
salad servers **45** 24
salad spoon **45** 67
salamander **364** 22
salamanders **364** 20-22
sal-ammoniac block **125** 6
sales area **99** 4
sales check **98** 44; **271** 7
salesclerk **98** 13
sales counter **271** 42, 61
salesgirl **97** 1; **98** 31; **99** 17; **271** 18, 63
saleslady **97** 1; **98** 31; **99** 17; **271** 18, 63
salesman **309** 29
sales premises **111** 1-19
sales shelf **99** 23
sales statistics **248** 46
salicional **326** 23-30
salientians **364** 23-26
salina *Map* **15** 32
salina *Spa* **274** 1-7
sallow **371** 24
salon, men's ~ **106** 1-42
salon mirror **105** 20; **106** 6
saloon, lower ~ **194** 37
saloon, upper ~ **194** 38
saloon car **193** 4, 25
salt **98** 40
salt, common ~ **1** 9
salta **276** 20
salta piece **276** 21
salt cake storage tank **172** 36
salt cellar **266** 77
salt mine **154** 57-68, 72
saltstick **97** 31
salt water outlet **145** 33
salt water pipe **145** 33
salt water tank **146** 17
salt works *Map* **15** 32
salt works *Spa* **274** 1-7
salt works attendant **274** 5
saltzstange **97** 31
salvage **227**
salvage tug **227** 5, 16
salvaging **227** 1
Salvator beer **93** 26
salving **227** 1
sampan **353** 31
sample beam **115** 36
sample sagger **161** 2
sample scoop **98** 72
samson post **223** 35
samson post, ventilator-type ~ **221** 58
samurai **353** 37
sanctuary **330** 32
sanctuary lamp **330** 49
sanctus bell **330** 46
sand *Map* **15** 6
sand *Bldg. Site* **118** 36; **119** 26
sandal **101** 51
sandal, ladies' ~ **101** 49
sandal court shoe **101** 27
sandbag **216** 50; **288** 65
sandbank **227** 3
sand bed **123** 8
sand belt, endless ~ **133** 15
sand box *Railw.* **212** 59, 76
sandbox *Playground* **273** 64
sandcastle **280** 35
sand delivery pipe **148** 38
sand deposit **216** 52
sand dome **210** 14
sander **129** 30
sander, orbital ~ **134** 53
sander, single-belt ~ **133** 30
sander control **211** 32
sander switch **211** 32
sandhill **273** 66
sand hills **15** 6
sanding **129** 28
sanding attachment, orbital ~ **134** 53
sanding belt, endless ~ **133** 15
sanding belt regulator **133** 14
sanding disc **134** 25
sanding dust extractor **133** 28
sanding machine, single-belt ~ **133** 30
sanding table **133** 35
sanding valve **210** 55
sanding wheel **133** 27
sand lizard **364** 27
sandpaper **128** 14; **129** 25; **135** 25
sandpaper block **128** 13; **129** 26
sand pipe **210** 15, 19
sandpit **273** 64
sand star **369** 11
sand table **173** 13
sand track racing **290** 24-28
sand trap *Paperm.* **173** 13
sand trap *Ball Games* **293** 81
sand tube **210** 15
sandwich **45** 39
sandwich, open ~ **45** 37; **266** 75
sandwich board **308** 50
sandwich man **308** 49

sanitary articles **99** 35
San-José scale **80** 35
Sanserif **342** 7
Sanserif type **342** 7
Sanskrit **341** 9
sap **120** 85; **370** 12
sappho **363** 4
sapwood **120** 85; **370** 12
sarcophagus **335** 53
sardine server **45** 78
sardines in oil **98** 19
Sargon's Palace **333** 29
sartorius **18** 45
Satan's mushroom **379** 12
satchel **260** 9
sate **137** 34
satellite **4** 45
satellite radio link **237** 51-52
satellite sounding **7** 33
satin stitch **102** 10
Saturn **4** 49
Saturn V **234** 1, 2
sauceboat **45** 17
sauce ladle **45** 18
saucepan **40** 16
saucer **44** 30
sauna, mixed ~ **281** 18
sauna stove **281** 21
sausage **98** 4; **99** 54
sausage, beef ~ **96** 11
sausage, pork ~ **96** 11; **99** 55
sausage, scalded ~ **96** 8
sausage filler **96** 49
sausage fork **96** 44
sausage meat **96** 41, 52
sausages **96** 6-11
sausages, manufacture of ~ **96** 31-59
sausage stuffer **96** 49
sausage tongs **308** 35
savings account **250** 4
savoy **57** 33
savoy cabbage **57** 33
saw, butcher's ~ **94** 19
saw, circular ~ **119** 19; **125** 24; **134** 50
saw, free-cutting ~ **84** 32
saw, two-handed ~ **120** 68
saw, vertical frame ~ **157** 2
sawbill **359** 15
saw blade **120** 62; **150** 16; **157** 3, 47; **260** 54
saw carriage **132** 71; **133** 38
saw chain **84** 35; **85** 14; **85** 15; **120** 16
saw frame **138** 25; **150** 17; **157** 8
saw guide **85** 16
saw handle **132** 4
sawing shed **120** 3
sawmill **144** 6; **157** 1
saw rasp **134** 6
saw set **132** 42
saw-sharpening machine **157** 42
saw tooth **96** 33
sawtooth roof **121** 20
saxboard **283** 43
saxifrage, rotundifoliate ~ **375** 1
saxophone **324** 69
scaffold **118** 25; **122** 34; **222** 18
scaffold, steel ~ **5** 18
scaffold, supporting ~ **14** 50
scaffold, tubular steel ~ **119** 46
scaffold board **122** 70
scaffolding **215** 62
scaffolding, tubular steel ~ **119** 46
scaffolding joint **118** 30
scaffold pole **118** 23
scaffold standard **118** 23
scalding colander **96** 45
scale *Map* **14** 29
scale *Chem.* **349** 35
scale *Fish etc.* **364** 11
scale *Decid. Trees* **371** 12
scale *Conifers* **372** 34, 42, 45, 50
scale, triangular ~ **151** 34
scale, wax ~ **77** 25
scale adjustment **116** 34
scale armour **329** 64
scaled prickle fungus **381** 24
scale insect **80** 35
scale louse **80** 35
scale pan *Kitch. Utensils* **40** 37
scale pan *Chem.* **349** 36
Scales *Astron.* **3** 19; **4** 59
scales *Doc.* **22** 66
scales *Kitch. Utensils* **40** 35
scales *Child. Rm.* **47** 33
scales *Supermkt.* **99** 88
scales *Photog.* **114** 58
scales *Music. Not.* **320** 45-49
scaling hammer **137** 38
scallop shell **309** 46
scalp **352** 15
scalpel **26** 43
scalper **340** 7
scaly ant-eater **366** 10
scanner **177** 39
scanner film **177** 72
scanning drum **177** 45
scanning head **177** 46, 63
scanning zone **243** 47
scantling **120** 10
scape **370** 52
scapula **16** 23; **17** 7
scar **11** 48
scarecrow **52** 27
scarf *Ladies' Wear* **31** 57
scarf *Men's Wear* **33** 65
scarf *Headgear* **35** 16
scarf *Bullfight. etc.* **319** 38
scarf joint, oblique ~ **121** 88
scarf joint, simple ~ **121** 87
scarifier **200** 20
scarlet pimpernel **61** 27
scarlet runner **52** 28; **57** 8
scarlet runner bean **57** 8
scarp **13** 57
scatter cushion **42** 27; **46** 17
scauper **340** 7
scaur **11** 48
scaw **11** 48
scene *Theatre* **316** 36
scene *Art* **334** 45
scene number **310** 35
scene painter **315** 35
scene-repeat key **243** 42
scenery **316** 35
scenery projector **316** 17
scene shifter **315** 28; **316** 46
scenic artist **315** 35
scenic railway **308** 39
scent, artificial ~ **289** 49
sceptre, fool's ~ **306** 59
schalmeyes **322** 14
schedule **204** 16
schedule, engineer's ~ **210** 52
Scheidt globe **349** 1
schilling **252** 13
schizocarp **370** 94
schnauzer **70** 35
schnorkel *Warships* **259** 72, 90
schnorkel *Swim.* **279** 11
schnorkel *Bathing* **280** 39
school **260**; **261**
school bag **260** 7
school book **47** 25
school children's wear **29** 31-47
school figure **289** 7
school horse **289** 3
school satchel **260** 9
schooner, four-masted ~ **220** 28
schooner, three masted ~ **220** 18
schooner, topsail ~ **220** 11-13
Schottel propeller **227** 20
Schwellwerk **326** 45
scion **54** 37
scion bud **54** 23, 34
scissor-blade **106** 35
scissor jump **295** 39; **298** 22
scissors *Shoem.* **100** 43
scissors *School* **260** 49
scissors *Gymn.* **296** 51
scissors *Athletics* **298** 22
scissors, angled ~ **22** 51
scissors, bull-nosed ~ **128** 34
scissors, curved ~ **26** 42
scissors movement **296** 51
scoop *Doc.* **22** 50
scoop *Hosp.* **26** 52
scoop *Graphic Art* **340** 8
scoop thermometer **92** 53
scooter **188** 47
scooters **188**
scoreboard **293** 34, 70
scorer **293** 71
scoring equipment, electrical ~ **294** 25-33
scoring equipment, electronic ~ **294** 32
scoring light **294** 28
scorper **340** 7
Scorpio **3** 38; **4** 60
Scorpion *Astron.* **3** 38; **4** 60
scorpion *Articulates* **358** 40
scorzonera **57** 35
Scots pine **372** 20
Scottish terrier **70** 17
scouring machine, open-width ~ **168** 8
scouring nozzle **216** 62
scouring tunnel **217** 62
scouring wheel **100** 6

scout **278** 11
scout camp **278** 8-11
scrag **95** 6
scrag end **95** 6
scramble racing **290** 24-28
scrambling motorcycle **189** 16
scrap box **141** 15
scraper *Butch.* **96** 42
scraper *Paperhanger* **128** 10
scraper *Painter* **129** 23
scraper *Graphic Art* **340** 63
scraper, pointed ~ **140** 63
scraper, triangle ~ **140** 63
scraper adjustment **340** 62
scraper and burnisher **340** 17
scraper blade **200** 17
scraper floor, movable ~ **62** 24
scrap iron charging box **147** 26
scrap iron feed **147** 65
scray entry, curved ~ **168** 47
scree **11** 47; **12** 45; **13** 29
screech owl **362** 17
screed **123** 41
screeding beam **201** 14
screeding board **201** 14
scree ledge **300** 4
screen *Hunt.* **86** 9
screen *Fish Farm.* **89** 10
screen *Bldg. Site* **118** 85
screen *Paperm.* **172** 57
screen *Refuse Coll.* **199** 11
screen *Post* **236** 40
screen *Inf. Tech.* **242** 84
screen *Swim.* **281** 17
screen *Films* **310** 16, 51; **312** 11
screen, all-matt ~ **115** 58, 59, 60, 65
screen, centrifugal ~ **172** 22, 56
screen, crystal glass ~ **179** 24
screen, fluorescent ~ **74** 40
screen, ground glass ~ **112** 24; **115** 58, 59, 60, 61, 65, 66; **177** 2, 34
screen, illuminated ~ **177** 20; **264** 30
screen, inner ~ **240** 20
screen, lead ~ **259** 70
screen, magnetic ~ **240** 20
screen, matt ~ *Optic. Instr.* **112** 24
screen, matt ~ *Photog.* **115** 61, 66
screen, protective ~ **154** 74
screen, rotary ~ **172** 2
screen, secondary ~ **172** 58
screen, vibrating ~ **158** 21
screen curtain **312** 10
screen frame, mobile ~ **168** 60
screen holder, hinged ~ **177** 3
screening **156** 14
screening, inner ~ **240** 20
screening, magnetic ~ **240** 20
screenings **158** 22
screen magazine **177** 9
screen printing **168** 59
screen printing operator **168** 65
screen table **168** 63
screen work **136** 4
screw *First Aid* **21** 16
screw *Metalwkr.* **140** 4
screw *Weaving* **165** 36
screw *Life-Sav.* **228** 26
screw, cheese-head ~ **143** 36
screw, cross-head ~ **143** 26
screw, feathering ~ **224** 19
screw, hexagonal socket head ~ **143** 27
screw, main ~ **148** 62
screw, self-tapping ~ **143** 26
screw, ship's ~ **221** 44; **222** 72; **223** 62
screw, slotted ~ **143** 36
screw, three-blade ~ **223** 62
screw-back **277** 4
screw base **127** 59
screw block **136** 8
screw clamp **120** 66
screw conveyor **92** 26
screw-cutting machine **125** 27; **126** 86
screw die **140** 61
screw dive **282** 44
screwdriver **109** 6; **126** 69; **127** 46; **134** 4; **140** 62
screwdriver, cross-point ~ **134** 5
screwgate **300** 47
screw groove **143** 38
screw joint **126** 42
screw log **224** 54
screw post **222** 71
screws **143** 13-50
screw slit **143** 38
screw slot **143** 38
screw tap **140** 60
screw thread **50** 50
screw wrench **126** 67
scrim **183** 33; **185** 20
scrim roll holder **185** 19
script *Films* **310** 45
script *Script* **341**; **342**
script, cuneiform ~ **341** 8
script, director's ~ **316** 44
script, Latin ~ **342** 12
script, producer's ~ **316** 44
script, Sinaitic ~ **341** 13
script, uncial ~ **341** 17
script girl **310** 39
scripts **341** 1-20
Scriptures **330** 11
scroll *Music. Instr.* **323** 17
scroll *Art* **333** 26; **334** 23
scroll, Vitruvian ~ **334** 39
scroll-opening roller **168** 13
scrollwork **336** 8
scrotum **20** 71
scrubber **156** 22, 23, 24
scrubbing agent **156** 37
scrubbing brush **50** 56
scrubbing oil tank **156** 43
scrub board **123** 21, 63
scrum **292** 20
scrummage **292** 20
scuba **279** 19
scull **283** 17, 35-38
sculptor **339** 1
sculpture **339** 32
sculpture, modern ~ **272** 64
scut **88** 19, 62
scutcher, double ~ **163** 14
scutcher lap **163** 47
scutcher lap holder **163** 48
scutch grass **61** 30
scutellum **82** 5; **358** 30
scythe **66** 12
scythe blade **66** 13
scythe sheath **66** 18
scythestone **66** 19
sea **13** 26; **14** 19-26
sea, epeiric ~ **14** 26
sea, epicontinental ~ **14** 26
sea, marginal ~ **14** 26
sea, open ~ **227** 4
sea anemone **369** 20
sea bear **367** 18
seabirds **359** 11-14
sea calf **367** 19
sea couch grass **61** 30
sea cucumber **369** 18
sea deity **327** 23
sea divinity **327** 23
sea dog **367** 19
sea fan **369** 8
sea feather **369** 14
sea fishing **90**
Sea Goat **3** 36; **4** 62
sea goddess **327** 23
sea grass **378** 54
sea hedgehog **357** 39; **369** 19
sea horse **364** 18
seakale beet **57** 28
seal **190** 69
seal, clay ~ **269** 39
seal, loam ~ **269** 39
sea ladder **221** 91
sea lead **89** 92
sea level **11** 11
sea lily **369** 3
sealing tape **126** 75
seals **367** 18-22
seam **144** 29
sea maid **327** 23
sea maiden **327** 23
seaman **327** 23
sea marks **224** 68-108
seam binding **103** 14; **104** 19
seamless engraving adjustment **177** 53
sea monster **327** 47
seam roller **128** 36
sea nymph **327** 23
sea otter **367** 17
sea ox **327** 47
sea pen **369** 14
seaplane **232** 1, 5
seaquake **11** 53
search **264** 31
searchlight **258** 28
Sea Serpent **3** 16
seaside pleasure boat **221** 15
sea star **357** 38; **369** 17
sea strait **14** 24
seat *Man* **16** 40
seat **24** 24; **41** 10; **44** 11; **65** 22; **71** 45; **212** 63; **271** 35; **273** 58; **283** 28; **303** 6; **307** 15; **312** 9; **315** 20
seat *Mach. Parts etc.* **143** 65

seat, back ~ **193** 22
seat, captain's ~ **235** 17
seat, child's ~ **187** 21
seat, circular ~ **281** 38
seat, coachman's ~ **186** 8
seat, commander's ~ **235** 17
seat, conical ~ **143** 67
seat, co-pilot's ~ **230** 37; **235** 18
seat, cox's ~ **283** 27
seat, double ~ **197** 19; **207** 63
seat, driver's ~ **186** 8; **191** 34; **210** 59
seat, engineer's ~ **210** 59
seat, fireman's ~ **210** 39
seat, folding ~ **193** 22; **207** 12
seat, instructor's ~ **257** 7
seat, observer's ~ **257** 7
seat, pilot's ~ **230** 36; **235** 18; **257** 6
seat, rear ~ **191** 31
seat, reclining ~ **191** 34; **207** 44, 64
seat, single ~ **197** 17; **207** 62
seat, sliding ~ **283** 41-50, 44
seat, student pilot's ~ **257** 6
seat, upholstered ~ **207** 44; **208** 25; **265** 10
seat cushion **42** 23
seated position **296** 31
seating **330** 28
seating group **42** 21-26
seat pillar **187** 24
seat stay **187** 19
seat stick **86** 10
seat tube **187** 18
seat upholstery **207** 65
sea urchin **357** 39; **369** 19
seawater desalination plant **146** 25
sea wave, seismic ~ **11** 53
sea wing **232** 3
secant **346** 50
secateurs **56** 50; **78** 12
second **299** 44
secondary **153** 16
secondary school **261**
second base **292** 43
second-class seating arrangement **211** 58
second-class section **207** 10; **208** 22
seconde engagement **294** 50
second-hand stall **308** 60
second indicator **110** 21
second man **300** 26
second-stage separation retro-rocket **234** 37
seconds timer **129** 39
secretary **209** 27
secretary, proprietor's ~ **248** 31
section *Forestry* **84** 2
section *Drawing Off.* **151** 28
section *Bookbind.* **183** 12
section *Railw.* **203** 29
section, hollow ~ **215** 5
section, middle ~ **215** 68
section, tubular ~ **215** 5
section line *Map* **15** 112
section line *Forestry* **84** 1
section line *Drawing Off.* **151** 27
section mark **342** 36
section of warp rib fabric **171** 14
sections **143**
sections, conic ~ **347** 11-29
sector **346** 54
securities **251** 11-19
security **251** 1-10
security, fixed-income ~ **251** 11-19
security, unlisted ~ **251** 5
security drawer **236** 22
sedan **193** 4, 25
sedge *Phys. Geog.* **13** 17
sedge *Indoor Plants* **53** 17
sedilia **330** 41
sediment *Phys. Geog.* **13** 69
sediment *Doc.* **23** 50
sediment filter, stainless steel ~ **79** 8
seed *Plant Propagn.* **54** 3
seed *Soft Fruit* **58** 23
seed *Drupes & Nuts* **59** 8
seed *Agr.* **63** 12
seed *Arable Crops* **68** 13, 15, 25
seed *Bot.* **370** 86
seed *Decid. Trees* **371** 20, 65
seed *Conifers* **372** 9, 10, 15, 28, 37, 54, 57, 60, 71
seed *Flowers etc.* **375** 25, 28
seed *Alp. Plants etc.* **378** 33, 34
seed *Trop. Plants* **382** 20, 34, 35, 39, 45
seed *Industr. Plants* **383** 15, 23, 24, 57
seed *South. Fruits* **384** 10, 20, 21, 47, 52, 58
seed, foraminate ~ **383** 57
seed, oleiferous ~ **383** 5
seedbed preparation **63** 31-41
seed capsule **61** 5
seed corn **63** 12
seed dressing machine **83** 52
seed dusting **83** 52
seed fish **89** 13
seed-harrow, combination ~ *Agr.* **63** 41
seed-harrow, combination ~ *Agr. Mach.* **65** 87
seed hopper **65** 75
seed leaf **370** 87
seedling *Plant Propagn.* **54** 6
seedling *Market Gdn.* **55** 23
seedling *Forestry* **84** 7, 9
seedling box **55** 51
seedling nursery **84** 6
seedling plant **54** 6
seedlip **63** 11
seed lobe **370** 87
seed pan **54** 2
seed pike **89** 11
seed potato **68** 39
seed sowing **54** 1
seed tuber **68** 39
seed vessel **57** 6; **378** 5; **383** 8
seed vessel, circumscissile ~ **370** 95
seesaw **273** 35; **307** 59
Seger cone **161** 6
seggar **161** 2
segment *Maths.* **346** 52
segment *Invertebr.* **357** 25
segment disc shutter **313** 8
seismograph, horizontal ~ **11** 39
seismology **11** 32-38
seismometer **11** 39
seizing **90** 5
selector **237** 42
selector, electronic ~ **237** 42
selector fork **192** 42, 45
selector head **192** 44
selector motor **237** 48
self-discharge freight car **213** 24
self-discharge wagon **213** 24
self-feeder **74** 13
self-heal **376** 16
self-rescue **21** 33
self-service restaurant **266** 45-78
self-service station **196** 1-29
self-threading guide **165** 18
self-time lever **115** 15
self-timer **115** 15
selvedge **166** 11; **171** 20, 24
selvedge shaft **171** 22
selvedge thread draft **171** 20
semaphore arm **203** 2
semaphore arm, supplementary ~ **203** 8
semaphore signal **203** 1, 7, 12
semibold **175** 3
semibreve **320** 13
semibreve rest **320** 21
semicircle **346** 46
semicolon **342** 19
semidome **334** 73
semiquaver **320** 17
semiquaver rest **320** 25
semitone **320** 50, 52
semi-trailer *Lorries etc.* **194** 30-33
semi-trailer *Station* **206** 59
semolina **98** 36
sending-off **291** 61
senna **380** 16
senna leaf **380** 16
sensing element **10** 22
sepal **58** 8, 44; **59** 12; **370** 58
separating funnel **349** 3
separating layer **7** 10
separating rail **164** 30
separation plant **199** 31
separation rocket motor, aft ~ **235** 62
separation rocket motor, forward ~ **235** 60
separator *Bldg. Site* **119** 81
separator *Offshore Drill.* **146** 28
separator *Cotton Spin.* **164** 43
separator *Paperm.* **172** 31
separator *Roulette* **275** 30
separator, centralized ~ **172** 15
septimole **321** 23
septolet **321** 23
septum **77** 43

septum, interventricular ~ **20** 52
septum, ventricular ~ **20** 52
septuplet **321** 23
sequestrum forceps **26** 45
sequoia **372** 69
seraglio, Sultan's ~ **306** 41
serial number *Stock Exch.* **251** 13
serial number *Money* **252** 36
series, arithmetical ~ **345** 11
series, geometrical ~ **345** 12
series, inner ~ **375** 32
series, outer ~ **375** 31
series of moulds **147** 36
Serpens **3** 20
Serpent *Astron.* **3** 20
serpent *Gymn.* **297** 48
serpent *Music. Instr.* **322** 13
serpent, nine-headed ~ **327** 33
serpent, paper ~ **308** 14
serrate **370** 44
serratus anterior **18** 42
serrulate **370** 44
server *Ball Games* **293** 51, 62
server *Church* **330** 40
service **293** 42
service area **293** 61
service bell panel **267** 28
service bridge **217** 72
service building **154** 36
service bunker **156** 3
service counter **250** 4
service court **293** 12
service girder, adjustable ~ **119** 78
service line **293** 6-7
service line judge **293** 27
service module **6** 2
service module main engine **234** 57
service pistol **264** 22
service riser **126** 7
service room **329** 27
service station **196** 1-29
service tray **105** 31
service vehicle **233** 22
servicing craft **258** 93
serviette **45** 9; **266** 47
serviette ring **45** 10
serving, jute ~ **153** 49
serving area **207** 79
serving cutlery **45** 69-70
serving fork **45** 70
serving hatch **266** 66
serving spoon **45** 74, 75
serving trolley **45** 32
servo-actuating mechanism **257** 22, 23
servo cylinder **192** 50
servo unit **192** 50
sesame plant **383** 45
sesquiplane **229** 13
set *Plant Propagn.* **54** 20
set *Blacksm.* **137** 34
set *Composing Rm.* **175** 48
set *Ball Games* **293** 37
set *Maths.* **348** 1, 3
set collar **143** 33
set designer **310** 43; **315** 37
set hammer **137** 33
set head **143** 57
set of rolls **148** 54-55
set piece **315** 30; **316** 47
sets **348**
set screw **127** 21
set square **151** 7
set square, adjustable ~ **151** 4
set square, steel ~ **108** 28
sett **137** 34
settee **42** 24
setting **54** 18
setting and hatching machine **74** 28
setting lever **115** 15
setting lotion **106** 23
setting rule **174** 14
setting stick **174** 13
set trigger **87** 12
set trigger, second ~ **87** 11
Seven Sisters **3** 26
seventh chord **321** 5
sewer, combined ~ **198** 27
sewing **183** 8, 34
sewing cord **183** 10
sewing frame **183** 9
sewing machine *Dressm.* **103** 8
sewing machine *Tailor* **104** 12
sewing machine *Bookbind.* **185** 16
sewing machine cotton **103** 12
sewing machine drawer **104** 18
sewing machine table **104** 17
sewing machine thread **103** 12
sewing mechanism **133** 5
sewing needle **185** 21
sewing silk **104** 10
sewing thread **183** 11
sex organs, female ~ **20** 79-88
sex organs, male ~ **20** 66-77
sextant **224** 1
sextolet **321** 23
sexton **330** 26, 58
sextuplet **321** 23
sgraffito **338** 41
shading panel **55** 9
shadow **34** 17
shadow mask **240** 17
shadow mask mount, temperature-compensated ~ **240** 22
shadow roll **289** 30
shaft *Farm Bldgs.* **62** 20
shaft *Agr. Mach.* **64** 59
shaft *Mach. Parts etc.* **143** 61
shaft *Nucl. Energy* **154** 69
shaft *Cotton Spin.* **164** 42
shaft *Weaving* **166** 4
shaft *Carriages* **186** 19, 30
shaft *Aircraft* **232** 56
shaft *Rowing* **283** 37
shaft *Ball Games* **291** 26
shaft *Sports* **305** 64
shaft *Art* **333** 27
shaft, intermediate ~ **232** 57
shaft, main ~ *Coal* **144** 24
shaft, main ~ *Car* **192** 40
shaft alley **223** 66
shaft bossing **223** 59
shaft chain **71** 20
shaft furnace **147** 1
shaft guide **166** 3
shaft strut **223** 61
shaft tunnel **223** 66
shag *Tobacc. etc.* **107** 25
shag *Birds* **359** 10
shake **321** 17, 18
shaker **324** 59
shallot **326** 18
shallows **224** 87, 97
shaman **353** 24
shampoo **106** 20
shampoo basin **105** 29; **106** 12
shampoo bottle **105** 32
shampooing head **50** 79
shampoo spray **105** 30; **106** 13
shampoo unit **105** 28; **106** 11
shank *Man* **16** 52
shank *Meat* **95** 14, 33
shank *Shoem.* **100** 68
shank *Metalwkr.* **140** 33
shank *Mach. Parts etc.* **143** 15, 53
shaper **150** 45
shapes game **48** 19
shaping, final ~ **162** 28, 36
shaping hammer **108** 40
shaping machine *Dairy.* **76** 35
shaping machine *Mach. Tools* **150** 45
shaping pad **104** 23
shard **161** 21
share *Agr. Mach.* **65** 7, 58, 65
share *Stock Exch.* **251** 11-19
share, chisel-shaped ~ **65** 58
share, diamond-shaped ~ **65** 58
share, pointed ~ **65** 65
share, three-bladed ~ **64** 67
share certificate **251** 11
share register **251** 14
share warrant **251** 11
shark **364** 1
sharp **320** 50
sharpie **284** 53
shave **136** 39
shave, clean ~ **34** 25
shaver, electric ~ **49** 37
shaving **120** 80
shaving cream **99** 33
shavings **132** 40; **135** 26
shawl **31** 71
shawm **322** 14
shawm, double ~ **322** 3
shearing train **148** 74, 75
shears **128** 34
shears, tinner's ~ **125** 1
sheatfish **364** 12
sheath *Arable Crops* **68** 9
sheath *Forestry* **84** 30
sheath, lead ~ **153** 39, 47
sheath, leather ~ **283** ps
sheathfish **364** 12
sheathing paper **122** 62
shed **166** 40
shedding tappet **166** 57
shed roof **37** 78; **121** 7
sheep **73** 13
sheepdog **70** 25

sheep pen **75** 9
sheer **259** 23
sheer strake **222** 44
sheet *Household* **50** 5
sheet *Offset Print.* **180** 17, 47
sheet *Ship* **219** 68
sheet *Office* **249** 57
sheet *Fire Brig.* **270** 18
sheet *Gymn.* **297** 11
sheet, blank ~ **180** 69; **181** 23, 30
sheet, corrugated ~ **122** 98
sheet, linen ~ **43** 9
sheet, plastic ~ **76** 28
sheet, printed ~ **180** 55, 57; **181** 25
sheet, single ~ **340** 27
sheet, unprinted ~ **180** 69; **181** 23, 30
sheet cloud **8** 3, 4, 8, 9, 10
sheet counter **181** 54
sheet delivery **249** 54
sheet feeder **180** 31, 48, 68, 74; **181** 24; **184** 16; **185** 25
sheet feeder, automatic ~ **181** 5
sheet-feeding station **184** 16
sheet glass **124** 5
sheet glass production **162** 1-20
sheeting support **119** 86
sheet metal **128** 17
sheet-metal screw **143** 26
sheet of glass **162** 10
sheet of stamps **236** 21
sheet pile **119** 17
sheet pile bulkhead **217** 5
sheet pile wall **119** 17; **217** 5
sheet piling **119** 17; **217** 5
sheet shears **125** 26
sheet zinc **122** 14
shelf **44** 19; **98** 14; **100** 36; **195** 14; **271** 27
shelf, continental ~ **11** 8
shelf, revolving ~ **39** 28
shelf, steel ~ **262** 12
shelf, wall-mounted ~ **248** 40
shelf for bottles **266** 10; **267** 64; **317** 4
shelf for glasses **266** 9; **267** 65; **317** 5
shelf unit **46** 1
shell *Cooper* **130** 23
shell *Shipbuild.* **222** 44-49
shell *Rowing* **283** 33, 48
shell *Ball Games* **293** 33
shell *Invertebr.* **357** 29
shell *Fish etc.* **364** 29
shell, soft ~ **59** 42
shell, steel ~ **154** 21
shell bit **135** 16
shell bossing **223** 59
shell membrane **74** 60
shell plating **222** 44-49
shells **283** 9-15
shelter **223** 17
shelving **248** 28
shepherd bird **361** 4
shepherd's club **376** 9
shepherd's purse **61** 9
shepherd's weatherglass **61** 27
sherd **161** 21
sherry glass **45** 84
shield *Game* **88** 55
shield *Plumb. etc.* **126** 33
shield *Ship* **218** 17
shield *Heraldry* **254** 5
shield *Ethnol.* **354** 10
shield, concrete ~ **154** 20
shield, concrete and lead ~ **1** 57
shield, protective ~ **2** 46
shield, round ~ **329** 57
shield, sliding ~ **2** 32
shield budding **54** 30
shielding, protective ~ **2** 46
shielding-gas supply **142** 34
shielding wall, lead ~ **2** 46
shield volcano **11** 13
shifting spanner **126** 68
shift key **249** 3
shift lock **249** 5
shift pattern **192** 47
shikara **337** 26
shin **95** 22, 28
shinbone **17** 25
shingle **34** 34
shin guard **142** 12; **291** 34
shin pad **292** 9; **302** 33
ship, five-masted ~ **220** 35
ship, four-masted ~ **220** 31
ship, full-rigged ~ **220** 24-27, 31, 35
ship, stranded ~ **228** 10
shipbuilding **222**
shipbuilding sheds **222** 3-4
shipbuilding yard **222** 1-43
'ship cleared through customs' **253** 36
ship-drawing office **222** 2
ship fix **224** 45
ship of the line **218** 51-60
shipper **206** 28
shipping traffic radio telephone **224** 28
ship run aground **227** 2
ship under construction **222** 30
shipyard **222** 1-43
shirt **30** 26; **291** 56
shirt, boy's ~ **29** 61
shirt, casual ~ **32** 38; **33** 37
shirt, check ~ **33** 50
shirt, knitted ~ **33** 36
shirt, short-sleeved ~ **33** 33
shirt-blouse **30** 40
shirt button **33** 34
shirts, men's ~ **32** 38-47
shirt top **30** 45
shirtwaist **319** 23
shirt-waister dress **30** 10
Shiva **337** 19
shoals **224** 87, 97
shoat **75** 42
shock absorber *Moon L.* **6** 32
shock absorber *Car* **191** 26; **192** 69
shock absorber *Railw.* **207** 4
shock absorber, telescopic ~ **188** 41; **189** 23
shock treatment **25** 26
shock wave **11** 35
shoe *Mills* **91** 14
shoe *Bldg. Site* **119** 50
shoe, bast ~ **122** 75
shoe, copped ~ **355** 42
shoe, finished ~ **100** 1
shoe, hemp ~ **122** 75
shoe, high-heeled ~ **101** 33
shoe, laced ~ **101** 31
shoe, peaked ~ **355** 42
shoe, piked ~ **355** 42
shoe, repaired ~ **100** 1
shoe, slater's ~ **122** 75
shoe brake **143** 97
shoe brush **50** 41
shoe buckle **101** 52
shoe care utensils **50** 39-43
shoelace **100** 64
shoemaker **100**
shoe polish **50** 39, 43
shoes **41** 16; **101**
shoe sieve **64** 19
shoe spray **50** 40
shoot **54** 37; **370** 19-25
shoot, female ~ **372** 46, 48
shoot, long ~ **78** 3
shoot, male ~ **372** 44, 49, 56
shoot, short ~ **372** 23, 31
shooting *Hunt.* **86** 47-52
shooting *Films* **310** 14-60, 26-60
shooting, exterior ~ **310** 18
shooting, outdoor ~ **310** 18
shooting box **305** 78
shooting brake **193** 15
shooting gallery **308** 58
shooting positions **305** 27-29
shooting range **305** 74
shooting script **310** 45
shooting seat **86** 10
shooting star **7** 25
shooting station **305** 78
shooting stick **86** 10
shop **195**
shop, goldsmith's ~ **215** 33
shop assistant **97** 1; **98** 13, 31; **99** 17; **271** 18
shop front **268** 42
shopkeeper **98** 41
shopper **50** 87
shopping bag **98** 45; **99** 3; **268** 19
shopping trolley **50** 87; **99** 1
shop shelf **47** 36
shop sign **268** 39
shop walker **271** 33
shop window **268** 10
shop window decoration **268** 12
shop window display **268** 11
shorthand **342** 13
shorthand pad **245** 29; **248** 32
shorthand writing **342** 13
short measure **294** 10
short/medium haul airliner **231** 4; **231** 11
short run **184** 1; **249** 59
shorts **33** 25; **291** 57
shorts, children's ~ **29** 25
shorts, ladies' ~ **31** 39
shorts, leather ~ **29** 32
short standing **75** 22

short stop **292** 42
short wave **7** 26
short-wave station **237** 54
short-wave therapy apparatus **23** 22, 39
shot *Athletics* **298** 49
shot *Sports* **305** 52
shote **75** 42
shot firer **158** 25
shotgun, over-and-under ~ **87** 33
shot number **310** 35
shot put **298** 48
shoulder *Phys. Geog.* **12** 41
shoulder *Man* **16** 22
shoulder *Horse* **72** 18
shoulder *Game* **88** 17, 38
shoulder *Meat* **95** 5, 9
shoulder *Composing Rm.* **175** 40
shoulder balance **295** 29
shoulderblade **16** 23; **17** 7
shoulder button **31** 15
shoulder cape **355** 39
shoulder girdle **17** 6-7
shoulder guard **142** 5
shoulder iron **38** 33
shoulder landing **298** 12
shoulder rest **255** 9, 31, 39
shoulder stand **295** 29
shoulder strap **260** 11
shoulder strap, frilled ~ **29** 14
shovel **55** 14; **137** 2; **200** 1; **255** 77
shovel, mechanical ~ **118** 81
shovel, wooden ~ **91** 24
shovel bucket **118** 82
show booth **308** 6
showcase **271** 13
shower *Meteorol.* **8** 19
shower *Meteorol. etc.* **9** 37
shower *Life-Sav.* **228** 30
shower *Swim.* **282** 2
shower, lukewarm ~ **281** 29
shower adjustment rail **49** 43
shower attachment, extendible ~ **126** 30
shower base **49** 44
shower bath **282** 2
shower cubicle **49** 39
shower curtain **49** 40
shower head, adjustable ~ **49** 41
shower nozzle **49** 42
'showers' **233** 46
show jumping **289** 8-14
showman **308** 10
show people, travelling ~ **308** 25-28
shredding **169** 6
shrew **366** 7
shrew mouse **366** 7
shrimp **369** 12
shrine **337** 21
shrine, Buddhist ~ **337** 21
shrink foil **76** 25
shrink ring **130** 24
shrink-sealing machine **76** 24
shroud **219** 16; **284** 18
shrub, anemophilous ~ **59** 44-51
shrub, ornamental ~ **272** 14
shrub, wind-pollinating ~ **59** 44-51
shrub bed **55** 37
shrubs, ornamental ~ **373; 374**
shuck **68** 33
shunter **206** 43
shunting engine **206** 43
shunting locomotive **206** 43
shutter *Market Gdn.* **55** 9
shutter *Mills* **91** 4
shutter, folding ~ **37** 30
shutter, louvred ~ **212** 84
shutter, rolling ~ **37** 28
shutter, side ~ **119** 55
shutter board **118** 41; **119** 18, 76
shutter catch **37** 31
shuttering **119** 54-76; **123** 10
shuttering, bottom ~ **119** 54
shuttering board **119** 76
shuttering strut **119** 13
shutter opening **304** 12
shutter release **114** 12, 31; **115** 18; **117** 6; **313** 24, 38
shutter release button **114** 12; **115** 18
shutter speed control **114** 35; **115** 19
shutter speed setting knob **115** 19
shutter weir **217** 65-72
shuttle *Needlewk.* **102** 20
shuttle *Weaving* **166** 9, 26
shuttle *Ball Games* **293** 44
shuttle box **166** 9
shuttlecock **273** 7; **293** 44
shuttlecock game **273** 6
shuttle eye **166** 29
shuttle tip, metal ~ **166** 25
sickle **56** 8
side *Man* **16** 32
side *Opticn.* **111** 13
side *Joiner* **132** 23
side *Weaves* **171** 32
side *Billiards* **277** 5
side *Art* **336** 40
side *Maths.* **346** 26, 27
side, subordinate ~ **252** 9
side, woven ~ **136** 18
side batten **222** 62
side blackboard **260** 35
sideboard *Dining Rm.* **44** 20
sideboard *Tablew. etc.* **45** 44
side board *Farm Bldgs.* **62** 25
sideboards **34** 24
sideburns **34** 24
sidecar **290** 30
sidecar body **189** 54
sidecar combination **290** 29
sidecar crash bar **189** 55
sidecar machine **189** 53
sidecar wheel **189** 57
sidecar windscreen **189** 58
sidecar windshield **189** 58
side cast, two-handed ~ **89** 32
side ceiling **222** 62
side comb **105** 6
side control **180** 5, 20
side drum **323** 51
side elevation **207** 1, 22-25, 37, 60, 74
side flat **310** 33
side frame **165** 12; **167** 20
side girder, longitudinal ~ **222** 52
side grafting **54** 36
side grip **134** 45
side horse **296** 5
side joint **111** 14
side lay control **180** 5, 20
sidelight **189** 56; **191** 20; **223** 15
sidelight, green ~ **286** 11
sidelight, headlight, and parking light switch **191** 62
sidelight, port ~ **286** 12
sidelight, red ~ **286** 12
sidelight, starboard ~ **286** 11
sideline **292** 17; **293** 2 *bis* 3, 4 *bis* 5; **293** 55
side margin control **180** 5, 20
sidemarker lamp **189** 56; **191** 20
side note **185** 68
side of pork **94** 23
side panel, removable ~ **188** 48
side parting **315** 1
side planking **62** 25
side pocket **33** 12
siderostat **5** 16
side rudder **218** 6
side shoot **370** 21
sideshow **308** 24
side slit **30** 49
side split **295** 14
side stake **206** 24
side stay **284** 18
sidestep **301** 27
sidestepping **299** 29
side stop **200** 34, 44
side straddle **295** 3
side strake **222** 45
side stringer **222** 50
side stroke **282** 36
side support *Shipbuild.* **222** 40
side support *Free Exerc.* **295** 25
side thrust kick **299** 19
side trappings **71** 16
side view **207** 1, 22-25, 37, 60, 74
sidewalk **37** 60; **198** 9
sidewall *Electrotyp. etc.* **178** 45
sidewall *Railw.* **213** 29
side wall *Music. Instr.* **323** 4, 25
side-whiskers **34** 24
side window blower **191** 61
siding **206** 50
Siemens-Martin open-hearth furnace **147** 21-30
sieve *Market Gdn.* **55** 13
sieve *Graphic Art* **340** 24
sieve, louvred-type ~ **64** 17
sieve, reciprocating ~ **64** 19
sieve, upright ~ **55** 13
sieve extension **64** 18
sifter **91** 26

sight **87** 65; **255** 45
sight, front ~ **87** 71; **255** 3, 23, 37; **305** 42
sight, optical ~ **305** 41
sight, telescopic ~ **87** 29; **255** 28; **305** 49
sight graticule **87** 31-32
sighting mechanism **255** 45
sighting notch *Hunt.* **87** 66
sighting notch *Army* **255** 22
sight scale division **87** 68
sign, chequered ~ **203** 30
sign, illuminated ~ **203** 38
signal **205** 42
signal, distant ~ **203** 7-24
signal, main ~ **203** 1, 1-6
signal, visual ~ **238** 30
signal and radar mast **221** 7
signal arm **203** 2
signal box **15** 24
signal box, electrically-operated ~ **203** 61
signal box, manually-operated ~ **203** 53
signal element **243** 60
signal flags **253** 22-34
signal generator **313** 30
signaling *see* signalling
signal knob **203** 62
signal lever **203** 56
signal light *Power Plant* **153** 3
signal light *Cotton Spin.* **164** 8
signal light *Railw.* **212** 15
signal light *Ship* **221** 125
signalling equipment **203**
signalling lamp **223** 7
signalling mast **225** 34
signal mast *Map* **14** 51
signal mast *Docks* **225** 34
signal position **203** 4, 5, 10, 11
signals, supplementary ~ **203** 25-44
signal stay **223** 11
signal tower **14** 51
signal tower, electrically-operated ~ **203** 61
signal tower, manually-operated ~ **203** 53
signal track **243** 59
signature *Bookbind.* **183** 12; **185** 69
signature *Stock Exch.* **251** 15, 16
signature, cross-folded ~ **185** 15
signature, parallel-folded ~ **185** 13
signature code **185** 69
signboard **118** 45
signet ring **36** 40
sign for day running **203** 36
sign for night running **203** 38
sign of parallelism **345** 21
sign of similarity **345** 22
signs, conventional ~ **15** 1-114
signs, zodiacal ~ **4** 53-64
signs of the zodiac **4** 53-64
signwriting brush **129** 41
sikar **337** 26
sikhara **337** 26
silencer **191** 29; **209** 12, 22, 24; **211** 49; **305** 93
silhouette **25** 39
silicon atom **1** 14
siliqua *Weeds* **61** 20, 23
siliqua *Bot.* **370** 93
siliqua *Alp. Plants etc.* **378** 33
siliqua *South. Fruits* **384** 46
siliqua, mature ~ **383** 4
siliqua, ripe ~ **383** 4
silk-cotton tree **383** 20
silk moth **358** 48
silk taffeta **35** 36
silkworm **358** 50
sill *Phys. Geog.* **11** 31
sill *Car* **193** 21
sill rail **120** 56
silo **225** 68
silo, above-ground ~ **62** 11
silo, polythene ~ **62** 43
silo cylinder **225** 69
silo pipe **62** 12
silver **254** 25
silver-disc pyrheliometer **10** 23
silver fir **372** 1
silverfish **81** 14
silverleaf **371** 23
silver owl **362** 17
silver poplar **371** 23
silverside **95** 34
silversmith **108**
sima **11** 4
simple interest formula **345** 7
simsim **383** 45
Sinanthropus **261** 18
sine **346** 32
singer **315** 22, 23
single, clinker-built ~ **283** 18
single-hand control **185** 7
single-loader **87** 1
singles **293** 4-5
single sculler **283** 16
single-shot rifle **305** 35
singles match **293** 4-5
singles sideline **293** 4-5
single-system recording **117** 8
singlet **296** 61
single-trip bottle **93** 29
sinister **254** 19,21,23
sink *Phys. Geog.* **11** 49; **13** 71
sink *Kitch.* **39** 35
sink *Forestry* **84** 28
sink *Bakery* **97** 68
sink *Coal* **144** 47
sink *Energy Sources* **155** 16
sink *School* **261** 6, 34
sink *Camping* **278** 6
sinker *Sea Fish.* **90** 10
sinker *Knitting* **167** 58
sinker *Navig.* **224** 73
sinker, oval ~ **89** 88
sinkhole **11** 49; **13** 71
sink unit **39** 33-36
Sinningia **53** 7
sinter terraces **11** 23
sinuate **370** 48
sinus, frontal ~ **17** 55
sinus, sphenoidal ~ **17** 54
siphon barometer **10** 1
siphon tube **10** 43
siren *Ship* **223** 3
siren *Fabul. Creat.* **327** 58
siren, ship's ~ **224** 32
sirenian **366** 23
Sirius **3** 14
sirloin **95** 17; **96** 4
sisal **35** 13
siskin **361** 8
site fence **118** 44
site hut **118** 48; **119** 44
site of battle **15** 93
site office **118** 48
sit harness **300** 57
situla, sheet-bronze ~ **328** 34
Siva **337** 19
six-day race **290** 2-7
six-day racer **290** 2
six-eight time **320** 34
six-four time **320** 35
sixte engagement **294** 48
sixteenth note **320** 17
sixteenth rest **320** 25
six-to-pica **175** 19
sixty-fourth note **320** 19
sixty-fourth rest **320** 27
size **128** 4
size press **173** 24
sizing **162** 53
sizing and edging machine **132** 57
sizing machine **165** 52
skateboard **273** 51
skate guard **302** 25
skate sailing **302** 27-28
skate sailor **302** 27
skeet **305** 70-78
skeet choke **305** 71
skeet shooting **305** 70-78
skeg **279** 3; **286** 61
skeletal **194** 30-33
skeleton *Man* **17** 1-29
skeleton *School* **261** 14
skeleton *Winter Sp.* **303** 22
skeleton, siliceous ~ **357** 8
skeleton construction **119** 1
skeleton rider **303** 23
skeleton toboggan **303** 22
skeleton tobogganing **303** 22-24
skep **77** 52
sketch for costume **315** 40
sketch pad **338** 35
skew notch **120** 54
skew notch, double ~ **121** 91
skew notch, single ~ **121** 90
ski, compact ~ **301** 1
ski, modern ~ **301** 46
ski bag **301** 28
ski bob **304** 16
ski cap **35** 39; **301** 10
skid chain **304** 10
skidder **85** 34
skidder, short-haul ~ **85** 27
skife knife **100** 51
skiff **283** 16
skiing **301** 1-72
skiing boot, cemented sole ~ **301** 12
skiing cap **35** 39; **301** 10
skiing goggles **301** 11
ski jumping **301** 35

ski jumping boot **301** 41
ski jumping ski **301** 38
ski lift **301** 57-63, 59
skim coulter **65** 11
skimmer **96** 43
skimmer, stepped ~ **286** 38-41
skimmer rod **148** 17
skimmers **286** 38-44
skim milk tank **76** 17
skin *Shipbuild.* **222** 44-49
skin *School* **261** 9
skin *Gliding* **287** 40
skin, light alloy ~ **235** 11
skin, outer ~ *Rowing* **283** 33, 48
skin, outer ~ *Ball Games* **293** 33
skin diver **279** 7
skin diving **279** 7-27
skip *Road Constr.* **200** 25
skip *Railw.* **213** 38; **214** 34
skip *Gymn.* **297** 42, 45
skip hoist *Iron & Steel* **147** 3
skip hoist *Road Constr.* **200** 14
ski pole **301** 5
skipping **273** 15
skipping rope **273** 16; **297** 43
skip rope **273** 16
skip-winding system **144** 25
skirt *Child. Clothes* **29** 52
skirt *Ladies' Wear* **31** 3, 24
skirt *Army* **255** 85
skirt *Motorboats etc.* **286** 66
skirt *Airsports* **288** 48
skirt, aft ~ **235** 63
skirt, girl's ~ **29** 46
skirt, grass ~ **306** 18
skirt, inverted pleat ~ **30** 51
skirt, loden ~ **30** 67
skirt, long ~ **30** 45
skirt, pleated ~ **30** 32
skirt, wrap-around ~ **31** 13
skirt, wrapover ~ **31** 13
skirting **123** 21
skirting board **123** 21, 63
skirt suit **31** 1
skirt suit, girl's ~ **29** 50
ski stick **301** 5
ski stop **301** 56
ski suit, ladies' ~ **301** 9
ski suit, one-piece ~ **301** 9
skittle frame **305** 1-11
skittles **305** 1-13
skiving knife **100** 51
ski wax **301** 21
ski-waxing equipment **301** 21-24
skull *Man* **17** 1, 30-41
skull *School* **261** 15, 17, 19, 21
skull *Rowing* **283** 35-38
skull *Chivalry* **329** 39
skull, Australopithecine ~ **261** 20
sky **3** 1-8
sky, northern ~ **3** 1-35
sky, southern ~ **3** 36-48
sky blue **343** 6
skylight **38** 2; **121** 8; **122** 12
skysail **220** 32
slab **120** 96
slab, reinforced concrete ~ **123** 28
slab, stone ~ **51** 17; **331** 61
slab, wooden ~ **324** 62
slab cake **97** 34; **99** 21
slacks **29** 49
slacks, lightweight ~ **31** 52
slack suit **30** 57
slade **65** 6, 66
slag escape **147** 9
slag ladle **147** 10
slag spout **148** 12
slalom **301** 29, 64
slalom canoe **283** 4
slalom ski **286** 60
slant track **243** 31
slapstick **306** 48
slat **229** 53
slat, extensible ~ **229** 38
slate *Roof* **122** 85
slate **309** 72
slate hammer **122** 73
slater *House Insects etc.* **81** 6
slater *Roof* **122** 71
slate roof **122** 61-89
slath **136** 21
slating batten **122** 17
slaughterer **94** 1
slaughterhouse *Slaughterho.* **94**
slaughterhouse *Bullfight. etc.* **319** 13
slaughterman **94** 1
slave, female ~ **306** 41
slave driver **218** 47
slave galley **218** 44-50
slave station **224** 41
sled **303** 1, 2
sled dog **353** 2
sledge **303** 1, 2
sledge dog **353** 2
sledge hammer **137** 22; **158** 6
sleeper *Bldg. Site* **119** 39
sleeper *Station* **205** 60
sleeper *Railw.* **207** 36
sleeper, concrete ~ **202** 37
sleeper, coupled ~ **202** 14, 38
sleeper, steel ~ *Railw.* **202** 36
sleeper, steel ~ *Hydr. Eng.* **217** 3
sleeper and strampler **29** 23
sleeping bag *Infant Care etc.* **28** 17
sleeping bag *Camping* **278** 30
sleeping car **207** 36
sleeping doll **47** 11
sleeve **30** 15
sleeve, batwing ~ **31** 16
sleeve, braided ~ **186** 24
sleeve, dagged ~ **355** 46
sleeve, full ~ **355** 60
sleeve, gallooned ~ **186** 24
sleeve, kimono ~ **30** 36
sleeve, petal-scalloped ~ **355** 46
sleeve, protective ~ **142** 6
sleeve, puffed ~ **31** 27; **355** 49, 60
sleeve, sliding ~ **192** 32, 35
sleeve, turned-up ~ **31** 62
sleeve, turnover ~ **30** 6
sleeve, turn-up ~ **30** 6
sleeve board **50** 20
sleeve protector **324** 17
sleigh, horse-drawn ~ **304** 25
sleigh bell **304** 26
slender funnel fungus **381** 25
slewing crab **222** 21
slew turntable **200** 22
sley **166** 41, 53
sley cap **166** 6
slice *Bakery* **97** 43
slice *Blacksm.* **137** 2
slice, sugared ~ **97** 43
slicer **96** 31
slicker **81** 14
slide *Inf. Tech.* **242** 42
slide *Playground* **273** 24
slide *Winter Countr.* **304** 17
slide *Music. Not.* **321** 16
slide *Music. Instr.* **322** 51; **323** 47; **326** 7, 33
slide, bed ~ **177** 59
slide bar **313** 10
slide calliper **85** 10
slide chair **202** 22
slide control **238** 47; **241** 8
slide-copying adapter **115** 88
slide-copying attachment **115** 87
slide holder **309** 43
slide projector **114** 76; **309** 42; **312** 23
slider **326** 7
slide rail **206** 38
sliding door **271** 50
sliding scale **349** 23
sliding weight **22** 68; **40** 36
sliding-weight scales **22** 66; **40** 35
sling *First Aid* **21** 2
sling *Mountain.* **300** 11
sling pump **101** 53
sling ring **87** 5
sling seat **300** 29
slip *Underwear etc.* **32** 13
slip *Plant Propagn.* **54** 20
slip *Roof* **122** 48
slip casting **161** 15
slip fault **12** 7
slip-off slope **13** 58
slipper *Shoes* **101** 41
slipper *Station* **206** 49
slipper animalcule **357** 9
slipper brake **206** 49
slip road **15** 16
slips **222** 11-26
slip sock, woollen ~ **101** 42
slipway **222** 11-18
slipway crane **222** 23
slipway floor **222** 17
slipway frame **222** 19
slipway portal **222** 11
slipways **222** 11-26
slit, side ~ **30** 49
slit gong **354** 18
slitter **181** 42
sliver **164** 15, 21
sliver, carded ~ **163** 38
sliver, carded and combed ~ **163** 72
sliver, coiled ~ **163** 35

sliver, doubled ~s **164** 12
sliver, thin ~ **164** 13
sliver can **164** 3, 20
sloe **374** 27
slope **347** 12
slope, continental ~ **11** 9
slope soaring **287** 27
slops **355** 34
slosh baffle system **235** 53
slot *Glass Prod.* **162** 9
slot *Weaving* **166** 32
slot *Garage* **195** 5
slot *Election* **263** 30
slot *Airsports* **288** 45
slotted board **2** 45
slouch hat **35** 21
slow motion control **243** 49
slow-running jet **192** 1
slowworm **364** 37
slubbing frame **164** 19
slug **174** 27
slug-casting machine **174** 19
slug-composing machine **174** 19
slug of clay **161** 10
sluice dam **217** 73-80
sluice gate **217** 53-56, 77
sluice valve **217** 53-56
slump fault **12** 7
slush **304** 30
slush pump **145** 16
smack **221** 49
small-arm **87** 2
small beer **93** 26
smallbore free rifle **305** 44
smallbore rifle **305** 48
smallbore standard rifle **305** 43
small cabbage white butterfly **80** 48
small ermine moth **80** 5
small of the back **16** 25
small of the butt **87** 7
small scabious **375** 29
small-shot cartridge **87** 49
small-shot charge **87** 51
smash **293** 17
smear **23** 15, 50
smelting section **147** 8
smith **137**; **138**
smith forging **139**
smock overall **31** 35
smock windmill **91** 29
smokebox door **210** 26
smoke canister **255** 83
smoke dispenser **255** 83
smoke extract **38** 81
smoke flap **352** 9
smoke house **96** 48
smoke outlet **38** 81; **210** 22; **353** 21
smoker's companion **107** 44
smokestack *Power Plant* **152** 15
smokestack *Railw.* **210** 22
smoke tube **210** 8
smoking requisites **107**
smoother **128** 11
smoothing blade **200** 18
smoothing plane **132** 15; **134** 1
snaffle **289** 12
snail **357** 27
snail, edible ~ **357** 27
snail shell **357** 29
snake, poisonous ~ **364** 40
snake, venomous ~ **364** 40
snake charmer **353** 45
snakes **364** 38-41
snakeweed **376** 10
snapdragon **51** 32
snap gauge **149** 59
snap lid **127** 24
snapping beetle **80** 37
snapping bug **80** 37
snare drum **323** 51
snath **66** 16
snathe **66** 16
snead **66** 16
sneath **66** 16
snedding machine **85** 18
snipe **88** 83
snorkel *Warships* **259** 72, 90
snorkel *Swim.* **279** 11
snorkel *Bathing* **280** 39
snout **73** 10; **88** 53; **364** 2
snow **8** 18; **9** 34; **304** 24; **353** 5
snow and ice climber **300** 15
snow and ice climbing **300** 14-21
snow and ice climbing equipment **300** 31-57
snow avalanche **304** 1
snowball *Winter Countr.* **304** 15
snowball *Shrubs etc.* **373** 10
snowball bush **373** 10
snowball fight **304** 14
snow blower **213** 17
snow bridge **300** 24
snow chain **304** 10
snow cornice **300** 20
snowdrift **304** 5
snowdrop **60** 1
snowfall **10** 48; **304** 4
snow fence **304** 6
snow forest climate **9** 56
snow gaiter **300** 55
snow goggles **300** 18
snow guard **38** 8
snow guard bracket **122** 16
snow hut **353** 4
snow ledge **300** 4
snowman **304** 13
snow plough, rotary ~ **213** 17
snow plough attachment **304** 9
snow plough signs **203** 34-35
snow push **304** 23
snowshirt **300** 6
snow shovel **304** 23
snowslide **304** 1
snow suit **29** 38
snuff **107** 20
snuff box **107** 20
soaking pit **148** 46
soaking pit crane **148** 47
soaking tub **136** 13
soap **49** 22
soap box **273** 33
soap dish **49** 21
soap dispenser **50** 27
soaring **287**
soccer **273** 10; **291**
sock **291** 58
sock, knee-length ~ **29** 53; **32** 32; **33** 42
sock, long ~ **32** 34
sock, surgical ~ **101** 50
socket *Hairdresser* **106** 15
socket *Plumb.* **125** 20
socket *Plumb. etc.* **126** 43
socket *Electr.* **127** 7
socket, double ~ **127** 6
socket, earthed ~ **127** 5, 6, 13
socket, four-way ~ **127** 8
socket, multi-outlet ~ **195** 39
socket, surface-mounted ~ **127** 13
socket, switched ~ **127** 7
socket, three-pin ~ **127** 66
socket, three-pole ~ **127** 13
socket, tinner's ~ **125** 20
socket, underfloor ~ **127** 22
socket outlet box **127** 25
socks, men's ~ **32** 32-34
soda bottle **42** 32
soda-lime absorber **27** 39
soda water **98** 87
soda water bottle **42** 32
sodium atom **1** 8
sodium chloride **1** 9; **170** 13
sodium ion **1** 11
sodium pump, primary ~ **154** 5
sodium pump, secondary ~ **154** 8
sodium sulphate storage tank **172** 36
sodium system, primary ~ **154** 2
sodium system, secondary ~ **154** 7
sofa **336** 17
sofa, two-seater ~ **246** 36
soffit **122** 27
soft corn **68** 31
soft pedal **325** 9
soil covering **200** 64
soil injector **83** 33
solan goose **359** 9
solar cell **155** 34
solar collector **155** 28, 32
solarium **281** 10
solar panel **10** 66
solar radiation shielding **10** 36
solar sensor **10** 69
solar spectrum **343** 14
solar system **4** 42-52
soldanella **378** 3
solder **108** 38
solder, tin-lead ~ **126** 76
soldering apparatus **125** 5-7
soldering borax **108** 39
soldering fluid **125** 7
soldering flux **108** 36
soldering gun *Goldsm. etc.* **108** 14
soldering gun *D.I.Y.* **134** 56
soldering iron *Plumb.* **125** 5
soldering iron *Plumb. etc.* **126** 73

soldering iron *D.I.Y.* **134** 19, 57
soldering iron, electric ~ **127** 45
soldering iron, high-speed ~ **134** 58
soldering stone **125** 6
solder wire, tin-lead ~ **134** 20
soldier, lead ~ **309** 52
soldier, tin ~ **309** 52
sole *Agr. Mach.* **65** 6, 66
sole *Shoem.* **100** 66
sole *Joiner* **132** 22
sole, cemented ~ **101** 11
sole, corrugated ~ **300** 43
sole, inner ~ **291** 31
sole, natural-colour ~ **101** 15, 38
sole, nylon ~ **291** 30
sole, plastic ~ **101** 2
sole, PVC ~ **101** 2
sole, rubber ~ **101** 38
sole, wooden ~ **101** 45
sole bar reinforcement **213** 12
sole leather **100** 31
sole-leather shears **100** 39
solenoid valve **139** 23
sole of the foot **19** 62
sole-plate *Household* **50** 7
sole-plate *Road Constr.* **200** 33
sole-plate *Railw.* **202** 5
sole press, automatic ~ **100** 14
sole stitcher **100** 26
sole-stitching machine **100** 26
sole trimmer **100** 5
solid-fuel rocket, recoverable ~ **235** 58
solidification **170** 35, 43
solid-newel staircase **123** 77
solid rocket booster **235** 58
solids **347** 30-46
solid stage **148** 26
solid-web girder **121** 72
solid-web girder bridge **215** 7
solifluction lobe **11** 51
solifluction tongue **11** 51
soling **284** 56
solleret **329** 55
solo machine **290** 27
solo seat **189** 19
solo skater **302** 1
solstice **3** 8
solution **345** 10
solution, viscous ~ **169** 15
solvent fumes **182** 25
Somali Current **14** 36
sombrero **35** 5
songbirds **360** 1,3,4,5,7,9,10; **361** 1-20
song thrush **361** 16
soot **38** 34
sordino **323** 10; **324** 68
Soricidae **366** 7
sort **174** 7, 28
sorter **172** 57
sorter, rotary ~ **172** 23
sorter, secondary ~ **172** 58
sorting machine **74** 38
sorting siding **206** 47
sorting table **64** 81
sound assistant **117** 68; **310** 57
soundboard *Music. Instr.* **323** 24; **324** 3
soundboard *Church* **330** 21
sound box **322** 18, 29; **323** 3; **324** 15, 63
sound camera **117** 22; **313** 26
sound camera, Super-8 ~ **117** 1
sound coding equipment **242** 11-14
sound connecting cord **117** 8
sound control console **238** 20, 41, 54; **239** 8
sound control desk **238** 20, 41, 54; **239** 8
sound control engineer **238** 19
sound control room **238** 27; **239** 7
sound dubbing **311** 34-36
sound echo **224** 63
sound editor **117** 96
sound effect **310** 30
sound effects box **238** 35
sound engineer **238** 19
sound film **117** 82
sound film cartridge, Super-8 ~ **117** 29
sound head *Cine Film* **117** 33
sound head *Audiovis.* **243** 35
sound head *Films* **312** 47
sound head housing **241** 59
sound hole **322** 22; **323** 6; **324** 5
sound impulse **224** 62
sounding balloon **7** 17
sounding board **330** 21
sound mixer **238** 26
sound mixing **311** 34-36
sound module **240** 14
sound OB van **239** 1-15
sound optics **312** 46
sound production control room **238** 27; **239** 7
sound projector **117** 81; **312** 24
sound recorder, portable ~ **310** 24
sound recording **311** 1-46
sound recording camera **310** 60; **311** 6
sound recording equipment **117** 7
sound recording level control **243** 11
sound recording selector switch **117** 13
sound recordist *Broadcast.* **238** 26
sound recordist *Films* **310** 23, 55; **311** 36
sound source **117** 27
sound source, external ~ **117** 8
sound technician **238** 26
sound track *Cine Film* **117** 82
sound track *Audiovis.* **243** 32
sound track system **117** 21
sound transmitter **224** 61
sound turntable, first ~ **117** 100
sound turntable, second ~ **117** 101
sound wave **224** 62
sound wave propagation **7** 14
soup ladle **45** 14
soup plate **44** 6; **45** 5
soup seasoning **98** 30
soup tureen **44** 8; **45** 15
soup vegetable **68** 25
source water inlet **155** 2
sour cherry **59** 5
souring chamber **159** 6
sour milk vat **76** 42
South America **14** 13
South Equatorial Current **14** 34
Southern Cross **3** 44
Southern Ocean **14** 22
Southern Triangle **3** 40
south point **4** 17
South Pole **14** 3
southwester **35** 30; **228** 5
souvenir plate **309** 48
sou'wester **35** 30; **228** 5
sow *Dom. Anim.* **73** 9
sow *Livestock* **75** 41
sow *Hunt.* **86** 32
sow *Game* **88** 48, 51
sow bug **81** 6
sower **63** 10
sowing **54** 1; **63** 10-12
sow pig **75** 42
spa **274**
space *Composing Rm.* **175** 5, 17
space *Music. Not.* **320** 44
space, popliteal ~ **16** 51
spaceband **174** 24
space bar **249** 2
space capsule **6** 9, 10; **234** 65
spacecraft **6** 1
space flight **234; 235**
spaceflight module **235** 70
Spacelab **235** 65
space laboratory **235** 65
spacer **119** 81
Space Shuttle-Orbiter **235** 1-45
space station **235** 65
space suit **6** 18-27
space suit helmet **6** 22
spacing bracket **126** 54
spacing clip **126** 57
spacing lines **10** 58
spacing material **174** 8
spade **56** 2; **331** 36
spade *Fish Farm.* **89** 82
spade *Army* **255** 55
spade, semi-automatic ~ **56** 12
spade piston **255** 56
spades **276** 39
spadix **370** 71; **378** 22
spadix, female ~ **384** 6
spadix, male ~ **383** 55; **384** 4
spa gardens **274** 1-21
spaghetti **98** 32
spale **136** 12
spale basket **136** 11

span *Bridges* **215** 14
span *Aircraft* **229** 2
span, clear ~ **215** 13
span, wire rope ~ **221** 102
Spandau **255** 32
Spanish chestnut **384** 48
Spanish paprika **57** 42
spanker **219** 30
spanker boom **218** 28; **219** 44
spanker boom topping lift **219** 48
spanker gaff **219** 45
spanker peak halyard **219** 49
spanker sheet **219** 69
spanker vang **219** 70
span of oxen **63** 16
spa orchestra **274** 20
spa promenade **274** 10
spar **230** 45
spar, diagonal ~ **287** 33
spar, integral ~ **257** 28
spar, main ~ **287** 30
spar buoy **224** 79
spar ceiling **222** 62
spare man **291** 11
spare part *Watchm.* **109** 22
spare part *Garage* **195** 32
spare rib **95** 47
spare tyre *Lorries etc.* **194** 4
spare tyre *Cyc. Racing* **290** 23
spare wheel **191** 25; **194** 33
spar-hawk **362** 12
spark arrester **210** 24
spark gap **153** 62
spark-ignition engine **190** 1, 2
sparking plug **190** 35; **242** 48
spark plug **190** 35; **242** 48
spark-plug cap **188** 27
Sparmannia **53** 9
sparring partner **299** 27
sparrow hawk **362** 12
sparrow owl **362** 19
spars **219** 32-45
spatula *Dent.* **24** 50
spatula *Hosp.* **25** 7
spatula *Art. Studio* **338** 15
spatula, plastic ~ **128** 44
spawn **89** 12
spawner **89** 13
speaker *Living Rm.* **42** 10
speaker *Election* **263** 5
speaker *Hotel* **267** 40
speaker *Disco* **317** 15
speaker *Nightclub* **318** 12
speaker, three way ~ **241** 14
speaking key **242** 24
spear, long-bladed ~ **354** 12
spear head, bronze ~ **328** 21
spear thrower **352** 40
special effects equipment **310** 59
special offer **96** 20; **271** 65
specialty shop **195** 1-55
specie **252** 1-28
speciestaler **252** 6
specimen insertion air lock **113** 33
specimen stage adjustment **113** 34
spectacle fitting **111** 1-4
spectacle frame *Opticn.* **111** 5, 10-14
spectacle frame *Ship* **223** 61
spectacle lens **111** 15
spectacles **111** 5, 9
spectator **308** 29
spectator barrier **292** 40
spectators' terrace *Airport* **233** 20
'spectators' terrace' *Airport* **233** 30
spectrograph **5** 33
speculum, aural ~ **22** 74
speculum, rectal ~ **23** 19
speculum, vaginal ~ **23** 13
speed ball **299** 22
speed change lever **149** 5
speed changer **241** 29
speed code number **203** 37
speed control **179** 29
speed indicator **203** 18
speed indicator, distant ~ **203** 19
speedo **188** 19, 34; **191** 38, 74
speedometer *Motorcycles etc.* **188** 19, 34, 40
speedometer *Motorcycle* **189** 40
speedometer *Car* **191** 38, 74
speedometer *Tram* **197** 31
speedometer *Railw.* **211** 35; **212** 9
speedometer *Navig.* **224** 54
speedometer, ship's ~ **224** 22
speedometer drive **192** 38, 39
speed recorder **210** 54
speed restriction, permanent ~ **203** 41, 42
speed restriction, temporary ~ **203** 39, 40
speed restriction sign **203** 36-38, 41, 44
speed restriction signs **203** 36-44
speed restriction warning sign **203** 43
speed selector **241** 29
speed skate **302** 20
speed skater **302** 26
speed skating set **302** 20
speedway **290** 24-28
speedwell **375** 22
speleothems **13** 80-81
spelling book **260** 17
spelt **68** 24
spelt, green ~ **68** 23
spencer **220** 1
sperm whale **367** 25
sphagnum mosses **13** 20, 22
sphenoid **17** 38
sphere **347** 41
sphere, celestial ~ **4** 23
sphere, plain ~ **36** 82
sphere, solar ~ **4** 36
spheres **36** 82-86
sphere unit **2** 38
spherical typing element **249** 15
sphincter, anal ~ **20** 63
sphinx *Fabul. Creat.* **327** 20
sphinx *Articulates* **358** 55
sphinx *Lepidopt.* **365** 9
sphinx, Egyptian ~ **333** 11
sphygmograph **26** 32
sphygmomanometer **25** 15
Spica **3** 18
spice **99** 67
spice jar **39** 32
spice rack **39** 31; **47** 29
spices **382**
spider legs **115** 91
spiders **358** 44-46
spider's web *Playground* **273** 46
spider's web *Articulates* **358** 47
spike *Arable Crops* **68** 2
spike *Mountain.* **300** 9
spike *Music. Instr.* **323** 22
spike *Industr. Plants* **383** 62, 66
spike, fleshy ~ **370** 71
spike, racemose ~ **370** 67
spikelet **68** 3, 10; **69** 23; **375** 41, 42
spill light **310** 51
spillway **217** 60
spin *Roulette* **275** 32
spin *Airsports* **288** 7
spinach **57** 29
spinal cord **17** 48; **18** 25
spindle *Watchm.* **109** 17
spindle *Mach. Tools* **149** 66; **150** 27
spindle *Cotton Spin.* **164** 43
spindle *Bookbind.* **183** 22
spindle *Bicycle* **187** 60, 80
spindle, horizontal ~ **150** 40
spindle, main ~ **149** 11
spindle, screwed ~ **149** 66
spindle catch **164** 49
spindle drive **164** 31
spindle oil **145** 61
spindle rail **164** 50
spindle rotation speed **150** 35
spindle shaft **164** 46
spindle speed **164** 38, 40
spindle top **126** 32
spine *Man* **17** 2-5
spine *Bookbind.* **183** 14; **185** 41
spine *Mammals* **366** 6
spine label **247** 38
spine of the book **183** 1
spinet **322** 45
spine tag **247** 38
spinet piano **325** 1
spinner *Fish Farm.* **89** 74, 75
spinner *Aircraft* **230** 33
spinner, long ~ **89** 76
spinneret *Synth. Fibres* **169** 14; **170** 41
spinneret *Articulates* **358** 46
spinneret hole **170** 41, 42
spinning **170** 57
spinning bath **169** 15
spinning jet **169** 14; **170** 41, 42
spiraea **374** 23
spiral *Photog.* **116** 2
spiral *Airsports* **288** 51
spiral *Gymn.* **297** 50
spiral design pottery **328** 13

spire **331** 6
spirit glass **45** 90
spirit lamp **24** 57
spirit level *Map* **14** 61
spirit level *Bldg. Site* **118** 55
spirit level *Plumb. etc.* **126** 79
spirit level *D.I.Y.* **134** 29
spirits **98** 56-59; **318** 19
spirograph **27** 36
Spirographis **357** 22
spirometer **23** 31
spirometry **27** 36-50
spit *Phys. Geog.* **13** 5
spit *Kitch. Utensils* **40** 33
spitz **70** 20
splashboard **186** 6
spleen **20** 12, 27
splenius of the neck **18** 51
splice, wet ~ **117** 89
splice graft **54** 39
splice grafting **54** 39
splicer **117** 89
splicing cement **312** 22
splicing head **133** 29
splint *First Aid* **21** 12
splint *Sawmill* **157** 16
splint, emergency ~ **21** 10
splint bone **17** 24
splinter **157** 16
split-image rangefinder **115** 55, 59, 64
splits **314** 20
splitter **94** 17
splitting hammer **85** 5
spoil **226** 47
spoiler **229** 39; **287** 38
spoiler, front ~ **193** 36
spoiler, inner ~ **229** 42
spoiler, rear ~ **193** 34; **290** 35
spoiler rim **193** 30
spoil heap **144** 19
spoke *Mach. Parts etc.* **143** 88
spoke *Bicycle* **187** 27
spoke *Motorcycle* **189** 24
spoke end **187** 29
spoke flange **187** 29
spoke nipple **187** 29
spokeshave **132** 27
spoke wheel **289** 25
sponge *Bathrm. etc.* **49** 6
sponge *School* **260** 42
sponge *Graphic Art* **340** 25
sponge *Invertebr.* **357** 13
sponge holder **23** 12
sponge tray **260** 41
spool **162** 55
spool box **312** 16
spool box, fireproof ~ **312** 25
spool holder **185** 17
spool knob **114** 27
spoon *Tablew. etc.* **45** 61
spoon *Fish Farm.* **89** 73
spoon, wooden ~ **40** 2
spoon bait **89** 73
spoon bit **135** 16
spoon bow **285** 30
spoon chisel **339** 18
spore **381** 8, 13
sporting coupé **193** 28
sporting gun **86** 4
sporting guns **87** 1-40
sporting rifle **86** 4
sporting rifles **87** 1-40; **305** 40-49
sport parachute **288** 45
sports, various ~ **305**
sportsboat, inflatable ~ **286** 1
sportsboats *Rowing* **283** 9-16
sportsboats *Motorboats etc.* **286** 1-5, 10-14
sports news item **342** 61
sports report **342** 60
sports reporter **299** 50
sports section **342** 57
spot **276** 32
spot, central ~ **115** 65
spot, clear ~ **115** 66
spot ball, white ~ **277** 13
spotlight **307** 3; **318** 24
spotlight catwalk **310** 53
spotted bruchus **81** 19
spotted woodpecker **359** 27
spotting position **297** 16
spot welder, foot-operated ~ **142** 29
spot welding **142** 22
spot welding electrode holder **142** 23
spout **91** 14
spout, swivel-mounted ~ **64** 37
spout hole **367** 26
spray *Doc.* **22** 60
spray *Pest Contr.* **83** 8
spray boom **83** 3
spray can **106** 23
spray canister **83** 44
spraydeck **283** 56
sprayer *Gdn. Tools* **56** 24
sprayer *Letterpress* **181** 10, 34
sprayer, semi-mounted ~ **83** 47
sprayer, tractor-mounted ~ **83** 2
spray fluid tank **83** 5, 50
spray gun *Pest Contr.* **83** 18
spray gun *Painter* **129** 32
spray gun *Letterpress* **181** 34
spray gun, airless ~ **129** 37
spraying **129** 28
spraying tube **83** 29
spray line, oscillating ~ **67** 1
spray nozzle *Household* **50** 13
spray nozzle *Intern. Combust. Eng.* **190** 54
spray pipe **172** 72
spray tank **83** 39
spray tube **83** 22
spray unit *Pest Contr.* **83** 58
spray unit *Offset Platem.* **179** 5, 6
spray unit, airless ~ **129** 36
spreader *Paperhanger* **128** 46
spreader *Ship* **223** 37
spreader *Sailing* **284** 13
spreader cylinder **62** 23
spreader unit **62** 22
spreading flap **200** 42
spring *Map* **15** 82
spring *Metalwkr.* **140** 46
spring *Knitting* **167** 38
spring *Carriages* **186** 15
spring, artesian ~ **12** 26
spring, rubber ~ **297** 13
spring attachment **11** 42
spring barrel **110** 38
springboard *Swim.* **282** 9, 10
springboard *Gymn.* **296** 12; **297** 8
springboard *Circus* **307** 36
springboard acrobat **307** 35
springboard artist **307** 35
springboard trampoline **297** 14
spring bolt **140** 37
spring bow compass **151** 64
spring buffer **214** 50
spring bumper **214** 50
spring chest **326** 12-14
springer **336** 22
spring extension **309** 28
spring fly **358** 12
spring form **40** 27
spring pin tool **109** 9
spring ring hinge **151** 65
spring snowflake **60** 1
spring suspension **83** 7
spring tine **65** 57
spring tine, double ~ **64** 42, 54
spring vice **140** 10
spring washer **143** 34; **202** 8
sprinkler **55** 19
sprinkler, oscillating ~ **56** 46
sprinkler, revolving ~ **56** 43; **62** 29; **67** 4, 32
sprinkler cart **62** 27
sprinkler hose **62** 30
sprinkler nozzle **67** 27
sprinkler stand **62** 28
sprinkler system **316** 6
sprinkling can **51** 21; **55** 26
sprinkling device **55** 19
sprinter **298** 5
spritsail **218** 43; **220** 5
sprocket **143** 90; **187** 38, 74
sprocket piece **121** 30
sprocket wheel **187** 38
sprout *Veg.* **57** 30
sprout *Bot.* **370** 19-25
spruce **372** 12
spruce cellulose **169** 1
spruce cone **372** 13
spruce fir **372** 12
spruce-gall aphid **82** 38
spruce needle **372** 19
spur *Dom. Anim.* **73** 26
spur *Game* **88** 82
spur *Mountain.* **300** 13
spurrey **69** 12
spurs **71** 50-51
spur vein **72** 28
spur wheel, helical ~ **143** 89
sputum **23** 25
spyhole *Hall* **41** 29
spyhole *Iron Foundry etc.* **148** 4
squadron marking **256** 2
square *Metalwkr.* **140** 57
square *Maths.* **346** 33; **347** 31
square, black ~ **276** 3
square, glazier's ~ **124** 20
square, iron ~ **120** 78
square, white ~ **276** 2

squared timber store **157** 32
square piano **325** 40
square root **345** 3
squash **57** 23
squat **295** 9
squat-style snatch **299** 1
squat vault **296** 53
squaw **352** 10
squaw corn **68** 31
squeegee *Photog.* **116** 49
squeegee *Text. Finish.* **168** 61
squeeze phase **75** 34
squeeze roller **165** 46
squirrel **366** 19
squirrel's bread **381** 16
stabilizer *Photog.* **116** 10
stabilizer *Motorcycles etc.* **188** 5
stabilizer *Railw.* **214** 55
stabilizer *Navig.* **224** 26
stabilizer *Air Force* **256** 22
stabilizer *Winter Sp.* **301** 49
stabilizer *Sports* **305** 58
stabilizer, horizontal ~ **229** 26; **230** 62; **256** 31; **288** 23
stabilizer, vertical ~ **229** 24; **230** 59; **231** 6; **232** 7; **256** 32; **288** 21
stabilizer and rudder, vertical ~ **229** 24-25; **230** 58
stabilizer bar **192** 71
stabilizing fin *Air Force* **256** 22
stabilizing fin *Swim.* **279** 3
stabilizing fin, aerodynamic ~ **234** 7
stabilizing layer **301** 49
stabilizing panel **288** 49
stabilizing surface **256** 22
stabilizing wing **117** 60
stable **62** 2; **75** 1
stable fly **81** 4
stableman **186** 27
staccato **321** 34
stack *Forestry* **84** 15
stack *Univ.* **262** 11
stack bearer **157** 37
stacker, intermediate ~ **236** 34
stacker truck **159** 18
stacking machine **162** 20
stack of logs **84** 16
staff **320** 43-44
staff compartment **207** 81
staff lavatory **207** 82
staff toilet **207** 82
staff washroom **207** 26
staff WC **207** 82
stag, rutting ~ **86** 12; **88** 4
stag beetle **358** 24
stag call **87** 46
stage *Films* **312** 8
stage *Theatre* **315** 14-27, 14
stage *Nightclub* **318** 22
stage, mechanical ~ **112** 10, 29; **115** 98
stage, microscopic ~ **112** 9
stage, revolving ~ **316** 31
stage, universal ~ **112** 17
stage base **112** 15
stage carpenter **316** 45
stagecoach **186** 39
stagecoach, English ~ **186** 53
stage curtain **312** 10
stage designer **315** 37
stage director **316** 30
stagehand **315** 28; **316** 46
stagehouse **316** 1-60
stage light **316** 14
stage lighting **318** 23
stage lighting unit **316** 14
stage manager **316** 30
stage plate **115** 95
stage rehearsal **315** 21-27
stage separation retro-rocket **234** 8
staghorn **377** 12
stag horn moss **377** 12
staghound **289** 47
staging *Photograv.* **182** 12
staging *Shipbuild.* **222** 18
stag jump **295** 40; **302** 7
stag leap **295** 40; **302** 7
stag's horn **377** 12
stag's horn moss **377** 12
staining dish **23** 50
staining vat **130** 15
staircase **37** 72; **118** 22
staircase, dog-legged ~ **123** 42-44
staircase, outside ~ **333** 33
staircase, quarter-newelled ~ **123** 75
staircase, spiral ~ **123** 76, 77
staircase, winding ~ **123** 76, 77
staircase bolt **123** 46
staircase construction **123**
staircase of locks **217** 17-25
staircase window **37** 81; **123** 65
stair light **41** 22
stairs, concrete ~ **123** 16
stair well **120** 46
stake *Wine Grow.* **78** 7
stake *Forestry* **84** 17
stake *Plumb.* **125** 23
stake *Basketm.* **136** 6
stake *Roulette* **275** 13
stake net **89** 94
stalactite **13** 80, 82
stalactite vault **337** 17
stalagmite **13** 81, 82
stalk **58** 13, 34, 61; **68** 6; **370** 20; **378** 31
stalk, herbaceous ~ **384** 30
stalking **86** 1-8
stall **75** 2
stallion **73** 2
stalls, front ~ **315** 19
stall turn **288** 4
stamen **58** 45; **59** 10, 39; **370** 57, 60; **372** 7, 18; **373** 2, 5; **374** 3
stamp *Doc.* **22** 29
stamp *Slaughterho.* **94** 24
stamp *Post* **236** 21, 61
stamp *Bank* **250** 24
stamp, impressed ~ **252** 35
stamp book **236** 20
stamp counter **236** 15
stanchion **221** 117
stanchion, hinged ~ **213** 6
stanchion, steel ~ **213** 6
stand *Hosp.* **25** 11; **26** 9, 29
stand *Overh. Irrign.* **67** 2
stand *Shoem.* **100** 54
stand *Opticn.* **111** 5
stand *Optic. Instr.* **112** 2
stand *Basketm.* **136** 10
stand *Composing Rm.* **175** 50
stand *Photomech. Reprod.* **177** 29
stand *Motorcycles etc.* **188** 51
stand *Circus* **307** 57
stand *Bullfight. etc.* **319** 8
stand, hydraulic ~ **310** 50
stand, raised ~ **86** 14, 14-17
standard *Bldg. Site* **119** 47, 59
standard *Forging* **139** 19
standard *Photomech. Reprod.* **177** 11
standard adjustment **114** 51
standard lamp **46** 37
Standard meridian **14** 5
standard of the German Federal President **253** 14
standby drive **214** 64
standing-in position **297** 16
standing matter **174** 11
standing matter rack **174** 9
standing position **305** 27
standing press **183** 20
standing room portion **197** 18
standing stone **328** 18
standing take-off pike dive **282** 40
standing type **174** 11
standing type rack **174** 9
standing wrestling **299** 6
standpipe *Farm Bldgs.* **62** 12
standpipe *Oil, Petr.* **145** 13
standpipe *Paperm.* **173** 12
standpipe *Space* **234** 25
standpipe *Fire Brig.* **270** 26
standpipe coupler **67** 5
stapelia **53** 15
staple fibre **169** 1-34
staple fibre lap **169** 31
staple fibre, viscose rayon ~ **169** 28-34
staple fibre layer **169** 31
staple length **170** 60
stapler **22** 25; **247** 4
staple shaft **144** 27
stapling machine **247** 4
star *Sailing* **284** 55
star *Films* **310** 27, 28
star, binary ~ **3** 29
star, circumpolar ~ **3** 5
star, double ~ **3** 29
star, principal ~ **3** 9
star, variable ~ **3** 11
star connection **153** 20
star finch **360** 3
starfish **357** 38; **369** 17
starling **361** 4
star map **3** 1-35
star network **153** 20
stars, fixed ~ **3** 9-48
Stars and Stripes **253** 18
Star-Spangled Banner **253** 18
start *Motorboats etc.* **286** 28, 29

start *Athletics* **298** 1-6, 3
starter **282** 30
starter, electric ~ **56** 39
starter and steering lock **191** 75
starter battery **212** 46
starter button, electric ~ **189** 52
starter motor *Intern. Combust. Eng.* **190** 44
starter motor *Railw.* **212** 30
starter pedal **188** 25
starter's flag **273** 34
starter switch **241** 30
starting and braking device, automatic ~ **168** 20
starting and finishing buoy **285** 14
starting and stopping handle **166** 8
starting and stopping lever **165** 17; **180** 80; **181** 32
starting block *Swim.* **282** 27
starting block *Athletics* **298** 1
starting dive **282** 29
starting gear ring **192** 31
starting handle **163** 17
starting lever **178** 20
starting line **286** 30
starting motor **190** 44
starting place **282** 27
starting position **295** 1
starting price **289** 37
starting resistance **135** 3
starting resistor **135** 3
starting rod **167** 22
starting signal **205** 47
start print button **249** 38
start-stop lever **163** 40
star wheel *Mach. Tools* **149** 43
star wheel *Graphic Art* **340** 39
Stassfurt salt **154** 66
Stassfurt seam **154** 65
stately home **15** 96
statement of account **247** 44
state of play **293** 38
static air tank **196** 19
station, coastal ~ **237** 53
station, lower ~ **214** 39
station, top ~ **214** 57
station, upper ~ **214** 57
stationary rings **296** 4
station bookstall **204** 26
station bookstand **204** 26
station clock **204** 30
station foreman **205** 41
station hall **204**
station mailbox **204** 11
station of the Cross **330** 54
station platform **205**
station post box **204** 11
station preset button **241** 4; **243** 17; **309** 20
station restaurant **204** 13
station selector button **241** 4; **243** 17; **309** 20
station sign **205** 28
station wagon **193** 15
statistics chart **248** 36
statue **215** 22; **272** 10; **334** 5; **339** 32
statue, stone ~ **272** 2
statuette, ivory ~ **328** 8
stave *Cooper* **130** 2
stave *Music. Not.* **320** 43-44
stay **219** 10
stay, triatic ~ **223** 11
stayer **290** 14
stay pole **152** 31
stay rope **299** 37
stay-warm plate **28** 28
stay wire **296** 10; **297** 5; **299** 37
St. Bernard dog **70** 37
steady, fixed ~ **150** 30
steam **50** 11
steam and recirculation water flow path **154** 51
steam boiler **152** 5
steam chest **210** 31
steam collector **210** 21
steam coupling hose **208** 20
steam dome **210** 12
steam extraction **103** 26
steam extractor **103** 25
steam-generating station **152** 1-28
steam generator **154** 9, 26, 44
steam heater **172** 38
steam hole **50** 14
steaming light **223** 40; **258** 55
steaming light mast **221** 51
steam iron **103** 20; **131** 3
steam line **154** 11
steam locomotives **210** 1-69
steam pipe **172** 64
steam pipe, high-pressure ~ **259** 63
steam press **104** 26
steam pressing unit **104** 26
'steam radio' **309** 16
steam reversing gear **210** 18
steam slit **50** 14
steam spray gun **131** 2
steam sterilizer **22** 39
steam storage locomotive **210** 68
steam trawler **221** 46
steam tube **210** 17
steam turbine **152** 23; **153** 23-30; **154** 14, 46, 52
steam turbine generator **259** 58
steel **94** 16
steel, finished ~ **148** 68
steel bender **119** 21
steel-casting ladle **147** 31
steel grit delivery pipe **148** 38
steel ingot **147** 33
steel lattice bridge **215** 34
steel-leg vice **126** 80
steel-wheel glass cutter **124** 26
steelworks **147** 21-69
steep face **12** 43
steeping **169** 4
steeping floor **92** 8, 28
steeping tank **92** 8
steeple **331** 2
steeplechase *Equest.* **289** 20-22
steeplechase *Athletics* **298** 7-8
steep liquor **92** 6
steering, hydraulic power ~ **65** 41
steering alignment **195** 17, 22
steering alignment, visual ~ **195** 41
steering and control position **224** 14
steering arm **192** 79
steering axle **64** 32
steering column **192** 56
steering column, controlled-collapse ~ **191** 57
steering drop arm **192** 58
steering gear **192** 56-59
steering head **187** 11
steering line *Rowing* **283** 52
steering line *Airsports* **288** 41
steering oar **218** 6
steering rudder **283** 51-53
steering runner **302** 45
steering system, rear-wheel ~ **64** 39
steering tube **187** 14
steering wheel **191** 37; **305** 89
steering wheel spoke **191** 58
steersman *Ship* **218** 2
steersman *Winter Sp.* **303** 20
stein **309** 53
steinbock **367** 7
Steinheim man **261** 17
stela **330** 43; **334** 33
stele **330** 43; **334** 33
stem *Forestry* **84** 19
stem *Tobacc. etc.* **107** 38
stem *Metalwkr.* **140** 33
stem *Ship* **218** 4; **221** 14, 83, 108; **258** 3
stem *Chem.* **350** 7
stem *Bot.* **370** 2
stem *Edib. Fungi* **381** 18
stem, bulbous ~ **222** 74
stem, prostrate ~ **58** 20
stem, straight ~ **285** 40
stem, wire ~ **325** 29
stem cutting **54** 25
stemless alpine gentian **378** 13
stemming sand bucket **158** 29
stem post **218** 4
stem rudder **218** 24
stem stitch **102** 4
stencil ejection **245** 9
stencil knife **129** 43
stencil lettering guide **151** 69
stencil magazine, vertical ~ **245** 8
stencil storage drawer **245** 10
stenography **342** 13
steno pad **245** 29; **248** 32
stenter **165** 54; **168** 21
stenter clip **168** 24
stenter pin **168** 24
step *Roof & Boilerr.* **38** 27
step *Hall* **41** 24
step *Carriages* **186** 13
step *Tram* **197** 15
step *Aircraft* **230** 42
step *Swim.* **281** 32, 37
step *Mountain.* **300** 17
step, bottom ~ **123** 18, 42

step, top ~ **123** 19
step, wedge-shaped ~ **123** 31
step bearing **91** 10
step-cut, hexagonal ~ **36** 62
step-cut, octagonal ~ **36** 52
step-cut, rectangular ~ **36** 50
step-cut, rhombus ~ **36** 59
step-cut, round hexagonal ~ **36** 64
step-cut, square ~ **36** 51
step-cut, trapezium ~ **36** 57
step-cut, triangular ~ **36** 60-61
step fault **12** 8
step irons **269** 28
stepladder **50** 35; **126** 2; **129** 5
steppe zone **9** 54
stepping stones **37** 45
steps *Dwellings* **37** 39
steps *Household* **50** 35
steps *Station* **204** 25; **205** 2
steps *Circus* **307** 20
steps, front ~ **37** 66
steps, wooden ~ **38** 25
stereobate **334** 4
stereo cassette deck **241** 33
stereo component system, three-in-one ~ **241** 52
stereo effect **310** 30
stereo equipment **42** 9; **317** 22-23
stereo microphone jack **241** 65
stereo microphone socket **241** 65
stereomicroscope, wide-field ~ **112** 61
stereoplanigraph **14** 66
stereo receiver **241** 52
stereoscope **14** 64
stereo sound **311** 35
stereo speakers **241** 13-14
stereo system **42** 9; **241** 13-48; **317** 22-23
sterilization room **26** 34-54
sterilizer **76** 12
sterilizer, small ~ **26** 35
stern **222** 66-72; **258** 26; **285** 29
stern, elliptical ~ **218** 25
stern, gilded ~ **218** 55-57
stern, lower ~ **218** 58
stern, round ~ **218** 25
stern, square ~ **285** 43
stern, upper ~ **218** 55
sterncastle **218** 23
stern fender **227** 29
stern frame **222** 70-71
stern gallery **218** 56
stern light **258** 62
stern light, white ~ **286** 14
stern loading door **221** 31
stern opening **221** 55; **226** 18
stern port **221** 55; **226** 18
stern post **218** 1
stern ramp **221** 88; **258** 91
stern towing point **221** 53
sternum **17** 8
stethoscope **23** 35
stetson hat **319** 37
steward *Ship* **221** 110
steward *Election* **263** 10
steward *Cyc. Racing* **290** 4
stick **322** 35; **323** 14, 56
stick, forked ~ **54** 13
stick, French ~ **97** 12
stick blade **302** 32
sticker *Slaughterho.* **94** 14
sticker *Music. Instr.* **325** 30; **326** 9
stick handle **302** 31
sticking knife **94** 14
sticking paper **260** 50-52
sticking plaster **21** 7; **22** 55
stiffener **215** 53
stiffening **101** 37
stifle **72** 33
stifle joint **72** 33
stigma *Soft Fruit* **58** 41
stigma *Drupes & Nuts* **59** 16
stigma *Articulates* **358** 32
stigma *Bot.* **370** 56
stile *Roof & Boilerr.* **38** 16
stile *Household* **50** 36
stile *Carp.* **120** 25
stile *Roof* **121** 40
stiletto **102** 12
stiletto beard **34** 13
stiletto heel **101** 28
stillhunting **86** 1-8
stilling basin **217** 61
stilling box **217** 61
stilling pool **217** 61
still life group **338** 27
stilt **359** 19
stilt bird **359** 19
stilt plover **359** 19
stilts **308** 49
stimulants **382**
sting **77** 11
stinging nettle **61** 33
stinging organs **77** 10-14
sting sheath **77** 12
stinkweed **379** 8
stipe **381** 18
stipple paint **129** 53
stippler **129** 18
stippling roller **129** 13
stipule **57** 5; **58** 48; **371** 73
stirrer *Dairy.* **76** 43
stirrer *Paperm.* **172** 47
stirrer *Chem.* **349** 18
stirrup *Horse* **71** 43
stirrup *Bldg. Site* **119** 70
stirrup iron **71** 43
stirrup leather **71** 42
stitch, flat ~ **102** 10
stitch, knotted ~ **102** 13
stitch, ornamental ~ **102** 3
stitch, overcast ~ **102** 8
stitch, Russian ~ **102** 9
stitching **183** 8, 34
stitching, decorative ~ **31** 5
stitching machine **100** 21
stitching wire feed mechanism **184** 18
stock *Plant Propagn.* **54** 33
stock *Hunt.* **87** 3,4,6,13
stock *Mills* **91** 2
stock *Joiner* **132** 24
stock *Paperm.* **173** 1, 2-10
stock *Stock Exch.* **251** 1-10
stock *Stock Exch.* **251** 11-19
stock, round ~ **139** 1
stock, square ~ **143** 9
stockbroker, sworn ~ **251** 4
stock certificate **251** 11
stock chest **172** 85; **173** 1
stock cube **98** 26
stock exchange **251** 1-10
stock exchange agent **251** 7
stock exchange attendant **251** 9
stocking **99** 26; **318** 32
stocking, knee-high ~ **32** 9
stockjobber **251** 6
stock ledger **251** 14
stock list **250** 8
stock preparation plant **172** 79-86
stocks **222** 11-26
stock saddle **71** 37-44
stogy **101** 39
stoker, travelling-grate ~ **152** 3
stola **355** 9
stole, fur ~ **318** 30
stollen **97** 11
stomach *Man* **16** 35-37; **20** 13, 41-42
stomach *Bees* **77** 16
stomiatid **369** 10, 13
stone *Agr.* **63** 9
stone *Mills* **91** 21
stone *Clocks* **110** 33
stone *Quarry* **158** 8
stone *Swim.* **281** 22
stone *Sculpt. Studio* **339** 5
stone *Shrubs etc.* **374** 12
stone, crushed ~ **158** 24
stone, dressed ~ **158** 30
stone, lower ~ **91** 23
Stone Age idol **328** 8
stone block **339** 5
stone catcher **64** 9
stone chippings **158** 23
stonecrop **51** 7; **61** 17; **375** 21
stone-crushing plant **158** 18
stone-dressing device **172** 70
stone fruit **59** 41, 43, 49; **370** 99
stone lithography **340** 25-26
stone marten **367** 14
stonemason **158** 34
stonemason's tools **158** 35-38
stone pine **372** 55
stones, faceted ~ **36** 42-71
stone spreader **200** 31
stone trap **64** 9
stool **24** 14; **27** 50; **260** 58
stop *Bookbind.* **185** 11
stop *Railw.* **214** 35
stop *Music. Instr.* **325** 44; **326** 6
stop *Chem.* **349** 37
stop and start lever **163** 31
stop and tail light **189** 9
stop and tail light unit **188** 38
stop bar **133** 11
stop bath **116** 10
stop board **203** 25, 33
stop boards **203** 31-32
stop button *Clocks* **110** 22

stop button *Office* **249** 73
stopclock **238** 62
stopclock, electronic ~ **238** 31
stopclock *Plumb. etc.* **126** 4
stopclock *Gas Weld.* **141** 7
stopclock *Water* **269** 48
stopcock, flange-type ~ **130** 21
stop-cylinder machine **181** 20
stop-cylinder press **181** 20
stop fillet **119** 62
stop key **243** 43
stop knob *Music. Instr.* **325** 44; **326** 6
stop knob *Chem.* **349** 38
stop lever **324** 42
stop line **268** 50
stop motion **166** 43
stop-motion device **168** 19
stopper *Overh. Irrign.* **67** 36
stopper *Iron & Steel* **147** 31
stopper *Music. Instr.* **326** 35
stopper *Chem.* **350** 44
stopper, ground glass ~ **349** 4
stopper, octagonal ~ **349** 4
stopping device **168** 19
stopping handle **164** 6, 32
stopping point **203** 25, 31-32
stop plate **157** 18
stop rod blade **166** 43
stops **342** 16-29
stop signal **203** 1
stop signal, electric ~ **203** 3
stop signals **203** 1-6
stop tab **326** 39
storage area **246** 5
storage bin **200** 35
storage box *Child. Rm.* **47** 2
storage box *D.I.Y.* **134** 34, 39
storage cell **77** 35
storage chamber **154** 71, 76
storage container **130** 17
storage cupboard **207** 27
storage door **39** 6
storage reservoir **217** 57
storage shelf **174** 10
storage siding **206** 50
storage tank *Brew.* **93** 13
storage tank *Oil, Petr.* **145** 72
storage tank *Paperm.* **172** 17, 41, 45, 46
storage tank *Docks* **225** 72
storage tank gauge **76** 10
storage unit *Dent.* **24** 8
storage unit *Composing Rm.* **176** 11
storage unit *Inf. Tech.* **242** 9
storage vessel **10** 46
store area **5** 17
storehouse **329** 13
storekeeper **98** 41
store room **223** 57
storey roof **337** 2
storm front **287** 24
storm-front soaring **287** 23
storm lantern **278** 29
storm signal **225** 35; **280** 4
stout **93** 26
stove, cylindrical ~ **309** 4
stove, tiled ~ **266** 34
stove bench **266** 36
stove door **309** 7
stovepipe **309** 5
stovepipe elbow **309** 6
stove screen **309** 8
stove tile **266** 35
stowage **227** 26; **228** 27
straddle **298** 23
straddle jump **298** 23
straddle position **296** 30
straddle seat **295** 18
straight ball **305** 17
straightedge *Paperhanger* **128** 39
straightedge *Metalwkr.* **140** 56
straightedge rule **179** 26
straight hang **296** 38
straight header **282** 12
straight inverted hang **296** 37
straight thrust **294** 7
strainer *Paperm.* **172** 54
strainer *Water* **269** 32
strainer, basket ~ **67** 12
strainer, rotary ~ **172** 23
strain insulator **152** 38
strait **14** 24
Strait of Gibraltar **14** 24
straits bridge **215** 57
strake, outside ~ **285** 50
stramonium **379** 8
stramony **379** 8
strampler **29** 23
strand **162** 54
strand of fruit **384** 8
strand of moulds **147** 36
strap *Clocks* **110** 5
strap *Bldg. Site* **119** 60, 65
strap *School* **260** 11
strap *Cyc. Racing* **290** 22
strap *Winter Sp.* **301** 3
strap hinge **140** 51
strap support **286** 59
stratification **12** 1
stratocumulus **8** 3
stratosphere **7** 8
stratosphere aircraft **7** 15
stratovolcano **11** 15
stratum, impermeable ~ *Phys. Geog.* **12** 28
stratum, impermeable ~ *Water* **269** 36
stratum, impervious ~ *Phys. Geog.* **12** 28
stratum, impervious ~ *Water* **269** 36
stratum, porous ~ **12** 29
stratum, water-bearing ~ *Phys. Geog.* **12** 22
stratum, water-bearing ~ *Water* **269** 2, 38
stratus **8** 4
straw *Agr.* **63** 34, 36
straw *Livestock* **75** 7
straw *Basketm.* **136** 30
straw *Station* **206** 23
straw *Restaurant* **266** 46
straw baler **63** 35
strawberry **58** 21
strawberry flan **97** 22
strawberry plant **58** 16
straw fiddle **324** 61
straw hive **77** 52
straw press **63** 35
straw shaker **64** 14
strawwalker **64** 14
straw yard system **74** 1-17
stream *Phys. Geog.* **13** 8
stream *Map* **15** 80
stream *Park* **272** 45
stream, subglacial ~ **12** 52
stream, underground ~ **269** 3
streamer **253** 9
streamer, paper ~ **306** 66
streamlining, integrated ~ **189** 44
street **37** 61; **198** 13
street, cross-section of a ~ **198**
street café **268** 59
streetcar **197**; **268** 46
streetcar schedule **268** 27
streetcar service **197** 13
streetcar stop **268** 25
streetcar stop sign **197** 36; **268** 26
streetcar track **268** 23
street cleaner **199** 41; **304** 8
street cleaning **199**
street-cleaning lorry **199** 41; **304** 8
street corner **198** 12
street lamp **37** 62; **268** 6
street lamp, suspended ~ **268** 49
street light **37** 62; **268** 6
street map **204** 15; **268** 2
street sign **268** 7
street sweeper **199** 5; **268** 20
stretcher *Fire Brig.* **270** 23
stretcher *Rowing* **283** 47
stretcher, emergency ~ **21** 23
stretcher, wedged ~ **338** 20
stretcher bar **202** 29
stretch girdle **32** 5
stretching **170** 46, 55
stretching, final ~ **170** 47
stretching, preliminary ~ **170** 45
stretching bond **118** 59
stretching course **118** 63
stretching machine **100** 18
streusel cake **97** 35
streusel slice **97** 43
stridulating apparatus **81** 8
stridulating mechanism **81** 8
strike *Phys. Geog.* **12** 2
strike *Composing Rm.* **175** 37
striker *Hunt.* **87** 21
striker *Ball Games* **291** 15
striker pad **255** 47
striking circle **292** 16
striking force control **249** 10
striking mechanism **325** 3
striking of coins **252** 40-44
striking surface *Tobacc. etc.* **107** 24
striking surface *Ball Games* **293** 31
striking weight **110** 28; **309** 60
string *Roof & Boilerr.* **38** 26
string *Sports* **305** 59
string *Music. Instr.* **322** 44, 55; **323** 9, 61; **325** 7

string, catgut ~ **324** 6, 14
string, chalked ~ **128** 45
string, fretted ~ **324** 24
string, gut ~ **324** 6, 14
string, nylon ~ **324** 14
string, open ~ **324** 25
string, outer ~ **123** 44
string, stopped ~ **324** 24
string, unfretted ~ **324** 25
string, wreathed ~ **123** 49
string briefs **32** 23
string course **335** 52
stringed instruments **323** 1-27; **324** 1-31
stringer *Roof & Boilerr.* **38** 26
stringer *Shipbuild.* **222** 50
stringer *Aircraft* **230** 47, 57
stringer *Sailing* **285** 55
stringer, outer ~ **123** 44
string fastener **324** 4
string holder **324** 4, 13
strings **293** 31
string vest **32** 22
strip **148** 66-75
stripe, magnetic ~ **117** 82
striped hyena **368** 1
strip flooring **123** 62
stripper *Paperhanger* **128** 1, 9
stripper *Nightclub* **318** 27
stripping **89** 11
stripping knife **128** 15; **134** 37
stripping table **179** 23
strip steel **143** 11
striptease act **318** 27-32
striptease artist **318** 27
striptease number **318** 27-32
strip window **37** 86
strobile **376** 19
stroke *Rowing* **283** 12
stroke *Music. Not.* **320** 6
stroke, plain ~ **277** 2
strokes **136** 1-4
stroller **28** 37
strong beer **93** 26
strong man **308** 27
strong room **250** 11
structural parts of ship **222** 44-61
structural system, Gothic ~ **335** 27-35
structure, geological ~ **154** 57-68
structure, longitudinal ~ **222** 44-56
structures, molecular ~ **1** 9-14
strut *Bldg. Site* **119** 63, 67
strut *Carp.* **120** 27, 54
strut *Roof* **121** 58, 69, 82
strut *Ship* **223** 61
strut *Aircraft* **229** 11
strut *Rowing* **283** 46
strut *Winter Sp.* **303** 5
strut, diagonal ~ *Bldg. Site* **118** 88
strut, diagonal ~ *Bridges* **215** 4
stub **84** 14
stub axle **192** 78
stubble beard **34** 23
stubble field **63** 33
stub wing **232** 3
stud *Carp.* **120** 25
stud *Roof* **121** 40
stud *Mach. Parts etc.* **143** 22
stud, ornamental ~ **253** 8
stud, rubber ~ **187** 84
stud, screw-in ~ **291** 28
student **262** 9, 10
student input device **242** 4
student response device **242** 4
studio *Broadcast.* **238** 18
studio *Art. Studio* **338** 1-43
studio, artist's ~ **338**
studio, sculptor's ~ **339**
studio apartment **37** 74
studio complex **310** 1-13
studio easel **338** 3
studio electrician **310** 37
studio flat **37** 74
studio lot **310** 1
studio microphone *Broadcast.* **238** 34
studio microphone *Films* **310** 31
studio skylight **338** 1
studio table **238** 29
studio window **238** 38
study in oils **338** 36
study step counter **242** 5
stuff **173** 1, 2-10
stuff box **173** 11
stuff chest **172** 85, 86; **173** 1, 13
stuffing box *Oil, Petr.* **145** 26
stuffing box *Railw.* **210** 33
stuffing box *Ship* **223** 64
stuff preparation plant **172** 79-86
stump **84** 14
stump of tooth **24** 27
stunner, electric ~ **94** 7
stunning device **94** 3
stupa **337** 21, 28
Stuttgart Planetarium **5** 17-28
sty **62** 8
style **58** 42; **59** 15; **68** 34; **370** 55; **373** 5; **378** 5
style jump **288** 50-51
styling scissors **106** 34
stylobate **334** 32
stylus **341** 25
stylus, conical ~ **241** 26
stylus, elliptical ~ **241** 26
stylus, steel ~ **341** 21
stylus force control **241** 24
stylus pressure control **241** 24
sub-base course, bituminous ~ **198** 2
sub-base course, gravel ~ **200** 60
sub-base course, hardcore ~ **200** 60
subcontra octave **321** 42
sub-drainage **200** 61
subfloor **123** 38, 73
subgrade grader **201** 1
sub-machine gun **255** 8
submarine **258** 64
substation, outdoor ~ **152** 29-35
substitute **291** 54; **292** 39
substitute flags **253** 30-32
substitute signal **203** 6
substructure *Oil, Petr.* **145** 2
substructure *Offshore Drill.* **146** 38
subtitle **185** 47
subtracting **344** 24
subtraction **344** 24
subtrahend **344** 24
succory **57** 40; **376** 25
sucker *House Insects etc.* **81** 37
sucker *Opticn.* **111** 23
sucker *Invertebr.* **357** 21
sucker rod **145** 25
sucking organ **358** 17
suction **162** 25, 28, 36
suction apparatus *Dent.* **24** 11
suction apparatus *Poultry Farm* **74** 41
suction box *Poultry Farm* **74** 41
suction box *Cotton Spin.* **164** 44
suction box *Paperm.* **173** 15
suction control **50** 72
suction control, fingertip ~ **50** 74
suction control, sliding ~ **50** 74
suction dredger **216** 59
suction electrode **23** 29
suction feeder **180** 72
suction head **217** 51
suction hose *Household* **50** 75
suction hose *Fire Brig.* **270** 67
suction hose, soft ~ **270** 30
suction pipe *Roof & Boilerr.* **38** 55
suction pipe *Docks* **226** 32
suction pipe *Water* **269** 5, 14, 41
suction pipe *Theatre* **316** 52
suction pipe, trailing ~ **216** 59
suction port **199** 43
suction pump **216** 62
suction roll **173** 16
suction slot **168** 43
suction tube **10** 37
sugar **98** 53-55
sugar, confectioner's ~ **98** 54
sugar, refined ~ **98** 55
sugar beet **68** 44
sugar beet eelworm **80** 51
sugar bowl **44** 32; **265** 20
sugar cane **382** 52
sugar loaf **99** 64
suit, asbestos ~ **270** 46
suit, casual ~ **33** 17
suit, denim ~ **31** 58; **33** 20
suit, extra-vehicular ~ **6** 18-27
suit, jersey ~ **29** 17
suit, men's ~ **33** 1
suit, one-piece ~ **29** 17
suit, quilted ~ **29** 38
suit, single-breasted ~ **33** 1
suit, two-piece ~ **29** 12
suitcase **194** 19; **204** 6; **205** 7
suitcase, light ~ **267** 15
suitcase, lightweight ~ **267** 15
suite, upholstered ~ **42** 21-26
suiting **104** 3
suits **276** 38-45

suits, German ~ **276** 42-45
suit trousers **33** 3
sulfate *see* sulphate
sulfide *see* sulphide
sulfur *see* sulphur
sulfuric *see* sulphuric
sulky **289** 24
sulphate pulp mill **172** 1-52
sulphur **351** 23
sulphur-crested cockatoo **363** 1
sulphuric acid **170** 23, 24
sulphuric acid, production of ~ **156** 34
sulphuric acid supply **156** 33
sultana **98** 8
sum **344** 23
Sumatra cigar **107** 2
summer **121** 67
summer beam **121** 67
summer blouse **31** 22
summer coat **31** 20
summer dike **216** 48
summer dress **31** 9
summerhouse **52** 14
summer quarters, animals' ~ **356** 11
summer slacks **31** 52
summer solstice **3** 8
summer wear **31**
summit **12** 40
sump *Coal* **144** 47
sump *Intern. Combust. Eng.* **190** 41
sump filter **192** 18
sun **4** 10-21, 29, 36-41, 42
sun bather **281** 12
sunbathing area *Dwellings* **37** 46
sunbathing area *Spa* **274** 12
sunbathing area *Swim.* **281** 11; **282** 4
sun bed **281** 5
sun blind **37** 71
sun canopy **274** 14
sun deck **223** 22
sundew **377** 14
sundial **110** 30
sun disc, winged ~ **333** 12
sundress, child's ~ **29** 13
sun filter **6** 22
sunflower **51** 35; **52** 7; **69** 20
sunflower oil **98** 24
sunglasses **6** 19; **111** 6; **301** 19
sunglass pocket **6** 19
sun hat **29** 16; **35** 37
sunlight **155** 18
sun lounge **37** 70
sun parlor **37** 70
sun ray lamp **281** 13
sun roof **37** 75
sunroof, steel ~ **193** 24
sun rose **377** 20
sun sensor **10** 69
sunshade *Dwellings* **37** 48, 71
sunshade *Town* **268** 61
sunshade *Park* **272** 58
sunshade *Films* **313** 3
sun spectacles **111** 6
sunspot **4** 37, 38
sun terrace **37** 75
supatap **126** 35
super *Bees* **77** 45
super *Theatre* **316** 39
Super-calender **173** 36
supercilium **19** 38
super grade gasoline **145** 55
super grade petrol **145** 55
superheater **152** 9
supermarket **99** 1-96
supernumerary **316** 39
superstructure *Weaving* **165** 6
superstructure *Ship* **221** 10, 69
superstructure, aft ~ **258** 22
superstructure, compact ~ **221** 33
superstructure, forward ~ **259** 45
superstructure deck **258** 10
superstructures **258** 10-28
Super-Vee racing car **290** 37
supplementary angle **346** 14
supply pipe *Butch.* **96** 50
supply pipe *Plumb. etc.* **126** 9
supply sprocket **312** 26
supply table **74** 51
supply vessel **221** 32
support *Plant Propagn.* **54** 33
support *Roof* **121** 83
support *Knitting* **167** 38
support *Offset Platem.* **179** 20
support *Shipbuild.* **222** 27
support *Circus* **307** 29, 45
support, adjustable ~ **67** 22
support, intermediate ~ **214** 29, 76
support, single-pylon ~ **214** 23
support, three-point ~ **349** 28
support, tubular steel ~ **214** 78
support cable **2** 30
supporters **254** 15-16
support guide rail **214** 79
supporting cable **214** 27, 38, 41, 44
supporting cable anchorage **214** 59
supporting cable brake **214** 71
supporting cable guide **214** 58
supporting cable guide rail **214** 79
supporting insulator **153** 54
supporting pulley **163** 46
supporting structure **337** 9
supporting wall **121** 77
support insulator **153** 54
support roll **270** 50
support truss **214** 80
suppressor **190** 35
surcoat **355** 25
surf **13** 27
surface, asphalt ~ **200** 58
surface, bituminous ~ **198** 5
surface, curved ~ **347** 40
surface, flat ~ **111** 39
surface, hatched ~ **151** 29
surface, icy ~ **304** 19
surface, lunar ~ **6** 13
surface, nap ~ **168** 31
surface, plane ~ **347** 31
surface, raised ~ **168** 31
surface, special ~ **111** 40, 41, 42
surface boundary layer **7** 7
surface chart **9** 1-39
surface condenser **152** 24
surface finisher **200** 43
surface-finish microscope **112** 37
surface hydrant **270** 35
surface not to be machined **151** 20
surfaces, plane ~ **346** 24-58
surface skimmers **286** 38-44
surface synoptic chart **9** 1-39
surface-to-air missile launcher **259** 50
surface-to-air rocket launcher **259** 50
surface to be machined **151** 21
surface to be superfinished **151** 22
surface wave **11** 36
surfacing **111** 36
surfboard **279** 1, 2; **280** 15; **284** 5
surfboarder **279** 5; **280** 14
surfer **279** 5; **280** 14
surfing **279** 1-6; **280** 13
surf riding **279** 1-6; **280** 13
surge baffle system **235** 53
surge diverter **152** 35
surgery **22** 32-74
surge tank **217** 40
surgical instruments **26** 40-53
surgical unit **26** 1-54
sur le cou-de-pied **314** 14
surroyal **88** 9
survey illumination **112** 52
surveying **14** 46-62
surveying, geodetic ~ **14** 46-62
surveying level **14** 48
surveyor's level **14** 48
suspect **264** 32
suspender *Underwear etc.* **32** 6
suspender *Bridges* **215** 41
suspender *Nightclub* **318** 28
suspenders **29** 26, 34; **32** 30; **33** 45
suspension **168** 16
suspension, steel and rubber ~ **207** 4
suspension and haulage cable **214** 21
suspension arm, lower ~ **192** 84
suspension bridge **215** 39
suspension bridge, primitive ~ **215** 15
suspension cable *Railw.* **214** 27, 38, 41, 44
suspension cable *Bridges* **215** 40
suspension cable anchorage *Railw.* **214** 59
suspension cable anchorage *Bridges* **215** 43
suspension cable bearing **214** 33
suspension cable brake **214** 71

suspension cable guide **214** 58
suspension cable guide rail **214** 79
suspension damper **192** 76
suspension file **248** 3
suspension file system **248** 2
suspension gear **214** 54
suspension gear bolt **214** 72
suspension line **288** 40
suspension line, double-cable ~ **214** 25, 30
suspension line gondola **214** 52
suspension lines, single-cable ~ **214** 15-24
suspension line support **214** 76
suspension rope **215** 17
suspension spring **192** 74
sustaining pedal **325** 8
suture material **22** 56; **26** 21
swab **137** 3
swab dispenser **22** 36
swage block *Goldsm. etc.* **108** 18
swage block *Blacksm.* **137** 17
swage block *Metalwkr.* **140** 14
swage head **143** 57
swallow **361** 20
swallowhole **11** 49; **13** 71
swallowtail **358** 52
swallow-tail twin crystal **351** 25
swamp **13** 24
Swan *Astron.* **3** 23
swan **272** 54; **359** 16
swan *Birds* **359** 16
swan-neck **37** 12; **122** 30
swan's neck **37** 12; **122** 30
swarf **149** 44
swarm cluster of bees **77** 53
swarming net **77** 54
swarm of bees **77** 53
swath **63** 23, 36
swathe **63** 23, 36
swather **63** 19
swather, rotary ~ **63** 26; **64** 40-45
swath rake **64** 44
swath reaper **63** 19
sweater **29** 43; **31** 51
sweater, short-sleeved ~ **33** 32
sweepback, positive ~ **229** 21
sweepback, semi-positive ~ **229** 20
sweeper, mechanical ~ **199** 39
sweet **98** 75, 80
sweet bread **97** 40
sweet calamus **377** 22
sweet cherry **59** 5
sweet chestnut **384** 48
sweet corn **68** 31
sweet flag **377** 22
sweet gale **373** 33
sweet pepper **57** 42
sweets **47** 31, 32
sweet sedge **377** 22
sweet syringa **373** 9
sweet william **60** 6
swell **325** 45
swell pedal, balanced ~ **326** 50
swift **359** 24
swimming **282**
swimming bath **281**
swimming bath attendant **281** 4; **282** 15
swimming belt **282** 19
swimming cap **280** 29, 44
swimming instruction **282** 16-20
swimming instructor **282** 16
swimming lane **282** 31
swimming pool **223** 23; **281** 1-9
swimming pool, open-air ~ **282** 1-32
swimming pool attendant **281** 4; **282** 15
swimming strokes **282** 33-39
swimming teacher **282** 16
swimming trunks **280** 43
swimsuit **280** 42
swing *Gymn.* **297** 39
swing *Athletics* **298** 30
swing, double ~ **273** 39
swing boat **308** 41, 42
swing bridge, flat ~ **215** 67
swing door **207** 18
swing-grippers **180** 33
swing pipe **172** 10
swing seat **273** 40
swing wing **256** 9
Swiss chard **57** 28
Swiss cheese **99** 41
Swiss roll **97** 19
Swiss stone pine **372** 29
switch *Electr.* **127** 7
switch *Garage* **195** 4, 12
switch *Aircraft* **230** 26
switch, main ~ *Joiner* **132** 58
switch, main ~ *Railw.* **211** 3, 31
switch, main ~ *Office* **249** 37
switch, manually-operated ~ **202** 16
switch, remote-controlled ~ **202** 27
switch, rotary ~ *Electr.* **127** 18
switch, rotary ~ *Office* **245** 28
switchback **308** 39
switch blade **202** 21
switchboard *Post* **237** 17, 22-26
switchboard *Office* **245** 13
switch engine **206** 43
switcher **206** 43
switches, single ~ **203** 45-48
switching box **237** 25
switching centre **237** 25, 41
switching device **269** 47
switching system **153** 5
switching system, automatic ~ **237** 25
switch knob **203** 62
switch lever *Mach. Tools* **149** 11; **150** 35
switch lever *Railw.* **203** 55
switch lock **202** 28
switch signal **197** 38; **202** 19
switch signal, electrically illuminated ~ **202** 33
switch signal lamp **202** 19
switch signals **203** 45-52
switch stand **202** 17
switch tongue **202** 21
switch tower **15** 24
switch tower, electrically-operated ~ **203** 61
switch tower, manually-operated ~ **203** 53
switch yard **206** 42
swivel *Fish Farm.* **89** 77
swivel *Oil, Petr.* **145** 10
swivel arm **26** 13; **104** 27; **105** 26
swivel chair **246** 1; **248** 25
swivel coupling **50** 69
swivel head **50** 60
swivel mechanism **65** 73
swivel motor **132** 69
swivel nozzle **235** 64
swivel saddle **188** 21
swivel tap **126** 36
swop platform **194** 23
sword **319** 32
sword antenna **256** 28
sword lily **60** 11
swordsman **319** 25
sword swallower **308** 26
S-wrench, adjustable ~ **126** 66
symbol, algebraic ~ **344** 9; **345** 5
symbols, geometrical ~ **345** 21-24
symbols, mathematical ~ **345** 15-24
symphisis, pubic ~ **20** 65
symphonia **322** 25
syncarp **384** 63
sync head **243** 34
synchro **153** 32
synchromesh gearbox, four-speed ~ **192** 28-47
synchronization **311** 37-41
synchronization start **117** 65
synchronization unit **117** 77
synchronizing cone **192** 33
synchronizing filter **311** 27
syncing **311** 37-41
syncline **12** 18
sync pulse cable **313** 29
sync start **117** 65, 69
sync track **243** 33
synthetic fibres **169**, **170**
syringe **22** 54, 65
syringe, hypodermic ~ **24** 53
syringe, multi-purpose ~ **24** 10
syrinx **322** 2
system, ancillary ~ **211** 34
system, planetary ~ **4** 42-52
system camera **115** 1-105
system-monitoring device **234** 17
system of accessories **115** 43-105
system of coordinates **347** 8, 11
system of flaps **229** 37

T

tabard **30** 50
tabby weave **171** 1
tabernacle **330** 42
table *Forging* **139** 20
table *Restaurant* **266** 74
table *Playground* **273** 2
table *Music. Instr.* **324** 3
table *Art* **336** 14, 16
table, auxiliary ~ *Blacksm.* **137** 14
table, auxiliary ~ *Mach. Tools* **150** 28
table, director's ~ **316** 42
table, flat ~ **36** 46, 72, 73, 74
table, producer's ~ **316** 42
table, revolving ~ **148** 41
table, rotary ~ **145** 15
tableau curtain **315** 2
table bed **277** 15
tablecloth **45** 2
table decoration **45** 19; **266** 78
table en cabochon **36** 47
table en cabochon, antique ~ **36** 76
table en cabochon, rectangular ~ **36** 77
table feed drive **150** 34
table lamp **46** 24; **246** 35
tableland **13** 46
table leg **44** 2
table linen **271** 57
table napkin **45** 9
table pedestal **26** 6
table piano **325** 40
table rise adjustment **133** 23
table runner **46** 35
table telephone, standard ~ **237** 6
table tennis **273** 1; **293** 45-55
table tennis ball **273** 5; **293** 48
table tennis bat **273** 4; **293** 45
table tennis net **273** 3; **293** 53
table tennis player **293** 49
table tennis racket **273** 4; **293** 45
table tennis table **293** 52
table top *Dining Rm.* **44** 3
table top *Arc Weld.* **142** 14
table-top tripod **115** 99
table tripod **115** 99
tableware **45**
tabulator clear key **249** 8
tabulator key **249** 7
tachograph **210** 54
tachometer *Weaving* **166** 2
tachometer *Knitting* **167** 43
tachometer *Letterpress* **181** 54
tachometer *Car* **191** 38
tachometer *Railw.* **212** 22
tachometer *Aircraft* **230** 8
tack **285** 25
tacking **285** 25-28
tackle **219** 1-72; **221** 27, 104
taffrail log **224** 54
tagetes **60** 20
tail *Horse* **72** 38
tail *Game* **88** 19, 47, 49, 58, 62, 67, 75, 80
tail *Roof* **122** 89
tail *Bookbind.* **185** 58
tail *Birds* **362** 8
tail *Mammals* **367** 29
tail, cruciform ~ **229** 28
tail, curly ~ **73** 12
tail, docked ~ **70** 12
tail, dolphin's ~ **327** 25
tail, falcate ~ **73** 25
tail, fish's ~ **327** 25, 43, 46, 49
tail, horizontal ~ **229** 26-27, 35; **230** 61; **257** 21
tail, normal ~ **229** 23
tail, prehensile ~ **364** 35
tail, raised ~ **229** 35
tail, serpent's ~ **327** 31
tail, tufted ~ **73** 6
tail, vertical ~ **229** 24-25; **230** 58
tailband **185** 42
tail bracing wire **232** 4
tailcoat **33** 13
tail end shaft **223** 60
tail fin *Aircraft* **229** 24; **230** 59; **231** 6; **232** 7
tail fin *Air Force* **256** 32
tail fin *Airsports* **288** 21
tail fin *Fish etc.* **364** 10
tail fluke **367** 29
tailgate **193** 16, 20; **195** 50
tailings auger **64** 21
tailings outlet **64** 22
tail line **122** 81
tail loading gate **232** 25
tail margin **185** 58
tail of kite **273** 43
tailor **104** 22; **271** 37
tailor's chalk **271** 39
tailor seat **295** 11
tailpiece **323** 7
tailpin **323** 22
tailplane **229** 26; **230** 62; **256** 31; **288** 23
tailpole **91** 32
tail propeller **232** 28
tail rotor **232** 14; **264** 4
tails **33** 13
tail shaft **223** 60
tail shapes **229** 23-36
tail skid **256** 23
tail slide **288** 5
tail sting **358** 43
tailstock *Turner* **135** 7
tailstock *Mach. Tools* **149** 29; **150** 5
tailstock *Photomech. Reprod.* **177** 62
tailstock barrel **149** 27
tailstock barrel adjusting handwheel **149** 30
tailstock barrel clamp lever **149** 28
tailstock centre **149** 26
tail unit, cruciform ~ **229** 28
tail unit, double ~ **229** 32, 34
tail unit, normal ~ **229** 23
tail unit, triple ~ **229** 36
tail unit shapes **229** 23-36
tail vice **132** 37
tail wheel **256** 27
take-down weight **167** 32
take number **310** 35
take-off **298** 26, 37
take-off, balloon ~ **288** 84
take-off board **298** 38
take-off shaft **65** 31
take-off stand **165** 41
taker-in **163** 53
take-up reel **117** 80
take-up spindle **312** 37
take-up spool *Photog.* **115** 25
take-up spool *Cine Film* **117** 32, 80
take-up sprocket **312** 27
taking lens **313** 2
talcum powder **99** 29
talkback equipment **238** 64
talkback microphone **238** 10, 53
talkback microphone, producer's ~ **238** 39
talkback speaker **238** 8, 52
talkback system **238** 64
talk button **242** 24
talk key **242** 24
talon *Stock Exch.* **251** 19
talon *Birds* **362** 7
talus **11** 47; **12** 45
tambour door **245** 5
tambourine *Disco* **317** 27
tambourine *Music. Instr.* **324** 45
tamer **307** 52
tamper **200** 26; **201** 13
tamping beam **200** 32; **201** 2
tandem **186** 50
tandem kayak **283** 5
tang **45** 52, 60
tangent *Music. Instr.* **322** 43
tangent *Maths.* **346** 32, 48
tangent screw **14** 56
tangerine **384** 23
tank *Cooper* **130** 1
tank *Lorries etc.* **194** 30
tank *Army* **255** 80
tank, bottom ~ **222** 38
tank, concrete ~ **310** 11
tank, side ~ **222** 37
tank, spherical ~ **145** 73; **221** 36
tank bottom valve **38** 49
tank car **213** 31
tank construction engineer **130**
tanker *Docks* **225** 73
tanker *Airport* **233** 22
tanker terminal **145** 74
tank farm **225** 61
tank for sterilized milk **76** 16
tank furnace **162** 1
tank inlet **38** 47
tank locomotive **210** 65
tank margin plate **222** 51
tank reel **116** 2
tank spiral, multi-unit ~ **116** 4
tank top **222** 54
tank top plating **222** 54
tank vent **234** 44
tank wagon **213** 31

tansy **380** 9
tap *Doc.* **23** 49
tap *Metalwkr.* **140** 60
tap *Power Plant* **153** 18
tap *Spa* **274** 17
tap *Disco* **317** 8
tap *Chem.* **349** 5, 22; **350** 44, 53
tap, outside ~ **37** 41
tap bar **148** 9
tap changer **211** 10
tapchanger driving mechanism **211** 13
tape *Ball Games* **293** 73
tape *Music. Instr.* **325** 36
tape, adhesive ~ **98** 47; **134** 38; **247** 29
tape, magnetic ~ **25** 46
tape, varnished-cambric ~ **153** 46
tape cassette **117** 76
tape counter **241** 64; **243** 9
tape deflector roller **241** 60
tape feed **243** 29
tape guide **243** 22
tape measure **103** 2; **271** 38
tape punch **176** 5
taper, wax ~ **77** 65
tape recorder **117** 70; **317** 21; **318** 17
tape recorder, four-track ~ **242** 13
tape recorder, portable ~ **309** 37
tape recorder, two-track ~ **242** 12
tape reel, open ~ **241** 57
taper thread, female ~ **126** 47
tape speed selector **241** 62
tapestry wallpaper **128** 18
tape threading indicator light **243** 14
tape wire **325** 35
tapeworm **81** 35
tap hole **147** 50
tapir **366** 26
tappet **166** 57
tappet shaft **166** 56
tapping **153** 18
tapping a spring **269** 24-39
tapping bar **148** 9
tapping hole **147** 50
tapping spout **148** 3
taproot, swollen ~ **370** 79
tap wrench **140** 30
tar **170** 4
tar and bitumen heater **200** 46
target *Inf. Tech.* **242** 84
target *Sports* **305** 30, 32, 66, 77
target, bobbing ~ **305** 33, 48
target, turning ~ **305** 33, 48
target archery **305** 52-66
target areas **294** 51-53
target cross **288** 56
target jack **305** 23
target rectangle **292** 34
targets **305** 30-33
tar-spraying machine **200** 46
tar storage tank **200** 47
tarsus *Man* **17** 26
tarsus *Birds* **362** 4
tartlet **97** 20
tasse **329** 49
tassel *Headgear* **35** 24
tassel *Arable Crops* **68** 35
tassel *Hist. Cost.* **355** 23
tasset **329** 49
tatting **102** 19
tatting shuttle **102** 20
tattoo **306** 44
tau cross **332** 59
Taurus **3** 25; **4** 54
taxi **268** 64
taxicab **268** 64
taxi rank **268** 63, 66
'taxis' **233** 32
taxi sign **268** 65
taxi stand **268** 63, 66
taxi telephone **268** 67
taxiway **233** 2
T-cut **54** 32
tea *Grocer* **98** 65-68
tea *Supermkt.* **99** 68-70, 69
tea *Trop. Plants* **382** 9
tea bag **98** 68
teacher **260** 21
teaching equipment **242; 242** 45-84
teaching laser **242** 81
teaching machine **242** 1
teaching material **261** 27
tea dance **267** 44-46
tea leaf **382** 9
team of oxen **63** 16
tea plant **382** 7
tea plate **39** 34
tear bag **88** 14
tear-off edge **247** 30
tea room **265** 1-26
teat *Infant Care etc.* **28** 20
teat *Livestock* **75** 19
teat cup **75** 30
teat cup cluster **75** 26
tea tree **382** 7
technical drawing **151** 16
technical laboratory **310** 9
Teclu burner **350** 4
tectogenis **12** 4-20
tedder, rotary ~ **63** 24; **64** 46-58
teddy bear **28** 46; **273** 26; **309** 12
teddy bear, rocking ~ **48** 30
tee **126** 44, 47
tee *Ball Games* **293** 90
teeing ground **293** 79
tee-iron **143** 3
teepee **352** 7
tee-square **151** 9
teeth **19** 16-18
teeth, false ~ **24** 25
teeth grinder **157** 43, 45
teething ring **28** 12
teeth of knock-over bit **167** 52
telecobalt unit **2** 28
telegraphy **237** 30
telemetry antenna **10** 70
telephone **22** 18; **41** 7; **238** 23; **246** 13; **248** 9
telephone, public ~ **236** 9; **237** 1, 3
telephone, toy ~ **47** 35
telephone adapter socket **249** 67
telephone answering and recording set **22** 13
telephone answering device **22** 13
telephone book **236** 12; **237** 5
telephone booth **204** 46; **236** 8; **237** 1; **251** 10; **268** 56
telephone box **204** 46; **236** 8; **237** 1; **251** 10; **268** 56
telephone cable **198** 15
telephone cable pipeline **198** 16
telephone casing **237** 15
telephone connection **242** 20
telephone cover **237** 15
telephone customer **237** 2
telephone directory **236** 12; **237** 5
telephone directory rack **236** 10
'telephone - emergency calls only' **233** 40
telephone exchange **237** 27-41
telephone exchange, internal ~ **245** 13
telephone index **22** 21
telephone instruments **237** 6-26
telephone kiosk **204** 46; **236** 8; **237** 1; **251** 10; **268** 56
telephone line, customers' ~ **198** 20
telephone line, subscribers' ~ **198** 20
telephone list, internal ~ **245** 17
telephone number **237** 38
telephone receiver **237** 7; **246** 16
telephones **237** 6-26
telephone service **237** 41
telephone subscriber **237** 2
telephone switchboard panel **238** 14
telephone user **237** 2
telephoto lens **117** 47
teleprinter **176** 31; **237** 31, 61, 66; **238** 12
telescope **14** 60; **42** 15; **224** 8
telescope, gimbal-mounted ~ **235** 68
telescope, monocular ~ **111** 18
telescope, reflecting ~ **113** 1
telescope, refracting ~ **113** 16
telescope, surveyor's ~ **14** 48
telescope magnifier **113** 38
telescope mountings **113** 16-25
telescope mounts **113** 16-25
telescope sight **87** 29; **255** 28; **305** 49
Teletype **176** 31
teletypewriter **237** 31
television **238; 239**
television cabinet **240** 2
television camera **10** 67; **112** 36; **154** 78; **240** 26

television disc system **243** 37-45
television engineering **240**
television mast **15** 33
television OB van **239** 1-15
television post-sync studio **238** 27-53
television programmes **342** 64
television receiver **242** 28
television receiver, domestic ~ **243** 6
television receiving aerial **239** 4, 5
television reception aerial **239** 4, 5
television set **42** 8; **46** 14; **242** 28
television sound **242** 27
television tube **240** 3
telex link **237** 65
telex message **237** 69
telex service **237** 41
telex tape **237** 68
Telford base **200** 60
teller **250** 2
tempera **338** 17
temperature **9** 8
temperature gauge **179** 4
temperature gauge, distant-reading ~ **210** 48
temperature graph **7** 37
temperature regulation flap **10** 65
temperature regulator **191** 84
temperature scale **7** 36
temperature selector **50** 8
tempest **284** 54
template **126** 83
template, circular ~ **141** 35
temple *Man* **16** 6
temple *Weaving* **166** 13
temple *Art* **337** 7
temple, Doric ~ **334** 1
temple, Etruscan ~ **334** 49
temple, funerary ~ **333** 7
temple buildings **337** 25
temple tower **333** 32; **337** 1, 26
temple wall **334** 6
temporalis **19** 3
tender *Railw.* **210** 38
tender *Warships* **258** 92
tender platform **210** 2
tendo calcanaeus **18** 48
tendril **57** 4
tendril, thorny ~ **58** 30
tennis **293** 1-42
tennis ball **293** 28
tennis court **293** 1
tennis net **293** 13
tennis player **293** 16
tennis racket **41** 13; **293** 29
tennis shoe **101** 36
tenon saw **132** 44
tenor clef **320** 11
tenor horn **323** 39
tenor trombone **323** 46
tenor viol **322** 23
tenpin bowling **305** 14-20
tens **344** 3
tension and slub-catching device **165** 13
tension bar **167** 49
tension cable, inclined ~ **215** 47
tension cable pulley **214** 43
tension compensator **165** 51
tension equalizer **165** 51
tension hoop **324** 56
tensioning device *Agr. Mach.* **64** 94
tensioning device *Railw.* **208** 18
tensioning lever **208** 18
tensioning screw **323** 53
tension roller *Joiner* **133** 13
tension roller *Letterpress* **181** 45
tension weight *Knitting* **167** 50
tension weight *Railw.* **214** 41, 42
tension weight shaft **214** 40
tent **80** 7
tent, four-pole ~ **307** 1
tentacle **357** 16, 31
tenter **165** 54; **168** 21
tenter clip **168** 24
tenter pin **168** 24
tent peg **278** 24
tent pole **278** 38; **307** 2; **352** 8
tent prop **307** 13
tenuto **321** 30
tepee **352** 7
teres major **18** 55
teres minor **18** 54
tergites **358** 31
term **344** 23
terminal *Docks* **226** 16
terminal *Airport* **233** 15
terminal box **211** 16
termination of speed restriction **203** 40
tern **359** 11
terrace **37** 36
terracette **13** 64
terrarium **356** 14
terrestrial meridian **14** 4
terrier **70** 15, 16, 17, 18, 27, 39
terry towel **49** 9
tessellation **338** 37
tessera **338** 39
tesseral crystal system **351** 1-17
test equipment **195** 17
testicle, right ~ **20** 72
testing and control station **237** 40
testing board **237** 29
testing desk **237** 29
testing device for waterproof watches **109** 26
testing kit **138** 14
testis **20** 72
test meter, universal ~ **127** 41
test oil and gas separator **146** 10
test separator **146** 10
test tube **350** 34
test tube rack **173** 8; **261** 31; **350** 35
tether **75** 15-16
tetradrachm **252** 1
tetragonal crystal system **351** 18-19
tetrahedrite **351** 1
tetrahedron **351** 1
text **237** 68
textbook **261** 28
thalamus **370** 53
thallus **378** 49
Thaumatolampas diadema **369** 4
T-head bolt **202** 10
theater *see* theatre
theatre *Astron.* **5** 26
theatre *Theatre* **315**; **316**
theatre, Greek ~ **334** 44
theatre, open-air ~ **272** 6
theatre projector **312** 24
theatre seat **315** 20
theatre ticket **315** 11
thé dansant **267** 44-46
theodolite **14** 52-62
theorbo **324** 1
thermal **287** 21
thermal protection shield **234** 5, 20
thermal soaring **287** 20
thermograph **10** 19, 51
thermometer *Meteorol. Instr.* **10** 25
thermometer *Infant Care etc.* **28** 29
thermometer *Text. Finish.* **168** 27
thermometer *Swim.* **281** 24
thermometer, ladle-type ~ **92** 53
thermometers **10** 53-54
thermometer screen **10** 49
thermometer shelter **10** 49
thermometric scale **7** 36
thermoplastic **130** 15
Thermos jug **40** 5
thermo time switch **190** 63
thickener **172** 24, 42, 44, 48, 62
thicknesser **132** 45
thicknessing machine **132** 45
thicknessing table **132** 46
thief **308** 16
thigh **16** 49; **17** 22
thigh bone **17** 22
thill **186** 19, 30
thiller **186** 28
thill horse **186** 28
thimble, graduated ~ **149** 64
thinner *Painter* **129** 16
thinner *Art. Studio* **338** 13
thinning **84** 37
thinning razor **105** 9; **106** 41
thinnings, small-sized ~ **84** 37
thinning scissors **105** 8; **106** 33
thinning shears **105** 8; **106** 33
third base **292** 47
third man **300** 27
thirty-second note **320** 18
thirty-second rest **320** 26
thistle **61** 32

Thomas converter **147** 55-69
thoracic shield **82** 4; **358** 29
thorax *Man* **16** 28-30; **17** 8-11
thorax *Articulates* **358** 29-30
thorn *Gdn. Flowers* **60** 18
thorn *Spa* **274** 2
thorn *Shrubs etc.* **374** 30
thorn apple **379** 8
thorn house *Map* **15** 32
thorn house *Spa* **274** 1
thousands **344** 3
thread *Overh. Irrign.* **67** 38
thread *Mach. Parts etc.* **143** 16, 68
thread *Glass Prod.* **162** 54
thread *Cotton Spin.* **164** 53
thread *Weaving* **165** 21
thread *Knitting* **167** 17, 36
thread *Bookbind.* **183** 11
thread, coarse ~ **149** 4
thread, female ~ **126** 41, 45
thread, glass ~ **162** 56, 57
thread, male ~ **126** 38, 51
thread, metal ~ **102** 30
thread, mycelial ~ **381** 2
thread, normal ~ **149** 4
thread, sleeved ~ **162** 57
thread chaser **135** 14
thread clearer **165** 20
thread container **22** 61
thread cop **185** 18
thread-cutting machine **125** 27; **126** 86
thread guide *Shoem.* **100** 30
thread guide *Knitting* **167** 3, 54, 64
thread head **187** 75
threading draft **171** 5
threading key **127** 30
thread interlacing **171** 26
thread pitch **149** 9
thread spool **185** 18
thread tapper **108** 15
threadworm **80** 51
three **302** 13
three-day event **289** 16-19
three-decker **218** 51-60
three-eight time **320** 36
three-four time **320** 37
three-masters **220** 18-27
three-phase generator **153** 26
three-phase plug **127** 14
three-two time **320** 38
threshing drum **64** 12
throat *Man* **16** 19; **19** 14-37, 24
throat *Horse* **72** 16
throat *Forestry* **84** 28
throatlash **71** 11; **72** 16
throatlatch **71** 11; **72** 16
throat piece **329** 42
throstle **361** 16
throttle control **230** 30; **288** 15
throttle lever **230** 30; **288** 15
throttle twist grip **188** 30; **189** 29
throttle valve *Hosp.* **27** 43
throttle valve *Car* **192** 9
through-the-lens reflex finder **117** 44
thrower **161** 9
throw-in **291** 53
throwing act **307** 43
throwing knife **354** 15
throwing ring **308** 47
throwing spear **328** 2
throwing stick **352** 40
thrush **360** 3
thrushes **361** 13-17
thrush nightingale **361** 17
thrust bearing **221** 29
thrust block **223** 67; **259** 60
thrust lever **257** 9
thrust mount, lower ~ **235** 6
thrust mount, upper ~ **235** 5
thrust nozzle **234** 35; **235** 37
thrust nozzle fuel tank **235** 45
thrust structure **234** 21
thrust vector control system **235** 43
thrust washer **190** 56
thrust weapon **294** 11, 36, 37
thuja **372** 39
thumb **19** 64
thumb hold **323** 45
thumb hole **305** 47
thumb nut **119** 75
thumb piston **326** 46
thundercloud **7** 2
thunderstorm **9** 38
thurible **332** 38
thurible bowl **332** 41
thurible chain **332** 39
thurible cover **332** 40
thwart **278** 17; **283** 28
thymele **334** 48
tiara, papal ~ **254** 37
Tibetan **353** 27
tibia **17** 25
tibialis anterior **18** 47
tick *Bedrm.* **43** 13
tick *Articulates* **358** 44
tick, drill ~ **43** 10
tick bean **69** 15
ticket **204** 36
ticket agent **204** 39
ticket-cancelling machine **197** 16
ticket clerk **204** 39
ticket counter **197** 33; **204** 35
ticket machine **268** 28
ticket office **204** 34
ticket printer, hand-operated ~ **204** 41
ticket-printing machine **204** 40
ticket-stamping machine **204** 40
tidal power plant **155** 37
tide level indicator **225** 37
tidemark **13** 35
tide table **280** 7
tie *Ladies' Wear* **30** 46
tie *Underwear etc.* **32** 41
tie *Bldg. Site* **119** 39
tie *Roof* **121** 59
tie *Station* **205** 60
tie *Music. Not.* **321** 24
tie, concrete ~ **202** 37
tie, coupled ~ **202** 14, 38
tie, diagonal ~ **121** 30
tie, double ~ **121** 50
tie, simple ~ **121** 49
tie, steel ~ **202** 36
tie beam **121** 53
tie belt **29** 55; **31** 19
tie fastening **101** 21
tiepin **36** 22
tier, lower ~ **228** 24
tier, upper ~ **228** 23
tierce engagement **294** 48
tiercel **86** 46
tie rod **65** 47
tier of oars **218** 12
tie shoe **101** 31
tie tube **119** 49
tie-up **171** 22, 23
tie-up of shafts **171** 9
tiger **307** 56; **368** 5
tightening screw **293** 33
tightrope **307** 41
tightrope dancer **307** 40
tights **29** 42; **32** 12
tilbury **186** 44
tilde **342** 35
tile *Bathrm. etc.* **49** 19
tile *Games* **276** 34
tile, flat interlocking ~ **122** 60
tile, interlocking ~ **122** 59
tile, plain ~ **122** 6, 46
tile beard **34** 16
tile cutter **122** 33
tile hammer **122** 20
tile roofings **122** 45-60
tiles **122** 45-60
tiling batten **122** 17
till **207** 86; **271** 5
till, electric ~ **271** 2
tillage **69** 1-28
tiller **218** 13; **284** 32; **286** 24
tiller extension **284** 31
tillering **68** 5
tilt **329** 71
tilt block **12** 9
tilting armour **329** 76
tilting device **147** 44, 59
tilting helmet **254** 4; **329** 77
tilting lance **329** 81
tilting shield **329** 79
tilting table **133** 17
tilting target **329** 79
tilt wing **232** 27
timbale **324** 57
timber **85** 42
timber, end-grained ~ **120** 92
timber, halved ~ **120** 88
timber, long ~ **120** 2
timber, round ~ **120** 35; **157** 30
timber, sawn ~ **157** 22
timber, small ~ **84** 37
timber, squared ~ **120** 10; **157** 36
timber, stacked ~ **84** 15
timber, standing ~ **84** 4
timber, undressed ~ **120** 83
timber, yarded ~ **84** 15
timber cutting **84** 15-37
timber dog **121** 97
timberjack **84** 18
timber joints **121** 84-98
timber planking **285** 50-57

time *Music. Not.* **320** 28-42
time *Maths.* **345** 7
time ball **280** 5
time indicator **289** 40
timekeeper **282** 24; **299** 47
timer *Doc.* **23** 40
timer *Hosp.* **27** 35
timer *Kitch.* **39** 21
timer *Watchm.* **109** 35
timer *Photog.* **116** 18
timer *Photograv.* **182** 20
timer *Billiards* **277** 17
timer, synchronous ~ **24** 52
timer switch, built-in ~ **243** 18
time scale *Meteorol. Instr.* **10** 17
time scale *Office* **249** 74
time scale stop **249** 75
time schedule **151** 12
time signatures **320** 28-42
timetable **204** 16, 18
timetable, driver's ~ **210** 52
timetable, official ~ **204** 50
time weight **110** 29; **309** 59
timing machine, electronic ~ **109** 27
timpano **323** 57
tin **129** 7
tin, molten ~ **162** 17
tinctures **254** 24-29
tine *Tablew. etc.* **45** 60
tine *Agr. Impl.* **66** 4
tine *Game* **88** 10, 31
tine bar **64** 53
tinner's snips **125** 1
tip, adjustable ~ **149** 47
tip, controlled ~ **199** 10
tip, cork ~ **107** 13
tip, gold ~ **107** 13
tip, oxide ceramic ~ **149** 47
tip, pointed ~ **253** 10
tip-cart, three-way ~ **62** 18
tip heap **144** 19
tipper **200** 7
tipper, three-way ~ **194** 24
tipper wagon **213** 37
tipping body *Lorries etc.* **194** 25
tipping body *Road Constr.* **200** 8
tipping bucket **214** 34
tipping car **147** 64
tipping cylinder **62** 19
tipping device **147** 44, 59
tipping truck **119** 28
tipping wagon **119** 28
tippler, three-way ~ **92** 34
tip tank **231** 9; **256** 30
tip-up seat **207** 12
tire *see* tyre
tired swimmer grip **21** 38
T-iron **143** 3
tissue, erectile ~ **20** 67
tit **360** 4; **361** 9
titan **327** 37
title block **151** 31
title bout **299** 35-50
title fight **299** 35-50
title page **185** 45
title panel **151** 31
titmouse **360** 4; **361** 9
tjalk **220** 6
T-joint **126** 44, 47
T-junction joint **126** 44, 47
toad **364** 23
toadstools **379** 10-13
toast **45** 34
toaster **40** 30
toat **132** 18
tobacco *Tobacc. etc.* **107** 25
tobacco *Trop. Plants* **382** 43
tobacco, raw ~ **83** 13
tobacco beetle **81** 25
tobacco factory **83** 11
tobacco leaf **382** 43
tobacco plant **382** 40
tobacco pouch **107** 43
tobacco presser **107** 47
toboggan **303** 1, 2, 13
toboggan, junior ~ **303** 3
toboggan cap **35** 39
toboggan slide **308** 40
toe, big ~ **19** 52
toe, first ~ **19** 52
toe, fourth ~ **19** 55
toe, great ~ **19** 52
toe, little ~ **19** 56
toe, second ~ **19** 53
toe, third ~ **19** 54
toecap **100** 58; **101** 16, 40
toecap remover **100** 52
toe clip **290** 21
toenail **19** 57
toe piston **326** 48
toe post sandal **101** 48
toe stand **295** 5
toestrap **284** 30
toe unit **301** 55
toffee **98** 77
toga **355** 13
toggle **340** 30
toggle action *Letterpress* **181** 16
toggle action *Bookbind.* **183** 30
toggle fastening **30** 66
toggle-joint action **181** 16; **183** 30
toggle-joint press **183** 26
toggle-lever press **183** 26
toilet **49** 12; **146** 29; **207** 16, 42, 72; **211** 59; **231** 31; **278** 5
toilet bowl **49** 13
toilet cistern **126** 14
toilet-cleaning vehicle **233** 22
toilet lid **49** 14
toilet pan **49** 13
toilet paper **49** 11
toiletries **99** 27-35
toilet roll holder **49** 10
toilets **317** 31
toilet seat **49** 15
toilet water **105** 37; **106** 9
tomahawk **352** 16
tomato **57** 12; **99** 82
tomato plant **55** 44
tomb **331** 23; **337** 16
tomb, giant's ~ **328** 16
tomb, megalithic ~ **328** 16
tomb, royal ~ **333** 1
tombola **306** 11
tombola booth **308** 44
tomb recess **331** 60
tombstone **331** 26
tom cat **73** 17
tom-tom **324** 48, 49
tondo **339** 36
tone **320** 51, 53
tone arm **241** 21
tone arm balance **241** 53
tone arm lift **241** 28
tone arm lock **241** 27
tone generator **238** 51
toner roll **249** 41
tongs *Atom* **2** 44
tongs *Glass Prod.* **162** 44
tongs *Graphic Art* **340** 50
tongs, concreter's ~ **119** 85
tongs, flat ~ **137** 24
tongs, round ~ **137** 25
tongue *Man* **17** 52; **19** 25
tongue *Tablew. etc.* **45** 52
tongue *Game* **88** 2
tongue *Shoem.* **100** 65
tongue *Shoes* **101** 32
tongue *Music. Instr.* **322** 52; **326** 19
tongue, foam rubber ~ **291** 24
tongue, forked ~ **327** 6
tonsil **19** 23
tonsil, palatine ~ **19** 23
tonsure **331** 57
tool **195** 43
tool, stone ~ **328** 1
tool bag **187** 25
tool bit holder **149** 45
tool box *D.I.Y.* **134** 35
tool box *Mach. Tools* **150** 13
tool box *Railw.* **212** 45
tool cabinet **134** 1-34
tool case **127** 49
tool cupboard **134** 1-34
tool grinder **137** 18
tool-grinding machine **137** 18
tool post **149** 21
tool rest **135** 5; **149** 22
tools **119** 77-89
tool shank **149** 49
tool shed **37** 32; **52** 3; **55** 1
tool slide **149** 22
tool trolley **195** 42
tooth *Man* **19** 28-37
tooth *Mach. Parts etc.* **143** 83
tooth *Composing Rm.* **174** 30
tooth *Office* **249** 31
tooth, bicuspid ~ **19** 18
tooth, canine ~ **19** 17
tooth, molar ~ **19** 18, 35
tooth, porcelain ~ **24** 29
tooth, premolar ~ **19** 18
toothbrush, electric ~ **49** 29
tooth chisel **339** 13
toothed **370** 45
tooth glass **49** 28
toothing, external ~ **143** 96
toothing, internal ~ **143** 95
toothing, spiral ~ **143** 92-93
toothing plane **132** 17
tooth mug **49** 28
toothpaste **99** 31
toothpick holder **266** 23

tooth pulp **19** 32
tooth-root elevator **24** 48
tooth scaler **24** 45
top **12** 40; **193** 10; **323** 24
top, collapsible ~ *Carriages* **186** 52
top, collapsible ~ *Car* **193** 10
top, convertible ~ **193** 10
top, elasticated ~ **32** 33
top, fireclay ~ **108** 9
top, fixed ~ **186** 14
top, folding ~ **194** 10
top, hard ~ **193** 27
top, humming ~ **309** 71
top, leather ~ **35** 19
top, marble ~ **265** 12
top, shirred ~ **29** 15
top clearer **164** 22
topgallant stay **219** 12
top gases **145** 38
top hat **35** 36; **186** 25; **289** 6
top light, white ~ **286** 10
top lighting, incident ~ **112** 63
topmark **224** 78, 90
topmark buoy **224** 80
topmast **223** 39
topmast stay **219** 11
topography, fluvial ~ **13** 1-13
topper **64** 85
topping **266** 54
topping knife **64** 87
top rail **221** 122
top ring **89** 52
top roller, light ~ **164** 18
tops **145** 38
topsail schooner, three-masted ~ **220** 19
top side *Meat* **95** 37
top side *Paperm.* **173** 31
top slide **149** 22, 42
top stroke **277** 3
top tube **187** 16
torch **127** 26
torch lighter **141** 27
torero **319** 21, 25
torii **337** 11
torpedo boat **258** 69, 75
torpedo housing, underwater ~ **259** 36
torpedo tube **258** 78; **259** 79
torque converter **190** 70
torque converter bearing **211** 54
torque converter lever **65** 34
torque wrench **195** 45
torril door **319** 11
torsional clamp **287** 39
torso **339** 7
Torsteel **119** 82
torten **97** 22-24
tortrix moth **80** 9
torus *Art* **334** 28, 30
torus *Bot.* **370** 53
totalizator **289** 35
totalizator window **289** 34
tote **289** 35
totem **352** 2
totem pole **352** 1
tote window **289** 34
toucan **363** 6
touch line **291** 9
touch-me-not **377** 11
touch-tone button **242** 25
touch-tone pad **242** 25
toupee wig **355** 8
toupet **34** 2
touring bicycle **187** 1
touring boat **283** 26-33
touring cycle **187** 1
touring cycle handlebar **187** 2
touring kayak **283** 61, 70
touring moped **188** 24
tourist **272** 28
tourist guide **272** 27
tournament **329** 71
tournament pennon **254** 33
tournament saddle **329** 87
tourneur **275** 3
tourney **329** 71
tourniquet, emergency ~ **21** 15
tourniquet, surgeon's ~ **26** 48
tow **170** 57, 58, 59, 60
towage **227**
towel **106** 25; **281** 25
towel, paper ~ **40** 1; **106** 5
towel rail **49** 8
tower *Bldg. Site* **119** 34
tower *Bridges* **215** 42
tower *Airport* **233** 17
tower *Gliding* **287** 12
tower, central ~ **335** 6
tower, lattice steel ~ **152** 36
tower, stepped ~ **333** 32
tower, terraced ~ **333** 32
tower clock **331** 7
tower crane **47** 39; **119** 31
tower platform **329** 8
tower roof, pyramidal ~ **335** 7
tower slewing crane **119** 31
tower spotlight **316** 21
tower tomb **333** 21
tow hook **227** 27
towing **216** 27
towing engine *Rivers* **216** 29
towing engine *Salvage* **227** 7
towing engine *Warships* **258** 86
towing gear **227** 6, 6-15, 13
towing hawser **216** 24; **227** 8, 15
towing line **286** 47
towing log **224** 54
towing machine **227** 7; **258** 86
towing mast **216** 28
towing path **216** 30
towing plane **287** 2
towing track **216** 30
towing vehicle **194** 21, 29
towing winch **227** 7; **258** 86
tow line **216** 24; **227** 8, 15; **286** 47
town **15** 51; **268**
town banner **218** 22
town centre **268**
tow path **216** 30
tow rope *Rivers* **216** 24
tow rope *Salvage* **227** 8, 15
tow rope *Gliding* **287** 4
tow rope guide **227** 9
toy, soft ~ **46** 13; **47** 6, 7, 41
toy, wooden ~ **260** 80
toy duck **28** 10
toys **48** 21-32
toy shop **47** 27
T position **288** 62
trace **71** 22, 24, 35
trace monitor **25** 54
tracer **153** 45
tracer element **153** 45
tracery **335** 39-40
tracery window **335** 39-41
trachea **17** 50; **20** 4
tracing head **141** 37
tracing leg **302** 2
tracing wheel **129** 42
track *Atom* **2** 37
track *Hunt.* **86** 8
track *Cine Film* **117** 82
track *Railw.* **202** 1-38
track *Station* **205** 59-61
track *Army* **255** 87
track *Equest.* **289** 23
track *Cyc. Racing* **290** 2
track *Winter Sp.* **301** 60
track, cinder ~ **298** 6
track, indoor ~ **290** 1
track, sand ~ **290** 24
track, synthetic ~ **298** 6
track, unfenced ~ **15** 102
track and field events **298**
track and signal indicator **203** 64
track-clearing vehicle **213** 17
track diagram control layout **203** 65
track diagram control panel **203** 66
tracker action **326** 6-16
track format **243** 28
trackhound **70** 42, 43
track indicator **65** 81
track inspection railcar **213** 32
track racer **290** 2
track rider **290** 2
track rider, motor-paced ~ **290** 14
track rod **65** 47
track-rod ball-joint **192** 80
tracksuit **33** 27
tracksuit bottoms **33** 29
tracksuit top **33** 28
trackwalker **202** 44
tract **330** 57
traction motor **211** 6
traction motor blower **211** 15
tractive effort indicator **211** 26
tractive unit **194** 21, 29
tractor **62** 38; **64** 46; **65** 20; **67** 17; **85** 43; **194** 21, 29; **273** 55
tractor, narrow-track ~ **78** 21
tractor driver **62** 39
tractor unit **85** 43
trader, itinerant ~ **308** 51
trades **9** 48, 49
tradesman **98** 41
trade winds **9** 48, 49
traffic control **264** 9
traffic control cuff **268** 31
traffic helicopter **264** 1

traffic light post **268** 53
traffic lights **268** 52
traffic patrol **264** 9
traffic policeman **268** 30
traffic sign **268** 66
trail **86** 8
trail, scented ~ **289** 49
trailer *Farm Bldgs.* **62** 40
trailer *Agr.* **63** 27, 38
trailer *Blacksm.* **138** 10
trailer *Lorries etc.* **194** 22
trailer *Station* **206** 3, 35
trailer *Camping* **278** 52
trailer, collapsible ~ **278** 3
trailer, folding ~ **278** 3
trailer, tip-up ~ **56** 42
trailer frame **138** 28
trailering **278**
trailer wagon **200** 25
trailing arm **191** 27; **192** 66
trailing cable hanger **133** 39
trailing cable support **133** 39
trailing edge *Sailing* **284** 45
trailing edge *Gliding* **287** 37
trailing link arm **192** 81
trail rope **288** 69
train **355** 80
train, electric ~ **197**
train, interurban ~ **197**
train, local ~ **208** 1-12
train, short-distance ~ **208** 1-12
train, suburban ~ **205** 25
train control system, inductive ~ **211** 7, 38; **212** 14, 38
train deck **221** 80
trainee pastry cook **265** 6
trainer **101** 35
train ferry *Map* **15** 12
train ferry *Ship* **221** 74
train heating generator **212** 39
train heating system **212** 17, 18
train heating system transformer **212** 40
train heating voltage indicator **211** 27
training apparatus **299** 20-24
training equipment **299** 20-24
training ship **258** 95
training shoe **101** 35
train plate, bottom ~ **110** 37
'trains' **233** 34
train schedule **204** 50
train service, local ~ **208** 1-30
trainset **209** 1
trainset, experimental ~ **209** 23
train set, wooden ~ **47** 37; **48** 29; **273** 27
trajectory **89** 36
tram **197**; **268** 46
tramline **268** 23
trammel **125** 11
trampoline **297** 10
tram service **197** 13
tram stop **197** 35; **268** 25
tram stop sign **197** 36; **268** 26
tram timetable **268** 27
transept **335** 3
Trans-Europe Express **209** 1-22
Trans-Europe Express, electric ~ **205** 34
transfer blanket **249** 40
transfer cylinder **180** 36
transfer drum **180** 36
transfer entry **250** 25
transfer port **242** 57
transformer *Clocks* **110** 8
transformer *Power Plant* **153** 9-18
transformer *Railw.* **211** 10
transformer, high-tension ~ **211** 4
transformer, mobile ~ **152** 30, 39
transformer, transportable ~ **152** 30, 39
transformer connection **153** 19
transformer station *Brew.* **92** 21
transformer station *Hydr. Eng.* **217** 46
transformer tank **152** 40
transforming section **23** 56
transillumination **112** 60
transistor, actuating ~ **195** 19
Transitional **342** 5
'transit passengers' **233** 27
transit shed **225** 9
transmission **209** 18
transmission, multi-speed ~ **65** 36
transmission cable **326** 53
transmission line **154** 16
transmission line, high-voltage ~ **152** 32
transmission oil **209** 15; **212** 36, 43
transmission oil temperature gauge **212** 20
transmissometer **10** 60
transmitted-light microscope **112** 14
transmitter **10** 59, 62
transmitting antenna **288** 88
transom *Dwellings* **37** 35
transom *Ship* **221** 42
transom *Sailing* **284** 35; **285** 49
transom *Motorboats etc.* **286** 26
transom stern **221** 42; **258** 26; **259** 11; **285** 48
transparency **242** 42
transparency arm **177** 44
transparent gage **59** 25
transplanting *Plant Propagn.* **54** 5
transplanting *Forestry* **84** 10
transport aircraft, medium-range ~ **256** 14
transport and communications aircraft **256** 24
transport and rescue helicopter **256** 18
transporter, suction ~ **74** 49
transporter container-loading bridge **225** 46; **226** 2
transporter loading bridge **225** 20
transport helicopter **232** 21
transport lug **152** 48
transport roller *Cine Film* **117** 34
transport roller *Joiner* **132** 72
transport sprocket **115** 26
transport vehicle **62** 18
transtainer **226** 2
transtainer crane **226** 2
transversal chicane **301** 68
transverse motion **149** 17
trap *Bathrm. etc.* **49** 27
trap *Hunt.* **86** 20
trap *Plumb. etc.* **126** 26
trapdoor **38** 13
trapeze *Sailing* **284** 12
trapeze *Circus* **307** 6
trapeze artist **307** 7
trapeze platform **307** 5
trapezium **346** 37
trapezius **18** 52
trap opening **316** 32
trapper **306** 8
trapping **86** 19-27, 19
trappings *Horse* **71** 16
trappings *Chivalry* **329** 74
trash bin *Doc.* **22** 70
trash bin *Butch.* **96** 46
trash can **199** 3
trash conveyor **64** 80
travel agency **271** 24
travel centre **204** 28
traveler *see* traveller
traveling *see* travelling
traveller *Cotton Spin.* **164** 51, 55
traveller *Sailing* **284** 27
Travellers' Aid **204** 45
travelling bag **205** 10
travelling box **77** 44
travelling salesman **209** 29
traverse **152** 37
traversing handle **255** 48
trawler **90** 11; **221** 86
trawl fishing **90** 11-23
trawling **90** 11-23
trawl warp **90** 12
tray *Living Rm.* **42** 30
tray *Pest Contr.* **83** 17
tray *Game* **88** 8
tray *Café* **265** 3, 14
tray *Restaurant* **266** 19, 45, 63
tray *Fair* **308** 52
tray, revolving ~ **204** 37
tray, round ~ **44** 24
tray counter **266** 64
tray for purchases **271** 15
tray thermometer **116** 13
tread **50** 38; **123** 32, 47
tread, rubber ~ **187** 85
treading water **282** 39
treadle *Poultry Farm* **74** 63
treadle *Dressm.* **103** 11
treadle *Tailor* **104** 13
treadle control **168** 48
treadle lever **166** 58

treadle sewing machine **309** 1
treadling diagram **171** 10
tread sledge **304** 29
treasury notes **252** 29-39
treble belly bridge **325** 11
treble bridge **325** 11
treble clef **320** 8
treble control **241** 31
treble coupler **324** 41
treble plume **254** 30
treble register **324** 41
treble stop **324** 41
treble string **325** 10
treble tuning **241** 43
treble viol **322** 23
tree **272** 59, 61; **370** 1
tree, conical ~ **272** 13
tree, globe-shaped ~ **272** 12
tree, pyramidal ~ **52** 16; **272** 19
tree brush **56** 23
tree cake **97** 46
tree calliper, steel ~ **84** 21
tree felling **84** 15-37
tree frog **364** 24
tree guard **118** 80
tree nursery *Map* **15** 111
tree nursery *Market Gdn.* **55** 3
tree nursery *Forestry* **84** 6, 10
tree of life **372** 39
tree pruner **56** 11
trees, coniferous ~ *Map* **15** 1
trees, coniferous ~ *Conifers* **372** 1-71
trees, deciduous ~ **371** 1-73
trees, mixed ~ **15** 14
trees, non-coniferous ~ **15** 4
trees, ornamental ~ **373**; **374**
trees, young ~ **84** 10-11
tree scraper **56** 14
tree stake **52** 31
tree stump **84** 14
tree toad **364** 24
treetop **272** 60; **370** 4
tree trunk **84** 19; **370** 2, 7
tree trunk, hollowed-out ~ **218** 7
trefoil arch **336** 32
trellis **89** 5
trellis, wire ~ **78** 9
trembling poplar **371** 21
trenchcoat **33** 57
trestle *Overh. Irrign.* **67** 7
trestle *Carp.* **120** 18, 19
trestle *Shipbuild.* **222** 27
trestle, paperhanger's ~ **120** 52
trestle rope **122** 67
triad **321** 1-4
triakis-octahedron **351** 10
trial **290** 24-28
trial frame **111** 3
trial lens case **111** 45
triangle *Fish Farm.* **89** 85
triangle *Drawing Off.* **151** 7, 8
triangle *Railw.* **203** 13
triangle *School* **260** 37
triangle *Music. Instr.* **323** 49
triangle, acute-angled ~ **346** 28
triangle, equilateral ~ **346** 26
triangle, obtuse-angled ~ **346** 30
triangle, pipe clay ~ **350** 17
triangle, right-angled ~ **346** 32
triangle cut **36** 67
triangles, plane ~ **346** 26-32
triangle sign **203** 13
triangle symbol **345** 24
triangulation point **14** 49; **15** 71
triangulation station **14** 49; **15** 71
Triangulum Australe **3** 40
triceps brachii **18** 38
trick button **117** 84
trick ski **286** 56
triclinic crystal system **351** 26
Tricolour **253** 16
triforium **335** 33
trigger *Slaughterho.* **94** 6
trigger *Army* **255** 5
trigger guard **87** 10
trigger mechanism **255** 20
trigger valve **270** 62
triglyph **334** 15
trilby hat **35** 22
trill **321** 17, 18
trim **46** 5
trimaran **278** 16
trimmer *Carp.* **120** 41
trimmer *Roof* **121** 71
trimmer *Paperhanger* **128** 43
trimmer joist **120** 41
trimming, fur ~ **30** 59
trimming, lace ~ **31** 32
trimming, leather ~ **30** 18
trimming blade **85** 22
trimming knife **128** 38
trimming machine **85** 18
trimmings **266** 55
trimming tab **288** 25, 30
trimming table **132** 64
trimming tool **162** 43
trim tab **288** 25, 30
triplane **229** 6
triple-spar tail construction **257** 20
triplet **321** 23
trip mileage recorder **191** 74, 77
tripod *Photog.* **114** 42; **115** 99
tripod *Paperm.* **173** 6
tripod *Chem.* **349** 15; **350** 14
tripod, wooden ~ **313** 13
tripod bush **115** 30
tripod crane **222** 6
tripod lattice mast **258** 41
tripod leg **114** 43
tripod socket **115** 30
tripod spotlight **310** 52
trireme **218** 9-12
triton **327** 40
trochilus **334** 29
troika **186** 45
trolley *Blacksm.* **138** 35
trolley *Lorries etc.* **194** 42
trolley *Tram* **197**
trolley *Station* **206** 14
trolley *Town* **268** 46
trolley, electric ~ **205** 29
trolley, metal ~ **74** 31
trolley bus **194** 40
trolley bus trailer **194** 44
trolley service **197** 13
trolley shoe **194** 42
trolley shoe, aluminium alloy ~ **197** 24
trolley shoe, carbon ~ **197** 24
trolley stop **197** 35; **268** 25
trolley stop sign **197** 36; **268** 26
trolley wire **197** 41; **205** 58
trolley wire contact point **197** 40
trombone **323** 46
trombone slide **323** 47
tropaeolum **53** 4
trophus **358** 26
trophy **352** 15, 30
tropic of Cancer **3** 4
tropics **14** 10
tropopause **7** 9
troposphere **7** 1
trot **72** 41
trotter *Meat* **95** 38, 42, 48
trotter *Equest.* **289** 28
trotting silks **289** 26
troubadour **329** 70
trough *Phys. Geog.* **12** 18
trough *Mills* **91** 14
trough *Railw.* **202** 34
trough *Art* **336** 48
trough, equatorial ~ **9** 46
trough, outdoor ~ **62** 9
trough gutter **122** 83
trough mixer, double shaft ~ **159** 10
trough plane **12** 19
trough surface **12** 19
trough valley **13** 55
trough vault **336** 47
trouser leg **33** 6
trouser pocket **33** 47
trousers, boy's ~ **29** 60
trouser suit **30** 57
trouser turn up **31** 40
trout **364** 15
trout breeding **89** 14
trout fry **89** 16
trout pond **89** 6
trout rearing **89** 14
trowel *Gdn. Tools* **56** 6
trowel *Bldg. Site* **118** 52
trub **93** 2
trub removal **93** 1-5
truck *Bldg. Site* **119** [illegible]
truck *Power Plant* **152** 41
truck *Sawmill* **157** 16
truck *Refuse Coll.* **199** 38
truck *Railw.* **207** 4; **208** 4; **212** 2; **213** 13
truck *Docks* **226** 4, 19
truck *Flags* **253** 1
truck, electric ~ **205** 29; **206** 2, 34
truck, heavy ~ **194** 20; **200** 7
truck, large-capacity ~ **158** 14
truck, light ~ **194** 1, 5
truck, toy ~ **47** 38; **273** 62
truck farm **55** 1-51, 3
truck garden **55**; **55** 1-51, 3

trucks **194**
truck tire **273** 19
truck-to-truck handling **226** 7
truck-to-truck operation **225** 41
truck-to-truck system **225** 41
truck with trailer **213** 34
trudgen **282** 37
trudgen stroke **282** 37
truffle *Grocer* **98** 86
truffle *Edib. Fungi* **381** 9, 10, 11
trumpet **318** 6; **323** 43
trumpet, bronze ~ **322** 1
trumpet daffodil **60** 3
trumpeter **318** 7
trumpet narcissus **60** 3
truncheon *Heraldry* **254** 31
truncheon *Police* **264** 19
trunk *Man* **16** 22-41
trunk *Forestry* **84** 19
trunk *Car* **191** 24; **193** 23
trunk *Mammals* **366** 21
trunk *Bot.* **370** 2
trunk, horse's ~ **327** 45
trunk, main ~ **88** 11
trunk, woman's ~ **327** 24
trunk-bending forwards **295** 33
trunk-bending sideways **295** 32
trunk call **237** 3
trunk-hose, paned ~ **355** 34
trunk-hose, stuffed ~ **355** 31
trunk lid **191** 7
trunk line **15** 21
trunk pipeline **145** 35
trunk road **15** 17
trunks **32** 27
truss **215** 3
trussed arch bridge **215** 23
trussed-rafter roof **121** 34
truss element **215** 24
trusser **130** 12
truss joint **215** 37
truss post **121** 68
truss tower **155** 43
trying plane **132** 39
trysail **220** 1
try square **120** 69; **132** 6; **134** 26
try-your-strength machine **308** 11
tsetse fly **81** 43
T-shirt **31** 38
T-shirt, children's ~ **29** 27
T-square **151** 9
tsunami **11** 53
T-tail **229** 29; **256** 31-32; **287** 10
T-tail unit **229** 29; **256** 31-32; **287** 10
tub *Market Gdn.* **55** 48
tub *Wine Grow.* **78** 10
tub, wooden ~ **91** 27
tuba **323** 44
tubaphone **324** 61
tube *Hosp.* **25** 13; **26** 17
tube *Pest Contr.* **83** 31
tube *Opticn.* **111** 18
tube *Optic. Instr.* **113** 8
tube *Bicycle* **187** 30
tube *Music. Instr.* **323** 29; **326** 22
tube *Invertebr.* **357** 23
tube *Edib. Fungi* **381** 17
tube, diaphragmed ~ **10** 27
tube, eustachian ~ **17** 65
tube, fallopian ~ **20** 81
tube, steel ~ **155** 30
tube, telescopic ~ **65** 77
tube, uterine ~ **20** 81
tube bin **255** 72
tube cap **260** 52
tube centre section **113** 9
tube clamp **40** 20; **350** 30
tube clip **40** 20; **350** 30
tube connection **6** 26
tube holder **22** 46
tuber *Arable Crops* **68** 40
tuber *Bot.* **370** 79
tuberose **60** 9
tuberosity **80** 27
tube support **27** 47
tube valve **187** 31
tube well **269** 60
tubing **145** 20, 24
tub plant **55** 47
tuck and miss stitch **171** 44, 47
tuck jump **282** 14; **295** 36; **297** 40
tuck stitch, pulled-up ~ **171** 45, 48
tuck stitch, staggered ~ **171** 46
tue iron **137** 6
tuff **11** 19
tuff deposit **11** 26
tuft **73** 7
tufted lark **361** 19
tuft of grass **375** 44
tug *Shipbuild.* **222** 42
tug *Docks* **225** 15
tug *Salvage* **227** 5, 16
tug *Gliding* **287** 2
tulip poplar **374** 1
tulip tree **374** 1
tulle background **102** 16
tulle lace **102** 15
tulle work **102** 15
tumble drier **50** 28
tumbler **140** 38
tumbler, seaward ~ **226** 23
tumbler, shore-side ~ **226** 28
tumbler lever **149** 10
tumbler reverse lever **149** 14
tumbler spring **140** 42
tumbling separator, mechanical ~ **64** 75
tumulus **328** 16
tun **92** 45
tun, wooden ~ **91** 27
tundra climate **9** 57
tuner **241** 9, 37; **317** 22
tuner, automatic ~ **23** 38
tunic *Ladies' Wear* **30** 29
tunic *Ship* **221** 115
tunic *Hist. Cost.* **355** 12, 25
tunic, long ~ **355** 19
tunica **355** 12
tunic dress **30** 29
tunic top **30** 29
tuning control **241** 9
tuning crook **326** 21
tuning device **326** 30
tuning dial **241** 7
tuning flap **326** 30
tuning fork element **110** 9
tuning fork principle **110** 6
tuning fork watch **110** 6
tuning hammer **325** 20
tuning hole **326** 33
tuning key **325** 20
tuning knob **241** 9; **309** 21
tuning meter **241** 39, 54
tuning peg **323** 18; **324** 11; **325** 17
tuning pin **324** 23; **325** 17
tuning screw **323** 59
tuning slot **326** 33
tuning tongue **326** 30
tuning wedge **325** 21
tuning wire **326** 21
tunnel *Map* **15** 70
tunnel *Soft Fruit* **58** 63
tunnel *Station* **204** 23
tunnel *Railw.* **214** 6
tunnel, plastic ~ **55** 40
tunnel, underground ~ **198** 29
tunnel entrance **233** 6
tunnel kiln **161** 5
tunnelling machine **144** 32
tunnel vault **335** 19; **336** 38
tup *Blacksm.* **137** 10
tup *Forging* **139** 12, 26
turban **353** 46
turbine **67** 20; **209** 18; **232** 40, 47
turbine, high and low pressure ~ **259** 62
turbine, high-pressure ~ **232** 53
turbine, low-pressure ~ **232** 54
turbine, reversible ~ **155** 39
turbine, supercharged ~ **212** 51
turbine engine **232** 17, 24; **257** 15
turbine exhaust **146** 5
turbine house **152** 22; **217** 43
turbine inlet **155** 40, 41
turbine monitoring panel **153** 30
turbine transmission **209** 10
turbine unit **209** 24
turbogenerator **154** 34
turbogenerator set **154** 33
turbogenerator unit **153** 23-30
turbojet engine **231** 26
turbojet engines **232** 33-50
turbopropeller engine **231** 5; **232** 30, 51
turbopropeller plane **231** 4
turboprop engine **231** 5; **232** 30, 51; **256** 16
turboprop plane **231** 4
tureen **45** 15
turkey **73** 28
turkey cock **73** 28
turkey hen **73** 28

turkey leg **99** 59
Turkish delight **98** 84; **308** 18
turk's cap **377** 4
turk's cap lily **377** 4
turn *Athletics* **298** 24
turn *Music. Not.* **321** 21
turnbuckle **130** 4; **202** 31
turner *Brew.* **92** 24
turner *Turner* **135** 20
turnery **135** 1-26
turn indicator *Car* **191** 76
turn indicator *Aircraft* **230** 12
turn indicator light **189** 37, 45
turn indicator light, front ~ **191** 19
turning head, multiple ~ **149** 41
turning judge **282** 26
turning tools **135** 14,15,24
turnip moth **80** 42
turnout **203** 51, 52
turn slot **288** 46
turntable *Porcelain Manuf.* **161** 11
turntable *Electrotyp. etc.* **178** 26
turntable *Lorries etc.* **194** 31
turntable *Bridges* **215** 64
turntable *Docks* **226** 56
turntable *Audio* **241** 20
turntable *Army* **255** 73
turntable, small ~ **142** 41
turntable glazing machine **161** 16
turn-up **30** 35; **31** 54; **33** 35
turpentine separator **172** 14
turret *Mach. Tools* **149** 40
turret *Warships* **258** 47, 67. 70; **259** 31, 52, 71
turret *Chivalry* **329** 28, 35
turret, aft ~ **259** 44
turret, armoured ~ **255** 84
turret, forward ~ **259** 43
turret head **117** 46; **313** 32
turret lathe **149** 38
turtle dove **359** 23
tuck **88** 51; **366** 22; **367** 22
tutu **314** 29
tuyère **147** 20
TV set **42** 8; **46** 14
tween deck **223** 76
tweeter **241** 15
tweezers **109** 14; **174** 18
twig **370** 6
twilight area **4** 21
twin anti-aircraft gun **258** 31
twin anti-aircraft gun turret **259** 30
twin anti-aircraft missile launcher **259** 25, 33
twin anti-aircraft rocket launcher **259** 25, 33
twin columns **336** 6
twin edger **157** 57
twin engine, horizontally-opposed ~ **189** 47
twin etching machine **178** 30
twin hull **284** 65
twin launching catapult **259** 14
Twins **3** 28; **4** 55
twin seat **188** 42
twin seat, racing-style ~ **189** 14
twin set **31** 49
twin-spar wing construction **257** 27
twin tail unit **229** 32, 34
twist bit **134** 49; **140** 59
twist drill **134** 49; **140** 59
twist grip *Pest Contr.* **83** 19
twist grip *Motorcycles etc.* **188** 31
twist grip throttle control **188** 30; **189** 29
twist of tobacco **107** 18
twitch grass **61** 30
two-eight time **320** 28
two-four time **320** 29
two-high mill **148** 53
two-line brevier **175** 30
two-line primer **175** 31
two-pipe system **126** 22
two-seater **193** 28
two-stroke blending pump **196** 13
two-toed sloth **366** 11
two-two time **320** 30
two-way tap **350** 49
tympan **340** 37
tympanum **335** 26
type *Composing Rm.* **174** 7, 15, 44; **175** 1-17, 38
type *Letterpress* **181** 37
type *Office* **249** 15, 29
type *Money* **252** 12
type, black-letter ~ **342** 1, 2, 3
type, bold ~ **175** 2
type, bold condensed ~ **175** 10
type, boldfaced ~ **175** 2
type, extra bold ~ **175** 9
type, Gothic ~ **342** 1
type, heavy ~ **175** 2
type, italic ~ **175** 7
type, light face ~ **175** 8
type, Schwabacher ~ **342** 2
type, semibold ~ **175** 3
type area **185** 59
type bed **180** 78; **181** 17
typecase **174** 3
type casting **175** 32-37
type character **174** 7; **175** 38
type cleaner **247** 8
type-cleaning brush **247** 7
type-cleaning kit **247** 8
type disc **176** 20
type face **174** 31; **175** 42
type faces **342** 1-15
type forme **340** 32
typefounding **175** 32-37
type height **175** 44
type line **175** 43
type magazine **174** 21
type matrix **174** 47; **176** 16
type matter **174** 15; **175** 1-17; **181** 37
types **342** 1-15
typescript *Composing Rm.* **174** 6
typescript *Script* **342** 9
typesetter **174** 5
typesetting, computer-controlled ~ **176** 14
typesetting computer **176** 10
type size **175** 18, 46
types of ship **221**
typewriter **209** 28; **248** 22; **309** 79
typewriter, electric ~ **249** 1
typewriter rubber **247** 26
typewriting **342** 9
typhoon wheel **308** 46
typing compartment **209** 26
typing desk **245** 25; **248** 26
typing opening **249** 19
typing window **249** 19
typist **248** 21
typographer beetle **82** 22
tyre **191** 15
tyre, high-pressure ~ **187** 30
tyre, pneumatic ~ **187** 30; **305** 86
tyre, rubber ~ **273** 54
tyre, tubular ~ **290** 19, 23
tyre chain **304** 10
tyre pressure gauge **196** 17
tyre tread **189** 27

U

udder **75** 18
ulna **17** 14
ulnar side of the hand **19** 70
ultra large crude carrier **221** 1
umbel **383** 65
umbel, simple ~ **370** 72
Umbellula encrinus **369** 14
umbo **329** 58
umbra **4** 35
umbrella *Hall* **41** 15
umbrella *Station* **205** 12
umbrella *Art* **337** 22
umbrella *Invertebr.* **357** 15
umbrella, telescopic ~ **41** 12
umbrella stand **41** 14
umpire **292** 55, 65; **293** 19, 68
unau **366** 11
uncial **341** 17
underbrush **84** 5
undercarriage **194** 32
undercarriage, retractable ~ **232** 10
undercarriage housing **256** 15
undercarriage hydraulic cylinder **257** 41
undercarriage unit, forward-retracting ~ **257** 40
undercarriage unit, main ~ **230** 41; **231** 28; **256** 26; **257** 40; **288** 33
undercarriage unit, retractable ~ **231** 28
underclothes, ladies' ~ **32** 1-15
underclothes, men's ~ **32** 22-29
undercut *Forestry* **84** 28
undercut *Meat* **95** 13
undercut swing saw **157** 24, 64
underframe **207** 3; **208** 5
undergown **355** 37

undergrasp **296** 41
undergrowth **84** 5
underlip **72** 10
under-ridge tile **122** 5
undershirt **296** 61
underside **173** 34
underskirt **309** 85
understructure **191** 2
under tile **122** 57
underwater case **117** 57
underwater housing **117** 57
underwater massage bath **281** 31
underwater salvo missile launcher **259** 24
underwater salvo rocket launcher **259** 24
underwater swimmer **279** 7; **280** 37
underwater swimming **279** 7-27; **282** 38
underwater swimming set **279** 8-22
underwear **32**
underwear, ladies' ~ **32** 1-15
underwear, men's ~ **32** 22-29
underwing tank **256** 4
underwood **84** 5, 32
uneven bars **297** 3
ungulates **366** 25-31; **367** 1-10
ungulates, even-toed ~ **366** 28-31
ungulates, odd-toed ~ **366** 25-27
unicorn **254** 16; **327** 7
uniform **264** 7
uniform cap **264** 8
Union Jack **253** 15
union of sets **348** 5-6
unison **321** 6
unison interval **321** 6
unit, assistant's ~ **24** 9
unit, slide-in ~ **27** 32
unit indicator **174** 36
unit load **225** 49; **226** 9
unit load, foil-wrapped ~ **225** 42
units **344** 3
university **262** 1-25
university lecturer **262** 3
university library **262** 11-25
unloading unit **62** 42
unwind station **173** 39
up-and-down roundabout **308** 5
up-and-down slide **273** 52
upcurrent, frontal ~ **287** vp
upholstery **134** 59
upper, corduroy ~ **101** 26
upper, rubber ~ **300** 45
upper, soft-leather ~ **101** 46
upper, terry ~ **101** 23
upper arm hang **296** 58
upper board **326** 15
upper board groove **326** 14
uppercut **299** 32
upper fore topgallant sail **219** 59
upper fore topgallant yard **219** 36
upper fore topsail **219** 57
upper fore topsail yard **219** 34
upper hatch **6** 45
upper-leather shears **100** 42
upper main topgallant sail **219** 65
upper main topgallant yard **219** 42
upper main topsail **219** 63
upper main topsail yard **219** 40
Upper Muschelkalk **154** 58
Upper Permian **154** 62
upright *Gymn.* **296** 9
upright *Athletics* **298** 13, 33
upright *Music. Instr.* **325** 1
upright kneeling position **295** 7
upright piano **325** 1
upright spin **302** 9
upsett **136** 25
upsetting block **137** 16
upstart **297** 28
upward ventilator **154** 81
U-rail **214** 22
Uranus **4** 50
ureter **20** 32
urethra **20** 68
urethroscope **23** 20
urine sediment chart **23** 58
urn **328** 40; **331** 31
urn, cinerary ~ **328** 38
urn, domestic ~ **328** 38
urn, embossed ~ **328** 38
urn grave **328** 39; **331** 30
Ursa Major **3** 29
Ursa Minor **3** 34
ursine seal **367** 18
usher **315** 12
usherette **312** 4
uterus **20** 79
utility room door **118** 6
utility room window **118** 5
U-tube **349** 2
U-valley **13** 55
uvula **19** 22

vacancy **342** 70
vacuum **240** 21
vacuum back **177** 35
vacuum box **173** 15
vacuum chamber **2** 52; **83** 12; **159** 12
vacuum cleaner *Household* **50** 80
vacuum cleaner *Goldsm. etc.* **108** 43
vacuum cleaner, cylinder ~ **50** 68
vacuum cleaner, upright ~ **50** 58
vacuum equipment **145** 51
vacuum film holder **177** 8
vacuum frame **179** 13; **182** 2
vacuum line **74** 50; **75** 29
vacuum printing frame **179** 13
vacuum pump *Intern. Combust. Eng.* **190** 59, 60
vacuum pump *Water* **269** 8
vacuum pump switch **179** 19
vacuum ripening tank **169** 11
vacuum timing control **190** 9
vagina **20** 86
Valasian dulcimer **322** 34
Valenciennes **102** 18
valerian **380** 5
valley *Phys. Geog.* **13** 52-56
valley *Roof* **121** 15; **122** 11, 82
valley, dry ~ **13** 75
valley, synclinal ~ **13** 56
valley, U-shaped ~ **13** 55
valley, V-shaped ~ **13** 53, 54
valley bottom **13** 67; **215** 60
valley floor **13** 67
valley glacier **12** 49
valley rafter **121** 64
valley station **214** 39
valley station platform **214** 51
valley temple **333** 8
value **250** 18
value, note's ~ **320** 7
valve *Roof & Boilerr.* **38** 73
valve *Bicycle* **187** 31
valve *Airsports* **288** 77
valve *Ball Games* **291** 18
valve *Music. Instr.* **323** 40; **324** 66
valve, aortic ~ **20** 49
valve, atrioventricular ~ **20** 46, 47
valve, bicuspid ~ **20** 47
valve, mitral ~ **20** 47
valve, pulmonary ~ **20** 50
valve, sliding ~ **217** 55
valve, tricuspid ~ **20** 46
valve control house **217** 42, 63
valve horn **323** 41
valve house **217** 42, 63
valve housing **217** 54
valve line **288** 78
valve sealing cap **187** 32
valves of the heart **20** 46-47
valve tube **187** 31
vambrace **329** 47
vamp *Shoem.* **100** 60
vamp *Carnival* **306** 32
vamplate **329** 82
van, medium ~ **194** 7
Vandyke beard **34** 13
vane, curved ~ **91** 38
vane, flat ~ **91** 40
vang **284** 21
vanilla **382** 48
vanilla plant **382** 46
vanilla pod **382** 48
vans **194**
vaquero **306** 31
variable **345** 14
variable depth sonar **259** 40
variable focus lens **313** 23
variable platen action lever **249** 24
varifocal lens **313** 23
variometer **230** 14
varnish **338** 12
varnishing **129** 14
vas deferens **20** 74

vase, Greek ~ **334** 37
vase, hand-painted ~ **161** 18
vase, porcelain ~ **337** 5
vase, stone ~ **272** 35
vastus lateralis **18** 46
vastus medialis **18** 46
vat *Fish Farm.* **89** 4
vat *Paperm.* **172** 25; **173** 47
vat, concrete ~ **79** 3
vat, stainless steel ~ **79** 4
vatman **173** 46
vault **79** 1
vault, cloistered ~ **336** 41
vault, groined ~ **336** 42
vault, ribbed ~ **336** 43
vault, stalactitic ~ **337** 17
vault, stellar ~ **336** 44
vault, types of ~ **336** 38-50
vaulter *Athletics* **298** 29
vaulter *Circus* **307** 32
vaulting **298** 9-41
vaulting, Romanesque ~ **335** 17
vaulting horse **296** 1; **297** 1
vaulting pole **298** 28
V-belt **64** 78
V-belt drive **180** 58
V-cardan **67** 31
VCR cassette **243** 5
veal **95** 1-13
vee-belt drive **180** 58
vee-neck **31** 68
vee-tail **229** 31
Vega **3** 22
vegetable, frozen ~ **99** 61
vegetable basket **99** 81
vegetable crate **55** 43
vegetable dish **45** 25
vegetable garden **52**
vegetable oil **98** 23
vegetable patch **52** 26
vegetable plants **57**
vegetable plate **45** 33
vegetable platter **45** 33
vegetable plot **52** 26; **55** 39
vegetables **57**
vegetables, canned ~ **96** 27
vegetable spoon **45** 74
vegetarian meal **266** 62
vehicle **195** 47
vehicle, articulated ~ **194** 28
vehicle, electrically-powered ~ **188** 20
vehicle ferry **15** 47
vehicle ramp **206** 1
vehicles **186** 1-54
vehicles, horse-drawn ~ **186** 1-54
vehicle tanker **194** 28
veil **381** 5
veil, bridal ~ **332** 20
veil, widow's ~ **331** 39
vein **370** 29
vein, frontal ~ **18** 6
vein, iliac ~ **18** 18
vein, jugular ~ **18** 2
vein, portal ~ **20** 39
vein, pulmonary ~ **18** 12; **20** 56
vein, subclavian ~ **18** 8
vein, temporal ~ **18** 4
velum **381** 5
velum palati **19** 21
vena cava, inferior ~ **18** 15; **20** 57
vena cava, superior ~ **18** 9; **20** 53
venation **370** 29
vendor **308** 17
veneer **133** 2
veneer-peeling machine **133** 1
veneer-splicing machine **133** 3
V-engine **190** 1
vent *Phys. Geog.* **11** 28
vent *Airsports* **288** 82
vent, volcanic ~ **11** 17
ventilating tile **122** 7
ventilation control knob **26** 27
ventilation drum **74** 29
ventilation drum motor **74** 33
ventilation flap *Market Gdn.* **55** 41
ventilation flap *Railw.* **213** 16, 29, 30
ventilation shaft *Brew.* **92** 14
ventilation shaft *Coal* **144** 21
ventilation slit **50** 30
ventilation switch **191** 83
ventilation system **6** 26
ventilation system, automatic ~ **191** 30
ventilation window **55** 10
ventilator *Bathrm. etc.* **49** 20
ventilator *Poultry Farm* **74** 10, 17
ventilator *Railw.* **207** 9
ventilator *Ship* **221** 41
ventilator *Water* **269** 27
ventilator *Disco* **317** 30
ventilator *Zoo* **356** 17
ventilator, hinged ~ **55** 10
ventilator grill **258** 43
ventilator lead **223** 41
ventilator opening **258** 43
ventilators **55** 10-11
vent mast **221** 38
vent pipe **155** 11
vent prop **55** 18
ventral part **95** 39
ventricle **20** 51
vents **55** 10-11
venturi **192** 8
venturi throat **190** 15
Venus **4** 44
Venus's flytrap **377** 14
Venus's slipper **376** 27
verge **37** 8; **121** 3
verger **330** 26, 58
Vermes **357** 20-26
vermouth **98** 62
vernier *Metalwkr.* **140** 55
vernier *Navig.* **224** 5
vernier calliper gauge **140** 52; **149** 67
vernier depth gauge **140** 54; **149** 72
vernier scale **149** 69
vert **254** 29
vertebra, cervical ~ **17** 2
vertebra, coccygeal ~ **17** 5; **20** 60
vertebra, dorsal ~ **17** 3
vertebra, lumbar ~ **17** 4
vertebra, thoracic ~ **17** 3
vertex *Man* **16** 1
vertex *Maths.* **346** 26; **347** 16, 28
vertex refractionometer **111** 33
vertical backward somersault **297** 17
vertical deflection module **240** 8
vertical drive head **150** 38
vertical flick spin **288** 6
vertical milling spindle **150** 37
vertical piano **325** 1
vertical/short take-off and landing aircraft **232** 26-32
vertical speed indicator **230** 14
vertical tangent screw **14** 54
vesicle, germinal ~ **74** 66
vesicle, seminal ~ **20** 77
vessel, completed ~ **162** 29, 37
vessel, damaged ~ **227** 2; **228** 10
vessel, funerary ~ **328** 34
vessels, ecclesiastical ~ **332** 34-54
vessels, liturgical ~ **332** 34-54
vessel with spiral pattern **328** 13
vest *Infant Care etc.* **28** 23
vest *Underwear etc.* **32** 7
vest *Men's Wear* **33** 4, 15
vest *Gymn.* **296** 61
vest *Hist. Cost.* **355** 75
vest, envelope-neck ~ **29** 7
vest, knitted ~ **33** 53
vest, short-sleeved ~ **32** 28
vest, sleeveless ~ **29** 6; **32** 25
vest, wrapover ~ **29** 8
vest and shorts set **32** 21
vestibule *Railw.* **207** 21
vestibule *Hotel* **267** 1-26
vestments **330** 22; **332** 4
vestry **331** 13
vestry door **330** 17
VHF and UHF tuner **240** 6
VHF antenna **257** 25
VHF station selector button **241** 38
viaduct **215** 59
vibrating beam **201** 13
vibrating cylinder **119** 89
vibrating head **119** 89
vibrating poker **119** 89
vibration, macroseismic ~ **11** 38
vibration damper **190** 26
vibrator **201** 13
vicar **330** 22
vicarage **331** 20
vice **109** 28; **134** 10; **138** 24; **260** 47, 56
vice, front ~ **132** 30
vice, parallel-jaw ~ **140** 2
vice bar **260** 48

vice handle **132** 31
vice screw **132** 32
Victoria regia water lily **378** 17
video cassette **242** 18
video cassette recorder **243** 7
video cassette recorder system **243** 5-36
video coding station **236** 39
video controller **239** 11
video control room **239** 10
video data terminal **238** 2, 11
video disc **243** 38, 44, 58
video disc jacket **243** 45
video disc player **243** 37, 46
video head **243** 26, 36
video head movement, direction of ~ **243** 30
video long play video disc system **243** 46-60
video monitor **238** 2
video recorder, portable ~ **243** 4
video signal **243** 58
videotape recorder, portable ~ **243** 4
video telephone **242** 21
video telephone screen **242** 26
video track **243** 31
vielle à roue **322** 25
Vienna sausage **96** 8
view, front ~ **151** 17
view, lateral ~ **27** 3
view, side ~ **151** 18
viewer editor **117** 91
viewfinder, rectangular ~ **114** 14
viewfinder, right-angle ~ **115** 71
viewfinder, universal ~ **114** 41
viewfinder eyepiece *Photog.* **114** 2; **115** 22
viewfinder eyepiece *Films* **313** 6
viewfinder hood **114** 23; **115** 68
viewfinder image **115** 51
viewing lens **114** 25
viewing screen **117** 94
view point **15** 68
Viking ship **218** 13-17
village **15** 105
vine *Wine Grow.* **78** 2-9
vine *Pest Contr.* **83** 51
vinegar **98** 25
vine layer **83** 15
vine leaf **78** 4
vine pests **80** 20-27
vine root louse **83** 33
vine shoot **78** 2
vine stem **78** 6
vine tendril **54** 22
vineyard *Map* **15** 65
vineyard *Wine Grow.* **78** 1, 21
vineyard area **78** 1-21
vineyard tractor **83** 48
viniculture **78**
viniculturist **78** 13
viol **322** 23
viola **323** 27
viola da gamba **322** 23
viol bow **322** 24
violet **343** 9
violin **323** 1
violin, miniature ~ **322** 20
violin body **323** 3
violin bow **323** 12
violin-bow fibula **328** 27
violin bridge **323** 5
violin clef **320** 8
violinist **267** 45
violin string **323** 9
violoncello **323** 16
violone **322** 23; **323** 23
vipers **364** 40-41
Virgin **3** 18; **4** 58
virginal **322** 45
Virginia creeper **51** 5; **374** 16
Virgin Mary **330** 51
Virgo **3** 18; **4** 58
vis-à-vis **186** 51
viscose **169** 13-27, 15
viscose process **169** 1-34
viscose rayon **169** 1-12, 34
viscose rayon cake **169** 18
viscose rayon thread **169** 13-27
viscose spinning solution **169** 10, 28-34
viscous drive **190** 8
vise *see* vice
vision controller **239** 11
vision control room **239** 10
vision mixer **238** 63
vision-mixing console **238** 63
vision-mixing desk **238** 63
visitor **356** 6
visor *Forestry* **84** 23
visor *Heraldry* **254** 9
visor *Chivalry* **329** 40
visual display **23** 27
visual display unit **248** 16, 44
viticulture **78**
viticulturist **78** 13
vitreous body **19** 46
vixen **88** 42
VLP video disc **243** 51
V-neck **31** 68
vocal pouch **364** 25
vocal sac **364** 25
Voith transmission **209** 14; **212** 74
vol-au-vent **97** 18
volcanism **11** 13-28
volcano, active ~ **11** 15
volcano, composite ~ **11** 15
volcano, extinct ~ **11** 25, 28
volcano, subterranean ~ **11** 20
vole and mole trap **83** 37
volley **293** 41
volley, forehand ~ **293** 41
volleyball **293** 56-71, 58, 59
voltage meter **212** 17
voltage regulator, automatic ~ **153** 31
voltage transformer **153** 59
voltmeter **326** 38
volume, respiratory ~ **26** 28
volume control **117** 85; **241** 41
volume control, pupil's ~ **261** 43
volume control, student's ~ **261** 43
volume readout **196** 5
volumetric flask **350** 28
volume unit meters **241** 35-36
volute **333** 26; **334** 23
volute cushion **334** 24
VOR antenna **257** 26
VOR radio direction finder **230** 15
voter **263** 22
voter, qualified ~ **263** 24
votive candle **330** 53
voussoir **336** 22
V-seat **295** 13
V-support **295** 17
V-tail **229** 31
vulcanicity **11** 13-28
vulva **16** 39
V-valley **13** 53
V-way *Joiner* **132** 61
V-way *Composing Rm.* **175** 54

W

wad, felt ~ **87** 52
wafer *Bakery* **97** 45
wafer *Church* **332** 28
wafer, sacred ~ **332** 48
waffle **97** 45
waffle iron, electric ~ **40** 34
waggonette **186** 2
wagon **213** 18
wagon, flat ~ **206** 21, 24; **213** 5, 11, 40
wagon, large-capacity ~ **213** 28
wagon, open ~ **213** 33
wagon, special ~ **213** 33
Wagoner **3** 27
wagon load **206** 52
wagon truck **200** 25
wagtail **360** 9
waist *Man* **16** 31
waist *Shoem.* **100** 68
waist, corseted ~ **355** 53
waistband *Ladies' Wear* **31** 41
waistband *Men's Wear* **33** 23
waistcoat **33** 4, 15
waistcoat, denim ~ **31** 59
waistcoat, embroidered ~ **355** 75
waistcoat, knitted ~ **33** 53
waistcoat, quilted ~ **30** 16
waist longeron **235** 9
waist slip **32** 14; **309** 85
waiter **267** 47
waiter, head ~ **266** 30
waiting room *Doc.* **22** 1
waiting room *Station* **204** 14
waiting room *Airport* **233** 18
'waiting room' *Airport* **233** 28
waitress **265** 13; **266** 18
wake **223** 58
wake-robin **379** 9
waldhorn **323** 41
walk **71** 2; **72** 39

walk, gravel ~ **272** 18
walkie-talkie set **270** 41
walking stick **41** 5
walking-stick umbrella **205** 12
walkway *Dwellings* **37** 60
walkway *Street Sect.* **198** 9
walkway *Hydr. Eng.* **217** 72
wall *Map* **15** 95
wall *Carp.* **120** 29
wall *Equest.* **289** 8
wall *Ball Games* **291** 44
wall, brick ~ **118** 8; **123** 29; **260** 45
wall, concrete ~ **123** 1
wall, framed ~ **120** 48
wall, glass ~ **37** 16
wall, hollow-block ~ **118** 15
wall, inner ~ **329** 19
wall, mirrored ~ **317** 28
wall, outer ~ **121** 32, 77; **122** 37
wall, Rococo ~ **336** 9
wall, rubble concrete ~ **119** 7
wall, side ~ **42** 2; **46** 4; **222** 37
wall, slatted ~ **213** 29
wall, stone ~ **337** 23
wall, timber ~ **119** 25; **120** 9
wall barley **61** 28
wall bars **296** 20
wall brush, flat ~ **129** 17
wall calendar **22** 17; **245** 3; **248** 42
wall candelabrum **330** 16
wall chart **195** 32
wall clock **109** 32; **309** 87
wall connection **25** 23
wall cupboard **39** 8; **46** 30
wall desk **267** 16
wall espalier **52** 1
wall fountain **272** 15
wall gecko **364** 36
wall joist **120** 39
wall lamp **265** 9
wall lining, 'acoustic' ~ **310** 15
wall map **260** 44
wall memorial **331** 14
wall mirror **309** 3
wall-of-death rider **308** 54
wall outlet **127** 5
wall outlet, double ~ **127** 6
wallower **91** 11
wallpaper **128** 18, 19
wallpaper, synthetic ~ **128** 18
wallpaper-cutting board **128** 41
wallpapering **128** 18-53
wallpaper paste **128** 23
wallpaper-stripping liquid **128** 1
wallpaper-stripping machine **128** 9
wall pepper **51** 7
wall plaster **123** 60
wall plate **120** 40, 49
wall shelf **104** 8
wall shelf unit **104** 8
wall socket **39** 26; **127** 5
wall socket, double ~ **127** 6
wall stone **331** 14
wall string **123** 45
wall stringer **123** 45
wall switch **127** 16
wall unit **42** 1; **44** 17; **46** 1
wall ventilator **266** 15
walnut **59** 41, 43
walnut tree **59** 37-43, 37
walrus **367** 20
wane **120** 89
waney edge **120** 89
Wankel engine, two-rotor ~ **190** 5
wapiti **367** 2
ward, inner ~ **329** 2
ward, outer ~ **329** 31
wardrobe **43** 1
wardrobe door **46** 2
wardrobe trunk **267** 29
warehouse *Station* **206** 53
warehouse *Docks* **225** 23
warhead **255** 65
war horn, ivory ~ **354** 39
warm-air brush **106** 30
warm-air comb **105** 22; **106** 29
warm-air curtain **271** 43
warm-air regulator **191** 87
warm house **55** 4, 32
warm-up regulator **190** 50
warning cross **202** 41
warning light **191** 67, 72, 76, 80; **202** 46, 50; **224** 69; **230** 64; **270** 6
warning sign **280** 6
warp *Sea Fish.* **90** 12
warp *Weaving* **165** 43; **166** 39
warp *Knitting* **167** 24
warp *Weaves* **171** 14
warp *Hydr. Eng.* **217** 23
warp, wire ~ **90** 15
war paint **352** 13
warp beam **165** 29, 42; **166** 48; **167** 24
warp beam, sized ~ **165** 56
warping capstan **217** 22
warping machine **165** 22
warping machine frame **165** 27
warp-knitting machine **167** 23
warp let-off motion **166** 61
warp rib fabric **171** 14
warp rib weave **171** 13
warp thread **166** 39; **171** 1-29, 2, 17, 18
warp thread, lowered ~ **171** 8
warp thread, raised ~ **171** 7
warren **86** 23
warship, Roman ~ **218** 9-12
warships **258; 259**
washbasin **24** 15; **49** 24; **126** 27, 31; **278** 6
washbasin, double ~ **267** 32
washbasin pedestal **49** 27
washboard *Floor etc. Constr.* **123** 21, 63
washboard *Flea Market* **309** 70
wash-bottle **349** 8
washer *Photog.* **116** 15
washer *Mach. Parts etc.* **143** 17, 34
washer *Sawmill* **157** 21
washer *Bicycle* **187** 55
washer, lead ~ **122** 103
washing **169** 19; **170** 48, 56
washing and toilet facilities **278** 5-6
washing basin **309** 65
washing bottle **261** 32
washing drum **50** 24
washing floor **92** 3, 27
washing line **38** 23; **50** 33
washing machine **157** 21
washing machine, automatic ~ **50** 23
washing machines **50** 23-34
washing set **309** 64
washing trough **165** 49
washing unit, compressed-air ~ **92** 3
washing-up area **207** 28
washing-up brush **50** 51
wash liquor, weak ~ **172** 44
washroom **207** 15; **278** 5
washstand *Railw.* **207** 40
washstand *Flea Market* **309** 67
wash tank *Photog.* **116** 15
wash tank *Oil, Petr.* **145** 30
washtub **309** 69
wash water, weak ~ **172** 44
wasp **82** 35
wasp waist **355** 53
waste **144** 37
waste, medium-activity ~ **154** 72
waste, nuclear ~ **154** 57-68
waste, radioactive ~ **154** 57-68, 77
waste bin **22** 70; **96** 46
waste-gas heat exchanger **155** 9
wastepaper basket **46** 25; **248** 45
waste pipe *Bathrm. etc.* **49** 45
waste pipe *Street Sect.* **198** 26
waste steam exhaust **210** 22
waste tray, mobile ~ **26** 22
waste water discharge **156** 38
waste water outlet **217** 62
waste water pump *Paperm.* **172** 63
waste water pump *Refuse Coll.* **199** 20
watch, automatic ~ **110** 32-43
watch, waterproof ~ **109** 26; *279* 16
watchdog **62** 32; **70** 25
watches **110**
watchglass-fitting tool **109** 11, 29
watchkeeper **221** 126
watchmaker **109** 1
watchman **329** 9
watch strap **110** 5
watch strap, metal ~ **109** 19
watch-testing machine **109** 24
watch-timing machine **109** 25
watchtower **329** 35
water **48** 8

water, artesian ~ **12** 21
water, baptismal ~ **332** 12
water, entrapped ~ **13** 16
water, raw ~ **269** 4
water, rising ~ **12** 26
water, running ~ **89** 1
water, shallow ~ **224** 87, 97
water, underlying ~ **12** 32
water and brine separator **145** 32
water appliances **126** 12-25
water ballast **223** 78
water barrel **52** 4
water bath **132** 12; **349** 14
water bath, constant temperature ~ **23** 48
Water Bearer **4** 63
water bottle **290** 10
water buffalo **367** 8
water bug **358** 4
water butt **52** 4
water canister **83** 57
water cannon **270** 66; **316** 18
Water Carrier *Astron.* **4** 63
water carrier *Camping* **278** 32
water channel **334** 54
water circuit, auxiliary ~ **259** 63
water circuit, primary ~ **259** 65
water circuit, secondary ~ **259** 63
water-collecting tank **92** 5
watercolour **260** 27; **338** 18
water connection **179** 5
water container **103** 22
water cooler **189** 35
water-cooling system *Moon L.* **6** 26
water-cooling system *Iron Foundry etc.* **148** 28
watercress **378** 30
water cruet **332** 45
water elf **327** 23
water extractor **281** 39
waterfall **11** 45
waterfall, artificial ~ **272** 9
water feed pipe **103** 21
waterfowl **272** 51-54
waterfowling **86** 40
water gauge *Map* **15** 29
water gauge *Roof & Boilerr.* **38** 63
water gauge *Railw.* **210** 45
water gauge *Chem.* **349** 16
water glass **24** 13
water heater **145** 31
water heater, electric ~ **126** 13
water heater, gas ~ **126** 12
water heater, instantaneous ~ **126** 12-13
watering can **51** 21; **55** 26
water inlet *Fish Farm.* **89** 7
water inlet *Plumb. etc.* **126** 18
water inlet *Water* **269** 54
water inlet pipe **168** 11
water jet pipe **281** 40
water jet pump **23** 49
water jug **309** 66
water jump **289** 20
water level **13** 77
water lily **51** 18; **272** 56
waterline **258** 27; **285** 31
water main **198** 22
watermark **252** 31
water meter **269** 53
water-meter dial **269** 58
watermill *Map* **15** 77
watermill *Mills* **91** 35-44
water molecule **242** 67
water moth **358** 12
water newt **364** 20
water nixie **327** 23
water nymph *Fabul. Creat.* **327** 23
water nymph *Articulates* **358** 3
water outlet *Fish Farm.* **89** 8
water outlet *Energy Sources* **155** 23
water outlet *Water* **269** 57
water outlet pipe **116** 17
water overfall **91** 43
water ox **367** 8
water pipe *Market Gdn.* **55** 30
water pipe *Poultry Farm* **74** 7, 26
water pipe *Tobacc. etc.* **107** 42
water pipe *Power Plant* **152** 7
water pipe *Paperm.* **172** 65
water pipe *School* **261** 4
water plantain **378** 44
water plants **378** 14-57
water polo **282** 46-50
water polo ball **282** 48
water preheater **152** 10
waterproofing **123** 5
water pump **190** 61
waters, coastal ~ **286** 10-14
waters, inshore ~ **286** 10-14
water scorpion **358** 4
water ski **280** 16
water ski, types of ~ **286** 56-62
water skier **286** 45
water skiing **286** 45-62
water slater **358** 2
Water Snake *Astron.* **3** 16
water snake *Fish etc.* **364** 38
water supply **27** 46; **269**
water supply, individual ~ **269** 40-52
water supply pipe *Brew.* **92** 48
water supply pipe *Photog.* **116** 16
water table **13** 77; **269** 1, 42, 63
water tank *Market Gdn.* **55** 2, 29
water tank *Gas Weld.* **141** 17
water tank *Refuse Coll.* **199** 27
water tank *Railw.* **210** 66
water tank *School* **261** 33
water tank *Theatre* **316** 51
water tanker **233** 22
water tap **39** 36; **49** 26; **126** 31
water temperature **280** 8
water temperature gauge **191** 38, 66
water tender **270** 51
water tower *Map* **15** 81
water tower *Market Gdn.* **55** 2
water tower *Coal* **144** 14
water tower *Water* **269** 18
water trough **137** 8
water tub **281** 26
water-tube boiler **152** 5
water vole **366** 17
waterway engineering **217**
water wings **281** 7; **282** 18
Watling Street thistle **61** 32
wattle **73** 24
wave **13** 36; **287** 17
wave, seismic ~ **11** 36
waves, artificial ~ **281** 1-9
wave soaring **287** 16
wave system **287** 17
waxing cork **301** 23
waxing iron **301** 22
wax scraper **301** 24
wax separation **145** 50
waxworks **308** 68
waybill **206** 30
wayside flowers **375; 376**
WC **49** 12; **207** 16, 42, 72; **211** 59; **231** 31; **317** 31
weaponry **255** 1-98
weapons, heavy ~ **255** 40-95
weapon system radar **258** 35
weasel **367** 16
weather **8** 1-19
weather chart **9** 1-39; **342** 66
weather cloth **223** 17
weathercock **331** 3
weather map **9** 1-39; **342** 66
weather radar antenna **231** 18
weather report **342** 65
weather satellite **10** 64
weather ship **9** 7
weather station **9** 7; **225** 33
weather vane **121** 26; **331** 4
weave, plain ~ **171** 1, 4, 24
weaver **136** 5
weaves *Basketm.* **136** 1-4
weaves *Weaves* **171** 1-29
weaving **165; 166**
weaving draft **171** 29
weaving machine **166** 1, 35
web *Dom. Anim.* **73** 36
web *House Insects etc.* **81** 10
web *Paperm.* **173** 30, 45
web *Letterpress* **181** 43, 58
web *Railw.* **202** 3
web *Gymn.* **297** 11
web *Articulates* **358** 47
web *Birds* **359** 7
webfoot **359** 6
web-offset press **180** 1, 18
wedding ceremony **332** 14
wedding ring **36** 5; **332** 17
wedding ring box **36** 6
wedding ring sizing machine **108** 24
wedge **119** 15; **132** 19; **158** 7
wedge, hardwood ~ **121** 96
wedge, optical ~ **176** 22
wedge heel **101** 55
wedge stone **336** 22
weed **379** 8
weeding hoe **51** 22
weeds **61**
weekend house **37** 84-86

weeping willow **272** 63
weevil **80** 10, 49; **82** 42
weft feeler **166** 31
weft feeler, electric ~ **166** 14
weft pirn **166** 7
weft replenishment **166** 5
weft thread **171** 1-29, 3
weft thread, lowered ~ **171** 15
weft thread, raised ~ **171** 16
weft yarn **163** 2
weigela **373** 23
weigelia **373** 23
weighbridge **206** 41
weighbridge office **206** 40
weighing apparatus **92** 32; **170** 29
weighing bottle **349** 24
weighing bunker **225** 22
weighing machine **206** 31
weighing platform **22** 67
weigh office **199** 12
weight *Roof & Boilerr.* **38** 32
weight *Sea Fish.* **90** 10
weight *Clocks* **110** 32
weight *Railw.* **202** 18
weight *Athletics* **298** 49
weight, iron ~ **90** 21
weight belt **279** 14
weighting disc **165** 21
weightlifter **299** 2
weightlifting **299** 1-5
weights, lead ~ **89** 88-92
weir *Map* **15** 66
weir *Hydr. Eng.* **217** 65-72
weir *Rowing* **283** 60
weir sill **217** 79
welder electrode arm **142** 30
weld gauge **142** 36
welding bench **141** 13; **142** 21
welding glove, five-fingered ~ **142** 32
welding glove, three-fingered ~ **142** 8
welding goggles **141** 24
welding lead **142** 19
welding nozzle **141** 33
welding paste **141** 18
welding pressure adjustment **142** 31
welding rod **141** 12
welding table **142** 13
welding torch **141** 11, 19, 28
welding transformer **125** 29; **142** 1, 27
well *Astron.* **5** 24
well *Map* **15** 100
well *Carp.* **120** 46
well *Joiner* **132** 35
well *Oil, Petr.* **145** 17
well *Water* **269** 40
well, artesian ~ **12** 25
well, driven ~ **269** 60
well, glass-roofed ~ **271** 11
well casing **269** 64
well head **269** 65
wellington boot **101** 14
wellingtonia **372** 69
wels **364** 12
welt, knitted ~ **29** 65; **31** 70
welt, stretch ~ **31** 43
welt cutter **100** 48
welt pincers **100** 38
West Australian Current **14** 45
westerlies **9** 50
Western roll **298** 16
west point **4** 15
West Wind Drift **14** 44
westwork **335** 22
wet and dry bulb thermometer **10** 52
wet bulb thermometer **10** 35
wet felt, first ~ **173** 17
wet felt, second ~ **173** 18
wether **73** 13
wet oil tank **145** 30
wetsuit, neoprene ~ **279** 9
wetting trough **165** 44
Weymouth pine **372** 30
Whale **3** 11
whales **367** 23-29
wharve **164** 48
wheat **68** 1, 23
wheat and rye bread **97** 6, 8
wheat beer **93** 26
wheat flour **97** 52; **99** 63
wheatgerm bread **97** 48
wheatgerm oil **98** 24
wheel *Overh. Irrign.* **67** 24
wheel *Clocks* **110** 11
wheel *Bicycle* **187** 1
wheel *Aircraft* **230** 24
wheel, back ~ **186** 17
wheel, co-pilot's ~ **230** 25
wheel, front ~ **186** 4; **187** 26-32
wheel, light alloy ~ **189** 48
wheel, rear ~ **186** 17
wheel, rubber-tyred ~ **64** 32
wheel, ship's ~ **224** 15
wheel, spoked ~ **289** 25
wheel adjustment **64** 58
wheel alignment **195** 17, 21
wheel alignment, visual ~ **195** 41
wheel and axle drive **212** 28
wheel and axle set **212** 3; **213** 3
wheelarch doorway **278** 39
wheelbarrow **56** 47; **118** 37; **119** 42
wheelbarrow sprayer **83** 38
wheel brush, wire ~ **134** 24
wheel cover **322** 27
wheel cylinder **192** 54
wheel disc, plastic ~ **289** 25
wheeler **186** 47
wheel flange lubricator **211** 52
wheel guard *Tram* **197** 11
wheel guard *Music. Instr.* **322** 27
wheelhead slide **150** 3
wheelhorse **186** 47
wheelhouse **223** 18; **224** 14-38
wheel lock **187** 49
wheel mirror **195** 41
wheel nut **187** 53
wheel of fortune **308** 45
wheel plough **65** 1
wheel ratchet **110** 10
wheel rim **187** 28; **189** 25; **191** 16; **192** 77
wheelsman **224** 16
wheel tapper **205** 39
wheel-tapping hammer **205** 40
whelp **73** 16
whetstone **66** 19
whetting anvil **66** 11
whetting hammer **66** 9
whip *Bldg. Site* **118** 30
whip *Equest.* **289** 43
whip *Circus* **307** 53
whip antenna **258** 60
whip line **228** 3
whipper-in **289** 43
whipping unit **97** 70
whip stall **288** 5
whirler **179** 1
whirligig **308** 2
whirlpool, hot ~ **281** 31, 35
whirlpool separator **93** 2
whisk **39** 23
whiskers *Hairst. etc.* **34** 12
whiskers *Mammals* **367** 21
whisky **42** 31; **98** 56
whisky glass **267** 57
whistle *Kitch. Utensils* **40** 11
whistle *Railw.* **211** 9; **212** 49
whistle *Navig.* **224** 70
whistle lever **211** 40
whistle valve handle **210** 51
white *Poultry Farm* **74** 62, 67
white *Heraldry* **254** 25
white *Colour* **343** 11
white bear **368** 11
white clover **69** 2
white light, supplementary ~ **203** 15
white line **268** 72
white owl **362** 17
white oxeye daisy **376** 4
white pelican **359** 5
white pine **372** 30
white poplar **371** 23
white-tailed eagle **362** 5
white-tailed sea eagle **362** 5
white wagtail **360** 9
white water lily **378** 14
white water pump **172** 63
white wine glass **45** 82
whitewood **374** 1
wholemeal bread **97** 48
whole note **320** 13
whole rest **320** 21
whortleberry **377** 23
wick **107** 29
wickerwork **136** 4, 16
wicket **292** 70
wicket keeper **292** 73
wide screen camera **310** 47
width *Roof* **122** 91, 95
width *Composing Rm.* **175** 48
width adjustment **100** 19
width scale **157** 58
width-setting tree **100** 55
Wiener **96** 8
wig **105** 38; **315** 49
wig, full-bottomed ~ **34** 2
wig, partial ~ **355** 8
wig block **105** 39

wiggler **89** 72
wigwam **352** 7
wild animal cage **307** 49
wild animal tamer **307** 52
wild arum **379** 9
wild barley **61** 28
wild boar **86** 32; **88** 51
wild briar **373** 26
wild camomile **380** 1
wild cherry **59** 5
wild chicory **376** 25
wild endive **376** 25
wildfowling **86** 40
wild morning glory **61** 26
wild mustard **61** 18
wild oat **61** 29
wild orchid **376** 28
wild pear tree **58** 31
wild radish **61** 21
wild sow **86** 32; **88** 51
wild strawberry **58** 16
wild-water racing kayak **283** 69
willow rod **136** 15
willow stake **136** 14
Wilson chamber **2** 24
Wilson cloud chamber **2** 24
winch **270** 56
winched launch **287** 5
winch house **226** 54
wind arrow **9** 9
wind avalanche **304** 1
wind box **147** 69
windbreak **354** 35
wind chest **326** 12, 12-14
wind chest box **326** 12
wind cone **287** 11
wind cripple **13** 43
wind direction **9** 9-19; **285** 6
wind-direction indicator **10** 31
wind directions **285** 1-13
wind-direction shaft **9** 9
wind-direction symbols **9** 9-19
windflower **375** 5; **377** 1
wind gauge **10** 28
wind generator **55** 34; **155** 42
winding, low-voltage ~ **153** 16
winding, primary ~ **153** 15
winding, secondary ~ **153** 16
winding crown **110** 42
winding engine house **144** 2
winding gear **217** 74
winding handle **117** 50
winding inset **144** 26
wind knob **110** 23
windlass **223** 49; **258** 6
windmill *Map* **15** 31
windmill *Mills* **91** 1-34
windmill *Fair* **308** 15
windmill, Dutch ~ **91** 29
windmill, German ~ **91** 31
windmill arm **91** 1
windmill cap, rotating ~ **91** 30
windmill sail **91** 1
windmill vane **91** 1
window **2** 16; **6** 40; **25** 8; **28** 36, 49; **75** 31; **77** 50; **186** 10; **268** 14; **284** 38
window, circular ~ **335** 12
window, double casement ~ **37** 22
window, heated ~ **191** 80
window, lead glass ~ **154** 75
window, rear ~ **191** 32, 80
window, side ~ **231** 29
window, single casement ~ **37** 23
window, sliding ~ **207** 7
window, transparent ~ **278** 41; **284** 3
window box **268** 15
window breast **37** 24
window decoration **260** 68; **268** 12
window display **98** 1; **268** 11
window frame **133** 44
window glass **124** 5
window head **37** 25; **118** 9; **120** 57
window jamb **120** 51
window ladder **296** 21
window ledge **118** 12; **120** 33
window lintel **120** 57
window opening **120** 30
window painting **260** 26
window shutter **37** 30
window sill **37** 24; **118** 12; **120** 33
window vent **55** 10
windpipe **17** 50; **20** 4
wind power plant **155** 42
wind pump **15** 73; **55** 34
windrow **63** 36
wind screen **5** 15
windscreen, panoramic ~ **191** 21
windscreen wiper **191** 41; **197** 32
wind shaft **91** 5
windshield **5** 31
windshield, panoramic ~ **191** 21
windshield wiper **191** 41
wind sock **287** 11
wind speed **9** 10
wind-speed barb **9** 10
wind-speed feather **9** 10
wind-speed indicator **10** 29
wind-speed meter **10** 29
windsurfer **284** 1
windsurfing **284** 1-9
wind systems **9** 46-52
wind trunk **326** 11
wind vane **10** 32; **55** 36; **331** 4
wind wheel **55** 35
wine **99** 76; **266** 43
wine, bottled ~ **98** 60-64
wine, red ~ **98** 64
wine, sparkling ~ **98** 63
wine, white ~ **98** 60
wine bar **266** 30-44
wine bottle **79** 14
wine carafe **266** 32
wine cask **79** 2
wine cellar **79** 1-22
wine cooler **266** 42
wine cruet **332** 46
wineglass **44** 9; **45** 12, 82, 83; **79** 19; **266** 33; **317** 7
wine grower **78** 13
wine growing **78**
wine in bottles **98** 60-64
wine jug **79** 15
wine list **266** 31
wine press, horizontal ~ **79** 21
wine restaurant **266** 30-44
wine tasting **79** 16
wine vat **79** 3
wine vault **79** 1-22
wine waiter **266** 30
wing *House Insects etc.* **81** 8
wing *Game* **88** 76, 79
wing *Sea Fish.* **90** 16
wing *Aircraft* **230** 43
wing *Airsports* **288** 27
wing *Fabul. Creat.* **327** 15, 28, 51, 60
wing *Decid. Trees* **371** 57
wing *Conifers* **372** 9
wing, bat's ~ **327** 4
wing, central ~ **229** 8
wing, cranked ~ **229** 14
wing, elliptical ~ **229** 15
wing, front ~ **191** 3
wing, hind ~ **358** 33
wing, lower ~ **229** 9
wing, membranous ~ **82** 11
wing, middle ~ **229** 8
wing, multispar ~ **287** 29
wing, ogival ~ **229** 22
wing, rectangular ~ **229** 16
wing, rotary ~ **232** 12
wing, swept-back ~ **229** 20, 21
wing, tapered ~ **229** 17
wing, upper ~ **229** 7
wing case **82** 10
wing configurations **229** 1-14
Winged Horse **3** 10
winger **291** 16
wing mirror, left-hand ~ **191** 40
wing mirror, right-hand ~ **191** 56
wing nut **143** 42; **187** 39
wing of bridge **223** 16
wing rail **202** 25
wings **307** 12
wing shapes **229** 15-22
wing span **229** 2
wing suspension, inner ~ **257** 34
wing suspension, outer ~ **257** 35
wing tally **74** 55
wing tank **256** 4
wing tank, integral ~ **257** 29
wing tip **287** 42
wing-tip tank **231** 9; **256** 30
wing wall *Rivers* **216** 35
wing wall *Hydr. Eng.* **217** 80
winker **71** 26
winner **299** 39
winner's price **289** 39
winners' table **289** 38
winning peg **292** 77
winnowing **64** 15
winter boot **101** 1
winter coat **30** 61
winter dike **216** 32
winter dress **30** 12

winter green **57** 34
winter moth **80** 16
winter slacks **30** 19
winter sports **301; 302; 303**
winter wear **30**
wiper *Post* **237** 44
wiper *Graphic Art* **340** 13
wiper/washer switch and horn **191** 60
wire *Paperm.* **173** 14
wire *Fencing* **294** 31
wire, gold ~ **108** 3
wire, iron ~ **143** 12
wire, overhead ~ **194** 43
wire, silver~ **108** 3
wire and sheet roller **108** 1
wireless mast **15** 33
wireman **127** 1
wire side **173** 34
wire spool, spring-loaded ~ **294** 29
wire stripper and cutter **134** 15
wire strippers **127** 64
wireworm **80** 38
witch **306** 6
witchgrass **61** 30
withers *Dog* **70** 11
withers *Horse* **72** 17
witloof **376** 25
witness **332** 23
wobbler, double-jointed ~ **89** 70
wobbler, round ~ **89** 71
wobbler, single-jointed ~ **89** 69
wolf **367** 13
wolfsbane **379** 1
womb **20** 79
wood *Forestry* **84** 1-34
wood *School* **260** 82
wood *Ball Games* **293** 91
wood *Sculpt. Studio* **339** 27
wood, coniferous ~ **15** 1
wood, deciduous ~ **15** 4
wood, mixed ~ **15** 14
wood, open ~ **326** 31-33
wood, rough ~ **135** 21
wood anemone **377** 1
woodbind **374** 13
woodbine **51** 5; **374** 13, 16
wood carver **339** 28
wood carving **260** 77
wood chip paper **128** 18
wood chisel **339** 19
wood cut **260** 83
wood cutting *Forestry* **84** 15-37
woodcutting *Graphic Art* **340** 2
wood engraving **340** 1, 1-13
wood file **132** 2
wood grouse **88** 72
wood haulage way **84** 3
woodland strawberry **58** 16
woodlark **361** 18
wood louse **81** 6
woodpecker **359** 27
wood pulp, chemical ~ **172** 77, 78
wood pulp paper **128** 18
wood rasp **132** 1; **134** 8; **260** 55
wood screw **122** 101; **132** 41; **143** 45
wood screw thread **143** 47
wood sculptor **339** 28
woodsman **84** 18
wood tick **358** 44
wood-turning lathe **134** 51; **135** 1
woodwind instruments **323** 28-38
woodwinds **323** 28-38
woodworking adhesive **134** 36
woofer **241** 17
woolly apple aphid **80** 32, 33
woolly apple aphid colony **80** 34
woolly milk cap **379** 13
woolpack cloud **8** 1; **287** 22
work **118** 17
workbench **97** 60, 62; **100** 33; **104** 7; **108** 20; **109** 2; **111** 20; **124** 15; **125** 10; **137** 21; **140** 7; **260** 46
workbench, collapsible ~ **134** 41
workbench lamp **109** 12
workboard **136** 7
work clamp *Joiner* **132** 51
work clamp *Arc Weld.* **142** 35
worker *Bees* **77** 1, 6-9, 10-19
worker *Articulates* **358** 22
worker bee **77** 1
worker cell **77** 34
work folder **261** 27
working, open-cast ~ **158** 1
working area **162** 5
working bath **162** 5
working deck **221** 19, 34
working face **158** 3
working passage **75** 24
working platform **118** 17; **145** 5; **211** 42; **234** 28, 46
workings, underground ~ **144** 21-51
working surface, tiled ~ **261** 5
working top **39** 11
workpiece **104** 25; **133** 44; **139** 46; **140** 6; **141** 20; **142** 28; **148** 51; **150** 20
workpiece, blocked ~ **139** 28
workpiece, preshaped ~ **139** 28
work platform **118** 17; **211** 42; **234** 28, 46
workroom, dressmaker's ~ **103** 1-27
workroom, furrier's ~ **131** 1-25
workroom, tailor's ~ **104** 1-32; **268** 17
works **15** 37
workshop **62** 17; **146** 30; **310** 6; **315** 28-42
workshop, bootmaker's ~ **100** 1-68
workshop, carpenter's ~ **120** 4
workshop, cooper's ~ **130** 1-33
workshop, fitter's ~ **140** 1-22
workshop, glazier's ~ **124** 1
workshop, joiner's ~ **132** 1-73
workshop, locksmith's ~ **140** 1-22
workshop, mechanic's ~ **140** 1-22
workshop, optician's ~ **111** 20-47
workshop, orbital ~ **235** 66
workshop, shoemaker's ~ **100** 1-68
workshop, tank construction engineer's ~ **130** 1-33
workshop, turner's ~ **135** 1-26
workshop area **5** 17
workshop door **120** 5
workshop trolley **109** 22
work top **50** 31
worm **192** 59
worm-and-nut steering gear **192** 56-59
worm gear sector **192** 57
wormhole **58** 65
worms **357** 20-26
wormwood **380** 4
worshipper **330** 29
wort **92** 50, 51, 52
wort boiler **92** 52
wort cooler **93** 5
wort cooling **93** 1-5
wound **21** 8
wrap, coloured ~ **355** 10
wrapper *Tobacc. etc.* **107** 5
wrapper *Bookbind.* **185** 37
wrapping, jute ~ **163** 4
wrapping counter **271** 14
wrapping material **98** 46-49
wrapping paper **98** 46
wreath **123** 52
wreath, bridal ~ **332** 19
wreath of the colours **254** 2
wreath piece **123** 49
wreck **224** 84
wrecking crane **270** 47
wreck to port **224** 86
wreck to starboard **224** 85
wren **361** 12
wrench **134** 14
wrench, open-end ~ **134** 2
wrest **325** 20
wrestler **299** 7
wrestling **299** 6-12
wrestling, Greco-Roman ~ **299** 6-9
wrestling mat **299** 12
wrest pin **324** 23; **325** 17
wrest pin block **324** 22; **325** 18
wrest plank **324** 22; **325** 18
wrist *Man* **19** 76
wrist *Horse* **72** 22
wristband **296** 64
wrist joint **2** 41
wrist sling **300** 32
wristwatch, automatic ~ **110** 32-43
wristwatch, electronic ~ **110** 1
writing, English ~ **342** 10
writing, German ~ **342** 11
writing cane **341** 23
writing surface **47** 23; **246** 3

writing system, pictorial ~ **341** 1
writing unit **46** 21
wrought-iron craftsman **140** 1
wryneck **359** 27

X

xanthate **169** 10
X-contact **115** 14
xenon lamp **177** 17
xenon lamp housing **177** 42
X-radiation **1** 33, 56
X-ray **25** 39
X-ray apparatus **24** 21; **27** 6
X-ray cassette **27** 2
X-ray control unit, central ~ **27** 9
X-ray examination table **27** 1
X-ray generator **24** 22
X-ray head **27** 18
X-ray image intensifier **27** 16
X-ray support, telescopic ~ **27** 8
X-ray technician **27** 11
X-ray tube **27** 17, 18
X-ray unit **27** 1-35
xylography **340** 1-13
xylophone **324** 61

Y

yacht **273** 29; **278** 12; **284** 10-48
yacht classes **284** 49-65
yacht hull, types of ~ **285** 29-41
yachting **284**; **285**
yachting cap **35** 29
yacht stern **285** 42
yacht stern, types of ~ **285** 42-49
yacht tacking **285** 7
yankee corn **68** 31
yard **276** 27
yardmaster **206** 45
yard radio **212** 50; **213** 4
yarn **164** 53, 56; **167** 17, 36; **169** 17, 25
yarn, doubled ~ **164** 60
yarn, glass ~ **162** 56, 57
yarn, inlaid ~ **171** 43
yarn, sleeved ~ **162** 57
yarn, viscose rayon ~ **169** 1-34, 27
yarn count **164** 40
yarn-distributing beam **167** 25
yarn-dividing beam **167** 25
yarn feeder **167** 6
yarn-forming frame, intermediate ~ **164** 27
yarn guide *Shoem.* **100** 30
yarn guide *Knitting* **167** 3, 54, 64
yarn guide support post **167** 2
yarn length recorder **165** 28
yarn package **165** 15; **170** 48
yarn package container **165** 16
yarn-tensioning device **167** 5
yarrow **376** 15
yawing **230** 69
yawl **220** 10
y-axis **347** 3
Y-connection **153** 20
Y-cross **332** 61
yeast **93** 6
yeast, baker's ~ **97** 53
yeast bread **97** 11
yeast propagation **93** 6
yellow *Heraldry* **254** 24
yellow *Colour* **343** 2
yellow bunting **361** 6
yellow card **291** 63
yellow coral fungus **381** 32
yellow filter adjustment **116** 44
yellow flag **60** 8
yellow-flowered jasmine **373** 4
yellowhammer **361** 6
yellow iris **60** 8
yellow light **203** 16
yellow lupin **69** 17
yellow meal beetle **81** 23
yellow owl **362** 17
yellow prickle fungus **381** 31
yellow water flag **60** 8
yerba maté **382** 11
yew tree **372** 61
yoghurt maker **40** 44
yoke *Bldg. Site* **119** 64
yoke *Power Plant* **153** 14
yoke *Rowing* **283** 51
yoke, adjustable ~ **65** 14
yoke, bolted ~ **119** 74
yoke, front ~ **33** 19
yoke, kimono ~ **31** 18
yoke elm **371** 63
yoke mount, English-type ~ **113** 23
yoke mounting, English-type ~ **113** 23
yolk **74** 68
yolk sac **74** 64
Y-tube **350** 56
yucca **373** 24
yurt **353** 19
yurta **353** 19

Z

zap flap **229** 50
Z-drive motorboat **286** 2
zebra **366** 27
zebra crossing **198** 11; **268** 24
Zechstein, leached ~ **154** 62
Zechstein, lixiviated ~ **154** 62
Zechstein shale **154** 68
zenith *Astron.* **4** 11
zenith *Hunt.* **87** 77
zero **275** 18
zero adjustment **2** 7
zero isotherm **9** 41
zero level **7** 6, 20
ziggurat **333** 32
zimmerstutzen **305** 35
zinc plate **179** 9; **180** 53; **340** 52
zinc plate, etched ~ **178** 40
zinc plate, photoprinted ~ **178** 32
zink **322** 12
zinnia **60** 22
zip **31** 55; **33** 28; **260** 13
zip, front ~ **29** 18
zip, inside ~ **101** 6
zip code **236** 43
zircon **351** 19
zither **324** 21
zone, arid ~ **9** 54
zone, paved ~ **268** 58
zone, tropical ~ **9** 53
zoo **356**
zoological gardens **356**
zooming lever **117** 54; **313** 22, 36
zoom lens **112** 41; **240** 34; **313** 23
zoom lens, interchangeable ~ **117** 2
zoom stereomicroscope **112** 40
Zulu **354** 36

MORE OXFORD PAPERBACKS

OXFORD BOOKS

Oxford Books began in 1900 with Sir Arthur Quiller-Couch ('Q')'s *Oxford Book of English Verse.* Since then over 60 superb anthologies of poetry, prose, and songs have appeared in a series that has a very special place in British publishing.

THE OXFORD BOOK OF ENGLISH GHOST STORIES

Chosen by Michael Cox and R. A. Gilbert

This anthology includes some of the best and most frightening ghost stories ever written, including M. R. James's 'Oh Whistle, and I'll Come to You, My Lad', 'The Monkey's Paw' by W. W. Jacobs, and H. G. Wells's 'The Red Room'. The important contribution of women writers to the genre is represented by stories such as Amelia Edwards's 'The Phantom Coach', Edith Wharton's 'Mr Jones', and Elizabeth Bowen's 'Hand in Glove'.

As the editors stress in their informative introduction, a good ghost story, though it may raise many profound questions about life and death, entertains as much as it unsettles us, and the best writers are careful to satisfy what Virginia Woolf called 'the strange human craving for the pleasure of feeling afraid'. This anthology, the first to present the full range of classic English ghost fiction, similarly combines a serious literary purpose with the plain intention of arousing pleasing fear at the doings of the dead.

'an excellent cross-section of familiar and unfamiliar stories and guaranteed to delight' *New Statesman*

Also in Oxford Paperbacks:

The Oxford Book of Short Stories edited by V. S. Pritchett
The Oxford Book of Political Anecdotes
edited by Paul Johnson
The Oxford Book of Ages
edited by Anthony and Sally Sampson
The Oxford Book of Dreams edited by Stephen Brock

PAST MASTERS

General Editor: Keith Thomas

Past Masters is a series of concise and authoritative introductions to the life and works of men and women whose ideas still influence the way we think today.

'Put end to end, this series will constitute a noble encyclopaedia of the history of ideas.' Mary Warnock

SHAKESPEARE

Germaine Greer

'At the core of a coherent social structure as he viewed it lay marriage, which for Shakespeare is no mere comic convention but a crucial and complex ideal. He rejected the stereotype of the passive, sexless, unresponsive female and its inevitable concommitant, the misogynist conviction that all women were whores at heart. Instead he created a series of female characters who were both passionate and pure, who gave their hearts spontaneously into the keeping of the men they loved and remained true to the bargain in the face of tremendous odds.'

Germaine Greer's short book on Shakespeare brings a completely new eye to a subject about whom more has been written than on any other English figure. She is especially concerned with discovering why Shakespeare 'was and is a popular artist', who remains a central figure in English cultural life four centuries after his death.

'eminently trenchant and sensible . . . a genuine exploration in its own right' John Bayley, *Listener*

'the clearest and simplest explanation of Shakespeare's thought I have yet read' Auberon Waugh, *Daily Mail*

Also available in Past Masters:

Paine Mark Philp
Dante George Holmes
The Buddha Michael Carrithers
Confucius Raymond Dawson

OXFORD REFERENCE

Oxford is famous for its superb range of dictionaries and reference books. The Oxford Reference series offers the most up-to-date and comprehensive paperbacks at the most competitive prices, across a broad spectrum of subjects.

THE CONCISE OXFORD COMPANION TO ENGLISH LITERATURE

Edited by Margaret Drabble and Jenny Stringer

Based on the immensely popular fifth edition of the *Oxford Companion to English Literature* this is an indispensable, compact guide to the central matter of English literature.

There are more than 5,000 entries on the lives and works of authors, poets, playwrights, essayists, philosophers, and historians; plot summaries of novels and plays; literary movements; fictional characters; legends; theatres; periodicals; and much more.

The book's sharpened focus on the English literature of the British Isles makes it especially convenient to use, but there is still generous coverage of the literature of other countries and of other disciplines which have influenced or been influenced by English literature.

From reviews of *The Oxford Companion to English Literature Fifth Edition:*

'a book which one turns to with constant pleasure . . . a book with much style and little prejudice' Iain Gilchrist, *TLS*

'it is quite difficult to imagine, in this genre, a more useful publication' Frank Kermode, *London Review of Books*

'incarnates a living sense of tradition . . . sensitive not to fashion merely but to the spirit of the age' Christopher Ricks, *Sunday Times*

Also available in Oxford Reference:

The Concise Oxford Dictionary of Art and Artists
edited by Ian Chilvers
A Concise Oxford Dictionary of Mathematics
Christopher Clapham
The Oxford Spelling Dictionary compiled by R. E. Allen
A Concise Dictionary of Law edited by Elizabeth A. Martin